OFFICIAL (ISC)²® GUIDE TO THE

CISSP® CBK®

THIRD EDITION

OTHER BOOKS IN THE (ISC)²® PRESS SERIES

OFFICIAL (ISC)²®
GUIDE TO THE
CISSP® CBK®
THIRD EDITION

Edited by
Harold F. Tipton - CISSP-ISSAP, ISSMP
Steven Hernandez - CISSP, CAP, SSCP, CSSLP

CRC Press
Taylor & Francis Group
Boca Raton London New York

CRC Press is an imprint of the
Taylor & Francis Group, an **informa** business
AN AUERBACH BOOK

CRC Press
Taylor & Francis Group
6000 Broken Sound Parkway NW, Suite 300
Boca Raton, FL 33487-2742

© 2013 by Taylor & Francis Group, LLC
CRC Press is an imprint of Taylor & Francis Group, an Informa business

No claim to original U.S. Government works

Printed in the United States of America on acid-free paper
Version Date: 20121109

International Standard Book Number: 978-1-4665-6976-8 (Hardback)

Visit the Taylor & Francis Web site at
http://www.taylorandfrancis.com

and the CRC Press Web site at
http://www.crcpress.com

Contents

DOMAIN 1
ACCESS CONTROL

DOMAIN 2
TELECOMMUNICATIONS & NETWORK SECURITY

DOMAIN 3
INFORMATION SECURITY GOVERNANCE
& RISK MANAGEMENT

DOMAIN 4
SOFTWARE DEVELOPMENT SECURITY

DOMAIN 5
CRYPTOGRAPHY

DOMAIN 6
SECURITY ARCHITECTURE & DESIGN

DOMAIN 7
SECURITY OPERATIONS

DOMAIN 8
BUSINESS CONTINUITY &
DISASTER RECOVERY PLANNING

DOMAIN 9
LEGAL, REGULATIONS, INVESTIGATIONS, AND COMPLIANCE

Foreword

Foreword to CISSP CBK Study Guide - Third Edition

We are living in an advanced cyber era, with every aspect of our lives, from medical records to bank transactions, now being transmitted online. The plethora of data and information flooding cyber space is overwhelming and there simply aren't enough qualified information security professionals to protect it all.

(ISC)²'s mission is to support and provide members and constituents with credentials, resources, and leadership to secure information and deliver value to society. The not-for-profit, vendor-neutral organization was founded by a group of passionate volunteers in 1989 who wanted to create an information security industry standard for professionals. Their initial concept for industry excellence came to fruition with the creation of the Certified Information Systems Security Professional (CISSP®) credential. It was the first technology-related credential to be accredited by the International Organization for Standardizations (ISO) ISO/IEC Standard 17024, a global benchmark for the certification of personnel.

The CISSP continues to be recognized as the industry's Gold Standard. The true differentiator is the organization's stringent membership requirements – passing the examination, possessing the required number of years of in depth experience in at least 2 of the domains, being endorsed by another (ISC)² member in good standing, abiding by a Code of Ethics, and maintaining quality continuing professional education (CPE) credits.

The CISSP is not only recognized throughout the industry, it's also highly regarded by governments, academia, human resources, and business entities around the world. In fact, the CISSP has become a job requirement and/or candidate differentiator for information security management positions.

The ten domains of the CISSP CBK® comprehensively encompass the core competencies that an experienced information security professional should possess. The latest security topics such as cloud computing, mobile security, application security, and more are regularly integrated into the examination through a rigorous process of evaluation and updates. We require our members to obtain the industry's latest knowledge and skills, and we reinforce that sentiment through our own examination process.

83% of (ISC)² members are employed in a wide variety of technically diverse professions and 17% are employed in governance and policy making roles.

The Official (ISC)² Guide to the CISSP CBK is the only study tool that delves into all of the topics and subtopics contained in the CISSP CBK. The authors and editor of this new, comprehensive edition have provided an extensive supplement to the CBK review seminars that are designed to help candidates study for the CISSP credential.

Earning the CISSP is a major highlight in an information security professional's career path. (ISC)²'s elite network of professionals enjoy benefits such as: complimentary access to (ISC)²'s one-day conferences and networking receptions in cities around the world; discounts at industry conferences; access to a Career Center with current job listings; subscription to (ISC)²'s digital magazine – InfoSecurity Professional; a dedicated member services staff to address your questions and issues; and much more.

You will also be a member of a highly respected organization that is dedicated to reaching society and shaping the industry at large through community goodwill programs such as Safe and Secure Online, academic scholarships for students, and cutting-edge research –under the (ISC)^2 Foundation.

We wish you success in your journey to becoming a CISSP.

W. Hord Tipton
International Information System Security Certification Consortium, Inc.

Introduction

The Certified Information Systems Security Professional (CISSP) is an information assurance professional who has demonstrated a cross-disciplinary expertise ranging from architecture, design, management, risk and controls that assure the security of business environments. There are two main requirements that must be met in order to achieve the status of CISSP; one must take and pass the certification exam, and be able to demonstrate a minimum of 5 years of direct full-time security work experience in two or more of the 10 domains of the (ISC)² CISSP CBK. A firm understanding of what the 10 domains of the CISSP CBK are, and how they relate to the landscape of business is a vital element in successfully being able to meet both requirements and claim the CISSP credential. The mapping of the 10 domains of the CISSP CBK to the job responsibilities of the Information Security professional in today's world can take many paths, based on a variety of factors such as industry vertical, regulatory oversight and compliance, geography, as well as public versus private versus military as the overarching framework for employment in the first place. In addition, considerations such as cultural practices and differences in language and meaning can also play a substantive role in the interpretation of what aspects of the CBK will mean, and how they will be implemented in any given workplace.

It is not the purpose of this book to attempt to address all of these issues or provide a definitive proscription as to what is "the" path forward in all areas. Rather, it is to provide the official guide to the CISSP CBK, and in so doing, to lay out the information necessary to understand what the CBK is, and how it is used to build the foundation for the CISSP and its role in business today. To that end, it is important to begin any journey with a sense of place, specifically where you are, and where you want to end up; and as a result, what tools you will need to have in order to make the journey comfortable and successful. The most important tool that the intrepid traveler can have at their disposal is a compass, that trusty device that always allows one to understand in what direction they are heading, and get their bearings when necessary. The compass of the Information Security professional is their knowledge, experience, and understanding of the world around them. The thing that is amazing about a compass is that no matter where you stand on Earth, you can hold one in your hand and it will point toward the North Pole. While we do not need to know where the North Pole always is in Information Security, as a CISSP, you are expected to be able to provide guidance and direction to the businesses and users that you are responsible for. Being able to map the CISSP CBK to your knowledge, experience, and understanding is the way that you will be able to provide that guidance, and to translate the CBK into actionable and tangible elements for both the business and its users that you represent.

While there is a strong interaction amongst the ten domains of the CISSP, security mechanisms are covered in Access Control, Software Development Security, Cryptography, the Physical (Environmental) Security, and the Telecommunications and Network Security domains. Security policies are addressed in the Security Architecture & Design, the Information Security Governance and Risk Management, The Business Continuity and Disaster Recovery Planning and Security Operations domains. The people aspects of security encompass a cross section of domains, and are specifically covered in the Legal, Regulations, Investigations and Compliance domain.

1. The *Access Control* domain covers mechanisms by which a system grants or revokes the right to access data or perform an action on an information system.

Access Control systems include:

■ File permissions, such as "create," "read," "edit," or "delete" on a file server.

■ Program permissions, such as the right to execute a program on an application server.

■ Data rights, such as the right to retrieve or update information in a database.

These elements of Access Control systems are things that Information Security professionals interact with every day, as do the users of any systems that the business provides, such as Directory Services for logon authentication, File and Print systems that allow for the secure storage, retrieval, and manipulation of data in a variety of formats, as well as web services that expose data to front end interfaces for user consumption. Whenever a user attempts to access secured data from any legitimate or illegitimate interface, internal or external to the enterprise, the Access Control domain plays an active and indispensable part in the transactions that take place to ultimately either validate, or disqualify that user's access request. The ability to understand Identity Management, Data Access Controls, Information Classification, System Access Control Strategies, and Threats, are all key elements that go into the Access Control Domain.

2. The *Telecommunications and Network Security* domain encompasses the structures, techniques, transport protocols, and security measures used to provide integrity, availability, confidentiality and authentication for transmissions over private and public communication networks.

The Information Security professional is responsible for security at all levels of the business, whether it is with regards to a senior level executive's request to access controlled information, or the testing and deployment of an application security patch, or the documentation of the processes and procedures that are in place to safeguard remote access to the business's data. Identification of threat and risk, and the implementation of mitigation techniques and strategies to counteract and minimize their impacts also play an important part in the list of activities that the Information Security professional is responsible for carrying out and managing on a daily basis within the business. All of these things are part of the Telecommunications and Network Security domain in one way or another. The 7 layers of the OSI model that are used to describe the activities and structure of the network, and how information is structured, transmitted, formatted, and secured with a focus on providing for Confidentiality, Integrity, and Availability (CIA) are the roadmap for the Information Security professional in this domain, allowing them to understand at **ALL** levels of a system, from end to end, how to envision information and the security that needs to envelop it to ensure it is properly protected and safeguarded.

3. The *Information Security Governance and Risk Management* domain entails the identification of an organization's information assets and the development, documentation, implementation and updating of policies, standards, procedures and guidelines that ensure confidentiality, integrity, and availability. Management tools such as data classification, risk assessment, and risk analysis are used to identify threats, classify assets, and to rate their vulnerabilities so that effective security measures and controls can be implemented.

The Information Security professional is actively involved in all aspects of the Information and Security Governance and Risk Management domain as part of any of the functions that they carry out within the enterprise. Whether it is the creation of compelling business cases for senior management to illustrate the Core Information Security Principles of Confidentiality, Availability, and Integrity (CIA) inherent in a current business system, or new software platform, or the clear delineation of the required Security

Policies, Procedures, Standards, Guidelines, and Baselines needed to run and maintain current systems, as well as testing new systems and software for possible deployment and use, the Information Security professional actively champions the Information Security Governance and Risk Management domain in all that they do within the business. The Information Security professional is also responsible for ensuring that the business, and all of its users are acting ethically with regards to information management and security, and that any and all activities engaged in always safeguard people first, as well as safeguarding the information that they are accessing.

4. The *Software Development Security* domain refers to the controls that are included within systems and applications software and the steps used in their development, for example a Software Development Life Cycle (SDLC).

Software refers to system software (operating systems) and application programs such as agents, applets, software, databases, data warehouses, and knowledge-based systems. These applications may be used in distributed or centralized environments.

The elements of Software Development Security are not the direct purview of many Information Security professionals. Software development is a highly specialized skill, and most Information Security professionals are not software developers traditionally. As a result, on the surface it may appear to Information Security professionals as if they cannot be effective in this domain of the CBK, but nothing can be further from the truth. Software forms the working foundation of every system that the Information Security professional and users in any business anywhere in the world interact with on a daily basis. While users typically do not understand the answer to the question of "how" their software was created, they do understand how to use that software, but unfortunately, not always in a secure and responsible manner. Being able to provide guidance to users with regards to things such as Malicious Software types and identification,

Audit and Assurance Mechanisms, Database Controls, and Web Application Threats are all elements that the Information Security professional will put in place as part of the Software Development and Security domain.

5. The *Cryptography* domain addresses the principles, means, and methods of applying mathematical algorithms and data transformations to information to ensure its integrity, confidentiality and authenticity.

While many of the physical elements of the Cryptography domain are used by business all the time to safeguard data and to ensure data integrity, most users are unaware of these functions and how they operate. Whether it is the use of Symmetric or Asymmetric Cryptography to protect data and ensure confidentiality, or the use of Hash Functions or Digital Signatures to ensure message integrity, or the practice of Encryption Management to ensure data availability on demand for authenticated users of a system, the Information Security professional plays an active role in all aspects of the Cryptography domain, and its application to data security in the enterprise. The other components of the Cryptography domain, such as the concepts of Nonrepudiation, Authentication, and Access Control are also important areas that the Information Security professional will actively be involved with as they set up and manage Directory Service based authentication systems such as Active Directory, or Network Information Service (NIS) systems, as well as encryption key management solutions.

6. The *Security Architecture & Design* domain contains the concepts, principles, structures, and standards used to design, implement, monitor, and secure, operating systems, equipment, networks, applications, and those controls used to enforce various levels of confidentiality, integrity, and availability.

Information security architecture and design covers the practice of applying a comprehensive and rigorous method for describing a current and/or future structure and behavior for an organization's security processes, information security systems, personnel and organizational sub-units, so that these practices and processes align with the organization's core goals and strategic direction.

The Information Security professional needs to remember that they are charged with providing direction and guidance to the business and its users in the various areas of the CISSP CBK. The best way for them to be able to accomplish that goal consistently, across all of the 10 domains of the CBK, is to be aware of the actions and activities that they already engage in everyday that align with the CBK, and allow them to translate the CBK into tangible action and measurable results for the business and its users. The Security Architecture & Design domain is all about the What, Why and How of security. The Information Security professional needs to be able to use these questions to examine the needs of the business and its users for secure access to information, and then to develop systems that will foster the level of secure access required. Measurement of that system and ongoing maintenance of it is addressed through other domains of the CISSP CBK, but the foundation necessary to ensure success of those efforts is built by the Information Security professional as they create well-formed and sound Security Architectures and Designs.

7. The **Security Operations** domain is used to identify critical information and the execution of selected measures that eliminate or reduce adversary exploitation of critical information. It includes the definition of the controls over hardware, media, and the operators with access privileges to any of these resources. Auditing and monitoring are the mechanisms, tools and facilities that permit the identification of security events and subsequent actions to identify the key elements and report the pertinent information to the appropriate individual, group, or process.

The Information Security professional should always act to Maintain Operational Resilience, Protect Valuable Assets, Control System Accounts and Manage Security Services Effectively. In the day to day operations of the business, maintaining expected levels of availability and integrity for data and services is where the Information Security professional impacts Operational Resilience. The day to day securing, monitoring, and maintenance of the resources of the business, both human and material, illustrate how the Information Security professional is able to Protect Valuable Assets. Providing a system of checks and balances with regards to privileged account usage, as well as system access, allows the Information Security professional to act to Control Systems Accounts in a consistent way. The use of change and configuration management by the Information Security professional, as well as reporting and service improvement programs (SIP), ensures that the actions necessary to Manage Security Services Effectively are being carried out.

8. The ***Business Continuity and Disaster Recovery Planning*** domain addresses the preservation of the business in the face of major disruptions to normal business operations. BCP and DRP involve the preparation, testing and updating of specific actions to protect critical business processes from the effect of major system and network failures.

The Information Security professional may or may not have direct experience with an actual disaster and the recovery actions that would be necessary to bring the business back to full functionality, while ensuring the safety and integrity of the business systems and information, as well as the safety and well- being of the users in the systems. Whether the Information Security professional has this direct, first- hand experience of applying a BCP and/or a DRP to an actual event is not as critical as their knowledge of, and training in the specific processes and procedures that are in place for their business in the event of an emergency, or an event that will negatively impact the business and its users. In addition, solid grounding in Project Management skills and the ability to interface with other risk management areas such as records management, regulatory compliance, vendor management, and physical security in the context of a Risk Management Framework that is used to help all areas of the business respond to and deal with risk effectively is also a critical success factor for the Information Security professional.

Business Continuity Planning (BCP) helps to identify the organization's exposure to internal and external threats. BCP counteracts interruptions to business activities and should be available to protect critical business processes from the effects of major failures or disasters. It deals with the natural and man-made events and the consequences, if not dealt with promptly and effectively.

Business Impact Analysis (BIA) determines the proportion of impact an individual business unit would sustain subsequent to a significant interruption of computing or telecommunication services. These impacts may be financial, in terms of monetary loss, or operational, in terms of inability to deliver.

Disaster Recovery Plans (DRP) contain procedures for emergency response, extended backup operation and post-disaster recovery, should a computer installation experience a partial or total loss of computer resources and physical facilities. The primary objective of the disaster recovery plan is to provide the capability to process mission-essential applications, in a degraded mode, and return to normal mode of operation within a reasonable amount of time.

9. The *Legal, Regulations, Investigations and Compliance* domain addresses ethical behavior and compliance with regulatory frameworks. It includes the investigative measures and techniques that can be used to determine if a crime has been committed, and methods used to gather evidence (e.g., forensics). A computer crime is any illegal action where the data on a computer is accessed without permission. This includes unauthorized access or alteration of data, or unlawful use of computers and services. This domain also includes understanding the computer incident forensic response capability to identify the Advanced Persistent Threat (APT) that many organizations face today.

Information Security professionals operate in a variety of environments today, and as a result of this diversity, they must be aware of any and all legal and regulatory responsibilities that the business may be subject to with regards to computer crime, data access, data use, data manipulation, and unauthorized data destruction. Understanding how to organize the response of the business to a computer incident, and to be able to interface with any and all other areas of Risk Management and Information Security Management as required to coordinate the response and ongoing communication and coordination efforts of the business with regards to the forensic examination of evidence are important functions that the Information Security professional should be comfortable with.

10. The *Physical (Environmental) Security* domain addresses the threats, vulnerabilities, and countermeasures that can be utilized to physically protect an enterprise's resources and sensitive information. These resources include people, the facility in which they work, and the data, equipment, support systems, media, and supplies they utilize.

Physical security describes measures that are designed to deny access to unauthorized personnel (including attackers) from physically accessing a building, facility, resource, or stored information; and guidance on how to design structures to resist potentially hostile acts.

The Information Security professional should be exercising a "holistic" vision of the business and its resources when it comes to security. Taking into account both the physical and logical aspects of security design, as well as the entirety of the business's physical footprint, are all important elements of success for the Information Security professional to be measuring their approaches and actions against with regards to the Physical (Environmental) Security domain. While many Information Security professionals will not be involved with the initial site and facility design criteria, and even the location choices for the business that they are a part of, that does not mean that they should not be aware of these factors with regards to their impact on security. Further, Information Security professionals need to play an active part in creating a focus within the business on the efficacy of its physical security posture, and if necessary, to be the agent that drives changes as required to ensure that security is maintained at appropriate levels given the threats and risks that are present in the operating environment.

Editors

Steven Hernandez - Lead Editor

Steven Hernandez MBA, CISSP, CSSLP, SSCP, CAP, CISA is the Chief Information Security Officer and the Director of Information Assurance for the Office of Inspector General at the US Department of Health and Human Services. Hernandez has over seventeen years of information assurance experience in a variety of fields including international heavy manufacturing, large finance organizations, educational institutions, and Government agencies. Steven is affiliate faculty at the National Information Assurance Training and Education Center located at Idaho State University. Through his academic outreach, he has presented lectures over the past decade on numerous information assurance topics including risk management, information security investing, and the implications of privacy decisions to graduate and post graduate audiences. In addition to his credentials from (ISC)², Hernandez also holds six US Committee for National Security Systems certifications ranging from Systems Security to Organizational Risk Management. Steven also volunteers service to (ISC)²'s Government Advisory Board and Executive Writers Bureau. When not engaged in information assurance pursuits he enjoys relaxing with his family and their overly demanding dog.

Adam Gordon - *Technical Editor*

With over 20 years of experience as both an educator and IT professional, Adam holds numerous Professional IT Certifications including CISA, CISSP, CRISC, CHFI, CEH, SCNA, VCP, and VCI. He is the author of several books and has achieved many awards, including EC-Council Instructor of Excellence for 2006-07 and Top Technical Instructor Worldwide, 2002-2003. Adam holds his Bachelor's Degree in International Relations and his Master's Degree in International Political Affairs from Florida International University.

Adam has held a number of positions during his professional career including CISO, CTO, Consultant, and Solutions Architect. He has worked on many large implementations involving multiple customer program teams for delivery.

Adam has been invited to lead projects for companies such as Microsoft, Citrix, Lloyds Bank TSB, Campus Management, US Southern Command (SOUTHCOM), Amadeus, World Fuel Services, and Seaboard Marine.

In Memoriam
Harold F. (Hal) Tipton - *Original Editor*

Hal Tipton, was a past president of the International Information System Security Certification Consortium and a director of computer security for Rockwell International Corporation for about 15 years. He initiated the Rockwell computer and data security program in 1977 and then continued to administer, develop, enhance, and expand the program to accommodate the control needs produced by technological advances until his retirement from Rockwell in 1994.

Tipton was a member of the Information Systems Security Association (ISSA) since 1982 and became the president of the Los Angeles Chapter in 1984, and the president of the national organization of ISSA (1987–1989). He was added to the ISSA Hall of Fame and the ISSA Honor Role in 2000.

Tipton was a member of the National Institute for Standards and Technology (NIST), the computer and Telecommunications Security Council, and the National Research Council Secure Systems Study Committee (for the National Academy of Science). He received his BS in engineering from the U.S. Naval Academy and his MA in personnel administration from George Washington University; he also received his certificate in computer science from the University of California at Irvine. He was a certified information system security professional (CISSP), ISSAP, & ISSMP.

He last chaired the (ISC)² CBK Committees and the QA Committee and received the Computer Security Institute's Lifetime Achievement Award in 1994 and the (ISC)²'s Hal Tipton Award in 2001. As important as he was to the field of Information Systems Security, he was an even better man. Hal will be missed as a leader, visionary, pioneer, and most importantly – a great friend by all that had the honor to get to know him.

Contributors

Paul Baker, Ph.D., CPP, is a security manager with more than 30 years of extensive and comprehensive experience in all phases of law enforcement and industrial security. He holds a doctorate in strategic leadership from Regent University along with a master of science in criminal justice from Troy University. Dr. Baker began his security management journey in the U.S. Marine Corps and continued as a Maryland State Trooper working extensively on narcotics and intelligence. After his retirement in 2001, he embarked on the next phase of his security career, working as a physical security supervisor for the MITRE Corporation in Washington, D.C. He is currently employed as a security manager for Capital One Bank. Dr. Baker has been involved in numerous security assessment projects and has designed complete physical protection systems for a multitude of facilities.

Alec Bass, CISSP, is a senior security specialist in the Boston area. During his 25 year career, Alec has developed solutions that significantly reduce risk to the digital assets of high-profile manufacturing, communications, home entertainment, financial, research, and federal organizations. He has helped enterprises enhance their network's security posture, performed penetration testing, and administered client firewalls for an application service provider. Before devoting his career to information security, Alec supported the IT infrastructure for a multinational Fortune 200 company and fixed operating system bugs for a leading computer firm.

Peter Berlich, CISSP-ISSMP, is working as an IT security manager on a large outsourcing account at IBM Integrated Technology Services, coming from a progression of IT security- and compliance-related roles in IBM. Before joining IBM, he was global information security manager at ABB, after a succession of technical and project management roles with a focus on network security management. Peter is a member of the (ISC)² European Advisory Board and the Information Security Forum Council. He is the author of various articles on the subject of security and privacy management in publications such as *Infosecurity Today*.

Todd Fitzgerald, CISSP, CISA, CISM, is the director of information systems security and a systems security officer for United Government Services, LLC (UGS), Milwaukee, Wisconsin. Todd has written articles on information security for publications such as The Information Security Management Handbook, The HIPAA Program Reference Book, Managing an Information Security and Privacy Awareness and Training Program (Auerbach Publications) and magazines such as Information Security. Todd is frequently called upon to present at national and local conferences, and has received several security industry leadership awards.

Stephen Fried, CISSP, CISM, is a seasoned information security professional with over 25 years' experience in information technology. For the last 12 years, Stephen has concentrated his eff orts on providing effective information security leadership to large organizations. Stephen has led the creation of security programs for two Fortune 500 companies and has an extensive background in such diverse security issues as risk assessment and management, security policy development, security architecture, infrastructure and perimeter security design, outsource relationship security, off shore development, intellectual property protection, security technology development, business continuity, secure e-business design, and information technology auditing. A frequent speaker at conferences, Stephen is also active in many security industry organizations. He is a contributing author to the Information Security Management Handbook, and has also been quoted in magazines such as Secure Enterprise and CIO Decisions.

Bonnie A. Goins, CISSP, NSA IAM, GIAC, CISM, ISS, PCI QSA, is a nationally recognized subject matter expert in information security management. With over 17 years of experience in management consulting, and information technology and security, Bonnie is chosen by executive management for her depth of knowledge and experience in information technology and security strategy development and refinement; risk and security assessment methods; security program design, development, and implementation; regulatory compliance initiatives, such as HIPAA, Sarbanes–Oxley, PCI, GLBA, NERC/FERC, FISMA, and others; policy, procedure, and plan creation; technology and business process reengineering; secure network infrastructure design and implementation; business continuity and incident response initiatives; application security methods; and security/technology/regulatory training. Her experience extends over multiple verticals and includes healthcare, financial services, government, utilities, retail, higher education, telecommunications, manufacturing, public health, pharmaceuticals/biotech, and manufacturing.

Kevin Henry, CISSP-ISSEP, ISSMP, CAP, SSCP, is a well-known speaker and consultant in the field of information security and business continuity planning. He provides educational and consulting services to organizations throughout the world and is an official instructor for (ISC)². He is responsible for course development and delivery for several (ISC)² programs. Kevin has a broad range of experience in both technology and management of information technology and information security programs. He has worked for clients ranging from the largest telecommunications firms in the world to governments, military, and small home-based operations. He is a highly respected presenter at conferences, seminars, and educational programs worldwide. With over 20 years of telecommunications and government experience, he brings a relevant and interesting approach to information security and provides practical and meaningful solutions to the information security challenges, threats, and regulations we face today.

Rebecca Herold, CISSP, CISM, CISA, FLMI, is an information privacy, security, and compliance consultant, author, and instructor with over

16 years of experience assisting organizations of all sizes in all industries throughout the world. Rebecca has written numerous books, including Managing an Information Security and Privacy Awareness and Training Program (Auerbach Publications) and The Privacy Management Toolkit (Information Shield), along with dozens of book chapters and hundreds of published articles. Rebecca speaks often at conferences, and develops and teaches workshops for the Computer Security Institute. Rebecca is a resident editor for the IT Compliance Community and also an adjunct professor for the Norwich University Master of Science in information assurance program.

Micki Krause, CISSP, has held positions in the information security profession for the last 20 years. She is currently the chief information security officer at Pacific Life Insurance Company in Newport Beach, California. Micki has held several leadership roles in industry-influential groups including the ISSA and the (ISC)² and is a long-term advocate for professional security education and certification. In 2003, Krause received industry recognition as a recipient of the "Women of Vision" award given by Information Security magazine. In 2002, Krause was honored as the second recipient of the Harold F. Tipton Award in recognition of sustained career excellence and outstanding contributions to the profession. She is a reputed speaker, published author, and coeditor of the Information Security Management Handbook series.

Tyson Macaulay, the security liaison officer for Bell Canada, is responsible for technical and operational risk management solutions for Bell's largest enterprise clients. Tyson leads security initiatives addressing large, complex, technology solutions including physical and logical (IT) assets, and regulatory/legal compliance requirements. In this role, he leads worldwide engagements involving multinational companies and international governments. Tyson's leadership encompasses a broad range of industry sectors from the defense industry to high-tech start-ups. His expertise includes large-scale security implementations in both public and private sector institutions, working on projects from conception through development to implementation. Tyson is a respected thought leader with publications dating from 1993. His work has covered authorship of peer-reviewed white papers, IT security governance programs, technical and integration services, and incident management processes.

Kelley Okolita, MBCP, is currently the program manager for business continuity and disaster recovery for the Hanover Insurance Group. Widely recognized as an industry expert with more than 25 years' experience, Kelley developed and implemented programs that were put to the test and proved successful for a variety of recoveries both large and small including from the events of September 11, 2001 and Hurricane Katrina. Kelley is sought after as a speaker and subject-matter expert by organizations such as Gartner, Sungard, and IBM. She has published articles in professional magazines and journals and was selected by (ISC)² to be the expert to rewrite Chapter 3 for their CISSP study guide and ISSAP study guide. Kelley has had a 10-year affiliation with DRI International (DRII)—six years on the Certification Commission for DRII, two as a chair and two as a member of their board of directors. She continues to serve on various committees. She is also an alternate on the NFPA 1600 Technical Committee. She has spoken at conferences from North America to Australia to Singapore and is currently completing her book on enterprise-wide business continuity planning, which is to be published by Taylor & Francis.

Keith Pasley, CISSP, CISA, ITIL, GSNA, is an information security professional specializing in helping companies understand information security requirements, regulatory compliance to help maximize security technology to reduce costs and complexity. Keith has over 20 years of hands-on experience in the information technology industry, and has spent the last 13 years specializing in information security. In various roles, Keith has designed security architectures and implemented security strategies for government, education, and commercial sectors. Keith is a security researcher and a contributing author to such publications as the Information Security Management Handbook and the HIPAA Program Reference (both published by Auerbach Publications). Keith has also published online and in-print articles on various security-related subjects.

Marcus K. Rogers, Ph.D, CISSP, CCCI, is the director of the Cyber Forensics Program in the Department of Computer and Information Technology at Purdue University. He is a professor, a faculty scholar, and a research faculty member at the Center for Education and Research in Information Assurance and Security. Dr. Rogers is a member of the quality assurance board for (ISC)²'s SCCP designation; the international chair of the Law, Regulations, Compliance and Investigation Domain of the Common Body of Knowledge (CBK) committee; the chair of the Ethics Committee Digital & Multimedia Sciences Section—American Academy of Forensic Sciences; and the chair of the Certification Committee Digital Forensics Certification Board. Dr. Rogers is the editor in chief of the Journal of Digital Forensic Practice and serves on the editorial board of several other professional journals. He is the author of numerous book chapters and journal publications in the field of digital forensics and applied psychological analysis.

Ken M. Shaurette, CISSP, CISA, CISM, is an experienced security and audit professional with a strong understanding of complex computing environments, legislative and regulatory requirements, and security solutions. He is a founding member and a past president of the Western Wisconsin InfraGard Chapter; a past president of ISSA-Milwaukee (International Systems Security Association); the current president and founding member of ISSA-Madison; a past chairman MATC Milwaukee Security Specialist Curriculum Advisory Committee; a member of Herzing University's Department of Homeland Security Degree; and a member of the Western Wisconsin Association of Computer Crime Investigators. Ken has published security information in several books and trade magazines. In his spare time, he finds time to work as a director of IT services for Financial Institution Products Corporation (FIPCO®), a subsidiary of the Wisconsin Bankers Association. He can be reached via e-mail at kshaurette@charter.net.

Robert M. Slade is an information security and management consultant from North Vancouver, British Columbia, Canada. Initial research into computer viral programs developed into the writing and reviewing of security books, and eventually into conducting review seminars for CISSP candidates. Slade also promotes the Community Security Education project, attempting to increase security awareness for the general public as a means of reducing overall information security threats. More information than anyone would want to know about him is available at http://victoria. tc.ca/techrev/rms.htm or http://en.wikipedia.org/wiki/Robert_Slade. It is next to impossible to get him to take "bio" writing seriously.

James S. Tiller, CISSP, CISA, is an accomplished executive with over 14 years of information security and information technology experience and leadership. He has provided comprehensive, forward-thinking solutions encompassing a broad spectrum of challenges and industries. Jim has spent much of his career assisting organizations throughout North America, Europe, and most recently Asia, in meeting their security goals and objectives. He is the author of Th e Ethical Hack: Framework for Business Value Penetration Testing and A Technical Guide to IPsec Virtual Private Networks (Auerbach Publications). Jim has been a contributing author to the Information Security Management Handbook for the last five years, in addition to several other publications. Currently, Jim is the vice president of Security North America for BT Global Services.

Additional images, tables, illustrations and grammatical edits provided by *Andrew Schneiter.*

Additional illustrations by *Andrea Graves*.

Domain 1

Access Controls

THE FIELD OF INFORMATION SECURITY is complex, dynamic, and infinitely challenging. This single discipline contains elements of advanced technology, human behavior, business strategy, statistical analysis, mathematics, and a host of other technical and personal skills. In fact, the field can be so complex that to categorize it for the CBK® takes ten distinct domains, each with its own unique skill and knowledge requirements. Despite all this complexity, however, the fundamental purpose of all information security efforts remains the same; to protect the confidentiality, integrity, and availability of information assets. Furthermore, the most fundamental way of doing this is to ensure that only those who have a specific need for an asset, combined with specific authoritative permission, will be able to access that asset. That, in a nutshell, is access control.

TOPICS

Control access by applying the following concepts, methodologies, and techniques:

- Policies
- Types of controls: preventive, detective, corrective, etc.
- Techniques, e.g., nondiscretionary, discretionary, and mandatory
- Identification and authentication
- Decentralized and distributed access control techniques
- Authorization mechanisms
- Logging and monitoring
- Understand access control attacks
- Assess effectiveness of access controls
- Identity and access provisioning lifecycle

OBJECTIVES

According to the (ISC)^2 Candidate Information Bulletin, an information security professional should fully understand:

- Access control concepts, methodologies, and implementation within centralized and decentralized environments across the enterprise's computer systems.

- Access control techniques and detective and corrective measures should be studied to understand the potential risks, vulnerabilities, and exposures.

Key Access Control Concepts

Before beginning a comprehensive overview of the access control domain, it is important to have an understanding of some key concepts that will be important throughout the chapter. These concepts form the basis for understanding how access control works, why it is a key security discipline, and how each individual component to be discussed in this chapter relates to the overall access control universe.

The most fundamental and significant concept to master is a precise definition of what is meant by the term "access control." For the rest of this chapter and throughout this book, the following definition is used:

> **Access Control** is the process of allowing only authorized users, programs, or other computer systems (i.e. networks) to observe, modify, or otherwise take possession of the resources of a computer system. It is also a mechanism for limiting the use of some resources to authorized users.

In summary, access controls are the collection of mechanisms, processes or techniques that work together to protect the assets of an organization. They help protect against threats and mitigate vulnerabilities by reducing exposure to unauthorized activities and providing access to information and systems to only authorized people, processes or systems.

Although access control is a single domain within the CISSP Common Body of Knowledge (CBK), it is the most pervasive and omnipresent aspect of information security. Access controls encompass all operational levels of an organization:

- **Facilities:** Access controls protect entry to, and movement around, an organization's physical locations to protect personnel, equipment, information, and, other assets inside that facility.

- **Support systems:** Access to support systems (such as power, heating, ventilation and air conditioning (HVAC) systems; water; and fire suppression controls) must be controlled so that a malicious entity is not able to compromise these systems and cause harm to the organization's personnel or the ability to support critical systems.

■ *Information systems:* Multiple layers of access controls are present in most modern information systems and networks to protect those systems, and the information they contain, from harm or misuse.

■ *Personnel:* management, end users, customers, business partners, and nearly everyone else associated with an organization should be subject to some form of access control to ensure that the right people have the ability to interface with each other, and not interfere with the people with whom they do not have any legitimate business.

Additionally, almost all physical and logical entry points to the organization and its information systems need some type of access control. Given the pervasive nature and importance of access controls throughout the practice of security, it is necessary to understand the four key attributes of access control that enable good security management. Specifically, access controls enable management to:

■ Specify which users can access a system or facility
■ Specify what resources those users can access
■ Specify what operations those users can perform
■ Enforce accountability and non for those users' actions

Each of these four areas, although interrelated, represents an established and individual approach to defining an effective access control strategy. The information in this chapter will assist the security professional in determining the proper course of action to satisfy each of the attributes as it applies to a particular system, process, or facility.

Joining the C-I-A

The common thread among information security objectives is that they address at least one (if not all three) of the core security principles:

confidentiality, integrity, and availability (more commonly referred to as the C-I-A).

- **Confidentiality** refers to efforts made to prevent unauthorized disclosure of information to those who do not have the need, or right, to see it.

- **Integrity** refers to efforts made to prevent unauthorized or improper modification of systems and information. It also refers to the amount of trust that can be placed in a system and the accuracy of information within that system. For example, many systems and applications will check data that come into the system for syntactic and semantic accuracy to ensure that incoming data do not introduce operational or processing errors, thus affecting its overall integrity.

- **Availability** refers to efforts made to prevent disruption of service and productivity.

The goals of information security are to ensure the continued C-I-A of an organization's assets. This includes both physical assets (such as buildings, equipment, and, of course, people) and information assets (such as company data and information systems.) Access controls play a key role in ensuring the confidentiality of systems and information. Managing access to physical and information assets is fundamental to preventing exposure of data by controlling who can see, use, modify, or destroy those assets. In addition, managing an entity's admittance and rights to specific enterprise resources ensures that valuable data and services are not abused, misappropriated, or stolen. It is also a key factor for many organizations that are required to protect personal information in order to be compliant with appropriate legislation and industry compliance requirements.

The act of controlling access inherently provides features and benefits that protect the integrity of business assets. By preventing unauthorized or inappropriate access, organizations can achieve greater confidence in data and system integrity. Without controls to manage who has access to specific resources, and what actions they are permitted to perform, there are a few alternate controls to ensure that information and systems are not modified by unwanted influences. Access controls (more specifically, records of access activity) also offer greater visibility into determining who or what may have altered data or system information, potentially affecting the integrity of those assets. Access controls can be used to match an entity (such as a person or a computer system) with the actions that entity takes against valuable assets, allowing organizations to have a better understanding of the state of their security posture.

Finally, access control processes go hand in hand with efforts to ensure the availability of resources within an organization. One of the most basic rules to embrace for any valuable asset, especially an asset whose criticality requires that it must be available for use over elongated periods of time, is that only people with a need to use that particular asset should be allowed access to that asset. Taking this stance ensures that the resource is not blocked or congested by people who have no business using it. This is why most organizations only allow their employees and other trusted individuals into their facilities or onto their corporate networks. In addition, restricting access to only those who need to use a resource reduces the likelihood that malicious agents can gain access and cause damage to the asset or that non-malicious individuals with unnecessary access can cause accidental damage.

Determining a Default Stance

An organization's access control strategy is directly influenced by its overall approach and philosophy concerning information security. For example, educational institutions and public social organizations generally promote more open and unfettered access to systems and information. They would most likely have fewer restrictions and controls on what information and services users can access. Their philosophy is based on allowing access to any information unless there is a specific need to restrict that access. Such an access philosophy is often referred to as **allow-by-default**. More formally, this philosophy dictates that any access that is not specifically denied is permitted. Even though such an organization may have security measures in place (like firewalls, for example), those devices are configured to allow access to a resource unless a specific resource is defined as requiring more restricted access. This approach provides a much more open environment for sharing information and resources, but at the potential cost of losing control over the confidentiality, integrity, and availability of the information and resources that organization manages. *Figure 1.1* shows a conceptual view of an allow-by-default environment.

In this illustration, the firewall is configured to allow most network protocols (e.g. FTP, HTTP, and SMTP) through to the organization's intranet. However, peer to peer (P2P) protocols (such as file sharing and instant messaging programs) are blocked at the firewall, presumably because the organization has determined they pose an unacceptable risk vs. the benefit they offer.

Other organizations have a much stricter access control philosophy. These include most commercial enterprises, government systems, and military installations. Their philosophy is one of **deny-by-default**, or, more

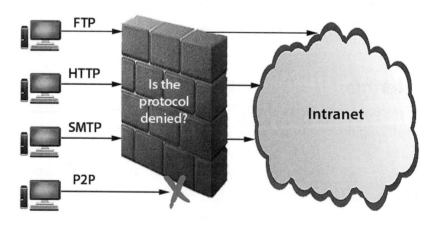

Figure 1.1 - **Conceptual view of an allow by default network environment**

formally, any access that is not specifically permitted is denied. In contrast to the allow-by-default approach, deny-by-default will block all attempts to access information and resources unless that access is specifically permitted. This approach provides an environment that protects information resources much more strongly, but at a cost of requiring much greater management and administration of those resources. In addition, workers in a deny-by-default environment may find that access to, and sharing of, information in such an environment is much more difficult. *Figure 1.2* shows a conceptual view of an allow-by-default environment.

In this diagram, the more restrictive environment blocks most protocols from entering the intranet. The exception is the SMTP protocol (used by most e-mail systems), which is allowed to pass through the firewall. This would allow e-mail traffic to travel in and out of the organization. In practice, few organizations follow pure allow-by-default or deny by default practices. Some areas of an organization may be more permissive (e.g., employee recreational information or cafeteria meal schedules), while other areas such as employee health and salary information or company financial records may be much more restrictive. Nevertheless, most organizations will have one or the other of these core philosophies as their underlying guiding principle for access control. Defining a core philosophy is very

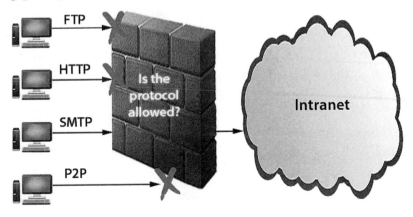

Figure 1.2 - **Conceptual view of an deny by default network environment**

important for a successful access control strategy, as it sets the tone for all other access control decisions to follow.

Defense in Depth

The practice of implementing appropriate access control mechanisms is also the first line of defense in an organization's *defense-in-depth* strategy. Defense in depth is the practice of applying multiple layers of security protection between an information resource and a potential attacker. If one of those layers should fail the successive layers will continue to function and protect the resource against compromise. A sound access control strategy provides the first layer of protection. By carefully managing all attempts to access a resource and blocking those that are not preauthorized, it ensures that all the other layers protecting that resource have a much greater chance of successfully protecting it. Defense in depth is applicable to both the physical and virtual environments. For example, imagine a modern office complex where top-secret data are stored, as depicted in *Figure 1.3*. In such an environment, a tall perimeter fence might provide the first layer of defense to keep intruders out. If an intruder gets through the fence, the building may have an armed guard at the front door. Should the intruder manage to knock out and disarm the guard, he may find that the building requires an access card to get past the main lobby. If the intruder can find an access card (perhaps from the security guard he just knocked out), and get into the main part of the building, he may find that all the cabinets with secret data are locked and the key is nowhere to be found! The goal in all of this is to ensure that access to target assets (in this case the secret data) is protected by multiple layers of controls.

A properly protected virtual environment, such as that depicted in *Figure 1.4*, should present similar challenges. If that same intruder decided to break into the company's data center over the Internet he may find that the company's network is protected by a strong firewall. However, this intrepid villain does not let that stop him and manages to find a hole through the firewall to the company's payroll server. The server, however,

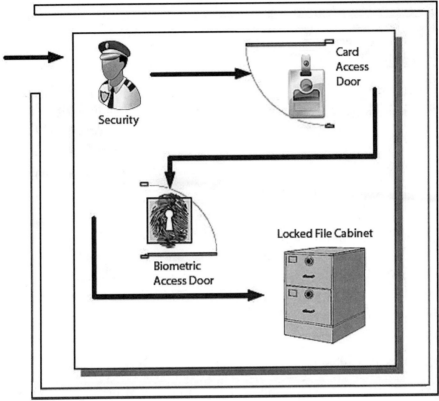

Security

Card
Access
Door

Locked File Cabinet

Biometric
Access Door

Figure 1.3 - **Physical defense in depth**

requires a password. If the attacker keeps going he will find that the applications on the server also require passwords, the system is protected by a host-based Intrusion Prevention System (more on that later), and the database files are encrypted. As it was with the physical security example, the more layers of protection placed between an attacker and a potential target the less likely it is that the failure of any single control will cause compromise or loss of the asset. Access controls can be found in many places within a computing environment. For example, firewalls employ rules that permit, limit, or deny access to various network services. By reducing the exposure to threats, controls protect potentially vulnerable system services, ensuring that network's availability. By reducing exposure to unwanted and unauthorized entities, organizations can limit the

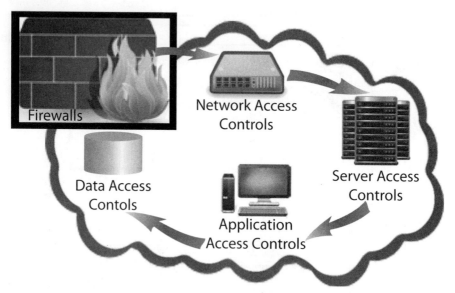

Figure 1.4 - **Network defense in depth**

number of threats that can affect the availability of systems, services, and data.

Access Control: A General Process

There are many different approaches to implementing an access control scheme—almost as many as there are security professionals. However, there is a general approach that is applicable to almost any situation and provides a useful framework for determining access controls. The three-step process is:

1. Defining resources

2. Determining users

3. Specifying the users' use of the resources

Step 1: Defining Resources

The first step to enable an effective access control strategy is to specifically define the resources that exist in the environment for users to access. Essentially, this step answers the fundamental security question, "What are you trying to protect?" While this may seem intuitive, this is not a step that should be overlooked, nor should its importance or potential complexity be underestimated. The definition of what exactly constitutes a "resource" to an organization may take considerable discussion, but once it is decided it will clarify and simplify the process of identifying those resources that are important enough for the organization to protect.

The proper definition of the available resources in your organization must also be coupled with a determination as to how each of those resources may be accessed. Do users need a specific organizational status to access a particular resource, or is it enough just to be a member of a specific project? Accessing information on a company's benefit plans may simply require a person to be an employee, whereas accessing quarterly financial projects may specifically require a person to be part of the finance organization. Addressing these issues during this step will also lay the foundation for effectively implementing role-based or domain-based access controls, which will be discussed later in this chapter.

It is also essential to bind a user, group, or entity to the resources each is accessing. Resources can include data, applications, services, servers, storage, processes, printers, or anything that represents an asset to the organization that can be utilized by a user. Every resource, no matter how mundane, is an asset that must be afforded protection from unwanted influences and unauthorized use. This includes important resources like internally developed software, manufacturing systems, employee personnel files, or secret product formulas. However, it may also include often-overlooked resources like printers, fax machines, and even office supplies. The actual amount of protection to give each resource may be based on a cost–benefit analysis of the effort required to provide the protection or it may be based on a particular risk or threat model favored by the organization. Once the required resources are determined, then controls can be defined to specify the level of access.

Step 2: Determining Users

The next step in managing access control is defining who can access a given resource. The concept of identifying who are permitted access and providing the credentials necessary for their role is fundamental to security and ancient in practice. In early tribal cultures, a rite of passage consisted of obtaining a specific garment, marking, or even a scar signifying you were approved for various activities within the tribe, which translated to access. As populations grew and became more sophisticated, new methods were developed to provide access to an approved community. Over 4000 years ago, the Egyptians developed the first lock-and-key systems. Wooden locks were operated by a wooden key that controlled pins to disengage a bolt and permit access to the protected object. The key would be provided only to those who had been identified as needing access. Although seemingly primitive by today's standards (after all, how long would a wooden lock protect a modern file cabinet?), the technology and social conventions of the day allowed this to be quite an effective mechanism in ancient Egypt. Today security professionals continue the tradition of using the latest in available technology to protect valuable assets.

A typical environment must manage employees, contractors, consultants, partners, clients, or even, on occasion, competitors that organizations need to identify as requiring access of one kind or another. The act of specifying which users can have access to a system is typically driven by an operational demand, such as providing access to an accounting system so that users in the financial department can record and pay bills. Access control decisions are often based on organizational, social, or political considerations as well. One's personal or functional status within the organization may dictate the type or scope of access to organizational assets that may be allotted. A company CEO is rarely denied access to any organizational asset he may request; despite the fact that his explicit need to have that information may not be readily apparent. While this may not be the preferable method of determining access rights, a real-world information security manager should be prepared to deal with such situations.

The most significant aspect of determining which users will be provided access is a clear understanding of the needs of the user and the level of trust given to that person or entity. An identification process must exist that takes into consideration the validity of the access need in the light of business needs, organizational policy, legal requirements, information sensitivity, and security risk. It is important to understand that with each new user or community, the threat profile of an organization changes. For example, an organization may determine that one of its partners needs access to a given system. Upon providing that access, the potential threats to the organization now include that partner organization. Not only must the relationship be founded on trust, established by legal or other mechanisms between the two entities, but it must also now consider the increase in the number of users, thereby increasing the potential sources of threat. The more sophisticated the access control system, the greater the number of options to support various access demands in a secure fashion. It is not uncommon for organizations to have several different access control strategies to accommodate various needs, resulting in the provisioning of multiple unique access solutions. However, this is not considered as a security best practice, and the objective is to have a consistent access control strategy to avoid too much complexity. The more the complexity that exists in any system, including access control systems, the more likely it is that unexpected interactions will cause security flaws to be exposed. Simplicity is the key to any effective security system. The overall goal, then, is to strike an effective balance between the need to manage the complex access needs of an organization and the need to keep the access control system as simple as possible to understand and manage.

Step 3: Specifying Use

The final step in the access control process is to specify the level of use for a given resource and the permitted user actions on that resource. Take, for example, the files and data resident on a typical computer. Most file systems provide multiple levels of permissions, such as read, write, and execute. Depending on the file system used to store data, there may be methods of permitting much more granular controls. These may include the ability to provide access to a specific user, but only permitting him or her to perform a certain task. For example, a user with the role of "data backup" will be allowed to perform administrative functions such as "copy to tape," but not to erase or alter the information. (Access permissions will be covered in greater detail later in this chapter.) Additionally, a user may have the need to run an application, and therefore be provided execute privileges. However, he may not have write privileges, to ensure that he cannot modify the application. The same philosophy can be applied to any resource, and access controls should be used to support an organization's business functionality. For example, to restrict a user's ability to access specific printers based on a particular organizational structure. This would, as an example, allow a department to restrict high-cost color printing to only the members of the graphics or marketing departments. Not only would this properly restrict access to valuable and expensive resources, it might also aid the organization's cost allocation efforts by ensuring that charges for those resources are allocated only to those who must use them. As another example, an organization that needs to restrict printing and duplication of sensitive or classified documents may allow any user to send a print job to a particular printer, but require another level of approval from an authorized official to actually print the document in order to avoid policy violations.

Ultimately, once a user is identified and authenticated, an access control system must be sensitive to the level of authorization for that user to use the identified resources. Therefore, it is not enough to simply identify and authenticate a user in order to access resources. It is also necessary to control what actions are permitted for a specified resource based on the user's role (unless, of course, "unlimited access" is the organizational policy).

Access Control Principles

Access Control Policy

The first element of an effective access control program is to establish an access control policy and associated standards and procedures. An access control policy specifies the guidelines for how users are identified and authenticated and the level of access granted to resources. The existence of an access control policy ensures that decisions governing the access to enterprise assets are based on a formalized organizational directive. The absence of a policy will result in inconsistencies in provisioning, management, and administration of access controls. The policy will provide the framework for the definition of necessary procedures, guidelines, standards, and best practices concerning the oversight of access management.

Separation of Duties

It is often possible to enable effective access controls by altering the way people perform their work functions. The primary objective of separation of duties is the prevention of fraud and errors. This objective is achieved by distributing the tasks and associated privileges for a specific process among multiple people. It acts as a deterrent to fraud or concealment because collusion with another individual is required to complete a fraudulent act, ensuring that no individual acting alone can compromise the security of a system or gain unauthorized access to data. Of course, just because separation of duties is established for a given process does not mean that fraud is impossible to carry out; it just means that it is more difficult. People are generally averse to include others in the planning of criminal acts, so forcing collusion to happen in order to carry out such an act reduces the overall risk of its occurrence.

The first action to employ separation of duties in a process or work function is defining the individual elements of that process. Processes are typically a collection of tasks that must be performed to achieve an objective. Examples of common processes include performing backups, copying

17

files, or granting system access. Work functions can also encompass highly complex and potentially vital (or dangerous) business elements that should not be in the control of any one person. A common example is the process of creating and approving requisitions for purchasing expensive items. The person who requests the expenditure should not also be allowed to approve the expenditure. This prevents a single person from creating and receiving fraudulent payments. A less common, though more dangerous, example from the military is the ability to launch nuclear missiles. One person may have the ability to arm the missile but not execute the launch sequence. Another person may have the ability to launch the missile but not arm its payload. Finally, neither person can do anything without receiving proper authorization from the President. In this case, all three people are needed in order to successfully launch an armed missile. This safeguard ensures that a single person with a political agenda (or just having a particularly bad day) will not be able to start a global nuclear war.

To determine the applicability of separation of duties, two distinct factors must be addressed: the sensitivity of the function under consideration and the elements within a process that lend themselves to distribution. Sensitivity of the function takes into consideration the criticality of the job performed and potential exposure to fraud, misuse, or negligence. It will be necessary to evaluate the importance of a given transaction and its relationship to enterprise security risk, operations, and, of course, C-I-A factors. It is important to be aware that seemingly mundane tasks may also sometimes require separation of duties practices. For example, a single user performing both backup and restore procedures would have the ability to manipulate or destroy the backup data to cover unauthorized activity, change information, or destroy valuable resources undetected.

There are other activities within an organization that are not only important when considering separation of duties, but their technical and procedural architecture also assists in establishing these controls as well. For example, in application development there are typically separate development, testing, and production environments. The integrity of libraries used for the development is critical, and it is important that live systems and proprietary information should not be used within the testing environment to mitigate the risk of exposing sensitive information. Therefore, the development environment needs to follow strict separation of duties throughout the process in order to ensure that code and data follow strict change management processes and access by personnel between these areas is restricted. This reduces the risk of changes being made to the code once it has been tested and ensures the integrity of the tested code and that the production code is maintained.

The second factor when determining the applicability of separation of duties is understanding what elements within a function are prone to abuse, which ones are easily segmented without significantly disrupting operations, and what skills are available to the pool of users performing the different elements of the function. These can be summarized as

1. Element identification, importance, and criticality
2. Operational considerations
3. User skills and availability

Element Identification, Importance, and Criticality

Each function will have one or more elements that must be performed to complete the transaction. Some elements within a function, known as milestone elements, may lend themselves to offer opportunities for fraud or abuse. Such cases would then require a different user with unique privileges to complete that element. To ensure that a process runs as efficiently as possible within a separation of duties environment, it may be possible to collect different elements into groups that together represent a milestone element. The key is to evaluate each element and the role it plays in performing the function. Once each element is assessed against the potential for abuse, they can begin to be distributed to various users.

In the event that a collection of elements within a function does not offer a clear point of segmentation, it may be necessary to incorporate a new milestone element as a validation and approval point within the function. For example, at a specific point in a process, a manager can send an e-mail, apply a digital signature, or add a validation mark to the data. That additional notification or mark must be present for the primary user to continue the remaining processes.

Operational Considerations

One of the key attributes of a successful security program is integrating effectively within the business or operational goals of the organization. When considering separation of duties, the impact to the function and its role in the business are essential to overall success. When implemented poorly, or without taking overall business goals into account, security-related processes like separation of duties can hinder the process and make it prone to circumvention.

The impact to the operations must be taken into account whenever establishing separation of duties practices for a function. The security manager must consider the impact to the efficient operation of the function as well as the meaningful alternative options in the event there is a system failure or outage. It is important not to sacrifice security, but rather to have alternate compensating controls that can meet the objectives for security.

In addition, the cost of implementing separation of duties within a business process must be weighed against the overall risk that process represents to the organization and whether the benefits of separation outweigh the time and effort costs to the organization. In the separation of duties example of arming and launching nuclear missiles, it can be nearly universally agreed that the cost of implementing separation in such a circumstance is greatly outweighed by the risk and potential harm that could come from a non-separated nuclear environment. Conversely, most would agree that implementing separation of duties in a cafeteria's tuna sandwich-making process would not make a great deal of sense. While it is true that a malevolent sandwich maker could intentionally inflict illness or even death upon unsuspecting patrons, the actual incidence of such an occurrence is relatively low and the addition of the extra personnel required for such a low-risk situation would be very costly to the organization.

User Skills and Availability

Clearly, separation of duties requires multiple participants, and each of those participants must have the appropriate skills and training to perform the specific element of a given function. Additionally, there must be enough personnel to perform all the elements that have been distributed. In organizations that have small staffs, pure separation of duties may not be feasible. For example, a common separation practice is to ensure that those who develop software programs should not have access to the production environments where those programs are run. Those who run and maintain the production environment should be a separate and distinct group from the development team. This separation prevents a rogue developer from introducing malicious code directly into a production system. Unfortunately, many small development shops and start-up companies cannot afford the extra personnel that such a separation environment requires. Staffing those extra positions may just mean the difference between a successful business and bankruptcy. Given the tradeoff between the benefits of separation (prevention against malicious code) and the cost of separation (double the salary expense), a reasonable business owner might opt against separation, preferring instead to instill other mitigating controls to reduce the risk, such as a strong change management process and code reviews.

The following concepts are important in ensuring appropriate application in policy and practice:

> *Least Privilege:* The principle of least privilege is one of the most fundamental characteristics of access control for meeting security objectives. Least privilege requires that a user or process be given no more access privilege than necessary to perform a job, task, or function. The objective is to limit users and processes to access only

21

resources and tools necessary to perform assigned functions. This often requires limits not only on what resources can be accessed, but also includes limiting the actions that can be performed by the user even if they have authorized access to the resource. For example, a user may be restricted to only read-only, update, and execute permission on a system without the ability to create or delete files and databases. Ensuring least privilege requires identifying what the user's job is, determining the minimum set of privileges required to perform that job, and restricting the user to a domain with those privileges and nothing more. Denying users access privileges that are not necessary for the performance of their duties ensures that those privileges cannot be used to circumvent the organization's security policy.

Need to Know: A companion concept to least privilege is the notion of need to know. If the goal of least privilege is to reduce access to a bare minimum, need to know defines that minimum as a need for that access based on job or business requirements. For example, although the CIO in an organization has the appropriate rank in the organization to view upcoming quarterly financial forecasts, the organization's comptroller may decide that the CIO does not have a need to know that information and, thus, restrict access to it. Need to know is also used heavily in situations where operational secrecy is a key concern, such as in military operations. Military leaders often keep operational plans on a need to know basis to reduce the number of people who know about the plans and reduce the risk that someone will leak that information to the enemy.

Compartmentalization: Finally, compartmentalization completes the least privilege picture. Compartmentalization is the process of separating groups of people and information such that each group is isolated from the others and information does not flow between groups. For example, an organization might compartmentalize (both logically and physically) a team working on mergers and acquisitions so that the information that team is working on will not leak to the general employee population and lead to a potential insider trading problem. Compartmentalization is helpful in situations where information needs to stay contained within a single group or area and strong protections need to be taken to keep that information from leaking outside the area.

Security Domain: A security domain is an area where common processes and security controls work to separate all entities involved in these processes from other entities or security domains. For example, all systems and users managing financial information might be separated into their own security domain, and all systems involved in e-commerce activity might get their own security domain. A security domain is based on trust between resources or services in areas or systems that share a single security policy and a single management structure. The trust is the unique context in which a program is operating. There may be multiple security domains within an organization and an entity may, at times, belong to more than one security domain based on its responsibilities and functions at any given time. The separation between domains can be either physically or logically managed. Security domains support a hierarchical relationship where subjects can access objects in equal or lower domains; therefore, domains with higher privileges are protected from domains with lesser privileges.

In *Figure 1.5*, three distinct and separate security domains exist on the server, and only those individuals or subjects authorized can have access to the information on a particular domain.

A subject's domain, which contains all of the objects that the subject can access, is kept isolated. Shared objects may have more than one access by subjects, and this allows this concept to work. For example, if a hundred subjects have access to the same object, that object has to appear in a hundred different domains to allow this isolation.

Information Classification

Many organizations have thousands, even millions, of data files containing valuable information on all aspects of the organization's business. Information is created in great volumes on a daily basis from a variety of transactional systems, as well as aggregated into databases and data warehouses to provide decision-making support. The information is stored on backup tapes, copied to portable USB drives, and burned to CDs and DVDs for portability. Information is stored on portable computers and network drives, and in e-mail systems to support the sharing of information.

The same information is printed and filed, and stored off site for business continuity and disaster recovery purposes. A file will typically have multiple versions, will be stored in multiple locations, and is capable of being accessed by different individuals in each of these locations. Fundamental security questions are raised in this type of environment. Where is the organization's information? How should the information be handled and protected? Who should have access to it? Who owns the information? Who makes the decisions around these parameters? These questions form the impetus for implementing an information classification strategy. Information classification is the practice of evaluating the risk level of the organization's information to ensure that the information receives the appropriate level of protection. The application of security controls to information has a cost of time, people, hardware, software, and ongoing maintenance resources that must be considered.

Applying the same level of control to all of the company's assets wastes resources and money by overprotecting some information and underprotecting other information. In an effort to simplify security budget management, security dollars are often spent uniformly to protect all assets at the same level. Not all assets have the same value or need the same level of protection. The budget could be better allocated, and the security of the organization better managed, by providing only basic protection to assets of little value and providing increased protection to those assets considered

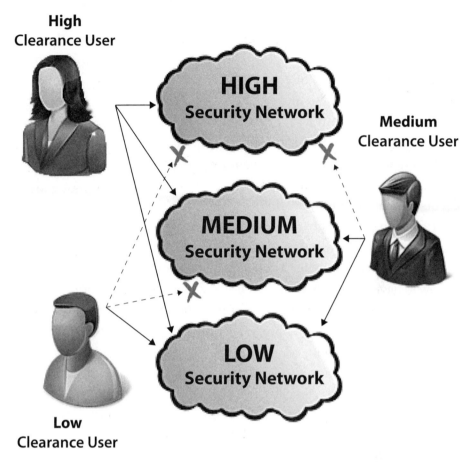

High
Clearance User

HIGH
Security Network

Medium
Clearance User

MEDIUM
Security Network

LOW
Security Network

Low
Clearance User

Figure 1.5 - **Three distinct and separate security domains exist on the server. Only those individuals or subjects authorized can have access to the information on a particular domain.**

to be of greater value or higher sensitivity. By applying protection controls to the information based upon the classification, the organization gains efficiencies and thus reduces the overall cost of information security. The primary objective of information classification, therefore, is to group an organization's information assets by levels of sensitivity and criticality. Once this is done, the organization then applies the appropriate level of protection controls to each asset in accordance with the classification assigned to it.

25

Information Classification Benefits

There are many benefits in classifying information within an organization. First, classification helps to establish ownership of the information, which provides a central point of control for all aspects of security and access to the information. This increases the likelihood that the information will be used in the proper context and those accessing the information will be properly authorized. Information classification also increases the confidentiality, integrity, and availability of information by focusing an organization's limited security funds on the resources requiring the highest level of protection and providing lesser controls for the information with less risk of loss. By understanding the information and its location, the organization can identify areas that may need higher levels of protection. Information classification can also have a positive effect on the knowledge and awareness of security within an organization. A classification program allows for greater understanding of the value of the information to be protected, and provides a clearer direction for the handling of sensitive information. In addition, a periodic review of the classification scheme and controls helps personnel maintain awareness of the importance of protecting information. Finally, the process itself helps create a greater organizational awareness of the need to protect company information.

Information classification can also have an operational benefit to the organization. Critical information can be identified to support business recovery scenarios by focusing the recovery efforts on the most critical areas. Placement of information with higher levels of classification on more reliable storage and backup mechanisms helps reduce recovery times. Organizations can also reduce the expense of inefficient storage for non-sensitive information in data storage or physical file cabinets through the use of a well-planned information classification program.

Establishing an Information Classification Program

Establishing an information classification strategy and developing plans for implementation may seem a bit onerous for an organization that has never had such a program before. However, once the work of defining the classification levels and determining the classification of the individual information has been completed, the value to the organization is well worth the effort. The following sections walk through the steps of establishing and sustaining an information classification program. Although the exact path each organization takes may be a bit different, the steps identified are a good representation of the major steps involved in programs of this type. The exact sequence or the steps included may also vary or be combined, depending upon the size, complexity, and culture of the organization. The basic steps are

1. Determine inforation classification program objectives.
2. Establish organizational support.
3. Develop an information classification policy and supporting procedures.
4. Develop information classification process flows and procedures.
5. Develop tools to support the process.
6. Identify process or application owners.
7. Identify information owners and delegates.
8. Distribute standard templates.
9. Classify information and applications.
10. Develop auditing procedures.
11. Load classification information into a central repository.
12. Train users.
13. Periodically review and update information classifications.

Step 1: Determine Information Classification Program Objectives

It is helpful to document the specific program objectives to give the program a clear vision of its goals and to help define and explain the program to others in the organization. Defining clear objectives also helps to contain the scope of the effort and determine when deliverables are completed, so that these accomplishments may be celebrated to sustain those involved in later phases of the project. The objectives are also important for obtaining the support of those needed to both endorse and carry out the program.

It is very important when defining the overall program objectives to clearly establish that information classification is a program, not a project. A project is a series of tasks that lead to a known end state. A program, on the other hand, is a change in organization process and behavior that will have long-term lasting impact to the organization. Implementing information classification in an organization will change the way the organization thinks about and manages information permanently and, thus, has no defined end state to speak of. It is truly a program in all meaningful respects and should always be referred to as such.

Step 2: Establish Organizational Support

Senior management support is essential to the start-up and continued operation of the information classification program. The program should be socialized with senior management by using business-focused benefits, as well as highlighting enhancements to the effectiveness of the organization. There may be a perception within the organization that all information should be treated as confidential and is adequately secured by physical barriers to the facility, firewalls, and other security controls protecting the environment. This view promotes the concept that all information should be protected equally. Unfortunately, the reality is that information resources should be given the appropriate protection based on their overall risk and threat profile: no more and no less. The security professional should work through the cost/benefit discussion with senior management to illustrate how the appropriate application of security controls is the most effective approach to benefit the business. Although security professionals understand the importance of information classification, without the proper positioning of the effort, the organization's senior management and end users may perceive the effort as another project requiring their resources, with little payback to individual departments. Some examples of the benefits that the organization may realize as a result of these efforts include:

- Ensuring confidentiality of information by restricting who can access or copy the information

- Increased accuracy and integrity of information by controlling who can modify or update the information

- Increased availability of information by restricting the ability to overwrite or erase important or critical data

- Avoiding damage to the organization's reputation by reducing the risk of unauthorized disclosures

- Reduction in costs of overprotection

- Ability for managers to enforce accountability

- Protection of intellectual property and trade secrets

- Protection of customer or consumer confidential information

- Compliance with industry regulation or legal requirements to protect personally identifiable information

Step 3: Develop an Information Classification Policy and Supporting Procedures

The information classification policy communicates the requirement to the organization to classify the information assets. The policy also communicates the primary purpose of information classification, which is to ensure that the appropriate protections are applied according to the level of sensitivity, risk, and criticality. The policy statement is a description of the requirement, including the scope of users and systems to which the policy applies, as well as what is expected of those affected by the program. The policy should describe the overall information classification framework and the meaning of each level or categorization within the framework.

The policy may also indicate the responsibilities of users and management in handling the information. Policies are generally written at a high level, with the details reserved for supporting procedures. The procedures communicate how to determine the classification of a particular information item, as well as how that information should be subsequently handled and protected. Involvement with business or application owners, as well as the IT department, is important in determining the various procedure and control matrices. This establishes business owners' buy-in to the procedures, and provides an operational perspective for determining how the information should be managed.

Step 4: Develop Information Classification Process Flow and Procedures

Documented procedures assist in the ongoing operation of classifying information. Because the organization may have many files that have not been looked at through the information classification lens, the start-up effort to develop these flows and procedures may require a large amount of resources. Ongoing efforts will also require that the information is reviewed and updated on a periodic basis. The initial gathering of the information classifications and the process utilized must be driven by a documented procedure so that all of the parties involved in the effort are aware of their individual roles and requirements to complete the classification. Flowcharts in addition to the documented written processes can be helpful, as individuals receive and retain information through different means. The documentation of the process also helps ensure that the classification process is handled uniformly throughout the organization.

Step 5: Develop or Acquire Tools to Support Process

Various tools, such as word processing documents, spreadsheets, databases, and presentations, support the collection process. Standardized templates facilitate collection as well as the ability to generate reports by data type to ensure that the designations are consistent across the enterprise and follow the prescribed information classification policy and associated standards. Once the chosen media and forms are distributed to the individuals completing the information, the results can be exported to a database for consolidation, review, and ongoing maintenance.

Step 6: Identify Process or Application Owners

The business owner of each application provides the functional requirements for what data is necessary for the business. The owner will have the most intimate knowledge of the data and how they are used. Apart from the business owner, the systems or information technology owner may act primarily as a data custodian of the information and must understand the processing, technical, storage, and security protections of the information. Both individuals contribute to an understanding of the classification requirements and is identified as part of the process. The relationship between the information owner, system owner and application owner will greatly influence the ability to make changes and identify stakeholders. When an information system owner and information owner are one and the same they generally have a greater motivation to make system security enhances which protect the information they must protect.

Step 7: Identify Information Owners and Delegates

Information owners are those people in the organization who understand the information in their area of the business and have the ultimate responsibility for making decisions about the usage of the information. They may manage the responsibility or assign designees or information delegates that are empowered to make the day-to-day operational decisions as to who is allowed to read, modify, or delete the business information. The owners and delegates are the primary individuals who are involved in the classification process, as they have the greatest business knowledge of the information in question.

Step 8: Distribute Standard Templates

Providing standard information classification templates to data owners promotes uniform data gathering and makes the subsequent tasks of tracking and analysis of the information much easier. The templates may be part of the tools developed in Step 5. These templates should be distributed to the information owners or delegates to collect the classification information on the data managed by their departments.

Step 9: Classify Information and Applications

Once the templates have been distributed, the data owners (or their delegates) use the information classification policy and standards to classify the information. Typically there are three to four levels of information classification used by most organizations:

- **Public:** Information that may be disclosed to the general public without concern for harming the company, employees, or business partners. No special protections are required, and information in this category is sometimes referred to as unclassified. For example, information that is posted to a company's public Internet site, publicly released announcements, marketing materials, cafeteria menus, and any internal documents that would not present harm to the company if they were disclosed would be classified as public. While there is little concern for confidentiality, integrity and availability should be considered.

- **Internal Use Only:** Information that could be disclosed within the company, but could harm the company if disclosed externally. Information such as customer lists, vendor pricing, organizational policies, standards and procedures, and internal organization announcements would need baseline security protections, but do not rise to the level of protection as confidential information. In other words, the information may be used freely within the company but any unapproved use outside the company can pose a chance of harm.

- **Confidential:** Information that, if released or disclosed outside of the organization, would create severe problems for the organization. For example, information that provides a competitive advantage is important to the technical or financial success (like trade secrets, intellectual property, or research designs), or protects the privacy of individuals would be considered confidential. Information may include payroll information, health records, credit information, formulas, technical designs, restricted regulatory information, senior management internal correspondence, or business strategies or plans. These may also be called top secret, privileged, personal, sensitive, or highly confidential. In other words this information is ok within a defined group in the company such as marketing or sales, but is not suited for release to anyone else in the company without permission.

■ *Restricted:* Information that requires the utmost protection or, if discovered by unauthorized personnel, would cause irreparable harm to the organization would have the highest level of classification. There may be very few pieces of information like this within an organization, but data classified at this level requires all the access control and protection mechanisms available to the organization. Even when information classified at this level exists, there will be few copies of it around, and tracking who has this information, when they received it, and when they returned it are extremely important. Information of this type includes merger and acquisition information, financial forecasts, or anything that (if publicly known) would materially affect the market status or stock price of the company. In other works information of this type is typically only suitable for a select few individuals such as "C" level executives and cause grave damage to the company if released outside of this group.

An important point to consider is that this process may take a long time to complete, especially if you are analyzing and classifying a large environment with complex data relationships. When faced with such a seemingly daunting task, data owners will often react by arguing against the process based on the cost of the analysis alone or relegating the project to back-burner status where it will receive little, if any, attention. It is important to work with all the data owners and senior management to ensure that the program remains on track. There are some steps you can take to reduce the amount of time required for the initial classification effort. For example, a data owner may have a database with thousands of intermingled data elements fitting into all three classification levels. Rather than classifying each individual data element and applying appropriate controls at the element level, the owner may elect to reorganize the database into public and nonpublic data sets and apply the appropriate controls in aggregate to each data set. While the process of such aggregation may lead to the oversimplification problem mentioned earlier, if applied judiciously it can lead to enormous time savings during the classification process and cost savings during the implementation of protection controls.

During the planning and design of the classification program some consideration should be given to the classification of aggregate data. This is information that would not be considered sensitive when taken alone, but, when combined with other data, suddenly becomes sensitive and worthy of additional protection. For example, a bank routing number (the number found at the bottom of a check that uniquely identifies a U.S. financial institution) by itself would not be considered particularly sensitive by a data owner. Routing numbers are public information easily found through a simple Internet search. However, when that routing number is combined with an individual account number at that bank, the combination of the two suddenly becomes very sensitive, because a thief can use that combination to access that individual's bank account. Data owners need to be aware of the dangers of aggregate data and account for them during the classification of their information.

In many circumstances one organization will be managing information on behalf of another organization. For example, many companies outsource their payroll processing to third parties and many banks outsource their IT systems (including account management) to third-party service providers. In these cases, the company that owns the information and the service provider may each have its own classification systems. It is important that each party understand the other's classification system and the information owner must ensure that the classification assigned to its information by the service provider (as well as the underlying protection mechanisms for that classification) meets its needs for adequate information protection.

Step 10 Develop Auditing Procedures

Once information is classified, classifications rarely change unless the information has been misclassified, the information that previously required protection is now public knowledge, or time has made wider disclosure of the information less harmful to the organization. In most cases, if there was a reason to protect the information initially to a certain level, then the information will continue to be protected at this same level through its useful life. However, new data are always being generated and needs to be classified. Existing data should also be periodically reviewed to ensure that the classifications are correct. Information classification auditing is the process of reviewing the classifications to ensure the accuracy of the information, thus ensuring that the appropriate security protections continue to be applied. An information classification audit often relies on performing "spot" tests such as observations of sensitive information left unprotected in work spaces (also known as a clean desk/clear screen check) and checking of trash receptacles for discarded sensitive information as a method to measure compliance with the information classification policy.

Step 11: Load Clssification Information into a Central Repository.

The classification information obtained through the classification procedures and templates is loaded into a central repository to support the analysis of the collections, as well as to serve as the database for the ongoing updating of the classifications. A database tool provides the ability to examine the information from multiple perspectives, such as listing all of the data types owned by a particular data owner, all of the data types of a particular classification level, or what data types are associated with which applications. Depending on the amount of assets being classified and the complexity of the classification scheme, the database may grow to considerable size. Careful planning is important to ensure adequate space and processing capacity for the future.

Step 12: Train Users

If the end user or employee does not understand what information is public, internal user only, or confidential, or if the user does not understand the requirements and differences in how to handle each type of information, then the investment in information classification will have limited success. It is critical that the user community gets proper training in the classification program because they (the users) are the ones who will work with the program on a daily basis. The training program must convey the purpose and importance of the program and provide the proper motivation for users to support the classification effort. Training should include information on the overall policies and the various classification levels the organization will use. Most importantly, the training should give practical examples of different types of information the users will come in contact with and how to properly handle and protect that information using the official standards and protection controls.

Step 13: Periodically Review

Periodically review and Update Information Classifications: Information within an organization rarely remains static. To ensure that the organization continues to match current threats with appropriate information protections, the classifications assigned to information must be reviewed on a periodic basis. It is most likely that the classifications will not change dramatically, but adjustments may be needed. Scheduling auditing procedures on a periodic basis increases the quality of the information classification program, as does providing the capability to update and add new information classifications outside of the normal cycle.

Labeling and Marking

The labeling and marking of media with classification levels provides the ability to manage the information contained within the media with the handling instructions appropriate to the respective classification. For example, a backup tape may be labeled with a serial number and "Company Confidential" to indicate how the information should be treated. Organizations may decide not to label individual information, but rather control all the information within a business area or location according to restrictions based upon a single classification type. For example, all backup tapes in the tape library may be classified as "Confidential" and have appropriate controls placed on the whole library.

Labeling and marking information also apply to all forms of systems and media that manage or display classified information. This includes application displays, printouts, and reports generated from organization systems. All these must have the appropriate classification verbiage displayed or printed alongside the information to ensure that all who come in contact with that information know the classification level and are able to take the appropriate protective measures.

Information Classification Assurance

Periodically testing the information classifications provides assurance that the activities are being properly performed. The audit procedures will uncover those data types that need to be added or reclassified. Random audits of user areas, such as checking desktops for confidential documents not returned to file drawers, information left overnight in open shredding bins, files in electronic file folders accessible by anyone within the organization, confidential information posted to a public Web site, or information left on copiers, printers, and fax machines, can provide information regarding organizational compliance. Encouraging end users to report security incidents related to mishandling of classified information can also be a source to provide assurance. The information security manager should work closely with the organization's internal audit manager to establish information classification reviews as part of the standard audit program. In this way, the audit group can assist in ensuring the continual monitoring of the classification program including the assurance that new information is classified appropriately as it enters the environment.

Access Control Requirements

As simple as it may seem, implementing an effective access control system—whether for a single application or for an entire enterprise—takes careful planning, research, foresight, and (of course) a great deal of persuasive skill to bring together all the disparate interests in the organization to agree on the best way to move forward. However, none of this can proceed without first considering the basic requirements that any access control system must meet. While each enterprise or application will have its own specific access control needs, there are some basic considerations that all security professionals must look for in an access control system, process, or technology. This section will discuss several of those requirements.

Reliability

First and foremost, any access control system under consideration must be reliable enough to give consistent results every time. The reliability of a system has both physical and logical components. Both are important to consider when determining the best path for an organization to take. An access control system must operate within the same physical environmental constraints under which its users operate. This means that all the environmental factors that assist or hinder its users will have the same effect on the access control system. Factors such as heat, humidity, complexity, wear and tear on components, and user attitude will all have an effect on the long-term viability of the environment. For example, if a badge reading system is used in a busy area (like a hospital emergency room or fire house) it will most likely be subject to physical abuse as users hurry to swipe their cards through the reader, perhaps knocking or banging it repeatedly in the process. It will get heavily abused as frustrated and busy users take out their frustration on the reader. Likewise, an access control system located at a boat marina or at a military facility in the desert will be subject to heat and moisture extremes that must be considered and tested before final acceptance.

While the physical aspects of reliability are important, they can usually be addressed by better material selection, manufacturing quality, and testing. What is often more difficult to determine during the research and product selection stage is the product's ability to work reliably and accurately over a long period of time. The product must have the ability to minimize false positives and negatives, make accurate authentication and authorization decisions, follow organizational policies (as defined within the product) unambiguously, and function predictably according to the expectations of the organization. Reliability of the system is a fundamental requirement, for without it the organization cannot place any confidence in the system or its results. An access control system that fails may even cause a complete denial of service to the organization. The inability to trust in the accuracy and reliability of an access control system will cause the entire access control infrastructure to collapse.

Transparency

Security (more specifically, the implementation of most security controls) has long been a sore point with users who are subject to security controls. Historically, security controls have been very intrusive to users, forcing them to interrupt their work flow and remember arcane codes or processes (like long passwords or access codes), and have generally been seen as an obstacle to getting work done. In recent years, much work has been done to remove that stigma of security controls as a detractor from the work process adding nothing but time and money. When developing access control, the system must be as transparent as possible to the end user. The users should be required to interact with the system as little as possible, and the process around using the control should be engineered so as to involve little effort on the part of the user.

For example, requiring a user to swipe an access card through a reader is an effective way to ensure a person is authorized to enter a room. However, implementing a technology (such as RFID) that will automatically scan the badge as the user approaches the door is more transparent to the user and will do less to impede the movement of personnel in a busy area. In another example, asking a user to understand what applications and data sets will be required when requesting a system ID and then specifically requesting access to those resources may allow for a great deal of granularity when provisioning access, but it can hardly be seen as transparent.

A more transparent process would be for the access provisioning system to have a role-based structure, where the user would simply specify the role he or she has in the organization and the system would know the specific resources that user needs to access based on that role. This requires less work and interaction on the part of the user and will lead to more accurate and secure access control decisions because access will be based on predefined need, not user preference. When developing and implementing an access control system special care should be taken to ensure that the control is as transparent to the end user as possible and interrupts his work flow as little as possible.

Scalability

Setting up an access control system for five people can be hard. Setting up an access control system for 5,000—or 50,000—people is really hard. Ensuring the same system originally developed for five will work just as well for 50,000 can be next to impossible. When establishing an access control system, the security professional should always assume that the system will grow beyond original expectations and ensure the capacity of the technology and the process scales accordingly. Advances in cloud computing and "software as a service" has reduced scalability concerns from many organizations; however, prudent planning should be conducted to ensure an organization's information systems can accommodate future growth.

Several models and "rules" exist for capacity planning. These rules and models make certain assumptions about the industry, user base and type of information or processes the system supports. Information security professionals need to understand their industry, the types of information and processes they are supporting and what kind of growth or contraction can be expected in information system use.

Initial capacity estimates may suffice for a project's original needs and purposes, but the security professional should assume that the system will grow well beyond original estimates and should plan, as much as reasonably possible, to ensure that any given solution has the ability to scale with that growth.

Integrity

Maintaining the integrity of the system includes many facets. Most notably, assuring that only authorized personnel have access to the administrative functions of the system. An attacker gaining the ability to manage the configuration of the access control system would have the ability to establish valid user credentials, alter or erase log and audit data, cause denial-of-service situations, or establish operational rules to selectively allow or deny users access to the protected system. Ensuring that only authorized personnel have access to administer the system goes a long way toward ensuring the integrity of the access control function. Regular testing of the access control function will ensure that the service maintains its integrity over time. As the system remains in continuous use it may begin to lose sensitivity, components may begin to wear out, or continuous administrative updates may introduce conflicts or obsolescence in the access rule set. Regular administrative care and testing will ensure that the system continues to operate within expected functional parameters and that any deviations from those parameters are caught early and corrected.

Maintainability

The access control system should require a minimum of maintenance to function properly over an extended period of time. Naturally, the physical components of the system may wear out over time, such as card readers, keypads, or support systems, and the cost and effort to maintain these components should be calculated into the overall business case for the system. However, the personnel effort to maintain the system should not be underestimated or overlooked.

Depending on the type of technology in use, the administrative effort required to keep the system in proper working order can be considerable or require specialized skills that may be expensive to acquire or maintain.

Overall, however, an effective access control system is one that requires a minimum of maintenance oversight or continuous tuning. Administrative effort and fine tuning should be concentrated on updating rule sets, managing user populations, and policy development. The management of these functions should also require as little effort as possible. The administrative controls over the system should be straightforward to understand and simple to operate. A system that is overly complicated to understand or difficult to maintain is one that will either quickly fall into disorder or be replaced with a system that is easier to manage.

Authentication Data Security

Equally as important as the access control system is to an organization are the controls that protect the authentication data itself. The authentication data include user identities, passwords, biometric information, access capabilities, and a host of other sensitive information which, if obtained by an attacker, would provide a roadmap for infiltrating and navigating around an organization's information systems. The protections around the authentication database should be researched and tested before the system is implemented. Data encryption should be in place, system- and file-level access controls should be present, and strong authentication for administrative functions should be investigated.

Auditability

Even if the access control system operates perfectly within expected parameters and there are no apparent instances of system failure or unauthorized access, a complete audit trail of system activities is necessary to provide documented assurance that the system is functioning properly. The system should have the ability to provide a complete record of all access control activity. This includes authentication requests, data access attempts, changes to privilege levels, and exercise of administrative capabilities. It is extremely important that this activity is recorded for successful activity as well as failures. Too often, systems record only failed instances of the above activity. Unfortunately, if an attacker succeeds in gaining authorized access to the system, or if an authorized insider attempts to perform nefarious acts the system that only records event failures will fail to capture the activity of these individuals. This will lead to an inability to understand precisely what these individuals did within the system and a failure to properly investigate and prosecute (organizationally or legally) their activities.

Types & Categories of Access Controls

In the development of an access control architecture for an enterprise, it is necessary to fully understand the different categories and types of potential controls. This section will describe those different categories and discuss how each fits into the overall access control universe. This will also establish a foundation for later discussion on access control technology, practices, and processes.

There are literally hundreds of different access approaches, control methods, and technologies, both in the physical world and in the virtual electronic world. Each method addresses a different type of access control or a specific access need. For example, access control solutions may incorporate identification and authentication mechanisms, filters, rules, rights, logging and monitoring, policy, and a plethora of other controls. However, despite the diversity of access control methods, all access control systems can be categorized into seven primary categories. The seven main categories of access control are

1. **Directive:** Controls designed to specify acceptable rules of behavior within an organization

2. **Deterrent:** Controls designed to discourage people from violating security directives

3. **Preventive:** Controls implemented to prevent a security incident or information breach

4. **Compensating:** Controls implemented to substitute for the loss of primary controls and mitigate risk down to an acceptable level

5. **Detective:** Controls designed to signal a warning when a security control has been breached

6. **Corrective:** Controls implemented to remedy circumstance, mitigate damage, or restore controls

7. **Recovery:** Controls implemented to restore conditions to normal after a security incident

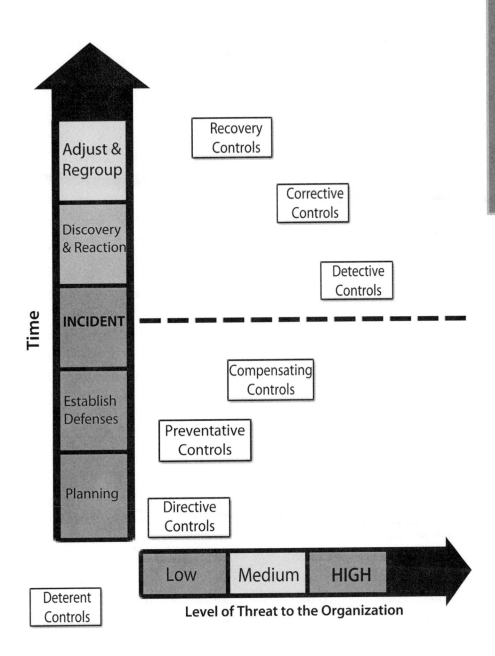

Figure 1.6 - **Continuum of controls relative to the time line of a security incident**

Figure 1.6 shows a continuum of controls relative to the time line of a security incident:

Directive Controls

Directive controls, sometimes referred to as administrative controls, provide guidance to personnel as to the expected behavior with respect to security within the organization. Directive controls provide users with the general guidelines they must follow if they are to be permitted access to information or systems. Directive controls are not only applicable to an organization's employees but contractors, guests, vendors, and anyone else who will have access to the organization's information systems must additionally abide by them.

The most common examples of directive controls are the organization's security policies and procedures. These documents provide the basis for information security throughout the organization and provide personnel with the model that must be adhered to as they perform their work. Although directive controls are generally implemented in the form of documented statements of organizational intent, they should not be considered optional or modifiable by organization personnel.

Directive controls have the weight of law within the organization and should be as strongly followed as any technical or procedural limitation. Many organizations compile their directive controls into a single acceptable use policy (AUP). The AUP provides a concise listing of the proper (and, in many cases improper) procedures, behaviors, and processes that all personnel must follow in order to gain and maintain access to information and systems within the organization. It is considered a best practice for all employees to agree to and sign the AUP before being granted access to any organizational resource. If the employee is unable (or unwilling) to abide by the terms of the AUP, no access will be granted. Many organizations require their employees to sign the AUP annually, either as part of the regular security awareness training or as part of the annual performance review process.

Deterrent Controls

Access controls act as a deterrent to threats and attacks by the simple fact that the existence of the control is enough to keep some potential attackers from attempting to circumvent the control. This is often because the effort required to circumvent the control is far greater than the potential reward if the attacker is successful, or, conversely, the negative implications of a failed attack (or getting caught) outweigh the benefits of success. For example, by forcing the identification and authentication of a user, service, or application, and all that it implies, the potential for incidents associated with the system is significantly reduced because an attacker will fear association with the incident. If there are no controls for a given access path, the number of incidents and the potential impact become infinite. Controls inherently reduce exposure to risk by applying oversight for a process. This oversight acts as a deterrent, curbing an attacker's appetite in the face of probable repercussions.

The best example of a deterrent control is demonstrated by employees and their propensity to intentionally perform unauthorized functions, leading to unwanted events. When users begin to understand that by authenticating into a system to perform a function, their activities are logged and monitored, and it reduces the likelihood they will attempt such an action. Many threats are based on the anonymity of the threat agent, and any potential for identification and association with their actions is avoided at all costs. It is this fundamental reason why access controls are the key target of circumvention by attackers. Deterrents also take the form of potential punishment if users do something unauthorized. For example, if the organization policy specifies that an employee installing an unauthorized wireless access point will be fired, that will deter most employees from installing wireless access points.

The effect deterrent controls have on a potential attacker will vary with both the type of control and the motivation of the attacker. For example, many organizations post a warning message to computer users during the login process indicating that their activities may be monitored. While this may deter a casual user from performing unauthorized activities, it will not stop a determined attacker from his goals. Likewise, implementing a multifactor authentication mechanism on an application will greatly reduce system compromises through such mechanisms as password guessing, but a sophisticated attacker may then turn to the use of a vulnerability scanning tool to determine if the system can be compromised through a host or network vulnerability. As the sophistication and the determination of an attacker rises, so does the sophistication and cost of an effective deterrent to prevent that attacker from attempting his attack.

Preventative Controls

Preventative access controls keep a user from performing some activity or function. Preventative controls differ from deterrent controls in that the control is not optional and cannot (easily) be bypassed. Deterrent controls work on the theory that it is easier to obey the control rather than to risk the consequences of bypassing the control. In other words, the power for action resides with the user (or the attacker). Preventative controls place the power of action with the system, obeying the control is not optional. The only way to bypass the control is to find a flaw in the control's implementation.

Compensating Controls

Compensating controls are introduced when the existing capabilities of a system do not support the requirement of a policy. Compensating controls can be technical, procedural, or managerial. Although an existing system may not support the required controls, there may exist other technology or processes that can supplement the existing environment, closing the gap in controls, meeting policy requirements, and reducing overall risk. For example, the access control policy may state that the authentication process must be encrypted when performed over the Internet. Adjusting an application to natively support encryption for authentication purposes may be too costly. Secure Socket Layer (SSL), an encryption protocol, can be employed and layered on top of the authentication process to support the policy statement. Other examples include a separation of duties environment, which offers the capability to isolate certain tasks to compensate for technical limitations in the system and ensure the security of transactions. In addition, management processes, such as authorization, supervision, and administration, can be used to compensate for gaps in the access control environment.

Keep in mind that it is typically not be possible to completely eliminate the risk in a given area while still allowing functionality. The use of compensating controls allows an organization to reduce that risk down to a level that is acceptable, or at least more manageable. Finally, compensating controls can be temporary solutions to accommodate a short-term change, or support the evolution of a new application, business development, or major project. Changes and temporary additions to access controls may be necessary for application testing, data center consolidation efforts, or even to support a brief business relationship with another company. The critical points to consider when addressing compensating controls are:

- Do not compromise stated policy requirements.
- Ensure that the compensating controls do not adversely affect risk or increase exposure to threats.
- Manage all compensating controls in accordance with established practices and policies.
- Compensating controls designated as temporary should be removed after they have served their purpose and another, more permanent control should be established.

Detective Controls

Detective controls warn when something has happened, and are the earliest point in the post-incident timeline. Access controls are a deterrent to threats and can be aggressively utilized to prevent harmful incidents through the application of least privilege. However, the detective nature of access controls can provide significant visibility into the access environment and help organizations manage their access strategy and related security risk. As mentioned previously, strongly managed access privileges provided to an authenticated user offer the ability to reduce the risk exposure of the enterprise's assets by limiting the capabilities that authenticated user has. However, there are few options to control what a user can perform once privileges are provided. For example, if a user is provided write access to a file and that file is damaged, altered, or otherwise negatively impacted (either deliberately or unintentionally), the use of applied access controls will offer visibility into the transaction. The control environment can be established to log activity regarding the identification, authentication, authorization, and use of privileges on a system. This can be used to detect the occurrence of errors, the attempts to perform an unauthorized action, or to validate when provided credentials were exercised. The logging system as a detective device provides evidence of actions (both successful and unsuccessful) and tasks that were executed by authorized users.

Detection aspects of access control can range from evidentiary, such as post incident investigations, to real-time alerting of inappropriate activities. This philosophy can be applied to many different characteristics of the security environment. Access detection can be triggered by intrusion detection systems (IDSs), virus controls, applications, Web filtering, network operations, administration, logs and audit trails, and security management systems. Visibility into the environment is a key factor in ensuring a comprehensive security posture and the ability to promptly detect problems in the environment.

Corrective Controls

When a security incident occurs, elements within the security infrastructure may require corrective actions. Corrective controls are actions that seek to alter the security posture of an environment to correct any deficiencies and return the environment to a secure state. A security incident signals the failure of one or more directive, deterrent, preventative, or compensating controls. The detective controls may have triggered an alarm or notification, but now the corrective controls must work to stop the incident in its tracks. Corrective controls can take many forms, all depending on the particular situation at hand or the particular security failure that needs to be dealt with.

The sheer number of corrective actions possible makes them difficult to successfully quantify. They can range from "quick fix" changes like new firewall rules, router access control list updates, and access policy changes to more long-term infrastructure changes like the introduction of certificates for wireless 802.1x authentication, movement from single-factor to multifactor authentication for remote access, or the introduction of smart cards for authentication. The difficulty in quantification is founded on the fact that access controls are universal throughout the environment. Nevertheless, it is important that a consistent and comprehensive management capability exists that can coordinate and employ corrective changes throughout the enterprise to enable policy compliance.

Recovery Controls

Any changes to the access control environment, whether in the face of a security incident or to offer temporary compensating controls, need to be accurately reinstated and returned to normal operations. There are several situations that may affect access controls, their applicability, status, or management. Events can include system outages, attacks, project changes, technical demands, administrative gaps, and full-blown disaster situations. For example, if an application is not correctly installed or deployed, it may adversely affect controls placed on system files or even have default administrative accounts unknowingly implemented upon install. Additionally, an employee may be transferred, quit, or be on temporary leave that may affect policy requirements regarding separation of duties. An attack on systems may have resulted in the implantation of a Trojan horse program, potentially exposing private user information, such as credit card information and financial data. In all of these cases, an undesirable situation must be rectified as quickly as possible and controls returned to normal operations.

	Directive	Deterrent	Preventative	Detective	Corrective	Recovery	Compensating
Administrative	Policy	Policy	User registration procedure	Review violation reports	Termination	DR Plan	Supervision
							Job rotation
							Logging
Logical	Config standards	Warning banner	Password based login	Logs	Unplug, isolate, & terminate connection	Backups	CCTV
			IPS	IDS			
Physical		Beware of Dog sign	Fence	Sentry	Fire extinguisher	Rebuild	Keystroke monitoring
	Authorized Personnel Only signs, traffic lights			CCTV			Layered defense

*Figure 1.7 - **Control examples for types and categories.***

Access Control Types

The access control categories discussed in the previous section serve to classify different access control methods based on where they fit into the access control time continuum shown in *Figure 1.6*. However, another way to classify and categorize access controls is by their method of implementation. For any of the access control categories, the controls in those categories can be implemented in one of three ways:

- *Administrative Controls:* Sometimes called Management Controls, these are procedures implemented to define the roles, responsibilities, policies, and administrative functions needed to manage the control environment.

- *Logical (Technical) Controls:* These are electronic hardware and software solutions implemented to control access to information and information networks.

- *Physical Controls:* These are controls to protect the organization's people and physical environment, such as locks, fire management, gates, and guards. Physical controls may be called "operational controls" in some contexts.

The categories discussed earlier can be mapped against these three access control types to demonstrate various control examples and options as shown in *Figure 1.7*.

Physical Controls

Physical security covers a broad spectrum of controls to protect the physical assets (primarily the people) in an organization. Physical Controls are sometimes referred to as "operational" controls in some risk management frameworks. These controls range from doors, locks, and windows to environment controls, construction standards, and guards. Typically, physical security is based on the notion of establishing security zones or concentric areas within a facility that require increased security as you get closer to the valuable assets inside the facility. Security zones are the physical representation of the defense-in-depth principle discussed earlier in this chapter. Typically, security zones are associated with rooms, offices, floors, or smaller elements, such as a cabinet or storage locker. The design of the physical security controls within the facility must take into account the protection of the asset as well as the individuals working in that area. For example, the fire control and suppression systems must account for the health safety of personnel in potential fire zones. One must consider fires, floods, explosions, civil unrest, or other man-made or natural disasters when planning the physical layout of a facility. Emergency strategies must be included in the physical controls to accommodate the safe exiting of personnel and adherence to safety standards or regulations. Adequate exits and emergency evacuation routes must be available in all areas and sensitive areas or information must be able to be secured quickly in case those areas must be evacuated. Human safety is the priority in all decisions of physical security.

The physical access controls in each zone should be matched with the level of security required for that zone. For example, an employee may work in the data center of a large financial institution—a very sensitive area. The employee may have a special badge to access the parking lot and the main entrance where guards are posted and recording access. To access the specific office area, he or she may need a different badge and PIN to dis-engage the door lock. Finally, to enter the data center, the card and PIN are combined with a biometric device that must be employed to gain access. As one gets closer and closer to the valuable asset—the data center—the protections get progressively stronger.

The most prevalent and visible aspect of physical security is often the perimeter of a facility. A typical perimeter should be without gaps or areas that can be easily broken into or entered undetected. The perimeter starts with the surrounding grounds. Hills, ditches, retention walls, fences, concrete posts, and high curbs can all act as deterrents to attack. Depending on the sensitivity of the facility, guards, attack dogs, and other aggressive measures can be applied. The construction of the facility may include special walls, reinforced barriers, and even certain foliage strategically placed near doors, windows, and utilities. All this can be augmented by cameras, alarms, locks, and other essential controls.

However, security is not the only consideration when designing a facility. The overall design of the facility must balance function of the building with the security needs of the organization. For example, a company's headquarters building will need good security to protect private areas, stored records, and personnel against malicious acts. But it must also serve as the company's face to the public and present a welcoming atmosphere to visitors. Protections at such a facility might include guards at the front desk (unarmed), locked doors, and badge readers to restrict entry. However, the company's data center facility would most likely have much more stringent measures to keep intruders out, such as a tall razor-wire fence, armed guards, biometric entry controls, and mantrap doors. As with all architecture, form follows function.

If an organization leases space in a facility (as opposed to owning the facility) there may be limits on what modifications can be made to accommodate the company's security needs. Any special security requirements must be negotiated with the facility's owner before the lease agreement is signed. If the organization is sharing the facility with other tenants, additional thought must be given to security and access control measures, since much of the facility (those portions not occupied by the organization) will be accessible to non-organization personnel. Areas of special concern to the information security professional will include heating ventilation and air conditioning (HVAC) equipment, electrical power panels and wiring closets—all of which may be readily accessible to contractors and other tenants of the facility.

Finally, the oversight of physical controls must adhere to the same basic principles as other forms of controls: separation of duties and least privilege. For example, it may be necessary to segment the job role of various guards to ensure that no single point of failure or collusion potentially allows threat agents to enter unchecked.

Physical Entry

Secure areas should be protected by appropriate entry controls to ensure that only authorized personnel are allowed access. The provisioning of credentials must take into consideration the needs of the individual, his or her job function, and the zone accessed. As discussed previously, the person requiring access must successfully pass an investigative process prior to being provided access. In defining physical entry controls, the following should be considered:

- Visitors should be appropriately cleared prior to entry and supervised while on the premises. Moreover, the date, time, and escort should be recorded and validated with a signature. Visitors should only be provided access to the areas that do not contain sensitive information or technologies and should be provided with instructions concerning security actions and emergency procedures.

- Access to controlled areas, such as information processing centers and where sensitive data may reside, should be restricted to authorized persons only. Authentication controls, such as badges, swipe cards, smart cards, proximity cards, PINs, and (potentially) biometric devices, should be employed to restrict access.

- Everyone within the controlled perimeter must wear some form of identification and should be encouraged to challenge others not wearing visible identification. Be aware, however, that most cultures encourage politeness and deference in social interactions, particularly where strangers are involved. Challenging an unknown person does not come easily to many people and this may be a large culture change for most organizations. Awareness and education programs on this topic are advised.

- Different styles of identification should be employed to allow others to quickly ascertain the role of an individual. For example, employees may be given white badges and visitors given blue badges. This makes it easier to identify who is an employee and who is not to ensure that all nonemployees are escorted in the building. In another example, a red ID badge may signify access to the fourth floor of an office building. If someone appeared on the fourth floor wearing a blue badge, others would be able to determine appropriate actions. Action may include verifying they are escorted, notifying security, or escorting them to the nearest exit.

- All access rights and privileges should be regularly reviewed and audited. This should include random checks on seemingly authorized users, control devices, approval processes, and training of employees responsible for physical security.

There may be occasional need for temporary facility access to sensitive areas for visitors, contractors, or maintenance personnel. Preparations and procedures should be defined in advance for these situations; special identification should be required for all temporary personnel, and they should be escorted by facility personnel at all times. This will make it easier for regular facility personnel to identify the temporary visitors in unauthorized areas and ensure that they are not able to cause any damage to the facility or obtain any confidential information.

Administrative Controls

Administrative controls represent all the actions, policies, processes, and management of the control system. These include any aspect of the access control environment that is necessary to oversee and manage the confidentiality, availability, and integrity of the access controls, and manage the people who use it, set policy on use, and define standards for operations.

Administrative controls can be broad and can vary depending on organizational needs, industry, and legal implications. Nevertheless, they can be broken into six major groups:

- Policies and procedures
- Personnel security, evaluation, and clearances
- Security policies
- Monitoring
- User management
- Privilege management

Policies and Procedures

The first aspect of administrative (managerial) oversight is the operations management of the control environment and how it should align with the enterprise architecture. Access control is realized by aligning the capabilities of many systems and processes, collaborating to ensure that threats are reduced and incidents prevented. Therefore, other operational elements of the environment must be addressed in some fashion within the access control strategy. These include but are not limited to:

- Vulnerability management and patch management
- Product life-cycle management
- Network management

When changes to the environment are required to accommodate a need, they must be defined, approved, tested, applied, verified, deployed, audited, and documented. Changes can be minor, such as a static route being added to a network, or more significant, such as the redesign of a storage solution. Every organization must have a change control process to ensure that there is a formalized methodology for making and documenting changes to the environment.

Given the scope of access control, it is important that the change control process includes aspects of the access strategy and policy. In some cases, this is obvious, such as adding a new virtual private network (VPN) gateway for remote access. Clearly this will affect the access control environment. Some changes, such as network redesign, which can affect various established access paths to information, are much less obvious, but can have significant impacts to access controls.

Many organizations have business continuity and disaster recovery (BCP/DRP) plans to ensure that the organization can maintain critical operations in case of a catastrophic event or failure. BCP/DRP plans can be simplistic, such as ensuring there are regular backups performed, or highly complex solutions incorporating multiple data centers. The scope and complexity of the BCP/DRP plan are typically defined by the business environment, risks, and system criticality.

Regardless of the type of BCP/DRP plan, the availability of access controls during an event is essential and must be incorporated into the plan. For example, if a system failure occurs and an alternate system is temporarily employed without the expected, original controls, the exposure to critical data can be significant. All too often, security is a secondary consideration in disaster recovery operations. If an event was to occur, a company could have its most valuable assets completely exposed. However, critical systems are most important in the context of BCP/DRP. Therefore, a system included in the BCP/DRP plan is important and the information on that system is valuable.

One of the first steps to ensure security incorporated into the BCP/DRP plan is defining the access controls for the temporary systems, services, and applications to be used during disaster recovery. This includes the access control system itself. For example, a Remote Authentication Dial In User Service (RADIUS) server may seem unimportant on the surface, but its absence in a disaster could be detrimental to security. In addition, a disaster scenario, by definition, is an unusual event with many extenuating arrangements that will need to be made to enable the organization to continue its work. Subsequently, there may be different access needs defined than what the organization would normally have in place. The notion of "acceptable security" may be very different during a disaster than it would be under ordinary circumstances, so proper planning and consideration of alternative access control needs and methods must be considered and incorporated into the BCP/DRP plan.

Traditional networks and applications are typically engineered to provide a high level of performance to users, systems, and services. The network is the cardiovascular system of most companies, and if its performance is low, the productivity of the organization will suffer. The same holds true for the access control environment. If it takes a user an excessive amount of time to logon, this could have a negative impact to operations and potentially encourage users to find ways to bypass the access control system. To reduce the time associated with access controls, the performance optimization processes for the network and system environments should include the performance of controls overseeing authentication and access.

Like change control, configuration management represents the administrative tasks performed on a system or device to ensure optimal operations. Configurations can be temporary or permanent to address a multitude of the organization's operations and security needs, and configuration management of devices, systems, services, and applications can greatly affect the access control environment. Changes to a system's configuration must take into account what, if any, impacts on user access may occur after the configuration is modified.

Given the common separation of the security group from the IT group, it is not uncommon for the IT group to make a seemingly innocuous modification to a system configuration and impact the access controls associated with that system. Therefore, it is important to ensure that the resources responsible for configuration management, such as network administrators, system owners, and application developers, are aware of the security control environment and the importance of their domain of influence on the security of the organization. This often ties in closely with any change management processes an organization might have in place, so it is a natural fit for processes to be enacted that tie in access control considerations as part of any change management or configuration management program.

Vulnerability management will typically include activities such as identifying system vulnerabilities, recommending potential remediation, and implementing system patches to accommodate a security issue, update a system service, or add features to a system or application. When patches are installed, there may be key system modifications that can negatively affect the security of the system, server, or application. Patches must be applied through the change control system to provide a comprehensive record of system modifications and accurate documentation. Ensuring that the current state of a system is well-documented allows organizations to gain more visibility into the status of their environment in the event a new vulnerability is published. This promotes rapid assessments to evaluate potential risks in the face of an attack or vulnerability. In addition, data from the change control system utilized during the application of patches offer documentation of the current state of a system that can be consulted prior to applying new patches or installing new software.

A key attribute of vulnerability management is the importance of minimizing the time for deploying patches or other system updates in order to mitigate a vulnerability. Vulnerabilities surface in a multitude of ways. For example, a vulnerability may be published by a vendor who has discovered a security issue and provides a patch. Usually, at this point, both attackers and organizations are made aware of the vulnerability. While companies are exercising due diligence in applying fixes, attackers are developing methods and tools to exploit the vulnerability. In contrast, an incident may have occurred that exposes the vulnerability in a system and constitutes an immediate threat. The most dangerous example of this kind of threat is zero day attacks, where an attacker identifies and exploits the vulnerability before that vulnerability is known to the vendor or the general user community. The attackers can exploit the vulnerability on a massive scale, understanding that time is on their side. It is very common for attackers to discover a vulnerability, develop tools and tactics to exploit it, then execute those exploits before anyone knows of the vulnerability or how to defend against it. Vulnerable organizations must find alternative measures to compensate for the threat while vendors rush to produce a patch, each consuming time as the attacks expand.

Given the complexity of each potential scenario, time is always a critical element in protecting assets. The ability to use time effectively to deploy a patch or employ compensating controls until a patch is published directly corresponds to the level of risk and the overall security posture of the organization. Emphasis on efficient testing and deployment of system patches or compensating controls should be the core of any vulnerability management program.

However, time must be balanced against effective deployment. Initially, the documentation provided by the configuration management and change control processes can be investigated to determine which systems are vulnerable and represent the greatest risk, then prioritized accordingly. As the process continues, other affected systems are addressed by a manual or automated (or combination) patch management process that is used to deploy the update throughout the organization. The vulnerability management program must then verify that the patch was, in fact, implemented as expected. Although this may seem inherent to the objective, it cannot be assumed. In the case of manual deployment, users and system owners may not respond accordingly or in a timely fashion. Even if timely deployment is executed, the patch may have failed. This is somewhat compensated for in automated deployment; nevertheless, both scenarios require validation of an effective installation.

The installation of a patch or control does, by itself, represent the complete mitigation of an identified vulnerability. Many systems are unique to a specific environment, representing the potential that a change mitigating one vulnerability unintentionally introduces another. Or, in some cases, it is assumed that the implementation of a patch or control eliminated the vulnerability altogether. Therefore, a vulnerability management system must not only address the testing, deployment, and verification that the patch was implemented as expected, but also include testing to ensure that the target vulnerability was mitigated and new problems were not introduced by the process. In the final analysis, vulnerability management is a comprehensive and integral process that every security program must develop, maintain, and test regularly.

In every organization there comes a time to upgrade or replace devices and systems. Reasons for the upgrade vary, but can include product obsolescence, the availability of newer technology with previously unavailable desirable features, or the need for advanced operational capabilities. Baselines must be established within the access control architecture that define the minimum access control requirements for all new systems to ensure that appropriate and acceptable controls are established. By doing so, the organization has a clear foundation by which to evaluate products for implementation without sacrificing security or expected controls. Do not assume that all new products have the security capabilities the organization needs. Each organization's needs vary and each environment may be different from that for which the product was designed. It is important to test all new products for access control functionality.

Finally, many networks are supported by a separate management network that allows administrators to manage devices without affecting the production environment. This is another form of separation of duties, where the production network and the management network have separate purposes, separate network connectivity, and separate access and control requirements. Given the ability to change aspects of the network environment, it is necessary to have strong access controls established on the management network to reduce risk to systems and network devices. If network management is performed using the same network as general production traffic, strong authentication and authorization are required to ensure that unauthorized personnel cannot modify network devices.

Personnel Security, Evaluation, and Clearances

One of the more overlooked aspects of access control is a review of the requirements of people requesting access to a resource. Prior to granting access of any kind, the credentials of the person requesting the access should be checked for validity and his need for access thoroughly evaluated. This does not mean that every user needs to have a complete background check prior to checking her e-mail. Clearly, the level of validation of an individual should be directly proportional to the sensitivity of the assets and the level of permissions available to the user. Nevertheless, it is critical that processes exist to evaluate users and ensure that they are worthy of the level of trust that is requested and, ultimately, granted.

First and foremost, security requirements—at some level—should be included in all defined job roles and responsibilities. Job roles defined by the organization should have alignment to defined policies and be documented appropriately. They should include any general responsibilities for adhering to security policies, as well as any specific responsibilities concerning the protection of particular assets related to the given role.

Once the security requirements for a role are defined and clearly documented, the process for validation of individuals to obtain credentials for a role can be defined and exercised. The definition of a screening process is typically related to the sensitivity of the assets being accessed. However, there may be contractual demands, regulatory compliance issues, and industry standards that define how a person is screened to reach a certain level of access. The best example of this type of screening comes from the military and the allocation of clearances. Depending on the clearance level requested, a person may be subjected to intense background checks, friend and family interviews, credit checks, employment history, medical history, polygraph examinations, and a plethora of other potentially unpleasant probing. Of course, once attained, the clearance translates to a level of trustworthiness and, therefore, access.

A typical organization will need only a standard process and some additional factors in the light of applicable legal requirements or regulations. These may include a credit check and criminal background checks that simply assure management that an applicant has not falsified information during the application process. Typical aspects of staff verification may include but are not limited to:

- Satisfactory character references
- Confirmation of claimed academic and professional qualifications
- Independent identity validation, such as a passport
- A credit check for those requiring access to financial systems
- Federal, state, and local law enforcement records check
- An online search of publicly available information on social media sites

The relevance of credit checks and other personal history can be valuable in determining a person's propensity for unlawful acts. Personal or financial problems, changes in behavior or lifestyle, recurring absences, and evidence of stress or depression might lead an employee to fraud, theft, error, or other security implications. The type of background check performed may vary based on the type of employee and his or her placement in the organization. For example, a file clerk or receptionist may need only a basic background check, whereas an applicant for a senior officer position may require a more extensive background investigation.

In the event the employee is temporary, the access provided must take into consideration the potential exposure of proprietary information given the transient position. Organizations that use staffing agencies to supply temporary help should require those agencies to perform employee validation checks and provide a reliability report on the temporary workers supplied to the organization. The requirements for background checks should be incorporated into the underlying contract with the staffing agency and its implementation should be reviewed and audited on a regular basis. Management should also evaluate the supervision and provisioning of access to new or inexperienced staff. It should not be necessary to provide a new employee with the keys to the kingdom until he or she has satisfied a probationary period.

Employees should also be periodically reevaluated to ensure that significant changes to key elements about them or their lives have not occurred that would alter their security worthiness. Also, it is important to remember that all information collected about an individual is private and confidential and should be afforded security controls like any other sensitive material. Finally, confidentiality or nondisclosure agreements should be read and signed annually by all employees to ensure there is no doubt on the part of employees that the information they will have access to is confidential, secret, protected, and valuable to the organization.

Security Policies

The organization's requirements for access control should be defined and documented in its security policies. Access rules and rights for each user or group of users should be clearly stated in an access policy statement. The access control policy should minimally consider:

- Statements of general security principles and their applicability to the organization
- Security requirements of individual enterprise applications, systems, and services
- Consistency between the access control and information classification policies of different systems and networks
- Contractual obligations or regulatory compliance regarding protection of assets
- Standards defining user access profiles for organizational roles
- Details regarding the management of the access control system

Monitoring

The ability to monitor the access control environment effectively is essential to the overall success and management of the security program. It is one thing to apply controls, but it is another to validate their effectiveness and ongoing status. The capacity for ensuring that controls are properly employed and working effectively and for being aware of unauthorized activity is enabled by the existence of monitoring and logging within the environment. This is not unique to access controls, security, or even IT; it is an essential aspect of business to monitor activity.

Systems should be monitored to detect any deviation from established access control policies and record all successful and unsuccessful authentication processes, credential assertion, user management, rights usage, and access attempts. The procedures and technology should also monitor the ongoing status of controls to ensure conformity to policies and expectations. This last point is typically overlooked and represents a significant potential to mask or hide unauthorized activities. For example, if the control activities are monitored, yet the status of controls is not, attackers can disable various controls, grant themselves access, and then re-enable the controls without detection. The logging and monitoring of the activities will then not raise any suspicion because they are now valid operations, thanks to the attacker.

Systems and activity logs are (typically) electronic records of any activity that has occurred within a system or application. They provide the documented record of what has happened and can be extremely useful when investigating an operational or security incident. Logs and their contents are important to security management and maintenance of an effective access control solution. A log can include:

- User IDs used on systems, services, or applications.
- Dates and times for logon and logoff.
- System identities, such as IP address, host name, or media access control (MAC) address. It may also be possible to

determine the network location of a device through local area network (LAN) logging, wireless access point identification, or remote-access system identification, if applicable.

- Logging of both successful and rejected authentication and access attempts. Knowing when and where people are utilizing their rights can be very helpful to determine if those rights are necessary for a job role or function. It is also helpful to know where access rights are denied to have a better understanding of what a user is trying to do. This can help determine if you have a user who does not have adequate rights to perform his or her job.

Audit logs should be retained for a specified period, as defined by organizational need and (potentially) regulatory requirements. In the latter case, this is preordained and not open to interpretation. However, there are cases where no legal or regulatory demands exist. If this is the case, the retention time will probably be defined by organizational policy and the size of available storage. The security of the logs is critical. If a log can be altered to erase unauthorized activity, there is little chance for discovery, and if discovered, there may be no evidence. Logs must also be protected from unauthorized reading as well as writing, as they can contain sensitive information such as passwords (for instance, when users accidentally type the password into a user ID prompt). Log security is also critical if the logs are needed as evidence in a legal or disciplinary proceeding. If logs are not secure and can be proven as such before, during, and after an event, the logs may not be accepted as valid legal evidence due to the potential for tampering. The fundamental approach to logs is that they must be an accurate reflection of system activity and, as such, must be secured and maintained for an appropriate period of time in order to provide a reference point for future investigative activity.

Once the events are properly logged, it is necessary to periodically review the logs to evaluate the impact of a given event. Typically, system logs are voluminous, making it difficult to isolate and identify a given event for identification and investigation. To preserve potential evidence, many organizations will make a copy of the log (preserving the original) and use suitable utilities and tools to perform automated interrogation and analysis of the log data. There are several tools available that can be very helpful in analyzing a log file to assist administrators in identifying and isolating activity. Once again, separation of duties plays an important role in reviewing logs. Logs should never be initially reviewed or analyzed by the "subject" of the logs. For example, a system administrator should not perform the log review for a system he manages. Otherwise, it may be possible for the person to "overlook" evidence of her unauthorized activity or intentionally manipulate the logs to eliminate that evidence. Therefore, it is necessary to separate those being monitored from those performing the review.

User Access Management

An organization must have a formal procedure to control the allocation of credentials and access rights to information systems and services. The procedure should cover all stages in the life cycle of user access, from the initial registration of new users to the final decommissioning of accounts that are no longer required. To provide access to resources, the organization must first establish a process for creating, changing, and removing users from systems and applications. These activities should be controlled through a formal process, based on policy, which defines the administrative requirements for managing user accounts. The process should define expectations, tasks, and standards concerning the user management. For example, elements of the process should include:

- Approval of user access, including information from human resources, the user's manager, or a business unit that has approved the creation of the user account. The owner of the system who is providing information or services should concur with the approval request. Approval processes should also address the modification of user accounts and their removal.

- Standards defining unique user IDs, their format, and any application-specific information. Additionally, information

69

about the user should be included in the credential management system to ensure the person is clearly bound to the user ID defined within the system.

- A process for checking that the level of access provided is appropriate to the role and job purpose within the organization and does not compromise defined segregation of duties requirements. This is especially important when a user's role and job function change. A process must exist to evaluate existing privileges compared to the new role of the user and ensure changes are made accordingly.

- Defining and requiring users to sign a written statement indicating that they understand the conditions associated with being granted access and any associated liabilities or responsibilities. It is important to understand that user confirmation should occur whenever there is a change in rights and privileges, not simply upon creation of the account.

- A documentation process to capture system changes and act as a record of the transaction. Keeping a log of the administrative process and relative technical information is essential to an effective access control system. The information will be used in assessments, audits, change requests, and as evidence for investigative purposes.

- Access modification and revocation procedures to ensure that users who have left the organization or changed job roles have their previously held access privileges immediately removed to ensure elimination of duplications and removal of dormant accounts.

- Specific actions that may be taken by management if unauthorized access is attempted by a user or other forms of access abuse are identified. This must be approved by the organization's human resources and legal departments.

A more in-depth look at user management will be found later in this chapter when identity management is discussed.

In addition to overall user management, it is necessary to define policies, procedures, and controls regarding passwords. The use of passwords is a common practice for validating a user's identity during the authentication process. Given that, in most traditional authentication solutions, the password is the only secret in the transaction, great care should be considered in how passwords are created and managed by users and systems.

A process governing user password should consider the following:

■ Users should be required to sign a statement agreeing to keep their passwords safe and confidential and to not share, distribute, or write down their passwords.

■ All temporary passwords should be permitted to be used only once—to reset the user's password to something that only he or she knows.

■ Passwords should never be stored unprotected and in clear text.

■ Passwords should have a minimum and maximum length and require the use of various characters and formats to increase their complexity and reduce their susceptibility to brute force and guessing attacks.

■ Passwords should be changed regularly.

■ Accounts should be locked for a period of time if excessive failed password attempts occur (typically within three to five tries).

■ A history of passwords should be maintained to prevent users from repeating old passwords as they are changed.

■ Passwords should not be disclosed to support personnel, and those personnel should not ask users for their passwords.

There is some debate over the security realized by a username and password combination used for authentication. For example, depending on the system, a longer, more complex password can actually make it more prone to compromise if it results in the user writing it down. The potential for exposure of passwords, poor password selection by users, and the sheer number of passwords most users need to track lay the foundation for potential compromises.

However, alternatives to passwords (such as will be examined later in this chapter) can be expensive, cumbersome, and annoying to end users, potentially negating any security or business benefit they may provide. Before moving away from the use of passwords toward an alternative technology or method, the security professional must always consider the value of the information or system that the passwords are protecting. Current password technology and processes (including the use of minimum complexity standards, lockouts, and reuse restrictions) will provide the organization with a certain minimal level of security protection. If, in the opinion of the organization, that level of protection is sufficient to protect the resources behind the password, then password technology is sufficient. If, however, the organization feels that password protection does not adequately protect the resources behind the password, then it must seek out alternative authentication methodologies.

Nevertheless, and despite all the negative connotations passwords have in the security space, passwords are today's de facto baseline standard. The best approach to ensure consistency and control is:

- Clearly defined password policies
- Well-implemented system controls
- Understanding of the technical considerations
- Comprehensive user training
- Continuous auditing

Privilege Management

The importance of access privileges demands that their allocation, administration, and use should have specific processes and considerations. The lack of effective privilege management can result in core failures in otherwise sophisticated access control systems. Many organizations will focus exclusively on identification, authentication, and modes of access. Although all these are critical and important to deterring threats and preventing incidents, the provisioning of rights within the system is the next layer of control. The typical cause of problems in the allocation of rights is due primarily to the vast number of access options available to administrators and managers. The complexity of potential access configurations leads to inadequate and inconsistent security. This aspect of privilege management demands clear processes and documentation that defines and guides the allocation of system rights.

In the development of procedures for privilege management, careful consideration should be given to the identification and documentation of privileges associated with each system, service, or application, and the defined roles within the organization to which they apply. This involves identifying and understanding the available access rights that can be allocated within a system, aligning those to functions within the system, and defining user roles that require the use of those functions. Finally, user roles need to be associated with job requirements. A user may have several job requirements, forcing the assignment of several roles and result in a collection of rights within the system. Be careful, however, of the consequences of aggregate access rights. Many systems have rules of precedence that dictate how access rules are applied. Should a rule that restricts access conflict with, and be overridden by, a rule that allows access, the unintended consequence is that the user will be granted more access permission than was intended. Remember the primary mantra of least privilege: only rights required to perform a job should be provided to a user, group, or role.

An authorization process and a record of all privileges allocated should be maintained. Privileges should not be granted until the authorization process is complete and validated. If any significant or special privileges are needed for intermittent job functions, these should be performed using an account specifically allocated for such a task, as opposed to those used for normal system and user activity. This enables the access privileges assigned to the special account to be tailored to the needs of the special function rather than simply extending the access privileges associated with the user's normal work functions. For example, an administrator of a UNIX system might have three accounts: one for daily routines, another for specific job requirements, and "root" (the all-omniscient access ID on UNIX systems) for rare occurrences where complete system access must be utilized.

Logical (Technical) Controls

Logical controls are those mechanisms employed within the digital and electronic infrastructure of an organization that enforce that organization's security policy. Given the pervasive nature of technology, logical access controls may take on a wide variety of forms and implementations. Logical controls can include elements such as firewalls, filters, operating systems, applications, and even routing protocols. Logical controls can be broadly categorized in the following groups:

- Network access
- Remote access
- System access
- Application access
- Malware control
- Encryption

Network Access

Network access controls are those employed within the communication infrastructure to restrict who may connect to, and use, that infrastructure. Usually, this is implemented through access control lists, remote-access solutions, virtual local area networks (VLANs), access control protocols, and security devices like firewalls and intrusion detection or intrusion prevention systems. The role of network access controls is usually to limit communications between two networks or resources. For example, a firewall will limit what protocols and protocol features are permitted from a given source to a defined destination.

However, there are other network-level controls that can be used to employ security services that increase the level of access management in the environment. The most common example is a proxy system: a device or service that is located in the middle of the communication between a user and an application and employs controls that monitor and regulate the traffic between the user and the application. Proxy systems can apply specific logic in managing service-level communications within the network. For example, a proxy system may control access to Web-based services via the hypertext transfer protocol (HTTP). Just as a firewall would block specific ports, a proxy system would block or control certain aspects of the HTTP session to limit exposure. Many proxy systems are used to authenticate sessions for internal users attempting to access the Internet and potentially filter out unwanted Web site activity, such as Java applets, active server page (ASP) code, plug-ins, or access to inappropriate Web sites.

VLANs can be utilized to segment traffic and limit the interaction from one network to another. VLANs are used in situations where many systems are on the same physical network but they need to be logically separated to enforce the access control requirements of the organization. Conversely, VLANs can be used to virtually connect systems in multiple physical locations to appear as if they are all on the same logical network segment.

Wireless networks can also employ several access control mechanisms, such as MAC filtering, multiple forms of authentication, encryption, and limitations on network access.

Network Access Control (NAC) provides is the ability to restrict access to systems based on network-wide policy. Prior to allowing a system to join the network, the NAC service queries the system to ensure it is adhering to established policies. Policies can be as simple as ensuring an antivirus package is present on the system and as complex as validating the system is up to date with security patches. In the event the system does not meet security policy, it may be denied access or redirected to a secure area of the network for further testing or to allow the user to implement the necessary changes required prior to gaining full access the network.

Remote Access

In today's environment, users working from outside the traditional office space make up a significant portion of the user community. Remote access solutions offer services to remote users requiring access to systems and data. One of the more commonly utilized technical solutions is the virtual private network (VPN). VPNs allow users to authenticate themselves and establish a secure communications channel over an insecure medium like the Internet. Typically, a VPN device is placed on the organization's Internet connection or behind a firewall to allow remote users to access the network, authenticate, and establish a protected session with various internal systems.

VPN access controls typically use authentication mechanisms in combination with encryption methods. For example, a VPN solution can be configured to permit access by users with the appropriate specific (company branded) client software or version of a browser, limit access to certain portions of the network, limit the types of services permissible, and control session time windows. In addition, because the connection is occurring over an insecure and publicly accessible network like the Internet, most VPN solutions employ multifactor authentication to positively identify the user. Multifactor authentication will be covered in more detail later in the chapter.

System Access

The term "system" comprises a wide variety of technologies and components, but the definition most often used is one or more computers that provide a service or assist in a process. When most people think of a system they think of their personal computer, and that provides a good model for discussing system access controls. The most prevalent system access control is the user ID and password combination. Almost all modern systems have this unless it has been specifically disabled for a particular reason. The user ID/password combination may be replaced in some systems by other forms of authentication, such as a smartcard or a one-time password token. Nevertheless, all these methods serve the same purpose: to restrict system access to authorized users.

All computer systems have an underlying operating system that controls all its functions and regulates how the various components of the system interact. There are literally hundreds of different operating systems, but most users (including security professionals) work primarily in one of the three major publicly available operating systems: Microsoft Windows®, Apple's OS X, and UNIX (including the many variants of Linux and OS X). Mobile operating systems such as Google's Android and Apple's iOS are also quickly becoming operating systems security professionals must be familiar with. Each of these operating systems has internal controls and layers built in that manage access control between components of the system. In particular, they all tightly control programs that directly access the hardware components of the system, such as the kernel (the part of the system that interfaces between the OS and the system hardware) and various device drivers that allow application programs to use devices like key-boards and printers. The ability to directly manipulate the system hardware is a powerful tool and must be tightly controlled by the operating system to prevent misuse by malicious programs.

Finally, almost all operating systems have some sort of file system to store information for later retrieval. The file system will also have controls to restrict who may access various files and directories. Some of these controls are imposed by the operating system itself, while others may be assigned by individual users to protect their personal files. These controls are very important to ensure that information is not disclosed to unauthorized individuals who may have access to the system.

Application Access

Applications will usually employ user and system access controls to deter threats and reduce exposure to security vulnerabilities. However, applications can also incorporate mechanisms to supplement other controls and ensure secure operations. For example, applications can monitor user sessions, apply inactivity time-outs, validate data entry, and limit access to specific services or modules based on user rights and defined user roles. Moreover, the application itself can be designed and developed to reduce exposure to buffer overflows, race conditions (where two or more processes are waiting for the same resource), and loss of system integrity.

The architecture of an application plays a significant role in its ability to thwart attack. Object-oriented programming, multitiered architectures, and even database security are important to controlling what services are provided to users and what tasks can be performed. Access controls associated with all aspects of an application are important to sound security. Many applications are complicated and offer a wide range of services and access to potentially sensitive information. Additionally, applications may be critical to the operational needs of the business. Therefore, their sensitivity to disruption must be considered when designing or using the access control features of the application.

Applications can also be segmented into modules or layers to further enforce access control policies. For example, a typical e-mail application can be segmented into modules for composing a message, managing address book information, connecting to net-work resources, and managing mail delivery and retrieval. Doing this allows the application designer to specify how each module can be accessed, what services each module will present to the user and to other applications, and what privileges each provides to the user. For example, the address book management module may be accessible from an e-mail application but not by any other application to prevent the possibility of a virus examining and using a user's address book. It is important to manage the interaction between application modules within an application as well as the interaction between these modules and other applications to ensure that malicious users or programs do not try to use them to perform unauthorized activities. A more detailed discussion of application security issues is found in Chapters 4 and 6.

Malware Control

Malicious code, such as viruses, worms, Trojans, spyware, and even spam, represent potential security threats to the enterprise. Weaknesses in systems, applications, and services offer opportunities for worms and viruses to infiltrate an organization, causing outages or damage to critical systems and information. Technical controls can be applied to reduce the likelihood of impact from such malicious programs. The most prevalent of these controls are antivirus systems that can be employed on the network perimeter, servers, and end-user systems to detect and potentially eliminate viruses, worms, or other malicious programs. Other technical solutions include file integrity checks and intrusion prevention systems that can detect when a system service or file is modified, representing a risk to the environment.

Cryptography

Although covered in greater detail in the cryptography chapter of this book, encryption has an important role in the access control domain. Encryption can be used to ensure the confidentiality of information or authenticate information to ensure integrity. These two characteristics are highly leveraged in the identification and authentication processes associated with access control. Authentication protocols will employ encryption to protect the session from exposure to intruders, passwords are typically hashed (put through a one-way mathematical function that cannot be reversed) to protect them from disclosure, and session information may be encrypted to support the continued association of the user to the system and services used. Encryption can also be used to validate a session. For example, a server can be configured such that if session information is not encrypted, the resulting communication is denied. The most predominant aspect of cryptography in access control is the employment of cryptographic mechanisms to ensure the integrity of authentication protocols and processes.

Encryption can also be used as a compensating control to improve security when the available access control functions are not granular enough to provide adequate security. For example, it may be necessary for several employees of a company to share a particularly sensitive financial spreadsheet. Unfortunately, all of these people are located in different offices in different parts of the country, and the only way for them to share this file is to use the company's general shared drive that was set up for all employees to transfer information between offices. While access to the drive is restricted to only internal company users, there is no way to specify that only particular users can access a specific file. In this case, the file can be encrypted and the key to decrypt the file can be disclosed only to the employees who need to see the spreadsheet. This will allow the file to be placed on the general shared drive while still restricting access to only those who need to see the file.

Cryptography is commonly used within applications to protect sensitive data. Information such as credit card numbers may be encoded so that they are not visible (except perhaps the last few digits) to personnel who do not need to see the entire number. Examples of this may be seen in reports or printouts, in the storage of such information in a database, or in the layout of a screen that is displayed to the user. Consider the use of encryption in those situations where the available access controls are not sufficient to provide the appropriate granularity of protection for sensitive information.

Access Control Techniques

Thus far in the chapter the discussion of access controls has been relegated to the processes and technology used to identify, authenticate, and authorize users and applications. However, all this must translate into specific controls associated with the security of data. In a defense-in-depth environment each layer of defense requires its own access controls and security capabilities.

Defining security controls for the systems and applications that host data is a good start, but special attention must also be paid to methods of organizing and protecting the data itself. This section will discuss various methods of providing data-based protection.

Discretionary and Mandatory Access Controls

One of the most fundamental data access control decisions an organization must make is the amount of control it will give system and data owners to specify the level of access users of that data will have. In every organization there is a balancing point between the access controls enforced by organization and system policy and the ability for information owners to determine who can have access based on specific business requirements. The process of translating that balance into a workable access control model can be defined by three general access frameworks:

- Discretionary access control
- Mandatory access control
- Nondiscretionary access control

Discretionary Access Controls (DACs)

Controls placed on data by the owner of the data. The owner determines who has access to the data and what privileges they have. Discretionary controls represent a very early form of access control and were widely employed in VAX, VMS, UNIX, and other minicomputers in universities and other organizations prior to the evolution of personal computers. Today, DACs are widely employed to allow users to manage their own data and the security of that information, and nearly every mainstream operating system, from Microsoft and Apple to mobile operating systems and Linux supports DAC. The advantage of a DAC-based system is that it is primarily user-centric. The data owner has the power to determine who can (and cannot) access that data based on the business requirements and constraints affecting that owner. While the owner never has the ability to ignore or contradict the organization's access control policies, he or she has the ability to interpret those policies to fit the specific needs of his or her system and his or her users.

Mandatory Access Controls (MACs)

Controls determined by the system and based primarily on organization policy. The system applies controls based on the clearance of a user and the classification of an object or data. With DACs the user is free to apply controls at their discretion, not based on the overall value or classification of the data. In contrast, MAC requires the system itself to manage access controls in accordance with the organization's security policies. MACs are typically used for systems and data that are highly sensitive and where system owners do not want to allow users to potentially contradict or bypass organizationally mandated access controls. Assigning the security controls of an object based on its classification and the clearance of subjects provides for a secure system that accommodates multilayered information processing.

MAC is based on cooperative interaction between the system and the information owner. The system's decision controls access and the owner provides the need-to-know control. Not everyone who is cleared should have access, only those cleared and with a need to know. Even if the owner determines a user has the need to know, the system must ascertain that the user is cleared or no access will be allowed. To accomplish this, data need to be labeled as to its classification, allowing specific controls to be applied based on that classification.

Access Capabilities	
No Access	No access permission granted
Read (R)	Read but make no changes
Write (W)	Write to file. Includes change capability
Execute (X)	Execute a program
Delete (D)	Delete a file
Change (C)	Read, write, execute, and delete. May not change file permission.
List (L)	List the files in a directory
Full Control (FC)	All abilities. Includes changing access control permissions.

Access Permission	
Public	R - L
Group	R - X
Owner	R - W - X - D
Admins	FC
System	FC

Figure 1.8 - **An example of access permissions. Access permissions are applied to an object based on the level of clearance given to a subject.**

As demonstrated in *Figure 1.8*, access permissions are applied to an object based on the level of clearance given to a subject. The example provided represents only a few of the possible permissions that can be assigned to an object. For example, "list" is a permission seen in common operating systems that permits users to only list the files in a directory, not read, delete, modify, or execute those files.

Moreover, a single object can have multiple access permissions depending on the user or group that needs to access that object. As demonstrated in *Figure 1.9*, users can be assigned to groups, such as administrators or printer users. Anyone in the group administrators has full control over the user directories for Bruce, Sally, and Bob. However, users in the printer users group can only access local printers but not any of the user directories.

83

```
┌─────────────────────────────────────────────────┐
│         ACCESS CONTROL LIST (Users)             │
│                                                 │
│  Mary:                                          │
│                                                 │
│     UserMary Directory - FullControl            │
│     UserBob Directory - Write        ┌──────────────────────────────────────┐
│     UserBruce Directory - Write      │      ACCESS CONTROL LIST (Groups)    │
│     Printer 001 - Execute            │                                      │
│                                      │  Group Administrators:               │
│  Bob:                                │                                      │
│                                      │     Members- Ted, Alice              │
│     UserMary Directory - Read        │     UserBruce Directory - Full Control│
│     UserBob Directory - Full Control │     UserSally Directory - Full Control│
│     UserBruce Directory - Write      │     UserBob Directory - Full Control │
│     Printer 001 - Execute            │     UserMary Directory - Full Control│
│                                      │                                      │
│  Bruce:                              │  Group Printer Users:                │
│                                      │                                      │
│     UserMary Directory - No Access   │     Members – Bruce, Sally, Bob      │
│     User Bob Directory - Write       │     UserBruce Directory – No Access  │
│     UserBruce Directory - Full Control│    UserSally Directory - No Access  │
│     Printer 001 - Execute            │     UserBob Directory - No Access    │
│                                      │     PrinterDevice P1 – Print         │
│  Sally:                              │     PrinterDevice P2 – Print         │
│                                      │     PrinterDevice P3 – Print         │
│     UserMary Directory - No Access   └──────────────────────────────────────┘
│     UserBob Directory - No Access               │
│     UserBruce Directory - No Access             │
│     Printer 001 - No Access                     │
│                                                 │
└─────────────────────────────────────────────────┘
```

Figure 1.9 - **Access permissions and group roles. Users can be assigned to groups, such as Administrators or Printer Users. Anyone in the group Administrators has full control over the user directories for Bruce, Sally and Bob. However, users In the PrinterUsers group can only access local printers but not any of the user directories.**

The third access control framework, nondiscretionary access control, is also based on the assignment of permissions to read, write, and execute files on a system. However, unlike discretionary access control, which allows the file owner to specify those permissions, nondiscretionary access control requires the administrator of a system to define and tightly control the access rules for files in the system.

Data Access Controls

Data access controls can be implemented in a number of different ways depending on the access needs, organization requirements, and available technology capabilities. This section will discuss the more common methods of implementing effective data access control.

The term access control list (ACL) is used in many forms to communicate how a collection of controls is assigned based on a particular set of parameters. ACLs will typically have two basic pieces of data: a keyword pattern and an action to take if the keyword is matched. The pattern of the keyword will vary based on the application. For example, if the ACL is located in a network router the keyword will be an IP address or network designation and the action will consist of instructions on whether to block the traffic from (or to) that network or allow it to pass through. If the ACL is attached to a file on a server, the keyword will be a user ID or system group and the action will be an indication of whether that user or group will be allowed to access the requested file. There will be many such keyword/action pairs in an ACL and the system will continue searching down the list until it finds a match. If no match is found, all ACL systems include a default action (usually "block" or "permit"). That default action will be based primarily on the organization's overall security stance. In other words, whether it belongs to the "deny by default" or "allow by default" philosophy security will determine the ultimate fate of unspecified actions.

ACLs are often used in the provisioning of permissions within a system based on organization policy. In most cases, ACLs within a system are applied to actions by the user, but they can also be tied to group permission. For example, an administrator may create a set of users, assign them to a group, and apply a set of files and directory permissions to that group. Within the system that information is translated into an ACL that is then employed when access to that file or directory is requested.

85

Access Control Matrix

An access control matrix (ACM) is an ACL in the form of a table. Subjects and objects are identified and the permissions applied to each subject/object combination are specified in the matrix. As shown in *Figure 1.10*, an ACM can be used to quickly summarize what permissions a subject has for various system objects. This is a simple example, and in large environments an ACM can become quite complex. But, it can be extremely helpful during system or application design to ensure that security is applied properly to all subjects and objects throughout the application.

Subject	A	B	C	D	E	F	G	H	I	J	K	X
1	●			●								●
2						●			●			
3	●						●					
4					●			●				●
5		●										
6							●					
7			●					●				

Figure 1.10 - **An Access Control Matrix (ACM) is an ACL in the form of a table. Subjects and objects are identified and the permissions applied to each subject/object combination are specified in the matrix. Here, an ACM can be used to quickly summarize what permissions a subject has for various system objects. This is a simple example. In large environments an ACM can become quite complex.**

Rule-Based Access Control

In a rule-based system, access is based on a list of predefined rules that determine what accesses should be granted. The rules, created or authorized by system owners, specify the privileges granted to users (e.g., read, write, and execute) when the specific condition of a rule is met. For example, a standard ACL may specify simply that user Bob is allowed to access the file labeled "Financial Forecast," but a rule-based system would additionally specify that Bob can only access that file between 9:00 AM and 5:00 PM Monday through Friday. A mediation mechanism enforces the rules to ensure only authorized access by intercepting every request, comparing it to user authorizations, and making a decision based on the appropriate rule. Rule-based controls are most commonly a form of DAC, because the system owner typically develops the rules based on organization or processing needs.

Role-Based Access Control

A role-based access control (RBAC) model, as shown in *Figure 1.11*, bases the access control authorizations on the roles (or functions) that the user is assigned within an organization. The determination of what roles have access to a resource can be governed by the owner of the data, as with DACs, or applied based on policy, as with MACs.

Access control decisions are based on job function, previously defined and governed by policy, and each role (job function) will have its own access capabilities. Objects associated with a role will inherit privileges assigned to that role. This is also true for groups of users, allowing administrators to simplify access control strategies by assigning users to groups and groups to roles.

There are several approaches to RBAC. As with many system controls, there are variations on how they can be applied within a computer system. As demonstrated in *Figure 1.11*, there are four basic RBAC architectures:

1. ***Non-RBAC***: Non-RBAC is simply a user-granted access to data or an application by traditional mapping, such as with ACLs. There are no formal "roles" associated with the mappings, other than any identified by the particular user.

2. ***Limited RBAC***: Limited RBAC is achieved when users are mapped to roles within a single application rather than through an organization-wide role structure. Users in a limited RBAC

Non-RBAC Management

Users are mapped to applications

Limited RBAC Management

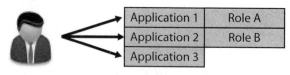

Users are mapped to application roles

Users ALSO mapped to applications that have not developed Role Based Access

Hybrid RBAC Management

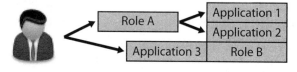

Users are mapped to multi-application roles

Only select application access rights are moved to the multi-application role

Full RBAC Management

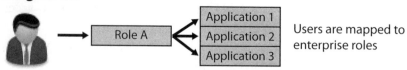

Users are mapped to enterprise roles

Figure 1.11 - **Role-Based Access Control architecture**

system are also able to access non-RBAC-based applications or data. For example, a user may be assigned to multiple roles within several applications and, in addition, have direct access to another application or system independent of his or her assigned role. The key attribute of limited RBAC is that the role for that user is defined within an application and not necessarily based on the user's organizational job function.

3. ***Hybrid RBAC***: Hybrid RBAC introduces the use of a role that is applied to multiple applications or systems based on a user's specific role within the organization. That role is then applied to applications or systems that subscribe to the organization's role-based model. However, as the term "hybrid" suggests, there are instances where the subject may also be assigned to roles defined solely within specific applications, complimenting (or, perhaps, contradicting) the larger, more encompassing organizational role used by other systems.

4. ***Full RBAC***: Full RBAC systems are controlled by roles defined by the organization's policy and access control infrastructure and then applied to applications and systems across the enterprise. The applications, systems, and associated data apply permissions based on that enterprise definition, and not one defined by a specific application or system.

The primary benefit of an RBAC-based access system is that it is easily modeled after the organization's own organization or functional structure. Just as employees have roles within the political hierarchy of the organization, so, too, do they have roles in the functional hierarchy of an information system. In addition, accounting for the movement of personnel around an organization and adjusting their information access accordingly is greatly simplified in an RBAC-based system. The administrator simply removes the old role designation from the user (instantly removing access to all information the old role required) and assigns that user to a new role, automatically granting that user access to all the information assigned to that new role.

89

Content-Dependent Access Control

Some access control decisions are affected by the actual content of the data rather than on overall organizational policy. For example, consider the typical payroll database where personnel from multiple levels require access. Managers should be able to view payroll information for their own staff but not for their peers or any other employees. This means that even though the user may be able to access the database in question, their ability to view the data within the database may be restricted according to the value of the data—in other words they may only be able to see records with the same department number as the department they belong to. The typical role-based functions may be applied to the database (e.g., manager, employee, administrator, etc.) but the logical structure of the data will be constantly changing.

Personnel move between departments, managers change assignments (and staff) and company reorganizations often mean that personnel can move from one division to another rapidly. In that type of environment the roles "manager" and "worker" may be valid, but the personnel that fall into those categories may change often over time. For that reason, some systems use content-dependent access control. Content-dependent access control is based on the actual content of the data rather than on general role definitions. It requires the access control mechanism (via an arbiter program within the software application or system used to access the data) to investigate the data to make decisions on how to apply the access rules in the system. With a content-dependent model the policy and access rules do not change, but the actual data a user may be able to see as a result of applying those changes may change over time as the data itself changes.

Constrained User Interface

Another method for controlling access is by restricting users to specific functions based on their role in the system. This is typically implemented by limiting available menus, data views, encryption, or by physically constraining the user interfaces. This is common on devices such as an automated teller machine (ATM). In the previously mentioned payroll database example, someone in an "employee" role would only have options for "view paycheck" and "change tax info," whereas a manager using the same system might be give the additional options of "grant a raise" and "promote employee" (but not for himself, of course!) The advantage of a constrained user interface is that it limits potential avenues of attack and system failure by restricting the processing options that are available to the user. On an ATM machine, if a user does not have a checking account with the bank he or she will not be shown the "Withdraw money from checking" option. Likewise, an information system might have an "Add/Remove Users" menu option for administrators, but if a normal, non-administrative user logs in he or she will not even see that menu option. By not even identifying potential options for non-qualifying users, the system limits the potentially harmful execution of unauthorized system or application commands.

Many database management systems have the concept of "views." A database view is an extract of the data stored in the database that is filtered based on predefined user or system criteria. This permits multiple users to access the same database while only having the ability to access data they need (or are allowed to have) and not data for another user. The use of database views is another example of a constrained user interface.

Capability Tables

Capability tables are used to match subjects (like users or processes) and their capabilities (like read, write, and update) against system objects (like files, directories, and devices) and the ability to use those capabilities on those objects. *Figure 1.12* shows a good example of how this works.

Subject	Procedure A	File X	File Y
Process A		Read	Read/Write
Joe	Execute	Write	

Figure 1.12 - **A good example of how a capability table works.**

Each row in the table holds the capabilities for a specific subject (like a process or a user). Each column represents an object in the environment. As you move across the columns for a particular row you can see what capability each subject can apply to each particular object. For example, Process A (subject) has read-only access to File X and read/write capability to File Y. Joe, on the other hand, can execute Process A and write to File X but has no ability to access File Y.

Temporal (Time-Based) Isolation

There are often times when certain activities on a system are considered either acceptable or unacceptable based not on who performs those activities, but rather on when they are performed. Temporal or timed-based access controls are those employed at a given time for a predetermined duration. If a request is made for access to data or a resource outside the defined time window, the access is denied. For example, a bank may want its employees to only access its loan application system during business hours (when, presumably, they are in the office) and not at night or on the weekends (when they would be at home or elsewhere). Likewise, an organization could establish their information processing service such that only confidential data will be processed in the morning, when all their workers possessing a "Confidential" clearance are scheduled to work. All secret data will then be processed in the afternoon, when workers with a "Secret" clearance are on the schedule. Attempts to access confidential data in the afternoon or secret data in the morning would be denied.

This concept can also extend to system processing, where certain types of jobs may only be run during certain parts of the day or on certain days of the year. For example, a business would not want its end-of-month processing to be run in the middle of the month, so it may restrict access to that process such that it can only be run from the 1st to the 5th days of any month. There is one important caveat to using temporal access controls: if the organization is spread across several time zones care must be taken to ensure that the time differences between locations are accounted for in both the process and the supporting technology. For example, if an organization defines "secret" access as being available only between 8:00 AM and 11:00 AM and has offices in both New York and Hong Kong the organization must define which location will serve as the reference point. Otherwise, it is possible that secret information will be accessible for a total of six hours (three in New York and three in Hong Kong) rather than the intended three

Identification and Authentication

To this point the chapter has focused on access control principles and the threats to the control environment. The section that follows covers details regarding specific access controls and essential control strategies. Areas include:

- Identification, authentication, and authorization
- Access control services
- Identity management
- Access control technologies

Identification, Authentication, and Authorization

Identification is the assertion of a unique identity for a person or system and is the starting point of all access control. Without proper identification it is impossible to determine to whom or what to apply the appropriate controls. Identification is a critical first step in applying access controls because all activities and controls are tied to the identity of a particular user or entity.

The downstream effects of proper identification include accountability (with a protected audit trail) and the ability to trace activities to individuals. They also include the provisioning of rights and privileges, system profiles, and availability of system information, applications, and services. The objective of identification is to bind a user to the appropriate controls based on that unique user instance. For example, once the unique user is identified and validated through authentication, his or her identity within the infrastructure will be used to allocate resources based on predefined privileges.

Authentication is the process of verifying the identity of the user. Upon requesting access and presenting unique user identification, the user will provide some set of private data that only the user should have access to or knowledge of. The combination of the identity and information only known by, or only in the possession of, the user acts to verify that the user identity is being used by the expected and assigned entity (e.g., a person). This, then, establishes trust between the user and the system for the allocation of privileges.

Authorization is the final step in the process. Once a user has been identified and properly authenticated, the resources that user is allowed to access must be defined and monitored. Authorization is the process of defining the specific resources a user needs and determining the type of access to those resources the user may have. For example, Deanna, Jennifer, and Matthew may all be identified and authenticated into the same system, but Deanna is only authorized to access the payroll information, Jennifer is only authorized to access product source code, and Matthew is only authorized to view the company's internal Web sites.

The relationship between these three important concepts is simple:

- Identification provides uniqueness
- Authentication provides validity
- Authorization provides control

Identification Methods

The most common form of identification is a simple user name, user ID, account number, or personal identification number (PIN). These are used as a point of assignment and association to a user entity within a system. However, identification may not be limited to human users and may include software and hardware services that may need to access objects, modules, databases, or other applications to provide a full suite of services. In an effort to ensure that the application is authorized to make the requests to potentially sensitive resources, the system can use digital identification, such as a certificate or one-time session identifier to identify the application. There are several common forms of identification used by organizations, and the type used may vary depending on the process or the situation.

Identification Badges

An identification badge is the most common form of physical identification and authorization in organizations. The badge represents that the badge holder is officially recognized and has some status within the organization. Most badges contain the name or logo of the organization, the name of the badge holder, and a picture of the holder printed on the face. In some cases, because of the cost of badge printing, organizations will print personalized badges only for employees. Visitors or temporary personnel will be given a generic badge, perhaps in a different color, to signify that they are permitted on the premises but do not belong to the organization.

The typical process behind an ID badge requires that the user wear the badge at all times while on company premises. Employees and security personnel will be able to observe the badge, check the picture on the badge against the badge wearer, and then make a determination as to whether the person legitimately belongs on the premises or not. If the name, picture, and badge holder do not all match, the employee should summon security or escort the badge holder off the premises.

Unfortunately, this process fails all too often. Most people, even security guards, fail to make a very close comparison of the badge against the holder. During the morning rush into a facility most employees simply wave the badge in the air to indicate they have one and are allowed to pass. While this is not a universal problem—government and military facilities generally pay close attention to badge holders and their credentials—it is common enough to conclude that identification badges are not a foolproof security mechanism.

Another type of badge, the access badge, provides a much stronger security mechanism. Access badges are used to enter secured areas of a facility and are used in conjunction with a badge reader to read information stored on the badge. A central monitoring facility will read the badge information, match that information against a list of authorized personnel for that area, and make a determination for or against access. A failing of access badges is that, because they are not physically tied with a specific person, employees often share their badges with others who may need temporary access to a secured area. While certainly not endorsed by the organization, and most often directly counter to security policy, this practice is widespread. To counter this problem, many organizations combine the identification badge with the access badge to provide a stronger tie between the badge holder and the individual ID card.

User ID

The common user ID—the standard entry point to most information systems—provides the system with a way of uniquely identifying a particular user amongst all the users of that system. No two users on a single system can have the same user ID, as that would cause confusion for the access control system and remove the ability to track any activity to an individual. It is important to note that the user ID should only be used as a system identifier, not an authenticator. The user ID simply tells the system that this user wants to be identified by that ID, not that this user has the legitimate right to access the system under that ID or be given access to any system resources. It is only when the user ID is combined with some other authentication mechanism, such as a password, security token, or a digital certificate, that a judgment can be made as to the legitimacy of the user and access can be permitted or denied.

Account Number/PIN

Much like a user ID, an account number provides a unique identity for a particular user within a system or an enterprise. Most ordinary users will encounter account numbers as part of a financial services application or transaction. In such transactions, the personal identification number (PIN), provides the authentication information needed to determine whether the user has the legitimate right to use that account number and access the information under that account.

MAC Address

All computers that participate in a network must have some method of uniquely identifying themselves to that network so that information can be sent to and from the network connection associated with the proper computer. The most common form of machine address in use today is the media access control (MAC) address. The MAC address is a 48-bit number (typically represented in hexadecimal format) that is supposed to be globally unique, meaning that every network device in the world is supposed to have a unique MAC address. In the early days of network computing, the MAC address was embedded into the hardware of the device during its manufacture and was not changeable by end users (or attackers). When that was the case, the MAC address was a good way to identify (and authenticate) particular devices with a high degree of certainty. Unfortunately, most modern network-enabled devices allow the MAC address to be set in software, meaning that anyone with administrative access to the device can alter the MAC address of that device to anything of his choosing. Thus, the MAC address is no longer considered a strong identifier or authenticator.

IP Address

Computers using the TCP/IP network protocol are also assigned an internet protocol (IP) address. Whereas the MAC address provides a way of identifying the physical location of a system, the IP address gives the logical location of a device on the IP network. IP addresses are organized into logical groups called subnetworks or subnets. A device's IP address must be unique among all the systems on that device's same subnet, but there are circumstances where devices on different subnets can have identical IP addresses. As was the case with MAC addresses, a device's IP address is assigned in software by the administrator of a system. As such, IP address is not a very strong indicator of a system's identity. It is possible to use the IP address as one data point amongst many to narrow down a system's unique network location or identity, but it should not be used alone for such purposes.

Radio Frequency Identification (RFID)

In recent years, a great deal of research has been done to determine ways to uniquely identify objects and be able to read that identification without physically interacting with the object itself. This can be very useful in cases where it is advantageous to identify items quickly or without the need for physical inspection. The most popular technology to come out of this research is the radio frequency identification (RFID), tag. The RFID tag is a small label that can be embedded in almost any object, including product shipping pallets, passports, consumer goods, and even human beings. The tag contains identifying information for the object, such as a UPC code or a person's name. When the tag comes in the proximity of an RFID reader, the reader reads the information from the tag and determines the identity of the object. RFID tags are extremely small, so they add no discernible size or weight to the object being tagged, and because they can be read from a distance of several feet the reader does not need close physical contact with the tagged object.

The use of RFID in some applications has raised some privacy concerns for some people. For instance, RFID tags are now included in all newly issued passports for several countries such as the U.S. and Australia. Unfortunately, because the tags can be read from a distance, many fear that their private passport information can be taken from the tag without their consent. In addition, many are advocating the injection of RFID tags into humans to allow authorities to positively identify those people if they are kidnapped or killed. Again, privacy advocates fear that RFID-injected people can have their personal tag information read without their consent by an intruder with a tag reader in a crowded public place, raising identity theft concerns. In the final analysis, RFID technology has been a big breakthrough in the manufacturing and consumer goods industries where it is helping to reduce inventory and product tracking costs. The values and risks to privacy and breach must be considered when using an RFID badge.

E-Mail Address

The use of a person's e-mail address as an identification mechanism or user ID has become increasingly popular in recent years, particularly for Internet e-commerce and portal sites. Part of the reason for this is that an e-mail address is globally unique. If a user's e-mail address is janet@jmail.com, nobody else can legitimately use that address to send or receive e-mail. Based on that assumption, many Web sites use the user's e-mail address as the unique user ID and allow the user to select a password for authentication. Web sites using this convention will additionally use that e-mail address to send correspondence to the user for administrative or informational purposes. One common mechanism in current use is to have a new user to register on the site to enter his e-mail address as a user ID. The site will then send a confirmation e-mail to that address and wait for a reply from the user before completing the registration process. The theory behind this process is that if a user has access to the e-mail account specified by the entered address there is a high degree of certainty that the user is legitimate.

However, this assumption may not be valid in many situations. The uniqueness of an e-mail address is enforced solely by convention. There are no technical restrictions preventing the use of another person's e-mail address as an identifier and, the aforementioned verification mechanism notwithstanding, there is no way to formally verify the legitimacy of a particular e-mail address or that a particular individual is the owner of that address. In addition, it is a simple matter to spoof (or falsify) the sender's e-mail address in most common e-mail systems in use today, and spammers, fraudsters, and phishing perpetrators regularly use this method as a way of masking the true origin of their attacks. It is convenient for a person to use an e-mail address as identification because it is easy to remember, but if an organization wishes to use this as an identification method it should not place absolute trust in its legitimacy and should certainly use other authentication methods to tie the use of that address to a particular user.

User Identification Guidelines

There are three essential security characteristics regarding identities: uniqueness, nondescriptiveness, and secure issuance. First and foremost, user identification must be unique so that each entity on a system can be unambiguously identified. Although it is possible for a user to have many unique identifiers, each must be distinctive within an access control environment. In the event there are several disparate access control environments that do not interact, share information, or provide access to the same resources, duplication is possible. For example, a user's ID at work may be "mary_t," allowing her to be identified and authenticated within the corporate infrastructure. She may also have a personal e-mail account with her Internet service provider (ISP) with the user ID of "mary_t." This is possible because the corporate access control environment does not interact with the ISP's access control environment. However, there are potential dangers with using the same ID on multiple systems. Users are prone to duplicating certain attributes, such as passwords, to minimize their effort. If an attacker discovers Mary's ISP ID and password, he or she may rightly conclude that she is using the same ID and password at work. Therefore, any duplication, although possible in certain circumstances, represents a fundamental risk to the enterprise.

User identification should generally be nondescriptive and should try as much as possible to disclose as little as possible about the user. The ID should also not expose the associated role or job function of the user. Common practice is to issue user IDs that are a variant of the user's name, for example, "bsmith" or "bob.smith." Once this scheme is identified by an attacker it becomes easy to begin enumerating through possible variations on the theme to discover other valid user IDs in the organization. In addition, a person's job function should never be used as the basis for a user ID. If a user ID were to be named "cfo," an attacker would be able to focus energy on that user alone based on the assumption that he is the CFO of the company and would probably have privileged access to critical systems. However, this is practiced quite often. It is very common

101

to have user IDs of "admin," "finance," "shipment," "Web master," or other representations of highly descriptive IDs. The naming of these IDs is voluntary and self-imposed by the organization.

There are some IDs, however, that cannot be easily changed. The most predominant is the username "root." It is the name given to the administrative account with unlimited access rights on a UNIX system. Everyone, including attackers, knows what the username "root" represents, and it is for this very reason that attaining root's password is so desirable. Unfortunately, in most UNIX systems, changing the user or masking that role is impossible. In Microsoft operating systems it is possible to change the username of the default "administrator" account (nearly the equivalent of "root" in UNIX) to some other nondescript name, and should be considered a best practice.

Clearly, any highly privileged system account, such as "root" and "administrator," represents a target for attackers, and it can be difficult to mask its role. However, traditional users, who may have a broad set of privileges throughout the enterprise, can be more difficult for attackers to isolate as a target. Therefore, establishing a user ID that is independent of the user's name, job function, or role will act to mask the true privileges of the user. Ideally, user IDs should be randomly assigned or include some randomized elements to prevent ID guessing and enumeration by attackers. While renaming is a best practice and will prevent rudimentary attempts at access it can be defeated by identifying the "Security IDs." Defense in depth must be practiced to ensure an appropriate level of defense is implemented vs. the burden to the user and risk.

Clearly, any highly privileged system account, such as "root" and "administrator," represents a target for attackers, and it can be difficult to mask its role. However, traditional users, who may have a broad set of privileges throughout the enterprise, can be more difficult for attackers to isolate as a target. Therefore, establishing a user ID that is independent of the user's name, job function, or role will act to mask the true privileges of the user. Ideally, user IDs should be randomly assigned or include some randomized elements to prevent ID guessing and enumeration by attackers.

Finally, the process of issuing identifiers must be secure and well documented. The quality of the identifier is in part based on the quality of how it is issued. If an identity can be inappropriately issued, the entire security system can break down. The identifier is the first, and arguably the most important, step in acquiring access. An organization must establish a secure process for issuing IDs, including the proper documentation and approval for all ID requests. The process must also account for notification of the user's management and any system owners for systems the user may have access to. The organization must deliver the user ID to the end user in a secure manner. This can be as simple as delivery in a sealed envelope or as complicated as using digitally signed and encrypted communications channels. Finally, the entire process must be logged and documented properly to ensure that the process can be verified and audited.

Identity Management

Identity management is a much-used term that refers to a set of technologies intended to offer greater efficiency in the management of a diverse user and technical environment. Modern enterprises must deal with the difficulties of managing the identity and access restrictions of employees, contractors, customers, partners, and vendors in a highly complex and dynamic organization. Identity management systems are designed to centralize and streamline the management of user identity, authentication, and authorization data.

Identity management addresses all aspects of controlling access, with a core focus on centralized management. Given the complexity of modern organizations and the diversity of business requirements, many access control infrastructures grow convoluted and difficult to manage. They manage multiple independent access control systems, often one per application. Rarely are they all integrated; at best there may be pockets of integration between several applications. Along with this multiplicity of access control systems comes a complex web of administrative responsibilities, making the administrator's job even more complex with each new application. Enterprises operate a vast array of IT infrastructure components, including:

- Network operating systems
- Multiple servers running multiple operating systems
- User directories
- Human resources, payroll, and contract management systems
- A variety of line-of-business applications
- Customer relationship management (CRM) systems
- Electronic commerce applications
- Enterprise resource management systems planning (ERP)

As shown in *Figure 1.13*, almost every system must track valid users and control their permissions for a given system. The diversity of these systems—each with its own administration software, and management processes—and the fact that users typically access multiple systems, makes managing this user data difficult at best, and a financial and operational burden to most organizations.

One of the primary tasks within an identity management infrastructure is the need to provision, maintain, and manage user IDs. This includes gathering the initial account information to populate the system and create an account record for that user. The information may be submitted by the user through filling out a standard form or an in-person interview, or it may come directly from the user as part of a self-help service. Once account information is gathered, the system must be able to account for the granting and revocation of access rights as the user (and the associated IDs) goes through its natural life cycle.

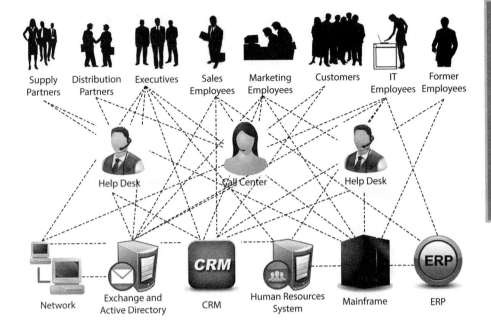

Supply Partners | Distribution Partners | Executives | Sales Employees | Marketing Employees | Customers | IT Employees | Former Employees

Help Desk | Call Center | Help Desk

Network | Exchange and Active Directory | CRM | Human Resources System | Mainframe | ERP

Figure 1.13 - **In complex environments, almost every system must track valid users and control their permissions.**

Efficiency in this process is a key performance factor. The goal of an identity management system is to consolidate access rights into an easily managed record of identity and access for each user in the system. This will work to reduce errors and increase control over IDs and access in the organization. It will also eliminate redundant and unnecessary access. "Once and done" is the mantra for this activity. Setting up user access on multiple systems is repetitive. Doing so with the individual tools provided with each system is needlessly costly. Therefore, all design and development for the identity management system should be aimed at reducing redundancy and streamlining the provisioning and management processes as much as possible.

Timeliness of the process is important to the business. If there is too much of a time lag during the front-end provisioning and management processes, that will translate directly to lost user productivity. If there is a time lag during the access removal or decommissioning stages, that will translate into increased security risk to the organization. Identity management systems promote timeliness by centrally managing the identity and access control for distributed systems throughout the enterprise.

Identity Management Challenges

Typically, when an employee is hired, a new user profile is created and stored in a human resources database and a request for access to various systems and applications is created. If the organization has predefined roles associated with particular jobs the new user request will be compared to a company's role authorization policies. If the organization does not have such a role-based system, a management-defined list of access rights will be created. The request is then routed for the necessary approval, and (if approval is granted) sent to the IT department. Finally, the IT department submits the approved request to various system administrators to provision user access rights. The user is provisioned, and the approval is recorded in a history file or log file.

This scenario assumes, of course, the best of all possible worlds, where processes work perfectly every time and all participants are prepared to do their part at any time. In actual practice, there are a number of problems that can arise during the identity management process:

- Requests for access rights can be backlogged, halting user productivity. There will be a limited number of people to process these requests and often this is not an individual's (or a group's) full-time job. As a result, these requests are often delayed or held until enough requests are pending for someone to allocate time to process them.

- Cumbersome policies cause errors. If the requested access involves different systems and complex levels of access there is a high likelihood that there will be errors in the implementation of the request. This will result in delayed access (at best) or the assignment of inappropriate access to the user (at worst).

- Request forms are not fully completed. This can cause

numerous delays in processing. Very often, the forms are not clear or the requestor is confused as to specifically what they need to request.

- The number of resources across the enterprise may be growing. This may lead to an increasing number of access requests continually flowing into the processing system. Given the chronic resource shortage in most organizations, this will become a perpetual problem.

- Precise audit trails of requests and approvals are rarely maintained. If there is a question about what access was requested, who approved it, or what was ultimately granted, an audit trail is the only definitive method of determining this. Unfortunately, many organizations do not keep accurate records of this process, particularly during the approval stages.

- Many system profiles and users are dormant or associated with departed employees, making them invalid. The process of removing access when no longer needed is just as important as granting it in the first place. However, many organizations fail to implement processes to regularly review existing access to determine if it is still needed.

Some people in the organization, particularly those in the upper levels of management, often bypass defined processes and protocols put in place to manage the flow of provisioning requests in an attempt to get their requests implemented more quickly. Even employees at lower levels in the organization may attempt to call a helpful friend in IT rather than go through the standard process. If allowed to continue, this practice leads to inaccurate record keeping as some provisioning will not be properly recorded.

Key management challenges regarding identity management solutions also include:

- *Consistency:* User profile data entered into different systems should be consistent. This includes name, user ID, contact

107

information, termination date, etc. The fact that each system has its own user profile management system makes this difficult.

- **Usability:** When users access multiple systems, they need to manage multiple user IDs, multiple passwords, and multiple sign-on screens. This complexity is burdensome to users, who consequently have problems accessing systems and incur productivity and support costs.

- **Reliability:** User profile data should be reliable, especially if it is used to control access to sensitive data or resources. Too often the process used to update user information on every system does not produce data that are complete, timely, and accurate.

- **Scalability:** Enterprises manage user profile data for large numbers of people. There are typically tens of thousands of internal users and hundreds or thousands of partners or clients. Many identity management systems cannot scale to support the data volumes and peak transaction rates produced by large user populations.

The need for more effective identity management is clear given the chronic limitations of existing system storage and processing capacity, increasing cost for managing growing user populations, and burgeoning inefficiencies that stem from growing business demands on existing systems. The potential negative impacts include loss of business productivity and increasing security risk.

Identity management systems can also help an organization to meet its obligations to comply with the seemingly endless (and expanding) laws, regulations, and customer requirements with respect to proper security management. While no current legislation mandates the implementation of an "identity management system," most laws that cover (at least in part) security and privacy issues have as a basic requirement that organizations will do what they can to manage access privileges across the enterprise and ensure that access to data (particularly private consumer data) is restricted to only those that need it. The ability to accurately manage user IDs, control their life cycle, and remove access accurately and quickly goes a long way toward demonstrating compliance with appropriate legislative, industry, and customer requirements.

Finally, all organizations must manage IDs for a variety of constituents, potentially including employees, contractors, business partners, customers, maintenance personnel, and visitors. An effective identity management system allows the organization to appropriately segment these various user populations and assign the appropriate type and level of access to each group. Access can be managed on a group basis to enforce organizational policies that may restrict the systems or services nonemployees may access. A comprehensive identity management strategy and implementation allows for tight control over access while also allowing for granularity and flexibility in managing such access.

Centralized Identity Management

One of the basic decisions an organization will need to make when establishing an identity management program is whether to enforce centralized or decentralized identity and access control management. In a centralized system, all access decisions, provisioning, management, and technology is concentrated in a central location (physically or virtually). One entity (an individual, a department, or a management system) manages the service for the entire enterprise and that entity sets all the policies, standards, and operational parameters. From a technology standpoint, all authentication and authorization requests are sent to the central service. Examples of centralized access control systems include RADIUS and Terminal Access Controller Access-Control System Plus (TACACS+).

Figure 1.14 shows a conceptual diagram of how a centralized identity management and access control model might be configured.

The benefits of such a scheme stem primarily from the ability of the single team to enforce uniform, organization-wide control over the allocation and

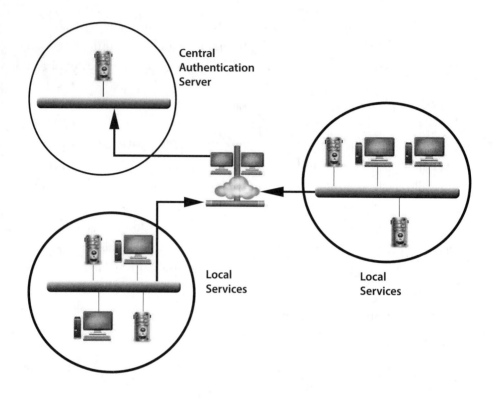

Figure 1.14 - **Centralized access control model.**

use of IDs across the organization. This promotes consistency of policy and use no matter where in the organization a particular user may reside or operate. Changes in the system can happen quickly and be distributed uniformly to all points using the service, limiting the risk exposure that may exist when a user is removed from one part of the system but removal from other areas is delayed. In a compliance-driven organization, a centralized service also demonstrates uniform control over all enterprise access processes.

Decentralized Identity Management

The primary drawback to a centralized system is that many organizations (particularly large international firms) just cannot operate a central service on the scale that is required by such an enterprise. The access needs of each local

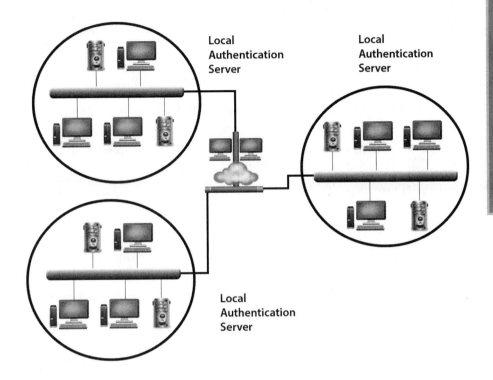

Figure 1.15 - **Decentralized access control model.**

or regional office may differ substantially enough that a central policy may not be the most effective way to manage the process. In addition, political or legal considerations may dictate that each office or region maintain some level of control over the access administration for that area. In such situations, a decentralized identity and access management system may be called for.

In a decentralized control model, ID management, authentication, and authorization decisions are spread throughout the environment to local organizations. "Local" is a subjective term depending on the organization, but it typically refers a single office, a group of offices in a single region, or an individual business unit. In this model, control decisions are distributed to the people closer to the resources or processes users need to access, for

111

example, department managers or system owners who are then responsible for implementing the appropriate access controls on their systems.

The benefit of a decentralized model is that it allows access decisions to be made by the people or organizations that are closest to the assets needing protection and can much better address local access policies and requirements. Local management and administrators typically have a much better sense of the requirements of their local users and will be in a much better position to understand who really needs access to their resources. Thus, they will be able to better define and manage the system based on those requirements. The drawback to a decentralized system is that it becomes harder to enforce enterprise-wide policies and standards for ID and access management. Unless a clear policy and process defining who has ultimate responsibility for setting, managing, and following organization access policies and standards is set a decentralized system may quickly lead to an inconsistent patchwork of access controls, standards, and processes. A decentralized system may also be more expensive for the organization, since multiple systems and technology components will have to be purchased and managed within the organization. Another potential problem is that a decentralized model may lead to overlapping or conflicting rights between resources, which may expose gaps in security controls. *Figure 1.15* shows a conceptual diagram of how a decentralized access control model might be configured.

Authentication Methods

Once an identity is established it must be authenticated. There exist numerous technologies and implementation of authentication methods however they almost all fall under three major areas. There are three fundamental types of authentication:

- *Authentication by knowledge*—something a person knows
- *Authentication by possession*—something a person has
- *Authentication by characteristic*—something a person is

Logical controls related to these types are called "factors." Something you know can be a password or PIN, something you have can be a token fob or smart card, and something you are is usually some form of biometrics. Single-factor authentication is the employment of one of these factors, two-factor authentication is using two of the three factors, and three-factor authentication is the combination of all three factors. The general term for the use of more than one factor during authentication is multifactor authentication.

Single-factor authentication is typically implemented with a user ID and password combination. Note that in this case the password is the relevant "factor," not the user ID. The user ID is merely an identifier to allow the system to know who is trying to authenticate. General security industry consensus is that single-factor authentication using only a password does not provide a high level of security because the typical reusable (static) password is easily compromised and, therefore, provides very limited security. There are a plethora of technical solutions that provide the framework to authenticate users based on passwords. Given the broad use of passwords, most technical solutions will provide this service, and the universal acceptance and historical foundation for the use of passwords as an authenticator means it will remain a staple of authentication mechanisms for a long time to come.

Two-factor authentication usually introduces an additional level of technical controls that the user must have in his possession in the form of a physical or programmatic device. Typically, this is a token, fob, or smart device that substantiates the user's identity by being incorporated into the authentication process. The incorporation can include one-time (or "single use") passwords, such as a time-sensitive number generators, or the existence of a digital certificate and private encryption key.

Three-factor authentication will include elements of all three factors and, as such, will include something about the user, such as a biometric feature. Available biometrics include a number of options, such as fingerprints, retina scanning, hand geometry, facial features, or even body temperature. This will typically involve the use of a device that interfaces with a person during the authentication process.

In recent years a potential fourth authentication factor has made an appearance on the landscape: geolocation or somewhere you are. Current network and mobile technology enables the identification of the apparent geographic source of a communication based on its IP address or (in some cases) GPS coordinates. This helps detect attackers using credentials from unexpected locations, such as outside of the corporate network or in a foreign country. The term "apparent location" is used because the use of IP address is not a foolproof method of geographic identification. IP addresses can be easily spoofed (or falsified) to mask the real source of a communication. Alternatively, a non-malicious user can be working on a remote network (say, for example, in Mumbai) using IP address space assigned to the company's headquarters in Milwaukee. Nevertheless, geolocation is being increasingly seen as a contender for an additional factor to increase the assurance applied to an authentication.

Authentication by Knowledge

A representation of single-factor authentication, what a person knows, is typically used in conjunction with a user ID or other unique identifier. As discussed previously, in common use this is predominantly a password. A password is typically a short (5–15 characters) string of characters that the user must remember to authenticate against their unique identifier. Passwords can be simple words or a combination of two or more easily remembered words, include numbers or special characters, and range in length and complexity. The more diverse or complicated the password is, the more difficult it will be for an attacker to guess or crack. Given that password crackers will typically start with a common language or technical dictionary or a predefined collection of words, the use of common words as passwords has grown significantly less secure. What was once feasible as a password is now considered a vulnerability.

Standard words, perhaps with some capitalization, are not considered secure by today's standards: BoB, Phoenix, airplane, doGWalk are examples of basic words. Unfortunately, passwords of this type represent the most common forms used. Good system administrators are now incorporating password complexity requirements into the password creation process so that the system will not accept such simple passwords. However, applying this type of administrative control is not always possible.

Combination passwords mix dictionary words to create a password that is easy for the user to remember: Air0ZiPPEr, Bean77Kelp, and OcEaNTaBlE12 are examples of combination passwords. The inclusion of numbers can help add some complexity to the password. This example represents what a user will create to meet the system requirements for passwords, but these are still somewhat easy for a password cracker to discover.

Complex passwords include many different types of characters to introduce a significant level of complexity: Z(1@vi|2, Al!e&N-H9z, and W@!k|nGD2w*^ are examples of complex passwords. Unfortunately, these examples can be difficult for the average user to remember, potentially forcing them to write the password down where it can be discovered.

There are several practices to help users produce strong passwords that can be easily remembered. A good alternative to passwords is a passphrase. They are longer to enter but typically easier to remember and harder to attack. A passphrase will support all types of characters and spaces, allowing the user to create an easier to remember password without sacrificing integrity. Once a phrase is identified, it is simple to incorporate special characters to replace letters, furthering the complexity. Examples include

- ***A list of names:*** "Bobby CarolAnn Stuart Martha Mark" is an example of a 33-character passphrase that is very easy for the user to remember, but can be difficult for a password cracker to discover.

- ***A song or phrase:*** "A long time ago in a galaxy far, far away …"

■ *The initial letters of an easily remembered phrase:* "The Red
   Fox Jumps over the Lazy Dog!" becomes "TRFJotLD!"

The confidentiality of the password or passphrase is critical. Passwords must never be sent over a network or stored in cleartext. Unfortunately, old services such as file transfer protocol (FTP) and telnet do not protect the password from exposure during authentication. It is important to ensure that applications and network-enabled services apply various controls to ensure passwords are not exposed. If the protocol or service does not have encryption capabilities, there are alternative services and protocols that add a layer of encryption to help protect the application. Additionally, the storage of passwords must be protected. Password crackers can be used to attack a password file offline and unbeknownst to the system owner. Therefore, the security of the system maintaining the user credentials is paramount.

To protect passwords on a system from being exposed, they are typically hashed. A hash function takes an arbitrary amount of data as input and, through the use of a mathematical algorithm, will produce a unique, fixed-length representation of the data as output. The most important aspect of the hash function is that it is considered a one-way function. This means that a hash result cannot be deciphered to produce the original data. Although there are several types of attacks that can be performed to take advantage of weaknesses in various hash algorithms or how they are employed, in nearly all cases the hash cannot be directly manipulated to produce the original data. Of course, password cracking programs can hash different passwords until a match with the original password hash in a file is found. This is not a weakness of the philosophical attributes of hashing data. It is simply performing an act that a normal system operation would perform, just thousands or potentially millions of times. However, the time to discovery of a password by means of a password cracker is directly related to the complexity of the user's password and the employment of the hashing algorithm. During a brute force attack, longer and more complex passwords will take longer to discover than simple short passwords.

Graphical Passwords

As the methods of infiltrating end-user systems to steal information have gotten more complex, many organizations are looking for ways to stay ahead of these attacks to provide more security for end users. A common threat for end users is the keystroke logger. As the name implies, keystroke loggers record every key typed on the victim's computer, including any IDs or passwords the user may enter to log into various information systems. A keystroke logger may be a small hardware device inserted between the keyboard and the computer or it may be a piece of software secretly installed on the user's system.

In an effort to combat this threat, many sites are turning to graphical passwords. In a graphical password system, the system displays a picture, image, or other visual device rather than requiring the user to enter their password into the keyboard. The most common example of this is the use of a graphical keyboard displayed on the screen during the login process. To enter a password the user will click on the appropriate "keys" on the keyboard image to simulate the entry of the password at the keyboard. Many keystroke loggers will record only that the mouse was clicked but not be able to capture specifically what information the click represents. In other implementations, a user is presented with a series of random images, one of which has been preselected by the user. If the user selects the correct image during the authentication process the authentication passes. A keystroke logger on a system will not know what image was clicked and, thus, cannot capture this information.

Graphic passwords are a good step forward in the effort to keep users' identification and authentication information secure. However, keystroke loggers continue to advance and the latest ones have the ability to identify the image or data that was selected by the user. They use screen location information and screen captures to record specifically what the user has selected. Based on this, graphical passwords are a good step forward in the fight to keep user information secure, but they must constantly keep evolving in order to keep up with the latest attack methods.

117

Authentication by Possession

In addition to a unique identity, a user may be provided a token or some form of physical device that can be used in lieu of, or in addition to, a traditional password. The objective is to add another layer of confidence that the user is who he or she claims to be by the assurance a physical device offers. The added security comes from the fact that the user must have possession of the device in order to complete the authentication. There are two basic authentication-by-possession methods: asynchronous and synchronous.

An asynchronous token device is a challenge–response technology. A dialogue is established between the authentication service and the remote entity trying to authenticate. Without possession of the asynchronous token device, a correct answer to the challenge cannot be generated.

As demonstrated in *Figure 1.16*, the user makes a request for access to a system or service. The system sends a "challenge" back to the user, which is typically a number that must be entered into the token.

The user enters the number along with a PIN or some other code ("something you know") to go along with the device's "something you have" and the device calculates a response to the challenge. The user enters the response and sends it back to the system. The system, for its part, knows what response it is expecting because it sent the original challenge, it knows the user's PIN, and it performs the same calculation the device performs. If the user's response matches the calculated response the authentication passes.

Although very similar to asynchronous authentication, synchronous token authentication is based on an event, location, or time-based synchronization between the requestor and authenticator. The most common and widely adopted version is time-based, although smart cards and smart tokens can store special credentials that promote event and location authentication schemes (covered in more detail later). *Figure 1.17* shows the synchronous authentication process.

118

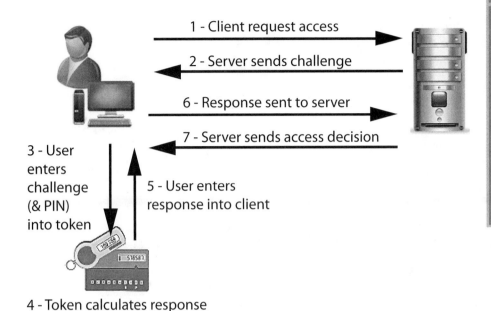

1 - Client request access

2 - Server sends challenge

6 - Response sent to server

7 - Server sends access decision

3 - User enters challenge (& PIN) into token

5 - User enters response into client

4 - Token calculates response

Figure 1.16 - **Asynchronous authentication.**

In a time-based model, a user will be issued a token or smart device that utilizes an embedded key to produce a unique number or string of characters in a given timeframe, such as every 60 seconds. The key is based on a combination of the time and a random number called a "seed." When the user makes a request for authentication, he or she is challenged to enter his or her user ID and the information (typically a number) that is currently displayed on the token. The system may also require the use of a password or PIN to enhance the authentication. The authenticating system will know which token is issued to that user and, based on the timing of the authentication request will know the data that should appear on the device. If the data entered by the user are the same as that expected by the system, the authentication is valid and the user is allowed to pass.

Static Authentication Devices

There are physical devices, in addition to traditional number-generation tokens, that can contain credentials for authentication. The credentials,

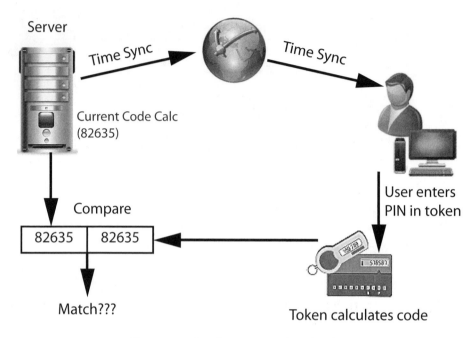

Server

Time Sync

Time Sync

Current Code Calc
(82635)

User enters
PIN in token

Compare

82635	82635

Match???

Token calculates code

Figure 1.17 - **Synchronous authentication**

which exist only on the device, are used during the authentication process and their use count as proof the user has possession of the device. There are two forms of such authentication devices; memory cards and smart cards. The main difference between memory cards and smart cards is the availability of processing power. A memory card holds information, but cannot process information. A smart card holds information, but also has the necessary hardware and logic to actually process information.

Memory Cards

A memory card holds a user's authentication information, so that this user needs only type in a user ID or PIN and presents the memory card to the system. If the entered information and the stored information match and are approved by an authentication service, the user is successfully authenticated. A common example of a memory card is a swipe card used to provide entry to a building. The user enters a PIN and swipes the memory card through a card reader. If this is the correct combination, the reader flashes green and the individual can open the door and enter the building.

Memory cards can also be used with computers, but they require a reader to process the information. The reader adds cost to the process, especially when one is needed for every computer. Additionally, the overhead of PIN and card generation adds additional overhead and complexity to the whole authentication process. However, a memory card provides a more secure authentication method than using only a password because the attacker would need to obtain the card and know the correct PIN. Administrators and management need to weigh the costs and benefits of a memory card implementation as well as the security needs of the organization to determine if it is the right authentication mechanism for their environment. USB authentication devices are replacing memory cards in many applications due to their near universal Interoperability, ruggedness and low cost.

One of the most prevalent weaknesses of memory cards is that data stored on the card are not protected. Unencrypted data on the card (or stored on the magnetic strip) can be extracted or copied. Unlike a smart card, where security controls and logic are embedded in the integrated circuit, memory cards do not employ an inherent mechanism to protect the data from exposure. Therefore, very little trust can be associated with confidentiality and integrity of information on the memory cards.

Smart Cards

A smart card is a credit card-size plastic card that has an embedded semiconductor chip that accepts, stores, and sends information. It can hold more data than memory cards. The term "smart card" is somewhat ambiguous and can be used in a multitude of ways. The International Organization for Standardization (ISO) uses the term integrated circuit card (ICC) to encompass all those devices where an integrated circuit (IC) is contained within an ISO 1 identification card piece of plastic. The card is

85.6 × 53.98 × 0.76mm and is essentially the same as a bank or credit card. The IC embedded is, in part, a memory chip that stores data and provides a mechanism to write and retrieve data. Moreover, small applications can be incorporated into the memory to provide various functions. The semiconductor chip can be either a memory chip with nonprogrammable logic or a microprocessor with internal memory. In an increasingly online environment, where critical information and transactions are exchanged over open networks, security is critical. New technologies allow smart cards, readers, and tools incorporating public key infrastructure (PKI) technologies to provide everything from authentication to network and information security functions on a single card platform. Some of the more common uses for smart cards today include

- Secure log-on
- Secure e-mail/digital signatures
- Secure Web access/remote access
- Virtual private networks (VPNs)
- Hard disk encryption

Information on a smart card can be divided into several sections:

- Information that is read only
- Information that is added only
- Information that is updated only
- Information with no access available

Typically, to use a smart card for accessing computer and network resources, a user inserts the smart card into a reader and enters the PIN associated with that card to unlock the card's services. In such a scenario, the first factor of security is providing something you have—a smart card. The second factor in this case is providing something you know—the PIN. With a smart card, there is an added level of integrity. The PIN provides access to the information on the card (not simply displayed, as with a token), and the key on the device is used during the authentication process. When used in combination with digital certificates, the system can participate in a larger enterprise infrastructure to provide integrity of the authentication process. A major advantage to smart cards is that the log-on process is done by the reader instead of at the host. Therefore, the identifier and password are not exposed to attackers while in transit to the host.

This last point is very important because it highlights the concept of a trusted path. A trusted path is a communications channel through which all information passing is assumed to be secure. The longer the trusted path, or the more links in the communication chain along the trusted path, the more opportunity there is for the security of that path to be compromised. Reducing the length of the path, or the number of links in the path, reduces the opportunity for security failures along the path. Therefore, by managing the authentication process within the smart card reader instead of sending the information to a remote authentication server, the trusted path for authentication is reduced and the opportunity for an attacker to compromise user information between the reader and a remote authentication service is eliminated.

There are different types of security mechanisms used in smart cards. Access to the information contained in a smart card can be controlled based on identity (e.g., everybody, only the cardholder, or a specific third party) and how the information can be accessed (e.g., read only, add only, modifiable, or erasable).

There are several memory types, some of which can be implemented into a smart card, for example:

- *Read-Only Memory (ROM):* ROM, or, more specifically, the data contained within ROM, is predetermined by the manufacturer and is unchangeable. Although ROM was used early in the evolution of smart cards, the inability to change the information in the memory makes it far too restrictive for today's requirements.

- *Programmable Read-Only Memory (PROM):* This type of memory can be modified, but requires the application of high voltages to enact fusible links in the IC. The high voltage requirements made it unusable for an ICC, but many have tried.

- *Erasable Programmable Read-Only Memory (EPROM):* EPROM was widely used in early smart cards, but the architecture of the IC operates in a one-time programmable mode (OTP), restricting the services offered by the ICC. Moreover, it requires ultraviolet light for erasing the memory, making it difficult for the typical organization to manage cards.

- *Electrically Erasable Programmable Read-Only Memory (EEPROM):* EEPROM is the current IC of choice because it provides user access and the ability to be rewritten, in some cases, up to a million times. This provides the capabilities smart cards need to be usable in today's environment. Typically, the amount of memory will range from 8 to 256KB.

- *Random-Access Memory (RAM):* Unlike ROM-based memory, whose data remains intact when power is removed, RAM-based memory loses its data when not powered. For some smart cards that have their own power source, RAM may be used to offer greater storage and speed. However, at some point the data will be lost—this can be an advantage or disadvantage, depending on your perspective. If a loss of electrical power might indicate a sign of attack or danger, losing the information on a smart card might be considered a prudent security measure.

Memory alone does not make a card "smart." In the implementation of an IC, a microcontroller (or central processing unit) is integrated into the chip, effectively managing the data in memory. Control logic is embedded into the memory controller providing various services, including security. Therefore, one of the most interesting aspects for smart cards, and their use in security-related applications, is the fact that controls associated with the data are intrinsic to the construction of the IC.

To demonstrate, when power is applied to the smart card, the processor can apply logic in an effort to perform services and control access to the EEPROM. The logic controlling access to the memory ensures that data, such as a private key, are not exposed outside the card. Smart cards can be configured to only permit certain types of data (such as public key certificates and private keys) to be stored on the device but never accessed directly by external applications. For example, a user may request a certificate and a corresponding public and private key pair from his organization. Once the keys and certificate are provided to the user, the user may store the certificate and private key on the smart card. In such situations, some organizations will establish a certificate policy that only allows the private key to be exported once. Therefore, the private key is stored permanently on the smart card. However, smart cards will typically contain all the logic necessary to generate the keys during a certificate request process. In this scenario, the user initiates a certificate request and chooses the smart card as the cryptographic service provider. Once the client system negotiates programmatically with the certificate authority, the private key is generated and stored directly on the smart card in a secure fashion. When organizations select this strategy, the keys are not exportable outside the card and are forever tied to the owner of the card.

A very similar process is utilized to leverage the private key material for private key processes, such as digitally signing documents. Data are prepared by the system and issued to the smart card for processing. This allows the system and user to leverage the key material without exposing the sensitive information, permitting it to remain in a protective state on the smart card. To allow these functions and ensure the protection of the data, programs are embedded in portions of the memory that the processor utilizes to offer advanced services.

It is important to understand that a smart card is effectively a computer, with many of the same operational challenges. The IC incorporates the processor and memory, the logic embedded in the processor supports

125

various services, applications built into the processor and housed on the EEPROM are available for on-demand use, protocol management interfaces with other systems, and data are managed on the card. All these and more exist in a very small substrate hidden in the card and will only become more complex as technology advances.

In order to exchange data with systems and services, the card must interface with a reader. There are two basic types of smart cards, and the difference is based on how they interact with other systems—contact cards, which use physical contact to communicate with systems, or contactless cards, which interface using proximity technology. Newer cards incorporate all these features including a magnetic strip, contact chip and contactless (RFID) features. *Figure 1.18* illustrates two types of card technologies.

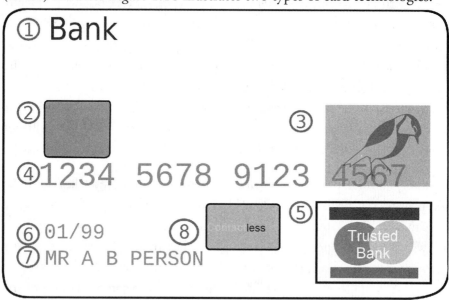

Figure 1.18 - **Credit Card technologies: Contact and Contactless**

1. Issuing bank logo	5. Card brand logo
2. EMV chip on "smart cards"	6. Expiration Date
3. Hologram	7. Card Holder Name
4. Credit Card number	8. Contactless Chip

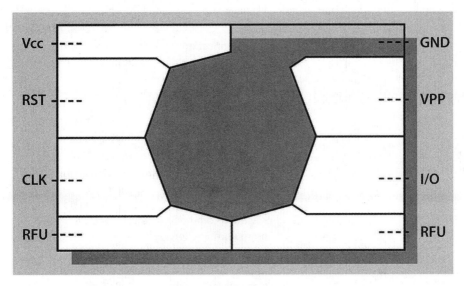

Figure 1.19 - **Typical Smart Card contact plate.**

Contact cards are fairly self-explanatory. Based on ISO 7816-2, a contact ICC provides for eight electrical contacts (only six are currently used) to interact with other systems or devices. The contacts on a smart card, as shown in *Figure 1.19*, provide access to different elements of the embedded IC. *Figure 1.20* explains the uses for each contact.

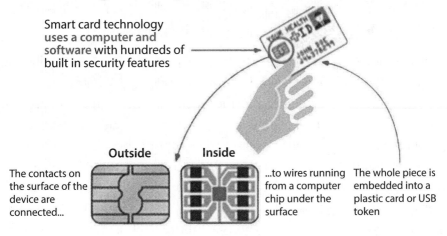

How a Smart Card works
Courtesy of www.aph.gov.au

Contact Designation	Use
Vcc	Power connection through which operating power is supplied to the microprocessor chip in the card.
RST	Reset line through which the interface device (IFD) can signal to the smart card's microprocessor chip to initiate its reset sequence of instructions.
CLK	Clock signal line through which a clock signal can be provided to the microprocessor chip. This line controls the operation speed and provides a common framework for data communication between the IFD and the ICC.
RFU	Reserved for future use.
GND	Ground line providing common electrical ground between the IFD and the ICC.
Vpp	Programming power connection used to program EEPROM of first-generation ICCs.
I/O	Input/output line that provides a half-duplex communication channel between the reader and the smart card.
RFU	Reserved for future use

Figure 1.20 - **Typical smart card pinouts.**

In contrast to contact cards, contactless cards do not require the user to place the card into a reader. Instead, the user simply holds the card in close proximity to the reader and the reader can detect the card and the information stored on it. For this reason, contactless cards are often called proximity cards. They are increasing in adoption because of durability, number of applications in use, speed, and convenience. They eliminate the need to physically interact with the reader, reducing the exposure and damage that contact cards have with the plate or magnetic strip on the card. Finally, a contactless card offers a multitude of uses and opportunity for integration, such as with cell phones or PDAs.

Other possession-based authentication devices are beginning to appear on the market as well. Many of these devices can attach to the universal serial bus (USB) port on most modern computers. These devices can contain many of the same data elements as smart cards, such as user IDs, passwords, access credentials, encryption keys, and other private information. When the device is inserted into the USB slot on a computer, the system or application takes the information it needs directly from the device. For additional two-factor security it may also require the user to enter some information from the keyboard.

These devices also have benefits beyond initial authentication. For example, they can be periodically polled or queried by the system to ensure it is still present. If it is not, the system can assume that the user has moved to another place and the system or application can lock itself until the user returns and reinserts the device. In addition, because many of these devices have data storage capabilities, systems or applications can also store credentials or confidential user information on them for later use. For this reason, care should be taken to protect the devices against loss or unauthorized use. These devices often have built-in encryption capabilities to protect the information from extraction by unauthorized persons.

Authentication by Characteristic (Biometrics)

The ability to authenticate a user based on physical attributes or other characteristics unique to that person is possible due to biometric technology. Biometrics is the use of specific biological indicators of the human body or behavioral characteristics that can be used to calculate uniqueness. There are two types of biometrics: physiological and behavioral.

A physiological biometric uses information about a unique physical attribute of the user, such as a fingerprint. The user interfaces with a biometric scanning device to provide the information. The device performs a measurement (potentially several times), makes a final determination as to the validity and ownership of the biometrics, and compares the results with the information stored in the control system. There are several biometrics that are more commonly used, the most common being human fingerprints. Fingerprints are unique to each person and have been used for years by law enforcement agencies to identify people. One of the earliest forms of easily accessible biometric systems was based on fingerprint analysis. Today, fingerprint biometric thumb readers can be easily purchased and quickly utilized with standard PCs. Moreover, the technology has become so commonplace that USB memory fobs have incorporated fingerprint readers into the data stick to authenticate its use.

Hand geometry techniques attempt to discern several attributes about the size, shape, and layout of a person's hand to gather enough information to draw conclusions about the person's identity. The system may measure tension in the tendons in the hand, temperature, finger length, bone length, and hand width, among other aspects. Palm or hand scans can be best described as a combination of the capabilities of both hand geometry and fingerprint analysis. The user's hand is typically placed flat on a special surface where, again, several points of information are collected and combined to make a determination on the user's identity.

Not all biometric information resides in the hands, however. The face and eyes offer other aspects of individuality that can be harnessed by a biometric device to determine and authenticate identity. There are two primary aspects of the human eye that can be investigated: the retina and the iris. Each is unique to an individual and to each eye. The retina, located in the back of the eye, has blood vessels that can be scanned to identify distinctive patterns. The iris is the colored material surrounding the pupil that governs the amount of light permitted to enter the eye. Again, each one has granularity characteristics that can uniquely identify the individual. Finally, the entire face can be used by a system to visually verify facial geometry and heat signatures that correspond to a person's skull structure and tissue density. Because each face is unique (even for identical twins) the layout and other facial characteristics make unique identification possible.

Vascular Scans

Another method of incorporating unique physical characteristics to enhance the authentication process is the use of vascular scanning technology. In a vascular scan, the scanning device studies the veins in the user's hands or face. The scanner will examine and analyze the patterns and thickness of the veins, which are believed to be unique for each person. The advantage of vascular scanning is that it is relatively nonintrusive to the end user, requiring only the placement of the hand near a scanning device. The disadvantage is that physical injury or deformity to the hands can render the system unable to accurately scan or analyze a particular hand. Vascular scanning technology is still relatively new, but it is gaining some acceptance in some high-security areas.

Unlike physiological characteristics, which attempt to establish identity by matching physical characteristics of a person, behavioral characteristics measure the way a person acts and performs in various situations. The act of determining unique characteristics about a person from patterns in their actions has emerged as one of the more viable approaches to biometrics. One common behavioral characteristic currently in use is the analysis of a person's voice pattern. Voice patterns and voice recognition are regularly used for identification and authentication. Voice pattern matching investigates how a user speaks. In recent history, advancements in speech recognition technology have increased the technology's viability. Typically, a user will enroll in a voice recognition system by speaking several different words or phrases, including the user's name. The system will attempt to determine the unique sounds produced by that particular human during speech. During subsequent authentication, the user repeats the phrases again and the system matches the results with the expected pattern recorded and analyzed from the original user.

With the addition of voice recognition, the system can identify what is said as well as how it is spoken. Therefore, a passphrase can be used in combination with a person's name to authenticate on multiple levels.

Again, as with other forms of multifactor authentication, other elements may be used, such as a PIN, smart card, swipe card, or even another biometric system, such as fingerprint input.

Another of the more promising new methods of behavioral authentication is keystroke dynamics. Keystroke pattern analysis is based on the fact that each person has a unique and distinguishable typing pattern and these patterns can be measured and identified during the entry of other authentication information. For example, a user is prompted for a traditional username and password. He enters the information, but in addition to checking the validity of the entered password, the system also measures how the user typed the password. If the password is correct, but the typing pattern is wrong, he may be denied access.

Signature dynamics has also emerged as an effective biometric solution. Much like voice patterns, a biometric system can measure the visual layout of the signature as well as the stroke speed, acceleration and deceleration, and pen pressure. Law enforcement and forensics experts have been leveraging the science of handwriting dynamics for many years. They inspect the physical nature of the signature to identify known characteristics that indicate forgeries. For example, if the paper (or material) shows signs that intense pressure was applied, it could indicate a copy or extreme intensity, representative of someone uncomfortable during the signing (a rarity for normal signing processes.) Moreover, pauses or slow movement in specific areas typically associated with fast or light areas of the signature can be identified by an investigator: again, signs of a forgery. These same principles are utilized by a pressure-sensitive digital interface to detect a divergence from expected signing practices.

Biometric Accuracy

For all the advancements in biometric technology in recent years, and its promise to offer advanced identification and authentication techniques, it is still far from perfect. Ironically, the biggest imperfection comes from the variability of the humans (and their surrounding environment) that biometrics seek to measure. Technical measures, like passwords, tokens, and smart devices, offer a high degree of accuracy and confidence in the transaction based on the limited variability in their measurement. A password can be hashed and verified, and the measurement process (the algorithm) is static. Tokens, especially synchronous tokens, are based on the strict measurement of time. When an error occurs in token-based authentication, it is typically because the time synchronization between the token and the server has shifted. This is a common and sometimes expected error, and the authentication failure tends toward denial of access. In the case with smart cards, there is no measurement dynamic and the card adheres to established technical and physical standards.

In stark contrast, the field of biometrics is essentially a technical and mathematical estimation. The measurement and subsequent analysis of biometric information collected by a scanning device can be affected by hundreds of environmental variables. Temperature, humidity, pressure, and even the medical or mental condition of the individual can cause significant physiological changes to the body that the measurement process must try to cope with. If a person is ill or a woman is pregnant, biometric results from those individuals may vary significantly from pre-established norms and iris scans, facial recognition, and hand geometry may fail. Therefore, the accuracy of the biometric mechanism—its ability to separate authentic users from imposters—is essential to understanding the risk of its use for any given application.

There are three categories of biometric accuracy measurement (all represented as percentages):

- *False Reject Rate (a Type I Error):* When authorized users are falsely rejected as unidentified or unverified.

- *False Accept Rate (a Type II Error):* When unauthorized persons or imposters are falsely accepted as authentic.

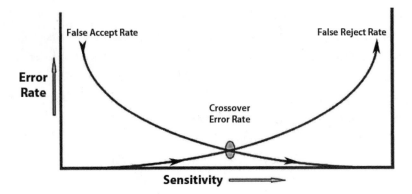

Figure 1.21 - **Crossover error rate is one of three categories of biometric accuracy measurements.**

- **Crossover Error Rate (CER):** The point at which the false rejection rates and the false acceptance rates are equal. The smaller the value of the CER, the more accurate the system.

As demonstrated in *Figure 1.21*, the sensitivity level of the biometric system translates into varying levels of false rejection and false acceptance. The lower the sensitivity, the more prone the system is to false acceptance. With low sensitivity, the system may offer a broad margin of error or disparity in the determination of the measured metrics. The low sensitivity also may not enable the system to acquire enough meaningful data to discern the authorized user from the unauthorized user. On the other hand, if the system is overly sensitive, it may apply too much granularity to the process, resulting in a level of investigation that is highly susceptible to environmental changes or minor biological changes in the person and increase the false rejection rate. A good balance between the two is difficult to obtain. Not sensitive enough, and everyone will be authorized; too sensitive, and no one gets through. Neutrality is achieved by tuning the system sensitivity so that the rates intersect at a midpoint. The lower the intersection point between the two rates, the more accurate the system is overall.

It is very important to understand the relationships and measurements between the two rates, because the trends in either direction are not

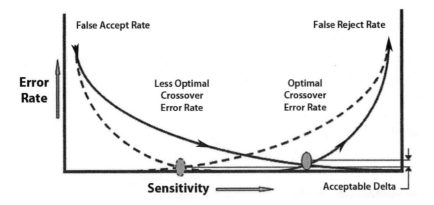

Figure 1.22 - **Comparison of crossover error rates.**

mathematically consistent. Using the example chart in *Figure 1.22*, if the lowest attainable intersection has an error rate of 20%, regardless of sensitivity adjustments, the system is clearly failing consistently at an unacceptable level.

In this case, 1 in 5 people are getting through the system improperly. Also, the key to proper tuning of the system is to attain the lowest possible intersection rate at the greatest possible sensitivity. However, there are other factors that must be taken into consideration as well.

It would appear that the crossover rate on the lower left side of the figure would be optimal, since it has the lowest error rate of the two crossover points shown. However, this low CER is achieved by tuning the system to a relatively low sensitivity. At this setting, it is likely that the system may not be sensitive enough to detect changes in body condition or environmental factors. However, the figure shows that by adjusting the sensitivity upward by nearly a third, the CER is raised only slightly. Therefore, the truly optimal CER location is in the bottom right of the graph. The amount to adjust the sensitivity and the maximum acceptable level of change in the CER is something the organization will need to determine based on its overall risk tolerance.

The correct conclusion here is that the ability to tune the system and make determinations on what is optimal for a specific solution is directly relative to the level of risk and the importance of the controls. In short, the crossover error rate must always be appropriate to the application and to the desired acceptable risk level of the organization.

Biometric Considerations

In addition to the access control elements of a biometric system, there are several other considerations that are important to the integrity of the control environment. These are:

- Resistance to counterfeiting
- Data storage requirements
- User acceptance
- Reliability and accuracy
- Target user and approach

First and foremost, biometric systems must be resistant to counterfeiting. Unlike in the movies, where the villain can use a severed finger to gain unauthorized access to a super-secure room, most biometric systems employ simple metrics, such as heat, blood pressure, or pulse rate to add further confidence in the process and resist such forgery attempts. However, a very popular activity is the mimicking of a human thumb to fool a fingerprint reader. The perpetrator can place a thin layer of gummy bear jelly modified with the image of a valid fingerprint on his finger to gain unauthorized access. The thin coating, with the fingerprint of the authorized user incorporated, allows heat, pressure, and other simple metrics to be fooled because there is a real finger behind the coating. If the imposter knows the user's PIN and has his or her physical credentials, success is possible, if somewhat unlikely.

Nonetheless, a highly determined and sophisticated attacker could identify biometric weaknesses and take advantage of them by counterfeiting what is measured. Although arguably very complicated, it is feasible and, therefore, must be considered. Beyond the tuning of the system to the upper, optimal range and adding other identification and authentication requirements, an organization implementing a biometric system is at the mercy of the biometric product vendor to incorporate added investigative controls.

A biometric system must be trained for a given user during enrollment (also called association). For example, a user may have to talk into a microphone, look into a scanner, or provide a fingerprint several times before the system can obtain enough data to make future decisions. During this process, the system is gathering highly sensitive and private information about the physical attributes of the user. Information gathered by biometric systems will be either an electronic representation (e.g., an image or picture) of the face, hand, eye, finger, or some other physical characteristic of a person, or a mathematical representation of the data gathered. The security of data storage here is paramount. Not unlike securing the hashed passwords on a system so that it does not fall into the hands of an attacker with a password cracker, the biometric information about a user's physical attributes can be used against the system or even the user. An attacker gaining access to the biometric data in the storage system would potentially have the ability to use those images to somehow gain access to the system or the facility. At the very least, the privacy and personal security of the users enrolled in the biometric system will be threatened. When designing and implementing a biometric system the security professional must pay careful attention to the security of the system's information database to protect the system, the organization, and the user's privacy.

User acceptance can also be a significant barrier to meaningful adoption of biometrics. People have understandable concerns about lasers scanning the insides of their eyes and the potential exposure of very private information, such as health status. For example, a biometric system may be able to detect a drug addiction, disease, or pregnancy, perhaps even before the user is aware of these conditions. The ability to detect this private information is a concern to potential users. In some scenarios, the process is a requirement of a job position or role within an organization, so that any user concerns are irrelevant (that is, if the user desires to remain employed by that organization.) In other cases, attempts to incorporate biometric systems to simplify customer interaction, such as with automated teller machines, where the participation is optional, have met with limited success and poor user adoption, in part because of the aforementioned concerns. Finally, user acceptance may be hindered by the intrusiveness of the system. Some people may not find it intrusive to place their thumb on a reader, while others may be uncomfortable with perceptions of the sanitary condition of such a device. Placing your hand on a device or looking into a system requires close personal interaction that may exceed an individual's threshold of personal space.

In addition to accuracy, the reliability of the system is important. For example, passport control points in airports, theme park admissions, or other areas that can utilize biometrics for the public often have these systems operating in locations that expose the system to the elements. For example, Sea World in Florida uses hand geometry biometrics for annual members. Members receive a picture identification card that is swiped at the entry point, and they insert their hand into the reader. The system will be used by thousands of people in a given year, and these devices are outside, exposed to the hot, humid air. The reliability of the system to perform, and perform at an acceptable level of accuracy, must be considered.

The speed of the solution is another important factor to consider. The standard enrollment process should take no more than two minutes per person and a system should be able to reliably obtain enough information in that time period for future authentication requirements. In the event the system takes longer, it may affect user acceptance, raise questions of capability, and reduce user confidence in the system. Moreover, the average authentication rate—speed and throughput—is six to ten seconds.

A reliable system should be able to attain these levels of performance or its use should be reconsidered.

When considering the role of biometrics, its close interactions with people, and the privacy and sensitivity of the information collected, the inability to revoke the physical attribute of the credential becomes a major concern. A token, fob, or smart card can be confiscated or the device assigned to a user can be changed. In contrast, a person cannot get new fingerprints or retinas if the authentication system is compromised. This limitation requires significant trust in the biometric system. If a user's biometric information were to be captured in transit or counterfeited via a falsified reader, there are few options to the organization to detect that the attack has occurred and revoke the physical credential. The binding of the authentication process to the physical characteristics of the user can complicate the revocation or decommissioning processes.

Finally, biometric technology in practice excels in authentication-based applications, such as building access. This is because the data points gathered during the biometric process are easily compared against the same data points collected during the enrollment process. The results are deterministic and leave relatively little room for chance or interpretation. In contrast, biometrics does not yet work extraordinarily well in applications where identification is the primary purpose, such as scanning the faces in a crowd for suspected terrorists. This is because the variability in the scan data (such as changing light sources, hair and makeup changes, and position relative to the camera) leave too much room for interpretation and make positive matching much more difficult.

Authentication Method Summary

This section has covered a large amount of information about identification and authentication techniques, technology, and processes. However, how do these solutions compare? As demonstrated in *Figure 1.23*, the capabilities and level of confidence increases as more factors and techniques are included in the identification and authentication process.

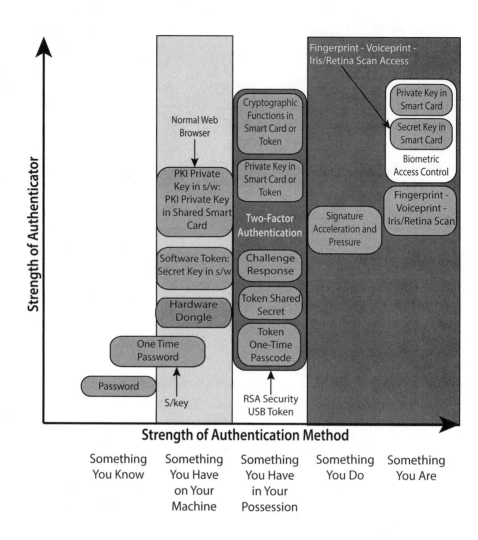

Figure 1.23 - **Comparison of authentication methods.**

The strength of individual authentication methods will vary, but generally, biometrics tends to provide higher security than any of the others. "Strength" can be defined as the assurance that the authentication produced by the method is valid. The best way to interpret *Figure 1.23* is to simply understand that as you move from left to right, you increase the strength provided by the authentication method. Something you are provides more security than something you know because it is much harder to impersonate or duplicate something you are.

In the end, however, authentication is but a single part of the overall access control (and security) picture. There are many trade-offs involved with identifying and implementing a particular authentication method and chances are that a large enterprise will select several to fit various needs within the organization. Some of the more prevalent considerations include:

- *The value of the protected asset.* An asset with higher value will require a more complex (and expensive) authentication method. Assets with lesser value can suffice with more basic methods.

- *The level of threat to the asset.* There may be many threats, both real and perceived, against the asset in question. The security manager must make an assessment to determine the actual threats of concern.

- *Potential countermeasures.* Once the level of threat is determined, possible countermeasures to address that threat must be considered. Each countermeasure will reduce the threat in some way, and the best method (or combination of methods) must be determined.

- *The cost of countermeasures.* Adjusting the authentication method may be one countermeasure to reduce the risk to the asset, but there may be others to consider. Each will have its own associated cost that must be weighed as part of an overall risk management solution.

- *Feasibility and inconvenience to users.* As has been shown, each method entails a certain level of participation (and annoyance) to its users. The security manager must weigh inconvenience, potential work flow disruption, and resulting user resistance when determining the best authentication method for an organization.

Authentication is an important step in an organization's overall access control strategy. As such, the method used must be chosen carefully and thoughtfully to ensure it is the best fit for the organization.

Session Management

With the increase in web based applications and cloud computing access controls must be viewed light of sessi on management. "Session management" is a term used to describe how a single instance of identification and authentication are applied to resources. For example a "desktop" session manager may allow a user to maintain a particular set of open applications, files and functions while simultaneously starting another desktop session with a different set of applications, files and functions. Many Unix and Linux operating systems offer this capability. Web browsers also rely on sessions to manage access to web applications and resources often through the use of cookies or other session monitoring and tracking technologies. While session management provides ease of use and flexibility for the end user it also provides an avenue of attack.

Desktop Sessions

Desktop sessions can be controlled and protected through several means including but not limited to the following:

- Screensavers
- Timeouts
- Automatic Logouts
- Session/Login limitation
- Schedule Limitations

Screensavers

Most operating systems have a "screensaver" function. This function was originally designed to help prevent "burn in" of Cathode Ray Tube (CRT) display monitors. As technology as advanced displays are subject to "burn in" of different types and energy efficiency concerns have driven the screensaver to become an energy conservation tool. In addition to saving energy many desktop screensavers can be configured to "lock" the session of the user. This is a form of a "timeout" session lock technology which is designed to automatically lock the session of user who may have left the session without locking it or logging out. This is helpful in preventing unauthorized access while ensuring the user can still access their session upon return.

Timeouts and Automatic Logouts

As noted prior, screensavers are a type of "timeout" control. Timeout controls can exist in many ways and are often cascaded to further restrict the access of an unattended session as time passes. For example when an unintended desktop session has been ongoing for fifteen minutes the screen saver may activate and require a user name and password to access the system. After two hours the system may automatically log off the user and close the session. After eight hours the system may shut itself down. These are all forms of timeouts which must balance the risk of access and exposure with the impact to the user and mission.

Session/Logon Limitation

Session and logon limitation focus on usability and security trade-offs. For example, if a company has a highly mobile workforce they may want to consider allowing multiple sessions from the same username. An example is if a user has some work on their desktop they need to keep running over night and they also need to work on a report using their laptop while in their home office. It is possible they will need two network sessions and perhaps two desktop sessions if virtual desktops are used. However, organizations must be cautious in how multiple sessions are implemented as each session can provide an additional point of attack for adversary and many more sessions to monitor by the security operations team and the end user.

Schedule Limitations

Some desktop sessions may be limited by time. For example if a Kiosk is available in the lobby of an organization for general use during normal hours does it make sense to have it allow sessions during non-business hours? Or should cash register allow the creation of sessions outside of normal operating hours? Typically session management should follow the concept of "least privilege" and only allow the creation of sessions within the most restrictive schedule and resources required to meet the mission.

Logical Sessions

As more information systems become service based through the web browser understanding web-based sessions, their weaknesses and how to protect them is critical for information security professionals to understand. Basic sessions are created between authenticated users, services, applications, and devices on a routine and regular basis in almost all information systems. For example, a typical banking online banking scenario may follow this sequence:

1. A user starts a web browser and navigates to their bank's website

    a. There is now a session created between the user's browser and the bank's webserver.

2. The user clicks on the "secure login" link to get to the bank login page

    a. The user has now secured the session typically using Secure Sockets Layer (SSL)

3. The user enters a user name and password and authenticates.

    a. This information is passed through the encrypted session where if intercepted it would be very difficult to decrypt.

4. The user conducts banking business and "logs off" of the banking website

    a. This will close the encrypted connection and ensure no other activities could occur under the user's credentials until another session is established.

If an attacker can hijack a session they may be able to receive all information the user expects be confidential. Session hijacking is common when sensitive Information may be gained with little exposure and the attacker can easily insert themselves into the session establishment process. In general here is how the attack would proceed:

1. A user starts a web browser and navigates to their bank's website

   a. An attacker has inserted themselves between the user and the bank.

   b. The attacker creates a session between the user and themselves by passing the bank information to the user so it seems to be legitimate.

   c. There is now a session created between the user's browser and the attacker and the attacker bank's webserver.

2. The user clicks on the "secure login" link to get to the bank login page

   a. The attacker intercepts the request and sends a login page for the bank with invalid certificates. As many users are unaware of what invalid certificates represent they often accept them.

   b. The user has now secured a session between the attacker and the attacker to the bank typically using Secure Sockets Layer (SSL)

3. The user enters a user name and password and authenticates.

   a. The attacker is able to view the user credentials as they are being decrypted at the attacker's session endpoint. The attacker is now able to pass those credentials to the bank impersonating the user.

4. The user conducts banking business and "logs off" of the banking website

   a. At this point the attacker has the credentials of the user and may be able to log into the users account and transfer money out of the account.

Session hijacking attacks are a form of "man-in-the-middle" attacks. There are several ways attacks such as this can be minimized and prevented. Logical sessions and session security will be explored in greater detail in the telecommunications and networking security chapter of this book.

Accountability

Ultimately one of the drivers behind strong identification, authentication, auditing and session management is accountability. Accountability is fundamentally about being able to determine who or what is responsible for an action and can be held responsible. A closely related information assurance topic is non-repudiation. Repudiation is the ability to deny an action, event, impact or result. Non-repudiation is the process of ensuring a user may not deny an action. Accountability relies heavily on non-repudiation to ensure users, processes and actions may be held responsible for impacts.

The following contribute to ensuring accountability of actions:

- Strong identification
- Strong authentication
- User training and awareness
- Comprehensive, timely and thorough monitoring
- Accurate and consistent audit logs
- Independent audits
- Policies enforcing accountability
- Organizational behavior supporting accountability

Strong Identification

For accountability to be successful an action must be attributable to a single Individual, process, device or object. Without the ability to directly associate an action with an individual repudiation of the action can arise. One of the most prevalent examples of this is the use of shared accounts. When several people have access to a single account the ability to directly associate an action performed through the account with an individual diminishes rapidly as users are able to blame others with plausible deniability.

Strong Authentication

Weak authentication not only makes it easier for an attacker to take control of an account with no accountability but also allows users to blame weak authentication on account abuses. Strong authentication such as biometrics helps ensure non-repudiation by strongly associating something only one individual has to an account. While not perfect, strong authentication with strong identification greatly increases accountability.

User Training and Awareness

Users need to be trained and have a basic awareness of the penalties for misuse of accounts, information and systems. Informed users are less likely to intentionally or unintentionally abuse accounts, access or information if they are aware of the consequences. A well-structured and repeated security awareness program is generally accepted as a baseline for ensuring users understand consequences and acceptable behaviors.

Monitoring

Monitoring must be sufficient to detect problems and violations with accounts, access, information egress and system operation. If an organization does not have visibility into an information system, it is unlikely the organization will know when accountability issues surface. Monitoring technologies such as data loss prevention (DLP), intrusion detection systems (IDS) and firewalls can be implemented to increase visibility and therefore strengthen accountability.

Audit Logs

Audit logs are necessary in the event an action must be traced back to a user. Audit logs from DLP, IDS, servers, firewalls and other network devices should be collected and consolidated as much as feasible. Often these logs are collected into a Security Information and Event Management (SIEM) system. SIEMs are used in conjunction with analytical tools to correlate information and help "tell the story" of what happened. They are highly useful in helping ensure accountability.

Independent Audits

Independent audits help ensure accountability by bringing in an unbiased third party to review accounts, actions and impacts. Independent audits, investigations or reviews are required to establish accountability when collusion may have occurred between several parties. Routine independent audits can also set a tone throughout the organization that corrupt practices are not tolerated.

Policy

An organization's policy must recognize the need for accountability and provide expectations of behavior and define sanctions and rewards for accountability related behaviors. Some organizations have an "integrity" award for outstanding acts of accountability in difficult situations. Without a policy, accountability cannot be enforced consistently and fairly throughout an organization.

Organizational behavior

Arguably the most significant aspect of ensuring accountability is the culture of the organization. An organization that does not set the "tone at the top" for accountability expectations is unlikely to receive the support necessary to implement accountability controls throughout the organization. Additionally, if violations of accountability are not met with timely and consistent treatment, further instances of accountability violations can be expected.

Decentralized/Distributed Access Control Techniques

Once the policies, standards, and processes for access control have been defined the next step is to implement the various technology components that will support the organization's access control needs. This section describes the access control technology options that an organization needs to create for an effective access control management service.

Identity management technologies attempt to simplify the administration of distributed, overlapping, and sometimes conflicting data about the users of an organization's information technology systems. The foundation of a comprehensive identity management solution is the implementation of appropriate processes and technologies to consolidate and streamline the management of user IDs, authentication, and access information consistently across multiple systems. A typical enterprise will have many users with various access requirements for a diverse collection of data and application services. To bind the user to established policies, processes, and privileges throughout the infrastructure, several types of technologies are utilized to ensure consistency and oversight. Technologies utilized in identity management solutions include but are not limited to:

- Password management
- Account management
- Profile management
- Directory management
- Single sign-on

Password Management

Passwords are the most common authentication technology in use today, so password management should be a primary concern for an organization. The complexity and use of passwords was discussed previously in this chapter, but the policies, standards, and complexity need to be managed

149

consistently throughout the organization. Because passwords may be compromised over time, it is prudent for users to periodically change their passwords. Most modern systems can be configured to require users to change their password at defined intervals. The reason for this is that if a password is compromised this will limit the amount of damage that can be done through that compromised ID to the amount of time left before the next change interval. Most enterprise organizations enforce a password change interval ranging from 30 to 90 days. A shorter length is better for security reasons, but a longer period of time is more convenient for users and does not force them to re-memorize their password as often. As with most security issues, the optimal time to expire a password will be an individual organizational compromise between business needs and security needs.

When users have multiple passwords, on multiple disparate systems, all expiring on different dates, they tend to write them down, store them insecurely (e.g., in a "password.txt" file on the desktop or on a sticky note underneath their keyboard), or replicate the same password across multiple systems. In the absence of a password management system incorporated into an organization-wide identity management solution, a user may set the same password for several systems as a matter of convenience or simply rotate a set of three or four, making it very easy to remember, but equally easy for an attacker to guess and exploit.

To protect against an attacker trying to guess a password multiple times, many systems incorporate a password lockout mechanism for excessive invalid attempts. In such a system, if a user unsuccessfully tries to log into a system multiple times (three to five attempts are common) the ID is locked and the user has to contact support personnel to get it unlocked. The benefits of this process is that it limits the amount of damage password guessing can have on a user's login. The drawback is that users are notorious for forgetting their password and end up calling the help desk often, especially if they have been away from the computer for an extended period of time (perhaps on vacation, where remembering a password is the last thing on a person's mind.) In fact, password reset calls are almost always the single largest category of calls for most help desk services. Any process or technology that can dramatically reduce the number of password reset calls to the help desk will have the added benefit of saving a lot of money for the organization.

A password management system is designed to manage passwords consistently across the enterprise. This is usually achieved by a central tool synchronizing passwords across multiple systems. However, other features might include assisting users with routine password management tasks. For example, users who forget their password or trigger a lockout from too many failed attempts may be offered alternative authentication mechanisms to gain specific access to utilities to reset their password. It is not uncommon for an organization to issue multifactor authentication tokens to be used, in part, for providing access to utilities so users can self-manage their accounts and passwords on other, potentially older or nonintegrated systems. Other alternative methods include voice response units for resetting passwords, the use of personal questions to validate a user's identity, or in-person verification. In the event that an alternative authentication mechanism does not exist, password management systems typically allow administrators or support staff to quickly reset forgotten or disabled passwords.

Another common feature of a password management system, and regularly employed on large Internet sites, is a self-registration process that incorporates personal data questions whose answers are private to that user, allowing him to manage his account and reset the password without the intervention of an administrator or help desk staffer.

Account Management
One of most costly, time-consuming, and potentially risk-laden aspects of access control is the creation, modification, and decommissioning of user

accounts. Many organizations consume inordinate amounts of resources to ensure the timely creation of new system access, the adjustments of user privileges to reflect changes in responsibilities, and the termination of access once a user leaves the organization.

Although Web-based access management tools address this problem for a Web-based environment, most enterprises are heterogeneous, with multiple types and versions of systems and applications, each with potentially different account management strategies, capabilities, and tools. For example, ERP systems, operating systems, network devices, mainframes, and database servers typically all have difficulty in interacting with a single centralized account directory. Moreover, for those that can achieve such integration, there may be limitations to the degree of control available within the system.

As a result, account management processes must typically be performed on each system directly. Account management systems attempt to streamline the administration of user identity across multiple systems. They normally include one or more of the following features to ensure a central, cross-platform security administration capability:

- A central facility for managing user access to multiple systems simultaneously. This ensures consistency between all systems and eases the administrative burden of managing access on these systems separately. This also reduces the risk of erroneous manual entry of user data, potentially resulting in the provisioning of inappropriate access.

- A workflow system where users can submit requests for new, changed, or terminated systems access, and these requests are automatically routed to the appropriate people for approval. Approved requests then trigger the creation of accounts and the allocation of other resources.

- Automatic replication of data, particularly user records, between multiple systems and directories. This ensures that user access permissions are propagated uniformly and promptly throughout the environment and reduces the likelihood of error through manual replication.

- A facility for loading batch changes to user directories. There are often occasions where large numbers of user changes need to be loaded in the database. This may come as a result of organizational restructuring, large employee hires, or large-scale employee terminations. The ability to load these changes in bulk will save time and increase accuracy over loading these changes individually.

- Automatic creation, change, or removal of access to system resources based on policies, and triggered by changes to information elsewhere (e.g., in an HR system or corporate directory.) By eliminating human intervention and manual processing, changes can happen more rapidly and reduce the window of opportunity for obsolete access permissions to be exploited.

One of the biggest obstacles to the implementation of an account management system is the time and cost of full-scale deployment. Some systems can take literally years to deploy fully in a large enterprise. The complexity of account management systems can also overwhelm project teams as they struggle to determine the best method for deploying the system. Implementation teams should start small and gain experience and success on a smaller scale before proceeding to full-scale deployment.

Interface issues can also be a big project killer for many organizations. A fully automated account management system must interface with each system, application, and directory in the enterprise (sometimes numbering in the hundreds), each based on its own technology platform and almost none of which will be designed to interface with the account management service. The process of building all those interfaces will be a daunting, time-consuming, and costly task to overcome and will require the resources of a dedicated team of programmers.

Profile Management

Profiles are a collection of information associated with a particular identity or group. In addition to the user ID and password, a user profile may include personal information, such as name, telephone number, e-mail address, home address, date of birth, etc. A profile can also contain information related to privileges and rights on specific systems. However, any information specific to a user is going to change over time, and the process to manage that change is an important component of an overall identity management process. When a change is required to a profile, the process should be easy to manage and be automatically propagated to key systems, such as the corporate directory and the individual systems a user logs into. Most customer relationship management (CRM) systems include some facility to manage user profiles, either administratively or using a self-service method. This capability is also available in some access management systems and password management systems. It is helpful to allow users to enter and manage those parts of their own profiles where new data are either not sensitive or do not have to be validated. This helps to reduce the cost and time to implement these changes and increase their accuracy.

Directory Management

A corporate directory is a comprehensive database designed to centralize the management of data about an assortment of company entities. A typical directory will contain a hierarchy of objects storing information about users, groups, systems, servers, printers, etc. The directory is stored on one or more servers that may replicate the data, in part or in whole, to other directory servers to ensure scalability and availability. Applications will normally access data stored in a directory by means of a standard directory protocol.

The primary benefit of a directory service is that it provides a centralized collection of user data that can be used by many applications to avoid replication of information and simplify the architecture. Using directories, it is possible to configure several applications to share data about users, rather than having each system manage its own list of users, authentication data, etc. This simplifies the overall management of user data, improves the consistency of user data as it is used between systems, and promotes uniform security control in the environment.

A key limitation of directories and their role in simplifying identity management is the difficulty of integration with legacy systems. Mainframes, older applications, and outdated systems often do not natively support the use of an external system to manage their own users without the development of interface facilities or translation code. These interfaces can be difficult and expensive to develop and, in some cases, technically impossible, limiting their effectiveness, and reducing the ability to use a directory service to manage enterprise-wide resources.

Directory Technologies

When considering the use of a centralized directory service for the enterprise, there are a number of technologies that should be considered. These technologies are all supported by international standards and most products that require directory services will be able to interface natively with one or more of them. The three most common directory standards are X.500, the Lightweight Directory Access Protocol (LDAP), Active Directory, and X.400.

X.500: The X.500 set of communications protocols was developed by the International Telecommunications Union (ITU-T) in the late 1980s. It is also known as ISO/IEC 9594. The protocol suite was developed by telecommunications companies to facilitate a standard method of developing electronic directories for use over telecommunications networks. The suite was originally developed to work with the OSI network communications model, although most current implementations allow it to operate over TCP/IP as well.

X.500 actually consists of four separate protocols:

- The directory access protocol (DAP). This is the primary protocol for access information in an X.500 directory.

- The directory system protocol (DSP)

- The directory information shadowing protocol (DISP)

- The directory operational bindings management protocol (DOP)

Information in an X.500 directory is organized as a hierarchical database of information. The key field in the database is called the distinguished name (DN). The DN provides the full path through the X.500 database where a particular entry may be found. X.500 also supports the concept of a relative distinguished name (RDN). The RDN provides the name of a specific entry without the full path component attached.

LDAP

Although it is a comprehensive suite of protocols for managing directory information, X.500 can be complex to implement and complicated to administer. It also originally required the implementation of the OSI protocol stack for operation. For that reason, organizations wanted a simpler directory protocol that could operate in a TCP/IP environment. In the early 1990s, the lightweight directory access protocol (LDAP) was developed. Based on X.500's DAP, LDAP provides a simpler implementation of directory services for enterprises.

LDAP uses a hierarchical tree structure for directory entries. Like X.500, LDAP entries support the DN and RDN concepts. DN attributes are typically based on an entity's DNS name. Each entry in the database has a series of name/value pairs to denote the various attributes associated with each entry. Common attributes for an LDAP entry include the following:

- *DN:* distinguished name
- *CN:* common name
- *DC:* domain component
- *OU:* organizational unit

LDAP operates in a client/server architecture. Clients make requests for access to LDAP servers and the server responds back to the client with results of that request. Standard requests the client can make include connecting and disconnecting to the LDAP service, searching a directory entry, comparing information in the directory, and adding, deleting, or modifying directory information.

LDAP typically runs over unsecured network connections using TCP port 389 for communications. If advanced security is required, version 3 of the LDAP protocol supports the use of TLS to encrypt communications. Alternately, many implementations run LDAP over an SSL connection via TCP port 636.

Active Directory

Active Directory, commonly referred to simply as AD, is an implementation of the LDAP protocol for Microsoft-based environments. Through the use of additional plug-in services, LDAP directories can also be utilized by many other systems, including UNIX, Linux, and even mainframe environments. AD provides central authentication and authorization capabilities for users and system services on an enterprise-wide level. AD implementations also have the ability to enforce organizational security and configuration policies across an enterprise. For that reason, many organizations use their AD implementations to enforce user and system-level security policies in a uniform and highly auditable manner.

AD uses LDAP for its naming structure. Like LDAP, AD uses a hierarchical framework to store information. AD directories are organized into forests and trees. A forest is a collection of all the objects and their associated attributes, and trees are logical groupings of one or more AD security domains within a forest. Domains in AD are identified by their DNS name. Objects in an AD database are grouped by Organizational Units.

X.400

X.400 is a set of ITU-T guidelines for the exchange of e-mail, known in X.400 parlance as Message Handling Systems (MHS). X.400 was originally developed in the early 80s and designed to run on OSI-based networks. As with X.500, most X.400 systems currently in use have the ability to run in TCP/IP-based environments as well.

The X.400 protocol supports two primary functions: message transfer and message storage. X.400 addresses consist of a series of name/value pairs separated by semicolons. Typical elements of an address specification include:

O (organization name)

OU (organizational unit names)

G (given name)

I (initials)

S (surname)

C (country name)

The implementation of security features was an early part of the X.400 specification, and early implementations included features related to message privacy and message integrity. These features were implemented in X.400 far earlier than in the next most common messaging protocol, SMTP. However, while X.400-based systems initially became popular in many parts of the world, they have been largely supplanted in recent years by SMTP-based e-mail systems.

Single Sign-On

Single sign-on (SSO) is a term used to describe a unified login experience (from the viewpoint of the end user) when accessing one or more systems. Single sign-on is often referred to as reduced sign-on or federated ID management. Some network enterprise systems provide users with access to many different computer systems or applications for their daily work. This wide range of access may require the user to have a user ID and password for each available resource. Users who often log into many systems will prefer to sign into one master system, and thereafter be able to access other systems without being repeatedly prompted to identify and authenticate themselves. There are numerous technical solutions that offer SSO to users, but most are associated with the centralization of user data, such as a centralized directory service. As previously discussed, many legacy systems do not support an external means to identify and authenticate users. Therefore, a SSO solution for these systems will need to store the credentials outside of the various applications and have them automatically entered on behalf of the user when an application is launched. *Figure 1.24* shows the architecture for a typical SSO system.

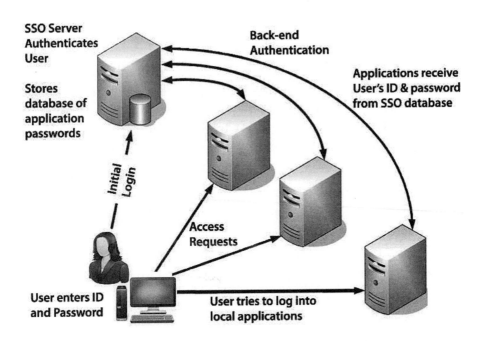

Figure 1.24 - **Architecture for a typical single sign-on (SSO) system**

Classic single sign-on systems provide a central repository of user credentials, such as user IDs and passwords associated with a suite of applications. Users launch various applications through the SSO client software, which opens the appropriate application program and sends the appropriate keystrokes to that program, thus simulating the user to type his own user ID and password. However, there are some limitations and challenges presented by the use of a legacy SSO solution. First, given that the applications are completely unaware of the "slight of hand" used by most SSO systems, when a user must change his or her password within the application, it must also be changed in the SSO system. The user must change the stored password in the application, but because the systems are not synchronized, the changed password must then be stored in the SSO system to maintain the synchronization between the two.

Today, many of these solutions utilize a smart card, secured by a PIN, to store the user's array of credentials in the memory of the card. The smart card loaded with user credentials is coupled with system software that detects when the user is prompted for authentication information. Upon detection, the user may be asked whether to learn the authentication data for the new application or ignore it in the future. If the system is told to learn it, it collects the identification and authentication information for that application from the user, stores it securely on the smart card, and populates the fields in the application on behalf of the user. From that point forward, the user must only remember the main SSO passphrase to unlock the smart card, so that the system can gain access to the collection of identification and authorization materials for that application. There are also solutions that store the user's credentials on a central system or directory. Once authenticated to the primary SSO system, the user credentials are provided to the end system for downstream use.

There are many advantages to SSO solutions:

- **Efficient log-on process:** Users require fewer passwords to remember and are interrupted less when performing their job.

■ *No need for multiple passwords:* The introduction of a SSO system translates into a single-use credential for users. While individual systems still require unique passwords, to the user there is only one master SSO password.

■ *Users may create stronger passwords:* With the reduced number of passwords to remember, users can remember a single, very strong password or passphrase that can also be changed often.

■ *Standards can be enforced across entire SSO system:* Access control policies and standards, such as inactivity time-outs and attempt thresholds, are easier to enforce through an SSO system because the system manages the enforcement across all applications. Inactivity time-outs are used to protect against a user being away from his workstation but still logged on for an extended period, thereby leaving the workstation available to an intruder to continue with the user's session. Attempt thresholds are used to protect against an intruder attempting to obtain an authentic user ID and password combination by brute force (trying all combinations). After a certain number of invalid access attempts (typically three to five) the account is locked.

■ *Centralized administration:* Most SSO solutions offer administrators a central administrative interface to support the enterprise.

Cost is a limiting factor in SSO development. The price of smart devices or simply the SSO software itself can become cost-prohibitive for a large or complex environment. If the solution is based on a centralized SSO system that users log into to collect their IDs and passwords, there are additional costs to ensure continuous availability of the system. If the entire user population utilizes the SSO system to gain access to enterprise applications and it was to fail (a classic single point of failure example), activity would come to a rapid halt.

One of the more prevalent concerns with centralized SSO systems is the fact that all of a user's credentials are protected by a single password: the SSO password. If someone was to crack that user's SSO password, they would effectively have all the keys to that user's kingdom. Likewise, many SSO systems store all the user credential and authentication information in a single database. Therefore, it is of critical importance that the SSO system be as hardened as possible against attack. In addition, strong monitoring and detection capabilities need to be implemented for the SSO systems to ensure that any problems are caught and addressed as quickly as possible.

Inclusion of unique platforms may also be challenging: SSO is complex and requires significant integration to be effective. It is not uncommon for a large enterprise to utilize hundreds, if not thousands, of applications running on a wide variety of operating systems, each with their own approach to user management. Therefore, significant planning and analysis should be performed prior to embarking on developing and deploying an SSO solution.

Script-Based Single Sign-On

If an integrated SSO solution is not available or practical, or if there are a lot of customized applications in use within the organization, an organization can implement its own solution by developing an array of customized scripts. These scripts manipulate the applications, interacting with them as if they were the user, and injecting user ID, password, and other authentication information as needed. The scripts manage all the login and authentication interaction with the application on behalf of the user. This approach may be advantageous for an organization that wants, or needs, SSO functionality but whose options are limited by the pervasiveness of legacy technology or highly customized applications to which modern SSO systems will not interface. By developing its own system, the organization can create highly customized service specifically tailored to its needs. Unfortunately the cost of developing such a system, as well as the ongoing maintenance of the system, can be extremely high. In addition, such systems become very complex, adding to the maintenance problem.

Kerberos

The name Kerberos comes from Greek mythology: it is the three-headed dog that guarded the entrance to Hades. The Kerberos security system guards a network with three elements: authentication, authorization, and auditing. Kerberos is essentially a network authentication protocol. It is designed to provide strong authentication for client/server applications by using secret key cryptography.

Kerberos is effective in open, distributed environments where users must have a unique ID for each application on a network. Kerberos verifies that users are who they claim to be and the network services they use are contained within their permission profile. It has four basic requirements for access control:

- *Security:* A network eavesdropper should not be able to obtain information that can be used to impersonate a user.

- *Reliability:* Resources must be available for users when they are needed.

- *Transparency:* Users should not be aware of the authentication process, and it should be as nonintrusive as possible.

- *Scalability:* The service must support a large number of clients and servers.

The Kerberos Process

Kerberos is based on interaction between three systems: the requesting system (or the principal), the endpoint destination server (where the application or information resource resides), and the Kerberos or Key Distribution Center (KDC). A principal is any entity that interacts with the Kerberos server, such as a user workstation, an application, or a service. The KDC will serve two functions during the authentication transaction— as an authentication server (AS) and as a ticket-granting server (TGS).

163

Kerberos is based on symmetrical encryption and a secret key shared amongst the participants: the KDC maintains a database of the secret keys of all the principals on the network. While acting as the AS, it will authenticate a principal via a pre-exchanged secret key. Once a principal is authenticated, the KDC operates as a TGS, providing a ticket—a piece of electronic data validated by the TGS—to the principal to establish trusted relationships between principals on the network. For example, a KDC maintains the secret keys for two principles on a network, a server and a workstation, both of which trust the KDC. When a user on the workstation authenticates to the AS and receives a ticket, that ticket will be accepted by the server because of the trust relationship between the server and the KDC.

Principals are preregistered with a secret key in the KDC, a process typically achieved through registration. When a user or system is added to the Kerberos realm, it is provided the realm key, a common key used for initial trusted communications. During the introduction into the realm, a unique key is created to support future communications with the KDC. For example, when a Windows workstation joins a domain (or a realm) or a user joins the domain, a unique key is created and shared via the realm's key, which is managed by the KDC. In the case of a user, it is common for Kerberos to utilize a hash of the user's password as the unique user key.

Once the user is incorporated into the Kerberos realm, he or she can then be authenticated by the AS. At this point, the system authenticates the user and the TGS provides him or her with a ticket-granting ticket (TGT). Possession of the TGT indicates that the client has successfully completed authentication and has the right to request service tickets (STs) on the KDC network. TGTs are valid for a certain period, typically between eight and ten hours, after which they expire and the user must reauthenticate to the KDC. However, once the TGT has been issued, there is no further use of passwords or other log-on factors when interacting with other systems within the Kerberos realm.

As demonstrated in *Figure 1.25*, a client (the workstation or application a user is working on) will request authentication from the AS. Once the client is authenticated, it will receive a TGT and a session encryption key. Later, the client may request access to an application server by requesting a ticket from the TGS. The client will need to produce the ticket received during the authentication process—the TGT—in order to receive a ticket to the application server. Upon validating the TGT, the TGS will generate a unique session key to be used between the client and the application server and will encrypt the session key with both the client's secret key and the application server's secret key. The KDC will pack up the data in a ST and send it to the client. If the client is legitimate, it will be able to decrypt the session key and send it, along with the encrypted application server's key, to the application server. The application server will receive the ticket from the client and decrypt the session key. Once all this is complete, the

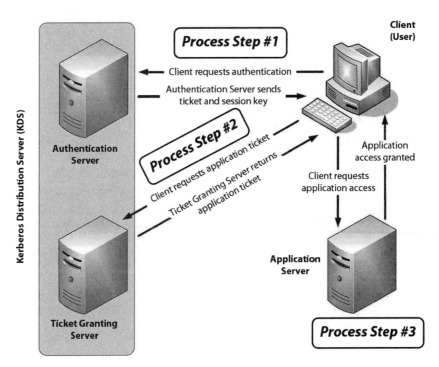

Figure 1.25 - **The Kerberos Architecture.**

client and the application server are authenticated and now have the shared session key that can be used for encrypted communications between them.

Given that the client and the application server have established secret keys with the KDC, the KDC can generate unique session keys and encrypt them with its stored secret keys from the systems requesting secure interactions. The client is sent the service ticket first to avoid DoS attacks against the application server; otherwise, the server could be overloaded with encrypted session requests. The session key is effectively encrypted twice, once with the client's secret key and once with application server's secret key. This forces both systems to authenticate themselves (by possession of the correct secret key) to obtain the unique session key. Once each has the session key, each now has matching key material that can be used in follow-on symmetrical encrypted communications.

There are a few key points to remember about Kerberos tickets:

- The user is authenticated once via a traditional log-on process and verified by means of message encryption to request and acquire service tickets. The user does not have to reauthenticate as long as the TGT is valid.

- When the user is authenticated to the AS, it simply receives a TGT. This, in and of itself, does not permit access. This is analogous to possession of a passport, which certifies that you are a legal citizen of your country but does not necessarily automatically grant you the ability to enter another country. Therefore, when the user obtains a TGT that only allows him to legitimately request access to a resource. It does not automatically mean he will receive that access.

- The TGT allows the user to request a service ticket from the TGS, authenticating the user through encryption processes and building a ST for the user to present to the target resource system.

- The possession of the ST signifies that the user has been authenticated and can be provided access (assuming the user passes the application server's authorization criteria).

■ Kerberos processes are extremely time sensitive and often require the use of Network Time Protocol (NTP) Daemons to ensure times are synchronized. Failure to maintain a synchronized time infrastructure will lead to authentication failures. This can be an attractive vector for a DOS attack.

The primary goal of Kerberos is to ensure private communications between systems over a network. However, in managing the encryption keys, it acts to authenticate each of the principals in the communication based on the possession of the secret key, which allows access to the session key. Kerberos is an elegant solution and used in many platforms as the basis for broad authentication processes.

However, no solution is perfect, and there are some issues related to the use of Kerberos. For starters, the security of the whole system depends on careful implementation: enforcing limited lifetimes for authentication credentials minimizes the threats of replayed credentials, the KDC must be physically secured, and it should be hardened, not permitting any non-Kerberos activity.

More importantly, the KDC can be a single point of failure, and therefore should be supported by backup and continuity plans. It is not uncommon for there to be several KDCs in a Kerberos architecture, each sharing principal information, such as keys, to support the infrastructure if one of the systems were to fail.

The length of the keys (secret and session) is very important. For example, if the key is too short, it is vulnerable to brute-force attacks. If it is too long, systems can be overloaded with encrypting and decrypting tickets and network data. Finally, the Achilles' heel of Kerberos is the fact that encryption processes are ultimately based on passwords. Therefore, it can fall victim to traditional password-guessing attacks.

One of the biggest roadblocks to implementing Kerberos in a processing environment is the need to embed Kerberos system calls into any application that needs to use the system. This process, known as "Kerberizing" an application, allows the application to attach to the Kerberos environment, exchange encryption keys and tickets, and communicate securely with other Kerberos-enabled devices and services. The system calls needed are part of the Kerberos library that must be compiled into every application, and that may cause a problem for some applications. While adding Kerberos library calls to source code may be possible with custom-developed applications, it is not practical in environments that rely on commercial, off-the-shelf (also known as COTS) software. If an organization does not have the ability to embed Kerberos calls into its applications its ability to use Kerberos will be limited.

Secure European System for Applications in a Multi-Vendor Environment (SESAME)

SESAME is a European research and development project, funded by the European Commission and developed to address some of the weaknesses found in Kerberos. The primary weakness was the limitation to Kerberos' scalability due to the need to manage symmetric keys across the environment. The more entities that exist in a Kerberos environment, the more keys that need to be managed. As the environment grows larger the key management problems become more and more complex. The second weakness in Kerberos has to do with the storage of user privilege information on the server a user wishes to use. Again, as the environment grows larger those access permissions need to be located on each server the user needs to access.

SESAME is actually an extension of Kerberos, but overcomes these two primary limitations by offering single sign-on services (like Kerberos) with distributed access controls across the environment. This alleviates the need to replicate authorization data between servers. In addition, SESAME uses both symmetric and asymmetric cryptographic techniques for protection of interchanged data, alleviating some of Kerberos' key management issues. Key attributes of SESAME include:

- Single Sign-On with added distributed access controls using symmetric and asymmetric cryptographic techniques for protecting interchanged data

- Role-based access control

- The use of a privileged attribute certificate (PAC), similar in functionality to a Kerberos ticket

- The use of the Kerberos V5 protocol to access SESAME components

- The use of public key cryptography for the distribution of secret keys

Perimeter-Based Web Portal Access

If an organization has a directory such as LDAP in place, it is possible to quickly leverage the directory data to manage user identity, authentication, and authorization data on multiple Web-based applications using a Web portal tied to a web access management (WAM) solution. These solutions replace the sign-on process in affiliated Web applications, typically by using a plug-in service on the Web server hosting the portal to the member applications. When users authenticate for the first time into the Web portal environment, the portal (more specifically, the WAM) maintains that user's authentication state as the user navigates between applications. Moreover, these systems normally also allow for the definition of user groups and the ability to manage access privileges by group on the managed systems.

These systems provide effective user management and single sign-on in Web environments. They do not, in general, support comprehensive management of the entire access control environment or legacy systems. Nevertheless, WAM has offered a meaningful solution for Web environments to help organizations manage multiple Internet users accessing a collection of Web-based applications. For this reason, WAM tools have been rapidly adopted by organizations seeking more efficient methods for managing a large number of users for a select group of applications.

Federated Identity Management

Single sign-on services are a great productivity boon to both users and organizations. When implemented properly they can also improve the application security of the organization implementing the service. However, most SSO implementations typically involve the management of users across multiple applications within a single enterprise, where the users are all part of the same organization and their identity and access privileges can be verified and managed by a single security infrastructure. A single organization manages the identity and authenticity information for each of its users and takes responsibility for the security and integrity of that process.

However, it is becoming more common that multiple organizations have the need to share the same applications and users between them. For example, an automobile manufacturer and a parts supplier may need to share each other's systems and information. Users from the manufacturer will need access to the supplier to check inventory levels, place orders, and check on order status. Users from the supplier will need to access the manufacturer's systems to check on part requirements, update order status information, and manage contract provisions. To provide this type of access each company would normally have to manage the authentication and verification of the other company's users' identity before provisioning their access to internal systems. Unfortunately, each company does not have access to the other company's employee records (nor should they) and cannot easily track the employee life cycle of the other company to determine whether or not the user is still a valid company employee.

The solution to problems such as this is the use of a federated identity management infrastructure. In a federated environment each organization in the federation subscribes to a common set of policies, standards, and procedures for the provisioning and management of user identification, authentication, and authorization information, as well as a common process for access control for systems these users must access. Each participating organization then establishes a trust relationship with the other organizations such that users from any of the organizations—once authenticated—can access resources from any of the other organization's systems that participate in the federation. They can do this because all the organizations share an agreed-upon standard for security and access control provisioning. Each organization trusts that the other will hold up their end of the process and that users from a "foreign" organization go through the same rigorous vetting process that users from the "home" organization must go through.

Federated ID management systems use one of two basic processes for linking the member organizations' processes together. The first is a cross-certification model. In this model, each organization must individually certify that every other participating organization is worthy of its trust. The organizations review each other's processes and standards and their due diligence efforts determine whether the other organizations meet or exceed their own standards. Once this verification and certification process is complete the organizations can then begin to trust other organizations' users. *Figure 1.26* shows a graphical representation of a cross-certification trust model.

While the cross-certification model may be sufficient for some organizations, there are some drawbacks that must be considered before implementing such a plan. The first issue is that once the number of participating organizations goes beyond a few, the number of trust relationships that must be managed grows rapidly. For example, a cross-certification between two companies (A and B) requires that two trust relationships must be managed (A trusts B and B trusts A). If three companies participate (A, B, and C) the number of trust relationships grows to six (A trusts B, B trusts A, A trusts C, C trusts A, B trusts C and C trusts B). Once the number of participants grows to five there are twenty trust relationships that must be managed (the reason for this is left as a mathematical exercise for the reader). Along with this comes the process for

171

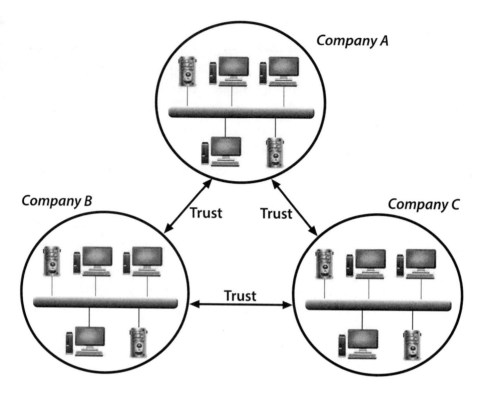

Figure 1.26 - **The cross-certification trust model.**

verifying the trustworthiness of the other participating organizations. The process must be thorough and can take considerable time and resources to accomplish. Thus, once the number of participants in a cross-certification model grows beyond a small number, the complexity of the model may grow too burdensome or expensive to manage for many organizations.

An alternative to the cross-certification model is the trusted third party or bridge model. In this model, each of the participating organizations subscribe to the standards and practices of a third party that manages the verification and due diligence process for all participating companies. Once that third party has verified the participating organization, they are automatically considered trustworthy by all the other participants. Later, when a user from a one of the participants attempts to access a resource from another participant, that organization only needs to check that the user has

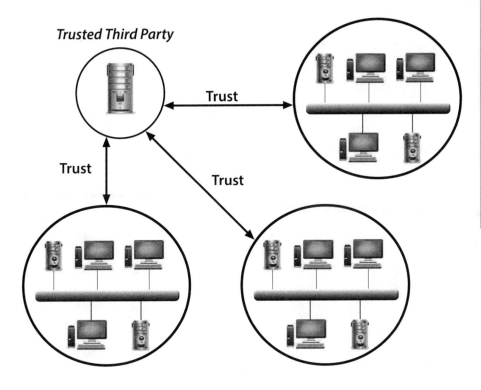

Figure 1.27 - **The Third Party Certification trust model.**

been certified by the trusted third party before access is allowed. The third party, in effect, acts as a bridge between the participating organizations for identity verification purposes. The trusted third-party model is a good solution for organizations that need to enter into a federation with a large number of other organizations. *Figure 1.27* shows a diagram of a typical third-party certification model.

Once In-Unlimited Access

Some organizations do not need to tightly manage user access or restrict resources in a very granular manner. For example, a public service organization may have several services or Web sites that contributors are allowed to access. Alternatively, an organization may have a special area of their intranet that is available to all employees without the need to identify or authenticate to each application individually. Some of the affected applications may not require authentication at all. In such a circumstance, the organization may employ a once in-unlimited access (OIUA) model. In this model, the user authenticates once, and then has access to all the resources participating in the model. This differs from a pure SSO model in that SSO typically manages authentication and access control behind the scenes from the user. In an OIUA model, the systems behind the initial authentication do not have any authentication mechanism to speak of. The fact that the user is able to access the system in the first place means that the user is authorized. How that initial authentication is managed varies with each implementation. In some cases it is as simple as having access to the organization's intranet, the assumption being that if the user got on the network in the first place he was authorized to be there.

The OIUA model suffers from one obvious drawback: the assumption on the part of each participating system that the user identification and authentication was properly handled before the user accesses the system. In many OIUA systems, there is no certificate or token that is passed between the authentication service and the back-end applications, and so true verification of the user's legitimacy is lacking. An unauthorized individual, such as a contractor or support person, accessing the organization's intranet can access the OIUA systems just as easily as a regular employee can. For some organizations, and depending on the type of systems affected by this model, that may not be a concern. Nevertheless, the security professional would be wise to thoroughly check the information contained in each participating system and the type of organizational resources those systems allow users to access before approving the use of a OIUA model. If the model serves a legitimate business purpose, the participating systems should be strongly isolated from the OIUA systems (logically and physically) before proceeding to offer this service to users.

Logging and Monitoring

A comprehensive access control strategy will include the monitoring and secure logging of identification, authentication, and authorization processes. It should also include a log of actions taken by, or on behalf of, the user (both successful and unsuccessful) with all the appropriate and pertinent information associated with the transaction. Moreover, a properly configured system will also log attempted actions by an authenticated user who does not have the necessary privileges for the requested task. Therefore, when properly employed, an access control system can provide substantiation of user activities, linking a user to a transaction or an attempt to access, modify, or delete information.

Logs store essential information about system activity and can also trace the steps that an attacker took to compromise a system. Therefore, the security of logs is important to ensure the integrity of the information; this is especially true if the information is going to be used for forensics investigations or legal proceedings. Logs have to be protected against unauthorized access and changes. If an attacker is able to manipulate or erase log data, successfully investigating an incident would be impossible. Likewise, if an attacker is able to access and read the system or application logs he or she will be able to determine what, if any, of his or her activities are known by the target and adjust his or her methods accordingly. Therefore, the security of the storage and archive systems used to store log data is critical to the integrity of the information collected.

A big issue to face when setting up logging and auditing in an environment is the volume of data that need to be managed. Depending on the extent of the logging, the system could easily fill up gigabytes or terabytes daily. The expected data volume needs to be anticipated in order to ensure that adequate space is available. In addition, the audit logs on a busy system may well exceed the administrative time and skills necessary to review and investigate events that seem suspicious. Therefore, it may be necessary to use some type of event filtering or "clipping level" to properly determine the amount of log detail captured.

After a certain threshold of log data is reached, the amount of information in the logging management system will be too great to review or analyze manually. There are automated tools available that can be used to process and analyze log information. Many of these also perform correlation of the logs from multiple systems to help determine relationships between systems to better determine exactly what was performed during an attack.

Following are some best practices to consider when establishing a log collection and management process:

- Control the volume of data. Log as much as is necessary and feasible, but be mindful of available storage and processing capacity, including analytical staffing requirements.

- Do not allow rollover of logs. Rollover is the act of erasing the earliest entries in a log when the log is full to make room for newer entries. Rollover is favored by administrators because it prevents the logs from filling up and consuming all available storage. Unfortunately, erasing log entries may result in losing valuable data. Ensure that logs are copied to permanent storage then cleared on a regular basis to ensure that there is always enough disk space for log storage.

- Evaluate and implement auditing tools to reduce the complex task of log analysis.

- Establish log review and investigative procedures in advance.

- Train personnel in pertinent log review.

- Protect the audit logs from unauthorized access and changes. Ensure the storage and archive process and facilities are secure.

Audit Trail Monitoring

An audit trail is the data collected from various systems' event logging activity. The purpose of an audit trail is to have enough information to faithfully reconstruct events that happened on the system and to be able to present that reconstructed record as legal evidence. It is a record of system activities that can be investigated to determine if network devices, systems, applications, services, or any computer system that produces a log is operating within expected parameters. Virtually any system can be configured to produce a log of system activities. Of course, not all possible events that can be logged are applicable to security. However, there are many system attributes that can be very helpful for collecting information and gaining awareness of the system and overall infrastructure status.

The function of audit trails is to alert staff of suspicious activity for further investigation. For example, an administrator may see evidence of a user unexpectedly logging into a mission-critical system outside of normal working hours. Upon further investigation, by checking the logs from other devices, the administrator may determine that the access came from a VPN connection over the Internet. This collection of information can be used to validate whether the access was legitimate or expected. Moreover, the investigation can look at other logs produced from the system in question to determine if other questionable actions were performed by that same user.

The audit trail can also provide details on the extent of intruder activity. During a typical attack, the attacker will often traverse several systems, such as routers, firewalls, and applications, potentially leaving behind a record of activity. This information can be used to reconstruct the path of the attack, what tools may have been used, the actions of the attacker, and the effects of the attack. If the information is properly collected and secured, and a chain of custody of log data can be accurately managed, the information can be used for legal proceedings to help prove guilt or innocence.

Audit Event Types
There are many event types that can be audited given the diversity and broad spectrum of technology employed in a typical organization.

177

However, with respect to information security and access controls, there are five key types that are the foundation of security auditing:

Network Events

The network can play a critical role during attacks. As useful as the network is to an organization in performing business processes, it is equally valuable to threat agents: it is the common field of operations providing opportunity to all users. Devices responsible for supporting communications can also provide ample information about events or activities on the network. Network layer information can be helpful in determining and isolating threat activity, such as a worm or a denial-of-service (DoS) attack. It can also be helpful in detecting whether users are using software or services not permitted by policy, such as instant messaging programs or peer-to-peer applications. Network logs can show the source and destination address of network traffic, what application the traffic was using, whether or not packets were allowed or blocked by the network devices, and how much traffic a system received in a given time period.

System Events

System events are an important part of the audit trail as they provide a clear understanding of the system activity. These can include reporting when files are deleted, changed, or added, when software is installed, or when privileges are changed. System logs can also help determine if a worm or virus is present through evidence of unexpected activity on the system. In addition, any changes to the configuration of a system should be reported. If the organization has a strong change management process those change events should correspond to changes approved through that process. If they do not, that may be an indication of unauthorized activity on the system.

Application Events

Application events encompass a broad range of possibilities for monitoring activity. Many of these are dependent on the specific services offered by an application. For example, it may be possible to determine if a Web server is being attacked through evidence of URL manipulation in the Web server logs. Given the diversity of applications and possible attributes of each that can be audited and logged, the objective is to audit activities that help isolate key functions to at least gain an initial perspective of application activity. The person reviewing application logs will need to have a deep understanding of each application and the potential problems that may show up in the logs. If an organization builds its own applications it might be possible to have the development team build specific security-oriented log entries into the application.

User Actions

User event logs are an extremely important resource needed to understand the user activity and behavior in a system. User activity lies at the heart of almost all system events, so understanding what a user on a system has done is essential to reconstructing events during an incident investigation. Information such as log-on and log-off times, use of privileged access, applications executed, and data files accessed are some of the essential basics of user monitoring.

Keystroke Activity

Logging the keystrokes a user enters on a system can be extraordinarily helpful in investigating suspicious activity, as it provides a clear record of all information typed into the computer, including IDs and passwords, system commands, and application data. However, keystroke logging can also be controversial in some environments and employees may become upset at what they perceive to be an invasion of their privacy (even if company policy allows it).

A lot of information about user activities can also be found from command history files found on some operating systems. Although not technically keystroke logging, these files will give a running account of the commands a user entered into the system. On UNIX systems, these

179

files are found in the user's $HOME directory and will have names like ".history," ".sh_history," or ".bash_history."

Intrusion Detection and Prevention

In the classic defense-in-depth model, a complete and secure access control environment employs multiple layers of policy, technology, and process working together to ensure that the desired security posture is maintained. Although firewalls, remote-access devices, applications, and innumerable other technical solutions play an integral role in access control, intrusion detection and prevention systems provide another important layer in a defense-in-depth strategy.

An intrusion detection system (IDS) is a technology that alerts organizations to adverse or unwanted activity. An IDS can be implemented as part of a network device, such as a router, switch, or firewall, or it can be a dedicated IDS device monitoring traffic as it traverses the network. When used in this way, it is referred to as a network IDS, or NIDS. IDS can also be used on individual host systems to monitor and report on file, disk, and process activity on that host. When used in this way it is referred to as a host-based IDS, or HIDS.

IDS attempts to detect activities on the network or host that which are evidence of an attack, and warn administrators or incident-response personnel of the discovery, but does not take any action on the problems found. An organization may want more proactive response when unusual traffic or activity is identified. The automated response capabilities of an IDS may vary based on its placement in the infrastructure and the existence and integration of other access control technologies. An IDS is informative by nature and provides real-time information when suspicious activities are identified. It is primarily a detective device and, acting in this traditional role, is not used to directly prevent the suspected attack.

In contrast, an intrusion prevention system (IPS), is a technology that monitors activity like an IDS but will automatically take proactive preventative action if it detects unacceptable activity. An IPS permits a predetermined set of functions and actions to occur on a network or system; anything that is not permitted is considered unwanted activity and blocked. IPS is engineered specifically to respond in real time to an event at the system or network layer. By proactively enforcing policy, IPS can thwart not only attackers, but also authorized users attempting to perform an action that is not within policy. Fundamentally, IPS is considered an access control and policy enforcement technology, whereas IDS is considered network monitoring and audit technology.

It is important to understand that the distinction between IDS and IPS is growing thinner. Some IDS solutions are adopting preventative capabilities that allow them to act more proactively in the event of policy infringement. IPS systems are incorporating detection techniques to augment the policy enforcement capabilities. In fact, for many of today's product offerings the move from IDS functions to IPS capabilities is as simple as selecting the "block" option when specifying activities of interest in the device.

A critical operational requirement for establishing IDS capabilities is the need to tune IDS to the unique traffic patterns generated by the organization. For example, without proper tuning the activity associated with a company's custom-developed application may appear to an IDS as unwanted or suspicious activity, forcing the generation of multiple alerts. It is equally problematic if the IDS is not tuned to notice the difference between a custom application's activities and those of a real attack, producing no alerts. Tuning an IDS is somewhat of an art form and can become a significant gap in security if not performed correctly, potentially rendering the system worthless. It then becomes a noisy box people begin to ignore, or it sits quietly as networks and systems are attacked. Given the complexity that tuning represents and the potential for excessive false positives or false negatives, automated responses generated from IDS alerts represent an operational risk many organizations deem unacceptable.

181

Network Intrusion Detection System Architecture

NIDS are usually incorporated into the network in a passive architecture, taking advantage of promiscuous mode access to the network. This means that it has visibility into every packet traversing the network segment. This allows the system to inspect packets and monitor sessions without impacting the network or the systems and applications utilizing the network.

Typically, a passive NIDS is implemented by installing a network tap, attaching it to a hub, or mirroring ports on a switch to a NIDS dedicated port. Given that the NIDS is monitoring all the traffic traveling through that device, the NIDS must be able to handle traffic throughput equivalent to (or greater than) the combined traffic load for all the ports on that device or it will begin to drop packets. For example, if a 100-MB, 10-port switch is used and all the ports are mirrored to a single-GB port for the NIDS, the NIDS device must have the capacity to monitor and investigate GB traffic or else it will begin to lose information.

NIDS can also fail to provide adequate monitoring if the traffic it is monitoring is encrypted. The same encryption employed to ensure confidentiality of communication greatly reduces the ability for IDS to inspect the packet. The amount and granularity of information that can be investigated from an encrypted packet is related to the way the packet is encrypted. In most cases, only the data portion of a packet is encrypted leaving the packet headers in cleartext. Therefore, the IDS can gain some visibility into the communication participants, session information, protocol, ports, and other basic attributes. However, if the IDS needs to dig deeper into the packet to perform data analysis, it will eventually fail due to the encryption.

Many technologies now exist which can break session encryption and then re-establish it. Using these technologies it is possible for an organization to get greater insight into network packets. Organizations must be careful though as user training and privacy concerns must be taken into consideration and at times balanced with security requirements.

Because a NIDS analyzes a copy of each packet to analyze the contents and its role in a session, it does not interfere with existing communications and can perform various investigative functions against the collected data. On those occasions when an IDS detects an unwanted communication stream and is enabled to perform automated responses, it can attempt to terminate the connection.

This can be accomplished in a multitude of ways. For example, it can start blocking any packets coming from the source of the traffic, or it can utilize features of the TCP protocol and inject reset packets into the network, forcing the remote system to cancel the communications. In lieu of directly terminating the session, many IDS solutions can be integrated with firewalls, routers, and switches to facilitate dynamic rule changes to block specific protocols, ports, or IP addresses associated with the unwanted communications.

Host-Based Intrusion Detection System (HIDS)

HIDS is the implementation of IDS capabilities at the host level. Its most significant difference from NIDS is that related processes are limited to the boundaries of a single-host system. However, this presents advantages in effectively detecting objectionable activities because the IDS process is running directly on the host system, not just observing it from the network. This offers unfettered access to system logs, processes, system information, and device information, and virtually eliminates limits associated with encryption. The level of integration represented by HIDS increases the level of visibility and control at the disposal of the HIDS application.

There are also multihost IDSs that identify and respond to data from multiple hosts. The multihost HIDS architecture allows systems to share policy information and real-time attack data. For example, if a system were to experience an attack, the signature of the attack and associated remediation actions can be shared with other systems automatically in an attempt to establish a defensive posture.

183

The biggest drawback of HIDS, and the reason many organizations resist its use, is that it can be very invasive to the host operating system. HIDS must have the capability to monitor all processes and activities on the host system and this can sometimes interfere with normal system processing. HIDS can consume inordinate amounts of CPU and memory to function effectively, especially during an event. Although today's server platforms are powerful, diminishing some of these performance issues, workstations and laptops (good candidates for HIDS) may suffer from the overhead of performing analysis on all system activities.

IDS Analysis Engine Methods

Several analysis methods can be employed by an IDS, each with its own strengths and weaknesses, and their applicability to any given situation should be carefully considered. There are two basic IDS analysis methods: pattern matching (also called signature analysis) and anomaly detection. Some of the first IDS products used signature analysis as their detection method and simply looked for known characteristics of an attack (such as specific packet sequences or text in the data stream) to produce an alert if that pattern was detected. For example, an attacker manipulating an FTP server may use a tool that sends a specially constructed packet. If that particular packet pattern is known, it can be represented in the form of a signature that IDS can then compare to incoming packets. Pattern-based IDS will have a database of hundreds, if not thousands, of signatures that are compared to traffic streams. As new attack signatures are produced, the system is updated, much like antivirus solutions.

There are drawbacks to pattern-based IDS. Most importantly, signatures can only exist for known attacks. If a new or different attack vector is used, it will not match a known signature and, thus, slip past the IDS. Additionally, if an attacker knows that the IDS is present, he or she can alter his or her methods to avoid detection. Changing packets and data streams, even slightly, from known signatures can cause an IDS to miss the attack. As with some antivirus systems, the IDS is only as good as the latest signature database on the system. Therefore, regular updates are required to ensure that the IDS has the most recent signatures. This is especially critical for newly discovered attacks.

Alternately, anomaly detection uses behavioral characteristics of a system's operation or network traffic to draw conclusions on whether the traffic represents a risk to the network or host. Anomalies may include but are not limited to:

- Multiple failed log-on attempts
- Users logging in at strange hours
- Unexplained changes to system clocks
- Unusual error messages
- Unexplained system shutdowns or restarts
- Attempts to access restricted files

An anomaly-based IDS tends to produce more data because anything outside of the expected behavior is reported. Thus, they tend to report more false positives as expected behavior patterns change. An advantage to anomaly-based IDS is that, because they are based on behavior identification and not specific patterns of traffic, they are often able to detect new attacks that may be overlooked by a signature-based system. Often information from an anomaly-based IDS may be used to create a pattern for a signature-based IDS.

Stateful Matching Intrusion Detection

Stateful matching takes pattern matching to the next level. It scans for attack signatures in the context of a stream of traffic or overall system behavior rather than the individual packets or discrete system activities. For example, an attacker may use a tool that sends a volley of valid packets to a targeted system. Because all the packets are valid, pattern matching is nearly useless. However, the fact that a large volume of the packets was seen may, itself, represent a known or potential attack pattern. To evade attack, then, the attacker may send the packets from multiple locations with long wait periods between each transmission to either confuse the signature detection system or exhaust its session timing window. If the IDS service is tuned to record and analyze traffic over a long period of time it may detect such an attack. Because stateful matching also uses signatures, it too must be updated regularly and, thus, has some of the same limitations as pattern matching.

Statistical Anomaly-Based Intrusion Detection

The statistical anomaly-based IDS analyzes event data by comparing it to typical, known, or predicted traffic profiles in an effort to find potential security breaches. It attempts to identify suspicious behavior by analyzing event data and identifying patterns of entries that deviate from a predicted norm.

This type of detection method can be very effective and, at a very high level, begins to take on characteristics seen in IPS by establishing an expected baseline of behavior and acting on divergence from that baseline. However, there are some potential issues that may surface with a statistical IDS. Tuning the IDS can be challenging and, if not performed regularly, the system will be prone to false positives. Also, the definition of normal traffic can be open to interpretation and does not preclude an attacker from using normal activities to penetrate systems. Additionally, in a large, complex, dynamic corporate environment, it can be difficult, if not impossible, to clearly define "normal" traffic.

The value of statistical analysis is that the system has the potential to detect previously unknown attacks. This is a huge departure from the limitation of matching previously known signatures. Therefore, when combined with signature matching technology, the statistical anomaly-based IDS can be very effective.

Protocol Anomaly-Based Intrusion Detection

A protocol anomaly-based IDS identifies any unacceptable deviation from expected behavior based on known network protocols. For example, if the IDS is monitoring an HTTP session and the traffic contains attributes that deviate from established HTTP session protocol standards, the IDS may view that as a malicious attempt to manipulate the protocol, penetrate a firewall, or exploit a vulnerability.

The value of this method is directly related to the use of well-known or well-defined protocols within an environment. If an organization primarily uses well-known protocols (such as HTTP, FTP, or telnet) this can be an effective method of performing intrusion detection. In the face of custom or nonstandard protocols, however, the system will have more difficulty or be completely unable to determine the proper packet format. Interestingly, this type of method is prone to the same challenges faced by signature-based IDSs. For example, specific protocol analysis modules may have to be added or customized to deal with unique or new protocols or unusual use of standard protocols. Nevertheless, having an IDS that is intimately aware of valid protocol use can be very powerful when an organization employs standard implementations of common protocols.

Traffic Anomaly-Based Intrusion Detection

A traffic anomaly-based IDS identifies any unacceptable deviation from expected behavior based on actual traffic structure. When a session is established between systems, there is typically an expected pattern and behavior to the traffic transmitted in that session. That traffic can be compared to expected traffic conduct based on the understandings of traditional system interaction for that type of connection.

Like the other types of anomaly-based IDS, traffic anomaly-based IDS relies on the ability to establish "normal" patterns of traffic and expected modes of behavior in systems, networks, and applications. In a highly dynamic environment it may be difficult, if not impossible, to clearly define these parameters.

Intrusion Response

Upon detection of an adverse event or suspicious activity, the IDS or IPS can begin, if permitted to and configured accordingly, to interact with the system (or systems) to restrict or block traffic and collaborate with other IDS devices or logical access control systems.

Early versions of IDS integration for automated intrusion responses tied the IDS to the firewall, allowing it to instruct the firewall to implement specific rules targeted at the questionable traffic. This practice is still employed today and used when the attack can be clearly quantified and the proposed rules do not conflict with normal business operations. On the surface, injecting a rule in a firewall to stop an attack seems logical. However, firewalls may have hundreds of rules, and the positioning of the new rule in the rule set can have a negative impact on normal, mission-critical communications. Moreover, some firewall platforms will share all or portions of their rules with other firewalls in the organization. Therefore, an attack affecting the Internet connection to headquarters may be blocked without affecting local traffic, but when that change is replicated to firewalls at remote sites, the results can be catastrophic.

Much like firewall rule set modification, the IDS can also inject new access control lists in routers, VPN gateways, or VLAN switches to block or restrict traffic. Again, the placement of the rule in the system's existing ACL can have repercussions to other communications. Nevertheless, in some cases these concerns can be quelled by tuning the interaction between the IDS and other filtering devices and predefining acceptable rules and default placement. Finally, because an attack can potentially cause large losses to confidentiality, integrity, and availability, as well as lost productivity or revenue, temporary loss of other communications may be deemed an acceptable risk in the face of an aggressive attack.

Finally, in some cases, the IDS can be used in combination with custom applications to enact changes in systems logically distant from the attack. For example, a script can be activated by an alert from an IDS that temporarily disables a user account, increases the level of auditing on certain systems, or suspends an application from accepting new connections.

Alarms and Signals

The impetus for the use of IDS is to gain visibility into the activities on the network and alert administrators to potentially harmful behavior. The core capability of IDS is to produce alarms and signals that work to notify people and systems to adverse events. There are three fundamental components of an alarm capability:

1. Sensor
2. Control and communication
3. Enunciator

A sensor is the detection mechanism that identifies an event and produces the appropriate notification. The notification can be informational, simply alerting an administrator of the event, or it can be active, triggering a specific response activity to deal with the problem. Tuning sensors to the appropriate sensitivity is important. If it is not sensitive enough events will be missed, and if it is too sensitive there will be too many false alarms. In addition, there may be different types of sensors used for different purposes. A sensor tuned to monitor network traffic will be different than one monitoring CPU activity on a server.

Control and communication refers to the mechanism of handling alert information. For example, an alert may be sent as an e-mail, instant message, pager message, text message, or even an audible message to a phone or voice mail.

The enunciator is essentially a relay system. It may be necessary to notify local resources immediately and remote resources later. Also, the enunciator is the system that can employ business logic, such as determining the specific business unit that is affected by an event and alerting the management of that unit. In addition, the enunciator can construct the message to accommodate different delivery mechanisms. For example, it may have to truncate the message to send to a pager, format to support a specific type of e-mail system, compile a special text-to-voice message, or send a fax.

Establishing who within an organization receives an alert, as well as the timing and delivery mechanism, is critical. Once the appropriate people are identified, determining what types of alerts they should receive and the level of urgency for those alerts must be determined. For example, if an alert occurs and a message containing sensitive material needs to be delivered to the CSO, the security of that information must be considered. Therefore, the type of technology used for delivery can have a bearing on the amount and type of data sent. To further complicate the issue of secure delivery, when one communication transaction fails and a secondary method is attempted, the message format as well as the information it contains may need to be changed. For example, the CSO may determine that the most secure mode of notification during working hours is his or her private fax machine in his or her office. If acknowledgment is not received in a predetermined timeframe, the next mode of communication is a message to his or her cell phone. Given this, the format of the message must be adjusted to accommodate not only the receiving device, but the security of that device as well.

IDS Management

As IDS became an accepted enterprise security technology and adopted more readily, it began to suffer from ill-founded perceptions. Many organizations felt that it was simply a technology investment that needed little or no ongoing maintenance. Nothing is further from the truth. The success of an effective IDS or IPS service depends as much on the implementation and maintenance of the service as on the technology used. IDS and IPS are real-time devices which require ongoing operational support.

An IDS is designed to alert an administrator in the event something is detected. If it is not implemented properly, tuned accordingly, and the appropriate personnel trained, the organization will get little or no value from its investment. In a typical corporate IDS implementation, what at first appears as simply a product investment quickly turns into a full technology management process, including the services of a full-time IDS administrator.

Soon after, investments are needed for managing the data output from the systems, and technology for storage, retention, and security. Finally, with added awareness of what is occurring on the network, many organizations are motivated to acquire additional technology, such as more IDSs, correlation engines, and other security controls to address the onslaught.

If not properly managed, an IDS or IPS system can quickly become a gravity well of time, effort, and money. An IDS requires expert administration and overall management of the solution and the technology's success within the enterprise is directly proportional to the support of management to maximize the value of their investment. Upon implementing IDS, organizations must ensure they have a knowledgeable resource to select, install, configure, operate, and maintain the system. Management processes and procedures must be developed and employed to ensure that the system is regularly updated with signatures, evaluated for suspicious activities, and the IDS itself is not vulnerable to direct attack.

One of the more important, but overlooked, aspects of IDS is managing the output from the system. Many organizations employ IDS to gain a better understanding of what may be occurring on their networks and systems. Once the IDS detects an event, it is necessary for the organization to have an incident response process. Although an IDS can be configured to perform some automated functions to thwart an attack, complete reliance on the system is not realistic. IDS is designed to detect and, if possible, identify an attack. It is up to the people in the organization to work within their environment to follow through with the process of managing an incident. Therefore, though it is an effective technology, IDS is simply the tip of the security management and incident response spear.

Physically implementing an IDS is the first step in orchestrating a comprehensive incident management infrastructure designed to deal with potentially harmful events. In summary, the following are needed to ensure an effective IDS:

- Employ a technically knowledgeable person to select, install, configure, operate, and maintain the IDS.

- Regularly update the system with new signature attacks and evaluate expected behavior profiles.

- Be aware that the IDS may be vulnerable to attacks and protect it accordingly.

- Intruders may try to disable the IDS with false information or overload the system.

Security Information and Event Management

Security information and event management (SIEM) is a term used to describe a group of technologies which aggregate information about access controls and selected system activity to store for analysis and correlation. Logs and system information may be collected for a variety of reasons including but not limited to:

- Regulation or compliance requirements
- Internal accountability and nonrepudiation
- Risk management functions
- Performance monitoring and trending
- Event correlation and root cause analysis
- Incident response
- Investigations

SIEMs and log analysis tools are two areas rapidly merging into one functional space. In general a SIEM has the following characteristics:

- Store raw information from various systems logs
- Aggregate the information in a single repository
- Normalize the information to make comparisons more meaningful
- Analytical tools which can process, map and extract target information
- Alerting and reporting tools

SIEMs and the functions they provide are becoming indispensable to many organizations as they offer the ability to get "near real time" reporting on events and incidents as they occur in network and information systems. In spite of the insight and reporting provided SIEMs can be extremely complex and expensive to implement and maintain. They are often the central data system and decision support system for security operation centers "SOC" of large organizations. SIEMS also present a attractive target for attackers as these systems are not only the repositories for current health information about the organization's information systems but also are the systems often first turned to when there is suspicion of an attack or infiltration. While SEIMs offer a great advantage, they also require extensive protection to ensure they do not become a liability.

Access Control Attacks

Understanding Threats

Access control threats are the agents that have a direct negative impact on the confidentiality, integrity, and availability of information assets. Threats are the proverbial "Forces of Evil" that are out to attack the networks, systems, and applications that store and process an organization's data. In the absence of validated threats, an organization need not worry about protecting itself, since there would be nothing to protect against. Unfortunately, a world without threats does not exist, so information security professionals need to understand the various types of threats that are out there and how they work in order to understand and formulate the best defenses possible to protect against them. Popular threats can be best represented as including but not limited to the following:

- Denial of service
- Buffer overflows
- Mobile code
- Malicious software
- Password crackers
- Spoofing/masquerading
- Sniffers
- Eavesdropping
- Emanations
- Shoulder surfing
- Tapping
- Object reuse
- Data remnants
- Unauthorized targeted data mining
- Dumpster diving

- Backdoor/trapdoor
- Theft
- Intruders
- Social engineering

Denial of Service

Denial-of-Service (DoS) attacks represent one of the leading threats to the secure operation of an organization's technology infrastructure. DoS attacks can range from the consumption of specific system resources, preventing useful processing, and interruption of network resources to preventing communication, rendering a system service or application unusable, or a complete system outage.

In the early 1990s, DoS attacks were mostly relegated to protocol manipulation within the TCP/IP protocol. Known as SYN floods, attackers would make an overwhelming number of session initiation requests (SYN packets) to a server without ever completing the proper session setup sequence, consuming all available system resources and effectively making it impossible for a valid user or application to gain access to the server. This was an effective basic attack because it did not require any knowledge of specific applications or services running on the system, only the fact that the system was running the TCP/IP protocol.

Soon, attackers began to identify weaknesses in specific system services, allowing them to make specially formatted requests to these services that would force an error, resulting in the complete loss of the service. For example, one early attack called Teardrop exploited the way many operating systems managed fragmented IP packets. Teardrop employed a tool to manufacture overlapping fragmented packets that would exploit the flaw in the system, thus shutting it down.

In the late 1990s and into the twenty-first century, distributed denial of service (DDoS), became a significant threat to operations. Rather

195

than attack a server from a single location (and risk being detected and blocked), DDoS attacks target a server from hundreds or thousands of locations. Attackers build vast networks of commandeered systems (also known as botnets) by infecting vulnerable machines with software agents known as zombies. The zombies react to commands relayed typically over IRC channels from the "botherder" and, when instructed, simultaneously make numerous requests to a single system or application, such as a Web site. The zombie systems make millions of requests to the Web site at once, completely flooding the target system to the point where others cannot access it, or until it simply fails and shuts down.

DoS attacks are one of the oldest tools used by attackers and are still used quite often today. DoS methods are often used during spoofing attacks (discussed later in this chapter) to make a system unavailable so the attacker could assume that system's identity. Since the DoS victim cannot, in effect, "speak up," the attacker can launch attacks on other systems without fear of being discovered by impersonating the victim.

DoS attacks can also be used as a method of circumventing access controls. Using the last example, an attacker can launch a DoS attack against a system and then impersonate that system to other systems. If those systems have a trust relationship with the machine suffering the DoS attack the attacker may not ask for additional authentication before being given access. In addition, some forms of DoS attack leave the system in a depleted state and allow access without the usual network- and system-based controls in place. Finally, successful DoS attacks prevent access to the system by other users, threatening availability to the system's resources.

Buffer Overflows

A buffer is a portion of system memory that is used to temporarily store information for processing. Buffers are essential to computer operations for managing data input and output at all levels of system interaction. A buffer overflow is an attack that manipulates the system's ability to manage its buffers, causing system failures and outages, the failure to control an application state, the inability to control a running program, or the execution of code of an attacker's choosing. Buffer overflows can also be used to inject malicious software for processing on behalf of the attacker. In addition, because memory buffers are used in network interfaces, video systems, traditional RAM, or virtual memory on hard disks, all those areas are potentially vulnerable to a buffer overflow. Buffer overflows are often used to gain unauthorized access or to escalate privileges from an authorized account.

Buffer overflows are typically the result of poor application or system memory management. This can be related to poor coding of the application, services, BIOS (Basic input–output system: the basic, low-level machine instructions that manage computers) or operating system code managing the allocation and manipulation of memory. Buffer overflows are one of the oldest and most common forms of system exploit in use today. Ironically, they are also one of the simplest problems in all of security to prevent. Strict attention to the allocation and management of memory when developing an application, including the transfer of information into and out of system buffers, will ensure that any changes to memory buffers are checked for overflow conditions. Improved application testing in the development process can also result in a dramatic decrease in buffer overflow exposure.

Buffer overflows have important access control consequences because they can be used to bypass a system's built-in access control mechanisms. A specifically crafted piece of code can be inserted into a system or application's buffer, halt normal processing, and force the system to execute code of the attacker's choosing. This could result in the attacker gaining access to restricted system files or escalating his access rights to those of a system administrator.

Mobile Code

Mobile code is software that is transmitted across a network from a remote source to a local system and is then executed on that local system, often requiring little or no explicit action on the part of the user. The local system is often a personal computer, but can also be a PDA, mobile phone, Internet appliance, or some other "smart" device. Mobile code differs from traditional software in that it need not be installed or executed explicitly by the user. Examples of mobile code include ActiveX controls, Java applets, JavaScript code run from a Web page, and HTML-based e-mail. Mobile code is also known as downloadable code or active content, especially in the context of Web sites and e-mail systems.

The security implications of mobile code are significant because of the distribution capabilities, limited user awareness, and potential for harm. Mobile code is designed to be provided to an end-user device (such as a browser of a smart phone) to perform a function on behalf of that user. If a device is not configured properly, it can be fooled into running mobile code designed to alter, infect, or otherwise manipulate the system. Mobile code, if left unchecked, can be used to track user activity, access vital information, or install other applications without alerting the user. The problems are multiplied if the user is accessing corporate resources. Data can be copied to the local system, exposing it to unwanted threats, access credentials may be captured and later used by an attacker, or the device can be used to inject malicious software into the organization. The effects of mobile code can range from a simple nuisance, such as Web sites tracking Internet activity, to highly problematic situations, such as spyware that can be used for identify theft.

Mobile code is not entirely without security controls, however. Many of the current mobile code technologies have tried to embed security controls within their architectures with mixed success. The Java security model is probably the most advanced of the group, having been designed into the base Java architecture from its inception. Java constrains its executing code within a security model called the sandbox. When a Java application executes, it is tightly limited in its capabilities for accessing network resources and local data files, attempting to reduce the risk that a malicious Java application can be used to spread a malicious attack to other systems. There have been several security flaws discovered in various implementations of Java, but by and large it has lived up to its promise of effective security for mobile applications.

Microsoft's ActiveX technology relies on digital code signatures as its base security mechanism. Each ActiveX control must be digitally signed by the author. The browser verifies the validity of the signature and asks the user to make a judgment on whether or not the developer is trustworthy. Unfortunately, most end users do not have the security or technical knowledge to make an informed decision in such a circumstance, and most simply bypass the code and allow the control to execute.

In addition, ActiveX controls execute on the user's local system with all the access privileges and restrictions that user may have. If the user has administrative rights on the machine the ActiveX control will have those rights as well. This makes it much easier for ActiveX controls to perform malicious activity on a system or network. This is easily prevented using "limited" accounts however many users balk at the reduced functionality this can propose.

Mobile code represents a threat to access control because it can bypass the access control mechanisms of a system or device based on the actions of the individual user rather than being subject to organizational policy or system restrictions. Once this control is bypassed there can be numerous threats to confidentiality, integrity, and availability. This, of course, assumes that the mobile code is malicious. There are many legitimate reasons to use mobile code in a system environment. Examples include common browser plug-ins to view files of differing formats or online seminars that require ActiveX applications to produce sound and present information. However, an organization should make its users aware of the dangers inherent with mobile code installation and employ the appropriate policies and technologies to restrict its installation on end-user systems.

Malicious Software

Malicious software, commonly referred to as malware, is a term used to describe software, applications, applets, scripts, or any digital material that is deliberately designed to perform undesirable functions. There was a time when the term was limited to the general category of viruses, Trojan horse programs, and spyware. However, it is now typically used to cover just about anything that can be run on a computer system that represents a threat to the system, information, or other applications.

There are generally four major classes of malicious code that fall under the general definition of malware:

1. ***Virus:*** Parasitic code that requires human action or insertion, or which attaches itself to another program to facilitate replication and distribution. Virus-infected containers can range from e-mail, documents, and data file macros to boot sectors, partitions, and memory fobs. Viruses were the first iteration of malware and were typically transferred by floppy disks (also known as "sneakernet") and injected into memory when the disk was accessed or infected files were transferred from system to system.

2. ***Worm:*** Self-propagating code that exploits system or application vulnerabilities to replicate. Once on a system, it may execute embedded routines to alter, destroy, or monitor the system on which it is running, then move on to the next system. A worm is effectively a virus that does not require human interaction or other programs to infect systems.

3. ***Trojan Horse:*** Named after the Trojan horse of Greek mythology (and serving a very similar function), a Trojan horse is a general term referring to programs that appear desirable, but actually contain something harmful. A Trojan horse purports to do one thing that the user wants while secretly

performing other potentially malicious actions. For example, a user may download a game file, install it, and begin playing the game. Unbeknownst to the user, the application may also install a virus, launch a worm, or install a utility allowing an attacker to gain unauthorized access to the system remotely, all without the user's knowledge.

4. *Spyware:* Prior to its use in malicious activity, spyware was typically a hidden application injected through poor browser security by companies seeking to gain more information about a user's Internet activity. Today, those methods are used to deploy other malware, collect private data, send advertising or commercial messages to a system, or monitor system input, such as keystrokes or mouse clicks.

   a. *Malvertisments* are web advertisements which appear to be legitimate yet direct users to download malware onto systems. Many organizations choose to use web filtering or web proxy technologies to block advertising.

   b. *Malnets* are malware networks which typically consist of numerous infected websites, desktops, laptops and increasingly mobile devices. These nodes clustered together form a malnet which is used to launch further attacks and further propagate malware. Web filtering, web proxy and user awareness are the best defenses against malnets

The line between the different types of malicious code is growing thinner every day. Many threats have surfaced that combine the capabilities of the different malicious software types to make for significant security challenges. The various categories within the mobile code taxonomy (virus, worm, Trojan, malware, spyware, etc.) are an attempt to assign a definition to a highly dynamic threat. Attackers do not operate within the same construct. Spam can lead to spyware, which can help the proliferation of worms exploiting vulnerabilities to implant their payload of Trojan devices.

The idea that malicious software represents a significant threat to access controls cannot be overstated. Clearly, the exposure of information, loss of system integrity, and potential exposure of user credentials to unknown entities undermine the control environment. Malicious software often uses access control-circumventing techniques to attach itself to an end user's system, and then uses its embedded position to undermine the access control capabilities of that system and other systems to which it can spread. Malicious software can also expose administrator and system credentials stored on that system to an attacker.

Password Crackers

Assuming a user does not share it with another person, a password combined with a user name offers basic (very basic) authentication. However, as any security professional should know, passwords are prone to discovery, and thereby the strategy of providing security based solely on username and password combinations is weak. Given the fact that the typical password will range from 5 to 15 characters on average, there is a limit to the combination of characters available to use as a password. Add in the fact that some characters are rarely used (when was the last time anyone used the tilde "~" in a password?) and the number of practical combinations is smaller still. Of course, the size of the available character set influences the number of possibilities.

Passwords are typically stored by means of a one-way hash (an algorithm that produces a unique numeric representation of the password). When a password is entered into a system during authentication, the system hashes the entered data using the same algorithm employed during the initial creation of the password and compares it to the hash already on file. If they match, there is a high degree of certainty the password provided is the same as the one on file and, thus, the user is legitimate. In most cases, the password itself is never stored or saved in its plaintext (or unhashed) form. When a user sets a new password, it is immediately hashed and only the new hash is saved. *Figure 1.28* shows the process of comparing a user's password against the password database.

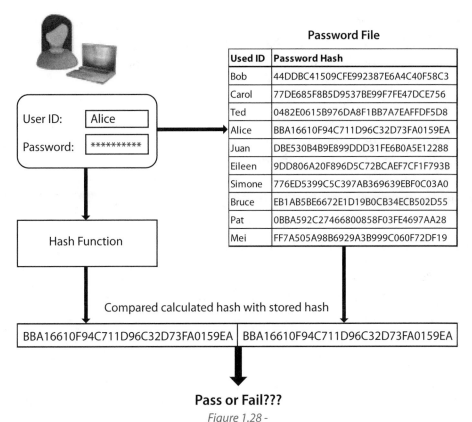

Password File

Used ID	Password Hash
Bob	44DDBC41509CFE992387E6A4C40F58C3
Carol	77DE685F8B5D9537BE99F7FE47DCE756
Ted	0482E0615B976DA8F1BB7A7EAFFDF5D8
Alice	BBA16610F94C711D96C32D73FA0159EA
Juan	DBE530B4B9E899DDD31FE6B0A5E12288
Eileen	9DD806A20F896D5C72BCAEF7CF1F793B
Simone	776ED5399C5C397AB369639EBF0C03A0
Bruce	EB1AB5BE6672E1D19B0CB34ECB502D55
Pat	0BBA592C27466800858F03FE4697AA28
Mei	FF7A505A98B6929A3B999C060F72DF19

User ID: Alice

Password: **********

Hash Function

Compared calculated hash with stored hash

| BBA16610F94C711D96C32D73FA0159EA | BBA16610F94C711D96C32D73FA0159EA |

Pass or Fail???

Figure 1.28 -
The process of comparing a user's password against the password database

The key factor in this scheme is the saving of the hashed password, and that is where password crackers come into play. If a file containing the hashed password is obtained by an attacker, he can perform brute-force attacks by comparing thousands of possible password combinations against the hash. Password crackers are tools that will use a predefined list (or create one dynamically) of possible combinations, hash them, and compare the hash to the one stored in the file.

With most password cracking attempts, it is only a matter of time before all possible character combinations are tested and the password is exposed. Of course, depending on the length and complexity of the password, the process could take minutes or years. However, human nature dictates that most people use passwords that are easily remembered, and, therefore, easily guessed by the system, reducing the required time for the tool to run successfully.

Password crackers are one of the few tools that are equally effective for security administrators and attackers alike. If the tool can discover the password, an attacker using the tool can use the password to break into the system. If an administrator is using the tool, he or she can issue a password change request to the user to get them to use a stronger password. Although there is much debate over the security of usernames and passwords, the role of the password cracker as a tool for the security administrator is well established as a mechanism to increase the security of the system.

Putting aside the administrative use of password crackers as a tool, the threat they represent to access controls is very high. Simply put, passwords, for some organizations, are the keys to the kingdom. If the access control strategy is based on passwords, their exposure would mean the demise of the control environment, rendering it useless. Moreover, the monitoring aspects of the control environment will not be very helpful in exposing the activity because, if performed discreetly, the attacker will be using stolen accounts of legitimate system users.

Early in the evolution of password crackers, the process of creating the hashes for a list of all potential passwords and then comparing them to the stolen collection of hashed passwords was very time-consuming. In 1980, Martin Hellman, best known for his work with Whitfield Diffie on the development of public key cryptography, discovered a method to save time by performing an exhaustive search of the hashed passwords and loading the results into memory, taking advantage of the close interaction between memory and the processor. This is possible because many popular operating systems generate password hashes by encrypting a fixed plaintext with the user's password as the key and storing the result as the password hash. If the password hashing scheme is poorly designed, the plaintext and the encryption method will be the same for all passwords. This technique was improved by Ron Rivest by 1982 with the introduction of a method to drastically reduce the number of memory lookups during cryptanalysis by organizing the resulting hashes in chains, with only the first and last elements loaded into memory. The results were a significant reduction in the time of processing passwords through optimizing the pre-calculated chains in memory.

In 2003 Philippe Oechslin developed a faster method of organizing the hash chains. The new chain structure developed from this method is called a rainbow chain or a rainbow table. To demonstrate the significance of rainbow table attacks, Oechslin successfully cracked 99.9% of 1.4GB of alphanumeric password hashes in 13.6 seconds, whereas previous processes would do the same in 101 seconds. The rainbow table attack has revolutionized password cracking and is being rapidly adopted by tool creators.

Spoofing/Masquerading

Spoofing or masquerading is the act of appearing to a system as if a communication from an attacker is actually coming from a known and trusted source. Early versions of spoofing were performed by manipulating the packets of data used in the IP protocol, the protocol used for Internet communications. Because IP provides little in the way of authentication or integrity checking, it is trivial to alter the source IP address of a transmission to appear as if it were coming from somewhere else. Attackers send packets to a server with the source address of a known (and trusted) system in the packet header. This would fool any filtering devices that were configured to permit activity to and from the server only for specific, trusted addresses and networks.

Because the TCP/IP protocol uses a specific sequence of packet transmissions to establish a connection and communicate between systems (the so-called three-way handshake of SYN-SYN/ACK-ACK packets), the difficult part is for the attacker to predict the response to the target server that would normally come from the host whose identity is being utilized. Session identifiers, such as TCP sequence numbers, have to be predetermined by the attacker to avoid detection by the target server.

In the 1980s, hacker Kevin Mitnick popularized the technique of IP spoofing, (originally identified by Steve Bellovin several years prior) as an attack method that used weaknesses within Internet network protocols to gain access to systems whose access controls are based on IP addresses and inherent trust relationships. Mitnick used this technique, along with social engineering, to gain access to systems to obtain various application source codes, including the source codes for the operating system running in the most popular cellular phones at that time.

Quickly, systems and firewalls learned to defeat and compensate for such an attack, making it much less common in today's computing environment. However, there are a multitude of other spoofing methods available to manipulate systems, allowing attackers to appear as valid participants within the network. For example, "phishing" is a process of fooling people to believe that an e-mail requesting a password change or request for personal information is coming from (for instance) a bank and not realize that it comes from an attacker masquerading as the trusted source. There are examples of attackers spoofing domain name servers to redirect Internet users to malicious sites engineered to inject malware or obtain information. Spoofing is also an effective technique used in part for man-in-the-middle attacks. In such an attack, a user may believe he or she is interacting with the expected destination, when in fact his or her communications are being redirected through an intermediary, impersonating each side of the communication to the other and collecting information from both sides.

Spoofing and masquerading have a profound effect on access control systems because they remove the assurance that a person is dealing with a trusted entity. To a target system, the attacking system looks, acts, and communicates like the actual trusted system. As such, the target system is likely to provide all the access rights and privileges that it would normally grant to a trusted system.

Sniffers, Eavesdropping, and Tapping: All communications, whether wired or wireless, need to travel from point to point over some medium, whether that medium is copper wire, fiber optic cable, or radio waves. These various transmission media all represent the potential for exposure. In the event an attacker was to insert a "listening point" into the communication medium, he could potentially collect all layers of the communication. The act of using such a listening point is called sniffing or eavesdropping.

Sniffers are typically devices that can collect information from a communication medium, such as a network. These devices can range from specialized equipment to basic workstations with customized software. A sniffer can collect information about most, if not all, attributes of the communication. The most common method of sniffing is to plug a sniffer into an existing network device like a hub or switch. A hub (which is designed to relay all traffic passing through it to all of its ports) will automatically begin sending all the traffic on that network segment to the sniffing device. On the other hand, a switch (which is designed to limit what traffic gets sent to which port) will have to be specially configured to send all traffic to the port where the sniffer is plugged in. Another method for sniffing is to use a network tap—a device that literally splits a network transmission into two identical streams; one going to the original network destination and the other going to the sniffing device. Each of these methods has its advantages and disadvantages, including cost, feasibility, and the desire to maintain the secrecy of the sniffing activity.

Interestingly, the same capability and methods are used by intrusion detection systems to monitor communications. So, like most things in security, sniffing is an activity that can be used for good and for evil. A protocol analyzer, for instance, is used by network maintenance technicians to identify network problems, but it allows the viewing of network traffic and can expose confidential information, such as logon routines. Accordingly, its use should be restricted to authorized technicians for maintenance purposes only. One thing is clear, however, and that is that sniffing bypasses any access control mechanisms on a system or application by seeing information passing between machines on a network. The attacker will let the two systems (or users) manage all the connection and authentication processes legitimately, and then monitor the traffic free of the need to identify or authenticate himself.

The best protection against sniffing, eavesdropping, and tapping is to encrypt transmissions between devices. If an attacker is listening to encrypted traffic, and assuming he or she does not have the decryption keys, he or she will be unable to determine the information that is passing through the sniffer. Of course, encrypting every transmission and communications link throughout even a moderately sized enterprise is neither practical nor inexpensive. However, all enterprises have a few links that often carry sensitive or confidential information. It may be worth the effort and expense to add encryption to those specific network links. Likewise, many applications have the ability to enable encryption as part of their network transmissions. If this option is available for a particular application and the security personnel in the organization fear that eavesdropping on that application may be a problem, they should investigate and implement encryption for that application.

Emanations

Every electronic device gives off its own unique electromagnetic signals. Emanation is the proliferation or propagation of those signals. By intercepting and interpreting the emanations coming from a particular device, an attacker can often reconstruct the information that is being displayed or processed on that device. Given the electromagnetic properties of some devices, there is the potential to acquire data from great distances. For example, sophisticated electromagnetic loops can be generated near communication lines to eavesdrop on communications without physically interacting with the wire. It is well known that various governments used this method to tap transoceanic communication lines during the Cold War. Other examples include utilizing sensitive devices to acquire signals propagating from computer monitors from other buildings or from the streets below to see what a user is doing. The technology even exists to use focused lasers to sense the vibrations from a building's exterior windows to listen to the conversations going on in that room.

There are stories (potentially urban legend) of acquiring communication signals from underground pipes that pass close to the communication line. The U.S. and U.K. governments began a program in the late 1960s, called TEMPEST, to study compromising emanations and research ways to limit them. Today, electronics manufacturers can submit their products for TEMPEST testing to determine if those products produce potentially compromising emanations. This is usually accomplished by shielding the cables, keyboards, and screens to prevent electromagnetic leakage.

The threat to access controls is very similar to that from the use of sniffers and taps. The attacker can obtain private information or gain better awareness of the communication architecture for further attacks without needing to go through any authentication or authorization processes and effectively bypassing all access control measures, both logical and physical. Defending against the threat from emanations can be difficult, but not impossible. Wireless antennae come in many formats with different irradiation patterns that can be utilized in different ways to reduce signal propagation or force the emanations to have a particular shape or pattern. There are three basic types of antennae: omnidirectional, semidirectional, and highly directional. Within these three basic groups there are several different antenna subtypes, such as mast, pillar, ground plate, patch, panel, sectorized, yagi, parabolic, and grid. Each type and subtype represents options for the designers of wireless networks to reduce exposure by focusing the signal.

Finally, there are materials that restrict the ability for radio waves to propagate through them. This involves the use of special paint on walls and special window coverings that can be placed on windows or other weak spots (electromagnetically speaking) to further disrupt the emanation of electromagnetic signals. The protection against emanations often is based on the principle of the penetration index which is the weakening of the emanations as the receiver is farther away from the source. For this reason, equipment that is processing very sensitive data should be located in the center of a building or ship and possibly protected by a Faraday cage which wraps the communications room in a wire mesh that will restrict signal leakage.

Shoulder Surfing

Shoulder surfing is the act of surreptitiously gathering information from a user by means of direct observation of the user's activity, typically (as the name suggests) by looking over their shoulder as they perform some action. A good example is watching someone type in their password while talking about what they did over the weekend or watching someone type in their telephone credit card number into a pay phone. People who travel frequently often spend a great deal of time in airports and hotel lobbies, filling the time by checking their e-mail or working on business documents. Shoulder surfing is a particularly prevalent in these environments, because people are often in close proximity to each other and the sensitive information on their screen is easily observed. There are many themes to this type of attack, ranging from watching people perform tasks to listening in on conversations. Essentially, this is a form of social engineering and seeks the opportunity to gain information through personal observation.

The impact to access controls is simply the exposure of potentially sensitive information to an unauthorized person. If an attacker were to see a user enter his ID and password, it would be trivial for that attacker to use that information to log in as that user later on. The most effective defense against shoulder surfing is to watch where you are and who is around you when performing sensitive actions. In some circumstances, organizations have employed multifactor authentication, making it much more difficult to acquire passwords. To avoid someone shoulder surfing a laptop user, screen filters are available that require a person to either look into the display directly (not from an angle) to see the contents or wear special glasses to depolarize the display stream. An organization should make the threat of shoulder surfing an important part of their employee security awareness program.

Object Reuse

Object reuse refers to the allocation or reallocation of system resources to a user or, more appropriately, to an application or process. Applications and services on a computer system may create or use objects in memory and in storage to perform programmatic functions. In some cases, it is necessary to share these resources between various system applications. However, some objects may be employed by an application to perform privileged tasks on behalf of an authorized user or upstream application. If object usage is not controlled or the data in those objects is not erased after use, they may become available to unauthorized users or processes.

There are two areas of concern with application object reuse: the direct employment of the object or the use of data input or output from the object. In the case of object use, it is necessary for the system managing the object to verify the requesting entity is authorized to use that object. In the event of object data use, the system should clear all residual data from the object prior to assigning the object to another process, ensuring that no process intentionally or unintentionally inherits or reads the data from another process.

More specifically, proper access control requires the controlled sharing of these resources between processes. For example, the printing process on a system needs to be controlled so that it prints only one user's output at a time. It may be a security violation if one user's secret output were mixed in with that of another user's public data and printed on the same physical sheet of paper. Fortunately, keeping print jobs separate is relatively simple. In addition, flushing (emptying) print queues and clearing printer device storage after a print job is complete is important to prevent similar data leakage from someone looking at the printer's storage area.

However, the controlled sharing of memory is more difficult to manage. Many systems allow several processes to execute in memory simultaneously. Sections of memory may be allocated to one process for a while, then de-allocated, then reallocated to another process. The constant reallocation of memory is a potential security vulnerability, because residual information may remain when a section of memory is reassigned to a new process after a previous process is completed. It is necessary for the operating system to erase the memory upon release and before being allocated to another process. However, good secure application programming practice calls for the application to specifically erase memory both when it is initially allocated and when it is no longer needed, not just leaving it for the operating system to do.

Object reuse is also applicable to system media, such as hard drives, magnetic media, RAM-based devices, or other forms of data storage. It is not uncommon for old media to be reassigned to a new system. When media is reused, it is considered a best practice to clean all data from the device prior to reassignment and preferably before it is removed from the old device in the first place. Removing all data from the storage device reduces the likelihood of exposing proprietary or confidential information. Degaussing and writing over media are examples of standard methods for handling object reuse to prevent unauthorized access to sensitive data when media is reassigned.

The threat to access controls is significant. Commonly available tools can be employed by an attacker to obtain nonzeroed, unallocated memory objects, effectively exposing information or allowing the assumption of privileges of the previous process without proper identification, authentication, and authorization. The threats associated with media are easily understandable. In the event devices are not degaussed or overwritten to eliminate the data, there is a significant risk to exposing sensitive information to unauthorized users.

Data Remanence

It is becoming increasingly commonplace for people to buy used computer equipment, such as a hard drive, or router, and find information on the device left there by the previous owner; information they thought had been deleted. This is a classic example of data remanence: the remains of partial or even the entire data set of digital information. Normally, this refers to the data that remain on media after they are written over or degaussed. Data remanence is most common in storage systems but can also occur in memory.

Hard drives are typically made up of magnetic platters organized into sectors (the smallest unit of accessible space on a hard drive) and clusters (groups of sectors). When a file is written to a hard drive, the file system will place the file in one or more sectors on the drive. Once a single sector in a cluster is written to, the operating system will allocate the entire cluster to that file. As data is written to a disk, it will be spread out to several clusters. Each cluster is reserved for a given file. Even if the actual data to be stored requires less storage than the cluster size, an entire cluster is still allocated for the file. The unused space in the cluster after the data are called the slack space. The file allocation table (FAT) on the drive maintains the physical location information for each file for later retrieval. *Figure 1.29* illustrates the use of sectors and clusters on a disk.

There are several scenarios that may occur in this scheme that can lead to data exposure. Deleting a file through the operating system's "delete" command typically does not remove it from the system. The process

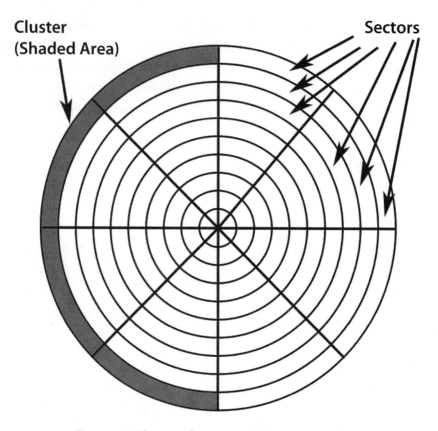

Figure 1.29 - **The use of sectors and clusters on a disk**

simply removes the information from the FAT, signifying to the system that those clusters are now available for use, but it leaves the actual data still physically on the drive. To the operating system it appears as if the data are gone, but in reality it is still sitting on the drive waiting to be found or until a new set of data is written to that space. The same basic principles apply during a disk format. The format process effectively clears the file allocation table but not the physical data.

Another potential source of data exposure comes from the slack space at the end of a file. In early computer systems, the slack space was filled with random portions of data pulled from memory. Soon, many came to realize that confidential information, including passwords stored in memory,

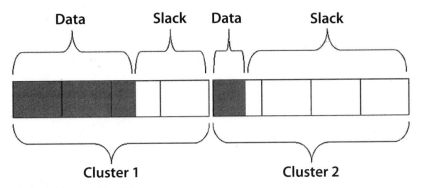

Figure 1.30 - **The dangers of data remaining in slack space**

could be found on the hard drive's slack space, even after the drive was supposedly formatted. In addition, when a sensitive data file is "deleted" and a new file is written to a portion of the reallocated cluster for that file, a portion of the original file will remain in the slack space until the cluster is completely overwritten. *Figure 1.30* demonstrates the dangers of data remaining in slack space.

Slack space can also be used by an attacker. Tools are available that can write data across multiple clusters using only the slack space from available file clusters. The data are completely hidden from the user and the operating system unless forensics tools are used to identify and extract the information. Attackers will use this capability to store information, tools, or malicious code on a victim's system. Depending on the frequency of data writes and deletes to the hard drive, the unwanted information may remain on the system for extended periods of time.

There are utilities that can be used to securely wipe the data from the hard drive by overwriting the file information with bytes of 1s or 0s, or a random combination of both. This wiping includes the unused slack space in clusters assigned to allocated files. However, some of these tools will not overwrite the file header, allowing someone to see the size, date, and location information of a file. This is another classic example of a security trade-off. The information that a file resided in that space is available, yielding some intelligence to an attacker. But the actual data are gone, preserving the confidentiality of the data. To ensure that the data are fully erased, make sure that the tool used to erase the file removes the data, the file's directory entry, and the file's FAT entry.

The most effective mechanism to destroy data, either a single file or an entire disk—short of grinding the disk into little pieces, which is still no guarantee—is to overwrite the data several times. This accomplishes two things: (1) it ensures enough randomization to avoid statistical analysis of the data, and (2) each write works to further mask the remnants of any electromagnetic representation of the original information. The more passes made through the disk with such a utility the harder it becomes to extract the information remaining on the disk. However, disk drives work by magnetically charging the surface of the disk to store information. Even if a portion of the disk is overwritten with new information (thus changing its magnetic properties) a portion of the original information still remains. As you successively overwrite the disk those original remnants get weaker and weaker, but advanced electromagnetic investigation (such as that available to some government agencies, if they are very interested in seeing the data) may still be able to read the original information.

As operating systems and application programs write to a drive, data are scattered all over the disk and data files may also be stored in the operating system's swap space (an area of the disk used as additional temporary memory for the operating system). Confidential data may also appear in other areas, such as the sent mail folder of an e-mail program, or previously deleted versions of data in slack space throughout the disk. To reduce exposure, remnants from all these areas should be identified and cleaned. There are several publicly available tools that identify these areas and keep them clean of remnant data.

The existence of data on a drive even after attempts have been made to erase it threatens the confidentiality and integrity of that data. Clearly, the exposure of data, even small parts, can represent an enormous risk to the organization, and the integrity of information can be affected by the manipulation of data physically on the disk. It is important to realize that the security controls applied to a file are several layers above disk operations. This means that even if the appropriate access controls are set within the operating system and the application, disk management tools can manipulate the hard disk directly to get at the data. Tools are readily available and can be easily employed to circumvent existing operating system and file system access controls at the hardware layer to change, obtain, or remove sensitive data.

Unauthorized Targeted Data Mining

Data mining is the act of collecting and analyzing large quantities of information to determine patterns of use or behavior and use those patterns to form conclusions about past, current, or future behavior. Data mining is typically used by large organizations with large databases of customer or consumer behavior. Retail and credit companies will use data mining to identify buying patterns or trends in geographies, age groups, products, or services. Data mining is essentially the statistical analysis of general information in the absence of specific data.

Attackers will typically perform reconnaissance against their target in an effort to collect as much information as possible to draw conclusions on operations, practices, technical architecture, and business cycles. This reconnaissance gathers small amounts of data which, by themselves, seem unimportant or nonsensitive, and it is for this reason that it is often easy to collect this information over the Internet or the phone. However, when combined in different ways and analyzed by a determined individual (a process known as aggregation), vulnerabilities or behavior patterns may surface in the data that can be exploited or used as the basis for an attack strategy. In the early days of the Internet, organizations rushed to put as much information about their companies as possible on their Web site to attract potential customers. This included information about the executive

217

staff, manufacturing practices, financial data, locations, technical solutions, and other data that could be used to guide attackers. Although this is much less prominent in today's communication practices, highly capable search engines, such as Google®, can be used to gather significant information about a target.

An effective access control strategy can limit the exposure of potentially harmful information. The security group within an organization should start by working closely with the marketing group to ensure public information placed on Web sites cannot be used against the company. Organizations must understand the potential impacts associated with data mining by unethically inclined entities.

Dumpster Diving

In·the early days of computer crime, when the Internet was not as prevalent and there was not as much readily available access to information as there is today, dumpster diving was the primary tactic used by information thieves to get corporate proprietary data, credit card numbers, and other personal information that could be gleaned from what people and companies throw away. Dumpster diving is simply the act of taking what people assume is trash and using that information, sometimes in combination with other data, to formulate conclusions or refine strategies for an attack.

This is especially problematic for companies who may throw away copies of proprietary data or other seemingly benign data that, when in the hands of an attacker, can provide substantial and valuable information. Many companies destroy documentation when it is no longer needed to mitigate the risk of exposing information. Conversely, many companies (misunderstanding the value of their intellectual property) assume there is little risk of disclosing proprietary information or simply ignore the risk and toss valuable business and employee information into the trash, increasing the exposure to a very basic and easily exploited vulnerability. Information commonly found in dumpsters ranges from phone numbers and e-mail lists to communication bills that have the service provider name and account details. A bill receipt containing account information can be used to help authenticate an attacker calling the service provider.

Even with sophisticated word processors and a computer on everyone's desk, people still print volumes of documentation, sometimes several times, to share with others or read later, only to throw it away without concern for the sensitivity of the data. It is not uncommon to find network designs, equipment purchase receipts, phone bills, phone books, human resource information, internal communications, configuration documentation, software documentation, project plans, and project proposals in a trash can or a dumpster in back of the building.

Most attackers do not want to risk physical contact with their target and the potential exposure of going through an organization's trash. The ability to go to the location, at the right time, and get information from the garbage exposes the attacker to a certain level of personal risk. But for those willing to take that risk the rewards can be substantial.

The ability for an unauthorized person to get near the trash repository of a site also shows a weakness in the physical access controls of that facility. As unglamorous as it may seem, even the garbage areas of a site need to be protected with proper access restrictions. In addition, the interior design of a facility needs to take steps to protect discarded information from falling into the wrong hands. Many organizations use special locked receptacles for personnel to discard proprietary information. These receptacles allow someone to place information into the receptacle but do not allow anyone to remove it once it is in there. Post office mail boxes work on the same principle. All this should be accompanied by a strong awareness campaign to educate employees on the importance of using these receptacles to protect discarded information.

Shredders play another important role in protecting confidential information. Organization policy should require the shredding of all physical information that is no longer needed, including paper, CD-ROMs, and DVD-ROMs. Many organizations will also specify this in their contracts with their suppliers. There are two basic types of shredders: strip cut and cross cut. As the name implies, strip cut shredders cut paper into long strips. While somewhat effective, it is possible for an information thief to piece the strips back together to see the original information. The more effective type of shredder is the cross cut shredder. In addition to cutting the paper into strips, a cross cut shredder will also cut the strips into smaller, confetti-like pieces, making it much harder for a thief to piece the original information back together. In highly sensitive situations safe and legal incineration of the media should be considered.

Backdoors and Trapdoors

During the development of an application, the creator or programmer has the ability to include special access capabilities hidden within the application. Referred to as backdoors or trap doors, applications may have hard-coded instructions that allow complete and unfettered access to those who know the existence of the backdoor. Often these are allegedly installed for support purposes, enabling the programmer to access the system by bypassing the front-end security controls in cases where the system fails, locking everyone out.

The most common method of backdoor access is the use of hidden accounts built within the application. These accounts can be used to gain authorized access without the knowledge of the system owner. Sometimes this occurs because the developer is attempting to support broad system functions and may not realize that the account can be used to gain access. For example, in 2003 Oracle released a new version of its software that had at least five privileged accounts created upon installation without the administrator's knowledge.

There are other cases where system integrators will create special rules or credentials that allow them to gain complete access to systems they have installed to support their customers. Unfortunately, these practices typically mean that the same methods, including the username and password combinations, are used for each customer. If the information was to be exposed or an employee was to leave with the information, every customer that has the backdoor implemented would be exposed to a plethora of threats. However, backdoors are seen primarily in independently developed applications and not in software or systems from established vendors. The threat to access controls from backdoors and trap doors is based on the existence of unknown credentials or configurations that will allow someone to circumvent established controls and gain full access to a system.

Logic Bombs

Attacks are typically thought of as real-time events, in that an attacker launches an attack and the results can be immediately seen or, at least, the effects take hold as soon as the attack is launched. There are some attacks, however, where the results of the attacks can be delayed for days, weeks, or even years. These attacks are called logic bombs because they rely on a logical progression of events before they unleash their aggression. Logic bombs are typically implemented as hidden code paths in application or system software. Typical attacks include continuously checking to see if a certain employee is removed from the HR database (thus indicating he has been fired) and, if that event occurs, wiping out the source code directories to the company's main product. Another example is to program a system such that if it does not receive a specific signal or code from an employee (one, perhaps, who is about to ask for a raise or promotion), stop all processing on the system and shut down the machine.

Logic bombs can be very difficult to find, particularly if they have been placed there by someone with intimate knowledge of the system or its source code. The best way to defend against logic bombs is to include a thorough code review on all software deployed throughout the enterprise. In true separation-of-duties fashion, the review should not be performed by the same person or team that wrote the original code, to reduce the likelihood of a conspiracy to overlook the logic bomb during the review. In addition, strong change management and release management processes must be enforced to reduce the likelihood that someone can insert the malicious code into the system after it is already in production.

Theft

Theft is a simple concept anyone can grasp. However, as the digital interaction between people and businesses expands, the exposure of valuable information continues to exceed the traditional physical notion of the term theft.

Physical theft includes anything of value an unauthorized entity can remove. Computers, documents, books, phones, keys, and any other material that can be moved can be stolen. It can also include theft of a service, such as power, cable television, or phone service. Physical theft of assets carries the risk that the owner of the asset will quickly notice it is missing. Digital theft, on the other hand, is typically less noticeable because, unless the thief has destroyed the information during the act of stealing it, the original data are still there even though the thief has a complete and perfect stolen copy.

Personal and private information about individuals and companies is shared, sold, transferred, and collected by other people and organizations for legitimate and illegitimate activities. Regardless of intent, as information is passed from entity to entity, the security of that data will grow weaker with each transfer. Even if the data are passed legitimately from entity to entity, it is difficult for the original data owner to ensure the proper access controls will be enforced as the data moves further and further down the line away from its original purpose and associated access controls.

While theft of products or services from organizations has been a traditional problem, recent years have seen a dramatic rise in theft of consumers' personal information. Many organizations store this information as a byproduct of their business processes, but many of these do not take the time or care to enact appropriate access controls and information protection controls. It is becoming increasingly common for attackers to gain access to an e-commerce site not to steal products or services, but rather the customers' credit card information and other personal information.

Theft and access controls are intertwined, as theft typically represents the failure of access control mechanisms. The fact that a theft was able to occur typically means that the access controls on that information were not sufficient to address the potential threat or the thief was somehow able to circumvent the access control mechanisms.

Social Engineering

Social engineering is the oldest form of attack used to bypass access controls and commit theft or fraud. Social engineering is the practice of misdirection to obtain information through social contact. Social engineering can take many forms, ranging from telephone calls to e-mail to face-to-face interaction. Additionally, the degree of personal interaction needed is variable. For example, a determined attacker may apply for a job that allows access to the establishment for on-site reconnaissance. Attackers may also assume the identity of employees or their colleagues to lure others into providing information.

On the other hand, an attacker may simply send an e-mail to a target (or thousands of targets) hoping for a response. E-mail is a potent medium that can be used effectively to extract information. It can be easy to obtain names of employees at a target company and deduce their e-mail address. If the target employee has published writings or documents on the Internet it is relatively easy to find subjects that interest the target and establish communication based on a common theme. For instance, if a network administrator has made a lot of postings to various news groups or personal Web logs, an attacker may be able to ascertain specific topics that interest him or her and determine his or her willingness to share information. Through subsequent e-mail interaction, the attacker may be able to gain insightful characteristics about the internal network he or she manages and other related security information.

A more prevalent approach used by attackers, and thankfully growing more difficult due to security awareness, is calling a company's help desk and asking for a password reset on an account. However, even with improved security practices, such as asking for an employee ID number or a mother's maiden name, it remains a simple barrier for a minimally skilled social engineer to overcome.

The best, and perhaps only, prevention against social engineering is an effective and continuous security awareness and education effort to all personnel within the organization. They must be continuously reminded of the threat of social engineering and armed with knowledge of some of the more common methods used to gain information. In addition, information about actual social engineering attempts made against the organization should be circulated amongst the staff so they will be better prepared if the attacker tries the same method again against a different employee.

E-Mail Social Engineering

E-mail can be a powerful persuasion device for attackers and con artists alike. E-mail has become a basic mode of communication for many people and is considered crucial for many companies to run a successful business. People have grown so accustomed to e-mail that they rarely question the integrity of an e-mail's source or content. To add to the problem, many people do not understand how e-mail is routed from one system to another, and eventually the technology and science take a back seat to magic, leaving people to assume if the sender is "dad@aol.com" it must actually be from Dad. Given that the general public is trusting of their e-mail and the direct access to people that e-mail service provides, e-mail is used over and over again under false pretenses to spread worms and viruses, commit theft or fraud, or just spread bad information.

It is a trivial task to make an e-mail appear as though it came from a known or trusted source. This can be especially powerful, for example, when sending an e-mail to someone from his or her management requesting the updated design for an executive presentation about the changes to security controls that are in progress. E-mails can be crafted to, for example, obtain remote-access phone numbers or gather information on applications in use. E-mail social engineering presents many problems to effective access control, but the primary problem is that it can be used to obtain enough personal or system information from a victim that the attacker can subsequently obtain or bypass legitimate authentication and authorization information. Either the social engineering will provide the attacker directly with a user ID or password, or he will gather enough information to charm his way past any support, technical, or business personnel standing in his way to get access to the systems or information he seeks. These attacks can take the forms of scams, or if a malicious attachment is involved, "phishing" or "whaling."

Help Desk Fraud

Finally, one of the more common and classic types of social engineering is calling the help desk posing as an employee in need of help. The traditional goal of a help desk attack is for the attacker to get a valid ID and password to an internal system. Fortunately, this technique is becoming harder and harder to use, because help desk employees are usually trained to follow a specific protocol for resetting and providing passwords, and many of these protocols do not include furnishing passwords over the phone.

A typical help desk will provide its employees with a predefined list of questions and actions to be executed by the help desk attendant to ensure the caller is authentic. In many cases, there are several options to the help desk employee to deal with different scenarios. For example, if the caller cannot retrieve e-mail to get the updated password, the help desk may be directed to use the caller's voice mail. Despite this, however, many social engineering attacks still include calls to the help desk seeking to obtain unauthorized information, and they still get results. Either the help desk employee does not follow the prescribed protocol or is simply fooled into thinking he or she has the necessary information to prove the identity of the caller.

A common tactic for the accomplished social engineer is the use of misdirection and controlled confusion during a conversation, such as introducing discussion items that are not part of the standard help desk protocol script. The attacker may take on the persona of an angry executive, pretend he or she is a complete neophyte to the computer, or begin asking the help desk employee random questions all in an attempt to confuse the employee into disclosing the information. Beyond trying to get passwords, which can be difficult, obtaining remote-access phone numbers or IP addresses of VPN devices can be helpful as well, and many help desk employees do not see the need to authenticate the caller to provide this seemingly useless information.

Nevertheless, well-trained help desks are usually prepared for controlling the provisioning of information and applications, but it is for this very reason that they can be an attractive target for social engineering attacks. They get calls asking for similar information all day long and are expected to provide answers using the predefined protocol, which can be weak. Additionally, for large help desks or companies that provide outsourced help desk services, there is usually a high degree of employee turnover, resulting in unfamiliarity with the protocol or security issues, introducing even more opportunities to glean information. The access control threats of help desk fraud are straightforward. The attacker will use social engineering techniques to either get enough information from the help desk to allow legitimate system access or trick the help desk staff into providing the access information directly.

Threat Modeling

In reviewing access control attacks and mitigating factors, several risk assessment methods can be considered. One of the most popular in the software development and system building communities is threat modeling. Threat modeling is a process of using scenario analysis with knowledge of threats and vulnerabilities to help determine what risks are present in a system or application and where to apply resources to ensure the best mitigation for the value.

Threat modeling approaches vary from organization to organization but generally follow an approach of:

- Defining the scope and objectives
- Understanding or modeling the system
- Development of threats
- Development of vulnerabilities
- Determining the impact and risk
- Develop the mitigation plan

Define the Scope and Objectives

An effective threat modeling exercise must determine what is within the scope of the modeling. If a web application is under review excluding the database it interfaces with may be a mistake. A further mistake may be excluding the data center and alternate data center if the primary site is located on a flood plain. There is a tradeoff between the size of the scope and the amount of effort required to provide meaningful recommendations. If the scope is to narrow the assessor may neglect significant information. If the scope is too large, resources available for mitigation are spent on assessment.

Understanding or Modeling the System

In understanding how the target system or application operates, collect as much information available about the system. Data flow diagrams, network

227

diagrams, recent vulnerability scans, recent incidents, development notes, vendor documentation, public vulnerability or patching information and any other information which may seem relevant. The assessor should interview system administrators, system security officers and end users for different perspectives about the system. Cost information about the operation, development and information contained in the system should also be understood as it will be required to make value based decision.

Development of Threats

The development of threats can be as much of an art as a science and will vary greatly depending on the threat information sources available. Earlier in this chapter, common threats are listed. In addition to those common threats, the following sources should be considered:

- Classified or national security information, which may be relevant to the system. This is primarily for government systems and critical infrastructure but some industries and organizations may have access to this information. While highly restrictive, this information can often provide some of the most potent threat information available.

- Public information about attacks on competitors or similar organizations.

- Does the organization know of any
  - Competitors who wish to do them harm?
  - Possible insider threats?
  - Recent incidents or odd behavior of the system or staff?

- Unintentional actions which could occur due to user error

Development of Vulnerabilities

Using automated tools, a vulnerability scan of the target system or application should be performed. In addition to the logical vulnerabilities, administrative and physical weaknesses should be reviewed as well. Questions such as the following should be considered:

- Is the organization financially weak?
- Does the organization leadership have rapid turnover?
- Is there backup administration for the system?
- Is the datacenter located in a flood zone or an area prone to weather disasters?

Determining Impacts and Risk

There are several qualitative and quantitative ways to determine impacts and risk. Often the qualitative route is the simplest and helps determine the overall impact and risk to the organization. A basic formula for risk is: "Impact x Threat Likelihood" where threat likelihood is the possibility an identified threat could exploit a vulnerability minus any identified countermeasures. The following tables from the United States National Institute of Standards and Technology helps visualize the process.

Once levels of risk are determined a value to mitigate each should be determined. Management should ultimately decide which risks are the best candidates for mitigation. For example, a high risk which can be mitigated for US$5,000 is a better choice than a low risk which costs US$50,000.

Develop a Mitigation Plan

Finally, the decisions of management and relevant stakeholders are memorialized in a plan. This plan should ideally identify residual risks, exposure, resources required to mitigate risks and timelines for mitigation. The plan should also identify responsible party for each risk mitigation and who accepted residual risk on behalf of the organization. The effectiveness of the mitigation activities will depend on management's ability to execute the plan.

Asset Valuation

In determining the value of information systems there are several components which must be accounted for. The physical cost of the equipment and the configuration time spent often represent only a fraction of the total cost of a system. The type of information on the system will also greatly impact the cost and exposure of a system. The following can greatly increase the value and cost of a system:

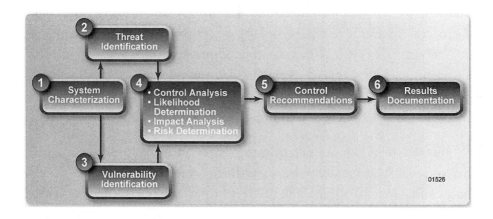

Threat Likelihood	Impact		
	Low (10)	Moderate (50)	High (100)
High (1.0)	10 x 1.0 = 10	50 x 1.0 = 50	100 x 1.0 = 100
Moderate (0.5)	10 x 0.5 = 5	50 x 0.5 = 25	100 x 0.5 = 50
Low (0.1)	10 x 0.1 = 1	50 x 0.1 = 5	100 x 0.1 = 10

Risk Scale: High (>50 to 100)   Moderate (>10 to 50)   Low (1 to 10)

01527a

Figure 1.31 - **A risk development table[1]** (Bowen 2006)

---

1   Bowen, Pauline, Josh Hash, and Mark Wilson. United States National Institute of Standards and Technology, "NIST Special Publication 800-100." Last modified 10, 2006. Accessed March 29, 2012. http://csrc.nist.gov/publications/nistpubs/800-100/SP800-100-Mar07-2007.pdf.

- Hardware
- Software
- Integration
- Opportunity cost
- Regulatory exposure
  - ◻ Civil
  - ◻ Criminal
- Information replacement
- Reputational exposure

Hardware

The replacement cost of hardware can be significant and can increase dramatically when the hardware is out of support or the vendor has gone out of business. The cost of hardware should be considered present replacement cost. In complex computing environments with multiple system interconnections consideration should also be given to the additional cost of integration if hardware platforms change.

Software

Much like hardware, software can go out of support and vendors can dissolve or merge with other companies. Custom developed code which no other copy exists can be extremely expensive to recode. Even with advances in hardware and technology, many modern systems use code and operating systems from 10 years ago or before. Often the cost of porting existing software is far In excess of maintaining the code in house.

Integration

Integration costs are often "sunk" invisible costs that are easily overlooked when considering the value of an asset. In terms of a replacement cost, a present day system or application should always consider the availability of a qualified integration team and the cost associated with the team.

Opportunity Costs

When a crucial business support system such as an e-commerce site for a major online retailer is down time is substantial money. If a business is generating revenue of US$1,000 dollars an hour from its website and that site goes down for 8 hours the math is quite simple. However, the loss of sales is only part of the equation. The marketing costs and overhead costs for those 8 hours are incurred so the loss may be much more. The value of uptime for a valuable system may far exceed the value of the system itself.

Regulatory Exposure

In a regulated environment, there are stiff penalties for breaching information. In the United States, The Health Insurance Portability and Accountability Act levies fines in the millions of dollars[1] against organizations who fail to protect health record information. Some laws such as the United States' Privacy Act[2] allow criminal sanctions for federal employees who flagrantly violate citizen privacy rights.

Information Replacement

The information an organization develops as part of its operations is most likely not going to be replaced overnight. In some cases, the information must be retained for legal reasons for years or longer. Some information cost millions of dollars to develop such as deep space information or stealth weapon technology. The cost of replacement could be substantial and in some instances the information may not be able to be replaced.

Reputational Exposure

Finally, what is the cost of losing a reputation? For a company it could be a loss in revenue and the turning point of losing market share to a competitor. For a country, it could be the loss of respect of the citizens or other nations that could weaken negotiating power. Reputation is extremely difficult and expensive to achieve and maintain. Unfortunately in many cases mere speculation is enough to start doubt.

1   http://www.hhs.gov/ocr/privacy/hipaa/news/cignetnews.html
2   http://www.justice.gov/opcl/privstat.htm

When determining asset valuation the following formula is useful in helping determine how much financial exposure an organization may experience from a single event:

SLE=AV x EF

Where:

> **SLE** is "single loss expectancy"
>
> **AV** is Asset value (from above)
>
> **EF** is Exposure factor

The exposure factor is probably the most difficult to estimate. It is the percentage value an asset will decline given a particular event. For example if a website going down will reduce the value of a company from US$100,000,000 to US$80,000,000 the exposure factor would be 20%.

Taking SLE, we can now also determine the expected monetary loss caused by risk over one year. This is expressed as:

ALE=SLE x ARO

Where, ARO is Annualized Rate of Occurrence. The annual rate of occurrence is the number of times during a year a specific event will trigger the SLE. The ALE is useful in helping justify additional controls to help protect the C-I-A of information and the information system. If the cost of protecting the system is less than the ALE, the countermeasure should be implemented.

Access Aggregation

Access aggregation is the act of collecting additional roles and responsibilities in an organization or information system. Take the following example:

1. A person starts out as a mail clerk in an organization and gets access to email and the mail system.

2. Two years later, this person is promoted to the human resources area as a classification clerk and gains access to the human resources information systems but never loses the mail system access.

3. Four years later, the individual takes a promotion as a staff manager in the finance division of the organization and is given information about a sensitive budget.

4. A few years later, the person transfers to the Information technology office and is given administrative access to the email servers.

The scenario described shows the concept of access aggregation. The individual has continued to retain access to systems which are no longer needed in their new positions. Often this is an oversight of the "onboarding/offboarding" process in organizations. This violates the concept of least privilege as the individual has access to numerous systems which they have no legitimate need for. The combination of systems may make it possible (and enticing!) to commit fraud as separation of duties also breaks down as access aggregation occurs. Information security professionals should work with human resources and information technology administrators to ensure de-provisioning of access is performed any time an human resource changes roles.

Assess Effectiveness of Access Controls

As part of an effective risk management program, an organization should employ a variety of methods to determine the effectiveness of its access controls. Vulnerability assessment, control assessment and penetration testing are all valuable methods of determining the effectiveness of an organization's access controls and their ability to mitigate risk.

Vulnerability Assessment

When seeking to determine the security position of an organization, the security professional will eventually turn to a vulnerability assessment to help identify specific areas of weakness that need to be addressed. A vulnerability assessment is the use of various tools and analysis methodologies to determine where a particular system or process may be susceptible to attack or misuse. Most vulnerability assessments concentrate on technical vulnerabilities in systems or applications, but the assessment process is equally as effective when examining physical or administrative business processes.

To begin the vulnerability assessment process, assessor must have a good understanding of the business, its mission and the system or application to be assessed. While it is possible to simply run an automated tool against the target system to produce a list of potential problems, understanding first what the system does and its relationship to the overall business process will assist the analyst in determining the overall risk of any discovered vulnerabilities. In addition, the security analyst must have a good understanding of the known and potential threats to the system as specifically identified by the business or by the assessor's general knowledge of the security landscape. A vulnerability in the absence of a validated threat will rate lower on the criticality scale when compared to a vulnerability that has a known threat poised to strike against it.

Threat and vulnerability information can come from many sources. The first place to begin is by discussing the system with the appropriate business owners and other interested stakeholders. They are the closest to both the system and the business landscape the system operates in, and will have a good under-standing of security issues they have had previously or similar problems that competitors or others in the industry may have faced. In addition, including appropriate business stakeholders in the vulnerability assessment process will build a better sense of partnership between the business group and the security team.

Once the business aspect of the system has been addressed, the analyst can turn to various sources of security industry information, including known vulnerability databases (like the US Government's National Vulnerability Database [NVD] http://nvd.nist.gov/ or the OWASP top 10 https://www.owasp.org/index.php/Main_Page), published vendor vulnerability information, and security mailing lists. If the assessor is using one or more automated tools, those tools will include many known vulnerabilities as part of their internal scanning database.

The next step is to examine the existing controls in place to protect the system or process. This includes any directive, preventative, deterrent, and detective controls that are in place in the organization. These controls may be specific to the system or business function or may be part of the organization's general control environment, such as security policies and standards, firewalls, antivirus systems, intrusion detection/prevention systems, and available authentication and access controls. The analyst will then match these existing controls against the known threats previously identified to determine if the existing control systems counteract the identified threats. Whatever gaps remain after this analysis will need to be addressed.

In most situations, the assessor will turn to the use of a variety of automated tools to assist in the vulnerability assessment process. These tools contain extensive databases of specific known vulnerabilities as well as the ability to analyze system and network configuration information to predict where a particular system might be vulnerable to different types of attacks. There are many different types of tools currently available to address a wide variety of vulnerability assessment needs. Some tools will examine a system from the viewpoint of the network, seeking to determine if a system can be compromised by a remote attacker exploiting available services on a particular host system. These tools will test for open ports listening for connections, known vulnerabilities in common services, and known operating system exploits.

These tools will also often attempt to determine if a system has the latest security patches in place. Other tools will examine individual applications to determine if they are susceptible to application exploits like buffer overflow, improper input handling, database manipulation attacks, or common Web-based vulnerabilities. Because the vulnerability landscape is constantly evolving as new exploits are discovered and others are patched, the security manager must establish a process to ensure that any scanning tools used for vulnerability analysis are kept up to date so as to always have the latest information against which to test.

Once the vulnerability scanning is complete the security analyst must examine the results for accuracy. It is rare that the results from a scanning tool are completely accurate. False positives are common because the tool may have incorrectly identified a target system or incorrectly analyzed the result data from the probes it performed. In addition, the analyst must match the scan results against what is already known about the business function of the system being analyzed. For example, many testing tools will report the use of the anonymous FTP service as a vulnerability, as this can be seen as a potential security problem. However, if the system in question is being officially operated as an anonymous FTP server for the organization, that result, although correct, would not be considered a vulnerability to the organization.

The security analyst must combine the information gathered during the discussions with the business areas with the information obtained from the scanning tools to make a final analysis of the actual vulnerabilities that must be addressed by the organization. It is also common to rate those vulnerabilities on some type of criticality scale (high/medium/low or 1–5 ratings are common) to give the organization a sense of the level of concern and immediacy to place on each particular finding. Many tools will give a ranking for each vulnerability. The assessor must remember those ratings are based on harm to the system and not the organization. The assessor must make the determination of risk to the organization based on input from the tools rather than relying solely on the ratings from the tool. Many organizations will also establish time limits for remediation actions—shorter time limits for more critical vulnerabilities and longer ones for less critical problems.

Once the final analysis is complete the assessor should discuss the findings with the business area to determine the appropriate course of remediation action to take. The actions should be based on the criticality of each reported vulnerability, the cost to remediate, the potential compensating controls that can be enacted, and the impact the remediation will have on the system and the business function that the system serves. In some circumstances the business group may elect to accept the risk of continued operation with the known vulnerability due to the cost of corrective measures or other business considerations. No matter what the resolution is, the assessor should ensure that all concerned understand—and agree to—the remediation plan. Assuming that an application or system group will always address all items in the report in a timely manner is a mistake. The system group will have a multitude of projects and deadlines they need to address, of which the vulnerability report is but one. The assessor may be asked and should continuously follow up with the system group to ensure they are addressing the vulnerabilities as agreed.

Vulnerability analysis is an important part of the security management process, and one that many organizations do not address consistently or effectively. It is a key component in the risk management process and, if performed effectively, can dramatically reduce the organization's overall risk and susceptibility to current, and future, security problems. Vulnerability analysis and management is also a core component in building an effective continuous monitoring program.

Penetration Testing

The next level in vulnerability assessments seeks to exploit existing vulnerabilities to determine the true nature and impact of a given vulnerability. Penetration testing goes by many names, such as ethical hacking, tiger teaming, red teaming and vulnerability testing. It is the use of exploitive techniques to determine the level of risk associated with a vulnerability or collection of vulnerabilities in an application or system. The primary goal of penetration testing is to simulate an attack on a system or network to evaluate the risk profile of an environment. This includes understanding the level of skill required, the time needed to exploit a given vulnerability, and the level of impact, such as depth of access and attainable privileges.

Penetration testing can be employed against any system or service. However, because of the time, expense, and resources required to properly execute a penetration test, most companies seek penetration testing to focus on Internet systems and services, remote-access solutions, and critical applications.

The key to successful and valuable penetration testing is clearly defined objectives, scope, stated goals, agreed-upon limitations, and acceptable activities. For example, it may be acceptable to attack an FTP server, but not to the point where the system is rendered useless or data are damaged. Having a clear framework and management oversight during a test is essential to ensure that the test does not have adverse effects on the target company and the most value is gained from the test.

Penetration Test Strategies

Strategies for penetration testing, based on specific objectives to be achieved, are a combination of the source of the test, how the company's assets are targeted, and the information (or lack thereof) provided to the tester. One of the first steps in establishing the rules of engagement for a penetration test is determining the amount of information to provide the tester about the target. No matter the scope or scale of a test, how information flows initially will set in motion other attributes of planning, ultimately defining factors by which the value of the test will be measured. Usually some form of information is provided by the target, and only in the most extreme cases is absolutely no information offered. Some cannot be avoided, such as the name of the company, while others can be easily kept from the testers without totally impeding the mechanics of the test.

External testing refers to attacks on the organization's network perimeter using procedures performed from outside the organization's systems, for example, from the Internet. To conduct the test, the testing team begins by targeting the company's externally visible servers or devices, such as the domain name server (DNS), e-mail server, Web server, or firewall.

Internal testing is performed from within the organization's technology environment. The focus is to understand what could happen if the network perimeter was successfully penetrated, or what an organization insider could do to penetrate specific information resources within the organization's network.

In a blind testing strategy, the testing team is provided with only limited information concerning the organization's information systems configuration. The penetration testing team must use publicly available information (such as the company Web site, domain name registry, and Internet discussion boards) to gather information about the target and conduct its penetration tests. Blind testing can provide information about the organization that may have been otherwise unknown, but it can also be more time-consuming and expensive than other types of penetration testing (such as targeted testing) because of the effort required by the penetration testing team to research the target. However, in blind testing the "attackers" (the test team) have little or no knowledge about the target company but the "defenders" (the company's IT and security teams) know the attack is coming and are prepared to defend against it.

Double-blind testing presents a more real-life attack scenario because the organization's IT and security teams are not notified or informed before the test and are "blind" to the planned testing activities. In addition to testing the strength of a network or application, double-blind testing can test the organization's security monitoring and incident identification, escalation, and response procedures. In double-blind testing engagements, very few people within the organization are made aware of the testing, perhaps only the project sponsor, and double-blind testing requires careful monitoring by the project sponsor to ensure that the testing procedures and the organization's incident response procedures can be terminated when the objectives of the test have been achieved or the test threatens to affect production systems or networks.

In a targeted testing environment (often referred to as the "lights on" approach) both the organization's IT team and the penetration testing team are made aware of the testing activities and are provided with information concerning the target and the network design. A targeted testing approach may be more efficient and cost-effective when the objective of the test is focused more on the technical setting, or on the design of the network, than on the organization's incident response and other operational procedures. A targeted test typically takes less time and effort to complete than blind testing, but may not provide as complete a picture of an organization's security vulnerabilities and response capabilities.

There are three basic categories of penetration test separated by how much information is provided to the tester or test team: zero knowledge, partial knowledge, and full knowledge. In zero knowledge testing the tester is provided no information about the target's network or environment. The tester is simply left to his abilities to discover information about the company and use it to gain some form of access. This is also called black box or closed testing, depending on who is scoping the test. Zero knowledge testing is particularly appropriate when executing a test from out-side the organization, as this is the position most attackers will be in when they start to attack an organization.

In a partial knowledge test scenario, the tester is provided with some knowledge about the environment. The information provided is high-level public (or near-pubic) information that would be trivial for a real attacker to find without much effort, including phone numbers and IP addresses to be tested, domain information, and application names. It is assumed that a competent attacker would be able to obtain this level of information rather quickly, so this information is given to the tester to speed up the testing process a bit. The interesting aspect of getting some information and not all is the assumption of scope. Organizations can use limited information to define boundaries of the test, as opposed to simply providing all the initial data to support the test. For example, exposing the organization's IP address range is an attempt to speed up the gathering of easily obtained information, while exposing the fact that the network has intrusion detection systems can shape the way the tester goes about performing the test.

Full knowledge testing provides every possible piece of information about the environment to the tester. This type of test is typically employed when there is greater focus on what can be done, as opposed to what can be discovered. The assumption is that an attacker can easily discover what is in the environment and the test needs to focus on how much damage can be done with that information. This is particularly appropriate when testing for internal penetrations. In that situation, the tester is taking the role of an informed insider (e.g., an employee or contractor) with existing inside knowledge of the environment, architecture, and information paths. The insider has all the knowledge he or she needs to find the target. The question the tester needs to answer is whether the target's defenses will withstand such an attack.

The organization must determine the area of the organization or the service to be tested. This is important when defining the scope of the test, because it will determine the boundaries and limits of acceptable testing practices. More than one target may be defined for a test, but each must be well defined and clearly understood by all involved.

Application Security Testing

The objective of application security testing is to evaluate the controls within an application and its information process flow. Topics to be evaluated may include the application's use of encryption to protect the confidentiality and integrity of information, the authentication of users, the integrity of the Internet user's session with the host application, and the management of the current processing state between parts of the application. Application testing will test the flow of information through the application and its susceptibility to interception or alteration. It will also test how the application handles input data and determine if user input can harm or crash the application. Finally, application testing will test for a wide range of common (as well as some uncommon) attack scenarios to gauge the level of resistance an application has to attacks of varying levels of sophistication.

Denial-of-Service (DoS) Testing

The goal of DoS testing is to evaluate the system's susceptibility to attacks that will render it inoperable or unable to provide needed services to the organization or external users. Decisions regarding the extent of DoS testing to be incorporated into a penetration testing exercise will depend on the relative importance of ongoing, continued availability of the information systems and related processing activities. When deciding to perform DoS testing, it is critical to ensure that these tests are not performed on live production systems unless that is a specific objective of the test and all system and information owners know about, and approve, this course of action. The potential for system disruption beyond a simple crash is very high with DoS testing, potentially leading to extended down time, angry customers, or lost revenue. In addition, make sure that everyone knows that a DoS test is being performed so that nobody (including system owners, users, and help desk staff) is caught unaware. Because DoS testing presents such a risk to systems, many testers will perform the attack steps leading up to the DoS but stop short of actually crashing the system. This saves a great deal of response and recovery time while still exposing a potentially risky situation on the system.

War Dialing

War dialing is a technique for systematically calling a range of telephone numbers in an attempt to identify modems, remote-access devices, and maintenance connections for computers that may exist within an organization's network. Well-meaning users can inadvertently expose the organization to significant vulnerability by connecting a modem to the organization's information systems or network devices. Once a modem or other access device has been identified, analysis and exploitation techniques are performed to assess whether this connection can be used to penetrate the organization's information systems network. In the Internet age, it may be difficult to understand that modems are still a primary source of network connectivity for many purposes, but they are still out there and there are plenty of them, very often connected to administrative ports on equipment for use by system administrators for emergency access, maintenance, or recovery purposes. Organizations would be wise not to underestimate their reach into the infrastructure or their potential for creating vulnerabilities in the environment.

Wireless Network Testing

The introduction of wireless networks, whether through formal, approved network architecture or the inadvertent actions of well-meaning users, creates additional security exposures. Sometimes referred to as war driving, attackers have become proficient in identifying wireless network access points within an organization simply by driving by, or walking around, office buildings with their wireless network equipment. The goal of wireless network testing is to identify security gaps or flaws in the design, implementation, or operation of the organization's wireless network. War driving also provides an advantage to attackers, who may be able to access and penetrate a network through the wireless connection even though they are not on the property of the organization they are breaking in to. Some security experts have likened the existence of a wireless on a corporate network to the equivalent of having a live network jack in the parking lot of the company.

Social Engineering:

Often used in conjunction with blind and double-blind testing, social engineering refers to techniques using social interaction, typically with the organization's employees, suppliers, and contractors, to gather enough information to be able to penetrate the organization's physical premises or systems. Such techniques could include posing as a representative of the IT department's help desk and asking users to divulge their user account and password information, posing as an employee and gaining physical access to restricted areas that may house sensitive information, or intercepting mail, courier packages, or even searching through trash for sensitive information on printed materials (also known as dumpster diving). Social engineering activities can test a less technical, but equally important, security component: the ability of the organization's people to contribute to (or prevent) unauthorized access to information and information systems.

PBX and IP Telephony Testing

Beyond war dialing, phone systems (traditional "POTS" service, corporate ISDN, and new IP-based telephone services) have traditionally been a highly vulnerable, yet often overlooked, method of gaining access to corporate resources. Attackers can gain access to voice mail systems to gather information and monitor activity. Moreover, phone systems can be manipulated to permit an attacker to make long-distance calls free and undetected, potentially furthering an attack on other organizations. It is also not uncommon for security services to leave secret information (e.g., passwords and account information) on voice mail systems, relying on the authentication mechanisms of the voice mail service to provide protection. If an attacker compromises the voice mail service that information can be lost.

IP telephony, or voice-over-IP (VoIP), is the use of traditional Internet protocol (IP) data networks to handle voice traffic. It can also include the integration of phone systems with network applications, databases, and other services, such as e-mail or workflow collaboration systems. While IP telephony systems share many of the same security vulnerabilities as traditional phone services, their integration with the IP protocol gives them an additional susceptibility to network-level attacks. Tests can be performed against these technologies to gain a better understanding of the risks the organization may face when combining voice and data on a single network, or whether a DoS attack on the data network would also render the VoIP system inoperable. The potential threat profile represented by combining the threats associated with IP networks and those of telephone systems is one any organization should take seriously.

Penetration Test Methodology

A methodology is an established collection of processes that are performed in a predetermined order to ensure the job, function, or, in this case, security test is accurately executed. There are many ways of performing a penetration test, perhaps as many as there are testers. However, there is a basic and logical methodology that has become best practice for performing such tests:

1. ***Reconnaissance/Discovery:*** Identify and document information about the target.
2. ***Enumeration:*** Gain more information with intrusive methods.
3. ***Vulnerability Analysis:*** Map the environment profile to known vulnerabilities.
4. ***Execution:*** Attempt to gain user and privileged access.
5. ***Document findings:*** Document the results of the test.

Step 1: Reconnaissance: As is the case with most military and espionage campaigns, penetration tests typically begin with a recon-naissance phase. Reconnaissance is the search for any available information on the target to assist in planning or executing the test. The search can include quick ping sweeps to see what IP addresses on a network will respond, scouring news groups on the Internet in search of disgruntled employees divulging useful information, or rummaging through the trash to find inside information on the business or the technical environment (also known as dumpster diving.) The ultimate goal of the reconnaissance phase is to gather as much information on the target as possible. This may include physical and virtual layouts, building and network topography, organizational strengths and weaknesses, operational patterns, technology in use, and practically anything else the tester may think will be useful in the coming attack. Reconnaissance can also include theft, lying to people, monitoring networks, impersonations, or even leveraging falsified friendships to collect data about a target. The search for information is only limited by the extremes to which a company and the tester are willing to go. The rule of thumb in the reconnaissance phase is that no piece of information is too small to be useful.

Step 2: Enumeration: Also known as network or vulnerability discovery, enumeration is the process of obtaining information directly from the target systems, applications, and networks. An interesting point to understand is that the enumeration phase represents a point within the penetration testing project where the line between a passive attack and an active attack begins to blur. At this point the tester is not just gathering information anymore; he or she is sending network probes or otherwise communicating with systems and network devices in order to gather more information. Some of these devices may be fragile or susceptible to even the slightest nudge from the tester. When setting up the test parameters, the enumeration phase should be thoroughly reviewed with the operations, support, and security teams to ensure there are no surprise alerts generated as a result of the test.

To build an accurate picture of a company's environment, there are several tools and techniques available to compile a list of information obtained from the systems. Most notably, port scanning is the most common and easily executed basic test to start with. A port scan is the manipulation of the basic communication setup between two networked systems to determine what services are being offered on the target system. Collecting information about available systems and services is the first step in formulating an attack plan. From here, the tester can build on the information found during the reconnaissance phase and define a path to attempt to compromise the system.

Step 3: Vulnerability Analysis: The information gathered by the reconnaissance and enumeration phases will yield a great deal of valuable information about the target environment. The next step is to analyze that data to determine potential vulnerabilities that may be exploited to successfully attack the target. This calls for a logical and pragmatic approach to analyzing data. During the enumeration phase, the tester performs an interpretation of the information collected (or provided), looking for relationships between systems, networks, and applications that may lead to exposures that can be exploited. The vulnerability analysis phase is a practical process of comparing the information collected with known vulnerabilities.

Most information about potential vulnerabilities can be collected from openly available sources, such as the Internet, public Web sites, hacker periodicals and mailing lists, news groups, vendor bug and patch data, and even the personal experience of the tester. These can be used to analyze information gleaned from the target to seek options for exploitation. All this information, properly analyzed, can be used to formulate a successful attack.

Because each organization and environment is different, the tester (and the attacker) must analyze the information carefully to identify potential avenues of attack that will work against that potential environment. The use of easily-obtained reconnaissance and analysis tools can help this effort a great deal. Such tools will systematically explore and analyze multiple categories of potential vulnerabilities, such as Web exploits, data handling exploits, buffer overflows, misconfigured systems, trust relationships, authentication errors, even missing patches or system updates. The analysis of potential vulnerabilities is critical, as it will pinpoint precise areas of weakness in the environment and optimize the tester's time when attempting to penetrate a system.

Step 4: Execution: A great deal of planning and evaluation are performed during the earlier testing phases to ensure that the test focuses on the areas of greatest vulnerability and criticality, ensuring ultimately that core business systems can be better protected. This planning must lead to the actual execution of some form of attack scenarios. Exploiting systems and applications can be as easy as running an automated tool or as intricate as manually executing specific steps to get a desired result. No matter the level of difficultly of the test, good testers follow a specific pattern during the exploitation phase of a test to ensure consistent and successful results.

During a penetration test, the details considered in the planning, reconnaissance, and analysis phases come to fruition and affect the outcome of every action taken by the tester. A sound methodology is needed to translate all the planning into an attack scenario to meet the objectives within the specified period and within the defined scope. The attack process is typically broken up into multiple threads of execution and groups of test scenarios. A thread is a collection of tasks that must be performed in a specific order to achieve a specific attack goal. Threads can be a single step or multiple steps used to gain access or compromise a system. Every thread is different, but many have similar steps that they share in common. Therefore, threads can be combined into groups to create a collection of access strategies. Groups are then reviewed, compared, and optimized to support a comprehensive attack strategy using different threads in a structured manner.

Each test is evaluated at multiple points throughout the process to ensure that the expected outcome is met. Occasionally during a test the tester will need to diverge from the established plan due to unexpected circumstances or an unexpected reaction from the target. Each divergence from plan is appraised to make two fundamental determinations:

- Are the test objectives of the thread or group not being met or are the test's results conflicting with the company's assumptions and stated goals? The objective is to ensure that each test falls within the bounds of what was established and agreed upon. On the other hand, if the test begins to produce results that were not considered during the planning, enumeration, and vulnerability analysis phases, the engagement needs to be reconsidered, or at minimum, the planning phase needs to be revisited. Meeting expectations is a primary goal of testing, and in the world of ethical hacking, it can represent a fundamental challenge when not planned properly or not executed to the plan.

- Is a system reacting in an unexpected manner, which is having an impact on the test? Live systems in a dynamic environment do not always react as predicted or expected. Keeping alert for unexpected responses from systems ensures that the target has not been negatively affected and the set scope and boundaries of the test have not been exceeded.

Step 5: Document Findings: The goal of penetration testing is to gain awareness and a detailed understanding of the state of the security environment. Information is collected throughout the test, producing information that can be used to draw conclusions and articulate findings. The tester will need to collate and analyze that information, document findings in a clear and concise manner, and provide an analysis of the results that can be used to improve the overall security profile of the environment. The goal of the document is to clearly present the findings, tactics used, and tools employed, and to produce an analysis of information collected from the test. Specific areas to cover in the documentation and analysis include but are not limited to:

- Vulnerabilities discovered in the target system(s)
- Gaps in security measures
- Intrusion detection and response capabilities
- Observation of log activity and analysis
- Suggested countermeasures

Although penetration testing is complex and potentially expensive to perform, it is well worth the effort to an organization that is serious about improving its security and maintaining strong controls against attack.

User Entitlement

User entitlement describes the action of provisioning resources to a user. For example a when a user logs onto a network he may notice he automatically receives several mapped drives without knowing what they are for or why they are there. This is an example of user entitlement. As users change roles in the organization, not only do they aggregate access but they also increase their user entitlement. Again, this not only violates the concept of least privilege but also separation of duties.

Steps that can reduce the user entitlement expansion include:

- Inventory critical or sensitive information and processes
- Identifying data and process owners of the inventoried information and processes
- Determine access rights based on the data/process owners
- Implement access controls based on the data/process owners
- Develop a monitoring plan to detect new information and processes without owners
- Develop a strong change management culture and process which enforces stewardship and ownership of data

Access Review & Audit

User access is subject to reviews and audits through a variety of mechanisms. As part of a continuous monitoring program, the access logs of information systems and in some cases facilities should be reviewed and audited to determine what access has been ongoing and which users have access. Access logs may be as simple as a sheet of paper for people to sign in at a server room or as complicated as a full federated simplified sign on system. Understanding the fundamentals of access control can help ensure users have access to the resources they need and prevent them for accessing resources they do not. Additionally, access reviews and audits ensure someone is looking for suspicious activity.

A data center is a prime example of a physical access control concern. A data center may host the most sensitive and valuable information an organization owns. If an attacker can gain physical access to the servers, they may be able to attack using a multitude of techniques and options unavailable if only attacking through the network. Worse yet, the intruder could be someone working for the company who is gathering information to take with them to another job. A former employee may have never been removed from the physical access system, and wishes to seek revenge.

To help counter these threats a review of the physical access controls systems is in order. First, the security practitioner should review a list of who has access to the facility. If logical controls are in place such as badge readers or other automated physical access control systems this may be a simple task. Next, the security professional should review all the individuals who have access. There should be a legitimate business reason why each person is on the list keeping with the principal of "least privilege." In the event a person is on the list without a reason their access should be suspended until their access requirements are determined. Finally, access logs should be reviewed to determine who has accessed the facility and at what time. Often data centers and secured facilities will require individuals to log the reason they entered the facility on a separate sheet. This sign in sheet should be audited against the access log from the access control system and discrepancies should be reviewed.

In the event an automated system is not in place, the next question to ask is "who may have a key to this facility?" or in some cases "who may have a combo to this door?" If the answer to the question is uncertain then locks should be re-keyed and combinations should be changed. Although not ideal, keys and cipher locks are commonplace in many secure environments. Combinations should be changed regularly and keys should be closely monitored and stamped with "do not duplicate" on them. Additionally special keys and locks can be purchased which are more difficult to duplicate but cost more.

Just as physical access systems require review and audit so does the logical access control of information systems. The access information can come from a variety of sources including system logs, file access logs, error logs and security logs to name a few. To ensure successful access audit trails:

- Do not overwrite the security or access logs of a system. Often system administrators will configure log files to overwrite after a certain size is reached. This often removes useful information from historical access events. Determine an appropriate retention period per regulation and business need and ensure the system can support it.
- When a log file is full, ensure it is archived off the system it was created.
- Consider using a SIEM to collect log information for review and access.
- Classify information and know where the most valuable information is processed, stored and transmitted.
- Conform to standard user profiles as much as possible for access as this creates expected access log results.
- Consider segregation of duties and ensure when reviewing access those functions which require more than one person to complete are functioning as intended.

- Review the access logs for users who may have left the organization.

The results form an access review or audit provides valuable feedback for the facility or system management. Information from the review should be used to consider how information systems are being used in the organization and where opportunities may exist to access controls of business processes. Sometimes the access control is not failing but human resources may forget to send a request to the helpdesk to remove access from a system. In cases such as this, business processes should be reviewed to determine if automated controls might prevent future events from occurring.

Identity and Access Provisioning Lifecycle

Throughout this chapter, several aspects of access control and identity management have been discussed. There concepts culminate into an overall "lifecycle" of access control to resources. The lifecycle is the workflow of how a user obtains access, uses it and finally loses it. The lifecycle contains the following:

1. Provisioning

2. Review

3. Revocation

Provisioning

When a new user or an existing user requires additional access to a resource the process that enables the access is called provisioning. Provisioning entails determining the organizational requirements for access to information and applying the appropriate access rights to the account of the user. When provisioning the elements of least privilege, separation of duties and access aggregation must be considered. The user should only be provided with access and information required to perform necessary functions. The provisioning of access should also determine if any aspect of new access would somehow violate a separation of duties process such as creation of a payment and authorization of a payment. Finally, the provisioning of resources should be considered in light of the access aggregation; does granting additional access mean access in another area should be revoked?

Review

As noted in the "access review and auditing" section of this chapter, access must be monitored on a basis commensurate with risk and access. Reviewing access can take the form of automated checks, manual audits and several other methods. Access found to be excessive or inconsistent with a user's role or organizational function should be reviewed for modification or restriction. Access aggregation issues are often identified as part of the review process.

Revocation

Access rights typically must come to an end for one reason or another. For example, when a user leaves an organization typically all access is revoked. In some circumstances like an extended leave of absence, a revocation of access may only be temporary. Through the process of access review revocation will typically be invoked when a user is found to have aggregated unnecessary access or access with is incommensurate with the role of the user.

More to Know The following articles and documents contain more information about access control and identity management. They are freely available on the Internet.

NISTIR 7316, Assessment of Access Control Systems
https://csrc.nist.gov/publications/nistir/7316/NISTIR-7316.pdf

Federal Identity, Credential, and Access Management Roadmap
http://www.idmaagement.gov/documents/FICAM_Roadmap_Implementation_Guidance.pdf

Strategies to Mitigate Targeted Cyber Intrusions
http://www.dsd.gov.au/infosec/top-mitigations/top35mitigationstrategies-list.htm

Summary and Conclusion

There is a lot more that can be discussed here, and such a discussion could fill an entire reference book alone. Nevertheless, this chapter has explored the most important facets of access control. Specifically, the following key themes should be impressed upon the security professional:

- Access controls enable the confidentiality, integrity, and availability of an organization's assets.

- Access control is the first line of defense in a defense-in-depth strategy.

- Least privilege and separation of duties are effective means to enforce access controls.

- Information classification enables the organization to apply specific access controls based on the criticality and sensitivity of the asset.

- The seven access control categories address specific points of risk to the organization that change over time.

- Access controls can be administrative, technical, or physical.

- Identification provides uniqueness, authentication provides validity, and authorization provides control

- The three authentication factors—something you know, something you have, and something you are—applied in various combinations enable strong access control mechanisms.

- Vulnerability assessments can indicate where a system may be weak, while penetration testing validates that assessment.

- Effective identity management can be a strong boost for effective access controls.

- The security professional must keep up with knowledge on the latest threat and attack techniques, as well as the latest available preventative and detective technologies.

- Identity management and user access lifecycle management is a crucial area of understanding for the security professional.

As stated in the introduction, access control provides the foundation to the start of an effective and well-managed information security program. The information contained in this chapter will give the information security professional the ideas and approaches that are necessary to start building such a program.

Review Questions

1. A preliminary step in managing resources is

    A. Conducting a risk analysis

    B. Defining who can access a given system or information

    C. Performing a business impact analysis

    D. Obtaining top management support

2. Which best describes access controls?

    A. Access controls are a collection of technical controls that permit access to authorized users, systems, and applications.

    B. Access controls help protect against threats and vulnerabilities by reducing exposure to unauthorized activities and providing access to information and systems to only those who have been approved.

    C. Access control is the employment of encryption solutions to protect authentication information during log-on.

    D. Access controls help protect against vulnerabilities by controlling unauthorized access to systems and information by employees, partners, and customers.

3. _____ requires that a user or process be granted access to only those resources necessary to perform assigned functions.

    A. Discretionary access control

    B. Separation of duties

    C. Least privilege

    D. Rotation of duties

4. What are the seven main categories of access control?

    A. Detective, corrective, monitoring, logging, recovery, classification, and directive

    B. Directive, deterrent, preventative, detective, corrective, compensating, and recovery

    C. Authorization, identification, factor, corrective, privilege, detective, and directive

    D. Identification, authentication, authorization, detective, corrective, recovery, and directive

5. What are the three types of access control?

    A. Administrative, physical, and technical

    B. Identification, authentication, and authorization

    C. Mandatory, discretionary, and least privilege

    D. Access, management, and monitoring

6. Which approach revolutionized the process of cracking passwords?

    A. Brute force

    B. Rainbow table attack

    C. Memory tabling

    D. One-time hashing

7. What best describes two-factor authentication?

    A. A hard token and a smart card

    B. A user name and a PIN

    C. A password and a PIN

    D. A PIN and a hard token

8. A potential vulnerability of the Kerberos authentication server is

    A. Single point of failure

    B. Asymmetric key compromise

    C. Use of dynamic passwords

    D. Limited lifetimes for authentication credentials

9. In mandatory access control the system controls access and the owner determines

    A. Validation

    B. Need to know

    C. Consensus

    D. Verification

10. Which is the least significant issue when considering biometrics?

    A. Resistance to counterfeiting

    B. Technology type

    C. User acceptance

    D. Reliability and accuracy

11. Which is a fundamental disadvantage of biometrics?

    A. Revoking credentials

    B. Encryption

    C. Communications

    D. Placement

12. Role-based access control .

    A. Is unique to mandatory access control

    B. Is independent of owner input

    C. Is based on user job functions

    D. Can be compromised by inheritance

13. Identity management is

    A. Another name for access controls

    B. Technologies and processes intended to offer greater efficiency in the management of a diverse user and technical environment

    C. Technologies and processes focused on the provisioning and decommissioning of user credentials

    D. Technologies and processes used to establish trust relationships with disparate systems

14. A disadvantage of single sign-on is

    A. Consistent time-out enforcement across platforms

    B. A compromised password exposes all authorized resources

    C. Use of multiple passwords to remember

    D. Password change control

15. Which of the following is incorrect when considering privilege management?

    A. Privileges associated with each system, service, or application, and the defined roles within the organization to which they are needed, should be identified and clearly documented.

    B. Privileges should be managed based on least privilege. Only rights required to perform a job should be provided to a user, group, or role.

    C. An authorization process and a record of all privileges allocated should be maintained. Privileges should not be granted until the authorization process is complete and validated.

    D. Any privileges that are needed for intermittent job functions should be assigned to multiple user accounts, as opposed to those for normal system activity related to the job function.

16. Threat modeling is the process of

    A. Determining which threats to neutralize first

    B. Developing access controls that compensate for vulnerabilities

    C. A risk assessment approach in which decisions are based on risk and value.

    D. Scenario analysis targeted towards determining the best approach for threat elimination.

17. When reviewing user entitlement the security professional must be **MOST** aware of

    A. Identity management and disaster recovery capability

    B. Business or organizational processes and access aggregation

    C. The organizational tenure of the user requesting entitlement

    D. Automated processes which grant users access to resources

18. Which formula represents ALE or annual loss exposure?

    A. ALE=SLE x ARO

    B. SLE=ARO x ALE

    C. SLE=ARO x EF

    D. ALE=EF x SLE

19. In constructing a continuous monitoring system, numerous feeds from several systems must be correlated and analyzed. Which of the following **BEST** provides this capability?

    A. Intrusion Prevention System (IPS)

    B. Identity Management and Access Control System

    C. Intrusion Detection System (IDS)

    D. Security Information and Event Management (SIEM)

20. A guard dog patrolling the perimeter of a data center is what type of a control?

    A. Recovery

    B. Administrative

    C. Logical

    D. Physical

Domain 2

Telecomunications & Network Security

THE TELECOMMUNICATIONS AND NETWORK SECURITY DOMAIN encompasses the structures, transmission methods, transport formats, and security measures used to provide confidentiality, integrity, and availability for transmissions over private and public communications networks and media. Network security is often described as the cornerstone of IT security. The network is a central asset, if not the most central, in most IT environments. Loss of network assurance (the combined properties of confidentiality, integrity, and availability) on any level can have devastating consequences, while control of the network provides an easy and consistent venue of attack. Conversely, a well-architected, well-protected, and guarded network provides powerful protection and will stop many attacks in their tracks.

Network security like all security controls and safeguards is best and most effectively applied proactively. Waiting for impacts to materialize and applying controls and safeguards under crisis conditions will always cost more and be less effective than planned and managed deployments of network security policy, procedures, and technologies. The challenge associated with proactivity is that it requires a solid business base: why should resources be applied without evidence of a need (such as a loss or breach)? Clues to addressing this challenge are contained throughout this chapter in the form of threats and risks that can be qualitatively measured to establish metrics and support a proactive business case.

In the past, most attention has been paid to perimeter defense through firewalls and similar tools. As disappearance of network boundaries becomes a business requirement facilitated through hastened introduction of new technologies and convergence of technologies onto an IP backbone (more on this to follow), a constant struggle exists between ease of use and security. It is widely recognized that the inside of a network must be as resilient as its perimeter, that tools alone are ineffective if not combined with proper process, and that the availability of a network, while being the most obvious element of the network assets, is not the only element. Increasingly, attacks on the network are aimed not only at availability but also at compromising the knowledge and "semantic" assets of the network through stealthy confidentiality and integrity attacks.

This chapter focuses heavily on the Open System Interconnect (OSI) model as a point of reference and Transmission Control Protocol/Internet Protocol (TCP/IP) as the most commonly used protocol stack. Other protocol stacks will be discussed and reviewed as needed. Excellent books and Internet resources exist to learn the basics of networking, and this chapter covers basic network concepts insofar as they are required for the self-sufficiency of this book and useful for obtaining an understanding of network security concepts.

It is not possible to give a complete and comprehensive overview of all possible attack scenarios. For the purposes of this chapter, we focus on the most important security risks and those that will be instructive to the readers to gain an understanding of network security concepts and enable them to enhance their understanding and gain in-depth knowledge in self-study.

Finally, an underlying theme in this chapter will be the convergence of multiple information assets onto a single network in what is called "IP convergence." IP convergence occurs as information and communications assets such as business data, voice-telephony, physical security controls (door strikes and cameras), industrial controls, and pretty much anything else that requires network services migrate to IP. IP convergence makes the network event more sensitive to security events and makes the job of secure telecommunications even more vital; as the diversity of the network declines so does the diversity of defense.

OBJECTIVES

According to the (ISC)² Candidate Information Bulletin, a CISSP candidate is expected to demonstrate an understanding of:

- Communications and network security as it relates to data communications in local area networks (LANs)and wide area networks (WANs)
- Remote access
- Internet, intranet and extranet configurations
- Use of firewalls, network equipment, and protocols such as TCP/IP, VPN
- Techniques for preventing and detecting network-based attacks

Secure Network Architecture and Design

Network communication is usually described in terms of layers. Several layering models exist; the most commonly used are:

- OSI reference model, structured into seven layers (physical layer, data-link layer, network layer, transport layer, session layer, presentation layer, application layer)

- TCP/IP or Department of Defense (DoD) model (not to be confused with the TCP/IP protocols), structured into four layers (link layer, network layer, transport layer, application layer)

One feature that is common to both models and highly relevant from a security perspective is encapsulation. This means that not only do the different layers operate independently from each other but they are also isolated on a technical level. Short of technical failures, the contents of any lower- or higher-layer protocol are inaccessible from any particular layer. Without restricting the generality of the foregoing, we are going to use the OSI model as a general point of reference herein.

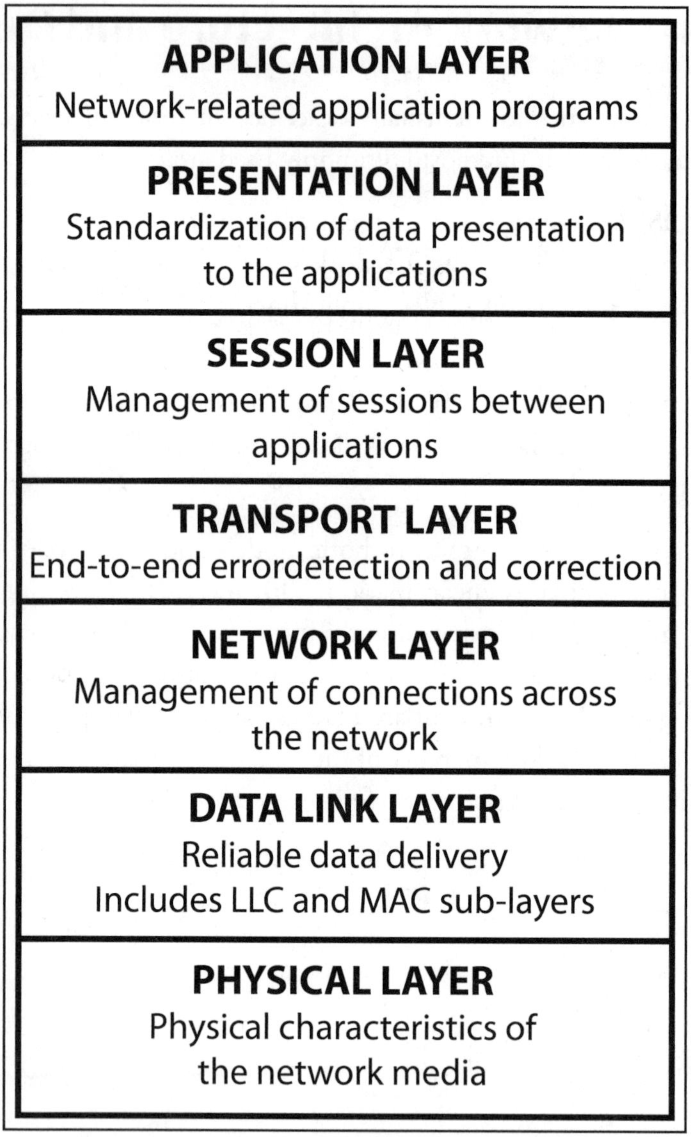

APPLICATION LAYER
Network-related application programs

PRESENTATION LAYER
Standardization of data presentation
to the applications

SESSION LAYER
Management of sessions between
applications

TRANSPORT LAYER
End-to-end errordetection and correction

NETWORK LAYER
Management of connections across
the network

DATA LINK LAYER
Reliable data delivery
Includes LLC and MAC sub-layers

PHYSICAL LAYER
Physical characteristics of
the network media

Figure 2.1 - **The Seven Layer OSI Reference Model**

(From Levi, B., UNIX Administration: A Comprehensive Sourcebook for Effective Systems
and Network Management, CRC Press, Boca Raton, FL, 2002. With permission.)

OSI and TCP/IP

The seven-layer OSI (Open System Interconnect) model was defined in 1984 and published as an international standard (ISO/IEC 7498–1). The last revision to this standard was in 1994. Although sometimes considered complex, it has provided a practical and widely accepted way to describe networking. In practice, some layers have proven to be less crucial to the concept (such as the presentation layer), while others (such as the network layer) have required more specific structure, and applications overlapping and transgressing layer boundaries exist. See *Figure 2.1.*

- *Layer 1* - the physical layer, describes the networking hardware, such as electrical signals, and bits and bytes, such as network interfaces and cabling.

- *Layer 2* - the data-link layer, describes data transfer between machines, for instance, by an Ethernet.

- *Layer 3* - the network layer, describes data transfer between networks, for instance, by the Internet Protocol (IP).

- *Layer 4* - the transport layer, describes data transfer between applications, flow control, and error detection and correction, for instance, by TCP.

- *Layer 5* - the session layer, describes the handshake between applications, for instance, authentication processes.

- *Layer 6* - the presentation layer, describes the presentation of information, such as ASCII syntax.

- *Layer 7* - the application layer, describes the structure, interpretation, and handling of information. In security terms, it is relevant because it relies on all underlying layers. From the point of view of the (ISC)² Common Body of Knowledge, the application layer is covered in the "Operations" section.

Each layer processes messages in a modular fashion, without concern for how the other layers on the same host process the message. For example, the layer that interacts directly with applications (layer 7) can communicate with its remote peer without knowing how the data is routed over the network (layer 3) or the hardware that is required (layers 1 and 2). When an application transmits data over a network, the data enters the top layer and moves to each successive lower level (moving down the stack) until it is transmitted over the network at layer 1. The remote host receives the data at layer 1 and moves to successive higher layers (moves up the stack) until it reaches layer 7 and then to the host's application.

Layer 1: Physical Layer - At the physical layer, bits from the data-link layer are converted into electrical signals and transmitted on a physical circuit. Physical topologies are defined at this layer. Because the required signals depend on the transmitting media (e.g., required modem signals are not the same as ones for an Ethernet network interface card), the signals are generated at the physical layer. Not all hardware consists of layer 1 devices. Even though many types of hardware, such as cables, connectors, and modems operate at the physical layer, some operate at different layers. Routers and switches, for example, operate at the network and data-link layers, respectively.

Layer 2: Data-Link Layer - The data-link layer prepares the packet that it receives from the network layer to be transmitted as frames on the network. This layer ensures that the information that it exchanges with its peers is error-free. If the data-link layer detects an error in a frame, it will request that its peer resend that frame. The data-link layer converts information from the higher layers into bits in the format that is expected for each networking technology, such as Ethernet, Token Ring, etc. Using hardware addresses, this layer transmits frames to devices that are physically connected only. As an analogy, consider the path between the end nodes on the network as a chain, and each link as a device in the path. The data-link layer is concerned with sending frames to the next link.

The Institute of Electrical and Electronics Engineers (IEEE) data-link layer is divided into two sublayers:

Logical Link Control (LLC): Manages connections between two peers. It provides error and flow control and control bit sequencing.

Media Access Control (MAC): Transmits and receives frames between peers. Logical topologies and hardware addresses are defined at this sublayer. An Ethernet's 48-bit hardware address is often called a MAC address as a reference to the name of the sublayer.

Layer 3: Network Layer - It is important to clearly distinguish between the functions of the network and data-link layers. The network layer moves information between two hosts that are not physically connected. On the other hand, the data-link layer is concerned with moving data to the next physically connected device. Also, whereas the data-link layer relies on hardware addressing, the network layer uses logical addressing that is created when hosts are configured.

Internet Protocol (IP) from the TCP/IP suite is the most important network layer protocol. IP has two functions:

Addressing: IP uses the destination IP address to transmit packets through networks until the packets' destination is reached.

Fragmentation: IP will subdivide a packet if its size is greater than the maximum size allowed on a local network.

IP is a connectionless protocol that does not guarantee error-free delivery. Layer 3 devices, such as routers, read the destination layer 3 address (e.g., destination IP address) in received packets and use their routing table to determine the next device on the network (the next hop) to send the packet.

If the destination address is not on a network that is directly connected to the router, it will send the packet to another router.

Routing tables are built either statically or dynamically. Static routing tables are configured manually and change only when updated. Dynamic routing tables are built automatically as routers periodically share information that reflect their view of the network, which changes as routers go on- and offline. When traffic congestion develops, this allows the routers to effectively route packets as network conditions change. Some examples of other protocols that work at Layer 3 are as follows:

> ***Routing Information Protocol (RIP) versions 1 and 2:*** The RIPv1 standard is defined in RFC 1058. Routing Information Protocol (RIP) is a standard for exchange of routing information among gateways and hosts. RIP is most useful as an "interior gateway protocol". RIP uses distance vector algorithms to determine the direction and distance to any link in the internetwork. If there are multiple paths to a destination, RIP selects the path with the least number of hops. However, because hop count is the only routing metric used by RIP, it does not necessarily select the fastest path to a destination.
>
> RIP v1 allows routers to update their routing tables at programmable intervals. The default interval is 30 seconds. The continual sending of routing updates by RIP v1 means that network traffic builds up quickly. To prevent a packet from looping infinitely, RIP allows a maximum hop count of 15. If the destination network is more than 15 routers away, the network is considered unreachable and the packet is dropped.
>
> The RIPv2 standard is defined in RFC 1723. RIPv2 provides the following advances over RIPv1:
>
> □ Carries a subnet mask.
>
> □ Supports password authentication security.

- ▫ Specifies the next hop address.
- ▫ Does not require that routes be aggregated on the network boundary.

Open Shortest Path First (OSPF) versions 1 and 2: The OSPF V1 standard is defined in RFC 1131. Open Shortest Path First, is an interior gateway routing protocol developed for IP networks based on the shortest path first or link-state algorithm. Routers use link-state algorithms to send routing information to all nodes in an internetwork by calculating the shortest path to each node based on a topography of the Internet constructed by each node. Each router sends that portion of the routing table (keeps track of routes to particular network destinations) that describes the state of its own links, and it also sends the complete routing structure (topography).

The advantage of shortest path first algorithms is that their use results in smaller, more frequent updates everywhere. They converge quickly, thus preventing such problems as routing loops and Count-to-Infinity (when routers continuously increment the hop count to a particular network). This makes for a more stable network. The disadvantage of shortest path first algorithms is that they require large amounts of CPU power and memory.

OSPF V2 is defined in RFC 1583 and updated by RFC 2328. It is rapidly replacing RIP on the Internet. It is used to allow routers to dynamically learn routes from other routers and to advertise routes to other routers. Advertisements containing routes are referred to as Link State Advertisements (LSAs) in OSPF. OSPF routers keep track of the state of all the various network connections (links) between itself and a network it is trying to send data to. This makes it a link-state routing protocol.

OSPF supports the use of classless IP address ranges and is very efficient. OSPF uses areas to organize a network into a hierarchal structure; it summarizes route information to reduce the number of advertised routes and thereby reduce network load and uses a designated router (elected via a process that is part of OSPF) to reduce the quantity and frequency of Link State Advertisements.

OSPF selects the best routes by finding the lowest cost paths to a destination. All router interfaces (links) are given a cost. The cost of a route is equal to the sum of all the costs configured on all the outbound links between the router and the destination network, plus the cost configured on the interface that OSPF received the Link State Advertisement on.

Border Gateway Protocol (BGP): BGP was created to replace the Exterior Gateway Protocol (EGP) protocol to allow fully decentralized routing. This allowed the Internet to become a truly decentralized system. BGP performs interdomain routing in Transmission-Control Protocol/Internet Protocol (TCP/IP) networks. BGP is a protocol for exchanging routing information between gateway hosts (each with its own router) in a network of autonomous systems. BGP is often the protocol used between gateway hosts on the Internet. The routing table contains a list of known routers, the addresses they can reach, and a cost metric associated with the path to each router so that the best available route is chosen.

Hosts using BGP communicate using the Transmission Control Protocol (TCP) and send updated router table information only when one host has detected a change. Only the affected part of the routing table is sent. BGP-4, the latest version, lets administrators configure cost metrics based on policy statements.

BGP is specified in several Request For Comments (RFCs):

- **RFC 4271** - Describes the current iteration of BGP4.
- **RFC 1771** - Describes BGP4, the current version of BGP.

□ **RFC 1654** - Describes the first BGP4 specification.

□ **RFC 1105, RFC 1163, and RFC 1267** - Describes versions of BGP prior to BGP4.

Internet Control Message Protocol (ICMP): Internet Control Message Protocol (ICMP) is documented in RFC 792.

ICMP messages are classified into 2 main categories:

□ ICMP Error Messages

□ ICMP Query Messages

ICMP's goals are to provide a means to send error messages for non-transient error conditions, and to provide a way to probe the network in order to determine general characteristics about the network.

Some of ICMP's functions are to:

1. ***Announce network errors***, such as a host or entire portion of the network being unreachable, due to some type of failure. A TCP or UDP packet directed at a port number with no receiver attached is also reported via ICMP.

2. ***Announce network congestion***. When a router begins buffering too many packets, due to an inability to transmit them as fast as they are being received, it will generate ICMP Source Quench messages. Directed at the sender, these messages should cause the rate of packet transmission to be slowed.

3. ***Assist Troubleshooting***. ICMP supports an Echo function, which just sends a packet on a round--trip between two hosts. Ping, a common network management tool, is based on this feature. Ping will transmit a series of packets, measuring average round--trip times and computing loss percentages.

4. ***Announce Timeouts***. If an IP packet's TTL field drops to zero, the router discarding the packet will often generate an ICMP packet announcing this fact. TraceRoute is a tool which maps network routes by sending packets with small TTL values and watching the ICMP timeout announcements.

For a listing of protocols associated with Layer 3 of the OSI model, see below:

- **IPv4/IPv6** - Internet Protocol
- **DVMRP** - Distance Vector Multicast Routing Protocol
- **ICMP** - Internet Control Message Protocol
- **IGMP** - Internet Group Multicast Protocol
- **OSPF** - Open Shortest Path First
- **BGP** - Border Gateway Protocol
- **PIM-SM** - Protocol Independent Multicast Sparse Mode
- **PIM-DM** - Protocol Independent Multicast Dense Mode
- **IPsec** - Internet Protocol Security
- **IPX** - Internetwork Packet Exchange
- **RIP** - Routing Information Protocol
- **DDP** - Datagram Delivery Protocol
- **RSMLT** - Routed-SMLT
- **SPB** - Shortest Path Bridging
- **APT** - Apple Talk Protocol
- **PDCP** - Packet Data Convergence Protocol
- **NDP** - Nortel Discovery Protocol
- **S-IS** - Intermediate System to Intermediate System

Layer 4: Transport Layer - The transport layer creates an end-to-end transport between peer hosts. User Datagram Protocol (UDP) and Transmission Control Protocol (TCP) are important transport layer protocols in the TCP/IP suite. UDP does not ensure that transmissions are received without errors, and therefore is classified as a connectionless unreliable protocol. This does not mean that UDP is poorly designed. Rather, the application will perform the error checking, instead of the protocol.

Connection-oriented reliable protocols, such as TCP, ensure integrity by providing error-free transmission. They divide information from multiple applications on the same host into segments to be transmitted on a network. Because it is not guaranteed that the peer transport layer receives segments in the order that they were sent, reliable protocols reassemble received segments into the correct order. When the peer layer receives a segment, it responds with an acknowledgment. If an acknowledgment is not received, the segment is retransmitted. Lastly, reliable protocols ensure that each host does not receive more data than it can process without loss of data.

TCP level data transmissions, connection establishment, and connection termination maintain specific control parameters that govern the entire process. The control bits are listed as follows:

- **URG**: Urgent Pointer field significant
- **ACK**: Acknowledgement field significant
- **PSH**: Push Function
- **RST**: Reset the connection
- **SYN**: Synchronize sequence numbers
- **FIN**: No more data from sender

These control bits are used for many purposes, chief among them is the establishment of a guaranteed communication session via a process referred to as the TCP three way handshake, illustrated here:

1. First, the client sends a SYN segment. This is a request to the server to synchronize the sequence numbers. It specifies its initial sequence number (ISN), which is incremented by 1, and that is sent to the server. To initialize a connection, the client and server must synchronize each other's sequence numbers.

2. Second, the server sends an ACK and a SYN in order to acknowledge the request of the client for synchronization. At the same time, the server is also sending its request to the client for synchronization of its sequence numbers. There is one major difference in this transmission from the first one. The server transmits an acknowledgement number to the client. The acknowledgement is just proof to the client that the ACK is specific to the SYN the client initiated. The process of acknowledging the client's request allows the server to increment the client's sequence number by one and uses it as its acknowledgement number.

3. Third, the client sends an ACK in order to acknowledge the request from the server for synchronization. The client uses the same algorithm the server implemented in providing an acknowledgement number. The client's acknowledgment of the server's request for synchronization completes the process of establishing a reliable connection.

For a listing of protocols associated with Layer 4 of the OSI model, see below:

- **ATP** - AppleTalk Transaction Protocol
- **CUDP** - Cyclic UDP
- **DCCP** - Datagram Congestion Control Protocol
- **FCP** - Fiber Channel Protocol
- **IL** - Internet Link Protocol

- □ **NBF** - NetBIOS Frames protocol

- □ **RDP** - Reliable Datagram Protocol

- □ **SCTP** - Stream Control Transmission Protocol

- □ **SPX** - Sequenced Packet Exchange

- □ **SST** - Structured Stream Transport

- □ **TCP** - Transmission Control Protocol

- □ **UDP** - User Datagram Protocol

- □ **UDP Lite** - User Datagram Protocol Lite

- □ **µTP** - Micro Transport Protocol

Layer 5: Session Layer - This layer provides a logical persistent connection between peer hosts. A session is analogous to a conversation that is necessary for applications to exchange information. The session layer is responsible for creating, maintaining, and tearing down the session. Three modes are offered:

(Full) Duplex: Both hosts can exchange information simultaneously, independent of each other.

Half Duplex: Hosts can exchange information, but only one host at a time.

Simplex: Only one host can send information to its peer. Information travels in one direction only.

For a listing of protocols associated with Layer 5 of the OSI model, see below:

- □ **ADSP** - AppleTalk Data Stream Protocol

- □ **ASP** - AppleTalk Session Protocol

- □ **H.245** - Call Control Protocol for Multimedia Communication

- □ **ISO-SP** - OSI session-layer protocol (X.225, ISO 8327)

- **iSNS** - Internet Storage Name Service
- **L2F** - Layer 2 Forwarding Protocol
- **L2TP** - Layer 2 Tunneling Protocol
- **NetBIOS** - Network Basic Input Output System
- **PAP** - Password Authentication Protocol
- **PPTP** - Point-to-Point Tunneling Protocol
- **RPC** - Remote Procedure Call Protocol
- **RTCP** - Real-time Transport Control Protocol
- **SMPP** - Short Message Peer-to-Peer
- **SCP** - Session Control Protocol
- **SOCKS** - the SOCKS internet protocol, see Internet socket
- **ZIP** - Zone Information Protocol
- **SDP** - Sockets Direct Protocol

Layer 6: Presentation Layer - The applications that are communicating over a network may represent information differently, such as using incompatible character sets. This layer provides services to ensure that the peer applications use a common format to represent data. For example, if a presentation layer wants to ensure that Unicode-encoded data can be read by an application that understands the ASCII character set only, it could translate the data from Unicode to a standard format. The peer presentation layer could translate the data from the standard format into the ASCII character set.

The Presentation Layer has a complex architecture that is represented below:

Services

- Data conversion
- Character code translation

□ Compression

□ Encryption and Decryption

Sublayers

The presentation layer can be composed of two sublayers: common application service element (CASE) and specific application service element (SASE).

CASE

The common application service element sublayer provides services for the application layer and request services from the session layer. It provides support for common application services, such as:

□ **ACSE** - Association Control Service Element

□ **ROSE** - Remote Operation Service Element

□ **CCR** - Commitment Concurrency and Recovery

□ **RTSE** - Reliable Transfer Service Element

SASE

The specific application service element sublayer provides application specific services (protocols), such as:

□ **FTAM** - File Transfer, Access and Manager

□ **VT** - Virtual Terminal

□ **MOTIS** - Message Oriented Text Interchange Standard

□ **CMIP** - Common Management Information Protocol

□ **MMS** - Manufacturing Messaging Service

□ **RDA** - Remote Database Access

- **DTP** - Distributed Transaction Processing

Protocols

For a listing of protocols associated with Layer 6 of the OSI model, see below:

- **AFP** - Apple Filing Protocol
- **ICA** - Independent Computing Architecture
- **LPP** - Lightweight Presentation Protocol
- **NCP** - NetWare Core Protocol
- **NDR** - Network Data Representation
- **Telnet** (a remote terminal access protocol)
- **XDR** - eXternal Data Representation
- **PAD** - X.25 Packet Assembler/Disassembler Protocol
- **MIME** - Multipurpose Internet Mail Extensions
- **NNTP** - Network News Transfer Protocol
- **FTP** - File Transfer Protocol

Layer 7: Application Layer - This layer is the application's portal to network-based services, such as determining the identity and availability of remote applications. When an application or the operating system transmits or receives data over a network, it uses the services from this layer. Many well-known protocols, such as Hypertext Transfer Protocol (HTTP), File Transfer Protocol (FTP), and Simple Mail Transfer Protocol (SMTP), operate at this layer. It is important to remember that the application layer is not the application, especially when an application has the same name as a layer 7 protocol. For example, the FTP command on many operating systems initiates an application called FTP, which eventually uses the FTP protocol to transfer files between hosts.

For a listing of protocols associated with Layer 7 of the OSI model, see below:

- **DHCP** - Dynamic Host Configuration Protocol
- **DHCPv6** - Dynamic Host Configuration Protocol v6
- **DNS** - Domain Name System
- **HTTP** - Hypertext Transfer Protocol
- **IMAP** - Instant Message Access Protocol
- **IRC** - Internet Relay Chat
- **LDAP** - Lightweight Directory Access Protocol
- **MGCP** - Media Gateway Control Protocol
- **XMPP** - Extensible Messaging and Presence Protocol
- **SMTP** - Simple Mail Transfer Protocol

TCP/IP Reference Model

The U.S. Department of Defense developed the TCP/IP model, which is very similar to the OSI model, but with fewer layers as shown in *Figure 2.2*. The link layer provides physical communication and routing within a network. It corresponds to everything required to implement an Ethernet. It is sometimes described as two layers, a physical layer and a link layer. In terms of the OSI model, it covers layers 1 and 2. The network layer includes everything that is required to move data between networks. It corresponds to the IP protocol, but also Internet Control Message Protocol (ICMP) and Internet Group Management Protocol (IGMP). In terms of the OSI model, it corresponds to layer 3.

The transport layer includes everything required to move data between applications. It corresponds to TCP and UDP. In terms of the OSI model, it corresponds to layer 4. The application layer covers everything specific to a session or application, in other words, everything relating to the data

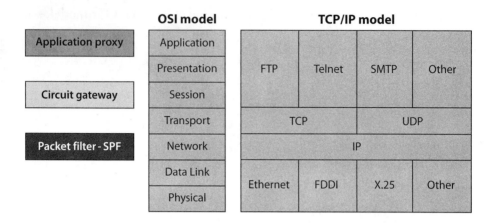

Figure 2.2 - **The TCP/IP Reference Model, with comparison to OSI stack**

(From Held, G., A Practical Guide to Content Delivery Networks, Auerbach Publications, Boca Raton, FL, 2006. With permission.)

payload. In terms of the OSI model, it corresponds to layers 5 through 7. Owing to its coarse structure, it is not well suited to describe application-level information exchange.

As with the OSI model, data that is transmitted on the network enters the top of the stack, and each of the layers, with the exception of the physical layer, encapsulates information for its peer at the beginning and sometimes the end of the message that it receives from the next highest layer. On the remote host, each layer removes the information that is peer encapsulated before the remote layer passes the message to the next higher layer. Also, each layer processes messages in a modular fashion, without concern for how the other layers on the same host process the message.

IP Networking

Internet protocol (IP) is responsible for sending packets from the source to the destination hosts. Because it is an unreliable protocol, it does not guarantee that packets arrive error-free or in the correct order. That task is left to protocols on higher layers. IP will subdivide packets into fragments when a packet is too large for a network.

Hosts are distinguished by the IP addresses of their network interfaces. The address is expressed as four octets separated by a dot (.), for example, 216.12.146.140. Each octet may have a value between 0 and 255. However, 0 and 255 are not used for hosts. The latter is used for broadcast addresses, and the former's meaning depends on the context in which it is used. Each address is subdivided into two parts: the network number and the host. The network number, assigned by an external organization, such as the Internet Corporation for Assigned Names and Numbers (ICANN), represents the organization's network. The host represents the network interface within the network.

Originally, the part of the address that represented the network number depended on the network's class. As shown in *Table 2.1*, a Class A network used the leftmost octet as the network number, Class B used the leftmost two octets, etc.

Class	Range of First Octet	Number of Octets for Network Number	Number of Hosts in Network
A	1–127	1	16,777,216
B	128–191	2	65,536
C	192–223	3	256
D	224–239	Multicast	
E	240–255	Reserved	

Table 2.1- **Network Classes**

The part of the address that is not used as the network number is used to specify the host. For example, the address 216.12.146.140 represents a Class C network. Therefore, the network portion of the address is represented by the 216.12.146, and the unique host address within the network block is represented by 140.

289

127.0.0.0, which is the Class A network address block, is reserved for a computer's loopback address. Usually the address 127.0.0.1 is used. The loopback address is used to provide a mechanism for self-diagnosis and troubleshooting at the machine level. This mechanism allows a network administrator to treat a local machine as if it were a remote machine, and ping the network interface to establish whether or not it is operational.

The explosion of Internet utilization in the 1990s caused a shortage of unallocated IP addresses. To help remedy the problem, classless interdomain routing (CIDR) was implemented. CIDR does not require that a new address be allocated based on the number of hosts in a network class. Instead, addresses are allocated in contiguous blocks from the pool of unused addresses.

To ease network administration, networks are typically subdivided into subnets. Because subnets cannot be distinguished with the addressing scheme discussed so far, a separate mechanism, the subnet mask, is used to define the part of the address that is used for the subnet. Bits in the subnet mask are 1 when the corresponding bits in the address are used for the subnet. The remaining bits in the mask are 0. For example, if the leftmost three octets (24 bits) are used to distinguish subnets, the subnet mask is 11111111 11111111 11111111 00000000. A string of 32 1s and 0s is very unwieldy, so the mask is usually converted to decimal: 255.255.255.0. Alternatively, the mask is expressed with a slash (/) followed by the number of 1s in the mask. The above mask would be /24.

IPv6

After the explosion of Internet usage in the mid-1990s, IP began to experience serious growing pains. It was obvious that the phenomenal usage of the Internet was stretching the protocol to its limit. The most obvious problems were a shortage of unallocated IP addresses and serious shortcomings in security. IPv6 is a modernization of IPv4 that includes:

A much larger address field: IPv6 addresses are 128 bits, which supports 2 hosts. Suffice it to say that we will not run out of addresses. Computing how many hosts will be supported by IPv6 and comparing the result to some other large constant will be left as an exercise for the student.

Improved security: As we will discuss below, IPSec must be implemented in IPv6. This will help ensure the integrity and confidentiality of IP packets, and allow communicating partners to authenticate with each other.

A more concise IP packet header: Hosts will require less time to process each packet, which will result in increased throughput.

Improved quality of service: This will help services obtain an appropriate share of a network's bandwidth.

Transmission Control Protocol (TCP)

The Transmission Control Protocol provides connection-oriented data management and reliable data transfer.

TCP, and UDP, map data connections through the association of port numbers with services provided by the host. TCP and UDP port numbers are managed by the Internet Assigned Numbers Authority (IANA). A total of 65,536 (216) ports exist. These are broken into three ranges:

- *Well-Known Ports:* Ports 0 through 1023 are considered to be well known. Ports in this range are assigned by IANA and, on most systems, can only be used by privileged processes and users.

- *Registered Ports:* Ports 1024 through 49151 can be registered with IANA by application developers but are not assigned by them. The reason for choosing a registered instead of a well-known port can be that on most systems, the user may not have the privileges to run an application on a well-known port.

- *Dynamic or Private Ports:* Ports 49152 through 65535 can

be freely used by applications; one typical use for these ports is initiation of return connections for requested data or services.

Attacks against TCP include sequence number attacks, session hijacking, and SYN floods. More information about attacks can be found later in this chapter.

User Datagram Protocol (UDP)

The User Datagram Protocol provides a lightweight service for connectionless data transfer without error detection and correction. For UDP, the same considerations for port numbers as described for TCP in the section on Transmission Control Protocol apply.

A number of protocols within the transport layer have been defined on top of UDP, thereby effectively splitting the transport layer into two.

Protocols stacked between layers 4 and 5 include Real-time Protocol (RTP) and Real-time Control Protocol (RTCP) as defined in RFC 3550,MBone, a multicasting protocol, Reliable UDP (RUDP), and Stream Control Transmission Protocol (SCTP) as defined in RFC 2960.

As a connectionless protocol, UDP services are easy prey to spoofing attacks.

Internet–Intranet

The Internet, a global network of independently managed, interconnected networks, is has changing changed life on Earth. People from anywhere on the globe can share information almost instantaneously using a variety of standardized tools like Web technologies or e-mail.

An **intranet** on the other hand is a network of interconnected internal networks within an organization, which allows information to be shared within the organization and sometimes with trusted partners and suppliers. For instance, during a project, staff in a global company can easily access and exchange documents, thereby working together almost as if they were in the same office. As with the Internet, the ease with which information can be shared comes with the responsibility to protect it from harm. Intranets will typically host a wide range of organizational data. For this reason, access to these resources is usually coupled with existing internal authentication services even though they are technically on an internal network, such as a Directory service coupled with Multi-factor authentication.

Extranet

An extranet differs from a DMZ (demilitarized network zone) in the following way: an extranet is made available to authenticated connections that have been granted an access account to the resources in the extranet. Conversely, a DMZ will host publicly available resources that must support unauthenticated connections from just about any source, such as DNS servers and e-mail servers. Due to the need for companies to share large quantities of information, often in an automated fashion, typically one company will grant the other controlled access to an isolated segment of its network to exchange information through the use of an extranet.

Granting an external organization access to a network comes with significant risk. Both companies have to be certain that the controls, both technical and nontechnical (e.g., operational and policy), effectively minimize the risk of unauthorized access to information. Where access must be granted to external organizations, additional controls such as deterministic routing can be applied upstream by service providers. This sort of safeguard is relatively simple to employ and has significant advantages because the ability for malicious entities to target an extranet for compromise leading to internal network penetration is abbreviated.

Companies that access extranets often treat the information within these networks and their servers as "trusted:" confidential and possessing integrity (uncorrupted and valid). However, these companies do not have control of each other's security profile. Who knows what can happen to a company if it access supposed trusted information from an extranet from an organization whose network has been compromised. To mitigate this, some companies demand that certain security controls are in place before granting access to an extranet.

Dynamic Host Configuration Protocol (DHCP)

System and network administrators are busy people and hardly have the time to assign IP addresses to hosts and track in which addresses are allocated. To relieve administrators from the burden of manually assigning addresses, many organizations use Dynamic Host Configuration Protocol (DHCP) to automatically assign IP addresses to workstations (servers and network devices usually are assigned static addresses).

Dynamically assigning hosts configuration is fairly simple. When a workstation boots, it broadcasts a DHCPDISCOVER request on the local LAN, which could be forwarded by routers. DHCP servers will respond with a DCHPOFFER packet, which contains a proposed configuration, including an IP address. The DHCP client selects a configuration from the received DHCPOFFER packets and replies with a DHCPREQUEST. The DHCP server replies with a DHCPACK (DHCP acknowledgment), and the workstation adapts the configuration. Receiving a DHCP-assigned IP address is referred to as receiving a lease.

A client does not request a new lease every time it boots. Part of the negotiation of IP addresses includes establishing a time interval for which the lease is valid and timers that reflect when the client must attempt to renew the lease. As long as the timers have not expired, the client is not required to ask for a new lease.

Within the DHCP servers, administrators create address pools from which addresses are dynamically assigned when requested by a client. In addition, they can assign specific hosts to have static (i.e., permanent) addresses through the use of client reservations.

Because the DHCP server and client do not always authenticate with each other, neither host can be sure that the other is legitimate. For example, in a DHCP network, an attacker can plug his or her workstation into a jack and receive an IP address, without having to obtain one by guessing or social engineering. Also, a client cannot be certain that a DHCPOFFER packet is from a DHCP server, instead of an intruder masquerading as a server.

To counteract these concerns, in June 2001 the IETF published RFC 3118, which specifies how to implement Authentication for DHCP Messages. This standard describes an enhancement that replaces the normal DHCP messages with authenticated ones. Clients and servers check the authentication information and reject messages that come from invalid sources. The technology involves the use of a new DHCP option type, the Authentication option, and operating changes to several of the leasing processes to use this option. Although these vulnerabilities are not trivial, the ease of administration of IP addresses usually makes the risk from the vulnerabilities acceptable, except in very high security environments.

Internet Control Message Protocol (ICMP)

The Internet Control Message Protocol (ICMP) is used for the exchange of control messages between hosts and gateways and is used for diagnostic tools such as ping and traceroute. ICMP can be leveraged for malicious behavior, including man-in-the-middle and denial-of-service attacks.

Ping of Death

Ping is a diagnostic program used to determine if a specified host is on the network and can be reached by the pinging host. It sends an ICMP echo packet to the target host and waits for the target to return an ICMP echo reply. Amazingly, an enormous number of operating systems would crash or become unstable upon receiving an ICMP echo greater than the legal packet limit of 65,536 bytes.

Before the ping of death became famous, the source of the attack was difficult to find because many system administrators would ignore a harmless-looking ping in their logs.

ICMP Redirect Attacks

A router may send an ICMP redirect to a host to tell it to use a different, more effective default route. However, an attacker can send an ICMP redirect to a host telling it to use the attacker's machine as a default route. The attacker will forward all of the redirected traffic to a router so that the victim will not know that his or her traffic has been intercepted. This is a good example of a man-in-the-middle attack. Some operating systems would crash if they received a storm of ICMP redirects.

Ping Scanning

Ping scanning is a basic network mapping technique that helps narrow the scope of an attack. An attacker can use one of many tools such as Very Simple Network Scanner for Windows based platforms and NMAP for Linux based platforms to ping all of the addresses in a range. If a host replies to a ping, then the attacker knows that a host exists at that address.

Traceroute Exploitation

Traceroute is a diagnostic tool that displays the path a packet traverses between a source and destination host. Traceroute can be used maliciously to map a victim network and learn about its routing. In addition, there are tools, such as Firewalk, that use techniques similar to those of traceroute to enumerate a firewall rule set.

Internet Group Management Protocol (IGMP)

IGMP is used to manage multicasting groups, which are a set of hosts anywhere on a network that are interested in a particular multicast. Multicast agents administer multicast groups, and hosts send IGMP messages to local agents to join and leave groups. There are three versions of IGMP, as highlighted below:

> ***Version 1:*** Multicast agents periodically send queries to a host on its network to update its database of multicast groups'

membership. Hosts stagger their replies to prevent a storm of traffic to the agent. When replies no longer come from a group, agents will stop forwarding multicasts to that group.

Version 2: This version extends the functionality of version 1. It defines two types of queries: a general query to determine membership of all groups and a group-specific query to determine the membership of a particular group. In addition, a member can notify all multicast routers that it wishes to leave a group.

Version 3: This version further enhances IGMP by allowing hosts to specify from which sources they want to receive multicasts.

Routing Information Protocol (RIP)

Routing Information Protocol is a dynamic routing protocol that is designed for small networks. Routers in a RIP network regularly merge their view of the network by exchanging their routing table with their neighbors. The number of hops is used to determine the best path for packets. However, RIP cannot route to a network or host that is more than 15 hops away. RIP has several shortcomings, including:

A. Routers exchange their entire route table every 30 s (by default), which can cause network congestion.

B. RIP only works in classful networks. In other words, RIP cannot be used in networks with different subnet masks.

C. There is no way for a router to verify the trustworthiness of a route update from its neighbors, which could allow an attacker to manipulate route tables with bogus route updates.

RIP version 2 (RIPv2) was implemented to address some of RIP's limitations. For example, RIPv2 can be used in a network with different subnet masks. Also, routers authenticate with each other, originally with a plaintext password, and later, using RFC 2082, keyed Message Digest 5 (MD5) authentication.

Virtual Router Redundancy Protocol (VRRP)

Organizations that demand that their network have 99.999 percent availability cannot tolerate critical routers as single points of failure. The most acceptable option is for a secondary router to automatically take the place of another router when it fails; i.e., failover. VRRP is a protocol that supports automatic failover. A virtual router is configured that appears to the rest of the network as a physical router.

Configured with the virtual router are physical routers, a primary router, and at least one secondary. The primary router performs all of the routing on behalf of the virtual router. If the primary router fails, one of the secondary routers will automatically perform the routing for the virtual router. As long as hosts forward packets to the virtual router, it will not matter which physical router is doing the work. Primary and secondary routers are often placed in separate data centers to improve resilience against disasters, and aid with Business Continuity Planning (BCP) and Disaster Recovery Planning (DRP) (*see Chapter 8*).

Remote Procedure Calls

Remote procedure calls (RPCs) are a general concept of executing objects across hosts, with a client sending a set of instructions to an application residing on a different host on the network. Generically, several (mutually incompatible) services in this category exist, such as distributed computing environment RPC (DCE RPC) and Sun's Open Network Computing RPC (ONC RPC, also referred to as SunRPC or simply RPC). It is important to note that RPC does not in fact provide any services on its own; instead, it provides a brokering service, by providing (basic) authentication and a way to address the actual service.

Common Object Request Broker Architecture (CORBA) and Microsoft Distributed Component Object Model (DCOM) can be viewed as RPC-type protocols. Generically, RPC services are not limited to layer 5.

RPC used over the open Internet was at one time common, but usage in this manner has been almost totally overwhelmed by the resulting vulnerabilities. Security problems with RPC include its weak authentication mechanism, which can be leveraged for privilege escalation by an attacker.

Directory Services

Domain Name Service (DNS)

Domain Name System is one of the most prominent and the most visible to the end user of all network services. The reason for this is DNS's role in creating the system that supports the use and resolution of e-mail and World Wide Web (WWW) addresses, which have become a ubiquitous element of our everyday life.

By virtue of this fact, DNS has become a prominent target of attack, aggravating weaknesses inherent in the protocol. By manipulating DNS, it is certainly possible to divert, intercept, or prevent the vast majority of end-user communications without having to resort to attacking any end-user devices, or endpoints.

As shown in *Figure 2.3*, the Domain Name System as a whole is a distributed, hierarchical database. Through its caching architecture, it

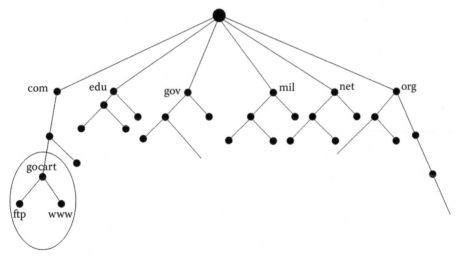

Figure 2.3 - **The DNS database structure**
(From Held, G., *ABCs of IP Addressing*, Auerbach Publications, Boca Raton, FL, 2002. With permission.)

299

possesses a remarkable degree of robustness, flexibility, and scalability, due to the fact that the use of a multi-tiered resolver hierarchy for redundancy and security allows for one or more DNS resolvers to go offline while still maintaining the integrity of the system as a whole.

DNS's central element is a set of hierarchical name (domain) trees, starting from a so-called top-level domain (TLD). A number of so-called root servers manage the authoritative list of TLD servers. To resolve any domain name, each Domain Name Server in the world must hold a list of these root servers.

Various extensions to DNS have been proposed, to enhance its functionality and security, for instance, by introducing authentication through the use of DNSSEC, multicasting, or service discovery. See *Table 2.2*.

Ports	53/TCP, 53/UDP
Definition	RFC 882
	RC 1034
	RFC 1035

Table 2.2 - **DNS Quick Reference**

Lightweight Directory Access Protocol (LDAP)

LDAP (see *Table 2.3*) is a client/server-based directory query protocol loosely based upon X.500, commonly used for managing user information. As opposed to DNS, for instance, LDAP is a front end and not used to manage or synchronize data per se.

Back ends to LDAP can be directory services, such as NIS (see Network Information Service (NIS), NIS +), Microsoft's Active Directory Directory Service, Sun's iPlanet Directory Server (renamed to Sun Java System Directory Server), and Novell's eDirectory.

LDAP provides only weak authentication based on host name resolution. It would therefore be easy to subvert LDAP security by breaking DNS (see section on Domain Name Service).

Ports	389/TCP, 389/UDP
Definition	RFC 1777

Table 2.3 - **LDAP Quick Reference**

LDAP communication is transferred in cleartext and therefore is easily intercepted. One way to address the issues of weak authentication and cleartext communication is deployment of LDAP over SSL, providing authentication, integrity, and confidentiality.

Network Basic Input Output System (NetBIOS)

The NetBIOS application programming interface (API) was developed in 1983 by IBM. NetBIOS was later ported to TCP/IP (NetBIOS over TCP/IP, also known as NetBT); however, implementations running on top of NetBEUI or Internetwork Packet Exchange (IPX) are still in use.

Under TCP/IP, NetBIOS is running over TCP on ports 137 and 138 and over UDP on port 139. In addition, it uses port 135 for remote procedure calls (see Remote Procedure Calls). See *Table 2.4.*

Ports	135/UDP
	137/TCP
	138/TCP
	139/UDP
Definition	RFC 1001
	RFC 1002

Table 2.4 - **NetBIOS Quick Reference**

Network Information Service (NIS), NIS +

NIS and NIS + are directory services developed by Sun Microsystems, which are mostly used in UNIX environments. They are commonly used for managing user credentials across a group of machines, for instance, a UNIX workstation cluster or client/server environment, but can be used for other types of directories as well.

NIS

NIS is using a flat namespace in so-called domains. It is based on RPC and manages all entities on a server (NIS server). NIS servers can be set up redundantly through the use of slave servers.

NIS is known for a number of security weaknesses. The fact that NIS does not authenticate individual RPC requests can be used to spoof responses to NIS requests from a client. This would, for instance, enable an attacker to inject fake credentials and thereby obtain or escalate privileges on the target machine. Retrieval of directory information is possible if the name of a NIS domain has become known or is guessable, as any client can associate themselves with a NIS domain.

Conversely, the fact that a NIS server is an attractive target of attacks cannot be considered a weakness of NIS as such; it is, in fact, an architectural issue with all client/server platforms. A number of guides have been published on how to secure NIS servers. The basic steps here are to secure the platform a NIS server is running on, to isolate the NIS server from traffic outside of a LAN, and to configure it in a way that limits the probability for disclosure of authentication credentials, especially system privileged ones.

NIS +

NIS + is using a hierarchical namespace. It is based on Secure RPC (see Remote Procedure Calls). Authentication and authorization concepts in NIS + are more mature; they require authentication for each access of a directory object. However, NIS + authentication in itself will only be as strong as authentication to one of the clients in a NIS + environment, as NIS + builds on a trust relationship between different hosts.

The most relevant attacks against a correctly configured NIS + network come from attacks against its cryptographic security. NIS + can be run at different security levels; however, most levels available are irrelevant for an operational network.

Common Internet File System (CIFS)/Server Message Block (SMB)

CIFS/SMB (see *Table 2.5*) is a file-sharing protocol prevalent on Windows systems. A UNIX/Linux implementation exists in the free Samba project. SMB was originally designed to run on top of the NetBIOS protocol (see Network Based Input Output System); it can, however, be run directly over TCP/IP.

Ports	445/TCP
	See also NetBIOS (Network Basic Input Output System)
Definition	Proprietary

Table 2.5 - **CIFS/SMB Quick Reference**

CIFS is capable of supporting user-level and tree/object-level (share-level) security. Authentication can be performed via challenge/response authentication as well as by transmission of credentials in cleartext. This second provision has been added largely for backward compatibility in legacy Windows environments.

The main attacks against CIFS are based upon obtaining credentials, be it by sniffing for cleartext authentication or by cryptographic attacks.

Network File System (NFS)

Network File System is a client/server file-sharing system common to the UNIX platform. It was originally developed by Sun Microsystems, but implementations exist on all common UNIX platforms, including Linux, as well as Microsoft Windows. NFS (see *Table 2.6*) has been revised several times. NFS Versions 2 and 3. NFS version 2 was based on UDP, and version 3 introduced TCP support. Both are implemented on top of RPC (see Remote Procedure Calls). NFS versions 2 and 3 are stateless protocols, mainly due to performance considerations. As a consequence, the server must manage file locking separately.

Ports	See RPC (Section "Directory services")
Definition	RFC 1094
	RFC 1813
	RFC 3010
	RFC 3530

Table 2.6- **NFS Quick Reference**

Secure NFS (SNFS) offers secure authentication and encryption using Data Encryption Standard (DES) encryption. In contrast to standard NFS, secure NFS (or rather secure RPC) will authenticate each RPC request. This will increase latency for each request as the authentication is performed and introduces a light performance premium, mainly paid for in terms of computing capacity.

Secure NFS uses DES encrypted time stamps as authentication tokens. If server and client do not have access to the same time server, this can lead to short-term interruptions until server and client have resynchronized themselves.

NFS Version 4 is a stateful protocol that uses TCP port 2049. UDP support (and dependency) has been discontinued. NFS version 4 implements its own encryption protocols on the basis of Kerberos and has discontinued use of RPC. Foregoing RPC also means that additional ports are no longer dynamically assigned, which enables use of NFS through firewalls.

Another approach to securing NFS where it must be deployed is to tunnel NFS through Secure Shell (SSH), which can be integrated with operating system authentication schemes.

Simple Mail Transfer Protocol (SMTP) & Enhanced Simple Mail Transfer Protocol (ESMTP)

SMTP is a client/server protocol utilized to route e-mail on the Internet. Using port 25/TCP; information on mail servers for Internet domains is managed through DNS, using mail exchange (MX) records. Although SMTP takes a fairly simple approach to authentication, it is fairly robust in the way it deals with unavailability; an SMTP server will try to deliver e-mail over a configurable period.

From a protocol perspective, SMTP's main shortcomings are nonexistent authentication and the lack of encryption. Identification is performed by the sender's e-mail address. A mail server will be able to restrict sending access to certain hosts, which should be on the same network as the mail server, as well as set conditions on the sender's e-mail address, which should be one of the domains served by this particular mail server. Otherwise, the mail server may be configured as an open relay, although this is not a recommended practice traditionally, as it poses a variety of security concerns.

To address the weaknesses identified in SMTP, an enhanced version of the protocol, ESMTP, was defined. ESMTP is modular in that client and server can negotiate the enhancements used. ESMTP does offer authentication, among other things, and allows for different authentication mechanisms, including basic and several secure authentication mechanisms.

File Transfer Protocol (FTP)

Before the advent of the World Wide Web and proliferation of Hypertext Transfer Protocol (HTTP), which is built on some of its features, FTP (*see Table 2.7*) was the protocol for publishing or disseminating data over the Internet.

Ports	20/TCP (data stream)
	21/TCP (control stream)
Definition	RFC 959

Table 2.7 - **FTP Quick Reference**

FTP is a stateful protocol that requires two communication channels. One control channel on port 21 under TCP, over which state information is exchanged, and a data channel on port 20, through which payload information is transmitted.

In its original form, FTP uses simple username/password authentication, and credentials as well as all data are transmitted in cleartext (visible to anyone able to intercept or "sniff" the traffic). This makes the protocol subject to a wide range of attacks against confidentiality, integrity and availability.

Although this authentication weakness can be addressed through the use of encryption, this approach carries with it the need for additional requirements to be imposed on the client. These requirements and methods are briefly outlined below:

1. **Secure FTP with TLS** is an extension to the FTP standard that allows clients to request that the FTP session be encrypted. This is done by sending the "AUTH TLS" command. The server has the option of allowing or denying connections that do not request TLS. This protocol extension is defined in the proposed standard RFC 4217.

2. **SFTP, the "SSH File Transfer Protocol",** is not related to FTP except that it also transfers files and has a similar command set for users. SFTP, or secure FTP, is a program that uses Secure Shell (SSH) to transfer files. Unlike standard FTP, it encrypts both commands and data. It is functionally similar to FTP, but because it uses a different protocol, standard FTP clients cannot be used to talk to an SFTP server.

3. **FTP over SSH** refers to the practice of tunneling a normal FTP session over an SSH connection. Because FTP uses multiple TCP connections, it is particularly difficult to tunnel over SSH. With many SSH clients, attempting to set up a tunnel for the control channel (the initial client-to-server connection on port 21) will protect only that channel; when data is transferred, the FTP software at either end will set up new TCP connections (data channels), which bypass the SSH connection and thus have no confidentiality or integrity protection.

FTP offers two principal modes of data transfer: ASCII and binary. In ASCII mode, a conversion of layer 6 representation, depending on the target platform, is performed, whereas this conversion is omitted in binary mode.

Transfer Modes

Although the control channel is always opened by the client, there are two different modes for the data channel:

- *Active mode (PORT mode)*, where the server initiates the data connection to the client. This mode has obvious drawbacks in firewalled environments, as incoming connections to the client can (and should) be blocked. A number of firewall products still support active mode.

- *Passive mode (PASV mode)*, where the client initiates the data connection to the server. Even though RFC 959 does not mandate implementation of passive FTP, the majority of FTP servers offer this type of connection.

Anonymous FTP

Before the advent and proliferation of HTTP, publication of information to an unspecific user group was fulfilled by FTP services offering guest authentication to anyone who so desired. These services were called anonymous FTP due to the fact that the guest user would be mapped to the FTP log-in ID "anonymous," whereas the user would pseudo-authenticate (and thereby identify) himself with his e-mail address.

In practice, the user could have been using any password or e-mail address, whereas using one's true e-mail address would still have been considered common courtesy.

Although Web browsers still support the (social) protocol as such, the use of anonymous FTP has widely fallen by the wayside. There are three main reasons.

1. With HTTP, anonymous publication of information can be handled in a much more efficient and seamless manner.

2. Disclosure of e-mail addresses on the part of the user (or a requirement to do so) is widely regarded as an unsafe and privacy-violating practice that will expose the user to address harvesting by spammers.

3. Guest access can expose the FTP server to security risks.

Trivial File Transfer Protocol (TFTP)

TFTP is a simplified version of FTP, which is used when authentication is not needed and quality of service is not an issue. TFTP runs on port 69/UDP. It should therefore only be used in trusted networks with low latency.

Ports	69/UDP
Definition	RFC 1350

Table 2.8 - **TFTP (R2) Quick Reference**

In practice, TFTP is used mostly in LANs for the purpose of pulling packages, for instance, in booting up a diskless client, or when using imaging services to deploy client environments.

Hypertext Transfer Protocol (HTTP)

HTTP is the Layer 7 foundation of the World Wide Web (WWW). HTTP (see *Table 2.9*), originally conceived as a stateless, stripped-down version of FTP, was developed at the European Organization for Nuclear Research (CERN) to support the exchange of information in Hypertext Markup Language (HTML).

Ports	80/TCP; other ports are in use, especially for proxy services
Definition	RFC 1945
	RFC 2109
	RFC 2616

Table 2.9 - **HTTP Quick Reference**

HTTP's popularity caused the deployment of an unprecedented number of Internet facing servers, not a small number of which were deployed with out-of-the-box, vendor preset configurations—most of which at the time were geared at convenience, rather than security.

As a result, a whole number of previously closed applications were suddenly marketed as "Web enabled." By implication, not much time was spent on developing the Web interface in a secure manner and authentication was simplified to become a browser-based style.

HTTP will work from within most networks, shielded or not, and thereby lends itself to tunneling an impressive number of other protocols, even though HTTP neither supports quality of service nor bidirectional communication natively— although workarounds were quickly developed to deal with Quality of Service (QoS) concerns and bi-directional communication needs.

HTTP does not support encryption and has a fairly simple authentication mechanism based on domains, which in turn are normally mapped to directories on a Web server. Although HTTP authentication is extensible, it is most often used in the classic username/password style.

HTTP Proxying

Anonymizing Proxies

Because HTTP is transmitting data in cleartext and generates a slew of logging information on Web servers and proxy servers, the resulting information can be readily used for illegitimate activities, such as industrial espionage.

To address this significant concern, a number of commercial and free services are available that allow the anonymization of HTTP requests. These services are mainly geared at the privacy market but have also attracted a criminal element seeking to obfuscate activity.

A relatively popular free service is JAP(also referred to as project AN.ON, or Anonymity.Online / JAP is referred to as JonDo within the commercially available solution JonDonym anonymous proxy server); a number of commercial services exist that interested readers may want to familiarize themselves with.

Open Proxy Servers

Like open mail relays, open proxy servers allow unrestricted access to GET commands from the Internet. They can therefore be used as stepping stones for launching attacks, or simply to obscure the origin of illegitimate requests.

More importantly, an open proxy server bears an inherent risk of opening access to protected intranet pages from the Internet. (A misconfigured firewall allowing inbound HTTP requests would need to be present on top of the open proxy to allow this to happen.)

As a general rule, HTTP proxy servers should not allow queries from the Internet. It is a best practice to separate application gateways (sometimes implemented as reverse proxies) from the proxy for Web browsing, as both have very different security levels and business importance. (It would be even better to implement the application gateway as an application proxy and not an HTTP proxy, but this is not always possible.)

Content Filtering

In many organizations, the HTTP proxy is used as a means to implement content filtering, for instance, by logging or blocking traffic that has been defined as, or is assumed to be nonbusiness related for some reason.

Although filtering on a proxy server or firewall as part of a layered defense can be quite effective to prevent, for instance, virus infections (though it should never be the only protection against viruses), it will be only moderately effective in preventing access to unauthorized services (such as certain remote-access services or file sharing), as well as preventing the download of unwanted content.

HTTP Tunneling. HTTP tunneling is technically a misuse of the protocol on the part of the designer of such tunneling applications. It has become a popular feature with the rise of the first streaming video and audio applications and has been implemented into many applications that have a market need to bypass user policy restrictions. Usually, HTTP tunneling is applied by encapsulating outgoing traffic from an application in an HTTP request and incoming traffic in a response. This is usually not done to circumvent security, but rather, to be compatible with existing firewall rules and allow an application to function through a firewall without the need to apply special rules, or additional configurations.

Many of the most prevalent and successful malicious software packages including viruses, worms, and especially botnets will use HTTP as the means to transmit stolen data or control information from infected hosts through firewalls.

Suitable countermeasures include filtering on a firewall or proxy server and assessing clients for installations of unauthorized software. However, a security officer will have to balance the business value and effectiveness of these countermeasures with the incentive for circumvention that a restriction of popular protocols will create.

Implications of Multi-Layer Protocols

Multi-layer protocols have ushered in an era of new vulnerabilities which were once unthinkable. In the past, several "networked" solutions were developed to provide control and communications with industrial devices. These often proprietary protocols evolved over time and eventually merged with other networking technologies such as Ethernet and Token Ring. Several vendors now use the TCP/IP stack to channel and route their own protocols. These protocols are used to control coils, actuators and machinery in multiple industries such as energy, manufacturing, construction, fabrication, mining and farming to name a few. Insecurities in these systems often have real world visibility and impact. Given the fact that the life expectancy of many of the devices under control is 20 years or longer, it is easy to see how systems can become outdated. Often critical infrastructure such as power grids are controlled using multi-layer protocols. The following table from the Idaho National Laboratory illustrates some of the differences and related challenges of control systems vs. standard information technology.[1]

SECURITY TOPIC	INFORMATION TECHNOLOGY	CONTROL SYSTEMS
Anti-virus/Mobile Code	Common Widely used	Uncommon/Impossible to deploy effectively
Support Technology Lifetime	2-3 Years Diversified vendors	Up to 20 years Single vendor
Outsourcing	Common Widely Used	Operations are often outsourced, but not diverse to various providers
Application of Patches	Regular Scheduled	Rare, Unscheduled Vendor specific
Change Management	Regular Scheduled	Highly managed and complex
Time Critical Content	Generally delays accepted	Delays are unacceptable
Availability	Generally delays accepted	24x7x365 (continuous)
Security Awareness	Moderate in both private and public sector	Poor except for physical
Security Testing/Audit	Part of a good security program	Occasional testing for outages
Physical Security	Secure (server rooms, etc.)	Remote/Unmanned Secure

---

1   http://www.inl.gov/technicalpublications/Documents/3375141.pdf Pg 8

SCADA

The term most often associated with multi-layer protocols is Supervisory Control and Data Acquisition or SCADA. Another term used in relation with multi-layer protocols is "Industrial Control System" or ICS. In general, SCADA systems are designed to operate with several different communication methods including modems, WANS and various networking equipment. The following figure shows a general layout of a SCADA system[2]:

As the figure demonstrates, a great complexity of devices and information exist in SCADA systems. Most SCADA systems minimally contain the following:

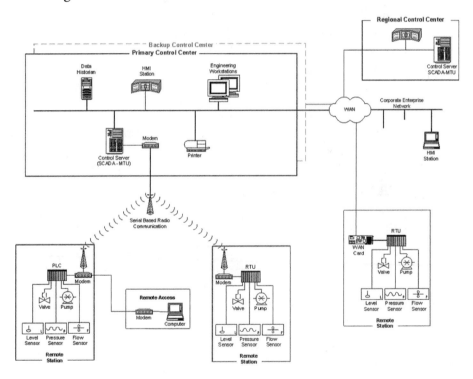

Figure 2.4 - **Diagram of a Generic SCADA ICS**

2   http://csrc.nist.gov/publications/nistir/ir7442/NIST-IR-7442_2007CSDAnnualReport.pdf

- **Control Server:** A control server hosts the software and often the interfaces used to control actuators, coils and PLCs through subordinate control modules across the network.

- **Remote Terminal Unit (RTU):** The RTU supports SCADA remote stations often equipped with wireless radio interfaces and are used in situations where land based communications may not be possible.

- **Human-Machine Interface (HMI):** The HMI is the interface where the humans (operators) can monitor, control and command the controllers in the system.

- **Programmable Logic Controller (PLC):** The PLC is a small computer which controls relays, switches, coils, counters and other devices.

- **Intelligent Electronic Devices (IED):** The IED is a sensor which can acquire data and also provide feedback to the process through actuation. These devices allow for automatic control at the local level.

- **Input/Output (IO) Server:** The IO server is responsible for collecting process information from components such as IEDs, RTUs and PLCs. They are often used to interface third-party control components such as custom dashboards with a control server.

- **Data Historian:** The data historian is like the Security Event and Incident Management (SEIM) for industrial control systems. It is typically a centralized database for logging process information from a variety of devices.

Given the unique design of SCADA systems, and the critical infrastructures that they control, it is little wonder they are a new focus of attacks. Organizations responsible for implementing or protecting SCADA systems should be aware of the following attacks:

- Network Perimeter Vulnerabilities

- Protocol Vulnerabilities throughout the stack

- Data Base Insecurities
- Session Hijacking and Man-in-the-middle-attacks
- Operating System and Server weaknesses
- Device and Vendor "Backdoors"

Modbus

Modbus and Fieldbus are standard industrial communication protocols designed by separate groups. The focus of the design around these protocols is not security; rather it is uptime and control of devices. Many of these protocols send information in clear text across transmission media. Additionally many of these protocols and the devices they support require little or no authentication to execute commands on a device. Strict logical and physical controls should be implemented to ensure these protocols are encapsulated and isolated from any public or open network.

Securing Network Components

In addition to providing throughput, a network's architecture should also help protect its assets. Listed below are the key concepts concerning isolating networks in different domains of trust.

Secure Routing/Deterministic Routing

While it is possible to establish corporate wide area networks (WANs) using the Internet and VPN technology, it is not desirable. Relying on the Internet to provide connectivity means that there is little ability to control the routes that traffic takes or to remedy performance issues. Deterministic routing means that WAN connectivity is supplied based upon a limited number of different routes, typically supplied by a large network provider. Deterministic routing means that traffic only travels by pre-determined routes that are known to be either secure or less susceptible to compromise. Similarly, deterministic routing from a large carrier will make it much easier to address performance issues and to maintain the service levels required by the applications on the WAN. If the WAN is supporting converged applications like voice (VOIP) or video (for security monitoring or videoconferencing), then deterministic routing becomes even more essential to the assurance of the network.

Boundary Routers

Boundary routers primarily advertise routes that external hosts can use to reach internal ones. However, they should also be part of an organization's security perimeter by filtering external traffic that should never be allowed to enter the internal network. For example, boundary routers may prevent external packets from the Finger service from entering the internal network because that service is used to gather information about hosts.

A key function of boundary routers is the prevention of inbound or outbound IP spoofing attacks. In using a boundary router, spoofed IP addresses would not be routable across the network perimeter. Examples of IP spoofing attacks are:

Non-Blind Spoofing

This type of attack takes place when the attacker is on the same subnet as the victim. The sequence and acknowledgement numbers can be sniffed, eliminating the potential difficulty of calculating them accurately. The biggest threat of spoofing in this instance would be session hijacking. This is accomplished by corrupting the datastream of an established connection, then re-establishing it based on correct sequence and acknowledgement numbers with the attack machine.

Blind Spoofing

This is a more sophisticated attack, because the sequence and acknowledgement numbers are unreachable. Several packets are sent to the target machine in order to sample sequence numbers. While not the case today, machines in the past used basic techniques for generating sequence numbers. It was relatively easy to discover the exact formula by studying packets and TCP sessions. Today, Operating Systems implement random sequence number generation, making it difficult to predict sequence numbers accurately. If, however, the sequence number was compromised, data could be sent to the target.

Man In the Middle Attack

Both types of spoofing are forms of a common security violation known as a man in the middle (MITM) attack. In these attacks, a malicious party intercepts a legitimate communication between two friendly parties. The malicious host then controls the flow of communication and can eliminate or alter the information sent by one of the original participants without the knowledge of either the original sender or the recipient.

Security Perimeter

The security perimeter is the first line of protection between trusted and untrusted networks. In general, it includes a firewall and router that help filter traffic. Security perimeters may also include proxies and devices, such as an intrusion detection system (IDS), to warn of suspicious traffic. The defensive perimeter extends out from these first protective devices, to include proactive defense such as boundary routers, which can provide early warning of upstream attacks and threat activities.

It is important to note that while the security perimeter is the first line of defense, it must not be the only one. If there are not sufficient defenses within the trusted network, then a misconfigured or compromised device could allow an attacker to enter the trusted network.

Network Partitioning

Segmenting networks into domains of trust is an effective way to help enforce security policies. Controlling which traffic is forwarded between segments will go a long way to protecting an organization's critical digital assets from malicious and unintentional harm. See *Figure 2.5*.

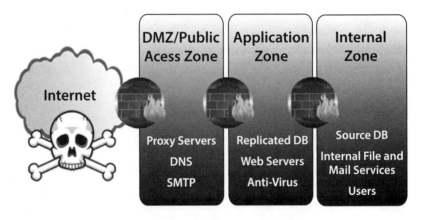

Figure 2.5 - **Network Partitioning**

Dual-Homed Host

A dual-homed host (*Figure 2.6*) has two network interface cards (NICs), each on a separate network. Provided that the host controls or prevents the forwarding of traffic between NICs, it can be an effective measure to isolate a network.

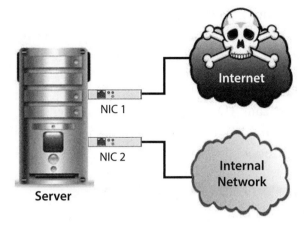

Figure 2.6 - **A Dual-Homed Host has two network interface cards (NICs), each on a separate network**

Bastion Host

Bastion hosts serve as a gateway between a trusted and untrusted network that gives limited, authorized access to untrusted hosts. For instance, a bastion host at an Internet gateway could allow external users to transfer files to it via FTP. This permits files to be exchanged with external hosts without granting them access to the internal network in an uncontrolled manner.

If an organization has a network segment that has sensitive data, it can control access to that network segment by requiring that all access must be from the bastion host. In addition to isolating the network segment, users will have to authenticate to the bastion host, which will help audit access to the sensitive network segment. For example, if a firewall limits access to the sensitive network segment, allowing access to the segment from only the bastion host will eliminate the need for allowing many hosts access to that segment. For instance, terminal servers are a form of bastion host, which allow authenticated users deeper into the network.

A bastion host may also include functionality called a "data diode." In the world of electronics, a diode is a device that only allows current to flow

319

in a single direction. A data diode only allows information to flow in a single direction; for instance it enforces rules that allow information to be read, but nothing may be written (changed or created or moved).

Demilitarized Zone (DMZ)

A demilitarized zone (DMZ), also known as a screened subnet, allows an organization to give external hosts limited access to public resources, such as a company Web site, without granting them access to the internal network. See *Figure 2.7*. Typically, the DMZ is an isolated subnet attached to a firewall (when the firewall has three interfaces—internal, external, and DMZ—this configuration is sometimes called a three-legged firewall). Because external hosts by design have access to the DMZ (albeit controlled by the firewall), organizations should only place in the DMZ hosts and information that are not sensitive.

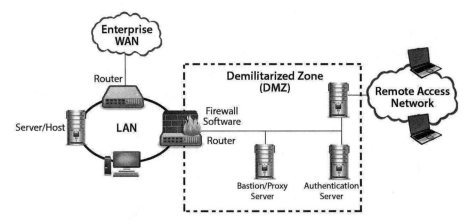

Figure 2.7 - **A Demilitarized Zone (DMZ) allows an organization to give external hosts limited access to public resources, such as a company Web site, without granting them access to the internal network.**

(From Fung, K.T., *Network Security Technologies*, Auerbach Publications, Boston, MA, 2004. With permission.)

Hardware

Modems

Modems (modulator/demodulator) allow users remote access to a network via analog phone lines. Essentially, modems convert digital signals to analog and vice versa. A modem that is connected to the user's computer converts a digital signal to analog to be transmitted over a phone line. On the receiving end, a modem converts the user's analog signal to digital and sends it to the connected device, such as a server. Of course, the process is reversed when the server replies. The server's reply is converted from digital to analog and transmitted over the phone line, and so on.

To address the problem of bandwidth reduction caused by errors in converting analog signals to digital, a new modem standard was created. Because most organizations that support modem access can do so without analog lines, V.90, and later V.92, was created. The new standards assume that a remote user's connection is the only one that is analog. With only one analog connection, the above conversion errors are reduced, which yields greater bandwidth.

Because the upstream transmission (i.e., from the user) is converted from analog to digital, the transfer speed is equivalent to that of a traditional modem. However, the downstream transmission is not converted from analog to digital, and therefore has the potential of speeds approaching the maximum of 56 Kbps. The slower upstream speed is often not noticeable because much less data is transferred in that direction. For instance, consider a Web-browsing session. The upstream data is typically generated by mouse clicks and keystrokes, which does not need a lot of bandwidth. It is the download of information from the Web server that requires and receives that extra bandwidth.

V.92 offers improved performance over V.90, including reducing the time required for connection, the ability not to disconnect when the user's line receives a call-waiting signal, and increased bandwidth in both directions.

Modems allow remote users to access a network from almost any analog phone line worldwide. While this provides easy access to telecommuters, road warriors, etc., it also provides easy access for intruders, who know they can sneak in an organization's backdoor while the security staff protects the Internet gateway. In fact, many organizations have implemented policies that forbid modems on the network for just this reason.

In order to mitigate some of the risks that exist from the legacy analogue work of communications, vendors have developed and taken to market "telephony firewalls" which act not unlike IP firewalls but for analog signals. These firewalls will sit at the demarcation point between the public switched telephone network (PSTN) and the internal organizational network, whether it is an IP phone system or an analog phone systems. Telephony firewalls will monitor both incoming and outgoing analog calls to enforce rule-sets. For instance, modem calls into the company phone exchange are only allowed from certain phone numbers. Or, no modem communications are allowed—only voice and fax communications. In this way, even if rogue or forgotten modems exist on the analog phone network they can be managed.

Concentrators

Concentrators multiplex connected devices into one signal to be transmitted on a network. For instance, a Fiber Distributed Data Interface (FDDI) concentrator multiplexes transmissions from connected devices to a FDDI ring.

Front-End Processors

Input and output involve moving parts, such as fingers typing and disks spinning, which are quite slow compared to the speed of CPUs (central processing units). Servicing input and output, therefore, reduces a computer's throughput. Some hardware architectures employ a hardware front-end processor that sits between the input/output devices and the main computer. By servicing input/output on behalf of the main computer, front-end processors reduce the main computer's overhead.

Multiplexers

A multiplexer overlays multiple signals into one signal for transmission. Using a multiplexer is much more efficient than transmitting the same signals separately. Multiplexers are used in devices from simple hubs (see below) to very sophisticated dense-wave division multiplexers (DWDMs) that combine multioptical signals on one optical fiber.

Hubs and Repeaters

Hubs are used to implement a physical star topology. All of the devices in the star connect to the hub. Essentially, hubs retransmit signals from each port to all other ports. Although hubs can be an economical method to connect devices, there are several important disadvantages:

- All connected devices will receive each other's broadcasts, potentially wasting valuable resources processing irrelevant traffic.
- All devices can read and potentially modify the traffic of other devices.
- If the hub becomes inoperable, then the connected devices will not have access to the network.

As the distance between the sender and receiver increases, the signal's quality can degrade due to attenuation. To allow longer distances while preserving signal quality, repeaters are used to re-amplify signals. For example, a repeater can be used to increase the length of an Ethernet bus to accommodate a physically larger network.

Switches and Bridges

As Local Area Networks (LAN)s grow in number of users, bandwidth utilization, and physical dimensions, they can reach thresholds that prevent the LAN from expanding. Bandwidth is exceeded, cable lengths cannot be increased because of signal attenuation, and the LAN can be too large to manage.

On the other side of the coin, how would one interconnect LANs without reconfiguring the networks so that they can communicate?

One possible solution to both issues is to use bridges. Bridges are layer 2 devices that filter traffic between segments based on Media Access Control (MAC) addresses. In addition, they amplify signals to facilitate physically larger networks. A basic bridge filters out frames that are not destined for another segment. Consider the network shown in *Figure 2.8*.

When a client PC on segment A transmits to a server on segment A, the bridge will read the destination's MAC address and not forward the traffic to segments B and C, relieving them of the burden of traffic that is not

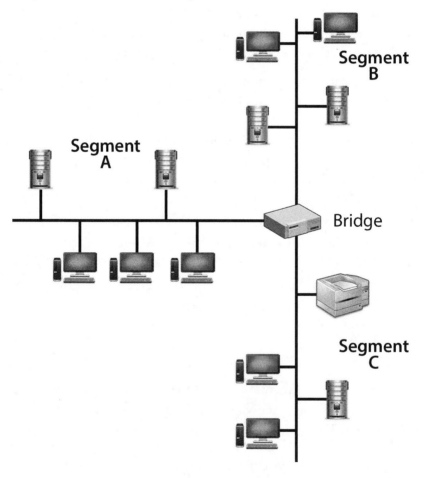

Figure 2.8 - **Network segments connected with a Bridge**

destined to a device on these segments. In this simple example, this might not seem important, but if the segments had hundreds of devices on long network segments, the bridge would greatly reduce unnecessary traffic and allow the network to physically grow without signal attenuation.

Bridges can connect LANs with unlike media types, such as connecting a Unshielded Twisted Pair (UTP) segment with a segment that uses coaxial cable.

Bridges do not reformat frames, such as converting a Token Ring frame to Ethernet. This means that only identical layer 2 architectures can be connected with a simple bridge (e.g., Ethernet to Ethernet, etc.). Network administrators can use encapsulating bridges to connect dissimilar layer 2 architectures, such as Ethernet to Token Ring. These bridges encapsulate incoming frames into frames of the destination's architecture.

Other specialized bridges filter outgoing traffic based on the destination MAC address. In the network in *Figure 2.8*, suppose the bridge were a filtering bridge. When a user on segment A sends traffic to a server on segment B, the bridge will forward the transmission to segment B only, reducing unnecessary traffic on segment C.

Again, in the network in *Figure 2.8*, if a server on segment A sends out a broadcast on the wire, would segments B and C receive the broadcast? Because broadcasts are for all devices, the bridge will forward the broadcast. This is an important point to keep in mind about bridges: they do not filter broadcasts.

Bridges do not prevent an intruder from intercepting traffic on the local segment. A common type of bridge for many organizations is a wireless bridge based upon one of the IEEE 802.11 standards. While wireless bridges offer compelling efficiencies, they can pose devastating security issues to organizations by effectively making all traffic crossing the bridge visible to anyone connected to the LAN. Wireless bridges must absolutely apply link-layer encryption and any other available native security features such as access lists to ensure secure operation.

325

Switches solve the same issues posed at the beginning of this section, except the solutions are more sophisticated and more expensive. Essentially, a basic switch is a multiport device to which LAN hosts connect. Switches forward frames only to the device specified in the frame's destination MAC address, which greatly reduces unnecessary traffic. To illustrate, see *Figure 2.9.*

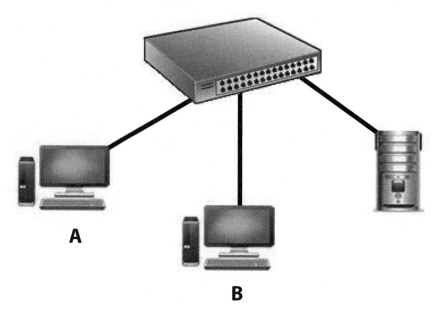

Figure 2.9 - **Simple switched network.**

In this very simple LAN, client A transmits traffic to the server. When the switch receives the traffic, it relays it out of the port to which the server is connected. Client B does not receive any of the traffic. On the other hand, if the switch were a hub, client B would receive the traffic transmitted between client A and the server.

Because client B does not receive the traffic between the other client and server, the likelihood of client B intercepting the traffic is reduced (there are sophisticated attacks that could trick a switch, especially a poorly configured one, into sending traffic to client B).

Switches can perform more sophisticated functions to increase network bandwidth. Due to the increased processing speed of switches, models exist that can make forwarding decisions based on IP address and prioritization of types of network traffic. Like hubs and bridges, switches forward broadcasts.

Hubs are little used in current network architectures because they are both inefficient and insecure. Inefficient because they forward all traffic onto all hosts, which can severely tax networks that host many converged applications like voice, video, and business applications. Insecure because a network managed with hubs allows anyone with physical access to intercept all the traffic. To the extent that hubs are present in a network, they should be considered for replacement as legacy equipment.

Routers

outers forward packets to other networks. They read the destination layer 3 address (e.g., destination IP address) in received packets, and based on the router's view of the network, it determines the next device on the network (the next hop) to send the packet. If the destination address is not on a network that is directly connected to the router, it will send the packet to another router.

Routers can be used to interconnect different technologies. For example, connecting a Token Ring and Ethernet networks to the same router would allow IP Ethernet packets to be forwarded to a Token Ring network.

Transmission Media

Wired

It is tempting to underestimate the importance of cables in a network. Yet, without the cables, there would not be a network, just stand-alone components. One can think of cables as the glue that holds a network together.

Selecting proper cables in a network design is imperative. If inappropriate ones are used, the results can lead to network failures. Cables have to withstand much that threatens the confidentiality, integrity, and availability of the information on the network. Consider the risk of someone tapping into a cable to intercept its signal, or electromagnetic interference from nearby devices, or simply the dangers of a cable breaking. This, considered with the technical parameters of cables, shows that the correct cable must be used for each application.

Here are some parameters that should be considered when selecting cables:

- **Throughput:** The rate that data will be transmitted. Certain cables, such as fiber optic, are designed for hauling an incredible amount of data at once.

- **Distance between devices:** The degradation or loss of a signal (attenuation) in long runs of cable is a perennial problem, especially if the signal is at a high frequency. Also, the time required for a signal to travel (propagation delay) may be a factor. A bus topology that uses collision detection may not operate correctly if the cable is too long.

- **Data sensitivity:** What is the risk of someone intercepting the data in the cables? Fiber optics, for example, makes data interception more difficult than copper cables.

- **Environment:** It is a cable-unfriendly world. Cables may have to be bent when installing which contributes to degradation of conduction and signal distortion. The amount of electromagnetic interference is also a factor because cables in an industrial environment with a lot of interference may have to be shielded. Similarly, cables running through areas with wide temperature fluctuations and especially exposure to ultra-violet (sunlight) will degrade faster and be subject to degrading signals.

Twisted Pair

Pairs of copper wires are twisted together to reduce electromagnetic interference and cross talk. Each wire is insulated with a fire-resistant material, such as Teflon. The twisted pairs are surrounded by an outer jacket that physically protects the wires. The quality of cable, and therefore its appropriate application, is determined by the number of twists per inch, the type of insulation, and conductive material. To help determine which cables are appropriate for an application or environment, cables are assigned into categories (*Table 2.10*).

Category 1	Less than 1 Mbps	Analog voice and basic interface rate (BRI) in Integrated Services Digital Network (ISDN)
Category 2	<4 Mbps	4 Mbps IBM Token Ring LAN
Category 3	16 Mbps	10 Base-T Ethernet
Category 4	20 Mbps	16 Mbps Token Ring
Category 5	100 Mbps	100 Base-TX and Asynchronous Transfer Mode(ATM)
Category 5e	1,000 Mbps	1000 Base-T Ethernet
Category 6	1,000 Mbps	1000 Base-T Ethernet

Table 2.10 - **Cable Categories**

Unshielded Twisted Pair (UTP)

UTP has several drawbacks. Because it does not have shielding like shielded twisted-pair cables, UTP is susceptible to interference from external electrical sources, which could reduce the integrity of the signal. Also, to

329

intercept transmitted data, an intruder can install a tap on the cable or monitor the radiation from the wire. Thus, UTP may not be a good choice when transmitting very sensitive data or when installed in an environment with much electromagnetic interference (EMI) or radio frequency interference (RFI). Despite its drawbacks, UTP is the most common cable type. UTP is inexpensive, can be easily bent during installation, and, in most cases, the risk from the above drawbacks is not enough to justify more expensive cables.

Shielded Twisted Pair (STP)

Shielded twisted pair is similar to UTP. Pairs of insulated twisted copper are enclosed in a protective jacket. However, STP uses an electronically grounded shield to protect the signal. The shield surrounds each of the twisted pairs in the cable, surrounds the bundle of twisted pairs, or both. The shield protects the electronic signals from outside. Although the shielding protects the signal, STP has disadvantages over UTP. STP is more expensive and is bulkier and hard to bend during installation.

Coaxial Cable

Instead of a pair of wires twisted together, coaxial cable (or simply, coax) uses one thick conductor that is surrounded by a grounding braid of wire. A non-conducting layer is placed between the two layers to insulate them. The entire cable is placed within a protective sheath.

The conducting wire is much thicker than the twisted pair, and therefore can support greater bandwidth and longer cable lengths. The superior insulation protects coaxial cable from electronic interference, such as EMI and RFI. Likewise, the shielding makes it harder for an intruder to monitor the signal with antennae or install a tap. Coaxial cable has some disadvantages. The cable is expensive and is difficult to bend during installation. For this reason, coaxial cable is used in specialized applications, such as cable TV.

Patch Panels

Even moderate-size data centers have many interconnected devices, such as switches, routers, servers, workstations, and even test equipment. It is a challenge for network administrators to organize the cables that connect these devices, and to easily modify how they are connected.

As an alternative to directly connecting devices, devices are connected to the patch panel. Then, a network administrator can connect two of these devices by attaching a small cable, called a patch cord, to two jacks in the panel. To change how these devices are connected, network administrators only have to reconnect patch cords. Patch panels and wiring closets must be secured since they offer an excellent place to tap into the network and egress the product. Wiring must be well laid out, neat and records kept in a secure location; otherwise, it is much easier to hide a tap in a mess of wires. Shared wiring closets should be avoided.

Wireless

Direct-Sequence Spread Spectrum (DSSS)

Direct-sequence spread spectrum is a wireless technology that spreads a transmission over a much larger frequency band, and with corresponding smaller amplitude. By spreading the signal over a wider band, the signal is less susceptible to interference at a specific frequency. In other words, the interference affects a smaller percentage of the signal. During transmission, a pseudorandom noise code (PN code) is modulated with the signal. The sender and receiver's PN code generators are synchronized, so that when the signal is received, the PN code can be filtered out.

Frequency-Hopping Spread Spectrum (FHSS)

This wireless technology spreads its signal over rapidly changing frequencies. Each available frequency band is subdivided into sub-frequencies. Signals rapidly change (hop) among these sub-frequencies in an order that is agreed upon between the sender and receiver.

The benefit of FHSS is that the interference at a specific frequency will affect the signal during a short interval. Conversely, FHSS can cause interference with adjacent DSSS systems.

Orthogonal Frequency Division Multiplexing (OFDM)

A signal is subdivided into sub-frequency bands, and each of these bands is manipulated so that they can be broadcasted together without interfering with each other.

Frequency Division Multiple Access (FDMA)

Frequency division multiple access is used in analog cellular only. It subdivides a frequency band into sub-bands and assigns an analog conversation to each sub-band. FDMA was the original "cellular" phone technology and has been de-commissioned in many locations in favor of GSM or CDMA-based technologies.

Time Division Multiple Access (TDMA)

Time division multiple access multiplexes several digital calls (voice or data) at each sub-band by devoting a small time slice in a round-robin to each call in the band. Two sub-bands are required for each call: one in each direction between sender and receiver.

Mobile Cellular Telephony

Code Division Multiple Access (CDMA), CDMA 2000, Wideband CDMA

CDMA is a spread-spectrum wireless technology that is mostly used for cellular technology. Like DSSS, it spreads each call over a large frequency band and is tagged with a pseudorandom noise code to differentiate between the calls. Qualcomm is a driver of this technology and is able to multiplex approximately three times as many calls as other technologies.

CDMA 2000 offers an improved capability of ten times the number of calls and transmission rates of 153.6 Mbps.

Wideband CDMA (W-CDMA) uses a wider band than CDMA, which increases the throughput of the carrier. W-CDMA is sometimes considered a form of third-generation (3G) mobile telephony and lumped into a broader specification known as UMTS—Universal Mobile Telephony Service. UMTS has been deployed with varying degrees of success in Europe and Asia, but has not seen consumer deployment in North American.

Global Service for Mobile Communications (GSM)

GSM is the most popular cellular technology in the world. A frequency band is subdivided in simplex channels; each can support as many as eight callers using time division multiplexing.

Mobile subscribers are associated and identify themselves with their so-called International Mobile Subscriber Identifier (IMSI), a (usually) 15-digit number coded into the user's Subscriber Identity Module (SIM) card and containing information about home country and network.

Because the user (or mobile phone) authenticates with the network, but not the network with the mobile phone, a man-in-the-middle attack can be performed using a device called an IMSI catcher, which the attacker can use to masquerade as a base station. Such devices are regularly used by law enforcement agencies.

The IMSI catcher can use a control command in GSM to deactivate encryption for a call from the targeted device. (Currently, commercially available mobile phones do not display whether encryption is activated for a connection.) Thus, mobile phone calls can be intercepted with relatively low effort for a well-resourced entity. Similarly, GSM phones can be easily cloned for the purposes of either fraud or call interception with tools and instruction available over the Internet.

Wireless Local Area Networks

Wireless networks allow users to be mobile while remaining connected to a LAN (*Figure 2.10*). Unfortunately, this allows unauthorized users greater

333

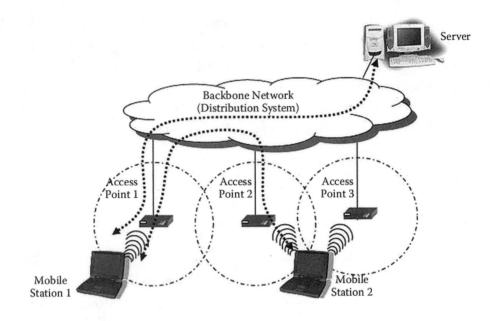

Figure 2.10 - **IEEE 802.11 Structured Network Architecture**

(From Zahariadis, T., and Douligeris, C., *WLAN technologies, in Handbook of Wireless Local Area Networks: Applications, Technology, Security, and Standards,* Mohammad Ilyas and Syed Ahson, Eds., Auerbach Publications, Boca Raton, FL, 2005. With permission.)

access to the LAN as well. In fact, many wireless LANs can be accessed off of the organization's property by anyone with a wireless card in a laptop, which effectively extends the LAN into areas where there are no physical controls.

Authentication

It is impractical for an organization to hide its access point's signal from unauthorized users. Instead, authentication should be the first real line of defense. Unfortunately, many wireless authentication mechanisms are weak because they do not provide sufficient assurance that the client and access point are who they claim to be.

Open System Authentication

Open system authentication is the most basic form of wireless authentication. The wireless client is permitted to join the network if its

Service Set Identifier (SSID) matches that of the wireless network. The wireless client sends a frame containing its SSID to the access point. Upon successful authentication (matching SSIDs), the client is associated with the wireless LAN.

Shared-Key Authentication

In shared-key authentication, Wired Equivalent Privacy (WEP) is used to encrypt a shared secret between the access point and the wireless client. After the client identifies its MAC address to the access point, the access point responds with a frame containing a randomly generated challenge using the WEP key stream generator. The client responds with the challenge encrypted with WEP. If the access point decrypts the challenge and it is the same as the one that it sent to the client, the client is authenticated.

There is a serious flaw with shared-key authentication. Because an "exclusive or" (XOR) is used in the authentication, an attacker can intercept the challenge and response and recover the key stream. Because of this, shared-key authentication is not considered effective.

MAC Address Tables

Authenticating based on MAC address is not very effective. Because it is very easy to spoof a MAC address, there is little assurance that the client is an authorized workstation, instead of an intruder who is advertising a bogus MAC address.

Service Set Identifier (SSID) Broadcasting

The service set identifier is defined in IEEE 802.11 as a name for the wireless LAN, not as an authentication mechanism. Specifying the SSID of the wireless LAN to which you want to connect ensures that you connect to the correct one when several are in the same vicinity. That is the primary reason not to use the default SSID. If neighboring LANs use access points from the same manufacturer and both use the default SSID, then users could easily attempt to connect to the wrong wireless LAN.

Wireless client cards can broadcast a probe to ask wireless LANs that receive the probe to respond with the SSID they are supporting. Network administrators often configure wireless LANs to ignore these requests unless their specific SSID has been named in the probe request. Similarly, wireless LANs will broadcast beacons that advertise the SSID of the network so clients know when they are within range. The downside of beaconing is that you also make your wireless network a target for attackers and freeloaders looking for a free connection.

Disabling beaconing is useful, if rudimentary, safeguard for wireless LANs, but a patient attacker can still observe the SSID as soon as another client who knows the SSID comes into range and probes the wireless network.

SSID Naming Conventions

Although SSIDs are not for authentication, an organization should not advertise that it is the owner of the wireless LAN. In general, organizations should not use SSIDs that can be easily identified with them, such as company name, product, mascot, etc.

Placement and Configuration of Access Points

Wireless access points should be placed and their power levels set to make it more difficult for unauthorized clients to receive a signal; e.g., do not place an access point by a window. However, organizations should not count on hiding their access point's signal, especially from an intruder with a unidirectional antenna. Besides being unrealistic, that would be an example of security by obscurity—a fundamental fallacy.

Access point placement should focus on ensuring that authorized users can receive a strong signal from an access point. Keep access points away from electronically noisy machines that could interfere with an access point's transmission. Many microwaves interfere with access points.

Encryption

Wired Equivalent Privacy (WEP)

Wired equivalent privacy uses a shared secret between the client and access point. Before each packet is transmitted, a CRC-32 checksum is appended to it and both are encrypted using RC4 with the shared secret and initialization vector. The encrypted packet with the initialization vector is transmitted. The recipient reverses the process. If the client has the same shared secret, then the packet will be decrypted.

Due to flaws in the RC4 implementation in WEP, and the reuse of initialization vector values, WEP transmissions can be decrypted by an attacker in a very short time.

WiFi Protected Access (WPA)

After it was announced that WEP could not effectively protect traffic from eavesdropping, the WiFi Alliance had to replace WEP, but IEEE 802.11i was not ready. As a stopgap measure, it released WPA. This system uses an improved implementation of RC4 with 128-bit keys. The initialization vector was expanded from 24 to 48 bits, which supports many more shared secrets. To make an intruder's task of cracking the encryption of intercepted traffic much more difficult, WPA uses the Temporal Key Integrity Protocol (TKIP). Instead of using the same key for the entire session, TKIP uses a different key for each packet. WEP's CRC-32 checksum was replaced with a message integrity check, dubbed Michael. Michael protects the packet's header and data and uses a frame counter to thwart replay attacks.

Another advantage of WPA is that both the client and network authenticate each other (mutual authentication). In addition to the network verifying that the client is authorized for network access, the client can be assured that he or she is not communicating with an imposter, posing as a network.

When IEEE 802.11i was completed, WPA2 was certified. Although WPA did not have any significant security flaws, RC4 was replaced by the

Advanced Encryption Standard (AES), a stronger encryption algorithm. Also, TKIP and Michael were replaced by the Counter-Mode/CBC-Mac Protocol (CCMP), which manages encryption keys and message integrity.

WPA2 supports IEEE 802.1X authentication, which is based on the Extensible Authentication Protocol (EAP) framework. The framework allows the authenticating partners to negotiate the authentication method during the authentication phase. EAP authentication methods include the following:

- *EAP-TLS (EAP, Transport Layer Security):* Both the client and authentication server mutually authenticate over a TLS session with digital certificates. In addition to ensuring that the client is authorized to access the network, the client can be confident that he or she is communicating with the desired network, not an imposter. This method is the most secure because an attacker must steal both a digital certificate and its password. However, organizations that have many clients may find there is too much overhead in administering the client certificates for EAP-TLS to be feasible.

- *EAP-TTLS (EAP, tunneled TLS):* Like EAP-TLS, digital certificates are used. However, to establish an encrypted tunnel, the authentication server only presents a certificate to the client. Once the tunnel is established, the client authenticates to the authentication server using an EAP or legacy mechanism that is easier to administer than client-side digital certificates. The lack of client-side certificates makes EAP-TTLS easier to administer than EAP-TLS, but the less robust client authentication makes EAP-TTLS less secure than EAP-TLS. Of course, the extent of how much less secure depends on the strength of the client authentication.

- *EAP-PEAP (EAP, protected EAP):* EAP-PEAP is very similar to EAP-TLS. To establish an encrypted tunnel, the authentication server authenticates to the client with a digital certificate, and the client employs a non-digital certificate mechanism to authenticate to the server. However, EAP-PEAP requires that the client authenticates with an EAP method. As with EAP-TTLS, EAP-PEAP is easier to administer than EAP-TLS, but the lack of a client-side certificate makes this method less secure than EAP-TLS.

During 802.1X authentication, a client (called a supplicant) contacts an authenticator (an access point, for wireless authentication). The authenticator blocks all traffic from the client to the network, except for what is required for authentication. The authenticator sends an EAP challenge to the client and forwards the challenge and client's EAP response to an authentication server on the wired network. The authentication server, a Remote Authentication Dial In User Services (RADIUS) server, establishes the appropriate authentication method and sends the corresponding challenge to the client via the access point. The client sends the response back to the authentication server via the access point. If the authentication is successful, a session key is generated and the authenticator removes the network traffic restriction.

Instead of EAP, homes or organizations without RADIUS can use preshared 32-byte keys between the access point and clients. In low-risk environments, the use of preshared keys is cost-effective. However, due to the relatively weak authentication and lack of accountability (all clients use the same key), businesses should avoid this option, if feasible.

WiFi Protected Access (WPA2)

WPA2, created by the IEEE 802.11i working group, addresses the many problems with wireless security. It supersedes the weak WEP and the stopgap WPA. It uses 802.1x access control to start an EAP authentication method and Counter-Mode/CBC-Mac Protocol (CCMP) for encryption.

WPA2 implements the final IEEE 802.11i amendment to the 802.11 standard (as opposed to WPA, which only implements a subset of IEEE 802.11i).

WiFi Variants

WiFi comes in number of different flavors, and most network managers will probably be in a position of supporting at least a couple.

IEEE 802.11b

This amendment to IEEE 802.11 was ratified in 1999. It continued the usage of CSMA/CA and direct-sequence spread spectrum (DSSS). The bandwidth was increased to 5.5 and 11 Mbps, and continued the support of the original 1- and 2-Mbps rates. The slower rates can be used when signal quality is poor. Use of DSSS ensured that transmissions were resilient to interference due to the number of chips used per broadcasted bit. There are 14 transmission channels in the 2.4-GHz band, each 5 MHz wide. Channel 14 is used in Japan only.

IEEE 802.11b was the first ratified version of WiFi and by virtue of a large head start has a large deployed base. IEEE 802.11b is definitely "legacy" at this time but the existing install base is such that it will be around for years to come. This presents a security "caution" to any manager that must deal with IEEE 802.11b because much of this equipment was built and deployed with weak security capabilities such as WEP and WPA and may not have been patched. Similarly, some older 802.11 clients (or bridges) might not support the security patches and will need to be replaced to support adequate security.

IEEE 802.11a

IEEE 802.11a was ratified in 1999. Because the 2.4 GHz band specified in IEEE 802.11b was already in heavy use by other applications from microwave ovens to medical equipment, 802.11a was specified for the 5-GHz range. The higher frequency has the disadvantage that more access points are required because attenuation from objects like walls or furniture is greater and therefore the access point and client must be nearer to each other. This amendment employs orthogonal frequency division multiplexing (OFDM) using 20-MHz channels subdivided into

52 subcarriers (48 are used for data). The maximum transmission speed is 52 Mbps. IEEE 802.11a is not compatible with IEEE 802.11b.

IEEE 802.11g

This standard, which was ratified in 2003, combines the frequency band of 802.11b (2.4 GHz) with the increased speed of 802.11a (52 Mbps). IEEE 802.11g is fully compatible with IEEE 802.11b. Cards are available to compensate for the incompatibility of some of the standards. Both IEEE 802.11g and IEEE 802.11b are very popular.

Bluetooth

Bluetooth is a short-range, low-power wireless specification (IEEE 802.15.1) intended to replace short cables and wires connecting devices together for ad hoc functions; for instance, the hand-free set for a mobile phone or a modem wire from phone to computer. Bluetooth devices are designed to communicate over a distance of 10 m (30 ft), but longer ranges are possible. Class 1 Bluetooth devices contain a 100-mW transmitter and are known to bridge distances of up to 1 km. Devices transmit at the 2.4-GHz band using frequency-hopping spread spectrum (FHSS).

Bluetooth's security features are limited. Services related to session encryption and authentication of associating devices are included within the specification, but may be set by manufacturer default to "open." To make matters worse, many owners of Bluetooth devices are not aware of the technology's vulnerabilities. Some of the vulnerabilities include:

- ■ *Blue Jacking:* Allows an anonymous message to be displayed on the victim's device.
- ■ *Buffer Overflow:* An attacker can remotely exploit bugs in software on Bluetooth-enabled devices.
- ■ *Blue Bug Attack:* An attacker can use the AT commands on a victim's cell phone to initiate calls, send SMS messages, etc.

Address Resolution Protocol (ARP)

Given a layer 3 IP address of a device, ARP determines the device's layer 2 MAC address. ARP tracks IP addresses and their corresponding MAC addresses in a dynamic table called ARP cache. To determine a device's address, ARP first looks in its cache to see if the MAC address is already known. If it is not, ARP sends out a broadcast asking all devices to return the MAC address, if they know it. The returned MAC address is added to the cache.

Because ARP does not require authentication, an attacker could place bogus entries in the ARP cache to carry out other attacks, such as a man-in-the-middle. Adding bogus entries in ARP cache is called ARP poisoning.

Point-to-Point Protocol (PPP)

PPP is used to connect a device to a network over a serial line to a network. Generally, this protocol is used to connect a remote workstation over a phone line. For example, Internet Service Providers (ISPs) use Point to Point Protocol (PPP) to allow dial-up users access to the Internet. PPP supports authentication, including the following protocols:

Password Authentication Protocol (PAP) - A simple insecure protocol that transmits in plaintext.

Challenge Handshake Authentication Protocol (CHAP) - A protocol that uses a three-way handshake. The server sends the client a challenge, which includes a random value (a nonce) to thwart replay attacks. The client responds with a MD5 hash of the nonce and the password. The authentication is successful if the client's response is the one that the server expected.

Extensible Authentication Protocol (EAP) - An authentication framework whereby the authentication partners establish the authentication method during the authentication phase. For details, see the section on WPA in Chapter 4.

PPP replaced the Serial Line Internet Protocol (SLIP) in many uses (SLIP is detailed in RFC 1055).

Broadband Wireless

A customer cannot subscribe to Digital Subscriber Line (DSL) service (DSL was originally referred to as Digital Subscriber Loop Service) if his or her premises are too far from the Central Office (CO). If using a cable modem or satellite is not an option, then these users cannot enjoy high-speed Internet access. To solve this and other problems, the IEEE has defined the IEEE 802.16 standard, which has been adopted as WiMAX commercially. WiMAX is currently considered a "fixed mobile" wireless solution, meaning that the receiving units (client devices) are highly portable but not while in use; i.e., they do not roam from base station to base station like a cell phone. Full mobility for WiMAX is currently being tested. WiMAX offers speeds in the 2Mbps to 10Mbps range.

The standard covers technology that allows users to connect to wireless base stations (access points) miles from where they are located and obtain access to a metropolitan area network (MAN). Base stations can be easily deployed on top of a building, which ensures complete coverage.

The IEEE amended the standard with IEEE 802.16a, which addresses issues such as improved access when a base station and user are not in line of site.

The new technology promises many features. The channel sizes are flexible, which allows providers to comply with local broadcast regulations. Broadband wireless will support protocols and services such as Asynchronous Transfer Mode (ATM), Multiprotocol Layer Switching (MPLS), and higher level applications like Internet, voice, and low-definition video. Finally, security is part of the WiMAX standard, using AES to protect the confidentiality of wireless data with authentication options which include the Extensible Authentication Protocol (EAP).

WiMAX allows a user to directly connect to a Metropolitan Area Network (MAN), which could finally resolve the problem of the last mile, not by replacing the CAT-3 cables of the local loop, but by not using cables at all. Wireless local loop removes two major obstacles:

The bandwidth limitation of a CAT-3 cable, designed for analog voice, is replaced by high-speed wireless.

The limit on the length of the CAT-3 cable, especially for provisioning DSL, is replaced with the ability to connect to a wireless base station from many miles away.

Wireless local loops will also allow underdeveloped and rural areas to use broadband without the limitations of an analog voice telephone system.

Wireless Optics

As an alternative to running fiber cables between buildings that are in line of sight, an organization can use infrared light or lasers to transmit data. In principle, two laser transceivers are aimed at each other to communicate at speeds comparable to fiber-optic systems, which also utilize lasers. Wireless optics has advantages over microwave because wireless optics transmissions are harder to intercept, and a license is not required for deployment.

Unfortunately, wireless optics can be unreliable during inclement weather, especially heavy fog, which can outweigh its benefits until the technology is improved.

Fiber

Fiber Optics

Fiber optics takes a very different approach to cabling. Instead of using a metal conductor to transmit and receive electrical signals, fiber optics uses glass or plastic to transmit light. Fiber optics consists of three components: a light source, the optical cable, and a light detector.

The light source transmits the optical signal on the fiber cable. There are two types of light sources:

- *Light-Emitting Diodes (LEDs):* Sophisticated cousins to the ubiquitous LEDs found in consumer electronics. LEDs are less expensive than diode lasers, but offer less bandwidth over a shorter distance. Typically LEDs are used in LANs.

- *Diode Lasers:* A much more expensive alternative, especially because they require more expensive fiber cables and light detectors. This optical source is used by carriers on their backbone.

Modern fiber optics systems may also employ wavelength division multiplexing (WDM) to increase the capacity of the network connects. WDM actually uses different light frequencies on the same fiber to generate unique light streams in a single fiber. Each of these streams can carry distinct network information and each has unique capacity unrelated to one another because, for all intents and purposes, they are invisible to each other. Using WDM, the capacity of fiber optic networks can be increased dramatically, easily up to 32 times!

Optical fiber is made from a very narrow glass or plastic fiber that is surrounded by a cladding that is designed to reflect transmitted light back into the fiber. The cladding in turn is covered by a protective sheath. There are two types of optical fiber:

- *Multimode Fiber:* Light is transmitted in slightly different modes (paths) in fibers that are about 50 to 100 microns in diameter. Due to the relatively large diameter, the light disperses too much when using medium and long cable lengths.

- *Single-Mode Fiber:* Single-mode fiber is about 10 microns in diameter. As the name implies, the transmitted light will take a direct path down the center of the fiber. This allows for greater bandwidth and longer cable lengths. Single-mode fiber is suitable for carrier backbones.

Light detectors convert transmitted optical signals back into electrical energy.

Fiber optics has clear advantages over copper cables. Fiber optics can support 40 gigabits or more per second, which far exceeds coaxial cable or twisted-pair and longer cable distances without amplification. From a security perspective, fiber optics' immunity to electromagnetic interference (EMI) and radio frequency interference (RFI) is important. Because fiber optics emit extremely small amounts of energy from the cable, data cannot be as easily intercepted as information is transported through electric current in wires.

Network Access Control Devices

Firewalls

Firewalls are devices that enforce administrative security policies by filtering incoming traffic based on a set of rules. Often firewalls are thought of as protectors of an Internet gateway only. While a firewall should always be placed at Internet gateways, there are also internal network considerations and conditions where a firewall would be employed, such as network zoning. Additionally, firewalls are also these days more threat-management appliances with a variety of other security services embedded, such as proxy services and Intrusion Prevention Services (IPS), which seek to monitor and alert proactively at the network perimeter.

Firewalls should be placed between entities that have different trust domains. For instance, if an engineering department LAN segment is on the same network as general LAN users, there would be two trust domains: general LAN users and engineers with the organization's intellectual property. Installing a firewall where the two trust domains meet would help protect the intellectual property from the general LAN user population, as shown in *Figure 2.11*.

Firewalls will not be effective right out of the box. Firewall rules must be defined correctly and not inadvertently grant unauthorized access. Like all hosts on a network, administrators must install patches to the firewall and disable all unnecessary services. Also, firewalls offer limited protection against vulnerabilities caused by applications flaws in server software on other hosts. For example, a firewall will not prevent an attacker from manipulating a database to disclose confidential information.

Firewalls can be fiendishly complex to administer and manage. The requirement to patch them frequently, monitor their logs and alter their rules to accommodate internal business requirements can overwhelm managers and technical staff alike. For this reason, outsourcing of the complete

347

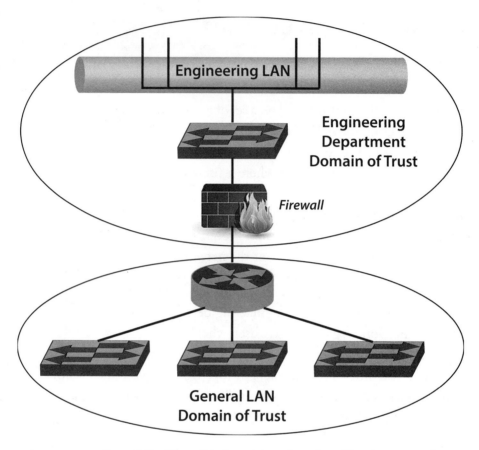

Figure 2.11 - **Firewall between two domains of trust.**

management and maintenance of firewalls has become a significant and well established industry, with organizations from governments to banks to donut shops outsourcing this critical but complex and mundane security task.

Filtering

As mentioned previously, firewalls filter traffic based on a rule set. Each rule instructs the firewall to block or forward a packet based on one or more conditions. For each incoming packet, the firewall will look through its rule set for a rule whose conditions apply to that packet, and block or forward the packet as specified in that rule. Below are two important conditions used to determine if a packet should be filtered.

By Address

Firewalls will often use the packet's source or destination address, or both, to determine if the packet should be filtered. For example, in the case shown in *Figure 2.11*, to grant a trusted user access to the engineering LAN segment, a rule can be defined to forward a packet whose source address is from a trusted user's host on the general LAN.

By Service

Packets can also be filtered by service. The firewall inspects the service the packet is using (if the packet is part of the TCP or UDP, the service is the destination port number) to determine if the packet should be filtered. For example, firewalls will often have a rule to filter the Finger service to prevent an attacker from using it to gather information about a host.

Address and service are often combined in rules. If the engineering department wanted to grant anyone on the LAN access to its Web server, a rule could be defined to forward packets whose destination address is the Web server's and the service is HTTP (TCP port 80).

Network Address Translation (NAT)

Firewalls can change the source address of each outgoing (from trusted to untrusted network) packet to a different address. This has several applications, most notably to allow hosts with RFC 1918 addresses access to the Internet by changing their non-routable address to one that is routable on the Internet. A non-routable address is one that will not be forwarded by an Internet router and therefore remote attacks using non-routable internal addresses cannot be launched over the open Internet.

Anonymity is another reason to use NAT. Many organizations do not want to advertise their IP addresses to an untrusted host, and thus unnecessarily give information about the network. They would rather hide the entire network behind translated addresses. NAT also greatly extends the capabilities of organizations to continue using IPv4 address spaces.

Port Address Translation (PAT)

An extension to NAT is to translate all addresses to one routable IP address and translate the source port number in the packet to a unique value. The port translation allows the firewall to keep track of multiple sessions that are using PAT.

Static Packet Filtering

When a firewall uses static packet filtering, it examines each packet without regard to the packet's context in a session. Packets are examined against static criteria, for example, blocking all packets with a port number of 79 (finger). Because of its simplicity, static packet filtering requires very little overhead, but has a significant disadvantage. Static rules cannot be temporarily changed by the firewall to accommodate legitimate traffic. If a protocol requires a port to be temporarily opened, administrators have to choose between permanently opening the port and disallowing the protocol.

Stateful Inspection or Dynamic Packet Filtering

Stateful inspection examines each packet in the context of a session, which allows it to make dynamic adjustments to the rules to accommodate legitimate traffic and block malicious traffic that would appear benign to a static filter. Consider FTP. A user connects to an FTP server on TCP port 21 and then tells the FTP server on which port to transfer files. The port can be any TCP port above 1023. So, if the FTP client tells the server to transfer files on TCP port 1067, the server will attempt to open a connection to the client on that port. A stateful inspection firewall would watch the interaction between the two hosts, and even though the required connection is not permitted in the rule set, it would allow the connection to occur because it is part of FTP.

Static packet filtering, in contrast, would block the FTP server's attempt to connect to the client on TCP port 1067 unless a static rule was already in place. In fact, because the client could instruct the FTP server to transfer files on any port above 1023, a static rule would have to be in place to permit access to over 65,536 ports (see section on Transmission Control Protocol).

Proxies

A proxy firewall mediates communications between untrusted end-points (servers/hosts/clients) and trusted end-points (servers/hosts/clients). From an internal perspective, a proxy may forward traffic from known, internal client machines to untrusted hosts on the Internet, creating the illusion to the untrusted host that the traffic originated from the proxy firewall, thus hiding the trusted internal client from potential attackers. A typical interaction with a server through a proxy is shown in *Figure 2.12*.

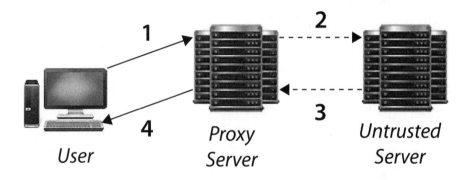

1. User's request goes to the proxy server.
2. Proxy server forwards the request to the untrusted host. To the untrusted host it will appear as if the request originated from the proxy server.
3. The untrusted host responds to the proxy server.
4. The proxy server forwards the response to the user.

Figure 2.12 - **Accessing a server through a proxy.**

To the user, it appears that he or she is communicating directly with the untrusted server. Proxy servers are often placed at Internet gateways to hide the internal network behind one IP address and to prevent direct communication between internal and external hosts.

Circuit-Level Proxy

A circuit-level proxy creates a conduit through which a trusted host can communicate with an untrusted one. This type of proxy does not inspect any of the traffic that it forwards, which adds very little overhead to the communication between the user and untrusted server. The lack of application awareness also allows circuit-level proxies to forward any TCP and UDP port. The disadvantage is that traffic will not be analyzed for malicious content.

Application-Level Proxy

An application-level proxy relays the traffic from a trusted end-point running a specific application to an untrusted end-point. The most significant advantage of application-level proxies is that they analyze the traffic that they forward for protocol manipulation and various sorts of common attacks such as buffer overflows. Application-level proxies add overhead to using the application because they scrutinize the traffic they forward.

Web proxy servers are a very popular example of application-level proxies. Many organizations place one at their Internet gateway and configure their users' Web browsers to use the Web proxy whenever they browse an external Web server (other controls are implemented to prevent users from bypassing the proxy server). The proxies typically include required user authentication, inspection of URLs to ensure that users do not browse inappropriate sites, logging, and caching of popular Web pages. In fact, Web proxies for internal users are one of the prime manners in which acceptable usage policies can be enforced, because external sites can be blacklisted by administrators and logs of user traffic kept for later analysis if required for evidentiary purposes.

Personal Firewalls

The firewalls that we have discussed so far protect a network or a segment of one. But what protects users from hosts that are behind a firewall? For example, the firewall in Figure 2.11 does not protect a user on the engineering LAN segment from someone on the same segment.

Following the principle of security in depth, personal firewalls are installed on workstations, which protect the user from all hosts on the network. It is critical for home users with DSL or cable modem access to the Internet to have a personal firewall installed on every PC, especially if they do not have a firewall protecting their network.

Because personal firewalls are employed by general users, they are easy to install and configure. Firewall rules are created with a nontechnical interface that does not require expertise in networking or security. Although they do not provide the flexibility of the best enterprise firewalls, they provide all of the essential functions of a firewall, such as stateful inspection, logging.

End-Point Security

The end-points of a network are often the most attractive targets as the rest of the network matures in defensive capabilities. Vulnerable workstations, printers and other end-points represent launching pads for numerous new attacks across the network. Workstations should be hardened and users should user limited accounts whenever possible in accordance with the concept of "least privilege." Workstations should minimally have:

- Up to date antivirus and antimalware software
- A configured and operational host-based firewall
- A hardened configuration with unneeded services disabled
- A patched and maintained operating system

While workstations are clearly the end point most will associate with end point attacks the landscape is changing. Mobile devices such as smart phones, tablets and personal devices are beginning to reflect more and more of the average organization's endpoints. With the additional diversity of devices there becomes a requirement to also increase the diversity and agility of an organization's endpoint defenses. For mobile devices such as smart phones and tablets organizations should consider:

- Encryption for the whole device or if not possible encryption for sensitive information on the device
- Remote management capabilities including:
  - Remote wipe
  - Remote geolocate
  - Remote update
  - Remote operation
- User policies and agreements which ensure an organization can manage the device

Secure Communication Channels

VPN

Virtual Private Network (VPN)

A VPN (*Figure 2.13*) is an encrypted tunnel between two hosts that allows them to securely communicate over an untrusted network; e.g., the Internet. Remote users employ VPNs to access their organization's network, and depending on the VPN's implementation, they may have most of the same resources available to them as if they were physically at the office. As an alternative to expensive dedicated point-to-point connections, organizations use gateway-to-gateway VPNs to securely transmit information over the Internet between sites or even with business partners.

IPSec Authentication and Confidentiality for VPNs

IP Security (IPSec) is a suite of protocols for communicating securely with IP by providing mechanisms for authenticating and encryption. Implementation of IPSec is mandatory in IPv6, and many organizations are using it over IPv4. Further, IPSec can be implemented in two modes, one that is appropriate for end-to-end protection and one that safeguards traffic between networks.

Standard IPSec only authenticates hosts with each other. If an organization requires users to authenticate, they must employ a nonstandard proprietary IPSec implementation, or use IPSec over L2TP (Layer 2 Tunneling Protocol). The latter approach uses L2TP to authenticate the users and encapsulate IPSec packets within L2TP.

Because IPSec interprets the change of IP address within packet headers as an attack, NAT does not work well with IPSec. To resolve the incompatibility of the two protocols, NAT-Transversal (a.k.a. NAT-T) encapsulates IPSec within UDP port 4500 (see RFC 3948 for details).

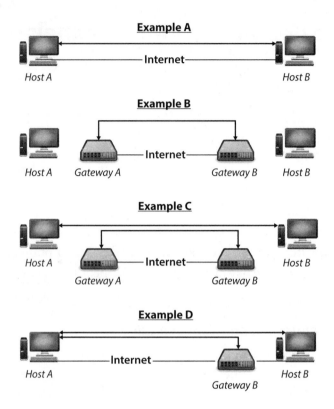

Figure 2.13 - **VPN Types**

- In **Example A**, two hosts establish secure peer communications over the Internet

- **Example B** illustrates a typical gateway-to-gateway VPN with the VPN terminating at the gateways to provide connectivity for internal hosts.

- **Example C** combines Examples A and B to allow secure communications from host to host in an existing gateway-to-gateway VPN.

- **Example D** details the situation when a remote host connects to an ISP, receives an IP address, and then establishes a VPN with the destination network's gateway. A tunnel is established to the gateway, and then a tunnel- or transport-mode communication is established to the internal system. In this example, it is necessary for the remote system to apply the transport header prior to the tunnel header. Also, it will be necessary for the gateway to allow IPSec connectivity and key management protocols from the Internet to the internal system.

(From Tiller, J.S., IPSec virtual private networks, *Information Security Management Handbook*, 6th edn., Tipton H.F., and Krause, M. Eds., Auerbach Publications, Boca Raton, FL, 2005. With permission.)

Authentication Header (AH)

he authentication header is used to prove the identity of the sender and ensure that the transmitted data has not been tampered with. Before each packet (headers + data) is transmitted, a hash value of the packet's contents (except for the fields that are expected to change when the packet is routed) based on a shared secret is inserted in the last field of the AH. The endpoints negotiate which hashing algorithm to use and the shared secret when they establish their security association. To help thwart replay attacks (when a legitimate session is retransmitted to gain unauthorized access), each packet that is transmitted during a security association has a sequence number, which is stored in the AH. In transport mode, the AH is shimmed between the packet's IP and TCP header. The AH helps ensure integrity, not confidentiality. Encryption is implemented with the encapsulating security payload.

Encapsulating Security Payload (ESP)

The encapsulating security payload encrypts IP packets and ensures their integrity. Both services are optional; however, at least one must be used. ESP contains four sections:

- **ESP header:** Contains information showing which security association to use and the packet sequence number. Like the AH, the ESP sequences every packet to thwart replay attacks.

- **ESP payload:** The payload contains the encrypted part of the packet. If the encryption algorithm requires an initialization vector (IV), it is included with the payload. The endpoints negotiate which encryption to use when the security association is established. Because packets must be encrypted with as little overhead as possible, ESP typically uses a symmetric encryption algorithm.

- **ESP trailer:** May include padding (filler bytes) if required by the encryption algorithm or to align fields.

■ ***Authentication:*** If authentication is used, this field contains the integrity check value (hash) of the ESP packet. As with the AH, the authentication algorithm is negotiated when the endpoints establish their security association.

Security Associations

A security association (SA) defines the mechanisms that an endpoint will use to communicate with its partner. All SAs cover transmissions in one direction only. A second SA must be defined for two-way communication. Mechanisms that are defined in the SA include the encryption and authentication algorithms, and whether to use the AH or ESP protocol.

Deferring the mechanisms to the SA, as opposed to specifying them in the protocol, allows the communicating partners to use the appropriate mechanisms based on risk.

Transport Mode and Tunnel Mode

Endpoints communicate with IPSec using either transport or tunnel mode. In transport mode, the IP payload is protected. This mode is mostly used for end-to-end protection, for example, between client and server. In tunnel mode, the IP payload and its IP header are protected. The entire protected IP packet becomes a payload of a new IP packet and header. Tunnel mode is often used between networks, such as with firewall-to-firewall VPNs.

Internet Key Exchange (IKE)

Internet key exchange allows communicating partners to prove their identity to each other and establish a secure communication channel, and is applied as an authentication component of IPSec. IKE uses two phases:

Phase 1: In this phase, the partners authenticate with each other, using one of the following:

■ ***Shared Secret:*** A key that is exchanged by humans via telephone, fax, encrypted e-mail, etc.

- *Public Key Encryption:* Digital certificates are exchanged.

- *Revised mode of Public Key Encryption:* To reduce the overhead of public key encryption, a nonce (a Cryptographic function that refers to a number or bit string used only once, in security engineering) is encrypted with the communicating partner's public key, and the peer's identity is encrypted with symmetric encryption using the nonce as the key.

Next, IKE establishes a temporary security association and secure tunnel to protect the rest of the key exchange.

Phase 2: The peers' security associations are established, using the secure tunnel and temporary SA created at the end of phase 1.

High Assurance Internet Protocol Encryptor (HAIPE)

Based on IPSec, HAIPE possess additional restrictions and enhancements; for instance, the ability to encrypt multicast data using high-assurance hardware encryption which requires that the same key be manually loaded on all communicating devices. HAIPE is an extension of IPSec that would be used for highly-secure communications such as those employed by military applications.

Tunneling

Point-to-Point Tunneling Protocol (PPTP)

Point-to-Point Tunneling Protocol (PPTP) is a VPN protocol that runs over other protocols. PPTP relies on generic routing encapsulation (GRE) to build the tunnel between the endpoints. After the user authenticates, typically with Microsoft Challenge Handshake Authentication Protocol version 2 (MSCHAPv2), a Point-to-Point Protocol (PPP) session creates a tunnel using GRE.

PPTP came under much fire in the 1990s. Cryptographers announced weaknesses in the protocol, including flaws with MSCHAPv1 (the authentication protocol) and the encryption implementation, and the use of user passwords as keys. Microsoft released PPTPv2, which addressed many of its predecessor's weaknesses, such as using an improved version of MSCHAP for authentication, but PPTPv2 is still vulnerable to offline password-guessing attacks.

A key weakness of PPTP is the fact that it derives its encryption key from the user's password. This violates the cryptographic principle of randomness and can provide a basis for attacks. Password-based VPN authentication in general violates the recommendation to use two-factor authentication for remote access.

Layer 2 Tunneling Protocol (L2TP)

Layer 2 Tunneling Protocol (L2TP) is a hybrid of Cisco's Layer 2 Forwarding (L2F) and Microsoft's PPTP. It allows callers over a serial line using PPP to connect over the Internet to a remote network. A dial-up user connects to his ISP's L2TP access concentrator (LAC) with a PPP connection. The LAC encapsulates the PPP packets into L2TP and forwards it to the remote network's layer 2 network server (LNS). At this point, the LNS authenticates the dial-up user. If authentication is successful, the dial-up user will have access to the remote network.

LAC and LNS may authenticate each other with a shared secret, but as RFC 2661 states, the authenticating is effective only while the tunnel between the LAC and LNS is being created.

L2TP does not provide encryption and relies on other protocols, such as tunnel mode IPSec, for confidentiality.

TLS/SSL

Secure Shell (SSH)

Users often want to log on to a remote computer. Unfortunately, most early implementations to meet that need were designed for a trusted network. Protocols/programs, such as TELNET, RSH, and rlogin, transmit unencrypted over the network, which allows traffic to be easily intercepted.

Secure shell (SSH) was designed as an alternative to the above insecure protocols and allows users to securely access resources on remote computers over an encrypted tunnel. SSH's services include remote log-on, file transfer, and command execution. It also supports port forwarding, which redirects other protocols through an encrypted SSH tunnel. Many users protect less secure traffic of protocols, such as X Windows and VNC (virtual network computing), by forwarding them through a SSH tunnel. The SSH tunnel protects the integrity of communication, preventing session hijacking and other man-in-the-middle attacks.

Another advantage of SSH over its predecessors is that it supports strong authentication. There are several alternatives for SSH clients to authenticate to a SSH server, including passwords and digital certificates. Keep in mind that authenticating with a password is still a significant improvement over the other protocols because the password is transmitted encrypted.

There are two incompatible versions of the protocol, SSH-1 and SSH-2, though many servers support both. SSH-2 has improved integrity checks (SSH-1 is vulnerable to an insertion attack due to weak CRC-32 integrity checking) and supports local extensions and additional types of digital certificates such as Open PGP. SSH was originally designed for UNIX, but there are now implementations for other operating systems, including Windows, Macintosh, and OpenVMS.

SOCKS

SOCKS is a popular circuit proxy server with several commercial and freeware implementations. The heart of SOCKSv5 (the current version) is RFC 1928, which does not require that developers include encryption of traffic in their implementations. Users employ the SOCKS client to access a remote server. The client initiates a connection to the SOCKS proxy server, which accesses the remote server on behalf of the user. If the implementation supports encryption, then the server can act as a VPN, protecting the confidentiality of the traffic between the SOCKS and remote servers. Because SOCKS is concerned with maintaining a circuit, it can be used with almost any application.

A key advantage of SOCKS and SSL VPNs is the possibility to use proxy servers. This is a feature most other VPNs are lacking. A SOCKS server may require that a user authenticates before providing services.

SSL/TLS VPNs

SSL 3.0 (Secure Socket Layer) and TLS 1.1 (Transport Layer Security) are essentially fully compatible, with SSL being a session encryption tool originally developed by Netscape and TLS 1.1 being the open standard IETF version of SSL 3.0.

SSL VPNs are another approach to remote access that is gaining momentum. Instead of building a VPN around the IPSec and the network layer, SSL VPNs leverage SSL/TLS (see section on Transport Layer Security) to create a tunnel back to the home office. Remote users employ a Web browser to access applications that are in the organization's network. Even though users employ a Web browser, SSL VPNs are not restricted to applications that use HTTP. With the aid of plug-ins, such as Java, users can have access to back-end databases, and other non-Web-based applications.

SSL VPNs have several advantages over IPSec. They are easier to deploy on client workstations than IPSec, because they require a Web browser only, and almost all networks permit outgoing HTTP. SSL VPNs can be operated through a proxy server. In addition, applications can restrict users' access based on criteria, such as the network that the user is on, which is useful for building extranets with several organizations.

IPSec VPNs, on the other hand, grant access directly to a network. A user is usually given access to applications and devices as if he or she were located at the office. Of course, this is a double-edged sword. Just as an authorized user has access to many devices on the internal network, so will an intruder who can steal IPSec VPN access. Currently, SSL VPNs do not support network-to-network tunnels. A significant disadvantage of IPSec VPNs is that a VPN client must be installed and updated on every workstation, while an SSL VPN can be established using just about any modern Web browser.

VLAN

A Virtual LAN is a LAN in which the hosts are not necessarily on the same physical media but are part of the same logical routing subnet. For example, an organization has a research team which is distributed all over the world but needs to maintain confidentiality between its sites. One option would be to build a completely separate infrastructure which would take considerable time and cost. A better option would be to use encryption through routers which would only pass encrypted traffic to each other. This would create a VLAN over an existing physical infrastructure which would be more cost efficient than building out new infrastructure. In such a situation, tight controls must be around network configuration changes and operations. A mistake in a single router could expose the entire VLAN and defeat the purpose of creating one.

Voice

Modems and Public Switched Telephone Networks (PSTN)

The PSTN is a circuit-switched network that was originally designed for analog voice communication. When a person places a call, a dedicated circuit is created between the two phones. Although it appears to the callers that they are using a dedicated line, they are actually communicating through a complex network. As with all circuit-switched technology, the path through the network is established before communication between the two endpoints begins, and barring an unusual event, such as a network failure, the path remains constant during the call. Phones connect to the PSTN with CAT 3 copper wires to a central office (CO), which services an area of about 1 to 10 km.

The central offices are connected to a hierarchy of tandem offices (for local calls) and toll offices (toll calls), with each higher level of the hierarchy covering a larger area. Including the COs, the PSTN has five levels of offices. When both endpoints of a call are connected to the same CO, the traffic is switched within the CO. Otherwise, the call must be switched between a toll center and a tandem office. The greater the distance between the calls, the higher in the hierarchy the calls are switched. For example, in *Figure 2.14*, a call between callers 1 and 2 is switched within their central office. However, a call between callers 1 and 3 must be switched within the leftmost primary toll office. To accommodate the high volume of traffic, toll centers communicate with each other over fiber-optic cables.

Today, the PSTN is also used for data communication over wide area networks. Users can use a modem to access a network over a phone line (see Modems in this chapter). Or, a digital subscriber line (DSL) can be used to access the Internet over a phone line. To meet the demands for improved reliability necessary for data communication, phone companies have converted most of the communication within the PSTN to digital. The most notable exception is the connection between the user and the CO—"the last mile"—which is still analog.

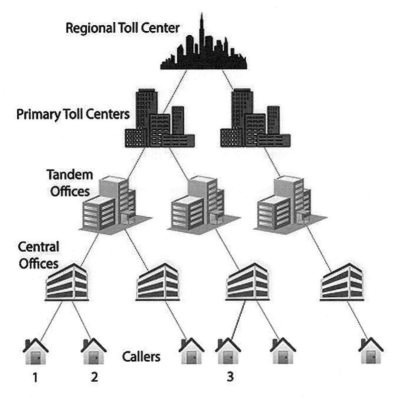

Figure 2.14 - **The Public Switched Telephone Network (PSTN)**

Previously, the PSTN was vulnerable to tone-frequency attacks. There was a subculture of phone hackers (phreaks) that attempted to make toll calls for free, manipulate public and private phone switches, gain unauthorized access to voice mail systems, etc. For example, in the 1960s, phone hackers discovered that AT&T signaled a 2600-Hz tone on all free toll lines and devised methods of reproducing that tone to make free long-distance calls. Phreaking as an art form has basically been made obsolete with the near ubiquitous deployment of digital switches and IP-based communications. To the extent phreaking exists, it is to exploit poorly configured company phone systems with key-pad commands to gain access to free long distance. However, most modern telecommunications carriers have entirely phased out analog (tone base) controls in favor of

365

IP-based, digital controls, which are not available through public network entry points like phones.

War Dialing

Although modems allow remote access to networks from almost anywhere, they could be used as a portal into the network by an attacker. Using automated dialing software, he or she can dial the entire range of phone numbers used by the company to identify modems. If the host, to which the modem is attached, has a weak password, then the attacker can easily gain access to the network. Worse yet, if voice and data share the same network, then both voice and data could be compromised.

The best defense to this attack is not to leave unattended modem turned on, and keep an up-to-date inventory of all modems so none get orphaned and left to operate without the knowledge of the organization. All modems should require some form of authentication, at least a single factor but industry standard has moved to two-factor authentication for modem connections due to the risks of these devices. If modems are necessary, then organizations must ensure that the passwords protecting the attached host are strong, preferably with the help of authentication mechanisms, such as RADIUS, one-time passwords, etc.

Users with modems that are connected to a network, especially the Internet, could be an easy target of attack. Sensitive information on the connected workstation could be stolen, or the workstation could become infected by malicious software, such as viruses, worms, or programs that allow an attacker to remotely control the workstation.

To greatly reduce the risk of accessing a network remotely, workstations should be protected with personal firewalls and antivirus software with current virus signatures. Security patches should also be installed as soon as possible. More importantly, users should learn and practice safe habits while connected to a network. For instance, do not open suspicious e-mail attachments; download software from trusted Web sites only, etc.

POTS

Plain old telephone service (POTS) is commonly found in the "last mile" of most residential and business telephone services. Once called "Post Office Telephone Service" in some countries the name has mostly been retired due to the proliferation of phones in homes and businesses. POTS typically represents a bi-directional analog telephone interface which was designed to carry the sound of the human voice. POTS lacks the mobility of cellular phones and the bandwidth of several competing products, however it is one of the most reliable systems available with an uptime close to or exceeding 99.999%. POTS is still often the telecom method of choice when high reliability is required and bandwidth is not. Typical applications include alarm systems and "out of band" command links for routers and other network devices.

PBX

A Private Branch Exchange (PBX) is an enterprise class phone system typically used in businesses or large organizations. A PBX often includes an internal switching network and a controller which is attached to telecommunications trunks. Many PBX had default manufacturer configuration codes, ports, and control interface which can be exploited. A PBX is often targeted by war dialers who can then use the PBX to route long distance calling or eavesdrop on the organization. Analog POTS PBXs are largely being replaced with VoIP based or VoIP enabled PBXs.

VoIP

Voice-over-IP (VoIP)

Although the possibility of transmitting voice over Internet connections has existed for a long time, the widespread acceptance of broadband home access created a market for Voice-over-IP solutions. In essence, Internet and telephony are switching roles—while previously the telephone network was a ubiquitous commodity that would carry Internet dial-up traffic, the Internet is taking over the role of the principal commodity.

Increasingly VoIP is replacing internal corporate telephony networks. While the benefits, such as negligible connection cost at a comparable initial investment and a larger degree of configurability, are obvious, VoIP networks are impacted by security risks in ways that would have left traditional telephony systems unaffected, such as being assailable by viruses and hacking and being dependent on electric power at all communication endpoints. In addition, VoIP systems are significantly more complex and need higher expertise to operate. For public services, questions of interconnectivity and interoperability come into focus. From a legal perspective, the situation is still unclear as to whether VoIP networks should be regulated in the same way as the public switched telephone network (PSTN).

One common requirement is the availability of gateways to public emergency services such as 911 when employing VoIP services. Due to the ability of VoIP devices to technically function from any IP address they can be highly mobile, following their users. This presents a serious challenge for emergency response services because IP addresses do not come with geo-spatial coordinates (longitude/latitude or even street address); therefore, a central VoIP support desk has to be maintained to inform emergency responders of the location of a given VoIP phone–based customer records and billing information. It has already come to pass that ambulances respond to life-and-death calls only to arrive at a location hundreds of miles from where they are needed because the VoIP phone had been moved. For large, corporate deployments of VoIP services, a means of tracking VoIP devices and mapping these devices to physical location is a key part of overall service-management and often a regulatory requirement related to workplace health and safety.

Another common requirement is access for lawful interception, which, while legitimate from a public policy perspective, raises concerns from a security perspective because of the potential design of backdoors into existing systems, which could then be exploited by third parties. However, the more pressing issue with lawful interception is to do with the provision of intercept services for legitimate purposes. VoIP traffic is still basically IP traffic and mixes with all the other IP traffic on a network. To intercept VoIP calls requires powerful and sophisticated network analysis tools that can extract VoIP packets from a potential torrent of data flowing at gigabit speeds, re-assemble these packets and extract the media stream within them, in real time.

Deployment of VoIP services may raise security concerns for its carrier network, for instance, with regard to enabling interconnectivity with other VoIP applications in a secure manner. Last but not least, a form of backup communication channel should be available with any VoIP installation, to have independent communication channels available in case of a disaster or network outage.

Readers may also want to familiarize themselves with protocols such as H.323.

Session Initiation Protocol (SIP)

As its name implies, SIP is designed to manage multimedia connections. It is not a comprehensive protocol suite and leaves much of the actual payload data transfer to other protocols, for instance, Real-Time Transport Protocol (RTP). A number of phone companies have begun offering SIP services to end users. SIP has been included in applications such as Microsoft Windows Messenger and open-source clients have been developed.

SIP is designed to support digest authentication structured by realms, similar to HTTP (basic username/password authentication has been removed from the protocol as of RFC 3261). In addition, SIP provides integrity protection through MD5 hash functions. SIP supports a variety of encryption mechanisms, such as TLS.

Privacy extensions to SIP, including encryption and caller ID suppression, have been defined in extensions to the original Session Initiation Protocol

369

(RFC 3325). On a related note, a SIP client may also act as a server that can receive requests from another machine. This may be considered a general risk for the machine the software is deployed to, because as with any server software, there is a risk of security gaps such as buffer overflows that can be exploited over the network.

Ports	5060/TCP, 5060/UDP
Definition	RFC 2543
	RFC 3261
	RFC 3325

Table 2.11 - **SIP Quick Reference**

Proprietary Applications and Services

Readers will want to familiarize themselves with proprietary VOIP implementation and applications, such as Skype. Most commercial instant messaging and chat services are also equipped with Voice-over-IP capabilities.

Multimedia Collaboration

Peer-to-Peer Applications and Protocols

Peer-to-peer applications have gained popularity—or notoriety, depending on one's point of view—due to their controversial role in sharing of intellectual property, mainly multimedia files. For reasons of bandwidth consumption, unacceptable conduct, and legal implications, the auditing of peer-to-peer applications in a business environment is highly advisable.

Arguably, the first popular P2P application was Napster, whose demise was brought about by legal disputes that the company lost, based among other things on the fact that it was operating a set of servers through which intellectual property violations had been committed. Other more recent and popular P2P applications include Limewire, eMule, Kazaa, Shareaza, Morpheus, Bittorrent, and many others.

The security risks associated with P2P begin with applications for which they are generally intended and end with their adoption for propagation and management of massive botnets. Generally, P2P applications, while possessing many legitimate applications, are associated with piracy and abuse of copyright and other forms of intellectual property. Legal risks due to the nature of content that is often found in P2P networks can hit an organization even if it did not approve of the use of P2P applications.

P2P applications are often designed to open an uncontrolled channel through network boundaries (normally through tunneling). See Figure 2.15. They therefore provide a way for dangerous content, such as botnets, spyware applications, and viruses, to enter an otherwise protected network. Because P2P networks can be established and managed using series of multiple, overlapping master and slave nodes they can be very difficult to shut down. If one master node is detected and shutdown, the "bot herder" who controls the P2P botnet can make one of the slave nodes a master and use that as a redundant staging point for botnet operations.

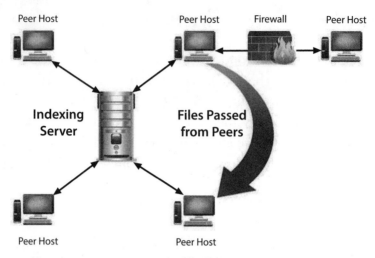

Figure 2.15 - **Peer-to-Peer (P2P) architecture**

P2P usage, legitimate or otherwise, has become so popular that many ISP have taken the step of "throttling" traffic on their subscriber networks. Specifically, if P2P traffic is observed, usually based upon packet analysis or port usage, the bandwidth available to that IP address will be limited to whatever the ISP prescribes. Throttling is done in order to prevent a user address from consuming a disproportionate amount of bandwidth. What is "disproportionate" is a matter of opinion for the ISP, but a single user of P2P applications can easily consume 100 times the amount of bandwidth of a non-P2P user on any given day.

Remote Meeting Technology

Several technologies and services exist which allow organizations and individuals to meet "virtually." These applications are typically web-based and either install extensions in the browser or client software on the host system. These technologies also typically allow "desktop sharing" as a feature. This feature can not only allow the viewing of a user's desktop but also the control of the system by a remote user.

Great care must be taken in determining a provider for remote meeting technology as the provider's software and servers should be suspect. Additionally, any options for encryption and authentication during the meeting should be considered by the participants as should the information being exchanged during the meeting.

Some organizations use dedicated equipment such as cameras, monitors and meeting rooms to host and participate in remote meetings. These devices are often a combination of IP and in some cases POTS technology. They are also subject to the same risks including but not limited to:

- War Dialing
- Vendor backdoors
- Default passwords
- Vulnerabilities in the underlying operating system or firmware

Instant Messaging

Instant messaging systems can generally be categorized in three classes: peer-to-peer networks, brokered communication, and server-oriented networks. See *Figure 2.16*. All these classes will support basic "chat" services on a one-to-one basis and frequently on a many-to-many basis.

Most instant messaging applications do offer additional services beyond their text messaging capability, for instance, screen sharing, remote control, exchange of files, and voice and video conversation. Some applications allow command scripting.

Instant messaging and chat is increasingly considered a significant business application used for office communications, customer support, and "presence" applications. Instant message may frequently be deployed with a bundle of other IP-based services such as VOIP and video conferencing support.

It should be noted that many of the risks mentioned here apply also to online games, which today offer instant communication between participants. For instance, multiplayer role-playing games, such as multiuser domains (MUDs), rely heavily on instant messaging that is similar in

373

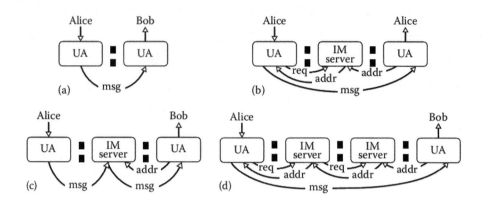

Figure 2.16 - **Setting up an instant-messaging connection:**

   a) Directly

   b) Through a central server

   c) Centralized, including messaging

   d) Through different servers

(From Wams, J.M.S and van Steen, M., Internet messaging, *The Practical Handbook of Internet Computing,* Singh, M.P., Ed., CRC Press, Boca Raton, FL, 2005. With permission.)

nature to Internet Relay Chat (IRC), even though it is technically based on a variant of the TELNET protocol.

A large collection of real-time communication protocols and applications exist to support instant messaging. Originally instant messaging required that client software be installed on the desktop, but current versions of instant message are based upon javaScript and ActiveX—requiring only a modern Web browser for clients, which then connect to an instant messaging server through HTTP. In the next section we will focus on applications based on open protocols.

Open Protocols, Applications, and Services

Extensible Messaging and Presence Protocol (XMPP) and Jabber

Jabber is an open instant messaging protocol for which a variety of open-source clients exist. A number of commercial services based on Jabber exist.

Ports	5222/TCP, 5222/UDP
Definition	RFC 3920
	RFC 3921

Table 2.12 - **XMPP Quick Reference**

Jabber has been formalized as an Internet standard under the name Extensible Messaging and Presence Protocol (XMPP), as defined in RFC 3920 and RFC 3921.

Jabber is a server-based application. Its servers are designed to interact with other instant messaging applications. As with IRC, anybody can offer a Jabber server. The Jabber server network can therefore not be considered trusted.

Although Jabber traffic can be encrypted via TLS, this does not prevent eavesdropping on the part of server operators. However, Jabber does provide an API to encrypt the actual payload data.

Jabber itself offers a variety of authentication methods, including cleartext and challenge/response authentication. To implement interoperability with other instant messaging systems from the server, however, the server will have to cache the user's credentials for the target network, enabling a number of attacks, mainly on behalf of the server operator, but also for anyone able to break into a server.

Internet Relay Chat (IRC)

Of the widely deployed chat systems on the Internet, IRC was arguably the first. IRC is still popular in academia, but has lost its dominant position to commercial services; however, IRC channels and servers are still very much available and popular with people wishing to share information and files on an anonymous basis. IRC supported good anonymity because they typically operate through terminal or telnet connections which leave no logs related to file transfers since the session is, in theory, just text on the screen.

Ports	194/TCP , 194/UDP
Definition	RFC 1459

Table 2.13 - **IRC Quick Reference**

Communication is organized in public discussion groups (channels) and private messaging between individual users.

IRC is a client/server-based network. IRC is unencrypted, and therefore an easy target for sniffing attacks. The basic architecture of IRC, founded on trust among servers, enables special forms of denial-of-service attacks. For instance, a malicious user can hijack a channel while a server or group of servers has been disconnected from the rest (net split).

IRC is also a common platform for social engineering attacks, aimed at inexperienced or technically unskilled users.

Although original clients were UNIX based, IRC clients are now available for many platforms, including Windows, Apple Macintosh, and Linux.

Proprietary Applications and Services. Readers will want to familiarize themselves with proprietary applications such as IBM Lotus Instant Messaging and Web Conferencing (Sametime), as well as commercial services such as:

- AOL Instant Messaging and ICQ, based on the proprietary Open System for Communication in Real-Time (OSCAR) protocol
- Google Talk, based on open Jabber/XMPP
- Microsoft MSN Messenger/Windows Messenger, based on the proprietary Mobile Status Notification Protocol (MSNP)
- Yahoo! Messenger, based on a proprietary protocol

All of these applications and services are server based. Interoperability between these services can be achieved through a server-based approach via XMPP or through multiple protocol clients. As usual, security of all of these applications rests in the strength of the protocol, quality of the implementation, trustworthiness of the operator, and behavior of the user. If these applications are to be used in a business context, stringent architectural and policy measures need to be put in place to prevent security gaps.

This is all the more important as many instant messaging applications by design support a variety of communication channels, offer the ability to tunnel through HTTP, and offer online awareness services that can be misused for technical or social attacks. While there are many business and personal benefits and efficiencies to be gained from adopting instant messaging/chat/IRC technologies, there are also many risks. These risks are faced both by private citizens and business trying to protect the integrity of their logical assets (networks, servers, workstations, data and intellectual property):

Authenticity: User identification can be easily faked in instant messaging and chat applications by

- Choosing a misleading identity upon registration or changing one's nickname while online
- Manipulating the directory service if the application requires one
- Manipulating either the attacker's or the target's client to send or display a wrong identity

Although these risks are inherent to all kinds of communication networks (and are also common in e-mail), they present an increased risk in real-time communication, where a user potentially has less time to analyze the communication presented to him or her. Similarly, the recent advent and rapid growth of social-networking sites like Facebook, Myspace, LinkedIn and others present amply opportunity to create false identity and try and dupe others for criminal purposes.

Confidentiality: Many chat systems transmit their information in cleartext. Similar to unencrypted e-mail, information can be disclosed by sniffing on the network. A different form of confidentiality breach may occur based upon the fact that chat applications can generate an illusion and expectation of privacy, e.g., by establishing "closed rooms." Depending on the kind of infrastructure used, all messages can however be read in cleartext by privileged users such as the chat system's operators.

File transfer mechanisms embedded in instant messaging clients can be considered an uncontrolled channel for information—especially file—leakage. Due to the large number of other, similarly uncontrollable channels, the resulting additional risk should not be overestimated, while of course the overall risk may still be high.

Scripting: Certain chat clients, such as IRC clients, can execute scripts that are intended to simplify administration tasks, such as joining a chat channel. Because these scripts are executed with the user's privileges with relatively unsophisticated (no sandbox) or nonexistent protection, they are an attractive target for social engineering or other attacks. Once the victim has been tricked into executing commands, he can leave his computer wide open for other attacks.

Social Engineering: Related to spam and phishing e-mail, in social engineering attackers can exploit human nature and good will to claim illicit legitimacy, for instance, by claiming to belong to a certain company or social group. Again, social networking applications and services provide many opportunities to masquerade as a legitimate member of a group for criminal and fraudulent purposes. As the social setting is informal and community oriented, there might even be social pressure to behave in an insecure manner, for instance, to demonstrate trust.

The lack of authenticity (and subsequently of non-repudiation) should be a concern, especially in business situations where instant messaging and chat systems can be used to give online support or enable other forms of customer interaction. Instant messaging is one of the primary avenues utilized by a person engaging in social engineering because it mixes the "live" nature of human communications with very little authentication and no tell-tale emotional indicators like body language or voice tonality.

Spam over Instant Messaging (SPIM): With the proliferation of instant messaging clients and social networking sites, a particular form of SPIM through pop-up windows ran rampant for a while. The easiest countermeasure is to disable the service. A current scourge of the major social networking sites is SPIM and SPAM, which are propagated through the nominally internal messaging systems that are intended to mitigate Internet SPAM by keeping messaging services proprietary and internal to the service and its members. Unfortunately, as is always the case, con artists and criminals have learned to route around this defense by opening up thousands of bogus accounts within these social networking sites and bombarding members through the internal messaging systems directly.

Tunneling Firewalls and Other Restrictions: Similar to streaming audio and video applications, corporate firewalls were perceived as an obstacle in establishing direct contact with Internet peers. The easy, but arguably illegitimate, solution for developers was to enable tunneling through the protocol that would always be available HTTP.

Depending on the client, it can even be possible to enable incoming connections by polling an external server. (This technique has been widely exploited in another type of application, a certain kind of remote-access software.) Control of HTTP tunneling can happen on the firewall or the proxy server. It should, however, be considered that in the case of peer-to-peer protocols, this would require a "deny by default" policy, and blocking instant messaging without providing a legitimate alternative is not likely to foster user acceptance and might give users incentive to utilize even more dangerous workarounds.

379

It should be noted that inbound file transfers can also result in circumvention of policy or restrictions in place, in particular for the spreading of viruses. An effective countermeasure can be found in on-access antivirus scanning on the client, which should be enabled anyway.

Remote Access

Remote Authentication Dial-in User Service (RADIUS)

RADIUS is an authentication protocol used mainly in networked environments, such as ISPs, or for similar services requiring single sign-on for layer 3 network access, for scalable authentication combined with an acceptable degree of security. On top of this, RADIUS provides support for consumption measurement such as connection time. RADIUS authentication is based on provision of simple username/password credentials. These credentials are encrypted by the client using a shared secret with the RADIUS server.

Ports	1812/TCP, 1812/UDP
	1813/TCP, 1813/UDP
Definition	RFC 2865

Table 2.14 - **RADIUS Quick Reference**

RADIUS is generally considered to be sufficiently secure. An ISP, in particular, will want to balance the risk of unauthorized access (and theft of bandwidth) with deployment cost of RADIUS. Fortunately, RADIUS is relatively easy to deploy and supported by a large number of devices in the market; its resulting cost reduction will offset the ISP's risk.

Conversely, RADIUS may not be sufficiently secure for higher security authentication and authorization requirements, such as access to a corporate network. In these cases, the added security offered by two-factor authentication in combination with RADIUS is clearly desirable.

RADIUS is victim to a number of cryptographic attacks and can be successfully attacked with a replay attack. RADIUS also suffers from a lack of integrity protection and the fact that just specific fields are transmitted encrypted.

Simple Network Management Protocol (SNMP)

SNMP is designed to manage network infrastructure.

Ports	161/TCP, 161/UDP
	162/TCP, 162/UDP
Definition	RFC 1157

Table 2.15 - **SNMP Quick Reference**

SNMP architecture consists of a management server (called the manager in SNMP terminology) and a client, usually installed on network devices such as routers and switches called an agent. SNMP allows the manager to retrieve "get" values of variables from the agent, as well as "set" variables. Such variables could be routing tables or performance-monitoring information.

Although SNMP has proven to be remarkably robust and scalable, it does have a number of clear weaknesses. Some of them are by design; others are subject to configuration parameters.

Probably the most easily exploited SNMP vulnerability is a brute-force attack on default or easily guessable SNMP passwords known as "community strings" often used to manage SNMP device. This may sound like a moot point, but given the scale of deployment, combined sometimes with perhaps relative inexperience of network administrators, it is certainly a realistic scenario, and a potentially severe but easily mitigated risk at that.

Until version 2, SNMP did not provide any degree of authentication or transmission security. Authentication consists of an identifier called a community string, by which a manager will identify itself against an agent (this string is configured into the agent) and a password sent with a command. As a result, passwords can be easily intercepted, which could then result in commands being sniffed and potentially faked.

Similar to the previous problem, SNMP version 2 did not support any form of encryption, so that passwords (community strings) where passed as cleartext. SNMP version 3 addresses this particular weakness with encryption for passwords, but is not in wide deployment yet (though it is widely available from vendors of network devices).

Remote-Access Services

The services described under this section, TELNET, rlogin, and the X Window System (X11), while present in many UNIX operations, and, when combined with NFS and NIS, provide the user with seamless remote working capabilities, do in fact form a risky combination if not administrated properly. Conceptually, because they are built on mutual trust, they can be misused to obtain access and to horizontally and vertically escalate privileges in an attack. Their authentication and transmission capabilities are insecure by design; they therefore had to be retrofitted (as X11) or replaced altogether (TELNET and rlogin by SSH).

TCP/IP Terminal Emulation Protocol (TELNET)

TELNET is a command line protocol designed to give command line access to another host. Although implementations for Windows exist, TELNET's original domain was the UNIX server world, and in fact, a TELNET server is standard equipment for any UNIX server. (Whether it should be enabled is another question entirely, but in small LAN environments, TELNET is still widely used.)

- TELNET offers little security, and indeed, its use poses serious security risks in untrusted environments.
- TELNET is limited to username/password authentication.
- TELNET does not offer encryption.

Once an attacker has obtained even a normal user's credentials, he has an easy road toward privilege escalation, as he cannot only transfer data from and to a machine, but also execute commands. As the TELNET server is running under system privileges, it is an attractive target of attack in itself; exploits in TELNET servers pave the way to system privileges for an attacker.

Ports	23/TCP
Definition	RFC 854
	RFC 855

Table 2.16 - **TELNET Quick Reference**

It is therefore reasonable to discontinue use of TELNET over the Internet and on Internet facing machines. In fact, the standard hardening procedure for any Internet facing server should include disabling its TELNET service, which under UNIX systems would normally run under the name of telnetd, and using SSHv2 for remote administration and management where required.

Remote Log-in (rlogin), Remote Shell (rsh), Remote Copy (rcp)

In its most generic form, rlogin is a protocol used for granting remote access to a machine, normally a UNIX server. Similarly, rsh grants direct remote command execution while rcp copies data from or to a remote machine.

Ports	513/TCP
Definition	RFC 1258

Table 2.17 - **RLogin Quick Reference**

If a rlogin daemon (rlogind) is running on a machine, rlogin access can be granted in two ways, by a central configuration file or by a user configuration. By the latter, a user may grant access that was not permitted by the system administrator. The same mechanism applies to rsh and rcp, while they are relying on a different daemon (rshd).

Authentication can be considered host/IP address based. Although rlogin grants access based on user ID, it is not verified; i.e., the ID a remote client claims to possess is taken for granted if the request comes from a trusted host. The rlogin protocol transmits data without encryption and is hence subject to eavesdropping and interception.

The rlogin protocol is of limited value—its main benefit can be considered its main drawback: remote access without supplying a password. It should only be used in trusted networks, if at all. A drastically more secure replacement is available in the form of SSH for rlogin, rsh, and rcp.

Screen Scraper

A screen scraper is a program which can extract data from output on a display intended for a human. Screen scrapers are used in a legitimate fashion when older technologies are unable to interface with modern ones. In a nefarious sense this technology can also be used to capture images from a user's computer such as PIN pad sequences at a banking website when implemented by a virus or malware.

Virtual Applications and Desktops

Virtual Network Terminal Services

Virtual terminal service is a tool frequently used for remote access to server resources. Virtual terminal services allow the desktop environment for a server to be exported to a remote workstation. This allows users at the remote workstation to execute desktop commands as though they were sitting at the server terminal interface in person. See *Table 2.18*.

Ports	80/TCP, 443/UDP
Definition	Vendor Specific

Table 2.18 - **VNTS Quick Reference**

The advantage of terminal services such as Citrix, Microsoft Network Virtual Terminal or public domain VNC services is that they allow for complex administrative commands to be executed using the native interface of the server, rather than a command-line interface, which might be available through SSH or telnet. Terminal services also allow for the authentication and authorization services integrated into the server to be leverage for remote users, in addition to all the logging and auditing features of the server.

Terminal services allow a remote user to manage a host without exposing that host to any potential malicious code that might be present on the remote machine; this is because only the terminal interface is exported, file systems are shared or joined between the system. While the various virtual terminal services run on different ports, most will also be available for tunneling through HTTP-SSL for security and to allow them to pass through zoning firewalls with a minimum of fuss and administration.

Like all sophisticated pieces of software, terminal services are subject to frequent vulnerability alerts from the vendors and must be patched. Unfortunately, patching virtual terminal services can be tricky because of interdependencies with native Web servers, which in turn will have interdependencies with the applications resident on the server.

Telecommuting

Telecommuting is growing in popularity with some organizations telecommuting the majority of the time with the majority of their employees. With a mobile mindset comes unique challenges the information security professional must address. Common controls such as visitor control, physical security and network control are mostly lost with teleworkers. Strong VPN connections between the teleworker and the organization need to be established and full device encryption should be the norm for protecting sensitive information. If the user works in public places or a home office the following should also be considered:

■ Is the user trained to use secure connectivity software and methods such as VPN?

■ Does the user know which information is sensitive or valuable and why someone might wish to steal or modify it?

■ Is the user's physical location appropriately secure for the type of work and type of information they are using?

■ Who else has access to the area? While a child may seem trusted the child's friends may not be.

Data Communications

A network's physical topology relates to how network components are connected with each other. The appropriate topology for a network can be determined by assessing the available protocols, how end nodes will be used, available equipment, financial constraints, and the importance of fault tolerance.

Analog Communication

Analog signals use electronic properties, such as frequency and amplitude, to represent information. Analog recordings are a classic example: A person speaks into a microphone, which converts the vibration from acoustical energy to an electrical equivalent. The louder the person speaks, the greater the electrical signal's amplitude. Likewise, the higher the pitch of the person's voice, the higher the frequency of the electrical signal.

Analog signals are transmitted on wires, such as twisted pair, or with a wireless device. In radio communication, for example, the electrical representation of the person's voice would be modulated with a carrier signal and broadcasted.

Digital Communication

Whereas analog communication uses complex waveforms to represent information, digital communication uses two electronic states (on and off). By convention, 1 is assigned to the on state and 0 to off. Electrical signals that consist of these two states can be transmitted over cable, converted to light and transmitted over fiber optics, and broadcasted with a wireless device. In all of the above media, the signal would be a series of one of two states: on and off.

It is easier to ensure the integrity of digital communication because the two states of the signal are sufficiently distinct. When a device receives a digital transmission, it can determine which digits are 0s and which are 1s (if it cannot, then the device knows the signal is erroneous or corrupted). On the other hand, analog complex waveforms make ensuring integrity very difficult.

Network Topology

Bus

A bus is a LAN with a central cable (bus) to which all nodes (devices) connect. All nodes transmit directly on the central bus. Each node listens to all of the traffic on the bus and processes only the traffic that is destined for it. This topology relies on the data-link layer to determine when a node can transmit a frame on the bus without colliding with another frame on the bus. A LAN with a bus topology is shown in *Figure 2.17*.

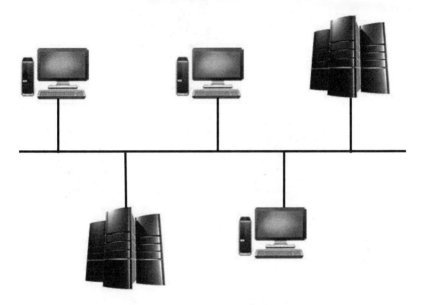

Figure 2.17 - **Network with a Bus topology**

Advantages of buses include

- Adding a node to the bus is easy.
- A node failure will not likely affect the rest of the network.

Disadvantages of buses include:

- Because there is only one central bus, a bus failure will leave the entire network inoperable.

389

Tree

Tree topology is similar to a bus. Instead of all of the nodes connecting to a central bus, the devices connect to a branching cable. Like a bus, every node receives all of the transmitted traffic and processes only the traffic that is destined for it. Furthermore, the data-link layer must transmit a frame only when there is not a frame on the wire. A network with a tree topology is shown in *Figure 2.18*.

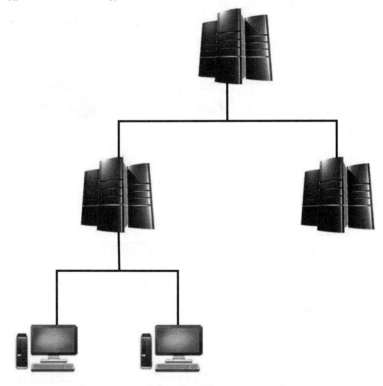

Figure 2.18 - **Network with a Tree topology**

Advantages of a tree include:

- Adding a node to the tree is easy.
- A node failure will not likely affect the rest of the network.

Disadvantages of a tree include:

- A cable failure could leave the entire network inoperable.

Ring

Ring is a closed-loop topology. Data is transmitted in one direction. Each device receives data from its upstream neighbor only and transmits data to its downstream neighbor only. Typically rings use coaxial cables or fiber optics. A Token Ring network is shown in *Figure 2.19*.

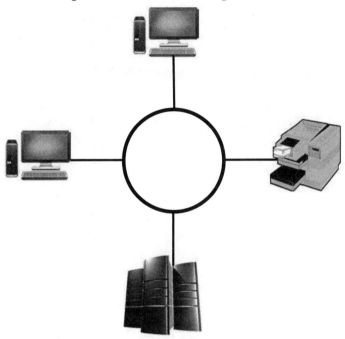

Figure 2.19 - **Network with a Ring topology**

Advantages of rings include:

■ Because rings use tokens, one can predict the maximum time that a node must wait before it can transmit (i.e., the network is deterministic).

■ Rings can be used as a LAN or network backbone.

Disadvantages of rings include:

■ Simple rings have a single point of failure. If one node fails, the entire ring fails. Some rings, such as fiber distributed data interface (FDDI), use dual rings for failover.

391

Mesh

In a mesh network, all nodes are connected to every node on the network. A full mesh network is usually too expensive because it requires many connections. As an alternative, a partial mesh can be employed in which only selected nodes (typically the most critical) are connected in a full mesh and the remaining nodes are connected to a few devices. As an example, core switches, firewalls, and routers and their hot standbys are often all connected to ensure as much availability as possible. A full mesh network is shown in *Figure 2.20*.

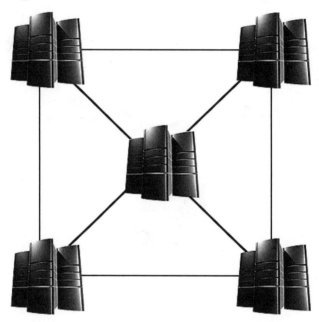

Figure 2.20 - **Network with a Mesh topology.**

Advantages of a mesh include:

- Mesh networks provide a high level of redundancy.

Disadvantages of a mesh include:

- Mesh networks are very expensive because of the enormous amount of cables that are required.

Star

All nodes in a star network are connected to a central device, such as a hub, switch, or router. Modern LANs usually employ a star typology. A star network is shown in *Figure 2.21*.

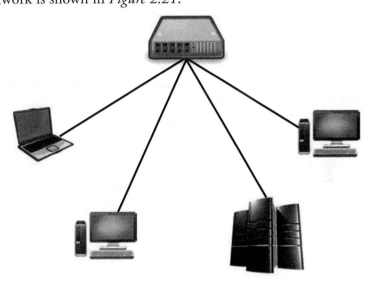

Figure 2.21 - **Network with a Star topology**

Advantages of a star include:

■ Star networks require fewer cables than full or partial mesh.

■ Star networks are easy to deploy, and nodes can be easily added or removed.

Disadvantages of a star include:

■ The hub is a single point of failure. If the hub is not functional, all of the connected nodes lose network connectivity.

There are many points that must be considered about transmitting information from sender to receiver. For example, will the information be expressed as an analog or digital wave? How many recipients will be there? If the transmission media will be shared with others, how can one ensure that the signals will not interfere with each other?

Unicast, Multicast, and Broadcast Transmissions

Most communication, especially that directly initiated by a user, is from one host to another. For example, when a person uses a browser to send a request to a Web server, he or she sends a packet to the Web server. A transmission with one receiving host is called unicast.

A host can send a broadcast to everyone on its network or subnetwork. Depending on the network topology, the broadcast could have anywhere from one to tens of thousands of recipients. Like a person standing on a soapbox, this is a noisy method of communication. Typically, only one or two destination hosts are interested in the broadcast; the other recipients waste resources to process the transmission. However, there are productive uses for broadcasts. Consider a router that knows a device's IP address but must determine the device's MAC address. The router will broadcast an Address Resolution Protocol (ARP) request asking for the device's MAC address.

Notice how one broadcast could result in hundreds or even thousands of packets on the network. Intruders often leverage this fact in denial-of-service attacks.

Public and private networks are used more often than ever for streaming transmissions, such as movies, videoconferences, and music. Given the intense bandwidth to transmit these streams, and the sender and recipients are not necessarily on the same network, how does one transmit the stream to only the interested hosts? The sender could send a copy of the stream via unicast to each receiver. Unless there is a very small audience, unicast delivery is not practical because the multiple simultaneous copies of the large stream on the network at the same time could cause congestion. Delivery with broadcasts is another possibility, but every host would receive the transmission, even if they were not interested in the stream.

Multicast was designed to deliver a stream to only interested hosts. Radio broadcasting is a typical analogy for multicasting. To select a specific radio show, you tune a radio to the broadcasting station. Likewise, to receive a desired multicast, you join the corresponding multicast group.

Multicast agents are used to route multicast traffic over networks and administer multicast groups. Each network and subnetwork that supports multicasting must have at least one multicast agent. Hosts use Internet Group Management Protocol (IGMP) to tell a local multicast agent that it wants to join a specific multicast group. Multicast agents also route multicasts to local hosts that are members of the multicast's group and relay multicasts to neighboring agents.

When a host wants to leave a multicast group, it sends an IGMP message to a local multicast agent.

Multicasts do not use reliable sessions. Therefore, the multicasts are transmitted as best effort, with no guarantee that datagrams are received.

As an example, consider a server multicasting a videoconference to desktops that are members of the same multicast group as the server (*Figure 2.22*). The server transmits to a local multicast agent. Next, the multicast agent relays the stream to other agents. All of the multicast agents transmit the stream to local hosts that are members of the same multicast group as the server.

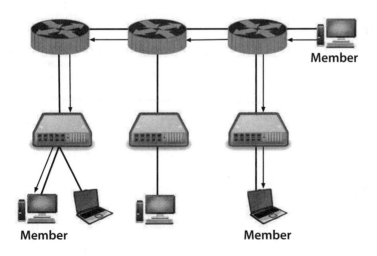

Figure 2.22 - **Multicast transmission**

395

Circuit-Switched Networks

Circuit-switched networks establish a dedicated circuit between endpoints. These circuits consist of dedicated switch connections. Neither endpoint starts communicating until the circuit is completely established. The endpoints have exclusive use of the circuit and its bandwidth. Carriers base the cost of using a circuit-switched network on the duration of the connection, which makes this type of network only cost-effective for a steady communication stream between the endpoints. Examples of circuit-switched networks are the plain old telephone service (POTS), Integrated Services Digital Network (ISDN), and Point-to-Point Protocol (PPP).

Packet-Switched Networks

Packet-switched networks do not use a dedicated connection between endpoints. Instead, data is divided into packets and transmitted on a shared network. Each packet contains meta-information so that it can be independently routed on the network. Networking devices will attempt to find the best path for each packet to its destination. Because network conditions could change while the partners are communicating, packets could take different paths as they transverse the network and arrive in any order. It is the responsibility of the destination endpoint to ensure that the received packets are in the correct order before sending them up the stack.

Switched Virtual Circuits (SVCs), Permanent Virtual Circuits (PVCs)

Virtual circuits provide a connection between endpoints over high-bandwidth, multiuser cable or fiber that behaves as if the circuit were a dedicated physical circuit. There are two types of virtual circuits, based on when the routes in the circuit are established. In a permanent virtual circuit, the carrier configures the circuit's routes when the circuit is purchased. Unless the carrier changes the routes to tune the network, respond to an outage, etc., the routes do not change. On the other hand, the routes of a switched virtual circuit are configured dynamically by the routers each time the circuit is used.

Carrier Sense Multiple Access

As the name implies, Carrier Sense Multiple Access (CSMA) is an access protocol that uses the absence/presence of a signal on the medium that it wants to transmit on as permission to speak. Only one device may transmit at a time; otherwise, the transmitted frames will be unreadable. Because there is not an inherent mechanism that determines which device may transmit, all of the devices must compete for available bandwidth. For this reason, CSMA is referred to as a contention-based protocol. Also, because it is impossible to predict when a device may transmit, CSMA is also nondeterministic.

There are two variations of CSMA based on how collisions are handled. LANs using Carrier Sense Multiple Access with Collision Avoidance (CSMA/CA) require devices to announce their intention to transmit by broadcasting a jamming signal. When devices detect the jamming signal, they know not to transmit; otherwise, there will be a collision. After sending the jamming signal, the device waits to ensure that all devices have received that signal, and then broadcasts the frames on the media. CSMA/CA is used in the IEEE 802.11 wireless standard.

Devices on a LAN using Carrier Sense Multiple Access with Collision Detection (CSMA/CD) listen for a carrier before transmitting data. If another transmission is not detected, the data will be transmitted. It is possible that a station will transmit before another station's transmission had enough time to propagate. If this happens, two frames will be transmitted simultaneously, and a collision will occur. Instead of all stations simply retransmitting their data, which will likely cause more collisions, each station will wait a randomly generated interval before retransmitting. CSMA/CD is part of the IEEE 802.3 standard.

Polling

A network that employs polling avoids contention by allowing a device (a slave) to transmit on the network only when it is asked by a master device.

397

Polling is used mostly in mainframe protocols, such as Synchronous Data Link. The point coordination function, an optional function of the IEEE 802.11 standard, uses polling as well.

Token Passing

Token passing takes a more orderly approach to media access. With this access method, only one device may transmit on the LAN at a time, thus avoiding retransmissions.

A special frame, known as a token, circulates through the ring. When a device wishes to transmit on the network, it must possess the token. The device replaces the token with a frame containing the message to be transmitted and sends the frame to its neighbor. When each device receives the frame, it relays it to its neighbor if it is not the recipient. The process continues until the recipient possesses the frame. That device will copy the message, modify the frame to signify that the message was received, and transmit the frame on the network.

When the modified frame makes a trip back to the sending device, the sending device knows that the message was received. Token passing is used

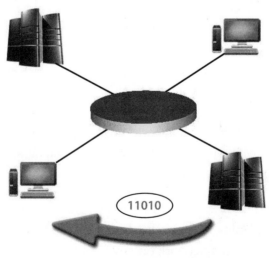

Figure 2.23 - **LAN token passing**

in Token Ring and FDDI networks. An example of a LAN using token passing is in *Figure 2.23*.

Ethernet (IEEE 802.3)

Ethernet, which is defined in IEEE 802.3, played a major role in the rapid proliferation of LANs in the 1980s. The architecture was flexible and relatively inexpensive, and it was easy to add and remove devices from the LAN. Even today, for the same reasons, Ethernet is the most popular LAN architecture. The physical topologies that are supported by Ethernet are bus, star, and point to point, but the logical topology is the bus.

With the exception of full-duplex Ethernet (which does not have the issues of collisions), the architecture uses CSMA/CD. This protocol allows devices to transmit data with a minimum of overhead (compared to Token Ring), resulting in an efficient use of bandwidth. However, because devices must retransmit when more than one device attempts to send data on the medium, too many retransmissions due to collisions can cause serious throughput degradation.

The Ethernet standard supports coaxial cable, unshielded twisted pair, and fiber optics as transmission media.

Ethernet was originally rated at 10 Mbps, but like 10-megabyte disk drives, users quickly figured out how to use and exceed its capacity and needed faster LANs. To meet the growing demand for more bandwidth, 100 Base-TX (100 Mbps over twisted pair) and 100 Base-FX (100 Mbps over multimode fiber optics) were defined. When the demand grew for even more bandwidth over unshielded twisted pair, 1000 Base-T was defined, and 1000 Base-SX and 1000 Base-LX were defined for fiber optics. These standards support 1,000 Mbps.

Token Ring (IEEE 802.5):

Originally designed by IBM, Token Ring was adapted with some modification by the IEEE as IEEE 802.5. Despite the architecture's name,

Token Ring uses a physical star topology. The logical topology, however, is a ring. Each device receives data from its upstream neighbor and transmits to its downstream neighbor. Token Ring uses ring passing to mediate which device may transmit. As mentioned in the section on token passing, a special frame, called a token, is passed on the LAN. To transmit, a device must possess the token.

To transmit on the LAN, the device appends data to the token and sends it to its next downstream neighbor. Devices retransmit frames whenever the token is not the intended recipient. When the destination device receives the frame, it copies the data, marks the frame as read, and sends it to its downstream neighbor. When the packet returns to the source device, it confirms that the packet has been read. It then removes the frame from the ring. Token ring is now considered a "legacy" technology that is rarely seen and only then because there has been no reason to upgrade away from it. Token ring has almost entirely been replaced with Ethernet technology.

Fiber Distributed Data Interface (FDDI)

FDDI is a token-passing architecture that uses two rings. Because FDDI employs fiber optics, FDDI was designed to be a 100-Mbps network backbone. Only one ring (the primary) is used; the other one (secondary) is used as a backup. Information in the rings flows in opposite directions from each other. Hence, the rings are referred to as counterrotating.

FDDI is not considered a legacy technology and has been supplanted by more modern transport technologies; initially Asynchronous Transfer Mode (ATM) but more recently Multiprotocol Label Switching (MPLS).

Multiprotocol Label Switching (MPLS)

As we move further and further into the IP world, the notion of disparate and critical Quality of Service (QoS) requirements is driving the deployment of Multiprotocol Label Switching (MPLS). MPLS (*Figure 2.24*) has attained a significant amount of popularity at the core of the carrier networks as of late because it manages to couple the determinism, speed, and QoS

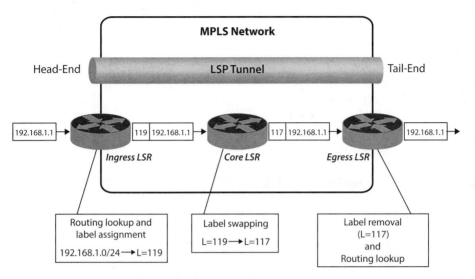

Figure 2.24 - **MPLS forwarding operation**

(From Tan, N.-K., ***MPLS for Metropolitan Area Networks***,
Auerbach Publications, New York, 2004. With permission.)

controls of established switched technologies like ATM and Frame Relay, with the flexibility and robustness of the Internet Protocol world. (MPLS is developed and propagated through the Internet Engineering Task Force (IETF.)) Additionally, the once faster and higher bandwidth ATM switches are being outperformed by Internet backbone routers. Equally important, MPLS offers simpler mechanisms for packet-oriented traffic engineering and multi-service functionality with the added benefit of greater scalability.

MPLS is often referred to as "IP VPN" because of the ability to couple highly deterministic routing with IP services. In effect, this creates a VPN-type service that makes it logically impossible for data from one network to be mixed or routed over to another network without compromising the MPLS routing device itself. MPLS does not include encryption services; therefore, any MPLS service called "IP VPN" does not in fact contain any cryptographic services. The traffic on these links would be visible to the service providers. Because MPLS is a comparatively new service, the following guidelines may be considered during the negotiation of MPLS

401

bandwidth and associated service level agreements (SLAs) to ensure that services live up to the assurance requirements for the assets relying upon the network:

- **Site Availability:** make certain MPLS is available for all desired locations; i.e., all the planned remote connections (offices) have MPLS service available in that area.

- **End-to-End Network Availability:** inquire about peering relationships for MPLS for network requirements that cross Tier 1 carrier boundaries.

- **Provisioning:** how fast can new links in new sites be provisioned.

Local Area Network (LAN)

LANs service a relatively small area, such as a home, office building, or office campus. In general, LANs service the computing needs of their local users. LANs consist of most modern computing devices, such as workstations, servers, and peripherals connected in a star topology or internetworked stars. Ethernet is the most popular LAN architecture because it is inexpensive and very flexible. Most LANs have connectivity to other networks, such as dial-up or dedicated lines to the Internet, access to other LANs via WANs, and so on.

Virtual Local Area Networks (VLANs)

For IT to be successful, it must provide effective computing resources for the business. However, a business rarely aligns itself to make IT's job easier, which includes physically locating users with similar computing requirements in the same area. For instance, engineers who mostly access the same servers could be scattered throughout a campus on different subnetworks.

Virtual local area networks (VLANs) allow network administrators to use switches to create software-based LAN segments that can be defined based on factors other than physical location. Devices that share a VLAN communicate through switches, without being routed to other subnetworks, which reduces overhead due to router latency (as routers become faster, this is less of an advantage). Furthermore, broadcasts are not forwarded outside of a VLAN, which reduces congestion due to broadcasts.

Placing devices that often communicate with each other in the same VLAN allows them to do so more efficiently. For example, the engineers in the above scenario can be placed in a dedicated VLAN with their servers. The throughput between the devices in the VLAN is increased because the traffic is not routed. Also, the broadcasts from the devices are isolated to the VLAN, which improves throughput for the entire LAN.

Because VLANs are not restricted to the physical location of devices, they help make networks easier to manage. When a user or group of users changes their physical location, network administrators can simply change the membership of ports within a VLAN. Likewise, when additional devices must communicate with members of a VLAN, it is easy to add new ports to a VLAN. VLANs can be configured based on switch port, IP subnet, MAC address, and protocols.

It is important to remember that VLANs do not guarantee a network's security. At first glance, it may seem that traffic cannot be intercepted because communication within a VLAN is restricted to member devices. However, there are attacks that allow a malicious user to see traffic from other VLANs (so-called VLAN hopping). Therefore, a VLAN can be created so that engineers can efficiently share confidential documents, but the VLAN does not significantly protect the documents from unauthorized access.

Integrated Services Digital Network (ISDN)

Before the days of DSL and cable modems, users wanted remote access with higher bandwidth than dial-up. ISDN provides such bandwidth by using a set of protocols and specialized equipment (see *Figure 2.25*). ISDN uses two types of channels: the B channel (bearer) is used for voice and data (at 64 kbps) and the D channel (delta) is used for signaling (at 16 kbps) and can also be used for data. The D channels are used to establish, maintain,

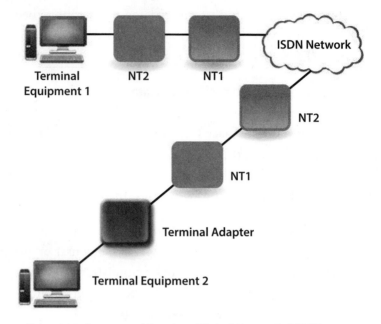

Figure 2.25 - **Integrated Services Digital Network (ISDN)**

and tear down connections with a remote site. Voice and data traffic are sent on the B channel. Each B channel can support a separate call or can be multiplexed (B channel bonding) to combine the bandwidth into a single channel.

SDN comes in two varieties, basic rate interface (BRI) and primary rate interface (PRI). BRI supports two B channels and one D channel. Each B channel will support separate 64-kbps sessions or can be multiplexed into one 128-kbps session.

PRI is ISDN's high-end. When all of the B channels are bonded, the ISDN connection provides the bandwidth of a leased line. In North America, PRI supports 23 B channels and 1 D channel that can support as many as 23 sessions or, combined, 1 1.55-Mbps session (a full T1). In Europe and Australia, PRI supports 30 B channels and 1 D channel. The B channels can support 30 sessions or, bonded, 1 2.0-Mbps channel (a full E1).

The following are common ISDN devices:

- **Terminal equipment 1 (TE1):** Computer, fax, etc., is ISDN ready.

- **Terminal equipment 2 (TE2):** Computer, fax, etc., cannot be directly attached to an ISDN network. To connect to ISDN, a TE2 must connect to a terminal adapter.

- **Network termination 1 (NT1):** Marks the end of the phone company and the beginning of the customer's network.

- **Network termination 2 (NT2):** Acts as a concentrator. NT2 devices are typically not used in the home.

- **Terminal adapter (TA):** Interfaces with TE2 devices to allow them to access an ISDN network.

Some organizations use PRI ISDN as a low-cost backup for a leased line.

ISDN as a technology is at end-of-life and being decommissioned in many service locations; however, ISDN has been deployed for many remote connectivity applications that are not scheduled for de-commissioning for years to come. For this reason ISDN will remain in service to support "legacy" applications for several more years.

Point-to-Point Lines

A point-to-point line connects two endpoints, most often over a WAN. In a wired WAN, point-to-point uses high-bandwidth fiber cable, but unlike FDDI, the traffic is dedicated to the endpoints. Point-to-point lines are an expensive option.

T1, T3, etc

T1 carrier is a popular WAN method in North America and Japan. Using time division multiplexing, T1 multiplexes 24 channels over copper cable. In a 193-bit frame, each of the channels in a round-robin transmits 8 bits (seven data and one control bit). One bit for synchronization is appended to the beginning of the frame. A T1 frame is shown in *Figure 2.26*.

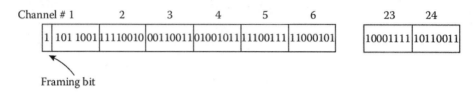

Framing bit

Figure 2.26 - **Structure of a T1 frame**

Eight thousand T1 frames are transmitted every second. Therefore, the transmission rate is 1.544 Mbps (8,000 frames/sec × 193 bits/frame).

Fractional T1 is available for organizations with a modest T1 budget. Customers may purchase fewer than 24 channels, which could be much less expensive than a full T1. Channels that are not purchased do not carry data. To meet the demand for more WAN bandwidth, multiple T1 channels are multiplexed into technologies with more throughput. In general, customers use T1 and T3. A summary of T channels is shown in *Table 2.19.*

Channel	Multiplex Ratio	Bandwidth (Mbps)
T1	1 T1	1.544
T2	4xT1	6.312
T3	7xT2	44.736
T4	6xT3	274.176

Table 2.19 - **T-Carrier Bandwidth**

Fractional T3 is available at a reduced cost for organizations that do not need all T3 channels. As with fractional T1, fractional T3 channels that are not purchased do not carry data.

E1, E3, etc

E-carrier, used in Europe, employs a similar concept as T-carrier. Using time division multiplexing, 32 channels take their turn transmitting 8 bits of data in a frame. E1 transmits 8,000 frames per second (the same rate as T1). The throughput for E1 is therefore 2.048 Mbps.

As with T-carrier, E1 channels are multiplexed into E-carrier technology with more bandwidth. Each successive E-carrier level contains four times the channels as the previous one. *Table 2.20* shows the bandwidth of E1 to E4.

Channel	Bandwidth (Mbps)
E1	2.048
E2	8.848
E3	34.304
E4	139.264

Table 2.20 - **E-Carrier Bandwidth**

Customers typically use E1 and E3. In addition, fractional E-carrier lines are available for organizations that do not require the entire capacity of E1 or E3 line.

OC1, OC12, etc

Like T- and E-carriers, 8,000 frames are transmitted per second. However, a SONET (synchronous optical network) frame is larger and more complex, as shown in *Figure 2.27*.

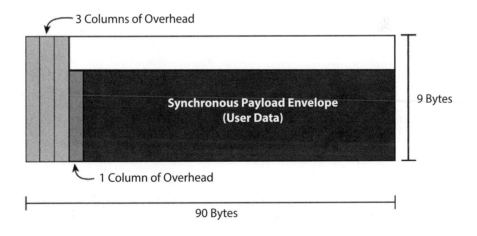

Figure 2.27 - **A SONET frame**

A SONET frame is a 90 × 9 byte matrix (810 bytes) with overhead in the first three columns. The overhead includes information for network management and the pointer to the start of user data. The rest of the frame is devoted to user data, known as the synchronous payload envelope (SPE), which can start at any byte within that area. However, the first column of the SPE is used as overhead.

SONET's basic transfer rate, optical carrier-1 (OC1) is 51.84 Mbps (810 bytes × 8 bits/byte × 8,000 bytes/s). Time division multiplexing of SONET signals is used to generate levels of SONET with a faster bandwidth. *Table 2.21* shows the potential speed of various OC levels.

OC Level	Bandwidth (Mbps)
OC-1	51.84
OC-3	155.52
OC-9	466.56
OC-12	622.08
OC-18	933.12
OC-24	1244.16
OC-36	1866.24
OC-48	2488.32
OC-192	9953.28

Table 2.21 - **E-Carrier Bandwidth**

Digital Subscriber Lines (DSL)

To meet the ever-growing demand by home users for more affordable bandwidth, telephone companies offer digital subscriber lines (DSLs) that use CAT-3 cables and the local loop. Fortunately for telephone companies, this technology requires relatively little change to their equipment. The local loop, the weakest link of the PSTN, can support a relatively high transmission rate. Traditionally, all frequencies above 4 KHz are filtered to optimize the network for human speech. When the filter is removed from the line, the line has the capacity for frequencies as high as 1.1 MHz, which is ample for the desired throughput of DSL.

There are several methods of implementing DSL, including:

- **Asymmetric Digital Subscriber line (ADSL):** Downstream transmission rates are much greater than upstream ones, typically 256 to 512 kbps downstream and 64 kbps upstream.

- **Rate-Adaptive DSL (RADSL):** The upstream transmission rate is automatically tuned based on the quality of the line.

- **Symmetric Digital Subscriber Line (SDSL):** Uses the same rates for upstream and downstream transmissions.

- **Very High Bit Rate DSL (VDSL):** Supports much higher transmission rates than other DSL technologies, such as 13 Mbps downstream and 2 Mbps upstream.

Due to ADSL's popularity, we will focus on it here. ASDL, like V.90 modems, dedicates more bandwidth for downstream transmission (from CO to user) than upstream, which matches the bandwidth requirements of most home users. For example, a user's mail client requires very little bandwidth to ask a mail server if the user has new mail. On the other hand, downloading mail could require much more network resources. A typical ADSL network is shown in *Figure 2.28*.

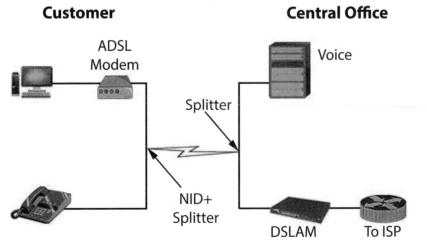

Figure 2.28 - **An ADSL network**

The network interface device (NID), which is usually installed on a customer's outside wall, marks the end of the telephone company's responsibility. The phone line is attached to the NID. Splitters are installed at both ends of the phone line to separate voice and data traffic.

How does a home computer transmit at high speeds on an old local loop over CAT-3 cable? The leading method is to use discrete multitone (DMT). The 1.1-MHz bandwidth of the local loop is subdivided into 256 channels. Voice is transmitted over one channel; 250 channels are allocated for ADSL, and 5 unused channels help isolate ASDL and voice. Because downstream transmission is favored over upstream, many more channels are allocated for downstream. All channels are modulated by an ASDL modem before transmitting over the local loop. At the CO, the ASDL channels are forwarded to a digital subscriber line access multiplexer (DSLAM), which demodulates the signal and sends the resulting bits to an ISP.

There are two significant issues with all variations of DSL:

1. There is a limit to the length of the phone line between the CO and the customer. The precise limit depends on several factors, including the quality of the cable and transmission rates. In other words, the customer cannot be too far from the CO.

2. DSL allows the users to be connected to the Internet for much longer time intervals. Certainly, this is very convenient for the user, but extended time exposed to the hostile Internet greatly increases the risk of being attacked. To mitigate this serious risk, it is imperative that the host has a firewall, vendor security patches are installed, and dangerous and unused protocols are disabled.

Cable Modem

As with DSL, cable modems allow home users to enjoy high-speed Internet connectivity. Instead of sending data through the phone company, cable modems use their cable provider as an ISP. The user connects their PC

Ethernet NIC to a cable modem, which is connected via coaxial cable to the cable provider's network. Most major cable providers supply cable modems that comply with Data-Over-Cable Service Interface Specifications (DOCSIS), which helps ensure compatibility. See *Figure 2.29.*

At a high level, when a cable modem is powered on, it is assigned upstream and downstream channels. Next, it establishes timing parameters by determining how far it is from the head end (the core of the cable network). The cable modem makes a Dynamic Host Configuration Protocol (DHCP) request to obtain an IP address. To help protect the cable provider from piracy and its users from their data being intercepted by other cable users, the modem, and head end exchange cryptography keys. From that point forward, all traffic between the two ends is encrypted.

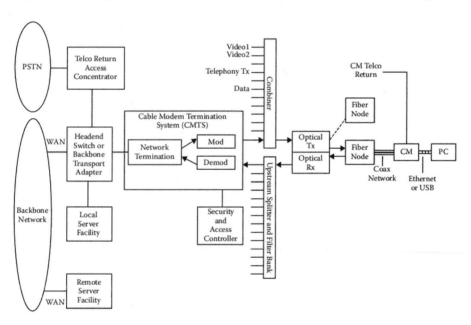

Figure 2.29 - **Data-Over-Cable reference architecture (after DOCSIS 2.0 RFI specification)**

(From Howard, D. et al., Last mile HFC access, *Broadband Last Mile: Access Technologies for Multimedia Communications,* Jayant, N. Ed., Dekker, Boca Raton, FL, 2005. With permission.)

Like DSL, cable modems make it practical for home users to remain connected to the Internet for an extended time, which exposes cable modem users to the same risks as DSL users. Cable modem users must take the same precautions as DSL users: ensure that PCs on the home network have a personal firewall, install vendor security patches, and disable dangerous and unused protocols.

X.25

X.25 is a protocol from a very different era of networking. In the 1970s, when it was developed, users had dumb terminals (essentially a cathode ray tube monitor and keyboard) that were connected to a large computer. Also, networks were very unreliable, and a lot of resources had to be invested in error checking and correction.

X.25 allows users and hosts to connect through a modem to remote hosts via a packet-switched network. As with all packet-switched networks, the user's stream of data is subdivided into packets and forwarded through the X.25 network to the destination host. Although it may seem as if the user has a dedicated circuit over the WAN, actually, packets could take different paths along the way. Because networks were very unreliable when X.25 was developed, packets go through rigorous error checking, which add much overhead—too much by today's standards.

Most organizations now opt for DSL and ATM, instead of X.25, for packet switching. Like ISDN, X.25 is largely de-commissioned now and available for the purposes of supporting legacy applications only.

Frame Relay

Frame Relay is an economical alternative to circuit-switched networks and dedicated lines between networks that have significant idle time. Because Frame Relay uses packet-switching technology, organizations are charged for used bandwidth, which is less expensive than maintaining a dedicated line or the cost of a circuit that is based on the duration of the connection. A Frame Relay network is shown in *Figure 2.30*.

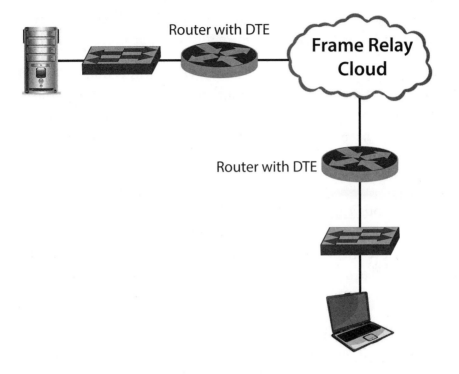

Figure 2.30 - **A Frame Relay network**

The heart of a Frame Relay network is the Frame Relay cloud of switches on the provider's premises. All Frame Relay customers share the resources in the cloud, which are assumed to be reliable, and do not require the intense error checking and correcting of X.25. This significantly increases the throughput over X.25. Devices within the cloud are considered data circuit-terminating equipment (DCE).

Devices that connect to the Frame Relay cloud, which are generally customer owned and on the customer's premises, are considered data terminal equipment (DTE). Communication between endpoints is connection oriented over permanent virtual circuits or switched virtual circuits. Organizations use a permanent virtual circuit when the connection between the DTEs will be active most of the time. For occasional

413

connections, a switched virtual circuit is more cost-effective because the connection will be disconnected when it is completed.

Frame Relay provides a mechanism that guarantees a customer-specified throughput through the cloud, called the committed information rate (CIR). For example, if 10 Kbps is specified, the provider will ensure that 10 Kbps will be available. In addition, the provider will permit bursts of higher throughput if the resources are available in the cloud. Naturally, higher CIRs are more expensive.

Asynchronous Transfer Mode (ATM)

ATM is a connection-oriented protocol designed to transmit data, voice, and video over the same network at very high speeds, such as 155 Mbps. This is facilitated by using small, fixed-length 53-byte cells for all ATM traffic.

Another hallmark of ATM is the use of virtual circuits. Cells transferred between circuit endpoints use the same path. To initiate a circuit, a cell is sent to the destination. As this cell transverses the network, all devices in the cell's path allocate necessary resources to prepare for the eventual transfer of data. As with IP, ATM does not guarantee the delivery of cells.

Virtual circuits can be either permanent or switched. Switched virtual circuits are torn down after the connection is terminated. Permanent virtual circuits, on the other hand, remain active.

Traffic engineering is an aspect of ATM. All virtual circuits are classified in one of the following categories:

- *Constant Bit Rate (CBR):* The circuit's cells are transmitted at a constant rate.
- *Variable Bit Rate (VBR):* The circuit's cells are transmitted within a specified range. This is often used for bursty traffic.
- *Unspecified Bit Rate (UBR):* The circuit's cells receive bandwidth that has not been allocated by circuits in other

categories. This is ideal for applications that are not interactive, such as file transfers.

- *Available Bit Rate (ABR):* The circuit's throughput is adjusted based on feedback from monitoring the available network bandwidth.

2

Telecommunications & Network Security

415

Network Attacks

Attacks can be directed at the network itself, i.e., the network's availability or one of its other services—especially security services—is at risk. In the past, it was considered that the network itself was not the necessary objective of an attack (*Figure 2.31*), but this is no longer the case. Under IP Convergence, the network has come to be the central nervous system of most organizations, controlling both physical and logical elements of the business. Physical elements can include the data and communications that control and manage massive productions systems and critical safety controls on pumps, furnaces, boilers, reaction chambers, and a wide range of other very "physical" elements which can cause serious property damage or loss of life. Physical elements can also include the access controls on buildings and the cameras and intercoms that monitor and record physical threats and alert security staff to emergencies. Logical elements include not only the data flowing around the network like e-mail and files, but all telephony calls and information services like TV might also be relying completely on the same network. Crippling or controlling the network in modern organizations and business, without attacking a specific application, can have the same impact as successfully attacking all the resident applications.

The Network as an Enabler or Channel of Attack

One must distinguish between two subtly different situations here: where an attacker uses certain network characteristics to support his attack, for instance, by intelligence gathering, and where an attack is borne across the network. This chapter will focus primarily on attacks that can be borne through the network; however, it will also still discuss attacks against the network itself, which have cascading impacts to the applications and assets riding on the network.

Use of a network is not necessarily based on a breach of the network, for instance, in the case of a virus infection the breach may have occurred on a user's laptop connected to the Internet. Although it is true that in such

Legacy Stand-Alone Network

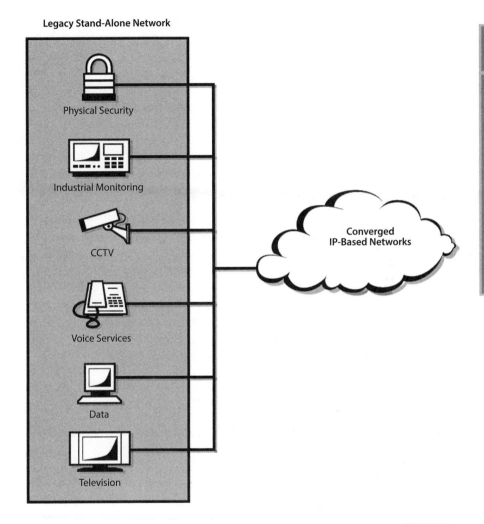

Figure 2.31 - **Converged IP-based networks**

a case a deficiency in the network's architecture was exploited, its own infrastructure and the security services that were designed into it have not technically been breached.

The Network as a Bastion of Defense

The network is a key, if not the most valuable, strategic component supporting the objective of IT security: protecting the information and knowledge. It is therefore paramount to implement strong and coherent network security architecture across an entire organization. As described elsewhere, such measures will typically be built around a complete Information Security Management System (ISMS) including social, organizational, procedural, and technical activities.

Measures will be based on the organization's security policy and typically include configuration and change management, monitoring and log reviews, vulnerability and compliance testing and scanning (including detection scans on the network), security reviews and audits, backup and recovery, as well as awareness and training measures. They need to be balanced, appropriate, and affordable to the organization and commensurate with its business objectives and level of risk acceptance and target assurance level. Key concepts include:

- **Definition of Security Domains** - This could be defined by level of risk or by organizational control. A prime example is the tendency of decentralized organizations to manage their IT—and thereby also their network security—locally, and to different degrees of success.

- **Segregation of Security Domains** - Control of traffic flows according to risk/benefit assessment, and taking into account formal models, such as the Bell–La Padula model, the Biba integrity model, or the Clark–Wilson model.

- **Incident Response Capability** - Including but not limited to:

  - An inventory of business-critical traffic (this could, for instance, be e-mail or file and print servers, but also DNS and DHCP, telephony traffic—VOIP, building access control traffic and or facilities management traffic. Remember—modern building controls, physical security controls and process controls are converging onto IP)

  - An inventory of less critical traffic (such as HTTP or FTP)

  - A way to quickly contain breaches (for instance, by shutting off parts of the network or blocking certain types of traffic)

  - A process for managing the reaction.

Protecting network assets, such as firewalls, routers and switches in all ways as would be normal for an IT system, but likely in a more stringent manner and to a far higher degree of security. Contingency or network "diversity" in case of overload or failure of the primary network connection, alternate network connections are in place to absorb the load/traffic automatically without loss of services to applications and users.

Network Security Objectives and Attack Modes

Although security objectives are specific to each organization, a number of key themes may be distinguished, which will be prioritized by each organization differently, but often the order in which they are listed here is the one chosen. A number of secondary objectives, such as interoperability and, in particular, ease of use, are undercurrents to these themes. A user expects the network (in particular, network security) to be fully transparent and not interfere with business processes and will not easily accept restrictions.

It is a common perception that network security is the end to all other security measures; i.e., that firewalls only will protect an organization. This is a flawed perception; perimeter defense (defending the edges of the network), is merely part of the solution. Perimeter defense is part of a wider concept known as "defense in depth," which simply holds that security must be a multi-layer effort including the edges but also hosts, applications, network elements (routers, switches, DHCP, DNS, wireless access points), people, and operational processes. See *Figure 2.32.*

Furthermore, protective measures will not actually prevent an attack, which is far better than having to repel and attack with the subsequent risks of failure! Neither will detect, response, and recovery strategies stop an attack. Ideally to counter an attack network security must also be proactive—anticipate and oppose the attack against the infrastructure by interdicting and disrupting an attack preemptively or in self-defense. This requires intelligence on the threat, active surveillance at the perimeter and beyond, and the ability to intercede upstream or disable a threat agent's tools.

419

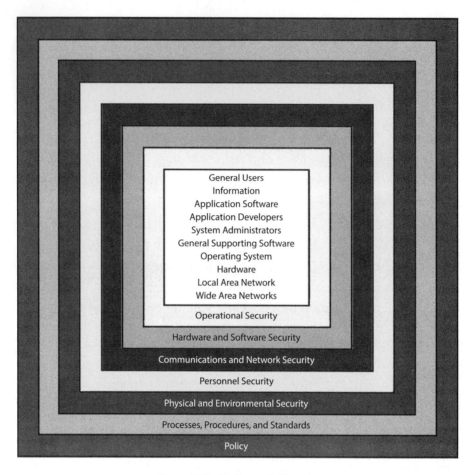

General Users
Information
Application Software
Application Developers
System Administrators
General Supporting Software
Operating System
Hardware
Local Area Network
Wide Area Networks

Operational Security

Hardware and Software Security

Communications and Network Security

Personnel Security

Physical and Environmental Security

Processes, Procedures, and Standards

Policy

Figure 2.32 - **Defense in Depth**

Techniques associated with proactivity can be undertaken independently by organizations with a willingness and resources to do so. Others such as upstream intercession (assuming an external source of the threat such as DDOS, spam/phish or botnet attacks) can be accomplished fairly easily and affordably through cooperation with telecommunications suppliers and Internet service providers (ISP). Finally, the most effective proactive network defense (*Figure 2.33*) is related to the ability to disable attack tools before they can be deployed and applied against you. Such tactics have historically been considered too imprecise and legally dubious for

Mind Map of the Proactive Defense

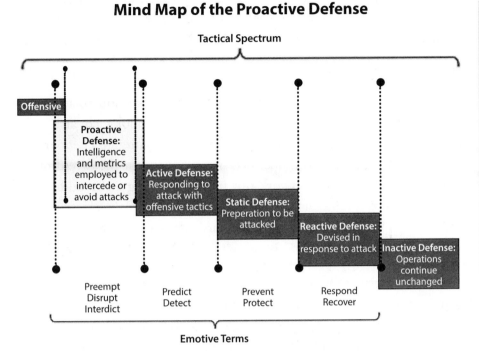

Figure 2.33- **Proactive Defense**

use, but the level of risk to security associated with network-based attacks has led to the adoption of a counteroffensive doctrine by the United States Strategic Defense Command headed by the U.S. Air Force.

Confidentiality

In the context of telecommunications and network security, confidentiality is the property of nondisclosure to unauthorized parties. Attacks against confidentiality are by far the most prevalent today because information can be sold or exploited for profit in a huge variety of (mostly criminal) manners. The network, as the carrier of almost all digital information within the enterprise, provides an attractive target to bypass access control measures on the assets using the network and access information while it is in transit. Among the information that can be acquired is not just the payload information, but also credentials, such as passwords. Conversely, an attacker might not even be interested in the information transmitted, but simply in the fact that communication has occurred. An overarching class of attacks carried out against confidentiality is known as "eavesdropping".

Eavesdropping (Sniffing)

To access information from the network, an attacker must have access to the network itself in the first place (see the "Methodology of an attack" section). An eavesdropping computer can be a legitimate client to the network or an unauthorized one. It is not necessary for the eavesdropper to become a part of the network (for instance, having an IP address); it is often far more advantageous for an attacker to remain invisible (and inaddressible) on the network. This is particularly easy in wireless LANs, where no physical connection is necessary.

Countermeasures to eavesdropping include encryption of network traffic on a network or application level, traffic padding to prevent identification of times when communication happens, rerouting of information to anonymize its origins and potentially split different parts of a message, and mandating trusted routes for data such that information is only traversing trusted network domains.

Integrity

In the context of telecommunications and network security, integrity is the property association with corruption or change (intentional or accidental). A network needs to support the integrity of its traffic. In many ways, the provisions taken for protection against interception, to protect confidentiality will also protect the integrity of a message. Attacks against integrity are often a step to compromising confidentiality or availability as opposed to the overall objective.

Although the modification of messages will often happen at the higher network layers (i.e., within applications), networks can be set up to provide robustness or resilience against interception and change of a message (man-in-the-middle attack) or replay attacks. Ways to accomplish this can be based on encryption or checksums on messages, as well as on access control measures for clients that would prevent an attacker from gaining the necessary access to send a modified message into the network.

Conversely, many protocols, such as SMTP, HTTP, or even DNS, do not provide any degree of authentication. Consequently, it becomes relatively easy for the attacker to inject messages with fake sender information into a network from the outside through an existing gateway. The fact that no application can rely on the security or authenticity of underlying protocols has become a common design factor in networking.

Availability

In the context of telecommunications and network security, availability is the property of the network service related to its uptime, speed, and latency. Availability of the service is commonly the most obvious business requirement especially with highly converged networks, where multiple assets (data, voice, physical security) are riding on the same network. For this very reason, network availability has also become a prime target for attackers and a key business risk. While a variety of availability threats and risks are addressed in this chapter, an overarching class of attack on availability is known as "denial of service".

Attacks on the transport layer of the OSI model (layer 4) seek to manipulate, disclose, or prevent delivery of the payload as a whole. This can, for instance, happen by reading the payload (as would happen in a sniffer attack) or changing it (which could happen in a man-in-the-middle attack). While disruptions of service can be executed at other layers as well, the transport layer has become a common attack ground via ICMP.

Domain Litigation

Domain names are subject to trademark risks, related to a risk of temporary unavailability or permanent loss of an established domain name. For the business in question, the consequences can be equivalent to the loss of its whole Internet presence in an IT-related disaster. Businesses should therefore put in place contingency plans if they are concerned with trademark disputes of any kind over a domain name used as their main Web and e-mail address. Such contingency plans might include setting up a second domain unrelated to the trademark in question (based, for instance, on the trademark of a parent company) that can be advertised on short notice, if necessary.

Cyber squatting and the illegitimate use of similar domains, containing common misspellings or representing the same second-level domain under a different top-level domain is occurring more frequently as the range of domains continues to expand. The only way to protect a business from this kind of fraud is the registration of the most prominent adjacent domains or by means of trademark litigation. A residual risk will always remain, relating not only to public misrepresentation, but also to potential loss or disclosure of e-mail.

Open Mail Relay Servers

An open mail relay server is an SMTP service that allows inbound SMTP connections for domains it does not serve; i.e., for which it does not possess a DNS MX record. An open mail relay is generally considered a sign of bad system administration. See *Figure 2.34.*

Open mail relays are a principal tool for distribution of spam, as they allow an attacker to hide his identity. A number of blacklists for open mail relay servers exist that can be used for blacklisting open mail relays; i.e., a legitimate mail server would not accept any e-mail from this host because it has a high likelihood of being spam. Although using blacklists as one indicator in spam filtering has its merits, it is risky to use them as an exclusive indicator. Generally, they are run by private organizations and individuals according to their own rules, they are able to change their policies on a whim, they can vanish overnight for any reason, and they can rarely be held accountable for the way they operate their lists.

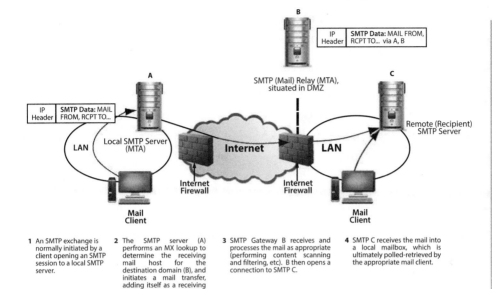

1 An SMTP exchange is normally initiated by a client opening an SMTP session to a local SMTP server.

2 The SMTP server (A) performs an MX lookup to determine the receiving mail host for the destination domain (B), and initiates a mail transfer, adding itself as a receiving host in the mail message header.

3 SMTP Gateway B receives and processes the mail as appropriate (performing content scanning and filtering, etc). B then opens a connection to SMTP C.

4 SMTP C receives the mail into a local mailbox, which is ultimately polled-retrieved by the appropriate mail client.

Figure 2.34 - Representative SMTP exchange

(From Young, S. and Aitel, D., *Hacker's Handbook: The Strategy behind Breaking into and Defending Networks*, Auerbach Publications, Boca Raton, FL, 2004. With permission.)

Spam

Spam benefits from the low cost of e-mail, as opposed to phone calls or letters. It can be sent in massive amounts with little additional cost and a low risk of retribution. Over the years, sending spam has become a professional and highly profitable business. This means that spammers are highly organized and structured. In general, spam is not limited to e-mail; it can also occur in newsgroups, Web logs (blogs), or through instant messaging (Spam over Instant Messaging (SPIM)).

Spam often promotes illegitimate or fraudulent businesses and shady Web sites. It is often crafted in such a way as to trick the user into thinking that either he has been addressed personally, for instance, by inclusion of personal names or e-mail addresses, or that he has accidentally received an important e-mail intended for someone else. Spam relies on illegitimate and security breaching means for its distribution. Because spam is nowhere

425

welcome and the majority of providers have acceptable use policies in place that disallow the sending of UCE, spammers have to resort to illegitimate distribution and redistribution of their e-mail and to obfuscation of its origin.

Spam is almost always sent with invalid (faked) sender addresses or from addresses that have been compromised and are used for sending spam without the legitimate owner's knowledge or permission. Spam can be sent through open mail relays.

Spam appears to be increasingly sent via virus-infected, back-doored hosts (zombie networks). Where this is the case, a security breach is exploited and the spammer may be a party in performing it. The average amount of spam a user receives can easily outnumber his or her normal e-mail. It has therefore become common practice to implement spam filters in e-mail gateways to protect network and server capacity, save working time on behalf of the recipient, and reduce the risk of actual e-mail accidentally being discarded.

By far the most common way of suppressing spam is e-mail filtering on an e-mail gateway. A large variety of commercial products exist, based on a variety of algorithms. Filtering based on simple keywords can be regarded as technically obsolete; (1) the method is prone to generate false-positives, and (2) spammers are having an easy day working around this type of filter. More sophisticated filters, based, for instance, upon statistical analysis or analysis of e-mail traffic patterns, have come to market. Filtering can happen on an e-mail server (mail transfer agent (MTA)) or in the client (mail user agent (MUA)).

As an administrator of a mail server, the server can be configured to limit or slow down an excessive number of connections (tar pit). A mail server can be configured to honor blacklists of spam sources either as a direct blocking list or as one of several indicators for spam. Organizations need to take precautions against becoming a spam haven; i.e., their mail servers and hosts need to be secured to avoid becoming a relay point for spam.

Organizations sending spam—whether deliberately or involuntarily—may face dire consequences and retribution, starting with being cut off from their own mail and Internet access partly or in its entirety.

Scanning Techniques

Port Scanning

Port scanning (*Figure 2.35*) is the act of probing for TCP services on a machine. It is performed by establishing the initial handshake for a connection. Although not in itself an attack, it allows an attacker to test for the presence of potentially vulnerable services on a target system.

Port scanning can also be used for fingerprinting an operating system by evaluating its response characteristics, such as timing of a response, details of the handshake. Protection from port scanning includes restriction of network connections; e.g., by means of a host-based or network-based firewall or by defining a list of valid source addresses on an application level.

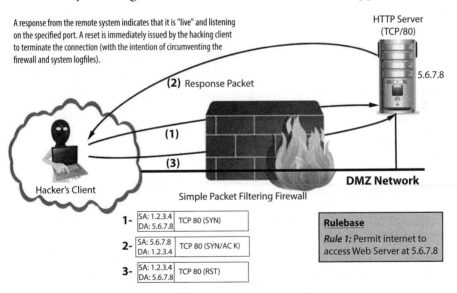

Figure 2.35 - **Example of TCP port scan**

(From Young, S., and Aitel, D., *Hacker's Handbook: The Strategy Behind Breaking into and Defending Networks*, Auerbach Publications, Boca Raton, FL, 2004. With permission.)

FIN, NULL, and XMAS Scanning

In FIN scanning, a stealth scanning method, a request to close a connection is sent to the target machine. If no application is listening on that port, a TCP RST or an ICMP packet will be sent. This attack commonly only works on UNIX machines, as Windows machines behave in a slightly different manner, deviating from RFC 793 (always responding to a FIN packet with an RST, thereby rendering recognition of open ports impossible) and thereby not being susceptible to the scan. Firewalls that put a system into stealth mode (i.e., suppressing system responses to FIN packets) are available. In NULL scanning, no flags are set on the initiating TCP packet; in XMAS scanning, all TCP flags are set (or "lit," as in a Christmas tree). Otherwise, these scans work in the same manner as the FIN scan.

TCP Sequence Number Attacks

To detect and correct loss of data packets, TCP attaches a sequenced number to each data packet that is transmitted. If a transmission is not reported back as successful, a packet will be retransmitted. By eavesdropping on traffic, these sequence numbers can be predicted and fake packets with the correct sequence number can be introduced into the data stream by a third party. This class of attacks can, for instance, be used for session hijacking. Protection mechanisms against TCP sequence number attacks have been proposed based on better randomization of sequence numbers as described in RFC 1948.

Methodology of an Attack

Security attacks have been described formally as attack tree models. Attack trees are based upon the goal of the attacker, the risks to the defender, and the vulnerabilities of the defense systems. They are a specialized form of decision tree that can be used to formally evaluate system security (*Figure 2.36*). The following methodology describes not the attack tree itself (which is a defender's view), but the steps that an attacker would undergo to successfully traverse the tree toward his or her target.

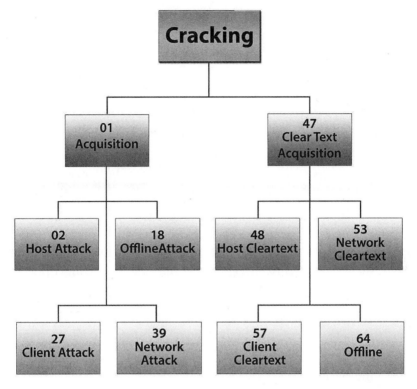

Figure 2.36 - **Attack Tree**

(From Houser, D.D., Blended Threat Analysis: Passwords and Policy, in *Information Security Management Handbook*, 6th edition, Tipton, H.F. and Krause, M. Eds., Auerbach Publications, Boca Raton, FL, 2006. With permission.)

Target Acquisition

An attack usually starts with intelligence gathering and surveillance to obtain a collection of possible targets, for instance, through evaluating directory services and network scanning.

It is therefore important to limit information on a network and make intelligence gathering as difficult as possible. This would include installation of split network security zones (internal nodes are only visible on the inside of a network), network address translation, limiting access to directories of persons and assets, using hidden paths, nonstandard privileged usernames, etc. Importantly, all of these obscurity measures do not have an inherent security value. They serve to slow the attacker down but will not in themselves provide any protection beyond this point; These measures are referred to as delaying tactics.

Target Analysis

In a second step, the identified target is analyzed for security weaknesses that would allow the attacker to obtain access. Depending on the type of attack, the discovery scan has already taken this into account, e.g., by scanning for servers susceptible to a certain kind of buffer overflow attack. Tools available for the target acquisition phase are generally capable of automatically performing a first-target analysis.

The most effective protection is to minimize security vulnerabilities, for instance, by applying software patches at the earliest possible opportunity and using an effective configuration management. In addition, target analysis should be made more difficult for the attacker. For example, system administrators should minimize the system information (e.g., system type, build, and release) that an attacker could glean, making it more difficult to attack the system.

Target Access

In the next step, an attacker will obtain some form of access to the system. This can be access as a normal user or as a guest. The attacker could be exploiting known vulnerabilities or common tools for this, or bypass technical security controls altogether by using social engineering attacks.

To mitigate the risk of unauthorized access, existing user privileges need to be well managed, access profiles need to be up to date, and unused accounts should be blocked or removed. Access should be monitored and monitoring logs need to be regularly analyzed; however, most malware will come with root kits ready to subvert basic operating system privilege management.

Target Appropriation

As the second but last level of an attack, the attacker can then escalate his or her privileges on the system to gain system-level access. Again, exploitation of known vulnerabilities through existing or custom tools and techniques is the main technical attack vector; however, other attack vectors, such as (again and always) social engineering, need to be taken into account.

Countermeasures against privilege escalation, by nature, are similar to the ones for gaining access. However, because an attacker can gain full control of a system through privilege escalation, secondary controls on the system itself (such as detecting unusual activity in log files) are less effective and reliable. Network (router, firewall, and intrusion detection system) logs can therefore prove invaluable. Logs are so valuable, in fact, that an entire discipline within IT security has developed known as Security Event Management (SEM) or sometimes Security Event and Incident Management (SEIM). As noted earlier, SEM/SEIM is a security service that is available from several different vendors as both software and as an appliance.

To detect the presence of unauthorized changes, which could indicate access from an attacker or backdoors into the system, the use of host-based or network-based intrusion detection systems can provide useful detection services. However, it is important to keep in mind that because an IDS relies on constant external input in the form of attack signature updates to remain effective, these systems are only as " good " as the quality and timeliness of the updates being applied to them. The output from the host-based IDS (such as regular snapshots or file hashes) needs to be stored in such a way that they cannot be overwritten from the source system in order to insure integrity.

Last but not least, the attacker may look to remotely maintain control of the system to regain access at a later time or to use it for other purposes, such as sending spam or as a stepping stone for other attacks. To such an end, the attacker could avail himself of prefabricated "rootkits" to sustain control over time. Such a rootkit will not only allow access, but also hide its own existence from traditional cursory inspection methods.

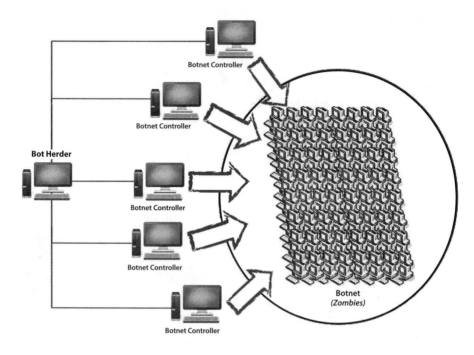

Figure 2.37 - **Architecture of a Botnet**

"Bots" and "botnets" are responsible for most of the activity leading to unauthorized, remote control of compromised systems today. Machines that have become infected, and are now considered to be "Bots", are essentially zombies controlled by shadowy entities from the dark places on the Internet. Bots and botnets are the largest source of spam e-mail and can be coordinated by "botherders" to inflict highly effective denial of services attacks, all without the knowledge of the system owners. *See Figure 2.37.*

Network Security Tools and Tasks

Tools make a security practitioner's job easier. Whether aids in collecting input for risk analysis or scanners to assess how well a server is configured, tools automate processes, which saves time and reduces error. Do not fall into the trap of reducing network security to collect and use tools however.

Intrusion Detection Systems

Intrusion detection systems (IDS) monitor activity and send alerts when they detect suspicious traffic. See *Figure 2.38*. There are two broad classifications of IDS: host-based IDS, which monitor activity on servers and workstations, and network-based IDS, which monitor network activity. Network IDS services are typically stand-alone devices or at least independent blades within network chassis. Network IDS logs would be accessed through a separate management console that will also generate alarms and alerts.

Currently, there are two approaches to the deployment and use of Intrusion Detection Systems. An appliance on the network can monitor traffic for attacks based on a set of signatures (analogous to antivirus software), or the appliance can watch the network's traffic for a while, learn what traffic patterns are normal, and send an alert when it detects an

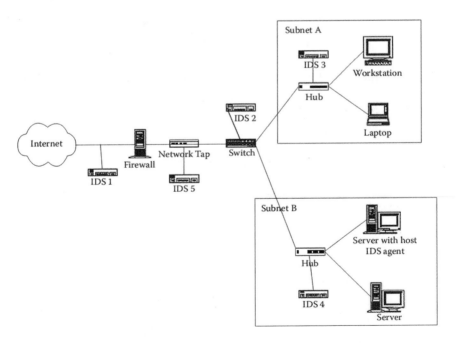

*Figure 2.38 - **Architecture of an Intrusion Detection System (IDS)***

anomaly. Of course, the IDS can be deployed using a hybrid of the two approaches as well.

Independent of the approach, how an organization uses an IDS determines whether the tool is effective. Despite its name, the IDS should not be used to detect intrusions because IDS solutions are not designed to be able to take preventative actions as part of their response. Instead, it should send an alert when it detects interesting, abnormal traffic that could be a prelude to an attack. For example, someone in the engineering department trying to access payroll information over the network at 3 a.m. is probably very interesting and not normal. Or, perhaps a sudden rise in network utilization should be noted.

The above implies that an organization understands the normal characteristics of its network. Considering modern networks' complexity and how much they change, that task is much easier said than done. Additionally, while there are literally thousands and thousands of IDS devices and services deployed in organizations around the world, the most typical operating condition for these IDS services is outright neglect: misconfiguration, full logs and disks, alerts turned off because they became a nuisance or un-intelligible to untrained operators. Basically, most IDS services are merely "running" not working. In most cases the best way to manage IDS services is to outsource to qualified manage security service provider, or integrate the IDS with a larger SEIM service. "Snort" is a free and open-source intrusion detection system. In addition, a large number of commercial tools are available.

Security Event Management (SEM)/
Security Event and Incident Management (SEIM)

SEM/SEIM is a solution that involves harvesting logs and event information from a variety of different sources on individual servers or assets, and analyzing it as a consolidated view with sophisticated reporting. Similarly, entire IT infrastructures can have their logs and event information centralized and managed by large-scale SEM/SEIM deployments. SEM/SEIM will not only aggregate logs but will perform analysis and issue alerts (e-mail, pager, audible, etc.) according to suspicious patterns.

SEM/SEIM solutions as concepts are not necessarily new. They have been around since shortly after 2000 at least; however, they are very complex technologies requiring significant skill on behalf of both the vendor (builder) and the integrator. This is because SEM/SEIM systems have to understand a wide variety of different applications and network element (routers/switches) logs and formats; consolidate these logs into a single database and then correlate events looking for clues to unauthorized behaviors that would be otherwise inconclusive if observed in a single log file.

Aggregation and consolidation of logs and events will also potentially require additional network resources to transfer log and event data from distinct servers and arrays to a central location. This transfer will also need to occur in as close to real time as possible if the security information is to possess value beyond forensics!

SEM/SEIM systems can benefit immensely from Security Intelligence Services (SIS). The output from security appliances is esoteric, and lacks the real-world context required for predictive threat assessments. It falls short of delivering consistently relevant intelligence to businesses operating in a competitive marketplace. SIS uses all-source collection and analysis methods to produce and deliver precise and timely intelligence guiding not only the "business of security" but the "security of the business." SIS are built upon accurate security metrics (cyber and physical), market analysis,

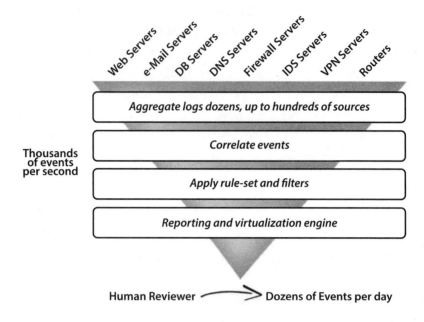

Figure 2.39 - **SEIM services**

technology forecasting, and are correlated to real-world events, giving business decision makers time and precision. SIS provides upstream data from proactive cyber defense systems monitoring darkspace and darkweb.

Scanners

A network scanner can be used in several ways:

- Discovery of devices and services on a network, for instance, to establish whether new or unauthorized devices have been connected. Conversely, this type of scan can be used for intelligence gathering on potentially vulnerable services.

- Test of compliance with a given policy, for instance, to ensure certain configurations (deactivation of services) have been applied.

- Test for vulnerabilities, for instance, as part of a penetration test, but also in preparation for an attack.

Discovery Scanning

A discovery scan can be performed with very simple methods, for example, by sending a ping packet (ping scanning) to every address in a subnet. More sophisticated methods will also discover the operating system and services of a responding device.

Compliance Scanning

A compliance scan can be performed either from the network or on the device; for instance, as a security health check. If performed on the network, it will usually include testing for open ports and services on the device.

Vulnerability Scanning and Penetration Testing

A vulnerability scan tests for vulnerability conditions generally by looking at responding ports and applications on a given server and determining patch levels. A vulnerability scan will infer a threat based upon what might be available as an avenue of attack. Vulnerability scans on a device (network or otherwise) have been performed on both operational and test assets because a vulnerability scan can usually be performed in a nondisruptive manner. But even a test for certain vulnerabilities might affect the target's availability or performance. When new vulnerabilities have been published or are exploited, targeted scanner tools often become available from software vendors, antivirus vendors, independent vendors, or the open-source community. Care must be taken when running scans in a corporate environment so that the load does not disrupt operations or cause applications and services to fail.

A penetration test is the follow-on step after a vulnerability scan, where the observed vulnerabilities are actually exploited or are attempted. It is often the case that an inferred vulnerability, when tested, is not actually a vulnerability. For instance, a service might be open on a port and appear un-patched, but upon testing it turns out that the administrator have implemented a secure configuration that mitigates the vulnerabilities.

437

Penetration tests always have a high potential to bring down the asset against which they are being performed, and for this reason should never be conducted on operational systems. Penetration tests should be conducted on test platforms and in test environments; in addition, a clear waiver from the asset owner should be obtained prior to testing.

Scanning Tools

This is not the place to describe the functionality of the many available scanning tools in detail. However the following tools are commonplace and worth understanding:

- **Nessus** - A vulnerability scanner
- **Nmap** - A discovery scanner that will allow for determining the services running on a machine, as well as other host characteristics, such as a machine's operating system

In addition, a large number of commercial tools exist. Consult the respective vendor's information on the Web.

Network Taps

A "network tap" is a device that has the ability to selectively copy all data flowing through a network in real time for analysis and storage. See *Figure 2.40*. Network taps may be deployed for the purposes of network diagnostics and maintenance or for purposes of forensic analysis related to incidents or suspicious events. Network taps will generally be fully configurable and will function at all layers from the physical layer up. In other words, a tap should be capable of copying everything from layer 2 (Ethernet, for instance) upward, including all payload information within the packets. Additionally, a tap can be configured to vacuum up every single packet of data, or perhaps just focus on selected application traffic from selected sources.

Increasingly network taps are being deployed for the purposes of compliance with legal requirements related to retaining records of transactions and detecting fraud. In a world of converged information assets with data, voice, instant messaging, and other communications assets all riding on the IP network, organizations might find themselves with little choice but to retain a complete copy of all traffic for later analysis if required. Network taps are available in a wide variety of forms and from a variety of commercial vendors.

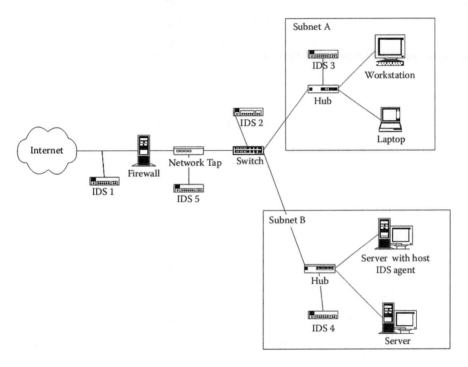

Figure 2.40 - **A network tap is a device that simply sits on a network in "monitor" or "promiscuous" mode and makes a copy of all the network traffic, possibly right down to the Ethernet frames.**

(From Macaulay, T., *Securing Converged IP Networks*, Auerbach Publications, Boca Raton, FL, 2006. With permission.)

IP Fragmentation Attacks and Crafted Packets

Teardrop

In this attack, IP packet fragments are constructed so that the target host calculates a negative fragment length when it attempts to reconstruct the packet. If the target host's IP stack does not ensure that fragment lengths are set within appropriate boundaries, the host could crash or become unstable. This problem is fixed with a vendor patch.

Overlapping Fragment Attack

Overlapping fragment attacks are used to subvert packet filters that only inspect the first fragment of a fragmented packet. The technique involves sending a harmless first fragment, which will satisfy the packet filter. Other packets follow that overwrite the first fragment with malicious data, thus resulting in harmful packets bypassing the packet filter and being accepted by the victim host. A solution to this problem is for TCP/IP stacks not to allow fragments to overwrite each other.

Source Routing Exploitation

Instead of only permitting routers to determine the path a packet takes to its destination, IP allows the sender to explicitly specify the path. An attacker can abuse source routing so that the packet will be forwarded between network interfaces on a multihomed computer that is configured not to forward packets. This could allow an external attacker access to an internal network.

Source routing is specified by the sender of an IP datagram, whereas the routing path would normally be left to the router to decide. The best solution is to disable source routing on hosts and to block source-routed packets.

Smurf and Fraggle Attacks

Both attacks use broadcasts to create denial-of-service attacks. A Smurf attack misuses the ICMP echo request to create denial-of-service attacks.

In a Smurf attack, the intruder sends an ICMP echo request with a spoofed source address of the victim. The packet is sent to a network's broadcast address, which forwards the packet to every host on the network. Because the ICMP packet contains the victim's host as the source address, the victim will be overwhelmed by the ICMP echo replies, causing a denial-of-service attack.

The Fraggle attack uses UDP instead of ICMP. The attacker sends a UDP packet on port 7 with a spoofed source address of the victim. Like the Smurf attack, the packet is sent to a network's broadcast address, which will forward the packet to all of the hosts on the network. The victim host will be overwhelmed by the responses from the network.

NFS Attacks

NFS versions 2 and 3 have several drawbacks from a security perspective, due to their rather basic authentication mechanisms and to the fact that a file system protocol must possess some form of state management, for which some workarounds have to be introduced on top of the stateless protocol to enable, for instance, file locking. An attacker would have several opportunities to attack NFS, be it from a client, a server, or a network perspective.

The first step in setting up an NFS connection will be the publication (exporting) of file system trees from the server. These trees can be arbitrarily chosen by the administrator. Access privileges are granted based upon the client IP address and directory tree. Within the tree, the privileges of the server file system will be mapped to client users.

Several points of risk exist:

- Export of parts of the file system that were not intended for publication or with inappropriate privileges; for instance, by accident or through the existence of UNIX file system hard links (which can be generated by the user). This is of particular concern if parts of the server root file system are

441

made accessible. One can easily imagine scenarios where a password file can be accessed and the encrypted passwords contained therein are subsequently broken by an off-the-shelf tool. Regular review of exported file system trees is an appropriate mitigation.

- Using an unauthorized client. Because NFS identifies the client by its IP address or (indirectly) a host name, it is relatively easy to use a different client than the authorized one, by means of IP spoofing or DNS spoofing. At the very least, resolution of server host names should therefore happen via a file (/etc/hosts on UNIX), not through DNS.

- Incorrect mapping of user IDs between server and client. Any machine not controlled by the server administrator can be used to propagate an attack, as NFS relies on user IDs as the only form of authorization credential. An attacker, having availed himself of administrative access to a client, could generate arbitrary user IDs to match those on the server. It is paramount that user IDs on server and client are synchronized; e.g., through the use of NIS/NIS + (see Network Information Service).

- Sniffing and access request spoofing. Because NFS traffic, by default, is not encrypted, it is possible to intercept it, either by means of network sniffing or by a man-in-the-middle attack. Because NFS does not authenticate each RPC call, it is possible to access files if the appropriate access token (file handle) has been obtained, for instance, through sniffing. NFS itself does not offer appropriate mitigation, however the use of secure NFS may. [1]

- SetUID files. The directories accessed via NFS are used in the same way local directories are. On UNIX systems, files with the SUID bit can therefore be used for privilege escalation on the client. NFS should therefore be configured in such a way as to not respect SUID bits.

---

[1]   Secure NFS (SNFS) offers secure authentication and encryption on the basis of secure RPC, which authenticates each RPC request.

Network News Transport Protocol (NNTP) Security

From a security perspective, the main shortcoming in NNTP is authentication. Confidentiality of the message is much less of a concern, as the information is indeed intended for publication; however, the proper identification and authentication of the sender remains a strong concern.

One of the earlier solutions users found to this problem was signing messages with Pretty Good Privacy (PGP). However, this did not prevent impersonation or faked identities, as digital signatures were not a requirement, and indeed would be unsuitable for the repudiation problem implied. To make matters worse, NNTP offers a cancellation mechanism to withdraw articles already published. Naturally, the same authentication weakness applies to the control messages used for these cancellations, allowing users with even moderate skills to delete messages at will.

On a related note, NNTP feeds have been plagued with spam for more than a decade (in essence, since Usenet spam became economically viable). A number of mechanisms to deal with this problem have evolved. It can be safely said that all technical measures are just add-ons to what is mostly a social self-regulation mechanism. The original Usenet way of dealing with unwanted information was maintenance of client-based blacklists by the user, so-called killfiles.

Some newsgroups have been set up as moderated to prevent misuse, mostly by partisan participants, but naturally the mechanism also works against spam, even though it comes at an increased workload to the moderator of a newsgroup. Over time, a convention evolved, after which messages classified as spam by well-defined criteria (excessive repetitions or cross-posting of identical or highly similar messages) were legitimate targets for cancellations. The problem of authentication has never been adequately addressed in NNTP, and it might even be undesirable to do so: in a certain way, Usenet as a social construct may well depend on the ability to post anonymously or under pseudonyms.

443

Finger User Information Protocol

Finger is an identification service that allows a user to obtain information about the last log-in time of a user and whether he or she is currently logged into a system. The "fingered" user has the possibility to have information from two files in their home directory displayed (the .project and .plan files).

Developed as early as 1971, Finger is implemented as an UNIX daemon, fingerd. Finger has become less popular for several reasons:

- Finger has been the subject of a number of security exploits.

- Finger is raising privacy and security concerns; it can easily be abused for social engineering attacks.

- The user's self-actuation (an important social aspect in early UNIX networks) happens through Web pages today.

For all practical purposes, the Finger protocol has become obsolete. Its use should be restricted to situations where no alternatives are available.

Ports	79/TCP
Definition	RFC 742
	RFC 1288

Table 2.22 - **Finger Quick Reference**

Network Time Protocol (NTP)

NTP synchronizes computer clocks in a network. This can be extremely important for operational stability (for instance, under NIS), but also for maintaining consistency and coherence of audit trails, such as in log files.

A variant of NTP exists in Simple Network Time Protocol (SNTP), offering a less resource intensive, but also less exact form of synchronization. From a security perspective, our main objective with NTP is to prevent an attacker from changing time information on a client or a whole network by manipulating its local time server.

NTP can be configured to restrict access based upon IP address. From NTP version 3 onward, cryptographic authentication has become available, based upon symmetric encryption, but to be replaced by public key cryptography in NTP version 4.

To make a network robust against accidental or deliberate timing inaccuracies, a network should have its own time server and possibly a dedicated, highly accurate clock. As a standard precaution, a network should never depend on one external time server alone, but synchronize with several trusted time sources. Thus, manipulation of a single source will have no immediate effect. To detect desynchronization, standard logging mechanisms can be used with NTP to ensure synchronicity of time stamping.

Ports	123/TCP, 123/UDP
Definition	RFC 778
	RC 891
	RC 956
	RC 958
	RFC 1305

Table 2.23 - **NTP Quick Reference**

DDoS

Denial-of-Service Attack

The easiest attack to carry out against a network, or so it may seem, is to overload it through excessive traffic or traffic which has been "crafted" to confuse the network into shutting down or slowing to the point of uselessness. See *Figure 2.41*.

Countermeasures include, but are not limited to multiple layers of firewalls, careful filtering on firewalls, routers and switches, internal network access controls (NAC), redundant (diverse) network connections, load balancing, reserved bandwidth (quality of service, which would at least protect systems not directly targeted), and blocking traffic from an attacker on an upstream router. Bear in mind that malicious agents can and will shift IP address or DNS name to sidestep the attack, as well as employing potentially thousands of unique IP addresses during the execution of an attack. Enlisting the help of upstream service providers and carriers is ultimately the most effective countermeasure, especially if the necessary agreements and relationships have been established proactively or as part of agreed service levels.

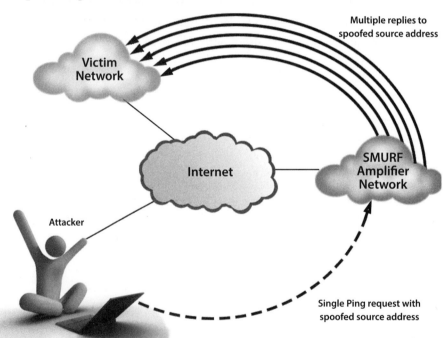

Figure 2.41 - **A Denial-of-Service attack. The attacker uses spoofed PING packets to floor a network by using a vulnerable intermediary network**

(From Thorsheim, P., Comparing firewall technologies, in *Information Security Management Handbook*, 6th edition, Tipton, H.F. and Krause, M. Eds., Auerbach Publications, Boca Raton, FL, 2006. With permission.)

It is instructive to note that many protocols contain basic protection from message loss that would at least mitigate the effects of denial-of-service attacks. This starts with TCP managing packet loss within certain limits, and ends with higher level protocols, such as SMTP, that will provide robustness against temporary connection outages (store and forward) [2].

For the attacker, there are a number of ways to execute denial-of-service attacks while minimizing his own cost:

- ■ *Distributed denial-of-service attack:* Using a network of remote-controlled hosts known as "botnets" (typically workstations that have been compromised by a virus or other form of "malware"), the target is subjected to traffic from a wide range of sources that are very hard to block. The downside of this type of attack to both the attacker and network service provider is that the attack may already throttle upstream network channels, taking out more than just its intended target.

- ■ Distributed denial-of-service attacks have been used as a means of extortion, but also as a political instrument (referred to by their initiators as online demonstration), where activists would instigate users to frequently reload a certain Web site at a certain point in time.

Countermeasures are similar to those of conventional denial-of-service attacks, but simple IP or port filtering might not work.

Utilizing weaknesses in the design of TCP/IP to clog the network stack on the target system instead of the network itself, for instance, through SYN flood attacks. Such attacks can be executed over minimal bandwidth and can be hard to trace by their very nature (no complete transaction channel is ever established, and consequently, no logging occurs).

---

2   The concept of store and forward allows for the reception of a data packet upstream from the end point, and the queuing of that data for a period of time if necessary, in order to ensure delivery of the data to the end point once it is located.

SYN Flooding

A SYN flood attack is a denial-of-service attack against the initial handshake in a TCP connection. Many new connections from faked, random IP addresses are opened in short order, overloading the target's connection table.

Countermeasures include tuning of operating system parameters (concretely, the size of the backlog table) according to vendor specifications. Another solution, which requires modification to the TCP/IP stack, is SYN cookies [3]— changing TCP numbers in a way that makes faked packets immediately recognizable.

Daniel J. Bernstein, the primary inventor of this approach, defines them as "particular choices of initial TCP sequence numbers by TCP servers. The difference between the server's initial sequence number and the client's initial sequence number is

- **Top 5 bits:** t mod 32, where t is a 32 bit time counter that increases every 64 seconds;

- **Next 3 bits:** An encoding of an MSS selected by the server in response to the client's MSS;

- **Bottom 24 bits:** A server-selected secret function of the client IP address and port number, the server IP address and port number, and t.

A server that uses SYN cookies does not have to drop connections when its SYN queue fills up. Instead it sends back a SYN+ACK, exactly as if the SYN queue had been larger. When the server receives an ACK, it checks that the secret function works for a recent value of t, and then rebuilds the SYN queue entry from the encoded MSS. "

One of the most successful variants of SYN flooding can be carried out by the botnets discussed earlier. Botnets have the ability to direct potentially

---

3   Bernstein, Daniel J., "SYN cookies". N.p., 1996. Web. 29 May 2012. <http://cr.yp.to/syncookies.html>.

thousands of SYN requests to hosts at the same time, overwhelming not only the hosts but also the network connections that they rest upon. Under such circumstances, there are no host-configuration countermeasures available because a host without a network is as good as dead anyway. While SYN flooding might be the mode of attack, it is not being employed in any cunning manner with spoofed IP addresses from possibly a single malicious host; it is being applied as a pure brute-force form of attack.

Countermeasures include protecting the operating system through securing its network stack. This is not normally something the user or owner of a system has any degree of control over; it is a task for the vendor.

Finally, the network needs to be included in a corporation's disaster recovery and business contingency plans. For local area networks, one may set high recovery objectives and provide appropriate contingency, based upon the fact that any recovery of services is likely to be useless without at least a working local area network (LAN) infrastructure. As wide area networks are usually outsourced, contingency measures might include acquisition of backup lines from a different provider, procurement of telephone or Digital Subscriber Loop (DSL) lines, etc.

Spoofing

IP Address Spoofing and SYN-ACK attacks

Packets are sent with a bogus source address so that the victim will send a response to a different host. Spoofed addresses can be used to abuse the three-way handshake that is required to start a TCP session. Under normal circumstances, a host offers to initiate a session with a remote host by sending a packet with the SYN option. The remote host responds with a packet with the SYN and ACK options. The handshake is completed when the initiating host responds with a packet with the ACK option.

An attacker can launch a denial-of-service attack by sending the initial packet with the SYN option with a source address of a host that does not exist. The victim will respond to the forged source address by sending a packet with the SYN and ACK options, and then wait for the final packet to complete the handshake. Of course, that packet will never arrive because the victim sent the packet to a host that does not exist. If the attacker sends a storm of packets with spoofed addresses, the victim may reach the limit of uncompleted (half-open) three-way handshakes and refuse other legitimate network connections.

The above scenario takes advantage of a protocol flaw. To mitigate the risk of a successful attack, vendors have released patches that reduce the likelihood of the limit of uncompleted handshakes being reached. In addition, security devices, such as firewalls, can block packets that arrive from an external interface with a source address from an internal network.

E-Mail Spoofing

As SMTP does not possess an adequate authentication mechanism, e-mail spoofing is extremely simple. The most effective protection against this is a social one, whereas the recipient can confirm or simply ignore implausible e-mail.

Spoofing e-mail sender addresses is extremely simple, and it can be done with a simple TELNET command to port 25 of a mail server and by issuing a number of SMTP commands.

E-mail spoofing is frequently used as a means to obfuscate the identity of a sender in spamming, whereas the purported sender of a spam e-mail is in fact another victim of spam, whose e-mail address has been harvested by or sold to a spammer.

DNS Spoofing

To resolve a domain name query, such as mapping a Web server address to an IP address, the user's workstation will in turn have to undertake a series of queries through the Domain Name Server hierarchy. Such queries can be either recursive (a name server receiving a request will forward it and return the resolution) or iterative (a name server receiving a request will respond with a reference).

An attacker aiming to poison a DNS server's (name server) cache (information related to previous queries, which is stored for reuse in future queries for speed and efficiency) by injecting fake records, and thereby falsifying responses to client requests, will need to send a query to this very name server. The attacker now knows that the name server will shortly send out a query for resolution.

In the first case, the attacker has sent a query for a domain, whose primary name server he controls. The response from this query will contain additional information that was not originally requested, but which the target server will now cache. The second case is a dissimilar method that can also be used in iterative queries. Using IP spoofing, the attacker will send a response to his own query before the authoritative (correct) name server has a chance to respond.

In both cases, the attacker has used an electronic conversation to inject false information into the name server's cache. Not only will this name server now use the cached information, but the false information will propagate to other servers, making inquiries to this one. Due to the caching nature of DNS, attacks on DNS servers as well as countermeasures always have certain latency, determined by the configuration of a (domain) zone.

There are two principal vulnerabilities here, both inherent in the design of the DNS protocol: it is possible for a DNS server to respond to a recursive query with information that was not requested, and the DNS server will not authenticate information. Approaches to address or mitigate this threat have only been partly successful.

Later versions of DNS server software are programmed to ignore responses that do not correspond to a query. Authentication has been proposed but attempts to introduce stronger (or even "any") authentication into DNS (for instance, through the use of DNSSEC) have not found wide acceptance. Authentication services have been delegated upward to higher protocol layers. Applications in need of guaranteeing authenticity cannot rely on DNS to provide such but will have to implement a solution themselves.

The ultimate solution to DNS security issues for many organizations is to establish DNS servers dedicated to their domains and vigorously monitor them. An "internal" DNS server will also be established, which only accepts queries from internal networks and users, and therefore it is considered to be substantially more difficult for outsiders to compromise and use as a staging point for penetrating internal networks.

Manipulation of DNS Queries

Technically, the following two techniques are only indirectly related to DNS weaknesses. However, it is worth mentioning them in the context of DNS because they seek to manipulate name resolution in other ways.

"Pharming" is the manipulation of DNS records; for instance, through the "hosts" file on a workstation. A hosts file (*/etc/hosts* on many UNIX machines, *C:\Windows\System32\drivers\etc* on a Windows machine) is the resource first queried before a DNS request is issued. It will always contain the mapping of the host name local host to the IP address 127.0.0.1 (loopback interface, as defined in RFC 3330) and potentially other hosts. A virus may add addresses of antivirus software vendors with invalid IP addresses to the hosts file to prevent download of virus pattern files. Alternately, Internet banking sites might have their IP addresses substituted for rogue, imposters' sites which will attempt to trick the user into providing login information. A further form of DNS pharming is to compromise a DNS server itself and thereby re-direct all users of the DNS server to imposter Web sites even though their workstation itself may be free from compromise.

Social engineering techniques will not try to manipulate a query on a technical level, but can trick the user into misinterpreting a DNS address that is displayed to him in a phishing e-mail or in his Web browser address bar. One way to achieve this in e-mail or Hypertext Markup Language (HTML) documents is to display a link in text where the actual target address is different from what is displayed. Another way to achieve this is the use of non-ASCII character sets (for instance, Unicode—ISO/IEC 10646—characters) that closely resemble ASCII (i.e., Latin) characters to the user. This may become a popular technique with the popularization of internationalized domain names.

Information Disclosure

Smaller corporate networks do not split naming zones, i.e., names of hosts that are accessible only from an intranet are visible from the Internet. Although knowing a server name will not enable anyone to access it, this knowledge can aid and facilitate preparation of a planned attack as it provides an attacker with valuable information on existing hosts (at least with regard to servers), network structure, and, for instance, details such as organizational structure or server operating systems (if the OS is part of the host name, etc.).

A business should therefore operate split DNS zones wherever possible and refrain from using telling naming conventions for their machines. In addition, a domain registrar's database of administrative and billing domain contacts (Whois database) can be an attractive target for information and e-mail harvesting.

Namespace-Related Risks

Besides the technical risks described, a number of other risks exist that, although not strictly security related, can lead to equivalent exposure.

Session Highjack

Session hijacking is the act of unauthorized insertion of packets into a data stream. It is normally based on sequence number attacks, where sequence numbers are either guessed or intercepted. Different types of session hijacking exist:

- ■ *IP spoofing:* Based on a TCP sequence number attack, the attacker would insert packets with a faked sender IP address and a guessed sequence number into the stream. The attacker would not be able to see the response to any commands inserted.

- ■ *Man-in-the-middle attack:* The attacker would sniff or intercept packets, removing legitimate packets from the data stream and replacing them with his own. In fact, both sides of a communication would then communicate with the attacker instead of each other.

Countermeasures against IP spoofing can be executed at layer 3 (see IP Address Spoofing and Syn-Ack Attacks). As TCP sessions only perform an initial authentication, application layer encryption can be used to protect against man-in-the-middle attacks.

SYN Scanning

As traditional TCP scans became widely recognized and were blocked, various stealth scanning techniques were developed. In TCP half scanning (also known as TCP SYN scanning), no complete connection is opened; instead, only the initial steps of the handshake are performed. This makes the scan harder to recognize; for instance, it would not show up in application log files. However, it is possible to recognize and block TCP SYN scans with an appropriately equipped firewall.

More to Know The following articles and documents contain more information about network security and telecommunications. The following are freely available on the Internet:

http://www.cyber.st.dhs.gov/docs/NIST%20Guide%20to%20Supervisory%20 and%20Data%20Acquisition-SCADA%20and%20Industrial%20Control%20 Systems%20Security%20%282007%29.pdf

http://www.inl.gov/technicalpublications/Documents/3375141.pdf

http://csrc.nist.gov/publications/nistpubs/800-13/sp800-13.pdf

http://www.etsi.org/WebSite/Standards/ETSIDeliverables.aspx

Summary and Conclusion

Interconnected systems are becoming increasingly more ubiquitous and complex in modern society. As the interconnectedness between systems and individuals grows so does the complexity of security and the size of the attack surface. While this chapter has covered a high level of several network and telecom basics, security professionals should continue to read further into trending topics such as critical infrastructure security and implications of newer protocols such as IPv6. The network wired or wireless will always exist as a tempting target for attack and exfiltration of information. Therefore, it should always be a concern for the security professional.

Review Questions

1. In the OSI reference model, on which layer would Ethernet (IEEE 802.3) be placed?

    A. Layer 1—Physical layer

    B. Layer 2—Data-link layer

    C. Layer 3—Network Layer

    D. Layer 4—Transport Layer

2. Which tactic would **BEST** be considered a part of a proactive network defense?

    A. Redundant firewalls

    B. Business Continuity planning

    C. Disallowing P2P traffic

    D. Perimeter surveillance and intelligence gathering

3. In which situation is the network not the target of the attack?

    A. A denial-of-service attack on servers on a network

    B. Hacking into a router

    C. A virus outbreak saturating network capacity

    D. A man-in-the-middle attack

4. Which of the following is **MOST** effective against a distributed denial-of-service attack?

    A. Secret fully qualified domain names (FQDNs)

    B. Redundant network layout

    C. Traffic filtering

    D. Network Address Translation (NAT).

5. What is the optimal placement for network-based intrusion detection systems (NIDS)?

    A. On the network perimeter, to alert the network administrator of all suspicious traffic

    B. On network segments with business-critical systems

    C. At the network operations center (NOC)

    D. At an external service provider

6. Which of the following end-point devices would MOST likely be considered part of a converged IP network?

    A. file server, IP phone, security camera

    B. IP phone, thermostat, cypher lock

    C. security camera, cypher lock, IP phone

    D. thermostat, file server, cypher lock

7. Which of the following is an advantage of fiber-optic over copper cables from a security perspective?

    A. Fiber optics provides higher bandwidth.

    B. Fiber optics are more difficult to wiretap.

    C. Fiber optics are immune to wiretap.

    D. None—the two are equivalent; network security is independent from the physical layer.

8. Which of the following devices should be part of a network's perimeter defense?

    A. A boundary router, A firewall, A proxy Server

    B. A firewall, A proxy server, A host based intrusion detection system (HIDS)

    C. A proxy server, A host based intrusion detection system (HIDS), A firewall

    D. A host based intrusion detection system (HIDS), A firewall, A boundary router

9. Which of the following is a principal security risk of wireless LANs?

    A. Lack of physical access control

    B. Demonstrably insecure standards

    C. Implementation weaknesses

    D. War driving

10. Which of the following configurations of a WLAN's SSID offers adequate security protection?

    A. Using an obscure SSID to confuse and distract an attacker

    B. Not using any SSID at all to prevent an attacker from connecting to the network

    C. Not broadcasting an SSID to make it harder to detect the WLAN

    D. An SSID does not provide protection

11. IPSec

    A. provides mechanisms for authentication and encryption.

    B. provides mechanisms for nonrepudiation.

    C. will only be deployed with IPv6.

    D. only authenticates clients against a server.

12. A Security Event Management (SEM) service performs the following function:

    A. Gathers firewall logs for archiving

    B. Aggregates logs from security devices and application servers looking for suspicious activity

    C. Reviews access controls logs on servers and physical entry points to match user system authorization with physical access permissions

    D. Coordination software for security conferences and seminars.

13. Which of the following is the principal weakness of DNS (Domain Name System)?

    A. Lack of authentication of servers, and thereby authenticity of records

    B. Its latency, which enables insertion of records between the time when a record has expired and when it is refreshed

    C. The fact that it is a simple, distributed, hierarchical database instead of a singular, relational one, thereby giving rise to the possibility of inconsistencies going undetected for a certain amount of time

    D. The fact that addresses in e-mail can be spoofed without checking their validity in DNS, caused by the fact that DNS addresses are not digitally signed

14. Which of the following statements about open e-mail relays is incorrect?

    A. An open e-mail relay is a server that forwards e-mail from domains other than the ones it serves.

    B. Open e-mail relays are a principal tool for distribution of spam.

    C. Using a blacklist of open e-mail relays provides a secure way for an e-mail administrator to identify open mail relays and filter spam.

    D. An open e-mail relay is widely considered a sign of bad system administration.

15. A botnet can be characterized as

    A. An network used solely for internal communications

    B. An automatic security alerting tool for corporate networks

    C. A group of dispersed, compromised machines controlled remotely for illicit reasons.

    D. A type of virus

16. A mesh network topology is rarely implemented in modern networks due to

    A. cost

    B. poor redundancy

C. throughput

D. optical fiber limits

17. In installing an 801.11N wireless access point, which of the following provides the strongest wireless encryption?

A. WPA

B. WEP

C. PKI

D. WPA2

18. A new installation requires a network in a heavy manufacturing area with substantial amounts of electromagnetic radiation and power fluctuations. Which media is best suited for this environment if little traffic degradation is tolerated?

A. Coax cable

B. Wireless

C. Shielded twisted pair

D. Fiber

19. Multi-layer protocols such as Modbus used in industrial control systems

A. often have their own encryption and security like IPv6

B. are used in modern routers as a routing interface control

C. Are often insecure by their very nature as they were not designed to natively operate over today's IP networks

D. Have largely been retired and replaced with newer protocols such as IPv6 and NetBIOS

20. A security professional needs to administer a server remotely. Assuming they can access the server from their location which is the BEST approach for access?

A. TELNET

B. SSHv2

C. FTP

D. TFTP

Domain 3

Information Security Governance & Risk Management

THE INFORMATION SECURITY GOVERNANCE AND RISK MANAGEMENT domain of the Certified Information Systems Security Professional (CISSP)® Common Body of Knowledge (CBK)® addresses the framework and policies, concepts, principles, structures, and standards used to establish criteria for the protection of information assets to instill holistically the criteria and assess the effectiveness of that protection. It includes issues of governance, organizational behavior, and security awareness.

Information security management establishes the foundation of a comprehensive and proactive security program to ensure the protection of an organization's information assets. Today's environment of highly interconnected, interdependent systems necessitates the requirement to understand the linkage between information technology and meeting business objectives. Information security management communicates the risks accepted by the organization due to the currently implemented security controls, and continually works to cost effectively enhance the controls to minimize the risk to the company's information assets. Security management encompasses the administrative, technical, and physical controls necessary to adequately protect the confidentiality, integrity, and availability of information assets. Controls are manifested through a foundation of policies, procedures, standards, baselines, and guidelines.

Information security management practices that manage risk include such tools as risk assessment, risk analysis, data classification, and security awareness. Information assets are classified, and through risk assessment, the threats and vulnerabilities related to these assets are categorized, and the appropriate safeguards to mitigate risk of compromise can be identified and prioritized.

Risk management minimizes loss to information assets due to undesirable events through identification, measurement, and control. It encompasses the overall security review, risk analysis, selection and evaluation of safeguards, cost–benefit analysis, management decision, and safeguard identification and implementation, along with ongoing effectiveness review. Risk management provides a mechanism to the organization to ensure that executive management knows current risks, and informed decisions can be made to use one of the risk management principles: risk avoidance, risk transfer, risk mitigation, or risk acceptance, all described in more detail later in this chapter.

Security management is concerned with regulatory, customer, employee, and business partner requirements for managing data as they flow between the various parties to support the processing and business use of the information. Confidentiality, integrity, and availability of the information must be maintained throughout the process.

TOPICS

- Understand and align security function to goals, mission, and objectives of the organization
- Understand and apply security governance
- Understand and apply concepts of confidentiality, integrity, and availability
- Develop and implement security policy
- Define and implement information classification and ownership
- Manage the information lifecycle
- Manage third-party governance
- Understand and apply risk management concepts
- Manage personnel security
- Manage the security function
- Develop and implement information security strategies
- Assess the completeness and effectiveness of the security program

OBJECTIVES

According to the (ISC)² Candidate Information Bulletin, a CISSP candidate is expected to demonstrate an understanding of:

- The planning, organization, and roles of individuals in identifying and securing an organization's information assets

- The development and use of policies stating management's views and position on particular topics and the use of guidelines, standards, and procedures to support the policies

- Security awareness training to make employees aware of the importance of information security, its significance, and the specific security-related requirements relative to their position

  - The importance of confidentiality, proprietary, and private information

  - Employment agreements

  - Employee hiring and termination practices

- Risk management practices and tools to identify, rate, and reduce the risk to specific resources

Understand and Align Security Function

Information security management practices protect the assets of the organization through the implementation of physical, administrative, managerial, technical, and operational controls. Information assets must be managed appropriately to reduce the risk of loss to confidentiality, integrity, or availability. Just as financial assets are managed through finance departments, human assets (people) are managed and cared for by the human resources department and so are the associated codes of conduct and employment policies and practices. Failure to protect information assets from loss, destruction, or unexpected alteration can result in significant losses of productivity, reputation, or financial loss. Information and the systems supporting the mission of an organization are assets which must be protected.

Information security management ensures that appropriate policies, procedures, standards, and guidelines are implemented to ensure business operations are conducted within an acceptable level of risk. Security exists to support and enable the vision, mission, and business objectives of the organization. Effective security management requires judgment based upon the risk tolerance of the organization, the costs to implement the security controls, and the benefit to the business. Although attaining 100% security of information is an admirable goal, in practice this is unrealistic. Even if this goal were attainable through an effective security program that includes all the best security practices for managing risk and a budget that would support all of the activities, it would not be long before a new vulnerability or exploit was discovered which could put the information at risk. As a result, the program must be proactive and ongoing.

Because most organizations are in a competitive environment that requires continuous product innovation and reduction of administrative costs, funding information security at the "100% security level" is

467

cost-prohibitive and impracticable for most organizations. Therefore, effective security management requires risk management that includes a strong understanding of the business objectives of the organization, the management's tolerance for risk, the costs of the various security alternatives, and, subsequently, the due diligence to match the appropriate security controls to the business initiatives. The security professionals who lead the information security program are relied upon for their knowledge of security and risk management principles. Senior management ultimately makes the final decision on the level of security expenditures and the risk it is willing to accept.

Security professionals should view their role as risk advisors to the organization, as they should not be the final decision makers in risk management. There may be situations where a risk is viewed as low, and therefore, the management is willing to accept a risk due to reasons that the security professional may not know. For example, the decision to accept operating in a regional office without a sprinkler system may be appropriate if the company has been operating in that office for ten years without a fire and management has undisclosed plans to relocate the office within the next six months.

Alternatively, there may be government mandates to comply with new regulations or audit findings that have a higher priority. Senior management must weigh all of the risks to the business, and choosing whether to implement specific security controls represents one of those risk management activities. This is why security professionals must be effective at communicating risks and possible security solutions. There will always be residual risk accepted by an organization, and effective security management will minimize this risk to a level that fits within the organization's risk tolerance or risk profile.

Security management is the glue that ensures that the risks are identified and an adequate control environment is established to mitigate the risks.

Security management ensures the interrelationships among assessing risk, implementing policies and controls in response to the risks, promoting awareness of the expectations, monitoring the effectiveness of the controls, and using this knowledge as input to the next risk assessment. These relationships are shown in *Figure 3.1.*

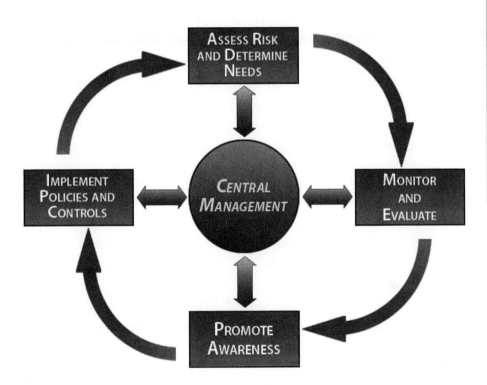

Figure 3.1 - **Security and Risk Management Relationships**

Understand and Apply Security Governance

The increased corporate governance requirements have caused companies to examine their internal control structures more closely to ensure that controls are in place and operating effectively. Organizations are increasingly competing in the global marketplace, which is governed by multiple laws and supported by various best practices (i.e., NIST, ITIL, ISO 27000, COSO, and COBIT). Appropriate information technology investment decisions must be made that are in alignment with the mission of the business. Information technology is no longer a back-office accounting function in most businesses, but rather is a core operational necessity to the business, which must have the proper visibility to the board of directors and management's attention of the program.

This dependence on information technology mandates ensuring the proper alignment and understanding of the risk to the business. Substantial investments are made in these technologies (which must be appropriately managed), company reputations are at risk for insecure systems, and the trust in the systems needs to be demonstrated to all parties involved, including the shareholders, employees, business partners, and customers. Information security governance provides the mechanisms for the board of directors and management to have the proper oversight to manage the risk to the enterprise to an acceptable level.

Although there is no universally accepted definition for security governance at this juncture, the intent of governance is to guarantee that the appropriate information security activities are being performed to ensure that the risks are appropriately reduced, the information security investments are appropriately directed, and the executive management has visibility into the program and is asking the appropriate questions to determine the effectiveness of the program.

The IT Governance Institute (ITGI)[1], in their publication entitled Board Briefing on IT Governance, 2nd edition, defines IT governance as being "the responsibility of the board of directors and executive management. It is an integral part of enterprise governance and consists of the leadership and organizational structures and processes that ensure that the organization's IT sustains and extends the organization's strategies and objectives." [2]

The ITGI proposes that information security governance should be considered a part of IT governance, and that the board of directors should

- Be informed about information security
- Set direction to drive policy and strategy
- Provide resources to security efforts
- Assign management responsibilities
- Set priorities
- Support changes required
- Define cultural values related to risk assessment
- Obtain assurance from internal or external auditors
- Insist that security investments are made measurable and reported on for program effectiveness.

Additionally, the ITGI suggests that the management should

- Write security policies with business input
- Ensure that roles and responsibilities are defined and clearly understood
- Identify threats and vulnerabilities
- Implement security infrastructures and control frameworks (standards, guidelines, baselines, and procedures)
- Ensure that policy is approved by the governing body

---

1   http://www.itgi.org
2   http://www.isaca.org/restricted/Documents/26904_Board_Briefing_final.pdf
(Page 10)

- Establish priorities and implement security projects in a timely manner
- Monitor breaches
- Conduct periodic reviews and tests
- Reinforce awareness education as critical
- Build security into the systems development life cycle.

These concepts are further delineated throughout this chapter.

Organizational Processes

Understanding the mission of an organization and the processes which support it are critical for the success of a security program. In many ways, an organization is like a living animal. It may go through several phases of growth, decline and illness during its lifetime. Understanding of the business transformational events and entities ensures the security professional maintains situational awareness of what is occurring in the boardroom, and/or the management decisions being made on a day to day basis throughout the enterprise. For example, the following are common activities organizations undergo which may impact the security professional:

- *Acquisitions and Mergers:* Organizations combine for many reasons. Some mergers are friendly with both parties realizing a gain from the merger, while others may be described as "hostile." In either situation, the information security professional must be aware of the following items and plan accordingly:

    - Additional data types which may need more protection than the existing security program provides.

    - New staff and roles with enhanced requirements for security awareness and training.

    - Threats from former employees or possibly threats the new organization will face that the old one did not.

    - Vulnerabilities when systems are merged.

    - Potentially new policies, standards and procedures to support compliance with any laws, regulations and requirements that the organization will need to be aware of.

    - External business partners and interconnections which will need review and assessment.

- *Divestitures and Spinoffs:* The opposite of an acquisition or a merger, a divesture may involve the spinoff of a part of an organization, or possibly the complete liquidation of an existing organization. These are tense times in an organization and the information security professional should be concerned with the following situations and plan accordingly:

◘ Data loss and data leak due to employees leaving for the spinoff or another company

◘ System interconnections, protocols and ports left open after the function they were serving is no longer applicable

◘ Loss of visibility into the network and system logs if both organizations did not keep security monitoring tools and capabilities

◘ New threats from employees who may have been laid off or forced out of the organization

◘ The need to revise policies, standards and procedures to recognize any new governance bodies in the organization and reflect the organization change if applicable

■ ***Governance Committees:*** A governance committee is responsible for recruiting and maintaining the governance board for an organization. The committee is also typically responsible for determining missing qualifications and characteristics needed to enhance the efficiency and effectiveness of the board. The information security professional should learn how the board functions and as much as possible attempt to:

◘ Ensure the committee understands at a high level the importance of information security and risk management.

◘ Ensure committee recruitment exercises for new board members include requirements for information security and risk aptitude where needed.

◘ Maintain a working relationship with committee members and be available to respond to specific risk, privacy and information security questions.

Security Roles and Responsibilities

Many different individuals within an organization contribute to successful information protection. Security is the responsibility of everyone within the company. Every end user is responsible for understanding the policies and procedures that are applicable to their particular job function and adhering to any and all security control expectations. Users must have knowledge of their responsibilities and be trained to a level that is adequate to reduce the risk of loss to an acceptable level. Although the exact titles and scope of responsibility of the individuals may vary from organization to organization, the following roles support the implementation of security controls. An individual may be assigned multiple roles for the organization. It is important to provide clear definition and communication of roles and responsibilities including accountability through the distribution of policies, job descriptions, training, and management direction, as well as providing the foundation for execution of security controls by the workforce.

End User

The end user is responsible for protecting information assets on a daily basis through adherence to the security policies that have been communicated. The end users represent many "windows" to the organization, and through their actions security can either be strengthened through compliance or compromised through their actions. For example, downloading unauthorized software, opening attachments from unknown senders, or visiting malicious Web sites could introduce malicious code (e.g., virus, Trojans, and spyware) into the environment. End users can also be the front-line eyes and ears of the organization and report security incidents for investigation. Creating this culture requires that this role and responsibility is clearly communicated and understood by all.

Executive Management

Executive management maintains the overall responsibility for protection of the information assets. The business operations are dependent upon information being available, accurate, and protected from individuals without a need to know. Financial losses can occur if the confidentiality, integrity, or availability of the information is compromised. They must be aware of the risks that they are accepting for the organization. Risk must be identified through risk assessment so that management can make informed decisions.

Security Officer

The security officer directs, coordinates, plans, and organizes information security activities throughout the organization. The security officer works with many different individuals, such as executive management, management of the business units, technical staff, business partners, auditors, and third parties such as vendors. The security officer and his or her team are responsible for the design, implementation, management, and review of the organization's security policies, standards, procedures, baselines, and guidelines.

Information Systems Security Professional

Drafting of security policies, standards and supporting guidelines, procedures, and baselines is coordinated through these individuals. Guidance is provided for technical security issues, and emerging threats are considered for the adoption of new policies. Activities such as interpretation of government regulations and industry trends and analysis of vendor solutions to include in the security architecture that advances the security of the organization are performed in this role.

Data/Information/Business Owners

A business executive or manager is typically responsible for an information asset. These are the individuals that assign the appropriate classification to information assets. They ensure that the business information is protected with appropriate controls. Periodically, the information asset owners need to review the classification and access rights associated with information assets. The owners, or their delegates, may be required to approve access to the information. Owners also need to determine the criticality, sensitivity, retention, backups, and safeguards for the information. Owners or their delegates are responsible for understanding the risks that exist with regards to the information that they control.

Data/Information Custodian/Steward

A data custodian is an individual or function that takes care of the information on behalf of the owner. These individuals ensure that the information is available to the end users and is backed up to enable recovery in the event of data loss or corruption. Information may be stored in files, databases, or systems whose technical infrastructure must be managed, by systems administrators. This group administers access rights to the information assets.

Information Systems Auditor

IT auditors determine whether users, owners, custodians, systems, and networks are in compliance with the security policies, procedures, standards, baselines, designs, architectures, management direction, and other requirements placed on systems. The auditors provide independent assurance to the management on the appropriateness of the security controls. The auditor examines the information systems and determines whether they are designed, configured, implemented, operated, and managed in a way ensuring that the organizational objectives are being achieved. The auditors provide top company management with an independent view of the controls and their effectiveness.

Business Continuity Planner

Business continuity planners develop contingency plans to prepare for any occurrence that could have the ability to impact the company's objectives negatively. Threats may include earthquakes, tornadoes, hurricanes, blackouts, changes in the economic/political climate, terrorist activities, fire, or other major actions potentially causing significant harm. The business continuity planner ensures that business processes can continue

477

through the disaster and coordinates those activities with the business areas and information technology personnel responsible for disaster recovery.

Information Systems/Information Technology Professionals

These personnel are responsible for designing security controls into information systems, testing the controls, and implementing the systems in production environments through agreed upon operating policies and procedures. The information systems professionals work with the business owners and the security professionals to ensure that the designed solution provides security controls commensurate with the acceptable criticality, sensitivity, and availability requirements of the application.

Security Administrator

A security administrator manages the user access request process and ensures that privileges are provided to those individuals who have been authorized for access by application/system/data owners. This individual has elevated privileges and creates and deletes accounts and access permissions. The security administrator also terminates access privileges when individuals leave their jobs or transfer between company divisions. The security administrator maintains records of access request approvals and produces reports of access rights for the auditor during testing in an access controls audit to demonstrate compliance with the policies.

Network/Systems Administrator

A systems administrator (sysadmin/netadmin) configures network and server hardware and the operating systems to ensure that the information can be available and accessible. The administrator maintains the computing infrastructure using tools and utilities such as patch management and software distribution mechanisms to install updates and test patches on organization computers. The administrator tests and implements system upgrades to ensure the continued reliability of the servers and network devices. The administrator provides vulnerability management through either commercial off the shelf (COTS) and/or non-COTS solutions to test the computing environment and mitigate vulnerabilities appropriately.

Physical Security

The individuals assigned to the physical security role establish relationships with external law enforcement, such as the local police agencies, state police, or the Federal Bureau of Investigation (FBI) to assist in investigations. Physical security personnel manage the installation, maintenance, and ongoing operation of the closed circuit television (CCTV) surveillance systems, burglar alarm systems, and card reader access control systems. Guards are placed where necessary as a deterrent to unauthorized access and to provide safety for the company employees. Physical security personnel interface with systems security, human resources, facilities, and legal and business areas to ensure that the practices are integrated.

Administrative Assistants/Secretaries

This role can be very important to information security; in many companies of smaller size, this may be the individual who greets visitors, signs packages in and out, recognizes individuals who desire to enter the offices, and serves as the phone screener for executives. These individuals may be subject to social engineering attacks, whereby the potential intruder attempts to solicit confidential information that may be used for a subsequent attack. Social engineers prey on the goodwill of the helpful individual to gain entry. A properly trained assistant will minimize the risk of divulging useful company information or of providing unauthorized entry.

Help Desk Administrator

As the name implies, the help desk is there to field questions from users that report system problems. Problems may include poor response time, potential virus infections, unauthorized access, inability to access system resources, or questions on the use of a program. The help desk is also often where the first indications of security issues and incidents will be seen. A help desk individual would contact the computer security incident response team (CIRT) when a situation meets the criteria developed by the team. The help desk resets passwords, resynchronizes/reinitializes tokens and smart cards, and resolves other problems with access control.

These functions may alternatively be performed through self-service by the end user, e.g., an intranet-based solution that establishes the identity of the end user and resets the password, or by another area, such as the security administration, systems administrator, etc., depending upon the organizational structure and separation of duties principles in place. A help desk area is also a prime target for social engineering attacks, and as such, should receive additional attention in security awareness training.

Organizations may have other roles related to information security to meet particular needs. Individuals within the different roles will require different levels of training. The end user may require basic security awareness training, including the activities that are acceptable, how to recognize that there may be a problem, and what the mechanism is for reporting the problem to the appropriate personnel for resolution. The security administrator will need more in-depth training on the access control packages to manage the log-on IDs, accounts, and log file reviews. The systems/network administrator will need technical security training for the specific operating system (e.g., Windows, UNIX, Linux, etc.) or network components (e.g., firewall, routers, switches) to competently set the security controls. Establishing clear, unambiguous security roles has many benefits to the organization beyond providing information as to the responsibilities to be performed and who needs to perform them. These benefits include:

- Demonstrable executive management support for information security
- Increased employee efficiency by reducing confusion about who is expected to perform which tasks
- Team coordination to protect information as it moves from department to department
- Lower risks to company reputation/brand recognition due to security problems
- Capability to manage complex information systems and networks

- Personal accountability for information security
- Reduction of turf battles between departments
- Security objectives balanced with business objectives
- Support of disciplinary actions for security violations up to and including termination
- Facilitation of increased communication for resolution of security incidents
- Demonstrable compliance with applicable laws and regulations
- Shielding of management from liability and negligence claims
- Road map for auditors to determine whether necessary work is performed effectively and efficiently
- Continuous improvement efforts (i.e., ISO 9000) [3]
- Overall risk management
- Provision of a foundation for determining the level of security and awareness training required

Information security is a team effort requiring the skill sets and cooperation of many different individuals. Executive management may have overall responsibility, and the security officer/director/manager may be assigned the day-to-day task of ensuring that the organization is complying with the defined security practices. However, every person in the organization has one or more roles to play in order to ensure proper and appropriate protection of the information assets within the organization.

---

3   Detailed information on all ISO standards can be found here: http://www.iso.org/iso/home.html

Legislative and Regulatory Compliance

Organizations must operate in environments where laws, regulations and compliance requirements must be met. Information security professionals must understand the laws and regulations of the country and industry they are working in. An organization's governance and risk management processes must take into account these requirements from an implementation and a risk perspective. These laws and regulations often offer specific actions which must be met for compliance, or in some cases, what must be met for a "safe harbor" provision. A safe harbor is typically a set of "good faith" conditions which if met, may temporarily or indefinitely protect the organization from the penalties of a new law or regulation.

For example, in the United States, federal executive agencies are required to adhere to the Federal Information Security Management Act (FISMA.) FISMA mandates the use of specific actions, standards and requirements for agencies to ensure sensitive information and vital mission services are not disrupted, distorted or disclosed to improper individuals. Agencies often take the requirements from FISMA and use them as the baseline for their information security policy and adopt the standards required by FISMA as their own. In doing so they not only meet the requirements of the law but can also provide proof to external parties that they are making a good faith effort to comply with the requirements of the law.

Compliance stemming from legal or regulatory requirements is best addressed by ensuring an organization's policies, procedures, standards and guidance are consistent with any laws or regulations which may govern it. Furthermore, it is advisable that specific laws and their requirements are sited in an organization's governance program and information security training programs. As a general rule, laws and regulations represent a "moral minimum" which must be adhered to and should never be considered wholly adequate for an organization without a thorough review. Additional requirements and specificity can be added to complement the requirements of law and regulation but they should never conflict with them. For example, a law may require sensitive financial information to be encrypted and an organization's policy could state that in accordance with the law all financial information will be encrypted. Furthermore, the agency may specify a standard strength and brand of encryption software to be used in order to achieve the required level of compliance with the law, while also providing for the additional layers of protection that the organization wants in place.

3

Information Security
Governance & Risk Management

Privacy Requirements Compliance

Privacy laws and regulations pose "confidentially" challenges for the information security professional. Personally identifiable information is becoming an extremely valuable commodity for marketers, as demonstrated by the tremendous growth of social networking sites based on demography, and the targeted marketing activities that come with them. While valuable, this information can also become a liability for an organization which runs afoul of information privacy regulations and laws.

For example, the European Data Protection Directive only allows for the processing of personal data under specific circumstances such as:

1. When processing is necessary for compliance with a legal action

2. When processing is required to protect the life of the subject

3. When the subject of the personal data has provided consent

4. When the processing is performed within the law and scope of "public interest."

The four requirements listed above reflect only a small portion of the directive. The directive further states what rights the subject has, such as objecting at any time to the processing of their personal data if the use is for direct marketing purposes. Recently, several internet search companies and social media companies have been cited for not complying with this law. These organizations have been accused of using the personal data of the subject for direct marketing efforts without the subject's permission. The information security professional working in a marketing firm in the European Union must understand the impact of these requirements on how information will be processed, stored, and transmitted in their organization.

Control Frameworks

To aid in ensuring security and privacy requirements are met, many organizations adopt control frameworks to provide a governance program which is:

1. **Consistent:** A governance program must be consistent in how information security and privacy is approached and applied. If two similar situations or requests result in different outcomes, stakeholders will lose faith in the integrity of the program and its usefulness.

2. **Measurable:** The governance program must provide a way to determine progress and set goals. Organizations who implement frameworks which can be measured are more likely to improve their security posture over time. Most control frameworks contain an assessment standard or procedure to determine compliance and in some cases risk as well.

3. **Standardized:** As with measurable above, a controls framework should rely on standardization so results from one organization or part of an organization can be compared in a meaningful way.

4. **Comprehensive:** The selected framework should cover the minimum legal and regulatory requirements of an organization and be extensable to accommodate additional organization specific requirements.

5. **Modular:** A modular framework is more likely to withstand the changes of an organization as only the controls or requirements needing modification are reviewed and updated.

An example of a control framework is the United States National Institute of Standards and Technology's Special Publication 800-53[4] (NIST SP 800-53). SP 800-53 is a control framework of over 300 controls in over 17 families and three classes. The framework includes the ability to scope and tailor controls to an organization's specific mission or requirements.

NIST SP 800-53 is mandatory for United States federal agencies and their contractors. While frameworks such as these may seem daunting, they are designed to be applicable to almost every organization.

Another example is the International Standard Organization (ISO) 27001 Standard. Like NIST SP 800-53, ISO 27001 is designed to cover organizations of all sizes and types. The annex A of ISO 27001 contains the control framework with objectives and specifics about each control. ISO is a global framework adopted by numerous industries in most countries. Frameworks often map to each other as well. For example NIST SP 800-53 has been mapped to the ISO 27001 standard. While there is considerable overlap, there are some areas which are not an exact fit. *Figure 3.2* demonstrates a sample control framework comparison.

The information security professional must exercise care and judgment when implementing a controls framework to ensure the proper fit for an organization.

	NIST SP 800-53 CONTROLS	ISO/IEC 27001 (Annex A) CONTROLS
AU-12	Audit Generation	A.10.10.1, A.10.10.4, A.10.10.5
AU-13	Monitoring for Information Disclosure	None
AU-14	Session Audit	None
CA-1	Security Assessment and Authorization Policies and Procedures	A.5.1.1, A.5.1.2, A.6.1.1, A.6.1.3 A.6.1.4, A.8.1.1, A.10.1.1, A.15.1.1, A.15.2.1
CA-2	Security Assessments	A.6.1.8, A.10.3.2, A.15.2.1, A.15.2.2
CA-3	Information System Connections	A.6.2.1, A.6.2.3, A.10.6.1, A.10.8.1, A.10.8.2, A.10.8.5, A.11.4.2
CA-4	Withdrawn	---
CA-5	Plan of Action and Milestones	None
CA-6	Security Authorization	A.6.1.4, A.10.3.2
CA-7	Continuous Monitoring	A.6.1.8, A.15.2.1, A.15.2.2
CM-1	Configuration Management Policy and Procedures	A.5.1.1, A.5.1.2, A.6.1.1, A.6.1.3, A.8.1.1, A.10.1.1, A.10.1.2, A.12.4.1, A.12.5.1, A.15.1.1, A.15.2.1
CM-2	Baseline Configuration	A.12.4.1, A.10.1.4
CM-3	Configuration Change Control	A.10.1.1, A.10.1.2, A.10.3.2, A.12.4.1, A.12.5.1, A.12.5.2, A.12.5.3
CM-4	Security Impact Analysis	A.10.1.2, A.10.3.2, A.12.4.1, A.12.5.2, A.12.5.3
CM-5	Access Restrictions for Change	A.10.1.2, A.11.1.1, A.11.6.1, A.12.4.1, A.12.4.3, A.12.5.3
CM-6	Configuration Settings	None
CM-7	Least Functionality	None
CM-8	Information System Component Inventory	A.7.1.1, A.7.1.2
CM-9	Configuration Management Plan	A.6.1.3, A.7.1.1, A.7.1.2, A.8.1.1, A.10.1.1, A.10.1.2, A.10.3.2, A.12.4.1, A.12.4.3, A.12.5.1, A.12.5.2, A.12.5.3
CP-1	Contingency Planning Policy and Procedures	A.5.1.1, A.5.1.2, A.6.1.1, A.6.1.3, A.8.1.1, A.9.1.4, A.10.1.1, A.10.1.2, A.14.1.1, A.14.1.3, A.15.1.1, A.15.2.1
CP-2	Contingency Plan	A.6.1.2, A.9.1.4, A.10.3.1, A.14.1.1, A.14.1.2, A.14.1.3, A.14.1.4, A.14.1.5
CP-3	Contingency Training	A.8.2.2, A.9.1.4, A.14.1.3
CP-4	Contingency Plan Testing and Exercises	A.6.1.2, A.9.1.4, A.14.1.1, A.14.1.3, A.14.1.4, A.14.1.5
CP-5	Withdrawn	

Figure 3.2 - **NIST SP 800-53 and ISO 27001 Sample Control comparison**

(Joint Task Force Transformation Initiative Interagency Working Group 08, 01, 2009)

Due Care

Due care is an important topic for the information security professional to understand. It is primarily a legal team used to describe the care a "reasonable person" would exercise under given circumstances. In other words, it is used to also describe what an individual's or organization's legal duty is considered to be. The lack of due care is often considered negligence, and in most countries is actionable under law. If an organization is legally mandated to comply with regulations or information security requirements knowingly or unknowingly neglecting those requirements could lead to legal exposure from a due care perspective.

Due Diligence

Due diligence is similar to due care with the exception that it is a preemptive measure made to avoid harm to other persons or their property. If performed correctly, due diligence leads to due care when needed and avoids other situations where due care may need to be exercised. Due diligence is a practice which should be adopted by the information security professional as a core tenant of their career. Examples of due diligence in an organization include, but are not limited to:

- Background checks of employees
- Credit checks of business partners
- Information system security assessments
- Risk assessments of physical security systems
- Penetration tests of firewalls
- Contingency testing of backup systems

In each of the above examples the organization is either attempting to avoid a situation which may lead to harm to the organization or other individuals. While at times due diligence can be expensive, the cost of a single data breach or lawsuit may be large enough to shut down an organization and destroy a career[4].

---

4   Burglary Triggers Medical Records Firm's Collapse (http://blogs.wsj.com/bank-ruptcy/2012/03/12/burglary-triggers-medical-records-firm%E2%80%99s-collapse/)

Understand and Apply Concepts of Confidentiality, Integrity and Availability

The information security program must ensure that the core concepts of availability, integrity, and confidentiality are supported by adequate security controls designed to mitigate or reduce the risks of loss, disruption, or corruption of information. Each of the security principles of the CIA triad are defined as follows:

Confidentiality

Confidentiality supports the principle of "least privilege" by providing that only authorized individuals, processes, or systems should have access to information on a need-to-know basis. The level of access that an authorized individual should have is at the level necessary for them to do their job. In recent years, much press has been dedicated to the privacy of information and the need to protect it from individuals, who may be able to commit crimes by viewing the information. Identity theft is the act of assuming one's identity through knowledge of confidential information obtained from various sources.

An important measure to ensure confidentiality of information is data classification. This helps to determine who should have access to the information (public, internal use only, or confidential). Identification, authentication, and authorization through access controls are practices that support maintaining the confidentiality of information. A sample control for protecting confidentiality is to encrypt information. Encryption of information limits the usability of the information in the event it is accessible to an unauthorized person.

Integrity

Integrity is the principle that information should be protected from intentional, unauthorized, or accidental changes. Information stored in files, databases, systems, and networks must be relied upon to accurately process transactions and provide accurate information for business decision making. Controls are put in place to ensure that information is modified through accepted practices.

Sample controls include management controls such as segregation of duties, approval checkpoints in the systems development life cycle, and implementation of testing practices that assist in providing information integrity. Well-formed transactions and security of the update programs provide consistent methods of applying changes to systems. Limiting update access to those individuals with a need to access limits the exposure to intentional and unintentional modification.

Availability

Availability is the principle that ensures that information is available and accessible to users when needed. The two primary areas affecting the availability of systems are

1. Denial-of-Service attacks and
2. Loss of service due to a disaster, which could be man-made (e.g., poor capacity planning resulting in system crash, outdated hardware, and poor testing resulting in system crash after upgrade) or natural (e.g., earthquake, tornado, blackout, hurricane, fire, and flood).

In either case, the end user does not have access to information needed to conduct business. The criticality of the system to the user and its importance to the survival of the organization will determine how significant the impact of the extended downtime becomes. The lack of appropriate security controls can increase the risk of viruses, destruction of data, external penetrations, or denial-of-service (DOS) attacks. Such events can prevent the system from being used by normal users.

Sample controls include an up-to-date and active malicious code system, tested incident management, and disaster recovery planning or business continuity planning that ensure that the department functions using alternate processes when an outage to the computer system occurs for a defined period. Disaster recovery ensures that all or parts of information technology processing systems can be recovered. Disaster recovery and business continuity work together to minimize the impact of critical events.

When considering the design and implementation of a network, system, application, or management process, evaluation of the impact to confidentiality, integrity, and availability should be understood. Will it enhance any of the core security principles? Different security controls apply to different core security principles. For example, the selection of a backup tape procedure, software, and hardware to perform backups would be most oriented toward the availability aspect of information security, whereas the selection of a security token utilizing strong, two-factor authentication would be most related to the enhancement of the confidentiality of information through improving authentication; an identity management system would best support access control to ensure only appropriate personnel have update functions commensurate with their job supporting the integrity principle.

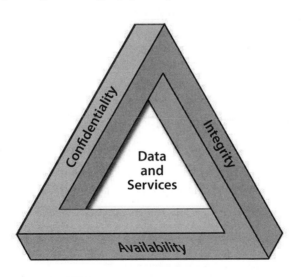

Develop and Implement Security Policy

Imagine the day-to-day operation of an organization without any policies. Individuals would have to make decisions about what is right or wrong for the company based upon their personal values or their own past experience. While many small companies and startups operate in this fashion, this could potentially create as many values as there are people in the organization. Policies establish the framework for the security program that ensures that everyone has a common set of expectations and communicates the management's goals and objectives.

Procedures, standards, guidelines, and baselines (illustrated in *Figure 3.3*) are components that support the implementation of the security policy. A policy without mechanisms supporting its implementation is analogous to an organization having a business strategy without action plans to execute the strategy. Policies communicate the management's expectations, which are fulfilled through the execution of procedures and adherence to standards, baselines, and guidelines.

Security officers and their teams have typically been charged with the responsibility of creating the security policies. The policies must be written and communicated appropriately to ensure that they can be understood by the end users. Policies that are poorly written, or written at too high of an education level (common industry practice is to focus the content for general users at the sixth- to eighth-grade reading level), will not be understood.

While security officers may be responsible for the development of the security policies, the effort should be collaborative to ensure that the business issues are addressed. The security officers will get better corporate support by including other areas in policy development. This helps build buy-in by these areas as they take on a greater ownership of the final product and reduces rework later should they need to provide vital input.

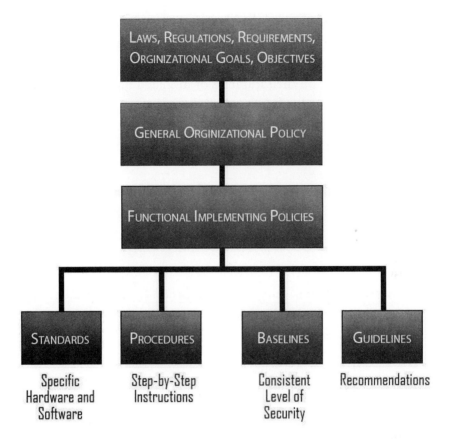

Figure 3.3 - **Relationships among policies, standards, procedures, baselines and guidelines**

Consider including areas such as HR, legal, compliance, various IT areas and specific business area representatives who represent critical business units. When policies are developed solely within the IT department and then distributed without business input, they are likely to miss important business considerations.

Once policy documents have been created, the basis for ensuring compliance is established. Depending on the organization, additional documentation may be necessary to support policy. This support may come in the form of additional controls described in standards, baselines, or procedures to help personnel with compliance. An important step after documentation is to make the most current version of the documents readily accessible to those who are expected to follow them. Many organizations place the documents on their intranets or in shared file folders to facilitate their accessibility. Such placement of these documents plus awareness actions, training if needed, checklists, forms, and sample documents can make awareness and ultimately compliance more effective.

Security Policies

Policies form the foundation of an organization's expectations for its employees. Information security policy is crucial in ensuring an organization conveys the significance of information security and also is able to enforce information security should the need arise. Writing policies does not have to be a mystery, and there are several guidelines for creating good security policies practiced in the industry including the following:

- *Formally define a policy creation and policy maintenance practice:* A clearly defined process for initiating, creating, reviewing, recommending, approving, and distributing policies communicates the roles and responsibilities of all parties. Tools to help include process flows, flowcharts, and written documentation.

- *Policies should survive for two or three years:* Even though they should be reviewed and approved at least annually, policies should survive for two or three years.

- *Do not be too specific in policy statements:* Policies are high-level statements defining the security objectives of the organization. The underlying methods and technologies for implementing the controls that support the policies may change. These should be in other related documents such as procedures, standards, guidelines, and baselines. By doing this the policy statements will need less frequent change, and the executive management or a board of directors that must review and approve policy annually does not need to review that information. This avoids frequent updates, keeps policy concise, and reduces frequent redistribution to the organization, which can lead to confusion.

- *Use forceful, directive wording:* Compliance with policies is expected. As such, statements including such words as *must*, *will*, and *shall* communicate this requirement. Weak directive words such as *should*, *may*, or *can*, must not be used in policies as they would suggest an option of not following them. This

495

latter type of wording fits better in guidelines or areas where there are options.

- **Technical implementation details do not belong in a policy:** Policies must be technology-independent. Technology controls may change over time as an organization's risk profile changes and new vulnerabilities are found.

- **Keep each policy as short as possible:** Policies published online should be limited in length to two or three pages maximum per policy. The intent for the policies is for the end user to understand, and not to create long documents for the sake of documentation.

- **Provide references in policy to the supporting documents:** If the implementation of the policy is placed online, then providing hyperlinks in policy to the related procedures, standards, guidelines, and baselines is an effective method for ensuring that the appropriate procedures are followed. Some of the internal security procedures would not be appropriate for general knowledge, such as the procedure for monitoring intrusions or reviewing log files, and these need to be accessible by the security department and properly secured from general distribution.

- **Thoroughly review before publishing:** Proofreading of policies by multiple individuals allows errors to be caught that may not be readily seen by the author.

- **Conduct management review and sign-off.** Senior management must endorse the policies if they are to be effectively accepted by all management levels, and subsequently the end users of the organization.

- **Employees should acknowledge policies:** All users should sign an acknowledgement that they have read and understand the policies. While this does not ensure that they have read or understand the policies, it will help to protect the organization if a user's behavior violates the policy. Typically this may be part of an information security awareness or training program.

- **Do not use technical jargon in policy language.** Policies are targeted to nontechnical users. Technical language is acceptable in technical documentation, but not in high-level security policies.

- **Review incidents and adjust policies:** Review the security incidents that have occurred. These may indicate the need for a new policy, a revision to an existing policy, or the need to redistribute the current policy to reinforce compliance.

- **Periodically review policies:** Set a regular review schedule and ensure it is followed. The formalized review process will provide a mechanism to ensure that the security policies remain in alignment with business objectives. Time is not the only action which should trigger a review. Changes in mission, systems, interconnections and business strategy should all necessitate a policy review.

- **Define policy exception rules:** A policy exception defines situations where a policy might not be enforced and requires that procedures document the exception and any special alternatives or monitoring that might be put in place to track the exception.

- **Develop sanctions for noncompliance.** Effective policies have consistent sanctions as deterrents and enable action when the policies are not followed. These sanctions may include "disciplinary action up to and including termination." Stronger language can also be added to warn of prosecution for serious offenses.

Policies provide the foundation for a comprehensive and effective security program. The policies define various roles and responsibilities in the organization and assign the necessary authority for security activities and compliance. By communicating the company policies as directives, accountability and personal responsibility for adhering to the security practices are established. The policies can be utilized for determining or interpreting conflicts that may arise. The policies also define the elements, scope, and functions of the security management framework.

497

Types of Security Policies

Security policies may consist of different types, depending upon the specific need for the policy. The different security policies will work together to meet the objectives of a comprehensive security program. Different policy types include the following:

- ■ *Organizational or program policy:* This policy is issued by a senior management individual or group, who creates the authority and scope for the security program. The purpose of the program is described, and the assigned responsibility is defined for carrying out the information security mission. The goals of confidentiality, integrity, and availability are addressed in the policy. Specific areas of security focus may be stressed, such as the protection of confidential information for a credit card or health insurance company, or the availability focus for a company maintaining mission-critical, high-availability systems. The policy should be clear as to the facilities, hardware, software, information, and personnel that are in scope for the security program. In most cases, the scope will be the entire organization. In larger organizations however, the security program may be limited in scope to a division or geographic location. The organization policy sets out the high-level authority to define the appropriate sanctions for failure to comply with the policy.

- ■ *Functional, issue-specific policies:* While the organizational security policies are broad in scope, the functional or issue-specific policies address areas of particular security concern requiring clarification. The issue-specific policies may be focused on the different domains of security and address areas such as access control, contingency planning, segregation of duties (SOD), principles, and so forth. They may also address specific technical areas of existing and emerging technologies, such as use of the Internet, e-mail and corporate communication systems, wireless access, or remote system access. For example, an acceptable use policy may define the responsibilities of the end user for using the corporate computer systems for business purposes only, or may allow the person some incidental personal use, provided the restriction of ensuring that usage is free from viruses, spyware, the downloading of inappropriate pictures or software, or the sending of chain letters through e-mail. These policies will depend upon the business needs and the tolerance for risk. They contain the statement of the issue, the statement of the organization's position on the issue, the applicability of the issue, the compliance requirements, and the sanctions for not following the policy.

■ *System-specific policies:* Areas where it is desired to have clearer direction or greater control for a specific technical or operational area may have more detailed policies. These policies may be targeted for a specific application or platform. For example, a system-specific policy may address which departments are permitted to input or modify information in the check-writing application for the disbursement of accounts payable payments.

The more detailed and issue-specific a policy is, the higher the likelihood that the policy will require more frequent changes. Typically, high-level organizational security policies are broad statements, establish corporate security philosophy, and can survive for several years, while those focused on the use of technology will change much more frequently as technology matures and new technology is added to the environment. Even if an organization is not currently utilizing a technology, policies can explicitly strengthen the message that the technology is not to be used and is prohibited. For example, a policy regarding removable media such as USB storage devices or one regarding the use of wireless devices or camera phones would reinforce management's intentions with regards to these technologies.

Standards/Baselines

Whereas policies define what an organization needs, standards take this a step further and define the specific requirements. Standards provide the agreements that provide interoperability within the organization through the use of common protocols. Adherence to standards is typically mandatory in most organizations.

Standards provide a more technical perspective. They lay out the hardware and software mechanisms, which the organization may have selected for controlling security risks. Standards are prevalent in many facets of daily life, such as the size of the tires on automobiles, specifications of the height, color, and format of a STOP sign, and the RJ45 plug on the end of an Ethernet cable. Standards provide consistency in implementation as well as permit interoperability while reducing confusion. An organization may set several specific security standards. For example, when selecting a control for remote-access identification and authentication, an organization could decide to utilize log-in IDs and passwords, strong authentication through a security token, or a virtual private network (VPN) solution over the Internet. The standard would be specific to the authentication tool or mechanism implemented.

A standard might state: "Remote connectivity requires biometric compatible multifactor tokens" or it might be more general in stating that multifactor authentication is required, but does not require that biometrics be included. The standard might even establish the specific solution that the organization has standardized on for a control such as the antivirus product.

Standards can improve the operation of the security controls and increase efficiency by requiring consistency across the organization. It is more costly to support multiple software packages that do essentially the same thing. Imagine if each user was told to go to the local computer store and purchase their favorite antivirus product. Some users would ask the salesperson's opinion, some would buy the least expensive, and others might get the most expensive, assuming this would provide the greatest protection. Without a consistent standard for antivirus products, the organization might not get the level of protection required. Individual products may not consistently get virus signatures updated and the organization would never know for sure if a workstation was protected. Additionally, each of these different products would have different installation, update, and licensing considerations, contributing to complex management. It makes sense to have consistent products chosen for the organization versus leaving the product choice to every individual or department.

Determination of which standards best meet the organization's security needs is driven by the security policies agreed upon by management. The standards provide the specification for the technology to effectively enable the organization to be successful in meeting the requirements set by policy. If, in the example of remote access, the organization was restricting information over the Internet or had many users in rural areas with limited Internet access, then the VPN standard over the Internet may not be a plausible solution. Conversely, for end users transmitting large amounts of information, the dial-up solution may be impractical. The policy defines the boundaries within which the standards must operate.

Standards may also refer to those guidelines established by a standards organization and accepted by management. Standards creators include organizations such as the United States' National Institute of Standards and Technology (NIST), International Organization for Standardization (ISO), Institute of Electronics and Electrical Engineers (IEEE), American National Standards Institute (ANSI), the United States' National Security Agency (NSA), and others.

Baselines

Baselines can describe how to best implement the security configuration or standard of a software or environment to ensure that it is consistent throughout the organization. Different software packages, hardware platforms, and networks have different ways to best ensure they are configured securely. Products and secure environments may have many different options and settings that can be configured to provide the best security protection. An analysis of the available configuration settings and their subsequent settings forms the basis for a consistent implementation of a standard. For example, turning off the Telnet service may be specified in the hardening baseline document for network servers. A procedure would describe how to turn off the service. Exceptions to the baseline may need to be documented in the event that the baseline cannot be followed in a particular department or environment, along with the business justification. Baselines are the specific rules describing how to implement the best security controls in support of policy and standards.

Testing of the current security controls on a periodic basis ensures that the baselines have been implemented as documented. The baselines themselves should be reviewed periodically to make sure that they are sufficient to address emerging threats and vulnerabilities. In large environments with multiple individuals performing systems administration and responding to urgent requests, there is an increased risk that one of the baseline configurations may not be implemented properly. Internal testing identifies these vulnerabilities and provides a mechanism to review why the control was or was not properly implemented. Failures in training, adherence to baselines and associated procedures, change control, documentation, or skills of the individual performing the changes may be identified through the testing.

Procedures

Procedures are step-by-step instructions to support compliance with the policies and standards. The procedure may provide step-by-step instructions for how to best implement the policy and who does what to accomplish various security tasks. The procedure provides clarity and a common understanding of the prescribed operations required to effectively support the policies on a consistent basis. Develop procedures with the input of each of the areas that might be impacted. This reduces the risk that important steps, communication, or required deliverables will get left out.

Companies must be able to provide assurance that they have exercised due diligence in the support and enforcement of company policies. This means that the company has made an effort to be in compliance with the policies and has communicated these expectations to the workforce. Documenting procedures communicated to the users, business partners, and anyone utilizing the systems, as appropriate, minimizes the legal liability of the corporation.

The documentation of procedures is more than an exercise. The process itself can create a common understanding among the developers regarding the methods used to accomplish the task. Individuals from different organizational units may be very familiar with their work area, but not as familiar with the impact of a procedure on another department. This is a common problem where organizations sometimes appear as a large multidisciplinary mass, and the individuals working in different departments only understand their portion of the organization and may not understand the other parts of the organization. The exercise of writing down a single, consistent procedure has the added effect of establishing agreement among impacted parties. Many times at the beginning of the process, individuals will think they understand the process and realize that departments were executing different, individual processes to accomplish a task.

Guidelines

Guidelines are discretionary or optional recommendations that can be used to enable individuals who make judgments with respect to security actions. Guidelines provide implementation recommendations or suggested steps for complying with the implementation of policy, standard, or how best to implement a configuration baseline.

Guidelines are also the recommendations, best practices, and templates documented in the frameworks created by other organizations such as the Control Objectives for Information and Related Technology (COBIT),[1] the Capability Maturity Model (CMM),[2] and ISO27000 (formally known as ISO17799 or BS7799). Ultimately, any standard procedure or policy which is not mandatory for an organization or individual may be viewed as a guideline. Guidelines are by definition optional; however, some standards or policies may make them mandatory.

---

1   Please see the following for detailed information on COBIT: http://www.isaca.org

2   Please see the following for detailed information on CMM: http://www.sei.cmu.edu/cmmi/start/faq/related-faq.cfm

Documentation

Each of these documents can be closely related to the others and may be developed as the result of new regulations, external industry standards, new threats and vulnerabilities, emerging technologies, upgraded hardware and software platforms, or risk assessments. Often organizations will combine the information into single documents for ease of management. Policies must not be combined with other documentation. It is also best to keep standards as standalone documents. This is to ensure only the appropriate level of management must be involved in changing a policy or a standard. Management must review and approve policy, and by keeping them concise, will make the review job easier and less confusing. Management, especially executive management or a board of directors, is not typically interested in procedures, guidelines, and technical configuration baselines. Policies as described in this chapter should be designed for less frequent change than the supporting processes, standards, or guidelines making it often less necessary to distribute and communicate policy changes. At a minimum, even if policy is not changed, it should be reviewed and approved on an annual basis.

Policy Analogy

A useful analogy to help remember the differences between policies, standards, guidelines, and procedures is to think of a company that builds cabinets and has a "hammer" policy. The different components may be as follows:

> *Policy:* "All boards must be nailed together using company-issued hammers to ensure end-product consistency and worker safety."

Notice that the policy provides the flexibility that permits the company to define the hammer type as changes in technology or safety issues warrant. In this example, the purpose ("ensure end-product consistency") is also communicated to the employees.

Standard: "Eleven-inch fiberglass hammers will be used. Only hardened-steel nails will be used with the hammers. Automatic hammers are to be used for repetitive jobs only that are > 1 hour." A standard may establish the maximum automatic power hammer settings or even the model of the hammer.

Standards are the technical specifics that clarify the expectations that make sense for the current environment and represent management's decision.

Guideline: "To avoid splitting the wood, a pilot hole may be drilled first."

The guideline is only a suggestion or recommendation and may not apply in all cases or in the analogy with all types of wood. The guideline is not a requirement, but rather a suggested practice to minimize wood splitting.

Procedure: "(1) Position nail in upright position on board. (2) Strike nail with full swing of hammer. (3) Repeat until nail is flush with board.

The procedure describes the process for using the hammer and the nail to get the best results and be successful. Following this procedure, with the appropriate standard hammers, and practicing guidelines where appropriate, will keep the employee compliant with the policy.

Manage the Information Life Cycle

Information has a life which consists of creation, use, and finally destruction. Several important information security actives surround the lifecycle of information to protect it, ensure it is available to only those who require access to it, and finally to destroy it when it is no longer needed. Several concepts of information ownership need to be understood by the information security professional as part of their duties.

When information is created someone in the organization must be directly responsible for it. Often this is the individual or group which created, purchased or acquired the information to support the mission of the organization. This individual or group is considered the "information owner." The information owner typically has the following responsibilities:

- Determine the impact the information has on the mission of the organization

- Understand the replacement cost of the information (if it can be replaced)

- Determine who in the organization or outside of it has a need for the information and under what circumstances the information should be released

- Know when the information is inaccurate or no longer needed and should be destroyed

Clearly the information owner must work with the information security program and officer to ensure the protection, availability and destruction requirements can be met. To standardize the types of information and protection requirements many organizations use classification or categorization to sort and mark the information. Classification is concerned primarily with access while categorization is primarily concerned with impact.

Classification is most often referred to when discussing military or government information however several organizations may use systems which are similar in function. The purpose of a classification system is to ensure information is marked in such a way that only those with an appropriate level of clearance can have access to the information. Many organizations will use the terms "Confidential", "close hold", "restricted" or "sensitive" to mark information. These markings may limit access to specific members such as board members or possibly certain sections of an organization such as the Human Resources area.

Categorization is the process of determining the impact of the loss of confidentiality, integrity or availability of the information to an organization. For example public information on a webpage may be low impact to an organization as it requires only minimal uptime, it doesn't matter if the information is changed and it is globally viewable by the public. However a startup company may have a design for a new clean power plant which if it was lost or altered may cause the company to go bankrupt as a competitor may be able to manufacture and implement the design faster. This type of information would be categorized as "high" impact.

Several classification and categorization systems exist. The information security professional should minimally be familiar with a few and understand which are common in the country and industry they practice.

For an example of classification see:

- Canada's "Security of Information Act[1]"
- China's Law on "Guarding State Secrets[2]"
- The United Kingdom's "Official Secrets Acts[3]"

---

1   http://laws-lois.justice.gc.ca/eng/acts/O-5/

2   http://www.asianlii.org/cn/legis/cen/laws/gssl248/

3   http://www.legislation.gov.uk/ukpga/1989/6/section/8

An excellent example of categorization may be found in the United States' National Institute of Standards and Technology's (NIST) Federal Information processing standard 199[4] and NIST's special publication 800-60[5] "Guide for Mapping Types of Information and Information Systems to Security Categories.) The United States federal civilian government is required to categorize information using these standards and guidelines.

Classification and categorization is used to help standardize the defense baselines for information systems and the level of suitability and trust an employee may need to access information. By consolidating data of similar categorization and classification organizations can realize economy of scale in implementing appropriate security controls. Security controls are then tailored for specific threats and vulnerabilities.

Finally all information must eventually come to an end. Organizations often hoard old information assuming it will be valuable at some point when really most information outlives its value and usefulness in a matter of years or months. Organizations should document retention schedules for information in their administrative policies. These schedules should mandate the destruction of information after a set date, period or non-use trigger. The advantages of taking this approach are:

- Storage costs are reduced
- Only relevant information is kept and this can speed up searching and indexing
- Litigation holds and eDiscovery is less likely to encounter erroneous, pre-decisional or deliberative information.

---

4   http://csrc.nist.gov/publications/fips/fips199/FIPS-PUB-199-final.pdf

5   http://csrc.nist.gov/publications/nistpubs/800-60-rev1/SP800-60_Vol1-Rev1.pdf

Manage Third-Party Governance

With the growing adoption of "Cloud" computing the information security professional must understand the contractual and governance implications of managing risk of a third-party provider. In general, third party solutions can be viewed in three ways:

1. Infrastructure as a service (IaaS)

2. Platform as a service (PaaS)

3. Software as a Service (SaaS)

IaaS focuses on providing "bare metal", or basic computing resources such as processors, memory, storage or transmission media to a customer. The customer is responsible for providing an operating system, data, applications, databases and the majority of the security controls. PaaS offerings typically provide an operating system or a database to the customer. The customer has little visibility into the hardware layer, is responsible for the application and data, and shares a security control balance with the provider. Finally, SaaS means the customer is only providing the data for the most part and the provider is responsible for the vast majority of the security controls.

When using a third party, organizations must be cautious to ensure service level agreements (SLAs) are not confused with the assurance provided by due diligence actives such as on-site assessments, document exchanges and process or policy reviews. SLAs are an important concept in any third party governance program or contract. SLAs define the agreed upon level of performance and compensation or penalty between the provider and the customer. However, simply having an SLA does not mean a provider will always comply with the SLA. For example, assume a provider is selling processing time to customer X for one U.S. dollar an hour. The SLA customer X has with the provider states that if processing is not available they will penalize the provider 1 U.S. dollar an hour. Therefore, the net cost to the provider for an hour of down time is two U.S. dollars; one for the lost revenue and one for the penalty. Should the provider be less than honest and another customer offers to pay five U.S. dollars per hour for the processing power, the provider may use customer X's processing power and still make a net gain of three U.S. dollars. This is a very simple example, but illustrates that SLAs do not equate to explicit assurance.

Greater assurance can only be gained through inspection, review and assessment. A security professional may be asked to review the information security documentation of a third party information system and then perform an assessment to determine their compliance with a specific control framework or regulation. An independent assessment gives the security professional and the customer an opportunity to view the information system provider as they really are. Findings such as a very high utilization rate with no firewalls may indicate a provider who is very inexpensive and has many customers but may have cut some corners on security to save costs. The security professional must ensure the assessment or inspection covers the information security and privacy areas most important to the organization.

Additionally, organizations must be cautious about the countries and individuals who own, operate and have jurisdiction over the third-party provider's system. Individuals who may not be suitable to access the customer's information may have access if proper controls are not implemented. Furthermore sensitive organizational information may be released to a non-friendly government without the consent or knowledge of the organization. Working with legal counsel, the information security professional has a duty to determine what legal exposure an organization may face depending on a third party system's hosting country.

511

Understand and Apply Risk Management Concepts

Risk, as defined in the *American Heritage Dictionary*, is "the possibility of loss." *Random House Dictionary* defines risk management as "the technique or profession of assessing, minimizing, and preventing accidental loss to a business, as through the use of insurance, safety measures, etc." (ISC)² defines risk management as "a discipline for living with the possibility that future events may cause harm." Further, (ISC)² states that "risk management reduces risks by defining and controlling threats and vulnerabilities." Refer to *Figure 3.4*, which illustrates the activities associated with the United States' National Institute of Standards and Technology (NIST) Risk Assessment Methodology. While this is a specific framework, it encompasses the general risk management process.

Risk Management Concepts

An organization will conduct a risk assessment (the term *risk analysis* is sometimes interchanged with risk assessment) to evaluate:

- Threats to its assets

- Vulnerabilities present in the environment

- The likelihood that a threat will be realized by taking advantage of an exposure (or probability and frequency when dealing with quantitative assessment)

- The impact that the exposure being realized will have on the organization

- Countermeasures available that can reduce the threat's ability to exploit the exposure or that can lessen the impact to the organization when a threat is able to exploit a vulnerability

- The residual risk (e.g., the amount of risk that is left over when appropriate controls are properly applied to lessen or remove the vulnerability)

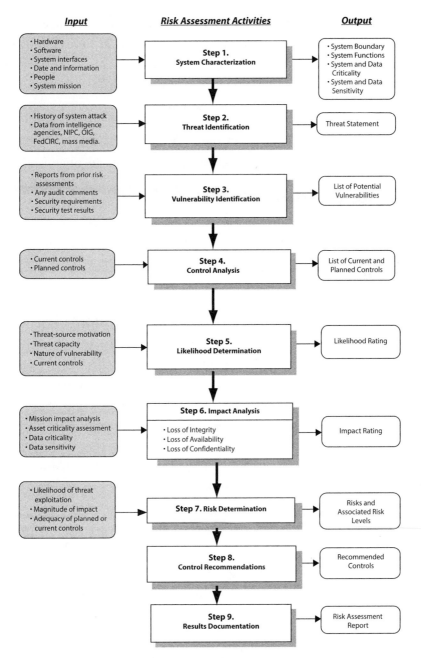

Figure 3.4 - **The NIST Risk Assessment Methodology flowchart**[1]

_____

1   http://csrc.nist.gov/publications/nistpubs/800-30/sp800-30.pdf

An organization may also wish to document evidence of the countermeasure in a deliverable called an exhibit or in some frameworks this is called "evidence." An exhibit can be used to provide an audit trail for the organization and, likewise, evidence for any internal or external auditors that may have questions about the organization's current state of risk.

Why undertake such an endeavor? Without knowing what assets are critical and which would be most at risk within an organization, it is not possible to protect those assets appropriately. For example, if an organization is bound by HIPAA regulations,[1] but does not know to what extent electronic personally identifiable information may be at risk, the organization may make significant mistakes in securing that information, such as neglecting to protect against certain risks, or applying too much protection against low-level risks.

Security and Audit Frameworks and Methodologies

Multiple frameworks and methodologies have been created to support security, auditing, and risk assessment of implemented security controls. These resources are valuable to assist in the design and testing of a security program. The following frameworks and methodologies have each gained a degree of acceptance within the auditing or information security community. Although several of them were not specifically designed to support information security, many of the processes within these practices help security professionals identify and implement controls to support confidentiality, integrity, and availability.

COSO

The Committee of Sponsoring Organizations of the Treadway Commission (COSO)[2] was formed in 1985 to sponsor the National Commission

---

1 Please see the following for detailed information on HIPPA: http://www.hhs.gov/ocr/privacy/

2 Please see the following for detailed information on COSO: http://www.coso.org/

on Fraudulent Financial Reporting, which studied factors that lead to fraudulent financial reporting and produced recommendations for public companies, their auditors, the Securities Exchange Commission, and other regulators. COSO identifies five areas of internal control necessary to meet the financial reporting and disclosure objectives. These include (1) control environment, (2) risk assessment, (3) control activities, (4) information and communication, and (5) monitoring. The COSO internal control model has been adopted as a framework by some organizations working toward Sarbanes–Oxley Section 404 compliance.

ITIL

The IT Infrastructure Library (ITIL)[3] is a set of 34 books published by the British government's Stationary Office between 1989 and 1992 to improve IT service management. The framework contains a set of best practices for IT core operational processes such as change, release and configuration management, incident and problem management, capacity and availability management, and IT financial management. ITIL's primary contribution is showing how the controls can be implemented for the service management IT processes. These practices are useful as a starting point for tailoring to the specific needs of the organization, and the success of the practices depend upon the degree to which they are kept up to date and implemented on a daily basis. Achievement of these standards is an ongoing process, whereby the implementations need to be planned, supported by management, prioritized, and implemented in a phased approach.

COBIT

Control Objectives for Information and related Technology (COBIT)[4] is published by the IT Governance Institute and integrates the following IT and risk frameworks:

---

3   Please see the following for detailed information on ITIL: http://www.itil-officialsite.com/
4   Please see the following for detailed information on COBIT: http://www.isaca.org/CO-BIT/Pages/default.aspx

515

- CobiT 4.1
- Val IT 2.0
- Risk IT
- IT Assurance Framework (ITAF)
- Business Model for Information Security (BMIS)

The COBIT framework examines the effectiveness, efficiency, confidentiality, integrity, availability, compliance, and reliability aspects of the high-level control objectives. The framework provides an overall structure for information technology control and includes control objectives that can be utilized to determine effective security control objectives that are driven from the business needs. The Information Systems Audit and Control Association (ISACA) dedicates numerous resources to the support and understanding of COBIT.

ISO 27000 (Formally Known as ISO17799/BS7799)

The BS 7799/ISO 17799[5] standards can be used as a basis for developing security standards and security management practices. The U.K. Department of Trade and Industry (DTI) Code of Practice (CoP) for information security, which was developed with the support of the industry in 1993, became British Standard 7799 in 1995. BS 7799 was subsequently revised in 1999 to add certification and accreditation components, which became Part 2 of BS 7799. Part 1 of BS 7799 became ISO 17799 and was published as ISO 17799:2005, as the first international information security management standard by the International Organization for Standardization (ISO) and International Electrotechnical Commission (IEC). ISO 17799 was modified in June 2005 and renamed ISO/IEC 17799:2005. It contains 134 detailed information security controls based upon the following 11 areas:

1. Information security policy
2. Organizing information security

---

5   Please see the following for detailed information on ISO 27000: http://www.27000.org/

3. Asset management

4. Human resources security

5. Physical and environmental security

6. Communications and operations management

7. Access control

8. Information systems acquisition, development, and maintenance

9. Information security incident management

10. Business continuity management

11. Compliance

The ISO standards are grouped together by topic areas and the ISO/IEC27000 series has been designated as the information security management series. For example, the 27002 Code of Practice has replaced ISO/IEC 17799:2005, "Information Technology—Security Techniques—Code of Practice for Information Security Management." This is consistent with how ISO has named other topic areas, such as the ISO 9000 series for quality management.

ISO/IEC 27002:2005 was released in October 2005 and specifies the requirements for establishing, implementing, operating, monitoring, reviewing, maintaining, and improving a documented information security management system, taking into consideration the company's business risks. This management standard was based on BS 7799, Part 2 and provides information on building information security management systems and guidelines for auditing the system.

Risk Assessment Methodologies

NIST SP 800–30, 800-39 and 800–66

These methodologies are qualitative methods established for the use of the United States federal government and the global general public, but are particularly used by regulated industries, such as health care. SP 800–66[6] is written specifically with HIPAA clients in mind (though it is possible to use this document for other regulated industries as well). 800-39 focuses on organizational risk management and 800-30 focuses on information system risk management.

The list of the NIST SP 800-30 Risk Assessment methodology process follows:

1. System characterization
2. Vulnerability identification
3. Threat identification
4. Countermeasure identification
5. Likelihood determination
6. Impact determination
7. Risk determination
8. Additional countermeasures recommendations
9. Document results

CRAMM

As described on the CRAMM (CCTA Risk Analysis and Management Method) Web site, residing on Siemens Insight Consulting's Web site, "CRAMM provides a staged and disciplined approach embracing both technical (e.g., IT hardware and software) and nontechnical (e.g., physical and human) aspects of security. To assess these components, CRAMM is divided into three stages: asset identification and valuation, threat and vulnerability assessment, and countermeasure selection and recommendation." [7] The implementation of this methodology is much like the other methods listed in this chapter.

---

6   Please see the following for detailed information on all NIST SP 800 series publications: http://csrc.nist.gov/publications/PubsSPs.html

7   Please see the following for the quoted overview of the CRAMM methodology: http://www.cramm.com/overview/howitworks.htm

Failure Modes and Effect Analysis

Failure modes and effect analysis [8] was born in hardware analysis, but can be used for software and system analysis. It examines potential failures of each part or module, and examines effects of failure at three levels:

1. Immediate level (part or module)
2. Intermediate level (process or package)
3. System-wide

The organization would then "collect total impact for failure of given modules to determine whether modules should be strengthened or further supported."

FRAP

The Facilitated Risk Analysis Process (FRAP)[9] makes a base assumption that a narrow risk assessment is the most efficient way to determine risk in a system, business segment, application or process. The process allows organizations to prescreen applications, systems, or other subjects to determine if a risk analysis is needed. By establishing a unique prescreening process, organizations will be able to concentrate on subjects that truly need a formal risk analysis. The process has little outlay of capital and can be conducted by anyone with good facilitation skills.

OCTAVE

As defined by its creator, Carnegie Mellon University's Software Engineering Institute, OCTAVE "is a self-directed information security risk evaluation."[10] OCTAVE is defined as a situation where people from an organization manage and direct an information security risk evaluation for their organization. The organization's people direct risk evaluation

---

8   Please see the following for detailed information on Failure Modes and Effects Analysis: http://asq.org/learn-about-quality/process-analysis-tools/overview/fmea.html

9   Please see the following for detailed information on FRAP: http://csrc.nist.gov/nissc/2000/proceedings/papers/304slide.pdf

10   Please see the following for detailed information on OCATVE: http://www.cert.org/octave/

activities and are responsible for making decisions about the organization's efforts to improve information security. In OCTAVE, an interdisciplinary team, called the analysis team, leads the evaluation.

Figure 3.5 illustrates that the OCTAVE approach is driven by operational risk and security practices. Technology is examined only in relation to security practices.

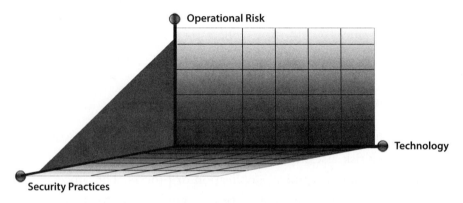

Figure 3.5 - **The Octave approach is driven by operational risk and security practices**

The OCTAVE criteria are a set of principles, attributes, and outputs. Principles are the fundamental concepts driving the nature of the evaluation. They define the philosophy that shapes the evaluation process. For example, self-direction is one of the principles of OCTAVE. The concept of self-direction means that people inside the organization are in the best position to lead the evaluation and make decisions.

The requirements of the evaluation are embodied in the attributes and outputs. Attributes are the distinctive qualities, or characteristics, of the evaluation. They are the requirements that define the basic elements of the OCTAVE approach and what is necessary to make the evaluation a success from both the process and organizational perspectives. Attributes are derived from the OCTAVE principles. For example, one of the attributes of OCTAVE is that an interdisciplinary team (the analysis team) staffed by personnel from the organization lead the evaluation. The principle behind the creation of an analysis team is self-direction.

Finally, outputs are the required results of each phase of the evaluation. They define the outcomes that an analysis team must achieve during each phase. It is recognized that there is more than one set of activities that can produce the outputs of OCTAVE. It is for this reason that one does not specify one set of required activities.

Security Officers Management and Analysis Project (SOMAP)

The Security Officers Management and Analysis Project (SOMAP) is a Swiss nonprofit organization with a primary goal to run an open information security management project and maintain free and open

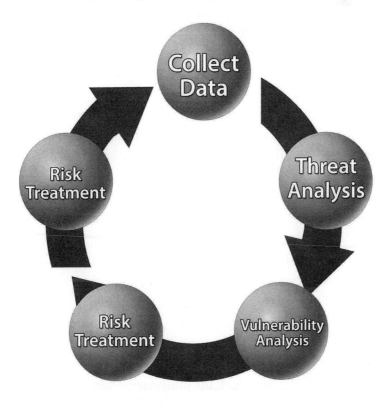

Figure 3.6 - **The SOMAP Risk Assessment Workflow**

tools and documentation under the GNU license. SOMAP has created a handbook and a guide and a risk tool to help with understanding risk management. In the SOMAP risk assessment guide the qualitative and quantitative methodologies are discussed. SOMAP identifies the importance of choosing the best methodology based on the goals of the organization.

SOMAP illustrates risk assessment workflow as illustrated in *Figure 3.6* More information, including the handbook, guide and available tools can be obtained from www.somap.org.

Spanning Tree Analysis

Spanning tree analysis "creates a 'tree' of all possible threats to or faults of the system. 'Branches' are general categories such as network threats, physical threats, component failures, etc." When conducting the risk assessment, organizations "prune 'branches' that do not apply."

VAR (Value at Risk)

In a paper presented by Jeevan Jaisingh and Jackie Rees of the Krannert Graduate School of Management at Purdue University a new methodology for information security risk assessment titled value at risk (VAR) was introduced. The VAR methodology provides a summary of the worst loss due to a security breach over a target horizon. Many of the information security risk assessment tools are qualitative in nature and are not grounded in theory. VAR is identified as a theoretically based, quantitative measure of information security risk. It is believed that by using VAR the best possible balance between risk and cost of implementing security controls can be achieved. Many organizations identify an acceptable risk profile for their company. Determine the cost associated with this risk so that when the dollar value at risk for the organization exceeds that dollar amount, the organization can be alerted to the fact that an increased security investment is required. The VAR framework for information security risk assessment appears in *Figure 3.7*.

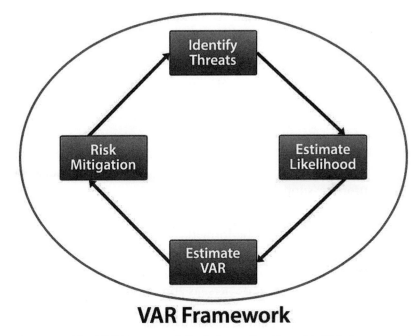

VAR Framework

Figure 3.7 - **The VAR Framework for information Security Risk Assessment**

Qualitative Risk Assessments

Organizations have the option of performing a risk assessment in one of two ways: qualitatively or quantitatively. Qualitative risk assessments produce valid results that are descriptive versus measurable. A qualitative risk assessment is typically conducted when:

- The risk assessors available for the organization have limited expertise in quantitative risk assessment; that is, assessors typically do not require as much experience in risk assessment when conducting a qualitative assessment.

- The timeframe to complete the risk assessment is short.

- Implementation is typically easier.

- The organization does not have a significant amount of data readily available that can assist with the risk assessment and, as a result, descriptions, estimates, and ordinal scales (such as high, medium, and low) must be used to express risk.

- The assessors and team available for the organization are long-term employees and have significant experience with the business and critical systems.

The following methods are typically used during a qualitative risk assessment:

- Management approval to conduct the assessment must be obtained prior to assigning a team and conducting the work. Management is kept apprised during the process to continue to promote support for the effort.

- Once management approval has been obtained, a risk assessment team can be formed. Members may include staff from senior management, information security, legal or compliance, internal audit, HR, facilities/safety coordination, IT, and business unit owners, as appropriate.

The assessment team requests documentation, which may include, dependent upon scope:

- Information security program strategy and documentation

- Information security policies, procedures, guidelines, and baselines

- Information security assessments and audits

- Technical documentation, to include network diagrams, network device configurations and rule sets, hardening procedures, patching and configuration management plans and procedures, test plans, vulnerability assessment findings, change control and compliance information, and other documentation as needed

- Applications documentation, to include software development life cycle, change control and compliance information, secure coding standards, code promotion procedures, test plans, and other documentation as needed

- Business continuity and disaster recovery plans and

corresponding documents, such as business impact analysis surveys

- Security incident response plan and corresponding documentation
- Data classification schemes and information handling and disposal policies and procedures
- Business unit procedures, as appropriate
- Executive mandates, as appropriate
- Other documentation, as needed

The team sets up interviews with organizational members, for the purposes of identifying vulnerabilities, threats, and countermeasures within the environment. All levels of staff should be represented, to include

- Senior management
- Line management
- Business unit owners
- Temporary or casual staff (i.e., interns)
- Business partners, as appropriate
- Remote workers, as appropriate
- Any other staff deemed appropriate to task

It is important to note that staff across all business units within scope for the risk assessment should be interviewed. It is not necessary to interview every staff person within a unit; a representative sample is usually sufficient.

Once interviews are completed, the analysis of the data gathered can be completed. This can include matching the threat to a vulnerability, matching threats to assets, determining how likely the threat is to exploit the vulnerability, and determining the impact to the organization in the event an exploit is successful. Analysis also includes a matching of current and planned countermeasures (i.e., protection) to the threat–vulnerability pair.

When the matching is completed, risk can be calculated. In a qualitative analysis, the product of likelihood and impact produces the level of risk. The higher the risk level, the more immediate is the need for the organization to address the issue, to protect the organization from harm.

Once risk has been determined, additional countermeasures can be recommended to minimize, transfer, or avoid the risk. When this is completed, the risk that is left over—after countermeasures have been applied to protect against the risk—is also calculated. This is the residual risk, or risk left over after countermeasure application.

Quantitative Risk Assessments

As an organization becomes more sophisticated in its data collection and retention, and staff becomes more experienced in conducting risk assessments, an organization may find itself moving more toward quantitative risk assessment. The hallmark of a quantitative assessment is the numeric nature of the analysis. Frequency, probability, impact, countermeasure effectiveness, and other aspects of the risk assessment have a discrete mathematical value in a pure quantitative analysis.

Often, the risk assessment an organization conducts is a combination of qualitative and quantitative methods. Fully quantitative risk assessment may not be possible, because there is always some subjective input present, such as the value of information. Value of information is often one of the most difficult factors to calculate.

It is clear to see the benefits, and the pitfalls, of performing a purely quantitative analysis. Quantitative analysis allows the assessor to determine whether the cost of the risk outweighs the cost of the countermeasure. Purely quantitative analysis, however, requires an enormous amount of time and must be performed by assessors with a significant amount of experience. Additionally, subjectivity is introduced because the metrics may also need to be applied to qualitative measures. If the organization has the time and manpower to complete a lengthy and complex accounting evaluation, this data may be used to assist with a quantitative analysis; however, most organizations are not in a position to authorize this level of work.

Three steps are undertaken in a quantitative risk assessment: initial management approval, construction of a risk assessment team, and the review of information currently available within the organization. Single loss expectancy (SLE) must be calculated to provide an estimate of loss. SLE is defined as the difference between the original value and the remaining value of an asset after a single exploit. The formula for calculating SLE is as follows:

SLE = asset value (in $) × exposure factor (loss due to successful threat exploit, as a %)

Losses can include lack of availability of data assets due to data loss, theft, alteration, or denial of service (perhaps due to business continuity or security issues).

Next, the organization would calculate the annualized rate of occurrence (ARO). This is done to provide an accurate calculation of annualized loss expectancy (ALE). ARO is an estimate of how often a threat will be successful in exploiting a vulnerability over the period of a year.

When this is completed, the organization calculates the annualized loss expectancy (ALE). The ALE is a product of the yearly estimate for the exploit (ARO) and the loss in value of an asset after an SLE. The calculation follows

ALE = SLE x ARO

Note that this calculation can be adjusted for geographical distances using the local annual frequency estimate (LAFE) or the standard annual frequency estimate (SAFE).

Given that there is now a value for SLE, it is possible to determine what the organization should spend, if anything, to apply a countermeasure for the risk in question. Remember that no countermeasure should be greater in cost than the risk it mitigates, transfers, or avoids. Countermeasure cost per year is easy and straightforward to calculate. It is simply the cost of the countermeasure divided by the years of its life (i.e., use within the organization). Finally, the organization is able to compare the cost of the risk versus the cost of the countermeasure and make some objective decisions regarding its countermeasure selection.

Identify Threats and Vulnerabilities

Identify Vulnerabilities

NIST Special Publication 800–30 Rev. 1, page 8, defines a vulnerability as "an inherent weakness in an information system, security procedures, internal controls, or implementation that could be exploited by a threat source".

In the field, it is common to identify vulnerabilities as they are related to people, processes, data, technology, and facilities. Examples of vulnerabilities could include

- Absence of a receptionist, mantrap, or other physical security mechanism upon entrance to a facility

- Inadequate integrity checking in financial transaction software

- Neglecting to require users to sign an acknowledgment of their responsibilities with regard to security, as well as an acknowledgment that they have read, understand, and agree to abide by the organization's security policies

- Patching and configuration of an organization's information systems are done on an *ad hoc* basis, and, therefore, are neither documented nor up to date.

Unlike a risk assessment, vulnerability assessments tend to focus on the technology aspects of an organization, such as the network or applications. Data gathering for vulnerability assessments typically includes the use of software tools, which provide volumes of raw data for the organization and the assessor. This raw data includes information on the type of vulnerability, its location, its severity (typically based on an ordinal scale of high, medium, and low), and sometimes a discussion of the findings.

Assessors who conduct vulnerability assessments must be expert in properly reading, understanding, digesting, and presenting the information obtained from a vulnerability assessment to a multidisciplinary, sometimes nontechnical audience. Why? Data that are obtained from the scanning may not truly be a vulnerability. False-positives are findings that are reported when no vulnerability truly exists in the organization (i.e., something that is occurring in the environment has been flagged as an exposure when it really is not); likewise, false-negatives are vulnerabilities that should have been reported and are not. This sometimes occurs when tools are inadequately "tuned" to the task, or the vulnerability in question exists outside the scope of the assessment.

Some findings are correct and appropriate, but require significant interpretation for the organization to make sense of what has been discovered and how to proceed in remediation (i.e., fixing the problem). This task is typically suited for an experienced assessor or a team whose members have real-world experience with the tool in question.

Identify Threats

The National Institute of Standards and Technology (NIST), in Special Publication (SP) 800–30 Rev. 1, pages 7 – 8, defines threats as "any circumstance or event with the potential to adversely impact organizational operations and assets, individuals, other organizations, or the Nation through an information system via unauthorized access, destruction, disclosure, or modification of information, and/or denial of service. In the OCTAVE framework, threats are identified as the source from which assets in the organization are secured (or protected).

NIST, in Special Publication (SP) 800-30 Rev.1, page 8, defines a threat-source as "either (1) intent and method targeted at the intentional exploitation of a vulnerability or (2) a situation and method that may accidentally trigger a vulnerability."

Threat sources can be grouped into a few categories. Each category can be expanded with specific threats, as follows:

- *Human:* Malicious outsider, malicious insider, (bio)terrorist, saboteur, spy political or competitive operative, loss of key personnel, errors made by human intervention, cultural issues

- **Natural:** Fire, flood, tornado, hurricane, snow storm, earthquake

- **Technical:** Hardware failure, software failure, malicious code, unauthorized use, use of emerging services, such as wireless, new technologies

- **Physical:** Closed-circuit TV failure due to faulty components, perimeter defense failure

- **Environmental:** Hazardous waste, biological agent, utility failure

- **Operational:** A process (manual or automated) that affects confidentiality, integrity, or availability

Many specific threats exist within each category; the organization will identify those sources as the assessment progresses, utilizing information available from groups such as (ISC)² and SANS, and from government agencies such as the National Institute of Standards and Technology (NIST), the Federal Financial Institutions Examination Council (FFIEC), the Department of Health and Human Services (HHS), and others.

Selecting Tools and Techniques for Risk Assessment

It is expected that an organization will make a selection of the risk assessment methodology, tools, and resources (including people) that best fit its culture, personnel capabilities, budget, and timeline. Many automated tools, including proprietary tools, exist in the field. Although automation can make the data analysis, dissemination, and storage of results easier, it is not a required part of risk assessment. If an organization is planning to purchase or build automated tools for this purpose, it is highly recommended that this decision be based on an appropriate timeline and resource skill sets for creation, implementation, maintenance, and monitoring of the tool(s) and data stored within, long term.

Risk Assessment/Analysis

Risk assessment processes may vary between frameworks and industries but the basic approach and formulas remain largely the same. Risk is a function of threats, vulnerabilities, likelihood and impact. Risk assessments may also be qualitative, quantitative or a hybrid of the two. Qualitative risk assessments define risk in relative terms such as "high," "moderate," or low. Quantitative risk assessments attempt to provide specific measurements and impacts with dollar figures representing the expected loss. In many cases these methods are combined to get the best of both worlds.

Likelihood Determination

It is important to note that likelihood is a component of a qualitative risk assessment. Likelihood, along with impact, determines risk. Likelihood can be measured by the capabilities of the threat and the presence or absence of countermeasures. Initially, organizations that do not have trending data available may use an ordinal scale, labeled high, medium, and low, to score likelihood rankings. Another method is presented in *Figure 3.8*.

Once a value on the ordinal scale has been chosen, the selection can be mapped to a numeric value for computation of risk. For example, the selection of high can be mapped to the value of 1. Medium can likewise be mapped to 0.5, and low can be mapped to 0.1. As the scale expands, the numeric assignments will become more targeted.

Determination of Impact

Impact can be ranked much the same way as likelihood. The main difference is that the impact scale is expanded and depends upon definitions, rather than ordinal selections. Definitions of impact to an organization often include loss of life, loss of dollars, loss of prestige, loss of market share, and other facets. Organizations need to take sufficient time to define and assign impact definitions for high, medium, low, or any other scale terms that are chosen.

Likelihood and Consequences Rating

Likelihood		Consequence	
Rare (Very Low)	E	**Insignificant** (Low - No Business Impact)	1
Unlikely (Low)	D	**Minor** (Low - Minor Business Impact, some loss of confidence)	2
Moderate (Medium)	C	**Moderate** (Medium - Business is Interrupted, loss of confidence)	3
Likely (High)	B	**Major** (High - Business is Disrupted, major loss of confidence)	4
Almost Certain (Very High)	A	**Catastrophic** (High - Business cannot continue)	5

Likelihood Qualification – How to Arrive at a Likelihood Rating

How to Qualify Likelihood	Rating
Skill (High Skill Level Required ⇨ Low or No Skill Required)	1=High Skill Required ⇨ 5=No Skill Required
Ease of Access (Very Difficult to Do ⇨ Very Simple to Do)	1=Very Difficult ⇨ 5=Simple
Incentive (High Incentive ⇨ Low Incentive)	1=Low or No Incentive ⇨ 5=High Incentive
Resource (Requires Expensive or Rare Equipment ⇨ No Resources Required)	1=Rare/Expensive ⇨ 5=No Resource Required
Total (Add Rating and Divide by 4)	1=E 2=D 3=C 4=B 5=A

Figure 3.8 - **Rating Likelihood and Consequences**

Once the terms are defined, impact can be calculated. If an exploit has the potential to result in the loss of life (such as a bombing or bioterrorist attack), then the ranking will always be high. In general, groups such as the National Security Agency view loss of life as the highest-priority risk in any organization. As such, it may be assigned the top value in the impact scale. An example: 51 to 100 = high; 11 to 50 = medium; 0 to 10 = low.

Determination of Risk

Risk is determined as the byproduct of likelihood and impact. For example, if an exploit has a likelihood of 1 (high) and an impact of 100 (high), the risk would be 100. [11] As a result, 100 would be the highest exploit ranking available. These scenarios (high likelihood, high impact) should merit immediate attention from the organization.

	Consequence				
Likelihood	**Insignificant** *1*	**Minor** *2*	**Moderate** *3*	**Major** *4*	**Catastrophic** *5*
A *(almost certain)*	H	H	E	E	E
B *(likely)*	M	H	H	E	E
C *(possible)*	L	M	H	E	E
D *(unlikely)*	L	L	M	H	E
E *(rare)*	L	L	M	H	H
E	**Extreme Risk:** Immediate action required to mitigate the risk or decide to not proceed				
H	**High Risk:** Action should be taken to compensate for the risk				
M	**Moderate Risk:** Action should be taken to monitor the risk				
L	**Low Risk:** Routine acceptance of the risk				

Figure 3.9 - **Rating Likelihood and Consequences**

11 This can be represented by the following formula: (Likelihood * Impact = Risk or L*I = R)

As the risk calculations are completed, they can be prioritized for attention, as required. Note that not all risks will receive the same level of attention, based on the organization's risk tolerance and its strategy for mitigation, transfer, or avoidance of risk. *Figure 3.9* shows another view of risk.

Risk Avoidance

Risk avoidance is the practice of coming up with alternatives so that the risk in question is not realized. For example, have you ever heard a friend, or parents of a friend, complain about the costs of insuring an underage driver? How about the risks that many of these children face as they become mobile? Some of these families will decide that the child in question will not be allowed to drive the family car, but will rather wait until he or she is of legal age (i.e., 18 years of age) before committing to owning, insuring, and driving a motor vehicle.

In this case, the family has chosen to avoid the risks (and any associated benefits) associated with an underage driver, such as poor driving performance or the cost of insurance for the child. Although this choice may be available for some situations, it is not available for all. Imagine a global retailer who, knowing the risks associated with doing business on the Internet, decides to avoid the practice. This decision will likely cost the company a significant amount of its revenue (if, indeed, the company has products or services that consumers wish to purchase). In addition, the decision may require the company to build or lease a site in each of the locations, globally, for which it wishes to continue business. This could have a catastrophic effect on the company's ability to continue business operations.

Risk Transfer

Risk transfer is the practice of passing on the risk in question to another entity, such as an insurance company. Let us look at one of the examples that were presented above in a different way. The family is evaluating

535

whether to permit an underage driver to use the family car. The family decides that it is important for the youth to be mobile, so it transfers the financial risk of a youth being in an accident to the insurance company, which provides the family with auto insurance.

It is important to note that the transfer of risk may be accompanied by a cost. This is certainly true for the insurance example presented earlier, and can be seen in other insurance instances, such as liability insurance for a vendor or the insurance taken out by companies to protect against hardware and software theft or destruction. This may also be true if an organization must purchase and implement security controls in order to make their organization less desirable to attack.

It is important to remember that not all risk can be transferred. While financial risk is simple to transfer through insurance, reputational risk may almost never be fully transferred. If a banking system is breached there may be a cost in the money lost, but what about the reputation of the bank as a secure place to store assets? How about the stock price of the bank and the customers the bank may lose due to the breach?

Risk Mitigation

Risk mitigation is the practice of the elimination of, or the significant decrease in the level of risk presented. Examples of risk mitigation can be seen in everyday life and are readily apparent in the information technology world.

For example, to lessen the risk of exposing personal and financial information that is highly sensitive and confidential organizations put countermeasures in place, such as firewalls, intrusion detection/ prevention systems, and other mechanisms, to deter malicious outsiders from accessing this highly sensitive information. In the underage driver example, risk mitigation could take the form of driver education for the youth or establishing a policy not allowing the young driver to use a cell phone while driving, or not letting youth of a certain age have more than one friend in the car as a passenger at any given time.

Risk Assignment/Acceptance

Risk Acceptance

In some cases, it may be prudent for an organization to simply accept the risk that is presented in certain scenarios. Risk acceptance is the practice of accepting certain risk(s), typically based on a business decision that may also weigh the cost versus the benefit of dealing with the risk in another way.

For example, an executive may be confronted with risks identified during the course of a risk assessment for their organization. These risks have been prioritized by high, medium, and low impact to the organization. The executive notes that in order to mitigate or transfer the low-level risks, significant costs could be involved. Mitigation might involve the hiring of additional highly skilled personnel and the purchase of new hardware, software, and office equipment, while transference of the risk to an insurance company would require premium payments. The executive then further notes that minimal impact to the organization would occur if any of the reported low-level threats were realized. Therefore, he or she (rightly) concludes that it is wiser for the organization to forego the costs and accept the risk. In the young driver example, risk acceptance could be based on the observation that the youngster has demonstrated the responsibility and maturity to warrant the parent's trust in his or her judgment.

The decision to accept risk should not be taken lightly, nor without appropriate information to justify the decision. The cost versus benefit, the organization's willingness to monitor the risk long term, and the impact it has on the outside world's view of the organization must all be taken into account when deciding to accept risk. When accepting risk, the business decision to do so must be documented.

It is important to note that there are organizations that may also track containment of risk. Containment lessens the impact to an organization when an exposure is exploited through distribution of critical assets (i.e., people, processes, data, technologies, and facilities).

Risk Assignment

"Who is assigned and responsible for risk?" is a very serious question, with an intriguing answer: it depends. Ultimately, the organization (i.e., senior management or stakeholders) owns the risks that are present during operation of the company. Senior management, however, may rely on business unit (or data) owners or custodians to assist in identification of risks so that they can be mitigated, transferred, or avoided. The organization also likely expects that the owners and custodians will minimize or mitigate risk as they work, based upon policies, procedures, and regulations present in the environment. If expectations are not met, consequences such as disciplinary action, termination, or prosecution will usually result.

Here is an example: A claims processor is working with a medical health-care claim submitted to his organization for completion. The claim contains electronic personally identifiable health-care information for a person the claims processor knows. Although he has acknowledged his responsibilities for the protection of the data, he calls his mother, who is a good friend of the individual who filed the claim. His mother in turn calls multiple people, who in turn contact the person who filed the claim. The claimant contacts an attorney, and the employee and company are sued for the intentional breach of information.

Several things are immediately apparent from this example. The employee is held immediately accountable for his action in intentionally exploiting a vulnerability (i.e., sensitive information was inappropriately released, according to United States federal law— Health Insurance Portability and Accountability Act of 1996 (HIPAA)). While he was custodian of the data (and a co-owner of the risk), the court also determined that the company was co-owner of the risk, and hence also bore the responsibility for compensating the victim (in this example, the claimant).

Once the findings from the assessment have been consolidated and the calculations have been completed, it is time to present a finalized report to senior management. This can be done in a written report, or by presentation. Any written reports should include an acknowledgment to the participants, a summary of the approach taken, findings in detail (in either tabulated or graphical form), recommendations for remediation of the findings, and a summary. Organizations are encouraged to develop their own formats, to make the most of the activity, as well as the information collected and analyzed.

Countermeasure Selection

One of the most important steps for the organization is to appropriately select countermeasures to apply to risks in the environment. Many aspects of the countermeasure must be considered to ensure that they are a proper fit to the task. Considerations for countermeasures or controls include:

- Accountability (can be held responsible)
- Auditability (can it be tested?)
- Trusted source (source is known)
- Independence (self-determining)
- Consistently applied
- Cost-effective
- Reliable
- Independence from other countermeasures (no overlap)
- Ease of use
- Automation
- Sustainable
- Secure
- Protects confidentiality, integrity, and availability of assets
- Can be "backed out" in event of issue
- Creates no additional issues during operation
- Leaves no residual data from its function

From this list it is clear that countermeasures must be above reproach when deployed to protect an organization's assets.

It is important to note that once risk assessment is completed and there is a list of remediation activities to be undertaken, an organization must ensure that it has personnel with appropriate capabilities to implement the remediation activities, as well as to maintain and support them. This may

541

require the organization to provide additional training opportunities to personnel involved in the design, deployment, maintenance, and support of security mechanisms within the environment.

In addition, it is crucial that appropriate policies, with detailed procedures and standards that correspond to each policy item be created, implemented, maintained, monitored, and enforced throughout the environment. The organization should assign resources that can be accountable to each task and track tasks over time, reporting progress to senior management and allowing time for appropriate approvals during this process.

Tangible and Intangible Asset Valuation

All information has value. Value is typically represented by information's cost and its perceived value internally and externally to an organization. It is important to remember that over time, however, information may lose its value. Additionally, information may lose value if it is modified, improperly disclosed, or has not had its proper value calculated. It is of utmost importance, then, to periodically attempt to properly value information assets.

How, then, is information value to be determined? Similar to risk analysis, information valuation methods may be descriptive (subjective) or metric (objective) based. Subjective methods include the creation, dissemination, and collection of data from checklists or surveys. An organization's policies or the regulatory compliance requirements that it must follow can also help to determine information's worth. Metric or statistical measures may provide a more objective view of information valuation, due to the fact that they are based on specific quantitative measurements, as opposed to qualitative. Each of these methods has its uses within an organization.

One of the methods that uses consensus relative to valuation of information is the consensus/modified Delphi method. Participants in the valuation exercise are asked to comment anonymously on the task being discussed. This information is collected and disseminated to a participant other than the original author. This participant comments upon the observations of the original author. The information gathered is discussed in a public forum and the best course is agreed upon by the group (consensus).

Risk assessment also takes into account special circumstances under which assets may require additional protection, such as with regulatory compliance. Many times, these regulatory requirements are the means to completion of an appropriate risk assessment for the organization, as meeting the compliance objectives requires the risk assessment to be done.

543

Because no organization has limitless dollars, resources, and time, it can be difficult to persuade senior executives to undertake risk assessment, even in the face of regulatory requirements. How, then, might they be persuaded? One of the principle outcomes of risk assessment is the definition and identification of threats, vulnerabilities, and countermeasures present (or desired) within the organization. It would then be useful to "reuse" the data gathered during the risk assessment for other security initiatives, such as business continuity, security incident response, disaster recovery, and others. The act of reusing data gathered during a risk assessment, when possible and appropriate, can save the organization dollars, time, and resources and can be demonstrated to senior management as a tangible value, or return on investment (ROI).

Tangible Asset Valuation

Tangible assets are those which have a physical presence. These assets are valued based on the original cost of the assets minus depreciation. These assets are often depreciated to zero for accounting purposes. For risk assessment purposes, the information security professional needs to be aware of the original cost as well as the replacement cost of the items in question. As suppliers and vendors come into and leave the market, the cost of replacing a specific appliance, server or type of lock may change due to supply and demand. Additionally assets originally depreciated may gain in value if the supply is less than the demand. Certain assets may also become outdated and new assets may be required to replace the functionality or utility they provided. Ways to determine tangible asset value include:

- Original cost minus depreciation
- Actual market value through market research
  - Consider online auction sites which show what others are actually buying the asset for.
  - Call vendors and get updated quotes for replacement cost comparison
- Cost of switching to a competing asset or capability

Intangible Asset Valuation

Intangible assets are not physical. Examples of intangible property include, but are not limited to:

- Trademarks
- Patents
- Copyrights
- Business processes
- Brand recognition
- Intellectual property

Intangible assets may also be further classified as definite or indefinite:

- A definite intangible asset is an intangible asset with a definite expiration period. An example of a definite intangible asset is a patent. The patent has value only as long as it is enforceable. Once the patent expires it no longer has value.

- An indefinite intangible asset is an intangible asset with an indefinite expiration period. An example would be an organization's brand. The brand is expected to be maintained and preserved into the foreseeable future.

Intangible assets can be quite difficult to determine a value for. What is the value of the "CISSP®" trademark? It is valuable to the members who hold the credential and it has a value to (ISC)² the organization which owns the trademark. But what is the total value of the trademark? To approximate the value of an intangible asset the following methods are considered generally acceptable:

- *Cost:* The cost to create and to replace the asset. This approach must be used cautiously, as rarely does the value of intangible assets only equal the creation or acquisition cost.

- *Capitalization of historic profits:* If getting a patent, creating a brand or developing a new process directly led to increased profits, those profits can be considered part of the overall value of the asset.

- **Cost avoidance or savings:** If acquiring the trademark of a product service allowed an organization to avoid paying royalties those savings can be considered part of the asset's value.

The information security professional should seek the aid of a financial expert when attempting to determine the intangible value of an asset. These are some of the most complex and valuable assets an organization has and require thorough valuation efforts.

Manage Personnel Security

Individuals within an organization come to work every day to perform their jobs to the best of their ability. As such these individuals have the appropriate intentions and seek out information on the best ways to perform their jobs, the training required, and what the expectations of their jobs are. The media places much attention on the external threat by hackers; however, there is also the threat internally of erroneous or fraudulent transactions, which could cause information assets to be damaged or destroyed. Internal personnel are closest to the data and best understand the processes, along with control weaknesses that currently exist. Job controls such as the segregation of duties, job description documentation, mandatory vacations, job and shift rotation, and need-to-know (least privilege) access are implemented to minimize the risks to the data. Individuals must be qualified with the appropriate level of training, with the job roles and responsibilities clearly defined so that the interaction among departments can properly function.

Various activities should be performed prior to an individual starting in a position, such as developing job descriptions, contacting references, screening/investigating background, developing confidentiality agreements, and determining policies on vendor, contractor, consultant, and temporary staff access. The following actions describe some of these activities.

Employment Candidate Screening

Hiring qualified, suitable and trustworthy individuals depends upon implementing and adhering to personnel policies that screen out those individuals whose past actions may indicate undesirable behavior. Lower employee morale can result in reduced compliance with controls. Increased staff turnover can also result in lower levels of staff expertise over time. Termination policies and procedures are necessary to ensure that terminated employees no longer have access to the system, and therefore do not have the opportunity to damage files or systems or disrupt company operations. These are also necessary to ensure that policy is consistently applied to personnel. Although most individuals are hardworking, competent individuals with no intentions of wrongdoing, there can be a few individuals with less than desirable intentions. Poor personnel security increases the risks to information, making it imperative to implement the appropriate personnel security controls.

Job descriptions should contain the roles and responsibilities of the position and the education, experience, and expertise required to satisfactorily perform the job function. A well-written job description provides not only the basis for conversation with the applicant to determine if the skills are a good match, but also the barometer by which ongoing performance reviews can be measured. Individual job goals stated within the performance reviews should mirror the job description. Failure to align the correct job description with a position could result in the individual lacking skills for the job requirements. To ensure that individuals possess the security skills on an ongoing basis, the job skills must be periodically reassessed. Requirements for annual training, especially for those individuals requiring specialized security training, will ensure that the skills remain relevant and current. Roles and responsibilities as defined by policies can help identify specific security skills that are needed. The employee training and participation in professional activities should be monitored and encouraged. All job descriptions of the organization should have some reference to information security responsibilities, as these responsibilities are shared across the organization. Specific technology, platform requirements, and certifications required for security staff should be noted within the job posting.

The access and duties of an individual for a particular department should be assessed to determine the sensitivity of the job position. The degree of harm that the individual can cause through misuse of the computer system, through disclosing information, disrupting data processing, sharing internal secrets, modifying critical information, or committing computer fraud, should be input to the classification as well. Role-based access establishes roles for a job or class of jobs, indicating the type of information the individual is permitted to access. Job sensitivity may also be used to require more stringent policies related to mandatory vacations, job rotations, and access control policies. Excess controls for the sensitivity level of the position waste resources through the added expense, while fewer controls cause unacceptable risks.

Reference Checks

During the interviewing and hiring process, individuals attempt to determine the past work history of the applicant and their competencies, such as teamwork, leadership abilities, perseverance, ethics, customer service orientation, management skills, planning and specific technical and analytical capabilities. Much of the information provided is obtained by observing the individual in the interview process or from the information he or she has provided through the targeted questions. It is not always possible to determine the true work orientation of the prospective employee without other collaborating information. There are essentially two kinds of reference checks: personal and work. Personal accounting for the character of the person and work associated with verifying the work history.

Personal reference checks involve contacting those individuals supplied by the prospective employee. Many employers are reluctant to provide personal references for fear of future litigation. As such many employers may have policies that only allow information such as date of hire and date of termination to be released. No information on why a termination occurred is released other than potentially whether it was a friendly (employee choice) or unfriendly (company terminated) decision. This still does not necessarily provide a reflection on the employee behavior as it may have been the result of staff reduction having nothing to do with performance. After all, when a company provides a reference it can be perceived as placing a stamp of approval on the performance or character of the employee, even though the person providing the reference really has no control over the future work performance of the employee. Many individuals will provide references to place them in the best possible light and may place individuals such as presidents, vice presidents, doctors, lawyers, ministers, and so forth, on the list to create the appearance of greater integrity. Targeted questions will be used by an employer to ascertain the tendencies and capabilities of the candidate, such as leadership ability, oral and written communication skills, decision-making skills, ability to work with others, respect from peers, how the individual acted under stress, and managerial ability (budgeting, attracting talent, delivering projects). Multiple reference checks provide multiple perspectives and provide for corroboration of the desired behaviors. Employers need to balance the response of references with the knowledge that the references were provided by the applicant and may be biased in their opinions. Failure of a prospective employee to provide references may be an indicator of a spotty work record or the possibility of prior personnel actions/sanctions against the individual.

Background Investigations

Just as the personal reference checks provide the opportunity to obtain corroborating information on whether the applicant will potentially be a good addition to the company, background checks can uncover more information related to the ability of the organization to trust the individual. Organizations want to be sure of the individuals that they are hiring and minimize future lawsuits or exposure. Resumes are often filled with errors, accidental mistakes, or blatant lies to provide a perceived advantage to the applicant. Common falsifications include embellishment of skill levels, job responsibilities and accomplishments, certifications held, and the length of employment. The background checks can greatly assist the hiring manager in determining whether he or she has an accurate representation of the skills, experience, and work accomplishments of the individual. Commercial businesses typically do not have the time and money to conduct meaningful, thorough investigations on their own and hire outside firms that specialize in the various background checks. Background checks can uncover:

- Gaps in employment
- Misrepresentation of job titles
- Job duties
- Salary
- Reasons for leaving a job
- Validity and status of professional certification
- Education verification and degrees obtained
- Credit history
- Driving records
- Criminal history
- Personal references
- Social security number verification

Benefits of Background Checks
The benefits of background checks in protecting the company are self-evident; however, the following benefits may also be realized:

- Risk mitigation
- Increased confidence that the most qualified candidate was hired versus the one who interviewed the best

551

- Lower hiring cost
- Reduced turnover
- Protection of assets
- Protection of the company's brand reputation
- Shielding of employees, customers, and the public from theft, violence, drugs, and harassment
- Insulation from negligent hiring and retention lawsuits
- Safer workplace by avoiding hiring employees with a history of violence
- Discouraging of applicants with something to hide
- Identify criminal activity

Timing of Checks

An effective background check program requires that all individuals involved in the hiring process support the program prior to the candidate being selected for hire. This requires that the human resources department, legal, hiring supervisors, and recruiters understand and execute the screening process. Once the individual is hired into the organization, it is much harder to obtain the information without having a specific cause for performing the investigation. Employees should also be periodically reinvestigated consistent with the sensitivity of their positions. This should also be documented in policy including a frequency schedule.

Types of Background Checks

Many different types of background checks can be performed depending upon the position that the individual may be hired for. A best practice would be to perform background checks on all of the company's employees and to require external agencies through contract agreements to perform background checks on the contractors, vendors, and anyone coming in contact with the company assets, systems and information. If this is cost-prohibitive, the organization must decide on the positions on which it is most critical to conduct background checks. Banks, for example, are required to perform background checks on any employee who may come in contact with money. In a bank this is obviously nearly every employee. The types of checks range from minimal checks to full background investigations. The types of individuals upon whom an organization may focus the checks or decide to provide more extensive checks include

- Individuals involved in technology
- Individuals with access to confidential or sensitive information
- Employees with access to company proprietary or competitive data
- Positions working with accounts payable, receivables, or payroll
- Positions dealing directly with the public
- Employees working for healthcare industry-based organizations or organizations dealing with financial information
- Positions involving driving a motor vehicle
- Employees who will come in contact with children

There is a broad range of possible background checks available. The following are the most common background checks performed.

Credit History

Credit history is the primary vehicle used by financial institutions to ensure the repayment of consumer loans, credit cards, mortgages, and other types of financial obligations. Credit histories are used to screen for high default risks and to discourage default. Financial services firms use credit histories as primary leverage, providing a threat to place delinquent information on the individual's credit reports should he or she fall behind in payments. In the past, managers would run a credit report only on those individuals who were directly handling money; however, this has changed due to the interconnection of computers and the potential access to high-risk applications. Basic credit reports verify the name, address, social security number, and prior addresses of the applicant. These can be used to provide more extensive criminal searches or uncover gaps in employment. Detailed credit histories provide the employer with liens, judgments, and payment obligations that may give an indication as to the individual's ability to handle his or her financial obligations. However, these items must be evaluated in context, as the individual may have previously slipped into financial trouble and then reorganized his or her financial life, so that this would not present a risk to the prospective employer. Sometimes credit reports have limited or no information, which may be representative of a prospect's age (has not yet established a credit history), cash paid for purchases, assumption of a false identity, or a prospects' residence (lives in an area that relies on fringe lenders, which typically do not report to credit bureaus).

Employers need to ensure that they are using the information appropriately, according to their country's laws. In the United States, the Fair Credit Reporting Act (FCRA)[1] and laws under the Equal Employment Opportunity Commission (EEOC),[2] and some state laws will govern the actions by the organization. Legal counsel and human resources should be involved in the development of any policies and procedures related to the screening process.

Criminal History

Criminal records are more difficult to obtain than credit histories, as credit histories are exchanged through a system among banks, retail establishments, financial services firms, and credit-reporting bureaus. With more than 3,000 legal jurisdictions in the United States, it is not feasible to search each jurisdiction. Starting with the county of residence and searching in other prior addresses will provide a reasonable background check for the applicant. Most background checks examine felonies and overlook the misdemeanors (less serious crimes). Under the FCRA, employers can request full criminal records for the past seven years, unless the applicant earns more than $75,000 annually, in which case there are

---

1 Please see the following for detailed information on the Fair Credit Reporting Act: www.ftc.gov/os/statutes/031224fcra.pdf
2 http://www.eeoc.gov/

no time restrictions. Important information to be searched includes state and county criminal records, sex and violent offender records, and prison parole and release records.

Driving Records

Driving records should be checked for those employees who will be operating a motor vehicle on their job. These records can also reveal information about applicants who will not be driving vehicles as part of their employment, such as verification of the applicant's name, address, and social security number, and will include information on traffic citations, accidents, driving-under-the-influence arrests, convictions, suspensions, revocations, and cancellations. These may be indicators of a possible alcohol or drug addiction or a lack of responsibility.

Drug and Substance Testing

The use of illicit drugs is tested by most organizations, as drug use may result in lost productivity, absenteeism, accidents, employee turnover, violence in the workplace, and computer crimes. Individuals using drugs avoid applying or following through the process with companies that perform drug testing. There are many different screening tests available, such as screens for amphetamines, cocaine and PCP, opiates (codeine, morphine, etc.), marijuana (THC), phencyclidine, and alcohol. Independent labs are frequently employed by employers to ensure that proper testing is performed, as businesses are not in the drug testing business. Labs employ safeguards to reduce the likelihood of false-positives, or making a wrongful determination of drug use. In the United States, laws such as the Americans with Disabilities Act (ADA)[3] may provide protections for individuals undergoing rehabilitation.

Prior Employment

Verifying employment information such as dates employed, job title, job performance, reason for leaving, and if the individual is eligible for rehire

---

3   Please see the following for detailed information on the Americans with Disabilities Act: http://www.ada.gov/

can provide information as to the accuracy of the information provided by the applicant. This is not an easy process; as noted earlier, many companies have policies to not comment on employee performance and will only confirm dates of employment.

Education, Licensing, and Certification Verification

Diploma and degree credentials listed on the resume can be verified with the institution of higher learning. Degrees can be purchased through the Internet for a fee, without attendance in any classes, so care should be taken to ensure that the degree is from an accredited institution. Certifications in the technology field, such as the CISSP, or other industry- or vendor-specific certifications, can be verified by contacting the issuing agency. State licensing agencies maintain records of state-issued licenses, complaints, and revocations of licenses.

Social Security Number Verification and Validation

That a number is indeed a social security number can be verified through a mathematical calculation, along with the state and year that the number may have been issued. Verification that the number was issued by the Social Security Administration, was not misused, was issued to a person who is not deceased, or that the inquiry address is not associated with a mail-receiving service, hotel or motel, state or federal prison, campground, or detention facility can be done through an inquiry to the Social Security Administration.

Suspected Terrorist Watch List

Various services search the federal and international databases of suspected terrorists. Although the construction of these databases and the methods for identifying the terrorists are relatively new and evolving, industries of higher risk, such as the defense, biotech, aviation, and pharmaceutical industries, or those that conduct business with companies associated with known terrorist activities, would benefit from checking these databases.

Employment Agreements and Policies

Employment agreements are usually signed by the employee before he or she starts the new job or during the first day. These agreements will vary from organization to organization as to the form and content, but their purpose is to protect the organization while the individual is employed, as well as after the employee has left employment by the organization. For example, nondisclosure agreements contain clauses to protect the company's rights to retain trade secrets or intellectual property that the employee may have had access to even after the employee's departure from the organization. Code of conduct, conflict of interest, gift-handling policies, and ethics agreements may be required to ensure that the employee handles the continued employment in a manner that will be in the best interests of the organization and reduce the liability of the organization to lawsuits for unethical behavior by its employees.

Ongoing supervision and periodic performance reviews ensure that the individuals are evaluated on their current qualifications and attainment of security goals. Performance ratings for all employees should cover compliance with security policies and procedures. Compensation and recognition of achievements should be appropriate to maintain high morale of the department. Monitoring ongoing skill capabilities, training, and experience requirements reduces the risk that inappropriate controls are being applied to information security. A variety of policies, agreements and process are considered best practices in managing employee risk. The ultimate goal is to ensure the employee can do the function they were hired for while minimizing the susceptibility, environments and enticement of fraud, theft, abuse or waste. The following processes aid in ensuring an efficient and low risk workforce.

Job Rotation

Job rotations reduce the risk of collusion of activities between individuals. Companies with individuals working with sensitive information or systems where there might be the opportunity for personal gain through collusion can benefit by integrating job rotation with segregation of duties. Rotating the position may uncover activities that the individual is performing outside of the normal operating procedures, highlighting errors or fraudulent behavior. It may be difficult to implement in small organizations due to the particular skill set required for the position, and thus security controls and supervisory control will need to be relied upon. Rotating individuals in and out of jobs provides the ability to give backup coverage, succession planning, and job enrichment opportunities for those involved. It also provides diversity of skills to support separation of duties.

Separation of Duties (SOD)

One individual should not have the capability to execute all of the steps of a particular process. This is especially important in critical business areas, where individuals may have greater access and capability to modify, delete, or add data to the system. Failure to separate duties could result in individuals embezzling money from the company without the involvement of others. Duties are typically subdivided or split between different individuals or organizational groups to achieve separation. This separation reduces the chances of errors or fraudulent acts, as each group serves as a balancing check on the others and a natural control process occurs. Management is responsible for ensuring that the duties are well defined and separated within their business processes. Failure to do so can result in unintended consequences; for example:

- An individual in the finance department with the ability to add vendors to the vendor database, issue purchase orders, record receipt of shipment, and authorize payment could issue payments to falsified vendors without detection.
- An individual in the payroll department with the ability to authorize, process, and review payroll transactions could increase the salaries of coworkers without detection.
- A computer programmer with the ability to change production code could change the code to move money to a personal bank

account and then conceal his or her actions by replacing the production code and hiding or creating false logging.

- A programmer with the authority to write code, move it to production, and run the production job, skipping internal systems development procedures, could implement erroneous, even malicious code either inadvertently or deliberately.

Some organizations utilize a two-dimensional segregation of duties matrix to determine what positions should be separated within a department. Each position is written along the axes of the matrix, with an *x* placed where the two responsibilities should not reside with the same individual. This *x* indicates where the job duties should be subdivided among different individuals. It is critical to separate the duties between the IS department and the business units, as well as between those areas within the IS organization. For example, the management of the user departments is responsible for providing the authorization of systems access for the access rights of their employees. The information systems department, more specifically the area responsible for security administration, is responsible for granting the access. On a periodic basis, this access is also reviewed and confirmed by the business management. Within the IT department, the security administrator would be separated from the business analyst, computer programmer, computer operator, and so forth. These duties, which should not be combined within one person or group, are referred to as incompatible duties. Incompatible duties may vary from one organization to another. The same individual should not typically perform the following functions:

- Systems administration
- Network management
- Data entry
- Computer operations
- Security administration
- Systems development and maintenance

559

- Security auditing
- Information systems management
- Change management

In smaller organizations, it may be difficult to separate the activities, as there may be limited staff available to perform these functions. These organizations may have to rely on compensating controls, such as supervisory review or active monitoring, to mitigate the risk. Audit logging and after-the-fact review by a third party can provide an effective control in lieu of separating the job functions. Larger organizations need to ensure that appropriate separation, supervisory review, and development of formalized operational procedures are in place. The separated functions should be documented fully and communicated to the staff to ensure that only the assigned individuals will execute tasks associated with these functions. These actions can help prevent or detect erroneous work performed by the user. Larger-dollar-amount transactions should have more extensive supervisory review controls (i.e., director/vice president/president formal sign-off) before processing is permitted.

Individuals in the information systems department must be prohibited from entering data into the business systems. Data entry personnel must not be the same individuals verifying the data, and reconciliation of the information should not be performed by the individual entering the information. Separation of these duties introduces checks and balances on the transactions. As new applications are developed, mergers and acquisitions occur, and systems are replaced, care must be taken to ensure that the segregation of duties is maintained. Periodic management review ensures that the transaction processing environment continues to operate with the designed separation principles.

Least Privilege (Need to Know)

Least privilege refers to granting users only the accesses that are required to perform their job functions. Some employees will require greater access than others based upon their job functions. For example, an individual performing data entry on a mainframe system may have no need for Internet access or the ability to run reports regarding the information that they are entering into the system. Conversely, a supervisor may have the need to run reports, but should not be provided the capability to change information in the database. Well-formed transactions ensure that users update the information in systems consistently and through the developed procedures. Information is typically logged from the well-formed transactions. This can serve as a preventive or deterrent control because the user knows that the information is being logged and a detective control can discover how information was modified after the fact. Security controls around these transactions are necessary to ensure that only authorized changes are made to the programs applying the transaction. Access privileges need to be defined at the appropriate level that provides a balance between supporting the business operational flexibility and adequate security. Defining these parameters requires the input of the business application owner to be effective.

Mandatory Vacations

Requiring mandatory vacations of a specified consecutive-day period can provide similar benefits to using job rotations. If work is reassigned during the vacation period, irregularities may surface through the transaction flow, communications with outside individuals, or requests to process information without following normal procedures. Some organizations remove access to the remote systems during this period as well to ensure that the temporarily replaced employee is not performing work.

Employee Termination Processes

Employees join and leave organizations every day. The reasons vary widely, due to retirement, reduction in force, layoffs, termination with or without cause, relocation to another city, career opportunities with other employers, or involuntary transfers. Terminations may be friendly or unfriendly and will need different levels of care as a result.

Friendly Terminations

Regular termination is when there is little or no evidence or reason to believe that the termination is not agreeable to both the company and the employee. A standard set of procedures, typically maintained by the human resources department, governs the dismissal of the terminated employee to ensure that company property is returned, and all access is removed. These procedures may include exit interviews and return of keys, identification cards, badges, tokens, and cryptographic keys. Other property, such as laptops, cable locks, credit cards, and phone cards, are also collected. The user manager notifies the security department of the termination to ensure that access is revoked for all platforms and facilities. Some facilities choose to immediately delete the accounts, while others choose to disable the accounts for a policy defined period, for example, 30 days, to account for changes or extensions in the final termination date. The termination process should include a conversation with the departing associate about their continued responsibility for confidentiality of information.

Unfriendly Terminations

Unfriendly terminations may occur when the individual is fired, involuntarily transferred, laid off, or when the organization has reason to believe that the individual has the means and intention to potentially cause harm to the system. Individuals with technical skills and higher levels of access, such as the systems administrators, computer programmers, database administrators, or any individual with elevated privileges, may present higher risk to the environment. These individuals could alter files, plant logic bombs to create system file damage at a future date, or remove sensitive information. Other disgruntled users could enter erroneous data into the system that may not be discovered for several months. In these situations, immediate termination of systems access is warranted at the time of termination or prior to notifying the employee of the termination.

Managing the people aspect of security, from pre-employment to postemployment, is critical to ensure that trustworthy, competent resources are employed to further the business objectives that will protect company information. Each of these actions contributes to preventive, detective, or corrective personnel controls.

3

Information Security
Governance & Risk Management

563

Vendor, Consultant and Contractor Controls

Business partners and other third parties often bring personnel in to an organization. Therefore the organization must ensure controls are in place to prevent the loss of sensitive information and also mitigate any damage these individuals could intentionally or unintentionally perform to an organization. Much like organizational employee screening, there are several approaches one may take depending on the nature of the relationship between the vendor and the organization.

- If the third party is infrequently on site, or accessing systems, but has administrative access consider:

  - Escorting the individual while on site to monitor activities

  - Virtually monitoring the employee with screen sharing technology and record all actions performed

  - Ensure an appropriate non-disclosure agreement with specific sanctions has been signed by the individual and the individual's organization if applicable

  - Ensure the third party identifies who the specified personnel gaining access are and verify their identification upon access

- If the third party is on site for a more permanent basis and has administrative access consider:

  - Perform a background investigation and determine if any suitability issues arise

  - Virtually monitoring the employee with screen sharing technology and record all actions performed

  - Ensure an appropriate non-disclosure agreement with specific sanctions has been signed by the individual and the individual's organization if applicable

- ¤ Ensure the third party identifies who the specified personnel gaining access are and verify their identification upon access

- ■ Regardless of duration, if the third party has limited access to sensitive information consider:

  - ¤ Virtually monitoring the employee with screen sharing technology and record all actions performed

  - ¤ Ensure an appropriate non-disclosure agreement with specific sanctions has been signed by the individual and the individual's organization if applicable

Ensure someone with a legal background is involved in any contractual negotiations and understands the requirements listed above. Many successful penetration tests involve short visits by "vendors" or "repair people" who are actually attackers. Careful screening of third parties can help ensure only suitable and authorized individuals gain access to facilities and systems. Contracts must specify the requirements the vendors must meet to ensure they can plan and budget accordingly.

3

Information Security Governance & Risk Management

Develop and Manage Security Education, Training and Awareness

Policies define what the organization needs to accomplish at a high level and serves as a definitive statement of management's intention with regards to information security. Security awareness can be defined as helping establish an understanding of the importance of security within the organization, as well as how to comply with security policies. Given today's complex business environments, most organizations perceive value in promoting an awareness of security within their environments. There are many methods by which an organization can educate its members regarding security. Security awareness addresses the *why* of policy. If end users understand the *why*, they are more apt to follow the policy. Generally people follow policy more consistently if they understand *why* policy exists and how to comply, such as following procedures or implementing baselines.

Formal Security Awareness Training

Security awareness training is a method by which organizations can inform employees about their roles, and expectations surrounding their roles, in the observance of information security requirements. Additionally, training provides guidance surrounding the performance of particular security or risk management functions, as well as providing information surrounding the security and risk management functions in general. Finally, educated users aid the organization in the fulfillment of its security program objectives, which may also include audit objectives for organizations that are bound by regulatory compliance.

Training Topics

Security is a broad discipline, and as such, there are many topics that could be covered by security awareness training. Topics that can be investigated within the security awareness curriculum include:

- Corporate security policies
- The organization's security program

- Regulatory compliance requirements for the organization
- Social engineering
- Business continuity
- Disaster recovery
- Emergency management, to include hazardous materials, biohazards, and so on
- Security incident response
- Data classification
- Information labeling and handling
- Personnel security, safety, and soundness
- Physical security
- Appropriate computing resource use
- Proper care and handling of security credentials, such as passwords
- Risk assessment
- Accidents, errors, or omissions

A well-rounded security curriculum will include specialty classes and awareness aids for individuals performing specialized roles within the organization, such as those in IT, accounting, and others. The training may also align with job functions, roles, and responsibilities. The organization must also keep in mind that special attention should be paid to align training with security risk management activities. In doing so, the training may result in partial or complete offset of the risk within the organization.

Creating a Security Awareness Course

The following creates an outline for a security awareness course surrounding a corporate security policy. Assuming that this is the first formal course the organization has conducted, it is likely that personnel have not been formally introduced to the policy. This introduction would be an appropriate place to begin. A curriculum would proceed as follows:

What Is a Corporate Security Policy?

This item allows the organization to explain, in detail, a security measure it is undertaking to protect its environment.

Why Is Having a Corporate Security Policy Important?

This item provides the opportunity to share with employees that it is everyone's responsibility to protect the organization, its people, and its assets. This is also an appropriate place for senior management to voice their support of the corporate security policy, and the security management effort in general.

How Does This Policy Fit into My Role at the Organization?

Many employees are concerned about the effect that security may have on them. Some fear that they will not be able to accomplish tasks on time; others fear that their role may change. This is the right time to indicate to employees that although security considerations may add a bit to job performance, it is more than likely that they are already performing many of the security responsibilities set forth in the security policy. The policy adds formalization to the *ad hoc* security functions in practice; that is, these *ad hoc* practices are now documented and may be enhanced as well.

What about People Who Say They Do Not Have Any Security Functions Present in Their Current Role?

It is important to point out that these functions may be present in an *ad hoc* fashion, but that any process performed over time becomes at least partly automatic. This leads to decreased time to performance, in reality, over time. The instructor may ask the student whether there was a time in recent memory when he or she was asked to perform a new function as part of his or her job. The instructor can then point out that this is a similar situation.

Do I Have to Comply?

It is crucial for an organization to agree that all employees, including senior management, must comply with corporate security policies. If there are exceptions to the rule, then the policy may become unenforceable. This puts the organization in the position of having wasted dollars, time, and resources in the crafting of a policy with no "teeth."

What Are the Penalties for Noncompliance?

It is equally critical that an organization spells out in common and easily understood terms what the penalty is for noncompliance with a corporate security policy. Policies may indicate in their body that all personnel, contractors, and business associates are expected to adhere to the policies or this may be covered as an overall statement for all policies. Typically, failure to do so results in disciplinary action, up to and including termination or prosecution.

At this point, there are likely to be questions about what may happen in the event of an accidental violation. It is important to reiterate to the students that security violations (or incidents) should be reported immediately, so that the impact to the organization can be minimized.

What Is the Effect of This Corporate Policy on My Work? (Will It Make Things Harder?)

This item was discussed in detail above; the instructor may tie this back to impact on the individual's role.

What Type of Things Should I Be Looking For?

At this point, the employee's questions have been answered, relative to their responsibility to comply with the corporate security policy. This would be an appropriate time to discuss the policy's contents with the students. This can be done as a lecture, by example, or in a "spot the security problem" format.

When teaching a course of this type, the instructor should be sure to address topics that apply to all staff, including senior management, line management, business unit users, temporary or seasonal staff, contractors, business associates, and so on.

Awareness Activities and Methods

There are a variety of methods that can be used to promote security awareness. Some of the more common methods include:

- Formalized courses, as mentioned above, delivered either in a classroom fashion using slides, handouts, or books, or online through training Web sites suited to this purpose.

- Use of posters that call attention to aspects of security awareness, such as password protection, physical security, personnel security, and others.

- Business unit walk-throughs, to aid workers in identification of practices that should be avoided (such as posting passwords on post-it notes in a conspicuous place on the desktop) and practices that should be continued (such as maintaining a clean desk or using a locked screen saver when away from the computer).

- Use of the organization's intranet to post security reminders or to host a weekly or monthly column about information security happenings within the organization.

- Appointment of a business unit security awareness mentor to aid with questions, concerns, or comments surrounding the implementation of security within the environment; these individuals would interact together and with the organization's security officer. These mentors could also interact with the organization's internal audit, legal, information technology, and corporate business units on a periodic (monthly or quarterly) basis.

- Sponsor an enterprise-wide security awareness day, complete with security activities, prizes, and recognition of the winners.

- Sponsor an event with an external partner, such as Information Systems Security Association (ISSA), Information Systems Audit and Control Association (ISACA), SysAdmin, Audit, Network, Security (SANS) Institute, International Information Systems Security Certification Consortium ((ISC)²), or others; allow time for staff members to fully participate in the event.

- Provide trinkets for the users within the organization that support security management principles.

- Consider a special event day, week, or month that coincides with other industry or world awareness events such as Global Security Awareness Week (annually in September), Security Awareness Month (typically annually in October)

- Provide security management videos, books, Web sites, and collateral for employees to use for reference.

It is important to note that activities should be interesting and rewarding for the organization's people. To facilitate this interest, the program should be adaptable, and the content and format of the awareness materials should be subject to change on a periodic basis.

Job Training

Unlike general security awareness training, security training assists personnel with the development of their skills sets relative to performance of security functions within their roles. A typical security curriculum in a mature organization will include classes for individuals performing specialized roles within the organization, such as those in IT, accounting, and others.

Even within these business units, specialized training will occur. For example, in the IT area, it would be advisable for network staff responsible for maintenance and monitoring of the firewalls, intrusion detection/ prevention systems, and syslog servers to be sufficiently trained to perform these duties. Say senior management determined that there were no funds available for training. What would be the result? Typically, motivated staff will receive some on-the-job learning; however, it may not be sufficient to perform the job duties adequately. As a result, the organization is breached and sensitive information is stolen. Who would be at fault in this case? Senior management is always ultimately responsible in the organization for information security objectives. Senior management failed, in this case, to adequately protect the environment by refusing to properly train staff in their respective security duties. Any legal ramifications would fall squarely upon management's shoulders.

However, assume that the personnel in question indicated to management that although no paid training was available, they felt comfortable that they could perform the security functions for which they were responsible. To demonstrate, they performed the requisite functions for IT management to demonstrate capability. All is well until the organization is breached some months later and confidential information stolen. Senior management returns to information systems management and asks the director to investigate. During his or her investigation, he or she discovers that patching has not occurred for the past three months. When staff was asked about the incident, no satisfactory answer could be given. Who would be responsible for the breach in that event? Again, senior management is always ultimately responsible for information security within the organization; however, senior management held the network team accountable for failing to maintain patching levels and promptly fired them from their positions. Ensuring that a resource is properly trained can assist an organization in assigning accountability for the satisfactory completion of security tasks for which they are responsible.

The organization must also keep in mind that training should be closely aligned with security risk management activities. In doing so, the training may result in a partial or complete offset of the risk within the organization.

Professional Education

Security education (specifically, in this case, information security) revolves around the education of a potential or experienced security professional along career development lines, and as the SSCP administrative domain course points out, "provides decision-making and security management skills that are important for the success of an organization's security program." Security certifications versus vendor certifications may fit into this category. Certifications such as the Systems Security Certified Practitioner (SSCP), Certified Information Systems Security Professional (CISSP), Certified Information Systems Auditor (CISA), Certified Information Security Manager (CISM), Global Information Assurance

Certification (GIAC), and others are related to the discipline of security for the practitioner. The benefits of this training have already been presented. Costs of the training, relative to the benefits received by the personnel and organization, must be evaluated pre-training.

Equally important are curricula that have been introduced into universities, implemented as bachelors, masters, and Ph.D. programs. Many of these programs present both theory and hands-on course work to the student. Topics covered in these programs may include policy and procedures design and development, security assessment techniques, technical and application security assessment techniques, social engineering, malicious software identification and eradication, incident response, disaster recovery, security program development, and others. The benefit derived from this education is self-evident: a practitioner versus a technician is created. It is important to note, however, that education of this type is typically two to six years in duration and takes significant time for resources to successfully complete. An alternative may be to train professionals on a course-by-course basis in information security. This may be a practical alternative, given the needs within the organization.

Performance Metrics

It is important for the organization to track performance relative to security for the purposes of both enforcement and enhancement of security initiatives under way. It is also important for the organization to ensure that users acknowledge their security responsibilities by signing off after each class that they have heard and understand the material and will agree to be bound by the organization's security program, policies, procedures, plans, and initiatives. Measurement can include periodic walk-throughs of business unit organizations, as well as quizzes to keep staff up to date.

Manage the Security Function

Organizations exist as a system of coordinated activities to accomplish a set of pre-defined objectives. Both small and large organizations need formalized mechanisms to ensure the stability of their operations; however, the greater complexity and size of the organization often make formalization even more important to ensure consistency across the entity. Formalized, written policies, standards, procedures, and guidelines are created to provide for long-term stability, regardless of the incumbent occupying the position. Over time, those in leadership positions will change, as well as those individuals within the workforce being managed.

Organizational business processes are rationalized and logically grouped to efficiently and effectively perform the necessary work. Mergers and acquisitions frequently change the dynamics of the current operating organization, providing new opportunities to achieve synergies.

Work is typically broken down into subtasks, which are then assigned to an individual through specialization. When these tasks, such as systems security, database administration, or systems administration activities, are grouped together, one or more individuals that can focus on that particular skill set can perform them. This process of specialization creates greater efficiency within the organization, as it permits individuals to become very knowledgeable in a particular discipline and produces the results faster than if combined with other responsibilities.

Organizations are also managed in a hierarchical manner, with the lower levels of the organization having more defined, repetitive tasks with less discretion over the resource allocation of human and physical assets. In the higher levels of the organization, through the definition of the chain of command, there are higher levels of authority and greater capability to reassign resources as necessary to accomplish higher-priority tasks.

Organizational Structure Evolution

The security organization has evolved over the past several decades with several names, for example, data security, systems security, security administration, information security, and information protection. These names are reflective of the scope expansion for information security departments. Earlier naming conventions, such as data security, indicated the primary focus on the data that were stored in the mainframe on centralized storage in the data-center. As the technology evolved into distributed computing and the data progressively moved outward from the data-center "glass house" protections, the scope of protection changed and data became less the focus. It became more about information security and the scope increased to include other platforms. The focus in the 1970s was on the processing between computers and the mainframe infrastructure, which evolved data security into information security in the 1980s. This recognized the importance of better protecting the access and integrity of the information. In the 1990s, as information technology became more fundamental to business success than ever before, and consumers became more aware of privacy issues regarding the protection and use of their information, the concepts of enterprise security protection emerged. The 2000s ushered in the era of "smart" devices and almost ubiquitous network connectivity and connection with other people.

The primary focus of the organization assigned responsibility for protecting information security is to ensure the confidentiality, availability, and integrity of the information. The size of the organization and the types of individuals necessary to staff the organization will depend upon the size of the overall organization, geographic dispersion, centralized or decentralized systems processing, the risk profile of the company, and the budget available for security. Every organization will be slightly different, as they operate within different industries with different threat profiles. Some organizations may not be willing to take even the slightest risk if the information that needs to be protected, if disclosed, would be devastating

575

to the long-term viability of the business. Organizations such as the defense industry, financial institutions, and technical research facilities needing to protect trade secrets may fall into this category.

Today's Security Organizational Structure

There is no "one size fits all" for the information security department or the scope of the responsibilities. The location of where the security organization should report has also been evolving. In many organizations, the information systems security officer (ISSO) or chief information security officer (CISO) still reports to the chief information officer (CIO) or the individual responsible for the information technology activities of the organization. This is due to the fact that many organizations still view the information security function as an information technology problem and not a core business issue.

Alternatively, the rationale for this may be due to the necessity to communicate in a technical language, which is understood by information technology professionals and not typically well understood by business personnel. Regardless of the rationale for the placement, placing the individual responsible for information security within the information technology organization could represent a conflict of interest, as the IT department is motivated to deliver projects on time, within budget, and of high quality. Shortcuts may be taken on the security requirements to meet these constraints, if the security function is reporting to the individual making these decisions. The benefit of having the security function report to the CIO is that the security department is more likely to be engaged in the activities of the IT department and aware of the upcoming initiatives and security challenges.

There is a growing trend toward integrating the information and physical security functions. This is partially a result of the increased automation of physical controls and requirements around the physical aspects of security to protect information. This growing trend is focused around the security function being treated as a risk management function and, as such, being located outside of the IT organization. This provides a greater degree of independence as well as the focus on risk management versus management of user IDs, password resets, and access authorization with the reporting relationship outside of the IT organization which also introduces a different set of checks and balances on the security activities that are expected to be performed. The security function may report to some other function outside of information technology. The function should report as high up in the organization as possible, preferably at the C-level. This ensures that the proper message is conveyed to senior management, the company employees view the appropriate authority of the department, and funding decisions can be made while considering the needs across the company.

Responsibilities of the Information Security Officer

The information security officer is accountable for ensuring the protection of all of the business information assets from intentional and unintentional loss, disclosure, alteration, destruction, and unavailability. The security officer typically does not have the resources available to perform all of these functions and must depend upon other individuals within the organization to implement and execute the policies, procedures, standards, and guidelines to ensure the protection of information. In this capacity, the information security officer acts as the facilitator of information security for the organization.

The threat environment is constantly changing and, as such, it is incumbent upon the security officer to keep up with the changes. It is difficult for any organization to anticipate new threats, some of which come from the external environment and some from new technological changes. Prior to the September 11, 2001, terrorist attack in the United States, few individuals perceived that sort of attack as very likely. However, since then, many organizations have revisited their access control policies, physical security, and business continuity plans. New technologies, such as wireless, low-cost removable media (writeable DVDs and USB drives), and mobile computing devices such as laptops, tablets and smart phones have created new threats to confidentiality and disclosure of information, which need to be addressed. Although the organization tries to write policies to last for two or three years without change, depending upon the industry and the rate of change, these may need to be revisited more frequently.

The security officer and his team are responsible for ensuring that the security policies, procedures, baselines, standards, and guidelines are written to address the information security needs of the organization. However, this does not mean that the security department must write all the policies by themselves. Nor should the policies be written solely by the security department without the input and participation of the other departments within the organization, such as legal, human resources, information technology, compliance, physical security, the business units, and others that have to implement the policies. Approval of policy must be done at the executive level. Typically standards, procedures, and baselines do not require that level of approval.

The security officer must stay abreast of emerging technologies to ensure that the appropriate solutions are in place for the company based upon its risk profile, corporate culture, resources available, and desire to be an innovator. Security solutions will be prioritized differently depending on whether an organization is seen as being a leader, or follower (mature product implementation) with regards to technology and security solutions. Failure to stay abreast of technology enhancements could increase the costs to the organization by maintaining older, less effective products. Approaches to satisfying accepted practices may range from active involvement in security industry associations to interaction with vendors to subscribing to industry research groups to simply reviewing printed material and Internet news.

Compliance is the process of ensuring adherence to security policies. A policy or standard for hardening of the company's firewalls will not be very useful if the activity is not being performed. Governments are continuously passing new laws, rules, and regulations that establish requirements to protect nonpublic information or improve controls over critical processes, with an eye towards ensuring the safety of the resources and infrastructure covered by the regulatory regimes through the ongoing efforts of the enterprises that are the targets of the laws to ensure compliance. . Although many of the laws are overlapping in the security requirements, frequently the new laws provide a more stringent requirement focused around or on a particular aspect of information security. Timeframes to be in compliance with the law may not always come at the best time for the organization, nor may they line up with the budget funding cycles. The security officer must stay abreast of emerging regulatory developments to enable response in a timely manner. Planning and documentation are very critical with regards to proof of compliance. Periodic compliance, whether through internal or external inspection, ensures that the procedures, checklists, and baselines are documented and practiced. Compliance reviews are also necessary to ensure that end users and technical staff are trained and have read the security policies.

Security officers are often responsible for implementing and operating computer incident response teams (CIRTs.) CIRTs are groups of individuals with the necessary skills, including management, technical staff, infrastructure, and communications staff, for evaluating the incident, evaluating the damage caused by an incident, and providing the correct response to repair the system and collect evidence for potential prosecution or sanctions. CIRTs are activated depending upon the nature of the incident and the culture of the organization. Security incidents need to be investigated and followed up promptly, as this is a key mechanism in minimizing losses from an incident and reducing the chance of a recurrence.

The security officer provides the leadership for the information security awareness program by ensuring that the program is delivered in a meaningful, understandable way to the intended audience. The program should be developed to grab the attention of the participants to convey general awareness of the security issues and what reporting actions are expected when the end user notices security violations. Without promoting awareness, the policies will not get communicated and there will be much less assurance that they will be practiced within the company. An effective awareness program will have multiple components and methods of delivery, be ongoing, and be delivered throughout the year, not just as a one-time effort.

Security officers must be involved in the management teams and planning meetings of the organization to be fully effective. Project directions and decisions are made during these meetings, as well as the establishment of buy-in and prioritization for the security initiatives. These meetings will include board of director meetings (periodic updates), IT steering committees, manager meetings, and departmental meetings.

Central to the security officer's success within the organization is to understand the vision, mission, objectives/goals, and plans of the organization. This understanding increases the chances of success, allowing security to be introduced at the correct times during the project life cycle and better enables the organization to carry out the corporate mission. The security officer needs to understand the competitive pressures facing the organization, the strengths, weaknesses, threats, opportunities, and the regulatory environment within which the organization operates. All of this will increase the likelihood that appropriate security controls are applied to the areas with the greatest need, highest risk, thus resulting in an optimal allocation of the scarce security funding. The business strategies of each department are critical to their success. Integrating security into that strategy will determine the security officer's success.

Communicate Risks to Executive Management

The information security officer is responsible for understanding the business objectives of the organization, ensuring that a risk assessment is performed, taking into consideration the threats and vulnerabilities impacting the particular organization, and subsequently communicating the risks to executive management. The makeup of the executive management team will vary based on the type of industry or government entity, but typically includes individuals with C-level titles, such as the chief executive officer (CEO), chief operating officer (COO), chief financial officer (CFO), and chief information officer (CIO). The executive team also includes the first-level reporting to the CEO, such as the VP of sales and marketing, VP of administration, general counsel, and the VP of human resources.

The executive team is interested in maintaining the appropriate balance between acceptable risk and ensuring that business operations are meeting the mission of the organization. In this context, executive management is not concerned with the technical details of the implementations, but rather with what is the cost/benefit of the solution and what residual risk will remain after the safeguards are implemented. For example, the configuration parameters of installing a particular vendor's router are not as important as seeking answers to the following questions:

- What is the real perceived threat (problem to be solved)?
- What is the risk (impact and probability) to business operations?
- What is the cost of the safeguard?
- What will be the residual risk (risk remaining after the safeguard is properly implemented and sustained)?
- How long will the project take? Each of these must be evaluated along with the other items competing for resources (time, money, people, and systems).

The security officer has a responsibility to ensure that the information presented to executive management is based upon a real business need and the facts are represented clearly. Recommendations for specific controls should be risk based. Ultimately, it is the executive management of the organization that is responsible for information security. Presentations should be geared at a high level to convey the purpose of the technical safeguard, and not be a rigorous detailed presentation of the underlying technology unless requested.

Reporting Model

The security officer and the information security organization should report as high in the organization as possible to (1) maintain visibility of the importance of information security and (2) limit the distortion or inaccurate translation of messages that can occur due to hierarchical, deep organizations. The higher up in the organization, the greater the ability to gain other senior management's attention to security and the greater the capability to compete for the appropriate budget and resources. Where the security officer's reports in the organization have been the subject of debate for several years and depend upon the culture of the organization. There is no one best model that fits all organizations, but rather pros and cons associated with each placement choice. Whatever the chosen reporting model, there should be an individual designated within the organization that is given the responsibility for ensuring information security at the enterprise-wide level is established, in order to create accountability for resolving security issues when they arise.

Business Relationships

Wherever the security officer reports, it is imperative that he or she establishes credible and good working relationships with business executive management, middle management, and the end users. Information gathered and acted upon by executive management is obtained through their daily interactions with many individuals, not just other executives. Winning their support may be the result of influencing a respected individual within the organization, possibly several management layers below the executive. Similarly, the relationship between the senior executives and the security officer is important if the security strategies are to carry through to implementation. Establishing a track record of delivery and demonstrating the value of the protection to the business will build this relationship. If done properly, the security function becomes viewed as an enabler of the business versus a control point that slows innovation, provides roadblocks to implementation, and represents an overhead cost function. Reporting to an executive structure that understands the need and importance to the business for information security, is willing to work to actively represent security and battle for appropriate funding is critical to success.

Reporting to the CEO

Reporting directly to the CEO greatly reduces the filtering of messages that can occur if a message must pass through several layers, improves overall communication, as well as demonstrates to the organization the importance of information security. Firms that have high security needs, such as credit card companies, technology companies, and companies whose revenue stream depends highly upon Internet Web site commerce, such as eBay or Amazon, might utilize such a model. The downside to this model is that the CEO may be preoccupied with other business issues and may not have the interest or time to devote to information security issues.

Reporting to the Information Technology (IT) Department

In this model, the information security officer reports directly to the chief information officer (CIO), director of information technology, the vice president of information technology, or whatever is the title for the head of the IT department. Most organizations have utilized this relationship, as this was historically where the data security function was found in many companies. This was often due to security being viewed as only a technical problem. The advantage to this model is that the individual to which the security officer is reporting has an understanding of the technical issues often impacted by information security and typically has the clout with senior management to make the desired changes. It can also be beneficial because the information security officer and his department must spend a good deal of time interacting with other areas in the information systems department. This can build strength, trust and appropriate awareness of project activities and issues.

The downside of the reporting structure is the conflict of interest. When the CIO must make decisions with respect to time to market, resource allocations, cost minimization, application usability, and project priorities, the ability exists to slight the information security function. The typical CIO's goals are more oriented toward delivery of application products to support the business in a timely manner. Often the perception is that security controls may slow the time to get products completed and money to implement. As a result the security considerations may not be provided equal weight.

Reporting to a lower level within the CIO organization should be avoided, as noted earlier; the more levels between the CEO and the information security officer, the more challenges that must be overcome. Levels further down in the organization may also have their own domains of expertise that they are focusing on, such as computer operations, applications programming, or computing or networking infrastructure.

Reporting to Corporate Security

Corporate security in most organizations is focused on the physical security of the enterprise. Often the individuals in this environment have backgrounds as former police officers, military, or were associated in some other manner with the criminal justice system. This alternative may appear logical; however, the individuals from these organizations historically come from different backgrounds. Physical security is focused on criminal justice, protection, safety, and investigation services, while information security professionals usually have different training in business and information technology. These disciplines intersect in some areas, but are vastly different in others. A potential downside of being associated with the physical security group is that it could result in the perception of a police-type mentality. This could make it difficult to build effective business relationships with users. Establishing positive relationships with end users can increase their willingness to listen and comply with policy and any implemented security controls. It can also increase user acceptance and support for the security department in reporting policy violations.

Reporting to the Administrative Services Department

The information security officer may report to the vice president of administrative services, which in some organizations may also include the physical security, employee safety, and HR departments. As described in the benefits of reporting to the CIO, there is only one level between the CEO and the information security department. This model can also be viewed as an enterprise function due to the association with the human resources department. It is an attractive model because it can provide focus on security for all forms of information (paper, oral, and electronic). Compared to the functions residing in the technology department, where the focus may tend to be more on just electronic information, there can be benefits. A downside can be that the leaders of this area would have a limited knowledge of information technology and this could make it more difficult to understand both the business strategies and security requirements and to communicate technical solutions to senior executives and the CEO.

Reporting to the Insurance and Risk Management Department

Information-intensive organizations such as banks, stock brokerages, and research companies may benefit from this model. The chief risk officer is already concerned with the risks to the organization and the methods to control those risks through mitigation, acceptance, insurance, etc. The downside is that the risk officer may not be conversant in information systems technology, and the strategic focus of this function may give less attention to day-to-day operational security projects.

Reporting to the Internal Audit Department

This reporting relationship could be seen as a conflict of interest, since the internal audit department is responsible for evaluating the effectiveness and implementation of the organization's control structure, including the activities of the information security department. It would be difficult for the internal audit to provide an independent viewpoint. The internal audit department may have adversarial relationships with other portions of the company due to the nature of its role (to uncover deficiencies in departmental processes), and through association, the security department may be perceived in a similar light. It is advisable that the security department establishes close working relationships with the internal audit department to facilitate the control environment. The internal audit manager most likely has a background in financial, operational, and general controls and may have difficulty relating to the technical activities of the information security department. On the positive side, both areas are focused on improving the controls of the company. The internal audit department does have a preferable reporting relationship for audit issues through a dotted-line relationship with the company's audit committee on the board of directors. It is advisable for the information security function to have a similar path to report security issues to the board of directors as well, either in conjunction with the internal audit department or on its own.

Reporting to the Legal Department

Attorneys are concerned with compliance with regulations, laws, and ethical standards, performing due diligence, and establishing policies and procedures that are consistent with many of the information security objectives. The company's general counsel also typically has the respect or ear of the CEO. In regulated industries, this may be a very good fit.

An advantage is that the distance between the CEO and the information security officer is one level. On the downside, due to the emphasis on compliance activities, the information security department may end up performing more compliance-checking activities (versus security consulting and support), which are typically the domain of internal audit.

Determining the Best Fit

As indicated earlier, each organization must view the pros and cons of each type of potential reporting relationship and develop the appropriate relationship based upon the company culture, type of industry, and what will provide the greatest benefit to the company. Optimal reporting relationships will minimize conflicts of interest, increase visibility, ensure funding is appropriately allocated and ensure that communication is effective when the placement of the Information Security Department is determined.

Budget

The information security officer prepares a budget to manage the information security program and ensures that security is included in the various other departmental budgets, such as the help desk, applications development, and the computing infrastructure. Security is much less expensive and easier to justify when it is built into the application design versus added as an afterthought at or after implementation. Estimates range widely over the costs of adding security later in the life cycle; however, it is not just the added cost caused by not considering security through the development or acquisition life cycle. It can be perceived as delaying implementation when the time necessary to properly implement security was not factored into the implementation timeline and delays occur. The security officer must work with the application development managers to ensure that security is considered in the project cost during each phase of development (analysis, design, development, testing, implementation, and post-implementation). For systems security certification there should be at a minimum, walk-throughs held to ensure that the deliverables meet security requirements. To facilitate this, the security officer should not report to information system or application development management.

In addition to ensuring that new project development activities appropriately address security, ongoing functions such as access administration, intrusion detection, incident handling, policy development, standards compliance, support of external auditors, and evaluations of emerging technology need to be appropriately funded. The security officer will rarely receive all the funding necessary to complete all of the projects for which he or she and his or her team have envisioned, and must usually plan these activities over multiple years. The budgeting process requires examination of the current risks and ensuring that activities with the largest cost/benefit to the organization are implemented first. Projects greater than 12–18 months are generally considered to be long term and strategic in nature, and typically require more funding and resources or are more complex in their implementation. In the event these efforts require a longer timeframe, pilot projects to demonstrate near-term results on a smaller scale are preferable. The longer the payback period, the higher the rate of return (ROR) expected by executive management. This is due primarily to the higher risk level associated with longer-term efforts.

The number of staff, level of security protection required, tasks to be performed, regulations to be met, staff qualification level, training required, and degree of metrics tracking are also parameters that drive funding requirements. For example, if an organization must meet government regulations to increase the number of individuals with security certifications, such as the CISSP or other industry standard security certifications, then the organization may feel an obligation to fund internal training seminars to prepare the individuals. This will need to be factored into the budget. This may also be utilized to attract and retain security professionals to the organization through increased learning opportunities. As another example, the time required in complying with government mandates and laws may necessitate increased staffing to provide the appropriate ongoing tracking and responses to audit issues.

Metrics

Measurements can be collected that provide information on long-term trends and illustrate the day-to-day workload. Measurement of processes provides the ability to improve the process. For example, measuring the number of help desk tickets for password resets can be translated into workload hours and may provide justification for the implementation of new technologies for the end user to self-administer the password reset process. Tracking how viruses spread or the frequency of reporting may indicate a need for further education or improvement of the antivirus management process. Many decisions need to be made when collecting metrics, such as who will collect the metrics, what statistics will be collected, when they will be collected, and what are the thresholds where variations are out of bounds and should be acted upon. An important first decision is to determine what metrics will be used, and whether the metric gathering effort will provide the necessary evidence or value desired.

Resources

When considering the overall resource management of an information security function the information security professional should consider more than just budget to ensure the success of the information security program. In many organizations the following resources may play a role in directly supporting the information security function:

- System Administrators
- Database Administrators
- Network Administrators
- Policy/Privacy Officers
- Compliance Officers
- Legal Council
- Law Enforcement
- Quality Assurance Testers
- Helpdesk Technicians

Additionally, the information security program is indirectly supported by several functions including but not limited to:

- Budget Officers
- Procurement Specialists
- Business Analysts
- Administrative Professionals
- Enterprise Architects
- Software Developers

The size, complexity and mission of an organization greatly influence the resources available to the information security program and the information security officer. Understanding the mission of the organization and building relationship with supporting resources as

591

described above often makes the difference between a successful security program and an ineffectual one. The security officer rarely has the tools or the team to solely resolve an organization's most pressing challenges.

Develop and Implement Information Security Strategies

Strategic, tactical, and operational plans are interrelated, and each provides a different focus toward enhancing the security of the organization. Planning reduces the likelihood that the organization will be reactionary toward the security needs. With appropriate planning, decisions on projects can be made with respect to whether they support the long- or short-term goals and have the priority that warrants the allocation of more security resources.

Strategic Planning

Strategic plans are aligned with the strategic business and information technology goals. These plans have a longer-term horizon (three to five years or more) to guide the long-term view of the security activities. The process of developing a strategic plan emphasizes thinking of the company environment and the technical environment a few years into the future. High-level goals are stated to provide the vision for projects to achieve the business objectives. These plans should be reviewed on an annual basis or whenever major changes to the business occur, such as a merger, acquisition, establishment of outsourcing relationships, major changes in the business climate, introductions of new competitors, and so forth. Technological changes will be frequent during a five-year period, and so the plan should be adjusted. The high-level plan provides organizational guidance to ensure that lower-level decisions are consistent with executive management's intentions for the future of the company. For example, strategic goals may consist of

- Establishing security policies and procedures
- Effectively deploying servers, workstations, and network devices to reduce downtime
- Ensuring that all users understand the security responsibilities and reward excellent performance

593

- Establishing a security organization to manage security enterprise-wide
- Ensuring effective risk management so that risks are effectively understood and controlled

Tactical Planning

Tactical plans provide the broad initiatives to support and achieve the goals specified in the strategic plan. These initiatives may include deployments such as establishing an electronic policy development and distribution process, implementing robust change control for the server environment, reducing vulnerabilities residing on the servers using vulnerability management, implementing a "hot site" disaster recovery program, or implementing an identity management solution. These plans are more specific and may consist of multiple projects to complete the effort. Tactical plans are shorter in length, such as 6–18 months to achieve a specific security goal of the company.

Operational and Project Planning

Specific plans with milestones, dates, and accountabilities provide the communication and direction to ensure that the individual projects are completed. For example, establishing a policy development and communication process may involve multiple projects with many tasks:

1. Conduct security risk assessment
2. Develop security policies and approval processes
3. Develop technical infrastructure to deploy policies and track compliance
4. Train end users on policies
5. Monitor compliance

Depending upon the size and scope of the efforts, these initiatives may be steps of tasks as part of a single plan, or they may be multiple plans managed through several projects. The duration of these efforts is short term to provide discrete functionality at the completion of the effort. Traditional "waterfall" methods of implementing projects spend a large amount of time detailing the specific steps required to implement the complete project. Executives today are more focused on achieving some short-term, or at least interim, results to demonstrate the value of the investment along the way. Such demonstration of value maintains organizational interest and visibility to the effort, increasing the chances of sustaining longer-term funding. The executive management may grow impatient without realizing these early benefits.

Assess the Completeness and Effectiveness of the Security Program

As noted earlier in this chapter several frameworks and assessment methods are available to assess the completeness and effectiveness of an information security program. Some organizations have established an enterprise-wide security oversight committee, sometimes referred to as a "Security Council". This group can serve as a steering committee to provide oversight and direction to the information security program. The vision of the security council must be clearly defined and understood by all members of the council.

Oversight Committee Representation

For maximum effectiveness the oversight committee should consist of representatives from multiple organizational units. This will increase a sense of ownership for the security program enterprise-wide and improve support for the policies in the long term. The HR department is essential to provide knowledge of the existing code of conduct, employment and labor relations, termination and disciplinary action policies, and practices that are in place. The legal department is needed to ensure that the language of the policies states what is intended, and that applicable local, state, and federal laws are appropriately followed. The IT department provides technical input and information on current initiatives and the development of procedures and technical implementations to support the policies. The individual business unit representation is essential to understand how practical the policies may be in carrying out the mission of the business. Compliance department representation provides insight on ethics, contractual obligations, and investigations that may require policy creation. And finally, the security officer, who typically chairs the council, should represent the information security department and members of the security team for specialized technical expertise.

The oversight committee is a management committee and, as such, is populated primarily with management-level employees. It is difficult to obtain the time commitment required to review policies at a detailed level by senior management. Reviewing the policies at this level is a necessary step to achieve buy-in within management. However, it would not be good to use the senior management level in the early stages of development. Line management is very focused on their individual areas and may not have the organizational perspective necessary (beyond their individual departments) to evaluate security policies and project initiatives. Middle management appears to be in the best position to appropriately evaluate what is best for the organization, as well as possessing the ability to influence senior and line management to accept the policies. Where middle management does not exist, it is appropriate to include line management, as they are typically filling both of these roles (middle and line functions) when operating in these positions.

Many issues may be addressed in a single Security Council meeting, which necessitates having someone record the minutes of the meeting. The chairperson's role in the meeting is to facilitate the discussion, ensure that all viewpoints are heard, and drive the discussions to decisions where necessary. It is difficult to perform that function at the same time as taking notes. Recording the meeting is also helpful to capture key points that may have been missed in the notes, so that accurate minutes can be produced.

The relationship between the security department and the security oversight committee is a dotted-line relationship that may or may not be reflected on the organization chart. The value of the committee is in providing the business direction and increasing the awareness of the security activities that are impacting the organization on a continuous basis. How frequently the committee meets will depend upon the organizational culture (i.e., are monthly or quarterly oversight meetings held on other initiatives?), the number of security initiatives, and the urgency of decisions that need the input of the business units.

Security Council Vision Statement

A clear security vision statement should exist that is in alignment with, and supports, the organizational vision. Typically, these statements draw upon the security concepts of confidentiality, integrity, and availability to support the business objectives. Vision statements are not technical and focus on the strategic advantages to the business. People will be involved in the council from management and technical areas and have limited time to participate, so the vision statement must be something that is viewed as worthwhile to sustain their continued involvement. The vision statement is a high-level set of statements, brief, to the point, and achievable.

Mission Statement

Mission statements are objectives that support the overall vision. These become the road map to achieving the vision and help the council clearly view the purpose for its involvement. Some individuals may choose nomenclature such as goals, objectives, initiatives, etc. A sample mission statement is shown in *Figure 3.10.*

Effective mission statements do not need to be lengthy; as the primary concern is to communicate the goals so both technical and nontechnical individuals readily understand them. The vision and mission statements should also be reviewed on an annual basis to ensure that the council is still functioning according to the values expressed in the mission statement, as well as to ensure that new and replacement members are in alignment with the objectives of the council.

Security Program Oversight

By establishing common goals in the beginning, the members of the council will feel that they have some input and influence over the direction of the security program. This is important since many security decisions will impact the areas of operation of members of the committee. This also is the beginning of management's commitment, as the deliverables produced through the information security program now become recommended

The Information Security Council provides management direction and a sounding board for the ACME Company's information security efforts to ensure that these efforts are:

- Appropriately prioritized
- Supported by each organizational unit
- Appropriately funded
- Realistic given ACME's information security needs
- Balance security needs to be made between cost, response time, ease of use, flexibility, and time to market

The Information Security Council takes an active role in enhancing our security profile and increasing the protection of our assets through:

- Approval of organization-wide information security initiatives
- Coordination of various workgroups so that security goals can be achieved
- Promoting awareness of security initiatives within their organizations
- Discussion of security ideas, policies, and procedures and their impact on the organization
- Recommendation of policies to the ACME Company IT Steering Committee
- Increased understanding of the threats, vulnerabilities, and safeguards facing our organization
- Active participation in policy, procedure, and standard review

The ACME Company information technology steering committee supports the information security council by:

- Developing the strategic vision for the deployment of information technology
- Establishing priorities, arranging resources in concert with the vision
- Approval of the recommended policies, standards, and guidelines
- Approving major capital expenditures

Figure 3.10 - **Sample Security Council mission statement**

or approved by the security council versus the information security department. The primary responsibilities of the council will include:

- ***Decide on Project Initiatives***—Each organization has limited resources (time, money, and people) to allocate across projects to advance the business. The primary objective of information security projects is to reduce the organizational business risk through the implementation of reasonable controls. The council should take an active role in understanding the initiatives and the resulting business impact.

- ***Prioritize Information Security Efforts***—Once the security council understands the proposed project initiatives and the associated positive impact to the business, its members can be involved with the prioritization of the projects. This may be in the form of a formal annual process or through the discussion and expressed support for individual initiatives.

- ***Review and Recommend Security Policies***—Review of the security policies should include a line-by-line review of the policies, a general review of any standards, a cursory review of the procedures that are designed to support the policies, and monitoring of the security implementation plan to ensure it meets policy, standards, and baseline requirements. Through this activity, three key concepts are implemented that are important to sustaining commitment:

  - ¤ Understanding of the policy is enhanced,

  - ¤ Practical ability of the organization to support the policy is discussed, and

  - ¤ A sense of ownership is established to increase support of implementation activities.

- ***Review and Audit the Security Program***—Auditors provide an essential role for maintaining and improving information security. They provide an independent view of the design, effectiveness, and implementation of controls. The results of audits generate findings that require management response and corrective action plans to resolve the issue and mitigate the risk. Auditors often request information prior to the start of the audit to facilitate the review. Some audits are performed at a high level without substantive testing, while other audits will identify test samples to determine if a control is implemented and followed. The security department cooperates with the internal and external auditors to ensure that the control environment is adequate and functional.

- ***Champion Organizational Security Efforts***—Once the council understands and accepts the policies, it serves as the organizational champion behind the policies. Council members may have started by reviewing a draft of the policy created by the information systems security department, but the resulting product was only accomplished through their review, input, and participation in the process. Their involvement creates ownership of the deliverable and a desire to see the security policy or project succeed within the company.

- ***Recommend Areas Requiring Investment***—Members of the council have the opportunity to provide input from the perspective of their individual business units. The council serves as a mechanism for establishing broad support for security investments from this perspective. Resources within any organization are limited and allocated to the business units with the greatest need and the greatest perceived return on investment. Establishing this support enhances the budgetary understanding of the other business managers, as well as the chief financial officer, which is often essential to obtain the appropriate funding.

601

The following articles and documents contain more information about network security and telecommunications. The following are freely available on the Internet:

NIST Special Publication 800-39: Managing Information Security Risk: Organization, Mission, and Information System View
  (http://csrc.nist.gov/publications/nistpubs/800-39/SP800-39-final.pdf)

Security Officers Management and Analysis Project
  (http://www.SOMAP.org)

OpenFISMA
  (http://www.openfisma.org/user/login)

On-line Reference Database for NIST Special Publication 800-53 Security Controls
  (http://web.nvd.nist.gov/view/800-53/home)

Summary and Conclusion

Information security governance and risk management are core security activities which drive information security spending, policy, hiring and ultimately impact. Organizations have survived or failed due to how they approach information security governance and risk management. Throughout this chapter the following concepts have been addressed:

- The expectations of the CISSP in relation to information security governance and risk management.
- How the security function of an organization relates to its goals, missions and objectives.
- The security governance concept including information about:
  - Organizational processes
  - Security roles and responsibilities
  - Laws and Regulations
  - Privacy
  - Control frameworks
  - Due care and Due Diligence
- Concepts of confidentiality, integrity and availability
- How security policies and their associated procedures, standards, guidelines and baselines are developed and function
- The information lifecycle and how it relates to classification, categorization and information retention and destruction

- Management and governance of third party systems and the relationship of assurance with service level agreements and assessments
- Risk management concepts such as:
  - Security and audit frameworks
  - Risk assessment methodologies
  - Qualitative and quantitative risk assessments
- The identification of threats and vulnerabilities
- Risk assessments and analysis methods including qualitative, quantitative and hybrid
- Risk assignment to organizations and individuals
- How countermeasures are used to help mitigate vulnerabilities and risk
- The value determination of tangible and intangible assets
- Personnel security and suitability management techniques
- Information security awareness, training and education development, deployment and monitoring
- Organizational management of the security function and how different roles report throughout the organization
- Information security strategies, tactics and objectives creation, planning and deployment
- Ways of assessing the completeness and effectiveness of the security program

Review Questions

1. When determining the value of an intangible asset which is the BEST approach?

    A. Determine the physical storage costs and multiply by the expected life of the company

    B. With the assistance of a finance of accounting professional determine how much profit the asset has returned

    C. Review the depreciation of the intangible asset over the past three years.

    D. Use the historical acquisition or development cost of the intangible asset

2. Qualitative risk assessment is earmarked by which of the following?

    A. Ease of implementation and it can be completed by personnel with a limited understanding of the risk assessment process

    B. Can be completed by personnel with a limited understanding of the risk assessment process and uses detailed metrics used for calculation of risk

    C. Detailed metrics used for calculation of risk and ease of implementation

    D. Can be completed by personnel with a limited understanding of the risk assessment process and detailed metrics used for the calculation of risk

3. Single loss expectancy (SLE) is calculated by using:

    A. Asset value and annualized rate of occurrence (ARO)

    B. Asset value, local annual frequency estimate (LAFE), and standard annual frequency estimate (SAFE)

    C. Asset value and exposure factor

    D. Local annual frequency estimate and annualized rate of occurrence

4. Consideration for which type of risk assessment to perform includes all of the following:

    A. Culture of the organization, likelihood of exposure and budget

    B. Budget, capabilities of resources and likelihood of exposure

    C. Capabilities of resources, likelihood of exposure and budget

    D. Culture of the organization, budget, capabilities and resources

5. Security awareness training includes:

    A. Legislated security compliance objectives

    B. Security roles and responsibilities for staff

    C. The high-level outcome of vulnerability assessments

    D. Specialized curriculum assignments, coursework and an accredited institution

6. A signed user acknowledgment of the corporate security policy:

    A. Ensures that users have read the policy

    B. Ensures that users understand the policy, as well as the consequences for not following the policy

    C. Can be waived if the organization is satisfied that users have an adequate understanding of the policy

    D. Helps to protect the organization if a user's behavior violates the policy

7. Effective security management:

    A. Achieves security at the lowest cost

    B. Reduces risk to an acceptable level

    C. Prioritizes security for new products

    D. Installs patches in a timely manner

8. Availability makes information accessible by protecting it from:

    A. Denial of services, fires, floods, hurricanes, and unauthorized transactions

    B. Fires, floods, hurricanes, unauthorized transactions and unreadable backup tapes

    C. Unauthorized transactions, fires, floods, hurricanes and unreadable backup tapes

    D. Denial of services, fires, floods, and hurricanes and unreadable backup tapes

9. To avoid bias, the security officer could report to any of the following:

    A. CEO, application development or CFO

    B. Chief information officer, CFO or application development

    C. CFO, CEO or chief information officer

    D. Application development, CFO or CEO

10. Tactical security plans are BEST used to:

    A. Establish high-level security policies

    B. Enable enterprise/entity-wide security management

    C. Reduce downtime

    D. Deploy new security technology

11. Who is accountable for implementing information security?

    A. Everyone

    B. Senior management

    C. Security officer

    D. Data owners

12. Security is likely to be most expensive when addressed in which phase?

    A. Design

    B. Rapid prototyping

    C. Testing

    D. Implementation

13. Information systems auditors help the organization:

    A. Mitigate compliance issues

    B. Establish an effective control environment

    C. Identify control gaps

    D. Address information technology for financial statements

14. Long-duration security projects:

    A. Provide greater organizational value

    B. Increase return on investment (ROI)

    C. Minimize risk

    D. Increase completion risk

15. Setting clear security roles has the following benefits:

    A. Establishes personal accountability, reduces cross-training requirements and reduces departmental turf battles

    B. Enables continuous improvement, reduces cross-training requirements and reduces departmental turf battles

    C. Establishes personal accountability, establishes continuous improvement and reduces turf battles

    D. Reduces departmental turf battles, Reduces cross-training requirements and establishes personal accountability

16. Well-written security program policies are BEST reviewed:

    A. At least annually or at pre-determined organization changes

    B. After major project implementations

    C. When applications or operating systems are updated

    D. When procedures need to be modified

17. Orally obtaining a password from an employee is the result of:

    A. Social engineering

    B. Weak authentication controls

    C. Ticket-granting server authorization

    D. Voice recognition software

18. A security policy which will remain relevant and meaningful over time includes the following:

    A. Directive words such as shall, must, or will, technical specifications and is short in length

    B. Defined policy development process, short in length and contains directive words such as shall, must or will

C. Short in length, technical specifications and contains directive words such as shall, must or will

D. Directive words such as shall, must, or will, defined policy development process and is short in length

19. The ability of one person in the finance department to add vendors to the vendor database and subsequently pay the vendor violates which concept?

A. A well-formed transaction

B. Separation of duties

C. Least privilege

D. Data sensitivity level

20. Collusion is best mitigated through:

A. Job rotation

B. Data classification

C. Defining job sensitivity level

D. Least privilege

21. Data access decisions are **BEST** made by:

A. User managers

B. Data owners

C. Senior management

D. Application developers

Domain 4

Software Development Security

SOFTWARE DEVELOPMENT SECURITY involves processes and activities regarding the planning, programming, and management of software and systems. Somewhat recursively, the field also deals with those controls that may be installed within software systems to ensure the confidentiality, integrity, and availability of either the software or the data under processing. In addition, this domain concentrates on concepts involved in databases and database management, and Web applications because database applications are a major and unique field of applications and systems, and the World Wide Web is a ubiquitous and widely used interface to all manner of systems, and is particularly widely used for access to a variety of public database applications. As well as discussing the proper and secure means of designing and controlling applications maliciously created software, or malware is also reviewed.

TOPICS

- ■ Understand and apply security in the system life cycle
    - ▫ Systems Development Life Cycle (SDLC)
    - ▫ Maturity models
    - ▫ Operation and maintenance
    - ▫ Change management
    - ▫ Perform risk analysis
- ■ Understand the application environment and security controls
    - ▫ Security of the application environment
    - ▫ Security issues of programming languages
    - ▫ Security issues in source code, e.g., buffer overflow
    - ▫ Configuration management
- ■ Assess the effectiveness of application security
    - ▫ Certification and accreditation
    - ▫ Auditing and logging
    - ▫ Corrective actions

OBJECTIVES

According to the (ISC)² CISSP Candidate Information Bulletin, an information security professional should fully understand the security and controls of:

- The systems development process
- System life cycle
- Application controls
- Change controls
- Data warehousing
- Data mining
- Knowledge-based systems
- Program interfaces
- Concepts used to ensure data and application integrity, security, and availability

4

Software Development Security

Security in the Software Development Life Cycle

Current Threats and Levels

Although information security has traditionally emphasized system-level access controls, recent history has focused attention on applications since many information security incidents now involve software vulnerabilities in one form or another. Application vulnerabilities also allow an entry point to attack systems, sometimes at a very deep level. (Web application vulnerabilities have been frequently used in this manner.) Evidence is increasing that malware is much more than a mere nuisance: it is now a major security risk.

Major consultancies and information technology publications are noting that software security has become a major problem. Development of in-house systems, commercial and off-the-shelf software, and controls on the choice, maintenance, and configuration of applications must be given greater attention than has been the case in the past. Fortunately, a number of books have started to address this topic. Unfortunately, too few security professionals have a significant programming or systems development background. At the same time, training in programming and development tends to emphasize speed and productivity over quality, let alone considerations of security. From the perspective of many developers, security is an impediment and a roadblock. This perception is changing, and in the current development environment, the security professional needs to take care not to be seen as a problem to be avoided.

When examined, most major incidents, breaches and outages will be found to involve software vulnerabilities. Software is increasingly large and complex. In addition, software is becoming standardized, both in terms of the programs and code used as well as the protocols and interfaces involved. Although this provides benefits in training and productivity, it also means that a troublesome characteristic may affect the computing and business environment quite broadly. Also, legacy code and design decisions taken decades ago are still involved in current systems and interact with new technologies and operations in ways that may open additional vulnerabilities.

Software Development Security Outline

This chapter addresses the important security concepts that apply during software development, operation, and maintenance processes. Software includes both operating system software and application software.

The computing environment is layered. The foundation is the hardware of the computer system and the functions that are built into that hardware. In some cases, a layer of microcode or firmware is implemented to generate or ease the use of certain common operations. The operating system provides management of all computer hardware resources, as well as a number of software and data resources required for proper operation. In addition, the operating system manages a variety of utilities and functions that are necessary for overall system security and audit. The applications sit on top of the operating system and associated utilities. The user interacts with data and the network resources through these applications. In some cases, there are additional layers, very often in terms of the interface either with the user or between systems. In addition, these systems may now be built on a distributed basis, with portions or aspects of the programming running on a variety of different machines.

When examining applications security, the applications that users use to do their jobs and interact with the operating system must be considered. However, also be aware that the fundamental concepts of application development also apply to operating system software development, even though most users purchase an existing operating system. Thus, although most enterprises do not develop operating system code, they do design, develop, operate, and maintain proprietary applications relevant to their business needs. Analysis and mitigation of software vulnerabilities uses similar concepts in both cases, although the significance of vulnerabilities in operating system software is greater.

This chapter can never be exhaustive, and as with the material on security management, the information security professional must thoughtfully apply these concepts to the specifics of their own company or situation. Software must be considered both an asset, to be assessed early in the risk management process, and a tool, with vulnerabilities that may require the addition of mitigation or specific controls and safeguards to the system.

Operating system and application software consist of increasingly complex computer programs. Without this software, it would be impossible to operate the computer for the purposes required of it. In the early days of computers, users had to write code for each activity to be undertaken using a language native to the specific machine. To improve productivity, sets or libraries of code were developed that would implement many of the more common instructions. These standard files of functions, along with utilities to ease their use, became the forerunners of what is known as programming languages. In that early environment, the programmers would have been intimately familiar with those standard libraries, and likely would have created most of them themselves. In the current situation, developers frequently use utilities and libraries with functionality that exceeds that immediately required, and programmers may not fully understand the internal structure and operations of the tools, utilities, and modules that comprise a given structure.

The development of programming languages is referred to in terms of generations. There are specific concerns at each level of this progression, but particularly in more recent environments, where the tendency has been to have functions and operations masked from the user, and handled by the operating system in the background. Reliance on the programming environment and code libraries may prevent the developer from fully understanding the dependencies and vulnerabilities included in the final structure.

It should be noted that the CISSP is not required to be an expert programmer or know the inner workings of developing application software code, like the FORTRAN programming language, or how to develop Web applet code using Java. It is not even necessary that the CISSP know detailed security-specific coding practices such as the major divisions of buffer overflow exploits or the reason for preferring str(n)cpy to strcpy in the C language (although all such knowledge is, of course, helpful). Because the CISSP may be the person responsible for ensuring that security is included in such developments, the CISSP should know the basic procedures and concepts involved during the design and development of software programming. That is, in order for the CISSP to monitor the software development process and verify that security is included, the CISSP must understand the fundamental concepts of programming developments and the security strengths and weaknesses of various application development processes.

System assurance is an indispensable, and all too often disregarded, part of information systems security, and thus will be underscored in a major section of its own. In a similar fashion issues specific to the topic of malware, and the countermeasures against it are examined. A third major section covers database concepts, management systems, safeguards, and the particular aspects of data warehousing and data mining. Due to its increasing importance in the current application environment, the security of Web applications will be dedicated a section as well.

4

Software Development Security

Development Life Cycle

A project management tool that can be used to plan, execute, and control a software development project is the systems development life cycle (SDLC). The SDLC is a process that includes systems analysts, software engineers, programmers, and end users in the project design and development. Because there is no industry-wide SDLC, an organization can use any one, or a combination of SDLC methods. The SDLC simply provides a framework for the phases of a software development project from defining the functional requirements to implementation. Regardless of the method used, the SDLC outlines the essential phases, which can be shown together or as separate elements. The model chosen should be based on the project. For example, some models work better with long-term, complex projects, while others are more suited for short-term projects. The key element is that a formalized SDLC is utilized.

The number of phases can range from three basic phases (concept, design, and implement) on up. The basic phases of SDLC are:

- Project initiation and planning
- Functional requirements definition
- System design specifications
- Development and implementation
- Documentation and common program controls
- Testing and evaluation control, (certification and accreditation)
- Transition to production (implementation)

The system life cycle (SLC) extends beyond the SDLC to include two additional phases:

- Operations and maintenance support (post-installation)
- Revisions and system replacement
- Project Initiation and Planning

Projects start out with one or more ideas, a vision and the goal or the objective. These may address particular business needs (functional requirements) along with a proposed technical solution. This information is contained in a document that outlines the project's objectives, scope, strategies, and other factors, such as an estimate of cost or schedule. Management approval for the project is based on this project plan document. During this phase, security must also be considered. Note that security activities should be done in parallel with project initiation activities and, indeed, with every task throughout the project.

The security professional's mental checklist during the project initiation phase should include topics such as:

- Does particular information have special value or sensitivity, and therefore require special protection?
- Even if the original data is of low sensitivity, does the resultant information have higher value?
- Has the information owner determined the information's value?
- What are the assigned classifications or categorizations?
- Will application operation risk exposure of sensitive information?
- Will control of output displays or reports require special measures?
- Will data be processed, stored or transmitted in public or semipublic places?
- Are controlled areas required for operation?
- What systems and data sources interconnect with this system?
- What will this system do to the operations and culture of the organization?
- Could the company become dependent upon it, and will the system require special support in terms of the business's continuity of operations?

619

These questions should be readily recognizable as forming the basis of the risk management process, and all of the answers to these questions should have been determined during that procedure.

Functional Requirements Definition

The project management and systems development teams will conduct a comprehensive analysis of current and possible future functional requirements to ensure that the new system will meet end-user needs. The teams also review the documents from the project initiation phase and make any revisions or updates as needed. For smaller projects, this phase is often subsumed in the project initiation phase. At this point security requirements should be formalized as well.

System Design Specifications

This phase includes all activities related to designing the system and software. In this phase, the system architecture, system outputs, and system interfaces are designed. Data input, data flow, and output requirements are established and security features are designed, generally based on the overall security architecture for the company.

Development and Implementation

During this phase, the source code is generated, test scenarios and test cases are developed, unit and integration testing is conducted, and the program and system are documented for maintenance and for turnover to acceptance testing and production. As well as general care for software quality, reliability, and consistency of operation, particular care should be taken to ensure that the code is analyzed to eliminate common vulnerabilities that might lead to security exploits and other risks.

Documentation and Common Program Controls

These are controls used when editing the data within the program, the types of logging the program should be doing, and how the program versions should be stored. A large number of such controls may be needed, including tests and integrity checks for:

- Program/application
- Operating instructions/procedures
- Utilities
- Privileged functions
- Job and system documentation
- Components - Hardware, software, files, databases, reports, users
- Restart and recovery procedures
- Common program controls
- Edits such as syntax, reasonableness (sanity), range checks, and check digits
- Logs (who, what, when)
- Time stamps
- Before and after images
- Counts—useful for process integrity checks; includes total transactions, batch totals, hash totals, and balances.
- Internal checks—checks for data integrity within the program from when it gets the data to when it is done with the data.
- Parameter ranges and data types
- Valid and legal address references
- Completion codes
- Peer review—the process of having peers of the programmer review the code
- Program or data library when developing software applications:
  - Automated control system
  - Current versions—programs and documentation
  - Record of changes made
    - By whom, when authorized by, what changed
  - Test data verifying changes
  - User sign-offs indicating correct testing

621

- A librarian ensures program or data library is controlled in accordance with policy and procedures:
  - ¤ Controls all copies of data dictionaries, programs, load modules, and documentation and can provide version controls.
- Change control/management—ensures no programs are added unless properly tested and authorized.
- Erroneous/invalid transactions detected are written to a report and reviewed by developers and management.

Acceptance

In the acceptance phase, preferably an independent group develops test data and tests the code to ensure that it will function within the organization's environment and that it meets all the functional and security requirements. It is essential that an independent group test the code during all applicable stages of development to prevent a separation of duties issue. The goal of security testing is to ensure that the application meets its security requirements and specifications. The security testing should uncover all design and implementation flaws that would allow a user to violate the software security policy and requirements. To ensure test validity, the application should be tested in an environment that simulates the production environment. This should include a security certification package and any user documentation. This is the first phase of what is commonly referred to as the certification and accreditation (C&A) process, or the security authorization process, which will be detailed shortly.

Testing and Evaluation Controls

During the test and evaluation phase, the following guidelines can be included as appropriate to the environment:

Test data should include data at the ends of the acceptable data ranges, various points in between, and data beyond the expected and allowable data points. Some data should be chosen randomly to uncover off-the-wall problems. However, some data should specifically be chosen on a fuzzy basis (that is, close to expected proper or problem values) to concentrate on particular areas.

- Test with known good data, although never with live production data.

- *Data validation:* Before and after each test, review the data to ensure that data has not been modified inadvertently.

- *Bounds checking:* Field size, time, date, etc. Bounds checking prevents buffer overflows.

Sanitize test data to ensure that sensitive production data is not exposed through the test process. Test data should not be production data until preparing for final user acceptance tests, at which point special precautions should be taken to ensure that actions are not taken as a result of test runs.

When designing testing controls, make sure to test all changes. The program or media librarian should maintain implementation test data used to test modifications, and should retain copies that are used for particular investigations. Testing done in parallel with production requires that a separate copy of production data be utilized for the assessment. Use copies of master files, not production versions, and ensure either that the data has been sanitized or that the output of the test cannot generate production transactions. Management should be informed of, and acknowledge, the results of the test.

Certification and Accreditation (Security Authorization)

Certification is the process of evaluating the security stance of the software or system against a predetermined set of security standards or policies. Certification also examines how well the system performs its intended functional requirements. The certification or evaluation document should contain an analysis of the technical and nontechnical security features and countermeasures and the extent to which the software or system meets the security requirements for its mission and operational environment. A certifying officer then verifies that the software has been tested and meets all applicable policies, regulations, and standards for securing information systems. Any exceptions are noted for the accreditation or authorizing official.

Security activities verify that the data conversion and data entry are controlled, and only those who need to have access are allowed on the system. Also, an acceptable level of risk is determined. Additionally, appropriate controls must be in place to reconcile and validate the accuracy of information after it is entered into the system. It should also test the ability to substantiate processing. The acceptance of risk is based on the identified risks and operational needs of the application to meet the organization's mission.

Management, after reviewing the certification, authorizes the software or system to be implemented in a production status, in a specific environment, for a specific period. There are two types of accreditation: provisional and full. Provisional accreditation is for a specific period and outlines required changes to the applications, system, or accreditation documentation. Full accreditation implies that no changes are required for making the accreditation decision. Note that management may choose to accredit a system that has failed certification, or may refuse to accredit a system even if it has been certified correct. Certification and accreditation are related, but not simply two steps in a single process.

Transition to Production (Implementation)

During this phase, the new system is transitioned from the acceptance phase into the live production environment. Activities during this phase include obtaining security accreditation; training the new users according to the implementation and training schedules; implementing the system, including installation and data conversions; and, if necessary, conducting any parallel operations.

Revisions and System Replacement

As systems are in production mode, the hardware and software baselines should be subject to periodic evaluations and audits. In some instances, problems with the application may not be defects or flaws, but rather additional functions not currently developed in the application. Any changes to the application must follow the same SDLC and be recorded in a change management system.

Revision reviews should include security planning and procedures to avoid future problems. Periodic application audits should be conducted and include documenting security incidents when problems occur. Documenting system failures is a valuable resource for justifying future system enhancements.

Maturity Models

While there are a number of useful technologies in this regard, possibly the best protection to use is to recall the lessons taught in pretty much every course in programming and software development. The best tools are those requiring attention and thought to the process, such as using an SDLC methodology, or structured programming.

System Life Cycle and Systems Development

Software development and maintenance is the dominant expenditure in information systems. Because of the expenses associated with early software development, industry research began to provide the best methods for reducing costs, which subsequently led to the discipline of software engineering. Software engineering stated that software products had to be planned, designed, constructed, and released according to engineering principles. It included software metrics, modeling, methods, and techniques associated with the designing of the system before it was developed, tracking project progress through the entire development process.

Software development faces numerous problems that could result in higher costs and lower quality. Budget and schedule overruns are two of the largest problems for software development. Remember that Windows 95 was released about 18 months late, and it is estimated that the budget was exceeded by 25%. Software projects continue to escalate. Subsequent to Windows 95, Windows NT required 4 million lines of code, whereas Windows XP contains 45 million.

On the other side, if software development is rushed and software developers are expected to complete projects within a shortened time frame, the quality of the software product could be reduced. In its 4 million lines of code, Windows NT was estimated to contain approximately 64,000 bugs, many of which would have security implications. IT industry analysts have focused on software vulnerabilities as the greatest current issue to be addressed in the whole field of information security. These days, software development is treated as a project, more often than not, a large project. Like any other large project, software development benefits from a formal project management structure: a life cycle of systems development. A great many such structures have been proposed. No single management structure will equally benefit all possible programming projects, but the common elements of organization, design, communications, assessment, and testing will aid any project.

The Software Engineering Institute released the Capability Maturity Model for Software (CMM or SW-CMM) in 1991.[1] The CMM focuses on quality management processes and has five maturity levels that contain several key practices within each maturity level. The five levels describe an evolutionary path from chaotic processes to mature, disciplined software processes. The results of using CMM are intended to be higher quality software products produced by more competitive companies.

The CMM framework establishes a basis for evaluation of the reliability of the development environment. At an initial level, it is assumed that good practices can be repeated. If an activity is not repeated, there is no reason to improve it. Organizations must commit to having policies, procedures, and practices and to using them so that the organization can perform in a consistent manner. Next, it is hoped that best practices are repeatable, and can be rapidly transferred across groups. Practices need to be defined in such a manner as to allow for transfer across project boundaries. This can provide for standardization across the entire organization. At the penultimate level, quantitative objectives are established for tasks. Measures are established, done, and maintained to form a baseline from which an assessment is possible. This can ensure that the best practices are followed and deviations are reduced. At the final level, practices are continuously improved to enhance capability (optimizing).

---

1   http://www.sei.cmu.edu/cmmi/start/

The CMM has been used to address a variety of fields, including security and systems integration. When followed, the CMM provides a means of determining the current maturity of an organization, and key practices to improve the ability of organizations to meet goals for cost, schedule, functionality, and product quality in order to move to the next level. The model establishes a yardstick against which it is possible to judge, in a repeatable way, the maturity of an organization's software process and also compare it to the state of the practice of the industry. The model can also be used by an organization to plan improvements to its software development processes.

The International Organization for Standardization (ISO) has included software development in its ISO 9000 quality standards. Both the ISO and SEI efforts are intended to reduce software development failures, improve cost estimates, meet schedules, and produce a higher quality product.

Operation and Maintenance

During this phase, the system is in general use throughout the organization. The activities involve monitoring the performance of the system and ensuring continuity of operations. This includes detecting defects or weaknesses, managing and preventing system problems, recovering from system problems, and implementing system changes. The operating security activities during this phase include testing backup and recovery procedures, ensuring proper controls for data and report handling, and ensuring the effectiveness of security processes.

During the maintenance phase, periodic risk analysis and recertification of sensitive applications are required when significant changes occur. Significant changes include a change in data sensitivity or criticality, relocation or major change to the physical environment, new equipment, new external interfaces, new operating system software, and new application software. Throughout the operation and maintenance phase, it is important to verify that any changes to procedures or functionality do not disable or circumvent the security features. Also, someone should be assigned the task of verifying compliance with applicable service-level agreements according to the initial operational and security baselines.

4

Software Development Security

629

Change Management

To ensure the integrity of applications, care must be taken to ensure that the application is not changed in a gratuitous or negligent manner during maintenance and patching cycles. Most particularly, there must be controls in place to ensure that users cannot request changes that will breach security policies, and developers cannot implement modifications to the software with unknown effects. Change controls must be sufficient to protect against accidental or deliberate introduction of variations in code that would allow system failures, security intrusions, corruption of data, or improper disclosure of information.

The change management process should have a formal cycle, in the same manner as the SDLC. There should be a formal change request, an assessment of impact and resource requirements and approval decision, implementation (programming) and testing, implementation in production, and a review and verification within the production environment. The key points of change management are that there is a rigorous process that addresses quality assurance, changes must be submitted, approved, tested, and recorded, and there should be a backout plan in case the change is not successful.

The same process should be applied to patch management, when vendors supply patches, hot fixes, and service packs to commercial software. In addition, it should be noted that patches are frequently released to address security vulnerabilities, so they should be applied in a timely manner. This is particularly important given the evidence that black hat groups study released patches to craft new exploits. A strategy should be developed for patch management and should be kept in place as part of the software maintenance infrastructure. A team, responsible for the patch management process, should research (and authenticate) announcements and related information from vendor Web sites.

Research should also be conducted in other areas, such as user groups, where other experiences with patches may be reported. This requirement may need to be addressed for various systems and applications. Analysis should be conducted balancing the implications of the vulnerability addressed, the need for timely application, and the need for thorough testing. Test the patch, and then deploy it into production. The test environment should mirror the production environment as far as possible. A fallback position should be prepared so that the patch or system can be "rolled back" to a previous stage if the patch creates unforeseen problems. Patch less sensitive systems first, to ensure that an error in the patch does not immediately affect critical systems.

Environment and Security Controls

Software Development Methods

Several software development methods have evolved to satisfy different requirements.

Waterfall

The traditional waterfall life-cycle method is the oldest method for developing software systems. It was developed in the early 1970s and provided a sense of order to the process. [1] Each phase—concept, requirements definition, design, etc.—contains a list of activities that must be performed and documented before the next phase begins. From the perspective of business in general, the disadvantage of the waterfall model is that it demands a heavy overhead in planning and administration, and requires patience in the early stages of a project. These same factors are considered an advantage, in the security community, since they force deliberate consideration and planning. Because each phase must be completed before the next, it can inhibit a development team from pursuing concurrent phases or activities. This limit slows initial development, but ensures that ad hoc additions are minimized. Usually, this method is not good for projects that must be developed in quick turnaround time periods (generally less than 6 months). The waterfall model is considered the paradigm for the following styles, known as noniterative models. From the perspective of security, noniterative models are preferred for systems development.

- ■ *Structured Programming Development*—This is a method that programmers use to write programs allowing considerable influence on the quality of the finished products in terms of coherence, comprehensibility, freedom from faults, and security. It is one of the most widely known programming development models, and versions are taught in almost all

---

1   Royce, Winston (1970), "Managing the Development of Large Software Systems", Proceedings of IEEE WESCON 26 (August): 1–9, http://www.cs.umd.edu/class/spring2003/cmsc838p/Process/waterfall.pdf .

academic systems development courses. The methodology promotes discipline, allows introspection, and provides controlled flexibility. It requires defined processes and modular development, and each phase is subject to reviews and approvals. It also allows for security to be added in a formalized, structured approach.

■ *Spiral Method*—The spiral model is a sort of nested version of the waterfall method. The development of each phase is carefully designed using the waterfall model. A distinguishing feature of the spiral model is that in each phase of the waterfall there are four substages, based on the common Deming PDCA (Plan-Do-Check-Act) model; [2] in particular, a risk assessment review (Check). The estimated costs to complete and the schedules are revised each time the risk assessment is performed. Based on the results of the risk assessment, a decision is made to continue or cancel the project.

■ *Cleanroom*—Cleanroom was developed in the 1990s as an engineering process for the development of high-quality software. It is named after the process of cleaning electronic wafers in a wafer fabrication plant. (Instead of testing for and cleaning contaminants from the wafer after it has been made, the objective is to prevent pollutants from getting into the fabrication environment.) In software application development, it is a method of controlling defects (bugs) in the software. The goal is to write the code correctly the first time, rather than trying to find the problems once they are there. Essentially, cleanroom software development focuses on defect prevention rather than defect removal. To achieve this, more time is spent in the early phases, relying on the assumption that the time spent in other phases, such as testing, is reduced. (Quality is achieved through design, rather than testing and remediation.) Because testing can often consume the majority of a project timeline, the time saved during the testing phase can be substantial. In terms of security, if risk considerations are addressed up front, security becomes an integral part of the system, rather than an add-on.

2   Moen and Norman. "Evolution of the PDCA Cycle". http://pkpinc.com/files/ NA01MoenNormanFullpaper.pdf. Retrieved 1 October 2011.

Iterative Development [3]

The pure waterfall model is highly structured and does not allow for changes once the project is started, or revisiting a stage in light of discoveries made in a later phase. Iterative models allow for successive refinements of requirements, design, and coding. Allowing refinements during the process requires that a change control mechanism be implemented. Also, the scope of the project may be exceeded if clients change requirements after each point of development. Iterative models also make it very difficult to ensure that security provisions are still valid in a changing environment.

- *Prototyping*—The prototyping method was formally introduced in the early 1980s to combat the perceived weaknesses of the waterfall model with regard to the speed of development. The objective is to build a simplified version (prototype) of the application, release it for review, and use the feedback from the users' review to build a second, better version. This is repeated until the users are satisfied with the product. It is a four-step process: initial concept, design and implement initial prototype, refine prototype until acceptable, and complete and release final version.

- *Modified Prototype Model (MPM)*—This is a form of prototyping that is ideal for Web application development. It allows for the basic functionality of a desired system or component to be formally deployed in a quick time frame. The maintenance phase is set to begin after the deployment. The goal is to have the process be flexible enough so the application is not based on the state of the organization at any given time. As the organization grows and the environment changes, the application evolves with it, rather than being frozen in time.

- *Rapid Application Development (RAD)*—RAD is a form of rapid prototyping that requires strict time limits on each phase and relies on tools that enable quick development. This

3   Please see the following for a good overview of the various methods described in this section: http://www.ctg.albany.edu/publications/reports/survey_of_sysdev/survey_of_sysdev.pdf

may be a disadvantage if decisions are made so rapidly that it leads to poor design.

- *Joint Analysis Development (JAD)*—JAD was originally invented to enhance the development of large mainframe systems. Recently, JAD facilitation techniques have become an integral part of RAD, Web development, and other methods. It is a management process that helps developers to work directly with users to develop a working application. The success of JAD is based on having key players communicating at critical phases of the project. The focus is on having the people who actually perform the job (they usually have the best knowledge of the job) work together with those who have the best understanding of the technologies available to design a solution. JAD facilitation techniques bring together a team of users, expert systems developers, and technical experts throughout the development life cycle. While input from the users may result in a more functional program, the involvement of large numbers may lead to political pressures that militate against security considerations.

- *Exploratory Model*—This is a set of requirements built with what is currently available. Assumptions are made as to how the system might work, and further insights and suggestions are combined to create a usable system. Because of the lack of structure, security requirements may take second place to enhancements which may be added on an ad hoc basis.

Other Methods and Models

There are other software development methods that do not rely on the iterate/do not iterate division, such as the following:

- *Computer-Aided Software Engineering (CASE)* [4]—This is the technique of using computers and computer utilities to help with the systematic analysis, design, development,

---

[4]   http://ithandbook.ffiec.gov/it-booklets/development-and-acquisition/development-procedures/software-development-techniques/computer-aided-software-engineering.aspx

implementation, and maintenance of software. It was designed in the 1970s, but has evolved to include visual programming tools and object-oriented programming. It is most often used on large, complex projects involving multiple software components and many people. It may provide mechanisms for planners, designers, code writers, testers, and managers to share a common view of where a software project is at each phase of the life-cycle process. By having an organized approach, code and design can be reused, which can reduce costs and improve quality. The CASE approach requires building and maintaining software tools and training for the developers who use them.

■ *Component-Based Development* [5]—This is the process of using standardized building blocks to assemble, rather than develop, an application. The components are encapsulated sets of standardized data and standardized methods of processing data, together offering economic and scheduling benefits to the development process. From a security perspective, the advantage is (or can be) that components have previously been tested for security. This is similar to object-oriented programming (OOP) where objects and classes may be designed with security methods initially, and then instantiated.

■ *Reuse Model* [6]—In this model, an application is built from existing components. The reuse model is best suited for projects using object-oriented development because objects can be exported, reused, or modified. Again, the components may be chosen on the basis of known security characteristics.

■ *Extreme Programming* [7]—This is a discipline of software development that is based on values of simplicity, communication, and feedback. Despite the name, extreme programming is a fairly structured approach, relying on

---

5   http://www.users.globalnet.co.uk/~rxv/CBDmain/cbdfaq.htm
6   http://www.ctg.albany.edu/publications/reports/survey_of_sysdev?chapter=10
7   http://www.extremeprogramming.org/

subprojects of limited and defined scope and programmers working in pairs. The team produces the software in a series of small, fully integrated releases that fulfill the customer-defined needs for the software. Those who have worked with the method say that it works best with small teams: around a dozen programmers in total.

Model Choice Considerations and Combinations

Depending on the application project and the organization, models can be combined to fit the specific design and development process. For example, an application may need a certain set of activities to take place to achieve success, or the organization may require certain standards or processes to meet industry or government requirements. When deciding on the programming model, security must be a consideration. Many developers focus on functionality and not security; thus, it is important to educate those individuals responsible for the development and the managers who oversee the projects. If developers are brought into the project knowing there is a focus on security, they may better understand the importance of coding both functionality and security.

The Database and Data Warehousing Environment

Database systems have always been a major class of computer applications and have specific security requirements all their own. Indeed, some aspects of database security have proven quite intractable and still present unique challenges.

In the early history of information systems, data processing occurred on stand-alone systems that used separate applications that contained their own sets of data files. As systems expanded and more applications were run on the same machine, redundant files were gathered. Several complexities and conflicts also arose, mainly the possibility of having duplicate information within each application contained on the same system. For example, an employee's address might be duplicated in several

637

application systems within the organization, once in the payroll system and again in the personnel system. This duplication of information not only wasted storage space, but also led to the possibility of inconsistency in the data. If an employee moved and notified payroll (to make sure the payroll check still arrived), only the database in payroll would be updated. If the personnel department needed to send something to the employee, the address contained within its application would not show the change. Another danger might occur if the personnel department saw the change in the payroll system, considered it to be an error, and overwrote the newer payroll data with data from the personnel files.

To resolve the potential inconsistencies of having information replicated in several files on a system, databases were developed to incorporate the information from multiple sources. They are an attempt to integrate and manage the data required for several applications into a common storage area that will support an organization's business needs.

DBMS Architecture

Organizations tend to collect data from many separate databases into one large database system, where it is available for viewing, updating, and processing by either programs or users. A database management system (DBMS) is a suite of application programs that typically manage large structured sets of persistent data. It stores, maintains, and provides access to data using *ad hoc* query capabilities. The DBMS provides the structure for the data and some type of language for accessing and manipulating the data. The primary objective is to store data and allow users to view the data. DBMSs have transformed greatly since their introduction in the late 1960s. The earliest file access systems were limited based on the storage technology of the time: primarily tape. These later evolved into network databases in the 1970s. In the 1980s, relational databases became dominant. In the 1990s, object-oriented databases emerged. Because companies have become increasingly dependent upon the successful operation of the DBMS, it is anticipated that future demands will drive more innovations and product improvements.

Typically, a DBMS has four major elements: the database engine itself, the hardware platform, application software (such as record input interfaces and prepared queries), and users. The database element is one (or more) large, structured sets or tables of persistent data. Databases are usually associated with another element, the software that updates and queries the data. In a simple database, a single file may contain several records that contain the same set of fields and each field is a certain fixed width. The DBMS uses software programs that allow it to manage the large, structured sets of data and provide access to the data for multiple, concurrent users while at the same time maintaining the integrity of the data. The applications and data reside on hardware and are displayed to the user via some sort of display unit, like a monitor.

The major elements may be supported by a number of additional components. These may include virtual machine platforms, interfaces or middleware between the applications and the database engine itself, utilities in support of applications, and, increasingly, Web access as a front end. Remember that increasing the items involved increases complexity, at a possible cost to security. The data consists of individual entities and entities with relationships linking them together. The mapping, or organization of the data entities is based on a database model. The database model describes the relationship between the data elements and provides a framework for organizing the data. The data model is fundamental to the design because it provides a mechanism for representing the data and any correlations between the data.

The database model should provide for:

- *Transaction persistence:* The state of the database is the same after a transaction (process) has occurred as it was prior to the transaction, and the transaction should be durable.

- *Fault tolerance and recovery:* In the event of a hardware or software failure, the data should remain in its original state. Two types of recovery systems available are rollback and shadowing. Rollback recovery is when incomplete or invalid transactions are backed out. Shadow recovery occurs when transactions are reapplied to a previous version of the database. Shadow recovery requires the use of transaction logging to identify the last good transaction.

- **Sharing by multiple users:** The data should be available to multiple users at the same time without endangering the integrity of the data; that is, locking of data.

- **Security controls:** Examples include access controls, integrity checking, and view definitions.

DBMSs may operate on hardware that has been implemented to run only databases and often only specific database systems. This allows hardware designers to increase the number and speed of network connections, incorporate multiple processors and storage disks to increase the speed of searching for information, and also increase the amount of memory and cache.

When an organization is designing a database, the first step is to understand the requirements for the database and then design a system that meets those requirements. This includes what information will be stored, who is allowed access, and estimating how many people will need to access the data at the same time. The structuring of the database may also depend upon minimizing duplication of attributes and keys, maximizing flexibility, and balancing those demands against the need to reduce accesses in order to increase performance.

In most database developments, the database design is usually done by either a database design specialist or a combination of database administrators and software analysts. The database designers produce a schema that defines what the data is and how the data is stored, how it relates to other data, and who can access, add, and / or modify the data. The data in a database can be structured in several different ways, depending upon the types of information stored. Different data storage techniques can exist on practically any machine level, from a PC to mainframe, and in various architectures, such as stand-alone, distributed, or client/server.

Hierarchical Database Management Model

The hierarchical model is the oldest of the database models and is derived from the information management systems of the 1950s and 1960s. Even today, there are hierarchical legacy systems that are still being operated by banks, insurance companies, government agencies, and hospitals. This model stores data in a series of records that have field values attached. It collects all the instances of a specific record together as a record type. These record types are the equivalent of tables in the relational model, with the individual records being the equivalent of rows. To create links between the record types, the hierarchical model uses parent/child relationships through the use of trees. A weakness is that the hierarchical model is only able to cope with a single tree and is not able to link between branches or over multiple layers. For example, an organization could have several divisions and several subtrees that represent employees, facilities, and products. If an employee worked for several divisions, the hierarchical model would not be able to provide a link between the two divisions for one employee. The hierarchical model is no longer used in current commercially available DBMS products; however, these models still exist in legacy systems.

Network Database Management Model

The network database management model, introduced in 1971, is an extended form of the hierarchical data structure. It does not refer to the fact that the database is stored on the network, but rather to the method of how data is linked to other data. The network model represents its data in the form of a network of records and sets that are related to each other, forming a network of links. Records are sets of related data values and are the equivalent of rows in the relational model. They store the name of the record type, the attributes associated with it, and the format for these attributes. For example, an employee record type could contain the last name, first name, address, etc., of the employee. Record types are

4

Software Development Security

641

sets of records of the same type. These are the equivalent of tables in the relational model. Set types are the relationships between two record types, such as an organization's division and the employees in that division. The set types allow the network model to run some queries faster; however, it does not offer the flexibility of a relational model. The network model is not commonly used today to design database systems; however, there are some legacy systems remaining.

Relational Database Management Model

The majority of organizations use software based on the relational database management model. The relational database has become so dominant in database management systems that many people consider it to be the only form of database. (This may create problems when dealing with other table-oriented database systems that do not provide the integrity functions required in a true relational database.) The relational model is based on set theory [8] and predicate logic [9] and provides a high level of abstraction. The use of set theory allows data to be structured in a series of tables that have columns representing the variables and rows that contain specific instances of data. These tables are organized using normal forms. The relational model outlines how programmers should design the DBMS so that different database systems used by the organization can communicate with each other.

For our purposes, the basic relational model consists of three elements:

1. Data structures that are called either tables or relations

2. Integrity rules on allowable values and combinations of values in tables

3. Data manipulation agents that provide the relational mathematical basis and an assignment operator

Each table, or relation, in the relational model consists of a set of

---

8   http://plato.stanford.edu/entries/set-theory/
9   http://i.stanford.edu/~ullman/focs/ch14.pdf

attributes and a set of tuples (rows) or entries in the table. Attributes correspond to a column in a table. Attributes are unordered left to right, and thus are referenced by name and not by position. All data values in the relational model are atomic. Atomic values mean that at every row/column position in every table there is always exactly one data value and never a set of values. There are no links or pointers connecting tables; thus, the representation of relationships is contained as data in another table.

A tuple of a table corresponds to a row in the table. Tuples are unordered top to bottom because a relation is a mathematical set and not a list. Also, because tuples are based on tables that are mathematical sets, there are no duplicate tuples in a table (sets in mathematics by definition do not include duplicate elements). The primary key is an attribute or set of attributes that uniquely identifies a specific instance of an entity. Each table in a database must have a primary key that is unique to that table. It is a subset of the candidate key. Any key that could be a primary key is called a candidate key. The candidate key is an attribute that is a unique identifier within a given table. One of the candidate keys is chosen to be the primary key, and the others are called alternate keys.

Primary keys provide the sole tuple-level addressing mechanism within the relational model. They are the only guaranteed method of pinpointing an individual tuple; therefore, they are fundamental to the operation of the overall relational model. Because they are critical to the relational model, the primary keys cannot contain a null value and cannot change or become null during the life of each entity. When the primary key of one relation is used as an attribute in another relation, it is the foreign key in that relation.

The foreign key in a relational model is different from the primary key. The foreign key value represents a reference to an entry in some other table. If an attribute (value) in one table matches those of the primary key of some other relation, it is considered the foreign key. The link (or matches) between the foreign and primary keys represents the relationships between tuples. Thus, the matches represent references and allow one table to be referenced to another table. The primary key and foreign key links are the binding factors that holds the database together. Foreign keys also provide a method for maintaining referential integrity in the data and for navigating between different instances of an entity.

Integrity Constraints in Relational Databases

To solve the problems of concurrency and security within a database, the database must provide some integrity. The user's program may carry out many operations on the data retrieved from the database, but the DBMS is only concerned about what data is read/written from or to the database—the transaction. Users submit transactions and view each transaction as occurring by itself. Concurrency occurs when the DBMS interleaves actions (reads/writes of database objects) of various transactions. For concurrency to be secure, each transaction must leave the database in a consistent state if the database is consistent when the transaction begins.

The DBMS does not really understand the semantics of the data; that is, it does not understand how an operation on data occurs, such as when interest on a bank account is computed. A transaction might commit after completing all its actions, or it could abort (or be aborted by the DBMS) after executing some actions. A very important property guaranteed by the DBMS for all transactions is that they are atomic. Atomicity implies that a user can think of X as always executing all its actions in one step, or not executing any actions at all. To help with concurrency, the DBMS logs all actions so that it can undo the actions of aborted transactions. The security issues of concurrency can occur if several users who are attempting to query data from the database interfere with each other's requests.

The two integrity rules of the relational model are entity integrity and referential integrity. The two rules apply to every relational model and focus on the primary and foreign keys. These rules actually derive from the

Clark and Wilson integrity model discussed in the security architecture and design domain.

In the entity integrity model, the tuple must have a unique and non-null value in the primary key. This guarantees that the tuple is uniquely identified by the primary key value.

The referential integrity model states that for any foreign key value, the referenced relation must have a tuple with the same value for its primary key. Essentially, every table relation or join must be accomplished by coincidence of the primary keys or of a primary key and the foreign key that is the primary key of the other table. Each table participating in the join must demonstrate entity integrity and in the referenced relation must have a similar primary key/foreign key relationship. Another example of the loss of referential integrity is to assign a tuple to a nonexistent attribute. If this occurs, the tuple could not be referenced, and with no attribute, it would be impossible to know what it represented.

Note that null values in non-key attributes are not a formal matter of integrity for relational databases, even though semantically they may be a problem for the database itself.

Structured Query Language (SQL)

The relational model also has several standardized languages. One is called the Structured Query Language (SQL), in which users may issue commands. An advantage of having a standard language is that organizations can switch between different database engine vendor systems without having to rewrite all of its application software or retrain staff.

SQL was developed by IBM and is an International Organization for Standardization (ISO) and American National Standards Institute (ANSI) standard. (ANSI is a private, nonprofit organization that administers and coordinates the U.S. voluntary standardization and conformity assessment system.) Because SQL is a standard, the commands for most systems are similar. There are several different types of queries, such as those for predesigned reports (included in applications) and *ad hoc* queries (usually done by database experts).

The main components of a database using SQL are:

- **Schemas:** Describes the structure of the database, including any access controls limiting how the users will view the information contained in the tables.

- **Tables:** The columns and rows of the data are contained in tables.

- **Views:** Defines what information a user can view in the tables—the view can be customized so that an entire table may be visible or a user may be limited to only being able to see just a row or a column. Views are created dynamically by the system for each user and provide access control granularity.

The simplicity of SQL is achieved by giving the users a high-level view of the data. A view is a feature that allows for virtual tables in a database; these virtual tables are created from one or more real tables in the database. A view can be set up for each user (or group of users) on the system so that the user can then only view those virtual tables (or views). In addition, access can be restricted so that only rows or columns are visible in the view. The value of views is to have control over what users can see. For example, a database administrator can allow users to see their information in an employee database, but not the other employee salaries unless they have sufficient authorization.

This view removes many of the technical aspects of the system from the users, and instead places the technical burden on the DBMS software applications. As an example, assume that all employees in the personnel department have the same boss, the director of personnel. To avoid repeating the data for each employee, this type of data would be stored in a separate table. This saves storage space and reduces the time it would take for queries to execute.

SQL actually consists of three sublanguages. [10] The data definition language (DDL) is used to create databases, tables, views, and indices (keys) specifying the links between tables. Because it is administrative in nature, users of SQL rarely use DDL commands. DDL also has nothing to do with the population of use of the database, which is accomplished by data manipulation language (DML), used to query and extract data, insert new records, delete old records, and update existing records. System and database administrators utilize data control language (DCL) to control access to data. It provides the security aspects of SQL and is therefore our primary area of concern. Some of the DCL commands are:

- **COMMIT** (saves work that has been done)
- **SAVEPOINT** (identifies a location in a transaction to which you can later roll back, if necessary),
- **ROLLBACK** (restores the database to its state at the last **COMMIT**)
- **SET TRANSACTION** (changes transaction options such as what rollback segment to use).

There are other scripting and query languages that can be used in similar ways to create database interface applications that rely on an underlying database engine for function.

Object-Oriented Database Model

The object-oriented (OO) database model is one of the most recent database models. Similar to object-oriented programming languages, the OO database model stores data as objects. The OO objects are a collection of public and private data items and the set of operations that can be executed on the data. Because the data objects contain their own operations, any call to data potentially has the full range of database functions available. The object-oriented model does not necessarily require a high-level language like SQL, because the functions (or methods) are

10   See the following for an overview of all three sublanguages discussed: http://databases.about.com/od/Advanced-SQL-Topics/a/Data-Control-Language-Dcl.htm

contained within the objects. An advantage of not having a query language allows the object-oriented DBMS to interact with applications without the language overhead.

Relational models are starting to add object-oriented functions and interfaces, to create an object-relational model. An object-relational database system is a hybrid system: a relational DBMS that has an object-oriented interface built on top of the original software. This can be accomplished either by a separate interface or by adding additional commands to the current system. The hybrid model allows organizations to maintain their current relational database software and, at the same time, provide an upgrade path for future technologies.

Database Interface Languages

The existence of legacy databases has proven a difficult challenge for managing new database access requirements. To provide an interface that combines newer systems and legacy systems, several standardized access methods have evolved, such as:

- Open Database Connectivity (ODBC)
- Java Database Connectivity (JDBC)
- eXtensible Markup Language (XML)
- Object Linking and Embedding Database (OLE DB)
- ActiveX Data Objects (ADO)

These systems provide a gateway to the data contained in the legacy systems as well as the newer systems.

Open Database Connectivity (ODBC)

ODBC is the dominant means of standardized data access. It is a standard developed and maintained by Microsoft. Almost all database vendors use it as an interface method to allow an application to communicate with a database either locally or remotely over a network. It is an API that is used to provide a connection between applications and databases. It was designed so that databases could connect without having to use specific database commands and features.

ODBC commands are used in application programs, which translate them into the commands required by the specific database system. This allows programs to be linked between DBMSs with a minimum of code changes. It allows users to specify which database is being used, and can be easily updated as new database technologies enter the market. ODBC is a powerful tool; however, because it operates as a system entity, it can be exploited. The following are issues with ODBC security:

- The username and password for the database are stored in plaintext. To prevent disclosure of this information, the files should be protected. For example, if an HTML document was calling an ODBC data source, the HTML source must be protected to ensure that the username and password in plaintext cannot be read. (The HTML should call a common gateway interface (CGI) that has the authentication details, because HTML can be viewed in a browser.)

- The actual call and the returned data are sent as cleartext over the network.

- Verification of the access level of the user using the ODBC application may be substandard.

- Calling applications must be checked to ensure they do not attempt to combine data from multiple data sources, thus allowing data aggregation.

- Calling applications must be checked to ensure they do not attempt to exploit the ODBC drivers and gain elevated system access.

Java Database Connectivity (JDBC)

JDBC is an API from Sun Microsystems used to connect Java programs to databases. It is used to connect a Java program to a database either directly

649

or by connecting through ODBC, depending on whether the database vendor has created the necessary drivers for Java. Regardless of the interface used to connect the user to the database, security items to consider include how and where the user will be authenticated, controlling user access, and auditing user actions. Fortunately, Java has a number of provisions for security, but these must be deliberately implemented in order to secure the database calls and applications.

eXtensible Markup Language (XML)

XML is a World Wide Web Consortium (W3C) standard for structuring data in a text file so that both the format of the data and the data can be shared on intranets and the Web. A markup language, such as the Hypertext Markup Language (HTML), is simply a system of symbols and rules to identify structures (format) in a document. XML is called extensible because the symbols are unlimited and can be defined by the user or author. The format for XML can represent data in a neutral format that is independent of the database, application, and the underlying DBMS.

XML became a W3C standard in 1998, and many believe it is the *de facto* standard for integrating data and content. It offers the ability to exchange data and bridge different technologies, such as object models and programming languages. Because of this advantage, XML is expected to transform data and documents of current DBMSs and data access standards (i.e., ODBC, JDBC, etc.) by Web-enabling these standards and providing a common data format. Another, and probably more important, advantage is the ability to create one underlying XML document and display it in a variety of different ways and devices. The Wireless Markup Language (WML) is an example of an XML-based language that delivers content to devices such as cell phones, pagers, and personal digital assistants (PDAs). As with any of the other programs used to make database interface calls, XML applications must also be reviewed for how authentication of users is established, access controls are implemented, auditing of user actions is implemented and stored, and confidentiality of sensitive data can be achieved.

Object Linking and Embedding Database (OLE DB)

Object Linking and Embedding (OLE) is a Microsoft technology that allows an object, such as an Excel spreadsheet, to be embedded or linked to the inside of another object, such as a Word document. The Component Object Model (COM) is the protocol that allows OLE to work.

OLE allows users to share a single source of data for a particular object. The document contains the name of the file containing the data, along with a picture of the data. When the source is updated, all the documents using the data are updated as well. On the other hand, with object embedding, one application (the source) provides data or an image that will be contained in the document of another application (the destination). The destination application contains the data or graphic image, but does not understand it or have the ability to edit it. It simply displays, prints, or plays the embedded item. To edit or update the embedded object, it must be opened in the source application that created it. This occurs automatically when you double-click the item or choose the appropriate edit command while the object is highlighted.

OLE DB is a low-level interface designed by Microsoft to link data across various DBMSs. It is an open specification that is designed to build on the success of ODBC by providing an open standard for accessing all kinds of data. It enables organizations to easily take advantage of information contained not only in data within a DBMS, but also when accessing data from other types of data sources. (Note, however, that because it is based on OLE, OLE DB is restricted to Windows interface applications.)

Essentially, the OLE DB interfaces are designed to provide access to all data, regardless of type, format, or location. For example, in some enterprise environments, the organization's critical information is located outside of traditional production databases, and instead is stored in containers such as Microsoft Access, spreadsheets, project management planners, or Web applications. The OLE DB interfaces are based on the Component Object Model (COM), and they provide applications with uniform access to data

651

regardless of the information source. The OLE DB separates the data into interoperable components that can run as middleware on a client or server across a wide variety of applications. The OLE DB architecture provides for components such as direct data access interfaces, query engines, cursor engines, optimizers, business rules, and transaction managers.

When developing databases and determining how data may be linked through applications, whether through an ODBC interface or an OLE DB interface, security must be considered during the development stage. If OLE DB is considered, there are optional OLE DB interfaces that can be implemented to support the administration of security information. OLE DB interfaces allow for authenticated and authorized access to data among components and applications. The OLE DB can provide a unified view of the security mechanisms that are supported by the operating system and the database components.

Accessing Databases through the Internet

Many database developers are supporting the use of the Internet and corporate intranets to allow users to access the centralized back-end servers. Several types of Application Programming Interfaces (APIs) can be used to connect the end-user applications to the back-end database. Although a couple of APIs that are available are covered, ActiveX Data Objects (ADO) and Java Database Connectivity (JDBC), there are several security issues about any of the API technologies that must be reviewed. These include authentication of users, authorizations of users, encryption, protection of the data from unauthorized entry, accountability and auditing, and availability of current data.

One approach for Internet access is to create a tiered application approach that manages data in layers. There can be any number of layers; however, the most typical architecture is to use a three-tier approach: presentation layer, business logic layer, and data layer. This is sometimes referred to as the Internet computing model because the browser is used to connect to an application server that then connects to a database.

Depending on the implementation, it can be good or bad for security. The tier approach can add to security because the users do not connect directly to the data. Instead, they connect to a middle layer, the business logic layer, which connects directly to the database on behalf of the users. The bad side of security is that if the database provides security features, they may be lost in the translation through the middle layer. Thus, when looking at providing security, it is important to analyze not only how the security features are implemented, but also where they are implemented and how the configuration of the application with the back-end database affects the security features. Additional concerns for security are user authentication, user access control, auditing of user actions, protecting data as it travels between the tiers, managing identities across the tiers, scalability of the system, and setting privileges for the different tiers.

ActiveX Data Objects (ADO)

ADO is a Microsoft high-level interface for all kinds of data. It can be used to create a front-end database client or a middle-tier business object using an application, tool, or Internet browser. Developers can simplify the development of OLE DB by using ADO. Objects can be the building blocks of Java, JavaScript, Visual Basic, and other object-oriented languages. By using common and reusable data access components (Component Object Model (COM)), different applications can access all data regardless of data location or data format. ADO can support typical client/server applications, HTML tables, spreadsheets, and mail engine information. Note that many security professionals are concerned about the use of ActiveX, because there are no configurable restrictions on its access to the underlying system. Newer browsers implement sandboxing and stronger ActiveX controls to help mitigate this vulnerability.

Data Warehousing

A data warehouse is a repository for information collected from a variety of data sources. Because of the compilation of information from many sources, data warehouses eliminate the organization's original information structures and access controls to enable sharing of that information to more levels of employees. The data stored in a data warehouse is not used for operational tasks, but rather for analytical purposes. The data warehouse combines all of the data from various databases into one large data container. Because the data is collected into one central location for analysis, instead of several smaller databases, the combined data can be used by executives to make business decisions.

A current term associated with data warehouses is data marts. Data marts are smaller versions of data warehouses. While a data warehouse is meant to contain all of an organization's information, a data mart may contain the information from just a division or only about a specific topic. In most instances, the creation of a data mart is less time-consuming, and thus the data can be available for analysis sooner than if a data warehouse was created.

The following tasks illustrate a simplified process of building a data warehouse:

- Feed all data into a large, high-availability, and high-integrity database that resides at the confidentiality level of the most sensitive data.

- Normalize the data. Regardless of how the data is characterized in each system, it must be structured the same when moved into the data warehouse. For example, one database could categorize birth date as "month/day/year," another as "day/month/year," and still another as "year/month/day." The data warehouse must normalize the various data categories into only one category. Normalization will also remove redundancies in the data.

- Mine the data for correlations to produce metadata.

- Sanitize and export the metadata, results of analysis of the data, to its intended users.

- Feed all new incoming data and the metadata into the data warehouse.

In traditional database administration, rules and policies are implemented to ensure the confidentiality and integrity of the database, such as defining user views and setting access permissions. Security is even more critical for data warehouses. Rules and policies must be in place to control access to the data. This includes items such as defining the user groups and the type of data each group can access and outlining the user's security responsibilities and procedures. Another danger of data warehouses is if the physical or logical security perimeter of the database servers were breached, the unauthorized user could gain access to all of the organization's data.

In addition to confidentiality controls, security for the data also includes the integrity and availability of the information. For example, if the data warehouse were accidentally or intentionally destroyed, a valuable repository of the organization's historical and compiled data would also be destroyed. To avoid such a total loss, appropriate plans for backups must be implemented and maintained, as well as recovery options for hardware and software applications.

Metadata

The information about the data, called metadata (literally data about data or knowledge about data), provides a systematic method for describing resources and improving the retrieval of information. The objective is to help users search through a wide range of sources with better precision. It includes the data associated with either an information system or an information object for the purposes of description, administration, legal requirements, technical functionality, usage, and preservation. It is considered the key component for exploiting and using a data warehouse.

Metadata is useful because it provides:

- Valuable information about the unseen relationships between data

- The ability to correlate data that was previously considered unrelated

655

- The keys to unlocking critical or highly important data inside the data warehouse

Note that the data warehouse is usually at the highest classification or categorization level possible. However, users of the metadata are usually not at that level, and therefore, any data that should not be publicly available must be removed from the metadata. Generally this involves abstracting the correlations, but not the underlying data that the correlations came from.

The Dublin Core metadata element set was developed during the first metadata workshop in Dublin, OH, in 1995 and 1996. It was a response to the need to improve retrieval of information resources, especially on the Web. It continues to be developed by an international working group as a generic metadata standard for use by libraries, archives, governments, and publishers of online information. The Dublin Core standard has received widespread acceptance among the electronic information community and has become the *de facto* Internet metadata standard.

The Dublin Core Web site[11] posts several proposals that are open for comment and review from the community. A former security proposal that the Dublin Core metadata group was working on was for access controls. The proposal states that security classification and access rights are not the same. Security classification deals with any official security stamp to give a particular status to the resource[12]. Only some resources will have such a stamp. Access rights do not need official stamps and can be used more loosely for the handling of the resource; for example, a resource marked "public" in a content management system can be published, and a resource marked "not public" will not be published, although metadata about the resource could be published. The nature of the two qualifiers is different, but the values could be related; for example, if the security classification is "top secret," then access rights should contain a value reflecting this. The

---

11   http://dublincore.org/
12   http://dublincore.org/documents/usageguide/qualifiers.shtml

difference between access rights and audience is that audience contains values stating which segment of the user group the information in the resource is created for. Access rights state which user group has permission to access the resource; it does not say anything about the content (which audience does).

The proposed solution: "For full implementation of this refinement, a namespace is needed. Inclusion in DC will mean the availability of a practical, usable namespace[13]." For further information, refer to the Dublin Core metadata Web site. Data contained in a data warehouse is typically accessed through front-end analysis tools such as online analytical processing (OLAP), data mining or knowledge discovery in databases (KDD) methods.

Online Analytical Processing (OLAP)

OLAP technologies provide an analyst with the ability to formulate queries and, based on the outcome of the queries, define further queries. The analyst can collect information by roaming through the data. The collected information is then presented to management. Because the data analyst interprets aspects of the data, the data analyst should possess in-depth knowledge about the organization and also what type of knowledge the organization needs to adequately retrieve information that can be useful for decision making.

For example, a retail chain may have several locations that locally capture product sales. If the management decided to review data on a specific promotional item without a data warehouse, there would be no easy method of capturing sales for all stores on the one item. However, a data warehouse could effectively combine the data from each store into one central repository. The analyst could then query the data warehouse for specific information on the promotional item and present the results to those people in the management who are responsible for promotional items.

---

13   http://dublincore.org/groups/government/securityClassification.shtml

Data Mining

In addition to OLAP, data mining is another process (or tool), for discovering information in data warehouses by running queries against the data. A large repository of data is required to perform data mining. Data mining is used to reveal hidden relationships, patterns, and trends in the data warehouse. Data mining is a decision-making technique that is based on a series of analytical techniques taken from the fields of mathematics, statistics, cybernetics, and genetics. The techniques are used independently and in cooperation with one another to uncover information from data warehouses.

There are several advantages to using data-mining techniques, including the ability to provide better information to managers that outlines the organization's trends, its customers, and the competitive marketplace for its industry. There are also disadvantages, especially for security. The detailed data about individuals obtained by data mining might risk a violation of privacy. The danger increases when private information is stored on the Web or an unprotected area of the network, and thus becomes available to unauthorized users. In addition, the integrity of the data may be at risk. Because a large amount of data must be collected, transformed and loaded, the chance of errors through human data entry may result in inaccurate relationships or patterns. These errors are referred to as data contamination.

One positive security function of data mining is to use the tools to review audit logs for intrusion attempts. Because audit logs usually contain thousands of entries, data-mining tools can help to discover abnormal events by drilling down into the data for specific trends or unusual behaviors. Information system security officers can use a data-mining tool in a testing environment to try to view unauthorized data. For example, testers could log in with the rights assigned to a general user, then use a data-mining tool to access various levels of data. If during this test environment, they are able to successfully view sensitive or unauthorized data, appropriate security controls, such as limiting views, could be implemented. Note that these tools and utilities should be used carefully for the purposes of audit log reduction or the establishment of clipping levels: make attempts to ensure that valuable information is not lost as a result. Data mining is still an evolving technology; thus, standards and procedures need to be formalized so that organizations will be able to use their data for a variety of business decisions and uses. The challenge will be to address the business need while still complying with security requirements that will protect the data from unauthorized users.

Database Vulnerabilities and Threats

One of the primary concerns for the DBMS is the confidentiality of sensitive data. A major concern for most people is that many databases contain health and financial information, both of which are protected by privacy laws in many countries. Another primary concern for the DBMS is enforcing the controls to ensure the continued integrity of the data. A breach of data integrity through an invalid input or an incorrect definition could jeopardize the entire viability of the database. In such an instance, the work required to restore the database or manually write queries to correct the data could have a serious impact on operations. The threats to a DBMS include:

- *Aggregation:* The ability to combine nonsensitive data from separate sources to create sensitive information. For example, a user takes two or more unclassified pieces of data and combines them to form a classified piece of data that then becomes unauthorized for that user. Thus, the combined data sensitivity can be greater than the classification of individual parts. For years, mathematicians have been struggling unsuccessfully with the problem of determining when the aggregation of data results in data at a higher classification.

- *Bypass attacks:* Users attempt to bypass controls at the front end of the database application to access information. If the query engine contains security controls, the engine may have complete access to the information; thus, users may try to bypass the query engine and directly access and manipulate the data.

- *Compromising database views used for access control:* A view restricts the data a user can see or request from a database. One of the threats is that users may try to access restricted views or modify an existing view. Another problem with view-based access control is the difficulty in verifying how the software performs the view processing. Because all objects must have a security label identifying the sensitivity of the information in the database, the software used to classify the information must also have a mechanism to verify the sensitivity of the information. Combining this with a query language adds even more complexity. Also, the view just limits the data the user sees; it does not limit the operations that may be performed on the views. An additional problem is that the layered model frequently used in database interface design may provide multiple alternative routes to the same data, not all of which may be protected. A given user may be able to access information through the view provided, through a direct query to the database itself, or even via direct system access to the underlying data files. Further, any standard views set up for security controls must be carefully prepared in terms of the granularity of the control. Views can restrict access to information down to a field, and even content-based, level, and modifications to these regulations can significantly change the degree of material provided.

- *Concurrency:* When actions or processes run at the same time, they are said to be concurrent. Problems with concurrency include running processes that use old data, updates that are inconsistent, or having a deadlock occur.

- *Data contamination:* The corruption of data integrity by input data errors or erroneous processing. This can occur in a file, report, or a database.

- *Deadlocking:* Occurs when two users try to access the information at the same time and both are denied. In a database, deadlocking occurs when two user processes have locks on separate objects and each process is trying to acquire a lock on the object that the other process has. (Deadlock is also sometimes referred to as a deadly embrace.) When this happens, the database should end the deadlock by automatically choosing and aborting one process, allowing the other process to continue. The aborted transaction is rolled back and an error message is sent to the user of the aborted process. Generally, the transaction that requires the least amount of overhead to roll back is the transaction that is aborted. Deadlock can be viewed as a special issue of concurrency.

- *Denial of service:* Any type of attack or actions that could prevent authorized users from gaining access to the information. Often this can happen through a poorly designed application or query that locks up the table and requires intensive processing (such as a table scan where every row in the table must be examined to return the requested data to the calling application). This can be partially prevented by limiting the number of rows of data returned from any one query.

- *Improper modification of information:* Unauthorized or authorized users may intentionally or accidentally modify information incorrectly.

- *Inference:* The ability to deduce (infer) sensitive or restricted information from observing available information. Essentially, users may be able to determine unauthorized information from what information they can access and may never need to directly access unauthorized data. For example, if a user is reviewing authorized information about patients, such as the medications they have been prescribed, the user may be able to determine the illness. Inference is one of the hardest threats to control.

- *Interception of data:* If dial-up or some other type of remote access is allowed, the threat of interception of the session and modification of the data in transit must be controlled.

- *Query attacks:* Users try to use query tools to access data not normally allowed by the trusted front end (e.g., those views

4

controlled by the query application). Malformed queries using SQL or Unicode in such a way as to bypass security controls are also popular. There are many other instances where improper or incomplete checks on query or submission parameters can be used in a similar way to bypass access controls.

- ***Server access:*** The server where the database resides must be protected not only from unauthorized logical access, but also from unauthorized physical access to prevent the disabling of logical controls.

- ***Time of check/time of use (TOC/TOU):*** TOC/TOU can also occur in databases. An example is when some type of malicious code or privileged access could change data between the time that a user's query was approved and the time the data is displayed to the user.

- ***Web security:*** Many DBMSs allow access to data through Web technologies. Static Web pages (HTML or XML files) are methods of displaying data stored on a server. One method is when an application queries information from the database and the HTML page displays the data. Another is through dynamic Web pages that are stored on the Web server with a template for the query and HTML display code, but no actual data is stored. When the Web page is accessed, the query is dynamically created and executed and the information is displayed within the HTML display. If the source for the page is viewed, all information, including restricted data, may be visible. Providing security control includes measures for protecting against unauthorized access during a log-in process, protecting the information while it is transferred from the server to the Web server, and protecting the information from being stored on or downloaded to the user's machine.

- ***Unauthorized access:*** Allowing the release of information either intentionally or accidentally to unauthorized users.

DBMS Controls

The future of the database environment is becoming more technically complex. Organizations must find solutions to easily and quickly support their end users' requirements. This includes user-friendly interfaces to access data stored in different DBMSs, from many different locations, and on a variety of platforms. Additionally, users want to manipulate the data from their own workstation using their own software tools and then transmit updates to other locations in the network environment.

In addition, it is depressing to note that many of the most significant problems specific to the database environment, such as aggregation and inference attacks, have proven largely intractable to solutions.

Database security is a very specific and esoteric field of study. The challenge for both the security and database managers is to retain control over the organization's data and ensure business rules are consistently applied when core data is accessed or manipulated. The DBMS provides security controls in a variety of forms—both to prevent unauthorized access and to prevent authorized users from accessing data simultaneously or accidentally or intentionally overwriting information.

As a first line of security to prevent unauthorized users from accessing the system, the DBMS should use identification, authentication, authorization, and other forms of access controls. Most databases have some type of log-on and password authentication control that limits access to tables in the database based on a user account. Another initial step is to assign permissions to the authorized users, such as the ability to read, write, update, query, and delete data in the database.

Typically, there are fewer users with add or update privileges than users with read and query privileges. For example, in an organization's personnel database, general users would be allowed to change their own mailing address, office number, etc., but only personnel officers would be allowed to change an employee's job title or salary.

Lock Controls

The DBMS can control who is able to read and write data through the use of locks. Locks are used for read and write access to specific rows of data in relational systems, or objects in object-oriented systems.

In a multiuser system, if two or more people wish to modify a piece of data at the same time, a deadlock occurs. A deadlock is when two transactions try to access the same resource; however, the resource cannot handle two requests simultaneously without an integrity problem. The system will not release the resource to either transaction, thereby refusing to process both of the transactions. To prevent a deadlock so that no one can access the data, the access controls lock part of the data so that only one user can access the data. Lock controls can also be more granular, so that locking can be accomplished by table, row or record, or even field.

By using locks, only one user at a time can perform an action on the data. For example, in an airline reservation system, there may be two requests to book the last remaining seat on the airplane. If the DBMS allowed more than one user (or process) to write information to a row at the same time, then both transactions could occur simultaneously. To prevent this, the DBMS takes both transactions and gives one transaction a write lock on the account. Once the first transaction has finished, it releases its lock and then the other transaction, which has been held in a queue, can acquire the lock and make its action or, in this example, be denied the action.

These and related requirements are known as the ACID test, which stands for atomicity, consistency, isolation, and durability. These terms are defined below:

- **Atomicity** is when all the parts of a transaction's execution are either all committed or all rolled back—do it all or not at all. Essentially, all changes take effect, or none do. Atomicity ensures there is no erroneous data in the system or data that does not correspond to other data as it should.

- **Consistency** occurs when the database is transformed from one valid state to another valid state. A transaction is allowed only if it follows user-defined integrity constraints. Illegal transactions are not allowed, and if an integrity constraint cannot be satisfied, the transaction is rolled back to its previously valid state and the user is informed that the transaction has failed.

- **Isolation** is the process guaranteeing the results of a transaction are invisible to other transactions until the transaction is complete.

- **Durability** ensures the results of a completed transaction are permanent and can survive future system and media failures, that is, once they are done, they cannot be undone. Again, this is similar to transaction persistence.

For access control, the relational and object-oriented database models use either discretionary access control (DAC) or mandatory access control (MAC). Refer to the Access Control domain for more information about discretionary and mandatory access control.

Other DBMS Access Controls

Security for databases can be implemented either at the user level, by restricting the operations (views) available to a user or placing permissions on each individual data item, or in an object-oriented database, the object. Objects can be tables, views of tables, and the columns in those tables, or views. For example, in the SQL 92 standard, rights to objects can be individually assigned. However, not all databases provide this capability, as outlined in SQL 92. The types of actions available in SQL include select (allows the reading of data), insert (allows adding new data to a table), delete (allows removing data from a table), and update (allows changing data in a table). Thus, it is possible to grant a set of actions to a particular table for a specific object.

4

Software Development Security

665

View-Based Access Controls

In some DBMSs, security can be achieved through the appropriate use and manipulation of views. A trusted front end is built to control assignment of views to users. View-based access control allows the database to be logically divided into pieces that allow sensitive data to be hidden from unauthorized users. It is important that controls are in place so that a user cannot bypass the front end and directly access and manipulate the data. The database manager can set up a view for each type of user, and then each user can only access the view that is assigned to that user. Some database views allow the restriction of both rows and columns, while others allow for views that can write and update data as well as read (not just read-only).

Grant and Revoke Access Controls

Grant and revoke statements allow users who have "grant authority" permission to grant permission and revoke permission to other users. In a grant and revoke system, if a user is granted permission without the grant option, the user should not be able to pass grant authority to other users. This is, in a sense, a modification of discretionary access control. However, the security risk is that a user granted access, but not grant authority, could make a complete copy of the relation and subvert the system. Because the user, who is not the owner, created a copy, the user (now the owner of the copy) could provide grant authority over the copy to other users, leading to unauthorized users being able to access the same information contained in the original relation. Although the copy is not updated with the original relation, the user making the copy could continue making similar copies of the relation, and continue to provide the same data to other users. The revoke statement functions like the grant statement. One of the characteristics of the revoke statement is its cascading effect. When the rights previously granted to a user are subsequently revoked, all similar rights are revoked for all users who may have been granted access by the newly revoked user.

Security for Object-Oriented (OO) Databases

Most of the models for securing databases have been designed for relational databases. Because of the complexity of object-oriented databases, the security models for object-oriented databases are also more complex. Adding to this complexity, the views of the object-oriented model differ; therefore, each security model has to make some assumptions about the object-oriented model used for its particular database.

Metadata Controls

In addition to facilitating the effective retrieving of information, metadata can also manage restricted access to information. Metadata can serve as a gatekeeper function to filter access and thus provide security controls. One specialized form of metadata is the data dictionary, a central repository of information regarding the various databases that may be used within an enterprise. The data dictionary does not provide direct control of the databases, or access control functions, but does give the administrator a full picture of the various bodies of information around the company, potentially including the sensitivity and classification of material held in different objects. Therefore, the data dictionary can be used in risk management and direction of protective resources.

Data Contamination Controls

To ensure the integrity of data, there are two types of controls: input and output controls. Input controls consist of transaction counts, dollar counts, hash totals, error detection, error correction, resubmission, self-checking digits, control totals, and label processing. Output controls include the validation of transactions through reconciliation, physical-handling procedures, authorization controls, verification with expected results, and audit trails.

Online Transaction Processing (OLTP)

OLTP is designed to record all of the business transactions of an organization as they occur. It is a data processing system facilitating and managing transaction-oriented applications. These are characterized as a system used by many concurrent users who are actively adding and modifying data to effectively change real-time data. OLTP environments are frequently found in the finance, telecommunications, insurance, retail, transportation, and travel industries. For example, airline ticket agents enter data in the database in real-time by creating and modifying travel reservations, and these are increasingly joined by users directly making their own reservations and purchasing tickets through airline company Web sites as well as discount travel Web site portals. Therefore, millions of people may be accessing the same flight database every day, and dozens of people may be looking at a specific flight at the same time.

The security concerns for OLTP systems are concurrency and atomicity. Concurrency controls ensure that two users cannot simultaneously change the same data, or that one user cannot make changes before another user is finished with it. In an airline ticket system, it is critical for an agent processing a reservation to complete the transaction, especially if it is the last seat available on the plane. Atomicity ensures that all of the steps involved in the transaction complete successfully. If one step should fail, then the other steps should not be able to complete. Again, in an airline ticketing system, if the agent does not enter a name into the name data field correctly, the transaction should not be able to complete.

OLTP systems should act as a monitoring system and detect when individual processes abort, automatically restart an aborted process, back out of a transaction if necessary, allow distribution of multiple copies of application servers across machines, and perform dynamic load balancing.

A security feature uses transaction logs to record information on a transaction before it is processed, and then mark it as processed after it is done. If the system fails during the transaction, the transaction can be recovered by reviewing the transaction logs. Checkpoint restart is the process of using the transaction logs to restart the machine by running through the log to the last checkpoint or good transaction. All transactions following the last checkpoint are applied before allowing users to access the data again.

Knowledge Management

Knowledge management involves several existing research areas tied together by their common application environment, that is, the enterprise. Some topics listed under the knowledge management category are workflow management, business process modeling, document management, databases and information systems, knowledge-based systems, and several methodologies to model diverse aspects relevant to the knowledge in an enterprise environment. A key feature of knowledge management is application of artificial intelligence techniques to decision support.

A key term for knowledge management is *corporate memory* or *organizational memory*, because knowledge management systems frequently make use of data warehousing. The memory serves to store the accumulated enterprise knowledge that has to be managed. Corporate memory contains several kinds of information stored in databases, including employee knowledge, lists of customers, suppliers, and products, and specific documents relating to the organization. Essentially, it is all of the information, data, and knowledge about an organization that can be obtained from several different sources.

For data to be helpful, it must have meaning. The interpretation of the data into meaning requires knowledge. This knowledge is an integral aspect of interpreting the data. When an organization tries to understand the raw data from various sources, it can have a knowledgeable employee attempt to interpret the data into some meaning for the organization. To automate this process, knowledge-based systems (KBSs) are used along with problem-solving methods for inference. In the first case, the user knows or learns something, whereas in the KBS, the system contains the knowledge.

Knowledge discovery in databases (KDD) is a mathematical, statistical, and visualization method of identifying valid and useful patterns in data.

669

It is an evolving field of study to provide automated analysis solutions. The knowledge discovery process takes the data from data mining and accurately transforms it into useful and understandable information. This information is usually not retrievable through standard retrieval techniques, but is uncovered through the use of artificial intelligence (AI) techniques.

There are many approaches to KDD. A probabilistic method uses graphical representation models to compare different knowledge representations. The models are based on probabilities and data independencies. The probabilistic models are useful for applications involving uncertainty such as those used in planning and control systems. A statistical approach uses rule discovery and is based on data relationships. A learning algorithm can automatically select useful data relationship paths and attributes. These paths and attributes are then used to construct rules for discovering meaningful information. This approach is used to generalize patterns in the data and to construct rules from the noted patterns. An example of the statistical approach is OLAP. Classification groups data according to similarities. One example is a pattern discovery and data-cleaning model that reduces a large database to only a few specific records.

By eliminating redundant and non-important data, the discovery of patterns in the data is simplified. Deviation and trend analysis uses filtering techniques to detect patterns. An example is an intrusion detection system that filters a large volume of data so that only the pertinent data is analyzed.

Neural networks are specific AI methods used to develop classification, regression, association, and segmentation models based on the way neurons work in the human brain. A neural net method organizes data into nodes that are arranged in layers, and links between the nodes have specific weighting classifications. The neural net is helpful in detecting the associations among the input patterns or relationships. It is also considered a learning system because new information is automatically incorporated into the system. However, the value and relevance of the decisions made by the neural network are only as good as the experience it is given. The greater the experience, the better the decision. Note that neural nets have a specific problem in terms of an individual's ability to substantiate processing, in that the neural nets are subject to superstitious knowledge, which is a tendency to identify relations when no relations actually exist.

More sophisticated neural nets are less subject to this problem. The expert system uses a knowledge base (a collection of all the data, or knowledge, on a particular matter) and a set of algorithms or rules that infer new facts from knowledge and incoming data. The knowledge base could be the human experience that is available in an organization. Because the system reacts to a set of rules, if the rules are faulty, the response will also be faulty. Also, because human decision is removed from the point of action, if an error were to occur, the reaction time from a human would be longer. As always, a hybrid approach could combine more than one system, which provides a more powerful and useful system.

Security controls include:

- Protecting the knowledge base as you would any database.
- Routinely verifying the decisions based on what outcomes are expected from specific inputs.
- If using a rule-based approach, changes to the rules must go through a change control process.
- If the data output seems suspicious or out of the ordinary, perform additional and different .queries to verify the information.
- Making risk management decisions because decisions that are based on data warehouse analysis techniques may be incorrect.
- Developing a baseline of expected performance from the analytical tool.

Web Application Environment

Web pages are the most visible part of the enterprise, because they are designed to be seen from the outside. Therefore, they attract vandals, who delight in the manifest defacement of a public Web site. Even if the Web pages are not modified, it is possible that the invader can execute a Denial of Service (DoS) attack against the web site.

Because Web sites are also the primary interface for e-commerce, there is also the potential for fraud, or even outright theft. In some cases, this may simply be access to information or resources that should have a charge associated with their use, but some situations may allow attackers to order goods without payment, or even transfer funds. In some cases, transaction data is kept on the Web server, thus allowing the attacker direct access to information that may contain details about either the activities of the company or customer particulars, such as credit card numbers.

Because Web-based systems are tied to production and / or internal systems, for ease of maintenance, access to database information, or transaction processing, Web sites may also offer a vector for intrusion into the private networks themselves. If the Web server can be compromised, it offers the attacker a semi-trusted platform from which to mount probes or other activities. Again, such access may provide the interloper with intelligence about corporate sales and projects, but can also provide an avenue to the enterprise's proprietary intellectual property.

Most attacks are conducted at the application level, either against the Web server application itself, in-house scripts, or the common front-end applications that are used for e-commerce. The pace of change is quite rapid for this type of software, and quality checks do not always uncover vulnerabilities and security problems. Therefore, attacks on the application software are much more likely to succeed than attacks on the underlying platforms. (Once the application has been breached, an attack on the operating system is generally also possible.)

There are additional factors common to Web sites that make them vulnerable. For one thing, Web sites are designed to be widely accessible, and are usually heavily advertised as well. Therefore, a very large number of people will have information about the site's addresses. Web server software does make provisions for logging of traffic, but many administrators either turn off logging altogether or reduce the logging to minimal levels. The standard security tools of firewalls and intrusion detection systems can be applied, but are not particularly well suited to protecting such public sites. In the case of firewalls, a Web site must have a standard port or ports open for requests to be made. Intrusion detection systems (IDS) must be tuned and maintained to provide any useful information out of a flood of data: Web sites will see all kinds of traffic, from all kinds of sites, requesting connections, Web pages, submitting form information, or even updating search engine facts.

Web Application Threats and Protection

Specific protections that may be helpful include having a particular assurance sign-off process for Web servers, hardening the operating system used on such servers (removing default configurations and accounts, configuring permissions and privileges correctly, and keeping up to date with vendor patches), extending Web and network vulnerability scans prior to deployment, passively assessing IDS and advanced intrusion prevention system (IPS) technology, using application proxy firewalls, and disabling any unnecessary documentation and libraries.

In regard to administrative interfaces, ensure that they are removed or secured appropriately. Only allow access from authorized hosts or networks, and then use strong (possibly multifactor) user authentication. Do not hard code the authentication credentials into the application itself, and ensure the security of the credentials using certificates or similar high trust authenticators. Use account lockout and extended logging and audit, and protect all authentication traffic with encryption. Ensure that the interface is at least as secure as the rest of the application, and most often secure it at a higher level.

Because of the accessibility of Web systems and applications, input validation is critical. Application proxy firewalls are appropriate in this

673

regard, but ensure that the proxies are able to deal with problems of buffer overflows, authentication issues, scripting, submission of commands to the underlying platform (which includes issues related to database engines, such as SQL commands), encoding issues (such as Unicode), and URL encoding and translation. In particular, the proxy firewall may have to address issues of data submission to in-house and custom software, ensuring validation of input to those systems. (This level of protection will have to be custom programmed for the application.)

In regard to sessions, remember that HTTP (Hypertext Transfer Protocol) is a stateless technology, and, therefore, periods of apparent attachment to the server are controlled by other technologies, such as cookies or URL data, which must be both protected and validated. If using cookies, always encrypt them. You may wish to have time validation included in the session data. Do not use sequential, calculable, or predictable cookies, session numbers, or URL data for these purposes: use random and unique indicators.

Again, protection for Web applications is the same as for other programming. Use the same protections: validate all input and output, fail secure (closed), make your application or system as simple as possible, use secure network design, and use defense in depth. Specific points to consider in a Web system are not to cache secure pages, confirm that all encryption used meets industry standards, monitor your code vendors for security alerts, log any and all critical transactions and milestones, handle exceptions properly, do not trust any data from the client, and do not automatically trust data from other servers, partners, or other parts of the application.

Several organizations have developed frameworks for secure web development. One of the most common is the Open Web Application Security Project (OWASP)[14] OWASP has several guides available for web application development including:

---

14   https://www.owasp.org/

- Development Guide
- Code Review Guide
- Testing Guide
- Top Ten web application security vulnerabilities
- OWASP Mobile

Given the prevalence of web-based and cloud-based solutions, OWASP provides an accessible and thorough framework with processes for web application security. The information security professional should be familiar with the "top ten" web application vulnerabilities and also how to mitigate them.

Security of the Software Environment

Applications Development and Programming Concepts and Protection

The security of data and information is one of the most important elements of information system security. It is through software mechanisms that users process and access the data on the system. In addition, almost all technical controls are implemented in software, and the interfaces to all technical countermeasures are managed through software. The objective of information security is to make sure that the system and its resources are available when needed, that the integrity of the processing of the data and the data itself is ensured, and that the confidentiality of the data is protected. All of these purposes rely upon secure, consistent, reliable, and properly operating software.

Application development procedures are absolutely vital to the integrity of systems. If applications are not developed properly, data may be processed in such a way that the integrity of either the original data or the processed results is corrupted. In addition, the integrity of both application and operating system software itself must be maintained, in terms of both change control and attack from malicious software such as viruses. If special protection requirements (such as confidentiality) for the data controlled by a system are required, protective mechanisms and safeguards (like encryption) should be designed and built into the system and coded from the beginning, and not added on as an afterthought. Because operating system software is also responsible for many of the controls on access to data and systems, it is vital that these areas of programming be tightly protected.

Current Software Environment

Information systems are becoming more distributed, with a substantial increase in the use of open protocols, interfaces, and source code, as well as sharing of resources. Increased sharing requires that all resources be protected against unauthorized access. Many of these safeguards

676

are provided through software controls, especially operating system mechanisms. The operating system must offer controls that protect the computer's resources. In addition, the relationship between applications and the operating system is also important. Controls must be included in operating systems so that applications cannot damage or circumvent the operating system controls. A lack of software protection mechanisms can leave the operating system and critical computer resources open to corruption and attack.

Note also that information systems are becoming much more complex. Originally a given application might have been the only application running on a specific machine, aside from the hardwired functions resident in the central processing unit (CPU). Today an application may involve the hardware platform, CPU microcode, virtual machine server, operating system, network operating system and utilities, remote procedure calls, object request broker, engine servers (such as database and Web servers), engine application, multiple interface applications, interface utilities, API libraries, and multiple entities involved in a remote client interface. While many of these levels have been added in the name of interoperability and standardization, the complexity introduced does make assurance of security and compliance more difficult.

Some of the main security requirements for applications and databases are to ensure that only valid, authorized, and authenticated users can access the data; that permissions related to use of the data can be controlled and managed; that the system or software provides some type of granularity for controlling such permissions; that encryption or other appropriate logical controls are available for protecting sensitive information such as password storage; and that audit trails, sufficient to provide assurance of the functional security controls, can be implemented and reviewed.

It is becoming increasingly evident that many problems in access control, networking, and operations security are related to the development of software and systems. Whether caused by an improper system development, sloppy programming practices, or a lack of rigorous testing, it is clear that a number of vulnerabilities are present, and continue to be created, in the software that is in widespread use. Essentially, security in operating systems, applications, and databases focuses on the ability of the software to enforce controls over the storage and transfer of information in and between objects. Remember that the underlying foundation of the software security controls is the organization's security policy. The security policy reflects the security requirements of the organization. Therefore, if the security policy requires that only one set of users can access information, the software must have the capability to limit access to that specific group of users. Keep in mind that the ability to refer to a system as secure is based upon the reliable enforcement of the organization's security policy.

Open Source

The term *open source* has a number of competing definitions. However, most advocates would agree to the basic condition that the vendor releases the software source code so that users may modify the software either to suit their own situation or for further development. When the source is open, this also means that others can comment on or assist in debugging the code. Traditionally, vendors have relied on the secrecy of their proprietary code to protect the intellectual property of their product: hiding the source code and releasing only an executable version in machine or object code. There is a trend toward open-source codes in commercial software houses, and many successful business models support this activity, but most software companies still keep their source code secret, relying on proprietary code to prevent others from producing competing products.

Advocates of open-source software believe that security can be improved when the source code is available to the public. This is expressed in Linus's law [1]: With sufficiently many eyeballs looking at the code, all bugs will become apparent. Let other developers and programmers review the code

---

1   http://www.catb.org/~esr/writings/cathedral-bazaar/cathedral-bazaar/index.html

and help to find the security vulnerabilities. The idea is that this openness will lead to quick identification and repair of any issues, including those involved with security.

Other developers disagree. Will other programmers be able to find all of the security vulnerabilities? Just releasing the source code does not ensure that all security bugs will be found, and the automatic assumption of reliability can lead to a false sense of security. Devotees of proprietary systems note that dishonest programmers may find security vulnerabilities but not disclose the problem, or at least not until they have exploited it. There have been instances where those in the black hat community tried to blackmail software vendors when they found problems.

A final determination on this issue has not yet been made. However, in general, it is known that "security by obscurity" — the idea that if a system is little known, there is less likelihood that someone will find out how to break into it — does not work. Whether programs are available in source or only executable versions, it is known that observation, reverse engineering, disassembly, trial and error, and random chance may be able to find security vulnerabilities.

Full Disclosure

A related issue, frequently tied to the idea of the open-source model, is full disclosure. Full disclosure means that individuals who find security vulnerabilities will publicly disseminate the information, possibly including code fragments or programs that might exploit the problem. Many models of partial disclosure exist, such as first contacting the vendor of the software and asking that the vulnerability and a subsequent fix be released to the public, or the release only of information of the vulnerability and possible workaround solutions.

Rather than making policy regarding the purchase of open-source or proprietary software, for security purposes it may be better to look at how the software was designed. Was security included as an initial consideration when decisions were made about such issues as programming languages, features, programming style, and tests and evaluations?

The Software Environment

The situation in which software operates is fundamental to computer operations. This environment begins with the standard model of hardware resources, with items such as the central processing unit (CPU), memory, input/output (I/O) requests, and storage devices. The operating system is responsible for controlling these resources and providing security mechanisms to protect them, as well as providing resource access permissions and safeguards against misuse. The applications employed by the end users make requests or calls to the operating system, or sometimes directly to devices, to provide the required computer services. In some applications, security features are built into the software that allow the users more control over their information, such as access controls or auditing capabilities.

Vulnerabilities can be introduced in the application, such as when a buffer overflow attack takes advantage of improper parameter checking within the application. Note that because of layering in the software, protections imposed at one level may be bypassed by functions at another.

In addition, many applications now include some form of distributed computing. There are many varieties, levels, and forms of distribution you may encounter, ranging from simple cooperation of programs to standard interfacing, message passing (in object environments), layering (as noted above, in more extensive forms), middleware (particularly in database applications), clustering, or virtual machines. Distributed applications provide a particular challenge in terms of security due to the complexity of the information flow model.

Security Issues of Programming Languages

In the development phase, programmers have the option of writing code in several different programming languages. A programming language is a set of rules telling the computer what operations to perform. Programming languages have evolved in generations, and each language is characterized into one of the generations. Those in the lower level are closer in form to the binary language of the computer. Both machine and assembly languages are considered low-level languages. As the languages become easier and more similar to the language people use to communicate, they become higher level. High-level languages are easier to use than low-level languages and can be used to produce programs more quickly. In addition, high-level languages may be said to be beneficial because they enforce coding standards and can provide more security. On the other hand, higher level languages automate certain functions, and provide complicated operations for the program, implemented by the programming environment or tool, the internal details of which may be poorly understood by the programmer. Therefore, it is possible that high-level languages may introduce security vulnerabilities in ways that are not apparent to the developer.

Programming languages are frequently referred to by generations. The first generation is generally held to be the machine language, opcodes (operating codes), and object code used by the computer itself. These are very simple instructions that can be executed directly by the CPU of a computer. Each type of computer has its own machine language. However, the hexadecimal or binary code is difficult for people to understand, and so a second generation of assembly language was created, which uses symbols as abbreviations for major instructions. The third generation, usually known as high-level language, uses meaningful words (generally English) as the commands. COBOL, FORTRAN, BASIC, Java and C are examples of this type.

Above this point there may be disagreement on definitions. Fourth-generation languages, sometimes known as very high-level languages,

681

are represented by query languages, report generators, and application generators. Fifth-generation languages, or natural language interfaces, require expert systems and artificial intelligence. The intent is to eliminate the need for programmers to learn a specific vocabulary, grammar, or syntax. The text of a natural language statement very closely resembles human speech.

Process and Elements

Most of those working in the information systems security profession are not experienced programmers. Therefore, the following is a very quick and simplistic explanation of the concepts and processes of different types of programming. It is provided purely for background understanding for the other material in this domain.

Machine language does not consist of the type of commands seen in higher level languages. Higher level languages use words from normal human languages, and so, while a given program probably looks odd to the nonprogrammer, nevertheless, programmers see recognizable words such as *print, if, load, case,* and so forth, which give some indication of what might be going on in the program. This is not true of machine language.

Machine language is all just ones and zeroes. The patterns of ones and zeroes are directions to the computer. The directive patterns, called opcodes, are the actual commands that the computer uses. Opcodes are very short—in most desktop microcomputers generally only a single byte (8 bits) in length, or possibly two. Opcodes may also have a byte or two of data associated with them, but the entire string of command and argument is usually no more than 4 bytes, or 32 bits, altogether. This is the equivalent of a word of no more than four letters.

Almost all computers in use today are based on what is termed the von Neumann architecture (named after John von Neumann)[2]. One of

---

2   Please see the following for the 1946 paper, written with Arthur W. Burks and Hermann H. Goldstine, which was titled "Preliminary Discussion of the Logical Design of an Electronic Computing Instrument,", that was to become the basis for the development of the modern computer. https://www.fdi.ucm.es/profesor/mozos/EC/burks.pdf

the fundamental aspects of von Neumann architecture is that there is no inherent difference between data and programming in the memory of the computer. Therefore, one cannot tell whether the pattern 4Eh (00101110) is the letter *N* or a decrement opcode. Similarly, the pattern 72h (01110010) may be the letter *r* or the first byte of the "jump if below" opcode. Therefore, when viewing the contents of a program file, as seen in *Figure 4.1*, the viewer will be faced with an initially confusing agglomeration of random letters and symbols and incomprehensible garbage.

```
–d ds:100 11f
B8 19 06 BA CF 03 05 FA–0A 3B 06 02 00 72 1B B4
.........;...r..
09 BA 18 01 CD 21 CD 20–4E 6F 74 20 65 6E 6F 75 .....!. Not enou
–u ds:100 11f
0AEA:0100 B81906 MOV AX,0619
0AEA:0103 BACF03 MOV DX,03CF
0AEA:0106 05FA0A ADD AX,0AFA
0AEA:0109 3B060200 CMP AX,[0002]
0AEA:010D 721B JB 012A
0AEA:010F B409 MOV AH,09
0AEA:0111 BA1801 MOV DX,0118
0AEA:0114 CD21 INT 21
0AEA:0116 CD20 INT 20
0AEA:0118 4E DEC SI
0AEA:0119 6F DB 6F
0AEA:011A 7420 JZ 013C
0AEA:011C 65 DB 65
0AEA:011D 6E DB 6E
0AEA:011E 6F DB 6F
0AEA:011F 7567 JNZ 0188
```

Figure 4.1 - **Display of the same section of a program file, first as data and then as an assembly language listing**

Ultimately, understanding this chaotic blizzard of symbols is going to be of the greatest use to machine language programmers or software forensic specialists. Source code may be available, particularly in cases dealing with script, macro, or other interpreted programming. To explain some of those objects, the process of programming must be examined.

The Programming Procedure

In the beginning, programmers created object (machine or binary) files directly. (Some programmers have retained this skill. It is possible to enter data directly from the keyboard of a common desktop computer, using only printable characters, and create a usable program. However, this activity is now relegated to the level of a game and has little relation to modern, commercial software development.) The operating instructions (opcodes) for the computer and any necessary arguments or data were presented to the machine in the form that was needed to get it to process properly. Assembly language was produced to help with this process: Although there is a fairly direct correspondence between the assembly mnemonics and specific opcodes, at least the assembly files are formatted in a way that is relatively easy for humans to read, rather than being strings of hexadecimal or binary numbers. You will notice in the second part of Figure 4.1 a column of codes that might almost be words: MOV (move), CMP (compare), DEC (decrement), and ADD. Assembly language added these mnemonics because "MOV to register AX" makes more sense to a programmer than simply B8h or 10111000. An assembler program also takes care of details regarding addressing in memory so that every time a minor change is made to a program, all the memory references and locations do not have to be manually changed.

With the advent of high-level (or at least higher level) languages (the so-called third generation), programming language systems split into two types. High-level languages are those where the source code is somewhat more comprehensible to people. Those who work with C may dispute this assertion, of course: These languages, in the hands of skilled programmers, can produce highly functional programs from very little source code, but at the expense of legibility. The much maligned COBOL is possibly the best example. As you can see in *Figure 4.2*, the general structure of a COBOL program should be evident from the source code, even for those not trained in the language.

```
OPEN INPUT RESPONSE-FILE
    OUTPUT REPORT-FILE
    INITIALIZE SURVEY-RESPONSES
    PERFORM UNTIL NO-MORE-RECORDS
    READ RESPONSE-FILE
    AT END
    SET NO-MORE-RECORDS TO TRUE
    NOT AT END
    PERFORM 100-PROCESS-SURVEY
    END-READ
    END-PERFORM
    begin.
    display "My parents went to Vancouver and all they got"
    display "for me was this crummy COBOL program!".
```

Figure 4.2 - **Two sections of code from different COBOL programs. Note that the intention of the program is reasonably clear, as opposed to Figure 4.1.**

Compiled languages involve two separate processes before a program is ready for execution. The application must be programmed in the source (the text or human-readable) code, and then the source must be compiled into object code that the computer can understand: the strings of opcodes. Those who actually do programming will know that this is an overly simplified picture of a process that generally involves linkers and a number of other utilities, but the point is that the source code for languages like FORTRAN and Modula cannot be run directly; it must be compiled first.

685

```
<html>
<head>
<title>
Adding input
</title>
<!-- This script writes three lines on the page -->
<script>
document.write ("Hello, ");
document.write ("class.<br>This line ");
document.write ("is written by the JavaScript in the   header.");
document.write ("<br>but appears in the body of the   page,");
</script>
<body>
<!-- The following line is HTML, giving a line break and text -->
<br>This line is the first line that is written by HTML itself.<p>
Notice that this is the last line that appears until after the new
input is obtained.<p>
<!-- This script asks for input in a new window -->
<!-- Note that window, like document, is an object with methods -->
<script>
// Note that within scripts we use C++ style comments
// We declare a variable, studentName
var studentName;
// Then we get some input
studentName = window.prompt ("What is your name?", "student   name");
/* Although we can use C style
multi-line comments */
</script>
<!-- This script writes a single line of text -->
<script>
document.write ("Thank you for your input, " +   studentName);
</script>
</body>
</html>
```

Figure 4.3 - **A JavaScript applet that will work in all browsers. Note that this script uses much more internal commenting than is usually the case.**

Interpreted languages shorten the process. Once the source code for the program has been written, it can be run, with the help of the interpreter. The interpreter translates the source code into object code "on the fly," rendering it into a form that the computer can use. There is a cost in performance and speed for this convenience: compiled programs are native, or natural, for the CPU to use directly (with some mediation from the operating system) and so run considerably faster. In addition, compilers tend to perform some level of optimization on the programs, choosing the best set of functions for a given situation. However, interpreted languages have an additional advantage: because the language is translated on the machine where the program is run, a given interpreted program can be run on a variety of different computers, as long as an interpreter for that language is available. Scripting languages, used on a variety of platforms, are of this type.

JavaScript is a language most commonly used in Web pages. However, it is not Java and has no relation to Java. It was originally named LiveScript and was renamed as a marketing strategy. It is interpreted by the user's Web browser and allows control over most of the features of the Web browser. It has access to most of the contents of the Hypertext Markup Language (HTML) document and has full interaction with the displayed content. Depending upon the browser, it may have significant access to the system itself. As opposed to Java, which has sandbox restrictions for applets and an extensive security model, security management in JavaScript is minimal; it is either enabled or disabled.

JavaScript applets, such as the example in *Figure 4.3*, may be embedded in Web pages and then run in browsers that support the language regardless of the underlying computer architecture or operating system. (JavaScript is probably a bad example to use when talking about cross-platform operation, because a given JavaScript program may not even run on a new version of the same software company's browser, let alone one from another vendor or for another platform. But, it is supposed to work across platforms.) As with

687

most other technologies where two options are present, there are hybrid systems that attempt to provide the best of both worlds. Java, for example, compiles source code into a sort of pseudo-object code called bytecode. The bytecode is then processed by the interpreter (called the Java Virtual Machine, or JVM) for the CPU to run. Because the bytecode is already fairly close to object code, the interpretation process is much faster than for other interpreted languages. And because bytecode is still undergoing an interpretation, a given Java program will run on any machine that has a JVM. (Java does have a provision for direct compilation into object code, as do a number of implementations for interpreted languages such as BASIC.)

Java Security

Java provides examples of a number of other points related to the security of software and development. At the time the bytecode is interpreted, Java checks the use of variables and memory by the application. This check can be a good thing for security, or a bad thing. In general it is good, since programs use memory properly, and do not exceed set bounds. However, overreliance on such functions if developers do not use additional security checks in their code may result in sloppy practices that lead to other security problems.

For example, Java is usually held to be very good at garbage collection, the automatic review of memory locations, and the de-allocation of memory areas that are no longer required. This is good in that it ensures the program does not fill all available memory and then run into problems. However, the language has no way of determining the sensitivity of the information that might be stored in those memory locations. Therefore, it may be possible for sensitive information to be improperly disclosed. Languages that do not provide this garbage collection service require that the programmer make a conscious choice about memory allocation, and this choice may prompt the programmer to consider overwriting the memory location before returning it to the pool of available memory.

The Java programming language implements some specific security provisions. Some of these have been added to subsequent programming languages.

The three parts (sometimes referred to as layers) of the Java security approach are:

1. Verifier (or interpreter), which helps to ensure type safety. It is primarily responsible for memory and bounds checking.

2. Class loader, which loads and unloads classes dynamically from the Java runtime environment.

3. Security manager, which acts as a security gatekeeper protecting against rogue functionality.

The verifier is responsible for scrutinizing the bytecode (regardless of how it was created) before it can run on a local Java VM. Because many programs written in Java are intended to be downloaded from the network, the Java verifier acts as a buffer between the computer and the downloaded program. Because the computer is actually running the verifier, which is executing the downloaded program, the verifier can protect the computer from dangerous actions that can be caused by the downloaded program. The verifier is built into the Java VM and by design cannot be accessed by programmers or users.

The verifier can check bytecode at a number of different levels. The simplest check ensures that the format of a code fragment is correct. The verifier also applies a built-in theorem prover to each code fragment. The theorem prover can ensure that the bytecode does not have rogue code, such as the ability to forge pointers, violate access restrictions, or access objects using incorrect type information. If the verifier discovers rogue code within a class file, it executes an exception and the class file is not executed.

A criticism of the Java verifier is the length of time it takes to verify the bytecodes. Although the delay time is minimal, Web business owners thought that any delay, such as 10 to 20 seconds, would prevent customers from using their sites. This could be viewed as an example of a technology that is not quite ready for the argument (trade-off) between functionality and security. In most Java implementations, when the bytecode arrives at the Java VM, the class loader forms it into a class, which the verifier automatically examines. The class loader is responsible for loading the mobile code and determining when and how classes can be added to a running Java environment. For security purposes, the class loaders ensure that important parts of the Java runtime environment are not replaced by impostor code (known as class spoofing). Also for security purposes, class loaders typically divide classes into distinct namespaces according to origin. This is an important security element—to keep local classes distinct from external classes. However, a weakness was discovered in the class loader— in some instances, it was possible for the namespaces to overlap. This has subsequently been protected with an additional security class loader.

The third part of the model is the security manager, which is responsible for restricting the ways an applet uses visible interfaces (Java API calls). It is a single Java object that performs runtime checks on dangerous operations. Essentially, code in the Java library consults the security manager whenever a potentially dangerous operation is attempted. The security manager has veto authority and can generate a security exception. A standard browser security manager will disallow most operations when they are requested by untrusted code, and will allow trusted code to perform all of its operations. It is the responsibility of the security manager to make all final decisions as to whether a particular operation is permitted or rejected.

Java was originally designed for a distributed application environment, and so the security model implemented a sandbox that imposed strict controls on what distributed Java programs can and cannot do. An alternative to the sandbox approach of handling mobile code is to run only the code that is trusted. For example, ActiveX controls should be run only when you completely trust the entity that signed the control. Unfortunately, there have been problems with both the design and implementation of the ActiveX system. ActiveX has no sandbox restrictions on the activity of an ActiveX control: it can perform any action or function available to any executable program. There is no runtime check on the reliability or bounds restriction of the program.

In the Java sandbox model, the Web browser defines and implements a security policy for running downloaded Java code, such as an applet. A Java-enabled Web browser includes a Java verifier and runtime library along with classes (in Java, all objects belong to classes) to implement a security manager. The security manager controls the access to critical system resources and ensures that the Web browser's version of the security manager is implemented correctly. In the extreme, if a Java-enabled Web browser did not install a system security manager, an applet would have the same access as a local Java application. The sandbox is not the only example of the operation of the security manager. Any Java application or environment can implement, and tune, a specific security manager and particular restrictions, making additional controls possible for specialized environments or applications.

A weakness of the three-part model is that if any of the three parts fail to operate, the security model may be completely compromised. Since Java's introduction, several additional security features have been released, including the Java security package. This package is an API that includes both a cryptographic provider interface and APIs for common cryptographic algorithms. It provides the ability to implement cryptography and manage or modify default security protections for a specific application. This provides additional application security, but only if the developer chooses to implement it.

Other new Java releases focusing on security include:

- Java Certification Path API for building and validating certification paths and managing certificate revocation lists.

4

691

- Java GSS-API for securely exchanging messages between communication applications using Kerberos. Support for single sign-on using Kerberos is also included.

- Java Authentication and Authorization Service (JASS), which enables services to authenticate and enforce access controls upon users.

- **Java Cryptography Extension (JCE) provides a framework and implementation** for encryption, key generation, key agreement, and message authentication code (MAC) algorithms.

- Java Secure Socket Extension (JSSE) enables secure Internet connections. It implements a Java version of the Secure Sockets Layer (SSL) and Transport Layer Security (TLS) protocols and includes functionality for data encryption, server authentication, message integrity, and optional client authentication.

Object-Oriented Technology and Programming

Object-oriented programming (OOP) is considered by some to be a revolutionary concept that changed the rules in computer program development. It is organized around objects rather than linear procedures. OOP is a programming method that makes a self-sufficient object. The object is a block of preassembled programming code in a self-contained module, although it operates differently, and more independently, than a function or procedure in a procedural language. The module encapsulates both data and the processing instructions that may be called to process the data. Once a block of programming code is written, it can be reused in any number of programs. Examples of object-oriented languages are Eiffel, Smalltalk (one of the first), Ruby, Java (one of the most popular today), C++ (also one of the most popular today), Python, Perl, and Visual Basic. A number of recent object-oriented languages are, themselves, built on top of other, previous object-oriented languages, and may extend them in specialized ways.

When defining an object-oriented language, the following are some of the key characteristics:

Encapsulation (Also Known as Data Hiding)

A class defines only the data it needs to be concerned with. When an instance of that class (i.e., an object) is run, the code will not be able to accidentally access other data, which is generally seen as positive in terms of security.

Inheritance

The concept of a data class makes it possible to define subclasses of data objects that share some or all of the main (or super) class characteristics. If security is properly implemented in the high-level class, then subclasses should inherit that security. The same is true of objects derived not from a class, but from another object.

Polymorphism

Objects may be processed differently depending on their data type. Instantiating an object from a prior object ensures that the new object inherits attributes and methods from the original. Changing attributes and aspects of an object created in such a way may change the operation of the modified object. Unfortunately, this has implications for security that must be carefully assessed, since secure methods may be lost through polymorphism.

Polyinstantiation

Specific objects, instantiated from a higher class, may vary their behavior depending upon the data they contain. Therefore, it may be difficult to verify that inherited security properties are valid for all objects. However, polyinstantiation can also be used to prevent inference attacks against databases, because it allows different versions of the same information to exist at different classification levels.

Within an OOP environment, all predefined types are objects. A data type in a programming language is a set of data with values having predefined characteristics, such as integer, character, string, and pointer. In most programming languages, a limited number of such data types are built

4

Software Development Security

693

into the language. The programming language usually specifies the range of values for a given data type, how the values are processed by the computer, and how they are stored. In OOP, all user-defined types are also objects.

The first step in OOP is to identify all the objects you want to manipulate and how they relate to each other; this is often known as data modeling. Once the object is identified, it is generalized as a class of objects and defined as the kind of data it contains and as any logic sequences that can manipulate it. Each distinct logic sequence is known as a method. A real instance of a class is called an object or an instance of a class, and this is what is run in the computer. The object's methods provide computer instructions, and the class object characteristics provide relevant data. Communication with objects, and objects communication with each other, is established through interfaces called messages.

When building traditional programs, the programmers must write every line of code from the beginning. With OOP, programmers can use the predetermined blocks of code (objects). Consequently, an object can be used repeatedly in different applications and by different programmers. This reuse reduces development time and thus reduces programming costs.

Object-Oriented Security

In object-oriented systems, objects are encapsulated. Encapsulation protects the object by denying direct access to view or interact with what is located inside the object—it is not possible to see what is contained in the object because it is encapsulated. Encapsulation of the object does provide protection of private data from outside access. For security purposes, no object should be able to access another object's internal data. On the other hand, it could be difficult for system administrators to apply the proper policies to an object if they cannot identify what the object contains.

Polyinstantiation allows for iteratively producing a more defined version of an object by replacing variables with values (or other variables). Thus, multiple distant differences between data within objects are done to discourage low-level objects from gaining information at a high level of security. It is also the technique used to avoid covert channels based on inference by causing the same information to exist at different classification levels. Therefore, users at a lower classification level do not know of the existence of a higher classification level.

In object-oriented programming, polymorphism refers to a programming language's ability to process objects differently depending on their data type. The term is sometimes used to describe a variable that may refer to objects whose class is not known at compile time, but will respond at runtime according to the actual class of the object to which they refer. Even though polymorphism seems straightforward, if used incorrectly, it can lead to security problems. The problems stem from the data driving the object and a malicious user taking advantage of the feature.

One of the basic activities of an object-oriented design is establishing relationships between classes. One fundamental way to relate classes is through inheritance. This is when a class of objects is defined; any subclass that is defined can inherit the definitions of the general (or super) class. Inheritance allows a programmer to build a new class similar to an existing class without duplicating all the code. The new class inherits the old class's definitions and adds to them. Essentially, for the programmer, an object in a subclass need not have its own definitions of data and methods that are generic to the class it is a part of. This can help decrease program development time—what works for the superclass will also work for the subclass.

Multiple inheritances can introduce complexity and may result in security breaches for object accesses. Issues such as name clashes and ambiguities must be resolved by the programming language to avoid a subclass inheriting inappropriate privileges from a superclass.

4

Software Development Security

695

Distributed Object-Oriented Systems

As the age of mainframe-based applications began to wane, the new era of distributed computing emerged. Distributed development architectures allow applications to be divided into pieces that are called components, and each component can exist in different locations. This development paradigm allows programs to download code from remote machines onto a user's local host in a manner that is seamless to the user.

Applications today are constructed with software systems that are based on distributed objects, such as the Common Object Request Broker Architecture (CORBA), Java Remote Method Invocation (JRMI), Enterprise JavaBean (EJB), and Distributed Component Object Model (DCOM, restricted to Microsoft Windows). A distributed object-oriented system allows parts of the system to be located on separate computers within an enterprise network. The object system itself is a compilation of reusable self-contained objects of code designed to perform specific business functions.

How objects communicate with one another is complex, especially because objects may not reside on the same machine, but may be located across machines on the network. To standardize this process, the Object Management Group (OMG) created a standard for finding objects, initiating objects, and sending requests to the objects. The standard is the Object Request Broker (ORB), which is part of the Common Object Request Broker Architecture (CORBA).

Common Object Request Broker Architecture (CORBA)

CORBA is a set of standards that address the need for interoperability between hardware and software products. CORBA allows applications to communicate with one another regardless of where they are stored. The ORB is the middleware that establishes a client–server relationship between objects. Using an ORB, a client can transparently locate and activate a method on a server object either on the same machine or across a network.

The ORB operates regardless of the processor type or programming language.

Not only does the ORB handle all the requests on the system, but it also enforces the system's security policy. The policy describes what the users (and the system) are allowed to do and also what user (or system) actions will be restricted. The security provided by the ORB should be transparent to the user's applications. The CORBA security service supports four types of policies: access control, data protection, non-repudiation, and auditing.

The client application (through an object) sends a request (message) to the target object.

1. The message is sent through the ORB security system. Inside the ORB security system is the policy enforcement code, which contains the organization's policy regarding objects.

2. If the policy allows the requester to access the targeted object, the request is then forwarded to the target object for processing.

When reviewing CORBA implementations, consider the following:

- The specific CORBA security features that are supported
- The implementation of CORBA security building blocks, such as cryptography blocks or support for Kerberos systems
- The ease by which system administrators can use the CORBA interfaces to set up the organization's security policies
- Types of access control mechanisms that are supported
- Types, granularity, and tools for capturing and reviewing audit logs
- Any technical evaluations (i.e., Common Criteria)

CORBA is not the only method for securing distributed application environments. Java's Remote Method Invocation (JRMI) and Enterprise JavaBean (EJB) are similar.

4

Software Development Security

697

EJB is a Sun Microsystems model providing an API specification for building scalable, distributed, multitier, component-based applications. EJB uses Java's RMI implementations for communications. The EJB server provides a standard set of services for transactions, security, and resource sharing. One of the security advantages is the EJB allows the person assembling the components to control access. Instead of a component developer hard coding the security policies, the end user (i.e., system administrator or security officer) can specify the policy. Other security features are also available to the end user. A vulnerability of EJB is the noted weakness of the RMI. For example, the RMI is typically configured to allow clients to download code automatically from the server when it is not present. Thus, before the client can make a secure connection, it can still download code or a malicious attacker could masquerade as the client to the server and download code. Although improvements have been made to increase the security of RMI, all implementations must be reviewed for security features.

Security Issues in Source Code

There are many threats to software during design, development, and operation. Most of these fall into standard patterns, the most common ones are mentioned here. Note that the threats are not mutually exclusive, and that many overlap to a greater or lesser extent. A given threat may belong to more than one category, and it is important to identify all relevant characteristics. This is particularly important in regard to malware.

Buffer Overflow

The buffer overflow problem is one of the oldest and most common problems in software development and programming, dating back to the introduction of interactive computing. It can result when a program fills up the assigned buffer of memory with more data than its buffer can hold. When the program begins to write beyond the end of the buffer, the program's execution path can be changed, or data can be written into areas used by the operating system itself. This can lead to the insertion of malicious code that can be used to gain administrative privileges on the program or system.

Buffer overflows can be created or exploited in a wide variety of ways, but the following is a general example of how a buffer overflow works. A program that is the target of an attack is provided with more data than the application was intended to handle. This can be done by diverse means such as entering too much text into a dialog box, submitting a Web address that is far too long, or creating a network packet much larger than is necessary. The attacked program (target) overruns the memory allocated for input data and writes the excess data into the system memory. The excess data can contain machine language instructions so that when the next step is executed, the attack code, like a Trojan horse or other type of malicious code, is run. (Frequently, the early part of the excess data contains characters that are read by the CPU as "perform no operation," forming a "no-op sled." The malicious code is usually at the end of the excess data.)

An actual attack method is far more detailed and is highly dependent on the target operating system and hardware architecture. The desired result is to put the attack instructions into memory. These instructions usually do something such as patch the kernel in such a way as to execute another program at an elevated privilege level. Sometimes the malicious code will call other programs, or even download them over the network.

Citizen Programmers

Because desktop and personal computers (and even applications, now) come equipped with scripting and programming tools, allowing all computer users to create their own utilities is a common practice that can have extremely harmful consequences and may violate the principle of separation of duties. If this type of unsupervised programming is allowed, then a single user may have complete control over an application or process. While programmers traditionally have little or no training in security requirements, they will at least have basic understandings of issues of software quality, reliability, and interoperability. Casual users have no such training, and may create applications with both security and reliability problems. Visual Basic, included in the Microsoft Office suite, is often used by citizen programmers to develop their applications or extend existing ones. Citizen, or casual, programmers are unlikely to be trained in, or bound by, system development practices that involve proper application design, change control, and support for the application. Therefore, application development in such a manner is likely to be chaotic and lack any form of assurance in regard to security. It should be addressed as a matter of policy, enforcement, awareness and sanctions when needed.

Covert Channel

A covert channel or confinement problem is an information flow issue. It is a communication channel that allows two cooperating processes to transfer information in such a way that it violates the system's security policy. Even though there are protection mechanisms in place, if unauthorized information can be transferred using a signaling mechanism via entities or objects not normally considered to be able to communicate, then a covert channel may exist. In simplified terms, it is any flow of information, intentional or inadvertent, that enables an observer not authorized to have the information, to infer what it is or that it exists. This is primarily a concern in systems containing highly sensitive information.

There are two commonly defined types of covert channels: storage and timing. A covert storage channel involves the direct or indirect reading of a storage location by one process and a direct or indirect reading of the same storage location by another process. Typically, a covert storage channel involves a finite resource, such as a memory location or sector on a disk that is shared by two subjects at different security levels.

A covert timing channel depends upon being able to influence the rate that some other process is able to acquire resources, such as the CPU, memory, or I/O devices. The variation in rate may be used to pass signals. Essentially, the process signals information to another by modulating its own use of system resources in such a way that this manipulation affects the real response time observed by the second process. Timing channels are normally considerably less efficient than storage channels, because they have a reduced bandwidth, but they are usually harder to detect and control.

These examples relate only to a situation in which an insider is attempting to provide information to an outsider and is very restricted in application. In order to have a complete view of covert channels, one should envisage a broader concept that includes, for example, unintentional covert channels that enable an uncleared or unauthorized person to observe a system activity that enables the inference of facts of which that person should not be aware.

Malicious Software (Malware)

Malware comes in many varieties and is written for different operating systems and applications, as well as for different machines. Malware also

4

Software Development Security

uses a variety of attacks when attempting to compromise a system or exhilarate information.

Malformed Input Attacks

A number of attacks employing input from the user are currently known, and various systems detect and protect against such attacks. Therefore, a number of new attacks rely on configuring that input in unusual ways. For example, an attack that redirected a Web browser to an alternate site might be caught by a firewall through the detection of the Uniform Resource Locator (URL) of an inappropriate site. If, however, the URL was expressed in a Unicode format, rather than ASCII, the firewall would likely fail to recognize the content, whereas the Web browser would convert the information without difficulty. In another case, many Web sites allow query access to databases, but place filters on the requests to control access. When requests using the Structure Query Language (SQL) are allowed, the use of certain syntactical structures in the query can fool the filters into seeing the query as a comment, whereupon the query may be submitted to the database engine and retrieve more information than the owners intended. In another instance, a site that allows users to input information for later retrieval by other users, such as a blog, may fail to detect when such input comes in the form of active scripting. This is the basis of cross-site scripting attacks. (Buffer overflows are also a form of malformed input.)

Memory Reuse (Object Reuse)

Memory management involves sections of memory allocated to one process for a while, then deallocated, then reallocated to another process. Because residual information may remain when a section of memory is reassigned to a new process after a previous process is finished with it, a security violation may occur. When memory is reallocated, the operating system should ensure that memory is zeroed out completely or overwritten completely before it can be accessed by a new process. Thus, there is no residual information in memory carrying over from one process to another. While memory locations are of primary concern in this regard, developers should also be careful with the reuse of other resources that can contain information, such as disk space. The paging or swap file on the disk is frequently left unprotected and may contain an enormous amount of sensitive information if care is not taken to prevent this occurrence. (Note that memory or object reuse may be a form of covert channel, as discussed earlier.)

Executable Content/Mobile Code

Executable content, or mobile code, is software that is transmitted across a network from a remote source to a local system and is then executed on that local system. The code is transferred by user actions and, in some cases, without the explicit action of the user. The code can arrive to the local system as attachments to e-mail messages or through Web pages.

Mobile code has been called by many names: mobile agents, mobile code, downloadable code, executable content, active capsules, remote code, etc. Even though the terms seem the same, there are slight differences. For example, mobile agents are programs that can migrate from host to host in a network, at times and to places of their own choosing. They have a high degree of autonomy, rather than being directly controlled from a central point. Mobile agents differ from applets, which are programs downloaded as the result of a user action, then executed from beginning to end on one host. Examples include ActiveX controls, Java applets, and scripts run within the browser. All of these deal with the local execution of remotely sourced code.

One way of looking at mobile code is in terms of current security architectures. Typically, security in the operating system could answer the question "Can subject X use object Y?" The challenge with mobile code is how to resolve when one subject may be acting on behalf of another, or may be acting on its own behalf. Thus, security mechanisms must be put into place that resolve whether these requests should be allowed or denied. Many of the issues of mobile code are tightly connected to problems of malware.

703

Social Engineering

One method of compromising a system is to befriend users to gain information; especially vulnerable are individuals with system administrator access. Social engineering is the art of getting people to divulge sensitive information to others either in a friendly manner, as an attempt to be "helpful," or through intimidation. It is sometimes referred to as people hacking because it relies on vulnerabilities in people rather than those found in software or hardware. While social engineering has many proper uses in management and training, in regard to information security social engineering is really only a fancy name for lying.

Social engineering comes in many forms, but they are all based on the principle of representing oneself as someone who needs or deserves the information to gain access to the system. For example, one method is for attackers to pretend they are new to the system and need assistance with gaining access. Another method is when attackers pretend to be a system staff member and try to gain information by helping to fix a computer problem, even though there is not a problem. Typically, therefore, social engineering is not considered to be a concern of software development and management. However, there are two major areas where social engineering should be considered in system development and management.

The first is in regard to the user interface and human factors engineering. It has frequently, and sadly, been the case where users have misunderstood the intent of the programmer with regard to the operation of certain commands or buttons, and sometimes the misunderstanding has had fatal results. (In one famous case, a correction to dosage levels on the input screen of a medical radiation treatment machine did not change the radiation-level settings, and dozens of patients suffered fatal overdoses before the problem was found and rectified.) The second issue of social engineering is in regard to its use in malicious software. Most malware will have some kind of fraudulent component, in an attempt to get the user to run the program, so that the malicious payload can perform undetected.

Time of Check/Time of Use (TOC/TOU)

This is a common type of attack that occurs when some control changes between the time the system security functions check the contents of variables and the time the variables actually are used during operations. (A broader term for similar types of situations is a race condition, where multiple, independent processes are proceeding, but the ultimate results will be determined by which process completes first. In this state of affairs the program may behave inconsistently, with arbitrary and erroneous results.) For instance, a user logs on to a system in the morning and later is fired. As a result of the termination, the security administrator removes the user from the user database. Because the user did not log off, he still has access to the system and might try to get even.

In another situation, a connection between two machines may drop. If an attacker manages to attach to one of the ports used for this link before the failure is detected, the invader can hijack the session by pretending to be the trusted machine. (A way to prevent this is to have some form of authentication performed constantly on the line.)

Between-the-Lines Attack

Another similar attack is a between-the-lines entry. This occurs when the telecommunication lines used by an authorized user are tapped into and data falsely inserted. To avoid this, the telecommunication lines should be physically secured and users should not leave telecommunication lines open when they are not being used.

Trapdoor/Backdoor

A trapdoor or backdoor is a hidden mechanism that bypasses access control measures. It is an entry point into a program that is inserted in software by programmers during the program's development to provide a method of gaining access into the program for modification if the access control mechanism malfunctions and locks them out. (In this situation, it may also be called a maintenance hook.) They can be useful for error correction,

4

Software Development Security

705

but they are dangerous opportunities for unauthorized access if left in a production system. A programmer or someone who knows about the backdoor can exploit the trapdoor as a covert means of access after the program has been implemented in the system. An unauthorized user may also discover the entry point while trying to penetrate the system.

This list of software threats is to be used as a reminder of the types of threats that developers and managers of software development should be aware. It is not intended to be an inclusive list, as there are new threats developed every day.

Malicious Software (Malware)

Malware is a relatively new term in the security field. It was created to address the need to discuss software or programs that are intentionally designed to include functions for penetrating a system, breaking security policies, or carrying malicious or damaging payloads. Because this type of software has started to develop a bewildering variety of forms—such as backdoors, data diddlers, DDoS, hoax warnings, logic bombs, pranks, RATs, Trojans, viruses, worms, zombies, etc.—the term *malware* has come to be used for the collective class of malicious software. However, the term is often used very loosely simply as a synonym for virus, in the same way that virus is often used simply as a description of any type of computer problem.

Viruses are the largest class of malware, in terms of both numbers of known entities and impact in the current computing environment. Viruses will therefore be given primary emphasis in this discussion, but will not be the only malware type examined.

Programming bugs or errors are generally not included in the definition of malware, although it is sometimes difficult to make a hard and fast distinction between malware and bugs. For example, if a programmer left a buffer overflow in a system and it creates a loophole that can be used as a backdoor or a maintenance hook, did he do it deliberately? This question cannot be answered technically given the relative ease of use of a given vulnerability.

In addition, it should be noted that malware is not just a collection of utilities for the attacker. Once launched, malware can continue an attack without reference to the author or user, and in some cases will expand the attack to other systems. There is a qualitative difference between malware and the attack tools, kits, or scripts that have to operate under an attacker's control, and which are not considered to fall within the definition of malware. There are gray areas here as well, because RATs and DDoS zombies provide unattended access to systems, but need to be commanded to deliver a payload.

Malware can attack and destroy system integrity in a number of ways. Viruses are often defined in terms of their ability to attach to programs (or to objects considered to be programmable) and so must, in some way, compromise the integrity of applications. Many viruses or other forms of malware contain payloads (such as data diddlers) that may either erase data files or interfere with application data over time in such a way that data integrity is compromised and data may become completely useless.

In considering malware, there is an additional type of attack on integrity. As with attacks where the intruder takes control of your system and uses it to explore or assail further systems, to hide his own identity, malware (viruses and DDoS zombies in particular) are designed to use your system as a platform to continue further assaults, even without the intervention of the original author or attacker. This can create problems within domains and intranets where equivalent systems "trust" each other, and can also create "badwill" when organizations doing business with each other find out one is sending viruses to the other.

As noted, malware can compromise programs and data to the point where they are no longer available. In addition, malware generally uses the resources of the system it has attacked and can, in extreme cases,

4

exhaust CPU cycles, available processes (process numbers, tables, etc.), memory, communications links and bandwidth, open ports, disk space, mail queues, and so forth. Sometimes this can be a direct DoS attack, and sometimes it is a side effect of the activity of the malware. Malware such as backdoors and RATs are intended to make intrusion and penetration easier. Viruses such as Klez and SirCam send data files from your system to others (in these particular cases, seemingly as a side effect of the process of reproduction and spread). Malware can be written to do directed searches and send confidential data to specific parties, and can also be used to open covert channels of other types.

The fact that you are infected with viruses, or compromised by other types of malware, can become quite evident to others. This compromises confidentiality by providing indirect evidence of your level of security, and may also create public relations problems. It has long been known that the number of variants of viruses or other forms of malware is directly connected to the number of instances of a given platform. The success of a given piece of malware is also related to the relative proportion of a given platform in the overall computing environment.

The modern computing environment is one of consistency. The Intel platform has achieved dominance in hardware, and Microsoft has a near monopoly on the desktop. In addition, compatible application software (and the addition of functional programming capabilities in those applications) can mean that malware from one hardware and operating system environment can work perfectly well in another. The functionality added to application macro and script languages has given them the capability to either directly address computer hardware and resources or easily call upon utilities or processes that have such access. This means that objects previously considered to be data, and therefore immune to malicious programming, must now be checked for malicious functions or payloads.

In addition, these languages are very simple to learn and use, and the various instances of malware carry their own source codes, in plaintext and sometimes commented, making it simple for individuals wanting to learn how to craft an attack to gather templates and examples of how to do so, without even knowing how the technology actually works. This expands the range of authors of such software enormously.

Malware Types

Viruses are not the only form of malicious software. Other forms include worms, Trojans, zombies, logic bombs, and hoaxes. Each of these has its own characteristics. Some forms of malware combine characteristics of more than one class, and it can be difficult to draw hard and fast distinctions with regard to individual examples or entities, but it can be important to keep the specific attributes in mind. Viruses and Trojans are being used to spread and plant RATs, and RATs are being used to install zombies. In some cases, hoax virus warnings are being used to spread viruses. Virus and Trojan payloads may contain logic bombs and data diddlers.

Viruses

A computer virus is a program written with functions and intent to copy and disperse itself without the knowledge and cooperation of the owner or user of the computer. A final definition has not yet been agreed upon by all researchers. A common definition is "a program that modifies other programs to contain a possibly altered version of itself." This definition is generally attributed to Fred Cohen from his seminal research in the mid-1980s, although Dr. Cohen's actual definition is in mathematical form. The term *computer virus* was first defined by Dr. Cohen in his graduate thesis in 1984. [3] Cohen credits a suggestion from his advisor, Leonard Adleman (of RSA fame), for the use of the term.

Cohen's definition is specific to programs that attach themselves to other programs as their vector of infection. However, common usage now holds

---

3   http://all.net/books/Dissertation.pdf

viruses to consist of a set of coded instructions that are designed to attach to an object capable of containing the material, without knowledgeable user intervention. This object may be an e-mail message, program file, document, floppy disk, CD-ROM, short message system (SMS) message on cellular telephones, or any similar information medium.

A virus is defined by its ability to reproduce and spread.

A worm, which is sometimes seen as a specialized type of virus, is currently distinguished from a virus because a virus generally requires an action on the part of the user to trigger or aid reproduction and spread, while a worm spreads on its own. The action on the part of the user is generally a common function, and the user generally does not realize the danger of the action, or the fact that he or she is assisting the virus. The only requirement that defines a program as a virus is that it reproduces. There is no necessity that the virus carries a payload, although a number of viruses do. In many cases (in most cases of successful viruses), the payload is limited to some kind of message.

A deliberately damaging payload, such as erasure of the disk or system files, usually restricts the ability of the virus to spread, because the virus uses the resources of the host system. In some cases, a virus may carry a logic bomb or time bomb that triggers a damaging payload on a certain date or under a specific, often delayed, condition.

Types of Viruses

There are a number of functionally different types of viruses, such as a file infector, boot sector infector (BSI), system infector, e-mail virus, multipartite, macro virus, and script virus. These terms do not necessarily indicate a strict division. A file infector may also be a system infector. A script virus that infects other script files may be considered a file infector, although this type of activity, while theoretically possible, is unusual in practice. There are also difficulties in drawing a hard distinction between macro and script viruses.

■ *File Infectors*—A file infector infects program (object) files. System infectors that infect operating system program files (such as COMMAND.COM in DOS) are also file infectors. File infectors can attach to the front of the object file (prependers), attach to the back of the file and create a jump at the front of the file to the virus code (appenders), or overwrite the file or portions of it (overwriters). A classic example of this type of behavior is the file infector Jerusalem. A bug in early versions caused it to add itself over and over again to files, making the increase in file length detectable. (This has given rise to the persistent myth that it is characteristic of a virus to eventually fill up all disk space: by far, the majority of file infectors add minimally to file lengths.)

■ *Boot Sector Infectors*—Boot sector infectors (BSIs) attach to or replace the master boot record, system boot record, or other boot records and blocks on physical disks. (The structure of these blocks varies, but the first physical sector on a disk generally has some special significance in most operating systems, and usually is read and executed at some point in the boot process.) BSIs usually copy the existing boot sector to another unused sector, and then copy themselves into the physical first sector, ending with a call to the original programming. Examples are Brain, Stoned, and Michelangelo.

■ *System Infectors*—System infector is a somewhat vague term. The phrase is often used to indicate viruses that infect operating system files, or boot sectors, in such a way that the virus is called at boot time and has or may have preemptive control over some functions of the operating system. (The Lehigh virus infected only COMMAND.COM on MS-DOS machines: recent viruses in the Windows environment sometimes preferentially infect utility files in the system directory.) In other usage, a system infector modifies other system structures, such as the linking pointers in directory tables or the MS Windows system registry, in order to be called first when programs are invoked on the host computer.

4

Software Development Security

711

An example of directory table linking is the DIR virus family. Many e-mail viruses target the registry: MTX and Magistr can be very difficult to eradicate.

- ***Companion Virus***—Some viral programs do not physically touch the target file at all. One method is quite simple, and may take advantage of precedence in the system. In MS-DOS, for example, when a command is given, the system checks first for internal commands, then .COM, .EXE, and .BAT files, in that order, .EXE files can be infected by writing a .COM file in the same directory with the same filename. This type of virus is most commonly known as a companion virus, although the term spawning virus is also used.

- ***E-Mail Virus***—An e-mail virus specifically, rather than accidentally, uses the e-mail system to spread. Although virus-infected files may be accidentally sent as e-mail attachments, e-mail viruses are aware of e-mail system functions. They generally target a specific type of e-mail system, harvest e-mail addresses from various sources, and may append copies of themselves to all e-mail sent, or may generate e-mail messages containing copies of themselves as attachments. Some e-mail viruses may monitor all network traffic and follow up legitimate messages with messages that they generate. Most e-mail viruses are technically considered to be worms, because they often do not infect other program files on the target computer, but this is not a hard and fast distinction. There are known examples of e-mail viruses that are file infectors, macro viruses, script viruses, and worms. Melissa, Loveletter, Hybris, and SirCam are all widespread current examples, and the CHRISTMA exec is an older example of the same type of activity.

- E-mail viruses have made something of a change to the epidemiology of viruses. Traditionally, viruses took many months to spread, but stayed around for many years in the computing environment. Many e-mail viruses have become "fast burners" that can spread around the world, infecting hundreds of thousands or even millions of machines within hours. However, once characteristic indicators of these viruses become known, they die off almost immediately as users stop running the attachments.

- *Multipartite*—Originally the term multipartite was used to indicate a virus that was able to infect both boot sectors and program files. (This ability is the origin of the alternate term dual infector.) Current usage tends to mean a virus that can infect more than one type of object, or that infects or reproduces in more than one way. Examples of traditional multipartites are Telefonica, One Half, and Junkie, but these programs have not been very successful. In contrast, Nimda was quite successful, spreading as a classic worm, a file infector, using network shares and other means.

- *Macro Virus*—A macro virus uses macro programming of an application such as a word processor. (Most known macro viruses use Visual Basic for Applications in Microsoft Word: some are able to cross between applications and function in, for example, a PowerPoint presentation and a Word document, but this ability is rare.) Macro viruses infect data files and tend to remain resident in the application itself by infecting a configuration template such as MS Word's NORMAL. DOT. Although macro viruses infect data files, they are not generally considered file infectors: a distinction is made between program and data files. Macro viruses can operate across hardware or operating system platforms as long as the required application platform is present. (For example, many MS Word macro viruses can operate on both the Windows and Macintosh versions of MS Word.) Examples are Concept and CAP. Melissa is also a macro virus, in addition to being an e-mail virus: it mailed itself to potential victims as an infected document.

- *Script Virus*—Script viruses are generally differentiated from macro viruses in that they are usually stand-alone files that can be executed by an interpreter, such as Microsoft's Windows

713

Script Host (.vbs files). A script virus file can be seen as a data file in that it is generally a simple text file, but it usually does not contain other data, and often has some indicator (such as the.vbs extension) that it is executable. Loveletter is an example of a script virus.

Worms

A worm reproduces and spreads, like a virus, and unlike other forms of malware. Worms are distinct from viruses, though they may have similar results. Most simply, a worm may be thought of as a virus with the capacity to propagate independent of user action. In other words, they do not rely on (usually) human-initiated transfer of data between systems for propagation, but instead spread across networks of their own accord, primarily by exploiting known vulnerabilities in common software. The lack of requirement for user involvement means that worms have a significant speed advantage when spreading. Even fast burner viruses have required times measured in days to spread around the world, where worms can travel worldwide in hours, or even minutes.

Originally, the distinction was made that worms used networks and communications links to spread, and that a worm, unlike a virus, did not directly attach to an executable file. In early research into computer viruses, the terms *worm* and *virus* tended to be used synonymously, it being felt that the technical distinction was unimportant to most users. The first worm to garner significant attention was the Morris Internet Worm of 1988. Recently, many of the most prolific virus infections have not been strictly viruses, but have used a combination of viral and worm techniques to spread more rapidly and effectively. LoveLetter was an example of this convergence of reproductive technologies. Although infected e-mail attachments were perhaps the most widely publicized vector of infection, LoveLetter also spread by actively scanning attached network drives, infecting a variety of common file types. This convergence of technologies will be an increasing problem in the future. Code Red and a number of

Linux programs (such as Lion) are modern examples of worms. (Nimda is an example of a worm, but it also spreads in a number of other ways, so it could be considered to be an e-mail virus and multipartite as well.)

Hoaxes

Hoaxes are usually warnings about new viruses: new viruses that do not, of course, exist. Hoaxes generally carry a directive to the user to forward the warning to all addresses available to him. Thus, these descendants of chain letters form a kind of self-perpetuating spam. Hoaxes use an odd kind of social engineering, relying on people's desire to communicate, and on a sense of urgency and importance, using the ambition that people have to be the first to provide important new information.

It is wisest, in the current environment, to doubt all virus warnings, unless they come from a known and historically accurate source, such as a vendor with a proven record of providing reliable and accurate virus alert information, or preferably an independent researcher or group. It is best to check any warnings received against known virus encyclopedia sites. It is best to check more than one such site: in the initial phases of a fast burner attack, some sites may not have had time to analyze samples to their own satisfaction, and the better sites will not post information they are not sure about.

A recent example of a hoax, referring to SULFNBK.EXE, got a number of people to clear this legitimate utility off their machines. The origin was likely the fact that the Magistr virus targets Windows system software, and someone with an infection did not realize that the file is actually present on all Windows 98 systems. Thus, a new class of malicious hoax message has started to appear, attempting to make users actually cripple their own machines.

Trojans

Trojans, or trojan horse programs, are the largest class of malware, aside from viruses. However, use of the term is subject to much confusion, particularly in relation to computer viruses.

4

Software Development Security

715

A trojan is a program that pretends to do one thing while performing another unwanted action. The extent of the pretense may vary greatly. Many of the early PC Trojans merely used the filename and a description on a bulletin board. Log-in trojans, popular among university student mainframe users, mimicked the screen display and the prompts of the normal log-in program and could in fact pass the username and password along to the valid log-in program at the same time as they stole the user data. Some trojans may contain actual code that does what it is supposed to while performing additional acts not clearly documented or defined.

Some data security writers consider a virus to simply be a specific example of the class of trojan horse programs. There is some validity to this usage because a virus is an unknown quantity that is hidden and transmitted along with a legitimate disk or program, and any program can be turned into a trojan by infecting it with a virus. However, the term *virus* more properly refers to the added, infectious code rather than the virus/target combination. Therefore, the term *trojan* refers to a deliberately misleading or modified program that does not reproduce itself.

An additional confusion with viruses involves trojan horse programs that may be spread by e-mail. In years past, a trojan program had to be posted on an electronic bulletin board system or a file archive site. Because of the static posting, a malicious program would soon be identified and eliminated. More recently, trojan programs have been distributed by mass e-mail campaigns, by posting on Usenet newsgroup discussion groups, or through automated distribution agents (bots) on Internet Relay Chat (IRC) channels. Because source identification in these communications channels can be easily hidden, trojan programs can be redistributed through a number of channels, and specific identification of a malicious program has become much more difficult as a result.

Social Engineering
A major aspect of trojan design is the social engineering component. A recent e-mail virus, in generating its messages, carried a list of a huge variety

of subject lines, promising pornography, humor, virus information, an antivirus program, and information about abuse of the recipient's e-mail account. Sometimes the message is simply vague and relies on curiosity. It is instructive to examine some classic social engineering techniques. Formalizing the problem makes it easier to move on to working toward effective solutions, making use of realistic, pragmatic policies. Effective implementation of such policies, however good they are, is not possible without a considered user education program and cooperation from management.

Social engineering can range from simple lying (such as a false description of the function of a file), to bullying and intimidation (to pressure a low-level employee into disclosing information), to association with a trusted source (such as the username from an infected machine), to dumpster diving (to find potentially valuable information people have carelessly discarded), to shoulder surfing (to find out personal identification numbers and passwords).

A recent entry to the list of malicious attacks aimed at computer users is the practice of phishing. Phishing attempts to get the user to provide information that will be useful for identity theft-type frauds. Although phishing messages frequently use Web sites and try to confuse the origin and ownership of those sites, very little programming, malicious or otherwise, may be involved. Phishing is unadulterated social engineering or deception. However, some recent phishing attacks have incorporated technical aspects, such as the creation of unframed browser windows in order to overlay areas in the browser frame and recreate "browser chrome," [4] such as the padlock symbol denoting a site certificate and authentication/ encryption via the SSL protocol.

Remote-Access Trojans (RATs)

Remote-access trojans are programs designed to be installed, usually remotely, after systems are in production and not in development, as is

4   http://www.pcmag.com/encyclopedia_term/0,2542,t=browser+-chrome&i=38972,00.asp

717

the case with logic bombs and backdoors. Their authors would generally like to have the programs referred to as remote administration tools, to convey a sense of legitimacy. All networking software can, in a sense, be considered remote-access tools: file transfer sites and clients, World Wide Web servers and browsers, and terminal emulation software that allows a microcomputer user to log on to a distant computer and use it as if he were on-site. The RATs considered to be in the malware camp tend to fall somewhere in the middle of the spectrum. Once a client, such as BlackShades, Back Orifice, Netbus, Bionet, or SubSeven, is installed on the target computer, the controlling computer is able to obtain information about the target computer. The master computer will be able to download files from and upload files to the target. The control computer will also be able to submit commands to the victim, which basically allows the distant operator to do pretty much anything to the prey. One other function is quite important: all of this activity goes on without any alert being given to the owner or operator of the targeted computer.

When a RAT program has been run on a computer, it will install itself in such a way as to be active every time the computer is started subsequent to the installation. Information is sent back to the controlling computer (sometimes via an anonymous channel such as IRC) noting that the system is active. The user of the command computer is now able to explore the target, escalate access to other resources, and install other software, such as DDoS zombies, if so desired.

Once more, it should be noted that remote-access tools are not viral. When the software is active, the master computer can submit commands to have the installation program sent on, via network transfer or e-mail, to other machines. In addition, RATs can be installed as a payload from a virus or Trojan. Many RATs now operate in very specialized ways, making the affected computer part of a botnet (robot network). Botnets use large numbers of computers to perform functions such as distributing spam messages, increasing the number of messages that can be sent, and isolating

718

the actual sender from the targets of the messages. Recently it has been demonstrated that certain viruses have carried RAT programming payloads to set up spam botnets, and that such spam botnets have also been used to seed the release of new viruses. Rootkits, containing software that can subvert or replace normal operating system software, have been around for some time. RATs differ from rootkits in that a working account must be either subverted or created on the target computer to use a rootkit. RATs, once installed by a virus or Trojan, do not require access to an account.

DDoS Zombies

DDoS (distributed denial of service) is a modified DoS attack. DoS attacks do not attempt to destroy or corrupt data, but attempt to use up a computing resource to the point where normal work cannot proceed. The structure of a DDoS attack requires a master computer to control the attack, a target of the attack, and a number of computers in the middle that the master computer uses to generate the attack. These computers in between the master and the target are variously called agents or clients, but are usually referred to as running zombie programs. As you can see, DDoS is a specialized type of RAT or botnet.

Again, note that DDoS programs are not viral, but checking for zombie software not only protects your system, but also prevents attacks on others. However, it is still in your best interest to ensure that no zombie programs are active. If your computers are used to launch an assault on some other system, you could be liable for damages. The efficacy of this platform was demonstrated in early 2000, when a couple of teenagers successfully paralyzed various prominent online players in quick succession, including Yahoo, Amazon, and eBay. DDoS is generally considered to be the first instance of the botnet concept to work in an effective manner.

Logic Bombs

Logic bombs are software modules set up to run in a dormant state, but to monitor a specific condition or set of conditions and to activate their

719

payload under those conditions. A logic bomb is generally implanted in or coded as part of an application under development or maintenance. Unlike a RAT or trojan, it is difficult to implant a logic bomb after the fact. There are numerous examples of this type of activity, usually based upon actions taken by a programmer to deprive a company of needed resources if employment was terminated. A trojan or a virus may contain a logic bomb as part of the payload. A logic bomb involves no reproduction and no social engineering.

A variant on the concept of logic bombs involves what is known as the salami scam. The basic idea involves the siphoning off of small amounts of money (in some versions, fractions of a cent) credited to a specific account, over a large number of transactions. In most discussions of this type of activity, it is explained as the action of an individual, or small group, defrauding a corporation. However, a search of the RISKS-FORUM archives, for example, will find only one story about a fast food clerk who diddled the display on a drive-through window and collected an extra dime or quarter from most customers. Other examples of the scheme are cited, but it is instructive to note that these narratives, in opposition to the classic salami scam anecdote, almost always are examples of fraudulent corporate activity, typically collecting improper amounts from customers.

Spyware and Adware

It is extremely difficult to define which spyware and adware entities are malicious and which are legitimate marketing tools. Originally, many of the programs now known as spyware were intended to support the development of certain programs by providing advertising or marketing services. These were generally included with shareware, but were installed as a separate function or program that generated advertising screens or reported on user activities, such as other installed programs and user Web-surfing activities. Over time, a number of these programs became more and more intrusive, and frequently now have functions that will install without the user's knowledge, and in the absence of any other utility being obtained.

Companies involved with spyware and adware have been quite active in promoting the confusion of definitions and terms. Vendors and developers of anti-spyware programs have frequently found themselves targets of lawsuits alleging that the identification of programs as spyware is defamation.

Pranks

Pranks are very much a part of the computer culture, so much so that anyone can now buy commercially produced joke packages that allow you to perform "stupid Mac (or PC or Windows) tricks." There are numerous pranks available as shareware. Some make the computer appear to insult the user; some use sound effects or voices; some use special visual effects. A fairly common thread running through most pranks is that the computer is, in some way, nonfunctional. Many pretend to have detected some kind of fault in the computer (and some pretend to rectify such faults, of course making things worse). One entry in the virus field is PARASCAN, the paranoid scanner. It pretends to find large numbers of infected files, although it does not actually check for any infections.

Generally speaking, pranks that create some kind of announcement are not malware: viruses that generate a screen or audio display are actually quite rare. The distinction between jokes and trojans is harder to make, but pranks are intended for amusement. Joke programs may, of course, result in a DoS if people find the prank message frightening. One specific type of joke is the Easter egg, a function hidden in a program and generally accessible only by some arcane sequence of commands. These may be seen as harmless, but note that they do consume resources, even if only disk space, and also make the task of ensuring program integrity much more difficult. Repeated pranks may also serve to dissuade the end user from seeking help from the helpdesk when legitimately needed for a security reason.

Botnets

A botnet is a network of automated systems or processes (robots or bots) performing a specific function. A botnet is also dedicated to some form of malicious activity. Botnets have greatly magnified the power and speed of malicious operations, and have allowed for tuning and directing of operations in a way that was not possible with viral programs alone. The distributed nature of botnets, and related technologies such as fast-flux domain and IP (Internet Protocol) address reassignment (rapidly rotating domain names and IP addresses), have made it much more difficult to detect, analyze, and remove botnets and botnet activity.

Bot agent software can be installed on user machines in any number of ways. Trojan horse programs may be mailed, and the user incited, or socially engineered, to infect their own machine. This may or may not be associated with a virus carrier. Worms may examine machines for server software with specific vulnerabilities. Drive-by downloads, peer-to-peer file sharing software, and instant messaging clients all have functions that may allow remote submission of files and invocation of commands or programs. Once any of these methods can be made to work, any further desired software may be placed on the user machine and set in operation. Generally speaking, once botnet software has been installed on the infected machine it no longer requires personal intervention by the botherder, but will respond to automated communications through the command and control channel directed at a number of computers in the botnet. This includes promotion into, and demotion out of, the control channel itself.

In the earliest days of botnets, IRC was the command and control channel of choice. IRC provided a one-to-many communications channel that did not require either that the attacker contact each machine individually, or that the infected computers regularly establish a connection with a central location, such as a Web server, for instructions. IRC also provided a measure of anonymity for the attacker or botherder. A system of codes or passwords could be used to ensure that the botherder retained control of the botnet without losing it to someone else.

IRC is far from the only control channel that can be used. Peer-to-peer (P2P) networking and file transfer systems have the same decentralization and anonymization functions that made IRC so suitable, as well as built-in functions that can be used for updating and access to new systems. Instant messaging (IM) is another highly functional means that can be used for malicious control, generally with means to evade normal firewall restrictions. Even basic Internet management protocols, such as the Domain Name System (DNS) can be used to pass information in a distributed and generally anonymous manner.

Malware Protection

In almost any recent work on security, there will be a list of signs to watch for to determine a virus infection. Unfortunately, all such catalogs seem to have extremely limited utility. The characteristics mentioned tend to refer to older malware instances, and may also relate to a number of conditions that do not involve any malicious programming.

Training and explicit policies can greatly reduce the danger to users. Some guidelines that can really help in the current environment are

- Do not double-click on attachments.
- When sending attachments, provide a clear and specific description as to the content of the attachment.
- Do not blindly use the most widely used products as a company standard.
- Disable Windows Script Host, ActiveX, VBScript, and JavaScript. Do not send HTML-formatted e-mail.
- Use more than one scanner, and scan everything.

Whether these guidelines are acceptable in a specific environment is a business decision based upon the level of acceptable risk. But remember, whether risks are evaluated and whether policies are explicitly developed, every environment has a set of policies (some are explicit, while some are implicit) and every business accepts risk. The distinction is that some companies are aware of the risks that they choose to accept.

All antivirus software is essentially reactive, that is, it exists only because viruses and other programmed threats existed first. It is common to distinguish between virus-specific scanning or known virus scanning (KVS) on the one hand and generic measures on the other. The technological aspects of antivirus software can be described in terms of three main approaches.

Protective tools in the malware area are generally limited to antivirus software. To this day there are three major types, first discussed by Fred Cohen in his research: known signature scanning, activity monitoring, and change detection. [5] These basic types of detection systems can be compared with the common intrusion detection system (IDS) types, although the correspondence is not exact. A scanner is like a signature-based IDS. An activity monitor is like a rule-based IDS or an anomaly-based IDS. A change detection system is like a statistical-based IDS.

Scanners

Scanners, also known as signature scanners or known virus scanners, look for search strings whose presence is characteristic of a known virus. They frequently have capabilities to remove the virus from an infected object. However, some objects cannot be repaired. Even where an object can be repaired, it is often preferable (in fact, safer) to replace the object rather than repair it, and some scanners are very selective about which objects they repair.

Heuristic Scanners

A recent addition to scanners is intelligent analysis of unknown code, currently referred to as heuristic scanning. It should be noted that heuristic scanning does not represent a new type of antiviral software. More closely akin to activity monitoring functions than traditional signature scanning, this looks for suspicious sections of code that are generally found in viral programs. Although it is possible for normal programs to try to "go

---

5   http://all.net/books/Dissertation.pdf

resident," look for other program files, or even modify their own code, such activities are telltale signs that can help an informed user come to some decision about the advisability of running or installing a given new and unknown program. Heuristics, however, may generate a lot of false alarms and may either scare novice users, or give them a false sense of security after "wolf" has been cried too often.

Activity Monitors

An activity monitor performs a task very similar to an automated form of traditional auditing: it watches for suspicious activity. It may, for example, check for any calls to format a disk or attempts to alter or delete a program file while a program other than the operating system is in control. It may be more sophisticated and check for any program that performs direct activities with hardware, without using the standard system calls.

It is very hard to tell the difference between a word processor updating a file and a virus infecting a file. Activity monitoring programs may be more trouble than they are worth because they can continually ask for confirmation of valid activities. The annals of computer virus research are littered with suggestions for virus-proof computers and systems that basically all boil down to the same thing: if the operations that a computer can perform are restricted, viral programs can be eliminated. Unfortunately, so is most of the usefulness of the computer.

Change Detection

Change detection software examines system or program files and configuration, stores the information, and compares it against the actual configuration at a later time. Most of these programs perform a checksum or cyclic redundancy check (CRC) that will detect changes to a file even if the length is unchanged. Some programs will even use sophisticated encryption techniques to generate a signature that is prohibitively expensive, in processing terms, from the point of view of a piece of malware to execute an attack against.

4

Software Development Security

725

Change detection software should also note the addition of completely new entities to a system. It has been noted that some programs have not done this and allowed the addition of virus infections or malware. Change detection software is also often referred to as integrity-checking software, but this term may be somewhat misleading. The integrity of a system may have been compromised before the establishment of the initial baseline of comparison.

A sufficiently advanced change detection system, which takes all factors, including system areas of the disk and the computer memory, into account, has the best chance of detecting viral strains. However, change detection also has the highest probability of false alarms, because it will not know whether a change is viral or valid. The addition of intelligent analysis of the changes detected may assist with this failing.

Antimalware Policies

Creating policies or educating users in safe practices can reduce the risk of becoming infected, even when a virus enters the organization. There are many possible preemptive measures, such as avoiding the use of applications that are particularly vulnerable and denying entry to mail attachments that are likely to be vectors for inbound viruses. Such measures can be very effective at addressing aspects of antivirus damage that reactive antivirus software does not deal with very well.

Organizations can use access control software suites to minimize the possibility of a virus or Trojan gaining entry, by enforcing authentication of program files, disks, users, or any combination of the three. This approach is sometimes combined with virus-specific or generic scanning. Applying such a multilayered strategy can be much more effective than using only one of these approaches, but the strategy's success in avoiding threats has to be balanced against the probable impairment of performance that multilayering entails.

It should be noted that a significant difference exits between access control as it is used in malware control and access control as it is often understood by systems administrators. Access control systems determine the appropriate allocation of access privileges to individuals and grant systems access to authenticated individuals. In other words, if the system recognizes an individual, he or she is allowed to use that system to the extent that the user's privileges allow. Authenticating the individual is not enough in the malware arena, because viruses and worms are usually spread (unwittingly) by trusted individuals. Confirming the identity of the individual does not disclose anything about his or her good intentions, though most would usually hope that the human resources department has applied the appropriate checks. It tells still less about the individual's competence at following security guidelines, or the currency and acuity of his or her antivirus measures.

Some software places the user at higher risk of virus infection. This is a simple fact. As has been noted, the more widely an operating system is used, the more likely it is that someone has written a virus for it. The same is true for application platforms, such as e-mail programs or word processors. There are other factors that can increase or decrease risk. Certain software designs are more dangerous than others. Specific strategic factors render Windows more vulnerable than it needs to be. Many users resent the restrictions that a highly secure environment imposes on the pursuit of business or personal aims. Management often pays lip service to the importance of security in meetings and reports, but cuts corners on implementation. Computer users frequently resent the obtrusiveness of most security measures. (In this regard, it should also be noted that draconian security policies without good reason will frequently be ignored or circumvented.)

The basic types of antivirus programs have a great many variations. There are hundreds of thousands of PC viruses and variants known. When a scanner checks for those viruses and variants, checking for every byte of viral code each time would impose a huge processing overhead. To keep this overhead to a minimum, scanners check for the shortest search strings they can afford and deduce the presence of a given virus accordingly. Scanners may apply a number of heuristics according to the virus type. Therefore, on-access scanners, as well as those based on firewalls and network gateways, always have poorer detection capabilities than their on-demand, or manual, counterparts, and this difference sometimes accounts for as much as a 20% disparity in performance and accuracy. The memory resident and on-demand components of a modern antivirus suite may use the same definitions database and still not score identical results with the identical test set.

Malware Assurance

In order to facilitate protecting against malware, as well as raising user awareness, policies should be put in place that will effectively protect against common malware and malware vectors, without unduly restricting operations. Explain to users the reasons for the control measures and the specific exploits that they protect against. Policies and education are useful protections against malware, regardless of scanning and restriction technologies.

For technical antimalware systems, regularly review their effectiveness. If the organization uses on-demand or server-based scanners, have regular check scans with a manual scanner in addition to the automated scanning. Note that disinfection is not always effective or possible, and have a policy to prefer deletion of malware and replacement of infected items from an uncompromised backup.

Monitor activity, especially communications. Check for open ports and scan outgoing, as well as incoming, e-mail. This will not protect your system from infection, but it will provide a means of detecting various malware-related activities should some problem get past your defenses. It also acts as a check on botnet activities, and is not affected by rootkit or stealth capabilities in malware.

Software Protection Mechanisms

Security Kernels

A security kernel is responsible for enforcing a security policy. It is a strict implementation of a reference monitor mechanism. The architecture of a kernel operating system is typically layered, and the kernel should be at the lowest and most primitive level. It is a small portion of the operating system through which all references to information and all changes to authorizations must pass. In theory, the kernel implements access control and information flow control between implemented objects according to the security policy.

To be secure, the kernel must meet three basic conditions: completeness (all accesses to information must go through the kernel), isolation (the kernel itself must be protected from any type of unauthorized access), and verifiability (the kernel must be proven to meet design specifications).

The reference monitor, as noted previously, is an abstraction, but there may be a reference validator, which usually runs inside the security kernel and is responsible for performing security access checks on objects, manipulating privileges, and generating any resulting security audit messages.

A term associated with security kernels and the reference monitor is the trusted computing base (TCB). The TCB is the portion of a computer system that contains all elements of the system responsible for supporting the security policy and the isolation of objects. The security capabilities of products for use in the TCB can be verified through various evaluation criteria, such as the earlier Trusted Computer System Evaluation Criteria (TCSEC) and the current Common Criteria standard.

Many of these security terms—reference monitor, security kernel, TCB—are defined loosely by vendors for purposes of marketing literature. Thus, it is necessary for security professionals to read the small print and

729

between the lines to fully understand what the vendor is offering in regard to security features.

Processor Privilege States

The processor privilege states protect the processor and the activities that it performs. The earliest method of doing this was to record the processor state in a register that could only be altered when the processor was operating in a privileged state. Instructions such as I/O requests were designed to include a reference to this register. If the register was not in a privileged state, the instructions were aborted. The hardware typically controls entry into the privilege mode. For example, the Intel vPro processor prevents system code and data from being overwritten, although these protections are seldom directly used. The privilege-level mechanism should prevent memory access (programs or data) from less privileged to more privileged levels, but only if the controls are invoked and properly managed in software. The privileged levels are typically referenced in a ring structure.

To illustrate this point, many operating systems use two processor access modes: user (or process, problem, or program) mode and kernel (or supervisor) mode. User application code runs in user mode, and operating system code runs in kernel mode. The privileged processor mode is called kernel mode. The kernel mode allows the processor access to all system memory, resources, and all CPU instructions.

The application code should run in a non-privileged mode (the user mode) and have a limited set of interfaces available, limited access to system data, and no direct access to hardware resources. An advantage of the operating system having a higher privilege level than the application software is that problematic application software cannot disrupt the system's functioning. A major security failure in modern desktop processing is that operating systems and applications may be most effective if run in supervisor or kernel mode at all times.

When a user mode program calls a system service (such as reading a document from storage), the processor catches the call and switches the calling request to kernel mode. When the call is complete, the operating system switches the call back to user mode and allows the user mode program to continue. Under the most secure operating policy, the operating system and device drivers operate at ring level 0, also known as kernel-level or system-level privilege. At this privilege level, there are no restrictions on what a program can do. Because programs at this level have unlimited access, users should be concerned about the source of device drivers for machines that contain sensitive information.

Applications and services should operate at ring level 3, also known as user-level or application-level privilege. Note that if an application or service fails at this level, a trap screen will appear (also known as a general protection fault) that can be dismissed and the operating system does not care. The decision to have services run at the same privilege level as regular applications is based on the idea that if the service traps, the operating system should continue to operate.

A monolithic operating system exists as a large program consisting of a set of procedures; there are no restrictions on what procedures may be called by any other procedures. This means that the majority of the operating system and device driver codes share the kernel mode protected memory space. Once in kernel mode, the operating system and the device driver code have complete access to system space memory and can bypass security to access objects. Because most of the operating system code runs in kernel mode, it is critical that kernel mode components be carefully designed to ensure they do not violate security features. If a system administrator installs a third-party device driver, it operates in kernel mode and then has access to all operating system data. If the device driver installation software also contains malicious code, that code will also be installed and could open the system to unauthorized accesses.

A privileged state failure can occur if an application program fails. The safest place for an application to fail is to a system halt. For example, if an application has an error, it will fail to the operating system program, and the user can then use the operating system to recover the application and data. This vulnerability could also be exploited by allowing an attacker to crash an application to get to the operating system with the identity and privileges of the person who started the application.

Security Controls for Buffer Overflows

Another issue with privilege states is called ineffective parameter checking, which causes buffer overflows. A buffer overflow is caused by improper (or lacking) bounds checking on input to a program. Essentially, the program fails to see if too much data is provided for an allocated space of memory. Because programs are loaded into memory when run, when there is an overflow, the data has to go somewhere. If that data happens to be executable malicious code that is loaded, it may run as if it were the program, or make other changes to the execution environment that can be exploited by an attacker.

Buffer overflows must be corrected by the programmer or by directly patching system memory. They can be detected and fixed by reverse engineering (disassembling programs) and looking at the operations of the application. Hardware states and other hardware controls can make buffer overflows impossible, although enterprises seldom specify hardware at this level. Bounds enforcement and proper error checking will also stop buffer overflows.

Controls for Incomplete Parameter Check and Enforcement

A security risk exists when all parameters have not been fully checked for accuracy and consistency by the operating systems. The lack of parameter checking can lead to buffer overflow attacks. A recent parameter check attack involved an e-mail attachment with a name longer than 64 K in length. Because the application required attachment names to be less than 64 K, attachments that had longer names would overwrite program instructions.

To counter the vulnerability, operating systems should offer some type of buffer management. Parameter checking is implemented by the programmer, and involves checking the input data for disallowed characters, length, data type, and format. Certain programming commands or styles are preferable and should be encouraged or mandated. Other technologies to protect against buffer overflows include canaries (the use and monitoring of indicator data values at the end of buffer areas).

Memory Protection

Memory protection is concerned with controlling access to main memory. When several processes are running at the same time, it is necessary to protect the memory used by one process from unauthorized access by another. Thus, it is necessary to partition memory to ensure processes cannot interfere with each other's local memory and to ensure common memory areas are protected against unauthorized access. This extends beyond applications executing in the main computer memory: an operating system may use secondary memory (storage devices) to give the illusion of a larger main memory, or it may partition the main memory among users so that each user sees a virtual machine that has memory smaller than that on the real machine. Additional controls may be required in these situations.

The memory used by the operating system needs to be protected to maintain the integrity of privileged code and data. Because memory protection deals with addressing, many protection mechanisms protect memory by placing it outside the address space available to a process. There are four methods used to provide memory protection so that no user process can inadvertently or deliberately corrupt the address space of another process or the operating system itself.

The first method ensures all system-wide data structures and memory pools used by kernel mode system components can be accessed only while in kernel mode. Thus, user mode requests cannot access these pages. If they attempt to do so, the hardware will generate a fault, and then the memory manager will create an access violation. In early Windows operating systems, such as Windows 95 and Windows 98, some pages in the system address space were writable from user mode, thus allowing an errant application to corrupt key system data structures and crash the system.

Second, each process has a separate, private address space protected from being accessed by any request belonging to another process, with a few exceptions. Each time a request references an address, the virtual memory hardware, in conjunction with the memory manager, intervenes and translates the virtual address into a physical one. Because Windows 7 controls how virtual addresses are translated, requests running in one process do not inappropriately access a page belonging to another process.

Third, most modern processors provide some form of hardware-controlled memory protection, such as read or write access. The type of protection offered depends on the processor. For example, a memory protection option is page_noaccess. If an attempt is made to read from, write to, or execute the code in this region, an access violation will occur.

The fourth protection mechanism uses access control lists to protect shared memory objects, and they are checked when processes attempt to open them. Another security feature involves access to mapped files. To map to a file, the object (or user) performing the request must have at least read access to the underlying file object or the operation will fail.

Covert Channel Controls

A covert channel or confinement problem is an information flow that is not controlled by a security control. It is a communication channel allowing two cooperating processes to transfer information in a way that violates the system's security policy. Even though there are protection mechanisms in place, if unauthorized information can be transferred using a signaling mechanism or other objects, then a covert channel may exist. The standard example used in application security is a situation where a process can be started and stopped by one program, and the existence of the process can be detected by another application. Thus, the existence of the process can be used, over time, to signal information.

The only channels of interest are those breaching the security policy; those channels that parallel legitimate communications paths are not of concern. Although there are differences for each type of covert channel, there is a common condition—the transmitting and receiving objects over the channel must have access to a shared resource.

The first step is to identify any potential covert channels; the second is to analyze these channels to determine whether a channel actually exists. The next steps are based on manual inspection and appropriate testing techniques to verify if the channel creates security concerns.

Cryptography

Cryptographic techniques protect information by transforming the data through encryption schemes. They are used to protect the confidentiality and integrity of information. Most cryptographic techniques are used in telecommunications systems; however, because of the increase in distributed systems, they are becoming increasingly used in operating systems. Encryption algorithms can be used to encrypt specific files located within the operating system. For example, database files that contain user information, such as group rights, are encrypted using one-way hashing algorithms to ensure a higher protection of the data.

Password Protection Techniques

Operating system and application software use passwords as a convenient mechanism to authenticate users. Typically, operating systems use passwords

4

to authenticate the user and establish access controls for resources, including the system, files, or applications. Password protections offered by the operating system include controls on how the password is selected and how complex the password is, password time limits, and password length.

Password files stored within a computer system must be secured by the protection mechanisms of the operating system. Because password files are prone to unauthorized access, the most common solution is to encrypt password files using one-way encryption algorithms (hashing). These, however, are very susceptible to a dictionary attack if the passwords chosen appear in any dictionary. Another feature offered by an operating system for password security involves an overstrike or password-masking feature. This prevents others from reading the typed password through shoulder surfing.

Inadequate Granularity of Controls

If there is not enough granularity of security, users will get more access permission than needed. If the user is unable to access object A, but the user has access to a program that can access object A, then the security mechanisms could be bypassed. If the security controls are granular enough to address both program and user, then the disclosure may be prevented. Inadequate granularity of controls can be addressed by properly implementing the concept of least privilege, setting reasonable limits on the user. Also, the separation of duties and functions should be covered. Programmers should never be system administrators or users of the application. Grant users only those permissions necessary to do their job.

Users should have no access to server rooms or legacy programs; programmers and system analysts should not have write access to production programs, allowing them to change the installed program code. Programmers should have no ongoing direct access to production programs. Access to fix crashed applications should be limited to the time required to repair the problem causing the failure. Mainframe operators should not be allowed to do programming. Maintenance programmers should not have access to programs under development. Assignment of system privileges must be tightly controlled and a shared responsibility.

More specifically, granularity addresses the issue of fine control. As far as the operating system is concerned, an object is a file, not a structure within that file. Therefore, users granted access to a file can read the whole file. To restrict access to certain parts of the file, such as records or fields within a database, additional controls must be built into the database access application which will ensure that areas of concern are protected.

Control and Separation of Environments

The following environmental types can exist in software development:

- Development environment
- Quality assurance environment
- Application (production) environment

The security issue is to control how each environment can access the application and the data and then provide mechanisms to keep them separate. For example, systems analysts and programmers write, compile, and perform initial testing of the application's implementation and functionality in the development environment. As the application reaches maturity and moves toward production readiness, users and quality assurance people perform functional testing within the quality assurance environment. The quality assurance configuration should simulate the production environment as closely as possible. Once the user community has accepted the application, it is moved into the production environment. Blended environments combine one or more of these individual environments and are generally the most difficult to control.

Control measures protecting the various environments include physical isolation of environment, physical or temporal separation of data for each environment, access control lists, content-dependent access controls, role-based constraints, role definition stability, accountability, and separation of duties.

Time of Check/Time of Use (TOC/TOU)

If there are multiple threads of execution at the same time, a TOC/TOU is possible. The most common TOC/TOU hazards are file-based race conditions that occur when there is a check on some property of the file that precedes the use of that file. To avoid TOC/TOU problems, especially file-based issues, the programmer should avoid any file system call that takes a filename for an input, instead of a file handle or a file descriptor. When using file descriptors, it is possible to ensure that the file used does not change after it is first called. In addition, files that are to be used should be kept in their own directory, where the directory is only accessible by the universal ID (UID) of the program performing the file operation. In this manner, even when using symbolic names, attackers are not able to exploit a race condition unless they already have the proper UID.

If they have a proper UID, there is, of course, no reason to deliberately exploit the race condition. However, race conditions of all types should still be considered, since they result in inconsistencies in output. Race conditions in distributed systems, or those platforms using multiple processors or multicore processor architectures are of particular concern. Race conditions are not the only TOC/TOU situations, and some applications may require periodic or continual authentication, depending upon security and policy requirements.

Social Engineering

Some of the ways in which attackers can try to use social influence over users in order to subvert normal processes and technical controls for their own gain include subtle intimidation, bluster, pulling rank, exploiting guilt, pleading for special treatment, exploiting a natural desire to be helpful, or appealing to an underling's subversive streak. Social engineering in software, particularly malicious software, tends to be more simplistic, but all forms should be noted.

In regard to protection against social engineering attacks, users and help desk staff need a proper framework to work. The staff needs a good understanding of what the rules actually are, what their responsibilities are, and what recourse they have in the event of a grievance or problem. They also need to know that when they have a run-in with a difficult user, they will have the backing of management, as long as they conform to policy.

Social engineering attracts such a range of definitions, covering such a variety of activities (from password stealing to scavenging through garbage and waste for useful information to spreading malicious misinformation) as to be confusing at best. The question is, do accepted definitions of social engineering meet the needs of those tasked with addressing this class of threat? Some examples of the use of social engineering in malware are instructive. Eugene Kaspersky wrote a fix for the original version of Concept in the form of a Word template. The author of WM/Nuclear uploaded a version of the same document infected with the new virus. The infected file was quickly removed, but collectors had already taken copies that were soon freely available on VX sites, though Nuclear's spread was far more restricted than Concept's.

Hare-infected files were posted to Usenet on 26 and 29 June, 1996, and spread from there. The posts were forged, and the files posted were an assortment of alleged utilities. Warez Web sites and bulletin boards (where pirate software is to be found) and newsgroups that allow the posting of binary files (pirated and legitimate, pornographic or otherwise) have often been the injection site for malicious software.

The best method of preventing social engineering is to make users aware of the threat and give them the proper procedures for handling unusual or what may seem usual requests for information. For example, if a user were to receive a phone call from a "system administrator" asking for their

4

Software Development Security

password, users should be aware of social engineering threats and ask that the system administrator come to their office to discuss the problems in a face-to-face format. Even if the user is 100% sure that the person on the phone is the system administrator and the phone line could not be tampered with, it is almost impossible to imagine a situation under which a user should give a password to anyone else, particularly using the phone lines.

Backup Controls

Backing up operating system and application software is a method of ensuring productivity in the event of a system crash. Operation copies of software should be available in the event of a system crash. Also, storing copies of software in an off-site location can be useful if the building is no longer available. Data, programs, documentation, computing, and communications equipment redundancy can ensure that information is available in the event of an emergency. Requiring that the source code for custom-designed software is kept in escrow ensures that if the software vendor were to go out of business, the source code would be available to use or give to another vendor in the event upgrades or assistance is needed. Contingency planning documents help to provide a plan for returning operations to normal in the event of an emergency. Disk mirroring, redundant array of independent disks (RAID), etc., provide protection for information in the event of a production server crashing.

Software Forensics

Software, particularly malicious software, has traditionally been seen in terms of a tool for the attacker. The only value that has been seen in the study of such software is in regard to protection against malicious code. However, experience in the virus research field, and more recent studies in detecting plagiarism, indicates that evidence of intention can be gained, and cultural and individual identity, from the examination of software itself. Although most would see software forensics strictly as a tool for assurance, in software development and acquisition, it has a number of uses in protective procedures.

Outside of virus research, forensic programming is a little known field. However, the larger computer science world is starting to take note of software forensics. It involves the analysis of program code, generally object or machine language code, to make a determination of or provide evidence for the intent or authorship of a program.

Software forensics has a number of possible uses. In analyzing software suspected of being malicious, it can be used to determine whether a problem is a result of carelessness or was deliberately introduced as a payload. Information can be obtained about authorship and the culture behind a given programmer, and the sequence in which related programs were written. This can be used to provide evidence about a suspected author of a program or to determine intellectual property issues. The techniques behind software forensics can sometimes also be used to recover source code that has been lost.

Software forensics generally deals with two different types of code. The first is source code, which is relatively legible to people. Analysis of source code is often referred to as code analysis and is closely related to literary analysis. The second, analysis of object, or machine, code, is generally referred to as forensic programming.

Literary analysis has contributed much to code analysis and is an older and more mature field. It is referred to, variously, as authorship analysis, stylistics, stylometry, forensic linguistics, or forensic stylistics. Stylistic or stylometric analysis of messages and text may provide information and evidence that can be used for identification or confirmation of identity.

Physical fingerprint evidence frequently does not help identify a perpetrator in terms of finding the person a fingerprint is obtained. However, a fingerprint can confirm an identity or place a person at the scene of a crime, once a suspect is determined. In the same way, the evidence gathered from analyzing the text of a message, or a body of messages, may help to confirm that a given individual or suspect is the person who created

741

the fraudulent postings. Both the content and the syntactical structure of text can provide evidence that relates to an individual.

Some of the evidence discovered may not relate to individuals. Some information, particularly that relating to the content or phrasing of the text, may relate to a group of people who work together, influence each other, or are influenced from a single outside source. This data can still be of use to us, in that it will provide clues in regard to a group that the author may be associated with, and may be helpful in building a profile of the writer.

Groups may also use common tools. Various types of tools, such as word processors or databases, may be commonly used by groups and provide similar evidence. In software analysis, indications of languages, specific compilers, and other development tools can be found. Compilers leave definite traces in programs and can be specifically identified. Languages leave indications in the types of functions and structures supported. Other types of software development tools may contribute to the structural architecture of the program or the regularity and reuse of modules.

In regard to programming, it is possible to trace indications of cultures and styles in programming. A very broad example is the difference between design of programs in the Microsoft Windows environment and the UNIX environment. Windows programs tend to be large and monolithic, with the most complete set of functions possible built into the main program, large central program files, and calls to related application function libraries. UNIX programs tend to be individually small, with calls to a number of single-function utilities.

Evidence of cultural influences exists right down to the machine-code level. Those who work with assembler and machine code know that a given function can be coded in a variety of ways, and that there may be a number of algorithms to accomplish the same end. It is possible, for example, to note, for a given function, whether the programming was intended to accomplish the task in a minimum amount of memory space (tight code), a minimum number of machine cycles (high-performance code), or a minimal effort on the part of the programmer (sloppy code).

The syntax of text tends to be characteristic. Does the author always use simple sentences? Always use compound sentences? Have a specific preference when a mix of forms is used? Syntactical patterns have been used in programs that detect plagiarism in written papers. The same kind of analysis can be applied to source code for programs, finding identity between the overall structure of code even when functional units are not considered. A number of such plagiarism detection programs are available, and the methods that they use can assist with this type of forensic study. Errors in the text or program can be extremely helpful in our analysis and should be identified for further study.

When dealing with authorship analysis, it may be important to distinguish between issues of style and stylometry. Literary critics, and anyone with a writing background, may be prejudiced against technologies that ignore content and concentrate on other factors. Although techniques such as cusum analysis have been proven to work in practice, they still engender unreasoning opposition from many who fail to understand that material can contain features quite apart from the content and meaning.

It may seem strange to use meaningless features as evidence. However, Richard Forsyth reported on studies and experiments that found that short substrings of letter sequences can be effective in identifying authors. Even a relative count of the use of single letters can be characteristic of authors.

Certain message formats may provide additional information. A number of Microsoft e-mail systems include a data block with every message that is sent. To most readers, this block contains meaningless garbage. However, it may include a variety of information, such as part of the structure of the file system on the sender's machine, the sender's registered identity, programs in use, and so forth.

743

Other programs may add information that can be used. Microsoft's word processing program, Word, for example, is frequently used to create documents sent by e-mail. Word documents include information about file system structure, the author's name (and possibly company), and a global user ID. This ID was analyzed as evidence in the case of the Melissa virus. MS Word can provide even more data: comments and "deleted" sections of text may be retained in Word files and simply marked as hidden to prevent them from being displayed. Simple utility tools can recover this information from the file itself.

Mobile Code Controls

The concept of attaching programs to Web pages has very real security implications. However, through the use of appropriate technical controls, the user does not have to consider the security consequences of viewing the page. Rather, the controls determine if the user can view the page. Secured systems should limit mobile code (applets) access to system resources such as the file system, the CPU, the network, the graphics display, and the browser's internal state. Additionally, the system should garbage-collect memory to prevent both malicious and accidental memory leakage. The system must manage system calls and other methods that allow applets to affect each other as well as the environment beyond the browser.

Fundamentally, the issue of safe execution of code comes down to a concern with access to system resources. Any running program has to access system resources to perform its task. Traditionally, that access has been given to all normal user resources. Mobile code must have restricted access to resources for safety. However, it must be allowed some access to perform its required functions.

When creating a secure environment for an executable program, such as mobile code, it is important to identify the resources the program needs and then provide certain types of limited access to these resources to protect against threats. Examples of threats to resources include:

- Disclosure of information about a user or the host machine
- Denial-of-service (DoS) attacks that make a resource unavailable for legitimate purposes
- Damaging or modifying data
- Annoyance attacks, such as displaying obscene pictures on a user's screen

Some resources are clearly more dangerous to give full access to than others. For example, it is hard to imagine any security policy where an unknown program should be given full access to the file system. On the other hand, most security policies would not limit a program from almost full access to the monitor display. Thus, one of the key issues in providing for safe execution of mobile code is determining which resources a particular piece of code is allowed access. That is, there is a need for a security policy that specifies what type of access any mobile code can have. Two basic mechanisms can be used to limit the risk to the user:

- Attempt to run code in a restricted environment where it cannot do harm, such as in a sandbox.
- Cryptographic authentication can be used to attempt to show the user who is responsible for the code.

Sandbox

One of the control mechanisms for mobile code is the sandbox. The sandbox provides a protective area for program execution. Limits are placed on the amount of memory and processor resources the program can consume. If the program exceeds these limits, the Web browser terminates the process and logs an error code. This can ensure the safety of the browser's performance. A sandbox can be created on the client side to protect the resource usage from Java applets.

In the Java sandbox security model, there is an option to provide an area for the Java code to do what it needs to do, including restricting the bounds of this area. A sandbox cannot confine code and its behavior without some type of enforcement mechanism. In the Java arena, the Java security manager makes sure all restricted code stays in the sandbox. Trusted code resides outside the sandbox; untrusted code is confined within it. By default, Java applications live outside the sandbox and Java applets are confined within. The sandbox aims to ensure an untrusted application cannot gain access to system resources. Newer malware can detect sandboxes and some can break out of them.

This confined area is needed for applet security. As an example, if a user is viewing an applet showing an environmental picture show of endangered dolphins, the applet could also, unbeknownst to the user, search the hard drive for private information. A sandbox can prevent this type of intrusion by controlling the boundaries or limits of the program.

Programming Language Support

A method of providing safe execution of programs is to use a type-safe programming language (also known as strong typing), such as Java. A type-safe language or safe language is a program that will never go wrong in certain ways. These ensure that arrays stay in bounds, the pointers are always valid, and code cannot violate variable typing (such as placing code in a string and then executing it). From a security perspective, the absence of pointers is important. Memory access through pointers is one of the main causes for weaknesses (bugs) and security problems in C or C++. Java does an internal check, called static type checking, which examines whether the arguments an operand may get during execution are always of the correct type.

Configuration Management

For software, configuration management refers to monitoring and managing changes to a program or documentation. The goal is to guarantee integrity, availability, and usage of the correct version of all system components such as the software code, design documents, documentation, and control files.

Configuration management consists of reviewing every change made to a system. This includes identifying, controlling, accounting for, and auditing all changes. The first step is to identify any changes that are made. The control task occurs when every change is subject to some type of documentation that must be reviewed and approved by an authorized individual. Accounting refers to recording and reporting on the configuration of the software or hardware throughout any change procedures. Finally, the auditing task allows the completed change to be verified, especially ensuring that any changes did not affect the security policy or protection mechanisms that are implemented.

The best method of controlling changes is to have a configuration management plan that ensures that changes are performed in an agreed upon manner. Any deviations from the plan could change the configuration of the entire system and could essentially void any certification that it is a secure, trusted system. In a project, configuration management often refers to the controlling of changes to the scope or requirements of the project. Often called scope creep, a lack of configuration management can lead to a project never being completed or structured, because its requirements are continuously changing.

Information Protection Management

If software is shared, it should be protected from unauthorized modification by ensuring that policies, developmental controls, and life-cycle controls are in place. In addition, users should be trained in security policies and procedures. Software controls and policies should require procedures for changing, accepting, and testing software prior to implementation. These controls and policies require management approval for any software changes and compliance with change control procedures.

Assess the Effectiveness of Software Security

Certification and Accreditation

In the United States, federal agencies are mandated to conduct security certification of systems that process, store or transmit information on behalf of the government. Certification is the technical evaluation or assessment of security compliance of the information system within its operational environment: the endorsement by the users and managers that the system/application meets their functional requirements and in most cases the independent verification of the endorsement. The certification process is followed by accreditation or authorization. The accreditation or authorization process reviews the certification (or the assessment) information and grants the official authorization to place the information system into operational use: it is the formal approval by senior management. The U.S. National Institute of Standards and Technology (NIST) has developed a document (SP 800-37) [1] that recommends a security authorization process and procedures. Every US federal executive government system and application that goes into production must go through a process of certification and accreditation prior to implementation.

While the US government and its business associates are required to undergo a formal authorization process, there are several reasons a private organization may choose to as well:

- A certification and accreditation process ensures a control framework has been selected and is consistently being applied across the organization

- If implemented as part of a change management program the system authorization process is relatively low overhead

- Security authorization standards mandate the use of standards. Standardization across an organization can lead to gains in efficiency and lower unexpected changes.

- If implemented properly, a security authorization program

---

1   http://csrc.nist.gov/publications/nistpubs/800-37-rev1/sp800-37-rev1-final.pdf

includes all aspects of a system's security including physical, training, environment and interconnections that could be missed by purely technical approaches.

Auditing and Logging

Software is frequently delivered with vulnerabilities that are not discovered until after the software has been installed and is operational. Both UNIX and Microsoft products have numerous security weaknesses that have been discovered only after their release. However, this is not a new problem. Early operating systems also had security vulnerabilities. Because this is an ongoing problem, organizations must implement policies and procedures to limit the vulnerabilities that are inherent in the software by implementation of applicable vendor patches.

Information Integrity

Procedures should be applied to compare or reconcile what was processed against what was supposed to be processed. For example, controls can compare totals or check sequence numbers. This would check whether the right operation was performed on the right data.

Information Accuracy

To check input accuracy, data validation and verification checks should be incorporated into appropriate applications. Character checks compare input characters against the expected type of characters, such as numbers or letters. This is sometimes also known as sanity checking. Range checks verify input data against predetermined upper and lower limits. Relationship checks compare input data to data on a master record file. Reasonableness checks compare input data to an expected standard— another form of sanity checking. Transaction limits check input data against administratively set ceilings on specified transactions.

Information Auditing

Because vulnerabilities exist in the software life cycle, there is a likelihood that attacks will occur. Auditing procedures assist in detecting any abnormal activities. A secure information system must provide authorized personnel with the ability to audit any action that can potentially cause access to, damage to, or in some way affect the release of sensitive information. The level and type of auditing is dependent on the auditing requirements of the installed software and the sensitivity of data that is processed or stored on the system. The key element is that the audit data provides information on what types of unauthorized activities have taken place and who or what processes took the action.

The system resources should be protected when they are available for use. If security software or security features of software are disabled in any way, notification should be given to appropriate individuals. The ability to bypass security features must be limited to only those individuals who need that level of access, such as system administrators or information system security officers. Hardware and software should be evaluated for compatibility with existing or complementary systems.

Risk Analysis and Mitigation

As part of the Software Development Life Cycle (SDLC) an ongoing or "continuous" approach to risk assessment, analysis and mitigation is advisable. As noted prior a vast majority of vulnerabilities are either developed into the software at its inception or as a part of changing the software's configuration over time. A well-designed risk analysis and mitigation strategy will:

- Be integrated into the overall SDLC and the change management process of an organization.
- Use standardized methods of accessing risk and reporting risk to stakeholders:
  - Qualitative versus quantitative or hybrid approaches should be considered
  - Standards such as ISO, NIST, ANSI and ISACA should be considered for frameworks

- Be comprehensive in risk and focus not just on the technology but also the operational and managerial controls related to the system.

- Track and manage weaknesses discovered during assessment, change management and continuous monitoring

- Memorialize resultant risk decisions for prosperity and due diligence.

Corrective Actions

Findings must be reviewed and prioritized. Not all findings may need to be mitigated. For example, if a low risk finding has an extremely high cost or have a major impact on the operations of an organization it should be accepted. And it may seem obvious that a high risk finding with a low corrective cost should be the first to be mitigated. However, often this is not the case. Many times high risk findings may have substantial costs associated with mitigating the corrective action. In these circumstances senior management must make difficult decisions regarding either the acceptance of the risk or reprogramming funds to cover the high risk items.

The information security professional must be in a position to provide:

- The finding with supporting details as to how it was discovered.

- How the risk was determined and any supplemental information regarding threats, vulnerabilities, likelihood and impact.

- The remediation cost details and what exactly the mitigation will buy and how it will affect threats, vulnerabilities, likelihood or impacts.

- Be ready to define the impact of not remediating the weakness with scenarios, stories and examples of what could happen. Remember to include impacts in the public space and the reputation of the organization.

Testing and Verification

When mitigations are implemented they must be tested. In mature SDLC environments this is often done as part of the promotion between development environments by the quality assurance and testing teams. Security findings should be addressed by the development team the same as any other change request; with the condition that the security assessor or another independent entity verify and validate the flaw has indeed been remediated. Typically, in large organizations independent verification and validation (IV&V) teams work to determine if security findings and flaws are truly resolved. An internal audit group or information assurance team may also perform the IV&V function. Most importantly, the developer or system owner does not authoritatively declare the risk mitigated without the concurrence of an independent party.

The following articles and documents contain more information about Software Development Security. They are freely available on the Internet.

OWASP Top Ten Project
https://www.owasp.org/index.php/Category:OWASP_Top_Ten_Project

US Department of Homeland Security "Build Security In: Software Assurance Group"
https://buildsecurityin.us-cert.gov/bsi/home.html

(ISC)² Certified System Security Lifecycle Professional
https://www.isc2.org/csslpdomains/default.aspx

US National Institute of Standards and Technology Special Publication 800-64 "Security Considerations in the System Development Life Cycle"
http://csrc.nist.gov/publications/nistpubs/800-64-Rev2/SP800-64-Revision2.pdf

US National Institute of Standards and Technology Special Publication 800-37 "Guide for Applying the Risk Management Framework to Federal Information Systems: A Security Life Cycle Approach"
http://csrc.nist.gov/publications/nistpubs/800-37-rev1/sp800-37-rev1-final.pdf

CERT Top Ten Secure Coding Practices
https://www.securecoding.cert.org/confluence/display/seccode/Top+10+Secure+Coding+Practices

David A. Wheeler's "Secure Programming for Linux and Unix HOWTO"
http://www.tldp.org/HOWTO/Secure-Programs-HOWTO/index.html

Building Secure ASP.NET applications
http://msdn.microsoft.com/en-us/library/ff649100.aspx

Bizarre security vulnerability found in every x86-64 Intel processor
http://www.theverge.com/2012/6/18/3092949/security-vulnerability-x86-64-intel-processor

Summary and Conclusion

When implementing security in an application program environment, it is important to consider security throughout the entire life-cycle process, especially in the conceptual, requirements, and design phases.

In their book Building Secure Software, John Viega and Gary McGraw provide the following 10 items as a 90/10 strategy: Organizations can avoid 90% of the potential problems by following these 10 guidelines. This list is a good guide for security overall, so keep it in mind when approaching system development and acquisition.

1. Secure the weakest link
2. Practice defense in depth
3. Fail securely
4. Follow the principle of least privilege
5. Compartmentalize
6. Keep it simple
7. Promote privacy
8. Remember that hiding secrets is hard
9. Be reluctant to trust
10. Use your community resources

Review Questions

1. The key objective of application security is to ensure

    A. that the software is hacker proof

    B. the confidentiality, integrity and availability of data

    C. accountability of software and user activity

    D. prevent data theft

2. For an application security program to be effective within an organization, it is critical to

    A. identify regulatory and compliance requirements.

    B. educate the software development organization the impact of insecure programming.

    C. develop the security policy that can be enforced.

    D. properly test all the software that is developed by your organization for security vulnerabilities.

3. The best defense against session hijacking and man-in-the-middle (MITM) attacks is to use which of the following in the development of software?

    A.   Unique and random identification

    B.   Use prepared statements and procedures

    C.   Database views

    D.   Encryption

4. An important characteristic of bytecode is that it

    A. has increased secure inherently due to sandboxing

    B. manages memory operations automatically

    C. is more difficult to reverse engineer

    D. is faster than interpreted languages

4

Software Development Security

755

5. Two cooperating processes that simultaneously compete for a shared resource, in such a way that they violate the system's security policy, is commonly known as

    A. Covert channel

    B. Denial of Service

    C. Overt channel

    D. Object reuse

6. An organization has a website with a guest book feature, where visitors to the web site can input their names and comments about the organization. Each time the guest book web page loads, a message box is prompted with the message 'You have been P0wnd' followed by redirection to a different website. Analysis reveals that the no input validation or output encoding is being performed in the web application. This is the basis for which type of attack?

    A. Denial of Service

    B. Cross-site Scripting (XSS)

    C. Malicious File Execution

    D. Injection Flaws

7. The art of influencing people to divulge sensitive information about themselves or their organization by either coercion or masquerading as a valid entity is known as

    A. Dumpster diving

    B. Shoulder surfing

    C. Phishing

    D. Social engineering

8. An organization's server audit logs indicate that an employee that was terminated in the morning was still able to access certain sensitive resources on his system, on the internal network, that afternoon. The logs indicate that the employee had logged on successfully before he was terminated but there is no record of him logging off before he was terminated. This is an example of which type of attack?

A. Time of Check/Time of Use (TOC/TOU)

B. Logic Bomb

C. Remote-access trojans (RATS)

D. Phishing

9. The most effective defense against a buffer overflow attack is

A. disallowing dynamic construction of queries

B. bounds checking

C. encoding output

D. forced garbage collection

10. It is extremely important that as one follows a software development project, security activities are performed

A. before release to production, so that the project is not delayed

B. if a vulnerability is detected in your software

C. in each stage of the life cycle

D. when management mandates it

11. Audit logs are which type of control?

A. Preventive

B. Detective

C. Compensating

D. Corrective

12. Who can enforce the separation of duties by ensuring that programmers do not have access to production code?

A. Operations personnel

B. Software librarian

C. Management

D. Quality assurance personnel

13. The technical evaluation of assurance to ensure that security requirements have been met is known as?

A. Accreditation

B. Certification

    C. Validation

    D. Verification

14. Defect prevention rather than defect removal is characteristic of which of the following software development methodology?

    A. Computer Aided Software Engineering (CASE)

    B. Spiral

    C. Waterfall

    D. Cleanroom

15. A security protection mechanism in which untrusted code, which is not signed, is restricted from accessing system resources is known as?

    A. Sandboxing

    B. Non-repudiation

    C. Separation of Duties

    D. Obfuscation

16. A program that does not reproduce itself but pretends to be performing a legitimate action, while actually performing malicious operations in the background, is the characteristic of which of the following?

    A. Worms

    B. Trapdoor

    C. Virus

    D. Trojan

17. A plot to take insignificant pennies from a user's bank account and move them to the attacker's bank account is an example of

    A. Social Engineering

    B. Salami Attack

    C. Pranks

    D. Hoaxes

18. Role-based access control to protect confidentiality of data in databases can be **BEST** achieved through which of the following?

    A. Views

    B. Encryption

    C. Hashing

    D. Masking

19. The two most dangerous types of attacks against databases containing disparate non-sensitive information are

    A. Injection and scripting

    B. Session hijacking and cookie poisoning

    C. Aggregation and inference

    D. Bypassing authentication and insecure cryptography

20. A property that ensures only valid or legal transactions that do not violate any user-defined integrity constraints in DBMS technologies is known as?

    A. Atomicity

    B. Consistency

    C. Isolation

    D. Durability

21. Expert systems are comprised of a knowledge base containing modeled human experience and which of the following?

    A. Inference engine

    B. Statistical models

    C. Neural networks

    D. Roles

4

Software Development Security

Domain 5

Cryptography

CRYPTOGRAPHY IS A FASCINATING DOMAIN in the CISSP® CBK®. Few information security topics have the history, challenge, and technological advancements that cryptography enjoys. Throughout history, cryptography has been a crucial factor in military victories or failures, treason, espionage, and business advantage. Cryptography is both an art and a science—the use of deception and mathematics, to hide data, as in steganography, to render data unintelligible through the transformation of data into an unreadable state, and to ensure that a message has not been altered in transit. Another feature of some cryptographic systems is the ability to provide assurance of who sent the message, authentication of source, and proof of delivery.

TOPICS

- ■ Understand the application and use of cryptography
  - ▫ Data at rest, e.g., hard drive
  - ▫ Data in transit, e.g., "On the wire"
- ■ Understand encryption concepts
  - ▫ Foundational concepts
  - ▫ Symmetric cryptography
  - ▫ Asymmetric cryptography
  - ▫ Hybrid cryptography
  - ▫ Message digests
  - ▫ Hashing
- ■ Understand key management processes
  - ▫ Creation and distribution
  - ▫ Storage and destruction
  - ▫ Recovery
  - ▫ Key escrow
- ■ Understand digital signatures
- ■ Understand nonrepudiation
- ■ Understand methods of cryptanalytic attacks
  - ▫ Chosen plaintext
  - ▫ Social engineering for key discovery
  - ▫ Brute force
  - ▫ Ciphertext only
  - ▫ Known plaintext
  - ▫ Frequency analysis
  - ▫ Chosen ciphertext
  - ▫ Implementation attacks
- ■ Use cryptography to maintain network security
- ■ Use cryptography to maintain e-mail security
- ■ Understand public key infrastructure (PKI)
- ■ Understand certificate related issues
- ■ Understand information hiding alternatives, e.g., steganography, watermarking

OBJECTIVES

According to the (ISC)2 Candidate Information Bulletin, a CISSP candidate will be expected to know basic concepts within cryptography including:

- Public and private key algorithms in terms of their applications and uses
- Algorithm construction
- Key distribution and management
- Methods of attack
- The applications, construction, and use of digital signatures to provide authenticity of electronic transactions
- Nonrepudiation of the parties involved.

5

Cryptography

The Application and Use of Cryptography

The History of Cryptography

Cryptography has been around for many years, and yet the basic principles of cryptography have not changed. The core principle of most cryptographic systems is that they take a plaintext message and, through a series of transpositions or substitutions, convert it to ciphertext, as shown in *Figure 5.1*.

Plaintext   **Cryptograhic System**   **Ciphertext**

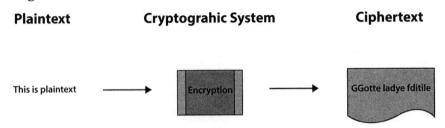

Figure 5.1 - **The Cryptographic Process**

The Early (Manual) Era

There is evidence of cryptographic-type operations going back thousands of years. In one case, there is an example in Egypt of one set of hieroglyphics that were encrypted with a simple substitution algorithm. The Spartans were known for the Spartan scytale—a method of transmitting a message by wrapping a leather belt around a tapered dowel. Written across the dowel, the message would be undecipherable once it was unwrapped from the dowel. The belt could then be carried to the recipient, who would be able to read the message as long as he had a dowel of the same diameter and taper.

There are further examples of the use and development of cryptographic methods throughout the past two centuries. Julius Caesar used the Caesar cipher—a simple substitution cipher that shifted the alphabet three positions. Developments in cryptographic science continued throughout the middle ages with the work of Leon Battista Alberti, who invented the idea of a cryptographic key in 1466, and the enhanced use of polyalphabetic ciphers by Blais de Vigenère. Their work will be examined in more detail when reviewing the methods of cryptography.

The Mechanical Era

From a paper-and-pencil world, cryptography developed into the mechanical era with the advent of cipher disks and rotors to simplify the manual processes of cryptography. Devices developed during this era were in regular use well into the twentieth century. These include the German Enigma machine, the Confederate Army's CipherDisk, and the Japanese Red and Purple machines. During this era, tools and machines were developed that greatly increased the complexity of cryptographic operations, as well as enabling the use of much more robust algorithms. Many of these devices introduced a form of randomization to the cryptographic operations and made the use of cryptographic devices available to nontechnical people.

One core concept developed in this era was the performance of the algorithm on the numerical value of a letter, rather than the letter itself. This was a natural transition into the electronic era, where cryptographic operations are normally performed on binary or hex values of letters, rather than on the written letter. For example, the alphabet could be written as follows:

$$A = 0, B = 1, C = 3 \ldots Z = 25$$

This was especially integral to the one-time pad and other cipher methods that were developed during this era.

The Modern Era

Today's cryptography is far more advanced than the cryptosystems of yesterday. Organizations are able to both encrypt and break ciphers that could not even have been imagined before human civilization had the power of computers. Today's cryptosystems operate in a manner so that anyone with a computer can use cryptography without even understanding cryptographic operations, algorithms, and advanced mathematics. However, it is still important to implement a cryptosystem in a secure manner. In fact, the majority of attacks against cryptosystems are not the result of weaknesses in cryptographic algorithms, but rather poor or mismanaged implementations. As cryptographic algorithms in use today are examined throughout this chapter, many of the advances of yesterday built into the functions of today—randomization, transposition, and cryptographic keys will be explained.

Emerging Technology

Quantum Cryptography[1]

A fundamental difference between traditional cryptography and quantum cryptography is that traditional cryptography primarily uses difficult mathematical techniques as its fundamental mechanism. Quantum cryptography, on the other hand, uses physics to secure data. Whereas traditional cryptography stands firm due to strong math, quantum cryptography has a radically different premise in that the security should be based on known physical laws rather than on mathematical difficulties.

Quantum cryptography (also known as *quantum key distribution*, or QKD) is built on quantum physics. Perhaps the most well-known aspect of quantum physics is the uncertainty principle of Werner Heisenberg. His basic claim is that a person cannot know both a particle's position and momentum with unlimited accuracy at the same time.

Specifically, quantum cryptography is a set of protocols, systems, and procedures by which it is possible to create and distribute secret keys. Quantum cryptography can be used to generate and distribute secret keys, which can then be used together with traditional crypto algorithms and protocols to encrypt and transfer data. It is important to note that quantum

---

1   Ben Rothke, An overview of quantum cryptography, in *Information Security Management Handbook*, 3rd ed., Vol. 3, Tipton, Harold F. and Krause, Micki, Eds., Auerbach Publications, New York, 2006, pp. 380–381.

cryptography is not used to encrypt data, transfer encrypted data, or store encrypted data.

The need for asymmetric key systems arose from the issue of key distribution. The challenge is that users need a secure channel to set up a secure channel. Quantum cryptography solves the key distribution problem by allowing the exchange of a cryptographic key between two remote parties with complete security, as dictated via the laws of physics. Once the key exchange takes place, conventional cryptographic algorithms are used. For that reason, many prefer the term QKD to quantum cryptography.

When used in a practical setting, the following is a basic overview of how quantum cryptography can be used:

1. Two remote parties need to exchange data electronically in a highly secure manner.

2. They choose standard crypto algorithms, protocols, systems, and transport technologies to exchange the data in an encrypted form.

3. They use a quantum cryptography channel to generate and exchange the secret keys needed by the algorithms.

4. They use the secret keys generated with quantum cryptography and the classical algorithms to encrypt the data.

5. They exchange the encrypted data using the chosen classical protocols and transfer technologies.

Within quantum cryptography, there are two unique channels. One is used for the transmission of the quantum key material via single-photon light pulses. The other channel carries all message traffic, including the cryptographic protocols, encrypted user traffic, and more. Within the laws of quantum physics, once a photon has been observed, its state is changed. This makes quantum cryptography perfect for security because any time that someone tries to eavesdrop on a secure channel, this will cause a disturbance to the flow of the photons. This can easily be identified to provide extra security.

5

Cryptography

767

Quantum algorithms are orders of magnitude better than current systems. It is theorized that quantum factorization can factor a number a million times longer than that used for RSA in a millionth of the time. In addition, it can crack a DES cipher in less than four minutes. The increased speed of a quantum computer comes from forming a superposition of numbers. Quantum computers are theoretically able to perform calculations on various superpositions simultaneously, which creates the effect of a massive parallel computation.

While still mainly theoretical, quantum computing and quantum key distribution will likely provide the next leap in encryption technology. Just as there is a massive distinction between the belts the Spartans used and the super computers of today; quantum key distribution could be a leap of the same magnitude.

Core Information Security Principles

The cryptography domain addresses the principles, means, and methods of disguising information to ensure its integrity, confidentiality, and authenticity. Unlike the other domains, cryptography does not completely support the standard of availability.

Availability

Cryptography supports all three of the core principles of information security. Many access control systems use cryptography to limit access to systems through the use of passwords. Many token-based authentication systems use cryptographic-based hash algorithms to compute one-time passwords. Denying unauthorized access prevents an attacker from entering and damaging the system or network, thereby denying access to authorized users.

Confidentiality

Cryptography provides confidentiality through altering or hiding a message so that ideally it cannot be understood by anyone except the intended recipient.

Integrity

Cryptographic tools provide integrity checks that allow a recipient to verify that a message has not been altered. Cryptographic tools cannot prevent a message from being altered, but they are effective to detect either intentional or accidental modification of the message.

Additional Features of Cryptographic Systems

In addition to the three core principles of information security listed above, cryptographic tools provide several more benefits.

Nonrepudiation

In a trusted environment, the authentication of the origin can be provided through the simple control of the keys. The receiver has a level of assurance that the message was encrypted by the sender, and the sender has trust that the message was not altered once it was received. However, in a more stringent, less trustworthy environment, it may be necessary to provide assurance via a third party of who sent a message and that the message was indeed delivered to the right recipient. This is accomplished through the use of digital signatures and public key encryption. The use of these tools provides a level of nonrepudiation of origin that can be verified by a third party.

Once a message has been received, what is to prevent the recipient from changing the message and contesting that the altered message was the one sent by the sender? The nonrepudiation of delivery prevents a recipient from changing the message and falsely claiming that the message is in its original state. This is also accomplished through the use of public key cryptography and digital signatures and is verifiable by a trusted third party.

Authentication

Authentication is the ability to determine if someone or something is what it declares to be. This is primarily done through the control of the keys,

5

Cryptography

because only those with access to the key are able to encrypt a message. This is not as strong as the nonrepudiation of origin, which will be reviewed shortly

Cryptographic functions use several methods to ensure that a message has not been changed or altered. These include hash functions, digital signatures, and message authentication codes (MACs). The main concept is that the recipient is able to detect any change that has been made to a message, whether accidentally or intentionally.

Access Control

Through the use of cryptographic tools, many forms of access control are supported—from log-ins via passwords and passphrases to the prevention of access to confidential files or messages. In all cases, access would only be possible for those individuals that had access to the correct cryptographic keys.

Data at Rest

The protection of stored data is often a key requirement for an organization's sensitive information. Backup tapes, off-site storage, password files, and many other types of sensitive information need to be protected from disclosure or undetected alteration. This is done through the use of cryptographic algorithms that limit access to the data to those that hold the proper encryption (and decryption) keys. (*Note*: Because password files are hashed instead of encrypted, there are no keys to decrypt them.) Some modern cryptographic tools also permit the condensing or compressing of messages, saving both transmission and storage space.

Data in Transit

One of the primary purposes throughout history has been to move messages across various types of media. The intent was to prevent the contents of the message from being revealed even if the message itself was intercepted in transit. Whether the message is sent manually, over a voice network, or via the Internet, modern cryptography provides secure and confidential methods to transmit data and allows the verification of the integrity of the message, so that any changes to the message itself can be detected. Advances in quantum cryptography also theorize the detection of whether a message has even been read in transit.

Link Encryption

Data are encrypted on a network using either link or end-to-end encryption. In general, link encryption is performed by service providers, such as a data communications provider on a Frame Relay network. Link encryption encrypts all of the data along a communications path (e.g., a satellite link, telephone circuit, or T-1 line). Because link encryption also encrypts routing data, communications nodes need to decrypt the data to continue routing. The data packet is decrypted and re-encrypted at each point in the communications channel. It is theoretically possible that an attacker compromising a node in the network may see the message in the clear. Because link encryption also encrypts the routing information, it provides traffic confidentiality better than end-to-end encryption. Traffic confidentiality hides the addressing information from an observer, preventing an inference attack based on the existence of traffic between two parties.

End-to-End Encryption

End-to-end encryption is generally performed by the end-user within an organization. The data are encrypted at the start of the communications channel or before and remains encrypted until it is decrypted at the remote end. Although data remain encrypted when passed through a network, routing information remains visible. It is possible to combine both types of encryption. See *Figure 5.2.*

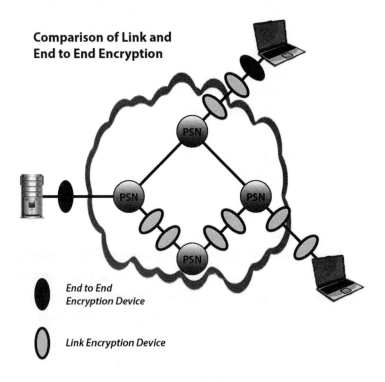

Figure 5.2 - **Comparison of Link and End-to-End encryption**

The Cryptographic Lifecycle

All cryptographic functions and implementations have a useful life. As computational power increases, and the ability to analyze cryptographic systems become more refined, cryptographic systems are constantly evaluated to ensure they still meet the security requirements originally specified. Information security professionals must stay abreast of current trends and discoveries in the cryptographic domain to ensure they provide accurate and timely assessments and recommendations. A cryptographic function or implementation is considered "broken" or no longer effective when one of the following conditions is met:

- For a hashing function:

  - Collisions or hashes can be reliably reproduced in an economically feasible fashion without the original source.

  - When an implementation of a hashing function allows a side channel attack.

- For an encryption system:

  - A cipher is decoded without access to the key in an economically feasible fashion

  - When an implementation of an encryption system allows for the unauthorized disclosure of information in an economically feasible fashion.

Cryptographic system life cycle phases are generally described in terms of strong, weakened and compromised. The United States National Institute of Standards and Technology uses the following terms to describe algorithms and key lengths in its special publication 800-131A[1]:

- "Acceptable is used to mean that the algorithm and key length is safe to use; no security risk is currently known.

---

1   http://csrc.nist.gov/publications/nistpubs/800-131A/sp800-131A.pdf

773

■ Deprecated means that the use of the algorithm and key length is allowed, but the user must accept some risk. The term is used when discussing the key lengths or algorithms that may be used to apply cryptographic protection to data (e.g., encrypting or generating a digital signature).

■ Restricted means that the use of the algorithm or key length is deprecated, and there are additional restrictions required to use the algorithm or key length for applying cryptographic protection to data (e.g., encrypting).

■ Legacy-use means that the algorithm or key length may only be used to process already protected information (e.g., to decrypt ciphertext data or to verify a signature), but there may be risk in doing so. Methods for mitigating this risk should be considered."

Algorithm/Protocol Governance

As cryptographic algorithms and protocols age they become compromised and replacements need to be put in place. This is a challenge as many organizations must determine how to migrate existing information systems and their cryptographic elements to new platforms. The information security professional must ensure governance processes are in place to support an organization's use of cryptography. The policies, standards and procedures relating to cryptography should minimally address:

■ Approved cryptographic algorithms and key sizes

■ Transition plans for weakened or compromised algorithms and keys

■ Procedures for the use of cryptographic systems in the organization and standards indicating what information and processes are subject to cryptographic requirements.

■ Key generation, escrow and destruction.

■ Incident reporting surrounding the loss of keys or the compromise of cryptographic systems.

Issues Surrounding Cryptography

The power of cryptography is increasingly misused by those with criminal intentions and is subject to export and law enforcement requirements. As part of risk analysis, it is important to understand how cryptography can be misused so that appropriate security mitigation can be applied. An example of misuse is the cryptologic time bomb. This is the case where, for example, a disgruntled employee or a rogue criminal organization installs a computer program that is designed to encrypt a company's computer files using strong encryption—using a key that only the attacker knows. The attacker will either attempt to hold the computer files until a ransom is paid or until some painful consequence occurs to the victim company.

Another issue with the potential misuse of cryptography is in the protection of intellectual property. Cryptographic protection is implemented for preventing software and media piracy. Although cryptography is used to allow or deny access to the video game market and DVDs, there are some general concerns expressed by privacy advocates about how such applications of cryptography could have macroeconomic effects if not used ethically. One scenario that could play out would be the case where a company could use encryption to create a new form of censorship based on the ability to track and identify electronic information. Such a system could be used to secretly inventory a computer anywhere on the Internet then make a catalog of software/hardware on a machine available for action by a third party, for example, barring someone with decryption software from playing a copy-protected DVD. So-called, digital rights management systems (DRMS) require a design and governance that can be used to both protect intellectual property and individual privacy while ensuring an individual's fair use of the intellectual property. Some governments impose restrictions on the use, export, or import of cryptographic hardware and software having high work factors.

International Export Controls

Most countries have some regulations regarding the use or distribution of cryptographic systems. Usually, this is to maintain the ability of law enforcement to do their jobs and to keep strong cryptographic tools out of the hands of criminals. Cryptography is considered in most countries to be on par with munitions, a weapon of war, and is managed through laws written to control the distribution of military equipment. Some countries do not allow any cryptographic tools to be used by their citizens; others have laws that control the use of cryptography, usually based on key length. This is because key length is one of the most understandable methods of gauging the strength of a cryptosystem.

International export controls are employed by governments to limit the shipment of products containing strong cryptography to countries that that government feels is trustworthy enough to use in a friendly way. For example, in the United States, the governmental agencies responsible for regulating and enforcing strong cryptography product shipment to other countries are the National Security Agency, the U.S. Department of State and the U.S. Department of Commerce.[2] In the United States, the process offers an opportunity for these agencies to determine if there is technology that should not be exported. Most countries concern over their national security related to cryptography is established as specific technologies that would be detrimental to their national defense and, therefore, need to be controlled through export regulations. As a result of export controls many vendors market two versions of their products, one that has strong encryption and another that has weaker encryption that is sold in other countries.

Law Enforcement

Privacy is a key issue in countries with a strong culture of freedom of speech and protection from unreasonable search and seizure, such as the United States. In some countries this is not an issue as the laws require all organizations and individuals to provide law enforcement with their cryptographic keys, use weak keys, or not allow private use of encryption.

---

2   http://www.bis.doc.gov/licensing/exportingbasics.htm

Electronic surveillance has become a powerful tool in the law enforcement arsenal. However, there is an increasing realization that new technology may be helping criminals more than law enforcement. However, in the European Union and several other countries, finding a way to guarantee law enforcement, the ability to legally access encrypted information without damaging the commercial viability of commercial cryptography, or the civil liberties of citizens is an enormous technological and legislative challenge.

In many countries, there is a general public acceptance of the use of telephone and mail interception with a warrant with the goal of protecting society. However, there is a general aversion of similar warranted access to encrypted communications. Additionally, security technology vendors do not like the idea of having to "build in" key recovery backdoors into their products for law enforcement. This is seen as both expensive and unpopular with customers.

Encryption is becoming more a generic technology, Integrated into an ever increasing number of applications and products. Voice and data are increasingly converging onto a single, Internet Protocol (IP) based transport network. Technology has reached the point where voice/data can be transmitted via Internet telephony, encrypted mobile phones, or stored on computers using disk encryption. The wide use of encryption technology can be seen in many news reports about terrorist attacks and serious domestic crimes includes findings that these technologies have been employed in perpetrating crime. The main technologic methods for lawful access to private data are key escrow, where a third party, possibly a government entity or service provider, holds a copy of the cryptographic keys, and brute force, where massive computer resources attack the key.

5

Cryptography

777

Encryption Concepts

Before exploring encryption and cryptographic further it is important the security professional understands several cryptographic key concepts and definitions. These terms should be thoroughly understood by the information security professional and are used frequently in the operational environment of most organizations' security function.

Key Concepts and Definitions

- *Key Clustering:* When different encryption keys generate the same ciphertext from the same plaintext message.

- *Synchronous:* Each encryption or decryption request is performed immediately.

- *Asynchronous:* Encrypt/ Decrypt requests are processed in queues. A key benefit of asynchronous cryptography is utilization of hardware devices and multiprocessor systems for cryptographic acceleration.

- A *Hash* function is a one-way mathematical operation that reduces a message or data file into a smaller fixed length output, or hash value. By comparing the hash value computed by the sender with the hash value computed by the receiver over the original file, unauthorized changes to the file can be detected, assuming they both used the same hash function. There should never be more than one unique hash for a given input and one hash exclusively for a given input.

- *Digital Signatures* provide authentication of a sender and integrity of a sender's message. A message is input into a hash function. Then the hash value is encrypted using the private key of the sender. The result of these two steps yields a digital signature. The receiver can verify the digital signature by decrypting the hash value using the signer's public key, then perform the same hash computation over the message, and then compare the hash values for an exact match. If the hash values are the same then the signature is valid.

■ *Asymmetric* is a term used in cryptography in which two different but mathematically related keys are used where one key is used to encrypt and another is used to decrypt. This term is most commonly used in reference to Public Key Infrastructure (PKI.)

■ A *Digital Certificate* is an electronic document that contains the name of an organization or individual, the business address, the digital signature of the certificate authority issuing the certificate, the certificate holder's public key, a serial number, and the expiration date. The certificate is used to identify the certificate holder when conducting electronic transactions.

■ *Certificate Authority (CA)* is an entity trusted by one or more users as an authority in a network that issues, revokes, and manages digital certificates.

■ *Registration Authority (RA)* performs certificate registration services on behalf of a CA. The RA, a single purpose server, is responsible for the accuracy of the information contained in a certificate request. The RA is also expected to perform user validation before issuing a certificate request.

■ *Plaintext* or *Cleartext* is the message in its natural format. Plaintext is readable to anyone and is extremely vulnerable from a confidentiality perspective.

■ *Ciphertext* or *Cryptogram* is the altered form of a plaintext message, so as to be unreadable for anyone except the intended recipients. An attacker seeing ciphertext would be unable to easily read the message or to determine its content.

■ The *Cryptosystem* represents the entire cryptographic operation. This includes the algorithm, the key, and key management functions.

■ *Encryption* is the process of converting the message from its plaintext to ciphertext. It is also referred to as *enciphering*. The two terms are used interchangeably in the literature and have similar meanings.

5

Cryptography

779

- **Decryption** is the reverse process from encryption. It is the process of converting a ciphertext message into plaintext through the use of the cryptographic algorithm and key that was used to do the original encryption. This term is also used interchangeably with the term *decipher*.

- The **Key** or **Cryptovariable** is the input that controls the operation of the cryptographic algorithm. It determines the behavior of the algorithm and permits the reliable encryption and decryption of the message. There are both secret and public keys used in cryptographic algorithms.

- **Nonrepudiation** is a security service by which evidence is maintained so that the sender and the recipient of data cannot deny having participated in the communication. Individually, it is referred to as the "nonrepudiation of origin" and "nonrepudiation of receipt."

- An **Algorithm** is a mathematical function that is used in the encryption and decryption processes. It may be quite simple or extremely complex.

- **Cryptanalysis** is the study of techniques for attempting to defeat cryptographic techniques and, more generally, information security services.

- **Cryptology** is the science that deals with hidden, disguised, or encrypted communications. It embraces communications security and communications intelligence.

- **Collision** occurs when a hash function generates the same output for different inputs.

- **Key Space** represents the total number of possible values of keys in a cryptographic algorithm or other security measure, such as a password. For example, a 20-bit key would have a key space of 1,048,576.

- **Work Factor** represents the time and effort required to break a protective measure.

- An *Initialization Vector (IV)* is a nonsecret binary vector used as the initializing input algorithm for the encryption of a plaintext block sequence to increase security by introducing additional cryptographic variance and to synchronize cryptographic equipment.

- *Encoding* is the action of changing a message into another format through the use of a code. This is often done by taking a plaintext message and converting it into a format that can be transmitted via radio or some other medium, and is usually used for message integrity instead of secrecy. An example would be to convert a message to Morse code.

- *Decoding* is the reverse process from encoding—converting the encoded message back into its plaintext format.

- *Transposition* or *Permutation* is the process of reordering the plaintext to hide the message. Transposition may look like this:

Plaintext	Transposition Algorithm	Ciphertext
HIDE	REORDER SEQUENCE 2143	IHED

- *Substitution* is the process of exchanging one letter or byte for another. This operation may look like this:

Plaintext	Substitution Process	Ciphertext
HIDE	Shift alphabet three places	KLGH

- The *SP-network* is the process described by Claude Shannon1 used in most block ciphers to increase their strength. SP stands for substitution and permutation (transposition), and most block ciphers do a series of repeated substitutions and

---

1   "A Mathematical Theory of Communication" is the influential 1948 article by mathematician Claude E. Shannon. It was renamed "The Mathematical Theory of Communication" in the book, printed in 1949, written with Warren Weaver (ISBN 0-252-72546-8). The book was released as a paperback in 1963 (ISBN 0-252-72548-4).

5

Cryptography

permutations to add confusion and diffusion to the encryption process. An SP-network uses a series of S-boxes to handle the substitutions of the blocks of data. Breaking a plaintext block into a subset of smaller S-boxes makes it easier to handle the computations.

■ ***Confusion*** is provided by mixing (changing) the key values used during the repeated rounds of encryption. When the key is modified for each round, it provides added complexity that the attacker would encounter.

■ ***Diffusion*** is provided by mixing up the location of the plaintext throughout the ciphertext. Through transposition, the location of the first character of the plaintext may change several times during the encryption process, and this makes the cryptanalysis process much more difficult.

■ The ***Avalanche Efect*** is an important consideration in all cryptography used to design algorithms where a minor change in either the key or the plaintext will have a significant change in the resulting ciphertext. This is also a feature of a strong-hashing algorithm.

Foundational Concepts

The information security professional must also be familiar with fundamental concepts and methods related to cryptography. Methods and concepts range from different ways of using cryptographic technologies to encrypt information to different standard encryption systems used in industry.

High Work Factor

The average amount of effort or work required to break an encryption system, that is to say, decrypt a message without having the entire encryption key or to find a secret key given all or part of a ciphertext, is referred to as the work factor of the cryptographic system. This is measured in some units such as hours of computing time on one or more given computer systems or a cost in dollars of breaking the encryption. If the work factor is sufficiently high, the encryption system is considered to be practically or economically unbreakable, and is sometimes referred to as "economically infeasible" to break. Communication systems using encryption schemes which are economically infeasible to break are generally considered secure. The work factor required to break a given cryptographic system can vary over time due to advancements in technology, such as improvements in the speed and capacity of computers. For example, while a 40-bit secret key encryption scheme can currently be broken by a fast personal computer in less than a few weeks or by a room full of personal computers in a matter of seconds, future advances in computer technology will likely substantially reduce this work factor.

Methods of Cryptography

Several common methods of cryptography exist including stream-based and block ciphers. The information security professional must have a basic understanding of both to ensure further understanding of encryption implementations.

Stream-Based Ciphers

There are two primary methods of encrypting data: the stream and block methods. When a cryptosystem performs its encryption on a bit-by-bit basis, it is called a stream-based cipher.

This is the method most commonly associated with streaming applications, such as voice or video transmission. Wired Equivalent Privacy (WEP), uses a streaming cipher, RC4, but is not considered secure due to a number of weaknesses that expose the encryption key to an attacker, weak key size and other vulnerabilities in WEP implementation. Newer wireless cryptography implements block ciphers such as Advanced Encryption Standard (AES), which provides stronger security. The cryptographic operation for a stream-based cipher is to mix the plaintext with a keystream that is generated by the cryptosystem. The mixing operation is usually an exclusive-or (XOR) operation—a very fast mathematical operation.

5

Cryptography

As seen in *Figure 5.3*, the plaintext is XORed with a seemingly random keystream to generate ciphertext. It is seemingly random because the generation of the keystream is usually controlled by the key. If the key could not produce the same keystream for the purposes of decryption of the ciphertext, then it would be impossible to ever decrypt the message.

Plaintext	Encryption Keystream	Ciphertext
A	xor randomly generated keystream	$
0101 0001	0111 0011	= 0010 0010

Figure 5.3 - **Cryptographic operation for a Stream-Based cipher.**

The exclusive-or process is a key part of many cryptographic algorithms. It is a simple binary operation that adds two values together. If the two values are the same, $0 + 0$ or $1 + 1$, then the output is always a 0; however, if the two values are different, $1 + 0$ or $0 + 1$, then the output is a 1.

From the example above, the following operation is the result:

Input plaintext	0101 0001
Keystream	0111 0011
Output of XOR	0010 0010

A stream-based cipher relies primarily on substitution—the substitution of one character or bit for another in a manner governed by the cryptosystem and controlled by the cipher key. For a stream-based cipher to operate securely, it is necessary to follow certain rules for the operation and implementation of the cipher:

1. The keystream should not be linearly related to the cryptovariable—Knowledge of the keystream output value

does not disclose the cryptovariable (encryption/decryption key).

2. Statistically unpredictable—given n successive bits from the keystream it is not possible to predict the n + 1st bit with a probability different from 1/2.

3. Statistically unbiased—there should be as many 0's as 1's, as many 00s as 01s, 10s, 11s, etc.

4. Long periods without repetition.

5. Functional complexity—each keystream bit should depend on most or all of the cryptovariable bits.

The keystream must be strong enough to not be easily guessed or predictable. In time, the keystream will repeat, and that period (or length of the repeating segment of the keystream) must be long enough to be difficult to calculate. If a keystream is too short, then it is susceptible to frequency analysis or other language-specific attacks. The implementation of the stream-based cipher is probably the most important factor in the strength of the cipher—this applies to nearly every crypto product and, in fact, to security overall. Some important factors in the implementation are to ensure that the key management processes are secure and cannot be readily compromised or intercepted by an attacker.

Block Ciphers

A block cipher operates on blocks or chunks of text. As plaintext is fed into the cryptosystem, it is divided into blocks of a preset size—often a multiple of the ASCII character size—64, 128, 192 bits, etc. Most block ciphers use a combination of substitution and transposition to perform their operations. This makes a block cipher relatively stronger than most stream-based ciphers, but more computationally intensive and usually more expensive to implement. This is also why many stream-based ciphers are implemented in hardware, whereas a block-based cipher is implemented in software.

Initialization Vectors (IV)—Why Needed

Because messages may be of any length, and because encrypting the same plaintext using the same key always produces the same ciphertext as described below, several "modes of operation" have been invented, which allow block ciphers to provide confidentiality for messages of arbitrary length (See *Table 5.1* for block cipher mode descriptions). The use of various modes answers the need for unpredictability into the keystream such that even if the same key is used to encrypt the same message the ciphertext will still be different each time.

Mode	How It Works	Usage
Electronic Code Book (ECB)	In ECB mode, each block is encrypted independently, allowing randomly accessed files to be encrypted and still accessed without having to process the file in a linear encryption fashion.	Very short messages (less than 64 bits in length), such as transmission of a DES key.
Cipher Block Chaining (CBC)	In CBC mode, the result of encrypting one block of data is fed back into the process to encrypt the next block of data.	Authentication
Cipher Feedback (CFB)	In CFB mode, each bit produced in the keystream is the result of a predetermined number of fixed ciphertext bits.	Authentication
Output Feedback (OFB)	In OFB mode, the keystream is generated independently of the message	Authentication
Counter (CTR)	In CTR mode, a counter—a 64-bit random data block—is used as the first initialization vector.	Used in high-speed applications such as IPSec and Asynchronous Transfer Mode (ATM)

Source: Tiller, J.S., Message authentication, in *Information Security Management Handbook*, 5th ed., Tipton, H.F. and Krause, M., Eds., Auerbach Publications, New York, 2004. With permission.

Table 5.1 - **Basic Block Cipher Modes**

To illustrate why an IV is needed when using block ciphers consider how they are used in various modes of operation using block ciphers. The simplest mode is the Electronic Code Book (ECB) mode where the plaintext is divided into blocks and each block is encrypted separately. However, in the Cipher-Block Chaining (CBC) mode, each block of plaintext is XORed with the previous ciphertext block before being encrypted. In the ECB mode, the same plaintext will encrypt to same ciphertext for the same key. This reveals patterns in the code.

In the CBC mode, each block is XORed with the result of the encryption of the previous block. This hides patterns. However, two similar plaintexts that have been encrypted using the same key will yield the same ciphertext up to the block containing the first difference. This problem can be avoided by adding an IV block, which starts the keystream randomization process for the first real block, to the plaintext. This will make each ciphertext unique, even when similar plaintext is encrypted with the same key in the CBC mode. There is no need for the IV to be secret, in most cases, but it is important that it is never reused with the same key. Reusing an IV leaks some information about the first block of plaintext, and about any common prefix shared by the two messages. Therefore, the IV must be randomly generated at encryption time.

Key Length

Key length is another important aspect of key management to consider when generating cryptographic keys. Key length is the size of a key, usually measured in bits or bytes, which a cryptographic algorithm used in ciphering or deciphering protected information. As discussed earlier, keys are used to control how an algorithm operates so that only the correct key can decipher the information. The resistance to successful attack against the key and the algorithm, aspects of their cryptographic security, is of concern when choosing key lengths. An algorithm's key length is distinct from its cryptographic security. Cryptographic security is a logarithmic measure of the fastest known computational attack on the algorithm, also measured in bits. The security of an algorithm cannot exceed its key length. Therefore, it is possible to have a very long key and yet it provides low security. As an example, three-key (56 bits per key) Triple DES (i.e., Triple Data Encryption Algorithm aka TDEA) can have a key length of 168 bits but, due to the meet-in-the-middle attack (discussed later), the effective security that it provides is at most 112 bits. However, most symmetric algorithms are designed to have security equal to their key length. A natural inclination is to use the longest key possible, which may make the key more difficult to break. However, the longer the key, the more computationally expensive the encrypting and decrypting process can be. The goal is to make breaking the key cost more (in terms of effort, time, and resources) than the worth of the information or mission being protected and, if possible, not a penny more (to do more would not be economically sound).

Block Size

The block size of a block cipher, like key length, has a direct bearing on the security of the key. Block ciphers produce a fixed length block of ciphertext. However, since the data being encrypted are arbitrary number of bytes, the ciphertext block size, may not come out to be a full block. This is solved by padding the plaintext up to the block size before encryption and unpadding after decryption. The padding algorithm is to calculate the smallest nonzero number of bytes, say N, which must be suffixed to the plaintext to bring it up to a multiple of the block size.

Encryption Systems

Various systems exist to encrypt and decrypt information. Many share common characteristics such as the ability to use a null cipher and substitution cipher. Many of these characteristics were implemented to enhance use cases and interoperability.

Null Cipher

A null cipher option may be used in cases where the use of encryption is not necessary but yet the fact that no encryption is needed must be configured in order for the system to work. In such cryptographic systems, various encryption options are configurable including the option to not use encryption. A Null cipher is used when testing/debugging, low security is needed, or when using authentication-only communications. For example, certain implementations of cryptographic schemes such as IPSec and SSL may offer the choice to authenticate only and not encrypt.

The term null cipher is also a reference to an ancient form of ciphering where the plaintext is mixed together with ***non-cipher*** material. Today it is regarded as a type of steganography, discussed later, which can be used to hide ciphertext. A simple example is

> "Interesting Home Addition to Expand behind Eastern Dairy Transport Intersection Meanwhile Everything."

If the first letter of each word is used, the message decodes into the secret message

> "I Hate Bed Time."

Null ciphers can of course be used in more complex systems but are mainly used today as a cipher "place holder" in configurations that offer this option when encryption is not needed. This historical definition of null cipher is also a form of what is known as "concealment cipher." Concealment ciphers include the plaintext within the ciphertext. The recipient must know which letters or symbols to exclude from the ciphertext in order to yield the plaintext. Another example of concealment cipher "technology" is invisible ink where a message is concealed and can only be disclosed by a special light or solution. The security of the message is completely tied to the secrecy of concealment method. Concealment ciphers, while fun to play with and analyze, are not used for any serious ciphering today.

Substitution Ciphers

The substitution cipher is something most have used. It involves the simple process of substituting one letter for another based upon a cryptovariable.

789

Substitution involves shifting positions in the alphabet of a defined number of characters. Many old ciphers were based on substitution, including the Caesar cipher and ROT-13.[2]

Playfair Cipher

The Playfair cipher was used well into the twentieth century and was a key element of the cryptographic systems used by the Allies in the Second World War. The sender and the receiver agreed on a key word, for example, *Triumph*. A table was then constructed using that word and then the rest of the alphabet—skipping over the letters already appearing in the key, and using I and J as the same letter. For the sake of clarity, the key word is highlighted in the table so that it can be easily found.

If the sender wanted to encrypt the message "Do not accept offer," it would be encrypted by first grouping the plaintext in two letter blocks and spacing the repeated letters in the plaintext with a filler letter, e.g., X.

T	R	I/J	U	M
P	H	A	B	C
D	E	F	G	K
L	N	O	Q	S
V	W	X	Y	Z

The plaintext would then be:

DO NO TA CX CX EP TO FX FX ER

---

2   Chris Hare, Cryptography 101, Data Security Management, 2002.

The table is read by looking at where the two letters of the block intersect. For example, if the first block, DO, was made into a rectangle, the letters at the other two corners of the rectangle would be FL, that is, the ciphertext for the block DO. The box created by the letters DO is in a border for clarity. The next plaintext block is NO, and because both of those letters are on the same row, and the ciphertext of the next letters—in this case, NO would be encrypted as OQ. If the input block had been OS, then the row would wrap and the output ciphertext would be QL, using the next letter after the O, and the next letter after the S being the L from the beginning of the row.

The letters FX fall in the same column, and for letters that fall in the same row the same applies—use the next lower letter and wrap to the top of the column if necessary. The block FX would be encrypted as either OI or OJ.

Transposition Ciphers

All of the above cryptosystems are based on the principle of substitution, that is, to substitute or exchange one value or letter for another. Cryptosystems that use transposition or permutation are instrumental for the information security professional to understand. These systems rely on concealing the message through the transposing of or interchanging the order of the letters.

The Rail Fence

In the simple transposition cipher known as the rail fence, the message is written and read in two or more lines. To send the message "Purchase gold and oil stocks," the message would be written in alternating diagonal rows as shown:

P	R	H	S	G	L	A	D	I	S	O	K	
	U	C	A	E	O	D	N	O	L	T	C	S

The ciphertext would read as follows:

PRHSGLADIGOKUCAEODNOLTCS

The problem with such a system is that because the letters are the same as the plaintext, no substitution has taken place, just a reordering of the letters; the ciphertext is still susceptible to frequency analysis and other cryptographic attacks.

Rectangular Substitution Tables

The use of rectangular substitution tables was an early form of cryptography. The sender and receiver decided on the size and structure of a table to hold the message, and then the order in which to read the message.

Using the same plaintext as the previous example ("Purchase gold and oil stocks"), and placing it in a rectangular substitution block results in the following.

P	U	R	C	H
A	S	E	G	O
L	D	A	N	D
O	I	L	S	T
O	C	K	S	

Reading the table in a top-down manner would produce the following ciphertext:

PALOOUSDICREALKCGNSSHODT

Of course, the sender and receiver could agree on reading the table any way—bottom up, diagonally—that suited them.

Monoalphabetic and Polyalphabetic Ciphers

The Caesar cipher is a simple substitution algorithm that merely shifted the plaintext over three places to create the ciphertext. This was a monoalphabetic system—the substitution was one alphabet letter for another. In the case of the Caesar cipher, the replacement alphabet was offset by three places:

A	B	C	D	E	F	G	H	I	J	K	...	Z
D	E	F	G	H	I	J	K	L	M	N	...	C

There is also the scrambled alphabet. In this case, the substitution alphabet is a scrambled version of the alphabet. It could look like this, for example:

A	B	C	D	E	F	G	H	I	J	K	...	Z
M	G	P	U	W	I	R	L	O	V	D	...	K

Using the scrambled alphabet above, the plaintext of BAKE would be substituted as GMDW. The problem with monoalphabetic ciphers, however, is that they are still subject to the characteristics of the plaintext language—an E, for example, would be substituted as a W throughout the ciphertext. That would mean the letter W in the ciphertext would appear as frequently as an E in plaintext. That makes a cryptanalytic attack of a monoalphabetic system fairly simple.

The use of several alphabets for substituting the plaintext is called polyalphabetic ciphers. It is designed to make the breaking of a cipher by frequency analysis more difficult. Instead of substituting one alphabet for another, the ciphertext is generated from several possible substitution alphabets. For Example:

Plaintext	A	B	C	D	E	F	G	H	I	J	K	...	Z
Substitution 1	M	G	P	U	W	I	R	L	O	V	D	...	K
Substitution 2	V	K	P	O	I	U	Y	T	J	H	S	...	A
Substitution 3	L	P	O	I	J	M	K	H	G	T	U	...	F
Substitution 4	N	B	V	C	X	Z	A	S	D	E	Y	...	W

Using this table, substitute the plaintext FEED as IIJC, using the substitution alphabets in sequence. The power of using multiple alphabets in this example is evident, as the repeated E in the plaintext is substituted for different results in the ciphertext. The ciphertext has a repeated I, and yet that is for different plaintext values.

Blais de Vigenère

Blais de Vigenère, a Frenchman, developed the polyalphabetic cipher using a key word and 26 alphabets, each one offset by one place. This is shown in the following table. The top row of the table would be the plaintext values and the first column of the table the substitution alphabets.

	A	B	C	D	E	F	G	H	I	J	K	L	...	Z
A	A	B	C	D	E	F	G	H	I	J	K	L	...	Z
B	B	C	D	E	F	G	H	I	J	K	L	M	...	A
C	C	D	E	F	G	H	I	J	K	L	M	N	...	B
D	D	E	F	G	H	I	J	K	L	M	N	O	...	C
E	E	F	G	H	I	J	K	L	M	N	O	P	...	D
F	F	G	H	I	J	K	L	M	N	O	P	Q	...	E
G	G	H	I	J	K	L	M	N	O	P	Q	R	...	F
H	H	I	J	K	L	M	N	O	P	Q	R	S	...	G
I	I	J	K	L	M	N	O	P	Q	R	S	T	...	H
J	J	K	L	M	N	O	P	Q	R	S	T	U	...	I
K	K	L	M	N	O	P	Q	R	S	T	U	V	...	J
L	L	M	N	O	P	Q	R	S	T	U	V	W	...	K
...	...	...	...	...	...	...	...	...	...	...	...	...	...	...
Z	Z	A	B	C	D	E	F	G	H	I	J	K	...	Y

The sender and the receiver of the message would agree on a key to use for the message—in this case one could use the word FICKLE, as the key. Just as in the running cipher shown below, one would repeat the key for the length of the plaintext.

To encrypt the message "HIKE BACK," it would be constructed as follows:

Plaintext	H	I	K	E	B	A	C	K
Key	F	I	C	K	L	E	F	I
Ciphertext	M	Q	M	O	M	E	H	S

The ciphertext is found by finding where the H of the plaintext—the top row of the table—intersects with the F row of the ciphertext. Again, one sees the power of a polyalphabetic system where repeated values in the plaintext do not necessarily give the same ciphertext values, and repeated ciphertext values correspond to different plaintext inputs.

Modular Mathematics and the Running Key Cipher

The use of modular mathematics and the representation of each letter by its numerical place in the alphabet are the key to many modern ciphers:

A	B	C	D	E	F	G	H	I	J	K	L	M	N	O	P	Q	...	Z
0	1	2	3	4	5	6	7	8	9	10	11	12	13	14	15	16	...	25

The English alphabet would be calculated as "mod 26" because there are 26 letters in the English alphabet. The use of mod 26 means that whenever the result of a mathematical operation is equal to or greater than 26, 26 is subtracted from the total as often as needed until it is less than 26.

Using the above values, the cryptographic operation operates as follows:

Ciphertext = plaintext + key (mod 26).

This is written as $C = P + K$ (mod 26). Ciphertext is the value of the plaintext + the value of the key (mod 26).

For example, the plaintext letter N has a value of 13 (it is the 13th letter in the alphabet using the table above). If the key to be used to encrypt the plaintext is a Q with a value of 16, the ciphertext would be 13 + 16, or the 29th letter of the alphabet. Because there is no 29th letter in the English alphabet, 26 is subtracted (hence the term *mod 26*) and the ciphertext becomes the letter corresponding to the number 3, a D.

Running Key Cipher

In the example below the use of a running key cipher is demonstrated. In a running key cipher the key is repeated (or runs) for the same length as the plaintext input. The key of FEED is selected to encrypt the plaintext CHEEK. The key is repeated as long as necessary to match the length of the plaintext input. To demonstrate the encryption of the word CHEEK, the table above and the key of FEED are used. The numbers under the letters represent the value or position of that letter in the alphabet.

Plaintext:					
CHEEK	C	H	E	E	K
	2	7	4	4	10
Key:					
FEED	F	E	E	D	F
	5	4	4	3	5

The key is repeated for the length of the plaintext.

The ciphertext is computed as follows:

Plaintext Key	C	H	E	E	K
	F	E	E	D	F
Value of Plaintext	2	7	4	4	10
Value of Key	5	4	4	3	5
Ciphertext Value	7	11	8	7	15
Ciphertext	H	L	I	H	P

One-Time Pads

The only cipher system asserted as unbreakable, that is, as long as it is implemented properly is the one-time pad. These are often referred to as Vernam ciphers after the work of Gilbert Vernam, who proposed the use of a key that could only be used once and that must be as long as the plaintext but never repeats.

The one-time pad uses the principles of the running key cipher, using the numerical values of the letters and adding those to the value of the key; however, the key is a string of random values the same length as the plaintext. It never repeats, compared to the running key that may repeat several times. This means that a one-time pad is not breakable by frequency analysis or many other cryptographic attacks.

The sender and the receiver must first exchange the key material. This is often done using cryptographic pads and sending them to both the sender and the receiver through a secure exchange mechanism, such as a diplomatic pouch or trusted courier.

A developed keystream for the one-time pad that looks like this:

ksosdfsherfn avaishdas vdsfvksdklvsidfva sckapocs

It is just a randomly chosen set of values—maybe generated through monitoring some seemingly random occurrence, such as atmospheric noise or the readings on a Geiger counter. In this case, a series of alphabetic values was chosen, but mathematical values could have been chosen and then added to the plaintext using mod 26.

The values of each letter are known from the prior example.

A	B	C	D	E	F	G	H	I	J	K	L	M	N	O	P	Q	...	Z
0	1	2	3	4	5	6	7	8	9	10	11	12	13	14	15	16	...	25

To send the message "Do not negotiate less than 5%." format the encryption as follows:

Plaintext Key	D	O	N	O	T	N	E	G
	K	S	O	S	D	F	S	H
Value of Plaintext	3	14	13	14	19	13	4	6
Value of Key	10	18	14	18	3	5	18	7
Ciphertext Value	13	32[1]	27[2]	6	22	18	22	13
Ciphertext	N	G	B	G	W	S	W	N

1 – (mod 26)=6
2 – (mod 26)=1

1. The first row represents the first eight characters of plaintext or "DONOTNEG." For the sake of brevity, only the first eight characters are shown in the example.

2. The second row of bolded letters represents the "key" or the developed keystream for the one time cypher pad "ksosdfsherfn avaishdas vdsfvksdklvsidfva sckapocs"

5

Cryptography

3. Plaintext values and key values are assigned.

4. Ciphertext values are assigned based on addition and Mod 26 as required.

5. The resultant cipher text is then determined using the result from step four.

Message Integrity Controls

An important part of electronic commerce and computerized transactions today is the assurance that a message has not been modified, is indeed from the person that the sender claims to be, and that the message was received by the correct party. This is accomplished through cryptographic functions that perform in several manners, depending on the business needs and level of trust between the parties and systems.

Traditional cryptography, such as symmetric algorithms, does produce a level of message authentication. If two parties share a symmetric key, and they have been careful not to disclose that key to anyone else, then when they transmit a message from one to another, they have assurance that the message is indeed from their trusted partner. In many cases, they would also have some degree of confidence in the integrity of the message, because any errors or modifications of the message in transit would render the message undecipherable. With chaining-type algorithms, any error is likely to destroy the remainder of the message.

Asymmetric algorithms also provide message authentication. Some, such as RSA, El Gamal, and ECC, have message authentication and digital signature functionality built into the implementation. These work with open messages and secure and signed messages using asymmetric key cryptography.

Symmetric Cryptography

To this point, some of the history of cryptography and some of the methods of cryptography has been covered, the following describes how cryptographic principles are actually used today in real implementations. There are two primary forms of cryptography in use today, *symmetric* and *asymmetric* cryptographies. Symmetric algorithms operate with a single cryptographic key that is used for both encryption and decryption of the message. For this reason, it is often called single, same, or shared key encryption. It can also be called secret or private key encryption because the main factor in secure use of a symmetric algorithm is to keep the cryptographic key secret.

Some of the most difficult challenges of symmetric key ciphers are the problems of key management. Because the encryption and decryption processes both require the same key, the secure distribution of the key to both the sender (or encryptor) of the message and the receiver (or decryptor) is a key factor in the secure implementation of a symmetric key system. The cryptographic key cannot be sent in the same channel (or transmission medium) as the data, so out-of-band distribution must be considered. Out of band means using a different channel to transmit the keys, such as courier, fax, phone, or some other methods (*Figure 5.4*).

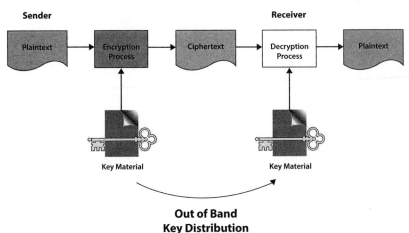

**Out of Band
Key Distribution**

Figure 5.4 - **Out-of-Band key distribution**

801

The advantages of symmetric key algorithms are that they are usually very fast, secure, and cheap.

The disadvantages include the problems of key management, as mentioned earlier, but also the limitation that a symmetric algorithm does not provide many benefits beyond confidentiality, unlike most asymmetric algorithms, which also provide the ability to establish nonrepudiation, message integrity, and access control. Symmetric algorithms can provide a form of message integrity—message will not decrypt if changed. Symmetric algorithms also can provide a measure of access control—without the key, the file cannot be decrypted.

This limitation is best described by using a physical security example. If 10 people have a copy of the key to the server room, it can be difficult to know who entered that room at 10 P.M. yesterday. There is limited access control in that only those people with a key are able to enter; however, it is unknown which one of those ten actually entered. The same with a symmetric algorithm; if the key to a secret file is shared between two or more people, then there is no way of knowing who was the last person to access the encrypted file. It would also be possible for a person to change the file and allege that it was changed by someone else. This would be most critical when the cryptosystem is used for important documents such as electronic contracts. If a person receiving a file can change the document and allege true copy had been received, repudiation problems arise.

Examples of Symmetric Algorithms

Algorithms such as the Caesar cipher, the Spartan Scytale, and the Enigma machine were all symmetric algorithms. The receiver needed to use the same key to perform the decryption process as he had used during the encryption process. The following covers many of the modern symmetric algorithms.

The Data Encryption Standard (DES)

The Data Encryption Standard was based on the work of Harst Feistal. Harst Feistal had developed a family of algorithms that had a core principle of taking the input block of plaintext and dividing it in half. Then each half was used several times through an exclusive-or operation to alter the other half—providing a type of permutation as well as substitution.

DES became the US standard in 1977 when it was adopted by several agencies of the U.S. federal government for deployment across all U.S. government departments for nonclassified but sensitive information. DES is used extensively even today in many financial, virtual private network (VPN), and online encryption systems. DES has been replaced as the standard by the AES, which is based on the Rijndael algorithm. The origin of DES was the Lucifer algorithm developed by Feistal; however, Lucifer had a 128-bit key. The algorithm was modified to make it more resistant to cryptanalysis, and the key length was reduced to 56 bits so that it could be fit onto a single chip. DES operates on 64-bit input blocks and outputs ciphertext into 64-bit blocks. There are 16 identical stages of processing, termed *rounds*. Before the main rounds, the block is divided into two 32-bit halves (because it is a Feistal cipher) and processed alternately using a 56-bit key.

When looking at a DES key, it is 64 bits in length; however, every eighth bit (used for parity) is ignored. Therefore, the effective length of the DES key is 56 bits. Because every bit has a possible value of either 1 or 0, it can be stated that the effective key space for the DES key is 2^{56}. This gives a total number of keys for DES to be 7.2×10^{16}. However, the modes of operation discussed next are used by a variety of other block ciphers, not just in DES. Originally there were four modes of DES accepted for use by the U.S. federal government (NIST); in later years, the CTR mode was also accepted (Table 5.1).

Basic Block Cipher Modes
The following basic block cipher modes operate in a block structure. (See http://csrc.nist.gov/groups/ST/toolkit/BCM/current_modes.html for a current list of block cipher modes approved by the U.S. government.)

- **Electronic Codebook Mode** - The ECB is the most basic block cipher mode (*Figure 5.5*). It is called codebook because it is similar to having a large codebook containing every piece of 64-bit plaintext input and all possible 64-bit ciphertext outputs. In a manual sense, it would be the same as looking up the input in a book and finding what the output would be depending on which key was used. When a plaintext input is received by ECB, it operates on that block independently and produces the ciphertext output. If the input was more than 64 bits long and each 64-bit block was the same, then the output blocks would also be the same. Such regularity would make cryptanalysis simple. For that reason, as seen in *Table 5.1*, ECB is only used for very short messages (less than 64 bits in length), such as transmission of a key. As with all Feistal ciphers, the decryption process is the reverse of the encryption process.

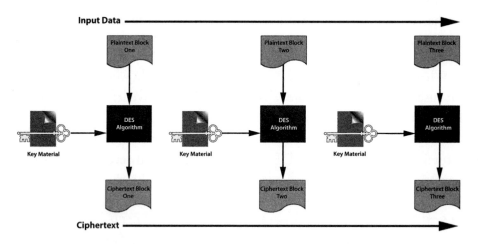

Figure 5.5 - **Electronic Codebook (ECB) is a basic mode used by block ciphers**

- **Cipher Block Chaining Mode** - The CBC mode is stronger than ECB in that each input block will produce a different output—even if the input blocks are identical. This is accomplished by introducing two new factors in the encryption process—an IV and a chaining function that XORs each input with the previous ciphertext. (*Note*: Without the IV, the chaining process applied to the same messages would create the same ciphertext.) The IV is a randomly chosen value that is mixed with the first block of plaintext. This acts just like a seed in a stream-based cipher. The sender and the receiver must know the IV so that the message can be decrypted later. The function of CBC can be seen in *Figure 5.6*.

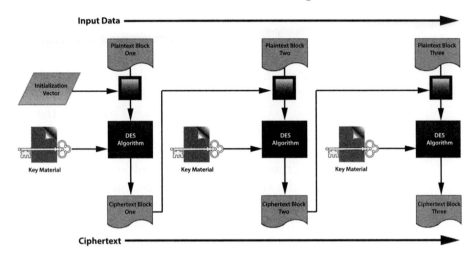

Figure 5.6 - **Cipher Block Chaining (CBC) mode**

- The initial input block is XORed with the IV, and the result of that process is encrypted to produce the first block of ciphertext. This first ciphertext block is then XORed with the next input plaintext block. This is the chaining process, which ensures that even if the input blocks are the same, the resulting outputs will be different.

- *The Stream Modes of DES* - The following modes of DES operate as a stream; even though DES is a block mode cipher, these modes attempt to make DES operate as if it were a stream mode algorithm. A block-based cipher is subject to the problems of latency or delay in processing.

805

This makes them unsuitable for many applications where simultaneous transmission of the data is desired. In these modes, DES tries to simulate a stream to be more versatile and provide support for stream-based applications.

- **Cipher Feedback Mode** - In the CFB mode, the input is separated into individual segments, the size of which can be 1-bit, 8-bit, 64-bit, or 128-bit (the four sub-modes of CFB)*—usually of 8 bits, because that is the size of one character (*Figure 5.7*). When the encryption process starts, the IV is chosen and loaded into a shift register. It is then run through the encryption algorithm. The first 8 bits that come from the algorithm are then XORed with the first 8 bits of the plaintext (the first segment). Each 8-bit segment is then transmitted to the receiver and also fed back into the shift register. The shift register contents are then encrypted again to generate the keystream to be XORed with the next plaintext segment. This process continues until the end of the input. One of the drawbacks of this, however, is that if a bit is corrupted or altered, all of the data from that point onward will be damaged. It is interesting to note that because of the nature of the operation in CFB, the decryption process uses the *encryption* operation rather than operate in reverse like CBC.

- **Output Feedback Mode**—The OFB mode is very similar in operation to the CFB except that instead of using the ciphertext result of the XOR operation to feed back into the shift register for the ongoing keystream, it feeds the encrypted keystream itself back into the shift register to create the next portion of the keystream (*Figure 5.8*).

- Because the keystream and message data are completely independent (the keystream itself is chained, but there is no chaining of the ciphertext), it is now possible to generate the entire keystream in advance and store it for later use. However, this does pose some storage complications, especially if it were to be used in a high-speed link.

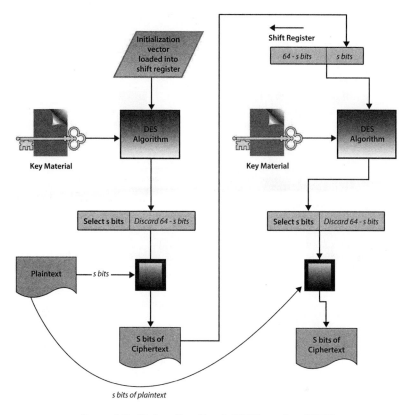

Figure 5.7 - **Cipher Feedback (CFB) mode of DES**

- ***Counter Mode***—The CTR mode is used in high-speed applications such as IPSec and ATM (*Figure 5.9*). In this mode, a counter—a 64-bit random data block—is used as the first IV. A requirement of CTR is that the counter must be different for every block of plaintext, so for each subsequent block, the counter is incremented by 1. The counter is then encrypted just as in OFB, and the result is used as a keystream and XORed with the plaintext. Because the keystream is independent from the message, it is possible to process several blocks of data at the same time, thus speeding up the throughput of the algorithm. Again, because of the characteristics of the algorithm, the encryption process is used at both ends of the process—there is no need to install the decryption process.

5

Cryptography

807

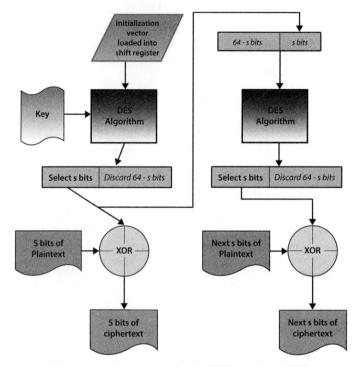

Figure 5.8 - **Output Feedback (OFB) mode of DES**

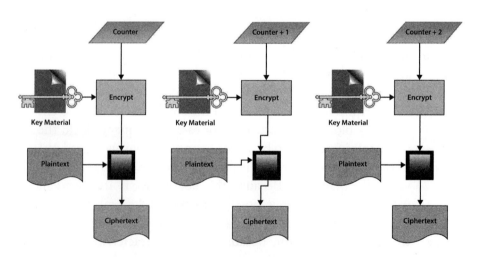

Figure 5.9 - **Counter (CTR) mode is used in high-speed applications such as IPSec and ATM**

Advantages and Disadvantages of DES

DES is a strong, fast algorithm that has endured the test of time; however, it is not suitable for use for very confidential data due to the increase in computing power over the years. Initially, DES was considered unbreakable, and early attempts to break a DES message were unrealistic. (A computer running at one attempt per millisecond would still take more than 1000 years to try all possible keys.) However, DES is susceptible to a brute-force attack. Because the key is only 56 bits long, the key may be determined by trying all possible keys against the ciphertext until the true plaintext is recovered. The Electronic Frontier Foundation (www.eff.org) demonstrated this several years ago. However, it should be noted that they did the simplest form of attack—a known plaintext attack; they tried all possible keys against a ciphertext knowing what they were looking for (they knew the plaintext). If they did not know the plaintext (did not know what they were looking for), the attack would have been significantly more difficult. Regardless, DES can be deciphered using today's computing power and enough stubborn persistence. There have also been criticisms of the structure of the DES algorithm. The design of the S-boxes used in the encryption and decryption operations was secret, and this can lead to claims that they may contain hidden code or untried operations.

Double DES

The primary complaint about DES was that the key was too short. This made a known plaintext brute-force attack possible. One of the first alternatives considered to create a stronger version of DES was to double the encryption process as shown in *Figure 5.10*. The first DES operation created an intermediate ciphertext, which will be referred to as "m" for discussion purposes.

This intermediate ciphertext, m, was then re-encrypted using a second 56-bit DES key for greater cryptographic strength. Initially there was a lot of discussion as to whether the ciphertext created by the second DES operation would be the same as the ciphertext that would have been created by a third DES key. In other words, double DES looks like this:

5

Cryptography

$$C = E_{K2}(E_{K1}(P))$$

Ciphertext created by double DES is the result of the plaintext encrypted with the first 56-bit DES key and then re-encrypted with the second 56-bit DES key. Is that equivalent to this?

$$C = E_{K3}(P)$$

Would the result of two operations be the same as the result of one operation using a different key? This is not the case as more serious vulnerabilities in double DES have emerged. The intention of double DES was to create an algorithm that would be equivalent in strength to a 112-bit key (two 56-bit keys). Unfortunately, this was not the case because of the "meet in the middle" attack, which is why the lifespan of double DES was very short.

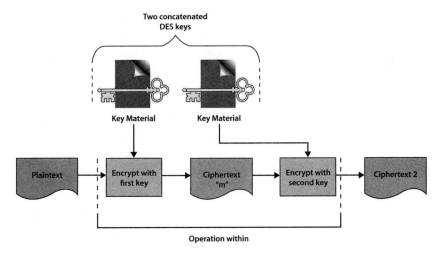

*Figure 5.10 - **Operations within Double DES (2DES) cryptosystems***

Meet in the Middle

The most effective attack against double DES was just like the successful attacks on single DES, based on doing a brute-force attack against known plaintext (*Figure 5.11*). The attacker would encrypt the plaintext using all possible keys and create a table containing all possible results. This intermediate cipher is referred to as "m" for this discussion[3]. This would mean encrypting using all 2^{56} possible keys. The table would then be sorted according to the values of m. The attacker would then decrypt the ciphertext using all possible keys until he found a match with the value of m. This would result in a true strength of double DES of approximately 2^{56} (twice the strength of DES, but not strong enough to be considered effective), instead of the 2^{112} originally hoped.[4]

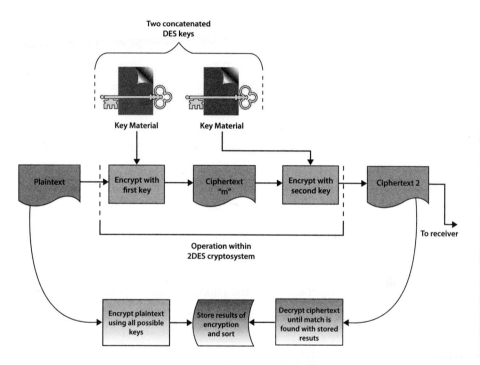

Figure 5.11 - **Meet-in-the-Middle attack on 2DES**

Triple DES (3DES)

The defeat of double DES resulted in the adoption of triple DES as the next solution to overcome the weaknesses of single DES. Triple DES was

3   In a known plaintext attack, the attacker has both the plaintext and the ciphertext, but he does not have the key, and the brute-force attack was an attack trying all possible keys. See "Attacks on hashing algorithms and message authentication codes" Section for more details on this

4   Note that most cryptographers consider the strength of single DES to be 2^{55}, not 2^{56} as might be expected. Because double DES is approximately twice the strength of DES, it would be considered to be 2^{56}

designed to operate at a relative strength of 2^{112} using two different keys to perform the encryption.

The triple DES operation using two keys is shown below:

$$C = E_{K1}(E_{K2}(E_{K1}(P)))$$

The ciphertext is created by encrypting the plaintext with key 1, re-encrypting with key 2, and then encrypting again with key 1.

This would have a relative strength of 2^{112} and be unfeasible for attack using either the known plaintext or differential cryptanalysis attacks. This mode of 3DES would be referred to as EEE2 (encrypt, encrypt, encrypt using two keys).

The preferred method of using triple DES was to use a decrypt step for the intermediate operation, as shown below:

$$C = E_{K1}(D_{K2}(E_{K1}(P)))$$

The plaintext was encrypted using key 1, then decrypted using key 2, and then encrypted using key 1.

Doing the decrypt operation for the intermediate step does not make a difference in the strength of the cryptographic operation, but it does allow backward compatibility through permitting a user of triple DES to also access files encrypted with single DES. This mode of triple DES is referred to as EDE2. Originally, the use of triple DES was primarily done using two keys as shown above, and this was compliant with ISO 8732 and ANS X9.17; however, some users, such as PGP and Secure/Multipurpose Internet Mail Extension (S/MIME), are moving toward the adoption of triple DES using three separate keys. This would be shown as follows:

$$C = E_{K3}(E_{K2}(E_{K1}(P)))$$ for the EEE3 mode

or

$$C = E_{K3}(D_{K2}(E_{K1}(P)))$$ for the EDE3 mode

There are seven different modes of triple DES, but the four explained above are the most common and of the most concern to the security professional.

Advanced Encryption Standard

In 1997, the National Institute of Standards and Technology (NIST) in the United States issued a call for a product to replace DES and 3DES. The requirements were that the new algorithm would be at least as strong as DES, have a larger block size (because a larger block size would be more efficient and more secure), and overcome the problems of performance with DES. DES was developed for hardware implementations and is too slow in software. 3DES is even slower, and thus creates a serious latency in encryption as well as significant processing overhead.

After considerable research, the product chosen to be the new AES was the Rijndael algorithm, created by Dr. Joan Daemon and Dr. Vincent Rijmen of Belgium. The name Rijndael was merely a contraction of their surnames. Rijndael beat out the other finalists: Serpent, of which Ross Anderson was an author; MARS, an IBM product; RC6, from Ron Rivest and RSA; and TwoFish, developed by Bruce Schneier. The AES algorithm was obliged to meet many criteria, including the need to be flexible, implementable on many types of platforms, and free of royalties.

Counter Mode with Cipher Block Chaining Message Authentication Code Protocol (CCMP)

CCMP is an encryption protocol that forms part of the 802.11i standard for wireless local area networks. The CCMP protocol is based on AES encryption using the CTR with CBC-MAC (CCM) mode of operation. CCMP is defined in the IETF RFC 3610[5] and is included as a component of the 802.11i IEEE standard.

---

5   http://tools.ietf.org/html/rfc3610

How CCMP Works

AES processing in CCMP must use AES 128-bit key and 128-bit block size. Per United States' Federal Information Processing Standard (FIPS) 197 standard, the AES algorithm (a block cipher) uses blocks of 128 bits, cipher keys with lengths of 128, 192, and 256 bits, as well as a number of rounds 10, 12, and 14 respectively. CCMP use of 128-bit keys and a 48-bit IV minimizes vulnerability to replay attacks. The CTR component provides data privacy. The Cipher Block Chaining Message Authentication Code component produces a message integrity code (MIC) that provides data origin authentication and data integrity for the packet payload data.

The 802.11i standard includes CCMP. AES is often referred to as the encryption protocol used by 802.11i, however AES itself is simply a block cipher. The actual encryption protocol is CCMP. It is important to note here that the 802.11i standard allows for Temporal Key Integrity Protocol (TKIP) encryption. Robust Security Network (RSN) is part of the 802.11i IEEE standard and negotiates authentication and encryption algorithms between access points and wireless clients. This flexibility allows new algorithms to be added at any time and supported alongside previous algorithms. The use of AES-CCMP is mandated for RSNs. AES-CCMP introduces a higher level of security from past protocols by providing protection for the MAC protocol data unit (MPDU) and parts of the 802.11 MAC headers. This protects even more of the data packet from eavesdropping and tampering.

Rijndael

The Rijndael algorithm can be used with block sizes of 128, 192, or 256 bits. The key can also be 128, 192, or 256 bits, with a variable number of rounds of operation depending on the key size. Using AES with a 128-bit key would do 10 rounds, whereas a 192-bit key would do 12 and a 256-bit key would do 14. Although Rijndael supports multiple block sizes, AES only supports one block size (subset of Rijndael). AES is reviewed below in

1st byte	5th byte	9th byte	13th byte
2nd byte	6th byte	10th byte	14th byte
3rd byte	7th byte	11th byte	15th byte
4th byte	8th byte	12th byte	16th byte

the 128-bit block format. The AES operation works on the entire 128-bit block of input data by first copying it into a square table (or array) that it calls state. The inputs are placed into the array by column so that the first four bytes of the input would fill the first column of the array.

Following is input plaintext when placed into a 128-bit state array: The key is also placed into a similar square table or matrix.

The Rijndael operation consists of four major operations.

1. ***Substitute bytes:*** Use of an S-box to do a byte-by-byte substitution of the entire block.

2. ***Shift rows:*** Transposition or permutation through offsetting each row in the table.

3. ***Mix columns:*** A substitution of each value in a column based on a function of the values of the data in the column.

4. ***Add round key:*** XOR each byte with the key for that round; the key is modified for each round of operation.

Substitute Bytes

The substitute bytes operation uses an S-box that looks up the value of each byte in the input and substitutes it with the value in the table. The S-box table contains all possible 256 8-bit word values and a simple cross-reference is done to find the substitute value using the first half of the byte (4-bit word) in the input table on the *x*-axis and the second half of the byte on

815

the *y*-axis. Hexadecimal values are used in both the input and S-box tables.

Shift Row Transformation

The shift row transformation step provides blockwide transposition of the input data by shifting the rows of data as follows. If one starts with the input table described earlier, the effect of the shift row operation can be observed. Please note that by this point the table will have been subjected to the substitute bytes operation, so it would not look like this any longer, but this table will be used for the sake of clarity.

		Columns		
Rows	1st byte	5th byte	9th byte	13th byte
	2nd byte	6th byte	10th byte	14th byte
	3rd byte	7th byte	11th byte	15th byte
	4th byte	8th byte	12th byte	16th byte

The first row is not shifted.

1st byte	5th byte	9th byte	13th byte

The second row of the table is shifted one place to the left.

6th byte	10th byte	14th byte	2nd byte

The third row of the table is shifted two places to the left.

11th byte	15th byte	3rd byte	7th byte

The fourth row of the table is shifted three places to the left.

16th byte	4th byte	8th byte	12th byte

The final result of the shift rows step would look as follows:

1	5	9	13
6	10	14	2
11	15	3	7
16	4	8	12

Mix Column Transformation

The mix column transformation is performed by multiplying and XORing each byte in a column together, according to the table in *Figure 5.12*.

1	5	9	13
6	10	14	2
11	15	3	7
16	4	8	12

$\oplus$

02	03	01	01
01	02	03	01
01	01	02	03
03	01	01	01

State table   Exclusive OR   Mix Columns table

Figure 5.12 - **Mix Column transformation**

The Figure 5.12 table is the result of the previous step, so when the first column (shaded in the state table), with the first row is worked using use multiplication and XOR in the mix column table (shaded), the computation of the mix columns step for the first column would be

$$(1*02)\ (6*03)\ (11*01)\ (16*01)$$

817

The second byte in the column would be calculated using the second row in the mix column table as

$$(6*01) \ (11*02) \ (16*03) \ (1*01)$$

Add Round Key

The key is modified for each round by first dividing the key into 16-bit pieces (4 4-bit words) and then expanding each piece into 176 bits (44 4-bit words). The key is arrayed into a square matrix, and each column is subjected to rotation (shifting the first column to the last (1, 2, 3, 4 would become 2, 3, 4, 1) and then the substitution of each word of the key using an S-box. The result of these first two operations is then XORed with a round constant to create the key to be used for that round. The round constant changes for each round, and its values are predefined. Each of the above steps (except for the mix columns, which is only done for nine rounds) are done for 10 rounds to produce the ciphertext. AES is a strong algorithm that is not considered breakable at any time in the near future and is easy to deploy on many platforms with excellent throughput.

International Data Encryption Algorithm (IDEA)

IDEA was developed as a replacement for DES by Xuejai Lai and James Massey in 1991. IDEA uses a 128-bit key and operates on 64-bit blocks. IDEA does eight rounds of transposition and substitution using modular addition and multiplication, and bitwise exclusive-or (XOR). The patents on IDEA expired in 2011.

CAST

CAST was developed in 1996 by Carlisle Adams and Stafford Tavares. CAST-128 can use keys between 40 and 128 bits in length and will do between 12 and 16 rounds of operation, depending on key length. CAST-128 is a Feistal-type block cipher with 64-bit blocks. CAST-256 was submitted as an unsuccessful candidate for the new AES. CAST-256 operates on 128-bit blocks and with keys of 128, 192, 160, 224, and 256 bits. It performs 48 rounds and is described in RFC 2612.

Secure and Fast Encryption Routine (SAFER)

All of the algorithms in SAFER are patent-free. The algorithms were developed by James Massey and work on either 64-bit input blocks (SAFER-SK64) or 128-bit blocks (SAFER-SK128). A variation of SAFER is used as a block cipher in Bluetooth.

Blowfish

Blowfish is a symmetrical algorithm developed by Bruce Schneier. It is an extremely fast cipher and can be implemented in as little as 5K of memory. It is a Feistal-type cipher in that it divides the input blocks into two halves and then uses them in XORs against each other. However, it varies from the traditional Feistal cipher in that Blowfish does work against both halves, not just one. The Blowfish algorithm operates with variable key sizes, from 32 up to 448 bits on 64-bit input and output blocks. One of the characteristics of Blowfish is that the S-boxes are created from the key and are stored for later use. Because of the processing time taken to change keys and recompute the S-boxes, Blowfish is unsuitable for applications where the key is changed frequently or in applications on smart cards or with limited processing power. Blowfish is currently considered unbreakable (using today's technology), and in fact, because the key is used to generate the S-boxes, it takes over 500 rounds of the Blowfish algorithm to test any single key.

Twofish

Twofish was one of the finalists for the AES. It is an adapted version of Blowfish developed by a team of cryptographers led by Bruce Schneier. It can operate with keys of 128, 192, or 256 bits on blocks of 128 bits. It performs 16 rounds during the encryption/decryption process.

RC5

RC5 was developed by Ron Rivest of RSA and is deployed in many of RSA's products. It is a very adaptable product useful for many applications, ranging from software to hardware implementations. The key for RC5 can

5

Cryptography

vary from 0 to 2040 bits, the number of rounds it executes can be adjusted from 0 to 255, and the length of the input words can also be chosen from 16-, 32-, and 64-bit lengths. The algorithm operates on two words at a time in a fast and secure manner.

RC5 is defined in RFC 2040 for four different modes of operation:

- RC5 block cipher is similar to DES ECB producing a ciphertext block of the same length as the input.

- RC5-CBC is a cipher block chaining form of RC5 using chaining to ensure that repeated input blocks would not generate the same output.

- RC5-CBC-Pad combines chaining with the ability to handle input plaintext of any length. The ciphertext will be longer than the plaintext by at most one block.

- RC5-CTS is called ciphertext stealing and will generate a ciphertext equal in length to a plaintext of any length.

RC4

RC4, a stream-based cipher, was developed in 1987 by Ron Rivest for RSA Data Security and has become the most widely used stream cipher, being deployed, for example, in WEP and SSL/TLS. RC4 uses a variable length key ranging from 8 to 2048 bits (1 to 256 bytes) and a period of greater than 10^{100}. In other words, the keystream should not repeat for at least that length.

The key is used to initialize a state vector that is 256 bytes in length and contains all possible values of 8-bit numbers from 0 through 255. This state is used to generate the keystream that is XORed with the plaintext. The key is only used to initialize the state and is not used thereafter. Because no transposition is done, RC4 is considered by some cryptographers to be theoretically weaker. The U.S. federal government through the NIST bans its use for protecting sensitive data for federal agencies and their contractors. If RC4 is used with a key length of at least 128 bits, there are currently no practical ways to attack it; the published successful attacks against the use of RC4 in WEP applications are related to problems with the implementation of the algorithm, not the algorithm itself. For example, the RC4 initialization vector length and reuse specification was never properly specified and therefore properly implemented in WEP. While RC4 is very strong with the initialization vector is large and random, in WEP the initialization vector implementation was small, began repeating itself and formed patterns. These patterns were then used to help break the encryption.

Advantages and Disadvantages of Symmetric Algorithms

Symmetric algorithms are very fast and secure methods of providing confidentiality and some integrity and authentication for messages being stored or transmitted. Many algorithms can be implemented in either hardware or software and are available at no cost to the user.

However, there are serious disadvantages to symmetric algorithms—key management is very difficult, especially in large organizations. The number of keys needed grows rapidly with every new user according to the formula $n(n - 1)/2$, where n is the number of users. An organization with only 10 users, all wanting to communicate securely with one another, requires 45 keys (10*9/2). If the organization grows to 1000 employees, the need for key management expands to nearly a half million keys.

Symmetric algorithms also are not able to provide nonrepudiation of origin, access control, and digital signatures, except in a very limited way. If two or more people share a symmetric key, then it is impossible to prove who altered a file protected with a symmetric key. Selecting keys is an important part of key management. There needs to be a process in place that ensures that a key is selected randomly from the entire keyspace, and that there is some way to recover a lost or forgotten key.

Because symmetric algorithms require both users (the sender and the receiver) to share the same key, there can be challenges with secure key distribution. Often the users must use an out-of-band channel such as mail, fax, telephone, or courier to exchange secret keys. The use of an out-of-band channel should make it difficult for an attacker to seize both the encrypted data and the key. The other method of exchanging the symmetric key is to use an asymmetric algorithm.

Asymmetric Cryptography

Due to the practical limitations of symmetric cryptography, asymmetric cryptography attempts to provide the best of all worlds. While initially more key management is required, the fundamentals of asymmetric cryptography provide an extensible and elastic framework in which to deploy cryptographic functions for integrity, confidentiality, authentication and nonrepudiation.

Asymmetric Algorithms

Whereas symmetric algorithms have been in existence for several millennia, the use of asymmetric (or public key) algorithms is relatively new. These algorithms became commonly known when Drs. Whit Diffie and Martin Hellman released a paper in 1976 called "New Directions in Cryptography."[6] The Diffie–Hellman paper described the concept of using two different keys (a key pair) to perform the cryptographic operations. The two keys would be linked mathematically, but would be mutually exclusive. For most asymmetric algorithms, if one half of this key pair was used for encryption, then the other key half would be required to decrypt the message.

When a person wishes to communicate using an asymmetric algorithm, they would first generate a key pair. Usually this is done by the cryptographic application or the PKI without user involvement to ensure the strength of the key generation process. One half of the key pair is kept secret, and only the key holder knows that key. For this reason, it is often called the private

---

6   Whit Diffie and Martin Hellman, New directions in cryptography, *IEEE Transactions on Information Theory*, IT-22, 1976.

key. The other half of the key pair can be given freely to anyone that wants a copy. In many companies, it may be available through the corporate Web site or access to a key server. That is why this half of the key pair is often referred to as the public key. Asymmetric algorithms are one-way functions, that is, a process that is much simpler to go in one direction (forward) than to go in the other direction (backward or reverse engineering). The process to generate the public key (forward) is fairly simple, and providing the public key to anyone who wants it does not compromise the private key because the process to go from the public key to the private key is computationally infeasible.

Confidential Messages

Because the keys are mutually exclusive, any message that is encrypted with a public key can only be decrypted with the corresponding other half of the key pair, the private key. Therefore, as long as the key holder keeps their private key secure, there exists a method of transmitting a message confidentially. The sender would encrypt the message with the public key of the receiver. Only the receiver with the private key would be able to open or read the message, providing confidentiality. See *Figure 5.13*.

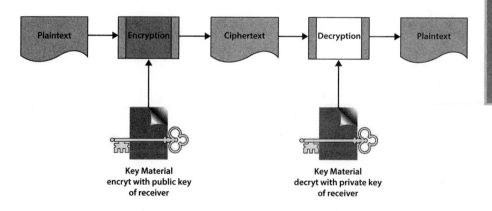

Figure 5.13 - **Using Public Key cryptography to send a confidential message.**

Open Message

Conversely, when a message is encrypted with the private key of a sender, it can be opened or read by anyone who possesses the corresponding public key. When a person needs to send a message and provide proof of origin (nonrepudiation), they can do so by encrypting it with their own private key. The recipient then has some guarantee that, because they opened it with the public key from the sender, the message did, in fact, originate with the sender. See *Figure 5.14.*

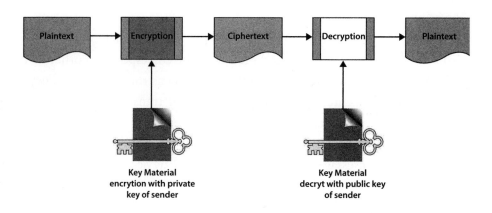

Figure 5.14 - **Using Public Key cryptography to send a message with proof of origin.**

Confidential Messages with Proof of Origin

By encrypting a message with the private key of the sender and the public key of the receiver, the ability exists to send a message that is confidential and has proof of origin. See *Figure 5.15.*

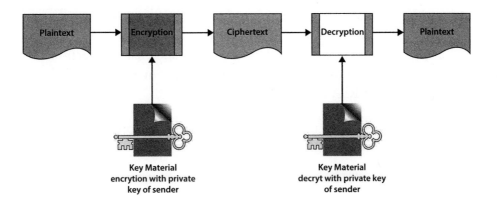

Figure 5.15 - **Using public key cryptography to send a message that is confidential and has a proof of origin**

RSA

RSA was developed in 1978 by Ron Rivest, Adi Shamir, and Len Adleman when they were at MIT. RSA is based on the mathematical challenge of factoring the product of two large prime numbers. A prime number can only be divided by 1 and itself. Some prime numbers include 2, 3, 5, 7, 11, 13, and so on. Factoring is defined as taking a number and finding the numbers that can be multiplied together to calculate that number. For example, if the product of $a*b = c$, then c can be factored into a and b. As $3*4 = 12$, then 12 can be factored into 3, 4 and 6, 2 and 12, 1. The RSA algorithm uses large prime numbers that when multiplied together would be incredibly difficult to factor. Successful factoring attacks have been executed against 512-bit numbers (at a cost of approximately 8000 MIPS years), and successful attacks against 1024-bit numbers appear increasingly possible in the near term, the U.S. government organization, NIST recommended moving away from 1024-bit RSA key size by the end of 2010[7]. The recommendation in part is stated as follows:

---

7   See chart on page 5, NIST SP 800–131A "Transitions: Recommendation for Transitioning the Use of Cryptographic Algorithms and Key Lengths" http://csrc.nist.gov/publications/nistpubs/800-131A/sp800-131A.pdf

"If information is initially signed in 2009 and needs to remain secure for a maximum of 10 years (i.e., from 2009 to 2019), a 1024 bit RSA key would not provide sufficient protection between 2011 and 2019 and, therefore, it is not recommended that 1024-bit RSA be used in this case."

RSA is the most widely used public key algorithm and operates on blocks of text according to the following formula:

$$C = P^e \bmod n$$

The ciphertext is computed from the plaintext to the exponent e mod n.

How to Generate RSA Key Pairs

Select p and q where both are prime numbers and p q:

$$p = 17 \text{ and } q = 11$$

Calculate $n = pq$:

$$n = 17 \ 11 = 187$$

Calculate $\leq (n) = (p - 1)(q - 1)$:

$$\leq(n) = (17 - 1)(11 - 1) = 16 \ 10 = 160$$

Select integer e where is e is relatively prime to $\leq(n) = 160$ and less than $\leq(n)$. Choose $e = 7$.

Determine d such that $de \leq 1 \bmod 160$ and $d < 160$:

$$d = 23 \text{ because } 23 \ 7 = 161 = 10 \ 160 + 1.$$

(d is calculated using Euclid's algorithm.)

Public key = {e, n} = {7, 187}
Private key = {d, n} = {23, 187}

To encrypt a plaintext of 88 using the public key (confidentiality), one would do the following mathematics:

$$C = P^e \bmod n$$

For the sake of simplicity, the modular arithmetic function will be broken into smaller pieces:

$C = 88^7 \bmod 187 = [(88^4 \bmod 187)\,(88^2 \bmod 187)\,88^1 \bmod 187)] \bmod 187$

$88^1 \bmod 187 = 88$

$88^2 \bmod 187 = 7744 \bmod 187 = 77$

$88^4 \bmod 187 = 59{,}969{,}536 \bmod 187 = 132$

$88^7 \bmod 187 = (88*77*132) \bmod 187 = 894{,}432 \bmod 187 = 11$

$C = 11$

To decrypt the ciphertext of 11, the formula $P = 11^{23} \bmod 187$ would be used.

Attacking RSA

The three primary approaches to attack the RSA algorithm are to use brute force, trying all possible private keys; mathematical attacks, factoring the product of two prime numbers; and timing attacks, measuring the running time of the decryption algorithm.

Diffie-Hellmann Algorithm

Diffie–Hellmann is a key exchange algorithm. It is used to enable two users to exchange or negotiate a secret symmetric key that will be used subsequently for message encryption. The Diffie–Hellmann algorithm does not provide for message confidentiality, but is extremely useful for applications such as Public Key Infrastructure. Diffie–Hellmann is based on discrete logarithms. This is a mathematical function based first on finding the primitive root of a prime number. Using the primitive root, one can put together a formula as follows:

$b \le a^i \bmod p \ \ 0 \text{ £ } i \text{ £ } (p - 1)$

where i is the discrete log (or index) for $a \bmod p$.

Key Exchange Using Diffie–Hellmann

The prime number (p) and primitive root (g) used in Diffie–Hellmann are common to most users. this example will use $p = 353$ and $g = 3$.

Each user A, B would choose a random secret key X that must be less than the prime number.

If A chose the secret key of 97, one could write its secret key as $X_A = 97$. The public key, Y_A, for user A would be calculated as $Y_A = g_A{}^x \bmod p$. Therefore, A would calculate $Y_A = 3^{97} \bmod 353 = 40$.

If B chose the secret key of 233, the public key, Y_B, for user B would be calculated as $Y_B = g_B{}^x \bmod p$. Therefore, B would calculate $Y_B = 3^{233} \bmod 353 = 248$.

A and B would then exchange the public keys that they had calculated.

Using the following formula, they would each compute the common session key:

A computes the common key, K, as

$$K = (Y_B)_A{}^X \bmod 353 = 248^{97} \bmod 353 = 160$$

B computes the common key as

$$K = (Y_A)^{XB} \bmod 353 = 40^{233} \bmod 353 = 160$$

The two parties A and B can now encrypt their data using the symmetric key of 160. This would be an example of a hybrid system.

El Gamal

The El Gamal cryptographic algorithm is based on the work of Diffie–Hellmann, but it included the ability to provide message confidentiality and digital signature services, not just session key exchange. The El Gamal algorithm was based on the same mathematical functions of discrete logs.

Elliptic Curve Cryptography (ECC)

One branch of discrete logarithmic algorithms is based on the complex mathematics of elliptic curves. These algorithms, which are too complex to explain in this context, are advantageous for their speed and strength. The elliptic curve algorithms have the highest strength per bit of key length of any of the asymmetric algorithms. The ability to use much shorter keys for ECC implementations provides savings on computational power and bandwidth. This makes ECC especially beneficial for implementation in smart cards, wireless, and other similar application areas. Elliptic curve algorithms provide confidentiality, digital signatures, and message authentication services.

Advantages and Disadvantages of Asymmetric Key Algorithms

The development of asymmetric key cryptography revolutionized the cryptographic community. Now it was possible to send a message across an untrusted medium in a secure manner without the overhead of prior key exchange or key material distribution. It allowed several other features not readily available in symmetric cryptography, such as the nonrepudiation of origin, access control, data integrity and the nonrepudiation of delivery.

The problem was that asymmetric cryptography is extremely slow compared to its symmetric counterpart. Asymmetric cryptography was a product that was extremely problematic in terms of speed and performance and would be impractical for everyday use in encrypting large amounts of data and frequent transactions. This is because asymmetric is handling much larger keys and computations—making even a fast computer work harder than if it were only handling small keys and less complex algebraic calculations. The ciphertext output from asymmetric algorithms may be much larger than the plaintext. This means that for large messages, they are not effective for secrecy; however, they are effective for message integrity, authentication, and nonrepudiation.

Hybrid Cryptography

The solutions to many of the problems with symmetric encryption lies in developing a hybrid technique of cryptography that combined the strengths of both symmetric cryptography, with its great speed and secure algorithms, and asymmetric cryptography, with its ability to securely exchange session keys, message authentication, and nonrepudiation. Symmetric cryptography is best for encrypting large files. It can handle the encryption and decryption processes with little impact on delivery times or computational performance.

Asymmetric cryptography can handle the initial setup of the communications session through the exchange or negotiation of the symmetric keys to be used for this session. In many cases, the symmetric key is only needed for the length of this communication and can be discarded following the completion of the transaction, so the symmetric key in this case will be referred to as a session key. A hybrid system operates as shown in Figure 5.16. The message itself is encrypted with a symmetric key, SK, and is sent to the recipient. The symmetric key is encrypted with the public key of the receiver and sent to the recipient. The symmetric key is decrypted with the private key of the receiver. This discloses the symmetric key to the recipient. The symmetric key can then be used to decrypt the message.

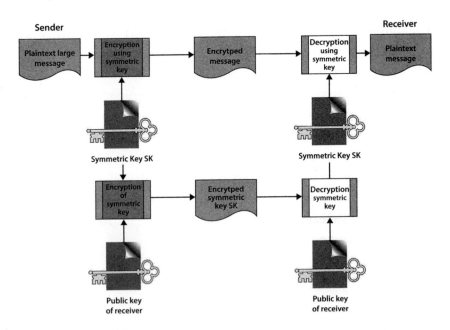

Figure 5.16 - **Hybrid system using asymmetric algorithm for bulk data encryption and an asymmetric algorithm for distribution of the symmetric key.**

Message Digests

A message digest is a small representation of a larger message. Message digests are used to ensure the authentication and integrity of information not the confidentiality. This chapter covers Message Authentication Code and HMAC.

Message Authentication Code

MAC (also known as a cryptographic checksum) is a small block of data that is generated using a secret key and then appended to the message. When the message is received, the recipient can generate their own MAC using the secret key, and thereby know that the message has not changed either accidentally or intentionally in transit. Of course, this assurance is only as strong as the trust that the two parties have that no one else has access to the secret key. A MAC is a small representation of a message and has the following characteristics:

- A MAC is much smaller than the message generating it.

- Given a MAC, it is impractical to compute the message that generated it.

- Given a MAC and the message that generated it, it is impractical to find another message generating the same MAC.

In the case of DES-CBC, a MAC is generated using the DES algorithm in CBC mode, and the secret DES key is shared by the sender and the receiver. The MAC is actually just the last block of ciphertext generated by the algorithm. This block of data (64 bits) is attached to the unencrypted message and transmitted to the far end. All previous blocks of encrypted data are discarded to prevent any attack on the MAC itself. The receiver can just generate his own MAC using the secret DES key he shares to ensure message integrity and authentication. He knows that the message has not changed because the chaining function of CBC would significantly alter the last block of data if any bit had changed anywhere in the message. He knows the source of the message (authentication) because only one other person holds the secret key. If the message contains a sequence number (such as a TCP header or X.25 packet), he knows that all messages have been received and not duplicated or missed.

HMAC

A MAC based on DES is one of the most common methods of creating a MAC; however, it is slow in operation compared to a hash function. A hash function such as MD5 does not have a secret key, so it cannot be used for a MAC. Therefore, RFC 2104 was issued to provide a hashed MACing system that has become the process used in IPSec and many other secure Internet protocols, such as SSL/TLS. Hashed MACing implements a freely available hash algorithm as a component (black box) within the HMAC implementation. This allows ease of the replacement of the hashing module if a new hash function becomes necessary. The use of proven cryptographic hash algorithms also provides assurance of the security of HMAC implementations. HMACs work by adding a secret key value to the hash input function along with the source message. The HMAC operation provides cryptographic strength similar to a hashing algorithm, except that it now has the additional protection of a secret key, and still operates nearly as rapidly as a standard hash operation.

Hashing

The hash function accepts an input message of any length and generates, through a one-way operation, a fixed-length output. This output is referred to as a hash code or sometimes it is called a message digest. It uses a hashing algorithm to generate the hash, but does not use a secret key.

There are several ways to use message digests in communications, depending on the need for the confidentiality of the message, the authentication of the source, the speed of processing, and the choice of encryption algorithms. The requirements for a hash function are that they must provide some assurance that the message cannot be changed without detection and that it would be impractical to find any two messages with the same hash value.

Five key properties of a hash function are:

1. ***Uniformly Distributed:*** The hash output value should not be predictable.

2. ***Weak Collision Resistant:*** Difficult to find a second input value that hashes to the same value as another input.

3. ***Difficult to Invert:*** Should be one way, should not be able to derive hash input x by reversing the hash function on output, y.

4. ***Strong Collision Resistant:*** Difficult to find any two inputs that hash to the same value

5. ***Deterministic:*** Given an input x, it must always generate the same hash value, y.

Simple Hash Functions

A hash operates on an input of any length (there are some limitations, but the message sizes are huge) and generates a fixed-length output. The simplest hash merely divides the input message into fixed-size blocks and then XORs every block. The hash would therefore be the same size as a block.

Hash = block 1 block 2 block 3 ... end of message

MD5 Message Digest Algorithm

MD5 was developed by Ron Rivest at MIT in 1992. It is the most widely used hashing algorithm and is described in RFC 1321. MD5 generates a 128-bit digest from a message of any length. It processes the message in 512-bit blocks and does four rounds of processing. Each round contains 16 steps. The likelihood of finding any two messages with the same hash code is estimated to be 2^{64}, and the difficulty of finding a message with a given digest is estimated to be 2^{128}. One common use of MD5 is to verify the integrity of digital evidence used in forensic investigations and ensure that the original media has not been altered since seizure. In the past two years, there have been several attacks developed against MD5 where it is now possible to find collisions through analysis. This is leading to many professionals recommending the abandonment of MD5 for use in secure communications, such as digital signatures. MD4 was developed in 1990 and revised in 1992. It only does three rounds of processing and fewer mathematical operations per round. It is not considered strong enough for most applications today. It also generated a 128-bit output. It is a predecessor to MD5.

Secure Hash Algorithm (SHA) and SHA-1

The original SHA was developed by NIST in the United States in 1993 and issued as Federal Information Processing Standard (FIPS) 180. A revised version (FIPS 180-1) was issued in 1995 as SHA-1 (RFC 3174). SHA was based on the MD4 algorithm, whereas SHA-1 follows the logic of MD5. SHA-1 operates on 512-bit blocks and can handle any message up to 2^{64} bits in length. The output hash is 160 bits in length. The processing includes four rounds of operations of 20 steps each. Recently, there have been several attacks described against the SHA-1 algorithm despite it being considerably stronger than MD5. NIST has issued FIPS 180-3, which recognizes SHA-1, SHA-224, SHA-256, SHA-384, and SHA-512 as a part of the Secure Hash Standard. The output lengths of the digests of these vary from 160 to 512 bits.

SHA-3

In November 2007, NIST issued an invitation for candidate algorithms for new hash algorithms for use in U.S. federal government cryptographic systems. NIST is conducting an open, public process to identify suitable candidates for the new hash algorithm, which is needed because of recent advances in the cryptanalysis of hash functions. NIST selected finalists in 2010 and hopes to have final selections in 2012[8]. The new hash algorithm will be named SHA-3, and it will augment the hash algorithms currently specified in FIPS 180-3, Secure Hash Standard.

HAVAL

HAVAL was developed at the University of Wollongong in Australia. It combines a variable length output with a variable number of rounds of

8   http://csrc.nist.gov/groups/ST/hash/sha-3/Round3/index.html

operation on 1024-bit input blocks. The output may be 128, 160, 192, 224, or 256 bits, and the number of rounds may vary from three to five. That gives 15 possible combinations of operation. HAVAL operates 60% faster than MD5 when only three rounds are used and is just as fast as MD5 when it does five rounds of operation.

RIPEMD-160

The European RACE Integrity Primitives Evaluation project developed the RIPEMD-160 algorithm in response to the vulnerabilities is found in MD4 and MD5. The original algorithm (RIPEMD-128) has the same vulnerabilities as MD4 and MD5 and led to the improved RIPEMD-160 version. The output for RIPEMD-160 is 160 bits, and it operates similarly to MD5 on 512-bit blocks. It does twice the processing of SHA-1, performing five paired rounds of 16 steps each for 160 operations.

Attacks on Hashing Algorithms and Message Authentication Codes

There are two primary ways to attack hash functions: through brute-force attacks and cryptanalysis. Over the past few years, research has been done on attacks on various hashing algorithms, such as MD-5 and SHA-1. Both cases are susceptible to cryptographic attacks. A brute-force attack relies on finding a weakness in the hashing algorithm that would allow an attacker to reconstruct the original message from the hash value (defeat the one-way property of a hash function), find another message with the same hash value, or find any pair of messages with the same hash value (which is called collision resistance). Oorschot and Weiner developed a machine that could find a collision on a 128-bit hash in about 24 days[9].

Cryptanalysis is the art and science of defeating cryptographic systems and gaining access to encrypted messages even when the keys are unknown. Side-channel attacks are examples of cryptanalyses. These attacks do not attack the algorithms but rather the implementation of the algorithms.

---

9   Read more about Oorschot and Weiner here: http://people.scs.carleton.ca/~paulv/papers/JoC97.pdf

Cryptanalysis is responsible for the development of "rainbow tables" which are used to greatly reduce the computational time and power needed to break a cipher at the expense of storage. A freely available password cracking program called "cain and abel[10]" comes with rainbow tables preloaded.

Rainbow tables are pre-computed tables or lists used in cracking password hashes. Tables are designed for specific algorithms such as MD5 and SHA-1 and can be purchased on the open market. "Salted" hashes provide a defense against rainbow tables. In cryptographic terms, "salt" is made of random bits and is an input to the one-way hash function with target plaintext as the only other input. The salt is stored with the resulting hash so hashing will use the same salt and get the same results. As the rainbow table did not include the salt when it was created, its values will never match the salted values.

The Birthday Paradox

The birthday paradox has been described in textbooks on probability for several years. It is a surprising mathematical condition that indicates the ease of finding two people with the same birthday from a group of people. If one considers that there are 365 possible birthdays (not including leap years and assuming that birthdays are spread evenly across all possible dates), then one would expect to need to have roughly 183 people together to have a 50% probability that two of those people share the same birthday. In fact, once there are more than 23 people together, there is a greater than 50% probability that two of them share the same birthday. Consider that in a group of 23 people, there are 253 different pairings ($n(n - 1)/2$). Once 100 people are together, the chance of two of them having the same birthday is greater than 99.99%.

So why is a discussion about birthdays important in the middle of hashing attacks? Because the likelihood of finding a collision for two messages and their hash values may be a lot easier than may have been believed.

10   More information about Cain and Abel may be found here: http://www.oxid.it/ cain.html

It would be very similar to the statistics of finding two people with the same birthday. One of the considerations for evaluating the strength of a hash algorithm must be its resistance to collisions. The probability of finding a collision for a 160-bit hash can be estimated at either 2^{160} or $2^{160/2}$, depending on the level of collision resistance needed.

This approach is relevant because a hash is a representation of the message and not the message itself. Obviously, the attacker does not want to find an identical message; he wants to find out how to (1) change the message contents to what he wants it to read or (2) cast some doubt on the authenticity of the original message by demonstrating that another message has the same value as the original. The hashing algorithm must be resistant to a birthday-type attack that would allow the attacker to feasibly accomplish his goals.

5

Cryptography

Key Management Processes

Perhaps the most important part of any cryptographic implementation is key management. Control over the issuance, revocation, recovery, distribution, and the history of cryptographic keys is of utmost importance to any organization relying on cryptography for secure communications and data protection.

The information security professional should know the importance of Kerckhoff's law. Auguste Kerckhoff wrote: "a cryptosystem should be secure even if everything about the system, except the key, is public knowledge."[1] The key, therefore, is the true strength of the cryptosystem. The size of the key and the secrecy of the key are perhaps the two most important elements in a crypto implementation.

Claude Shannon, the famous twentieth-century military cryptographer, wrote, "the enemy knows the system." The secrecy of the algorithm, the deftness of the cryptographic operations, or the superiority of our technology to protect our data and systems cannot be relied on solely. Always consider that the adversary knows the algorithms and methods used and act accordingly. A symmetric algorithm shares the same key between the sender and the receiver. This often requires out-of-band transmission of the keys—distribution through a different channel and separate from the data. Key management also looks at the replacement of keys and ensuring that new keys are strong enough to provide for the secure use of the algorithm. Users will often choose weak or predictable passwords and store them in an insecure manner. This same tendency would affect the creation of cryptographic keys if the creation was left to the user community.

People also forget passwords, necessitating the resetting of access to the network or a workstation; however, in the cryptographic world, the loss of a key means the loss of the data itself. Without some form of key recovery, it would be impossible to recover the stored data that were encrypted with a lost key.

---

1   Kerckhoff's Law, http://underbelly.blog-topia.com/2005/01/kerckhoffs-law.html.

Advances in Key Management

Key management has become increasingly important due to critical business requirements for secure information sharing and collaboration in high risk environments. As a result, developers are seeing the need to embed security, particularly cryptography, directly into the application or network device. However, the complexity and specialized nature of cryptography means increased risk if not implemented properly. To meet this challenge, a number of standardized key management specifications are being developed and implemented for use as a sort of key management "plug-in" for such products.

XML (Extensible Markup Language), the flexible data framework that allows applications to communicate on the Internet, has become the preferred infrastructure for e-commerce applications. All of those transactions require trust and security, making it mission-critical to devise common XML mechanisms for authenticating merchants, buyers, and suppliers to each other, and for digitally signing and encrypting XML documents such as contracts and payment transactions. XML-based standards and specifications have been in development for use in the field of key management systems. Such specifications and standards are then implemented within Web services libraries, provided by vendors or by open source collaborative efforts.

One such specification is the XML Key Management Specification 2.0 (XKMS)[2]. This specification defines protocols for distributing and registering public keys, suitable for use in conjunction with XML Digital Signatures[3] and XML Encryption[4]. XKMS, while very focused on key

---

2   "XML Key Management Specification (XKMS 2.0)", W3C, 28 June 2005, Available online: http://www.w3.org/TR/xkms2/; Last Accessed: 5 MAY 2008

3   "XML Signature Syntax and Processing (Second Edition)", W3C, 10 June 2008, Available online: http://www.w3.org/TR/xmldsig-core/; Last Accessed: 12 June 2008

4   "XML Encryption Syntax and Processing", W3C, 10 December 2002, Available online: http://www.w3.org/TR/xmlenc-core/; Last Accessed: 5 MAY 2008

5

Cryptography

management, works in conjunction with other specifications[5] that define protocols and services necessary to establishing and maintaining the trust needed for secure Web transactions. These basic mechanisms can be combined in various ways to accommodate building a wide variety of security models using a variety of cryptographic technologies. A goal of XKMS implementation is based on the assumption that simplicity helps developers avoid mistakes and, as such, increases the security of applications. The XKMS protocol consists of pairs of requests and responses. XKMS protocol messages share a common format that may be carried within a variety of protocols. However, XKMS messages transported via SOAP over HTTP is recommended for interoperability.

The two parts of the XML Key Management Specification 2.0 are the XML Key Information Service Specification (X-KISS) and the XML Key Registration Service Specification (X-KRSS). First, X-KISS describes a syntax that allows a client (i.e., application) to delegate part or all of the tasks required to process XML Signature < ds:KeyInfo > elements to a Trust service. A key objective of the protocol design is to minimize the complexity of applications that use XML Digital Signatures. By becoming a client of the trust service, the application is relieved of the complexity and syntax of the underlying PKI used to establish trust relationships, which may be based upon a different specification such as X.509/PKIX, SPKI, PGP, Diffie–Hellman, Elliptic Curve, and can be extended for other algorithms. The < ds:KeyInfo > element in a XML Digital Signature is an optional element that enables the recipient to obtain cryptography key-related data needed to validate the signature. The < ds:KeyInfo > element may contain the key itself, a key name, X.509 certificate, a PGP key identifier, chain of trust, revocation list info, in-band key distribution or key agreement data and so on. As an option, a link to the location where the full < ds:KeyInfo > data set can be found can also be provided.

---

5   For example, Security Assertion Markup Language (SAML) for communicating user authentication, entitlement, and attribute information and WS-Security et al. See http:// www.oasis-open.org/home/index.php for more details.

For example, if using certificates, DSA, RSA, X.509, PGP, SPKI are values that can be used in the < ds:KeyInfo > element of an XML Digital Signature. An application (client of the XKMS) would learn what public key cryptographic algorithm is being used for the transaction by reading from a directory server the < ds:KeyInfo > element of an XML Digital Signature using the X-KISS protocol of XKMS 2.0.

Secondly, X-KRSS describes a protocol for registration of public key information. The key material can be generated by the X-KRSS, on request to support easier key recovery, or manually. The registration service can also be used to subsequently recover a private key. An application may request that the Registration Service (X-KRSS) bind information to a public key. The information bound may include a name, an identifier or other attributes defined by the implementation. After first registering a key pair, the key pair is then usable along with the X-KISS or a PKI such as X.509v3.

The XKMS service shields the client application from the complexities of the underlying PKI such as

- Handling of complex syntax and semantics (e.g. X.509v3).
- Retrieval of information from directory/data repository infrastructure.
- Revocation status verification.
- Construction and processing of trust chains.

Additional information about the signer's public signing key ("< ds:KeyInfo >") can be included inside the signature block, which can be used to help the verifier determine which public key certificate to select.

Information contained in the < ds:KeyInfo > element may or may not be cryptographically bound to the signature itself. Therefore, < ds:KeyInfo > element data can be replaced or extended without invalidating the digital signature. For example, Valerie signs a document and sends it to Jim with a <

ds:KeyInfo > element that specifies only the signing key data. On receiving the message, Jim retrieves additional information required to validate the signature and adds this information into the < ds:KeyInfo > element when he passes the document on to Yolanda (see *Figure 5.17*).

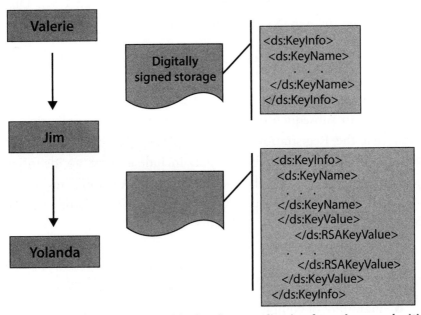

Figure 5.17 - **The XKMS service shields the client application from the complexities of the underlying PKI**

The X-KISS Locate service resolves a < ds:Keyinfo > element but does not require the service to make an assertion concerning the validity of the binding between the data in the < ds:Keyinfo > element. The XKMS service can resolve the < ds:Keyinfo > element using local information store or may relay the request to other directory servers. For example, the XKMS service might resolve a < ds:RetrievalMethod > element (*Figure 5.18*) or act as a gateway to an underlying PKI based on a non-XML syntax (e.g. X.509v3).

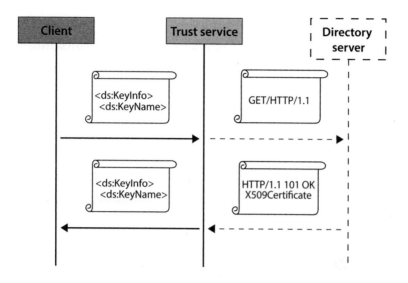

Figure 5.18 - **The SKMS service might resolve a <ds: Retrieval Method> element.**

Example: Encryption

Terry wants to send an encrypted email to Pat but does not know Pat's encryption key. Terry can use both the S/MIME and PGP secure e-mail formats. Terry's client uses Distinguished Names (DNs) to locate the XKMS service that provides a Locate service for keys bound to the domain example.com then sends an XKMS Locate request to the discovered XKMS service for a key bound to Pat@example.com and the S/MIME or PGP protocol. The application then verifies that the certificate obtained meets its trust criteria by standard certificate validation to a trusted root.

Pat receives the signed document from Terry, which specifies Terry's X.509v3 certificate but not the key value. Pat's e-mail client is not capable of processing X.509v3 certificates but can obtain the key parameters from the XKMS service by means of the Locate service. Pat's e-mail client sends the < ds:Keyinfo > element to the location service requesting that the corresponding < KeyValue > element be returned. The location service does not report the revocation status or the trust level of the certificate. However, the service takes the X.509v3 certificate from the < ds:Keyinfo > element and sends the key values.

Standards for Financial Institutions

ANSI X9.17 was developed to address the need of financial institutions to transmit securities and funds securely using an electronic medium. Specifically, it describes the means to ensure the secrecy of keys. The ANSI X9.17 approach is based on a hierarchy of keys. At the bottom of the hierarchy are data keys (DKs). Data keys are used to encrypt and decrypt messages. They are given short lifespans, such as one message or one connection. At the top of the hierarchy are master key-encrypting keys (KKMs).

KKMs, which must be distributed manually, are afforded longer lifespans than data keys. Using the two-tier model, the KKMs are used to encrypt the data keys. The data keys are then distributed electronically to encrypt and decrypt messages. The two-tier model may be enhanced by adding another layer to the hierarchy. In the three-tier model, the KKMs are not used to encrypt data keys directly, but to encrypt other key-encrypting keys (KKs). The KKs, which are exchanged electronically, are used to encrypt the data keys.

Segregation of Duties

Another aspect of key management is maintaining control over sensitive cryptographic keys that enforce the need to know principle as part of a business process. For example, in many business environments, employees are required to maintain separation or segregation of duties. In other words, in such environments no one person is allowed to have full control over all phases of an entire transaction without some level of accountability enforcement. The more negotiable the asset under protection, the greater the need for the proper segregation of duties. Especially in the area of cryptography, this is a business concern. Imagine the damage that could be done by a single dishonest person if allowed unchecked access to cryptographic keys that, for example, unlock high risk, high value, or high liquidity information such as customer financial accounts.

The segregation of duties is used as a cross-check to ensure that misuse and abuse of assets, due to innocent mistake or malicious intent, can be efficiently detected and prevented. This is an important confidentiality and integrity principle that is often misunderstood, judging by news reports of embezzlement schemes, primarily by employee insiders, that go undetected for long amounts of time. The segregation of duties is primarily a business policy and access control issue. However, it may not be possible for smaller organizations, due to personnel constraints, to perform the segregation of all duties, so other compensating controls may have to be used to achieve the same control objective. Such compensating controls include monitoring of activities, audit trails, and management supervision.

Two mechanisms necessary to implement high integrity cryptographic operations environments where separation of duties is paramount are dual control and split knowledge.

Dual Control

Dual control is implemented as a security procedure that requires two or more persons to come together and collude to complete a process. In a cryptographic system the two (or more) persons would each supply a unique key, that when taken together, performs a cryptographic process. Split knowledge is the other complementary access control principle to dual control.

Split Knowledge

Split knowledge is the unique "what each must bring" and joined together when implementing dual control. To illustrate, a box containing petty cash is secured by one combination lock and one keyed lock. One employee is given the combination to the combo lock and another employee has possession of the correct key to the keyed lock. In order to get the cash out of the box both employees must be present at the cash box at the same time. One cannot open the box without the other. This is the aspect of dual control.

5

Cryptography

845

On the other hand, split knowledge is exemplified here by the different objects (the combination to the combo lock and the correct physical key), both of which are unique and necessary, that each brings to the meeting. Split knowledge focuses on the uniqueness of separate objects that must be joined together. Dual control has to do with forcing the collusion of at least two or more persons to combine their split knowledge to gain access to an asset. Both split knowledge and dual control complement each other and are necessary functions that implement the segregation of duties in high integrity cryptographic environments (see *Figure 5.19*).

In cryptographic terms, one could say dual control and split knowledge are properly implemented if no one person has access to or knowledge of

Bad Examples	Problem	How to make dual control split knowledge "compliant."
Splitting a key "in half" to form two parts	Dual control but no split knowledge (assuming two people each with a unique key half). One person could determine the key by brute forcing the other key half space.	Each person maintains control of his or her half of the key. Protect each half with a unique pin or passphrase.
Storing key components on two cryptographic tokens with no further user authentication.	No enforcement of split knowledge (i.e., No unique authentication method for individual accountability)	Each person maintains control of his individual token/smartcard. Protect each smart card with unique pin/passphrase.
Storing a key on a single smartcard (or cryptographic token) that requires one or more passphrases to access.	No dual control enforcement. Single card cannot be maintained by two or more persons.	Distribute cryptographic token to each person. Protect token with unique pin/ passphrase.

Figure 5.19 - **Split knowledge and dual control complement each other and are necessary functions that implement segregation of duties in high-integrity cryptographic environments.**

the content of the complete cryptographic key being protected by the two processes. The sound implementation of dual control and split knowledge in a cryptographic environment necessarily means that the quickest way to break the key would be through the best attack known for the algorithm of that key. The principles of dual control and split knowledge primarily apply to access to plaintext keys. Access to cryptographic keys used for encrypting and decrypting data or access to keys that are encrypted under a master key (which may or may not be maintained under dual control and split knowledge) do not require dual control and split knowledge.

Dual control and split knowledge can be summed up as the determination of any part of a key being protected must require the collusion between two or more persons with each supplying unique cryptographic materials that must be joined together to access the protected key. Any feasible method to violate the axiom means that the principles of dual control and split knowledge are not being upheld.

There are a number of applications that implement aspects of dual control and split knowledge in a scalable manner. For example, a PGP commercial product based on the OpenPGP[6] standard has features for splitting public keys that are not part of the OpenPGP standard. These features use Blakely–Shamir secret sharing. This is an algorithm that allows the user to take a piece of data and break it into N shares, of which K of them are needed to retrieve the original data. Using a simple version of this approach, the user could break the data into three shares, two of which are needed to get the data back. In a more complex version, the user could require 3 of 6 or even 5 of 12 shares to retrieve the original data, with each key share protected with a unique passphrase known only to the key holder.

Such a solution uses the basic form of secret sharing and shares the private key. This process permits a key pair to be controlled by a group

6   Callas, Jon, "OpenPGP Message Format", IETF, Available Online: http://www.ietf.org/rfc/rfc2440.txt; Last Accessed: 4 April 2008

of people, with some subgroup required to reconstitute and use the key. Other systems are based on key holders answering a series of questions in order to recover passwords needed to unlock a protected plaintext key.

To recreate the key under protection, a user can create a set of questions that contain some information only the user would know. The key is split to those questions, with some set of them being required to synthesize the key. Not only does the user provide individualized security questions that are unique to each key holder, but also decides how many of the questions need to be answered correctly to retrieve the key under protection, by having it reconstructed from the split parts.

Creation and Distribution of Keys

Creation of Keys

The details of key creation using various algorithms were discussed earlier in this chapter. However, from a key management perspective there are a number of issues that pertain to scalability and cryptographic key integrity.

Automated Key Generation

Mechanisms used to automatically generate strong cryptographic keys can be used to deploy keys as part of key lifecycle management. Effective automated key generation systems are designed for user transparency as well as complete cryptographic key policy enforcement.

Truly Random

For a key to be truly effective, it must have an appropriately high work factor. That is to say, the amount of time and effort (work by an attacker) needed to break the key must be sufficient so that it at least delays its discovery for as long as the information being protected needs to be kept confidential. One factor that contributes to strong keys, which have a high work factor, is the level of randomness of the bits that make up the key.

Random

As discussed earlier, cryptographic keys are essentially strings of numbers. The numbers used in making up the key need to be unpredictable, so that an attacker cannot easily guess the key and then expose the protected information. Thus, the randomness of the numbers that comprise a key plays an important role in the lifecycle of a cryptographic key. In the context of cryptography, randomness is the quality of lacking predictability. Randomness intrinsically generated by a computer system is also called pseudo randomness. Pseudo randomness is the quality of an algorithm for generating a sequence of numbers that approximates the properties of random numbers. Computer circuits and software libraries are used to perform the actual generation of pseudo random key values. Computers and software libraries are well known as weak sources of randomness.

Computers are inherently designed for predictability not randomness. Computers are so thoroughly deterministic that they have a hard time generating high-quality randomness. Therefore, special purpose built hardware and software called "random number generators" or RNGs, are needed for cryptography applications. The U.S. federal government provides recommendations on deterministic random number generators through the NIST[7]. An international standard for random number generation suitable for cryptographic systems is sponsored by the International Organization for Standardization as ISO 18031[8]. A rigorous statistical analysis of the output is often needed to have confidence in such RNG algorithms. A random number generator based solely on deterministic computation done solely by computer cannot be regarded as a true random number generator sufficient in lack of predictability for cryptographic applications, since its output is inherently predictable.

7   NIST, "Recommendation for Random Number Generation Using Deterministic Random Bit Generators, SP800–90", Available Online: http://csrc.nist.gov/publications/nistpubs/800–90/SP800–90revised_March2007.pdf; Last Accessed: 4 April 2008.

8   "Security Techniques – Random Bit Generation, ISO/IEC 18031:2005", ISO, Available Online: http://www.iso.org; Last Accessed: 5 May 2008.

5

Cryptography

There are various methods for ensuring the appropriate level of randomness in pseudo random keys. The approach found in most business level cryptographic products use computational algorithms that produce long sequences of apparently random results, which are in fact completely determined by a shorter initial value, known as a seed or key. The use of initialization vectors and seed values that are concatenated onto computer generated keys increases the strength of keys by adding additional uniqueness to a random key material. The seed value or initialization vector is the number input as a starting point for an algorithm. The seed or IV can be created either manually or by an external source of randomness, such as radio frequency noise, randomly sampled values from a switched circuit, or other atomic and subatomic physical phenomenon. To provide a degree of randomness intermediate between specialized hardware on the one hand and algorithmic generation on the other, some security related computer software requires the user to input a lengthy string of mouse movements, or keyboard input.

Regarding manually created seed or initialization values, many may be familiar with this process if they have ever set up a wireless network with encryption using a WEP/WPA key. In most cases, when configuring wireless encryption on a wireless adapter or router the user is asked to enter a password or variable length "key" that is used by the wireless device to create cryptographic keys for encrypting data across the wireless network. This "key" is really a seed or initialization value that will be concatenated to the computer generated key portion that together comprise the keying material to generate a key consisting of appropriate amount of pseudo randomness to make it hard for an attacker to easily guess and thus "breaking" the key.

The important role randomness plays in key creation is illustrated by the following example. One method of generating a two-key encryption key set making a private component and a public component is comprised of the following steps:

1. Generate a first pseudo random prime number;

2. Generate a second pseudo random prime number;

3. Produce a modulus by multiplying first pseudo random number by a second pseudo random prime number;

4. Generate a first exponent by solving a first modular arithmetic equation;

5. Generate a second exponent that is a modular inverse to the first exponent, by solving a second modular arithmetic equation and securely storing either the first exponent or the second exponent in at least one memory location.

Key Length

Key length is another important aspect of key management to consider when generating cryptographic keys. Key length is the size of a key, usually measured in bits or bytes, which a cryptographic algorithm used in ciphering or deciphering protected information. Keys are used to control how an algorithm operates so that only the correct key can decipher the information. The resistance to successful attack against the key and the algorithm, aspects of their cryptographic security, is of concern when choosing key lengths. An algorithm's key length is distinct from its cryptographic security. Cryptographic security is a logarithmic measure of the fastest known computational attack on the algorithm, also measured in bits.

The security of an algorithm cannot exceed its key length. Therefore, it is possible to have a very long key and yet it provides low security. As an example, three-key (56 bits per key) Triple DES can have a key length of 168 bits but, due to the meet-in-the-middle attack, the effective security that it provides is at most 112 bits. However, most symmetric algorithms are designed to have security equal to their key length. A natural inclination is to use the longest key possible, which may make the key more difficult to break. However, the longer the key, the more computationally expensive the encrypting and decrypting process can be. The goal is to make breaking

5

Cryptography

the key cost more (in terms of effort, time, and resources) than the worth of the information being protected and, if possible, not a penny more (to do more would not be economically sound).

Asymmetric Key Length

The effectiveness of asymmetric cryptographic systems depends on the hard to solve nature of certain mathematical problems such as prime integer factorization. These problems are time consuming to solve, but usually faster than trying all possible keys by brute force. Thus, asymmetric algorithm keys must be longer for equivalent resistance to attack than symmetric algorithm keys.

RSA Security claims that 1024-bit RSA keys are equivalent in strength to 80-bit symmetric keys, 2048-bit RSA keys to 112-bit symmetric keys, and 3072-bit RSA keys to 128-bit symmetric keys. RSA claims that 2048-bit keys are sufficient until 2030. An RSA key length of 3072 bits should be used if security is required beyond 2030[9]. NIST key management guidelines further suggest that 15,360-bit RSA keys are equivalent in strength to 256-bit symmetric keys[10].

ECC can secure with shorter keys than those needed by other asymmetric key algorithms. NIST guidelines state that elliptic curve keys should be twice the length of equivalent strength symmetric key algorithms. For example, a 224-bit elliptic curve key would have roughly the same strength as a 112-bit symmetric key. These estimates assume no major breakthroughs in solving the underlying mathematical problems that ECC is based on.

Key Wrapping and Key Encrypting Keys

One role of key management is to ensure that the same key used in encrypting a message by a sender is the same key used to decrypt the

9   Kaliski, Burt, TWIRL and RSA Key Size, RSA Labs, Available Online: http://www.rsa.com/rsalabs/node.asp?id = 2004; Last Accessed: 4 April 2008.

10   "Recommendation for Key Management -SP800–57", NIST, Available Online: http://csrc.nist.gov/publications/nistpubs/800–57/SP800–57-Part1.pdf; Last Accessed: 4 April 2008

message by the intended receiver. Thus, if Terry and Pat wish to exchange encrypted messages, each must be equipped to decrypt received messages and to encrypt sent messages. If they use a cipher, they will need appropriate keys. The problem is how to exchange whatever keys or other information are needed so that no one else can obtain a copy.

One solution is to protect the session key with a special purpose long-term use key called a key encrypting key (KEK). KEKs are used as part of key distribution or key exchange. The process of using a KEK to protect session keys is called key wrapping. Key wrapping uses symmetric ciphers to securely encrypt (thus encapsulating) a plaintext key along with any associated integrity information and data. One application for key wrapping is protecting session keys in untrusted storage or when sending over an untrusted transport. Key wrapping or encapsulation using a KEK can be accomplished using either symmetric or asymmetric ciphers. If the cipher is a symmetric KEK, both the sender and the receiver will need a copy of the same key. If using an asymmetric cipher, with public/private key properties, to encapsulate a session key both the sender and the receiver will need the other's public key.

Protocols such as SSL, PGP, and S/MIME use the services of KEKs to provide session key confidentiality, integrity, and sometimes to authenticate the binding of the session key originator and the session key itself to make sure the session key came from the real sender and not an attacker.

Key Distribution

Keys can be distributed in a number of ways. For example, two people who wish to perform key exchange can use a medium other than that through which secure messages will be sent. This is called "out of band" key exchange. If the two or more parties will send secure messages via e-mail, they may choose to meet up with each other or send via courier. The concept of "out of band" key exchange is not very scalable beyond a few people.

A more scalable method of exchanging keys is through the use of a PKI key server. A key server is a central repository of public keys of members of a group of users interested in exchanging keys to facilitate electronic transactions. Public key encryption provides a means to allow members of a group to conduct secure transactions spontaneously. The receiver's public key certificate, which contains the receiver's public key, is retrieved by the sender from the key server and is used as part of a public key encryption scheme, such as S/MIME, PGP, or even SSL to encrypt a message and send it. The digital certificate is the medium that contains the public key of each member of the group and makes the key portable, scalable, and easier to manage than an out-of-band method of key exchange.

Key Distribution Centers

Recall the formula used before to calculate the number of symmetric keys needed for users: n $(n-1)/2$. This necessitates the setup of directories, public key infrastructures, or key distribution centers.

The use of a key distribution center (KDC) for key management requires the creation of two types of keys. The first are master keys, which are secret keys shared by each user and the KDC. Each user has his own master key, and it is used to encrypt the traffic between the user and the KDC. The second type of key is a session key, created when needed, used for the duration of the communications session, and then discarded once the session is complete. When a user wants to communicate with another user or an application, the KDC sets up the session key and distributes it to each user for use. An implementation of this solution is found in Kerberos. A large organization may even have several KDCs, and they can be arranged so that there are global KDCs that coordinate the traffic between the local KDCs.

Because master keys are integral to the trust and security relationship between the users and hosts, such keys should never be used in compromised situations or where they may become exposed. For encrypting files or communications, separate nonmaster keys should be used. Ideally, a master key is never visible in the clear, it is buried within the equipment itself, and it is not accessible to the user.

Key Storage and Destruction

The proper storing and changing of cipher keys are important aspects of key management and are essential to the effective use of cryptography for security. Ultimately, the security of information protected by cryptography directly depends on the protection afforded by the keys. All keys need to be protected against modification, and secret and private keys need to be protected against unauthorized disclosure. Methods for protecting stored keying material include trusted, tamperproof hardware security modules, passphrase protected smart cards, key wrapping the session keys using long-term storage KEKs, splitting cipher keys and storing in physically separate storage locations, protecting keys using strong passwords/passphrases, key expiry, and the like.

In order to guard against a long-term cryptanalytic attack, every key must have an expiration date after which it is no longer valid. The key length must be long enough to make the chances of cryptanalysis before key expiration extremely small. The validity period for a key pair may also depend on the circumstances in which the key is used. A signature verification program should check for expiration and should not accept a message signed with an expired key. The fact that computer hardware continues to improve makes it prudent to replace expired keys with newer, longer keys every few years. Key replacement enables one to take advantage of any hardware improvements to increase the security of the cryptosystem. Additional guidance for storage of cipher keys include[11]:

- All centrally stored data that is related to user keys should be signed or have a MAC applied to it (MACed) for integrity,

11   "Guideline for Implementing Cryptography In the Federal Government", NIST, Available Online: http://csrc.nist.gov/publications/nistpubs/800–21–1/sp800–21–1_ Dec2005.pdf; Last Accessed 5 May 2008

5

Cryptography

and encrypted if confidentiality is required (all user secret keys and CA private keys should be encrypted). Individual key records in a database—as well as the entire database—should be signed or MACed and encrypted. To enable tamper detection, each individual key record should be signed or MACed so that its integrity can be checked before allowing that key to be used in a cryptographic function.

- Backup copies should be made of central/root keys, since the compromise or loss of those components could prevent access to keys in the central database, and possibly deny system users the ability to decrypt data or perform signature verifications.

- Provide key recovery capabilities. There must be safeguards to ensure that sensitive records are neither irretrievably lost by the rightful owners nor accessed by unauthorized individuals. Key recovery capabilities provide these functions.

- Archive user keys for a sufficiently long crypto period. A crypto period is the time during which a key can be used to protect information; it may extend well beyond the lifetime of a key that is used to apply cryptographic protection (where the lifetime is the time during which a key can be used to generate a signature or perform encryption). Keys may be archived for a lengthy period (on the order of decades), so that they can be used to verify signatures and decrypt ciphertext.

Among the factors affecting the risk of exposure are[12]:

1. The strength of the cryptographic mechanisms (e.g., the algorithm, key length, block size, and mode of operation)

2. The embodiment of the mechanisms (e.g., FIPS 140-2 Level 4 implementation, or software implementation on a personal computer)

3. The operating environment (e.g., secure limited access facility, open office environment, or publicly accessible terminal)

---

12   "Recommendations for Key Management, SP800–57",NIST, Available Online: http://csrc.nist.gov/publications/nistpubs/800–57/sp800–57-Part1-revised2_Mar08–2007. pdf; Last Accessed 5 May 2008

4. The volume of information flow or the number of transactions

5. The security life of the data

6. The security function (e.g., data encryption, digital signature, key production or derivation, key protection)

7. The re-keying method (e.g., keyboard entry, re-keying using a key loading device where humans have no direct access to key information, remote re-keying within a PKI)

8. The key update or key derivation process

9. The number of nodes in a network that share a common key

10. The number of copies of a key and the distribution of those copies

11. The threat to the information (e.g., whom the information is protected from, and what are their perceived technical capabilities and financial resources to mount an attack).

In general, short crypto periods enhance security. For example, some cryptographic algorithms might be less vulnerable to cryptanalysis if the adversary has only a limited amount of information encrypted under a single key. Caution should be used when deleting keys that are no longer needed. A simple deletion of the keying material might not completely obliterate the information. For example, erasing the information might require overwriting that information multiple times with other non-related information, such as random bits, or all zero or one bits. Keys stored in memory for a long time can become "burned in." This can be mitigated by splitting the key into components that are frequently updated as shown in *Figure 5.20.*

5

Cryptography

Key Type	Cryptoperiod	
	Originator Usage Period (OUP)	Recipient Usage Period
1. Private signature key	1–3 years	
2. Public signature key	Several years (depends on key size)	
3. Symmetric authentication key	≤ 2 years	≤ OUP + 3 years
4. Private authentication key	1–2 years	
5. Public authentication key	1–2 years	
6. Symmetric data encryption keys	≤ 2 years	≤ OUP + 3 years
7. Symmetric key wrapping key	≤ 2 years	≤ OUP + 3 years
8. Symmetric and asymmetric RNG keys	Upon reseeding	
9. Symmetric master key	About 1 year	
10. Private key transport key	≤ 2 years[14]	
11. Public key transport key	1–2 years	

Figure 5.20 - **Recommended Crypto Periods for key types**

On the other hand, where manual key distribution methods are subject to human error and frailty, more frequent key changes might actually increase the risk of exposure. In these cases, especially when very strong cryptography is employed, it may be more prudent to have fewer, well-controlled manual key distributions rather than more frequent, poorly controlled manual key distributions. Secure automated key distribution, where key generation and exchange are protected by appropriate authentication, access and integrity controls may be a compensating control in such environments.

Users with different roles should have keys with lifetimes that take into account the different roles and responsibilities, the applications for which the keys are used, and the security services that are provided by the keys (user/data authentication, confidentiality, data integrity, etc.). Reissuing keys should not be done so often that it becomes excessively burdensome; however, it should be performed often enough to minimize the loss caused by a possible key compromise.

Handle the deactivation/revocation of keys so that data signed prior to a compromise date (or date of loss) can be verified. When a signing key is designated as "lost" or "compromised," signatures generated prior to the specified date may still need to be verified in the future. Therefore, a signature verification capability may need to be maintained for lost or compromised keys. Otherwise, all data previously signed with a lost or compromised key would have to be re-signed.

Cost of Certificate Replacement/Revocation

In some cases, the costs associated with changing digital certificates and cryptographic keys are painfully high. Examples include decryption and subsequent re-encryption of very large databases, decryption and re-encryption of distributed databases, and revocation and replacement of a very large number of keys; e.g., where there are very large numbers of geographically and organizationally distributed key holders. In such cases, the expense of the security measures necessary to support longer crypto periods may be justified; e.g., costly and inconvenient physical, procedural, and logical access security; and use of cryptography strong enough to support longer crypto periods even where this may result in significant additional processing overhead.

In other cases, the crypto period may be shorter than would otherwise be necessary, for example, keys may be changed frequently in order to limit the period of time the key management system maintains status information. On the other hand, a user losing their private key would require that the lost key be revoked so that an unauthorized user cannot use it. It would be a good practice to use a master decryption key (Additional decryption key in PGP), or another key recovery mechanism to guard against losing access to the data encrypted under the lost key. Another reason to revoke a certificate is when an employee leaves the company or, in some cases, when changing job roles, as in the case of someone moving to a more trusted job role, which may require a different level of accountability, access to higher risk data, and so on.

5

Cryptography

859

Key Recovery

A lost key may mean a crisis to an organization. The loss of critical data or backups may cause widespread damage to operations and even financial ruin or penalties. There are several methods of key recovery, such as common trusted directories or a policy that requires all cryptographic keys to be registered with the security department. Some people have even been using steganography to bury their passwords in pictures or other locations on their machine to prevent someone from finding their password file. Others use password wallets or other tools to hold all of their passwords.

One method is multiparty key recovery. A user would write her private key on a piece of paper, and then divide the key into two or more parts. Each part would be sealed in an envelope. The user would give one envelope each to trusted people with instructions that the envelope was only to be opened in an emergency where the organization needed access to the user's system or files (disability or death of the user). In case of an emergency, the holders of the envelopes would report to human resources, where the envelopes could be opened and the key reconstructed. The user would usually give the envelopes to trusted people at different management levels and different parts of the company to reduce the risk of collusion.

Key recovery should also be conducted with the privacy of the individual in mind. If a private individual used encryption to protect the confidentiality of some information, it may be legally protected according to local laws. In some situations, a legal order may be required to retrieve the key and decrypt the information.

Key Escrow

Key escrow is the process of ensuring a third party maintains a copy of a private key or key needed to decrypt information. Key escrow also should be considered mandatory for most organization's use of cryptography as encrypted information belongs to the organization and not the individual;

however often an individual's key is used to encrypt the information. There must be explicit trust between the key escrow provider and the parties involved as the escrow provider now holds a copy of the private key and could use it to reveal information. Conditions of key release must be explicitly defined and agreed upon by all parties.

5

Cryptography

Digital Signatures

A digital signature is intended to be comparable to a handwritten signature on an important document such as a contract. It is important to note that a digital signature is a mathematical representation and conveys specific meaning in binary data, and is not the same as a "digitized signature." A digitized signature is a representation of a handwritten personal signature as can be created using a scanner or fax machine.

The purpose of a digital signature is to provide the same level of accountability for electronic transactions where a handwritten signature is not possible. A digital signature will provide assurance that the message does indeed come from the person who claims to have sent it, it has not been altered, both parties have a copy of the same document, and the person sending the document cannot claim that he did not send it. A digital signature will usually include a date and time of the signature, as well as a method for a third party to verify the signature.

What is a digital signature? It is a block of data (a pattern of bits, usually a hash) that is generated based on the contents of the message sent and encrypted with the sender's private key. It must contain some unique value that links it with the sender of the message that can be verified easily by the receiver and by a third party, and it must be difficult to forge the digital signature or create a new message with the same signature.

Digital Signature Standard (DSS)

The DSS was proposed in 1991 as FIPS 186 using the Secure Hashing Algorithm (SHA). It has since been updated several times, most recently in 2009, when it was issued as FIPS 186-3 and expanded to include the Digital Signature Algorithm (DSA) based on RSA and ECC. Contrasted with RSA, a digital signature is based on a public key (asymmetric) algorithm, but it does not provide for confidentiality of the message through encryption and is not used for key exchange.

The DSS uses two methods of creating the signature: the RSA method and the DSS approach. In both cases, the operation starts with the creation of a hash of the message. The RSA approach then encrypts the hash with the private key of the sender, thus creating the signature. The DSS approach is to sign the hash using the DSA. The DSA is based on the discrete logarithmic algorithms used in El Gamal and Schnorr. The DSA chooses a random number to create a private and public key pair and encrypts the hash value with the private key and a universal key to create a two-part signature.

A digital signature can be created by encrypting the entire message with the private key of the sender; however, in most cases this is not practical because of the computational impact of encrypting a message using asymmetric algorithms. Therefore, in most cases the digital signature is created by encrypting a hash of the message with the sender's private key. If further confidentiality is needed, then the message can be encrypted with a symmetric algorithm; however, it is best to create the signature before encrypting the message—then the signature authenticates the message itself and not the ciphertext of the message.

Once a digital signature is created, it is appended to the message and sent to the receiver. The receiver decrypts the signature with the public key of the sender and can verify the message has not been altered and can establish the nonrepudiation of origin of the signature.

Uses of Digital Signatures

Digital signatures have become invaluable in protecting the integrity of financial transactions, e-commerce, and e-mail. They are also used by software vendors to ensure that software has not been compromised through the introduction of viruses or other manipulation. This is especially important when downloading a patch via the Internet to ensure that the patch is from a legitimate site, as well as ensuring the integrity of the download.

Digital signatures are used to sign digital certificates. A digital certificate is an electronic document that asserts authenticity and data integrity that is tied to a sender. A hash computation is performed over the certificate content; the hash value is then encrypted using the private key of the sender and then embedded into the certificate. The recipient decrypts the embedded hash value using the sender's public key. The receiver then uses the public key of the sender to verify the sender authenticity by performing the same hash computation over the certificate content as was done by the sender. If the hash results are the same, then sender authentication and data integrity of the certificate has been established. In many parts of the world, digital signatures have become recognized by the government and courts as a verifiable form of authentication.

Non-Repudiation

Non-repudiation is a service that ensures the sender cannot deny a message was sent and the integrity of the message is intact. NIST's SP 800-57 defines non-repudiation as:

> *"A service that is used to provide assurance of the integrity and origin of data in such a way that the integrity and origin can be verified by a third party as having originated from a specific entity in possession of the private key of the claimed signatory. In a general information security context, assurance that the sender of information is provided with proof of delivery and the recipient is provided with proof of the sender's identity, so neither can later deny having processed the information."*

Non-repudiation can be accomplished with digital signatures and PKI. The message is signed using the sender's private key. When the recipient receives the message, they may use the sender's public key to validate the signature. While this proves the integrity of the message, it does not explicitly define the ownership of the private key. A certificate authority must have an association between the private key and the sender (meaning only the sender has the private key) for the non-repudiation to be valid.

5

Cryptography

Methods of Cryptanalytic Attacks

Any security system or product is subject to compromise or attack. The following explains common attacks against cryptography systems.

Chosen plain-text

To execute the chosen attacks, the attacker knows the algorithm used for the encrypting, or even better, he may have access to the machine used to do the encryption and is trying to determine the key. This may happen if a workstation used for encrypting messages is left unattended. Now the attacker can run chosen pieces of plaintext through the algorithm and see what the result is. This may assist in a known plaintext attack. An adaptive chosen plaintext attack is where the attacker can modify the chosen input files to see what effect that would have on the resulting ciphertext.

Social Engineering for Key Discovery

This is the most common type of attack and usually the most successful. All cryptography relies to some extent on humans to implement and operate. Unfortunately, this is one of the greatest vulnerabilities and has led to some of the greatest compromises of a nation's or organization's secrets or intellectual property. Through coercion, bribery, or befriending people in positions of responsibility, spies or competitors are able to gain access to systems without having any technical expertise.

Brute Force

Brute force is trying all possible keys until one is found that decrypts the ciphertext. This is why key length is such an important factor in determining the strength of a cryptosystem. With DES only having a 56-bit key, in time the attackers were able to discover the key and decrypt a DES message. This is also why SHA-256 is considered stronger than MD5, because the output hash is longer, and, therefore, more resistant to a brute-force attack.

Graphical Processor Units (GPUs) have revolutionized brute force hacking methods. Where a standard CPU might take 48 hours to crack an eight character mixed password, a modern GPU can crack it in less than ten minutes. GPUs have a large number of "Arithmetic/Logic Units" (ALUs) and are designed to perform repetitive tasks continuously. These characteristics make them ideal for performing brute force attack processes. Due to the introduction of GPU based brute force attacks, many security professionals are evaluating password length, complexity and multifactor considerations.

Differential Cryptanalysis

Also called a side channel attack, this more complex attack is executed by measuring the exact execution times and power required by the crypto device to perform the encryption or decryption. By measuring this, it is possible to determine the value of the key and the algorithm used.

Linear Cryptanalysis

This is a known plaintext attack that uses linear approximations to describe the behavior of the block cipher. Linear cryptanalysis is a known plaintext attack and uses a linear approximation to describe the behavior of the block cipher. Given sufficient pairs of plaintext and corresponding ciphertext, bits of information about the key can be obtained and increased amounts of data will usually give a higher probability of success.

There have been a variety of enhancements and improvements to the basic attack. For example, there is an attack called differential-linear cryptanalysis, which combines elements of differential cryptanalysis with those of linear cryptanalysis.

Algebraic

Algebraic attacks are a class of techniques that rely for their success on block ciphers exhibiting a high degree of mathematical structure. For instance, it is conceivable that a block cipher might exhibit a group structure. If this were the case, it would then mean that encrypting a plaintext under

5

Cryptography

one key and then encrypting the result under another key would always be equivalent to single encryption under some other single key. If so, then the block cipher would be considerably weaker, and the use of multiple encryption cycles would offer no additional security over single encryption

Rainbow Table

Hash functions map plaintext into a hash. Since the hash function is a one-way process, one should not be able to determine the plaintext from the hash itself. To determine a given plaintext from its hash there are two ways to do that: 1) hash each plaintext until matching hash is found or 2) hash each plaintext but store each generated hash in a table that can used as a look up table so hashes do not need to be generated again. A rainbow table is a lookup table of sorted hash outputs. The idea here is that storing pre-computed hash values in a rainbow table that one can later refer to saves time and computer resources when attempting to decipher the plaintext from its hash value.

Ciphertext-Only Attack

The ciphertext-only attack is one of the most difficult because the attacker has so little information to start with. All the attacker starts with is some unintelligible data that he suspects may be an important encrypted message. The attack becomes simpler when the attacker is able to gather several pieces of ciphertext and thereby look for trends or statistical data that would help in the attack. Adequate encryption is defined as encryption that is strong enough to make brute-force attacks impractical because there is a higher work factor than the attacker wants to invest into the attack. Moore's law states that available computing power doubles every 18 months. Experts suggest this advance may be slowing[1]; however, encryption strength considered adequate today will probably not be sufficient a few years from now due to advances in CPU and GPU technology and new attack techniques. Security professionals should consider this when defining encryption requirements.

---

1   Read more about the slowing of Moore's law here: http://news.cnet.com/8301-10784_3-9780752-7.html

Know plaintext

For a known plaintext attack, the attacker has access to both the ciphertext and the plaintext versions of the same message. The goal of this type of attack is to find the link—the cryptographic key that was used to encrypt the message. Once the key has been found, the attacker would then be able to decrypt all messages that had been encrypted using that key. In some cases, the attacker may not have an exact copy of the message—if the message was known to be an e-commerce transaction, the attacker knows the format of such transactions even though he does not know the actual values in the transaction.

Frequency Analysis[2]

This attack works closely with several other types of attacks. It is especially useful when attacking a substitution cipher where the statistics of the plaintext language are known. In English, for example, some letters will appear more often than others will, allowing an attacker to assume that those letters may represent an E or S.

Chosen cipher-text

This is similar to the chosen plaintext attack in that the attacker has access to the decryption device or software and is attempting to defeat the cryptographic protection by decrypting chosen pieces of ciphertext to discover the key. An adaptive chosen ciphertext would be the same, except that the attacker can modify the ciphertext prior to putting it through the algorithm. Asymmetric cryptosystems are vulnerable to chosen ciphertext attacks.

For example, the RSA algorithm is vulnerable to this type of attack. The attacker would select a section of plaintext, encrypt it with the victim's public key, then decrypt the ciphertext to get the plaintext back. Although this does not yield any new information to the attacker, the attacker can

---

2   Read more about Frequency Analysis and Claude Shannon's work at: http://www.schneier.com/crypto-gram-9812.html

exploit properties of RSA by selecting blocks of data, when processed using the victim's private key, yields information that can be used in cryptanalysis. The weakness with asymmetric encryption in chosen ciphertext attacks can be mitigated by including a random padding in the plaintext before encrypting the data. Security vendor RSA Security recommends modifying the plaintext using process called optimal asymmetric encryption padding (OAEP). RSA encryption with OAEP is defined in PKCS #1 v2.1[3].

Birthday Attack

Because a hash is a short representation of a message, given enough time and resources, another message that would give the same hash value. However, hashing algorithms have been developed with this in mind, so that they can resist a simple birthday attack. The point of the birthday attack is that it is easier to find two messages that hash to the same message digest than to match a specific message and its specific message digest. The usual countermeasure is to use a hash algorithm with twice the message digest length as the desired work factor (e.g., use 160 bit SHA-1 to have it resistant to 2^{80} work factor).

Dictionary Attack

The dictionary attack is used most commonly against password files. It exploits the poor habits of users who choose simple passwords based on natural words. The dictionary attack merely encrypts all of the words in a dictionary and then checks whether the resulting hash matches an encrypted password stored in the sam file or other password file.

Replay Attack

This attack is meant to disrupt and damage processing by the attacker sending repeated files to the host. If there are no checks or sequence verification codes in the receiving software, the system might process duplicate files.

---

3   http://www.rsa.com/rsalabs/node.asp?id=2125

Factoring Attacks

This attack is aimed at the RSA algorithm. Because that algorithm uses the product of large prime numbers to generate the public and private keys, this attack attempts to find the keys through solving the factoring of these numbers.

Reverse Engineering

This attack is one of the most common. A competing firm buys a crypto product from another firm and then tries to reverse engineer the product. Through reverse engineering, it may be able to find weaknesses in the system or gain crucial information about the operations of the algorithm.

Attacking the Random Number Generators

This attack was successful against the SSL installed in Netscape several years ago. Because the random number generator was too predictable, it gave the attackers the ability to guess the random numbers so critical in setting up initialization vectors or a nonce. With this information in hand, the attacker is much more likely to run a successful attack.

Temporary Files

Most cryptosystems will use temporary files to perform their calculations. If these files are not deleted and overwritten, they may be compromised and lead an attacker to the message in plaintext.

Implementation Attacks

Implementation attacks are some of the most common and popular attacks against cryptographic systems due to their ease and reliance on system elements outside of the algorithm. The main types of implementation attacks include:

- Side-channel analysis
- Fault Analysis
- Probing Attacks

Side-channel attacks are passive attacks that rely on a physical attribute of the implementation such as power consumption/emanation. These attributes are studied to determine the secret key and the algorithm function. Some examples of popular side-channels include timing analysis and electromagnetic differential analysis.

Fault analysis attempts to force the system into an error state to gain erroneous results. By forcing an error, gaining the results and comparing it with known good results, an attacker may learn about the secret key and the algorithm.

Probing attacks attempt to watch the circuitry surrounding the cryptographic module in hopes that they complementary components will disclose information about the key or the algorithm. Additionally new hardware may be added to the cryptographic module to observe and inject information.

Network Security and Cryptography

Cryptography is a critical part of ensuring networks can remain secure. From Virtual Private Networks (VPN) to secure e-commerce through web browsers much of the internet's economic success can be attributed to the protection cryptography provides. As mobile devices and cloud computing play a larger role in the interconnected world, the security professional will see an increased focus on network security and advanced cryptographic approaches.

Virtual Private Networks

The goal of VPN technology is to provide confidentiality and data integrity of data transmission. IPSec and SSL are the dominant security protocols in current use. Both protocols use a combination of symmetric key encryption algorithms for bulk data encryption and asymmetric encryption for user authentication and hash algorithms for data integrity. The difference between the two protocols is the network communications layer each is designed to operate at. Beyond that, differences in capabilities between the two are rapidly converging.

The two types of basic VPN applications are site to site and remote access VPN. Site to site deploys two or more VPN servers or appliances that securely connect two or more private networks together. Remote access VPN securely connects a user computer to another user computer or VPN server. With any VPN, each VPN member must be configured to use the same cryptographic parameters (i.e., same encryption algorithm, hash function, etc.), Site to site VPN policy can be configured to control access to the private network based on authentication trust levels defined at each end of the VPN. A concern when considering remote access VPNs is endpoint security posture. Remote access VPN solutions are moving to a "inspect before allowing" model, or network admission/access control, before granting the remote user's computer access to the private network.

5

Cryptography

873

E-Commerce

The role of cryptography in e-commerce continues to be as an enabler of trust between business entities and between consumer and business. Data encryption plays a central role in securing online transactions. Encryption ensures transaction privacy to prevent unauthorized access to confidential transactions. Authentication protocols allow each party to an online transaction to verify each other's identity. Often this is accomplished using digital certificates or username/password across an encrypted transport such as SSL. To ensure that transactions have not been modified in transit by a third party, cryptographic hashing is used. Digital signatures are sometimes used to prevent a party from denying they ever received or sent a particular message or transaction, or nonrepudiation.

Tools

Two major tools assist in both VPN and e-commerce secure networking. IPSec and SSL/TLS have become synonymous with network security. These protocols form the vast majority of secure network traffic and e-commerce enablement.

IPSec

IPSec was developed to provide security over Internet connections and prevent IP spoofing, eavesdropping, and misuse of IP-based authentication. It operates with both IPv4 and IPv6. IPSec is documented in RFCs 2401, 2402, 2406, and 2408. IPSec uses HMAC-MD5-96 or HMAC-SHA-1-96 to provide an integrity check value for the message and part of the headers. This prevents the spoofing of the address portion of the headers. The reason they are called "-96" is that although the full MD5 or SHA-1 is used to calculate the integrity check value, only the first 96 bits (of 128 or 160, respectively) are used.

For Encapsulating Security Payload (ESP) mode of operations, IPSec uses three-key 3DES, RC5, IDEA, three-key 3IDEA, CAST, or Blowfish to encrypt the payload (message) and, depending on whether it is tunnel or transport mode, part of the header. Key management is an important part of IPSec, and it uses Oakley/ISAKMP for key exchange. Oakley uses a form of Diffie–Hellman with some added security to prevent the clogging of the key exchange process. This is done by forcing the sender to include a random number (nonce) in the original packet to the receiver. The receiver will then respond back to the address of the sender in the packet and not begin the decryption process until it receives an acknowledgment that the reply was received by the sender. If an attacker spoofed the sender's address, the sender would never get the response from the receiver, and this would prevent the receiver from doing unnecessary work and clogging up his system with spoofed requests. ISAKMP specifies the format of the process to negotiate security associations.

SSL/TLS

SSL is one of the most common protocols used to protect Internet traffic. It encrypts the messages using symmetric algorithms, such as IDEA, DES, 3DES, and Fortezza, and also calculates the MAC for the message using MD5 or SHA-1. The MAC is appended to the message and encrypted along with the message data. The exchange of the symmetric keys is accomplished through various versions of Diffie–Hellmann or RSA. TLS is the Internet standard based on SSLv3. TLSv1 is backward compatible with SSLv3. It uses the same algorithms as SSLv3; however, it computes an HMAC instead of a MAC along with other enhancements to improve security.

5

Cryptography

Application Security and Cryptography

E-Mail Security Using Cryptography

Cryptography has many uses in today's business environment, but perhaps one of the most visible is to protect e-mail. E-mail is the most common form of business communications for most organizations today, far outranking voice or personal contact in its importance for commerce.

There are several reasons why an organization may need to protect e-mail—to protect the confidentiality of message content and preserve intellectual property, to protect the integrity of the message itself, to verify the course of e-mails to ensure that the sender is who he claims to be, to provide access control, and to prevent the distribution or copying of e-mail message content.

The ability to forge e-mails, alter attachments, and masquerade as another user is a fairly simple process, and this underlines the requirement for secure e-mail.

E-mail Protocols and Standards

Privacy Enhanced Mail (PEM)

This group of protocols was the first defined in a group of RFCs (RFC 1421-RFC 1424) for encrypting e-mail. PEM was superseded by S/MIME. The PEM security enhancements provide three security services: message integrity, message origin authentication, and message confidentiality. Base64 encoding represents digital data using the base64 numbering system where each digit represents 6 bits of data. PEM represents the 64 digits of base64 with ASCII characters "A– Z," "a-z," "0–9," " +," and "/" with " = " being used to pad the last line or signify the end of data block. An encapsulation boundary is used to indicate beginning and end of a PEM encoded message. ("—-BEGIN PRIVACY ENHANCED MESSAGE—" "—-END PRIVACY ENHANCED MESSAGE—")

PEM was designed to be interoperable in a X.509 certificate–based PKI. The legacy use of PEM is currently found in SSL where PEM is used as a file format for representing public and private keys and signatures with file extension being ".pem." The PEM protocols rely on the trusted distribution of the public keys using X.509 certificates.

Pretty Good Privacy (PGP)

PGP was developed by Phil Zimmerman as a free product for noncommercial use that would enable all people to have access to state-of-the-art cryptographic algorithms to protect their privacy. PGP is also available as a commercial product that has received widespread acceptance by many organizations looking for a user-friendly, simple system of encryption of files, documents, and e-mail and the ability to wipe out old files through a process of overwriting them to protect old data from recovery. PGP also compresses data to save on bandwidth and storage needs.

PGP uses several of the most common algorithms—symmetric algorithms such as CAST-128 and 3DES for encryption of bulk data, RSA for key management and distribution of hash values, and SHA-1 to compute hash values for message integrity. It gives the user the option to choose which algorithm the user wishes to use, including others not mentioned here.

When sending e-mail, PGP will ensure compatibility with most e-mail systems, converting binary bits to ASCII characters, breaking large messages into smaller pieces, and encrypting each message with a session (symmetric) key that is only used once. A user needing a new key ring will select a passphrase and PGP will generate the key pair to be used. A user will establish trust in another user's public key through a web of trust relationship. Rather than establishing trust in a hierarchical format, where a root CA is trusted by everyone and everyone below that level trusts the higher authority, PGP establishes trust based on relationships, and one user can sign another user's key for a third party based on the level of trust that the third party has on the key signer.

Secure/Multipurpose Internet Mail Extension

S/MIME is the security enhancement for the MIME Internet e-mail standard format. S/MIME provides several features, including signed and encrypted mail messages. As a hybrid cryptographic application, S/MIME, similar to IPSec and SSL, uses hash functions, symmetric and asymmetric cryptographies. There are a variety of bulk encryption algorithms defined the most popular being AES. Asymmetric encryption, such as RSA, is used for digital signatures. Secure hash algorithms, such as SHA-1, are used to provide data integrity of the message body and message attributes.

Remote Access

The role of cryptography in remote access applications has only grown in importance as connectivity has grown in importance in both consumer and business environments. Compliance regulations are increasingly mandating the use of encryption when transmitting confidential information across open transports such as the public Internet. Encryption is used to protect the data that are sent between a remote access client and the remote access server. For environments where data confidentiality is required, such as financial institutions, law-enforcement, government agencies, and corporations, the network administrator can set the remote access server to require encrypted communications with the remote access clients. Users who connect to that server must encrypt their data or the connection attempt is denied. Encryption along with access controls and strong authentication forms the basis for fulfilling most confidentiality security requirements.

Public Key Infrastructure (PKI)

A PKI is a set of system, software, and communication protocols required to use, manage, and control public key cryptography. It has three primary purposes: publish public keys/certificates, certify that a key is tied to an individual or entity, and provide verification of the validity of a public key.

The CA "signs" an entities digital certificate to certify that the certificate content accurately represents the certificate owner. There can be different levels of assurance implied by the CA signing the certificate similar to forms of the physical identification of an individual can imply differing levels of trust. In the physical world, a credit card with a name on it has a differing level of authentication value than, say, a government-issued ID card. Any entity can claim to be anything it wants, but if the entity wants to provide a high level of assurance it should provide identifying content in its certificate that is easily confirmed by third parties that are trusted by all parties involved. In the digital world, a Dun and Bradstreet number, credit report, or perhaps another form of trusted third party reference would be provided to the CA before certifying by signing the entity's certificate with a marking indicating the CA asserts a high level of trust of the entity. Now all the entities that trust the CA can now trust that the identity provided by a certificate is trustworthy.

The functions of a CA may be distributed among several specialized servers in a PKI. For example, server RAs may be used to provide scalability and reliability of the PKI. RA servers provide the facility for entities to submit requests for certificate generation. The RA service is also responsible for ensuring the accuracy of certificate request content.

The CA can revoke certificates and provide an update service to the other members of the PKI via a certificate revocation list (CRL), which is a list of non-valid certificates that should not be accepted by any member of the PKI. The use of public key (asymmetric) cryptography has enabled

5

Cryptography

more effective use of symmetric cryptography as well as several other important features, such as greater access control, nonrepudiation, and digital signatures.

So often, the biggest question is, who can be trusted? How does one know that the public key being used to verify Terry's digital signature truly belongs to Terry, or that the public key being used to send a confidential message to Pat is truly Pat's and not that of an attacker who has set himself up in the middle of the communications channel?

Public keys are by their very nature public. Many people include them on signature lines in e-mails, or organizations have them on their Web servers so that customers can establish confidential communications with the employees of the organization, who they may never even meet. How does one know an imposter or attacker has not set up a rogue Web server and is attracting communications that should have been confidential to his site instead of the real account, as in a phishing attack?

Setting up a trusted public directory of keys is one option. Each user must register with the directory service, and a secure manner of communications between the user and the directory would be set up. This would allow the user to change keys—or the directory to force the change of keys. The directory would publish and maintain the list of all active keys and also delete or revoke keys that are no longer trusted. This may happen if a person believes that her private key has been compromised, or she leaves the employ of the organization. Any person wanting to communicate with a registered user of the directory could request the public key of the registered user from the directory.

An even higher level of trust is provided through the use of public key certificates. This can be done directly. Pat would send a certificate to Terry, or through a CA, which would act as a trusted third party and issue a certificate to both Pat and Terry containing the public key of the other party. This certificate is signed with the digital signature of the CA and can be verified by the recipients. The certification process binds identity information and a public key to an identity. The resultant document of this process is the public key certificate. A CA will adhere to the X.509 standards. This is part of the overall X.500 family of standards applying to directories. X.509 version 3 of the standard, is the most common. Figure 5.21 shows an example of a certificate issued by Verisign.

An X.509 certificate looks as follows:

Field	Description of Contents
Algorithm used for the signature	Algorithm used to sign the certificate
Issuer name	X.500 name of CA
Period of Validity: Start Date/End Date	
Subject's name	Owner of the public key
Subject's Public Key Information (algorithm, parameters, key)	Public key and algorithm used to create it
Issuer unique identifier	Optional field used in case the CA used more than one X.500 name
Subject's unique identifier	Optional field in case the public key owner has more than one X.500 name
Extensions	
Digital signature of CA	Hash of the certificate encrypted with the private key of the CA

Figure 5.21 - **A X.509 certification issued by Verisign**

5

Cryptography

Certificate Related Issues

Users will often need to communicate with other users that are registered with a different CA. Especially in a large organization; it may not be practical to use one CA for all users. Therefore, the CAs must also have a method of cross-certifying one another so that a public key certificate from one CA is recognized by users from a different CA. For large organizations that have implemented multiple CAs for scalability reasons, full trust between cross-certified CAs is often appropriate. However, for disparate organizations that have a specific and limited business relationship, establishing full trust between CAs is often not appropriate.

Business agreements and PKI policies are negotiated between the organizations. The agreements and policy define the trust levels and use policies that will be used as part of the cross-certified organizations. Then each CA signs each other's public key, or root certificate, thus establishing a certificate chain. This process of two or more CAs signing each other's root certificates is called "cross-certification."

There are three basic ways of constraining the trust between CAs: path length, name, and policy. The cross-certificate between two CAs (peer to peer cross certification) or the subordinate CA certificate (hierarchical cross-certification) is used to convey the constraint, and the client application automatically enforces the specified control when validating certificates.

Path length constraints can be used to control transitive trust. Organizations can control whether their CA should trust any cross-certification relationships that have been established by CAs with whom organizations have cross-certified. This control is important since all members of a hierarchical cross-certification trust each other.

In a peer to peer cross-certification, name constraints are used to limit trust to a subgroup of cross certified CAs based on their distinguished name (DN). For example, suppose all employees in a company are organized within organizational units such that each user's DN includes their organizational unit. Users in the finance department have DNs like cn = Bill Smith, ou = Finance, o = ABC Corp, c = US, while users in sales have DNs like cn = Valerie Jones, ou = Sales, o = ABC, c = US. If ABC Corp establishes a cross-certification relationship with ACMS Corp and vice versa, it can now limit such that only the finance groups within each CA trust each other.

Policy constraints can be used to limit trust only to those users in another CA who has certain policy values in their certificates. Here is an example of assurance levels again. Assurance refers to the degree of trust an individual places in who their certificates say they are. An organization may have different levels of assurance depending on the way a user is authenticated before issuing a certificate. A low-assurance policy could be associated with a user requesting an activation code over the phone. A high-assurance policy could be associated with a user requesting activation in person with proper identification. Access credentials may be issued to each user with one of these two assurance levels, depending on each user's authority and access control requirements. PKI policy networking provides the flexibility and control needed to establish and enforce limited trust relationships that mirror the business relationships between or within organizations.

As the number of cross-certified CAs grows, the number of peer-to-peer relationships grows. Cross-certifying n organization PKIs requires (n2-n/2 peer to peer relationships and (n2-n) certificates. Establishing these relationships requires a time consuming review of policies and practices. In large cross-certifying CA environments, a bridge CA can be used to establish trust with better scalability. A bridge CA does not issue end user/entity certificates. Unlike a root CA in a PKI hierarchy, a bridge CA is not intended as a trust point. All PKI users consider the bridge as an intermediary. The trust relationships between the bridge CA and the principal CAs are all peer-to-peer. It is easy to add new CAs, or entire PKIs, to a bridge connected PKI. The change is transparent to users because no change in trust points is required. In general, the use of a bridge CA will require less time spent reviewing policies and practices than comparable cross-certified PKI.[1]

1   *The Internet Encyclopedia* Volume 3, Hussein Bidgolli, ISBN 0–471–22203–8, 2003

Information Hiding Alternatives

Steganography

Steganography is the hiding of a message inside of another medium, such as a photograph, music, or other item. Steganography comes from the Greek expression of "hidden writing."

Steganography is not a new art—history tells of slaves having a message tattooed onto their head to carry it through enemy lines. The message itself was not encrypted, but its existence was hidden so that only the recipient would know to reveal the message through a radical haircut. Steganography was also used through the centuries through microdots, invisible ink, and regular letters between friends containing hidden meanings.

Modern stego tools will bury a message inside of a jpeg or other graphic image by "stealing" the least significant bit of every byte and using it to carry the secret message. This will not noticeably change the image, and a casual observer will not realize that a message is hidden inside the image, only to be revealed to the person with the correct stego tool. Most unfortunately, this has become a method of industrial espionage, where a mole (spy) within a company will send confidential information to a competitor via a generic e-mail address, hiding confidential corporate information within the message that would not be noticed even if the e-mail was being monitored.

Watermarking

Watermarking is the addition of identifiable information into a file or document. This is often done to detect the improper copying or theft of information. The watermark may or may not be visible and may affect the quality of the original file.

Code Words

Many government and military units carry code books with short code words that are used to shorten and/or hide communications. For instance, the U.S. Navy uses 'BZ' to congratulate a unit for a well done job or maneuver. The code books are usually weighted so they will sink rapidly in the ocean when jettisoned if a ship or aircraft is about to be captured by the enemy.

For many years now, radio transmissions have been an important part of air traffic control; however, people do not all speak with the same accent, and the radios themselves are often subject to noise, distortion, and interference. For the sake of understanding, it is often better to use a code word instead of a letter—a person may not understand whether the speaker said a B or a D, but if they say "Bravo" or "Delta," a B from the word *Bravo* or D from *Delta* can easily be distinguished.

More to Know

The following articles and documents contain more information about Cryptography. They are freely available on the Internet.

EU Council Regulation 438/2009 of 5 May 2009: Describes EU specific cryptographic import and export regulations
*http://eur-lex.europa.eu/LexUriServ/LexUriServ.
do?uri=OJ:L:2009:134:0001:0269:en:PDF*

NIST Special Publication 800-131A Transitions: Recommendation for Transitioning the Use of Cryptographic Algorithms and Key Lengths
http://csrc.nist.gov/publications/nistpubs/800-131A/sp800-131A.pdf

The Evolution of 802.11 Wireless Security INF 795 - Kevin Benton April 18th, 2010
http://itffroc.org/pubs/benton_wireless.pdf

Smart Card Alliance Smart Card FAQ
http://www.smartcardalliance.org/pages/smart-cards-faq

Information and Freeware versions of PGP
http://www.pgpi.org/doc/faq/pgpi/en/

http://www.pgpi.org/products/pgp/versions/freeware/

NIST's Cryptographic Toolkit
http://csrc.nist.gov/groups/ST/toolkit/index.html

The Australian Crypto FAQ
https://www.efa.org.au/Issues/Crypto/cryptfaq.html

EPIC Online Guide to Practical Privacy Tools
http://epic.org/privacy/tools.html/

US' National Security Agency National Cryptologic Museum
http://www.nsa.gov/about/cryptologic_heritage/museum/

5

Cryptography

Summary and Conclusion

Cryptography has enabled information technology use in environments never before possible.

The move towards telework and the secure communications required for remote work would not be possible without the advances in cryptography. Cryptography provides the information security professional with a rich menu of methods, devices, softwareandtechniquestohelpensuretheconfidentiality, integrity, authentication and nonrepudiation of information. While advances in computing power have rendered some cryptographic tools weakened or comprised, security professionals and researchers are constantly developing new tools to enhance security.

Cryptography will continue to play a vital role in the advancement of privacy, security, commerce and communications for the foreseeable future.

Review Questions

1. Asymmetric key cryptography is used for the following:

    A. Encryption of data, Access Control, Steganography

    B. Steganography, Access control, Nonrepudiation

    C. Nonrepudiation, Steganography, Encryption of Data

    D. Encryption of Data, Nonrepudiation, Access Control

2. Which of the following supports asymmetric key cryptography?

    A. Diffie–Hellman

    B. Rijndael

    C. Blowfish

    D. SHA-256

3. What is an important disadvantage of using a public key algorithm compared to a symmetric algorithm?

    A. A symmetric algorithm provides better access control.

    B. A symmetric algorithm is a faster process.

    C. A symmetric algorithm provides nonrepudiation of delivery.

    D. A symmetric algorithm is more difficult to implement.

4. When a user needs to provide message integrity, what option is BEST?

    A. Send a digital signature of the message to the recipient

    B. Encrypt the message with a symmetric algorithm and send it

    C. Encrypt the message with a private key so the recipient can decrypt with the corresponding public key

    D. Create a checksum, append it to the message, encrypt the message, then send to recipient

5. A CA provides which benefits to a user?

    A. Protection of public keys of all users

    B. History of symmetric keys

5

Cryptography

889

    C. Proof of nonrepudiation of origin

    D. Validation that a public key is associated with a particular user

6. What is the output length of a RIPEMD-160 hash?

    A. 160 bits

    B. 150 bits

    C. 128 bits

    D. 104 bits

7. ANSI X9.17 is concerned primarily with

    A. Protection and secrecy of keys

    B. Financial records and retention of encrypted data

    C. Formalizing a key hierarchy

    D. The lifespan of key-encrypting keys (KKMs)

8. When a certificate is revoked, what is the proper procedure?

    A. Setting new key expiry dates

    B. Updating the certificate revocation list

    C. Removal of the private key from all directories

    D. Notification to all employees of revoked keys

9. Which is true about link encryption?

    A. Link encryption is advised for high-risk environments, provides better traffic flow confidentiality, and encrypts routing information.

    B. Link encryption is often used for Frame Relay or satellite links, is advised for high-risk environments and provides better traffic flow confidentiality.

    C. Link encryption encrypts routing information, is often used for Frame Relay or satellite links, and provides traffic flow confidentiality.

    D. Link encryption provides better traffic flow confidentiality, is advised for high-risk environments and provides better traffic flow confidentiality.

10. Which is the sequence that controls the operation of the cryptographic algorithm?

    A. Encoder

    B. Decoder wheel

    C. Cryptovariable

    D. Cryptographic routine

11. The process used in most block ciphers to increase their strength is

    A. Diffusion

    B. Confusion

    C. Step function

    D. SP-network

12. Which of the following BEST describes fundamental methods of encrypting data:

    A. Substitution and transposition

    B. 3DES and PGP

    C. Symmetric and asymmetric

    D. DES and AES

13. Cryptography supports all of the core principles of information security except

    A. Availability

    B. Confidentiality

    C. Integrity

    D. Authenticity

14. A way to defeat frequency analysis as a method to determine the key is to use

    A. Substitution ciphers

    B. Transposition ciphers

    C. Polyalphabetic ciphers

    D. Inversion ciphers

5

Cryptography

15. The running key cipher is based on

    A. Modular arithmetic

    B. XOR mathematics

    C. Factoring

    D. Exponentiation

16. The only cipher system said to be unbreakable by brute force is

    A. AES

    B. DES

    C. One-time pad

    D. Triple DES

17. A message protected by steganography would most likely be found in a

    A. Public key

    B. Algorithm

    C. Private key

    D. Picture file

18. Which is the BEST choice for implementing encryption on a smart card?

    A. Blowfish

    B. Elliptic Curve Cryptography

    C. TwoFish

    D. Quantum Cryptography

19. An e-mail with an document attachment from a known individual is received with a digital signature. The e-mail client is unable to validate the signature. What is the **BEST** course of action?

    A. Open the attachment to determine if the signature is valid.

    B. Determine why the signature can't be validated prior to opening the attachment.

    C. Delete the e-mail

    D. Forward the e-mail to another address with a new signature.

20. The vast majority of Virtual Private Networks use

    A. SSL/TLS and IPSec.

    B. El Gamal and DES.

    C. 3DES and Blowfish.

    D. TwoFish and IDEA.

5

Cryptography

Domain 6

Security Architecture and Design

THE SECURITY ARCHITECTURE AND DESIGN domain addresses the concepts, principles, structures, frameworks, and standards used to design, implement, monitor, and secure individual systems and the IT enterprise. It focuses on the architecture of security services used to enforce various levels of confidentiality, integrity, and availability in key information assets. Security architecture and design focus on the translation of security requirements into usable designs for security controls. The scope of those designs may be enterprise in scope or may be focused on individual components within a single computing system. Several variations on the theme have been written about the topic of information security architecture and design. Explaining the "what," "why," and "how" of this domain will help frame the rest of the chapter.

What?

Security architecture:

- Provides the framework and foundation to enable secure communication, protect information resources, and ensure that IT delivery is confidential, available, and with integrity
- Identifies the basic services needed to provide security for current and future systems
- Models the rules of behavior as well as the technologies required to securely and effectively protect assets
- Documents these evolving models to connect the business drivers to the technical implementation of controls
- Is typically built using standardized methodologies founded on industry frameworks and international standards

Why?

Security architectures require considerable investment in time and resources while yielding many potential benefits. These benefits can include:

- Better coordination of investment in security technologies and practices
- Improved long-term planning for capital investment and operating budgets
- Interoperability with other components of system and enterprise architecture
- Greater adaptability, scalability, and coherence of security services
- Standardization of common functions across multiple systems

- Consistent application of security practices and solutions, including compliance with regulations
- Providing the means to ensure that the implementation of security controls is correct and verifiable

How?

There are many methodologies for developing an IT and security architecture. This chapter will discuss some examples of frameworks, models, and standards frequently used in secure design. Although most security architectures are built on common themes, they vary depending on the needs of the organization that sponsored them. Successful integration is predicated on the acceptance and adoption of the stakeholders and customers of the architecture. This is accomplished by ensuring that the security architecture addresses the business requirements of a system. Those requirements will often be different depending on the scope of the design effort: system security architecture will focus on requirements for individual systems while enterprise security architecture (ESA) will focus on multiple systems throughout the enterprise. The basic principles of secure design and the common methodologies and techniques used to create, implement, and verify these designs will be focused on. Finally, key concepts in system security architecture and ESA will be addressed. The security professional needs to understand how security architecture and design is performed and how different levels of architecture work together to secure information assets.

6

Security Architecture & Design

897

System security architecture is focused on designing security services within individual computing systems. Modern computing systems are complex creatures, comprised of a myriad of moving parts: computing platform hardware, firmware, operating system (OS), utilities, and a variety of specialized applications. Each moving part may either have a native control, the ability to implement a control, or none of the above.

In general, a well-architected solution will be able to combine security functions from each of the moving parts into a cohesive design. At the same time, it will need to strike a balance between security and the other needs of the computing system. This can be a very difficult balance to achieve: since security components can consume considerable resources, control is frequently sacrificed in favor of improved functionality, usability, or performance. It is a security architect's challenge to find the balance and ensure that necessary controls are implemented as designed.

There are a wide variety of computing platforms available and each platform will take a different approach to providing security services. The architecture of these platforms is fundamental to the ways that they approach security requirements. Most computing platforms will offer a wide variety of security controls to help protect sensitive assets that are being generated, transmitted, or stored by the system. The security architect may be responsible for determining what security controls will be implemented or they may be responsible for deciding what native controls will be used for a particular system in the enterprise.

The security architect must understand the basic building blocks that make up modern computing systems as well as some characteristics that distinguish types of systems from each other. Most importantly, they should be aware of the different ways that security can be implemented at the system level and be able to choose which mechanisms would be most appropriate in a given scenario.

TOPICS

- Understand the fundamental concepts of security models, e.g., confidentiality, integrity, and multi-level models
- Understand the components of information systems security evaluation models
  - Product evaluation models, e.g., common criteria
  - Industry and international security implementation guidelines, e.g., PCI-DSS, ISO
- Understand security capabilities of information systems, e.g., memory protection, virtualization, trusted platform module (TPM)
- Understand the vulnerabilities of security architectures
  - System, e.g., covert channels, state attacks, emanations
  - Technology and process integration, e.g., single point of failure, service-oriented architecture (SOA)
- Understand application and system vulnerabilities and threats
  - Web-based, e.g., XML, SAML
  - Client-based, e.g., applets
  - Server-based, e.g., data flow control
  - Database security, e.g., inference, aggregation, data mining
- Understand countermeasure principles, e.g., defense in depth

OBJECTIVES

A review of the ten domains of the Information Candidate Information Bulletin clearly shows that this domain is a compilation of the fundamentals from the other domains, incorporated and integrated into a representative set of controls. This chapter brings the many elements of architecture methodology, common techniques, and frequently used technologies used in secure design. It also focuses on information security architecture as physical or industrial security architecture is in the physical security domain.

According to the (ISC)² Candidate Information Bulletin, a CISSP® candidate should understand security models in terms of:

- Confidentiality, integrity, and information flow
- System models in terms of the common criteria
- Technical platforms in terms of hardware, firmware, and software
- System security techniques in terms of preventative, detective, and corrective controls.

Fundamental Concepts of Security Models

Creating and maintaining good security architecture is a difficult task. The role of the security architect is the translation of business requirements into solutions that provide security to key assets. Since both the assets requiring protection and the organization's preferred approach to protect them may be different, each design is unique. A strong design will require that the architect understands both the assets to be protected and management's priorities. The architect must also be prepared to adjust the design over time as key assets or those priorities change as well as verify that their designs have been implemented correctly. This requires the architect to be a good negotiator, artist, and analyst.

Common System Components

Modern computing systems are comprised of layers of hardware, firmware, and software that work together to provide computing services. Although the security architect may not need to be a specialist in system architecture, he or she should understand some of the most common system components and their respective roles. Given their importance for system security, the focus of discussion will be on four main components: processors, storage, peripherals, and the OS.

Each have specialized roles in the architecture. Processors are the brains behind a computer system and perform calculations as it solves problems and performs system tasks. Storage devices provide both long- and short-term storage of information. Peripherals (scanners, printers, modems, etc.) are devices that either input data or receive the data output by the processors. The OS provides the glue that binds all these elements together as well as providing the interface for applications, utilities, and the end-user. Security functions are often distributed across these components where most appropriate to ensure that the system can secure information assets most effectively.

Processors

Processing is the conversion of inputted raw data into useful output. Traditionally, processing was performed exclusively by a single processing unit (the central processing unit or CPU), responsible for ensuring that system instructions were performed and that interactions between memory, storage, and input/output devices were controlled. While this continues to be the case in smaller embedded systems, it is more common to find multiple processors that share the responsibility for processing in a computing system. While CPUs continue to play the most important role, there are also specialized processing units for graphics (graphics processing units or GPUs) and numerous coprocessors, including those used to offload cryptographic functions from the CPUs.

Traditionally, the CPU managed all of the system's devices as well as doing the actual data processing. In modern systems, the CPU still plays an important role but is no longer the sole source of processing power. It is paired with a computer's motherboard, which provides the supporting chipset that controls access to memory, storage, and input/output devices such as mice, keyboards, monitors, and other communications devices. The CPU, motherboard, and memory operate together, with the memory holding data and the next set of program instructions as the CPU uses its current instructions to perform calculations on the data.

Processors perform four main tasks: fetching, decoding, executing, and storing. When the CPU requires data, it retrieves it from memory. The CPU fetches information from memory, i.e., instructions and data; it decodes the instructions to decipher next steps; it executes the instructions, e.g., calculating numbers; and it stores the results of the instruction. Then the cycle repeats until there are no further instructions to be executed.

This simple process is sufficient for a system that is only running a single, serial set of instructions, but it may not be the most efficient way to provide processing to a complex program or many programs that must share a common processor. Ideally, the processor should be able to weave multiple sets of instructions together to make sure that they are taking full advantage of any processing power.

One way to take advantage of the capabilities of a processor is to split programs into multiple, cooperating processes. A multitasking system switches from one process to another quickly to speed up processing. To the user, it appears to be simultaneous execution even though only one process is running at any given time on the CPU. However, there needs to be a mechanism in place that will allow the OS to start running an application with the probability, but not the certainty, that the application will sooner or later return control to the OS.

Another way to achieve higher performance can be achieved by increasing the number of processors in a system where each processor can assume some of the load. Powerful computers such as servers have several processors handling different tasks, although there must be one processor to control the flow of instructions and data through the supplementary processors. This type of system is called a multiprocessing system.

Another common way to get higher performance is to split programs into threads. As the name implies, threads are a series of instructions that can be treated as a running thread. Normally, as a program is executing, a processor runs each line of code in sequence. However, there are times when a subsequent step is not dependent upon the completion of a previous step. If the programmer requests a new thread to be generated for the later step, the CPU can be asked to do something else at the same time the application continues doing its current task. An example might be a spreadsheet calculation running at the same time that the main application asks a user for input.

Multithreading, then, is the concept whereby the OS time slices the threads and gives one thread some time on the CPU, then switches to another thread and lets it run for a while. This routine continues until the first thread has its turn again. In essence, the threads are split up and given to the CPU in an interleaved manner. Each thread operates as though it has exclusive access to the CPU, even though it runs only for a short time and then stops until it runs again in a short time.

While multitasking, multiprocessing, and multithreading have obvious advantages, they can lead to some potential security vulnerabilities. It is vital that the system provide means to protect multiple processes/tasks/threads from the other processes/tasks/threads that may contain bugs or exhibit unfriendly actions. Techniques need to be implemented to measure and control resource usage. For example, when a system is running many different tasks, being able to measure each task's total resource usage is a desired piece of managing security in such a system. This information needs to be gathered without incurring a significant performance penalty and without changing the manner that tasks are written and executed. If this type of functionality is not available, a mischievous task might assign and seize enough memory to result in a denial-of-service attack, a crash, or a system slowdown. The bottom line, even though there are many advantages to implementing multiprocessing, multitasking, and multithreading, is that the more subtasks a system creates, the more things that can go awry.

Memory and Storage

In general, system architecture will focus heavily on memory and how memory is managed. Valuable or critical information assets are stored in memory. Sensitive or important programs are executed from memory. This makes memory the key for any system security architecture, and may explain why most security components within computing systems are so heavily focused on it. There are a few main types of memory, each requiring different approaches for protection.

Primary Storage

As data waits for processing by the processors, it sits in a staging area called primary storage. Whether implemented as memory, cache, or registers (part of the CPU), and regardless of its location, primary storage stores data that has a high probability of being requested by the CPU, so it is usually faster than long-term, secondary storage. The location where data is stored is denoted by its physical memory address. This memory register identifier remains constant and is independent of the value stored there. Some examples of primary storage devices include random-access memory (RAM), synchronous dynamic random-access memory (SDRAM), and read-only memory (ROM). RAM is volatile, that is, when the system shuts down, it flushes the data in RAM although recent research has shown that data may still be retrievable. Contrast this to ROM, which is nonvolatile storage that retains data even when electrical power is shut off.

The closer data is to the CPU, the faster it can be retrieved and thus processed. Data are sent to the CPU through various input devices (keyboards, modems, etc.), cache, main memory, and disk storage devices. As the data travels to the CPU, it moves from storage devices (disks, tapes, etc.) to main memory (RAM) to cache memory, finally arriving at the CPU for processing (*Figure 6.1*). The further data are from the CPU, the longer the trip takes. In fact, if one were to compare speed of access to data, retrieving data from disk storage takes the longest, retrieval from RAM is

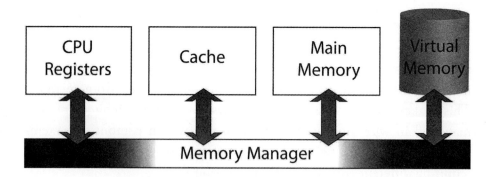

Figure 6.1 - **Common types of memory in most computing systems. One of the main tasks of memory management is to ensure that information is in an appropriate area of memory when it is needed as well as manage how information is moved between the different types of memory available to the memory manager.**

faster than disk storage, and cache memory retrieval takes the least amount of time. Cache memory can be described as high-speed RAM on the same chip as the processor. Optimally designed caches can reduce the memory access time because data moves from the slower RAM to the faster cache then to the CPU. This process speeds up the CPU's access to the data and thus improves the performance of program execution.

Secondary Storage

Secondary storage holds data not currently being used by the CPU and is used when data must be stored for an extended period of time using high-capacity, nonvolatile storage. Computer systems use multiple media types for storing information as both raw data and programs. This media differs in storage capacity, speed of access, permanency of storage, and mode of access. Fixed disks may store up to terabytes in personal computers and up to hundreds of petabytes in large systems.

Fixed-disk data access is done randomly and is slower than RAM access. However, data stored on fixed disks is permanent in that it does not disappear when power is turned off, although data can be erased and modified. Dismountable media devices can be removed for storage or shipping and include floppy diskettes, which are randomly accessed; magnetic tapes, with gigabytes of storage and either sequential or random access (DLT, SDLT, 8-mm DAT); optical compact disks (CDs), with 650 to 870 MB of storage per CD; high-capacity DVDs and Blu-rays, with 50 to 125 GB of storage. Both CDs and DVDs use random access. External hard drives and USB drives range from a few GB to Terabytes of information and are random access based.

Virtual Memory

Most OS's have the ability to simulate having more main memory than is physically available in the system. This is done by storing part of the data on secondary storage, such as a disk. This can be considered a virtual page. If the data requested by the system is not currently in main memory, a page fault is taken. This condition triggers the OS handler. If the virtual address is a valid one, the OS will locate the physical page, put the right information in that page, update the translation table, and then try the request again. Some other page might be swapped out to make room. Each process may have its own separate virtual address space along with its own mappings and protections.

One of the reasons that virtual memory was developed is that computer systems have a limited amount of physical memory, and often that amount of RAM is insufficient to run simultaneously all of the programs that users want to use. For example, with the Windows OS loaded and an e-mail program, along with a Web browser and word processor, physical memory may be insufficient to hold all of the data. If there were no such entity as virtual memory, the computer would not be able to load any more applications. With virtual memory, the OS looks for data in RAM that has not been accessed recently and copies it onto the hard disk. The cleared space is now available to load additional applications (but within the same physical memory constraints). This process occurs automatically, and the computer functions as though it has almost unlimited RAM available. Because hard disks are cheaper than RAM chips, virtual memory provides a good cost-effective solution.

There are potential downsides to using virtual memory, especially if it is not configured correctly. To take advantage of virtual memory, the system must be configured with a swap file. This swap or page file is the hard disk area that stores the data contained in the RAM. These pages of RAM, called page frames, are used by the OS to move data back and forth between the page file and RAM.

When it comes to accessing data, the read and write speeds of a hard drive are drastically slower than RAM access. In addition, because hard drives are not designed to constantly access tiny bits of data, if a system relies too much on virtual memory, there may be a sizable negative impact on performance. One solution is to install sufficient RAM to run all tasks simultaneously. Even with sufficient physical memory, the system may experience a small hesitation as tasks are changed. However, with the appropriate amount of RAM, virtual memory functions well. On the other hand, with an insufficient amount of RAM, the OS continuously has to swap data between the hard disk and RAM. This thrashing of data between the disk and RAM will also slow down a computer system.

Firmware

Firmware is the storage of programs or instructions in ROM. Typically, this software is embedded into hardware and is used to control that hardware. Because ROM is nonvolatile, these programs and instructions will not change if power is shut off, but instead become a permanent part of the system. User manipulation of the firmware should not be permitted.

Usually, firmware is upgradeable and is stored in electrically erasable programmable read-only memory (EEPROM.) This is handy in those instances where firmware may have bugs and an upgrade will fix the problems. The hardware itself is not upgradeable without substituting portions of it. Therefore, vendors attempt to store as many important controls as possible in the firmware in case changes need to be made. From the vendor's perspective, if a bug is discovered, it is preferable to notify the affected clients to upgrade the firmware than to replace the product. Examples of devices with firmware are computer systems, peripherals, and accessories such as USB flash drives, memory cards, and mobile phones.

Peripherals and Other Input/Output Devices

As was described earlier, data needs to be inputted and processed and output generated. The data is transferred between numerous locations—from disk to CPU or from the CPU to memory or from memory to the display adapter. It would be unrealistic to have discrete circuits between every pair of entities. For instance, throughput would be too slow. However, when a bus concept is implemented, a shared set of wires connects all the computer devices and chips. Certain wires transmit data; others send control and clocking signals. Addresses identifying specific devices or memory locations are transmitted and, when a device's address is transmitted, the corresponding device then transfers data across the wires to the CPU, RAM, display adapter, etc.

Data is the raw information fed to the computer, and programs are the collection of instructions that provide directions to the computer. To tell a system what tasks to perform, commands are entered into the system by the user. For ease of use, input takes various forms. Commands and responses can be entered locally via a keyboard or mouse, with menus and icons, or remotely from another system or peripheral.

The result of computer processing is considered output. This output is in binary or hexadecimal numbers, but for users to understand the output, it takes the form of alphanumeric characters and words that are interpreted by humans as video, audio, or printed text. Thus, output devices may be computer displays, speaker systems, laser printers, and all-in-one devices. Inputs are the signals received through an interface, and outputs are the signals sent from the interfaces. A person (or another computer system) communicates with the computer by using these interfaces (I/O devices.) In summary, the CPU and main memory, working in tandem, are the core processes of a computer, and the transfer of information from or to that duo, for example, retrieving from and storing data to a disk drive, is considered to be I/O.

Software programs called drivers control the input and output devices and the communication channels that are used for system I/O. Drivers enable the OS to control and communicate with hardware. Different signals require different interfaces that differ according to the communications channel of the I/O device. For example, a Universal Serial Bus (USB) device communicates through a USB cable attached to a USB port. The current USB standard supports higher speeds and large numbers of peripheral devices, such as removable disk drives, mice, printers, and keyboards.

Operating Systems

The Operating System is the software that controls the operation of the computer from the moment it is turned on or booted. The OS controls all input and output to and from the peripherals, as well as the operation of other programs, and allows the user to work with and manage files without knowing specifically how the data is stored and retrieved. In multiuser systems, the OS will manage user access to the processor and peripherals and schedule jobs.

Examples of Operating Systems are Microsoft Windows, Apple's Mac OS X, various versions of UNIX and Linux, and mainframe systems commonly using proprietary Operating Systems, such as IBM's MVS, developed by their manufacturers. Although functions performed by Operating Systems are similar, it can be very difficult to move files or software from one to another; many software packages run under only one OS, or have substantially different versions for different Operating Systems.

The system kernel is the core of an OS, and one of its main functions is to provide access to system resources, which includes the system's hardware and processes. The kernel supplies the vital services: it loads and runs binary programs, schedules the task swapping, which allows computer systems to do more than one thing at a time, allocates memory, and tracks the physical location of files on the computer's hard disks. The kernel provides these services by acting as an interface between other programs operating under its control and the physical hardware of the computer; this insulates programs running on the system from the complexities of the computer. For example, when a running program needs access to a file, it does not simply open the file. Instead, it issues a system call asking the kernel to open the file. The kernel takes over and fulfills the request, then notifies the program of the success or failure of the request. To read data from the file requires another system call. If the kernel determines the request is valid, it reads the requested block of data and passes it back to the program.

6

Security
Architecture & Design

How They Work Together

A program is a set of instructions, along with the information necessary to process those instructions. When a program executes, it spawns a process or an instance of that program. This process then requests any necessary resources (usually called handles or descriptors).

The OS allocates the required resources, such as memory, to run the program. A process progresses through phases from its initial entry into the system until it completes or exits. From the process' point of view, it is either running or not, and the status of each process is maintained in a process table.

When a process requests resources, it creates one or more independent threads. There is not a parent/child relationship between threads as there is for processes. This is because threads may be created and joined by many different threads in the process. Threads can be created by any thread, joined by any other, and have different attributes and options. A thread can be considered a lightweight process.

Upon creation, a process is allocated a virtual address space as well as control of a resource (a file, I/O device, etc.). This process (or task) has protected access to processors, other processes, files, and I/O resources. As it is executing, it becomes a lightweight process or thread. This thread is either running or ready to run. If it is not running, its context is saved. When it is executing, a thread has access to the memory space and resources of its processes. Thus, it takes less time to create a new thread than a process, because the newly created thread uses the current process' address space.

Communication overhead between threads is minimized because the threads share everything. Because address space is shared, data produced by one thread is immediately available to all other threads. Similar to multiple processes running on some systems, there can also be multiple threads running (when it is multithreading). Once the process has completed, all threads are closed by the OS and allocated resources are freed up and can be reallocated to other executing processes as needed.

Enterprise Security Architecture

Security architecture refers to the set of disciplines used to design solutions to address security requirements at a solution or system level. Enterprise Security Architecture (ESA) implements the building blocks of information security infrastructure across the entire organization. Rather than focus on individual functional and nonfunctional components in an individual application, it focuses on a strategic design for a set of security services that can be leveraged by multiple applications, systems, or business processes.

ESA is focused on setting the long-term strategy for security services in the enterprise. Its primary purpose is to establish the priorities for security services development and provide that input into information security program planning. It focuses on the design and implementation of common security services and the enforcement of security zones of control. These approaches are used to help ensure that enterprise security services are both effective and cost-sensitive.

Key Goals and Objectives

While ESA can be applied in many different ways, it is focused on a few key goals:

- *It represents a simple, long-term view of control:* With the heterogeneity of possible solutions, duplications and inefficiencies are endemic to many security architectures. To ensure that the organization gets the right level of control to address the most common risks, a good architecture must be comprehensive but also simple. It must also avoid unnecessary duplication of services or complexities that could compromise the business benefits of the security services. It must be able to address control requirements as they evolve over time.

■ *It provides a unified vision for common security controls:* By providing this common services model, the architecture looks at security controls from a holistic view, identifying potential gaps in those controls, and providing a long-term plan for improvement. As such, it is a fundamental part of good security management practices.

■ *It leverages existing technology investments:* Any proposed security should reuse existing technologies that are already deployed in the enterprise whenever practical. By focusing on what the organization has already deployed, the architecture can take full advantage of the internal skill sets, licensing and agreements to minimize the need for training or staff augmentation.

■ *It provides a flexible approach to current and future threats and also the needs of core functions:* If done well, the implementation of the architecture should be flexible enough to provide safeguards and countermeasures for current and emerging threats. It also, however, has to be flexible enough to allow the core applications within the organization to operate and integrate as intended.

The result should be an architecture that supports and integrates with:

1. An effective security program that recognizes that all information is not equal or constant in terms of value and risk over time.

2. An efficient security program that applies the right technology to protect the most critical assets combined with quality processes that reduce the risks to acceptable business levels.

3. A high quality security program that includes regular management reviews and technology assessments to ensure controls are working as intended and providing feedback so that technology and processes can adapt to changes in value and risks over time.

Intended Benefits

While every design may be different, all ESAs strive to:

- Provide guidance to IT architects and senior management, and enable these decision makers to make better security-related investment and design decisions;

- Establish future-state technology architecture for the security environment focused on a limited set of proposed security services;

- Support, enable, and extend security policies and standards;

- Describe general security strategies used to guide security-related decisions at technical architecture and solution levels;

- Leverage industry standards and models to ensure security best-practices are being applied;

- Present and document the various elements of the security architecture in order to ensure proper linkage and alignment with other architecture domains;

- Define technology security architecture in relationship with other technology domains;

- Provide an understanding of the impact on the security posture (better, worse, no change) of development and implementation within the other domains;

- Manage IT solution risk consistently across the project, while leveraging industry best-practices, and;

- Reduce costs and improve flexibility by implementing reusable, common security services.

Defining and Maintaining Enterprise Security Architecture

ESA starts with a basic understanding of the overall strategic direction of the organization, and the IT delivery strategies that are used to support them. Key business drivers and technology positions are also documented. Current policies and standards are used as input to requirement gathering (particularly with legal or regulatory compliance). As security hinges on the question of access of subjects (active parties asking for information) to objects (passive parties providing information), effort is made to capture common

6

Security
Architecture & Design

types of users, types of sensitive or critical assets, and how access between the two should be mitigated. To capture high-level priorities, generally accepted security and security architecture principles are discussed and documented. Other requirements are obtained through interviews with key stakeholders, documentation reviews, and current IT security management processes and procedures. All of these inputs are then used to provide a comprehensive set of requirements for security services. The success of any design can then be measured against its alignment with these standards.

Once these requirements have been documented, they are then used to derive a set of architectural models. A security architect starts with conceptual target models describing a number of sets of common security services. These services are defined according to their intended users, the systems and data they access, and how security must be applied in the contexts of use scenarios. Target models include high-level logical models for each set of common security services as well as walkthroughs using those models, combining user groups and scenarios. At the beginning, the security architect may choose to develop a limited set of target models intended to address the most critical business problems. Further models may be added in the future.

Component models and physical models are considerably more granular, addressing security components within individual systems. Component models describe security functionality in terms of generic components, component flows and nodes. Physical models showing security services in context are also developed during implementation. These types of models are developed as part of projects focused on the deployment of new services and incorporated into the ESA during development. As decisions are made, they are captured as architectural decisions. These are separate documents describing the issue at hand, the options that were considered, and the rationale for decisions that were made. This ensures that all decisions are open to continuous review.

While models assist in framing the final shape of the ESA, it is important that they be grounded in a practical, ordered set of transition activities that will move the organization from the current environment to the future state. With the development of the models, the current security controls environment is documented. A gap analysis is then performed, and steps to address those gaps prioritized based on business priorities and interdependencies. These are then articulated into a strategic roadmap, showing how those gaps will be addressed over an extended period, typically three to five years.

The security architect has to be prepared to address any issues, risks, and planned updates that may come up during the development of the designs. For example, a threat/risk assessment provides a method of quantifying the risks associated with IT and can be used to help validate the abilities of new security controls and countermeasures to address the identified risks. If new vulnerabilities have been discovered or introduced, it also provides a way to determine if changes are required to the overall ESA.

With a firm idea at the current threat/risk environment, security architects can set priorities for the solution-level design and implementation, and security designs can be revalidated to ensure that the high-level requirements and models can be kept up to date.

Common Security Services

A number of security functions are suitable as foundations for common security services in the enterprise. Most ESAs distinguish between different types of services. The following is a sample taxonomy of services that may be used as building blocks in ESA.

- ***Boundary Control Services***: These services are concerned with how and whether information is allowed to flow from one set of systems to another, or from one state to another. Boundary control systems are intended to enforce security zones of control by isolating entry points from one zone to

6

Security
Architecture & Design

917

another (choke points). As such, they provide a set of common points to access or transmit information across security zones. These systems will include the typical range of secure networking devices—firewalls, border routers, proxies and other boundary services—intended to protect more trusted/sensitive assets from less trusted/sensitive assets.

- **Access Control Services**: These services focus on the identification, authentication, and authorization of subject entities (whether human or machine) as they are deployed and employed to access the organization's assets. As a strategic set of services, they are intended to normalize identification and promote shared authentication throughout the enterprise. In general, these services will promote reduced-sign-on (RSO) or single-sign-on (SSO), but will also include RSO or SSO services themselves as common services. It will also include a number of other services surrounding the creation, handling, and storage of credentials in the enterprise. On the authorization side, these services focus on what valid user entities are allowed and not allowed to do within the enterprise given a set of rules enforced through automated systems. They will offer coarse-grained (system-level) authorization services that can be leveraged by other domains in the enterprise architecture.

- **Integrity Services**: Integrity services focus on the maintenance of high-integrity systems and data through automated checking to detect and correct corruption. As a set of common services, these can be leveraged by the enterprise at various levels but many are intended for systems that can be accessed directly by untrusted or less trusted user entities or systems. Integrity services typically focus on antivirus, content filtering, file integrity services, whitelisting, and intrusion prevention systems (IPS).

- **Cryptographic Services**: While cryptography is a common security tool used by many systems, cryptographic services focus on common services that can be deployed and reused by a variety of systems. This will involve a modest public key infrastructure (PKI) as well as the continued use of PKI functions through external providers. This may also include common hashing and encryption services, tools and technologies.

- *Audit and Monitoring Services*: These services will focus on the secure collection, storage, and analysis of audited events through centralized logging as well as the events themselves through intrusion detection systems (IDS) and similar services. Services will include log collection, collation, and analysis services through the deployment of security event information management (SEIM) solutions. Given the centralized infrastructure required, this is also the suitable place to consider centralized management systems.

Security Zones of Control

Maintaining a consistent and manageable level of risk is a significant challenge in a complex and largely distributed environment. Easy access to networks complicates the picture, especially when publicly accessible networks such as the Internet or outsourced environments are involved. There is a trade-off between security (applying mechanisms to lower risk) and user accessibility. Some information is highly sensitive or valuable and other information is much less so (e.g., public information on Web pages about historical buildings). The challenge is to apply the appropriate amount of security control without greatly affecting access to information.

The following questions help to understand the complexity:

- How are information assets protected in relation to the environment within which they exist?

- What is the appropriate level of authentication required to access the information asset? Is there a difference when accessing the asset over an untrusted network? Are there similar requirements inside the internal networks?

- How will confidentiality be protected? Does the required confidentiality level change depending on where or how the asset is accessed?

6

Security Architecture & Design

919

- How must the availability of protected resources be assured? Will access controls have a positive or negative effect on them?

- Are there assets with high integrity requirements? How will the integrity of assets be maintained as many entities are given access to them?

- How can the architect decide how to apply these trade-offs, when the information assets may have such different characteristics?

One method of addressing these questions is with security zones of control. A security zone of control is an area or grouping within which a defined set of security policies and measures are applied to achieve a specific level of security. Zones are used to group together those entities with similar security requirements and levels of risk and ensure each zone is adequately segregated from another zone.

The separation of the zones ensures that the capability of accessing or modifying information and systems in a more secure zone does not leak through to a less secure zone. Access between the zones is tightly controlled with control mechanisms such as firewalls, authentication services, and proxy services. The security zones of control become crucial, high-level design constructs in the security architecture. The following diagram (*Figure 6.2*) from the US National Institute of Standards and Technology (NIST) illustrates this concept using a subsystem guard (Joint Task Force Transformation Initiative Feb, 2010)[1].

Common Architecture Frameworks

No two security architects will likely produce the same design or approach the problem in the same way. To help one security architect understand the designs produced by another, any design must be created using

---

1   Joint Task Force Transformation Initiative, First. United States National Institute of Standards and Technology, "NIST Special Publication 800-37 Revision 1 | Guide for Applying the Risk Management Framework to Federal Information Systems, A Security Life Cycle Approach." Last modified Feb, 2010. http://csrc.nist.gov/publications/nistpubs/800-37-rev1/sp800-37-rev1-final.pdf. Page 13

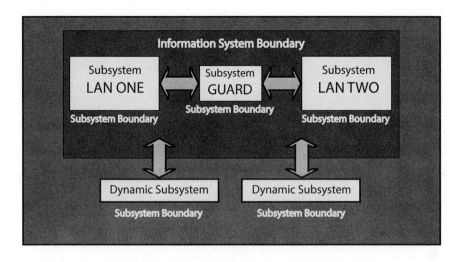

Figure 6.2 - **An example of a Subsystem guard**

standardized methodologies that will allow other security architects (as well as business owners, auditors, and others) to validate their design processes and deliverables. This will require the security architect to be transparent about the methods they are using. To ease the acceptance of their designs, security architects can take advantage of common architecture frameworks used across multiple industries and disciplines.

An architecture framework is a structure that can be used for developing a broad range of different architectures. It describes a method for designing a target state as an integrated set of systems or system components, provides a set of tools to ease architecture development and a common vocabulary. They also frequently include a set of recommended standards and operational practices. They may also include information on compliant vendor products, modules, or components that can be used as design elements within the framework. The following describes some common architecture frameworks used in enterprise architecture and a few for security architecture in particular.

921

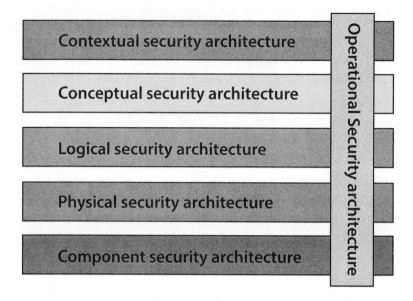

Figure 6.3 - **The SABSA Model for Security Architecture at a high level. It takes a very similar approach to the Zachman Framework by describing any architecture with different levels of detail and for different audiences.**

(Available online at http://www.sabsa-institute.org/the-sabsa-method/the-sabsa-model.aspx. With permission

Zachman Framework²

In the 1980s, John Zachman, a contributor to the federal enterprise architecture framework (FEAF) effort, developed a common context for understanding a complex architecture. His Zachman Framework allows for the communication and collaboration of all entities in the development of the architecture. While not specific to security architecture, it provides a logical structure for integrating the various perspectives such as the plan, design, and build aspects. As Zachman himself explained, "The Framework, as it applies to enterprises, is a logical structure for identifying and organizing the descriptive representations (models) that are important in the management of enterprises and to the development of the systems, both automated and manual, that comprise them."

---

2   Read more about the Zachman framework at: http://www.zachman.com/about-the-zachman-framework and http://www.eacoe.org/index.shtml

Sherwood Applied Business Security Architecture (SABSA) Framework

Intended to follow the same basic outline provided by Zachman, SABSA[3] is a holistic life cycle for developing security architecture that begins with assessing business requirements and subsequently creating a "chain of traceability" through the phases of strategy, concept, design, implementation, and metrics. It represents any architecture using six layers, each representing a different perspective for the design and construction and use of the target system (see *Figure 6.3*).

The Open Group Architecture Framework (TOGAF)

Originally inspired by earlier frameworks from the U.S. Department of Defense, the Open Group started to develop TOGAF[4] in the mid 1990's. It is an open framework for organizations wishing to design and build enterprise architecture. In its ninth version, TOGAF (*Figure 6.4*) provides a common set of terms, an architecture development method (ADM) that describes the step-by-step process employed by TOGAF architects, an architecture content framework (ACF) to describe standard building blocks and components as well as numerous reference models. It also provides advice on how organizations may best incorporate TOGAF into their enterprises.

---

3 Read more about the SABSA framework here: http://www.sabsa-institute.org/the-sabsa-method/the-sabsa-model.aspx

4 Read more about the TOGAF framework here: http://www.opengroup.org/togaf/

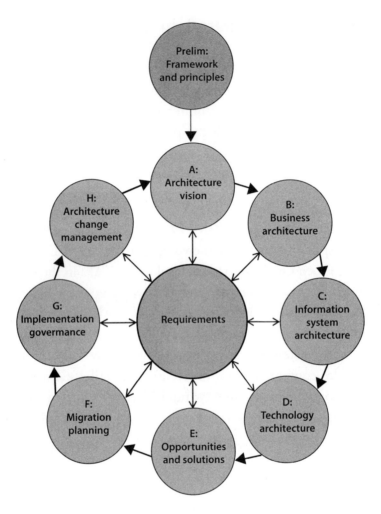

Figure 6.4 -**The TOGAF Architecture Development Method. It highlights the critical role that requirements analysis plays in each step of the model**

(From Marley, S., *Architectural Framework*, NASA /SCI, 2003.)

IT Infrastructure Library (ITIL)

ITIL was developed by the Central Computer and Telecommunications Agency (CCTA)[5] under the auspices of the British government as a collection of best practices for IT governance. ITIL defines the organizational

---

5   Read more about ITIL here: http://www.itil-officialsite.com/AboutITIL/WhatisITIL.aspx

structure and skill requirements of an IT organization as well as the set of operational procedures and practices that, direct IT operations and infrastructure, including information security operations. ITIL continues to evolve. What sets the current version of ITIL apart is the strong focus on end-to-end service delivery and management. ITIL v4 comprises five main activities or tasks: service strategy, service design, service transition, service operations, and continuous service improvement.

Each of these activities is addressed in a separate volume within ITIL. *Figure 6.5* illustrates the five main "books" that comprise ITILv4 and how they relate to each other:

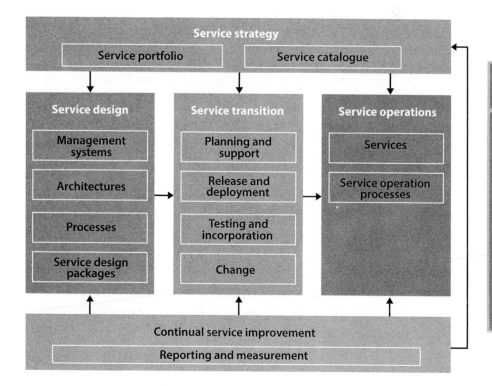

Figure 6.5 - **ITIL Version 4 summary. Note that ITIL constantly feeds back the results of more detailed architecture work in the service strategy, and continuous service improvement identifies opportunities for evolution across other parts of ITIL**

- ■ ***Service Strategy*** addresses new business needs by describing the range of services that are or will be deployed. The service portfolio includes all of the services that are provided by IT. These may include services that are entirely internal to the IT organization as well as services provided to its customers. The service catalogue is a limited subset of the service portfolio containing only services for customers of IT. These services are a particular focus within ITIL, since success or failure is generally measured by the ability to service the customer. Service strategy provides requirements for most other activities under ITIL, including service design, service transition, and service operations. Changes to service strategy may either originate from changes to business requirements or through Continual Service Improvement.

- ■ ***Service Design*** focuses on creating the services described within the service portfolio. In addition to the service design packages that describe the design of individual services and the metrics and service levels that will be used to govern them, this component within ITIL also focuses on management systems and architectures that guide or constrain design as well as the design processes that are in place. Service design packages are the key deliverable from service design, since these packages are the primary input into service transition.

- ■ ***Service Transition*** is primarily concerned with translating designs into operational services through a standard project management structure. It is also responsible for managing change to existing services. Planning and support focuses on providing the necessary structure for service transition, particularly when multiple services are being deployed. Release and deployment represents the core set of processes that guide the deployment of new or updated services through a phased deployment. Testing and incorporation addresses the need to ensure that newly deployed services meet the service design and service strategy requirements and that the service has been properly incorporated within the production environment. Change provides the structure and processes for change management. Once the services have been deployed, they are transferred into steady-state service operations. The key to this component in ITIL are the *service operation* processes that provide structure to service delivery and ensure that metrics are being captured.

■ These metrics are a key input into *Continual Service Improvement.* Through reporting and measurement, each service is validated against their individual key performance indicators and service levels. Based on the need to provide improvement, this ITIL component provides feedback into all other aspects of service management. It may propose recommendations to changes within the service strategy. It may recommend changes to any aspect of service design. It may provide input to the way that services are deployed or tested through service transition. Finally, it may provide input to service operations processes in service operations.

Types of Security Models

Most security models will focus on defining allowed interactions between subjects (active parties) and objects (passive parties) at a particular moment in time. For example, consider a simple example of a user trying to access a file on a computing system. As the active party, the user would be the subject while the file would be considered the object. The following types of security model approach the problem in slightly different ways.

■ *State Machine Model*[6]: State describes a system at a point in time. A state machine model, then, describes the behavior of a system as it moves between one state and another, from one moment to another. Typically, it uses mathematics to describe system states and the transition functions that define allowed or unpermitted actions. When used in security modeling, the purpose is to define which actions will be permitted at any point in time to ensure that a secure state (a point in time when things are secure) is preserved. The role of time in a

---

6   Read more about state machine models here: http://openlearn.open.ac.uk/mod/oucontent/view.php?id=397581&section=9.1

state machine model is very important. According to its rule set, which is determined by a security policy, a model system's secure state can only change at distinct points in time, such as when an event occurs or a clock triggers it. Thus, upon its initial start-up, the system checks to determine if it is in a secure state. Once the system is determined to be in a secure state, the state machine model will ensure that every time the system is accessed, it will be accessed only in accordance with the security policy rules. This process will guarantee that the system will transition only from one secure state to another secure state.

- *Multilevel Lattice Models[7]:* A multilevel security model describes strict layers of subjects and objects and defines clear rules that allow or disallow interactions between them based on the layers they are in. These are often described using lattices, or discrete layers with minimal or no interfaces between them. Most lattice models define a hierarchical lattice with layers of lesser or greater privilege. Subjects are assigned security clearances that define what layer they are assigned to and objects are classified into similar layers. Related security labels are attached to all subjects and objects. According to this type of model, the clearance of the subject is compared with the classification of the data to determine access. They will also look at what the subject is trying to do to determine whether access should be allowed.

- Noninterference models[8] may be considered a type of multilevel model with a high degree of strictness, severely limiting any higher-classified information from being shared with lower-privileged subjects even when higher-privileged subjects are using the system at the same time. In other words, these models not only address obvious and intentional interactions between subjects and objects, but also deal with the effects of covert channels that may leak information inappropriately.

7   Read more about Multilevel Lattice Security here: http://dimacs.rutgers.edu/Workshops/Lattices/slides/meadows.pdf

8   Read more about Noninterference Models here: http://www.cs.cornell.edu/andru/cs711/2003fa/reading/1990mclean-sp.pdf

- *Noninterference Model:* The goal of a noninterference model is to help ensure that high-level actions (inputs) do not determine what low-level users can see (outputs). Most of the security models presented are secured by permitting restricted flows between high- and low-level users. A noninterference model maintains activities at different security levels to separate these levels from each other. In this way, it minimizes leakages that may happen through covert channels, because there is complete separation between security levels. Because a subject at a higher security level has no way to interfere with the activities at a lower level, the lower-level subject cannot get any information from the higher level.

- *Matrix-Based Models:* While lattice-based models tend to treat similar subjects and objects with similar restrictions, matrix-based models focus on one-to-one relationships between subjects and objects. The best known example is the organization of subjects and objects into an access control matrix. An access control matrix is a two-dimensional table that allows for individual subjects and objects to be related to each other. It lists the subjects (such as users or processes) down the left-hand side, and all the resources and functions across the top in the table. A matrix is a concise way to represent the capabilities that subjects have when accessing particular objects. To make this easier, an individual subject may be put into groups or roles, and the matrix is built according to role or group membership. This provides ease of management and simplification. Most matrix-based models provide more than simple binary rules (such as allow or deny). Sometimes it is beneficial to specify how the access will be performed or what capabilities the subject will require. Perhaps some subjects are allowed read only, while others can read and write. The list of access methods will be what is appropriate to the organization. Typical access methods for content are read, write, edit, and delete. Recording this type of information requires extending the access control matrix to include the appropriate permissions in each cell. It

6

Security
Architecture & Design

is important to note that this model does not describe the relationship between subjects in the model, such as if one subject created another or gave another subject access rights.

■ *Information Flow Models[9]:* While most models are concerned with subject-to-object relationships, information flow models focus on how information is allowed or not allowed between individual objects. Information flow models are used to determine if information is being properly protected throughout a given process. They may be used to identify potential covert channels, unintended information flow between compartments in compartmented systems. For example, although compartment A has no authorized path to do so, it may send information to compartment B by changing a variable or condition that B can see. This usually involves cooperation between the owners of the compartments in a manner that is not intended or anticipated by the managers of the system. Alternatively, compartment B may simply gather intelligence about compartment A by observing some condition that is influenced by A's behavior.

Examples of Security Models

There are hundreds of security models. The following are few examples that have had a major impact on the ways that security services have been developed over the years.

Bell–LaPadula Confidentiality Model[10]

The Bell–LaPadula model is perhaps the most well-known and significant security model, in addition to being one of the oldest models used in the creation of modern secure computing systems. Like the Trusted Computer System Evaluation Criteria (or TCSEC), it was inspired by early U.S. Department of Defense security policies and the need to prove that confidentiality could be maintained. In other words, its primary goal is to prevent disclosure as the model system moves from one state (one point in time) to another.

---

9   Read more about Information flow models here: http://users.cis.fiu.edu/~smithg/papers/sif06.pdf

10   Read more about Bell-La Padula Here: http://www.acsac.org/2005/papers/Bell.pdf

It starts by describing four basic components in defining the main actors and how they are distinguished from each other. Subjects are the active parties, while objects are the passive parties. To help determine what subjects will be allowed to do, they are assigned clearances that outline what modes of access (read, write, or read/write) they will be allowed to use when they interact with objects assigned a classification level. The model system uses labels to keep track of clearances and classifications, and implements a set of rules to limit interactions between different types of subjects and objects.

Using this set of basic components, the Bell–LaPadula model explores the rules that would have to be in place if a subject is granted a certain level of clearance and a particular mode of access. They describe these as different properties, depending on whether the subject in question has the ability to read, write, or read/write objects in the model system. In the simple security property (*Figure 6.6*), Bell and LaPadula considered a subject with the ability to read information (but not write it).

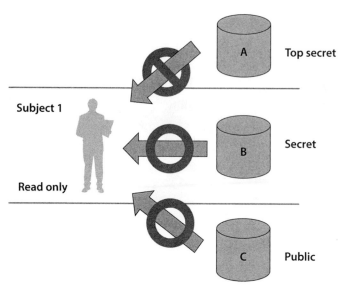

Figure 6.6 - The Simple Security Property according to Bell–LaPadula. Subject 1 has been assigned a clearance level of secret and the ability to read only from a set of objects. In order to prevent disclosure, the subject may read information from objects classified as public or secret, but is prevented from reading information classified as top secret.

931

To prevent disclosure, that subject would be able to read information from objects at a similar classification level or at lower levels, but would be barred from reading any information from objects classified at a higher level of confidentiality. For example, if an employee has a government security clearance of secret, they may be allowed to read secret and documents classified at lower levels. They would not be allowed to read top secret information as this would result in disclosure.

In the "* property" (so named as the story goes because the authors never replaced the asterisk with another term in the manuscript before it was published[11]), the same subject has the ability to write information, but not read it (*Figure 6.7*).

To prevent disclosure, the subject would be able to write information to objects at a similar classification level or higher levels, but would be

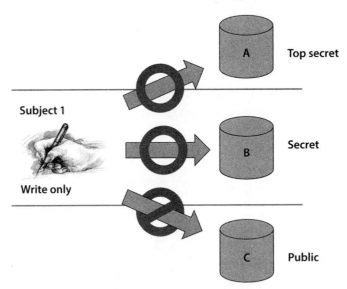

Figure 6.7 - **The * Property according to Bell–LaPadula.**

Subject 1 has been assigned a clearance level of secret and the ability to write only to a set of objects. In order to prevent disclosure, the subject may write information to objects classified as secret or top secret, but is prevented from writing information classified as public.

---

11   http://www.acsac.org/2005/papers/Bell.pdf page 3

barred from writing any information to objects classified at a lower level of confidentiality. This can seem very odd at first glance, but remember that the goal is to prevent disclosure. Writing something at a higher level will not result in disclosure, even if it makes it impossible for the original subject to read it! It also has some practical value in some cases. For example, an organization's president may wish a set of subordinate officers to make reports to their superiors in such a way that they cannot read each other's reports while still allowing their superiors to read and collate information across reports from their subordinates.

In the strong * property (*Figure 6.8*), they consider the same subject with the ability to read or write to objects in the model system. To be mathematically certain that the subject could never disclose information, they must be restricted to objects at a similar classification level and not be allowed to interact with any other objects in the model system.

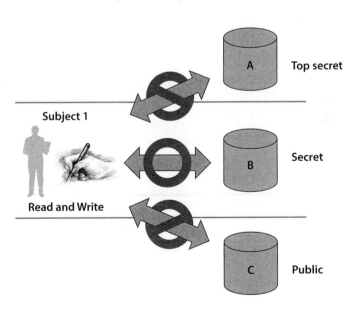

Figure 6.8 - **The Strong * Property according to Bell–LaPadula.**

Subject 1 has been assigned a clearance level of secret and the ability to read or write to a set of objects. In order to prevent disclosure, the subject may only access information classified at their own level, in this case objects classified as secret.

933

Bell–LaPadula is not without its limitations. It is only concerned with confidentiality, and makes no mention of other properties (such as integrity and availability) or more sophisticated modes of access. These have to be addressed through other models. More importantly, it does not address important confidentiality goals such as need-to-know, the ability to restrict access to individual objects based on a subject's need to access them. Since Bell–LaPadula does not provide a mechanism for a one-to-one mapping of individual subjects and objects, this also needs to be addressed by other models.

Biba Integrity Model[12]

Biba's model is just enough like Bell–LaPadula to possibly confuse the two. Like Bell–LaPadula, Biba is also a lattice-based model with multiple levels. It also uses the same modes of access (read, write, and read/write) and also describes interactions between subjects and objects. Where Biba differs most obviously is that it is an integrity model: it focuses on ensuring that the integrity of information is being maintained by preventing corruption. At the core of the model is a multilevel approach to integrity designed to

Property	BLP Model	Biba Model
ss-property	A subject cannot read/access an object of a higher classification (no read up)	A subject cannot observe an object of a lower integrity level
*-property	A subject can only save an object at the same or higher classification (no write down)	A subject cannot modify an object of a higher integrity level
Invocation property	Not Used	A subject cannot send logical service requests to an object of a higher integrity

Source –
Hare, C., Policy development, in Information Security Management Handbook, 6th edn., Tipton, H.F. and Krause, M., Eds., Auerbach Publications. New York 2007. 47&

Figure 6.9 - **BLP and Biba Model Properties**

12   Read more about the Biba Integrity Model here: http://www.dtic.mil/cgi-bin/GetTRDoc?AD=ADA166920 page 27

prevent unauthorized subjects from modifying objects. Access is controlled to ensure that objects maintain their current state of integrity as subjects interact with them. Instead of the confidentiality levels used by Bell–LaPadula, Biba assigns integrity levels to subjects and objects depending on how trustworthy they are considered to be. Like Bell–LaPadula, Biba considers the same modes of access but with different results. *Figure 6.9* compares the BLP and Biba models.

In the simple integrity property (*Figure 6.10* and *Figure 6.11*), a given subject has the ability to read information from different types of objects with differing levels of integrity or accuracy. In this case, less accurate information than what the subject would expect could result in corruption so the subject must not be allowed to read from less accurate objects, but can read from objects that are more accurate than the subject needs.

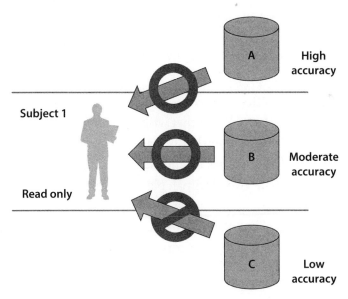

Figure 6.10 - **The Simple Integrity Property according to Biba**

In this example, Subject 1 has information that is moderately accurate and can read from a set of objects with varying degrees of accuracy. In order to prevent corruption, the subject may be able to read information with the same or higher level of accuracy, but not information that is less accurate since that may compromise the integrity of the information it already possesses

935

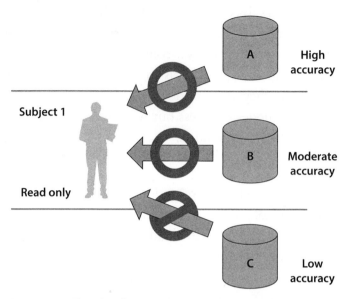

Figure 6.11 - **The Simple Integrity Property according to Biba.**

In this example, Subject 1 has information that is moderately accurate and can write to a set of objects with varying degrees of accuracy. In order to prevent corruption, the subject may be able to write information with the same or lower level of accuracy, but not information that is more accurate since that may compromise the integrity of the information in the more accurate object (Object A).

For example, consider a subject that wishes to add two numbers together. The subject needs information that is reasonably accurate to two decimal places, and has different values to choose from. Some of these values are accurate to more than two decimal places. Some are less accurate. To prevent corruption, the subject must only use information that is at least as accurate as two decimal places; information that is only accurate to one decimal place must not be used or corruption may occur.

In the * integrity property, a given subject has the ability to write information to different types of objects with differing levels of integrity or accuracy. In this case, the subject must be prevented from corrupting objects that are more accurate than it is. The subject should then be allowed to write to objects that are less accurate, but not to objects that are more accurate. To allow otherwise may result in corruption. Biba also addresses the problem of one subject getting a more privileged subject to work on their behalf. In the invocation property, Biba considers a situation where corruption may occur because a less trustworthy subject was allowed to take advantage of the capabilities of a more trustworthy subject by invoking their powers. According to Biba, this must be prevented or corruption could occur.

Clark–Wilson Integrity Model[13]

As it turns out, Biba only addresses one of three key integrity goals. The Clark–Wilson model improves on Biba by focusing on integrity at the transaction level and addressing three major goals of integrity in a commercial environment. In addition to preventing changes by unauthorized subjects, Clark and Wilson realized that high-integrity systems would also have to prevent undesirable changes by authorized subjects and to ensure that the system continued to behave consistently. It also recognized that it would need to ensure that there is constant mediation between every subject and every object if such integrity was going to be maintained.

To address the second goal of integrity, Clark and Wilson realized that they needed a way to prevent authorized subjects from making changes that were not desirable. This required that transactions by authorized subjects be evaluated by another party before they were committed on the model system. This provided separation of duties where the powers of the authorized subject were limited by another subject given the power to evaluate and complete the transaction. This also had the effect of ensuring external consistency (or consistency between the model system and the real world) since the evaluating subject would have the power to ensure that the transaction matched what was expected in reality.

To address internal consistency (or consistency within the model system itself), Clark and Wilson recommended a strict definition of well-formed transactions. In other words, the set of steps within any transaction would need to be carefully designed and enforced. Any deviation from that

---

13   Read more about the Clark-Wilson model here: http://www.cs.clemson.edu/course/cpsc420/material/Policies/Integrity%20Policies.pdf

6

Security Architecture & Design

expected path would result in a failure of the transaction to ensure that the model system's integrity was not compromised.

To control all subject and object interactions, Clark–Wilson establishes a system of subject–program–object bindings such that the subject no longer has direct access to the object. Instead, this is done through a program with access to the object. This program arbitrates all access and ensures that every interaction between subject and object follows a defined set of rules. The program provides for subject authentication and identification and limits all access to objects under its control.

Lipner Model

Lipner combines elements of Bell–LaPadula and Biba together with the idea of job functions or roles in a novel way to protect both confidentiality and integrity. The Lipner implementation, published in 1982, describes two ways of implementing integrity. One uses the Bell–LaPadula confidentiality model, and the other uses both the Bell–LaPadula model and the Biba integrity model together. Both methods assign security levels and functional categories to subjects and objects. For subjects, this translates into a person's clearance level and job function (e.g., user, operator, applications programmer, or systems programmer). For objects, the sensitivity of the data or program and its functions (e.g., test data, production data, application program, or system program) are defined according to its classification.

Lipner's first method, using only Bell–LaPadula model, assigns subjects to one of two sensitivity levels—system manager and anyone else—and to one of four job categories. Objects (i.e., file types) are assigned specific classification levels and categories. Most of the subjects and objects are assigned the same level; therefore, categories become the most significant integrity (i.e., access control) mechanism. The applications programmers, systems programmers, and users are confined to their own domains according to their assigned categories, thus preventing unauthorized users from modifying data (the first integrity goal).

Lipner's second method combines Biba's integrity model with Bell–LaPadula. This combination of models helps to prevent the contamination of high-integrity data by low-integrity data or programs. The assignment of levels and categories to subjects and objects remains the same as for Lipner's first method. Integrity levels are used to avoid the unauthorized modification of system programs; integrity categories are used to separate domains that are based on functional areas (e.g., production or research and development). This method prevents unauthorized users from modifying data and prevents authorized users from making improper data modifications.

Lipner's methods were the first to separate objects into data and programs. The importance of this concept becomes clear when viewed in terms of implementing the Clark–Wilson integrity model; because programs allow users to manipulate data, it is necessary to control which programs a user may access and which objects a program can manipulate.

Brewer–Nash (Chinese Wall) Model

This model focuses on preventing conflict of interest when a given subject has access to objects with sensitive information associated with two competing parties. The principle is that users should not access the confidential information of both a client organization and one or more of its competitors. At the beginning, subjects may access either set of objects. Once, however, a subject accesses an object associated with one competitor, they are instantly prevented from accessing any objects on the opposite side. This is intended to prevent the subject from sharing information inappropriately between the two competitors even unintentionally. It is called the Chinese Wall Model because, like the Great Wall of China, once on one side of the wall, a person cannot get to the other side. It is an unusual model in comparison with many of the others because the access control rules change based on subject behavior.

6

Security Architecture & Design

939

Graham–Denning Model

Graham–Denning is primarily concerned with how subjects and objects are created, how subjects are assigned rights or privileges, and how ownership of objects is managed. In other words, it is primarily concerned with how a model system controls subjects and objects at a very basic level where other models simply assumed such control.

The Graham–Denning access control model has three parts: a set of objects, a set of subjects, and a set of rights. The subjects are composed of two things: a process and a domain. The domain is the set of constraints controlling how subjects may access objects. Subjects may also be objects at specific times. The set of rights govern how subjects may manipulate the passive objects. This model describes eight primitive protection rights called commands that subjects can execute to have an effect on other subjects or objects. The model defines eight primitive protection rights:

1. ***Create object:*** the ability to create a new object

2. ***Create subject:*** the ability to create a new subject

3. ***Delete object:*** the ability to delete an existing object

4. ***Delete subject:*** the ability to delete an existing subject

5. ***Read access right:*** the ability to view current access privileges

6. ***Grant access right:*** the ability to grant access privileges

7. ***Delete access right:*** the ability to remove access privileges

8. ***Transfer access right:*** the ability to transfer access privileges from one subject or object to another subject or object

Harrison–Ruzzo–Ullman Model

This model is very similar to the Graham–Denning model, and it is composed of a set of generic rights and a finite set of commands. It is also concerned with situations in which a subject should be restricted from gaining particular privileges. To do so, subjects are prevented from accessing programs or subroutines that can execute a particular command (to grant read access for example) where necessary.

Capturing and Analyzing Requirements

Regardless of the framework used, the security architect needs to establish the business requirements from key stakeholders and reviewers before any design work can proceed. This may require the architect to work closely with sponsoring executives, business line management, business process owners, and IT management to capture and document the major requirements. Since these requirements will determine the success or failure of any design, it is important that they be firmly established at the beginning and agreed upon by the stakeholders.

A security architect should start with establishing key principles and guidelines for the design. Principles are defined as fundamental statements of belief, mandatory elements that will restrict the overall design and establish the key priorities for protection. To act as trustworthy guides to design, these must be negotiated with their sponsors and key stakeholders so that everyone understands the motivations and implications of the chosen principles. Not all potential principles end up being mandatory, and may become optional guidelines instead. As the design effort progresses, the architect should refer back to the chosen principles and guidelines to ensure continued alignment with them.

The security architect will also need to establish detailed requirements in addition to any principles or guidelines. There are two main types of requirements: functional and nonfunctional requirements (*Figure 6.12*).

- Functional requirements address what the design must do or accomplish. This includes what types of controls need to be included, what assets must be protected, what common threats must be addressed, and what vulnerabilities have been found. In other words, functional requirements will guide what security services will be included in the design.

941

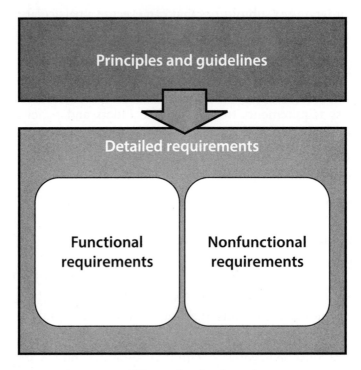

Figure 6.12 - **Different levels of requirements**

Principles and guidelines provide the high-level requirements for secure design by set-ting the design priorities while functional and non-functional requirements are more detailed. Together they are used to establish the goals and objectives for the design

■ Nonfunctional requirements focus on the qualities of the services, including any requirements for reliability and performance.

These detailed requirements can be captured in a number of different ways, depending on the scope of the architecture and the level of detail required. Paradoxically, requirements will need to be more detailed the smaller the scope, in order to allow it to be examined and validated more thoroughly. For example, the requirements for a design limited to a single system will be highly detailed to allow for improved ability to verify the design and to provide solid guidance to implementers of the system. On the other hand, requirements for ESA tend to be more general to provide greater flexibility.

Vulnerability assessments, risk assessments, and threat modeling may be used to capture detailed requirements. In some cases, detailed requirements will be captured by others and passed along to the security architect. Detailed product evaluation criteria requirements may be documented by product consumers. These detailed requirements are then passed along to product vendors for architecture and implementation. Third-party evaluation labs may then be employed to examine the product against the requirements, and certify whether or not it addresses the requirements and how much assurance the consumer should have that the product will perform the tasks required. Principles, guidelines, and detailed requirements must be signed off by an appropriate authority such as an executive sponsor or senior leader if they are to be used to guide the next phase: the creation of security designs.

Creating and Documenting Security Architecture

Once the requirements have been captured and signed off, the security architect can get down to the business of creating suitable designs based on those requirements. This will require the architect to be able to provide designs that appeal to a wide variety of stakeholders with varying degrees of depth and technical detail. It may also need to be presented in a variety of different deliverables, including technical specifications, modeling documents, presentations, and executive summaries.

Following the SABSA framework, a complete security architecture will be represented by six layers of designs. Each layer is a view intended to provide a different level of detail. *Figure 6.13* summarizes the six layers of views according to SABSA:

The security architect will be expected to produce all or some of these different layers depending on the scope of the architecture and the need for the design. In many cases, system security architecture will focus most on logical, physical, and component security architecture while ESA may focus more heavily on contextual, conceptual and logical security architectures. It will depend on their design goals. Since ESA tends to

Contextual security architecture	*The Business view:* Assets to be protected in context
Conceptual security architecture	*The Architect's view:* High-level view of services to protect the assets
Logical security architecture	*The Designer's view:* Node-level view of the services showing how services will be deployed and how they relate to each other at a high level
Physical security architecture	*The Builder's view:* Detailed, node-level view of all services and how they will be deployed against physical assets
Component security architecture	*The Tradesman's view:* Component view of individual security services
Operational security architecture	*The Facility Manager's view:* Security Operations view of all security services in scope

Figure 6.13 - **The different layers of security architecture using the SABSA model**

(From Sherwood, J., Clark, A., and Lynas, D., *Enterprise Security Architecture: A Business-Driven Approach,* CMP, San Francisco, CA, 2005. With permission.)

focus on long-term strategic planning, there is less need for the detail and precision required by system security architecture.

Given the amount of effort that may be required, security architects may rely on a variety of reference architectures to provide a starting point for their designs. Reference architectures provide templates for secure design based on industry best practices and recommended deployment models. The architect may also make use of a variety of modeling tools and languages to document their designs, including variations on the unified modeling language (UML) and systems modeling language (SysML). They will also illustrate how security services will work through the usage scenarios and walkthroughs.

They may also rely on a number of international standards and best practices as well as regulations and legislation that mandate good practices for information security. They can have a profound effect not only in shaping security requirements but also in how security architecture is developed.

Information Systems Security Evaluation Models

Once the design work is completed, any security architecture needs to be carefully evaluated to ensure that it has effectively addressed the documented requirements. This may be as simple as a peer review or may require a complex series of tests to ensure that the design is sound. Where it is necessary to prove that the design is correct, formal security models and verification techniques may be issued. Alternatively, vendor products may be evaluated using international, standardized, product evaluation criteria or can be tested in its intended deployment environment and certified before being run in production.

The following reviews each one of these approaches. Each provides different ways to verify that the security architecture is correct and meets the security requirements, although they are used in very different situations. They also have an impact on how security requirements and security architecture is documented and described.

Common Formal Security Models

Security policy documents the security requirements of an organization. Subsequently, a security model is a specification that describes the rules to be implemented to support and enforce the security policy. A formal security model describes and verifies the ability to enforce security policy in mathematical or measurable terms. A number of security models have been proposed over the years, and many have become fundamental models that have been used to design security services for many systems deployed today. The security policy can be thought of as the "what" (what are the requirements for security), while the security model can be thought of as the "how" (how are those requirements translated into implementable and auditable technical specifications). Given the demands of formal verification, most models are focused on system-level security architecture at the component level. In most cases, it would be too difficult or too time-consuming to formally verify all aspects of large-scale security architectures.

Evaluation Criteria

In most cases, formal security models have limited value in the real world and are narrowly focused on a small number of system components where formal verification is practical or desirable. Verifying their correct implementation will only give the architect a limited view of the security in a complex computing platform, so other mechanisms must be reviewed to verify the implementation of secure design in real-world vendor products. Vendors and their consumers need some assurance that security requirements have been met and will continue to be met over time. To accomplish this, they need a common way to describe security requirements, evaluate products against them in a consistent and repeatable manner, and report on the results.

To accomplish this, a number of product evaluation criteria have been published over the years. These criteria provide a shared mechanism to allow certified third-party evaluation labs to evaluate vendor products against a set of security requirements and publish their findings. Each criteria has taken different approaches to this task with later criteria building on the lessons learned through the use of earlier criteria.

Although there have been many product evaluation criteria developed in the last three decades, three are the focus of this chapter: TCSEC, ITSEC, and Common Criteria. Before explaining the evaluation criteria it is necessary to understand the basics of certification and accreditation.

Certification and Accreditation

A primary way to determine how well a system meets its security requirements is to perform an analysis of the system within its intended deployment environment. The objective is to determine how well a system measures up to a preferred level of security in the real world, and then make a decision whether to proceed with its use in the enterprise. During the certification phase, the product or system is tested to see whether it meets the documented requirements (including any security requirements). It considers the system in context, including the other systems around it, the network it is running on and its intended use. At the beginning of the process, the evaluation criteria must be chosen. With the criteria known, the certification process will test the system's hardware, software, and configuration in a production-like environment. The results of the evaluation become a baseline, which will be used to compare against the set of specific security requirements. If the certification is positive, the system enters the next phase of the evaluation.

In the accreditation phase, management evaluates the capacity of a system to meet the needs of the organization. If management determines that the needs of the system satisfy the needs of the organization, they will formally accept the evaluated system, usually for a defined period of time or set of conditions. If the configuration is changed or the accreditation expires, the new configuration must be certified. Recertification must normally be performed either when the time period elapses or when significant configuration changes are made.

6

Security
Architecture & Design

Product Evaluation Models

When evaluating product security the security architect has several pre-defined frameworks to choose from. Some frameworks such as the Trusted Computer System Evaluation Criteria were designed for classified systems while others such as Common Criteria are more generic and global in nature. The security architect must understand the industry, data types and mission of the organization they are serving to determine the best evaluation model.

Trusted Computer System Evaluation Criteria

First published in 1983 and updated in 1985, the TCSEC, frequently referred to as the Orange Book, was a United States Government Department of Defense (DoD) standard that sets basic standards for the implementation of security protections in computing systems. Primarily intended to help the DoD find products that met those basic standards, TCSEC was used to evaluate, classify, and select computer systems being considered for the processing, storage, and retrieval of sensitive or classified information on military and government systems. As such, it was strongly focused on enforcing confidentiality with no focus on other aspects of security such as integrity or availability. Although it has since been superseded by the common criteria, it influenced the development of other product evaluation criteria, and some of its basic approach and terminology continues to be used. *Figure 6.14 - Summary of Orange Book Evaluation Criteria Divisions* is a summary of Orange Book evaluation criteria divisions.

TCSEC differs most from other evaluation criteria by being both very specific and very prescriptive. Rather than provide a flexible set of security requirements, TCSEC defined very specific types of security controls that should be implemented in secure and defined levels of secure systems based on their ability to implement them. A great deal of emphasis was placed on the ability to enforce security in ways that could be formally verified to be correct and reliable. The more rigid and formal the system's enforcement of security policy, the higher the rating that the system could receive.

Evaluation Division	Evaluation Class	Degree of Trust
A - Verified Protection	**A1** - Verified Design	Highest
B - Mandatory Protection	**B3** - Security Domains **B2** - Structured Protection **B1** - Labeled Security Protection	
C - Discretionary Protection	**C2** - Controlled Access Protection **C1** - Discretionary Security Protection	
D - Minimal Protection	**D1** - Minimal Protection	Lowest

Source –
Herman, D.S., The common criteria for IT Security evaluation, in Information Security Management Handbook, 6th edn., Tipton, H.F. and Krause, M., Eds., Auerbach Publications. New York 2007. 1489

Figure 6.14 - **Summary of Orange Book Evaluation Criteria Divisions**

To assist with the evaluation of secure products, TCSEC introduced the idea of the Trusted Computing Base (TCB) into product evaluation. In essence, TCSEC starts with the principle that there are some functions that simply must be working correctly for security to be possible and consistently enforced in a computing system. For example, the ability to define subjects and objects and the ability to distinguish between them is so fundamental that no system could be secure without it. The TCB then are these fundamental controls implemented in a given system, whether that is in hardware, software, or firmware.

Each of the TCSEC levels describes a different set of fundamental functions that must be in place to be certified to that level. *Figure 6.15* describes the high-level requirements that any TCB would need to meet to achieve each division or class (essentially a subdivision):

The most important thing to note is the move from DAC to MAC between the C levels and B levels. Most commercial, general-purpose computing systems were never intended for MAC and could only achieve a C2 rating. The more rigid requirements for the higher B and A levels also

6

Security
Architecture & Design

949

Division	Class	Description
D	–	Evaluated but does not meet security requirements
C	C1	Discretionary Security Protection: ■ Basic Discretionary Access Control (DAC)
	C2	Controlled Access Protection: ■ Improved DAC ■ Individual accountability through login procedures and audit trails ■ Resource isolation ■ Essential system documentation and user manuals

B	B1	Labeled Security Protection:
		■ Mandatory Access Control (MAC) over some subjects and objects
		  ■ Informal statement of the security policy model
		  ■ Data sensitivity labels and label exportation
		■ All discovered flaws must be removed or otherwise mitigated

	B2	Structured Protection: ■ DAC and MAC enforcement extended to all subjects and objects ■ Security policy model clearly defined and formally documented ■ Covert storage channels are identified and analyzed ■ Objects are carefully structured into protection-critical and non-protection-critical ■ Design and implementation enable more comprehensive testing and review ■ Authentication mechanisms are hardened from compromise ■ Trusted management segregates administrator and operator privileges ■ Strict configuration management
	B3	Security Domains: ■ Can satisfy reference monitor requirements ■ Structured to exclude code not essential to security policy enforcement ■ Significant system engineering directed toward minimizing complexity ■ Trusted management provides security administrator function ■ Audits all security-relevant events ■ Automated imminent intrusion detection, notification, and response ■ Trusted system recovery procedures ■ Covert timing channels are identified and analyzed
A	A1	Verified Design: ■ Functionally identical to B3 but more formal design and verification

Figure 6.15 - **High-Level TCB Requirements**

had the effect of limiting the size and scope of the systems being evaluated, and made it highly impractical for them to be used in the development of highly complex, distributed systems.

Information Technology Security Evaluation Criteria (ITSEC)

TCSEC was not widely accepted outside of the United States due to some of its perceived limitations and relative inflexibility. It inspired a number of other national product evaluation criteria as a result. This lack of international standardization put a great deal of pressure on product vendors since they essentially had to build and document the same products in different ways to meet different criteria. From lessons learned from the use of TCSEC and other national product evaluation criteria, a more harmonized approach was proposed by a number of European nations and later ratified by the European Community.

In contrast to TCSEC, security requirements are not as proscribed in ITSEC. Instead, the consumer or the vendor has the ability to define a set of requirements from a menu of possible requirements into a Security Target (ST) and vendors develop products (the Target of Evaluation or ToE) and have them evaluated against that target. While it still assigned levels, it provided two sets of levels: functional levels and assurance levels. Unlike TCSEC, it also addressed a wider range of security needs, including integrity and availability requirements.

Functional levels (F1 to F10) are intended to describe the functional strength of a system under evaluation similar to what TCSEC did with its levels. They are really provided for guidance only since adherence to them was not a strict requirement and the consumer or vendor could still define their own.

Where ITSEC was significantly different from TCSEC is in the assignment of assurance levels (or E levels). Assurance can be defined as the level of confidence that the evaluator has that the product not only meets the functional requirements, but that it will continue to meet those requirements. In other words, it is really a statement of how much assurance the evaluator has that the product is trustworthy. To this end, ITSEC defined six different levels of assurance, each more difficult to achieve than the last. *Figure 6.16 - ITSEC Requirements E1 through E6* outlines the requirements for E1 through E6:

951

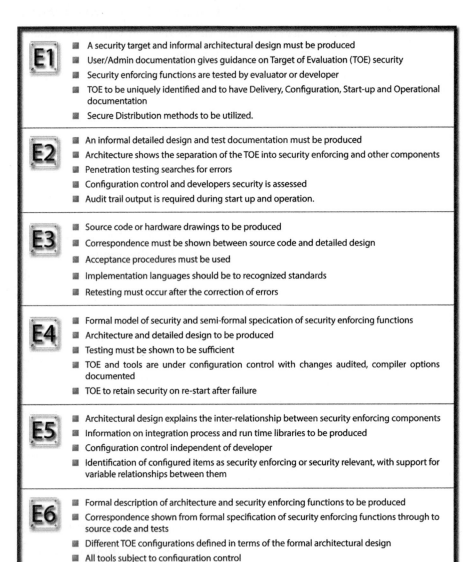

E1
- A security target and informal architectural design must be produced
- User/Admin documentation gives guidance on Target of Evaluation (TOE) security
- Security enforcing functions are tested by evaluator or developer
- TOE to be uniquely identified and to have Delivery, Configuration, Start-up and Operational documentation
- Secure Distribution methods to be utilized.

E2
- An informal detailed design and test documentation must be produced
- Architecture shows the separation of the TOE into security enforcing and other components
- Penetration testing searches for errors
- Configuration control and developers security is assessed
- Audit trail output is required during start up and operation.

E3
- Source code or hardware drawings to be produced
- Correspondence must be shown between source code and detailed design
- Acceptance procedures must be used
- Implementation languages should be to recognized standards
- Retesting must occur after the correction of errors

E4
- Formal model of security and semi-formal specication of security enforcing functions
- Architecture and detailed design to be produced
- Testing must be shown to be sufficient
- TOE and tools are under configuration control with changes audited, compiler options documented
- TOE to retain security on re-start after failure

E5
- Architectural design explains the inter-relationship between security enforcing components
- Information on integration process and run time libraries to be produced
- Configuration control independent of developer
- Identification of configured items as security enforcing or security relevant, with support for variable relationships between them

E6
- Formal description of architecture and security enforcing functions to be produced
- Correspondence shown from formal specification of security enforcing functions through to source code and tests
- Different TOE configurations defined in terms of the formal architectural design
- All tools subject to configuration control

Figure 6.16 - **ITSEC Requirements E1 through E6**[1]

1   source: http://www.cesg.gov.uk/servicecatalogue/CCITSEC/Pages/ITSEC-Assurance-Levels.aspx

In order to achieve a higher E-level, vendors would need to be prepared to provide more formal architecture and documentation and the product would need to be tested more carefully and thoroughly. Higher E-levels are intended then to provide the consumer with higher degrees of assurance. When picking between products with similar functionality, assurance levels could be used to pick the more appropriate option.

Common Criteria

Although ITSEC provided some international harmonization, it was not universally adopted and vendors continued to have to develop their products with multiple criteria in mind. The publication of the Common Criteria as the ISO/IEC 15408 standard provided the first truly international product evaluation criteria. It has largely superseded all other criteria, although there continue to be products in general use that were certified under TCSEC, ITSEC and other criteria. It takes a very similar approach to ITSEC by providing a flexible set of functional and assurance requirements, and like ITSEC, it is not very proscriptive as TCSEC had been. Instead, it is focused on standardizing the general approach to product evaluation and providing mutual recognition of such evaluations all over the world.

While flexibility can be desirable, it does make it difficult for vendors to develop products to a common set of requirements or for consumers to evaluate two or more products against a predefined common baseline. To help with this, common criteria introduced protection profiles (PP). These are a common set of functional and assurance requirements for a category of vendor products deployed in a particular type of environment. For example, the "Software based Personal Firewall for Home Internet Use" PP provides functional and assurance requirements that should be common to all such firewall systems. This could then be used as the basis for vendor development and subsequent product evaluation.

In many cases, however, these protection profiles may not be specific enough or may not cover the specific situation required by the consumer

6

Security Architecture & Design

953

so they may still choose to develop their own. The vendor product (referred to as a ToE) is then examined against this specific profile by a third-party evaluation lab using a common evaluation methodology (CEM).

Short Name	Long Name	Level of Confidence
EAL1	Functionally tested	Lowest
EAL 2	Structurally tested	
EAL3	Methodically tested and checked	
EAL4	Methodically designed, tested, and reviewed	Medium
EAL5	Semi-formally designed and tested	
EAL6	Semi-formally verified design and tested	
Source: Herrman, D.S. The common criteria for IT security evaluation, in *Information Security Management Handbook, 6th edn.*, Tipton, H.F. and Krause, M. Eds., Auerbach Publications, New York, 2007, 1496.		

Figure 6.17 - **Standard EAL Packages**

The result of that evaluation is a report that outlines whether the ToE met the requirements identified by the profile or not. It also assigns the evaluation an Evaluation Assurance Level (EAL) as shown in *Figure 6.17 - Standard EAL Packages.* The EAL level is intended to provide the consumer or the vendor with some idea of how confident they should be in the results of the evaluation, based on how much information was available to the evaluation lab and how carefully the system was examined. The EALs are as follows:

- **EAL 1:** The product is functionally tested; this is sought when some assurance in accurate operation is necessary, but the threats to security are not seen as serious.

- **EAL 2:** Structurally tested; this is sought when developers or users need a low to moderate level of independently guaranteed security.

- **EAL 3:** Methodically tested and checked; this is sought when there is a need for a moderate level of independently ensured security.

- **EAL 4:** Methodically designed, tested, and reviewed; this is sought when developers or users require a moderate to high level of independently ensured security.

- **EAL 5:** Semiformally designed and tested; this is sought when the requirement is for a high level of independently ensured security.

- **EAL 6:** Semiformally verified, designed, and tested; this is sought when developing specialized TOEs for high-risk situations.

- **EAL 7:** Formally verified, designed, and tested; this is sought when developing a security TOE for application in extremely high-risk situations.

EALs are frequently misunderstood to provide a simple means to compare security products with similar levels. In fact, products may be very different even if they are assigned the same EAL level, since their functionality may have little in common.

Industry and International Security Implementation Guidelines

Some industries and organizations are required to adhere to security standards or guidelines when implementing systems. These requirements and specifications should be captured by the security architect when defining the organization's macro security architecture. For example, if an organization accepts payment by credit cards they will be expected to conform to the security requirements of Payment Card Industry Data Security Standard (PCI-DSS). While these standards rarely are sufficient for a secure system, they represent the minimum mandatory requirements a security architect must address if applicable.

ISO/IEC 27001 and 27002 Security Standards[1]

The International Organization for Standardization (ISO) is the world's largest developer and publisher of international standards. ISO is a nongovernment organization of the national standards institutes of 157 countries, one member per country, with a Central Secretariat in Geneva, Switzerland, that coordinates the system. Its mission is to form a bridge between the public and private sectors, enabling consensus to be reached on solutions that meet both the requirements of business and the broader needs of society. The 27000 series of standards address information security practices.

The security standards 27001 and 27002 are universally recognized as the standards for sound security practices. Both standards were inspired by the earlier British Standard 7799 (BS7799). The first part of BS7799 inspired the publication of ISO/IEC 17799, which was renumbered as ISO/IEC 27002 in 2005. In turn, the second part of BS7799 strongly influenced the development of ISO/IEC 27001. Although they share common origins, these standards approach information security management in very different ways.

---

1   Read more about the ISO 27000 series here: http://www.27000.org/

ISO/IEC 27001:2005 is focused on the standardization and certification of an organization's information security management system (ISMS). An ISMS (*Figure 6.18*) is defined as the governance structure supporting an information security program. It addresses the tone at the top, roles and responsibilities, and maps business drivers to the implementation of appropriate controls vis-à-vis the risk management process. The following illustrates the elements common to a generic ISMS:

A MANAGEMENT SYSTEM

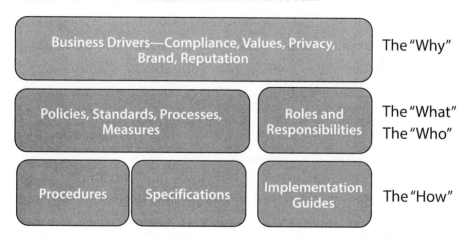

Figure 6.18 - **A generic Information Security Management System**

It starts with key business drivers and determines how the organization will respond to them and how responsibility will be shared within the organization.

ISO/IEC 27001:2005 provides instructions on how to apply the ISMS concept and to construct, run, sustain, and advance information security management. The core of the standard is focused on five key areas:

1. General requirements of the ISMS
2. Management responsibility
3. Internal ISMS audits
4. Management review of the ISMS
5. ISMS improvement

6

Security
Architecture & Design

957

ISO/IEC 27002 is often used in tandem with 27001. Rather than focus on security governance, it provides a "Code of Practice for Information Security Management," which lists security control objectives and recommends a range of specific security controls according to industry best-practice. Unlike 27001, this standard is more of a guideline than a standard, leaving it up to the organization to decide what level of control is appropriate, given the risk tolerance of the specific environment under the scope of the ISMS. The recommended control objectives are the "how"—they demonstrate the implementation of operational controls. A well-rounded information security program will likely include services that address each of these control objectives. ISO/IEC 27002 includes the following 11 focus areas:

1. **Security Policy** provides management guidance and support for information security.

2. **Organization and Information Security** provides a formal and defined security mechanism within an organization that includes information processing facilities and information assets accessed or maintained by third parties.

3. **Asset Management** protects the organization's assets by ensuring valuable data assets are identified and receive appropriate protection.

4. **Human Resources Security** minimizes the risks of human error, theft, and misuse of resources, provides information security threats and concerns to users, and disseminates information to support the corporate security policy.

5. **Physical and Environmental Security** prevents unauthorized physical access, damage, and interference to facilities and data.

6. **Communications and Operations Management** ensures the proper and secure operation of data processing facilities by protecting software, communications, data, and the supporting infrastructure, as well as ensuring proper data exchange between organizations.

7. **Access Control** limits access to data, mobile communications, telecommunications, and network services, as well as detects unauthorized activities.

8. **Information Systems Acquisitions, Development, and Maintenance** implements security controls into operations and development systems to ensure the security of application systems software and data.

9. **Information Security Incident Management** implements procedures to detect and respond to information security incidents.

10. **Business Continuity Management** mitigates an incident's impact on critical business systems.

11. **Compliance** ensures adherence to criminal and civil laws and statutory, regulatory, or contractual obligations, complies with organizational security policies and standards, and provides for a comprehensive audit process.

Each of these control objectives also includes numerous clauses describing specific controls along with recommendations on how they should be implemented in a typical enterprise.

Both standards can be used to guide security architecture and design. The big difference lies with certification. An organization's ISMS may be certified by a licensed third-party assessor under ISO/IEC 27001 but their control practices cannot be. The certification process allows the assessor to capture the essential elements of the organization's ISMS and publish their findings in the form of a statement of applicability. This document is intended not only to highlight the ISMS but allow different organizations to compare their ISMSs. For this reason, ISO/IEC 27001 certification is commonly used by service organizations to share information regarding the ISMS with current and potential customers.

Control Objects for Information and Related Technology (COBIT)

The COBIT is a framework for IT management that was created by the Information Systems Audit and Control Association (ISACA), and the IT Governance Institute (ITGI) in the early 1990s. COBIT provides a set of generally accepted processes to assist in maximizing the benefits derived using information technology (IT) and developing appropriate

6

Security Architecture & Design

IT governance. It describes security controls as recommended by the IT auditing community and is often thought of as the base minimum security services that every IT organization will need to implement. It is also frequently used as the basis for both internal and external audits.

The most recent version of COBIT (version 5) documents five principles that drive control objectives categorized in seven enablers. See *Figure 6.19*:

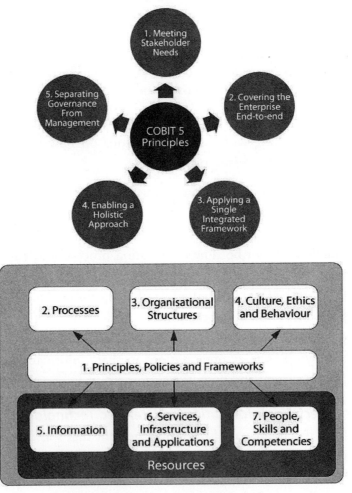

Figure 6.19 - **COBIT's 5 Principles and 7 Enablers (source:** ISACA n.d.)[1]

1   ISACA. n.d. http://www.isaca.org/popup/Pages/framefig12large.aspx (accessed 07 12, 2012).

COBIT is frequently used by security architects as a menu of core security services that must be implemented, and design documents will frequently use the COBIT structure to document security services. This can ease the effort required to provide audit support, and allow current control gaps to be addressed as part of the architecture.

Payment Card Industry Data Security Standard (PCI-DSS)

PCI-DSS was developed by the PCI Security Standards Council to enhance payment card data security. Much like COBIT and ISO 27002, the PCI-DSS provides the security architect with a framework of specifications to ensure the safe processing, storing, and transmission of cardholder information. PCI-DSS is focused on compliance with the standard that includes prevention, detection, and reaction to security incidents.

PCI-DSS[2] is targeted towards merchants and service providers but is mandated for the systems involved in handling an organization's payment card services. Six goals are further defined through twelve broad requirements as seen in *Figure 6.20*.

Goals	PCI DSS Requirements
Build and Maintain a Secure Network	1. Install and maintain a firewall configuration to protect cardholder data 2. Do not use vendor-supplied defaults for system passwords and other security parameters
Protect Cardholder Data	3. Protect stored cardholder data 4. Encrypt transmission of cardholder data across open, public networks
Maintain a Vulnerability Management Program	5. Use and regularly update anti-virus software or programs 6. Develop and maintain secure systems and applications
Implement Strong Access Control Measures	7. Restrict access to cardholder data by business need to know 8. Assign a unique ID to each person with computer access 9. Restrict physical access to cardholder data
Regularly Monitor and Test Networks	10. Track and monitor all access to network resources and cardholder data 11. Regularly test security systems and processes
Maintain an Information Security Policy	12. Maintain a policy that addresses information security for all personnel

Figure 6.20 - **PCI DSS requirements**[1]

---

1   PCI Security Standards Council, First. "PCI-DSS Quick Reference Guide." Last modified Oct, 2010. https://www.pcisecuritystandards.org/documents/PCI SSC Quick Reference Guide.pdf. Page 34

2   Read more about PCI-DSS here: https://www.pcisecuritystandards.org/security_standards/documents.php?view=&association=PCI+DSS&language=

Each requirement has several sub-objectives that must be met. For example, under "Protect Cardholder Data and "4. Encrypt transmission of cardholder data across open, public networks" the following objectives apply:

> **4.1** Use strong cryptography and security protocols such as SSL/TLS, SSH or IPSec to safeguard sensitive cardholder data during transmission over open, public networks (e.g. Internet, wireless technologies, Global System for Mobile communications [GSM], General Packet Radio Service [GPRS]). Ensure wireless networks transmitting cardholder data or connected to the cardholder data environment use industry best practices (e.g., IEEE 802.11i) to implement strong encryption for authentication and transmission. The use of WEP as a security control is prohibited

> **4.2** Never send unprotected Primary Account Numbers (PANs) by end user messaging technologies.

If a security architect were required to comply with PCI-DSS, they would look at existing secure infrastructure to determine if it were suitable from an encryption perspective to support the requirement. If not, they would research the best approach for either enhancing the existing infrastructure or acquiring suitable infrastructure. The recommendations made by the security architect must be correct as they will be implemented by the organization and assessed by an independent party to determine if the requirements are truly met. If flaws are found or the infrastructure does not encrypt and protect as required the architect may be faulted and the organization will need to revisit the infrastructure enhancement or acquisition. These mistakes prove to be costly and disrupt the mission of the organization. Understanding the architectural requirements and implementing them correctly saves considerable amounts of waste and rework.

Security Capabilities of Information Systems

While the requirements of security frameworks may seem daunting from an implementation perspective, there are a wide range of techniques and technologies available that the system security architect may choose. The challenge for the security architect is to provide security without compromising the primary function of the system. This can be extremely difficult in some types of computing environments where processing power is scarce and any security features may cause unacceptable delays in normal processing. At the same time, there are a wide variety of techniques available to protect systems across the many layers of hardware, firmware, and software that make up modern computing platforms.

Access Control Mechanisms

All systems need to be able to distinguish between individual subjects and objects managed by the system, and make appropriate decisions concerning how they will be allowed to interact with each other. The system will need some way to assign identifiers to both subjects and objects, and to authenticate all subjects before they are allowed to access resources on the system. This is one of the most fundamental controls required on a secure system and its correct operation is a requirement for many other security controls. For this reason, it is one of the key elements in a TCB that may be the subject of careful verification using security models and product evaluation criteria.

When no subject can gain access to any object without authorization, this is referred to as complete mediation. Complete mediation is normally the responsibility of the security kernel implementing the reference monitor concept. A reference monitor will examine all attempts by subjects to access objects to determine if it should be allowed or not. It consults with the security kernel database, which stores access controls lists and logs its decision into a secure audit log. Ideally, this function will be as simple as possible to allow for easier modeling, implementation, and formal verification. A reference monitor is considered to be in place only when such mediation is complete.

Secure Memory Management

From a security perspective, memory and storage are the most important resources in any computing system. If data in memory is damaged or corrupted, the system may not function or may function in inappropriate ways. If data in memory is disclosed, sensitive or confidential information may be revealed to less privileged subjects or unprivileged attackers. At the same time, few resources are more available—physically and logically—than memory, putting it constantly in harm's way.

Ideally, it would be possible to easily separate memory used by subjects (such as running processes and threads) from objects (such as data in storage). Unfortunately for security architects, most modern computing systems share a common approach to computing memory where subjects and objects share a common pool of memory, leaving it up to the system to distinguish between areas of memory that will be executed from areas of memory that will be used for storage only. This is one of the reasons why buffer overflows are so successful. With a common pool of memory, the security architect must resort to a variety of techniques to keep subjects isolated from objects and from each other. These techniques include the use of processor states, layering, and data hiding.

Technologies such as address space layout randomization (ASLR) involve randomly arranging position of data areas in memory to help protect against hard coded values in malware and viruses. While most modern operating systems support ASLR, the security architect must ensure programs and applications are designed and configured to take advantage of this security control.

Processor States

Processors and their supporting chipsets provide one of the first layers of defense in any computing system. In addition to providing specialized processors for security functions (such as cryptographic coprocessors), processors also have states that can be used to distinguish between more than less privileged instructions. Most processors support at least two states: a supervisor state and a problem state. In supervisor state (also known as kernel mode), the processor is operating at the highest privilege level on the system, and this allows the process running in supervisor state to access any system resource (data and hardware) and execute both privileged and non-privileged instructions. In problem state (also known as user mode), the processor limits the access to system data and hardware granted to the running process.

This is an extremely useful function for a variety of reasons. It allows the processor to give priority to processes that have access to supervisor state over those which do not. It also enables the processor to apply limitations on resources (which requires processor power in itself) only when it has to. Thus, processes that need rapid and relatively unlimited access to memory can get it, while processes that do not can be restricted when need be.

The use of processor states also has some important limitations. It requires that any process in supervisor state be highly trustworthy and isolated from processes that are not. A malicious process running in supervisor state has very little restrictions placed upon it and can be used to cause a lot of damage. Ideally, access to supervisor state is limited only to core OS functions that are abstracted from end-user interaction through other controls, but this is not always the case. For example, device drivers that control input/output devices are typically installed by end-users but are often granted access to supervisor state to help them run faster. This may allow a malformed driver to be used to compromise the system unless other controls are in place to mitigate this risk.

Layering

One of the ways that privileged parts of the system are protected is through the use of discrete layers that control interactions between more privileged and less privileged processes on the system. In computer programming, layering is the organization of programming into separate functional components that interact in some sequential and hierarchical way, with each layer usually having an interface only to the layer above it and the layer below it. This helps to ensure that volatile or sensitive areas of the system are protected from unauthorized access or change.

One of the most common ways this is done uses ring protection (*Figure 6.21*). It is frequently represented as a series of concentric rings where the innermost ring is assigned the lowest number and the outermost ring is assigned the highest number. For example, in a ring architecture with four rings, the innermost ring would be Ring 0 with the outermost ring being Ring 4. In ring protection, privilege level controls prevents direct memory access from less privileged to more privileged rings while memory access from more privileged to less privileged levels is permitted. Mechanisms called control gates manage transfers from a less privileged level to a more privileged ring. The most privileged ring (Ring 0 in our example) is associated with core system functions like the most sensitive parts of the OS kernel while the lowest privileged ring (Ring 3 in our example) is associated to end-user applications.

The rings are used to control interactions between different execution domains (or the range of objects available to a given subject) with different levels of privilege. This is done through the use of application programming interfaces (API) and similar mechanisms that allow less privileged processes to call on the services of more privileged processes in a different ring.

Process Isolation

Process isolation can also be used to prevent individual processes from interacting with each other, even when they are assigned to the same ring when ring protection is used. This can be done by providing distinct address spaces for each process and preventing other processes from accessing that area of memory. Naming distinctions is also used to distinguish between different processes. Virtual mapping is also used to assign randomly chosen areas of actual memory to a process to prevent other processes from finding those locations easily. Encapsulation of processes as objects can also be

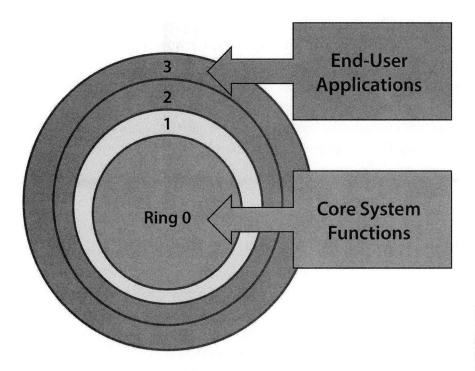

Figure 6.21 - **One example of ring protection in action**

The x86 architecture defines four rings (numbered 0 through 3) where more privileged functions, usually limited to kernel functions and some device drivers, are assigned to Ring 0 while less privileged applications are assigned to outer rings.

Functions assigned to lower rings can access all other higher rings, but applications assigned to Ring 3 can only access functions outside their own ring through very restricted gates or interfaces.

used to isolate them, since an object includes the functions for operating on it, the details of how it is implemented can be hidden. The system can also ensure that shared resources are managed to ensure that processes are not allowed to access shared resources in the same time slots.

Data Hiding

Data hiding maintains activities at different security levels to separate these levels from each other. This assists in preventing data at one security level from being seen by processes operating at other security levels.

Abstraction

Abstraction involves the removal of characteristics from an entity in order to easily represent its essential properties. For example, it is easier for a system administrator to grant group rights to a group of 25 people called "Human Resources" than to grant 25 individual rights to each HR member. Abstraction negates the need for users to know the particulars of how an object functions. They only need to be familiar with the correct syntax for using an object and the nature of the information that will be presented as a result.

Cryptographic Protections

Cryptography can be used in a variety of ways to protect sensitive system functions and data. By encrypting sensitive information and limiting the availability of key material, data can be hidden from less privileged parts of the system. For example, secure file systems make heavy use of cryptography to encrypt large amounts of data in storage to prevent it from being disclosed inappropriately. A Trusted Platform Module (TPM) [1] is an example of a specialized cryptoprocessor that provides for the secure generation, use and storage of cryptographic keys. Since each TPM is unique, it may also be used to provide hardware authentication using its keys.

Host Firewalls and Intrusion Prevention

While firewalls and IPS are normally associated with network partitioning and the enforcement of security zones of control, they are also frequently used to protect individual hosts from attack. Software or hardware-based firewalls can be implemented within individual hosts to control traffic to and from a particular system. Similarly, host intrusion prevention can be used to validate network traffic directed at a host and block it from executing if it is found to be malicious.

Audit and Monitoring Controls

Secure systems must also have the ability to provide administrators with an evidence of their correct operation. This is performed using logging

---

1   For more information about Trusted Platform Modules, please see the following: http://www.trustedcomputinggroup.org/resources/tpm_main_specification

subsystems that allow for important system, security and application messages to be recorded for analysis. More secure systems will provide considerable protection to ensure that these logs cannot be tampered with, including secure export of such logs to external systems.

Host intrusion detection (HIDS) and Network Intrusion Detection (NIDS) may also be considered a types of audit and monitoring controls. HIDS subsystems examine the operation of the system to detect anomalous events and alert security administrators accordingly. They will frequently analyze logs, running processes, and common services/daemons that may come under attack to determine if the system continues to be secure. NIDS performs similar functions but at the network layer.

Virtualization

Virtualization offers numerous advantages from a security perspective. Virtual machines are typically isolated in a sandbox environment and if infected can quickly be removed or shut down and replaced by another virtual machine. Virtual machines also have limited access to hardware resources and therefore help protect the host system and other virtual machines. Virtual machines do require strong configuration management control and versioning to ensure known good copies are available for restoration if needed. Virtual machines are also subject to all the typical requirements of hardware based systems including anti-malware software, encryption, HIDS, firewalls and patching. Given the existing requirements, plus the required overhead for the VM host, systems with consistent high resource utilization may not benefit through virtualization. Additionally, more malware and viruses are becoming virtual machine aware[2]. They are able to detect when they are in a virtual machine and "break out" to the host system. The security architect must be aware of these tradeoffs and plan accordingly for the system and enterprise security architecture.

6

Security
Architecture & Design

---

2 Read more about virtual machine aware malware here: http://www.kb.cert.org/vuls/id/649219

Vulnerabilities of Security Architectures

While every system is different, insecure systems tend to suffer from the same sorts of threats and vulnerabilities. Common vulnerabilities include poor memory management, the existence of covert channels, insufficient system redundancy, poor access control, and poor protection for key system components such as hardware resources and core OS functions. Common threats to system availability, integrity, and confidentiality include hardware failure, misuse of system privileges, buffer overflows and other memory attacks, denial of service, reverse engineering, and system hacking.

Since many vulnerabilities result from insecure design and most threats are well known, it is the responsibility of the security architect to ensure that their designs are addressing security requirements appropriately while also ensuring that the system can continue to perform its intended function.

System

Poorly designed systems are ripe for attack. The security architect must familiarize themselves with well-known attacks and vulnerabilities in their industry and the types of systems they work with. They should also possess an understanding of what kinds of threats and capabilities exist concerning the organization's mission and system. Countless attacks exist; however, some of the most challenging in terms of secure architecture are emanations, state attacks and covert channels.

Emanations

System emanations are unintentional electrical, mechanical, optical,[1] or acoustical energy signals that contain information or metadata about the information being processed stored or transmitted in a system. One of the

[1] Read more about optical emanations here: http://applied-math.org/acm_optical_tempest.pdf

earliest public descriptions released by the US National Security Agency describes it as:

> " Any time a machine is used to process classified information electrically, the various switches, contacts, relays, and other components in that machine may emit radio frequency or acoustic energy. These emissions, like tiny radio broadcasts may radiate through free space for considerable distances-a half mile or more in some cases.
>
> Or they may be induced on nearby conductors like signal lines, power lines, telephone lines, or water pipes and be conducted along those paths for some distance-and here we may be talking of a mile or more.
>
> When these emissions can be intercepted and recorded, it is frequently possible to analyze them and recover the intelligence that was being processed by the source equipment. The phenomenon affects not only cipher machines, but any information-processing equipment--teletypewriters, duplicating equipment, intercoms, facsimile, computers--you name it. But it has special significance for crypto-machines because it may reveal not only the plaintexts of individual messages being processed but also that carefully guarded information about the internal machine processes. Thus, conceivably, the machine could be radiating information which could lead to the reconstruction of our daily changing keying variables--and from a Comsec viewpoint, that is absolutely the worst thing that can happen to us. This problem of compromising radiation we have given the cover name TEMPEST."[2]

Governments, intelligence organizations, and militaries have spent years and countless resources researching emanations. Their research has focused on how to capture them and use or protect against them. TEMPEST is a set of standards designed to shield buildings and equipment to protect them

2   US NSA, First. "TEMPEST: A Signal Problem." Last modified Sept, 27, 2007. http://www.nsa.gov/public_info/_files/cryptologic_spectrum/tempest.pdf. Pages 1-2

against eavesdropping and passive emanations gathering attempts. One of the more common approaches was the "Red/Black" separation of equipment.

The Red/Black separation requirements meant installing physical security controls such as shielding between normal unclassified (nonsensitive) circuits and equipment and the classified ones. Once implemented and certified the operators must ensure the smallest of changes to the controls was reported as something as small as moving a component a few millimeters can invalidate the installation.

While this may initially seem to apply only to the counter intelligence situations, the prudent security architect will understand today's competitive market place and the possibility of industrial espionage and the criminal element. As the price of emanations monitoring capability goes down, the incentive to use it by dishonest individuals to steal intellectual property and other assets increases. For example, a research paper by Dmitri Asonov and Rakesh Agrawal[3] describes an emanation attack on an automatic teller machine (ATM.) They proposed the sound (audible emanation) from the ATM pad was different for each key pressed. They studied the keypad and determined they could "listen in" at distances of 15 meters and greater. They were able to determine about 79% of the key presses accurately. This means an attacker would be able to determine the banking PIN of a person, at a distance, without installing any additional equipment on the ATM. Many security architecture frameworks would miss this this vulnerability. A security architect designing banking systems with ATM's would take this vulnerability into account and possibly specify the keypad be made of a different material or determine a way to muffle or distort the sound.

State Attacks

State attacks are also known as "race conditions" which attempt to take advantage of how a system handles multiple requests. For example, during a logon process, the process is started at the kernel level of the processor and

---

3   http://rakesh.agrawal-family.com/papers/ssp04kba.pdf

then demoted to the standard level. Should a user login and then quickly interrupt the login process by pressing the escape key before the processor has time to demote the level they would have successful accomplished a state attack. The attacker escalated their privilege in violation of the system security policy by exploiting the timing of the login process.

Race conditions are also caused by poorly written code and the adoption of applications without assessing the security posture of the system and how it will integrate into the existing environment. A time of check to time of use (tocttou) is a common race condition bug in programming. The attack involves changing the system between the checking of a condition and the action that results from the check. While the coder and system developer are typically the roles involved in ensuring race conditions cannot exist, the security architect should be aware of the condition and ensure the selected control framework can test for the condition.

Covert Channels

Covert channels are communications mechanisms hidden from the access control and standard monitoring systems of an information system. Covert channels may use irregular methods of communication such as the free space sections of a disk or even the timing of processes to transmit information. The TCSEC identifies two types of covert channels:

- *Storage channels* that communicate via a stored object.

- *Timing channels* that modify the timing of events relative to each other.

The only way to mitigate covert channels is through the secure design of an information system. The security architect must understand how covert channels function and strive to eliminate them in any design which has associated requirements.

Technology and Process Integration

Different computing platforms have traditionally taken slightly different approaches to system and security architecture. The following describes the high-level architecture of common computing platforms and how they have addressed security concerns.

Mainframes and Other Thin Client Systems

The term mainframe originally referred to the very large computer systems housed in steel-framed boxes, and was used to differentiate them from the smaller mini- or microcomputers. These mainframes were used in Fortune 1000 companies to process commercial applications and were also employed by federal, state, and local governments. The term has been used in numerous ways over the years, but most often it describes the successive families of large-scale systems built by IBM and other companies.

Historically, a mainframe was associated with centralized rather than distributed computing. This means that most processing occurs within a large centralized system while clients (or terminals in the mainframe world) are limited to simple interaction and emulation. This type of thin client architecture puts the majority of processing and memory resources within the mainframe itself while peripherals (such as secondary storage and printing) are treated as separate, discrete systems. Centralizing processing power also has the effect of centralizing the responsibility for security, although discrete peripherals may also implement their own security features.

In today's modern mainframe environment, they are less likely to be used as discrete computing platforms. Instead, the base system is used to host a wide variety of other OS's as virtual hosts. By consolidating multiple vendor platforms and providing scalability, mainframes are an effective way to minimize costs. Multiple OS's can be running on a mainframe, most notably numerous instances of Linux. Other uses include data warehousing systems, Web applications, financial applications and middleware. Mainframes provide reliability, scalability, and maintainability, with the lower total cost of ownership (TCO) and credible disaster recovery.

Mainframes are not the only systems to provide a highly centralized model for processing. Other thin client systems have emerged to provide a similar centralized processing environment, limiting the client to keyboard and mouse emulation, graphics processing and basic networking functions. This has the benefit of centralizing most functions (including most security functions) while allowing the client to focus on user interaction and networking.

For example, central server-based processing can be combined with diskless workstations or other types of hardware thin clients. A diskless workstation is a computer without a hard drive in it, and sometimes without a DVD drive or a USB port. The workstation has a network card and video card, and may also have other expansion cards, such as a sound card. It relies on services provided by network servers for most of its operation, such as booting and running applications. This puts greater pressure on the central server infrastructure while minimizing the processing power required at the workstation level. Software-based thin client applications provide similar advantages. For example, an Internet browser may be considered a thin client.

From a security perspective, the advantage of this type of architecture is that it focuses the design and implementation of security services in a single, centralized environment. This can make it easier to design, implement, and verify security services as well as maintain them. Since patches and updates only need to be patched in a central location, most security vulnerabilities can be dealt with quickly and efficiently. At the same time, unpatched vulnerabilities will be inherited across the entire system. This makes any vulnerability much more pervasive and dangerous than in other computing platforms. It also requires very careful control of privileged and non-privileged subjects operating at the same time to ensure that one cannot interfere or leak information to the other.

Middleware

Middleware is a connectivity software that enables multiple processes running on one or more machines to interact. These services are collections

975

of distributed software that are present between the application running on the OS and the network services, which reside on a network node. The main purpose of middleware services is to help solve many application connectivity and interoperability problems.

In essence, middleware is a distributed software layer that hides the intricacies and heterogeneous distributed environment consisting of numerous network technologies, computer architectures, OS, and programming languages. Some of the services provided are directory services, transaction tracking, data replication, and time synchronization, services that improve the distributed environment. Some examples are workflow, messaging applications, Internet news channels, and customer ordering through delivery.

In recent years, considerable attention has been placed on middleware as a foundation for Service Oriented Architectures (SOA[4]). Organizations are recognizing that continued reliance on legacy systems impedes business imperatives such as growth, speed to market, business, and IT alignment. Moreover, upgrading to newer technologies is an expensive proposition, especially in a struggling economy. With these challenges in mind, organizations are migrating to a more usable and efficient IT architecture, which enables their customers to more closely interact with the company through Internet-based Web applications. In a SOA, disparate entities make their resources available to an entire population in a standardized way. In other words, SOA is a model for distributed computing, wherein applications call other applications over the network. Functionality is distributed over the network, utilizing the ability to find the functionality and the ability to connect to it.

The SOA provides for modularity, flexibility, and reusability. Moreover, it allows for consistent and collaborative governance, security, and management, including policy enforcement, authentication, encryption,

---

4   Read more about SOA vulnerabilities and mitigations here: http://www.nsa.gov/ia/_files/factsheets/SOA_security_vulnerabilities_web.pdf

and digital signature implementations, with the caveat that the security is designed and implemented correctly. The availability of middleware interfaces, however, can make them common targets for attack as many of the SOAs were not developed with end-to-end security as a requirement.

Embedded Systems

Embedded systems are used to provide computing services in a small form factor with limited processing power. They embed the necessary hardware, firmware, and software into a single platform that can be used to provide a limited range of computing services, usually around a single application. They typically feature a limited OS with the base minimum functionality required to meet its functional requirements. Other constrained devices such as mobile phones, media players, and networking devices such as routers and wireless devices take a similar approach.

From the security architect perspective, embedded systems have a number of potential advantages and disadvantages. Security services tend to be simple, testable, and verifiable, making the task of ensuring that security has been designed and implemented correctly much simpler. Unfortunately, security in such systems is typically limited to a few basic security features to help protect memory and privileged access to memory. While they may be able to support a wide range of security services, they have very limited processing power that must be shared by the core functions and security components. This frequently results in less-than-robust security features, particularly when richer functionality is the primary business driver. It is also frequently more difficult to patch security vulnerabilities in constrained embedded devices[5].

Pervasive Computing and Mobile Devices

The number of mobile devices has grown considerably in the past four or five years. Products vary from sophisticated mobile phones, such as fourth-generation (4G) handsets, to full-featured "ultrabooks" and tablets.

---

5   Read more about embedded device security here: http://www.csoonline.com/article/704346/embedded-system-security-much-more-dangerous-costly-than-traditional-software-vulnerabilities

These devices can now manage personal information, such as contacts, appointments, and to-do lists. Current tablets and cell phones connect to the Internet, function as global positioning system (GPS) devices, and run multimedia software. They can also support a wireless Bluetooth network and wireless wide area networks (WANs). They have memory card slots that accept flash media that can serve as additional storage for files and applications. Most all devices provide audio and video support, incorporating MP3 players, a microphone, a speaker, and headphone jacks along with a built-in digital camera. Integrated security features such as a biometric fingerprint reader can also be included.

These devices share common security concerns with other resource-constrained devices. In many cases, security services have been sacrificed to provide richer user interaction when processing power is very limited. Their mobility has made them a prime vector for data loss since they can be used to transmit and store information in ways that may be difficult to control.

Single Point of Failure

As technology such as virtualization makes technology more efficient and manageable, the security architect must also understand how single points of failure can arise. Using the example of virtualization, if one were to compare the before and after states from a point of failure perspective it would seem virtualization often adds a single point of failure to many enterprises. Before virtualization servers where typically individual hardware components all separate from one another. If the e-mail server went down it would rarely mean the network attached storage server would go down as well. If these systems were virtualized, and ran on the same host, that host becomes a single point of failure for both systems. If the host goes down all guests running on the host will go down as well. The security architect must identify single points of failure and determine alternatives so stakeholders can make informed decisions regarding the acceptance of the risk or mitigation strategies.

Software and System Vulnerabilities and Threats

Software and systems will continue to suffer from vulnerabilities. Web-based applications, clients, servers, and the technologies supporting them continue to require remediation actions. Sound design through a secure architecture can help mitigate and eliminate vulnerabilities before they develop.

Web-Based

In essence, Web applications are subject to all of the threats and protection mechanisms discussed elsewhere. However, Web applications are specifically vulnerable because of their accessibility.

Specific protections that may be helpful include having a particular assurance sign-off process for Web servers, hardening the operating system used on such servers (removing default configurations and accounts, configuring permissions and privileges correctly, and keeping up to date with vendor patches), extending Web and network vulnerability scans prior to deployment, passively assessing IDS and advanced intrusion prevention system (IPS) technology, using application proxy firewalls, and disabling any unnecessary documentation and libraries.

Ensure administrative interfaces are removed or secured appropriately. Only allow access from authorized hosts or networks, and then use strong (possibly multifactor) user authentication. Do not hard code the authentication credentials into the application itself, and ensure the security of the credentials using certificates or similar high trust authenticators. Use account lockout and extended logging and audit, and protect all authentication traffic with encryption. Ensure that the interface is at least as secure as the rest of the application, and most often secure it at a higher level.

Because of the accessibility of Web systems and applications, input validation is critical. Application proxy firewalls are appropriate in this regard, but ensure that the proxies are able to deal with problems of buffer overflows, authentication issues, scripting, submission of commands to the underlying platform (which includes issues related to database engines, such as SQL commands), encoding issues (such as Unicode), and URL encoding and translation. In particular, the proxy firewall may have to address issues of data submission to in-house and custom software, ensuring validation of input to those systems. (This level of protection will have to be custom programmed for the application.)

XML

Extensible Markup Language (XML) is a World Wide Web Consortium (W3C) standard for structuring data in a text file so that both the format of the data and the data can be shared on intranets and the Web. A markup language, such as the Hypertext Markup Language (HTML), is simply a system of symbols and rules to identify structures (format) in a document. XML is called extensible because the symbols are unlimited and can be defined by the user or author. The format for XML can represent data in a neutral format that is independent of the database, application, and the underlying DBMS.

XML became a W3C standard in 1998, and many believe it is the de facto standard for integrating data and content. It offers the ability to exchange data and bridge different technologies, such as object models and programming languages. Because of this advantage, XML is expected to transform data and documents of current DBMSs and data access standards (i.e., ODBC, JDBC, etc.) by Web-enabling these standards and providing a common data format. Another, and probably more important, advantage is the ability to create one underlying XML document and display it in a variety of different ways and devices. The security architect must be aware of XML's fundamental structure and how it allows an attacker to manipulate the XML parser. As in database security, the security architect must understand that XML is vulnerable to injection attacks. When reviewing the XML parser for an application, the architect must ensure input is validated and "normal" parameters are established in the design phases.

SAML

The Security Assertion Markup Language is an XML based standard used to exchange authentication and authorization information. SAML was developed by the security services technical committee of the Organization of the Advancement of Structured Information Standards (OASIS.) SAML is designed to allow federated systems with different identity management systems to interact through simplified sign on and single sign on exchanges. OASIS sites the following as advantages of SAML[1]:

- *Platform Neutrality* – SAML abstracts the security framework away from platform architectures and particular vendor implementations. Making security more independent of application logic is an important tenet of Service-Oriented Architecture.

- *Loose coupling of directories* – SAML does not require user information to be maintained and synchronized between directories.

- *Improved online experience for end users* - SAML enables single sign-on by allowing users to authenticate at an identity provider and then access service providers without additional authentication. In addition, identity federation (linking of multiple identities) with SAML allows for a better-customized user experience at each service while promoting privacy.

- *Reduced administrative costs for service providers* – Using SAML to "reuse" a single act of authentication (such as logging in with a username and password) multiple times across multiple services can reduce the cost of maintaining account information. This burden is transferred to the identity provider.

- *Risk Transference* – SAML can act to push responsibility for proper management of identities to the identity provider, which is more often compatible with its business model than that of a service provider."

---

1   https://www.oasis-open.org/committees/download.php/13525/sstc-saml-exec-overview-2.0-cd-01-2col.pdf page 3

While SAML is inherently designed to be secure, the security architect must ensure the implementation does not weaken the security of the language. For example, when passing SAML assertions if a system were to leave out the identifier of the authorization request or the identity of the recipient an attacker could be able to access a user's account without authorization[2].

OWASP

The Open Web Application Security Project (OWASP) is a nonprofit focused on improving the security of software. OWASP develops numerous free and useful products of interest to the security architect including:

- **OWASP Top 10 Project** [3]**:** Provides OWASP's opinion of the top ten web-based application security flaws and how to mitigate them.

- **OWASP Guide Project** [4]**:** Aimed at architects this is a comprehensive manual for designing secure web applications and services.

- **OWASP Software Assurance Maturity Model (SAMM** [5]**):** SAMM is a framework used to design software which is secure and tailored to an organization's specific risks.

- **OWASP Mobile Project** [6]**:** Provides a resource for developers and architects to develop and maintain secure mobile applications.

Given the prevalence of web-based and cloud-based solutions, OWASP provides an accessible and thorough framework with processes for web application security. The security architect should be thoroughly familiar with OWASP's work and how it may apply to the mission they serve.

---

2   http://www.kb.cert.org/vuls/id/612636

3   https://www.owasp.org/index.php/Category:OWASP_Top_Ten_Project

4   https://www.owasp.org/index.php/Category:OWASP_Guide_Project

5   http://www.opensamm.org/

6   https://www.owasp.org/index.php/OWASP_Mobile_Security_Project

Client-Based Vulnerabilities

The client platform is increasingly a staging ground for more advanced attacks towards servers and services. Additionally client platforms are also more diverse and mobile with tablets and smartphones becoming dominate devices for information access. Most tablets and smart phone rely on apps or applets to interface the device with a service or server. The security architect must be aware of what the organization's mobile (smartphones, tablets, removable media) and stationary (standard workstations and thin clients) system environment consists of. The architect must also either determine or make certain assumptions regarding the security posture of the end device data and services reach. For example, the European Network and Information Security Agency (ENISA) warned banks in 2012 to stop assuming customer's computers were free of malware and viruses. They further suggested banks consider offline verification before allowing large transactions[7].

Desktops, Laptops and Thin Clients

The security architect must take into account the basis of the client's machines when designing security architecture. Using the ENISA example, if the architect knows customers need to use the banks website, but the architect cannot force the customer to use a "clean" workstation, then the architect must design security with the assumption the client is infected. This could take the form of one time pad tokens or a variety of security measures to ensure loss and exposure is limited to the customer and the bank. The client level security architecture of an organization should ensure the organization's client systems minimally include:

- A supported and licensed operating system is running
- Updated, verified and supported anti-malware and anti-virus capabilities are installed
- A host based intrusion detection system is installed

---

7   http://www.enisa.europa.eu/media/press-releases/eu-cyber-security-agency-enisa-201chigh-roller201d-online-bank-robberies-reveal-security-gaps

- The whole drive or sensitive information on the drive is encrypted with strong encryption

- Whenever possible the client operates in a "limited" account which does not have administrative privileges.

- Whenever possible the client system is part of a continuous monitoring program which monitors for vulnerabilities and patches them when needed without the need for interaction of the end user.

- Changes to the operating system or new software are validated through an assessment process to determine any security impacts.

Mobile Devices

Tablets and smartphones are increasingly being used in the professional environment as the client platform of choice. Due to their intuitive interfaces, ease of portability and size mobile devices have become the platform of choice for many organizations and individuals. Additionally many users are demanding organizations allow their personal device onto the organization's network and systems in a "bring your own device" or BYOD movement. The security architect needs to be aware of cultural shifts such as the BYOD movement and realign the security architecture of an organization accordingly while keeping the architecture aligned with business needs.

The majority of mobile devices available were not explicitly built for enterprise security or control. In many cases they were designed with the average end user in mind and functionality the top priority. The security architect must understand the devices the end users are using and how to protect sensitive information on them. The architect could consider all of the following options when defining a mobile device security architecture:

- Integration with a mobile device management (MDM) system which allows for:
  - Remote
    - Whole device wipe
    - Account management
    - GPS/WIFI/Cellular location of the device
    - OS, application and firmware updates
    - Application management
    - Device authentication and enrollment
    - Information archive with integrity validation for legal hold situations
  - Secure
    - Web browser
    - Virtual private network (VPN) with web filtering or proxying
    - Organization application "store"
  - Whole device encryption with key escrow
  - "Jailbreak" or "root" access detection
- Secure encrypted container technology for organizational system access which includes:
  - Automatic deletion of any organizational information downloaded to the device
  - VPN for container traffic
  - Secure web browser for container
  - Secure application "store" for container
  - "Jailbreak" or "root" access detection

Server-Based Vulnerabilities

Servers present an enticing target for attackers. While hosting sensitive information and processing an organization's mission sensitive tasks, a server also supports several options which makes an attacker's attempts more effective. The security architect should consider the following when designing server security architecture:

- Determine how remote access will be established to the server:

  ▫ Many servers are located in data centers physically away from the operations of an organization. This requires the security architect to determine the most secure way to access the server for administration and changes.

  ▫ The security architect should consider out of band communications such as separate networks for administration of large groups or servers. Where physical separation is not practical logical separation should be considered.

  ▫ Strong multifactor authentication including one-time pads should be used to help prevent the use of brute force attacks and key logging.

  ▫ Built in remote access services should be evaluated to determine if they are sufficient to provide secure remote access. If they are not, they should be disabled.

- Determine how configuration management will be performed:

  ▫ Identify the individual, group or process responsible for change management and configuration management in the organization.

    • Ensure they are capable of monitoring and patching the server on an ongoing basis. If not, the security architect should recommend a monitoring and patching solution.

    • Identify the vulnerability management capability within the organization. If none exists, the security architect should recommend a vulnerability scanning and tracking solution.

    o Determine how updated code or new versions of software will be deployed on the server. Does a mature system development lifecycle include a development, test, stage and production promotion approach? If not the security architect should recommend a system development lifecycle approach that suits the organization.

- Determine the business continuity requirements and ensure the server security architecture includes backups, fail over sites and notification processes as determined by the mission the server supports.

Data Flow Control

The security architect must be familiar with how data flows into and out of servers. This is most often accomplished using a data flow diagram (DFD). *Figure 6.22 NIST Data Flow diagram* shows an example from the US National Institute of Standards and Technology for the process of analyzing a website's link structure. The diagram breaks down the basic operations into data, processes and windows a user or operator might see. The diagram also delineates the timing of different groups by website, session, analysis, and visualization. The security architect is interested in the controls between the various components that enforce the data flow to only the required recipients and how the communication is protected if required. The concept of least privilege should be employed to ensure data only flows to authorized recipients and processes. The architect should also review any technologies in use such as PERL, the parser, and the visualization tool kit to ensure they are supported under the existing security architecture and if not ensure they can be or find alternatives.

6

Security Architecture & Design

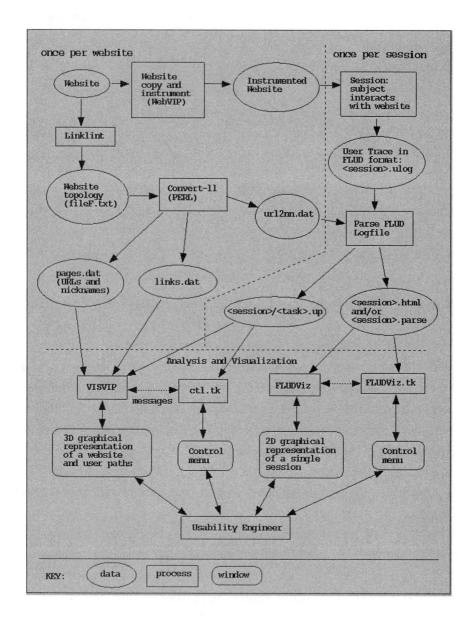

Figure 6.22 - **NIST Data Flow diagram** [1]

---

1   http://zing.ncsl.nist.gov/WebTools/dataflow.gif

Database Security

Database vulnerabilities go beyond vulnerabilities in the server platform to how the data stored within the database is controlled. The security architect must be aware of several topics surrounding database security including inference, aggregation, data mining and warehousing.

Warehousing

A data warehouse is a repository for information collected from a variety of data sources. Because of the compilation of information from many sources, data warehouses eliminate the organization's original information structures and access controls to enable sharing of that information to more levels of employees. The data stored in a data warehouse is not used for operational tasks, but rather for analytical purposes. The data warehouse combines all of the data from various databases into one large data container. Because the data is collected into one central location for analysis, instead of several smaller databases, the combined data can be used by executives to make business decisions.

A current term associated with data warehouses is data marts. Data marts are smaller versions of data warehouses. While a data warehouse is meant to contain all of an organization's information, a data mart may contain the information from just a division or only about a specific topic. In most instances, the creation of a data mart is less time-consuming, and thus the data can be available for analysis sooner than if a data warehouse was created.

The following tasks illustrate a simplified process of building a data warehouse:

- Feed all data into a large, high-availability, and high-integrity database that resides at the confidentiality level of the most sensitive data.

- Normalize the data. Regardless of how the data is characterized in each system, it must be structured the same when moved into

6

Security
Architecture & Design

the data warehouse. For example, one database could categorize birth date as "month/day/year," another as "day/month/year," and still another as "year/month/day." The data warehouse must normalize the various data categories into only one category. Normalization will also remove redundancies in the data.

- Mine the data for correlations to produce metadata.

- Sanitize and export the metadata, results of analysis of the data, to its intended users.

- Feed all new incoming data and the metadata into the data warehouse.

In traditional database administration, rules and policies are implemented to ensure the confidentiality and integrity of the database, such as defining user views and setting access permissions. Security is even more critical for data warehouses. From a security architecture perspective rules and policies must be in place to control access to the data. This includes items such as defining the user groups and the type of data each group can access and outlining the user's security responsibilities and procedures. Another danger of data warehouses is if the physical or logical security perimeter of the database servers were breached, the unauthorized user could gain access to all of the organization's data. The security architect must ensure data flow diagrams and access controls are carefully examined to determine if information leakage or breach may be an issue.

In addition to confidentiality controls, security for the data also includes the integrity and availability of the information. For example, if the data warehouse were accidentally or intentionally destroyed, a valuable repository of the organization's historical and compiled data would also be destroyed. To avoid such a total loss, the security architect must ensure appropriate plans for backups are defined and developed, as well as the security architecture for recovery options such as hardware and software applications.

Inference

Inference is the ability to deduce (infer) sensitive or restricted information from observing available information. Essentially, users may be able to determine unauthorized information from what information they can access and may never need to directly access unauthorized data. For example, if a user is reviewing authorized information about patients, such as the medications they have been prescribed, the user may be able to determine the illness. Inference is one of the hardest threats to control and the security architect will need to apply a deep understanding of the business models surrounding an organization's mission to mitigate this risk.

Aggregation

Aggregation is combining nonsensitive data from separate sources to create sensitive information. For example, a user takes two or more publicly available pieces of data and combines them to form a classified piece of data that then becomes unauthorized for that user. Thus, the combined data sensitivity can be greater than the sensitivity of individual parts. For years, mathematicians have been struggling unsuccessfully with the problem of determining when the aggregation of data results in data at a higher classification. The security architect must work with the data architect to understand the fields and types of information present in a database. The security architect must understand the possible combinations of information including which combinations may result in an escalation of sensitivity.

Data Mining

Data mining is a process of discovering information in data warehouses by running queries on the data. A large repository of data is required to perform data mining. Data mining is used to reveal hidden relationships, patterns, and trends in the data warehouse. Data mining is based on a series of analytical techniques taken from the fields of mathematics, statistics, cybernetics, and genetics. The techniques are used independently and in cooperation with one another to uncover information from data warehouses.

6

Security
Architecture & Design

There are several advantages to using data-mining including the ability to provide better information to managers that outlines the organization's trends, its customers, and the competitive marketplace for its industry. There are also disadvantages, especially for security. The detailed data about individuals obtained through data mining might risk a violation of privacy. The risk increases when private information is stored on the Web or an unprotected area of the network, and thus becomes available to unauthorized users. In addition, the integrity of the data may be at risk. Because a large amount of data must be collected, the chance of errors through human data entry may result in inaccurate relationships or patterns. These errors are referred to as data contamination. The security architect should reference integrity models such as Clark-Wilson and Biba when determining data mining security procedures.

Distributed Systems

Distributed systems are the opposite of centralized systems like mainframes and thin client implementations. Traditional client/server architectures are the most common example of a distributed system. In a traditional client/server architecture, responsibilities for processing have been balanced between centralized servers providing services to multiple clients and client machines that focus on user interaction and standalone processing where appropriate. For the most part, servers are responsible for serving, meaning that they provide services that will be leveraged by the clients in the environment. Clients are the primary consumers of server services, while also hosting services of their own primarily for their own individual use.

In distributed environments, users log into their own computer and data is saved locally or remotely at various sites. There is no central authority that administers user authentications and accounts or manages data storage. No central server is necessary, although servers may have an assortment of roles in such systems. Distributed environments support a wide range of diverse software applications, real-time data access, and varied media formats and data storage. In addition, distributed systems support diverse devices, such as desktops and laptop computers, cell phones, or other kinds of handheld devices. Finally, because there may be a wide range of resources accessed, updated, and stored, there needs to be a way to track user interactions with the system.

A distributed environment will typically need to share common protocols and interfaces. For example, file-sharing networks use a common or universal file format (e.g., network file system [NFS]) to allow an unknown array of files to be stored, recognized, and exchanged by any authorized user on the network. For more functional software, such as gaming or instant messaging, all involved users must have a common software application. This software is obtained in diverse ways, including propagating software around the network from one user to another.

Peer-to-peer systems are another type of distributed environment. These support peer-to-peer exchanges of data and software, typically with the minimal involvement of a centralized authority. Rather, each individual, or peer, logs on and is connected to all other peers in a network. This permits the viewing and exchanging of files with any other peer. Although many peer-to-peer implementations use central servers to set up the interconnected network of users, many peer-to-peer implementations use dynamic peer discovery. This enables them to discover all other peers connected to the system and running the same software. This collection of interconnected users provides a new type of functionality that does not need a central authority to negotiate transactions or store data.

One challenge of distributed systems is the need to coordinate resources that may be distributed on numerous systems. This is accomplished through common structures such as a central naming repository, which generates universally unique identifiers (UUIDs). When a user requests a resource, a search is done within a potentially large network to find a particular resource, thus requiring a precise specification of the resource.

6

Security
Architecture & Design

However, authorization may be the biggest challenge, as there is no central authority to trust. It is also significantly more difficult to control security vulnerabilities in a distributed environment, although such vulnerabilities may be less pervasive. Each system has some responsibility for enforcing security and protecting themselves from compromise.

Grid Computing

Grid computing is the sharing of CPU and other resources across a network in such a manner that all machines function as one large computer. Grid computers are often used for processor intensive tasks which are suitable to be processed by parallel tasks. Grid computing is often confused with "cluster computing." Both involve using two or more computers to solve problems but grid computing is heterogeneous while cluster computing is homogenous. Grid computers can have different operating systems, hardware and software. Grid systems are also associated with multi-tasking (a desktop computer may be part of a grid with spare CPU resources and also serve normal desktop functions) whereas a cluster is devoted to a single task. Finally, clusters are most often physically close together with a fast bus or network connecting the nodes while a grid is geographically dispersed.

Given the dispersed and shared nature of grid computing, the security architect involved in the design of a grid system should keep in mind some of the vulnerabilities this leads to:

- Unless dedicated private communication lines are funded between nodes much of the traffic for the grid will flow over public internet conduits. Encryption of information between nodes or the use of VPN technology may provide mitigation for this vulnerability.

- Given the geographic distance a grid has between nodes, user authentication may be completely logical. Therefore strong logical authentication controls must be implemented to ensure only authorized users access the grid. Consider specifying Kerberos, PKI or multifactor authentication methods as part of the grid's security architecture.

- Grid node software must be examined if joining a grid and designed security if hosting a grid. Special attention should be directed towards how the grid application isolates grid computing activity from other system activities.

Cloud Computing

Cloud computing is a vague and ambiguous term. Many vendors market their product as cloud although it may not match what another vendor considers cloud. For the sake of discussion, cloud computing has been formally defined by US NIST as:

".. a model for enabling ubiquitous, convenient, on-demand network access to a shared pool of configurable computing resources (e.g., networks, servers, storage, applications, and services) that can be rapidly provisioned and released with minimal management effort or service provider interaction. This cloud model is composed of five essential characteristics, three service models, and four deployment models.[8]"

NIST defines the five essential characteristics of cloud computing as:

- *On-Demand Self-Service:* A consumer can unilaterally provision computing capabilities, such as server time and network storage, as needed automatically without requiring human interaction with each service provider.

- *Broad Network Access:* Capabilities are available over the network and accessed through standard mechanisms that promote use by heterogeneous thin or thick client platforms (e.g., mobile phones, tablets, laptops, and workstations).

- *Resource Pooling:* The provider's computing resources are pooled to serve multiple consumers using a multi-tenant model, with different physical and virtual resources dynamically assigned and reassigned according to consumer

8   Mell, Peter, and Timothy Grance. US National Institute of Standards and Technology, "The NIST Definition of Cloud Computing." Last modified Sept 2011. http://csrc.nist.gov/publications/nistpubs/800-145/SP800-145.pdf. Page 2-3

demand. There is a sense of location independence in that the customer generally has no control or knowledge over the exact location of the provided resources but may be able to specify location at a higher level of abstraction (e.g., country, state, or datacenter). Examples of resources include storage, processing, memory, and network bandwidth.

- ***Rapid Elasticity:*** Capabilities can be elastically provisioned and released, in some cases automatically, to scale rapidly outward and inward commensurate with demand. To the consumer, the capabilities available for provisioning often appear to be unlimited and can be appropriated in any quantity at any time.

- ***Measured Service:*** Cloud systems automatically control and optimize resource use by leveraging a metering capability at some level of abstraction appropriate to the type of service (e.g., storage, processing, bandwidth, and active user accounts). Resource usage can be monitored, controlled, and reported, providing transparency for both the provider and consumer of the utilized service."[30]

NIST identifies three service models that represent different types of cloud services available:

- ***Software as a Service (SaaS):*** The capability provided to the consumer is to use the provider's applications running on a cloud infrastructure. The applications are accessible from various client devices through either a thin client interface, such as a web browser (e.g., web-based email), or a program interface. The consumer does not manage or control the underlying cloud infrastructure including network, servers, operating systems, storage, or even individual application capabilities, with the possible exception of limited user-specific application configuration settings.

- ***Platform as a Service (PaaS):*** The capability provided to the consumer is to deploy onto the cloud infrastructure consumer-created or acquired applications created using programming languages, libraries, services, and tools supported by the provider. The consumer does not manage or control the underlying cloud infrastructure including network, servers, operating systems, or storage, but has control over the deployed applications and possibly configuration settings for the application-hosting environment.

■ *Infrastructure as a Service (IaaS):* The capability provided to the consumer is to provision processing, storage, networks, and other fundamental computing resources where the consumer is able to deploy and run arbitrary software, which can include operating systems and applications. The consumer does not manage or control the underlying cloud infrastructure but has control over operating systems, storage, and deployed applications; and possibly limited control of select networking components (e.g., host firewalls)". [30]

Finally NIST describes four different deployment models:

■ *Private Cloud:* The cloud infrastructure is provisioned for exclusive use by a single organization comprising multiple consumers (e.g., business units). It may be owned, managed, and operated by the organization, a third party, or some combination of them, and it may exist on or off premises.

■ *Community Cloud:* The cloud infrastructure is provisioned for exclusive use by a specific community of consumers from organizations that have shared concerns (e.g., mission, security requirements, policy, and compliance considerations). It may be owned, managed, and operated by one or more of the organizations in the community, a third party, or some combination of them, and it may exist on or off premises.

■ *Public Cloud:* The cloud infrastructure is provisioned for open use by the general public. It may be owned, managed, and operated by a business, academic, or government organization, or some combination of them. It exists on the premises of the cloud provider.

6

Security
Architecture & Design

997

- **Hybrid Cloud:** The cloud infrastructure is a composition of two or more distinct cloud infrastructures (private, community, or public) that remain unique entities, but are bound together by standardized or proprietary technology that enables data and application portability (e.g., cloud bursting for load balancing between clouds)."[9]

As more organizations are leveraging SaaS, PaaS, and IaaS, the security architect must be aware of the limited ability they have to define specific security controls and functions. As cloud computing moves from infrastructure to platform to software the responsibility to implement effective security controls shifts away from the organization and towards the cloud service provider. Therefore, as cloud service models are being designed, the security architect must understand which controls may be modified or added and which may need compensating controls.

For example, assume an online retailer has decided to use Infrastructure as a Service to store their credit card holder's information. The retailer has several PCI-DSS requirements they must adhere to including encrypting the cardholder's information when in storage. As the cloud service provider is not offering encrypted storage, the security architect may advise encrypting the information prior to transmission of the cloud storage service. If the retailer instead decided to use a SaaS option in the form of a pre-designed and ready to use storefront software the approach would be different. The security architect would ensure as part of the contracting process the retailer has passed a PCI-DSS assessment and has appropriate encryption of cardholder information in place.

---

9   Mell, Peter, and Timothy Grance. US National Institute of Standards and Technology, "The NIST Definition of Cloud Computing." Last modified Sept 2011. http://csrc.nist.gov/publications/nistpubs/800-145/SP800-145.pdf. Page 3

Countermeasure Principles

Well-designed security architectures will include several forms of countermeasures. Countermeasures can be thought of as procedures, techniques, devices, or actions that mitigate a threat or vulnerability. The security architect is most involved in the development of countermeasures related to minimizing and eliminating vulnerabilities of information systems. The core tenant of ensuring appropriate countermeasures is defense in depth.

Defense in Depth

The practice of implementing appropriate access control mechanisms is also the first line of defense in an organization's defense-in-depth strategy. Defense in depth[1] is the practice of applying multiple layers of security protection between an information resource and a potential attacker. If one of those layers should fail the successive layers will continue to function and protect the resource against compromise. Defense in depth is applicable to both the physical and virtual environments. The goal is to ensure that access to assets is protected by multiple layers of controls. *Figure 6.23* illustrates the defense in depth concept.

When developing security architectures, the architect must understand the existing countermeasures in place and where they may fit in the security architecture of a system or an enterprise. For example, if an architect were designing a security architecture for an internal accounting system and knew all information system components were to be stored on site then the countermeasure in place for physical security may ease some of the requirements for logical security like encryption of local area network traffic. The layers of defense available (or not) will greatly shape the overall enterprise and system security architecture.

---

1   Read more about defense in depth here: http://www.nsa.gov/ia/_files/support/defenseindepth.pdf

Figure 6.23 - **Defense in Depth**

Maintaining Security Architecture

Even well-designed and implemented security services may become less effective over time. Threats are continuously evolving and new vulnerabilities are constantly being discovered. On a regular basis, security designs will need to be assessed and updated. Where the business requirements for security have changed, it may be necessary to start over from the beginning. A strong architectural design will need to be in place to gather feedback and manage such changes over time.

Feedback into the security architecture comes through security metrics. Security metrics allow the organization to measure the current state of security through the data provided by active security services. These metrics identify areas for potential improvement, whether that is an improvement in technical, people, or supporting processes. Reporting also provides valuable feedback from various stakeholders, and may indicate that changes to security architecture are desirable at the executive or management level.

Another common way to get feedback is through an organization's continuous service improvement practices following a framework such as ITIL. Typically, this will combine metrics and reporting with maturity modeling to determine where the organization is in their development and what the target state of information security practices should be. In general, organizations that have achieved a high maturity level that focuses on optimization and measurable improvement are considered the most mature, and represent the most advanced. A focus on process development shows an organization is on the right track.

While there are many maturity modeling methods available, most are based on the Software Engineering Institute's capability maturity model (or CMM[2]). Originally designed with application programming practices in mind, CMM allows an organization to assess the current state of their processes and chart out a future state where these practices are more robust and mature. CMM identified five key stages in maturity as illustrated in *Figure 6.24 CMM maturity models*:

During the initial stage, the process is not very well-defined and most activities are essentially reactive. This is common when starting to use new processes or perform new activities. During the managed stage, the process may still be largely reactive but at least it has been established at the individual project level. At the defined stage, the process is now generally proactive and universally established across the organization but

2   Read more about CMM here: http://www.brighthub.com/office/project-management/articles/69744.aspx

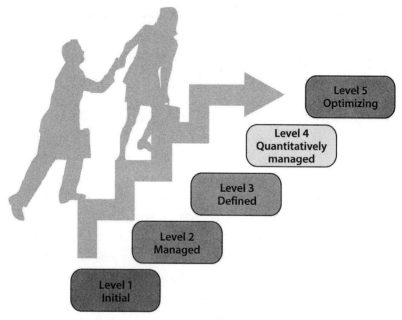

Figure 6.24 - **CMM Maturity Models**

it is not really measured for effectiveness. At the quantitatively Managed stage, the process is not only proactive and universally established, but it is possible to measure and control its effectiveness. At the final optimizing stage, measurements can be used to drive out continuous improvements in the quality and effectiveness of the process.

A similar approach is used by ISACA and ITGI [3] to measure the maturity of information security governance. The COBIT Maturity Model is used to rank organizations against both industry best practices and international standard guidelines, from a maturity perspective. This maturity model illustrates the typical current state of many organizations in dealing with information security governance. Rather than focus on specific gaps, it focuses on the ability to show improvement across the entire spectrum of information security. *Figure 6.25* illustrates the levels of maturity used by this model:

---

3   For more information on ISACA and ITGI please see the following:

A. ISACA: https://www.isaca.org/Pages/default.aspx

B. ITGI: http://www.itgi.org/

These may be used to guide the continuous development of security architecture in a number of ways. Typically, this model is used to establish the desired target maturity for specific security services, and form the basis to assess those services in the architecture.

Rating	COBIT MM Level	CMU-SEI CMM Equivalent[b]	Comments
0	Nonexistent		Complete lack of any recognizable processes. There is a general lack of awareness that an issue even exists
1	Initial/ad hoc	Initial/ad hoc	Organization recognizes that an issue exists, which needs to be addressed. However, there are no coherent security processes; issues are addressed on an ad hoc basis
2	Repeatable	Managed	Security processes have been developed to the extent that similar procedures are followed by different people undertaking the same tasks. There are no organizational standards. Security activities are mostly reactive. There is over-reliance on individuals, with high potential for errors and inconsistencies.
3	Defined	Defined	Some security processes have been standardized and documented, and communicated through awareness or training. However, the processes are not sophisticated and merely represent formalization of existing processes. Compliance is still left up to individuals; it is not likely that deviations and non-compliance will be detected.
4	Managed	Quantitatively managed	A formal and proactive approach for continuously reviewing and enhancing security objectives and controls exists. Security controls are derived based on sound risk management principles. Enterprise-wide integration of security is well under way. Monitoring for compliance and measurement for effectiveness has been implemented. However, automation and tools are being used in a limited or fragmented way.
5	Optimized	Optimizing	Processes have been refined to world class level, based on continuous improvement and alignment with best-practices. Security is well integrated within the organization, and involves multiple stakeholders, in order to improve quality and effectiveness, and allowing the organization to adapt quickly to changing threats and requirements.

[a] http://www.isaca.org/Knowledge-Center/cobit/Pages/FAQ.aspx#25

[b] Carnegie Mellon University Software Engineering Institute Capability Maturity Model.

Figure 6.25 - **COBIT Maturity Levels**

6

Security Architecture & Design

1003

The following articles and documents contain more information about Security Architecture and Design. They are freely available on the Internet:

NIST SP 800-124 Revision 1 (Draft), Guidelines for Managing and Securing Mobile Devices in the Enterprise
http://csrc.nist.gov/publications/drafts/800-124r1/draft_sp800-124-rev1.pdf

Australia's DCITA ITSEAG TISN, Secure Your Information: Information Security Principles for Enterprise Architecture
http://www.dbcde.gov.au/__data/assets/pdf_file/0016/70621/SIFT_Full_Report_020707.pdf

NIST SP 800-144, Guidelines on Security and Privacy in Public Cloud Computing
http://csrc.nist.gov/publications/nistpubs/800-144/SP800-144.pdf

Trusted Could Initiative Reference Architecture
https://research.cloudsecurityalliance.org/tci/

NISTIR 7497, Security Architecture Design Process for Health Information Exchanges
http://csrc.nist.gov/publications/nistir/ir7497/nistir-7497.pdf

US National Airspace System Security Cyber Architecture
http://www.mitre.org/work/tech_papers/2011/10_4169/10_4169.pdf

Download a free Virtual Machine software package here:
https://www.virtualbox.org/

Summary and Conclusion

Security Architecture and Design domain covers a wide range of topics focused on designing security into computing systems and across IT services throughout the enterprise. The security architect is expected to understand a number of key security architecture concepts and apply them against a number of common scenarios. Security architects capture and analyze requirements, design security services based on those requirements and verify the effectiveness of those designs.

Security architects understand the different architecture frameworks, standards, and best practices leveraged by numerous frameworks and methodologies, and how they may be used together to provide stronger designs.

6

Security
Architecture & Design

Review Questions

1. A holistic lifecycle for developing security architecture that begins with assessing business requirements and subsequently creating a 'chain of traceability' through phases of strategy, concept, design, implementation and metrics is characteristic of which of the following frameworks?

    A. Zachman
    B. SABSA
    C. ISO 27000
    D. TOGAF

2. Which of the following component of ITIL's Service Portfolio is primarily focused on translating designs into operational services through a project management standard?

    A. Service Strategy
    B. Service Design
    C. Service Transition
    D. Service Operations

3. Which of the following can **BEST** be used to capture detailed security requirements?

    A. Threat modeling, covert channels, and data classification
    B. Data classification, risk assessments, and covert channels
    C. Risk assessments, covert channels, and threat modeling
    D. Threat modeling, data classification, and risk assessments

4. Which of the following security standards is internationally recognized as the standards for sound security practices and is focused on the standardization and certification of an organization's Information Security Management System (ISMS)?

    A. ISO 15408
    B. ISO 27001

C. ISO 9001

D. ISO 9146

5. Which of the following describes the rules that need to be implemented to ensure that the security requirements are met?

   A. Security kernel

   B. Security policy

   C. Security model

   D. Security reference monitor

6. A two-dimensional grouping of individual subjects into groups or roles and granting access to groups to objects is an example of which of the following types of models?

   A. Multilevel lattice

   B. State machine

   C. Non-interference

   D. Matrix-based

7. Which of the following models ensures that a subject with clearance level of 'Secret' has the ability to write only to objects classified as 'Secret' or 'Top Secret' but is prevented from writing information classified as 'Public'?

   A. Biba-Integrity

   B. Clark–Wilson

   C. Brewer–Nash

   D. Bell–LaPadula

8. Which of the following is unique to the Biba Integrity Model?

   A. Simple property

   B. * (star) property

   C. Invocation property

   D. Strong * property

6

Security Architecture & Design

1007

9. Which of the following models is **BEST** considered in a shared data-hosting environment so that the data of one customer is not disclosed to a competitor or other customers sharing that hosted environment?

   A. Brewer–Nash

   B. Clark–Wilson

   C. Bell–LaPadula

   D. Lipner

10. Which of the following security models is primarily concerned with how the subjects and objects are created and how subjects are assigned rights or privileges?

    A. Bell–LaPadula

    B. Biba-Integrity

    C. Chinese Wall

    D.   Graham–Denning

11. Which of the following ISO standards provides the evaluation criteria that can be used to evaluate security requirements of different products with different functions?

    A.   a.   15408

    B.   b.   27000

    C.   c.   9100

    D.   d.   27002

12. In the Common Criteria, the common set of functional and assurance requirements for a category of vendor products deployed in a particular type of environment are known as

    A.   a.   Protection Profiles

    B.   b.   Security Target

    C.   c.   Trusted Computing Base

    D.   d.   Ring Protection

13. Which of the following evaluation assurance level that is formally verified, designed and tested is expected for high risk situation?

    A. EAL 1

    B. EAL 3

    C. EAL 5

    D. EAL 7

14. Formal acceptance of an evaluated system by management is known as

    A. Certification

    B. Accreditation

    C. Validation

    D. Verification

15. Which stage of the Capability Maturity Model (CMM) is characterized by having organizational processes that are proactive?

    A. Initial

    B. Managed

    C. Defined

    D. Optimizing

16. Which of the following BEST provides a method of quantifying risks associated with information technology when validating the abilities of new security controls and countermeasures to address the identified risks?

    A. Threat/risk assessment

    B. Penetration testing

    C. Vulnerability assessment

    D. Data classification

17. The use of proxies to protect more trusted assets from less sensitive ones is an example of which of the following types of security services?

    A. Access control

    B. Boundary control

    C. Integrity

    D. Audit and monitoring

6

Security Architecture & Design

18. Which of the following is the main reason for security concerns in mobile computing devices?

    A. The 3G protocol is inherently insecure

    B. Lower processing power

    C. Hackers are targeting mobile devices

    D. The lack of anti-virus software.

19. In decentralized environments device drivers that enable the OS to control and communicate with hardware need to be securely designed, developed and deployed because they are

    A. typically installed by end-users and granted access to the supervisor state

    B. typically installed by administrators and granted access to user mode state

    C. typically installed by software without human interaction.

    D. integrated as part of the operating system.

20. A system administrator grants rights to a group of individuals called "Accounting" instead of granting rights to each individual. This is an example of which of the following security mechanisms?

    A. Layering

    B. Data hiding

    C. Cryptographic protections

    D. Abstraction

Domain 7

Security Operations

THE SECURITY OPERATIONS DOMAIN can be challenging. If a security professional has considerable practical experience with day-to-day security operations, the domain will be easier to relate to. If experience is lacking it may be difficult as the concepts can be challenging to replicate through self-study. It is also essentially two domains in one: operations security and security operations. Operations security is primarily concerned with the protection and control of information processing assets in centralized and distributed environments. Security operations are primarily concerned with the daily tasks required to keep security services operating reliably and efficiently. Operations security is a quality of other services and are also a set of services in its own right.

TOPICS

- Understand security operations concepts
  - Need-to-know/least privilege
  - Separation of duties and responsibilities
  - Monitor special privileges, e.g., operations, administrators (e.g., operators, administrators)
  - Job rotation
  - Marking, handling, storing, and destroying of sensitive information and media
  - Record retention
- Employ resource protection
  - Media management
  - Asset management (e.g., equipment life cycle, software licensing)
- Manage incident response
  - Detection
  - Response
  - Reporting
  - Recovery
  - Remediation and review (e.g., root cause analysis)
- Implement preventative measures against attacks (e.g., malicious code, zero-day exploit, denial of service)
- Implement and support patch and vulnerability management
- Understand change and configuration management (e.g., versioning, baselining)
- Understand system resilience and fault tolerance requirements

OBJECTIVES

According to the (ISC)^2 Candidate Information Bulletin, an information security professional is expected to know:

- The resources that must be protected
- The privileges that must be restricted
- The control mechanisms available
- The potential for abuse of access
- The appropriate controls
- The principles of good practice.

Security Operations Concepts

Key Themes

There are four main themes discussed in this chapter: maintaining operational resilience, protecting valuable assets, controlling system accounts, and managing security services effectively. Each of these themes is fundamental to operations security.

Maintaining Operational Resilience

When it comes to day-to-day operations, few things are more important than maintaining the expected levels of service availability and integrity. Organizations require critical services to be resilient. When negative events affect the organization, operations staff are expected to ensure minimal disruption to the organization's activities. This includes anticipating such disruptions and ensuring that key systems are deployed and maintained to help ensure continuity. They are also expected to maintain processes and procedures to help ensure timely detection and response.

Protecting Valuable Assets

Security operations are expected to provide day-to-day protection for a wide variety of resources, including human and material assets. They may not be responsible for setting strategy or designing appropriate security solutions. At a minimum, they will be expected to maintain the controls that have been put into place to protect sensitive or critical resources from compromise.

Controlling System Accounts

In the current regulatory environment, there has been a renewed focus on maintaining control over users (subjects) that have access to key business systems. In many cases, these subjects have extensive or unlimited capabilities on a given system, privileges that could be misused or abused. Operations security will be expected to provide checks and balances against privileged accounts as well as maintain processes that ensure that there continues to be a valid business need for them.

Managing Security Services Effectively

No security operations will be effective without strong service management and the processes that are put into place to ensure service consistency. These include key service management processes common to most IT services such as change, configuration, and problem management. It will also include security-specific procedures such as user provisioning and Help Desk procedures. In today's security operations, there is also considerable focus on reporting and continuous service improvement practices. These themes are discussed in the detailed sections below.

Key Operational Processes and Procedures

Security Operations is expected to play a valuable role in supporting and leveraging a number of processes and procedures intended to provide for smooth operations. They help to ensure that changes are implemented with appropriate review and approval, that IT resources are configured to provide steady and reliable services that incidents are addressed quickly and effectively, and that problems are fixed. The security professional should be able to describe these processes at a high level and identify their role in them.

Controlling Privileged Accounts

Security operations must maintain strong control over the number and types of accounts used on systems. This requires careful supervision over the management of accounts that are given privileges on IT systems. Identity management controls the life-cycle process for every account in a system, from the provisioning of the account through to its eventual removal from the system. Access management refers to the assignment of rights or privileges to those accounts that will allow them to perform their intended function. Identity and access management (IAM)[1] solutions

1   For further information on Identity and Access Management (IAM) solutions, please see the following: http://www.csoonline.com/article/205053/the-abcs-of-identity-management

focus on harmonizing the provisioning of users and managing their access across multiple systems with different native access control systems. Within the Security Operations domain, the focus is on using these solutions most effectively while also ensuring that privileged accounts are carefully controlled and audited.

Need to-Know/Least Privilege

The principle of least privilege is one of the most fundamental characteristics of access control for meeting security objectives. Least privilege requires that a user or process be given no more access privilege than necessary to perform a job, task, or function. The objective is to limit users and processes to access only resources and tools necessary to perform assigned functions. This often requires limits not only on what resources can be accessed, but also includes limiting the actions that can be performed by the user even if they have authorized access to the resource. For example, a user may be assigned read-only, update, and execute permissions on a system without the ability to create or delete files and databases. Ensuring least privilege requires identifying what the user's job is, determining the minimum set of privileges required to perform that job, and restricting the user to a domain with those privileges and nothing more. Denying users access privileges that are not necessary for the performance of their duties ensures that those privileges cannot be used to circumvent the organization's security policy.

A companion concept to least privilege is the notion of need to know. If the goal of least privilege is reducing access to a bare minimum, need to know defines that minimum as a need for access based on job or business requirements. For example, although the CIO in an organization has the appropriate rank in the organization to view upcoming quarterly financial forecasts, the organization's comptroller may decide that the CIO does not have a need to know that information and, thus, restrict access to it. Need to know is also used heavily in situations where operational secrecy is a key concern, such as in military operations. Military leaders often keep operational plans on a need to know basis to reduce the number of people who know about the plans and reduce the risk that someone will leak that information to the enemy.

7

Security Operations

Managing Accounts Using Groups and Roles

Efficient management of users requires the assignment of individual accounts into groups or roles. This will allow rights and privileges to be assigned to groups or a role as opposed to individual accounts. Individual user accounts can then be assigned to one or more groups depending on the access and privileges they require. When groups can be set up according to job functions within the organization, role-based access control (RBAC) can be used. Under RBAC, individual users are assigned a single role that corresponds to the rights and privileges they require to do their jobs. Whether groups or roles are used, security administrators must devise the appropriate assignment of permissions and rights, depending on the access control strategy used.

Different Types of Accounts

On most systems, accounts with greater privilege are distinct from ordinary user accounts that require less privilege. Privileged entities possess extensive powers on a given system. While these privileges may be necessary, they could be misused by unscrupulous individuals or targeted by external attackers. Security operations is expected to maintain control and oversight of these privileged entities, including ensuring they are assigned for legitimate business use and that continued need is being regularly examined. This requires a defined regimen for how privileged entities are created on various systems as well as the processes in place to confirm that they are still required. While ordinary user accounts have less privilege, they also need to be controlled through good account management practices.

Privileged Accounts

Traditionally, there are four types of accounts with different privilege levels Identified as follows: root or built-in administrator accounts, service accounts, administrator accounts, and power user accounts.

- ***Root or built-in administrator accounts:*** These accounts are the all-powerful default administrative accounts used to manage a device or system. These accounts are generally shared by administrators for performing specialized administrative tasks. However, administrators should refrain from using these accounts, as a loss of accountability is possible when multiple individuals have access to an account password. These accounts should be renamed whenever possible and strictly controlled. Default passwords should be changed prior to adding the device or computer to the production network. Logs should be kept to record individual use of the root account and password as part of a change management and configuration management program. The logs should correlate with the system audit log regarding the account activity. In most modern systems, interactive login using the root or administrator account has been disabled in favor of individually assigned administrative accounts that can assume root powers when needed. If login as root is required, the administrators should log in at the device console in an area with restricted access. Remote log-in with root accounts should only occur when the session can be strongly encrypted and monitored. This prevents a compromise of the root password or session hijacking by a rogue node on the system. These accounts should always be considered for multi-factor authentication methods such as one-time pads.

- ***Service accounts:*** These accounts are used to provide privileged access used by system services and core applications. Systems use a variety of accounts to provide automated services, such as Web servers, e-mail servers, and database management systems. Such services require accounts to perform actions on the local system. Services might also have multiple internal accounts. Database management systems, such as Oracle, can have 10 or more internal default accounts at the initial installation. Management of service accounts can become challenging in a distributed environment where administrators must perform administrative functions remotely. Passwords for service accounts should be complex and must be strictly

7

Security Operations

1019

controlled to mitigate the risks of attack. Developing a strategy for changing service account passwords on a routine basis is necessary to provide continued integrity for the system.

- *Administrator accounts:* These accounts are assigned only to named individuals that require administrative access to the system to perform maintenance activities. Passwords for administrative accounts should be distributed in person. Administrators should acknowledge in writing receipt of their account and willingness to follow organizational usage policies for privileged accounts. Remove administrative accounts immediately from the system when individuals no longer require that level of access. It is common practice to revalidate continued business need on a regular basis to ensure that these accounts are still required. It is also important that all actions taken by an administrative account are audited. Given the power of these accounts, it is usually necessary to employ external logging systems since administrators may be able to tamper with log files. These accounts should always be considered for multi-factor authentication methods such as one-time pads.

- *Power users:* These accounts are granted greater privileges than normal user accounts when it is necessary for the user to have greater control over the system, but where administrative access is not required. For example, it is common to allow power users to install software on their own desktop systems. These accounts must be controlled, and should be revalidated regularly for continued business need. Power users should acknowledge in writing receipt of their account and willingness to follow organizational usage policies for privileged accounts. Remove power user accounts immediately from the system when individuals no longer require that level of access. It is common practice to revalidate continued business need on a regular basis to ensure that these accounts are still required. These accounts should always be considered for multi-factor authentication methods such as one-time pads.

Ordinary or Limited User Accounts

Ordinary or limited user accounts are what most users are assigned. They should be restricted only to those privileges that are strictly required, following the principle of least privilege. Access should be limited to specific objects following the principle of need-to-know.

Separation of Duties and Responsibilities

Accounts are assigned to individuals with particular job roles. In this domain, the security professional should be able to distinguish between the common types of job roles and how they are related in an operational environment.

System Administrators

System administrators enjoy the highest level of privilege on most systems, particularly in server environments. They are entrusted with managing system operations and maintenance, and helping ensure that the system is functioning properly for system users. They perform key maintenance and monitoring tasks on a wide range of systems, including workstations, servers, network devices, databases, and applications. Each of these components requires various levels of recurring maintenance to ensure continued operations. For example, system administrators require the ability to affect certain critical operations such as setting the time, boot sequence, system logs, and passwords.

System administrators may be responsible for managing different sorts of systems, including workstations, laptops, and servers. Specialized applications, such as database management systems, can be considered systems unto themselves. Sometimes an administrator is dedicated to the task of database management as the database administrator (DBA). The operational control concepts expressed for ordinary system administrators are also applicable to individuals assigned administrative duties for specialized applications.

7

Security Operations

Given the impact systems administrators can have on an organization, special care should be used when hiring them. The security professional should ensure the following actions are considered for a system administrator role:

- **Least Privilege:** The system administrator often does not require access to every system and function in an organization. Determine what access is needed and apply accordingly.

- **Monitoring:** If possible, the system administrator's actions should be logged and sent to a separate system that the system administrator does not control. The logs should be reviewed with change or configuration management requests to determine if only authorized actions are taking place.

- **Separation of Duties:** An administrator should not have the ability to engage in malicious activities without collusion.

- **Background Investigation:** A background investigation should be conducted to determine if the system administrator has abused the role in the past or may be vulnerable to blackmail or extortion attempts.

- **Job Rotation:** System administrators should be subject to job rotation. Job rotation ensures another individual must perform the original system administrator's duties and also review their work.

Operators

System operators represent a class of users typically found in data center environments where mainframe systems are used. They provide day-to-day operations of the mainframe environment, ensuring that scheduled jobs are running effectively and troubleshooting problems that may arise. They also act as the arms and legs of the mainframe environment, load and unloading tape and results of job print runs. Operators have elevated privileges, but less than those of system administrators. If misused, these privileges may be used to circumvent the system's security policy. As such, use of these privileges should be monitored through audit logs. Some of the privileges and responsibilities assigned to operators include:

- *Implementing the initial program load:* This is used to start the operating system. The boot process or initial program load of a system is a critical time for ensuring system security. Interruptions to this process may reduce the integrity of the system or cause the system to crash, precluding its availability.

- *Monitoring execution of the system:* Operators respond to various events, to include errors, interruptions, and job completion messages.

- *Volume mounting:* This allows the desired application access to the system and its data.

- *Controlling job flow:* Operators can initiate, pause, or terminate programs. This may allow an operator to affect the scheduling of jobs. Controlling job flow involves the manipulation of configuration information needed by the system. Operators with the ability to control a job or application can cause output to be altered or diverted, which can threaten the confidentiality.

- *Bypass label processing:* This allows the operator to bypass security label information to run foreign tapes (foreign tapes are those from a different data center that would not be using the same label format that the system could run). This privilege should be strictly controlled to prevent unauthorized access.

- *Renaming and relabeling resources:* This is sometimes necessary in the mainframe environment to allow programs to properly execute. Use of this privilege should be monitored, as it can allow the unauthorized viewing of sensitive information.

- *Reassignment of ports and lines:* Operators are allowed to reassign ports or lines. If misused, reassignment can cause program errors, such as sending sensitive output to an unsecured location. Furthermore, an incidental port may be opened, subjecting the system to an attack through the creation of a new entry point into the system.

7

Security Operations

1023

Given the impact operators can have on an organization, special care should be used when hiring them. The security professional should ensure the following actions are considered for an operator role:

- **Least Privilege:** The systems operator often does not require access to every system and function in an organization. Determine what access is needed and apply accordingly.

- **Monitoring:** If possible, the operator's actions should be logged and sent to a separate system that the operator does not control. The logs should be reviewed with change or configuration management requests to determine if only authorized actions are taking place.

- **Separation of Duties:** An operator should not have the ability to engage in malicious activities without collusion.

- **Background Investigation:** A background investigation should be conducted to determine if the operator has abused the role in the past or may be vulnerable to blackmail or extortion attempts.

Security Administrators

The role of security administrators is to provide oversight for the security operations of a system. The aspects of security operations in their purview include account management, assignment of file sensitivity labels, system security settings, and review of audit data. Operating systems and some applications, such as database management systems, and networking equipment contain a significant number of security settings. Security administrators are responsible for defining the security settings of a system. In some cases, the security administrator may also implement the settings in conjunction with the system administrator or appropriate application manager. It is necessary for the security administrator and system administrator to work together on security settings because an improper configuration can impact the proper operation of the system or network.

These administrators usually have fewer rights than system administrators. This is necessary to ensure that separation of duties is enforced. Security administrators provide a check and balance of the power assigned to system administrators with the ability to audit and review their activities.

Help Desk Personnel

Help desk personnel are responsible for providing front line support for all users. While they may be supplemented by automated systems, they are typically responsible for some aspects of account management. For example, they often are responsible for resetting user passwords when needed. This requires that they have sufficient privileges on the system to perform these functions. As helpdesk personnel often have the ability to reset passwords, they should be subject to monitoring and background investigations as feasible and necessary.

Ordinary Users

Ordinary users are individuals requiring access to information technology resources. Their access is limited to normal user activities.

Monitor Special Privileges

A security professional is expected to ensure accounts and their privileges are assigned appropriately and reviewed on a regular basis. Only authorized users should be granted access and for only the period of time that they require that access. This means validating their trustworthiness and occasionally revalidating their privileges.

Clearances, Suitability and Background Checks/Investigations

Individuals are granted clearances, suitabilities and other types of acceptable personal background designations according to their past actions, history of trustworthiness, and the level of access to sensitive information needed for their assigned duties. Security administrators participate in the background investigation process by ensuring that individuals have had an appropriate background check completed and any requisite clearance, suitability or designation assigned prior to providing the individual an account and password. Periodic background checks should also be conducted to ensure that the level of trust granted to an individual is appropriate for his or her assigned duty. Individuals should not be given access to areas of the system where they have demonstrated an unmitigated:

- recent and relevant serious lack of judgment
- repeated patterns of high-risk behavior relevant to the performance of the role
- illegal activity relevant to the performance of the role

For example, individuals convicted of committing financial fraud should not be granted access to financial systems and databases. On the other hand, a person convicted of reckless driving seven years ago may be suitable for the same position. A "whole person" concept viewed through the nexus of the role's responsibility is necessary to make sound and consistent background check decisions[2]. Background checks and investigations are a

---

2   Read more about the United States Military's approach to the "whole person" concept and clearances here: http://www.dhra.mil/perserec/adr/intro/introtext.htm

useful tool for determining the trustworthiness of an individual and the likelihood of their compliance with organization policy.

Account Validation

Reviews of account activity are necessary to determine the existence of inactive accounts. Those accounts found to be inactive due to the departure of an individual from the organization should be removed from the system. Accounts that are inactive due to extended leave or temporary duties should be disabled. Ideally, individuals or their supervisors would promptly report temporary or permanent departures of system users to the appropriate system or security administrator. However, this does not always occur, so the security practitioner must be vigilant in conducting periodic reviews of accounts for inactivity.

Job Rotation

Job rotations reduce the risk of collusion of activities between individuals. Companies with individuals working with sensitive information or systems where there might be the opportunity for personal gain through collusion can benefit by integrating job rotation with segregation of duties. Rotating the position may uncover activities that the individual is performing outside of the normal operating procedures, highlighting errors or fraudulent behavior. It may be difficult to implement in small organizations due to the particular skill set required for the position, and thus security controls and supervisory control will need to be relied upon. Rotating individuals in and out of jobs provides the ability to give backup coverage, succession planning, and job enrichment opportunities for those involved. It also provides diversity of skills to support separation of duties.

Marking, Handling, Storing and Destroying of Sensitive Information

As with physical assets, it is important that classified information assets are clearly marked and labeled. Ideally, the computing systems will in turn enforce those labels uniformly. This, however, is common only in systems using mandatory access control (MAC). Systems based on discretionary access control (DAC) do not typically enforce labels uniformly and labels may be lost as information assets are transferred from one system to another.

Information assets are harder to value since they may not have a declared value on the organization's financial statements. Such assets include all forms of information, including the many types of intellectual property. Even asset ownership can be harder to resolve in the case of information assets: it could be the creator of the asset or the organization who ultimately owns it.

Unlike physical assets, information assets can also be harder to delineate. Information assets with different values to the organization may exist on the same systems, but may need to be protected very differently. To help guide the valuation and protection of information assets information classification is often used.

Information classification refers to the practice of differentiating between different types of information assets, and providing some guidance as to how sensitive information will need to be protected. Traditional information classification schemes were based on confidentiality requirements. Assets would be classified according to their confidentiality (such as Top Secret, Secret or Public) and subjects would be granted clearances based on a matching set of clearance levels. Modern information classification schemes pull in multiple criteria including confidentiality, integrity, and availability requirements[3].

In both cases, the goal of information classification is to group similar assets together and protect them based on common classification levels.

---

3   Read more about information classification approaches here:

A.   http://csrc.nist.gov/publications/nistpubs/800-60-rev1/SP800-60_Vol1-Rev1.pdf

B.   http://www.enisa.europa.eu/activities/cert/support/incident-management/browsable/
policies/basic-policies-1/information-classification-policy

C.   https://www.rimp.gov.ab.ca/publications/pdf/infosecurityclassification.pdf

This allows protection solutions to be used across multiple assets with similar value to the organization and with similar security requirements. This helps to achieve economies-of-scale as well as ensuring that managing those solutions is more cost-effective.

Information classification also includes the processes and procedures to declassify information. For example, declassification may be used to downgrade the sensitivity of information. Over the course of time, information once considered sensitive may decline in value or criticality. In these instances, declassification efforts should be implemented to ensure that excessive protection controls are not used for non-sensitive information. When declassifying information, marking, handling, and storage requirements will likely be reduced. Organizations should have declassification practices well documented for use by individuals assigned with the task.

Media

Media used to store sensitive information requires physical and logical controls. The security professional must continually bear in mind that media lacks the means for digital accountability when the data is not encrypted. For this reason, extensive care must be taken when handling sensitive media. Logical and physical controls, such as marking, handling, storing, and declassification, provide methods for the secure handling of sensitive media.

Marking

Organizations should have policies in place regarding the marking of media. Storage media should have a physical label identifying the sensitivity of the information contained. The label should clearly indicate if the media is encrypted. The label may also contain information regarding a point of contact and a retention period. When media is found or discovered without a label it should be immediately labeled to the highest level of sensitivity until the appropriate analysis reveals otherwise.

1029

Handling

Only designated personnel should have access to sensitive media. Policies and procedures describing the proper handling of sensitive media should be promulgated. Individuals responsible for managing sensitive media should be trained on the policies and procedures regarding the proper handling and marking of sensitive media. Security professionals should never assume that all members of the organization are fully aware of, or understand security policies. It is also important that logs and other records be used to track the activities of individuals handling backup media. Manual processes, such as access logs, are necessary to compensate for the lack of automated controls regarding access to sensitive media.

Storing

Sensitive media should not be left lying about where a passerby could access it. Whenever possible, backup media should be encrypted and stored in a security container, such as a safe or strong box with limited access. Storing encrypted backup media at an off-site location should be considered for disaster recovery purposes. Sensitive backup media stored at the same site as the system should be kept in a fire-resistant box whenever possible. In every case, the number of individuals with access to media should be strictly limited and the separation of duties and job rotation concepts should be implemented where it is cost-effective to do so.

Destruction[4]

Media that is no longer needed, or is defective, should be destroyed rather than simply disposed of. A record of destruction should be used that corresponds to any logs used for handling media. Security practitioners should implement object reuse controls for any media in question when the sensitivity is unknown rather than simply recycling it.

---

4   Read more about media destruction recommendations at: http://csrc.nist.gov/publications/nistpubs/800-88/NISTSP800-88_with-errata.pdf

Record Retention[5]

Information and data should be kept only as long as it is required. Organizations may have to keep certain records for a period as specified by industry standards or in accordance with laws and regulations. Hard- and soft-copy records should not be kept beyond their required or useful life. Security practitioners should ensure that accurate records are maintained by the organization regarding the location and types of records stored. A periodic review of retained records is necessary to reduce the volume of information stored and ensure that only relevant information is preserved.

Record retention policies indicate how long an organization must maintain copies of information. For example, financial transactions related to a fraud case may need to be retained indefinitely or until ten years after a court judgment. Other information such as system logs may need to be retained for six months or longer to ensure appropriate forensics and incident response capabilities can use the information to reconstruct a past event. The security professional must ensure:

- The organization understands the retention requirements for different types of data throughout the organization.

- The organization documents in a records schedule the retention requirements for each type of information

- The systems, processes and individuals of the organization retain information in accordance with the schedule but not longer.

A common mistake in records retention is finding the longest retention period and applying it to all types of information in an organization without analysis. This not only wastes storage but also adds considerable "noise" when searching or processing information in search of relevant records. Records and information no longer mandated to be retained should be destroyed.

---

5   Read more about records retention here: http://www.acc.com/vl/public/Program-Material/loader.cfm?csModule=security/getfile&pageid=20241

7

Security Operations

Employ Resource Protection

It may seem obvious that security operations are focused on protecting valuable assets. It is never practical to protect all assets equally since the cost to protect them may exceed their value. The real challenge is finding out which assets are truly valuable to the organization. In most cases, security functions depend on asset owners to identify valuable assets and help ensure that they are being protected appropriately.

Tangible versus Intangible Assets

Assets may be either tangible or intangible. Tangible assets are physical and fall under the category of traditional property. Intangible assets are not physical and fall under the categories of intellectual property. Some assets may include both tangible and intangible elements. For example, a physical server box is a tangible asset while the information stored on that server is intangible. They are valued and protected in very different ways.

Protecting Physical Assets

Physical assets are easier to value since they have a declared value on the organization's financial statements. Such assets in an IT setting include all types of IT systems from end-user equipment (such as desktops and laptops) to high-end server equipment. These assets must be protected from potential theft and damage.

In the case of physical assets, the IT department is often playing both an owner and custodian role. It depends on who is ultimately paying for the gear and who is bearing the cost associated with maintenance and licensing. It is frequently the role of the security professional to confirm asset ownership and to consult with those owners to verify the declared value of those assets. It would then be the responsibility of security operations to ensure that the physical asset was being protected appropriately.

Facilities

Facilities require appropriate systems and controls to sustain the IT operation environment. Various utilities and systems are necessary to support operations and provide continuous protection. Fire detection and suppression systems are necessary for resource protection and worker safety. Heating, ventilation, and air conditioning systems provide appropriate temperature and humidity controls for user comfort and acceptable environmental operating ranges for equipment. Water and sewage systems are an integral part of any facility. IT systems cannot provide adequate availability without a reliable power supply and distribution system. Power should also be conditioned to remove spikes and fluctuations. Stable communications are a vital aspect of geographically distributed systems. Finally, an integrated facility access control and intrusion detection system forms the first line of defense regarding the IT operations security. Facilities should be marked plainly when possible to make identification of a data center more difficult.

Hardware

System hardware requires appropriate physical security measures to maintain the desired confidentiality, integrity, and availability. Physically secure data center facilities and locked server rooms are used to protect critical computing systems at common locations.

Access to these facilities should be limited to named individuals with a requirement for physical access following the principle of least privilege. Individuals who do not require frequent physical access to physical systems should not receive access to the facility. If occasional access is required, then temporary access should be granted and revoked when it is no longer required.

Operator consoles and workstations should also have limited access whenever possible. Users performing sensitive data operations should have their workstations located in a separate room with access limited to the

7

Security Operations

1033

individuals authorized to work in the room. Providing physical security to sensitive workstations can reduce the likelihood of an unauthorized individual from tampering with a workstation to bypass logical controls, remove media, or install malicious code or devices.

There are also a number of assets that will need to be protected outside of physically secure data center facilities or server rooms. Mobile assets such as laptops, phones, and PDAs need to be protected. This can include solutions such as cable locking devices.

Printing devices should be located near the authorized users. System policies should be established that prevent users from producing output to printers outside of their immediate area unless absolutely necessary. Users should be required through policy and instructed through training to immediately retrieve their output from printing devices to preclude unauthorized access to sensitive information. Where possible, users may also be required to authenticate to the printer prior to receiving output.

Network devices are also key hardware assets that need to be protected from compromise or misuse. They are usually stored in secure data center facilities with other IT assets as well as secured utility closets and riser rooms. Strong physical security controls including cameras should be considered for these areas.

Media Management

Organizational information resides on various media types. Security practitioners should keep in mind that media includes soft copy as well as hard copy. Soft-copy media can be found as magnetic, optical, and solid state. Magnetic media includes floppy disks, tapes, and hard drives. CD-ROMs and DVDs are examples of optical media. Solid-state media includes flash drives and memory cards. Hard-copy examples include paper and microfiche.

Media containing sensitive or confidential information should be encrypted. There are a wide variety of encryption options for media available, depending on what type of media is being used. Many hard drive manufacturers now support on-disk encryption, which automatically encrypts data when it is being written to the hard disk. Backup tape drives from some manufacturers also support encryption, mitigating some of the risk associated with lost or stolen tapes. Many programs that are used to burn DVDs or CDs provide similar functions. Even portable USB flash drives can support encryption solutions. The security professional should help select an appropriate solution for the media being used.

In some cases, sensitive information is transmitted between media storage locations. Electronic transport strategies such as system snapshots, shadowing, network backups, and electronic vaulting send bulk information from one part of a network to another. The information may travel a significant distance and pass many network segments before reaching the intended storage area. The data can be viewed by network sniffing devices within any segment where the traffic passes. For this reason, the data should be protected through the use of encryption to mitigate a compromise.

Particular types of media may require special protections. For example, product software must be carefully controlled. Original copies and installed versions of system and application software require appropriate protection and management for information assurance purposes. Weak controls on

7

Security Operations

1035

software can subject a system to compromise through the introduction of backdoors and malicious code such as Trojan horses, viruses, and worms. Protecting the integrity of system code is necessary to defend against these types of threats. The process of handling software from original media through installation, use, modification, and removal should follow the concepts of least privilege and separation of duties. The types of controls necessary include access control, change control management, and library maintenance.

Original copies of software media should be controlled through a software librarian. Establishing a software library where original copies of software are strictly controlled provides accountability and a form of integrity control. A librarian is necessary to catalog and securely store the original copies of test data, binaries, object files, and source code.

Installed software should have appropriate access controls in place to prevent unauthorized access or modification. Ordinary users should have read and execute permissions for executable content and other system binaries and libraries. Setting this level of access control can prevent accidental or unauthorized modification to system binaries. For example, some viruses infect executable content through modification of the binary. If the user does not have write, modify, or delete permissions to system binaries, then the virus will be unable to affect these files when executing in the context of an ordinary user.

Removable Media

Portable devices such as thumb drives and external hard drives are a growing threat to organizations in terms of data loss. Organizations that do not provide secure means of providing users encrypted removable media often find users will purchase their own and use it without encryption. This leads to several problems:

- The organization does not know when information is leaving the enterprise

- The organization does not know if the information is breached
- The user has little incentive to report breaches

To mitigate these situations the security professional should advise:

- The organization implement data loss prevention capability which includes:
  - ¤ Monitoring and restriction of USB and other external ports
  - ¤ Monitoring of DVD, Blu-ray and other writable disk drives
- A secure removable media solution which includes
  - ¤ Mandatory encryption with strong authentication
  - ¤ Monitoring and logging of information transferred to the media
  - ¤ An inventory capability
  - ¤ A remote wipe capability if required
  - ¤ A geo-locate capability if required

Providing users with a secure removable media solution has many benefits. The security professional can provide assurance to management that data is protected. Should removable media be lost the security professional can mitigate the impact of data loss. The implementation of an enterprise secure removable media may also enhance the productivity of the workforce.

Archival and Offline Storage

Backups and archives are two different types of methods used to store information. Backups are conducted on a regular basis and are useful in recovering information or a system in the event of a disaster. Backups contain information that is regularly processed by the system users. Information that is needed for historical purposes, but not in continual use, should be saved and removed from the system as an archive. Each type of record retention requires appropriate management to include strong physical access controls and periodic reviews for the relevance of the stored records.

Data stored in a backup or archive may need to be reloaded into the main production environment. In this case, it is not only appropriate that a suitable technical solution be in place but that there are procedures in place to ensure that recovery can be done quickly and effectively.

Recovery from backups, for example, may need to have well-defined and documented procedures to ensure that restorations are done in the right order. Using these procedures, it is possible to determine how long it will take to recover a system given particular backup solutions. It is also important, however, that all backup and archival media is tested regularly to see if it can still be used for restorations. For longer term retention purposes, it may be necessary to migrate backups and archives to new media on a regular basis depending on the viability of the media. The security professional should ensure the drives, media, software and support required to restore media is available or advise moving legacy archives and backups to modern and supported media if necessary.

Disposal/Reuse

When media is to be reassigned (a form of object reuse), it is important that all residual data is carefully removed. Simply deleting files or formatting media does not actually remove the information. File deletion and media formatting often simply remove the pointers to the information. Providing assurance for object reuse requires specialized tools and techniques according to the type of media on which the data resides.

Specialized hardware devices known as degaussers [1] can be used to erase data saved to magnetic media. The measure of the amount of energy needed to reduce the magnetic field on the media to zero is known as coercivity. It is important to make sure that the coercivity of the degausser

---

1   For more information on degaussing, please see the following resources:

A. http://www.nsa.gov/ia/_files/government/MDG/NSA_CSS-EPL-9-12.pdf

B. http://www.oss-spectrum.org/Attach2.htm

is of sufficient strength to meet object reuse requirements when erasing data. If a degausser is used with insufficient coercivity, then a remanence of the data will exist. Remanence is the measure of the existing magnetic field on the media; it is the residue that remains after an object is degaussed or written over. Data is still recoverable even when the remanence is small. While data remanence exists, there is no assurance of safe object reuse. Some degaussers can destroy drives. The security professional should exercise caution when recommending or using degaussers on media for reuse.

Software tools also exist that can provide object reuse assurance. These tools overwrite every sector of magnetic media with a random or predetermined bit pattern. Overwrite methods are effective for all forms of electronic media with the exception of read-only optical media. There exists a drawback to using overwrite software. During normal write operations with magnetic media, the head of the drive moves back-and-forth across the media as data is written. The track of the head does not usually follow the exact path each time. The result is a miniscule amount of data remanence with each pass. With specialized equipment, it is possible to read data that has been overwritten. To provide higher assurance in this case, it is necessary to overwrite each sector multiple times. Security practitioners should keep in mind that a one-time pass may be acceptable for noncritical information, but sensitive data should be overwritten with multiple passes. Overwrite software can also be used to clear the sectors within solid-state media such as USB thumb drives. It is suggested that physical destruction methods such as incineration or secure recycling should be considered for solid-state media that is no longer used.

The last form of preventing unauthorized access to sensitive data is media destruction. Shredding, burning, grinding, and pulverizing are common methods of physically destroying media. Degaussing can also be a form of media destruction. High-power degaussers are so strong in some cases that they can literally bend and warp the platters in a hard drive. Shredding and burning are effective destruction methods for non-rigid

7

Security Operations

magnetic media. Indeed, some shredders are capable of shredding some rigid media such as an optical disk. This may be an effective alternative for any optical media containing nonsensitive information due to the residue size remaining after feeding the disk into the machine. However, the residue size might be too large for media containing sensitive information. Alternatively, grinding and pulverizing are acceptable choices for rigid and solid-state media. Specialized devices are available for grinding the face of optical media that either sufficiently scratches the surface to render the media unreadable or actually grinds off the data layer of the disk. Several services also exist which will collect drives, destroy them on site if requested and provide certification of completion. It will be the responsibility of the security professional to help, select, and maintain the most appropriate solutions for media cleansing and disposal.

Asset Management

Asset management is a foundation of information security. If an organization cannot account for its hard drives, servers or systems it has no way of knowing if a data breach has occurred. Asset systems can also be used to drive access controls systems such as Network Authentication/Access Control (NAC.) Software and equipment are the two major areas of asset management the information security professional should review.

Software Licensing

Software is also an important asset to be protected. Original copies of licensed software must be controlled by the organization to prevent copyright infringement. Unscrupulous individuals within an organization may make illegal copies of software for their personal use. Security practitioners should assist their organizations in providing appropriate physical controls to prevent illegal duplication and distribution of licensed software. All software copies should be managed by a software or media librarian who is responsible for maintaining control over software assets, both physically and as information assets. Inventory scans of installed software should also be conducted by the organization to identify unauthorized installations or license violations.

Equipment Lifecycle

All equipment has a useful life to the organization. Often IT equipment will be depreciated by the accounting department until its value is zero. IT equipment may also become unsuitable if its performance is no longer capable of performing required tasks or if support is no longer available for it. The information security professional must ensure throughout the lifecycle of the equipment appropriate information security activities take place. The following illustrates common activities of the information security professional throughout the equipment lifecycle:

- Defining Requirements
    - Ensure relevant security requirements are included in any specifications for new equipment

- ◘ Ensure appropriate costs have been allocated for security features required
- ◘ Ensure new equipment requirements fits into the organizational security architecture
- ■ Acquiring and Implementing
  - ◘ Validate security features are included as specified
  - ◘ Ensure additional security configurations, software and features are applied to the equipment
  - ◘ Ensure the equipment is followed through any security certification or accreditation process as required
  - ◘ Ensure the equipment is inventoried
- ■ Operations and Maintenance
  - ◘ Ensure the security features and configurations remain operational
  - ◘ Review the equipment for vulnerabilities and mitigate if discovered
  - ◘ Ensure appropriate support is available for security related concerns
  - ◘ Validate and verify inventories to ensure equipment is in place as intended
  - ◘ Ensure changes to the configuration of the system are reviewed through a security impact analysis and vulnerabilities are mitigated
- ■ Disposal and Decommission
  - ◘ Ensure equipment is securely erased and then either destroyed or recycled depending on the security requirements of the organization
  - ◘ Ensure inventories are accurately updated to reflect the status of decommissioned equipment

Manage Incident Response

Security professionals manage the day-to-day operations of key security services as well as participate in cross-enterprise processes. The security professional must understand the many types of security technologies that are deployed. The security professional should also understand the role that security plays in operational processes such as change, configuration, incident and problem management.

Incident Management

When bad things happen, it is important they are detected quickly and addressed effectively. While it is ideal that all potential incidents be prevented from happening in the first place, organizations cannot prevent all possible threats, particularly those involving human threat agents. Security operations must have strong processes in place that allow security analysts to quickly detect and respond to security-related incidents.

A successful incident management program combines people, processes, and technology. For security-related incidents, this will require trained individuals who have experience dealing with security-related incidents, processes that will guide the response, and technologies that will enable the response to be performed quickly and efficiently.

For example, consider a security-related incident involving a single system that has become unreliable. The system is now continuously rebooting itself, declaring that the security kernel is not available. Network operations detects the outage and since it is security-related, security operations is called in. It turns out that the system in question is highly critical to the organization, and that it will need to be back up and running in a very short timeframe.

In this case, the priority is clear: get the system back up and running. At the same time, the security professional wants to preserve as much information as possible for investigative purposes. The system has been attempting to perform an emergency system restart (by rebooting itself) but it has been unable to return itself to normal service. While a warm reboot (or graceful reboot) is not likely going to work, perhaps a cold reboot which shuts the system down completely may be most suitable.

Will restoration from backup be required? Is there a redundant server available than can be brought online? What about the evidence of a potential attack that may be lost if we shut down the system? The possible questions and avenues of response are almost endless.

Incident management procedures are intended to guide all activities related to the incident, and guide the security practitioner down a pre-defined and (where possible) pre-approved path for resolution. They describe the actions that should be taken during the incident, roles and responsibilities of the various parties that may be involved, and who gets to make decisions around what will be done. These procedures are in constant development and must incorporate the lessons learned from previous incidents.

Security Measurements, Metrics, and Reporting

Security services also need to provide the ability to measure the effectiveness of security controls deployed in the enterprise. Such measurements provide a point-in-time gauge of the current state. They form the basis for metrics, which combine measurement with goals to be measured against. Such metrics can be used to determine if technology deployments are successful just as they can be used to determine if manual processes can be improved.

Most security technologies support measurements and metrics. Intrusion detection and prevention systems can provide information on attacks that were detected or blocked and provide trending over time. Firewalls can identify common sources of attacks through IP addresses and other means. E-mail security services can provide information on the amount of malware or spam that is being detected and blocked. Of course, all platforms can be measured according to their availability and reliability.

Many things can be used to drive metrics within the organization. The key to using them is to focus on the metrics that mean the most to the organization's executives, and to their overall mission. For example, one large retail organization focused their entire IT mission on a straightforward availability target. They had come to the conclusion that nothing was more important than ensuring that systems were available when they needed to be. All departments and their systems were measured against it. It drove technology investment and was the foundation for their incentive programs, both with internal staff and with their external partners.

Reporting is also fundamental to successful security operations. It can take a variety of forms depending on the intended audience. Technical reporting tends to be designed for technical specialists or managers with direct responsibility for service delivery. Management reporting will provide summaries of multiple systems as well as key metrics for each of the services covered by the report. Executive dashboards are intended for the executive who is interested in seeing only the highlights across multiple services, and provide simple summaries of current state, usually in a highly visual form like charts and graphs.

Reporting frequency will also vary. At an operational level, some measurements and metrics may be required yearly, monthly, weekly, or even daily, depending on how closely management wishes to monitor service delivery.

Managing Security Technologies

There are a large number of technical controls deployed at most enterprises. These controls need to be maintained and managed effectively if they are to be trusted to protect the enterprise. They will also be necessary to quickly alert the security professional when security incidents occur and assist them to respond more effectively. In security operations the focus is less on the technologies themselves and more on the ways that they are managed in an operational environment.

7

Security Operations

1045

Boundary Controls

An important technology for the security professional to understand is boundary controls. Boundary controls may be placed wherever there is a necessary division between more trusted and less trusted environments. Such boundaries may be deployed within the enterprise network using firewalls, routers, proxies, and other technologies to control the boundary between more trusted and less trusted network segments. Similar technologies can be deployed within individual systems. For example, the boundaries between kernel functions and end-user processes may be enforced through common anti-malware systems, ring protection and various process isolation techniques.

Security operations will focus on ensuring that these technologies have been deployed effectively and monitoring their use over time to ensure that they are still effective. Changes to firewall rules and router Access Control Lists (ACLs) need to be carefully examined to determine if they accomplish their intended purpose without affecting other rules or the stability of the platform. Secured systems will need to be examined regularly to ensure that system boundaries remain intact.

Detection

Intrusion detection and prevention systems are used to identify and respond to suspected security-related events in real-time or near-real-time. Intrusion Detection Systems (IDS) will use available information to determine if an attack is underway, send alerts, and provide limited response capabilities. Intrusion Prevention Systems (IPS) will use available information to determine if an attack is underway, send alerts but also block the attack from reaching its intended target.

Network-based intrusion systems focus on the analysis of network traffic while host-based intrusion systems focus on audit logs and processes inside a single system.

The distinction between IDS and IPS is very important since it materially affects both how the system must be deployed and its effect on the systems it is monitoring. If an IDS is used, it may be deployed out-of-band, meaning that it is not deployed in the middle of the communications path, and will not affect normal processing or cause latency. Any attacks, however, will likely reach their intended target. If an IPS is used, it must be deployed in-line (also known as in-band), meaning that it is deployed in the middle of the communications path. Because it is in-line, it will cause some latency and slow down normal processing to a slight extent. Detected attacks, however, will not likely reach their intended targets. On many modern systems, both IDS and IPS techniques can be used within the same device, allowing the security practitioner to decide whether to use one technique or the other.

Intrusion systems use a number of techniques to determine whether an attack is underway:

- **Signature- or pattern-matching systems** examine the available information (logs or network traffic) to determine if it matches a known attack.

- **Protocol-anomaly-based systems** examine network traffic to determine if what it sees conforms to the defined standard for that protocol; for example, as it is defined in a Request for Comment or RFC.

■ **Statistical-anomaly-based systems** establish a baseline of normal traffic patterns over time and detect any deviations from that baseline. Some also use heuristics to evaluate the intended behavior of network traffic to determine if it intended to be malicious or not. Most modern systems combine two or more of these techniques together to provide a more accurate analysis before it decides whether it sees an attack or not.

In most cases, there will continue to be problems associated with false-positives as well as false-negatives. False-positives occur when the IDS or IPS identifies something as an attack, but it is in fact normal traffic. False-negatives occur when the IPS or IDS fails to interpret something as an attack when it should have. In these cases, intrusion systems must be carefully "tuned" to ensure that these are kept to a minimum.

An IDS requires frequent attention. An IDS requires the response of a human who is knowledgeable enough with the system and types of normal activity to make an educated judgment about the relevance and significance of the event. Alerts need to be investigated to determine if they represent an actual event, or if they are simply background noise.

Anti-Malware Systems

Today, anti-malware systems may be deployed at various points throughout the enterprise. They are installed on individual hosts, on systems such as e-mail servers, and even at key points in the network in e-mail and Web gateways as well as unified threat management (UTM) devices, which combine anti-malware with other functions (such as firewall, intrusion detection/prevention, and content filtering).

To remain effective, anti-malware solutions require continual updates and must be monitored to ensure they are still active and effective. Each implementation should be monitored to ensure that updates are received and active. Likewise, the anti-malware engines should be configured to take advantage of automatic scanning for new media and e-mail attachments. Scanning should be scheduled and accomplished on a regular basis. It is best for the scanning to be done automatically during nonpeak usage times.

Security Event Information Management

Few solutions are more important to security operations than one that provides the ability to get a view into security-related events in real-time. System audit logs collect valuable information on the operation of the system but logs do not alert security professionals. They also do not provide ways to collate audit logs across multiple systems.

Security-related audit logs will typically log access attempts (including successes and failures), the use of privileges, service failures, and the like. Even on a single system, these logs can get to be very large. They may need to be tuned to ensure that you are only collecting the logs that you want using appropriate clipping levels. For example, successful login attempts may not be required for analysis and may be filtered out.

One disadvantage of system logs is that they provide a view into that single system. They do not provide a view into events that may be affecting multiple systems or where multiple systems have some information that may be required to detect an incident and track it back to its sources. Security Event Information Management (SEIM) solutions are intended to provide a common platform for log collection, collation, and analysis in real-time to allow for more effective and efficient response.

They can also provide reports on historical events using log information from multiple sources.

Log management systems are similar: they also collect logs and provide the ability to report against them, although their focus tends to be on historical analysis of log information, rather than real-time analysis. They may be combined with SEIM solutions to provide both historical and real-time functions.

7

Security Operations

In both cases, log information must be carefully managed, and security operations must maintain a disciplined practice of log storage and archiving. For most SEIM or log management systems, there is a practical limit to the amount of information they can analyze at once or generate reports against. For most systems, only a fraction of the logs will be stored online with the remaining logs moved into longer term storage or archival solutions. These solutions store online logs for 30 to 180 days, shift them into an online or near-line archive for up to a year, and then move any logs into longer term backup to cover the remainder of the retention period. At the end of that period, security operations are responsible for ensuring that old log information is properly disposed of using defined data disposal procedures and tools.

Modern reporting tools can also be used to transform security event information into useful business intelligence. Rather than focusing on basic log analysis, they tend to focus on higher level reporting on service metrics as well as reporting for compliance purposes.

Response

When an incident is detected a containment strategy must be decided. Containment may include disconnecting devices from the network, shutting systems down or redirecting traffic around an affected area of the network. The containment strategy should be driven by several criteria including:

- The need to preserve forensic evidence for possible legal action
- The availability of services the affected component provides
- The potential damage leaving the affected component in place may cause
- The time required for the containment strategy to be effective.
- The resources required to contain the affected component

Delaying containment when a system is compromised by a suspected attacker is often a poor choice as it can lead to further attacks on more information systems. Arguments may be made that the security professional could observe the attacker to learn more about what is happening, however that is best left to honeypots and experienced security engineers. There may also be legal implications if the organization knows about the compromised system and then the compromised system is used to attack another system.

The team should instead focus on obtaining a forensic image of the RAM and hard drive of the compromised system and then determine how to mitigate the vulnerability which caused the compromise. The security professional should consult an organization's legal team to determine if the image gathered must be suitable for law enforcement or be admissible in court. If needed for law enforcement or court, the security professional must avoid violating the chain of custody and is best assisted by law enforcement or an experienced forensics team while creating an image.

The initial incident and as much relevant information as possible should be documented in an incident management system. The incident should be updated as more information becomes available until the incident is deemed resolved by the security operations team. The documented incident is often one of the most important parts of reconstructing the attack and explaining what happened to third parties.

Reporting

Some organizations are required to report incidents which meet certain conditions. For example, United States civilian government agencies are required to report any breach of personally identifiable information to the US Computer Emergency Readiness Team (US-CERT) within an hour of discovery[1]. Security professionals must be aware of when an incident must be reported to upper management or law enforcement. Policies and procedures must be defined to determine how an incident is routed when criminal activity suspected. Additionally, policies and procedures need to be in place to determine how an incident escalates and should address:

- Does the media or an organization's external affairs group need to be involved?
- Does the organization's legal team need to be involved in the review?
- At what point does notification of the incident rise to the line management, middle management, senior management, the board of directors or the stakeholders?
- What confidentiality requirements are necessary to protect the incident information?
- What methods are used for the reporting? If email is attacked how does that impact the reporting and notification process?

Recovery

Recovery can range from the very basic of restoring an image to a machine to no recovery situations that involve the loss of sensitive information. The first step of recovery is eradication if possible. Eradication is the

---

1   http://www.whitehouse.gov/sites/default/files/omb/memoranda/fy2006/m06-19.pdf

process of removing the threat. For example, if an unpatched system were infected with malware, removal of the malware would be the eradication. Recovery is primarily interested in restoring or repairing a system back to a known good state. Recovery can be extremely complicated if the last known image or "good" state actually contained the vulnerability which caused the incident. In those cases a new image may need to be created and tested prior to application in the production environment.

Remediation and Review

Perhaps the most important part of incident response is the lesson learned. Organizations have an opportunity to analyze and understand what failed and try to ensure it does not happen again. There are various degrees of rigor an organization can take when reviewing an incident with a trade off in the time required for analysis and the impact of the results.

Root Cause Analysis

Fundamentally, Root Cause Analysis (RCA) is asking "why?" until there is only one answer. RCA is an intensive process involving numerous individuals from across different disciplines to determine why something happened and how to prevent it in the future. RCA involves reviewing system logs, policies, procedures, security documentation network capture traffic if available to first piece together the history of the event which caused the incident. Once the event is understood the RCA team can work backwards to determine what allowed the event to happen in the first place. Did a system not get patched? If this is true, why did the system not get patched? If the answer is "The patch management team couldn't patch it because the system was off" the next question is "why was it off?" If the answer is "the new Green IT policy mandates all systems be shut down and powered off when not in use." then the question needs to be "can we turn systems on when patching through wake-on-lan and have all systems check for patches on boot before connected to the internet?" If the answer is "yes," then a solution is reached. If not, then the team needs to keep asking "why?"

7

Security Operations

1053

While this is a very simple example of patching missing a machine it helps to illustrate the process. When incidents involve motivated attackers and multiple vulnerabilities and systems this process gets extremely complicated fast. Further complicating matters, individuals whose areas are targets for the analysis may resist providing information or cooperating for fear of appearing weak or mismanaged. RCA can quickly cross boundaries between technical, cultural, and organizational boundaries quickly. The security professional should work through the consensus of the RCA team and ensure senior management is supporting the analysis. Remediation actions from RCA are then reviewed by management for adoption and implementation or management may decide to accept the risk if the proposed recommendation costs more than the exposure or the likelihood of the event happening again is extremely small.

Problem Management

Incident and problem management are intimately related. While incident management is concerned primarily with managing an adverse event, problem management is concerned with tracking that event back to a root cause and addressing the underlying problem.

Problem management is seen as distinct from incident management for a number of reasons. First, their goals are slightly different. While incident management is focused on limiting the effect of an incident, problem management is about addressing defects that made the incident possible or more successful. Second, problem management tends to have a longer term view of incidents as they occur in the operational environment. It can take longer periods of time to track down the underlying defect since it may take specific conditions to be in place that may not occur frequently. For example, a defect associated with insufficient resources may only manifest when system load is particularly high.

Security Audits and Reviews

A security audit is typically performed by an independent third party to the management of the system. The audit determines the degree with which the required controls are implemented. A security review is conducted by the system maintenance or security personnel to discover vulnerabilities within the system. A vulnerability occurs when policies are not followed, misconfigurations are present, or flaws exist in the hardware or software of the system. System reviews are sometimes referred to as a vulnerability assessment.

Penetration testing is a form of security review where an attempt is made to gain access or compromise a system. Penetration tests can be conducted with physical access to the system or from the outside of the system and facility.

Security audits can be divided between internal and external reviews. Internal reviews are conducted by a member of the organization's staff that does not have management responsibility for the system. External reviews involve outside entities that evaluate the system based on the organizational security requirements. Entities performing an external review provide an independent assessment of the system. Security practitioners may find this review particularly appealing if the assessment supports prior security concerns that have been avoided by management. Managers should invite an independent review as a fresh perspective that may uncover unknown weaknesses within the system or associated processes.

7

Security Operations

Preventative Measure against Attacks

Resilience is an important quality for any production operation. It is concerned with ensuring that the IT environment is prepared for any potential threat to smooth, steady, and reliable service. It is the security professional's role to understand common threats to operations and help prepare for them.

Operations can be impacted by a variety of threats. These threats may be caused by individuals or environmental factors. A security practitioner who is aware of common threats will be more prepared to propose or implement controls to mitigate or limit the potential damage. Just as most security requirements can be summed up by the CIA triad (confidentiality, integrity, and availability), most threats are associated with their opposites: disclosure, corruption, and destruction.

Unauthorized Disclosure

The unauthorized release of information is a considerable threat. Disclosure may result when a hacker or cracker penetrates a system that contains confidential information. Sensitive information may be leaked through malware infection. It may also be intentionally disclosed by disgruntled employees, contractors, or partners. From an operations perspective, technical solutions intended to protect sensitive information need to be maintained and privileged users monitored to detect any potential disclosure.

Destruction, Interruption, and Theft

Malicious, unintentional, and uncontrollable irreparable damage can result in the destruction of system data and resources. Malicious activity on the part of malware and malicious users can cause the loss of a significant amount of information. Errors on the part of users can cause the accidental deletion of important data. Secure operations is intended to prevent destruction of sensitive assets, except of course when done intentionally as part of an information retention program.

Interruptions in service can also be extremely disruptive to normal business operations. Failure of equipment, services, and operational procedures can cause system components to become unavailable. Denial-of-service attacks and malicious code can also interrupt operations. Any loss of availability will need to be dealt with appropriately, either automatically through technology or manually through strong processes and procedures.

Theft is also a common threat. While large-scale thefts within a secure operation may be less likely, component theft is often common in many environments. You may be expected to help prevent these sorts of thefts as well as coordinate investigations into such problems.

Corruption and Improper Modification

Environmental factors as well as the acts of individuals can cause damage to systems and data. Sporadic fluctuations in temperature or line power can cause systems to make errors while writing data. Inappropriate or accidental changes to file or table permissions can cause unintended data corruption. You may be expected to help implement and maintain integrity protections on key systems as well as provide appropriate procedures to ensure that privileged access to high-integrity resources is tightly controlled and monitored.

7

Security Operations

Patch and Vulnerability Management

A key part of configuration and change management involves the deployment of software updates, which is also known as patch management. Flaws in vendor products are continuously discovered. The development and distribution of vendor patches results in a never-ending cycle of required updates to production systems. Managing these updates is not a trivial task for any organization. The patch management process must be formalized through change and configuration management to ensure that changes to existing configurations are carefully controlled.

Security-related patches will typically be issued following the discovery or disclosure of a security vulnerability. Vendors will frequently fix security problems in software or firmware through version updates. They may not specify the reason for the version change or what flaws were addressed in a given update. In this case, it is important to obtain vulnerability information from third-party services. Several sources of vulnerability and patch availability information can be obtained from resource centers such as

- **cve.mitre.org:** The Common Vulnerability and Exposures database that provides the standard naming and numbering convention for disclosed vulnerabilities

- **nvd.nist.gov:** An online database of known vulnerabilities managed by the US National Institute of Standards and Technology (NIST)

- **www.cert.gov:** An online resource for a wide variety of information on known vulnerabilities and remediation options

Given the large number of vulnerabilities found each year, the security professional must be able to examine systems for known vulnerabilities and recommend action. There are a variety of automated and manual tools that test devices, systems, and applications for known flaws. They work by probing the target environment and examining it against a database of known vulnerabilities. While many of these systems are highly automated, they must be kept up to date and may not contain all vulnerabilities being exploited in the wild. Additionally these systems may produce false positives. The security professional must be able to determine if the finding is truly a vulnerability or simply a mistake by the tool.

Once a discovery is made of a flawed item in the target system, a determination should be made whether to patch the item. A risk-based decision is required to determine the necessity of patching the problem. What will be the risk if the flaw is not patched? Is the system likely to be exposed to threats that may exploit the vulnerability? Will special privileges be required for the vulnerability to be exploited? Can the vulnerability be used to gain administrative privileges on the target? How easy is it to exploit the vulnerability? Will it require physical access to the system or can it be exploited remotely? The answers to these questions will influence how critical it will be to patch the system. The security professional is expected to evaluate the level of risk and determine if and when a suitable patch (or workaround) should be applied.

Upon determining the level of potential exposure, the security practitioner should consult with the management and the owners of the system to determine the chosen course of action. The security professional should work with administrators to determine if the update causes any undesirable affects. For example, some updates can change system configurations or security settings. Some vendor patches have been known to reset access control lists on various sensitive files, creating a subsequent vulnerability. In this regard, patch testing should address not only the proper functioning of the system, but also the effect the update may have on the overall security state and policy of the system.

Once the update is tested and residual issues addressed, a schedule should be established for system deployment. It is important that users be notified of system updates prior to deployment. This way, if an unanticipated error occurs, it can be corrected more readily. When possible, it is best to schedule updates during periods of low productivity, such as evenings or weekends. Again, this is primarily accomplished to accommodate unforeseen system crashes.

Prior to deploying updates to production servers, make certain that a full system backup is conducted. In the event of a system crash due to the update, the server and data can be recovered without significant loss of data. Additionally, if the update involved propriety code, it will be necessary to provide a copy of the server or application image to the media librarian.

Deploy the update in stages, when possible, to accomplish a final validation of the update in the production environment. This may not always be possible given the network configuration, but is desirable to limit unforeseen difficulties.

After the deployment, it is necessary to confirm that the updates are deployed to all of the appropriate machines. System management tools and vulnerability scanners can be used to automate the validation. Continue checking the network until every network component scheduled for the change has been validated. Redeploy updates as necessary until all systems receive the update.

The last step in the patch management process is to document the changes. This provides a record of what was accomplished, the degree of success, and issues discovered. Documentation should also be conducted when decisions are made to not patch a system. The reasons for the decision and the approving authority should be recorded. This serves the dual purpose of providing external auditors with evidence that the organization is practicing due diligence regarding system maintenance, and imparting a history of uniqueness within the system.

Vulnerability Management Systems

Sun Tzu once wrote, "If you know the enemy and know thyself, then you need not fear the result of a hundred battles." The two principal factors needed for an organization to "know thyself" involve configuration management and vulnerability scanning. Configuration management provides an organization with knowledge about all of its parts, while vulnerability scanning identifies the weakness present within the parts. Knowing what composes the system is the first critical step in understanding what is needed to defend it. Identifying vulnerabilities of a known system provides the security practitioner with the necessary knowledge to defend against the onslaught of all types of attackers.

Vulnerabilities arise from flaws, misconfigurations (also known as weaknesses), and policy failures. Flaws result from product design imperfections. The most common type of flaw in software is the buffer overflow. Flaws are usually fixed with a security patch, new code, or a hardware change. Misconfigurations represent implementation errors that expose a system to attack. Examples of misconfigurations include weak access control lists, open ports, and unnecessary services. Policy failures occur when individuals fail to follow or implement security as required. This includes weak passwords, unauthorized network devices, and unapproved applications.

Vulnerability scanning is conducted against network, host system, and application resources. Each type of scan is used to detect vulnerabilities specific to the type of scan. Network scans look for vulnerabilities on the network. Flaws in devices are found with scanning tools designed to perform tests that simulate an attack. Misconfigured network settings such as unauthorized services can be found during network scans.

Policy violations, which include unauthorized devices, workstations, and servers, are also found with a comprehensive network scanning tool. Host-based scans are conducted at the system console or through the use of agents on servers and workstations throughout the network. Host-based scans are critical for identifying missing security updates on servers and workstations. This type of scan can also identify when local policy or security

7

Security Operations

configurations, such as audit log settings, are not implemented correctly. A good host-based scanner can also identify unauthorized software or services that might indicate a compromised system or a blatant violation of configuration management within the organization. The last type of vulnerability scanning involves specialized application security scanners. These tools check for patch levels and implementations of applications. For instance, some application scanning tools can identify vulnerabilities in Web-based applications. Other tools are designed to work with large applications, such as a database management system, to identify default settings or improper rights for sensitive tables.

Change and Configuration Management

Systems experience frequent changes. Software packages are added, removed, or modified. New hardware is introduced, while legacy devices are replaced. Updates due to flaws in software are regular business activities for system managers. The rapid advancement of technology, coupled with regular discovery of vulnerabilities, requires proper change control management to maintain the necessary integrity of the system. Change control management is embodied in policies, procedures, and operational practices.

Maintaining system integrity is accomplished through the process of change control management. A well-defined process implements structured and controlled changes necessary to support system integrity and accountability for changes. Decisions to implement changes should be made by a committee of representatives from various groups within the organization such as ordinary users, security, system operations, and upper-level management. Each group provides a unique perspective regarding the need to implement a proposed change. Users have a general idea of how the system is used in the field. Security can provide input regarding the possible risks associated with a proposed change. System operations can identify the challenges associated with the deployment and maintenance of the change. Management provides final approval or rejection of the change based on budget and strategic directions of the organization. Actions of the committee should be documented for historical and accountability purposes.

The change management structure should be codified as an organization policy. Procedures for the operational aspects of the change management process should also be created. Change management policies and procedures are forms of directive controls. The following subsections outline a recommended structure for a change management process.

Requests

Proposed changes should be formally presented to the committee in writing. The request should include a detailed justification in the form of a business case argument for the change, focusing on the benefits of implementation and costs of not implementing.

Impact Assessment
Members of the committee should determine the impacts to operations regarding the decision to implement or reject the change.

Approval/Disapproval
Requests should be answered officially regarding their acceptance or rejection.

Build and Test
Subsequent approvals are provided to operations support for test and integration development. The necessary software and hardware should be tested in a nonproduction environment. All configuration changes associated with a deployment must be fully tested and documented. The security team should be invited to perform a final review of the proposed change within the test environment to ensure that no vulnerabilities are introduced into the production system. Change requests involving the removal of a software or a system component require a similar approach. The item should be removed from the test environment and have a determination made regarding any negative impacts.

Notification
System users are notified of the proposed change and the schedule of deployment.

Implementation
The change is deployed incrementally, when possible, and monitored for issues during the process.

Validation
The change is validated by the operations staff to ensure that the intended machines received the deployment package. The security staff performs

a security scan or review of the affected machines to ensure that new vulnerabilities are not introduced. Changes should be included in the problem tracking system until operations has ensured that no problems have been introduced.

Documentation

The outcome of the system change, to include system modifications and lessons learned, should be recorded in the appropriate records. This is the way that change management typically interfaces with configuration management.

Configuration Management

Organizational hardware and software require proper tracking, implementation testing, approvals, and distribution methods. Configuration management is a process of identifying and documenting hardware components, software, and the associated settings. A well-documented environment provides a foundation for sound operations management by ensuring that IT resources are properly deployed and managed. The security professional plays an important role in configuration management through the identification and remediation of control gaps in current configurations.

Detailed hardware inventories are necessary for recovery and integrity purposes. Having an inventory of each workstation, server, and networking device is necessary for replacement purposes in the event of facility destruction. All devices and systems connected to the network should be in the hardware list. At a minimum, configuration documentation should include in the hardware list the following information about each device and system:

1. Make
2. Model
3. MAC addresses

7

Security Operations

1065

4. Serial number

5. Operating system or firmware version

6. Location

7. BIOS and other hardware-related passwords

8. Assigned IP address if applicable

9. Organizational property management label or bar code

Software is a similar concern and a software inventory should minimally include:

1. Software name

2. Software vendor (and reseller if appropriate)

3. Keys or activation codes (note if there are hardware keys)

4. Type of license and for what version

5. Number of licenses

6. License expiration

7. License portability

8. Organizational software librarian or asset manager

9. Organizational contact for installed software

10. Upgrade, full or limited license

The inventory is also helpful for integrity purposes when attempting to validate systems, software and devices on the network. Knowing the hardware versions of network components is valuable from two perspectives. First, the security professional will be able to quickly find and mitigate vulnerabilities related to the hardware type and version. Most hardware vulnerabilities are associated with a particular brand and model of hardware. Knowing the type of hardware and its location within the network can substantially reduce the effort necessary to identify the affected devices. Additionally, the list is invaluable when performing a network scan to discover unauthorized devices connected to the network. A new device appearing on a previously documented network segment may indicate an unauthorized connection to the network.

A configuration list for each device should also be maintained. Devices such as firewalls, routers, and switches can have hundreds or thousands of configuration possibilities. It is necessary to properly record and track the changes to these configurations to provide assurance for network integrity and availability. These configurations should also be periodically checked to make sure that unauthorized changes have not occurred.

Operating systems and applications also require configuration management. Organizations should have configuration guides and standards for each operating system and application implementation. System and application configuration should be standardized to the greatest extent possible to reduce the number of issues that may be encountered during integration testing. Software configurations and their changes should be documented and tracked with the assistance of the security practitioner. It is possible that server and workstation configuration guides will change frequently due to changes in the software baseline.

7

Security Operations

System Resilience and Fault Tolerance Requirements

A large number of potential dangers cause systems to be unreliable. Thankfully, there are also a large number of ways that the security and reliability of key computing systems can be maintained.

The best way to ensure that systems are resilient is to ensure that they are designed to be resilient in the first place, and that you are selecting resilient solutions. Most systems are designed to accommodate common threats to smooth operations, and provide some ability to prevent common threats from being successful, or if they are, responding quickly to them to minimize disruption to the organization.

For example, systems are examined carefully during design and development to determine where common system failures will likely occur, and calculate the mean time to failure (MTF) for key system components. Components with moving parts such as fans, power supplies, and hard drives will most likely fail sooner than components with fewer moving parts. This is one of the main reasons why critical systems are deployed with redundant fans and power supplies or why we use drive configurations that take drive failure into account. The key principle is to avoid single points of failure where practical, and provide for automated and manual means to address any problems that can disrupt normal service.

It is also vital that systems have some ability to react automatically to common failures and do what they can to address the problem without human intervention. This will limit that amount of disruption. The following sections discuss some common ways by which systems can provide greater resilience to common threats.

Trusted Paths and Fail Secure Mechanisms

While there are a number of system security mechanisms that aid in protecting systems, there are a number of them that could be compromised and must be maintained by operations. Trusted paths provide trustworthy interfaces into privileged user functions and are intended to provide a way to ensure that any communications over that path cannot be intercepted or corrupted. For example, when a user logs in locally to a system, it is important that his credentials can be shared safely and securely through the paths taken from the user interface to the access control subsystem. Many attacks, however, are designed to specifically attack such trusted paths by redirecting input down an alternative channel where it can be intercepted, disclosed, or manipulated. The success of such attacks increases with the level of privilege, making attacks using privileged user accounts very dangerous.

Operations security must include measures to validate that trusted paths continue to operate as intended. Typical countermeasures include log collection and analysis, vulnerability scanning, patch management, and system integrity checking on a regular basis. A combination of these techniques is used to limit or detect any changes in the behavior of trusted paths.

Similarly, operations will be expected to ensure that fail-safe and fail-secure mechanisms are working correctly. While both are concerned with how a system behaves when it fails, they are often confused with each other. It is important for the security professional to distinguish between them:

- *Fail-safe* mechanisms focus on failing with a minimum of harm to personnel or systems.
- *Fail-secure* focuses on failing in a controlled manner to block access while the systems is in an inconsistent state.

For example, data center door systems will fail safe to ensure that personnel can escape the area when the electrical power fails. A fail-secure door would prevent personnel from using the door at all, which could put personnel in jeopardy. Fail-safe and fail-secure mechanisms will need to be maintained and tested on a regular basis to ensure that they are working as designed.

7

Security Operations

1069

Redundancy and Fault Tolerance

Redundant items are said to provide fault tolerance within a system. This means that a system can continue to operate in the event of a component failure. This can involve the use of spare components, leveraging redundant servers or networks, and / or redundant data storage.

Spares are components that are available in case that the primary component is damaged or becomes unavailable for some reason. Depending on how the spare is used will determine if it is a cold, warm, or hot spare:

- A *cold spare* is a spare component that is not powered up but is a duplicate of the primary component that can be inserted into the system if needed. Typically, cold spares will be stored nearby the system in question and will require someone to manually unpack it and insert it into the affected system.

- *Warm spares* are normally already inserted in the system but do not receive power unless they are required.

- *Hot spares* are not only inserted into the system but are powered on and waiting to be called upon as needed. In many cases, the system will be able to work with warm or hot spares automatically and without much human intervention required.

Spares may present their own problems. Cold spares are obviously not going to be much use in an unmanned facility, and will typically require that the system be shut down to be brought on line. Cold and warm spares may not successfully start up when needed, and cause further disruption. Hot spares may also fail more rapidly than cold or warm spares since they are powered up and will wear down like any powered equipment.

These are some of the reasons why most facilities do not rely solely on redundant components but make use of redundant systems instead. In a typical redundant configuration such as an active–passive pair, the primary system will provide all services while the passive system monitors the primary for any problems. If the primary fails for some reason, the secondary system can take over. Ideally, this means that there is little or no disruption in service caused by system failure. Assuming that the passive system is a duplicate of the primary, there is not even degradation in service.

Redundant networks are similar. In the case that the primary network is unavailable, a secondary path is available. For example, it is common to use a redundant connection to an alternate service provider to deal with the failure of the primary connection. It is also common to deploy core enterprise networks to allow for portions of the core to fail while still providing service. However, duplicate systems often come at over twice the price! The security professional must assure the cost of the system is less than the benefit derived.

Clustering may also be used, although it should not be confused with redundancy. In clustering, two or more "partners" are joined into the cluster and may all provide service at the same time. For example, in an active–active pair, both systems may provide services at any time. In the case of a failure, the remaining partners may continue to provide service but at a decreased capacity.

That degradation in service may not be acceptable in some environments, so often clusters will be deployed with "passive partners" that are intended to join into the active cluster in the case that one of the active systems fails. Naturally, a wide variety of components, systems, and networks can be configured with appropriate levels of fault tolerance and redundancy where needed, and where the additional cost is justified.

Power Supplies

If the power fails or becomes unreliable, then systems will obviously fail or become unreliable. Redundant (or dual) power supplies are common in systems where such failures cannot be tolerated (such as in core network switches, for example). Alternatively, failures that occur outside of an individual system can be dealt with using appropriate uninterruptible power

7

Security Operations

1071

supply (UPS) systems and alternative sources of power from the main grid (such as diesel-based generators common to many data center facilities).

Drives and Data Storage

One of the most common types of failure is drive failure. Normal hard drives consist of many rotating and moving parts that will eventually fail. Even the newer solid state disk (SSD) will eventually fail after so many write operations. To help address drive failure and minimize disruption of service or loss of data, a number of options have been developed over the years. The most appropriate solution will depend largely on where the data is stored and what type of media is being used.

In the simplest configuration, all data is stored on a hard drive or multiple hard drives housed within the system itself. In more complex situations, the data may be stored in large storage networks connected to the systems using controllers or in common storage attached to the network. The data may also be mirrored across multiple systems or portions of it stored on different systems and shared equally.

The security professional is expected to understand the common ways that data is stored and identify the most common ways that data can be protected. This includes understanding the basics of how hard disk storage is used in single systems, in storage area networks (SANs) and network attached storage (NAS). Each of these will require different approaches to providing system resilience.

A SAN consists of dedicated block level storage on a dedicated network. They can be made of numerous storage devices such as tape libraries, optical drives and disk arrays. They utilize protocols like iSCSI to appear to operating systems as locally attached devices.

A NAS is similar to a SAN but with a few very important distinctions. A SAN operates at the file level instead of the block level. A NAS is generally designed to simply store and serve files. Common uses of a NAS include

FTP servers and other types of file servers. They are typically on a shared network and cannot be mounted as local drives on a system, but they can often be mapped as network drives.

If performance enhancements and redundancy is required within a single system, it is very common to use multiple drives to accomplish this. On systems with multiple drives, these drives may be configured in a number of different ways, depending on what the system needs to do.

If all that is required is basic data storage, then a just-a-bunch-of-drives (JBOD) configuration may be most appropriate. If the disks are configured in this way, each disk may be used independently and in isolation from one another. In this case, data is stored on discrete disks and is not stored across multiple disks. Partitions are usually stored on single disks (and not across multiple disks). In the case that a drive fails, all the data from that drive is lost, but the other drives will continue to be available.

Where it may be desirable to use multiple disks for a single partition, this is referred to as concatenation. Concatenated disks will appear to the operating system as a single, continuous drive. This may be most appropriate where exceptionally large partitions are desirable, but drive failures may cause considerable problems since all the data on the failed drive would be lost.

To help systems use multiple drives in concert, redundant array of independent disk (RAID) levels have been standardized. RAID levels describe various ways that multiple disks can be configured to work together. Some RAID levels will provide enhanced performance while others provide enhanced reliability. Some are intended to provide both. The security professional should know each of these different levels as well as their advantages and disadvantages.

7

Security Operations

1073

- **RAID 0:** Writes files in stripes across multiple disks without the use of parity information. This technique allows for fast reading and writing to disk since all of the disks can be accessed in parallel. However, without the parity information, it is not possible to recover from a hard drive failure. This technique does not provide redundancy and should not be used for systems with high availability requirements. It does, however, represent the fastest RAID configuration and may be suitable in scenarios where resilience is not required. For example, it is common to use RAID 0 to store temporary data that will only be required for a short period of time.

- **RAID 1:** This level duplicates all disk writes from one disk to another to create two identical drives. This technique is also known as data mirroring. Redundancy is provided at this level; when one hard drive fails, the other is still available. This mirroring may even happen between drives on different hard drive controllers (which is called duplexing). RAID 1 is very costly from a drive space perspective since half of the available disk is given to the mirroring, and is typically only used between pairs of drives. It is commonly used to provide redundancy for system disks where the core operating system files are found.

- **RAID 2:** This RAID level is more or less theoretical and not used in practice. Data is spread across multiple disks at the bit level using this technique. Redundancy information is computed using a Hamming error correction code, which is the same technique used within hard drives and error-correcting memory modules. Due to the complexity involved with this technique (and the number of drives required to make it work), it is not used.

- **RAID 3 and 4:** These levels require three or more drives to implement. In these raid levels, we get striping of data like in RAID 0, but now we also get redundancy in the form of a dedicated parity drive. Parity information is written to a dedicated disk. If one of the data disks fails, then the information on the parity disk may be used to reconstruct the drive. The difference between RAID 3 and RAID 4 is in how the data is striped: data is striped across multiple disks at the byte level for RAID 3 and at the block level for RAID 4. It is a minor difference but it does mean that RAID 3 is more efficient with disk space but that RAID 4 is a little faster. In both cases, the parity drive is the Achille's heel since it can become a bottleneck and will typically fail sooner than the other drives.

- **RAID 5:** This level also requires three or more drives to implement, and is similar to RAID 4 is many respects. The big difference is in how parity information is stored. Rather than using a dedicated parity drive, data and parity information is striped together across all drives. This level is the most popular and can tolerate the loss of any one drive since the parity information on the other drives can be used to reconstruct the lost one. It is most commonly used for general data storage.

- **RAID 6:** This level extends the capabilities of RAID 5 by computing two sets of parity information. The dual parity distribution accommodates the failure of two drives. However, the performance of this level is slightly less than that of RAID 5. This implementation is not frequently used in commercial environments as it is usually possible to reconstruct a single failed drive before a second one fails.

RAID 0+1 and RAID 1+0: These are examples of nested RAID levels, combining two different RAID types together to try to get the advantages of both. In RAID 0+1, two different arrays of disk are at play. The first set of disks stripes all of the data across the available drives (the RAID 0 part) and those drives are mirrored to a different set of disks (the RAID 1 part). In RAID 1+0 (also known as RAID 10), two different arrays of disk are at play, but they are used a little differently. In this case, each drive in the first set is mirrored to a matching drive in the second set. When data is striped to one drive, it is immediately striped to another. In general, RAID 1+0 is considered to be superior to RAID 0+1 in all respects, both in terms of speed and redundancy.

7

Security Operations

Redundancy can also be provided for tape media. This is known as redundant array of independent tapes (RAIT). A RAIT is created with the use of robotics mechanisms to automatically transfer tapes between storage and the drive mechanisms. RAIT utilizes striping without redundancy. It is also common to use tape vaulting to make multiple copies of tapes that are used for backup and recovery.

Storage Area Networks (SANs) also provide additional options for performance, capacity, and redundancy. In SANs, large banks of disks are made available to multiple systems connecting to them via specialized controllers or via Internet Protocol (IP) networks. They offer the same RAID levels described above, but with some additional advantages. For example, SANs may be used to provide warm or hot spares for a variety of systems in a central location. They may also be used to provide additional drive capacity that can be allocated or reallocated on the fly. They can also provide additional redundancy by providing mechanisms to mirror data to separate drive arrays, speeding up any recovery, and may even allow for such mirroring to occur over long distances. This technique is commonly used by organizations with multiple data centers that wish to be able to serve equally from two or more locations.

NAS may also be used to provide storage for multiple systems across the network. They also generally support the same RAID levels above, and may be servers in their own right. There are also additional redundancy options available within application and database software platforms. For example, database shadowing may be used where a database management system updates records in multiple locations. This technique updates an entire copy of the database at a remote location.

Backup and Recovery Systems

Not all problems can be solved using fault tolerance and redundancy. In many cases, the only solution will be to restore the system to a previous state, presumably before the system became damaged or unreliable. Backup and recovery systems focus on copying data from one location to another so that it can be restored if it is needed. These backups typically include both critical system files as well as user data. Normally, backups occur at times of day when normal use is lower so that the backup processes do not impact normal use. This requires the planning of backups around selected backup windows where they will be least disruptive. If the backup window is large enough, a full backup where all the files are backed up may be chosen.

In some cases, the window may not be long enough to backup all the data on the system during each backup. In that case, differential or incremental backups may be more appropriate. In an incremental backup, only the files that changed since the last backup will be backed up. In a differential backup, only the files that changed since the last full backup will be backed up. In general, differentials require more space than incremental backups while incremental backups are faster to perform. On the other hand, restoring data from incremental backups requires more time than differential backups. To restore from incremental backups, the last full backup and all of the incremental backups performed are combined. In contrast, restoring from a differential backup requires only the last full backup and the latest differential.

Usually, a backup involves copying data from the production system to removable media, such as high-density tapes that can be transported and stored in different locations. It is common for at least three bulk copies of backup tapes to be available. The original will be stored on-site and can be used to quickly restore individual failed systems. Tape stored in a near-site facility (close by but in a different building) is typically used only when the primary facility has suffered a more general failure and where the local tapes have been damaged.

An off-site facility (typically a disaster recovery site) is a secure location at some distance from the primary facility. This provides assurance of a recovery in the event that the facility is destroyed in a catastrophe. The off-site location should be far enough away to preclude mutual destruction in

7

Security Operations

the event of a catastrophe, but not so far away as to introduce difficulties in transporting the media or retrieving it for recovery purposes. Unfortunately, the answer to off-site storage is a difficult challenge in areas prone to natural catastrophes. Geographical areas prone to natural disasters such as forest fires, earthquakes, tornados, typhoons, or hurricanes make it difficult to decide on an appropriate off-site location.

Such copies can be made using a number of different techniques including vaulting and journaling.

Electronic vaulting is accomplished by backing up system data over a network. The backup location is usually at a separate geographical location known as the vault site. Vaulting can be used as a mirror or a backup mechanism using the standard incremental or differential backup cycle. Changes to the host system are sent to the vault server in real-time when the backup method is implemented as a mirror. If vaulting updates are recorded in real-time, then it will be necessary to perform regular backups at the off-site location to provide recovery services due to inadvertent or malicious alterations to user or system data.

Vault servers can also be configured to act in a similar fashion as a backup device. As opposed to performing real-time updates, file changes can be transferred to the vault using an incremental or differential method. Off-line backups of the vault server may not be necessary if there is sufficient storage space for multiple backup cycles.

Journaling is a technique used by database management systems to provide redundancy for their transactions. When a transaction is completed, the database management system duplicates the journal entry at a remote location. The journal provides sufficient detail for the transaction to be replayed on the remote system. This provides for database recovery in the event that the database becomes corrupted or unavailable.

Staffing for Resilience

Technical solutions will only get so far and there is only so much that a system can do automatically without requiring human assistance. An important part of maintaining resilient operations is ensuring adequate and trained staff is available to keep everything running smoothly. An adequate level of staffing will depend on the individual organization. In general, the principle is to avoid single points of failure associated with critical individuals on the operations team. If two or more individuals are capable of providing similar services, then the operation will be less influenced by the unavailability of single individuals. Adequate staffing levels can also depend on when staff will be required. In a 24 × 7 operation, larger numbers of staff will be required to cover all shifts and services than would be required in a business-hours-only operation.

In any case, training and education is critical to successful operations. Operations staff need to have the appropriate skills to perform their duties effectively, and maintain those skills as technologies and processes change over time. Cross-training can also be used to encourage multiple individuals to be able to cover for each other. While mandatory vacations and job rotation have other security advantages, they also encourage skills to be shared between multiple individuals.

7

Security Operations

More to Know **The following articles and documents contain more information about Security Operations. They are freely available on the Internet:**

NIST SP 800-137 Information Security Continuous Monitoring for Federal information Systems and Organizations
http://csrc.nist.gov/publications/nistpubs/800-137/SP800-137-Final.pdf

ENISA Technical Guideline on Incident Reporting
http://www.enisa.europa.eu/activities/Resilience-and-CIIP/Incidents%20 reporting/Technical%20Guidelines%20on%20Incident%20Reporting/ incidents-reporting-to-enisa/technical-guideline-on-incident-reporting

NIST Computer Forensics Tool Testing Project
http://www.cftt.nist.gov/

Bill Wilson's Root Cause Analysis Site
http://www.bill-wilson.net/root-cause-analysis

CIO New Zealand: *Signs your vulnerability management program is Failing*
http://cio.co.nz/cio.nsf/tech/signs-your-vulnerability-management-program-is- failing

DefendAmerica - An Operational Security (OPSEC) Primer
http://www.au.af.mil/au/awc/awcgate/doe/opsec_primer.htm

Summary and Conclusion

Operations security and security operations are two halves of the same coin. Operations security is primarily concerned with the protection and control of information processing assets in centralized and distributed environments. Security operations are primarily concerned with the daily tasks required to keep security services operating reliably and efficiently. Operations security refers to a quality of other services that must be maintained. Security operations are a set of services in its own right.

The security professional should be able to put both into context, understand their main goals, and apply a common sense approach to typical scenarios. The focus here is to maintain operational resilience and protect valuable operational assets through a combination of people, processes, and technologies. At the same time, security services must be managed effectively and efficiently just like any other set of services in the enterprise.

7

Security Operations

Review Questions

1. In the event of a security incident, one of the primary objectives of the operations staff is to ensure that

    A. the attackers are detected and stopped.

    B. there is minimal disruption to the organization's mission.

    C. appropriate documentation about the event is maintained as chain of evidence.

    D. the affected systems are immediately shut off to limit to the impact.

2. Assuming a working IDS is in place, which of the following groups is **BEST** capable of stealing sensitive information due to the absence of system auditing?

    A. Malicious software (malware)

    B. Hacker or cracker

    C. Disgruntled employee

    D. Auditors

3. Which of the following provides controlled and un-intercepted interfaces into privileged user functions?

    A. Ring protection

    B. Anti-malware

    C. Maintenance hooks

    D. Trusted paths

4. The doors of a data center spring open in the event of a fire. This is an example of

    A. Fail-safe

    B. Fail-secure

    C. Fail-proof

D. Fail-closed

5. Which of the following ensures constant redundancy and fault-tolerance?

    A. Cold spare
    B. Warm spare
    C. Hot spare
    D. Archives

6. If speed is preferred over resilience, which of the following RAID configuration is the best choice?

    A. RAID 0
    B. RAID 1
    C. RAID 5
    D. RAID 10

7. Updating records in multiple locations or copying an entire database to a remote location as a means to ensure the appropriate levels of fault-tolerance and redundancy is known as

    A. Data mirroring
    B. Shadowing
    C. Backup
    D. Archiving

8. When the backup window is not long enough to backup all of the data and the restoration of backup must be as fast as possible, which of the following types of high-availability backup strategy is **BEST**?

    A. Full
    B. Incremental
    C. Differential
    D. Increase the backup window so a full backup can be performed

9. At a restricted facility, visitors are requested to provide identification and verified against a pre-approved list by the guard at the front

gate before being let in. This is an example of checking for

    A. Least privilege

    B. Separation of duties

    C. Fail-safe

    D. Psychological acceptability

10. The major benefit of information classification is to

    A. map out the computing ecosystem

    B. identify the threats and vulnerabilities

    C. determine the software baseline

    D. identify the appropriate level of protection needs

11. When sensitive information is no longer critical but still within scope of a record retention policy, that information is **BEST**

    A. Destroyed

    B. Re-categorized

    C. Degaussed

    D. Released

12. The main benefit of placing users into groups and roles is

    A. Ease of user administration

    B. Increased security

    C. Ease of programmatic access

    D. Increased automation

13. Which of the following **BEST** determines access and suitability of an individual?

    A. Job rank or title

    B. Partnership with the security team

    C. Role

    D. Background investigation

14. Reports must be specific on both the message and which of the following?

 A. Intended audience
 B. Delivery options
 C. Colors used
 D. Print layout

15. Which of the following can help with ensuring that only the needed logs are collected for monitoring?

 A. Clipping level
 B. Aggregation
 C. XML Parsing
 D. Inference

16. The main difference between a Security Event Information Management (SEIM) system and a log management system is that SEIM systems are useful for log collection, collation and analysis

 A. In real time
 B. For historical purposes
 C. For admissibility in court
 D. In discerning patterns

17. When normal traffic is flagged as an attack, it is an example of

 A. Fail-safe
 B. Fail-secure
 C. False-negative
 D. False-positive

18. The best way to ensure that there is no data remanence of sensitive information that was once stored on a DVD-R media is by

 A. Deletion
 B. Degaussing
 C. Destruction
 D. Overwriting

19. Which of the following processes is concerned with not only identifying the root cause but also addressing the underlying issue?

    A. Incident management

    B. Problem management

    C. Change management

    D. Configuration management

20. Before applying a software update to production systems, it is **MOST** important that

    A. Full disclosure information about the threat that the patch addresses is available

    B. The patching process is documented

    C. The production systems are backed up

    D. An independent third party attests the validity of the patch

Domain 8

Business Contiunity and Diaster Recovery Planning

THE BUSINESS CONTINUITY PLANNING (BCP) and Disaster Recovery Planning (DRP) domain addresses the preparation, processes, and practices required to ensure the preservation of the organization in the face of major disruptions to normal organization operations. BCP and DRP involve the identification, selection, implementation, testing, and updating of processes and specific prudent actions necessary to protect critical organization processes from the effects of major system and network disruptions and to ensure the timely restoration of organization operations if significant disruptions occur.

This chapter describes a process for building an enterprise-wide business continuity (BC) program. It discusses the evolution of the industry regulations that have influenced or in some cases mandated that organizations build programs within their organization that will ensure their continuation of their organization "no matter what."

Finally, it discusses the interrelationship between information security and BC and other risk management areas such as physical security, records management, vendor management, internal audit, financial risk management, operational risk management, and regulatory compliance (legal and regulatory risk) in the context of the overall BC risk management framework shown in *Figure 8.1.*

Risk Management Framework

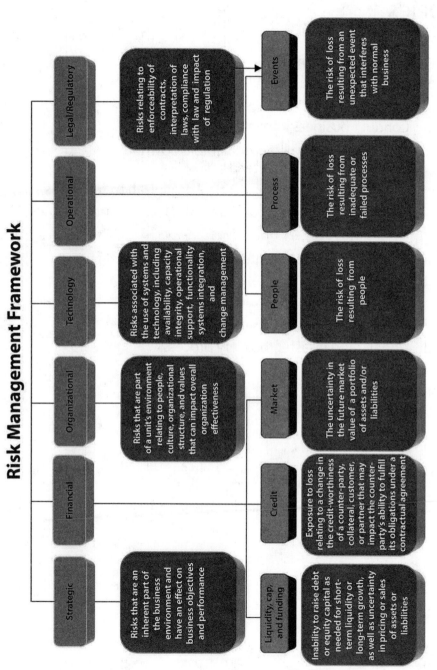

*Figure 8.1 - **BC Risk Management Framework***

TOPICS

- Understand business continuity requirements
  - Develop and document project scope and plan
- Conduct business impact analysis
  - Determine maximum tolerable downtime (MTD) and other criteria
  - Identify and prioritize critical organization functions
  - Assess exposure to outages, e.g., local, regional, global
  - Define recovery objectives
- Develop a recovery strategy
  - Implement a backup storage strategy, (e.g., offsite storage, electronic vaulting, tape rotation)
  - Recovery site strategies
- Understand disaster recovery process
  - Response
  - Personnel
  - Communications
  - Assessment
  - Restoration
  - Provide training
- Exercise, assess and maintain the plan, (e.g., version control, distribution)

OBJECTIVES

According to the (ISC)² Candidate Information Bulletin, a CISSP® candidate is expected to know:

- The difference between BCP and disaster recovery (DR)
- BCP in terms of project scope and planning
- Business Impact Analysis (BIA)
- Recovery strategies
- Recovery plan development
- Implementation
- Understand DR in terms of:
  - Recovery Plan Development
  - Implementation
  - Restoration.

Business Continuity Requirements

Project Initiation and Management

The first step in building the BC program is project initiation and management. During this phase, the following activities will occur:

- Obtain senior management support to go forward with the project

- Define a project scope, the objectives to be achieved, and the planning assumptions

- Estimate the project resources needed to be successful, both human resources and financial resources

- Define a timeline and major deliverables of the project

In this phase, the program will be managed like a project, and a project manager should be assigned to the BC and DR domain. Once the project is complete, the domain will transition to a program in order to maintain the viability of the recovery.

Senior Leadership Support

Before the project can even start, it must have committed senior management support. Without that support, the project will fail. To convince leadership that the organization needs to build an enterprise-wide BC and DR plan, the planner must sell the importance of the program to the leadership.

Senior leadership in any organization has two major goals: Execute the mission and protect the organization. Business continuity and DR have little to do with executing the mission (unless the organization's organization is DR!) and everything to do with protecting the organization. It is still a hard sell because unless the organization actually has a disaster; the value of the time, money and people resources to build the plan are going to be suspect, because it takes away from goal number one, execute the mission.

So, why does an organization need BC and DR? It started in the data center. Once computers became part of the organization landscape, even before the introduction of personal computers on individual desks, it quickly became clear that organizations could not return to manual processes if computers failed. The operational model had changed. The work people did with manual general ledgers in ledger books, or with their hands in a manufacturing environment was now done more consistently, with fewer errors and many times faster by computers. If those computer systems failed, there were not enough people to do the work; nor did the people in the organization still have the skills to do it manually anymore. This was the start of the DR industry. Still today, the term "disaster recovery" commonly means recovery of the technology environment.

It took some time for many industries to realize that it really did not matter if it recovered the data center if there were no people to use it. That is when the term BC began to replace DR as a more accurate reflection of the goal of the industry—to continue the organization.

To convince leadership of the need to build a viable DR and BCP, the planner needs to help them understand the risk they are accepting by not having one and the cost to the corporation if a disaster were to occur. The risks to the corporation are found in three areas; financial (how much money the corporation stands to lose), reputational (how badly the corporation will be perceived by its customers and its shareholders), and regulatory (fines or penalties incurred, lawsuits filed against them). There is also the potential that the leaders of the organization could be held personally liable, financially and even criminally, if it is determined that they did not use due care to adequately protect the corporation.

Financial risks can be quantified in many cases, and are generally used to help determine how much should be spent on the recovery program. One of the ways financial risk can be calculated is using the formula P * M = C:

- **Probability of harm (P):** the chance that a damaging event will occur times the

- **Magnitude of harm (M):** the amount of financial damage that would occur should a disaster happen =

- **Cost of prevention (C):** the price of putting in place a countermeasure preventing the disaster's effects. The cost of countermeasures should not be more than the cost of the event.

Reputational risk is harder to quantify. For example, if a company cannot satisfy the needs of its customers when required, it is not hard for the customer to find someone else who will. Reputational risk is about how the company is perceived by its customers and stockholders. There are many examples of a negative impact to stock price in the wake of a crisis that is not managed properly. Effective BC and DR programs can be the difference between a company surviving an event and a company ceasing to exist.

Additional Benefits of the Planning Process

In many organizations, contingency planning is a necessity that has turned out to be beneficial in more ways than ever expected. Contingency planning helps to ensure an organization's viability during and following a disaster. Another benefit of contingency planning is significant improvements in the daily operations of many organizations.

Researching and documenting contingency plans can discover numerous single points of failure (SPOF). A SPOF is any single input to a process that, if missing, would cause the process or several processes to be unable to function. Once identified, these SPOFs can often easily be eliminated or have their damaging potential reduced. Many organizations have also witnessed process improvements as a direct result of their contingency planning efforts, particularly while exercising their DR and BCPs.

There are many more benefits to contingency planning. Few other processes require that a data center staff or an organization think about what they do, how they do it, and how to make it better. Thinking about how to recover in a new environment, operating without the primary building, missing half the staff or working without connectivity all lead to improved performance and resilience.

Develop and Document Project Scope and Plan

When seeking senior leadership approval, it is important to gain agreement on the scope and goals of the planning effort. Will the plan cover just the technology recovery or will it cover the organizational operations as well? Will it address only the technology in the data center or will it address all the technology used to run the organization? Will it address recovery of the main office only or will all the offices be considered?

Every company needs a technology recovery plan. Whether the company is a small organization that conducts all of its business on a laptop or a major corporation with multiple data centers, technology is an integral part of how business is conducted in today's world. Without modern technology, it is unlikely that most organization operations could survive for long.

Planning for the recovery of the organization operations is also key to the survivability of the organization. Both the technology recovery and the organization recovery enable the organization to continue in the wake of an unexpected event. Another type of planning to consider is some type of workforce impairment event such as a pandemic, a labor strike, transportation issues, etc., where the building is fine, the data center is fine, but for some reason, the workforce is unable or unwilling to come to work.

The planner will need to agree with leadership on the scope of the planning effort as that will define the project resources the planner will need, the timeline to complete the project, and the deliverables the leadership team can expect as the project progresses. Generally, building a plan where none currently exists within a medium sized organization (1,000 - 3,000 staff with two data centers) with an experienced planner and a commitment from leadership to support the effort would follow a timeline as outlined below:

- *Emergency notification list*—1 month
  - ¤ To respond to an emergency with any success, the planner must first be able to reach the people in the planner organization who can and will respond.

- *Vital records backup and recovery*—within the first 6 months
  - ¤ To be able to recover from a disaster situation, the planner must have access to all records needed to operate the organization.

- *Business Impact Analysis*—first 6 months
  - ¤ Identify organization functions, the capabilities of each organization unit to handle outages, and the priority and sequence of functions and applications to be recovered, identify resources required for recovery of those areas and interdependencies

- *Strategy development*—6 to 9 months
  - ¤ Assessing various available strategies, performing cost benefit analysis, and making recommendations to leadership for approval

- *Alternate site selection*—9 to 12 months
  - ¤ Preparing Requests for Proposals (RFP's), performing site surveys, selecting vendor and/or build out and equip of internal site, negotiating contracts

- *Contingency plan development*—12 months
  - ¤ Including: emergency response, restoring of critical systems, and organization functions to normal organization operations

- Testing, plan maintenance, periodic audit—ongoing

Organizational Analysis

Senior leadership must support an organizational policy requiring compliance with the BCP/DRP development program to facilitate getting resources assigned from the various areas of the organization that will need to participate. The policy should state the following:

> "The senior leaders of each functional area of the company are responsible for ensuring that a BCP exists for their area of responsibility, for the contents of the plan itself, and for affirming their concurrence with the plan annually by signing off on the plan document."

Legal and Regulatory Requirements

The legal or regulatory requirements that the organization is subject to are industry specific and the number of regulations in this area have increased in times of global international uncertainty. Two of the most recent regulations introduced are Title IX of the Implementing the 9/11 Commission Recommendations Act of 2007[1] and British Standard, BS25999[2].

Title IX of "The Implementing The 9/11 Commission Recommendations Act Of 2007" (Public Law 110–53) addresses a diversity of other national security issues as well. It was signed into law by the President of the United States on August 3, 2007 and is applicable to United States organizations. The intent of the law is to implement the findings of the 9/11 Commission Report. The law recommends that private sector organizations validate their readiness to recover by comparing their programs against a yet unnamed standard. NFPA 1600[3] was recommended by the 9/11 Commission for a standard to be used. The DRII Professional Practices shown in Section "The Ten Professional Practice Areas" are the basis for BCP in NFPA 1600. While the US Government has endorsed this standard, it is voluntary.

---

1   http://intelligence.senate.gov/laws/pl11053.pdf

2   For more information on BS25999 please see the following: http://www.25999.info/

3   http://www.nfpa.org/assets/files/pdf/nfpa1600.pdf

The Ten Professional Practice Areas

Project Initiation and Management
Establish the need for a BCP, including obtaining management support and organizing and managing the BCP project to completion.

Risk Evaluation and Control
Determine the events and environmental surroundings that can adversely affect an organization, the damage that such events can cause, and the controls needed to prevent or minimize the effects of potential loss.

Business Impact Analysis
Identify the impacts that result from disruptions that can affect the organization and the techniques that can be used to quantify and qualify such impacts.

Developing Business Continuity Strategies
Determine and guide the selection of alternative organization recovery operating strategies to be used to maintain the organization's critical functions.

Emergency Response and Operations
Develop and implement procedures to respond to and stabilize the situation following an incident or event.

Developing and Implementing Business continuity Plans
Design, develop, and implement the BCP.

Awareness and Training Programs
Prepare a program to create an organizational awareness and enhance the skills required to develop, implement, maintain, and execute the BCP.

Maintaining and Exercising Business Continuity Plans
Preplan, coordinate, evaluate, test and exercise the plan, and document the results. Develop processes to maintain the currency of the plan in accordance with the strategic direction of the organization.

Public Relations and Crisis Communication

Develop, coordinate, evaluate, implement, and exercise public relations and crisis communication plans.

Coordination with Public Authorities

Establish applicable procedures and policies for coordinating response, continuity, and restoration activities with local authorities while ensuring compliance with applicable statutes or regulations.

BS 25999 Part 1[4] is an extension of PAS56[5] which provides guidance and is nonperformance based. BS 25999Part 2[6] has a certification body, specific requirements and is auditable. The intention is to create the ability to demonstrate compliance with the standard. Stage 1 is an audit including a desktop review and must be completed before moving to stage 2. Stage 2 is a conformance and certification audit where the planner must demonstrate implementation. If the implementation fails, it requires corrective action which must be agreed upon. If the planner successfully completes stages 1 and 2, the organization can then apply for BS 25999 certification. BS 25999 stage 2 is scheduled to be replaced in 2012 by ISO 22301[7]

Regulations for US Financial Institutions

The Federal Financial Institutions Examination Council (FFIEC) BCP Booklet [8] specifies, among other things, that BCP is about maintaining, resuming, and recovering the organization, not just the recovery of the technology and that the planning process should be conducted on an enterprise-wide basis. It also stipulates that a thorough Business Impact Analysis (BIA) and risk assessment are the foundation of an effective BCP,

4   For more information on BS25999 Part 1, please see the following: http://www.25999.info/bs25999-1.htm

5   For more information on PAS56 please see the following: http://www.pas56.com/

6   For more information on BS25999 Part 2, please see the following: http://www.25999.info/bs25999-2.htm

7   Read more about ISO 22301 here: http://pecb.org/iso22301/

8   For more information on the FFIEC BCP Booklet, please see the following: http://ithandbook.ffiec.gov/it-booklets/business-continuity-planning.aspx

that the effectiveness can be validated only through testing or practical application and that the BCP and test results should be subjected to an independent audit and reviewed by the board of directors.

In addition, appendix D of the FFIEC states that a company should be aware of the BCP activities of its third-party providers, key suppliers, and organization partners. When a company outsources information, transaction processing, and settlement activities, the company should review and understand service providers' BCP and ensure critical services can be restored within acceptable timeframes based upon the needs of the institution. If possible, it recommends the institution consider participating in their provider's testing process.

The *US Financial Integrity Regulatory Authority (FINRA) Rule 4370* [9] requires a BCP that addresses, at a minimum, that

- Data backup and recovery (hard copy and electronic) exists for mission critical systems.
- Financial and operational assessments are performed.
- Alternate communications between customers and the firm, and employees and the firm, have been identified and implemented.
- Business constituent, bank and counter-party impact are documented.
- Regulatory reporting and communications with regulators would continue.

Additional regulations on financial firms include but are not limited to

- National Association of Insurance Commissioners[10] (NAIC)
- National Futures Association Compliance Rule 2–38[11]

---

9   Read more about FINRA Rule 4370 here: http://www.finra.org/Industry/Issues/BusinessContinuity/
10   http://www.naic.org/
11   http://www.nfa.futures.org/nfamanual/NFAManual.aspx?RuleID=RULE%20 2-38&Section=4

■ Electronic Funds Transfer Act—"reasonable" standard of care (the care that a reasonable person would exercise under the circumstances; the standard for determining legal duty.)[12]

■ Basel Committee—Banks should have contingency plans and BCPs in place[13]

Other Regulations or Standards are

■ *The Australian Prudential Standard CPS 232*—July 2012[14]

  ❑ A regulated institution's BCM must, at a minimum, include:

  • BCM Policy

  • Business Impact Analysis (BIA) including risk assessment

  • Recovery objectives and strategies

  • Business Continuity Plan (BCP) including crisis management and recovery

  • Programs for:

    - Review and testing of the BCP

    - Training and awareness of staff in relation to BCM.

■ *Monetary Authority of Singapore* [15]—June 2003 "Business continuity Management ("BCM") is an over-arching framework that aims to minimize the impact to organizations due to operational disruptions. It not only addresses the restoration of information technology ("IT") infrastructure, but also focuses

---

12   For more information about the EFTA, please see the following: http://www.fdic.gov/regulations/laws/rules/6500-1350.html

13   For more information on the Basel Committee, please see the following: http://www.bis.org/bcbs/

14   http://www.apra.gov.au/CrossIndustry/Documents/Prudential%20Standard%20CPS%20232%20Business%20Continuity%20Management.pdf

15   http://www.mas.gov.sg/~/media/MAS/Regulations%20and%20Financial%20Stability/Regulatory%20and%20Supervisory%20Framework/Risk%20Management/BCMGuidelines.ashx

on the rapid recovery and resumption of critical organization functions for the fulfillment of organization obligations."

- **Standard for Business Continuity/Disaster Recovery Service Providers (SS507)**[16]—Singapore is the first country in the world to introduce a Standard and Certification program for BC/DR service providers. Developed by the Infocomm Development Authority of Singapore and the IT Standards Committee (ITSC), the standard specifies the stringent requirements for BC/DR service providers. These requirements benchmark against the top practices in the region and stipulate the operating, the monitoring, and the maintenance of BC/DR services offered.

- **HIPAA**[17]--- United States Health Information Privacy requires a data backup plan, a disaster recovery plan, and an emergency mode operations plan regarding privacy and portability of health insurance information.

Sarbanes–Oxley—Section 404
Management Assessment of Internal Controls

RULES REQUIRED—The Commission shall prescribe rules requiring each annual report required by Section 13(a) or 15(d) of the Securities Exchange Act of 1934 (15 U.S.C. 78m or 78o(d)) to contain an internal control report, which shall—

(1) state the responsibility of management for establishing and maintaining an adequate internal control structure and procedures for financial reporting; and

(2) contain an assessment, as of the end of the most recent fiscal year of the issuer, of the effectiveness of the internal control structure and procedures of the issuer for financial reporting.

---

16   http://www.itsc.org.sg/pdf/synthesis08/Two_SS507.pdf

17   http://www.hhs.gov/ocr/privacy/hipaa/understanding/coveredentities/index. html

(b) INTERNAL CONTROL EVALUATION AND REPORTING—With respect to the internal control assessment required by subsection (a), each registered public accounting firm that prepares or issues the audit report for the issuer shall attest to, and report on, the assessment made by the management of the issuer. An attestation made under this subsection shall be made in accordance with standards for attestation engagements issued or adopted by the Board. Any such attestation shall not be the subject of a separate engagement.

PCAOB (Public Company Accounting Oversight Board) is responsible for BCP:[18]

"Furthermore, management's plans that could potentially affect financial reporting in future periods are not controls. For example, a company's business continuity or contingency planning has no effect on the company's current abilities to initiate, authorize, record, process, or report financial data. Therefore, a company's business continuity or contingency planning is not part of internal control over financial reporting."

Legal Standards

Legal standards to consider include the liability of corporations, liability of organizational executives, liability to outside parties, standard of negligence, standard of care, prudent man doctrine, and informed organization judgment vs. gross negligence. There is significant case law in these areas including:

- ***Blake vs. Woodford Bank & Trust Co. (1977)***[19] Foreseeable workload—failure to prepare

---

18   http://pcaobus.org/Pages/default.aspx

19   http://www.casebriefs.com/blog/law/commercial-law/commercial-law-keyed-to-warren/payment-systems-checks-and-credit-cards/blake-v-woodford-bank-trust-co/

- *Sun Cattle Company, Inc. vs. Miners Bank (1974)*[20] Computer System Failure—Foreseeable Computer Failure

- *US vs Carroll Towing Company (1947)*[21], Judge Hand stated that "The owner's duty, as in other similar situations, to provide against resulting injuries is a function of three variables: (1) The probability that she will break away; (2) the gravity of the resulting injury, if she does; (3) the burden of adequate precautions. This relationship has been formalized by the law and economics school as such: an act is in breach of the duty of care if: $B < PL$ where B is the cost (burden) of taking precautions, and P is the probability of loss (L). L is the gravity of loss. The product of P x L must be a greater amount than B to create a duty of due care for the defendant."

- *Negligent Standard to Plan or Prepare (pandemic) 2003*— Canadian nurses who filed suit saying the federal government was negligent in not preparing for the second wave after the disease was first identified.

Resource Requirements

Once the scope of the planning effort has been agreed to, the next step is to determine resource requirements. The planning team needs to have representatives from both the organization operations and from the technology areas. The business continuity staff will determine the applications that need to be recovered and the timeframe they need to be recovered in. The technology staff will then determine what technology needs to be recovered to support that organization requirement. The individuals on the planning team need to be the same individuals who would execute the recovery if it happened for real.

---

20   Sun River Cattle Co, Inc. v. Miners Bank, 164 Mont. 287, 521 P.2d 679 (1974)

21   For more information on this case, please see the following sources:

    A. United States v. Carroll Towing Co., 159 F.2d 169, 173 (2d Cir. 1947).
    B. http://lawteaching.org/resources/lawreviewarticles/saintlouis/2001torts/kelley-patrick-ocr.pdf

The planning team will have tasks to complete in support of the project. The initial time the planning team will have to spend on the project will be in understanding the organization processes within their area and the impact to the firm if those processes got interrupted by an unexpected event. Additional tasks will follow as the planning process continues.

Financial resources will also need to be defined for the planning process. Resources may be spent hiring outside consultants to help facilitate the planning in the initial stages or for software tools to assist in data collection and plan development. Travel may need to be budgeted for the lead BC planner to go to each site to work with the planning teams in each site.

The lead planner should develop a project plan outlining each phase of the planning process, the resource requirements needed for each, the amount of time each phase will take to complete and the deliverables to be produced from each phase of the planning process. When developing a new plan or updating an old one, the following phases are recommended.

Planning Team and Critical Staff
The planner will need to identify and build contact lists for the planning team, leadership and critical staff. See a sample Emergency Notification List (ENL) in *Figure 8.2.*

Emergency Management Team – Home Office

Title	Name	Home Phone	Work Phone	Mobile Number
Emergency Management Team Leader	John Smith	(508) 555-3546	(508) 855-1234	(508) 555-3452
Human Resource Team Leader	Mary Flounder	(508) 555-6765	(508) 855-2779	(508) 555-9876

Figure 8.2 - **Sample Emergency Notification List**

Vital Records
Validating that all the records needed to rebuild the organization are stored offsite in a secure location that will be accessible

---

Common Vital Records
Legal Records

- Anything with a signature
- Customer correspondence (statements, letters back and forth, requests,etc.)
- Customer conversations (recorded interactions with customer service reps)
- Accounting records
- Justification proposals/documents
- Transcripts/minutes of meetings with legal signifigance
- Paper with value - Stock certificates, bonds, comercial paper, etc.
- Legal documents - Letters of incorporation, deeds, etc.

Figure 8.3 - **Legal Vital Records**

following a disaster. This includes backups of the electronic data as well as paper records. Most organizations understand their traditional vital records but the planner should also consider things like procedure manuals, forms, letterhead—unique assets crucial to routine activities. Some common vital records are shown in *Figure 8.3* and *Figure 8.4*.

Risk and Business Impact Analysis
The planning team will make recommendations about which risks the organization should mitigate and which systems and processes the plan will recover and when.

Strategy Development
In this phase, the planner will review the different types of strategies for the recovery of business areas and technology based on the recovery period identified for each. They will also prepare a cost benefit analysis on the viable strategies available and present a proposal to leadership to implement the selected strategies.

Common Vital Records

Business Records

- Databases and contact lists for employees, customers, vendors, partners, or others that your business unit deals with regularly or at a time of emergency (this includes your ENL)
- Business unit contingency plans
- Procedure/application manuals that your employees normally use and procedure manuals for operation in your alternate site if different from above
- Backup files from production servers/applications owned by your business unit that support your critical functions
- Reference documents used by your employees on a regular basis
- Calendar files or printouts - particularly if your business unit schedules appointments with customers
- Source code

Figure 8.4 - **Common Vital Records**

Alternate Site Selection and Implementation

During this phase, the planner will select and build out the alternate sites used to recover the areas of the organization or technology.

Documenting the Plan

This phase is where all the information collected up to this point is combined into a plan document. The plan will include documented procedures for each site where the company performs organization and for each type of technology and/or application to be recovered.

Testing, Maintenance, and Update

This final phase is where the planner will validate the recovery strategies implemented through testing and establish a maintenance schedule for the plan and an update schedule for the plan documentation.

Each of these phases as well as other components of the planning process will be discussed in detail later in the chapter.

Conduct Business Impact Analysis

The next step in the planning process is to have the planning team perform a BIA. The BIA will help the company decide what needs to be recovered, and how quickly. Mission functions are typically designated with terms such as critical, essential, supporting and nonessential to help determine the appropriate prioritization.

Identify and Prioritize Critical Organization Functions

Generally speaking, organizations do not hire staff to perform nonessential tasks. Every function has a purpose, but some are more time sensitive than others when there is limited time or resources available to perform them. A bank that has suffered a building fire could easily stop its marketing campaign but would not be able to stop check processing and deposits made by its customers. The organization needs to look at every function in this same light. How long can the company not perform this function without causing significant financial losses, significant customer unhappiness or losses or significant penalties or fines from regulators or lawsuits?

All organizational functions and the technology that supports them need to be classified based on their recovery priority. Recovery time frames for organization operations are driven by the consequences of not performing the function. The consequences may be the result of organization lost during the down period; contractual commitments not met resulting in fines or lawsuits, lost goodwill with customers, etc. *Figure 8.5* Sample BIA form is a simple BIA form for classifying functions and determining their time sensitivity code, which is shown in *Figure 8.6* Time sensitivity codes.. To use this form, the planner will need to adjust the factors to reflect the organization being evaluated. The planner will need to define for the planning team what a low, medium, or high impact is in that organization in each of the impact areas, as well as the time before impact is realized.

BIA Form

Functional Area	Function Name	Mailzone	Risk Code	Time Before Impact	Customer Impact	Regulatory Impact	Financial Impact	Rating Total	Recovery Time Sensitivity Code	Alt. Site
			F=Financial C=Customer R=Regulatory	0=Week 2 or more 1=Week 1 5=Up to 3 days 10=Day 1 20=4 hours 40=Immediate	0=None 1=Low 3=Medium 5=High	0=None 1=Low 3=Medium 5=High	0=None 1=0 to10K 2=>10K but < 100K 3=>100K but <500K 4=>500K but <1 Mil 5=>1Mil	Sum of 1 through 4		
Customer Service	Call Center	Z 45	C & F	40	5	1	3	49	AAA	Surviving sites then Smith Road
Customer Service	Customer Account Maint.	Z 37	C	1	3	0	0	4	D	Work from Home
Customer Service	Customer Monetary	Z 38	C & F & R	10	3	3	4	20	A	Smith Road

*Figure 8.5 - **Sample BIA form***

Business Function Recovery Time Sensitive Codes

Rating Total of 45 or More =
AAA Immediate Recovery

Must be performed in at least two geographically dispersed locations that are fully equipped and staffed

Rating Total of 25 to 45 =
AA Up to 4 hours to recover

Must have a viable alternate site that can be staffed and functioning within the four hour timeframe required

Rating Total of 15 to 24 =
A Same day recovery

Must be operational the same business day and must therefore have a viable alternate site that can be staffed and functioning within the same business day

Rating Total of 10 to 14 =
B Up to 3 days

Can be suspended for up to 3 business days, but must have a viable alternate site that can be staffed and functioning by the fourth business day

Rating Total of 7 to 10 =
C Week 1

Can be suspended for up to a week, but must have a viable alternate site that can be staffed and functioning by the second week following an interruption

Rating Total of 0 to 6 =
D Week 2 or greater downtime allowable

Can be suspended for greater than one week - A maximum number of days should be identified for this function

---

Figure 8.6 - **Time Sensitivity Codes**

Determine Maximum Tolerable Downtime and Other Criteria

All applications, like all organization functions, need to be classified as to their time sensitivity for recovery even if those applications do not support organization functions that are time sensitive. For applications, this is commonly referred to as Recovery Time Objective (RTO) or Maximum Tolerable Downtime (MTD). This is the amount of time the organization can function without that application before significant impact occurs.

Assess Exposure to Outages

Understanding the Organization

As part of the planning process, the planner will need to perform a risk assessment to determine which threats the organization has and where the planner will recommend spending mitigating dollars to attempt to reduce the impact of a threat.

There are three elements of risk: threats, assets, and mitigating factors. The first is threats themselves. A threat is an event or situation that if it occurred, would prevent the organization from operating in its normal manner, if at all. Threats are measured in probabilities such as "may happen 1 time in 10 years" and have duration of time where the impact is felt.

External Threats and Vulnerabilities

The most common threat that impacts a organization's ability to function normally is power availability. Power outages cause more organization interruption events than any other type of event. The second most common type of event is water, either too much water (flooding, plumbing leak, broken pipes, and leaky roof) or not enough (water main break). Other common events are severe weather, cable cuts resulting in network outages, fires, labor disputes, transportation mishaps, and for the data center, hardware failures.

Internal Threats and Vulnerabilities

Internal outages are typically caused by the following actions:

- Equipment fails prematurely
  - Could be due to improper installation
  - Could also be due to improper environment

- Equipment fails due to wear and tear
  - ◘ Most equipment has a "mean time between failures" rating
  - ◘ Running equipment beyond this average is risking failure
- Equipment goes down due to untested production changes or other human errors

Refer to the threat matrix in *Figure 8.7* Potential threats. Reviewing the list of threats, one will notice that some of them are events that are fairly localized while others, like a hurricane, have a more regional impact. Threats to be considered include both natural hazards such as tornados, earthquakes and hurricanes as well as man-made hazards such as transportation mishaps, chemical spills, and sabotage.

*Figure 8.7 - **Potential Threats***

Assets

The second element of risk is assets. If the organization does not own anything, then it would not be concerned about risks because it would have little or nothing to lose. The more assets the company has that would be impacted by an event, the more the organization will be concerned about how to manage the threats to those assets. Assets are comprised of many elements, information assets, financial assets, physical assets, human assets and when considering the impact of a risk, the planner must also consider additional costs to recover, fines or penalties the organization may incur and lost goodwill or competitive advantage.

The third element of risk is mitigating factors. Mitigating factors are the controls or safeguards the planner will put in place to reduce the impact of a threat. The planner cannot eliminate a threat. Nothing can prevent power outages from occurring. The planner can, however, mitigate the impact of a power outage on the organization by implementing battery backup UPS (uninterruptible power supply) systems and generators to provide power until the utility company returns power. The planner cannot eliminate the criminal element in society but the organization can prevent them from working for the company by performing background investigations and make it harder for them to gain access to a building by implementing access control systems. These are all examples of mitigating factors.

When the planner identifies a risk, the planner will need to make recommendations about how to respond to that risk. The planner can accept the risk, transfer the risk, attempt to avoid the risk altogether, or mitigate the risk.

- The planner can recommend accepting it. If the likelihood of occurrence is so small or the impact so minimal or the cost to mitigate it so substantial, the planner can recommend that the organization simply choose to accept the risk.

- The planner can recommend transferring it. This is where insurance comes into play. If a risk to too costly to mitigate against but too big to just accept, the planner can choose to recommend transferring the risk by purchasing an insurance policy. Similar to car insurance, organization interruption insurance is often used to transfer the risk of an event, which cannot be mitigated either because of cost or some other factor. Be aware that many insurance policies will not cover systems already compromised or lacking in security control evidence.

- The planner can take steps to avoid the risk altogether. Depending on the situation, risk avoidance might prove to be the most cost effective option available to deal with the risk being presented to the business. For example, if there is a large enterprise that has multiple offices and datacenters scattered geographically across the United States, they would be able to avoid risks pertaining to severe weather events simply by transferring operations to any of the unaffected offices and datacenters for the duration of the expected event. The business could then transfer operations back again to their normal offices and datacenters once the events impact has been neutralized in those affected areas.

- The planner can recommend mitigation against the risk. Preventing a disaster is always better than trying to recover from one. If the planner can recommend controls to be put in place to prevent the most likely of risks from having an impact on the organization's ability to do organization, then the planner will have to recover from fewer actual events. Risks are from both natural hazards such as hurricanes, earthquakes and tornados; man made risks such as human error, sabotage, arson; and workplace violence and technology risks such as hardware failures, mechanical failures, and software failures. The ones the planner will mitigate against are the ones most likely to occur. The planner would probably not choose to anchor equipment to a desktop or wall to mitigate against an earthquake if the organization is not located in a region where earthquakes are a common threat.

A BC and DR plan is one type of mitigation. In fact, a BC and DR plan is what we implement when all other mitigating factors fail. No matter how hardened an organization makes a facility, the building itself is still a Single Point of Failure (SPOF). Despite all the controls put in place to mitigate against a disaster, a disaster can still occur and the organization needs a plan to recover its important technology and organization operations so the organization can continue. What the organization recovers and when is determined during the next phase of the planning process.

Define Recovery Objectives

Once all the organization functions have been identified and a recovery time frame determined, the planning team then needs to identify all the resources necessary to perform each of those functions. Resources include applications systems, minimum staff requirements, phone requirements, desktop requirements, internal and external interdependencies, etc.

The recovery priority for application systems is identified during this process. It is the organization that decides what application systems need to come back on line when based on the recovery priority of the functions those applications support.

This technology review process is sometimes difficult for the organization to perform. The basic average desktop user knows they click on this icon and this application system launches. They have little comprehension of where the application resides (mainframe, midrange, server, desktop), where the data resides (central storage, a network server, or the desktop) or where the executable resides.

These are important considerations in building a recovery plan. If the application is colocated with the organization, then the recovery for that application must be part of the site recovery plan for that site. If it is not, then recovery could mean only providing network access to the application at the alternate site.

1115

For both organization functions and applications, the organization also needs to determine the amount of work in process that can be at risk in an event. The data that is on employee's desks when a fire occurs would be lost forever if that information was not backed up somewhere else. The information stored in file cabinets, incoming mail in the mailroom, the backup tapes that have not yet left the building, all are at risk.

The planning team needs to make decisions about all types of data because data is what runs the organization. How much data is acceptable to lose? A minute's worth? An hour's worth? A whole business day? This is commonly referred to as the recovery point objective (RPO). The point in time that the planner will recover to. Backup policies and procedures for electronic data and hard copy data need to comply with the RPO established by the organization.

Develop a Recovery Strategy

Recovery strategies are driven by the recovery timeframe required by the function or application to be recovered. Some strategies the planner may consider for organization operations are as follows:

- *Surviving Site:* A surviving site strategy is implemented so that while service levels may drop, a function never ceases to be performed because it operates in at least two geographically dispersed buildings that are fully equipped and staffed.

- *Self-Service:* An organization can transfer work to another of its own locations, which has available facilities and/or staff to manage the time sensitive workload until the interruption is over.

- *Internal Arrangement:* Training rooms, cafeterias, conference rooms, etc., may be equipped to support organization functions while staff from the impacted site travels to another site and resumes organization.

- *Reciprocal Agreements/Mutual Aid Agreements:* Other similar organizations may be able to accommodate those affected. For example, one law firm may be able to provide office space to another in the event of an outage. This could involve the temporary suspension of non-time sensitive functions at the organization operations not affected by the outage.

- *Dedicated Alternate Sites:* Built by the company to accommodate organization function or technology recovery.

- *Works from Home:* Many organizations today have the capability to have employees work from locations that are remote from a physical office environment.

- *External Suppliers:* A number of external organizations offer facilities covering a wide range of organization recovery needs from full data centers with a wide range of platforms, alternate site space in physical facilities, mobile units that can be transported to the company site, and temporary staff to provide services when the employees cannot.

■ **No Arrangement:** For low-priority business functions or applications it may not be cost justified to plan at a detailed level. The minimum requirement would be to record a description of the functions, the maximum allowable lapse time for recovery, and a list of the resources required.

Each of these strategies can be considered for the organization and technology recovery. Those which are recommended need to have a cost/benefit analysis (CBA) performed to determine if the costs of the strategy being recommended fits within the amount of risk or loss the organization is trying to avoid. The company should not spend $1,000,000 a year on a recovery strategy to protect $100,000 of income. Every organization does not need a dual data center recovery strategy. The strategy selected must fit the organizational need.

The cost of implementing the recovery strategy recommended needs to include the initial costs associated with building out the strategy as well as ongoing costs to maintain the recovery solution, and where applicable, the cost of periodic testing of the solution to ensure it remains viable.

Once the strategy has been agreed to and funded, the planner must then implement the various strategies approved. This may involve negotiating with vendors to provide recovery services for organization or technology, doing site surveys of existing sites to determine excess capacity, wiring conference rooms or cafeterias to support organization functions, buying recovery technology, installing remote replication software, installing networks for voice and data recovery, assigning alternate site seats to the various organization areas and the like.

Implement a Backup Storage Strategy

Backup strategies for data used to restore technology are varied and are driven by the RTO and the RPO needed to support the organizational requirements. Some organizations have begun tiering data based on its importance to the organization and frequency of use. The more time sensitive data is replicated offsite either synchronously or asynchronously to ensure its availability and its currency. Other data is backed up to tape and sent offsite once or more a day.

If the backup tapes are stored somewhere else besides an alternate site, then the time it takes to pack and transport those tapes must be included in the RTO. Depending on how many tapes are required, this could increase the time to recovery by hours or even days. To reduce the recovery time from 3 to 5 days minimum to 24 hours or less, the data that will be used to recover systems and applications must be stored at the recovery site.

It is vital that the data that is stored offsite include not only the application data but also the application source code, hardware and software images for the servers and end user desktops, utility software, license keys, etc.

Most organizations, no matter what strategy they employ for storing data offsite, start by performing full backups of all their data followed by periodic incremental backups. Incremental backups take copies of only the files that have changed since the last full or incremental backup was taken and then set the archive bit to "0." The other common option is to take a differential backup. A differential backup copies only the files that have had their data change since the last full backup and does not change the archive bit value.

If a company wants the backup and recovery strategy to be as simple as possible, then they should only use full backups. They take more time and hard drive space to perform but they are the most efficient in recovery. If that option is not viable, a differential backup can be restored in just two steps; by first laying down the full backup then the differential backup on top of it. Remember that a differential backup records every piece of data in a file that has changed since the last full backup.

An incremental backup takes the most time in restoration because the full backup must be performed first and then every incremental backup taken since the last full backup. If daily incremental backups are taken but only monthly full backups, and a recover is needed on the 26th day of the month, the full backup restore must be performed first and then 26 incremental backups must be laid on top in the same order that they were taken in.

Interdependencies, both internal and external need to be understood and documented. Interdependencies include all the inputs to a function or application and where they come from as well as all the outputs to a function or application and where they go to. They include external dependencies such as network service providers and the post office for mail delivery and internal dependencies such as firewalls and local area networks.

The RTO or MTD for a business process or for an application is going to determine the recovery strategy for the process or application. The more time that can elapse before the recovery needs to occur, the more recovery options are available. The more time sensitive an application or function is, the fewer options an organization will have in selecting a recovery strategy.

Recovery Site Strategies

Depending on how much downtime an organization has before the technology recovery must be complete, recovery strategies selected for the technology environment could be any one of the following:

- **Dual Data Center**—This strategy is employed for applications, which cannot accept any downtime without negatively impacting the organization. The applications are split between two geographically dispersed data centers and either load balanced between the two centers or hot swapped between the two centers. The surviving data center must have enough head room to carry the full production load in either case.

- **Internal Hot Site**—This site is standby ready with all the technology and equipment necessary to run the applications positioned there. The planner will be able to effectively restart an application in a hot site recovery without having to perform any bare metal recovery of servers. If this is an internal solution, then often the organization will run non-time sensitive processes there such as development or test environments, which will be pushed aside for recovery of production when needed. When employing this strategy, it is important that the two environments be kept as close to identical as possible to avoid problems with O/S levels, hardware differences, capacity differences, etc., from preventing or delaying recovery.

- **External Hot Site**—This strategy has equipment on the floor waiting, but the environment must be rebuilt for the recovery. These are services contracted through a recovery service provider. Again, it is important that the two environments be kept as close to identical as possible to avoid problems with O/S levels, hardware differences, capacity differences, etc., from preventing or delaying recovery. Hot site vendors tend to have the most commonly used hardware and software products to attract the largest number of customers to utilize the site. Unique equipment or software

1121

would generally need to be provided by the organization either at time of disaster or stored there ahead of time.

- **Warm Site**—A leased or rented facility that is usually partially configured with some equipment, but not the actual computers. It will generally have all the cooling, cabling, and networks in place to accommodate the recovery but the actual servers, mainframe, etc., equipment are delivered to the site at time of disaster.

- **Cold Site**—A cold site is a shell or empty data center space with no technology on the floor. All technology must be purchased or acquired at the time of disaster.

There are advantages and disadvantages for each of these recovery strategies.

Advantages of a dual data center:

- Little or no downtime
- Ease of maintenance
- No recovery required

Disadvantages of a dual data center:

- Most expensive option
- Requires redundant hardware, networks, staffing
- Distance limitations

Advantages of internal or external hot site:

- Allows recovery to be tested
- Highly available
- Site can be operational within hours

Disadvantages of internal or external hot site:

- Expensive—Internal solution more expensive than external
- Hardware and software compatibility issues in external sites

Advantages of warm and cold site:

- Less expensive
- Available for longer recoveries

Disadvantages of warm and cold site:

- Not immediately available
- Not fully testable without extensive work

Mobile Sites

Another option available is the *mobile site*, meaning the data center of an organization is housed in a mobile trailer or possibly a standard sea cargo shipping container. Should disaster strike, an organization can simply load up the cargo container data center and move it to another location which has the power, resources and connectivity required to continue operations. *Figure 8.8* below, shows what a container based mobile solution may look like[1]:

Figure 8.8 - **An example of a Container Data Center module.**

The advantages to this approach include:

- Highly mobile and relatively easy to transport.
- Modular approach to building data centers.
- Buildings are not required to house equipment.

---

1   http://www.nasa.gov/offices/ocio/ittalk/06-2010_cloud_computing.html

The disadvantages include:

- "cold site" capability must be built at determined locations.
- The density and design of the container make upgrading and customizing challenging.
- Maintaining a shipping contract or equipment to move the container in times of disaster can be expensive.

Processing Agreement

Organizations may also choose to create different processing agreements with other organizations. This can take many forms, but typically can be viewed as reciprocal agreements or outsourced agreements.

Reciprocal agreements

Reciprocal agreements are between organizations who choose to share the risk of an outage with each other. Each organization commits to host the data and processing of each other in the event of a disaster. While this seems like a logical solution, it is fraught with problems.

The reality of the situation is both organizations must agree to either maintain spare capacity for the other or agree to a reduced processing capability should one fail. Additionally, if there is a disparity in the number of outages affecting one party the other party could request compensation. There is also a concern regarding other organization's ability to comply with all the requirements of the first. For example, if the first organization is a health care provider in the US they will be subject to the requirements of the Health Insurance Portability and Accountability Act (HIPAA.) Whoever is the partner for a reciprocal agreement must also agree to adhere to the rules of HIPAA even if that is not their core business. This leads organizations seeking to be in reciprocal agreements often searching for partners in their own industry. If competition is a concern then it may be very difficult to find a willing partner for a reciprocal agreement.

Outsourcing

To avoid the problems with reciprocal agreements and the cost of building alternative sites some organizations may choose to outsource their contingency operations and disaster recovery. This can be cost effective as the business may only incur major costs if a plan is activated, but also carries risks in the form of unknown capabilities and the ability to ensure compliance with requirements. For example, while a service level agreement (SLA) may state a service will only be down for a certain period of time it does not provide assurance the provider can actually meet the SLA during a disaster.

The benefits of outsourcing include:

- Service as needed.
- All requirements and execution responsibilities are on a third party.
- Little to no capital costs.
- Greater geographical options for continuity and recovery.

The disadvantages include

- More proactive testing and assessment to ensure capability is ready.
- Contract disputes should the vendor be unable to perform.
- Vendor lock-in if proprietary systems are deployed.
- Can cost more than building the capability if frequent outages occur.

Multiple Processing Sites

Multiple processing sites can be a solution for an organization if the organization's facilities separated throughout a country or the world. Multiple processing sites can be an advantage if numerous locations are required to conduct business and there is sufficient bandwidth and latency between the locations. If multiple processing sites are used for the production environment they should be treated as an organizational "reciprocal" agreement. This means workloads must be categorized based on criticality to the organization and each location must be able to process, store and transmits another's workload. While this can be a very cost efficient arrangement, it takes careful planning and coordination to ensure success.

The Disaster Recovery Process

Disaster recovery is the process of restoring services from a contingency state. DR is typically performed and described in several areas including response, personnel, communications, assessment, restoration, and training. The process must be documented. During adverse events personnel should rely on documented plans and not on ad hoc solutions as judgment may be impaired during stressful events such as natural disasters.

Documenting the Plan

Once recovery strategies have been developed and implemented for each area, the next step is to document the plan itself. The plan includes plan activation procedures, the recovery strategies to be used, how recovery efforts will be managed, how human resource issues will be handled, how recovery costs will be documented and paid for, how recovery communications to internal and external stakeholders will be handled, and detailed action plans for each team and each team member. The plan then needs to be distributed to everyone who has a role.

The documentation for recovery of the technology environment needs to be detailed enough that a person with a similar skill set, having never executed the procedures before could use them to perform the recovery. Documentation tends to be a task put off until it is too late; however, there is no guarantee that the people who perform this function in the production environment or the person who restored the infrastructure and application at the last test is going to be available at the time of disaster. In addition, disasters tend to be chaotic times where many demands are happening at once. Without the proper documentation, a practiced recovery strategy can fall apart and add to the chaos. Restoring an application can be challenging, restoring an entire data center just destroyed by a tornado can be overwhelming if not impossible without good documentation.

Event Management Requirements

- Strategy must be consistent regardless of event
- Need to establish an assessment process
- Event ownership needs to be defined
- Management teams identified
- Response teams identified
- Process for gathering of key decision makers
- Methods of communication need to be defined

Figure 8.9 - **The goals of an Event Management process**

The documentation needs to be stored at the recovery facility and every time the recovery is tested, the documentation should be used by the recovery participants and updated as needed. Once the level of confidence is high on the documentation, have someone who has never performed the procedure attempt it with the subject matter expert observing them. It may slightly delay the recovery time at that particular test but once complete, confidence in the documentation will be strong.

In addition to the actual recovery procedures, the planner also needs to document the process that will be used to manage the recovery in any type of event. See *Figure 8.9* for the goals of an event management process and *Figure 8.10* for the requirements of an event management process. Event management is about communication and response and because those two things are needed even when the problem is not to the level of a disaster, event management can become part of the fabric of an organization and how it manages problems that arise.

Goals of Event Management

- Single source of information
- Triage
- Rapid Escalation
- Consistent Problem Management
- Rumor control
- Make sure *everyone* who need to know does
- Allow the problem solvers room to solve
- Playbook which documents key roles and reponsibilities

Figure 8.10 - **The requirements of an Event Management process**

The event management process has to have a trigger, something that causes the process to begin. The trigger is an event. An event is defined as anything that either already has or has the potential to cause a significant organization interruption. A hardware failure, a power outage, a network failure, a building evacuation are all examples of events.

Response

Once an event is identified, it must be reported to a central communications group who will then be responsible for initiating the communications to those who must respond to the event and to those who are impacted by the event. The group that gets this initial report from the problem finder needs to operate twenty-four hours a day and seven days a week (24x7) because problems happen 24x7. Everyone in the organization should have this central number available to them to report problems. Commonly, these communications would go to an organization's help desk, technology operations center, physical security staff, or whoever in the organization is responsible for alarm monitoring.

In support of this communication, emergency notification lists are built by event type because different events have different event owners. A facility event such as a power failure, a water leak, or a fire would be owned by the facility staff, whereas a network outage would be owned by the network communication staff. In addition, each event would impact different organization people depending on their physical location or the technology they used.

Any event that occurs would first be reported to an assessment team. The assessment team's sole purpose is to determine if the problem requires further escalation and if so, who else needs to know about this event and who else needs to help fix the problem.

If it is determined that the event requires further escalation and communication, the first escalation team for that event type would be contacted. The first escalation team consists of the event owner, the event responders, and anyone else who has determined that when this type of disruption occurs, it directly and immediately affects their ability to execute the business or mission performed in that environment.

Many organizations manage this communication with a conference call. The conference call acts as a virtual command center to manage the communications and response to the event. One conference bridge should be for managing the responders, the people responsible for fixing the problem and another conference bridge meeting is held where the event owner can communicate to those impacted by the event. They communicate what the problem is, the current status of the problem, how long it should be before it is resolved, what is impacted and if necessary, when the next update will be provided and how. However, do not forget the conference bridge or the phone systems may be affected by an event. In those situations, plan for alternate communications. Internal and external communications are often the processes that determine if a contingency plan is successful.

The organization's senior leadership team generally does not need to be a part of the initial response to an issue. However, at some point they need to be made aware that the issue exists and if the problem persists or has a significant impact, so they may be called in to make decisions on how to manage the organizational impacts and to coordinate the larger scale response if needed.

Every event that the firm has should be managed through this process. From a small event such as a plumbing leak that has impacted workstations on the floor below, to large events such as typhoons, hurricanes and tornadoes. If an organization will design and use a graduated contingency plan, it will be used and understood on a frequent basis. Everyone understands how he or she will be communicated to and where to go to get the right information or help needed when a catastrophic disaster occurs. Event management takes practice.

The event management plan is part of the BC and DR plan. Making a decision to execute the BCP or DR plan is one possible response to an event. The event management plan needs to identify who is authorized to declare a disaster, how a declaration is done, and when the decision to "declare" is made, how it will be communicated to the teams that need to respond.

The executive emergency management team is a team that consists of the senior executives within the organization who have an overall responsibility for the recovery of the organization and services to others. As needed during the emergency, these individuals will participate in the command centers, virtual or physical established for the recovery efforts and in the execution of the plan. The plan documents both a formal integrated response process for management and on-site coverage and support in emergencies.

The executive team does not directly manage the day-to-day operations of the organization under normal circumstances and is not expected to have day-to-day responsibilities in managing the recovery efforts from the emergency. However, the executive team will respond to and assist in the resolution of issues, which need their direction. They will be the spokesperson for the organization to the media and make decisions on how the organization will manage the business impacts of the event.

The executives of most organizations are concerned with strategic issues, not with tactical delivery. While the next team, the emergency management team, needs to be held accountable for the tactical response from the event; the executive team needs to focus on the strategic response. It is the executive team that will lead the organization through the crisis, not manage the crisis itself. *Figure 8.11* shows the difference between crisis management and crisis leadership.

Crisis Management vs. Crisis Leadership

Managing	vs.	Leading
React		Anticipate
Short-term		Long-term
Process		Principles
Narrow		Wide Focus
Tactical		Strategic

Figure 8.11 - **Crisis Management vs. Crisis Leadership**

The emergency management team is comprised of individuals who report directly to the command center and have responsibility to oversee the recovery and restoration process being executed by the emergency response teams. They are responsible for communicating the recovery status to the executive management team and making the necessary management decisions to support the recovery efforts. The emergency management team leader has overall responsibility for the recovery team and communications with the executive management team.

The objectives and the functions of the executive management team are:

- Make a preliminary assessment of the damage.
- Notify senior management on the current status, impact to organization and plan of action.
- Declare the disaster if necessary.
- Initiate the plan during the emergency situation.
- Organize and control the command centers as a central point of control of the recovery efforts.
- Organize and provide administrative support to the recovery effort.
- Administer and direct the problem management function.

Emergency response teams are comprised of individuals who are responsible for executing the recovery processes necessary for the continuity or recovery of critical organization functions in that site. These individuals report to the alternate sites for their critical functions to execute the recovery process. They report to the emergency management team through emergency response team leaders who have overall responsibility for the response teams' efforts in those locations. The response teams may be broken into sub-teams, each with their own leader to facilitate the recovery effort.

The primary responsibilities of the members of these teams are as follows:

- Retrieve offsite records and recovery information from offsite storage.
- Report to the alternate site identified in their procedures.
- Execute the organization recovery procedures for their area of responsibilities in the order of priority identified.
- Communicate the status of the recovery to the command centers as needed.
- Identify issues or problems to be escalated to the management team for resolution.

1133

- Establish shifts for recovery team members to support the recovery effort 24x7.
- Establish liaison with alternate site personnel if needed.
- Support efforts to return to normal operations.
- Reestablish support operations affected by the disaster
- Identify replacement equipment/software needed for the recovery effort and to return to normal operations.

Command centers are set up as a central location for communications and decision making during an emergency situation. Command centers are set up in response to the disaster and are equipped with a copy of the plan document and other resources which may be needed in a disaster. For insurance purposes, it is important that costs associated with the recovery effort be tracked as well as payment for purchases of needed supplies and replacement equipment be expedited. Procedures for handling finance issues must also be included in the plan.

If there are multiple locations for the organization, there needs to be an initial response plan for each site where the organization conducts business. That plan will document the following:

- What organization or technology operates at that site
- The recovery strategy in place for the organization or technology
- Who the decision makers are
- Where everyone should go if they cannot get back into the building
- The declaration process for declaring a disaster for that site
- The location of the alternate site
- Travel directions to get to the alternate site
- Seat assignments at the alternate site
- Hotels, transportation services, and supply options near the alternate site

For each recovery strategy, detail execution procedures need to be documented on how to execute the recovery strategy at the time of disaster. Again, these procedures need to be written in such a way that someone with a similar skill set or background, having never done them before, would be able to pick up the procedure and execute it.

When documenting the plan, do not forget some of the simple things often taken for granted when business is normal. Some areas to consider are actions such as planning for delivery of office supplies to the alternate site, setting up a package delivery account for the alternate site like UPS or Airborne, having a postage meter for the alternate site, and knowing where the post office is located.

If the organization uses some type of mail zone for internal delivery of mail between sites, make sure the plan sets one up for the alternate site as well. Be prepared to have a "switchboard operator" or an automated service at the alternate site until the company can publish a new phone directory for the employees working from the alternate site. This operator or service would manage a central phone number that can be published quickly to the appropriate stakeholders until the new phone numbers for individuals can be published.

Personnel

One common factor left out of many plans is human resource issues. Disasters are events which can greatly impact humans and it is important that the plan document the responsibility of the firm to the employees participating in the recovery. Organizations need to recognize that to respond to the organization's needs in a disaster situation, it must also recognize the hardships placed on the families of its response team. To be able to give the best to the company at the time when it is needed most, employees need to have a level of comfort that their family members are safe and the employee's absence during the recovery effort will not place undue hardship on them.

The level of support to team members will be clearly defined by the nature of the disaster itself. In the case of natural disaster where the employee's family may be at risk, it may provide for a temporary relocation of family members or allowing the family to accompany the employee to the recovery site. It may range from facilitating dependent care services, company-paid travel for employees to return home for a visit or for family members to travel to recovery locations, or cash advances to provide for family needs. This section of the plan also needs to document how the company will handle the injury or death of an employee that occurs during an event.

Do not forget to include administrative support as part of the recovery team. Planners do not often think of administrative support staff as being "time sensitive" but they are welcome additions in a recovery. They do things no one else has the time to do—answering phones, sending communications as requested to communicate to recovery staff, making travel arrangements for recovery staff, ordering food at recovery locations, keeping minutes of the status meetings, making copies, arranging courier service, keeping track of the locations of employees, and similar administrative and personnel related functions.

Communications

Employee Notification

Employees who are members of an emergency notification list will be contacted directly in the event of an emergency situation by the responsible management team member. The planner will need to document the process of how the organization will communicate with the remaining employees about the event and the recovery efforts.

A common method of doing this is having a contingency information line established for the general employee population to get information about what happened and the progress of the recovery. To keep this number handy, many organizations put it on a sticker on the back of their employee badges and on a magnet the employee is supposed to take home and put on their refrigerator. This same number can be used by the company to communicate office closures and early release or late start notifications in the event of severe weather.

The plan needs to document how the organization communications to all the stakeholders (*Figure 8.12*) will be managed.

Potential Stakeholders

- ☑ Employees and their families
- ☑ Contractors and business partners
- ☑ Facility and Site Managers
- ☑ Staff Managers (HR, IT, etc.)
- ☑ Senior Managers; Board of Directors
- ☑ Institutional investors and shareholders
- ☑ Insurance representatives
- ☑ Suppliers and Distributors
- ☑ Customers
- ☑ Goverment Regulators and Politicians
- ☑ Competitors
- ☑ Media representatives
- ☑ Unions
- ☑ Communities
- ☑ Internet users or bloggers
- ☑ Industry activist groups

Figure 8.12 - **Potential Stakeholders**

Employees who talk with customers or clients as a part of their normal organization day should be provided with a statement or list of statements regarding the recovery effort. It is important that EVERYONE tell the same story. Any customer or vendor not satisfied with the response provided should be referred to management or the organizational communications staff.

As the recovery progresses, the company will need to provide recovery status updates to all the stakeholders. It is important that the statements be honest and concise. It is also important to consider each stakeholder's various needs and concerns. Employees may be worried about their jobs, where stockholders may be more worried about the impact to the company stock and customers just want to know that their product or service will be there when they need it.

The planner will need to document a process for reporting and managing problems that will occur during the recovery. Even if the plan was tested yesterday and everything worked perfectly, unexpected problems may happen during the recovery. There needs to be a process in the plan to document them, triage them, escalate them, fix them, and report on them. If the company already has a formal problem management/change management process, use that in the plan. If not, invent one to use in a recovery and test the problem management process while testing recovery.

If the process for managing problems day to day is to have the problem reported to a central group and a ticket opened and assigned to a responder, use that process in recovery. Even during alternate site tests when organization users come to validate alternate site readiness or during a data center recovery exercise, make people call in a ticket before a problem is addressed.

During the course of the recovery efforts, it may be helpful to establish conference bridges to communicate recovery issues and to coordinate communications between the different recovery locations. Multiple conference bridges can be used for different parts of the recovery. Often it is best to keep the discussions between the technical groups and the organization partners separate because technical language barriers can cause confusion.

Assessment

During an event, a decision will need to be made regarding the severity of the event. A person or process within the contingency team will need to determine the impact of the event on the organization and its mission and determine the appropriate response. This is done by using tiers or categorizations of such as the following:

- **Non-Incident:** These events are typically caused by system malfunctions or human errors which result in limited to minor disruptions of service. There is a short period of downtime and alternate processing or storage facilities are not required.

- **Incident:** Events which cause an entire facility or service to be inoperative for a significant amount of time. These events require the enactment of the disaster recovery plan and reporting of information and status to senior management and may involve crisis management.

- **Severe Incident:** Significant destruction or interruption to an organization's mission, facility and personnel. These events require the enactment of the DR plan and may involve the building of a new primary facility. These events require senior management reporting and crisis management.

Restoration

The final parts of the documented plan are about restoration of the primary environment and transition back to normal operations. While other parts of the organization are focusing on the resumption of organization in the alternate site, part of the staff needs to focus on what needs to be done to restore the production environment of the primary facility.

Ownership of this process is dependent on what was impacted by the event. In most cases, it will be a coordinated effort between the facilities staff to restore the building to its original state or acquire and build out new space, the technology staff to repair or replace technology hardware, software or network components affected, and records management to recover lost or damaged records.

The organization's legal staff and insurance agent will play a role in the restoration and recovery from the event. No recovery efforts should begin until both have been contacted but the area of impact should be secured from further loss and, where possible, pictures taken of the damage before anything is removed, repaired, or replaced.

The transition back to normal operations is easier than the recovery for the simple fact that it is a planned event. The plan can be to return all at once or the plan can move operations back over time to control issues that may arise from the transition and prevent yet another event. General transition plans should be documented about the process to move back but detailed plans will need to be written to respond to the specific issues of the transition that results from the type of event that the organization is in recovery for. Moving an organizational operation back to its primary space is challenging but is usually easier than moving a data center. If the data center was impacted by this event, then the organization needs to manage the transition project like a data center move.

For example, an organization may be located in alternate sites for 15 months following the events of an earthquake and for two months following the events of a hurricane. After 9 weeks in the earthquake alternate site, an interim transition plan was executed where employees were distributed between two interim sites while the primary site was repaired and built out. The interim sites used spare equipment and furniture from storage and other sites to populate the space. When it was time to re-populate the data center, asset swaps were used vs. moving the technology that was used in the alternate sites.

Assets swaps involve negotiating with a vendor to provide the equipment to populate the new or restored data center. This allows the ability to burn-in and test the new equipment and the building infrastructure before the actual move. After the move back is completed, the equipment in the alternate site was given back to the appropriate vendor, moved back to storage, or sold. In the event equipment is sold or traded the organization must ensure proper decommission and sanitation processes are followed.

Provide Training

It does not matter how good the plan is if no one knows what is in it. It is important that every single person in the firm be able to know what to do in an emergency. Business continuity needs to be imbedded in the culture of the organization. To accomplish that, the planner must introduce training and awareness programs that involve all the stakeholders.

The type of training needed is different for different populations of the organization. The leadership team needs crisis management training. Their role in a recovery is not to execute the recovery but to lead the organization back to organization as normal. The technical teams need to know not just the procedures for executing the recovery but also the logistics of where they are going and how they will get there.

The planner will need to design awareness programs for different audiences. Various vehicles for the delivery of training and awareness programs can be utilized depending on the audience that needs to hear the message. The intranet portion of the organizational Web site is a good vehicle for communicating the plan to the general employee population.

The customers of an organization may want to know that the company has a plan and will be there for them no matter what. They should be aware of the planned course of action in the event of a disaster, alternate contact numbers and any changes in operational procedures they may expect. The organizational Web site available to the public may be a good means of communicating information to the customers of an organization.

The employees need to know basic information about the plan and their role in the plan. This includes assembly areas following evacuation, who the leadership team is, how they will be communicated to after an event, alternate site location including directions to get there and when they should report to the alternate site.

Conducting exercises are also a form of training for those who have a direct role in the recovery. Whether the exercise is a tabletop exercise, an actual exercise at the alternate site or just a call notification exercise, the team will practice their role during the exercises. The more the plan is exercised the more confident the recovery team will be if or when it happens for real.

Putting a section on the BCP program in a new employee orientation session is a great vehicle for introducing the program when an employee starts with the organization. The information provided can explain the overall scope of the plan, what they should expect if a disaster were to happen, and where they can go to get additional information on the program.

Exercise, Assess and Maintain the Plan

Once the plan has been completed and the recovery strategies fully implemented, it is important to test all parts of the plan to validate that it would work in a real event. It is often wise to stop using the word "test" for this and begin to use the word exercise. The reason to call them exercises is that when the word "test" is used, people think pass or fail. In fact, there is no way to fail a contingency test. If the planners knew that it all worked, they would not bother to test it. The reason to test is to find out what does not work so it can be fixed before it happens for real.

There are many different types of exercises that the planner can conduct. Some will take minutes, others hours or days. The amount of exercise planning needed is entirely dependent on the type of exercise, the length of the exercise, and the scope of the exercise the planner will plan to conduct. The most common types of exercises are call exercises, walkthrough exercises, simulated or actual exercises, and compact exercises.

A call exercise shown in *Figure 8.13* is how the planner takes the emergency notification list and attempts to call everyone on it to see how long it takes to reach them and to see if they are prepared to respond.

Call exercises can be conducted using the method of one person calling five people who each in turn call five people and so forth, or the organization can use some type of automated system for making calls. If the planner has an automated system, it is important to periodically use the old way to reach out to people just in case the automated system is not working at the time of a real event.

When conducting call exercises, it is common to have the participants reached to call into a conference bridge to acknowledge receipt of the communication and so that the team can communicate with each other as they would if this event was real. It is an opportunity to have people talk to each other and validate the teams' readiness to respond.

1143

What to Do:

Call everyone on the emergency notification list, validate their phone numbers are accurate, and that the team is prepared to respond

How to Do It:

Call their cell

Call them at home

Page them - If they do not respond within a certain timeframe, try again or try reaching their backup. Require a response.

Why Do It:

Validate the phone numbers are accurate

Find out how long it takes to reach everyone

Determine what percentage of people are unavailable

Exercise call notification procedure

Figure 8.13 - **Sample Call Notification exercise**

The next type of exercise is a tabletop or walkthrough exercise as shown in *Figure 8.14*. When the organization has a new plan, the best type of tabletop exercise to do is a walkthrough of the actual plan document with everyone who has a role in the plan. Even the planning team is unlikely to read the entire document and walking through the plan helps to ensure that everyone knows the whole story and everyone's role. Walking through the plan with the team will help to identify gaps in the plan so that they can be addressed.

Once the planner has conducted that type of walkthrough, they can begin scenario-based tabletop exercises. These exercises are where the planner will gather the team in a meeting and pretend that something has happened and the team members are supposed to respond as if it is a real event. The planner could pretend that there is a power outage and based on what is backed up by alternate power sources such as UPS and generators and what is not, how the technology or organization would be impacted, and how the team would exercise the portions of the plan to address that scenario.

What to Do:
    Walkthrough all or a portion of the recovery procedures with the team

How to Do It:
    Set up a date and time
    Contact team members and invite them
    Walkthrough the plan with the team members
    Take notes of comments and action items

Why Do It:
    Use as training and awareness for team members
    Identify plan weakness or deficiencies
    Improve recovery capabilities

Figure 8.14 - **Sample Walkthrough exercise**

Tabletop exercises are used to validate the plan within an actual scenario without having to actually execute the recovery procedures. The planner will "talk through" what the team would do, they will not do it. These types of exercises are especially helpful in working through the decision processes that will occur for the leadership team when faced with an event and for other teams to talk through recovery options based on the scenario being presented for the exercise.

The next type of exercise is a simulated or actual exercise shown in *Figure 8.15*. The only difference between a simulated exercise and an actual exercise is that the first rule of testing is the planner will never create a disaster by testing for one. The planner must make every effort to make certain that what is being tested will not impact the production environment whether organization or technical. For example, when testing the routing of call center calls from a primary site to an alternate site, don't take live calls. Wait till the call center is closed or set up a test 800 number and only route that one to test the routing, the messaging, the queues

1145

What to Do:
   Simulate execution or actually execute recovery procedures at the alternate site

How to Do It:
   Create test scenario
   Obtain management/leadership permission
   Team members respond to scenario by executing recovery procedures
   Take notes on comments and action items

Why Do It:
   Use as training and awareness for team members
   Identify plan weakness or deficiencies
   Improve recovery capabilities
   Validate alternate site readiness

Figure 8.15 - **Sample Simulated or Actual exercise**

and overflows, etc. at the alternate site. In that way, the planner limits the possibility of a live customer call coming into the alternate site or worse yet not going anywhere but getting lost in the cloud during a test.

The purpose of this type of exercise is to validate alternate site readiness, whether this is the alternate site for technology recovery or for organization operations, or both. The planner should run this exercise as much as possible the way it would happen if it happened for real. Clearly because exercises are planned events, the planner will have an opportunity to reduce the actual timeline by pre-staging certain things that the planner could not do if this were an unplanned event. Examples include pulling backup tapes or hard copy information from offsite storage and having it delivered to the alternate site and ensuring it is ready for use on the day of the exercise. What the planner should not do as part of the planning is plan for success. Remember, the reason for the exercise is to find out what does not work so it can be fixed before it happens for real.

An actual exercise should be considered successful if the required resources, equipment, and connectivity of voice and data are recovered to the satisfaction of the organization unit at the designated alternate site within the timeframe required. An actual exercise should also be considered successful if the above did not happen so the planner can fix it before a real incident. There truly is no way to fail a contingency plan exercise. The only time the planner will fail is if it happens for real and the organization does not recover. See *Figure 8.15* and *Figure 8.16* for some mandatory and highly recommended test strategies.

The final exercise is a compact exercise. This is where the planner will begin with a call exercise and continue right through an actual exercise. These are sometimes done as surprise exercises where very few people know in advance when they are going to happen. For example, a contingency planner could conduct a compact exercise, which begins with

---

Highly Recommended Alternate Site Components

☑ Was the management team, critical vendors, and interdependencies notified at time of test and did they participate?

☑ Was the problem mangement strategy tested during the test?

☑ Was the Production Network available on time and with sufficient bandwidth (for external sites)?

☑ Was network response time acceptable?

☑ Was all information required for recovery available and did backups have good data?

☑ Were all platforms and applications restored?

☑ Was the desktop image complete and current and restored in time required?

☑ Was the business able to print?

☑ Were end-user directions provided?

☑ Were there sufficient number of phones (inbound and outbound trunks available and tested)?

☑ Was voice recording tested? (if applicable)

☑ Were phone instructions provided to the business users?

☑ Was voice mail available at the alternate site?

Figure 8.16 - **Highly-recommended alternate site test components**

an unannounced evacuation of over 4000 employees from three buildings on the same campus. The general employee population is allowed to go back into the building but the BC and DR teams are not allowed back into the space. They have to gather their leadership team, get them to make a "decision" to go to the alternate site, assemble their teams, go to the alternate site, and then "execute" their recovery.

The local police, fire, and EMTs may participate in the exercise. Some members may pretend to be injured, while another may walk around with a movie camera pretending to be the media. Exercises such as these can be outstanding learning examples.

After every exercise the planner conducts, the exercise results need to be published and action items identified to address the issues that were uncovered by the exercise. Action items should be tracked until they have been resolved and, where appropriate, the plan updated. It is very unfortunate when an organization has the same issue in subsequent tests simply because someone did not update the plan.

Update and Maintenance of the Plan

All team members have an obligation to participate in the change control process. The plan document and all related procedures will need to be updated on an on-going basis such as after each exercise and after each material change to the production, IT, or organization environment. The procedures should be reviewed every three months and the formal audit of the procedures should be conducted annually. The exercise reports produced following each exercise should be provided to internal audit and internal audit should include review of the plan documentation and test results as part of their regular audit cycle. A sample data center exercise report in included in *Figure 8.17*.

Note the data center exercise report contains the following information on each platform and application recovered:

- The name of the technology or application restored
- The RTO for the application

June 2013 Disaster Recovery Exercise Report

Application/ Platform	RTO	Last Tested	Documented Plan Offsite	Recovery met RTO	Recovered Successfully	End User Validation	Batch 1 Success	Batch 2 Success	Support Team
Applications									
Call Center Application	24 Hours	8-Jun					N/A	N/A	Joe Smith
Corp. Fin. - ABC	72 Hours	8-Jun					N/A	N/A	Dave Brown
Corp. Fin. - Peoplesoft GL	72 Hours	8-Jun					N/A	N/A	Linda Jones
Corp. Fin. - Peoplesoft AP	72 Hours	8-Jun					N/A	N/A	Mark Sawin
Corp. Fin. - Treasury Ops	72 Hours	8-Jun					N/A	N/A	Scott Gray
Account Applications	24 Hours	8-Jun							Mike Beta
Corp. Serv. - Employee DB	72 Hours	8-Jun					N/A	N/A	Michael Green
Infrastructure									
AS400	24 Hours	7-Nov				N/A	N/A	N/A	Joe Myer
CAT Switch	12 Hours	7-Nov				N/A	N/A	N/A	Bob Gerawn
CICS	12 Hours	7-Nov				N/A	N/A	N/A	Chris Alpha
Cisco Routers	12 Hours	7-Nov				N/A	N/A	N/A	John Crank
Cleartrust	24 Hours	7-Nov				N/A	N/A	N/A	Tom Skye
DB2	12 Hours	7-Nov				N/A	N/A	N/A	Lucy James
DNS/DHCP Gateway	12 Hours	7-Nov				N/A	N/A	N/A	Ned Young
DS3	12 Hours	7-Nov				N/A	N/A	N/A	Dave Anderson
LAN	12 Hours	7-Nov				N/A	N/A	N/A	Sam Okra
Linux	24 Hours	7-Nov				N/A	N/A	N/A	Frank Perry
Mainframe IPL	12 Hours	7-Nov				N/A	N/A	N/A	Mike Night
RS6000	24 Hours	7-Nov				N/A	N/A	N/A	Jim Dyer
SUN	24 Hours	7-Nov				N/A	N/A	N/A	Liz Harris
Alt Site Network	2 Hours	7-Nov				N/A	N/A	N/A	Mike O'Toole
Windows	24 Hours	7-Nov				N/A	N/A	N/A	Lucas Kerry

Figure 8.17 - **Sample Data Center Exercise report**

- The date last tested
- Whether the application was recovered in the RTO during that test
- Whether the application was recovered at all even if it did not meet the RTO

- Whether current documented repeatable processes for recovery are stored offsite
- If the application had a batch cycle, was it run and was it successful
- Application owner

The plan needs to have version control numbers on it to make sure everyone is using the current version of the plan. The plan needs to be published to everyone who has a role and also needs to be stored in a secure offsite location that not only survives the disaster but is accessible immediately following the disaster.

Transitioning from Project to Program

The contingency planning program is an ongoing process. All of the tasks defined to originally build the program need to be repeated on a regular basis to ensure that the plan stays current with the organization and technology environment of the company through the years. In support of that, the program has annual requirements that need to be completed by the planning team in order to remain in compliance with the program. See the sample report card in *Figure 8.18*.

Business Continuity Program Status Report

Home Office Business Area	BCP Contact	ENL	Identity Functions	Alt Site Requirements	Technology Review	Inter-dependencies	Published Plan	Call Test	Walkthrough Test	Alternate Site Test
DC Operations	Dave Caster									
Help Desk	Mike Lamp									
Facilities	Priscilla Jones									
Finance	Jen Katto									
Operations	Pam Halperb									
Process Support	Jennifer Potts									
Mail Room	Joe Kalin									
Office General Council	Linda Logan									
Human Resources	Steve Riley									
Audit	Mary French									

Figure 8.18 - **Sample Report Card**

The following is a brief explanation of the contingency planning program and its components.

The contingency planning program is designed to serve as an aid in developing and maintaining viable organization function contingency plans.

The organizational contingency planning program provides for the continuation of the company's critical organization functions in the event of an organization interruption. The organizational program assists and prepares the various areas of the company to document and exercise emergency response and recovery plans.

The senior manager of each operating area has the responsibility for ensuring the organization's survival. To help facilitate this, each senior manager will appoint a business continuity planner to coordinate the contingency planning and response efforts of the organization functions performed by that functional area.

The emergency management organization (EMO) is formed to provide both a formal response process for management; and on-site coverage, support and expertise during large-scale emergencies. The EMO ensures that all locations and operating areas will receive an appropriate, coordinated response in the event of a serious outage of any type.

The EMO management team is the decision-making body of the EMO and is usually comprised of areas within the company that play a key role in responding to emergency situations including the following areas:

- Security
- Real estate
- Systems
- Human resources
- Organizational communications

- Compliance
- Risk and insurance management
- Organizational contingency planning
- Each of these groups has specific responsibilities in the event of an emergency, including:
- Responding to incidents and emergencies
- Determining the extent of the impending or actual emergency situation
- Establishing and maintaining communication with senior management
- Communicating with employees and customers
- Managing media communications, security, systems, facilities
- Coordinating and integrating business continuity planners

The organizational emergency operations center (EOC) has been established to provide a location, equipped with all of the necessary resources to manage the organization resumption process whenever the EMO is activated.

Roles and Responsibilities

The organizational contingency planning group develops, implements, and maintains a worldwide business contingency planning program for the company. This group provides leadership and guidance in maintaining integrated continuity of critical organization functions, and assists management in achieving timely recovery of organization operations in the event of organization interruption. The roles and responsibilities of the group are:

- Setting strategic direction and plans for all organization units to ensure BC and effective emergency management.
- Integrating the contingency planning process across organization units when the nature of the organization requires it.
- Providing consulting services and direction to senior level contingency managers.

- Coordinating and integrating the activation of emergency response organizations with the organization units.
- Providing periodic management reporting and status.
- Ensuring executive management compliance with the contingency planning program.
- Ensuring the identification and maintenance of all critical organization functions, and requirements.
- Procuring and managing the alternate sites used to support recovery of the operations of the company whether technical or organization.
- Developing, implementing, and maintaining policy and guidelines for all organization units to follow.
- Developing and maintaining testing and maintenance programs for all contingency planning organizations.
- Providing training, maintenance, and support for approved contingency planning tools.

The business continuity planners act as a focal point for their company in any situation involving contingency planning or emergency response. The planner plans the integration of a series of tasks, procedures, and information that direct actions at the time of a organization interruption in order to reduce confusion, improve communications, and achieve a timely continuation/resumption of organization. The roles and responsibilities of the business continuity planner include:

- Provide primary contact for their functional area to handle coordination response during a organization interruption.
- Act as a resource for contingency planning efforts within their area of responsibility.
- Secure appointment, training, and backup of all contingency planning and response teams.
- Assist in the design and maintenance of alternate sites.
- Maintain currency of all contingency planning documentation including all deliverables listed in *Figure 8.19* .

Program Requirements

	Current BCP Deliverable	Description/Specifics	Due Date
1	Management Engagement	- Appoint BCP - Established Goal for BCP - Present to President	Ongoing
2	BCP Engagement	- Attend monthly BCP meetings - Participates in training conferences - Actively work BCP deliverables list	Ongoing
3	Cell phones for key employees	- Maintain event management listings	Ongoing
4	Published ENL	- Publish and distribute emergency conference call in number and procedure to key personnel	Quarterly
5	Conference Bridge Procedures	- Establish and distribute emergency conference call in number and procedure to key personnel	Annually
6	Identify business functions and time sensitivity	- ID all functions the group performs - ID on core or mission critical function although the rating may be below A	Semi Annually
7	Alternate site requirements defined	- Document systems and personnel needed to perform functions	Semi Annually
8	Perform technology review	- Inventory and assess hardware and software used by the business function - Participate in validating technology recovery	Annually
9	Interdependencies defined	- ID any internal or external dependencies	Annually
10	Published Plan	- Signed off by leadership	Annually
11	Call Notification exercise	- Report results	Semi Annually
12	Walkthrough/Tabletop exercise	- Report results	Annually
13	Alternate site exercise	- Report results	Semi Annually

Figure 8.19 - **List of Ccontingency Planning documentation**

Business Continuity and Other Risk Areas

There is a significant interrelationship between information security and BC and other risk management areas such as physical security, records management, vendor management, internal audit, financial risk management, operational risk management, and regulatory compliance (legal/regulatory risk) in the context of an overall risk management framework.

It does not matter how strong the firewall is or how good the password enforcement is if the physical security practices are so poor that unauthorized individuals can easily gain access to the company space. It does not matter if the company has an alternate site if the records management practices are so poor that the data needed to recover the organization is not available offsite. All of these efforts are enterprise-wide in scope, they intersect each other at various points and the extent to which we do one well and another area poorly can impact all the other areas. Each of these areas needs to work collaboratively to effectively manage risk.

The following are free internet based resources related to disaster recovery and business continuity:

NIST Special Publication 800-34. Contingency Planning Guide for Information Technology Systems
http://csrc.nist.gov/publications/nistpubs/800-34-rev1/sp800-34-rev1_errata-Nov11-2010.pdf

Example IT system disaster recovery plan template
http://net.educause.edu/ir/library/word/SPC0561D.doc

Personal Continuity
http://www.continuitycompliance.org/what-is-personal-continuity/

Summary and Conclusion

In summary, the BC and DR domain is comprised of the process for determining risks, adopting counter measures to mitigate those risks and developing real, tested and executable plans for continuing the organization if the disaster occurs. BC and DR is more than just planning, it is executing, integrating with change management and using BC as part of routine operations. Organizations with well-defined and executed contingency programs are much more likely not only to survive during adverse events, but also outperform other organizations due to process maturity.

Review Questions

1. Which phrase best defines a business continuity/disaster recovery plan?

    A. A set of plans for preventing a disaster.

    B. An approved set of preparations and sufficient procedures for responding to a disaster.

    C. A set of preparations and procedures for responding to a disaster without management approval.

    D. The adequate preparations and procedures for the continuation of all organization functions.

2. Regardless of industry, which element of legal and regulatory requirements are all industries subject to?

    A. Sarbanes–Oxley

    B. HIPAA

    C. Due diligence

    D. BS25999

3. Which of the following statements **BEST** describes the extent to which an organization should address business continuity or disaster recovery planning?

    A. Continuity planning is a significant organizational issue and should include all parts or functions of the company.

    B. Continuity planning is a significant technology issue and the recovery of technology should be its primary focus.

    C. Continuity planning is required only where there is complexity in voice and data communications.

    D. Continuity planning is a significant management issue and should include the primary functions specified by management.

1157

4. Business impact analysis is performed to **BEST** identify:

    A. The impacts of a threat to the organization operations.

    B. The exposures to loss to the organization.

    C. The impacts of a risk on the organization.

    D. The cost efficient way to eliminate threats.

5. During the risk analysis phase of the planning, which of the following actions could **BEST** manage threats or mitigate the effects of an event?

    A. Modifying the exercise scenario.

    B. Developing recovery procedures.

    C. Increasing reliance on key individuals

    D. Implementing procedural controls.

6. The **BEST** reason to implement additional controls or safeguards is to:

    A. deter or remove the risk.

    B. identify and eliminate the threat.

    C. reduce the impact of the threat.

    D. identify the risk and the threat.

7. Which of the following statements **BEST** describes business impact analysis?

    A. Risk analysis and organization impact analysis are two different terms describing the same project effort.

    B. A business impact analysis calculates the probability of disruptions to the organization.

    C. A business impact analysis is critical to development of a business continuity plan.

    D. A business impact analysis establishes the effect of disruptions on the organization.

8. The term "disaster recovery" refers to the recovery of:

    A. organization operations.

    B. technology environment.

    C. manufacturing environment.

    D. personnel environments.

9. Which of the following terms **BEST** describes the effort to determine the consequences of disruptions that could result from a disaster?

A. Business impact analysis.

B. Risk analysis.

C. Risk assessment.

D. Project problem definition

10. The **BEST** advantage of using a cold site as a recovery option is that it

___

A. is a less expensive recovery option.

B. can be configured and made operational for any organization function.

C. is preconfigured for communications and can be customized for organization functions.

D. is the most available option for testing server and communications restorations.

11. The elements of risk are as follows:

A. Natural disasters and man made disasters

B. Threats, assets and mitigating controls

C. Risk and business impact analysis

D. business impact analysis and mitigating controls

12. The term "Recovery Time Objective" RTO means

A. The maximum time a service or system can be unavailable.

B. The amount of time a disaster recovery should take.

C. The time required to switch from a primary site to an alternate.

D. The time which must elapse before enacting a crisis communication plan.

13. The most efficient restore from tape back-up is:

A. Full backup

B. Incremental Backup

C. Partial Backup

D. Differential backup

14. One of the advantages of a hot site recovery solution is that it

    A. is less expensive

    B. is Highly highly available

    C. does not incur downtime

    D. no maintenance is required

15. Which of the following methods is not acceptable for exercising the business continuity plan?

    A. Table-top exercise.

    B. Call exercise.

    C. Simulated exercise.

    D. Halting a production application or function.

16. Which of the following is the primary desired result of any well-planned business continuity exercise?

    A. Identifies plan strengths and weaknesses.

    B. Satisfies management requirements.

    C. Complies with auditor's requirements.

    D. Maintains shareholder confidence

17. A business continuity plan is best updated and maintained:

    A. Annually or when requested by auditors.

    B. Only when new versions of software are deployed.

    C. Only when new hardware is deployed.

    D. During the configuration and change management process.

18. Which of the following is **MOST** important for successful business continuity?

    A. Senior leadership support.

    B. Strong technical support staff.

    C. Extensive wide area network infrastructure.

    D. An integrated incident response team.

19. Which of the following is the **BEST** alternate site approach if the recovery time objective of a service is two months?

    A. Cold site.

    B. Reciprocal agreement.

    C. Warm site.

    D. Hot site.

20. A service's recovery point objective is zero. Which approach BEST ensures the requirement is met?

    A. RAID 6 with a hot site alternative.

    B. RAID 0 with a warm site alternative

    C. RAID 0 with a cold site alternative

    D. RAID 6 with a reciprocal agreement.

Domain 9

Legal, Regulations, Investigations, and Compliance

THE LEGAL, REGULATIONS, INVESTIGATIONS, AND COMPLIANCE DOMAIN addresses general computer crime legislation and regulations, the investigative measures and techniques that can be used to determine if an incident has occurred, and the gathering, analysis, and management of evidence if it exists. The focus is on concepts and internationally accepted methods, processes, and procedures. This chapter will avoid in-depth discussions of country- or region-specific laws, legislation, and regulations. Although some regional examples are presented to clarify certain discussion points, these will be limited to the emphasis of principles common across most, if not all, jurisdictions.

The chapter is geared toward the conceptual issues and concerns and is not intended as a deep technical discussion of the domain. This conceptual level of depth is in keeping with the need to proverbially walk before running. Without a solid understanding of the concepts and issues, any deep technical discussions would be problematic and superficial. A secondary reason for the choice of depth is directly related to the sheer size of this topic; it is not unrealistic to find entire books devoted to each of the sections this chapter will attempt to address; thus, only a high-level examination is possible and appropriate.

Having qualified and constrained the scope of this chapter, it is time to delve into what exactly will be covered and what the security professional can expect to glean from the pages contained herein. The chapter has been logically broken down into broad categories, each with several subsections in coordination with the (ISC)^2 CISSP® Candidate Information Bulletin (CIB) The intention is not to turn readers into international law experts, but to introduce the context and backdrop for the remainder of the chapter. Under the major legal systems, at a high level, principles of common law; civil or code law; and customary, religious, and mixed legal systems will be examined. Similarities and differences between these systems that are important for information security professionals will be briefly introduced.

Areas to be focused on will include detection and investigation of information system-related events, incident response from a policy requirement and developing a response capacity are explored, as are proper evidence management and handling procedures. These sections go into more of the investigative aspects and examine digital investigations/cyber forensics (both network and computer forensics). These sections briefly discuss cybercrime scene analysis and cyber forensics protocol (e.g., identification, preservation, collection, analysis, examination, report, and presentation of digital evidence).

Other areas deal specifically with the law as it relates to information systems. The need for awareness of legislative and regulatory compliance is examined; this includes general information system legislative and regulatory principles (e.g., protection of property, intellectual property protection of persons, privacy, and licensing issues). The subtopics of cybercrime will also be reviewed: what is it, who is doing it, what effect it has on the information systems community and society in general, and, finally, issues related to the international harmonization of cybercrime laws and prosecution (e.g., jurisdiction, legislation) are addressed.

The chapter concludes with an overall discussion of the current and future roles of detective and investigative controls, and what needs to be done to ensure that these controls are flexible enough to keep pace with the constantly changing technology environment and the reality of increased regulatory and legislative compliance.

TOPICS

- **Understand legal issues that pertain to information security internationally**
    - Computer crime
    - Licensing and intellectual property, (e.g., copyright, trademark)
    - Import/export
    - Trans-border data flow
    - Privacy
- **Understand professional ethics**
    - (ISC)² Code of Professional Ethics
    - Support organization's code of ethics
- **Understand and support investigations**
    - Policy, roles and responsibilities (e.g., rules of engagement, authorization, scope)
    - Incident handling and response
    - Evidence collection and handling, (e.g., chain of custody, interviewing)
    - Reporting and documenting
- **Understand forensic procedures**
    - Media analysis
    - Network analysis
    - Software analysis
    - Hardware/embedded device analysis
- **Understand compliance requirements and procedures**
    - Regulatory environment
    - Audits
    - Reporting
- **Ensure security in contractual agreements and procurement processes (e.g., cloud computing, outsourcing, vendor governance)**

OBJECTIVES

According to the (ISC)² CIB, a CISSP® candidate is expected to know:

- The methods for determining whether a computer crime has been committed
- The laws that would be applicable for the crime
- The laws prohibiting specific types of computer crime
- Methods to gather and preserve evidence of a computer crime
- Ivestigative methods and techniques
- Ways to address compliance.

Legal Issues that Pertain to Information Security Internationally

Upon completing this chapter, readers will have a better understanding of the major legal systems found throughout the world. This understanding is required for several reasons: Information systems security is an international phenomenon; crimes committed using information systems or targeted at information systems know no geographical boundaries. It is also important that information security professionals do not have false preconceptions of legal systems they are not familiar with (i.e., all common law countries have identical laws). It will soon be rare to find a professional in this field who, during the course of an investigation, has not dealt with legal professionals from various countries or has been introduced to several different systems of law.

For the sake of this chapter, major legal systems are categorized as:

- Common law
- Civil or code law
- Customary law
- Religious law
- Mixed law

This taxonomy is consistent with the current legal literature in this area. Maritime law is not addressed in this discussion, although it is an excellent example of the harmonization of international law.

Common Law

The legal system referred to as common law traces its roots back to England, or more precisely, the development of a customary law system of both the Anglo-Saxons in Northern France and the early residents of England. Due to England's rich history of colonization, the common law framework can be found in many parts of the world that were once colonies or territories of the British empire (e.g., United States, Canada, United Kingdom, Australia, and New Zealand). The European continent has resisted the common law influence and is based primarily on a codified legal system, civil law. The common law system is based on the notion of legal precedents, past decisions, and societal traditions. The system is based on customs that predated any written laws or codification of laws in these societies. Prior to the twelfth century, customary law was unwritten and not unified in England; it was extremely diverse and was dependent on local norms and superstitions. During the twelfth century, the king of England created a unified legal system that was common to the country. This national system allowed for the development of a body of public policy principles.

A defining characteristic of common law systems is the adversarial approach to litigation, and the findings of fact in legal fictions. It is assumed that adjudicated argumentation is a valid method for arriving at the truth of a matter. This approach led to the creation of barristers (lawyers) who take a very active role in the litigation process. Another discriminating element of the common law system stems from its reliance on previous court rulings. Decisions by the courts are predicated on jurisprudence (case law), with only narrow interpretation of legislative law occurring. In this system, judges play a more passive role than in civil law systems and are not actively involved in the determination of facts. Although historically, common law was a non-codified legal system, this is no longer true; most, if not all, common law countries have developed statute laws and a codified system of laws related to criminal and commercial matters. Most descriptions of common law systems are quick to point out that the differences between civil and common law systems are becoming increasingly difficult to distinguish, with civil systems adopting a jurisprudence approach and common law systems increasingly relying on legislative statutes and regulations. Most common law systems consist of three branches of law: criminal law, tort law, and administrative law.

Criminal Law

Criminal law can be based on common law, statutory law, or a combination of both. Criminal law deals with behaviors or conduct that is seen as harmful to the public or society. In these cases, an individual has violated a governmental law designed to protect the public and, thus, the real victim is society. The government therefore prosecutes the transgressor on behalf of the public. Typically, the punishment meted out by the criminal courts involves some loss of personal freedom for the guilty party (e.g., incarceration, probation, death). However, monetary punishments in the way of fines or restitution to the court or victim are also common.

Tort Law

Tort law deals with civil wrongs (torts) against an individual or business entity. As the transgressions are not against the general public or society (in most cases), the law (government) provides for different remedies than in criminal cases. These remedies usually consist of money for the damages caused to the victim. These damages can be compensatory, punitive, or statutory. Interestingly enough, tort law can trace its origin to criminal law, and in some jurisdictions, offenses can fall into both the criminal and tort law categories (e.g., assault against an individual). Tort law can be divided into intentional torts, wrongs against a person or property, dignitary wrongs, economic wrongs, negligence, nuisance, and strict liability.

Administrative Law

Administrative law or, as it is known in some countries, regulatory law, is primarily an artifact of the Anglo-American common law legal system. However, some civil law systems have administrative courts to oversee social security law or grievances against the government itself (either national or local). This branch of common law is concerned with the governance of public bodies and the designation of power to administrative agencies, commissions, boards, administrative tribunals or professional associations (e.g., Securities Exchange Committee, Labor Relations Boards, Law Societies, Medical Boards, School Boards). These agencies are often controlled by other government agencies, but can come under the purview of the courts and are reviewed "under some principle of due process."

The objectives of administrative law include confining government power to its proper scope, curbing potential for abuse of power, ensuring that proper procedures are followed in the exercise of powers that affect the rights/interests of citizens and ensuring performance of mandatory statutory duties. Punishments under administrative law consist of fines, inability to practice a profession (delicensing) and, in some cases, incarceration.

Civil Law

Civil law traces its roots back to two beginnings. The first was the living law of the Roman Empire, which culminated with the compilation of the Code and Digest of Emperor Justinian. The second birth began as a result of Italian legal scholars and progressed through the codification of law in Europe, as exemplified with the Napoleonic Code of France and the French Civil Code of 1804.

The civil law system was, at one time, the most common legal system on the European continent.

The system became regionalized over time with Germany, Norway, Sweden, Denmark, and Switzerland developing their own national systems, unique from the French Napoleonic system. Due to this nationalization, civil law can be subdivided into French civil law, German civil law, and Scandinavian civil law. Civil law is not confined to Europe alone. Many Asian countries have legal systems based on the German model of civil law.

The distinguishing feature of civil law is thought to be the codification of law and heavy reliance on legislation as the primary source of law, as opposed to jurisprudence. This is not accurate, as there are several countries that follow an uncodified civil law legal system (e.g., Scotland and South Africa). However, when contrasted against the common law system, other differences become apparent. Civil law emphasizes the abstract concepts of law and is influenced by the writings of legal scholars and academics, more so than common law systems. The common law doctrine of stare decisis (lower courts are compelled to follow decisions of higher courts) is absent from the civil law system. The role of judges in civil law systems is also different than in common law systems. In civil law legal systems, judges are distinct from lawyers and are not attorneys who have graduated through the ranks. Judges also play a more active role in determining the facts of the case and in some instances, direct the actual investigations.

Customary Law

Custom or customary law systems are regionalized systems and reflect the society's norms and values based on programmatic wisdom and traditions. These countries have a rich history of traditions and customs that dictate acceptable behavior between the various members of society. These customs or norms over the years have become recognized as defining legitimate social contracts and have become part of the rule of law. It is rare to find a country whose rule of law is based solely on customary law. Most countries that have a strong law of custom also prescribe to another legal system, such as civil or common law (e.g., many African countries). This combination of legal systems is referred to as a mixed legal system. Punishment under customary law systems focuses on restitution to the victim by means of some kind of fine.

Religious Law

In a manner of speaking, all laws have been influenced by religion. The earliest societal rules of conduct that dictated the behavior of the people reflected the predominant religious teachings on morality. Over the years, many countries have attempted to separate the spiritual and secular lives of its citizens (e.g., First Amendment of the United States). Other countries not necessarily under the direct influence of Judaism or Christianity have not made the same cultural or societal distinction. Although there are technically several religious law systems, this discussion is confined to a very brief discussion of Muslim law as an example. This system was chosen because the Islamic faith is practiced by a large portion of the world's population. Many Muslim societies, such as those found in North Africa and the Middle East, follow Islamic laws or Sharia. Although Sharia has been the dominant system defining the rule of law, there is increasing pressure to adopt or, at the very least, incorporate more secular legal thinking and ideas (see "Mixed law" section).

Traditional Islamic law is separated into rules of worship and rules of human interaction and is guided by the Qur'arn and the "way," or Sunnah—the manner in which the prophet Muhammad lived his life. Sharia covers all aspects of a person's life, from religious practices, dietary choices, dress code, marriage/family life, and commerce, to domestic justice and sexual behavior. Law is not considered a man-made entity; it is decreed by divine will. Lawmakers and law scholars do not create laws; they attempt to discover the truth of law. Jurists and clerics play a central role in this system and have a high degree of authority within the society. Like the civilian systems, Sharia has been codified, but still remains open to interpretation and modification.

Mixed Law

With the new global economy, trade pacts such as the North American Free Trade Agreement (NAFTA), the creation of the European Union, etc., the introduction or blending of two or more systems of law is now becoming more common. Mixed law by definition is the convergence of two or more legal systems, usually civil law and common law, but increasingly customary, religious, and or civil or common law. The interaction of these legal systems can be the result of historical, economic, or political pressures. Examples of mixed systems can be found in Europe with Holland, in North America with Quebec and Louisiana, in Africa with South Africa, and in the United Kingdom with Scotland.

Liability

Another integral part of an information security professional's job function is understanding issues related to liability, negligence, and due care. In the world's increasingly litigious culture, these concepts become especially important, as we are seeing examples of shareholder lawsuits and third-party liability claims against organizations suffering information technology attacks and breaches. When organizations are weighing the costs versus the benefits of certain actions, inactions, or security controls, the ability to demonstrate reasonable corporate behavior and overall due diligence is an essential factor.

In law (i.e., tort), liability refers to being legally responsible. Sanctions in cases dealing with liability include both civil and criminal penalties. Liability and negligence are somewhat associated, as negligence is often used to establish liability. Negligence is simply acting without care, or the failure to act as a reasonable and prudent person would under similar circumstances. The exact definition of a reasonable and prudent person is somewhat more complicated, as the courts usually engage in legal fiction by prescribing qualities that this person has without reference to any real person. The "reasonable person" yardstick is determined by the circumstances in question, and is usually the center of heated debate during the litigation process.

Due care and due diligence are other terms that have found their way into issues of corporate governance. Due care can be thought of as the requirement that officers and other executives with fiduciary responsibilities meet certain requirements to protect the company's assets. These requirements include the safety and protection of technology and information systems that fall under the term corporate assets.[1]

Due diligence is a much more ethereal concept and is often judged against a continually moving benchmark. What used to constitute

---

[1] Another way of understanding these terms is to think of due care as doing the right thing and due diligence as evaluating the results of due care measures to ensure that they are performing as intended.

due diligence may no longer be valid. This dynamic nature requires a commitment to an ongoing risk analysis and risk management process and a good understanding of generally accepted business and information security practices, within the applicable industry, as well as international standards. The increase in government scrutiny of information system practices has resulted in the majority of companies allocating their security budgets to be compliant with the various current and pending regulatory requirements. Some estimates indicate that information security budgets will rise in direct response to the requirement for regulatory compliance. Though this is strictly speculative, it demonstrates the importance of controlling liability.

Computer Crime

An information security professional is focused on risks that arise not only from errors and omissions, but also from behavior that is both malicious and intentional. The fact that computer systems have become the target for criminals should come as no surprise. The very features that make technology, information systems, and the Internet attractive to businesses also make them attractive to criminals, both petty and professional or organized. As more digital assets (e.g., personal information, bank account numbers, credit card information) move online, the likelihood, impacts, and, correspondingly, risk that private citizens, companies, and governments will become victims of computer crime increases.

The phenomena of computer crime, or cybercrime, as it is often called has plagued society for several years. Some of the so-called new computer crimes are actually more traditional criminal activities that have benefited from the new technological advances, such as the Internet, color scanners and copiers, etc. Information system crimes are often divided into the following categories:

- Computer as a tool
- Computers as the target of crime
- Computers incidental to the crime

As a tool, computers merely allow criminals to become more efficient at practicing their criminal tradecraft, more able to target victims, or more easily able to share contraband. Examples of these types of crimes are fraud, counterfeit, theft, and child pornography. With our society's increasing dependence on technology, the characteristics of what constitutes evidence have drastically changed. A majority of all criminal investigations include evidence that is digital in nature. Here again, this is no surprise: society has become dependent on e-mail, PDAs, electronic calendars, etc. In this context, computers as incidental is almost a useless category because it is so generic that it encompasses all but very few types of criminal behavior.

Computers as the target refers to those criminal activities that have their origins in technology and have no analogous real-world equivalents. These crimes target information systems and the underlying architecture and represent some of the largest issues for information security. These activities denote concepts that legal systems have not had experience dealing with and have not effectively embodied into the statutes, regulations, etc. Within the classification of computer-targeted crime, several subcategories of activities exist. Examples of such directed activities include:

- Viruses
- Digital identity theft
- Computer hacking

Although this list is not at all exhaustive, it does capture some of the uniqueness of this type of criminal behavior. Just as the criminal activity seems unique, the type of offender seems to be exclusive as well. It is fair to say that individuals are attracted to specific types of crime for various reasons (e.g., personal choice, aptitude, social learning). Rather than trying to label offenders, for the sake of this discussion, it is more pragmatic to simply state that computer criminals have developed a distinctive tradecraft and that the various subclasses of computer crime require specific skills, knowledge, abilities, and access to technology.

The computer as incidental is a direct artifact of our wired society. Every person has a digital "footprint" that is very extensive and rather intrusive. Online activities, whether Internet based or cell phone are logged and recorded—often these are archived and open for anyone to look at without any court orders being required (e.g., news group postings or social network archives). Computers and computing technology (e.g., cell phones, smart phones) are often a repository of digital information related to our activities, geo-locations, conversations, preferences and so on. This type of information is often of interest during an investigation, including the non-technology-related cases such as murders, kidnappings, drug trafficking, custody disputes, etc.

1177

A word of caution is necessary: although the media has tended to portray the threat of cybercrime as existing almost exclusively from the outside, external to a company, reality paints a much different picture. Often the greatest risk of cybercrime comes from the inside, namely, criminal insiders. Information security professionals must be particularly sensitive to the phenomena of the criminal or dangerous insider, as these individuals usually operate under the radar, inside of the primarily outward/external facing security controls, thus significantly increasing the impact of their crimes while leaving few, if any, audit trails to follow and evidence for prosecution.

International Cooperation

The biggest hindrance to effectively dealing with computer crime is the fact that this activity is truly international in scope, and thus requires an international solution, as opposed to a domestic one based on archaic concepts of borders and jurisdictions. The concept of geographical borders is meaningless in the realm of cyber space; society is truly seeing the manifestation of a global village.

The World Wide Web is exactly that, worldwide; criminals in one country can victimize individuals clear across the world with a keystroke, Web site, spam attack, phishing scam, etc. Previous attempts based on domestic solutions (e.g., the introduction of criminal statutes, regulations) designed to stop activities that utilized the ubiquitous nature of the Internet and distributed information systems (e.g., online gambling, adult pornography) were inadequate and completely unsuccessful. The framers of these solutions failed to take into account the global reach of technology; the owners of these sites simply moved their operations to countries whose governments condoned, tolerated, or turned a blind eye to the activities. The desired effect of stopping or at the very least deterring the activity did not occur. In some cases, the activity thrived due to the unprecedented media exposure.

International responses to computer crime have met with mixed results. The Council of Europe (CoE) Convention on Cybercrime[2] is a prime example of a multilateral attempt to draft an international response to criminal behaviors targeted at technology and the Internet. Thirty countries, including Canada, the United States, and Japan, ratified the convention that came into effect July 1, 2004. The Convention on Cybercrime consists of 48 articles and in summary it requires parties to:

- Establish laws against cybercrime and offenses related to child pornography
- Ensure that their law enforcement officials have the necessary procedural authorities to investigate and prosecute cybercrime offenses effectively
- Provide international cooperation to other parties in the fight against computer- related crime

One of the Convention on Cybercrime's stated objectives is to assist international enforcement efforts by creating a framework for the domestication and cooperation between ratifying states. This objective directly addresses one of the most difficult problems faced when dealing with computer crime: jurisdictional disputes. Issues related to establishing jurisdiction, extradition of accused, and lack of domestication have hamstrung many past investigations. The ultimate success of the convention is still unknown, but it is definitely a step in the right direction.

---

2   http://conventions.coe.int/Treaty/EN/Treaties/Html/185.htm

Licensing and Intellectual Property

Although no one expects an information systems security professional to be a legal expert on all areas of technology-related law—as with the various legal systems—a working knowledge of legal concepts directly related to information technology is required to fully understand the context, issues, and risks inherent with information systems. Two general categories of information technology law have the largest impact on information systems: intellectual property and privacy regulations. This section only provides a brief summary of these concepts. Readers wishing to delve deeper into this area are strongly encouraged to refer to the relevant legislation and regulations in their respective countries.

Intellectual Property Laws

Intellectual property laws are designed to protect both tangible and intangible items or property. Although there are various rationales behind the state-based creation of protection for this type of property, the general goal of intellectual property law is to protect property from those wishing to copy or use it, without due compensation to the inventor or creator. The notion is that copying or using someone else's ideas entails far less work than what is required for the original development. According to the World Intellectual Property Organization (WIPO[3]):

> Intellectual property is divided into two categories: *Industrial property*, which includes inventions (patents), trademarks, industrial designs, and geographical indications of source; and *Copyright*, which includes literary and artistic works such as novels, poems and plays, films, musical works, artistic works such as drawings, paintings, photographs and sculptures, and architectural designs.

Patent

Simply put, a patent grants the owner a legally enforceable right to exclude others from practicing the invention covered for a specific time (usually 20

---

3   Read more about WIPO here: http://www.wipo.int/about-ip/en/iprm/

years). A patent is the "strongest form of intellectual property protection." A patent protects novel, useful, and nonobvious inventions. The granting of a patent requires the formal application to a government entity. Once a patent is granted, it is published in the public domain, to stimulate other innovations. Once a patent expires, the protection ends and the invention enters the public domain. WIPO, an agency of the United Nations, looks after the filing and processing of international patent applications.

Trademark

Trademark laws are designed to protect the goodwill an organization invests in its products, services or image. Trademark law creates exclusive rights to the owner of markings that the public uses to identify various vendor or merchant products or goods. A trademark consists of any word, name, symbol, color, sound, product shape, device, or combination of these that is used to identify goods and distinguish them from those made or sold by others. The trademark must be distinctive and cannot mislead or deceive consumers or violate public order or morality. Trademarks are registered with a government registrar. International harmonization of trademark laws began in 1883 with the Paris Convention, which prompted the Madrid Agreement of 1891. Like patents, WIPO oversees international trademark law efforts, including international registration.

Copyright

A copyright covers the expression of ideas rather than the ideas themselves; it usually protects artistic property such as writing, recordings, databases, and computer programs. In most countries, once the work or property is completed or is in a tangible form, the copyright protection is automatically assumed. Copyright protection is weaker than patent protection, but the duration of protection is considerably longer (e.g., a minimum of 50 years after the creator's death or 70 years under U.S. copyright protection). Although individual countries may have slight variations in their domestic copyright laws, as long as the country is a member of the international Berne

Convention[4], the protection afforded will be at least at a minimum level, as dictated by the convention; unfortunately, not all countries are members.

Trade Secret

The final area covered in this section is trade secrets. Trade secret refers to proprietary business or technical information, processes, designs, practices, etc., that are confidential and critical to the business (e.g., Coca-Cola's formula). The trade secret may provide a competitive advantage or, at the very least, allow the company to compete equally in the marketplace. To be categorized as a trade secret, it must not be generally known and must provide some economic benefit to the company. Additionally, there must be some form of reasonable steps taken to protect its secrecy. A trade secret dispute is unique, as the actual contents of the trade secret need not be disclosed. Legal protection for trade secrets depends upon the jurisdiction. In some countries, it is assumed under unfair business legislation, and in others, specific laws have been drafted related to confidential information. In some jurisdictions, legal protection for trade secrets is practically perpetual and does not carry an expiry date, as is the case with patents. Trade secrets are often at the heart of industrial and economic espionage cases and are the proverbial crown jewels of some companies.

Licensing Issues

The issue of illegal software and piracy is such a large problem it warrants discussion. More than one company has been embarrassed publicly, sued civilly, or criminally prosecuted for failing to control the use of illegal software or violating software licensing agreements. With high-speed Internet access readily available to most employees, the ability—if not the temptation—to download and use pirated software has greatly increased. According to a recent (2012) study[5] by the Business Software Alliance (BSA) and International Data Corporation (IDC), prevalence and frequency

---

4   Read more about the Berne convention here: http://www.wipo.int/treaties/en/ip/berne/trtdocs_wo001.html
5   http://www.bsa.org/globalstudy

of illegal software is exceedingly high, the weighted average was 42% worldwide. The same study found that for every two dollars worth of legal software purchased, one dollar's worth of software was pirated. Though not all countries recognize the forms of intellectual property protection previously discussed, the work of several international organizations and industrialized countries seems somewhat successful in curbing the official sanctioning of intellectual property rights violations (e.g., software piracy).

There are several categories of software licensing including freeware, shareware, commercial, and academic. Within these categories, there are specific types of agreements. Master agreements and end-user licensing agreements (EULAs) are the most prevalent though most jurisdictions have refused to enforce the shrink-wrap agreements that were commonplace at one time. Master agreements set out the general overall conditions of use along with any restrictions, whereas the EULA specifies more granular conditions and restrictions. The EULA is often a "click through" or radio button that the end user must click on to begin the install, indicating that he or she understands the conditions and limitations and agrees to comply.

Various third parties have developed license metering software to ensure and enforce compliance with software licensing agreements. Some of these applications can produce an audit report and either disable software attempting to run in violation of an agreement (e.g., exceeding the number of devices running software concurrently) or produce an automated alert. The use of carefully controlled software libraries is also a recommended solution. Ignorance is no excuse when it comes to compliance with licensing conditions and restrictions. The onus is clearly on the organization to enforce compliance and police the use of software or face the possibility of legal sanctions, such as criminal prosecution or civil penalties.

Import/Export

Some software such as encryption software may be illegal to import or export. Many software vendors are familiar with restrictions for their software but the prudent information security professional will ensure all software complies with local laws. Other considerations include United Nation sanctions which may prohibit technology of certain types or from certain countries being imported into a country.

Trans-Border Data Flow

As information moves from one server to another or from one cloud to another the location of the data and the hosting organization begins to matter. Information developed in one country, transmitted through another and finally stored in a third may be subject to three different jurisdictions and three different legal systems. In some situations even if information is stored in one country, if the organization who owns the sever is a member of a different country, the latter may be able to gain jurisdiction over the information.

Privacy

With the proliferation of technology, and the increasing awareness that most of our personally identifiable information (PII)[6] is stored online or electronically in some way, shape, or form, there is growing pressure to protect personal information. Almost monthly, there are media reports worldwide of databases being compromised, files being lost, and attacks against businesses and systems that house personal, private information. This has spurred concerns over the proper collection, use, retention, and destruction of information of a personal or confidential nature. This public concern has prompted the creation of regulations intended to foster the responsible use and stewardship of personal information. In the context of this discussion, privacy is one of the primary areas in which business, in almost all industries, is forced to deal with regulations and regulatory compliance.

---

6   For more information on PII, please see the following: http://csrc.nist.gov/
publications/nistpubs/800-122/sp800-122.pdf

The actual enactment of regulations or, in some cases, laws dealing with privacy depend on the jurisdiction. Some countries have opted for a generic approach to privacy regulations—horizontal enactment (i.e., across all industries, including government), while others have decided to regulate by industry—vertical enactment (e.g., financial, health, publicly traded).

Regardless of the approach, the overall objective is to protect a citizen's personal information, while at the same time balancing the business, governmental, and academic or research need to collect and use this information appropriately. Unfortunately, there is no one international privacy law, resulting in a mosaic of legislation and regulations. Some countries have been progressive in dealing with privacy and personal information, while others have yet to act in this area. Given the fact that the Internet has created a global community, our information and business transactions and operations may cross several different borders and jurisdictions—each with their own sovereign concerns, societal standards, and laws. Therefore, it is prudent to have a basic understanding of privacy principles and guidelines, and keep up to date with the changing landscape of privacy regulations that may affect business as well as personal information.

Privacy can be defined as the rights and obligations of individuals and organizations with respect to the collection, use, retention, and disclosure of personal information. Personal information is a rather generic concept and encompasses any information that is about or on an identifiable individual. Although international privacy laws are somewhat different in respect to their specific requirements, they all tend to be based on core principles or guidelines. The Organization for Economic Cooperation and Development (OECD[7]) has broadly classified these principles into the collection limitation, data quality, purpose specification, use limitation, security safeguards, openness, individual participation, and accountability.

---

7   http://oecdprivacy.org/

1185

The guidelines are as follows:

- There should be limits to the collection of personal data, and any such data should be obtained by lawful and fair means and, where appropriate, with the knowledge or consent of the data subject.

- Personal data should be relevant to the purposes for which they are to be used and, to the extent necessary for those purposes, should be accurate, complete, and kept up to date.

- The purposes for which personal data is collected should be specified not later than at the time of data collection, and the subsequent use limited to the fulfillment of those purposes or such others as are not incompatible with those purposes and as are specified on each occasion of change of purpose.

- Personal data should not be disclosed, made available, or otherwise used for purposes other than those specified above except.

  - With the consent of the data subject.

  - By the authority of law.

- Personal data should be protected by reasonable security safeguards against such risks as loss or unauthorized access, destruction, use, modification, or disclosure of data.

- There should be a general policy of openness about developments, practices, and policies concerning personal data. Means should be readily available for establishing the existence and nature of personal data, and the main purposes of their use, as well as the identity and usual residence of the data controller.

- An individual should have the right:

  - To obtain from a data controller, or otherwise, confirmation of whether the data controller has data relating to him

  - To have communicated to him, data relating to him:

- Within a reasonable time
- At a charge, if any, that is not excessive
- In a reasonable manner
- In a form that is readily intelligible to him

□ To be given reasons if a request made is denied, and to be able to challenge such denial

□ To challenge data relating to him and, if the challenge is successful, to have the data erased, rectified, completed, or amended.

□ A data controller should be accountable for complying with measures that give effect to the principles stated above.

It should be noted that the OECD is very cautious about not creating barriers to the legitimate transborder flow of personal information. The OECD also cautions members to be aware of, and sensitive to, regional or domestic differences and safeguard personal information from countries that do not follow the OECD guidelines or an equivalent.

Generally, these principles should form the minimum set of requirements for the development of reasonable legislation, regulations, and policy, and that nothing prevents organizations from adding additional principles. However, the actual application of these principles has proved more difficult and costly in almost all circumstances; there has been a vast underestimation of the impact of the various privacy laws and policies both domestically and with cross-border commerce. This is not an excuse to abandon, block, or fail to comply with applicable laws, regulations, or policies. However, information security professions need to appreciate that business practices have changed due to the need to be in compliance (often with international regulations), and that budgets must be appropriately increased to meet the demand.

Employee Monitoring and Surveillance

The monitoring of employees' use, and in some cases abuse, of information technology is a balancing act. Businesses and organizations must balance the need for security and the demonstration of due diligence with the privacy rights of the employees. Internationally, businesses are required to "police" the activities of their employees to prevent lawsuits by third parties aggrieved by an employee's online conduct, or to prevent a hostile work environment—that would again become fodder for a lawsuit. In some instances, businesses are required to search employee e-mails or blog postings in response to a legal request for discovery of any electronically stored information (ESI) filed as part of a lawsuit or other legal proceedings. Businesses also wish to ensure that employee productivity and efficiency is being maintained and that the risk of an internal breech or other IT security incident is greatly reduced.

Employee monitoring also carries some social baggage. Businesses run the risk of alienating the employees, eroding the employer and employee trust relationship, and having policies that ultimately result in disgruntled employees (who statistically are the highest risk to most businesses), or leave employees with the perception of a hostile workplace. Therefore, care must be taken to develop and implement policy that considers not only the technical and legal aspects, but also the employer–employee relationship.

However, the right to privacy of the employee is a legally entrenched concept in most countries either by constitutional amendments, charter right or precedent. It is so entrenched in some jurisdictions that businesses at times feel handicapped in their ability to protect themselves from their own supposedly trusted employees. There are numerous cases on record where employees have successfully sued their employers for violations of their privacy while in the workplace.

Despite the seemingly near impossible balancing act, the practice of employee monitoring and use of online and e-mail surveillance technologies (automated or manual) is common place. Recent studies indicate that the majority of companies monitor employee e-mails, Internet activities, and phone conversations. This has resulted in several countries developing governmental offices to oversee issues of privacy, and in most cases, drafting guidelines for the acceptable use and implementation of employee monitoring and surveillance.

While it is somewhat utopian to think that there would be international harmony regarding employee monitoring standards or guidelines, there is a body of work developed in Europe called the Directive on Data Protection that distills this issue down to seven basic principles[8]. These principles can be used as a checklist for organizations to determine whether employee monitoring (specific to e-mail and Internet use) is lawful and justified. While these principles are EU specific, they provide a good example of the considerations or restrictions being imposed by current or anticipated legislation and regulations in several countries (e.g., Canada, United States, United Kingdom).

The seven principles are:

- **NOTICE:** An organization must inform individuals about the purposes for which it collects and uses information about them, how to contact the organization with any inquiries or complaints, the types of third parties to which it discloses the information, and the choices and means the organization offers individuals for limiting its use and disclosure. This notice must be provided in clear and conspicuous language when individuals are first asked to provide personal information to the organization or as soon thereafter as is practicable, but in any event before the organization uses such information for a purpose other than that for which it was originally collected or processed by the transferring organization or discloses it for the first time to a third party.

---

8   Read more about the seven principals here: http://export.gov/safeharbor/eu/eg_main_018475.asp

- **CHOICE:** An organization must offer individuals the opportunity to choose (opt out) whether their personal information is (a) to be disclosed to a third party(1) or (b) to be used for a purpose that is incompatible with the purpose(s) for which it was originally collected or subsequently authorized by the individual. Individuals must be provided with clear and conspicuous, readily available, and affordable mechanisms to exercise choice.

- For sensitive information (i.e. personal information specifying medical or health conditions, racial or ethnic origin, political opinions, religious or philosophical beliefs, trade union membership or information specifying the sex life of the individual), they must be given affirmative or explicit (opt in) choice if the information is to be disclosed to a third party or used for a purpose other than those for which it was originally collected or subsequently authorized by the individual through the exercise of opt in choice. In any case, an organization should treat as sensitive any information received from a third party where the third party treats and identifies it as sensitive.

- **ONWARD TRANSFER:** To disclose information to a third party, organizations must apply the Notice and Choice Principles. Where an organization wishes to transfer information to a third party that is acting as an agent, as described in the endnote, it may do so if it first either ascertains that the third party subscribes to the Principles or is subject to the Directive or another adequacy finding or enters into a written agreement with such third party requiring that the third party provide at least the same level of privacy protection as is required by the relevant Principles. If the organization complies with these requirements, it shall not be held responsible (unless the organization agrees otherwise) when a third party to which it transfers such information processes it in a way contrary to any restrictions or representations, unless the organization knew or should have known the third party would process it in such a contrary way and the organization has not taken reasonable steps to prevent or stop such processing.

- **SECURITY:** Organizations creating, maintaining, using or disseminating personal information must take reasonable precautions to protect it from loss, misuse and unauthorized access, disclosure, alteration and destruction.

- **DATA INTEGRITY:** Consistent with the Principles, personal information must be relevant for the purposes for which it is to be used. An organization may not process personal information in a way that is incompatible with the purposes for which it has been collected or subsequently authorized by the individual. To the extent necessary for those purposes, an organization should take reasonable steps to ensure that data is reliable for its intended use, accurate, complete, and current.

- **ACCESS:** Individuals must have access to personal information about them that an organization holds and be able to correct, amend, or delete that information where it is inaccurate, except where the burden or expense of providing access would be disproportionate to the risks to the individual's privacy in the case in question, or where the rights of persons other than the individual would be violated.

- **ENFORCEMENT:** Effective privacy protection must include mechanisms for assuring compliance with the Principles, recourse for individuals to whom the data relate affected by non-compliance with the Principles, and consequences for the organization when the Principles are not followed. At a minimum, such mechanisms must include (a) readily available and affordable independent recourse mechanisms by which each individual's complaints and disputes are investigated and resolved by reference to the Principles and damages awarded where the applicable law or private sector initiatives so provide; (b) follow up procedures for verifying that the attestations and assertions businesses make about their privacy practices are true and that privacy practices have been implemented as presented; and (c) obligations to remedy problems arising out of failure to comply with the Principles by organizations announcing their adherence to them and consequences for such organizations. Sanctions must be sufficiently rigorous to ensure compliance by organizations.

It is essential to be familiar with these principles to provide direction for policies and procedures and to ensure that the activities of the information security professional during an investigation are ethical and lawful. A common approach to ensuring that the monitoring of employees is both lawful and does alienate workers is to use employee-signed acceptable usage policies that clearly and unambiguously discuss employee monitoring and the sanctions for violating the company policy. However, organizations must be careful that such polices do not conflict with others such as de minimis use and "bring your own device."

The exact protocols that can or should be used to conduct employee monitoring are outside the scope of this chapter. However, as several government entities have stated, the focus should be on the prevention of employee abuse and not solely on its detection.

Understand Professional Ethics

The consideration of computer ethics fundamentally emerged with the birth of computers. There was concern right away that computers would be used inappropriately to the detriment of society, or that they would replace humans in many jobs, resulting in widespread job loss. To fully grasp the issues involved with computer ethics, it is important to consider the history. The following provides a brief overview of some significant events.

Consideration of computer ethics is recognized to have begun with the work of MIT professor Norbert Wiener during World War II in the early 1940s, when he helped to develop anti-aircraft cannons that were capable of shooting down fast warplanes. This work resulted in Wiener and his colleagues creating a new field of research that Wiener called cybernetics, the science of information feedback systems. The concepts of cybernetics, combined with the developing computer technologies, led Wiener to make some ethical conclusions about the technology called information and communication technology (ICT), in which Wiener predicted social and ethical consequences.

Wiener published the book The Human Use of Human Beings in 1950, which described a comprehensive foundation that is still the basis for computer ethics research and analysis.

In the mid-1960s, Donn B. Parker, at the time with SRI International in Menlo Park, CA, began examining unethical and illegal uses of computers and documenting examples of computer crime and other unethical computerized activities. He published "Rules of Ethics in Information Processing" in Communications of the ACM in 1968, and headed the development of the first Code of Professional Conduct for the Association for Computing Machinery, which was adopted by the ACM in 1973.

1193

During the late 1960s, Joseph Weizenbaum, a computer scientist at MIT in Boston, created a computer program that he called ELIZA that he scripted to provide a crude imitation of "a Rogerian psychotherapist engaged in an initial interview with a patient." People had strong reactions to his program, some psychiatrists fearing it showed that computers would perform automated psychotherapy. Weizenbaum wrote Computer Power and Human Reason in 1976, in which he expressed his concerns about the growing tendency to see humans as mere machines. His book, MIT courses, and many speeches inspired many thoughts and projects focused on computer ethics.

Walter Maner is credited with coining the phrase "computer ethics" in the mid-1970s when discussing the ethical problems and issues created by computer technology, and taught a course on the subject at Old Dominion University. From the late 1970s into the mid-1980s, Maner's work created much interest in university-level computer ethics courses. In 1978, Maner published the Starter Kit in Computer Ethics, which contained curriculum materials and advice for developing computer ethics courses. Many university courses were put in place because of Maner's work.

In the 1980s, social and ethical consequences of information technology, such as computer-enabled crime, computer failure disasters, privacy invasion using computer databases, and software ownership lawsuits, were being widely discussed in America and Europe.

James Moor of Dartmouth College published "What Is Computer Ethics?" in Computers and Ethics, and Deborah Johnson of Rensselaer Polytechnic Institute published Computer Ethics, the first textbook in the field in the mid-1980s. Other significant books about computer ethics were published within the psychology and sociology field, such as Sherry Turkle's The Second Self, about the impact of computing on the human psyche, and Judith Perrolle's Computers and Social Change: Information, Property and Power, about a sociological approach to computing and human values.

Maner Terrell Bynum held the first international multidisciplinary conference on computer ethics in 1991. For the first time, philosophers, computer professionals, sociologists, psychologists, lawyers, business leaders, news reporters, and government officials assembled to discuss computer ethics. During the 1990s, new university courses, research centers, conferences, journals, articles, and textbooks appeared, and organizations like Computer Professionals for Social Responsibility, the Electronic Frontier Foundation, and the Association for Computing Machinery-Special Interest Group on Computers and Society (ACM-SIGCAS) launched projects addressing computing and professional responsibility. Developments in Europe and Australia included new computer ethics research centers in England, Poland, Holland, and Italy. In the U.K., Simon Rogerson, of De Montfort University, led the ETHICOMP series of conferences and established the Centre for Computing and Social Responsibility.

Regulatory Requirements for Ethics Programs

When creating an ethics strategy, it is important to look at the regulatory requirements for ethics programs. These provide the basis for a minimal ethical standard upon which an organization can expand to fit its own unique organizational environment and requirements. An increasing number of regulatory requirements related to ethics programs and training now exist.

The 1991 U.S. Federal Sentencing Guidelines for Organizations[1] (FSGO) outline minimal ethical requirements and provide for substantially reduced penalties in criminal cases when federal laws are violated if ethics programs are in place. Reduced penalties provide strong motivation to establish an ethics program. Effective November 1, 2004, the FSGO was updated with additional requirements:

---

1   Read more about FSGO here: http://www.ussc.gov/Guidelines/2011_guidelines/ Manual_HTML/Chapter_8.htm

In general, board members and senior executives must assume more specific responsibilities for a program to be found effective:

■ Organizational leaders must be knowledgeable about the content and operation of the compliance and ethics program, perform their assigned duties exercising due diligence, and promote an organizational culture that encourages ethical conduct and a commitment to compliance with the law.

■ The commission's definition of an effective compliance and ethics program now has three subsections:

◻ Subsection (a)—the purpose of a compliance and ethics program

◻ Subsection (b)—seven minimum requirements of such a program,

◻ Subsection (c)—the requirement to periodically assess the risk of criminal conduct and design, implement, or modify the seven program elements, as needed, to reduce the risk of criminal conduct

The purpose of an effective compliance and ethics program is to exercise due diligence to prevent and detect criminal conduct and otherwise promote an organizational culture that encourages ethical conduct and a commitment to compliance with the law. The new requirement significantly expands the scope of an effective ethics program and requires the organization to report an offense to the appropriate governmental authorities without unreasonable delay.

The U.S. Sarbanes–Oxley Act of 2002 introduced accounting reform and requires attestation to the accuracy of financial reporting documents:

■ Section 103, "Auditing, Quality Control, and Independence Standards and Rules," requires the board to

◻ Register public accounting firms

◻ Establish, or adopt, by rule, "auditing, quality control, ethics, independence, and other standards relating to the preparation of audit reports for issuers"

- New Item 406(a) of Regulation S-K requires companies to disclose:
  - ¤ Whether they have a written code of ethics that applies to their senior officers
  - ¤ Any waivers of the code of ethics for these individuals
  - ¤ Any changes to the code of ethics
- If companies do not have a code of ethics, they must explain why they have not adopted one.

The U.S. Securities and Exchange Commission approved a new governance structure for the New York Stock Exchange (NYSE) in December 2003. It includes a requirement for companies to adopt and disclose a code of business conduct and ethics for directors, officers, and employees, and promptly disclose any waivers of the code for directors or executive officers. The NYSE regulations require all listed companies to possess and communicate, both internally and externally, a code of conduct or face delisting.

In addition to these, U.S. organizations must monitor new and revised regulations from U.S. regulatory agencies, such as the Food and Drug Administration (FDA), Federal Trade Commission (FTC), Bureau of Alcohol, Tobacco, Firearms and Explosives (ATF), Internal Revenue Service (IRS), and Department of Labor (DoL), and many others throughout the world such as the EU Data Protection Directives. Ethics plans and programs need to be established within the organization to ensure that the organization complies with all such regulatory requirements regardless of the country they reside.

Topics in Computer Ethics

When establishing a computer ethics program and accompanying training and awareness program, it is important to consider the topics that have been addressed and researched. The following topics, identified in most computer ethics textbooks are good to use as a basis.

Computers in the Workplace

Computers can pose a threat to jobs as people feel they may be replaced by them. However, the computer industry already has generated a wide variety of new jobs. When computers do not eliminate a job, they can radically alter it. In addition to job security concerns, another workplace concern is health and safety. It is a computer ethics issue to consider how computers impact health and job satisfaction when information technology is introduced into a workplace.

Computer Crime

With the proliferation of computer viruses, spyware, phishing and fraud schemes, and hacking activity from every location in the world, computer crime and security are certainly topics of concern when discussing computer ethics. Besides outsiders, or hackers, many computer crimes, such as embezzlement or planting of logic bombs, are committed by trusted personnel who have authorization to use company computer systems.

Privacy and Anonymity

One of the earliest computer ethics topics to arouse public interest was privacy. The ease and efficiency with which computers and networks can be used to gather, store, search, compare, retrieve, and share personal information make computer technology especially threatening to anyone who wishes to keep personal information out of the public domain or out of the hands of those who are perceived as potential threats. The variety of privacy-related issues generated by computer technology has led to reexamination of the concept of privacy itself.

Intellectual Property

One of the more controversial areas of computer ethics concerns the intellectual property rights connected with software ownership. Some people, like Richard Stallman, who started the Free Software Foundation, believe that software ownership should not be allowed at all. He claims that all information should be free, and all programs should be available for copying, studying, and modifying by anyone who wishes to do so. Others, such as Deborah Johnson[2], author of the first major textbook on computer ethics, argue that software companies or programmers would not invest weeks and months of work and significant funds in the development of software if they could not get the investment back in the form of license fees or sales.

Professional Responsibility and Globalization

Global networks such as the Internet and conglomerates of business-to-business network connections are connecting people and information worldwide. Such globalization issues that include ethics considerations include:

- Global laws
- Global business
- Global education
- Global information flows
- Information-rich and information-poor nations
- Information interpretation

The gap between rich and poor nations, and between rich and poor citizens in industrialized countries, is very wide. As educational opportunities, business and employment opportunities, medical services, and many other necessities of life move more and more into cyberspace, the gaps between the rich and the poor may become even worse, leading to new ethical considerations.

Common Computer Ethics Fallacies

Although computer education is starting to be incorporated in lower grades in elementary schools, the lack of early computer education for most current adults led to several documented generally accepted fallacies

---

2   Deborah G. Johnson (1985), Computer Ethics, Prentice-Hall. (Second Edition 1994).

that apply to nearly all computer users. As technology advances, these fallacies will change; new ones will arise, and some of the original fallacies will no longer exist as children learn at an earlier age about computer use, risks, security, and other associated information.

There are more than described here, but Peter S. Tippett[3], developer of Norton Antivirus, identified the following computer ethics fallacies, which have been widely discussed and generally accepted as being representative of the most common.[4]

Computer Game Fallacy

Computer users tend to think that computers will generally prevent them from cheating and doing wrong. Programmers particularly believe that an error in programming syntax will prevent it from working, so that if a software program does indeed work, then it must be working correctly and preventing bad things or mistakes from happening. Even computer users in general have gotten the message that computers work with exacting accuracy and will not allow actions that should not occur. Of course, what computer users often do not consider is that although the computer operates under very strict rules, the software programs are written by humans and are just as susceptible to allowing bad things to happen as people often are in their own lives. Along with this, there is also the perception that a person can do something with a computer without being caught, so that if what is being done is not permissible, the computer should somehow prevent them from doing it.

Law-Abiding Citizen Fallacy

Laws provide guidance for many things, including computer use. Sometimes users confuse what is legal with regard to computer use with what is reasonable behavior for using computers. Laws basically define the

---

3   http://web.archive.org/web/20050830080428/http://www.cybertrust.com/about_ us/management.html
4   Harold Tipton, and Micki Krause, Information Security Management Handbook, 6th Edition, (Palm Harbor Florida: CRC Press, 2007), chap. 1.8.

minimum standard about which actions can be reasonably judged, but such laws also call for individual judgment. Computer users often do not realize they also have a responsibility to consider the ramifications of their actions and to behave accordingly.

Shatterproof Fallacy

Many, if not most, computer users believe that they can do little harm accidentally with a computer beyond perhaps erasing or messing up a file. However, computers are tools that can harm, even if computer users are unaware of the fact that their computer actions have actually hurt someone else in some way. For example, sending an e-mail insult to a large group of recipients is the same as publicly humiliating them. Most people realize that they could be sued for libel for making such statements in a physical public forum, but may not realize they are also responsible for what they communicate and for their words and accusations on the Internet.

As another example, forwarding e-mail without permission of the author can lead to harm or embarrassment if the original sender was communicating privately without expectation of his or her message being seen by any others. Also, using e-mail to stalk someone, to send spam, and to harass or offend the recipient in some way also are harmful uses of computers. Software piracy is yet another example of using computers to, in effect, hurt others.

Generally, the shatterproof fallacy is the belief that what a person does with a computer can do minimal harm, and only affects perhaps a few files on the computer itself; it is not considering the impact of actions before doing them.

Candy-from-a-Baby Fallacy

Illegal and unethical activity, such as software piracy and plagiarism, are very easy to do with a computer. However, just because it is easy does not mean that it is right. Because of the ease with which computers can make copies, it is likely almost every computer user has committed software piracy of one form or another. The Software Publisher's Association (SPA) and Business Software Alliance (BSA) studies reveal software piracy costs companies multibillions of dollars. Copying a retail software package without paying for it is theft. Just because doing something wrong with a computer is easy does not mean it is ethical, legal, or acceptable.

Hacker Fallacy

Numerous reports and publications of the commonly accepted hacker belief is that it is acceptable to do anything with a computer as long as the motivation is to learn and not to gain or make a profit from such activities. This so-called hacker ethic is explored in more depth in the following section titled "Hacking and Hactivism".

Free Information Fallacy

A somewhat curious opinion of many is the notion that information "wants to be free," as mentioned earlier. It is suggested that this fallacy emerged from the fact that it is so easy to copy digital information and to distribute it widely. However, this line of thinking completely ignores the fact the copying and distribution of data are completely under the control and whim of the people who do it, and to a great extent, the people who allow it to happen.

Hacking and Hacktivism

Hacking is an ambivalent term, most commonly perceived as being part of criminal activities. However, hacking has been used to describe the work of individuals who have been associated with the open-source movement. Many of the developments in information technology have resulted from what has typically been considered as hacking activities. Manuel Castells considers hacker culture as the "informationalism" that incubates technological breakthrough, identifying hackers as "the actors in the transition from an academically and institutionally constructed milieu of innovation to the emergence of self-organizing networks transcending organizational control".

A hacker was originally a person who sought to understand computers as thoroughly as possible. Soon hacking came to be associated with phreaking, breaking into phone networks to make free phone calls, which is clearly illegal.

The Hacker Ethic

The idea of a hacker ethic originates in the activities of the original hackers at MIT and Stanford in the 1950s and 1960s. Stephen Levy, journalist and author of several books on computers, technology, and privacy, outlined the so-called hacker ethic as follows:[5]

1. Access to computers should be unlimited and total.

2. All information should be free.

3. Authority should be mistrusted and decentralization promoted.

4. Hackers should be judged solely by their skills at hacking, rather than by race, class, age, gender, or position.

5. Computers can be used to create art and beauty.

6. Computers can change your life for the better.

The hacker ethic has three main functions:

1. It promotes the belief of individual activity over any form of corporate authority or system of ideals.

2. It supports a completely free-market approach to the exchange of and access to information.

3. It promotes the belief that computers can have a beneficial and life-changing effect.

Ethics Codes of Conduct and Resources

Several organizations and groups have defined the computer ethics their members should observe and practice. In fact, most professional

---

5   Stephen Levy, Hackers: Heroes of the Computer Revolution, (Garden City, NY: Anchor Press/Doubleday, 1984).

organizations have adopted a code of ethics, a large percentage of which address how to handle information. To provide the ethics of all professional organizations related to computer use would fill a large book. The following are provided to give an opportunity to compare similarities between the codes and, most interestingly, to note the differences (and sometimes contradictions) in the codes followed by the various diverse groups.

The Code of Fair Information Practices

In 1973 the U.S. Secretary's Advisory Committee on Automated Personal Data Systems for the U.S. Department of Health, Education and Welfare recommended the adoption of the following Code of Fair Information Practices to secure the privacy and rights of citizens:

1. There must be no personal data record-keeping systems whose very existence is secret.

2. There must be a way for an individual to find out what information is in his or her file and how the information is being used.

3. There must be a way for an individual to correct information in his or her records.

4. Any organization creating, maintaining, using, or disseminating records of personally identifiable information must assure the reliability of the data for its intended use and must take precautions to prevent misuse.

5. There must be a way for an individual to prevent personal information obtained for one purpose from being used for another purpose without his or her consent.

Internet Activities Board (IAB) (Now the Internet Architecture Board) and RFC 1087

RFC 1087 is a statement of policy by the Internet Activities Board (IAB) posted in 1989 concerning the ethical and proper use of the resources of the Internet. The IAB "strongly endorses the view of the Division Advisory Panel of the National Science Foundation Division of Network,

Communications Research and Infrastructure,"[6] which characterized as unethical and unacceptable any activity that purposely

1. Seeks to gain unauthorized access to the resources of the Internet

2. Disrupts the intended use of the Internet

3. Wastes resources (people, capacity, computer) through such actions

4. Destroys the integrity of computer-based information or

5. Compromises the privacy of users

Computer Ethics Institute (CEI)

In 1991 the Computer Ethics Institute held its first National Computer Ethics Conference in Washington, D.C. The Ten Commandments of Computer Ethics were first presented in Dr. Ramon C. Barquin's paper prepared for the conference, "In Pursuit of a 'Ten Commandments' for Computer Ethics." The Computer Ethics Institute published them as follows in 1992[7]:

1. Thou Shalt Not Use a Computer to Harm Other People.

2. Thou Shalt Not Interfere with Other People's Computer Work.

3. Thou Shalt Not Snoop around in Other People's Computer Files.

4. Thou Shalt Not Use a Computer to Steal.

5. Thou Shalt Not Use a Computer to Bear False Witness.

6. Thou Shalt Not Copy or Use Proprietary Software for Which You Have Not Paid.

7. Thou Shalt Not Use Other People's Computer Resources without Authorization or Proper Compensation.

---

6   http://www.faqs.org/rfcs/rfc1087.html

7   http://computerethicsinstitute.org/publications/tencommandments.html

8. Thou Shalt Not Appropriate Other People's Intellectual Output.

9. Thou Shalt Think about the Social Consequences of the Program You Are Writing or the System You Are Designing.

10. Thou Shalt Always Use a Computer in Ways That Insure Consideration and Respect for Your Fellow Humans.

National Conference on Computing and Values

The National Conference on Computing and Values[8] (NCCV) was held on the campus of Southern Connecticut State University in August 1991. It proposed the following four primary values for computing, originally intended to serve as the ethical foundation and guidance for computer security:

1. Preserve the public trust and confidence in computers.

2. Enforce fair information practices.

3. Protect the legitimate interests of the constituents of the system.

4. Resist fraud, waste, and abuse.

The Working Group on Computer Ethics

In 1991, the Working Group on Computer Ethics[9] created the following End User's Basic Tenets of Responsible Computing:

1. I understand that just because something is legal, it isn't necessarily moral or right.

2. I understand that people are always the ones ultimately harmed when computers are used unethically. The fact that computers, software, or a communications medium exists between me and those harmed does not in any way change moral responsibility toward my fellow humans.

---

8   http://southernct.edu/organizations/rccs/?p=1131&sub=1618

9   http://southernct.edu/organizations/rccs/?p=709

3. I will respect the rights of authors, including authors and publishers of software as well as authors and owners of information. I understand that just because copying programs and data is easy, it is not necessarily right.

4. I will not break into or use other people's computers or read or use their information without their consent.

5. I will not write or knowingly acquire, distribute, or allow intentional distribution of harmful software like bombs, worms, and computer viruses.

National Computer Ethics and Responsibilities Campaign (NCERC)

In 1994, a National Computer Ethics and Responsibilities Campaign (NCERC) was launched to create an "electronic repository of information resources, training materials and sample ethics codes"[10] that would be available on the Internet for IS managers and educators. The National Computer Security Association (NCSA) and the CEI cosponsored NCERC. The NCERC Guide to Computer Ethics was developed to support the campaign.

The goal of NCERC is to foster computer ethics awareness and education. The campaign does this by making tools and other resources available for people who want to hold events, campaigns, awareness programs, seminars, and conferences or to write or communicate about computer ethics. NCERC is a nonpartisan initiative intended to increase understanding of the ethical and moral issues unique to the use, and sometimes abuse, of information technologies.

---

10   http://privacyguidance.com/blog/2006/08/28/crime-really-doesnt-pay-computer-criminals-sentenced-to-prison-for-copyright-infringement-and-computer-attacks/

(ISC)² Code of Professional Ethics

The following is an excerpt from the (ISC)² Code of Ethics preamble and canons, by which all (ISC)² members must abide. Compliance with the preamble and canons is mandatory to maintain membership and credentials. Professionals resolve conflicts between the canons in the order of the canons. The canons are not equal and conflicts between them are not intended to create ethical binds.

Code of Ethics Preamble

Safety of the commonwealth, duty to our principals, and to each other requires that we adhere, and be seen to adhere, to the highest ethical standards of behavior. Therefore, strict adherence to this Code is a condition of certification.

Code of Ethics Canons

Protect society, the commonwealth, and the infrastructure

> Promote and preserve public trust and confidence in information and systems.

> Promote the understanding and acceptance of prudent information security measures

> Preserve and strengthen the integrity of the public infrastructure.

> Discourage unsafe practice.

Act honorably, honestly, justly, responsibly, and legally

> Tell the truth; make all stakeholders aware of your actions on a timely basis.

> Observe all contracts and agreements, express or implied.

> Treat all constituents fairly. In resolving conflicts, consider public safety and duties to principals, individuals, and the profession in that order.

Give prudent advice; avoid raising unnecessary alarm or giving unwarranted comfort. Take care to be truthful, objective, cautious, and within your competence.

When resolving differing laws in different jurisdictions, give preference to the laws of the jurisdiction in which you render your service.

Provide diligent and competent service to principals

Preserve the value of their systems, applications, and information.

Respect their trust and the privileges that they grant you.

Avoid conflicts of interest or the appearance thereof.

Render only those services for which you are fully competent and qualified.

Advance and protect the profession

Sponsor for professional advancement those best qualified. All other things equal, prefer those who are certified and who adhere to these canons. Avoid professional association with those whose practices or reputation might diminish the profession.

Take care not to injure the reputation of other professionals through malice or indifference.

Maintain your competence; keep your skills and knowledge current. Give generously of your time and knowledge in training others.

Support Organization's Code of Ethics

Peter S. Tippett has written extensively on computer ethics. He provided the following action plan to help corporate information security leaders to instill a culture of ethical computer use within organizations[11]:

1. Develop a corporate guide to computer ethics for the organization.

2. Develop a computer ethics policy to supplement the computer security policy.

3. Add information about computer ethics to the employee handbook.

4. Find out whether the organization has a business ethics policy, and expand it to include computer ethics.

5. Learn more about computer ethics and spreading what is learned.

6. Help to foster awareness of computer ethics by participating in the computer ethics campaign.

7. Make sure the organization has an E-mail privacy policy.

8. Make sure employees know what the E-mail policy is.

Fritz H. Grupe, Timothy Garcia-Jay, and William Kuechler[12] identified the following selected ethical bases for IT decision making

- *Golden Rule:* Treat others as you wish to be treated. Do not implement systems that you would not wish to be subjected to yourself. Is your company using unlicensed software although your company itself sells software?

- *Kant's Categorical Imperative:* If an action is not right for everyone, it is not right for anyone. Does management monitor call center employees' seat time, but not its own?

---

11   Harold Tipton, and Micki Krause, Information Security Management Handbook, 6th Edition, (Palm Harbor Florida: CRC Press, 2007), chap. 1.8.

12   First Fritz H. Grupe, Timothy Garcia-Jay, and William Kuechler Last, "Is it time for an IT Ethics Program?," Information Systems Management, 19, no. 3 (2002): 1-7,

- **Descartes' Rule of Change (also called the Slippery Slope):** If an action is not repeatable at all times, it is not right at any time. Should a Web site link to another site, "framing" the page, so users think it was created and belongs to the former?

- **Utilitarian Principle (also called Universalism):** Take the action that achieves the most good. Put a value on outcomes and strive to achieve the best results. This principle seeks to analyze and maximize the IT of the covered population within acknowledged resource constraints. Should customers using a Web site be asked to opt in or opt out of the possible sale of their personal data to other companies?

- **Risk Aversion Principle:** Incur least harm or cost. When there are alternatives that have varying degrees of harm and gain, choose the one that causes the least damage. If a manager reports that a subordinate criticized him in an e-mail to other employees, who would do the search and see the results of the search?

- **Avoid Harm:** Avoid malfeasance or "do no harm." This basis implies a proactive obligation of companies to protect their customers and clients from systems with known harm. Does your company have a privacy policy that protects, rather than exploits customers?

- **No Free Lunch Rule:** Assume that all property and information belong to someone. This principle is primarily applicable to intellectual property that should not be taken without just compensation. Has a company used unlicensed software? Or hired a group of IT workers from a competitor?

- **Legalism:** Is it against the law? Moral actions may not be legal, and vice versa. Might a Web advertising exaggerate the features and benefits of products? Are web sites collecting information illegally on minors?

- **Professionalism:** Is an action contrary to codes of ethics? Do the professional codes cover a case and do they suggest the path to follow? When you present technological alternatives to managers who do not know the right questions to ask, do you tell them all they need to know to make informed choices?

- **Evidentiary Guidance:** Is there hard data to support or deny the value of taking an action? This is not a traditional "ethics" value but one that is a significant factor related to IT's policy decisions about the impact of systems on individuals and groups. This value involves probabilistic reasoning where outcomes can be predicted based on hard evidence based on research. Does management assume that they know PC users are satisfied with IT's service or has data been collected to determine what they really think?

- **Client/Customer/Patient Choice:** Let the people affected decide. In some circumstances, employees and customers have a right to self-determination through the informed consent process. This principle acknowledges a right to self-determination in deciding what is "harmful" or "beneficial" for their personal circumstances. Are workers subjected to monitoring in places where they assume that they have privacy?

- **Equity:** Will the costs and benefits be equitably distributed? Adherence to this principle obligates a company to provide similarly situated persons with the same access to data and systems. This can imply a proactive duty to inform and make services, data, and systems available to all those who share a similar circumstance. Has IT made intentionally inaccurate projections as to project costs?

- **Competition:** This principle derives from the marketplace where consumers and institutions can select among competing companies, based on all considerations such as degree of privacy, cost, and quality. It recognizes that to be financially viable in the market, it is necessary to have data about what competitors are doing and understand and acknowledge the competitive implications of IT decisions. When presenting a build or buy proposition to management, is it fully aware of the risk involved?

- *Compassion/Last Chance:* Religious and philosophical traditions promote the need to find ways to assist the most vulnerable parties. Refusing to take unfair advantage of users or others who do not have technical knowledge is recognized in several professional codes of ethics. Do all workers have an equal opportunity to benefit from the organization's investment in IT?

- *Impartiality/Objectivity:* Are decisions biased in favor of one group or another? Is there an even playing field? IT personnel should avoid potential or apparent conflicts of interest. Do you or any of your IT employees have a vested interest in the companies that you deal with?

- *Openness/Full Disclosure:* Are persons affected by this system aware of its existence, aware of what data are being collected, and knowledgeable about how it will be used? Do they have access to the same information? Is it possible for a Web site visitor to determine what cookies are used and what is done with any information they might collect?

- *Confidentiality:* IT is obligated to determine whether data it collects on individuals can be adequately protected to avoid disclosure to parties whose need to know is not proven. Have security features been reduced to hold expenses to a minimum?

- *Trustworthiness and Honesty:* Does IT stand behind ethical principles to the point where it is accountable for the actions it takes? Has IT management ever posted or circulated a professional code of ethics with an expression of support for seeing that its employees act professionally?

How a Code of Ethics Applies to CISSPs

In 1998, Michael Davis, a professor of Philosophy at the Illinois Institute of Technology, described a professional ethics code as a "contract between professionals."[13] According to this explanation, a profession is a group of persons who want to cooperate in serving the same ideal better than

13   Davis, Michael. Center for the Study of Ethics, "Thinking Like an Engineer." Accessed July 31, 2012. http://ethics.iit.edu/publication/md_te.html.

they could if they did not cooperate. Information security professionals, for example, are typically thought to serve the ideal of ensuring the confidentiality, integrity, and availability of information and the security of the technology that supports the information use. A code of ethics would then specify how professionals should pursue their common ideals so that each may do his or her best to reach the goals at a minimum cost while appropriately addressing the issues involved.

The code helps to protect professionals from certain stresses and pressures (such as the pressure to cut corners with information security to save money) by making it reasonably likely that most other members of the profession will not take advantage of the resulting conduct of such pressures. An ethics code also protects members of a profession from certain consequences of competition, and encourages cooperation and support among the professionals.

Considering this, an occupation does not need society's recognition to be a profession. Indeed, it only needs the actions and activities among its members to cooperate to serve a certain ideal. Once an occupation becomes recognized as a profession, society historically has found reason to give the occupation special privileges (e.g., the sole right to do certain kinds of work) to support serving the ideal in question (in this case, information security) in the way the profession serves society.

Understanding a code of ethics as a contract between professionals, it can then be explained why each information security professional should not depend upon only his or her private conscience when determining how to practice the profession, and why he or she must take into account what a community of information security professionals has to say about what other information security professionals should do. What others expect of information security professionals is part of what each should take into account in choosing what to do within professional activities, especially if the expectation is reasonable. The ethics code provides a guide to what information security professionals may reasonably expect of one another, basically setting forth the rules of the game.

Just as athletes need to know the rules of football to know what to do to score, computer professionals also need to know computer ethics to know, for example, whether they should choose information security and risk reduction actions based completely and solely upon the wishes of an employer, or, instead, also consider information security leading practices and legal requirements when making recommendations and decisions.

A code of ethics should also provide a guide to what computer professionals may expect other members of our profession to help each other do. Keep in mind that people are not merely members of this or that profession. Each individual has responsibilities beyond the profession and, as such, must face his or her own conscience, along with the criticism, blame, and punishment of others, as a result of actions. These issues cannot be escaped just by making a decision because their profession told them to.

Information security professionals must take their professional code of ethics and apply it appropriately to their own unique environments. To assist with this, Donn B. Parker a consultant, information security researcher and fellow of the association for computing machinery describes the following five ethical principles that apply to processing information in the workplace, and also provides examples of how they would be applied.

1. ***Informed consent.*** Try to make sure that the people affected by a decision are aware of your planned actions and that they either agree with your decision, or disagree but understand your intentions. Example: An employee gives a copy of a program that she wrote for her employer to a friend, and does not tell her employer about it.

2. ***Higher ethic in the worst case***. Think carefully about your possible alternative actions and select the beneficial necessary ones that will cause the least, or no, harm under the worst

circumstances. Example: A manager secretly monitors an employee's email, which may violate his privacy, but the manager has evidence-based reason to believe that the employee may be involved in a serious theft of trade secrets.

3. *Change of scale test.* Consider that an action you may take on a small scale, or by you alone, could result in significant harm if carried out on a larger scale or by many others. Examples: A teacher lets a friend try out, just once, a database that he bought to see if the friend wants to buy a copy, too. The teacher does not let an entire classroom of his students use the database for a class assignment without first getting permission from the vendor. A computer user thinks it's okay to use a small amount of her employer's computer services for personal business, since the others' use is unaffected.

4. *Owners' conservation of ownership.* As a person who owns or is responsible for information, always make sure that the information is reasonably protected and that ownership of it, and rights to it, are clear to users. Example: A vendor, who sells a commercial electronic bulletin board service with no proprietary notice at log-on, loses control of the service to a group of hackers who take it over, misuse it, and offend customers.

5. *Users' conservation of ownership.* As a person who uses information, always assume others own it and their interests must be protected unless you explicitly know that you are free to use it in any way that you wish. Example: Hacker discovers a commercial electronic bulletin board with no proprietary notice at logon, and informs his friends, who take control of it, misuse it, and then uses it to offend other customers.

Understand and Support Investigations

One area that has traditionally been lacking in most organizations is proper evidence handling and management. The exact name given to this area ranges from computer forensics, digital forensics, and network forensics, to electronic data discovery, cyber forensics, and forensic computing. For the sake of clarity, the term digital investigations will be used to encompass all the components expressed in the other terms mentioned; thus, no one definition will be provided. Instead, digital investigations will include all domains in which the evidence or potential evidence exists in a digital or electronic form, whether in storage or on the wire. We intentionally omit digital multimedia from the mix, as this is a related, yet highly differentiated, field within the umbrella of digital forensic science. Unlike the media depiction, computer forensics/digital investigations is not some piece of software or hardware. It is based on a methodical, verifiable, and "auditable" sets of procedures and protocols.

Digital investigations fall under the larger domain of digital forensic science. In 2008, the American Academy of Forensic Sciences (AAFS) in the United States formally recognized digital forensic science as a discipline under the category of Digital and Multimedia Sciences; it was the first time in 28 years that a new section has been recognized by the AAFS. The Digital Forensic Science Research Workshop[1] (DFRWS) defines digital forensic science as

> *The use of scientifically derived and proven methods toward the preservation, collection, validation, identification, analysis, interpretation, documentation and presentation of digital evidence derived from digital sources for the purpose of facilitating or furthering the reconstruction of events found to be criminal, or helping to anticipate unauthorized actions shown to be disruptive to planned operations.*

---

1   http://www.dfrws.org/index.shtml

1217

As a forensic discipline, this area deals with evidence and the legal system and is really the marriage of computer science, information technology, and engineering with law. The inclusion of the law introduces concepts that may be foreign to many information security professionals. These include crime scene, chain of custody, best evidence, admissibility requirements, rules of evidence, etc. It is extremely important that anyone who may potentially be involved in an investigation be familiar with the basics of dealing with and managing evidence. There is nothing worse than finding the proverbial smoking gun only to learn that the evidence cannot be used, will be suppressed, or, even worse, the information security professional has violated the rights of the individuals in question and is now in worse trouble than the "bad guys." Although different countries and legal systems have slight variations in determining how evidence and the digital crime scene should be handled, there are enough commonalities that a general discussion is possible.

Like incident response, there are various computer forensics guidelines (e.g., International Organization of Computer Evidence (IOCE), Scientific Working Group on Digital Evidence (SWGDE), Association of Chief Police Officers (ACPO)). These guidelines formalize the computer forensic processes by breaking them into numerous phases or steps. A generic guideline includes:

- ***Identifying Evidence:*** Correctly identifying the crime scene, evidence, and potential containers of evidence.

- ***Collecting or Acquiring Evidence:*** Adhering to the criminalistic principles and ensuring that the contamination and the destruction of the scene are kept to a minimum. Using sound, repeatable, collection techniques that allow for the demonstration of the accuracy and integrity of evidence, or copies of evidence.

- ***Examining or Analyzing the Evidence:*** Using sound scientific methods to determine the characteristics of the evidence, conducting comparison for individuation of evidence, and conducting event reconstruction.

■ *Presentation of Findings:* Interpreting the output from the examination and analysis based on findings of fact and articulating these in a format appropriate for the intended audience (e.g., court brief, executive memo, report).

Crime Scene

Before identifying evidence, the larger crime scene needs to be dealt with. A crime scene is nothing more than the environment in which potential evidence may exist. The same holds for a digital crime scene. The principles of criminalistics apply in both cases: identify the scene, protect the environment, identify evidence and potential sources of evidence, collect evidence, and minimize the degree of contamination. With digital crime scenes, the environment consists of both the physical and the virtual, or cyber. The physical (e.g., server, workstation, laptop, PDA, digital music device) is relatively straightforward to deal with; the virtual is more complicated, as it is often more difficult to determine the exact location of the evidence (e.g., data on a cluster or GRID, or storage area networks (SANs)) or acquire the evidence, as is the case with "live" systems.

Live evidence is data that are very dynamic and exist in running processes or other volatile locations (e.g., RAM) that disappear in a relatively short time once the system is powered down. It is also more difficult to protect the virtual scene. The crime scene can provide additional information related to whom or what might be responsible for the attack or incident.

Locard's principle of exchange states that when a crime is committed, the perpetrators leave something behind and take something with them, hence the exchange. This principle allows us to identify aspects of the persons responsible, even with a purely digital crime scene. As with traditional investigations, understanding the means, opportunity, and motives (MOM), as well as the modus operandi (MO [method of operation] or the way the crime was committed), allows for a more thorough investigation or root cause analysis. As was mentioned in the "incident response" section, identifying the root cause correctly and quickly is extremely important when dealing with an incident, whether it is criminal or not.

Criminologists, sociologists, and psychologists generally agree that behavior is intentional and serves to fulfill some purpose (e.g., need fulfillment). Criminal behavior is no different, and thus neither is criminal computer behavior. Computer criminals and hackers rarely have significant differences related to motivation for attacking systems. Like traditional criminals, computer criminals have specific MOs (e.g., hacking software, type of system or network attacked) and leave behind signature behaviors (e.g., programming syntax, e-mail messages, bragging notices) that can be used to identify the attacker (or at least the tool), link other criminal behaviors together, and provide insight into the thought processes of the attackers. This information can be extremely useful in the event of an insider attack, as it can be used during the interview process to solicit more accurate responses from the accused. With an external attack, the information can assist law enforcement in piecing together other offenses by the same individual, assist in the interview and interrogation process, and provide strategies at trial when the accused will be the most defensive.

Given the importance of the evidence that is available at a crime scene, only those individuals with knowledge of basic crime scene analysis should be allowed to deal with the scene. The logical choice is members of the incident response or handling team. The need for a formal approach to this task, coupled with very thorough documentation, is essential. So too is the ability to deal with a scene in a manner that minimizes the amount of disruption, contamination, or destruction of evidence. Once a scene has been contaminated, there is no undo or redo button to push; the damage is done. In many jurisdictions, the accused or opposing party has the right to conduct its own examination and analysis, requiring as original a scene as possible.

General Guidelines

Most seasoned digital investigators have mixed emotions regarding detailed guidelines for dealing with an investigation. The common concern is that too much detail and formalism will lead to rigid checklists and negatively affect the creative aspects of the analysis and examination. Too little formalism and methodology leads to sloppiness, difficulty in recreating the investigative process, and the lack of an "auditable" process that can be examined by the courts. In response to this issue, several international entities (e.g., Scientific Working Group on Digital Evidence (SWGDE[2])) have devised general guidelines that are based on the IOCE/Group of 8 Nations (G8) principles for computer forensics and digital/electronic evidence:

- When dealing with digital evidence, all of the general forensic and procedural principles must be applied.

- Upon seizing digital evidence, actions taken should not change that evidence.

- When it is necessary for a person to access original digital evidence, that person should be trained for the purpose.

- All activity relating to the seizure, access, storage, or transfer of digital evidence must be fully documented, preserved, and available for review.

- An individual is responsible for all actions taken with respect to digital evidence while the digital evidence is in his possession.

- Any agency that is responsible for seizing, accessing, storing, or transferring digital evidence is responsible for compliance with these principles.

These principles form the foundation for the current international models most prominent today (e.g., United States National Institute of Standards and Technology (NIST), United States Department of Justice (DOJ)/ Federal Bureau of Investigations (FBI) Search and Seizure Manual,

---

2   Read more about SWGDE here: https://www.swgde.org/

NIST SP 800-86: Computer Forensic Guidelines, SWGDE Best Practices for Computer Forensics, ACPO Good Practices Guide for Computer Based Evidence, IACIS forensic examination procedures). These models are also responsive to the prevailing requirements of the court systems and updated on a frequent basis.

The sagest advice that can be given to anyone involved in a computer forensics investigation or any form of incident response is to act ethically, in good faith, attempt to do no harm, and do not exceed one's knowledge, skills, and abilities. The following "rules of thumb" were developed by the Australian Computer Emergency Response Team (AusCERT) and should be a part of an investigator's methodology:

- Minimize handling/corruption of original data.
- Account for any changes and keep detailed logs of your actions.
- Comply with the five rules of evidence.
- Do not exceed your knowledge.
- Follow your local security policy and obtain written permission.
- Capture as accurate an image of the system as possible.
- Be prepared to testify.
- Ensure your actions are repeatable.
- Work fast.
- Proceed from volatile to persistent evidence.
- Do not run any programs on the affected system.

As an information security professional, it is incumbent to stay current on the latest techniques, tools, processes, and requirements for admissibility of evidence. The entire area of computer forensics is coming under increased scrutiny by both the courts and the public and will undergo significant changes in the next few years as the field matures and develops, as did other more traditional forensic disciplines, such as DNA and latent fingerprint analysis.

Policy, Roles and Responsibilities

To have effective and efficient incident handling, a solid foundation must exist. In this instance, the foundation is comprised of a corporate incident handling and response policy, clearly articulated procedures and guidelines that take into consideration the various legal implications of reacting to incidents, and the management and handling of evidence (digital, physical, and document based). The policy must be clear, concise, and provide a mandate for the incident response/handling team to deal with any and all incidents. The policy must also provide direction for employees on the escalation process to follow when a potential incident is discovered, and how various notifications, contacts, and liaisons with third-party entities, the media, government, and law enforcement authorities are to be notified, by whom, and in what manner.

A properly staffed and trained response team is also required; the team can be virtual or permanent depending on the requirements of the organization. Virtual teams usually consist of individuals that, while assigned to the response team, have other regular duties and are only called upon if there is some need to start the incident handling capability. Some organizations have teams whose members are permanently assigned to the incident team and work in this capacity on a full-time basis. A third model can be described as a hybrid of the virtual and permanent, with certain core members permanently assigned to the incident team and others called up as necessary.

Although the actual makeup of the response team depends upon the structure of the organization, there are core areas that need to be represented: legal department (in lieu of in-house legal counsel, arrangements should be made with external counsel), human resources, communications, executive management, physical/corporate security, internal audit, IS security, and IT. Obviously, there needs to be representation by other pertinent business units as well as systems administrators and anyone else that can assist in the recovery and investigation of an incident. Once the team has been established, it must be trained and stay current with its training. This sounds easy enough at first glance, but the initial and ongoing training requires a budget and resources to cover for team members who are away at training; more than one organization has been stymied in its attempt to establish a response team because of the failure to anticipate realistic costs associated with training and education.

What has yet to be discussed or even hinted at, is dealing with the public or the media. This is not an oversight, as the whole domain of public relations and communications is an extremely sensitive issue at the best of times. When an event becomes an incident, the proper handling of public disclosure can either compound the negative impact or, if handled correctly, provide an opportunity to engender public trust in the organization. This is why communications, human resources, and only properly trained and authorized individuals should handle the communications and external notifications. In some countries or jurisdictions, legislation exists (or is being contemplated) that requires organizations to publicly disclose when they reasonably believe there has been an incident that may have jeopardized someone's private or financial information. Obviously, denial and "no comment" are not an effective public relations strategy in today's information culture.

Incident Response

Incident response, or more precisely incident handling, has become one of the primary functions of today's information security department, and thus of those professionals working in this capacity. This increased importance is a direct result of the fact that attacks against networks and information systems are evolving—total volume of attacks appear to be decreasing, yet the sophistication and attack vectors are changing. Although statistics related to the exact increase in volumes of attacks and the corresponding economic costs are impossible to calculate given the lack of universal reporting, the gross trends indicate significant changes in the last few years. The types of attacks seem to undergo almost continuous modifications. Today spam, phishing scams, worms, spyware, distributed denial-of-service attacks (DDoS), botnets, and other imaginative yet malicious attacks and mutations inundate personal computers, networks, and corporate systems on a daily basis.

Historically, incident response has been precisely that, a reaction to a trigger event. Incident response in its simplest form is the practice of detecting a problem, determining its cause, minimizing the damage it causes, resolving the problem, and documenting each step of the response for future reference. Although reactive controls are obviously necessary, lessons learned from the various attacks against information systems worldwide make it painfully obvious that preventive controls as well as detective controls are also required if we are to have any hope of recovering or maintaining business operations. Although various entities have developed detailed models for incident handling (e.g., Computer Emergency Response Team Coordination Center (CERT/CC), AusCERT, Forum of Incident Response Teams (FIRST), NIST, British Computing Society, and Canadian Communications Security Establishment (CSE)), there is a common framework to these models. The framework consists of the following components:

- Creation of a response capability
- Incident response and handling
- Recovery and feedback

Incident Handling and Response

If the appropriate groundwork has been laid, the next phase is the actual handling of an incident. Although there are various definitions of what constitutes an incident (usually any event that has the potential to negatively affect the business or its assets), it is ultimately up to the organization to categorize events that warrant the activation of the incident response escalation process. In most cases, this is described in some level of detail in the policies and guidelines.

1225

When an event becomes an incident, it is essential that a methodical approach be followed. This is necessary given the complexities of dealing with the dynamics of an incident; several tasks must be carried out in parallel as well as serially. Often the output of one phase or stage in the handling of an incident produces input for a subsequent phase. In some cases, previous steps need to be revisited in light of new information obtained as the investigation develops—the process should be viewed as iterative in nature. CERT/CC at Carnegie Melon University, one of the foremost authorities on incident response and incident handling, depicts the incident handling model as a circular process that feeds back into itself, thus capturing the various dynamics and dependencies of the incident life cycle. The incident response and the handling phase can be broken down further into triage, investigation, containment, and analysis and tracking.

Triage Phase

Regardless of what actual model of incident handling is prescribed to, there is usually some trigger event that kick starts the process. The consensus of the various models is that the first step is some type of triage process. A good analogy here (and one that is mentioned in several models) is that of a hospital emergency department receiving a new patient. Once the patient arrives, he or she is examined to determine the urgency of care required. Patients with life-threatening conditions receive priority, patients with less life-threatening conditions are placed into a queue, and patients with minor conditions may be directed to their own physicians or neighborhood clinics.

Triage encompasses the detection, identification, and notification subphases. Following the medical model, once an incident has been detected, an incident handler is tasked with the initial screening to determine the seriousness of the incident and to filter out false-positives. One of the most time-consuming aspects of information security can be dealing with false-positives (events that are incorrectly deemed to be incidents based on rules or some other rubric). If during the initial phase of the triage it is determined that it is a false-positive, the event is logged and the process returns to the pre-incident escalation level of readiness. However, if it is a real incident, then the next step is identifying or classifying the type of incident. This classification is dependent on the organization, but is commonly based on a hierarchy beginning with the general classifiers (e.g., apparent source = internal versus external) and progressing to more granular or specific characteristics (e.g., worm versus spam). This categorization is used to determine the level of potential risk or criticality of the incident, which in turn is used to determine what notifications are required. Here again, the policies, procedures, and guidelines that were developed before the incident provide direction for the incident handler to follow.

It is important to recognize that in the triage phase, the initial detection can come from automated safeguards or security controls, from employees, or some other third party (e.g., National CERT). Often, the end user will notice that his system is behaving oddly or that he has received some type of suspicious e-mail that was not blocked by the controls. If the end user is well educated and informed about the policy and procedures to follow when he notices something unusual or suspicious, the entire response escalation process becomes far more efficient and effective.

Investigative Phase

The next major phase deals directly with the analysis, interpretation, reaction, and recovery from an incident. Regardless of the specific model that is followed, the desired outcomes of this phase are to reduce the impact of the incident, identify the root cause, get back up and running in the shortest possible time, and prevent the incident from occurring again. All of this occurs against the backdrop of adhering to company policy, applicable laws and regulations, and proper evidence management and handling. This last point cannot be stressed enough. Various countries have enacted privacy laws that protect employees and others from frivolous monitoring of network and online activities by employers. Potential evidence must also be handled correctly according to rules of evidence and a chain of custody

1227

documented and maintained, or it runs the risk of being inadmissible in the case of civil or criminal sanctions, or even as grounds for terminating someone's employment (see "*Computer Forensics*" section).

Containment

After the notification, the next task is to contain the incident. Using the medical analogy yet again is similar to quarantining a patient until the exact nature of the disease or pathogen is determined. This quarantining prevents an outbreak if it turns out that the cause was some infectious agent, and allows medical staff to conduct directed analysis of the cause of the malady. In our case, the patient is a system, device, or subset of systems on the network. The containment is used to reduce the potential impact of the incident by reducing the number of other systems, devices, or network systems that can become infected.

The method of containment can vary depending on the category of the attack (e.g., external, worm), the asset affected (e.g., Web server, router), and the criticality of the data or the risk of infection to the rest of the network. Strategies include removing the system from the network by disconnecting it, virtually isolating the systems by way of network segmentation (e.g., switch, virtual local area network (VLAN)), or implementing a firewall or filtering router with the appropriate rule sets. It should be noted that in some cases, complete isolation or containment may not be a viable solution, or if the ultimate goal of the exercise is to track the event or capture additional evidence of further wrongdoing, other alternatives such as sniffing traffic, honeypots can be used. However, depending on the incident or attack, the act of containing a system can alert the attacker that he or she has been detected. This can result in the attacker deleting any trails he or she has left or, in extreme cases, escalating the damage in an attempt to overwhelm the victim's resources, thus allowing the attacker to escape or obfuscate the source of the attack.

While dealing with the process of containment, proper documentation and handling of any potential sources of evidence must be maintained. It is very difficult at the beginning of an incident to anticipate the outcome (e.g., criminal attack, error or omission); therefore, operating under the highest standard or "burden of proof" is prudent. If it turns out to be a false alarm or something not worth pursuing, the documentation and data can be used for training purposes as well as for postmortem or post-incident debriefing purposes.

Analysis and Tracking

The next logical step after isolation or containment is to begin to examine and analyze what has occurred, with a focus on determining the root cause. The idea of root cause goes deeper than identifying only symptoms. It looks at what is the initial event in the cause—effect chain. Root cause analysis also attempts to determine the actual source and the point of entry into the network. Different models portray this step in various forms, but the ultimate goal is to obtain sufficient information to stop the current incident, prevent future "like" incidents from occurring, and identify what or whom is responsible. This stage requires a well-trained team of individuals with heterogeneous or eclectic skills and a solid understanding of the systems affected, as well as system and application vulnerabilities. The ability to read and parse through large log files is also a skill that is in high demand during this phase as log files from routers, switches, firewalls, Web servers, etc. are often the primary source of initial information. Secondary sources of information are artifacts. An artifact is any file, object, or data directly related to the incident or left behind or created as part of the attack.

As with any form of analysis, individuals need a combination of formal training and sufficient real-world applied experience to make appropriate interpretations without the luxury of an unlimited timeframe. A side benefit of containment is that it "buys you time." By containing the potential spread, a bit of breathing room can be gained to continue with the analysis and tracking in a controlled manner, as opposed to the complete state of chaos that may ensue at the beginning of the incident response and handling process. One of the biggest enemies to the tracking process is the dynamic nature of many of the logs, both internal and external. Log files tend to a have very limited life expectancy, and depending upon the organization, logs may be purged or overwritten in as little as 24 hours. The proverbial clock starts ticking the minute the attack, worm, virus, etc., is launched, not necessarily at the point when it is first detected.

Tracking often takes place in parallel with the analysis and examination. When information is obtained, it is fed into the tracking process to weed out false leads or intentionally spoofed sources. To have an effective tracking or traceback, it is extremely important that the organization or team have a good working relationship with other entities, such as Internet Service Providers (ISP), other response teams, and law enforcement. These relationships can expedite the tracking process, and needless time-consuming hiccups can be avoided (e.g., not knowing whom to notify at the ISP to request log information). Despite the cultural myth that law enforcement is woefully inept at dealing with Internet and technology-based crimes, today many law enforcement agencies have specialized units dedicated to high-tech crime investigations, and these agencies can be extremely helpful in assisting with the tracking and tracing.

An important point to consider, as part of developing the incident handling policy and guidelines, is what to do once the root cause has been both identified and traced back to the source. As an aside, some policies forbid tracking and traceback and direct the response team to focus on the recovery and future prevention aspects. An alarming trend that is surfacing deals with the suggestion of striking back at the source. The ramifications regarding this are huge, not only legally but also ethically. Source addresses can be spoofed, and often the source turns out to be a compromised machine that the owner had no idea it had been used in an illegal manner. Although it is tempting to seek revenge after being wronged, it is better to take the moral high ground and seek redress through the proper legal channels.

Recovery Phase

The next major category deals with recovery, repair, and prevention of the affected systems and assets. The goal of this phase is to get the business back up and running (in a worst-case scenario), or, in the best case, bring the affected systems back into production, being sensitive to other activities that may be happening in unison (e.g., tracking and traceback).

Once the root cause analysis has provided sufficient information, the recovery process should begin. The exact strategy and techniques used are dependent on the type of incident and the characteristics of the "patient." The important consideration is to recover in a manner that has the maximum likelihood of withstanding another directed incident. There is little to be gained by simply recovering a system or device to the same level that it was at before the incident, as the probability that it will be attacked again is quite high. If it did not survive the first attack, it is not likely to survive a subsequent attack. The more prudent approach is to delay putting the system or device back into production until it is at least protected from the incident that affected it in the first place. This can be accomplished by upgrading the operating system, updating service packs, applying the appropriate patches (after they are thoroughly tested, of course), or, in more drastic cases, rebuilding the entire system or replacing the original with a different or newer product. Once the system or device appears to be ready to be reintroduced back into production, it should be tested for vulnerabilities and weaknesses. It is not advisable to have the same members who worked on the recovery and repair conduct this activity, to ensure some independence and objectivity. There is an abundance of first-rate vulnerability testing software, both open-source and retail software, available that can be used to test the systems.

As was stated earlier, incident response is a dynamic process, with very fuzzy lines between the various phases; often these phases are conducted in parallel and each has some natural dependencies on the other. Incident response and handling can be thought of as an iterative process that feeds back into itself until there is some form of closure to the incident.

What exactly constitutes incident closure is dependent upon a number of variables, the nature or category of the incident, the desired outcome of the organization (e.g., business resumption, prosecution, system restoration), and the success of the team in determining the root cause and source of the incident. It is advisable that the corporate policy or guidelines contain some sort of checklist or metric by which the team can determine when an incident is to be closed.

Evidence Collection and Handling

Chain of Custody

Two concepts that are at the heart of dealing effectively with digital/electronic evidence, or any evidence for that matter, are the chain of custody and authenticity/integrity. The chain of custody refers to the who, what, when, where, and how the evidence was handled—from its identification through its entire life cycle, which ends with destruction or permanent archiving. Any break in this chain can cast doubt on the integrity of the evidence and on the professionalism of those directly involved in either the investigation or the collection and handling of the evidence. The chain of custody requires following a formal process that is well documented and forms part of a standard operating procedure that is used in all cases, no exceptions.

Ensuring the authenticity and integrity of evidence is critical. If the courts feel the evidence or its copies are not accurate or lack integrity, it is doubtful that the evidence or any information derived from the evidence will be admissible. The current protocol for demonstrating authenticity and integrity relies on hash functions that create unique numerical signatures that are sensitive to any bit changes, e.g., SHA-256. Currently, if these signatures match the original or have not changed since the original collection, the courts will accept that integrity has been established.

Interviewing

A delicate component of any investigation is the actual interview of witnesses and suspects. Before conducting any interview, it is paramount that appropriate policies be reviewed, management is notified, and corporate legal counsel is contacted.

While interviewing witnesses may seem like a straightforward process, care must be taken to avoid invalidating the process. Interviewing (or interrogation) is both an art and a science and success relies on proper training experience and preparation. Witnesses can be easily influenced (often unconsciously), intimidated, or become uncooperative. Therefore only properly trained and experienced personnel should conduct a witness interview.

Suspect interviewing is fraught with potential legal "land mines" and investigators need to keep in mind such concerns as due process, the rights of the individual being questioned, and literally any other considerations that may be unique to the organization, jurisdiction or country. Any violations of policy, law, or other charter or constitutionally protected right of the suspect can lead to charges against the investigator, legal redress by the suspect (e.g., law suits against the company and the individuals conducting the interview), and the possible suppression of any evidence derived from the interview (e.g., written or verbal confessions).

It is prudent to never conduct an interview alone, and when possible, video tape the entire interview for later corroboration of events and context of the meeting. Information security professionals are strongly advised to seek expert assistance before conducting interviews. All interviews should be conducted under the supervision of a legal counsel.

Reporting and Documenting

Once an incident has been deemed closed, the incident handling process is not yet complete. One of the most important, yet overlooked, phases is the debriefing and feedback phase. It would be utopian to believe that despite having the best policy, team, etc., there is nothing to be learned from every incident that is handled. Issues invariably arise; accidents happen, or some previously unexpected variable creeps into the mix. As the saying goes, organizations often learn more from their mistakes than from their successes. This is why it is vital to have a formal process in place to document what worked well, what did not work well, and what was totally unexpected. The debriefing needs to include all the team members, including representatives from the various business units that may have been affected by the incident. The output from the feedback process should also be used to adapt or modify policy and guidelines.

A side benefit to the formalism of the debriefing/feedback is the ability to start collecting meaningful data that can be used to develop or track performance metrics for the response team. Metrics (e.g., number and type of incidents handled, mean time from detection of incident to closure) can be used when determining budget allocations, personnel requirements, and baselines, demonstrating due diligence and reasonableness, and for numerous other statistical purposes. One of the biggest challenges faced by information security professionals is the ability to produce meaningful statistics and metrics specific to the organization, or at the very least, the industry in general. By formalizing a process for capturing data specific to the organization, the incident team can finally reverse this trend.

Understand Forensic Procedures

The exact requirements for the admissibility of evidence vary across legal systems and between different cases (e.g., criminal versus tort). At a more generic level, evidence should have some probative value, be relevant to the case at hand, and meet the following criteria (often called the five rules of evidence):

- Be authentic
- Be accurate
- Be complete
- Be convincing
- Be admissible

Digital or electronic evidence, although more fragile or volatile, must meet these criteria as well. What constitutes digital/electronic evidence is dependent on the investigation; do not rule out any possibilities until they can be positively discounted. With evidence, it is better to have and not need than vice versa. Given the variance that is possible, the axiom to follow here is check with the respective judiciary, attorneys, or officer of the court for specific admissibility requirements.

The dynamic nature of digital electronic evidence bears further comment. Unlike more traditional types of evidence (e.g., fingerprints, hair, fibers, bullet holes), digital/electronic evidence can be very fragile and can be erased, partially destroyed, or contaminated very easily, and, in some circumstances, without the investigator knowing this has occurred. This type of evidence may also have a short life span and must be collected very quickly (e.g., cache memory, primary/random access memory, swap space) and by order of volatility (i.e., most volatile first). Sufficient care must also be taken not to disturb the timeline or chronology of events. Although time stamps are best considered relative and easily forged, the investigator needs to ensure that any actions that could alter the chronology (e.g., examining a live file system or accessing a drive that has not been write protected) are recorded or, if possible, completely avoided.

Media Analysis

Media analysis involves the recovery of information or evidence from information media such as hard drives, DVDs, CD-ROMs or portable memory devices. This media may have been damaged, overwritten, degaussed or reused to aid in hiding evidence or useful information. Numerous tools and techniques exist which can recover information from the media with differing success. Should a forensic image be required the information security professional may need to enlist the help of a media recovery specialist. These specialists often work in clean rooms and can rebuild a drive if needed and maintain a chain of custody while doing it if needed. However, they are very expensive so unless a forensically sound image is required several other tools and techniques should be considered[1].

Network Analysis

The term network forensics (analysis) was coined in 1997 by Markus Ranum[2] and refers to the analysis and examination of data from network logs and network activity for use as potential evidence. (The original definition used the term investigation but later authors amended this to "evidence" to emphasize the forensic aspect.) Like software forensics/analysis, network analysis or network forensics is now encompassed under the larger category of digital evidence.

The analysis of network activity is an innate function of any incident response situation and the process model is identical to what has been previously discussed in the "Incident response" section of this chapter. The critical features are proper evidence management and handling (i.e., chain of custody) with the concern that any derived evidence will be admissible in a legal proceeding.

---

1   Read more about Media Analysis here: http://www.cscjournals.org/csc/manuscript/
Journals/IJS/volume3/Issue2/IJS-13.pdf

2   Simson Farfinkel, and Gene Spafford, Web Security, Privacy & Commerce, (O'Reilly
Media, 2001)http://www.oreillynet.com/network/2002/04/26/nettap.html (accessed July 31,
2012).

Software Analysis

With the move toward a more generic term for investigations related to digital evidence, many of the historical sub areas have been subsumed under the category of "Digital Evidence." However, the field of software analysis or software forensics bears further discussion.

Software analysis or forensics refers to the analysis and examination of program code. The code being analyzed can take the form of source code, compiled code, (binaries) or machine code. Decompiling and reverse engineering techniques are often used as part of the process. Software analysis encompasses such investigative activities as malware analysis, intellectual property disputes, copyright infringements, etc. The objectives of the analysis include author identification, content analysis (payload), and context analysis.

Author identification, or more precisely author attribution, involves attempts to determine who created or authored the software/program in question (was it an individual or group effort). The code is examined for clues to programming style, program language, development toolkits used, embedded comments and addresses, etc. The underlying theory here is that writing code is similar to writing prose and each author has a unique style and eccentricities that allow the investigator to discriminate between various potential suspects. This is very similar to the scientific field of questioned document analysis, and both areas use many of the same techniques.

Content analysis involves the systematic analysis of the purpose of the code. In the case of Trojan horse programs, for example, the focus would be on determining what the actual attack was meant to do, what and where files were installed or altered on the infected systems, what communications channels were opened (ingress and egress), the identification of any upstream destination addresses, what information was being sent or stored locally for batch uploads, etc.

Content analysis is also used in cases related to intellectual property disputes. In these instances, a pain staking examination of the source code or decompiled binary is used to determine the similarity between two programs. The investigator is often asked to provide an expert opinion on how similar the programs are and on what basis the opinion is based.

Context analysis deals with developing a meta view of the impact of the suspicious software relative to the case or the environment it was found in. Understanding context can assist with the analysis and can be used to develop a realistic rating of the risk to the organization or victim.

Hardware/Embedded Device Analysis

The analysis of hardware and embedded devices often involves the analysis of mobile devices such as smart phones or personal digital assistants (PDAs.) The standard hardware and firmware found in a laptop or a desktop computer's motherboard, such as the CMOS chip used to control basic functions will also need to be forensically imaged and then examined. Special tools and techniques are required to image embedded devices. The information security professional must understand that many embedded devices cannot be read or copied without altering the very information they wish to obtain. The U.S. National Institute of Standards and technology recommends the following[3]:

- No actions performed by investigators should change data contained on digital devices or storage media.

- Individuals accessing original data must be competent to do so and have the ability to explain their actions.

- An audit trail or other record of applied processes, suitable for independent third-party review, must be created and preserved, accurately documenting each investigative step.

- The person in charge of the investigation has overall responsibility for ensuring the above mentioned procedures are followed and incompliance with governing laws.

3   Read more about hardware and embedded forensics here: http://csrc.nist.gov/publications/nistpubs/800-72/sp800-72.pdf

- Upon seizing digital evidence, actions taken should not change that evidence.

- When it is necessary for a person to access original digital evidence, that person must be forensically competent.

- All activity relating to the seizure, access, storage, or transfer of digital evidence must be fully documented, preserved, and available for review.

- An individual is responsible for all actions taken with respect to digital evidence while the digital evidence is in their possession.

Any agency that is responsible for seizing, accessing, storing, or transferring digital evidence is responsible for compliance with these principles.

Understand Compliance Requirements and Procedures

Compliance varies depending on the industry and country an organization is in. For example, in the United States health care companies are subject to the compliance requirements of the Health Insurance Portability and Accountability act (HIPAA[1].) This law requires organizations to comply with reporting information security breaches and several other controls. Failure to comply often means fines for an organization.

Regulatory Environment

The industry an organization operates in and the mission they perform defines their regulatory environment. Hospitals in the United States are subject to HIPAA and any organization working with privacy information in the EU is subject to the Data Protection Directive. Any merchant accepting major credit cards must comply with the Payment Card Industry (PCI) security standards. And any educational institution in the U.S. must comply with the Federal Educational Rights and Privacy act.

The information security professional must understand the minimum requirements for each regulation or requirement within an organization's operational environment. A requirements traceability matrix is useful in documenting each requirement, searching over overlapping requirements and then ensuring implemented controls meet the requirements.

Audits

Some regulations require audits. For example, in the U.S. federal agencies are subject to the Federal Information Security Management Act (FISMA.) FISMA requires agencies to self-audit and have an independent auditor review their information security implementation at least annually. The

---

1   http://www.hhs.gov/ocr/privacy/

information security professional needs to understand that while the requirements outlined in laws and standards provide protection they are rarely sufficient to ensure full protection or risk management of an information system. The information security professional must ensure proper scoping and tailoring get the appropriate number of controls at the correct level for the target system.

Reporting

Several regulations and laws around the world require agencies to either report on their compliance on a frequency such as once every three months or when certain conditions are met such as if a sensitive information breach occurred. The information security professional must understand what drives reporting requirements and when reports will need to be provided to outside entities and internal stakeholders.

Ensure Security in Contractual Agreements and Procurement Processes

When outsourcing any part of an organization or its information systems the information security professional must ensure the contractor is obligated to adhere to any legal, regulatory or compulsory requirements the organization must implement. When determining appropriate levels of controls and requirements the information security professional should always error on the side of clarity and disambiguation. Anything unclear or ambiguous in the contact can be interpreted against the information security professional. Using a requirements traceability matrix from a prior system with similar requirements is often the best way to start the process of outsourcing.

A contractor may not come to the negotiation with all the security controls and requirements met. In this case the information security professional must evaluate the impact of using the proposed service or system and report back to senior management what the exposure is and what the risk is. If the outsource option is a wonderful price and great service, senior management may be inclined to accept more risk. In the event an emergency or incident arises, the contract must clearly stipulate how information will be processed, stored and transmitted. The contract must also contain service level agreements with violation amounts and impacts clearly stipulated.

The following links contain more information about the legal, compliance and investigative nature of information security. The articles are feely available on the Internet:

NIST Guide to Integrating Forensic Techniques into Incident Response
http://csrc.nist.gov/publications/nistpubs/800-86/SP800-86.pdf

NIST Computer Forensics Tool Testing (CFTT) Project Web Site
http://www.cftt.nist.gov/

Free Forensic software links
http://forensiccontrol.com/resources/free-software/

Summary and Conclusion

It should be apparent that the domain of legal, regulations, compliance, and investigations covers a very large range of knowledge, skills, and abilities. The intent of this domain is to provide concepts, based on a fairly high level summary of the issues, topics, and processes that need to be a part of the repertoire of information security professionals. It is unreasonable to expect an individual to have a deep expertise in all the areas that were discussed. However, it is reasonable to expect a professional to have enough general knowledge to understand the issues and potential pitfalls and to know how to search out the appropriate expertise.

The legal, regulations, compliance, and investigation domain highlights the international nature of today's business environment and the necessity to have global cooperation to have truly effective information assurance and security. Cross-border commerce requires the understanding of various legal systems, legislation, and regulations. Today, no business, and in a sense, no network is an island; our business practices and stewardship of data and information may fall under the purview of several different regulations and laws, both foreign and domestic. Understanding compliance requirements, effectively assessing our abilities to comply, making the appropriate changes, and maintaining this compliance and due diligence on a go-forward basis are now integral parts of corporate governance.

Many of the controls and safeguards discussed fall into the traditional categories of detective/investigative and reactive controls. Historically, the focus has been on detecting attacks against information systems or infrastructures, and once detected, how to properly determine the who, what, when, where, why, and how with the objective of minimizing the impact and returning to a production state as quickly as possible. With the increased public and governmental focus on the protection of personal information, and the passing in several countries of privacy laws and regulations, the focus is now shifting to preventative and proactive approaches, e.g., policies, encryption. It is no longer reasonable to have a strictly reactive information security posture; businesses must demonstrate that they have put sufficient forethought into how to prevent system compromises or the unauthorized access to data, and if these are detected, how to disclose the incident to affected parties, e.g., the public.

As more attacks are launched on our systems, the synthesis of incident response and handling with digital evidence management and handling will become increasingly more important. One of the artifacts of having more and better detective/investigative controls has been the increase in the volume of incidents that need to be dealt with. As these incidents end up in the various court systems, care must be taken to ensure that from the very start of the incident, evidence is handled and managed properly, i.e., forensically sound practices. Digital evidence is coming under increased scrutiny, and what was allowable and admissible yesterday may not be tomorrow.

In the dynamic field of information security and assurance, knowledge is one of the greatest resources. We must be diligent to ensure that our knowledge, skills, and abilities meet the current and future demands. This can be accomplished with a commitment to ongoing education, training, and maintaining proficiency in our profession across all the domains that make up the foundation of information assurance and security. The domain of legal, regulations, compliance, and investigation does not exist in a vacuum. It is but one piece of the larger mosaic collectively referred to as information assurance and security. To have truly effective information assurance and security, a holistic multidisciplinary approach that weaves all the foundations (domains) together is necessary.

Review Questions

1. Where does the greatest risk of cybercrime come from?

    A. Outsiders

    B. Nation-states

    C. Insiders

    D. Script kiddies

2. What is the largest hindrance to fighting computer crime?

    A. Computer criminals are generally smarter than computer investigators.

    B. Adequate funding to stay ahead of the computer criminals.

    C. Activity associated with computer crime is truly international.

    D. There are so many more computer criminals than investigators that it is impossible to keep up.

3. Computer forensics is the marriage of computer science, information technology, and engineering with

    A. Law

    B. Information systems

    C. Analytical thought

    D. The scientific method

4. What principal allows an investigator to identify aspects of the person responsible for a crime when, whenever committing a crime, the perpetrator leaves residual traces while stealing information?

    A. Meyer's principal of legal impunity

    B. Criminalistic principals

    C. IOCE/Group of 8 Nations principals for computer forensics

    D. Locard's principle of exchange

5. Which of the following is part of the five rules of evidence?

    A. Be authentic, be redundant and be admissible.

    B. Be complete, be authentic and be admissible.

    C. Be complete, be redundant and be authentic.

    D. Be redundant, be admissible and be complete

6. What is not mentioned as a phase of an incident response?

    A. Documentation

    B. Prosecution

    C. Containment

    D. Investigation

7. Which **BEST** emphasizes the abstract concepts of law and is influenced by the writings of legal scholars and academics.

    A. Criminal law

    B. Civil law

    C. Religious law

    D. Administrative law

8. Which type of intellectual property covers the expression of ideas rather than the ideas themselves?

    A. Trademark

    B. Patent

    C. Copyright

    D. Trade secret

9. Which type of intellectual property protects the goodwill a merchant or vendor invests in its products?

    A. Trademark

    B. Patent

    C. Copyright

    D. Trade secret

10. Which of the following are computer forensics guidelines?

    A. IOCE, MOM and SWGDE.

    B. MOM, SWGDE and IOCE.

    C. IOCE, SWGDE and ACPO.

    D. ACPO, MOM and IOCE.

11. Which of the following are categories of software licensing?

    A. Freeware, Open Source, and Commercial

    B. Commercial, Academic and Open Source

    C. Academic, Freeware and Open Source

    D. Freeware, Commercial and Academic

12. What are the rights and obligations of individuals and organizations with respect to the collection, use, retention, and disclosure of personal information **BEST** related to?

    A. Privacy

    B. Secrecy

    C. Availability

    D. Reliability

13. Triage encompasses which of the following incident response subphases?

    A. Collection, transport, testimony

    B. Traceback, feedback, loopback

    C. Detection, identification, notification

    D. Confidentiality, integrity, availability

14. The integrity of a forensic bit stream image is determined by:

    A. Comparing hash totals to the original source

    B. Keeping good notes

    C. Taking pictures

    D. Encrypted keys

9

15. When dealing with digital evidence, the crime scene:

    A. Must never be altered

    B. Must be completely reproducible in a court of law

    C. Must exist in only one country

    D. Must have the least amount of contamination that is possible

16. When outsourcing IT systems

    A. all regulatory and compliance requirements must be passed on to the provider.

    B. the outsourcing organization is free from compliance obligations.

    C. the outsourced IT systems are free from compliance obligations.

    D. the provider is free from compliance obligations.

17. The (ISC)² code of ethics resolves conflicts between canons by:

    A. there can never be conflicts between canons.

    B. working through adjudication.

    C. the order of the canons.

    D. vetting all canon conflicts through the board of directors.

18. When dealing with digital evidence, the crime scene:

    A. Must never be altered

    B. Must be completely reproducible in a court of law

    C. Must exist in only one country

    D. Must have the least amount of contamination that is possible

19. To ensure proper forensics action when needed, an incident response program should:

    A. avoid conflicts of interest by ensuring organization legal council is not part of the process.

    B. routinely create forensic images of all desktops and servers.

    C. only promote closed incidents to law enforcement.

    D. treat every incident as though it may be a crime.

20. A hard drive is recovered from a submerged vehicle. The drive is needed for a court case. What is the best approach to pull information off the drive?:

    A. Wait for the drive to dry and then install it in a desktop and attempt to retrieve the information via normal operating system commands.

    B. Place the drive in a forensic oven to dry it and then use a degausser to remove any residual humidity prior to installing the drive in a laptop and using the OS to pull off information.

    C. While the drive is still wet use a forensic bit to bit copy program to ensure the drive is preserved in its "native" state.

    D. Contact a professional data recovery organization, explain the situation and request they pull a forensic image.

Domain 10

Physical (Enviromental) Security

THE PHYSICAL (ENVIROMENTAL) SECURITY DOMAIN provides a comprehensive evaluation of physical, environmental, and procedural risks that may exist within a facility, organization, or structure in which information systems are stored and managed. It also addresses security surveys, risk and vulnerability assessments, site planning, design criteria, physical protection methods, access control, protection equipment required, and the protection of environmental controls and infrastructure.

The information in this domain provides the necessary requirements to comprehend overall physical and environmental security and the threats associated with the protection of a secured facility.

Much of physical security is just common sense, but there are some twists and nuances that need to be clarified, along with significant advances in physical security technology. There are a multitude of concepts, ideas, and theories from different vocations: from criminology to architecture on how to reduce the incidence of crime and the protection of a facility. These concepts are straightforward but because it is easier to teach someone with an electrical engineering or a computer science background the basics of physical security than the other way around; interactions between physical and logical protection will be up to the systems person to manage.

The U.S. DoD Dictionary of Military and Associated Terms states, "Physical security is defined as the part of security concerned with physical measures designed to safeguard personnel; to prevent unauthorized access to equipment, installations, material, and documents; and to safeguard them against espionage, sabotage, damage, and theft. "

Organizations face new and complex physical security challenges across the full spectrum of operations. Although security technologies are not the answer to all organizational security problems, if applied appropriately, they can enhance the security envelope and in the majority of cases will save the organization money.

Obviously, when considering any physical security measure for an organization, it is important to balance its application with the desire of creating a "bunker" or "prison" atmosphere that is not conducive to the overall function of the organization. Nevertheless, at the same time if servers, laptops, and electronic equipment can be removed from the facility, all the information security policies and procedure mean nothing, and if direct physical access to equipment is allowed, technical security measures can be easily compromised. There must be an integration between information security and physical security.

TOPICS

- Understand site and facility design considerations
- Support the implementation and operation of perimeter security
- Support the implementation and operation of interior security
- Support the implementation and operation of operations and facility security
    - Communications and server rooms
    - Restricted and work area security
    - Data center security
    - Utilities and HVAC considerations
    - Water issues
    - Fire prevention, detection and suppression
- Support the protection and securing of equipment
- Personnel privacy and safety

OBJECTIVES

According to the (ISC)² Candidate Information Bulletin (CIB), a CISSP® candidate is expected to know:

- The elements involved in choosing a secure site
- Its design and configuration
- The methods for securing the facility against unauthorized access, theft of equipment and information
- The environmental and safety measures needed to protect people, the facility, and its resources

10

Physical (Enviromental) Security

Understand Site and Facility Design Considerations

A physical security program is designed to prevent the interruption of operations and provide for the security of information, assets, and personnel. Operational interruptions can occur from natural or environmental catastrophes like hurricanes, tornados, and floods as well as from industrial accidents like fires, explosions, or toxic spills, and intentional acts of sabotage, vandalism, or theft.

During the design phase of a site, it should be the standard operational procedure for a security professional to review all aspects of construction to include land use, site planning, stand-off distance, controlled access zones, entry control and vehicular access, signage, parking, loading docks' and service access, security lighting, and site utilities. Integrating security requirements into a comprehensive approach necessitates achieving a balance among many objectives such as reducing risk, architectural aesthetics, creating a safe work environment, and hardening of physical structures for added security.

It is important to remember that the nature of any threat is always changing. In other words, having direction is the best approach in dealing with physical security. Do not be reactive and start throwing money into security systems. Be insightful in identifying necessary security needs, and put a plan together along with a budget in order to achieve the overall objective.

In addition to the traditional problems of violence and crime, security professionals must now contend with international terrorism, environmental damage, energy disruptions, and potential pandemics. To these protracted and almost universal problems, one can add the prospect of unexpected and often violent natural events like earthquakes, floods, hurricane, fires, or tornadoes.

The Security Survey

Before any project begins, there must be an assessment made in order to put together an operational plan and a practical approach to securing the facility. This security assessment can also be called a security survey, a vulnerability assessment, or a risk analysis.

No one with any common sense starts a project without a plan. A ship's captain would never leave port without navigational tools, maps, global positioning systems, and a crew that was seasoned. The same goes for security professionals who will need the tools to initiate a security assessment. It makes no sense to simply deploy cameras around the organization without sound justification; this would be a waste of resources and money.

A security assessment is a comprehensive overview of the facility including physical security controls, policy, procedures, and employee safety. A good assessment requires the security professional to determine specific protection objectives. These objectives include threat definition, target identification, and facility characteristics.

The first question a security professional should be asking is "What is the threat?" Then start down the list of the potential threats to the organization or facility. Is it vandals, hackers, terrorists, internal employees, corporate spies or a combination? Stating the threat will identify how adversaries can impact assets and will provide the guidance to developing a sound physical protection system.

Target Identification

What is the most valuable asset that needs to be protected? Assets can be personnel, property, equipment, or information. To identify assets to be protected it is prudent to prioritize the assets or establish a matrix and identify the asset in conjunction with probability of attack, along with the question: what would be the impact and consequence of the loss of the asset? *Figure 10.1* illustrates a threat matrix.

1257

Sample of Defined Threat Matrix

Asset	Probability of Attack	Consequence Of Loss
Data Center Server	Medium	Very High
Portable Laptops (critical staff)	High	High
Copy Machine	Low	Low
Portable Laptops (non-essential personnel)	High	Low
PCU	Medium	High
Classified Containers	Low	High

Figure 10.1 - **A Threat Matrix**

Facility Characteristic

There are several things to look at from the standpoint of whether the facility is an existing structure or is new construction. The security professional will either be reviewing architectural drawings or doing a walkthrough of the facility. In the case of an existing structure, it is recommended that a team of security personnel walk the facility. Having several eyes on the project will assist in developing a good evaluation.

Walking with a team of security professionals though a facility will provide a static presentation of how to protect the facility. However, one of the best ways to build a comprehensive approach toward protecting the facility is by doing on-site interviews. Everyone has an opinion on security and it is often that the best insight and information on what needs to be protected and how it should be protected comes from interviewing the staff. One such astute and insightful person is the overnight security officer. He often has nothing but time and walks the facility without interruption, seeing things that are only clearly visible at night.

The American Institute of Architects[1] has established key security concerns that need to be addressed while performing the security assessment.

1   Grassie, Richard P. "Vulnerability Analysis and Security Assessment." *AIA Best Practices*, Last modified February 2007. http://www.aia.org/aiaucmp/groups/ek_members/documents/pdf/aiap016650.pdf.

1. Facility security control during and after hours of operation
2. Personnel and contract security policies and procedures
3. Personnel screening
4. Site and building access control
5. Video surveillance, assessment, and archiving
6. Natural surveillance opportunities
7. Protocols for responding to internal and external security incidents
8. Degree of integration of security and other building systems
9. Shipping and receiving security
10. Property identification and tracking
11. Proprietary information security
12. Computer network security
13. Workplace violence prevention
14. Mail screening operations, procedures, and recommendations
15. Parking lot and site security
16. Data center security
17. Communications security
18. Executive protection
19. Business continuity planning and evacuation procedures

Once these areas are reviewed and a thorough facilities evaluation and staff interview completed, it is time to develop and outline a physical protection system for the facility.

Vulnerability Assessment

The assessment of any vulnerability of a facility or building should be done within the context of the defined threats and the value of the organization's assets. That is, each element of the facility should be analyzed for vulnerabilities to each threat and a vulnerability rating should be assigned based on the criteria below. It would be foolish to install $10,000 worth of security equipment in order to protect $100 worth of assets. It should be noted that a vulnerability assessment might change the value rating of assets due to the identification of critical nodes or some other factor that makes the organization's assets more valuable. *Figure 10.2* is a sample vulnerability matrix.

Sample of Vulnerability Matrix

Main Facility	Vulnerability
Front Entrance	Medium
Receptionist	High
Access Control	Low
Response to Alarms	High
Closed Circuit Television	Medium
Classified Containers	Low

Figure 10.2 - **A Sample Vulnerability Matrix**

- ***Very High***—One or more major weaknesses have been identified that make the organization's assets extremely susceptible to an aggressor or hazard.

- ***High***—One or more significant weaknesses have been identified that make the organization's assets highly susceptible to an aggressor or hazard.

- ***Medium High***—An important weakness has been identified that makes the organization's assets very susceptible to an aggressor or hazard.

- ***Medium***—A weakness has been identified that makes the organization's assets fairly susceptible to an aggressor or hazard.

- ***Medium Low***—A weakness has been identified that makes the organization's assets somewhat susceptible to an aggressor or hazard.

- **_Low_**—A minor weakness has been identified that slightly increases the susceptibility of the organization's assets to an aggressor or hazard.

- **_Very Low_**—No weaknesses exist.

Site Planning

The single most important goal in planning a site is the protection of life, property, and operations. A security professional needs to make decisions in support of this purpose and these decisions should be based on a comprehensive security assessment of the threats and hazards so that planning and design countermeasures are appropriate and effective in the reduction of vulnerability and risk.

There is a natural conflict between making a facility as convenient as possible for operation and maintaining a secure facility. If it were only up to security in designing a facility, it would look like the fortified castle shown in *Figure 10.3*. However, with most applications and design requirements there needs to be cooperation between several departments. Convenience and accessibility should be considered during the different phases of the design review; however, the requirement for security should never be sacrificed for convenience. Proper security controls will reduce the flow rate and ease of entering and leaving a facility. These issues must be addressed in the initial planning to facilitate additional egress points or administrative requirements.

Once a process has been established, and there is buy-in from the organizational leadership, the acceptance of normal operations becomes the organizational standard. When there are changes to the design after the fact and personnel are used to doing something a certain way, there will be reluctance, questions, and push back.

To maximize safety and security, a design team should implement a holistic approach to site design that integrates security and function to

Figure 10.3 - **Facility designed by a security professional**
(Courtesy of Bosch Security Systems)

achieve a balance among the various design elements and objectives. Even if resources are limited, significant value can be added to a project by integrating security considerations into the more traditional design tasks in such a way that they complement the design.

The movement of people and materials throughout a facility is determined by the design of its access, delivery, and parking systems. Such systems should be designed to maximize efficiency while minimizing conflicts between the entry and exiting of vehicles and pedestrians. Designers should begin with an understanding of the organization's requirements based on an analysis of how the facility will be used.

Roadway Design

There is not a facility that does not have roadways and vehicular traffic. The idea of streets is often not thought of as a way to curtail unauthorized access or prevent sabotage and structural damage to the facility. Streets are generally designed to minimize travel time and maximize safety, with the end result typically being a straight path between two or more endpoints.

Although a straight line may be the most efficient course, designers should consider a roadway system to minimize vehicle velocity, thus using the roadway itself as a protective measure. This is accomplished through the use of several strategies.

First, straight-line or perpendicular approaches to the facility should not be used, because this gives a vehicle the opportunity to gather the speed necessary to ram and penetrate buildings. This can also occur by accident when a gas pedal sticks and the driver panics. Instead, approaches should be parallel to the perimeter of the building, with natural earthen berms, high curbs, trees or other measures used to prevent vehicles from departing the roadway. Existing streets can be retrofitted with barriers, bollards, swing gates, or other measures to force vehicles to travel in a serpentine path. Again, high curbs and other measures should be installed to keep vehicles from departing the roadway in an effort to avoid these countermeasures.

Crime Prevention through Environmental Design (CPTED)[2]

Crime Prevention through Environmental Design (CPTED) is a crime reduction technique that has several key elements applicable to the analysis of the building function and site design against physical attack. It is used by architects, city planners, landscapers, interior designers, and security professionals with the objective of creating a climate of safety in a community by designing a physical environment that positively influences human behavior.

CPTED concepts have been successfully applied in a wide variety of applications including streets, parks, museums, government buildings, houses, and commercial complexes.

The CPTED process provides direction to solve the challenges of crime with organizational (people), mechanical (technology and hardware), and natural design (architecture and circulation flow) methods.

---

2   For more information about CPTED, please see the following: http://www.cpted.net/

CPTED concepts can be integrated into expansion or reconstruction plans for existing buildings as well as plans for new buildings. Applying CPTED concepts from the beginning usually has minimal impact on costs and the result is a safer facility.

Landscape design features should be used to create the desired level of protection without turning the facility into a fortress. Elements such as landforms, water features, and vegetation are among the building blocks of attractive and welcoming spaces, and they can also be powerful tools for enhancing security. During site planning it would be beneficial to consider and install these techniques from a cost savings approach. The earth movers, graders, and landscapers have all been budgeted, so why not use CPTED techniques to supplement security concerns? Stands of trees, natural earthen berms, and similar countermeasures generally cannot replace setbacks, but they can offer supplementary protection. With careful selection, placement, and maintenance, landscape elements can provide visual screening that protects employee gathering areas and other activities from surveillance without creating concealment for covert activity.

However, dense vegetation in close proximity to a building can screen illicit activity and should be avoided. Additionally, thick ground cover or vegetation over four inches tall can be a security disadvantage; in setback clear zones, vegetation should be selected and maintained with the elimination of concealment opportunities in mind. Similarly, measures to screen visually detractive components such as transformers, trash compactors, and condensing units should be designed to minimize concealment opportunities for people and weapons.

The New Zealand Ministry of Justice's The Seven Qualities for Well-Designed, Safer Places[3] offers this advice: "Avoid using elements that create a poor image or a fortress-like appearance. Integrate any necessary security

---

3   http://www.justice.govt.nz/publications/global-publications/n/national-guidelines-for-crime-prevention-through-environmental-design-in-new-zealand-part-1-seven-qualities-of-safer-places-part-2-implementation-guide-november-2005/the-seven-qualities-for-well-designed-safer-places

Figure 10.4 - **Building designed with crime prevention in mind**
(Courtesy of Bosch Security Systems)

features into buildings or public spaces by designing them to be intrinsic, unobtrusive or a positive visual feature. Possible design techniques include:

- Treating gates and grilles as public art

- Making perimeter fences look attractive by allowing visibility through the fences, including simple design motifs or combining them with a hedge of thorny shrub varieties can 'target harden' boundary treatment

- Using open grilled designs or internal shutters instead of roller-shutter blinds

- Using different grades of toughened or laminated glass as a design alternative to various types of grille" (*Figure 10.4.*)

Many CPTED crime prevention techniques are common sense approaches. For example, businesses are encouraged to direct all visitors through one entrance that offers contact with a receptionist who can determine the purpose of the visit and the destination, provide sign in/sign out, and an ID badge prior to building access. These measures are nothing new to the retail business world. This approach encourages employees to make personal contact with everyone entering the store in order to keep track of people who want to be invisible and do not want to attract the attention of store employees while they perpetrate crimes.

Other CPTED concepts include the idea that a standard front with windows overlooking sidewalks and parking lots is more effective than encircling the facility with cyclone fences and barbed wire. A communal area with picnic seating, in which activities happen frequently has a greater deterrent effect. Trees also help, as they make shared areas feel safer. Access matters, too; defensible spaces should have single egress points, so that potential intruders are afraid of being trapped. For example, closed circuit television (CCTV) cameras best deter crime in facilities such as parking lots where there is a single exit.

Windows

Because of the ease with which most windows can be entered or glass broken, it makes them targets for most intruders; so, they need to be addressed as a potential vulnerability in the facility defenses. A standard home's installed glass windows can be shattered relatively easily when hit with force. Not only will the glass break but also it will leave sharp fragments that can cause severe lacerations.

Window systems such as glazing, frames, and anchorage to supporting walls on the exterior façade of a building should be used to mitigate the hazardous effects of flying glass during an explosion event. In an effort to protect occupants, the security professional should integrate the features of the glass, the connection of the glass to the frame, and anchoring of the frame to the building structure to achieve a balanced installation.

It is recommended that windows should not be placed adjacent to doors because, if the window is broken, the door can be reached and unlocked. Consider using laminated glass in place of conventional glass and placing window guards, such as grills, screens, or meshwork, across window openings to protect against covert entry. Windows on the ground level should not have the ability to open and should be protected with bars and alarm systems. The alarms available for a window include a magnetic switch, which when the magnets are separated, as when the window is opened, cause an alarm to sound. Windows up to the fourth floor should have this protection installed. Also, consider using steel window frames securely fastened or cement grouted into the surrounding structure.

Types of Glass

- ***Tempered glass*** is similar to the glass installed in car windshields. It will resist breakage and will disintegrate into small cubes of crystals with no sharp edges. Tempered glass is used in entrance doors and adjacent panels.

- ***Wired glass*** provides resistance to impact from blunt objects. The wire mesh is imbedded into the glass thereby providing limited protection.

- ***Laminated glass*** (Figure 10.5) is recommended for installation in street-level windows, doorways, and other access areas. It is

Figure 10.5 - **Laminated glass is recommended for installation in street-level windows, doorways and other access areas**
(Courtesy of Bosch Security Systems)

1267

made from two sheets of ordinary glass bonded to a middle layer of resilient plastic. When it is struck it may crack but the pieces of glass tend to stick to the plastic inner material. ***Bullet resistant (BR) glass*** (*Figure 10.6*) is typically installed in banks and high-risk areas. There are different layers of BR glass with the standard being 1 ¼-inch thick, which provides protection from a 9mm round.

*Figure 10.6 - B*ullet resistant (BR) glass is typically installed in banks and high-risk areas (Courtesy of Bosch Security Systems)

Glass Break

Glass break sensors are a good intrusion detection device for buildings with a lot of glass windows and doors with glass panes. Glass as an exterior protection barrier can be easily defeated. Windows can be quickly and easily broken. There are several basic types of glass-break sensors: acoustic sensors listen for an acoustic sound wave that matches the frequency of broken glass and shock sensors that feel the shock wave when glass is broken. The use of dual-technology glass break sensors—both acoustic and shock wave—is most effective. The reason is that if only acoustic sensors are used and an employee pulls the window blinds up, it can set off a false alarm; but if it is set to a dual-alarm system both acoustic and shock sensors will need to be activated before an alarm is triggered. There is not a significant price difference between a simple acoustic sensor and combination sensors (acoustic and shock). For the nominal component price increase, which is a fraction of the total installed cost, the increased capability can justify the higher price.

Garages

If the facility has an underground parking garage or an attached parking structure, the security professional must understand two primary safety threats: crime and vehicles hitting pedestrians.

Start by utilizing signage that can direct vehicles and pedestrian to the exits or the entrance to the facility. CCTV cameras should be used for monitoring events and emergency call boxes should be placed throughout the garage. Installing bright lights is one of the most effective deterrents to both accidents and attacks. Lighting levels of at least 10 to 12 foot-candles over parked cars and 15 to 20 foot-candles in walking and driving aisles is recommended.

It is also advisable to install high lighting levels to illuminate the exterior of the parking facility, particularly in areas that experience high pedestrian traffic. As a rule, exterior lights should be placed approximately 12 feet above ground, and they should point downward to illuminate wide areas along the ground. Another method for increasing visibility is to paint the walls of the structure white to reflect light. Lighting fixtures should also be strategically placed to bounce light off the walls and reduce dark corners where criminals or attackers could hide.

If the garage is under the facility, elevators or walk-ups should all empty into the lobby, outside of the controlled space. Having all employees and visitors pass through the controlled receptionist area will maintain the integrity of the facility. In this way, the elevators going into the core of the building will only be accessible from the lobby and not from the garage levels.

10

Physical (Enviromental) Security

Location Threats

Natural Threats

Natural hazards typically refer to events such as earthquakes, floods, tornado, and hurricanes. This requires preparation for these natural hazards by establishing a communication system in order to get information to employees and upper management. Information and periodic emergency training exercises are the best ways to be prepared and thereby reduce fear and anxiety. Organizations can also reduce the impact of disasters by flood proofing, installing emergency power systems, and securing items that could shake loose in an earthquake.

Types of Natural Threats

According to the United States Federal Emergency Management Agency (FEMA) "Are You Ready[4]?" series, the following are specific natural threats and ways to deal with each:

- A hurricane is a type of tropical cyclone, the generic term for a low-pressure system that generally forms in the tropics. A hurricane is accompanied by thunderstorms, and in the Northern Hemisphere, a counterclockwise circulation of winds near the earth's surface.

  - All Atlantic and Gulf of Mexico coastal areas are subject to hurricanes or tropical storms. Parts of the Southwest United States and the Pacific Coast experience heavy rains and floods each year from hurricanes spawned off Mexico. The Atlantic hurricane season lasts from June to November with the peak season from mid-August to late October.

  - Hurricanes can cause catastrophic damage to coastlines and several hundred miles inland. Winds can exceed 155 miles per hour. Hurricanes and tropical storms can also spawn tornadoes and create storm surges along the coast, and cause extensive damage from heavy rainfall.

---

4   http://training.fema.gov/EMIWeb/is/is22.asp

◘ Hurricanes are classified into five categories based on their wind speed, central pressure, and damage potential. Category Three and higher hurricanes are considered major hurricanes, though Categories One and Two are still extremely dangerous and warrant full attention.

■ Tornadoes are nature's most violent storms. Spawned from powerful thunderstorms, tornadoes can cause fatalities and devastate a neighborhood in seconds. A tornado appears as a rotating, funnel-shaped cloud that extends from a thunderstorm to the ground with whirling winds that can reach 300 miles per hour. Damage paths can be in excess of one mile wide and 50 miles long. Every state is at some risk from this hazard.

■ Earthquakes are one of the most frightening and destructive phenomena of nature. An earthquake is a sudden movement of the earth caused by the abrupt release of strain that has accumulated over a long time. For hundreds of millions of years, the forces of plate tectonics have shaped the earth, as the huge plates that form the earth's surface slowly move over, under, and past each other. Sometimes, the movement is gradual. At other times, the plates are locked together, unable to release the accumulating energy. When the accumulated energy grows strong enough, the plates break free. If the earthquake occurs in a populated area, it may cause many deaths and injuries and extensive property damage.

■ Floods are one of the most common hazards in the United States. Flood effects can be local, impacting a neighborhood or community, or can affect entire river basins and multiple states.

◘ However, all floods are not alike. Some floods develop slowly, sometimes over a period of days. Nevertheless, flash floods can develop quickly, sometimes in just a few minutes and without any visible signs of rain. Flash floods often have a dangerous wall of roaring water that carries rocks, mud, and other debris and can sweep away most things in their path. Overland flooding occurs outside a defined river or stream, such as when a levee is breached, but still can be destructive. Flooding can also occur when a dam breaks, producing effects similar to flash floods.

o Be aware of flood hazards no matter where you live, but especially if you live in a low-lying area, near water or downstream from a dam. Even very small streams, gullies, creeks, culverts, dry streambeds, or low-lying ground that appears harmless in dry weather can flood. Every state is at risk from this hazard.

Man-Made Threats

Threats from fire can be potentially devastating and can affect an organization beyond the physical damage. Not only fire, but also heat, smoke, and water can cause irreversible damage. This type of damage can keep a company from ever regaining its market share and is the leading cause of environmental failures for a company.

The fire protection system should maintain life safety protection and allow for safe evacuation from the building. A facilities fire protection water system should be protected from a single point of failure. The incoming line should be encased, buried, or located 50 feet away from high-risk areas. The interior mains should be looped and sectionalized. Water can be the main fire suppression tool; however, it will cause extreme damage to electronic equipment.

Fire requires three elements to burn: heat, oxygen, and a fuel source. Fire extinguishers and fire suppression systems fight fires by removing one of the three elements. Fire extinguishers are divided into four categories, based on different types of fires:

- **Class A** extinguishers are for ordinary combustible materials such as paper, wood, cardboard, and most plastics. The numerical rating on this type of extinguisher indicates the amount of water it holds and the amount of fire it can extinguish.

- **Class B** fires involve flammable or combustible liquids such as gasoline, kerosene, grease, and oil. The numerical rating for a class B extinguisher indicates the approximate number of square feet of fire it can extinguish.

- *Class C* fires involve electrical equipment, such as appliances, wiring, circuit breakers and outlets. Never use water to extinguish class C fires—the risk of electrical shock is far too great! Class C extinguishers do not have a numerical rating. The C classification means the extinguishing agent is nonconductive.

- *Class D* fire extinguishers are commonly found in a chemical laboratory. They are for fires that involve combustible metals, such as magnesium, titanium, potassium and sodium. These types of extinguishers neither have numerical rating nor are they given a multipurpose rating. They are designed for class D fires only.

Utility Concerns

Electrical

The primary security involvement dealing with electrical systems is to guarantee essential power to facility services, especially those required for daily operations and life safety. They should also consider the following recommendations:

- Emergency and normal electric panels, conduits, and switchgear should be installed separately, at different locations, and as far apart as possible. Electric distribution should also run at separate locations.

- Emergency generators should be located away from loading docks, entrances, and parking. More secure locations include the roof, protected grade level, and protected interior areas.

- Main fuel storage for generators should be located away from loading docks, entrances, and parking. Access should be restricted and protected to include locks on caps and seals.

Communications

Communication devices are also an integral part of the core facility utilities. Security professionals should consider having a second telephone service to maintain communications in case of an incident. For most operations, specific employees should be provided cellular telephones or the organization maintains a phone list of all critical employees and their cell phone numbers. In addition, a base radio communications system with a repeater antenna should be installed, and portable radios distributed on floors. This system is usually operated by building guards and the radio communications system can be used in cases of emergencies. A standard radio system can use more than one channel for operational purposes.

Utilities

Utility systems can suffer significant damage when subjected to the shock of extensive environmental hazards. Some of these utilities may be critical for safety of the facility. To minimize the possibility of critical failure due to hazards, apply the following measures:

- Where possible, provide underground, concealed, and protected utilities.

- Consider quick connects for portable utility backup systems if redundant sources are not available.

- Protect drinking water supplies from waterborne contaminants by securing access points, such as manholes. If warranted, maintain routine water testing to help detect waterborne contaminants.

- Minimize signs identifying critical utilities. Provide fencing to prevent unauthorized access and use landscape planting to conceal aboveground systems.

- Locate petroleum, oil, and lubricants storage tanks and operations buildings down slope from all other occupied buildings. Locate fuel storage tanks at least 100 feet from buildings.

- Locate utility systems at least 50 feet from loading docks, front entrances, and parking areas.

Support the Implementation and Operation of Perimeter Security

The primary goal of a physical protection program is to control access into the facility. In the concept of defense-in-depth, barriers are arranged in layers with the level of security growing progressively higher as one comes closer to the center or the highest protective area. Defending an asset with a multiple posture can reduce the likelihood of a successful attack; if one layer of defense fails, another layer of defense will hopefully prevent the attack, and so on. (*Figure 10.7*) This design requires the attacker to circumvent multiple defensive mechanisms to gain access to the targeted asset. Implementing defense in depth requires that the security practitioner understand the goals of security. Essentially, security can be distilled down to three basic elements: availability, integrity, and confidentiality. Availability addresses the fact that legitimate users require resources, which should be available to the users as needed. Integrity relates to the concept that information is whole, complete, and remains unchanged from its true state. Confidentiality can be defined as ensuring that data is available to only those individuals that have legitimate access to it.

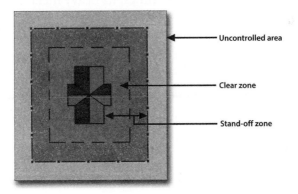

Figure 10.7 - **Defending an asset with a multiple posture can reduce the likelihood of a successful attack; if one layer of defense fails, another layer of defense will hopefully prevent the attack, and so on**

(Courtesy of Bosch Security Systems)

Consider, for example, the layers of security at a local bank, which employs many redundant measures to protect personnel and assets. The fortress-like appearance and protective reputation that is synonymous with banking is likely a deterrent factor to some would be bank robbers, but of course not all. The next line of defense that serves as both a deterrent and as a means for suspect apprehension and asset recovery are security cameras. This layer of security obviously has a level of failure; how many times have we seen video of bank robberies showing a suspect who was never caught. If the cameras are considered ineffective, the next layer is an armed security guard present both as a deterrent factor and to physically defend the bank. This too is not 100% effective as the security guard can be neutralized by the intruder.

If the security guard is overpowered, the next layer involves hardware such as bulletproof glass and electronically locked doors. Of course, not all branch offices are fortified in this manner, leaving the bank tellers vulnerable. In this case, the teller must rely on the silent alarm button, dye packs, and robbery training. Some branches also have double time-release doors where people are slightly delayed during ingress and egress. The vault itself has defense-in-depth through multiple layers of defense such as opening only at certain controlled times, its heavy metal construction, and multiple compartments that require further access.

The defense-in-depth principle may seem contradictory to the "secure the weakest link" principle, since we are essentially saying that defenses taken as a whole can be stronger than the weakest link. However, there is no contradiction; the principle "secure the weakest link" applies when components have security functionality that does not overlap. But when it comes to redundant security measures, it is indeed possible that the sum protection offered is far greater than the protection offered by any single component.

Of course, all of these defenses collectively do not ensure that the bank will never be successfully robbed, even at banks with this much security. If the attacker wants to rob the bank, he is going to give it his best effort.

Nonetheless, it is quite obvious that the sum total of all these defenses results in a far more effective security system than any one of these defenses alone. This does not mean that every known defensive measure should be indiscriminately applied in every situation. Using risk, vulnerability, and threat assessment, a balance has to be found between security provided by the defense-in-depth approach, and the financial, human, and organizational resources the management is willing to expend.

The key to a successful system is the integration of people, procedures, and equipment into a system that protects the targets from the threat. A well-designed system provides defense-in-depth, minimizes the consequences of component failures, and exhibits balanced protection. Physical protection is no different from information security and, in fact, it is a dovetail of the processes: An organization performs a threat analysis, and then designs a system that involves equipment and procedures, and then tests it. The system itself typically has a number of elements that fall into the essence of deter–detect—delay–respond.

Deter is meant to render a facility as an unattractive target so that an adversary abandons attempts to infiltrate or attack. Examples of deterrence are the presence of security guards, adequate lighting at night, signage, and the use of barriers such fencing or bars on windows. While deterrence can be very helpful in discouraging attacks by adversaries, it cannot stop an adversary who chooses to attack regardless of defenses. Similar to the bank robber who is dead set on robbing the bank, nothing is going to stop him from attempting to rob the bank. The deterrent value of a true physical protection system can be very high while at the same time providing protection for assets in the event of an attack.

Detect involves the use of appropriate devices, systems, and procedures to signal that an attempted or actual unauthorized access has occurred. It will have one or more layers of barriers and sensors, which will be utilized to keep out casual intruders, detect deliberate intruders, and make it difficult for them to defeat your defensive security easily. Delay involves having a perpetrator delayed by the use of layered defenses. It will delay the attack for a sufficient period to allow a response force time to confront and intercept.

Response requires communication to a response force that an unauthorized person is attempting to or has entered the facility. The response force is required to intercept the adversary before an attack has occurred or has been completed.

Security systems are best designed utilizing multiple barriers—"rings of protection"—encircling the protected asset. Layered barrier designs are advantageous when they require increased knowledge, skill, and talent to circumvent them. A group of attackers with the necessary skills must be assembled and since group secrecy is hard to maintain, the likelihood of being discovered is increased. Layered barriers also afford a greater time delay because each layer requires time to be circumvented. This helps to provide the necessary delay in the event that the response time is relatively slow.

The following critical building components should be located away from main entrances, vehicle circulation, parking, and maintenance areas. If this is not possible, harden as appropriate:

- Emergency generator, including fuel systems, day tank, fire sprinkler, and water supply
- Fuel storage
- Telephone distribution and main switchgear
- Fire pumps
- Building control centers
- Uninterrupted power supply (UPS) systems controlling critical functions
- HVAC systems if critical to building operation
- Elevator machinery and controls
- Shafts for stairs, elevators, and utilities
- Critical distribution feeders for emergency power

Gates and Fences

Barriers

Barriers can be comprised of natural or manufactured elements. The idea is to define an area that is designated to impede or deny access. A natural barrier can be a river, dense growth, a culvert, or a ditch. Fabricated or structural barriers can be a wall, a fence, doors or the building itself. Walls, fences, and gates have long been designated as the first line of defense for a facility. There are a multitude of barriers and they provide the same objective: keep intruders out, delay them and keep them at a safe distance. However, with sufficient time and effort any barrier can be breached. Thus the principle objective is to delay the intruder until law enforcement or a security team can respond.

Fences

As shown in *Figure 10.8*, fences are a perimeter identifier that are designed and installed to keep intruders out. However, most organizations do not like the feeling of a fenced-in compound and look for other remedies to secure their property. Depending on the organization, location and funding, a fence can consist of many variations and levels of protection.

The most commonly used fence is the chain linked fence and it is the most affordable. The standard is a six-foot high fence with two-inch mesh square openings. The material should consist of nine-gauge vinyl or galvanized metal. Nine-gauge is a typical fence material installed in residential areas. Additionally, it is recommended to place barbed wire strands angled out from the top of the fence at a 45° angle and away from the protected area with three strands running across the top. This will provide for a seven-foot fence. There are several variations of the use of "top guards" using V-shaped barbed wire or the use of concertina wire as an enhancement, which has been a replacement for more traditional three strand barbed wire "top guards."

The fence should be fastened to ridged metal posts set in concrete every six feet with additional bracing at the corners and gate openings. The

Figure 10.8 - **From left to right: Ornamental fence, security fence with 3 strands of barb wire, high-security fence with 3 rolls of razor wire, and another view of rolled razor wire**

(Courtesy of Bosch Security Systems)

bottom of the fence should be stabilized against intruders crawling under by attaching posts along the bottom to keep the fence from being pushed or pulled up from the bottom. If the soil is sandy, the bottom edge of the fence should be installed below ground level.

For maximum security design, the use of double fencing with roles of concertina wire positioned between the two fences is the most effective deterrent and cost-efficient method. In this design, an intruder is required to use an extensive array of ladders and equipment to breach the fences.

Most fencing is largely a psychological deterrent and a boundary marker rather than a barrier, because in most cases such fences can be rather easily penetrated unless added security measures are taken to enhance the security of the fence. Sensors attached to the fence to provide electronic monitoring of cutting or scaling the fence can be used.

Gates

Gates exist to facilitate and control access. Gates need to be controlled to ensure that only authorized persons and vehicles pass through. A variety of controls are used. It is best to minimize the number of gates and access points because any opening is always a potential vulnerability. Each gate requires resources whether it uses electronic access control or a guard. The fewest number of entry points, the better the control of the facility.

Walls

Walls serve the same purpose as fences. They are manufactured barriers but generally are more expensive to install than fences. Common types of walls are block, masonry, brick, and stone. Walls tend to have a greater aesthetic value, appealing to those who prefer a more gentle and subtle look. Regardless of the type of wall used, its purpose as a barrier is the same as a fence. To be most effective, walls ought to be 7 feet high with 3 to 4 strands of barbed wire on top. This will help deter scaling. Walls also have a disadvantage in that they obstruct the view of an area. Chain link and wire fencing allow for visual access from both sides.

Perimeter Intrusion Detection

Depending on the extent of security required to protect the facility, exterior or perimeter sensors will alert an organization to any intruders attempting to gain access across open space or attempting to breach the fence line. These may provide security ample opportunity to evaluate and intercept any threat. In general, open terrain sensors work best on flat, cleared areas. Heavily or irregular contoured areas are not conducive to open terrain sensing systems. Open terrain sensors include infrared, microwave systems, combination (dual technology), vibration sensors, video content analysis, and motion path analysis (CCTV) systems.

Infrared Sensors

Passive infrared sensors are designed for human body detection, so they are great for detecting when someone approaches. "Passive-infrared sensors detect the heat emitted by animate forms. Because all living things emit heat, a system of recording measurable changes in a specific area provides a means of detecting unauthorized intrusions. When the unit registers changes in temperature in its area of detection, it relays the information to a processor, which measures the change according to detection parameters. If the change falls outside the parameters, the processor sends a signal to the unit's alarm." Active infrared sensors transmit an infrared signal via a transmitter. The location for reception is at a receiver. Interruption of the normal IR signal indicates an intruder or object has blocked the path. The beam can be narrow in focus, but should be projected over a cleared path.

Microwave

Microwave sensors come in two configurations: bistatic and monostatic. With both bistatic and monostatic sensors, the sensors operate by radiating a controlled pattern of microwave energy into the protected area. The transmitted microwave signal is received, and a base level "no intrusion" signal is established. Motion by an intruder causes the received signal to be altered, setting off an alarm. Microwave signals pass through concrete and steel and must be applied with care if roadways or adjacent buildings are near the area of coverage. Otherwise, nuisance

Figure 10.9 - **Bistatic Microwave Sensor**

(Courtesy of Bosch Security Systems)

alarms may occur due to reflected microwave patterns. A bistatic sensor (*Figure 10.9*) sends an invisible volumetric detection field that fills the space between a transmitter and receiver. Monostatic microwave sensors use a single sensing unit that incorporates both transmitting and receiving functions. It generates a beam radiated from the transceiver and creates a well-controlled, three-dimensional volumetric detection pattern with adjustable range. Many monostatic microwave sensors feature a cutoff circuit, which allows the sensor to be tuned to cover only the area within a selected region. This helps to reduce nuisance alarms.

Coaxial Strain-Sensitive Cable

These systems use a coaxial cable woven through the fabric of the fence (*Figure 10.10*). The coaxial cable transmits an electric field. As the cable moves due to strain on the fence fabric caused by climbing or cutting, changes in the electric field are detected within the cable, and an alarm condition occurs. Coaxial strain-sensing systems are readily available and are highly tunable to adjust for field conditions due to weather and climate characteristics. Some coaxial cable systems are susceptible to electromagnetic interference and radio frequency interference.

Figure 10.10 - **Coaxial Strain-Sensitive cable**

(Courtesy of Bosch Security Systems)

1283

Time Domain Reflectometry (TDR) Systems

Time domain reflectometry (TDR) systems send induced radio frequency (RF) signals down a cable that is attached to the fence fabric. Intruders climbing or flexing a fence create a signal path flaw that can be converted to an alarm signal. When the conductor cable is bent or flexed, a part of the signal returns to the origination point. This reflected signal can be converted to an intrusion point by computing the time it takes for the signal to travel to the intrusion point and return. The cable can be provided in an armored cable, which requires more than a bolt cutter to sever the sensing cable. These systems require their own processor unit and can be configured in a closed loop, such that if the cable is cut, it can be detected by the other return path.

Video Content Analysis and Motion Path Analysis

Video content analysis and motion path analysis intrusion detection is sophisticated software analysis of the camera images. CCTV camera systems are increasingly being used as intrusion detection systems. Application of complex algorithms to digital CCTV camera images allows CCTV systems to detect intruders. The software programming is smart enough to detect pixel changes and differentiate and filter out normal video events (leaves blowing, snow falling) from true alarm events. The application of software rules can further evolve to differentiate between a rabbit hopping across a parking lot, to a person trespassing through the parking lot, which needs to be addressed. The application of complex software algorithms to CCTV digital images takes on the aspect of an artificial camera, whereby the camera and processors become "smart video" and start to emulate a human operator. The difference between a smart camera and a human operator is that it takes complex software programming and associated rules to allow the camera to differentiate and assess video events compared to the processing ability of the human mind.

The advantage of video content analysis and motion path analysis is that the camera systems do not get tired. They remain "alert" after monitoring hundreds of video events during a shift. Video content analysis systems can monitor more cameras, more effectively, with fewer operators at a reduced cost. This allows for the use of less dispatch center/command staff while letting technology assist with the human factor.

Lighting

Security lighting can be provided for overall facility illumination along with the perimeter to allow security personnel to maintain a visual assessment during times of darkness. It may provide both a real and psychological deterrent against intruders who will attempt to use the cover of darkness as a means of entry into a compound, parking lot, or facility. Lighting should enable security personnel and employees to notice individuals at night at a distance of 75 feet or more and to identify a human face at about 33 feet. These distances will allow the security personnel to avoid the individuals or take defensive action while still at a safe distance. Security lighting increases the effectiveness of guard forces and CCTV by increasing the visual range of the guards or CCTV during periods of darkness. It also provides increased illumination of an area where natural light does not reach or is insufficient. Lighting also has value as a deterrent to individuals looking for an opportunity to commit crime. Normally, security lighting requires less intensity than lighting in working areas. An exception is at doorways where increased illumination is required.

Lighting is relatively inexpensive to maintain and may reduce the need for security personnel while enhancing personal protection by reducing opportunities for concealment and surprise by potential attackers. Overall, it will be required to provide sufficient lighting at entry control points to ensure adequate identification of personnel. Also, wherever practical, place lighting devices as high as possible to give a broader and more natural light distribution. This requires fewer poles and is more aesthetically pleasing than standard lighting.

10

Physical (Enviromental) Security

Types of Lighting Systems

The type of site lighting system used depends on the overall security requirements. Four types of lighting are used for security lighting systems:

- **Continuous lighting** is the most common security lighting system. It consists of a series of fixed lights arranged to flood a given area continuously during darkness with overlapping cones of light.

- **Standby lighting** has a layout similar to continuous lighting; however, the lights are not continuously lit, but are either automatically or manually turned on when suspicious activity is detected or suspected by the security personnel or alarm systems.

- **Movable lighting** consists of manually operated, movable searchlights that may be lit during hours of darkness or only as needed. The system normally is used to supplement continuous or standby lighting.

- **Emergency lighting** is a backup power system of lighting that may duplicate any or all of the above systems. Its use is limited to times of power failure or other emergencies that render the normal system inoperative. It depends on an alternative power source such as installed or portable generators or batteries. Consider emergency/backup power for security lighting as determined to be appropriate.

Depending on the nature of the facility, protective lighting will be deployed to illuminate the perimeter of the facility along with any outside approaches. It will also be utilized in order to concentrate on the inner area and the buildings within the perimeter. The United States Code of Federal Regulations lists a specific requirement of 0.2 foot-candles (fc) for lighting protected areas within a perimeter.

Isolation zones and all exterior areas within the protected area shall be provided with illumination sufficient for the monitoring and observation requirements, but not less than 0.2 fc measured horizontally at ground level. 0.5 fc is acceptable for side landscapes and roadways. But from the standpoint of a regular security professions, who can determine what exactly a fc is? The basic idea for perimeter lighting (0.5 fc) will equate to using a 40W bulb in a 12×12 foot room. It gives off enough light to see, as it is a soft amber glow, but it will not totally illuminate the entire room.

Types of Lights

There are several types of lights that can be used within the protected area. They include fluorescent, mercury vapor, sodium vapor, and quartz lamps.

- *Fluorescent lights* are highly efficient and cost effective. However, they are temperature sensitive and while improving are not considered an effective outdoor lighting system. This light is better suited inside buildings and facilities.

- *Mercury Vapor lights* are the preferred security light which disperses a strong white-bluish cast. They have an extended lamp life; however the downside is they take an amount of time to full light when activated—typical to the lights at a stadium.

- *Sodium Vapor light* provides a soft yellow light and is more efficient than mercury vapor. This light is used in areas where fog can be a problem.

- *Quartz Lamps* emit a very bright white light and comes on immediately. They typically provide high wattage from 1500 to 2000 and can be used on perimeters and troublesome areas where high visibility and a day light scene is required.

According to the American Institute of Architects, interior lighting levels for elevators, lobbies, and stairwell range from 5 to 10 fc, exterior lighting requirements vary for different locations. Common lighting levels include the following:

- Building entrances (5 fc)
- Walkways (1.5 fc)

- Parking garages (5 fc)
- Site landscape (0.5 fc)
- Areas immediately surrounding the building (1 fc)
- Roadways (0.5 fc)

Adequate lighting for monitoring activities is important. In addition, lighting serves as a crime deterrent and discourages unwanted visitors while giving the building occupants a sense of security and safety. Lights used for CCTV monitoring generally require at least 1–2 fc of illumination, whereas the lighting needed for safety considerations in exterior areas such as parking lots or garages is substantially greater (at least 5 fc).

Infrared Illuminators

The human eye cannot see infrared (IR) light. Most monochrome CCTV (black/white) cameras can. Thus, invisible infrared light can be used to illuminate a scene, which allows night surveillance without the need for additional artificial lighting. See *Figure 10.11*. IR beam shapes can be designed to optimize CCTV camera performance and can provide covert surveillance, no visible lighting to alert or annoy neighbors. This is extremely effective in low-light areas and can provide the monitoring guard the ability to see in the dark.

Figure 10.11 - **An infrared camera is extremely effective in low-light areas and can provide the monitoring guard the ability to see in the dark**

(Courtesy of Bosch Security Systems)

Access Control

The primary function of an Access Control System (ACS) is to ensure that only authorized personnel are permitted inside the controlled area. This can also include the regulation and flow of materials into and out of specific areas. Persons subject to control can include employees, visitors, customers, vendors, and the public. Access control measures should be different for each application to fulfill specific security, cost, and operational objectives.

Control can begin at the facility property line to include such areas as parking lots. Exterior building entrances can then be controlled. Within the facility, any area can be controlled at the discretion of management. However, control is normally applied to be consistent with identified risk and the protective value that is desired. Protected areas include street level entrances, lobbies, loading docks, elevators, and sensitive internal areas containing assets such as customer data, proprietary information, and classified information.

The goal of an access control program is to limit the opportunity for a crime to be committed. If the potential perpetrator of a crime cannot gain access to financial assets, data files, computer equipment, programs, documentation, forms, operating procedures, and other sensitive material, the ability to commit a crime against the institution is minimized. Thus, only identified, authorized personnel should be permitted access to restricted areas. The basic components of an ACS include card readers, electric locks, alarms, and computer systems to monitor and control the ACS (*Figure 10.12*).

In order for the system to identify an authorized employee, an ACS needs to have some form of enrollment station used to assign and activate an access control device. Most often a badge is produced and issued with the employee's identifiers with the enrollment station giving the employee specific areas that will be accessible. In general, an ACS compares an individual's badge against a verified database. If authenticated, the ACS

10

Physical (Enviromental) Security

1289

sends output signals that allow authorized personnel to pass through a controlled area such as a gate or door. The system has the capability of

Figure 10.12 - **A card reader is one of the basic components of an access control system**
(Courtesy of Bosch Security Systems)

logging and archiving entry attempts (authorized and unauthorized).

Card Types

Magnetic Stripe (mag stripe) cards consist of a magnetically sensitive strip fused onto the surface of a PVC material, like a credit card. A magnetic stripe card is read by swiping it through a reader or by inserting it into a position in a slot. This style of card is old technology; it may be physically damaged by misuse and its data can be affected by magnetic fields. Magnetic stripe cards are easily duplicated.

Proximity Card (prox cards) use embedded antenna wires connected to a chip within the card. The chip is encoded with the unique card identification. Distances at which proximity cards can be read vary by the manufacturer and installation. Readers can require the card to be placed within a fraction of an inch from the reader to six inches away. This will then authenticate the card and will release the magnetic lock on the door.

Smart Cards are credential cards with a microchip embedded in them. Smart cards can store data such as access transactions, licenses held by individuals, qualifications, safety training, security access levels, and biometric templates. This card can double as an access card for doors and be used as an authenticator for a computer. The U.S. federal government has mandated smart cards to provide personal identity verification (PIV) to verify the identity of every employee and contractor in order to improve data and facility security. The card will be used for identification, as well as for facility and data access.

Additional security measures can be employed using keypads with PIN Codes or biometric readers. Coded devices use a series of assigned numbers commonly referred to as a PIN. This series of numbers is entered into a keypad and is matched to the numbers stored in the ACS. This provides additional security because if a badge is lost or stolen, it will not activate a control area without the proper PIN number, similar to an ATM bank card. Biometrics provides the same support as even if the card is stolen the reader must match a biometric to the biometric on the card to be successful.

Access Control Head End

The application software housed in the CPU provides the intelligent controller where all ACS activity is monitored, recorded, commanded, and controlled by the operator. Current state-of-the-art access systems allow each local security panel to hold the system logic for its associated devices. The CPU retains the system-specific programming to allow entry (access) for authorized personnel and deny access to unauthorized personnel.

Communication failure between the CPU and the local access control panels could result in new users not being permitted entry; however, the system is set so that the panel will recognize personnel already installed and will grant access to an authorized badge holder. These systems have advances that can integrate with CCTV and provide instant visual recognition along with visual alarm activation in order to provide the

10

Physical (Enviromental) Security

security console operator visual information before dispatching a security response team.

Closed Circuit TV

Closed Circuit Television (CCTV) is a collection of cameras, recorders, switches, keyboards, and monitors that allow viewing and recording of security events. The CCTV system is normally integrated into the overall security program and centrally monitored at the security central station.

Within the past several years there have been enhanced developments in the CCTV industry, particularly better picture resolution, microprocessor-based video switchers, and the ability to transmit video over networks with a compressed bandwidth ratio.

CCTV provides a highly flexible method of surveillance and monitoring. One advantage is its immediate output. There is never a question of whether the equipment works properly or not. In addition, it can be adapted through the use of remote control devices, recorders and computer imaging to guard against virtually any crime including burglary, unauthorized entrance, and employee theft. Uses of CCTV systems for security services include several different functions as described below:

- **Surveillance:** CCTV cameras can be used to give a viewer the capability to be made aware of or view visual events at multiple locations from a centralized remote viewing area. CCTV camera technology makes visual information available that would normally only be available through multiple (possibly roving) human resources.

- **Assessment:** When alerted by an alarm notification, CCTV cameras allow the security control center operators or other viewers to assess the situation and make a determination as to what type of response may or may not be required. An example would be an intrusion alarm at a remote facility. Visual assessment may indicate an unannounced maintenance crew at work. This situation will be handled differently than if the operator viewed an unknown individual removing a laptop from the facility.

- **Deterrence:** While more effective against unsophisticated burglars, as opposed to trained covert insurgents, CCTV cameras may deter burglary, vandalism, or intrusion due to fear of discovery and prosecution.

- **Evidentiary Archives:** Retrieval of archived images may be helpful in the identification and prosecution of trespassers, vandals, or other intruders.

Cameras

Color cameras offer more information, such as the color of a vehicle or a subject's clothing. Some ultra-low-light color cameras are able to automatically sense the ambient light conditions and switch from color to black and white in low-light conditions. Cameras must have auto-white balance to adjust for the changing color temperature of daylight and artificial lighting needed for night-time viewing. Black and white cameras are more sensitive under low-light or darkness conditions. Color cameras require a higher illumination level than black and white cameras to be effective. Typically, a high-quality color camera will work well down to 1.5 fc illumination, whereas a standard black and white camera might only require 0.5 fc. These lighting level requirements vary with the camera model and manufacturer, so be sure to specify the necessary illumination level that is required for camera observation, and coordinate carefully with the lighting levels for the particular area to be viewed.

Outdoor Cameras

Outdoor camera installations cost more than indoor cameras due to the need to environmentally house, heat, and ventilate the camera. When mounting a camera outdoors, the lighting requirements change depending on the time of day and the weather. Because of this, consider the following for outdoor cameras:

- Shrubs, trees, and other vegetation in a camera's line of sight may cause obstructed views. Security professionals need to be aware of this when determining where to place cameras. Also, motion detector systems can register a false positive when plants in the field-of-view move in windy conditions.

- Provide heater blower packages for cold weather applications.

- Always use auto-iris lenses with outdoor cameras. The iris automatically adjusts the amount of light reaching the camera and thereby optimizes its performance. The iris also protects the image sensor from getting damaged by strong sunlight.

- Always set the focus in low light with an auto-iris lens. If the adjustment is made in sunlight, it is very easy to focus, but at night the iris diameter increases and the image is not in focus anymore.

- Special dark focus filters called "neutral density" (ND) filters help reduce lighting by one or more stops of exposure. These filters do not affect the color of the image.

- Always try to avoid direct sunlight in an image. Direct sunlight blinds the camera and may permanently bleach the small color filters on the sensor chip, causing stripes in the image. If possible, position the camera so that it is looking away from the sun.

- When using a camera outdoors, avoid viewing too much sky. Due to the large contrast, the camera will adjust to achieve a good light level for the sky, and the landscape and objects that must be assessed might appear too dark. One way to avoid these problems is to mount the camera high above ground (*Figure 10.13*). Use a pole if needed. Given mounting choices, mount cameras facing away from rising or setting sun, realizing that this varies by season. This is especially important with a long focal length lens. These lenses amplify even the smallest movement of the mount. Building mounts are generally more stable than pole mounts.

Fixed Position Cameras

A fixed position camera cannot rotate or pan. A good application for fixed cameras is detection surveillance, because video motion detection can be more readily applied to the static field-of-view. The installation and cost of

Figure 10.13 - **A Wall-Mounted Camera**
(Courtesy of Bosch Security Systems.)

fixed cameras is lower because there is no associated motor/control wiring. Fixed cameras are good for review of pre-alarm conditions because there is a static view of the alarm area. Pre-alarm allows the review of video information for the time period immediately before the alarm occurred. Due to the static view, fixed cameras are not as well suited for tracking a dynamic event.

Pan/Tilt/Zoom (PTZ) Cameras

PTZ camera mounts allow the camera to rotate, pan, tilt, and zoom. Because of the drive motor, housing, and wiring for controls, PTZ cameras are typically three to four times more expensive than fixed cameras. However, the operator gets a much better view of the overall area than with a fixed camera. PTZ cameras are often used to view and assess alarm conditions. PTZ cameras are not well suited for pre-alarm assessment because they may not be focused on the alarm area at all times. When designing CCTV surveillance, consideration needs to be given to lost coverage within the camera sweep field-of-view when the camera zooms to a fixed location.

1295

Dome Cameras

Dome cameras (*Figure 10.14*) are actually a cheaper version of the PTZ camera when the total cost is considered (installation, parts, and maintenance). Dome cameras are mounted in a hardened plastic lower dome, which is commonly smoke colored to conceal the camera. The use of smoke-colored domes provides covert lens positioning, while the use of clear domes provides for better low-light performance. Dome cameras are a good design solution for applications where the camera needs to be protected from the environment or it is desired to conceal the axis and field-of-view of a scanning camera. A common application of dome cameras is in office buildings with suspended ceilings. The dome camera is more aesthetic looking than a standard camera unit. Improvements in product design have reduced the packing to integral units that now fit in the space of a quarter ceiling tile. PTZ features within dome cameras move substantially quicker than conventional cameras with a separate PTZ drive unit on them.

Figure 10.14 - **A Dome Camera.**
(Courtesy of Bosch Security Systems.)

Internet Protocol (IP) Cameras

An IP camera captures a video image digitally. The IP camera resides on a local area network (LAN). Video data is transmitted via the LAN to a video server that routes the video to end users and a mass storage server. While this may sound advantageous, there are pros and cons. IP cameras are the least secure CCTV system, but may have applications where remote viewing over a network is desired, or where a high bandwidth and low latency network may exist. With an IP camera system, a network connection between the sites is all that is required to view any camera image on the system. One drawback to IP cameras is that they cost more than a standard analog (non-IP) camera. Due to the security concerns with the Internet, IP cameras will generally not be used on high-risk projects. The possible exception would be CCTV surveillance of low priority assets at remote locations.

Lens Selection

Another important consideration during installation of a CCTV system is the proper choice of lenses. Focal length is the distance from the surface of the lens to the point of focus measured in millimeters. Lenses either have a fixed or variable focal length. Manually variable focal length lenses are called "Vari-Focal Camera Lenses." The focal length of a lens is usually given in millimeters (mm). Focal lengths of most CCTV camera lenses vary from 3.6mm to 16mm for fixed focal length lenses to well over 70mm for zoom lenses. For a security camera in a warehouse with a high visibility requirement, a 2.8 or 4mm lens (makes wide, somewhat distant view) is the best choice. If the requirement is to positively identify people 25 feet away from a camera, a short focal length lens 3.6mm would give such a large field of view (37 feet × 26 feet) that recognition would be uncertain. An 8mm or even 12mm lens would be far better (see *Figure 10.15*).

Lighting Requirements

One design parameter of CCTV systems is specification of a proper light-to-dark ratio in the space viewed. "Light-to-dark" ratio refers to the

Figure 10.15 - **Camera view with 3.6 mm lens (top left), 4.3 mm lens (top right), 6 mm lens (middle left), 12 mm lens (middle right), and 25 mm lens (bottom)**

(Courtesy of Bosch Security Systems.)

light intensity (as measured in foot-candles or LUX) of the lightest (most reflective surface) to the darkest (least reflective surface). A proper light-to-dark ratio for good CCTV picture clarity is 4:1. The maximum ratio is 8:1. When the ratio is too high, the shadows appear black and the viewer cannot distinguish any shapes in the shadows. While not always achievable, the designer should strive for a light-to-dark ratio of 4:1.

Some cameras will automatically switch from color during daytime to black/white at night, which permits viewing under low-light conditions. This can be an effective solution in situations where the existing illumination levels are too low during night conditions to permit color camera use, but color camera use is desired during daytime conditions. Numerous CCTV camera manufacturers offer auto switching cameras.

Resolution

Resolution refers to the "graininess" of an image. The clearer the picture, the more pixels it will have. In addition, the larger the file, the more bandwidth it will consume. 352×288, which is the default frame rate for CCTV digital video recorder (DVR) systems will generate a satisfactory image that can help with transmission costs because it is a quarter of the data associated with a 640 by 480 image. While several high definition (HD) cameras exist, which can operate at 720 and 1080 lines, the security professional must understand the bandwidth, storage, and processing resources that HD gear requires.

Frames Per Second (FPS)

CCTV cameras transmit video in image frames. The measure of the "smoothness" of the playback of the video is quantified in frames per second (fps). The more frames per second you choose, the more network capacity each camera will require and the more data storage you will need. For most security applications, 30 fps is higher than needed for evidentiary and investigative purposes. Additionally, CCTV cameras have the option to transmit video at two image rates: alarm condition and non-alarm condition. Making use of a lower non-alarm fps can reduce project cost by allowing a lower bandwidth transmission and storage recording of the CCTV system. The idea is to increase the frame rate to actual motion when an alarm or the operator wants to capture images in real time compared to having the DVR record an image every 2 seconds at a reduced frame rate. In general, the bandwidth required will be increased with the frame rate used.

Compression

Digital images and digital video can be compressed in order to save space on hard drives and make transmission faster. Typically, the compression ratio is between 10 and 100. There are several standard commercial compression algorithms, but the most common is MPEG-4. Moving Picture Experts Group (MPEG) is a compression technique for audio and video that balances compression against loss of detail in the image.

1299

The greater the compression, the more information is lost. MPEG can be provided in any resolution size. MPEG-4 allows a style of transmission where an "anchor" image is transmitted, and then another image is not transmitted until something in the image changes. This minimizes the number of images transmitted when there is no movement. MPEG-4 is a proven compression standard because it is economical and has all the clarity and ease of use.

Digital Video Recorder (DVR)

In current CCTV systems, the DVR has become the central focus of the CCTV system. The DVR is used principally for the download of camera images onto a hard drive for recording and storage of historical information. Older systems used VHS tapes, but have largely been phased out. This system required tapes to be changed every day for storage and when an incident occurred you had to sit in front of the monitor and review the entire tape. DVRs currently have memory storage capability starting at tens of gigabytes to several terabytes with options to expand using additional hardware to increase storage. DVRs typically come in an 8 port or 16 port version, meaning that 8 or 16 cameras can be recorded at one time. Most DVRs are provided with self-contained DVD burners for archiving or removal of stored data. Many security specifications require a CCTV system to be able to retain a minimum of 45 days of camera images. The amount of storage required for 45 days is dependent on a number of factors including number of cameras, compression ratio, resolution, and frame rate. Most systems can be configured to motion detections and will not fill up the database with useless images. For example, is it necessary for the DVR to record the loading dock area from midnight until 4 am if there is no activity? Once there is motion in front of the camera then the system will begin recording. This does not mean that the monitoring officer cannot see the real-time images, it just will not store images that have no significant reason for maintaining. Again, this is a feature that each security professional can determine whether or not they wish to utilize.

Monitor Displays

Single Image Display

A single CCTV camera image is displayed. It is typical for a receptionist or a guard to monitor an entry door position where they are assigned duties.

Split Screen

Split screen is most commonly used to describe displaying multiple CCTV camera images on a single display. The display screen is typically split into a square pattern. Typically, if a 16 port DVR is used, then the screen can be installed to monitor 16 specific views. It is recommended that a second screen be utilized to allow the officer, guard, or receptionist to pull one view off the split screen for specific viewing or allow a flip sequencing of selected views to change every second in a larger view.

Matrix Displaying for Large Format Displays

LCD and flat-screen plasma displays (*Figure 10.16*) lend themselves to programming to show several camera images. The configuration is best done in a square matrix. A square matrix avoids distorting or stretching the camera image in one direction or the other, as would occur in a 5 by 7 matrix configuration for "alarm call-up" with additional monitors for a fixed view or switching images.

Figure 10.16 - **Large Format Displays in a control center**
(Courtesy of Bosch Security Systems.)

1301

Guards

Security officers are the physical presence and the deterrence to unauthorized entry into a facility along with being the response force to an alarm activation. With all the alarm technology, it still requires human intervention to respond to an alarm, make contact with an intruder, interact with employees, and provide first aid when necessary.

Security officers are required to conduct foot patrols of building interiors, exteriors, and parking areas. Some officers are assigned a fixed or stationary position at entrances and other designated areas in order to prevent unauthorized entrance or the introduction of prohibited items. Another security officer responsibility is to control access into the facility by checking employee identification badges, issuing temporary badges, and registering visitors. Officers are required to respond to fire, security and medical emergencies, and render assistance when needed as well as submit written or verbal reports regarding significant events to security management. They also escort designated visitors, usually construction or maintenance contractors, who require nonbusiness hour access to facilities or access to areas where classified or proprietary information is accessible. They must report potentially hazardous conditions and items in need of repair, including inoperative lights, leaky sprinkler heads, leaky faucets, toilet stoppages, broken or slippery floor surfaces, trip hazards, etc.

Proprietary

The advantages of proprietary security include the quality of personnel, degree of control over the security program, employee loyalty to the company, and prestige for both the employee and the company. A proprietary security force would be provided better training, which would be more specific to the operation and better training equates to better performance. There would be a sense of employee loyalty, which will create a stronger sense of ownership. Officers see themselves as a part of the team and are willing to go the extra mile for the benefit of the company and other employees. They see themselves with a stake in the long-term success of the company. Proprietary guards benefit from esprit de corps and a sense of community. Because it is possible to pay better wages to proprietary employees, turnover might be lower in proprietary guard organizations.

Utilizing proprietary security allows companies to design, field, and manage a security program to meet its particular needs. Many managers feel that they have a much greater degree of control over personnel when they are directly on the firm's payroll. Employee loyalty is much greater in a proprietary system. Contract security personnel are often moved around between different clients, making it hard for them to develop relationships and a sense of loyalty to a particular client. In the end, it is the contract company, not the client whom they protect, that signs their paychecks.

However, proprietary security operations have their disadvantages, including cost, administration, staffing, impartiality, and expertise. The administration required to operate a proprietary security operation include recruiting, screening, and training security personnel, as well as maintaining logs, audits, and other security program components. There is little question that the administrative workload is substantially decreased when a contract service is employed.

A considerable disadvantage of a proprietary service is the time it would take a firm to establish its own program. From selecting a head of security, filing of numerous positions, and the specific training that would be needed. Businesses would spend a considerably larger amount of money and time on in-house services where they would have to offer competitive wages and benefits to compete with other businesses and security firms. Another disadvantage is the possibility that more permanent in-house guards have the potential to form friendships and become somewhat partial to other employees, which could result in favoritism and a lack in their performance of duty.

Contract

Contract security can adapt staffing levels more easily than a proprietary system, as the need for staff rises and falls due to sudden or unexpected circumstances. The cost of hiring, training, and equipping proprietary staff makes rapidly increasing or decreasing staff levels more cumbersome than if contract services were used. With contract guard services, the cost for salary, insurance, administrative costs, uniforms, and benefits are all rolled up in one hourly price. This is helpful for budgeting purposes and there are no hidden costs.

Contract security employees are seen as impartial, because they are paid by an outside company to enforce a set of policies, and are not as likely to deviate from procedures due to personal relationships or pressure. There is no bond between the employees and the guard company and if there is found to be a quid pro quo system starting to develop, a phone call to the account manager can replace the guard easily.

Contract security companies focus on security as a business, not a supporting function of business. This gives them an advantage over proprietary operations. When clients hire a security service, they also hire the management of that service to guide them in their overall security program. It may take time for a company to develop a proprietary security organization with the wide-ranging level of experience that comes with a contract security company.

When it comes to staffing needs, guard companies already have a process established for the recruitment and hiring of staff. Their business is to have bodies available for assignment. This relieves the company of paying overtime when proprietary employees leave or take vacation. With a contract guard service, when you need three guards, you ask for three guards. When you do not need three anymore, you ask for two. Another big benefit is that if a contract officer does not work out, he or she can easily be replaced. You just call your account manager and ask for a replacement.

Contract security costs less than proprietary security because, typically, proprietary personnel earn more than contract personnel, due to the prevailing wage at their company. Contract personnel generally have fewer benefits than proprietary personnel do. Start-up costs for proprietary systems also make contract security services cheaper.

Hybrid

Sometimes contract security officers make sense. Sometimes, proprietary guards make sense. Sometimes, mixing both together at the same institution makes better sense. The hybrid system allows an organization to maintain more control over its security program, while achieving the cost savings and administration reduction associated with contract security. The use of hybrid systems is considered a workable solution, as it affords the benefits of both contract and proprietary security, while possibly mitigating the downsides of both.

Alarm Monitoring

After all the cameras, alarms systems, and locks are installed throughout a facility the question remains "who will monitor and respond to the alarms?" All alarm, CCTV and access control signals are tied into a central station. An organization will typically have a central station located on their property and monitored by a proprietary or contract guard service.

The central center (*Figure 10.17*), also known as the security console center, security control center, or dispatch center, is an area that serves as a central monitoring and assessment space for access control, CCTV, and intrusion detection systems. In this space, operators assess alarm conditions and determine the appropriate response, which may entail dispatching of security forces. Normally, the central station is staffed by trained personnel 24 hours a day, seven days a week.

Maintaining a 24/7 security control center requires at the minimum two officers per shift. They are responsible for monitoring alarms, access control, CCTV and fire. They will be required to dispatch officers to investigate alarms, disturbances, and unknown events.

1305

Figure 10.17 - **The Central Center, also known as the Security Console Center, security control center or dispatch center is an area that serves as a central monitoring and assessment space for access control, CCTV, and intrusion detection systems**

(Courtesy of Bosch Security Systems)

In this circumstance, a hybrid scenario is a practical application in the use of proprietary officers within the security control center and contract officers out on the floor. Inside the control center an organization needs a higher level of commitment to the company and performance continuity in knowledge and action. The contract officers can be crossed trained for times when there is a staffing issue dealing with the control center propriety staff. This would be a support element that could be counted on for vacation, sickness, or temporary duties. While the contractor management does not like being an employment warehouse, the contracted officer can be viewed as a potential replacement in the event a proprietary position becomes available.

Many organizations utilize the UL 1981[1] standard when dealing with high security facilities for designating staffing levels at a central station. UL 1981 requires monitoring facility staffing be such that all alarm signals be acknowledged and the appropriate dispatch or verification action be

---

1   http://ulstandardsinfonet.ul.com/scopes/scopes.asp?fn=1981.html

initiated not more than a defined period after the monitoring facility receiver acknowledges to the alarm panel at the protected site that the alarm signal has been received.

Design Requirements

The control center will be located on the main floor or in the basement of the facility, as long as the area is not below ground level and there is no chance of flooding. Entry will be controlled and only authorized personnel will be allowed inside the center. The control center will be provided with primary and secondary sources of power. The secondary power should consist of a battery backup or UPS system that will provide for a normal load of at least 24 hours. It is also recommended that an engine drive generator system be used as a complement to the rechargeable battery system in order to keep uninterrupted power to the control center.

Support the Implementation of Internal Security

Interior Intrusion Detection Systems

Within the facility, it is still necessary to maintain levels of security. The layered approach provides for additional security measures while inside the perimeter of the facility. Specifically, not all employees need access to the sensitive areas, such as the phone closets, or need access into the data center. It is not practical or economical to have guards stationed at every security point within the facility; however, an access control system can provide the necessary security controls throughout the building.

A card reader can control access into a specific room. This can be controlled through the access control software, which will be maintained within the security control center. If the individual has access to the room, the employee will place his badge up to the reader and it will release the electric lock and allow entry. Other elements necessary for this control of interior access are as follows:

- **Balanced Magnetic Switch (BMS):** This device uses a magnetic field or mechanical contact to determine if an alarm signal is initiated. One magnet will be attached to the door and the other to the frame; when the door is opened the field is broken. A BMS differs from standard magnetic status switches in that a BMS incorporates two aligned magnets with an associated reed switch. If an external magnet is applied to the switch area, it upsets the balanced magnetic field such that an alarm signal is received. Standard magnetic switches can be defeated by holding a magnet near the switch. Mechanical contacts can be defeated by holding the contacts in the closed position with a piece of metal or taping them closed. Balanced magnetic switches are not susceptible to external magnetic fields and will generate an alarm if tampering occurs. These switches are used on doors and windows (*Figure 10.18*).

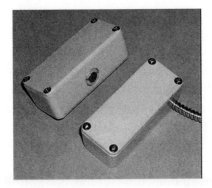

Figure 10.18 - **Balanced Magnetic Switch (BMS), used on doors and windows, uses a magnetic field or mechanical contact to determine if an alarm signal is initiated**
(Courtesy of Bosch Security Systems.)

- *Motion Activated Cameras:* A fixed camera with a video motion feature can be used as an interior intrusion point sensor. In this application, the camera can be directed at an entry door and will send an alarm signal when an intruder enters the field of view. This device has the added advantage of providing a video image of the event, which can alert the security officer monitoring the camera and he can make a determination of the need to dispatch a security force. Typically one camera can be associated with several doors along a hallway. If a door is forced open the alarm will trigger the camera to begin recording and can give the monitoring officer a video view starting one minute before the alarm was tripped, so as to allow the operator all the possible information before dispatching a security response. This system uses technology to supplement the guard force. It can activate upon motion and can give a control center operator a detailed video of actual events during alarm activation.

- *Acoustic Sensors:* This device uses passive listening devices to monitor building spaces. An application is an administrative building that is normally only occupied in daylight working hours. Typically, the acoustic sensing system is tied into a password-protected building entry control system, which is monitored by a central security monitoring station. When someone has logged into the building with a proper password,

1309

the acoustic sensors are disabled. When the building is secured and unoccupied, the acoustic sensors are activated. After hours intruders make noise which is picked up by the acoustic array and an alarm signal is generated. The downside is the false alarm rate from picking up noises such as air conditioning and telephone ringers. This product must be deployed in an area that will not have any noise. Acoustic sensors act as a detection means for stay-behind covert intruders. One way to use the system is as a monitoring device, when it goes into alarm the system will open up an intercom and the monitoring officer can listen to the area. If no intruder is heard then the alarm is cancelled.

■ **Infrared Linear Beam Sensors:** Many think of this device from spy movies, where the enduring image of secret agents and bank robbers donning their special goggles to avoid triggering an active infrared beam is recalled. This is the device found in many homes on garage doors. A focused infrared (IR) light beam is projected from an emitter and bounced off of a reflector that is placed at the other side of the detection area (Figure 10.19). A retroreflective photoelectric beam sensor built into the emitter detects when the infrared beam is broken by the passing of a person or the presence of an object in the path of the infrared beam. If the beam is broken the door will stop or the light will come on. This device can also be used to notify security of individuals in hallways late at night, when security is typically at its reduced coverage.

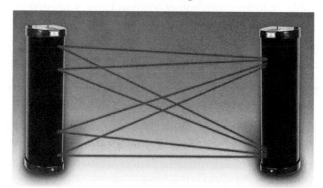

Figure 10.19 - **Infrared Linear Beam sensors** (Courtesy of Bosch Security Systems)

■ ***Passive Infrared (PIR) Sensors:*** A PIR sensor (*Figure 10.20*) is one of the most common interior volumetric intrusion detection sensors. Because there is no beam it is called passive. A PIR picks up heat signatures (infrared emissions) from intruders by comparing infrared receptions to typical background infrared levels. Infrared radiation exists in the electromagnetic spectrum at a wavelength that is longer than visible light. It cannot be seen but it can be detected. Objects that generate heat also generate infrared radiation and those objects include animals and the human body. The PIR is set to determine a change in temperature, whether warmer or colder, and distinguish an object that is different from the environment that it is set in. Typically, activation differentials are three degrees Fahrenheit. These devices work best in a stable environmentally controlled space.

Figure 10.20 - **A Passive Infrared (PIR) sensor is one of the most common interior volumetric intrusion detection sensors. Because there is no beam it is called passive**

(Courtesy of Bosch Security Systems)

A PIR is a motion detector and will not activate for a person who is standing still because the electronics package attached to the sensor is looking for a fairly rapid change in the amount of infrared energy it is seeing. When a person walks by, the amount of infrared energy in the field of view changes rapidly and is easily detected. The sensor should not detect slower changes, like the sidewalk cooling off at night.

PIRs come in devices that project out at a 45° angle and can pick up objects 8 to 15 meters away. There are also 360° PIRs, which can be used in a secured room, so when there is entry the PIR will activate. These motion detection devices can also be programmed into an alarm key pad located within the protected space. When motion is detected, it can be programmed to wait for a prescribed time while the individual swipes their badge or enters their pass code information into the keypad. If identification is successful the PIR does not send an intruder notification to the central station.

While not only a security application, PIRs are often used as an automatic request to exit (REX) device for magnetically locked doors. In this application, the REX (*Figure 10.21*) acts as the automatic sensor for detecting an approaching person in the exit direction for magnetically locked doors and deactivates the alarm.

- **Dual-Technology Sensors:** These provide a common sense approach for the reduction of false alarm rates. For example, this technology uses a combination of microwave and PIR sensor circuitry within one housing. An alarm condition is only generated if both the microwave and the PIR sensor detect an intruder. Since two independent means of detection are involved, false alarm rates are reduced when configured into this setting. Integrated, redundant devices must react at the same time to cause an alarm. More and more devices are coming with dual-technology that will reduce the need for multiple devices and will significantly reduce the false alarm rates.

Figure 10.21 - **An automatic Request to Exit (REX) device [located over the Exit sign] provides for magnetically locked doors acting as an automatic sensor for detecting an approaching person in the exit direction and deactivates the alarm as the person exits**

(Courtesy of Bosch Security Systems.)

Escort and Visitor Control

All visitors entering the facility should sign in and sign out on a visitor's log to maintain accountability of who is in the facility, the timeframe of the visit, who they visited, and in the case of an emergency have accountability of everyone for safety purposes.

All visitors should be greeted by a knowledgeable receptionist who in turn will promptly contact the employee that they are there to visit or meet with. There should be some type of controlled waiting area within the lobby so the receptionist can keep track of the visitor and can direct the employee to them, in the event they have never met previously.

1313

Visitors are given temporary badges, but this badge does not double as an access card. The temporary badge will be issued at an entry control point only after the visitor identifies the purpose of the visit and receives approval by the employee being visited. In some organizations only certain employees may approve visitor access along with the day and time of the visit. In many operations, the visitor is escorted at all times while inside the facility. When the visitor arrives, he will present a form of photo identification, such as a driver's license to the receptionist for verification. Some visitor badges are constructed of paper and may have a feature that causes a void line to appear after a preset time period. Typically, the pass is dated and issued for a set period, usually one day. In most cases a visitor will wear a conspicuous badge that identifies them as a visitor and clearly indicates whether an escort is required (often done with color-coded badges). If an escort is required the assigned person should be identified by name and held responsible for the visitor at all times while on the premises. A visitor management system can be a pen and paper system that records basic information about visitors to the facility. Typical information found in an entry includes the visitor's name, reason for the visit, date of visit, and the check in and check out times.

Other types of visitor management systems use a computer-based system or specific visitor software product. They can either be manually inserted into the system by the receptionist' or, on a higher-end visitor management system, the visitor provides the receptionist' with identification, such as a driver's license, or a government or military ID. The receptionist then swipes the person's identification through a reader. The system automatically populates the database with ID information and recognizes whether the ID is properly formatted or false. The receptionist who is registering the guest identifies the group to which the person belongs— guest, client, vendor, or contractor. Then the badge is printed.

It is best for the employee to come to the lobby area and greet the visitor personally. This is more than a common courtesy because it provides the necessary security in proper identification, escorting and controlling the movement of the visitor. Some companies initiate a sound security practice by properly identifying the visitor and signing them into a visitor management system, but then allow the visitor to wander the halls of the company trying to find their contact. This completely defeats the prior work of identifying and badging the visitor.

Building and Inside Security

Doors

Door assemblies include the door, its frame, and anchorage to the building. As part of a balanced design approach, exterior doors should be designed to fit snugly in the doorframe, preventing crevices and gaps, which also helps prevent many simple methods of gaining illegal entry. The doorframe and locks must be as secure as the door in order to provide good protection.

Perimeter doors should consist of hollow steel doors or steel-clad doors with steel frames. Ensure the strength of the latch and frame anchor equals that of the door and frame. Permit normal egress through a limited number of doors, if possible, while accommodating emergency egress. Ensure that exterior doors into inhabited areas open outward. Locate hinges on the interior of restricted areas. Use exterior security hinges on doors opening outward to reduce their vulnerability.

If perimeter doors are made of glass, make sure that the material is constructed of a laminate material or stronger. Ensure that glass doors only allow access into a public or lobby area of the facility. High security doors will then need to be established within the lobby area where access will be controlled. All doors that are installed for sensitive areas such as telephone closets, network rooms, or any area that has access control will require the door to have an automatic door closing device.

10

Physical (Enviromental) Security

Door Locks

Electric Locks

The electric lock is a secure method to control a door. An electric lock actuates the door bolt. For secure applications dual locks can be used. In some cases, power is applied to engage the handle, so the user can retract the bolt instead of the electric lock door operator actually retracting the bolt. Most electric locks can have built-in position switches and request-to-exit hardware. Although offering a high security level, electric locks are expensive. A special door hinge, that can accommodate a wiring harness and internal hardware to the door, is required. For retrofit applications, electric locks usually require the purchase of a new door.

Electric Strikes

The difference between an electric strike and an electric lock is in the mechanism that is activated at the door. In an electric-lock door, the bolt is moved. In an electric-strike, door the bolt remains stationary and the strike is retracted. As in electric locks, electric strikes can be configured for fail-safe or fail-secure operation. The logic is the same. In fail-safe configuration, the strike retracts when de-energized on loss of power. This allows the door to be opened from the public side. In fail-secure configuration, the strike remains in place causing the door to be locked from the public side requiring manual key entry to unlock the door from the public side. Again, as with electric locks, unimpeded access is allowed for in the direction of exit by manual activation of the door handle or lever when exiting from the secure side. For retrofit situations, electric strikes rarely require door replacement and can often be done without replacing the doorframe.

Magnetic Locks

The magnetic lock is popular because it can be easily retrofitted to existing doors (*Figure 10.22*). The magnetic lock is surface-mounted to the door and doorframe. Power is applied to magnets continuously to hold the door closed. Magnetic locks are normally fail-safe.

Magnetic locks do have a security disadvantage. In requirements for the U. S. Life Safety Codes[1], doors equipped with magnetic locks are required to have one manual device (emergency manual override button) and an automatic sensor (typically a passive infrared sensor (PIR) or request to exit (REX) device) to override the door lock signal when someone approaches the door in the exit direction. All locks are controlled by a card reader that when activated will release the secured side portion of the door and allow entry into the facility. While enhancing overall building safety, the addition of these extra devices allows possible compromise of the door lock. In the scenario, where a REX is used with magnetic locks, it not only turns off the alarm when the individual exits but also deactivates the locking device. This can be a problem if an adversary can get something through or under the door to cause the REX to release the magnetic lock.

Figure 10.22 - **Magnetic Lock (Courtesy of Bosch Security Systems)**

---

1   http://www.nfpa.org/aboutthecodes/AboutTheCodes.asp?DocNum=101&cookie_
test=1

Anti-Passback

In high security areas, a card reader is utilized on both entry and exit sides of the door. This keeps a record of who went in and out. Anti-passback is a strategy where a person must present a credential to enter an area or facility, and then again use the credential to "badge out." This makes it possible to know how long a person is in an area, and to know who is in the area at any given time. This requirement also has the advantage of instant personnel accountability during an emergency or hazardous event. Anti-passback programming prevents users from giving their cards or PIN number to someone else to gain access to the restricted area. In a rigid anti-passback configuration, a credential or badge is used to enter an area and that same credential must be used to exit. If a credential holder fails to properly "badge-out," entrance into the secured area can be denied.

Turnstiles and Mantraps

A common and frustrating loophole in an otherwise secure ACS can be the ability of an unauthorized person to follow through a checkpoint behind an authorized person, called "piggybacking" or "tailgating."

The traditional solution is an airlock-style arrangement called a "mantrap," in which a person opens one door and waits for it to close before the next door will open (*Figure 10.23*). A footstep-detecting floor can be added to confirm there is only one person passing through. A correctly constructed mantrap or portal will provide for tailgate detection while it allows roller luggage, briefcases, and other large packages to pass without causing nuisance alarms. People attempting to enter side-by-side are detected by an optional overhead sensing array. The mantrap controller prevents entry into secured areas if unauthorized access is attempted.

Another system that is available is a turnstile, which can be used as a supplemental control to assist a guard or receptionist while controlling access into a protected area. Anyone who has gone to a sporting event has gone through a turnstile. In this approach, the individual's badge is used to control the turnstile arm and allow access into the facility. See *Figure 10.24*.

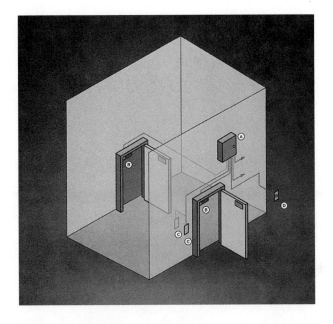

Figure 10.23 - **A Mantrap** (Courtesy of Bosch Security Systems.)

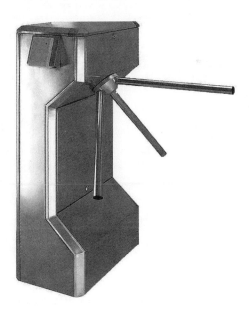

Figure 10.24 - **A Turnstile can be used as a supplemental control to assist a guard or receptionist while controlling access into a protected area.**

1319

A higher-end turnstile is an optical turnstile, which is designed to provide a secure access control in the lobby of a busy building. This system is designed as a set of parallel pedestals that form lanes, which allow entry or exit. Each barrier is equipped with photoelectric beams, guard arms, and a logic board. See *Figure 10.25.*

To gain access to the interior of the building, an authorized person uses his access card at the optical turnstile. When the access card is verified the guard arm is dropped, the photoelectric beam is temporarily shut off and the cardholder passed without creating an alarm. The concept behind these options is to create a secure perimeter just inside the building to ensure only authorized people proceed further into the building, thereby creating the secure working environment.

Figure 10.25 - **A higher end turnstile is an optical turnstile, which is designed to provide a secure access control in the lobby of a busy building**

(Courtesy of Bosch Security Systems)

Keys, Locks, and Safes

Types of Locks

Key locks are one of the basic safeguards in protecting buildings, personnel, and property and are generally used to secure doors and windows. According to UL standard 437[2], door locks and locking cylinders must resist attack through the following testing procedures: the picking test, impression test (a lock is surreptitiously opened by making an impression of the key with a key blank of some malleable material—wax or plastic—which is inserted into the keyway and then filed to fit the lock), forcing test, and salt spray corrosion test for products intended for outdoor use. The door locks and locking cylinders are required by UL standards to resist picking and impression for ten minutes.

Rim Lock

A rim lock, shown in *Figure 10.26*, is a lock or latch typically mounted on the surface of a door. It is typically associated with a dead bolt type of lock.

Figure 10.26 - **A Rim Lock is a lock or latch typically mounted on the surface of a door**
(Courtesy of Bosch Security Systems)

---

2   http://ulstandardsinfonet.ul.com/tocs/tocs.asp?doc=s&fn=0437.toc

Mortise Lock

A mortise lock, shown in *Figure 10.25*, is a lock or latch that is recessed into the edge of a door, rather than being mounted to its surface. This configuration has a handle and locking device all in one package.

Figure 10.27 - **A Mortise Lock is a lock or latch that is recessed into the edge of a door, rather than being mounted to its surface**

(Courtesy of Bosch Security Systems.)

Locking Cylinders

The pin tumbler cylinder is a locking cylinder that is composed of circular pin tumblers that fit into matching circular holes on two internal parts of the lock (*Figure 10.28*). The pin tumbler functions on the principle that the pin tumblers need to be placed into a position that is entirely contained with the plug. Each pin is of a different height, thus accounting for the varying ridge sizes of the key. When the pins are properly aligned, the plug can be turned to unlock the bolt.

Cipher Lock

A cipher lock, shown in *Figure 10.29*, is controlled by a mechanical key pad, typically 5 to 10 digits that when pushed in the right combination the lock will releases and allows entry. The drawback is someone looking over a shoulder can see the combination. However, an electric version of the cipher lock is in production in which a display screen will automatically

Figure 10.28 - **A Pin Tumbler Cylinder is a locking cylinder that is composed of circular pin tumblers that fit into matching circular holes on two internal parts of the lock**

(Courtesy of Bosch Security Systems)

move the numbers around, so if someone is trying to watch the movement on the screen they will not be able to identify the number indicated unless they are standing directly behind the victim.

Remember locking devices are only as good as the wall or door that they are mounted in and if the frame of the door or the door itself can be easily destroyed then the lock will not be effective. A lock will eventually be defeated and its primary purpose is to delay the attacker.

Figure 10.29 - **A Cipher Lock is controlled by a mechanical key pad with digits that when pushed in the right combination will release the lock and allow entry**

(Courtesy of Bosch Security Systems.)

1323

Hi-Tech Keys

Not all lock and key systems are standard metal composite. There have been developments in key technology that offer convenient, reliable access control.

"Intelligent keys" are keys with a built-in microprocessor, which is unique to the individual key holder and identifies the key holder specifically. The lock, which also contains a minicomputer and the key exchange data, allows the lock to make valid access decisions based on the parameters established for the key holder. For example, the key will know if the employee is allowed access into the facility after normal business hours; if not, the key will not work. Also, it will keep track of whose key is being used to access specific locked doors and when the attempts are taking place. When an employee resigns from the organization, the relevant key is disabled.

"Instant keys" provide a quick way to disable a key by permitting one turn of the master key to change a lock. This method of changing a lock can save both time and money in the event a master key is lost. According to a manufacturer, a 50-story bank building can be rekeyed in six hours by two security guards. The system can go through 10 to 15 changes before having to be re-pinned.

Safes

Safes are often the last bastion of defense between an attacker and an asset. Several types of safes not only protect against theft but also fire and flood. A safe (*Figure 10.30*) is defined as a fireproof and burglarproof iron or steel chest used for the storage of currency, negotiable securities, and similar valuables.

The categories for safes depend on the amount of security needed. Underwriters Laboratory lists several classifications of safe; the following is one such classification:

Tool-Resistant Safe Class TL-15. This type of combination lock safe is designed to meet the following requirements: It must be resistant to

Figure 10.30 - **A safe is a fireproof and burglarproof iron or steel chest used for the storage of currency, negotiable securities, and similar valuables**

(Courtesy of Bosch Security Systems)

entry (by opening the door or making a six-inch hand hole through the door) for a net working time of 15 minutes using any combination of the following tools: mechanical or portable electric hand drills not exceeding one-half-inch size, grinding points, carbide drills (excluding the magnetic drill press and other pressure-applying mechanisms, abrasive wheels, and rotating saws), and common hand tools such as chisels, drifts, wrenches, screwdrivers, pliers, and hammers and sledges not to exceed the eight-pound size, pry bars and ripping tools not to exceed five feet in length, and picking tools that are not specially designed for use against a special make of safe. A TL-15[3] safe must:

- Weigh at least 750 pounds or be equipped with anchors and instructions for anchoring in larger safes, in concrete blocks, or to the floor of the bank premises.

- Have metal in the body that is solid cast or fabricated open-hearth steel at least 1 inch thick with a tensile strength of 50,000 pounds per square inch (psi) and that is fastened to the floor in a manner equal to a continuous 1/4-inch penetration

3   http://ulstandardsinfonet.ul.com/scopes/scopes.asp?fn=0687.html

weld of open-hearth steel having an ultimate tensile strength of 50,000psi.

■ Have the hole to permit insertion of electrical conductors for alarm devices not exceed a 1/4-inch diameter and be provided in the top, side, bottom, or back of the safe body, but must not permit a direct view of the door or locking mechanism.

■ Be equipped with a combination lock meeting UL Standard No. 768 requirements for Group 2,1, or 1R locks.

■ Be equipped with a relocking device that will effectively lock the door if the combination lock is punched.

The UL classifications mean that a Tool-Resistant Safe Class TL-30 will take 30 minutes to break into the safe using tools. A TRTL-30 safe means it will take 30 minutes for a combination of tools and torches to break into the safe. The categories go up to a safe that can resist tools, torches, and explosives.

Vaults

A vault (*Figure 10.31*) is defined as a room or compartment designed for the storage and safekeeping of valuables and has a size and shape that permits entrance and movement within by one or more persons. Vaults generally are constructed to withstand the best efforts of man and nature to penetrate them.

The UL has developed standards for vault doors and vault modular panels for use in the construction of vault floors, walls, and ceilings. The standards are intended to establish the burglary-resistant rating of vault doors and modular vault panels according to the length of time they withstand attack by common mechanical tools, electric tools, cutting torches, or any combination thereof. The ratings, based on the net working time to affect entry, are as follows:

■ *Class M*—one-quarter hour
■ *Class 1*—one-half hour
■ *Class 2*—one hour
■ *Class 3*—two hours

Figure 10.31 - **A Vault is a room or compartment designed for the storage and safe-keeping of valuables and has a size and shape that permits entrance and movement within by one or more persons**

(Courtesy of Bosch Security Systems.)

Containers

A container is a reinforced filling cabinet that can be used to store proprietary and sensitive information. The standards for classified containers are typically from a government. For example, the U.S. Government lists a class 6 container (*Figure 10.32*) as approved for the storage of secret, top secret, and confidential information. The container must meet the protection requirements for 30 man-minutes against covert entry and 20 hours against surreptitious entry with no forced entry.

Key Control

Key control, or more accurately the lack of key control, is one of the biggest risks that businesses and property owners face. Strong locks and stronger key control are the two essentials in a high security locking system. In most

1327

cases, master and sub-master keys are required for most building systems so that janitorial and other maintenance personnel may have access. Thus, the control of all keys becomes a critical element of the key lock system: all keys need to be tightly controlled from the day of purchase by designated personnel responsible for the lock system.

Without a key control system an organization cannot be sure who has keys or how many keys may have been produced for a given property. Not having a patent-controlled key system leads to unauthorized key duplication, which can lead to unauthorized access or employee theft. Most key control systems utilize patented keys and cylinders. These lock cylinders employ very precise locking systems that can only be operated by the unique keys to that system. Because the cylinders and the keys are patented, the duplication of keys can only be done by factory-authorized professional locksmiths.

The key blanks and lock cylinders are made available only to those same factory authorized professional locksmiths. Procedures may be in place to allow the organization to contract another security professional, should the need arise.

All high-security key control systems require specific permission to have keys originated or duplicated. These procedures assure the property owner or manager that they will always know who has keys and how many they possess. If an employee leaves and returns the keys, the organization can be reasonably assured that no copies of the keys were made. Most systems have cylinders that will retrofit existing hardware, keeping the cost of acquisition lower. Some systems employ different levels of security within the system, still giving patented control, but not requiring ultra-high security where it is not needed. These measures are again aimed at cost control.

Most systems can be master keyed; some will coordinate with existing master key systems. There are systems available that allow interchangeable core cylinders for retrofitting of existing systems.

Figure 10.32 - **A Class 6 Container is approved for the storage of secret, top secret, and confidential information**

(Courtesy of Bosch Security Systems.)

Locks, keys, doors, and frame construction are interconnected and all must be equally effective. If any single link is weak, the system will break down.

The *Medeco Guide for Developing and Managing Key Control*[4] states:

---

4   http://www.medeco.com/Other/Medeco/Downloads/Key_Control/Key_Control.pdf pg 3

2. The following represent the basic and most critical elements of key control and shall be included, as a minimum, in the key control specification.

   2.1. Facility shall appoint a Key Control Authority or Key Control Manager to implement, execute, and enforce key control policies and procedures.

   2.2. A policy and method for the issuing and collecting of all keys shall be implemented.

   2.3. Keys and key blanks shall be stored in a locked cabinet or container, in a secured area.

   2.4. A key control management program shall be utilized. A dedicated computer software application is preferred.

   2.5. All keys shall remain the property of the issuing facility.

   2.6. A key should be issued only to individuals who have a legitimate and official requirement for the key.

      2.6.1. A requirement for access alone, when access can be accomplished by other means (such as unlocked doors, request for entry, intercoms, timers, etc.), shall not convey automatic entitlement to a key.

   2.7. All keys shall be returned and accounted for.

   2.8. Employees must ensure that keys are safeguarded and properly used.

Support the Implementation and Operation of Facilities Security

Biometrics

Biometric devices rely on measurements of biological characteristics of an individual, such as a fingerprint, hand geometry, voice, or iris patterns. Biometric technology involves data that is unique to the individual and is difficult to counterfeit. Selected individual characteristics are stored in a device's memory or on a card, from which stored reference data can be analyzed and compared with the presented template. A one-to-many or a one-to-one comparison of the presented template with the stored template can be made and access granted if a match is found.

However, on the negative side, some biometric systems may periodically fail to perform or have a high rejection rate. The sensitivity of readers could make system readers susceptible to inadvertent reader damage or intentional sabotage. Some systems may be perceived by the user as a safety or health risk. Also, some of the systems may require a degree of skill on the part of the user for proper operation, and others may be perceived as unacceptable by management for a combination of reasons.

There are two types of failures in biometric identification:

False Rejection—Failure to recognize a legitimate user. While it could be argued that this has the effect of keeping the protected area extra secure, it is an intolerable frustration to legitimate users who are refused access because the scanner does not recognize them.

False Acceptance—Erroneous recognition, either by confusing one user with another or by accepting an imposter as a legitimate user.

10

Physical (Enviromental) Security

1331

Failure rates can be adjusted by changing the threshold ("how close is close enough") for declaring a match, but decreasing one failure rate will increase the other.

Biometric Readers

Biometric readers verify personal biological metrics of an individual. Biometric readers may be used in addition to credential devices or with a PIN code. This type of security technology is more likely found in high security areas such as a government Sensitive Compartmented Information Facility (SCIF) or a data center.

Current gains in large-scale production of some types of biometric readers have brought biometrics close in cost to conventional card readers. Although biometric scanners are typically not as fast as other readers, these technologies are still evolving.

Fingerprint

Fingerprint reader technology scans the loops, whorls, and other characteristics of a fingerprint and compares it with stored templates (*Figure 10.33*). When a match is found, access is granted. The advantage of fingerprint technology is that it is easily understood. The disadvantages are that the systems can be disrupted if cuts or sores appear on fingers or if grease or other medium contaminates the fingers and the scanning plates. Some systems create two templates for two different fingers, in the event that one finger is altered by injury or other means. Early fingerprint readers were compromised by picking up a valid fingerprint from a reader with a manufactured "finger." To combat this shortcoming of the technology, sensors were equipped with the ability to sense a pulse and temperature.

Facial Image

This technology measures the geometric properties of the subject's face relative to an archived image. Specifically, the center of the subject's eyes must be located and placed at precise locations.

Figure 10.33 - **A Fingerprint Reader scans the loops, whorls, and other characteristics of a fingerprint and compares it with stored templates. When a match is found, access is granted**

(Courtesy of Bosch Security Systems.)

Hand Geometry

This technology assesses the hand's geometry: height, width, and distance between knuckle joints and finger length. Advantages of hand geometry are that the systems are durable and easily understood. The speed of hand recognition tends to be more rapid than fingerprint recognition. Hand recognition is reasonably accurate because the shape of all hands is unique. A disadvantage is that they tend to give higher false accept rates than fingerprint recognition. This technology cannot determine when fingernails have been applied and it reads only geometric measurements of the hand.

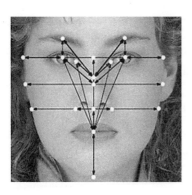

1333

Voice Recognition

Voice recognition identifies the voice characteristics of a given phrase to that of one held in a template. Voice recognition is generally not performed as one function, and is typically part of a system where a valid PIN must be entered before the voice analyzer is activated. An advantage of voice recognition is that the technology is less expensive than other biometric technologies. Additionally, it can be operated hands-free. A disadvantage is that the voice synthesizer must be placed in an area where the voice is not disturbed by background sounds. Often a booth or a security portal has to be installed to house the sensor in order to provide the system an acceptable quiet background.

Iris Patterns

Iris recognition technology scans the surface of the eye and compares the iris pattern with stored iris templates. Iris scanning is the most accurate and secure biometric technology. A benefit of iris recognition is that it is not susceptible to theft, loss, or compromise, and irises are less susceptible to wear and injury than many other parts of the body. Newer iris scanners allow scanning to occur from up to ten inches away. A disadvantage of iris scanning is that some people are timid about having their eye scanned. Throughput time for this technology should also be considered. Typical throughput time is two seconds. If a number of people need to be processed through an entrance in a short period of time, this can be problematic.

Retinal Scanning

Retinal scanning analyses the layer of blood vessels at the back of the eye which is unique to each person. Scanning involves using a low-intensity LED light source and an optical coupler that can read the patterns with great accuracy. It does require the user to remove glasses, place his eye close to the device, and focus on a certain point. The user looks through a small opening in the device and must keep his head still and eye focused for several seconds during which time the device will verify his identity. This process takes about 10 seconds.

Retina scan devices are probably the most accurate biometric available today. The continuity of the retinal pattern throughout life and the difficulty in fooling such a device also make it a great long-term, high-security option. Unfortunately, the cost of the proprietary hardware as well the stigma of users thinking it is potentially harmful to the eye makes retinal scanning a bad fit for most situations. Typically, this application is used in high-end security applications, such as military bases and nuclear power plants.

Signature Dynamics

First, the signer writes out a handwritten signature on a special electronic pad, such as the ePad by Interlink or a Palm Pilot. The shape of the signature is then electronically read and recorded, along with such unique features as the pressure on the pen and the speed at which the signature was written in order to identify the signer's unique writing; for example, did the "t" get crossed from right to left and did the "i" get dotted at the very end.

The advantage of signature dynamics is that it works like a traditional signature. Signers do not need special knowledge of computers nor any unusual tools to make a signature. At the same time, the system allows the notary to record unique identifying features to help prevent and detect forged signatures. For example, if a forger attempted to copy the signature of another person and wrote slowly to try and create a visually identical style of writing, an analyst could compare it with the data to detect the slower writing speed and recognize it as a different signer.

Vascular Patterns

This is the ultimate palm reader. Vascular patterns are best described as a picture of the veins in a person's hand or finger. The thickness and location of these veins are believed to be unique enough to an individual to be used to verify a person's identity. The NTSC Subcommittee on Biometrics reports that researchers have determined that the vascular pattern of the human body is unique to the specific individual and does not change as people age. Claims for the technology include

- **Difficult to Forge:** Vascular patterns are difficult to recreate because they are inside the hand, and for some approaches, blood needs to flow to register an image.

- **Contact-less:** Users do not touch the sensing surface, which address hygiene concerns and improves user acceptance.

- **Many and Varied Uses:** It is deployed at ATMs, hospitals, and universities in Japan. Applications include ID verification, high security physical access control, high security network data access, and POS access control.

- **Capable of 1:1 and 1:Many Matches:** Users' vascular patterns are matched against personalized ID cards/smart cards or against a database of many scanned vascular patterns.

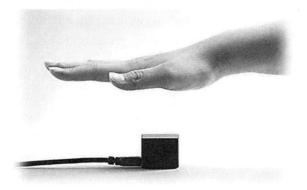

Keystroke Dynamics

Keystroke dynamics, also known as keyboard dynamics, looks at the way a person types at a keyboard. Specifically, the keystroke rhythms of a user are measured to develop a unique template of the users typing pattern for future authentication. Raw measurements available from most every keyboard can be recorded to determine dwell time (the amount of time you hold down a particular key) and flight time (the amount of time between the next key down and the next key up.)

Communications and Server Rooms

Securing the Area

Communication rooms or closets must maintain a high level of security. Access must be controlled into this area and only authorized personnel should be allowed to work on this equipment. No matter what transmission mode or media is selected, it is important that a method for securing communications be included. This includes physical protection, such as providing a rigid metallic conduit for all conductors, as well as technical protection, such as encrypting communication transmissions.

Protection from Lightning

A lightning strike to a grounding system produces an elevated ground or ground potential rise (GPR). Any equipment bonded to this grounding system, and also connected to wire-line communications will most likely be damaged from outgoing current seeking remote ground. Personnel working at this equipment are susceptible to harm, because they will be in the current path of this outgoing current. The equipment damage from a lightning strike may not be immediate. Sometimes the equipment is weakened by stress and primed for failure at some future time. This is called latent damage and leads to premature "mean time before failure" (MTBF) of the equipment.

The best engineering design, for open ended budgets, is the use of dielectric fiber optic cable for all communications. Obviously, a fiber optic cable is non-conductive, provided that it is an all dielectric cable with no metallic strength members or shield, making isolation no longer a requirement. This is because physical isolation is inherent in the fiber optic product itself. This all dielectric fiber optic cable must be placed in PVC conduit to protect it from rodents.

However, if budgets are tight, the engineering design solution to protect this equipment is to isolate the wire-line communications from remote ground. This is accomplished using optical isolators or isolation transformers. This equipment is housed together, mounted on a non-conducting surface in a non-conducting cabinet, and is called the high voltage interface (HVI).

The HVI isolates the equipment during a GPR and prevents any current flow from a higher potential grounding system to a lower potential grounding system. This totally protects any equipment from damage or associated working personnel from harm. No ground shunting device ever made, no matter how fast acting, will ever completely protect equipment from a GPR. Ground shunting devices are connected to the elevated ground and during a GPR offer an additional current path in the reverse direction from which they were intended to operate. Obviously, this flow of current, even away from the equipment, will immediately cause equipment damage and harm to working personnel.

Server Rooms

A server room needs a higher level of security than the rest of the facility. This should encompass a protected room with no windows and only one controlled entry into the area. Remember that once servers are compromised, the entire network is at risk. While some server attacks are merely annoying, others can cause serious damage. In order to protect the organization, it is paramount to protect your servers. Physical access to a system is almost a guaranteed compromise if performed by a motivated attacker. Therefore, server room security must be comprehensive and constantly under review.

Rack Security

It would be unusual for everyone in a room full of racks to have the need to access every rack; rack locks can ensure that only the correct people have access to servers and only telecommunications people have access to telecommunications gear. "Manageable" rack locks that can be remotely configured to allow access only when needed—to specific people at specific times—reduce the risk of an accident, sabotage, or unauthorized installation of additional equipment that could cause a potentially damaging rise in power consumption and rack temperature.

Restricted and Work Area Security

Depending on the configuration and operations structure of the data center, administrators and operators can be within the secured portion of the data center or can be in an auxiliary area. In most cases the latter is true, for the simple fact that there just isn't enough room within the data center to maintain equipment and personnel. Additionally, server rooms are noisy and cold, not ideal conditions for human beings.

Individuals who maintain sensitive information must present the common sense attitude of being security minded within the confines of the facility. Not everyone who works on sensitive information needs to be inside a secured room. For areas not considered a high security area, there are still requirements to maintain a responsible profile. Store and maintain sensitive information in security containers, which can be a filing cabinet with locking bars and a padlock. Maintain a clean desk approach, which encourages personnel to lock up information when they are finished for the day.

Maintain strong password protection for workstations. Never have computer screens facing toward the window without blinds or some type of protective film. Privacy filters and screen protectors keep prying eyes off sensitive work. Have a shredding company destroy trash containing all proprietary and customer confidential information. This will eliminate outsiders from obtaining confidential information through dumpster diving.

Restricted Work Areas

In highly restricted work areas such as government SCIFs, there is a requirement to increase the security blanket to ensure tighter access to these areas. The physical security protection for a SCIF is intended to prevent as well as detect visual, acoustical, technical, and physical access by unauthorized persons.

An organization may not be required to maintain government-classified information, however the company's livelihood and your employment is tied to proprietary information that requires the same level of security.

SCIF walls will consist of 3 layers of 5/8 inch drywall and will be from true floor to true ceiling. There will typically be only one SCIF entrance door, which will have an X-09 combination lock along with access control systems. According to the United States Director of Central Intelligence Directive 1/21 DCID1-21[1], all SCIF perimeter doors must be plumbed in their frames and the frame firmly affixed to the surrounding wall. Door frames must be of sufficient strength to preclude distortion that could cause improper alignment of door alarm sensors, improper door closure or degradation of audio security. All SCIF primary entrance doors must be equipped with an automatic door closer."

Basic HVAC requirements have any duct penetration into the secured area that is over 96 square inches include man bars to prevent a perpetrator from climbing through the ducts.

White noise or sound masking devices need to be placed over doors, in front of plenum or pointed toward windows to keep an adversary from listening to classified conversations. Some SCIFs use music or noise that sounds like a constant flow of air to mask conversation. All access control must be managed from within the SCIF. Intrusion detection is sent out to a central station with the requirement that a response force will respond to the perimeter of the SCIF within 15 minutes.

Data Center Security

When discussing the need to secure the data center, security professionals immediately think of sabotage, espionage, or data theft. While the need is obvious for protection against intruders and the harm caused by intentional infiltration, the hazards from the ordinary activity of personnel working

---

1   http://www.fas.org/irp/offdocs/dcid1-21.pdf

in the data center present a greater day-to-day risk for most facilities. Personnel within the organization need to be segregated from access areas where they have no "need to know" for that area. The security director will have physical access to most of the facility but has no reason to access financial or HR data. The head of computer operations might have access to computer rooms and operating systems, but not the mechanical rooms that house power and HVAC facilities. It comes down to not allowing wandering within your organization.

As data centers and web hosting sites grow, the need for physical security at the facility is every bit as great as the need for cyber security of networks. The data center is the brains of the operation and as such only specific people should be granted access. The standard scenario for increased security at a data center would consist of the basic security-in-depth: progressing from the outermost (least sensitive) areas to the innermost (most sensitive) areas. Security will start with entry into the building, which will require passing a receptionist or guard, then using a proximity card to gain building entry. For access into the computer room or data center, it will now require the same

Figure 10.34 - **A Card Reader with PIN and biometric features for additional security**

(Courtesy of Bosch Security Systems)

1341

proximity card along with a PIN (*Figure 10.34*), plus a biometric device. Combining access control methods at an entry control point will increase the reliability of access for authorized personnel only. Using different methods for each access level significantly increases security at inner levels, because each is secured by its own methods plus those of outer levels that must be entered first. This would also include internal door controls.

For a data center, the use of an internal mantrap or portal would provide increased entry and exit control. A portal (*Figure 10.35*) allows only one person in at a time and will only open the inner door once the outer door is closed. The portal can have additional biometrics within the device that must be activated before the secured side door opens.

Figure 10.35 - **A Secure Portal allows only one person in at a time and will only open the inner door once the outer door is closed** (Courtesy of Bosch Security Systems)

The "two-person" rule is a strategy where two people must be in an area together, making it impossible for a person to be in the area alone. Two-man rule programming is optional with many access control systems. It prevents an individual cardholder from entering a selected empty security area unless accompanied by at least one other person. Use of the two-person rule can help eliminate insider threats to critical areas by requiring at least two individuals to be present at any time. It is also used for life safety within a security area; if one person has a medical emergency there will be assistance present.

Utilities and HVAC Considerations

Utilities and Power

Because they often host mission-critical servers, data centers are built with both battery and generator backups. If the power cuts out, the batteries take over, just as they might in a home user's uninterruptible power supply. The generators also begin and start producing power before the batteries fail. Areas that contain back–up generators and power supplies need similar protection. This area can be controlled with key access or a card access reader and electric door strikes can be installed for entry into this area. This area is also a person-specific area; there is no need to give everyone access to the generator room. This room will maintain back up power for the entire facility in the event of a power outage emergency.

Uninterruptible Power Supply (UPS)

This is a battery backup system, which maintains a continuous supply of electric power to connected equipment by supplying power from a separate source when utility power is not available. A UPS has internal batteries to guarantee that continuous power is provided to the equipment even if the power source stops providing power. Of course, the UPS can only provide power for a while, typically a few minutes, but that is often enough to ride out power company glitches or short outages. Even if the outage is longer than the battery lifetime of the UPS, this provides the opportunity to execute an orderly shutdown of the equipment.

10

Physical (Enviromental) Security

1343

Generator

Generator power should be activated automatically in the event of a utility failure by the transfer switch. The data center load is maintained by the UPS units; however, often this is a short time as the generator should be active and up to speed within 10 seconds of a power failure. A generator (*Figure 10.36*) is typically run on diesel fuel and can be located outside of the facility or inside a parking garage. The generator room needs to be protected from unauthorized access either by access control devices or key-locked doors. The generator will operate as long as fuel is supplied. Some generators have a 300-gallon capacity and a facilities manager will have a contract with a local distributor to supply fuel. Most operation centers have more than one generator and test them once a month. If it is located outside, it needs protective barriers placed around it to protect it from a vehicle running into it.

Figure 10.36 - **A Backup Generator is activated automatically in the event of a utility failure by the transfer switch.** (Courtesy of Bosch Security Systems)

HVAC

HVAC stands for heating, ventilation, and air-conditioning. Heat can cause extensive damage to computer equipment by causing processors to slow down and stop execution or even cause solder connections to loosen and fail. Excessive heat degrades network performance and causes downtime. Data centers and server rooms need an uninterrupted cooling system. Generally, there are two types of cooling: latent and sensible.

Latent cooling is the ability of the air-conditioning system to remove moisture. This is important in typical comfort-cooling applications, such as office buildings, retail stores, and other facilities with high human occupancy and use. The focus of latent cooling is to maintain a comfortable balance of temperature and humidity for people working in and visiting such a facility. These facilities often have doors leading directly to the outside and a considerable amount of entrance and exit by occupants.

Sensible cooling is the ability of the air-conditioning system to remove heat that can be measured by a thermometer. Data centers generate much higher heat per square foot than typical comfort-cooling building environments, and are typically not occupied by large numbers of people. In most cases, they have limited access and no direct means of egress to the outside of the building except for seldom used emergency exits.

Data centers have a minimal need for latent cooling and require minimal moisture removal. Sensible cooling systems are engineered with a focus on heat removal rather than moisture removal and have a higher sensible heat ratio; they are the most useful and appropriate choice for the data center. Cooling systems are dove tailed into the power supply overhead. If there is a power interruption, this will affect the cooling system. For the computers to continue operation, they need to be cooled. Portable air-conditioning units can be used as a backup in case of HVAC failure but good design should ensure cooling systems are accounted for as backup devices.

Air Contamination

Over the past several years there has been an increasing awareness dealing with anthrax and airborne attacks. Harmful agents introduced into the HVAC systems can rapidly spread throughout the structure and infect all persons exposed to the circulated air.

To avoid air contamination place intakes at the highest practical level in the facility. For protection against malicious acts, the intakes should also be covered by screens so that objects cannot be tossed into the intakes or into air wells from the ground. Such screens should be sloped to allow thrown objects to roll or slide off the screen, away from the intake. Many existing buildings have air intakes that are located at or below ground level. For those that have wall-mounted or below-grade intakes close to the building, the intakes can be elevated by constructing a plenum or external shaft over the intake.

The following is a list of guidelines necessary to enhance security in this critical aspect of facility operations:

- Restrict access to main air intake points to persons who have a work-related reason to be there
- Maintain access rosters of pre-approved maintenance personnel authorized to work on the system
- Escort all contractors with access to the system while on site
- Ensure that all air intake points are adequately secured with locking devices

All buildings have air intake points that either are roof-mounted, exterior wall-mounted or in a free-standing unit on the ground outside of the building. Due to "sick building syndrome" where one person infects several with a cold or flu through a buildings HVAC system, many governments require all new buildings to mix a certain percentage of fresh air in with re-circulated air in the HVAC system. The volume of fresh air taken in is based on the square footage of the building and the number of employees working inside.

One method of reducing the risk of biological agents circulating throughout a building is installation of UV light filters in the HVAC system's supply and return ducts. UV light inhibits the growth and reproduction of germs, bacteria, viruses, fungi, and mold. UV light is the portion of the electromagnetic spectrum that lies beyond the "purple" or visible edge of the spectrum. The sun acts as a natural outdoor air purification system, controlling airborne bacteria with UV rays. UV light penetrates the microorganism and breaks down molecular bonds causing cellular or genetic damage. The germs are either killed or sterilized, leaving them unable to reproduce. In either case, live bacterial counts can be significantly reduced and kept under control.

Water Issues

Along with excessive heat, water is a detriment to computer equipment. A data center may have a gas suppression fire system, but what about the floors above? Are they on a standard water sprinkler system and what would happen if the sprinklers are activated or begin leaking? Proper planning moves equipment away from water pipes that might burst, basements that might flood, or roofs that might leak. However, there are other water leaks that are more difficult to recognize and detect. Blocked ventilation systems can cause condensation if warm, moist air is not removed quickly. If vents are located above or behind machines, condensation can form small puddles that no one sees. Stand-alone air conditioners are especially vulnerable to water leaks if condensation is not properly removed. Even small amounts of water near air intakes will raise humidity levels and fill servers with moisture.

Fire Prevention, Detection and Suppression

To protect your server room from fire the organization needs to have smoke detectors installed and linked to a panel with enunciators that will warn people that there is smoke in the room. Also, it should be linked to a fire suppression system that can help put out the fire with no damage to equipment from the gas itself.

Fire Detection

A smoke detector is one of the most important devices to have due to its ability to warn of a pending fire, coupled with a good signaling device.

A detector in proper working condition will sound an alarm and give all occupants a chance to make it out alive. There are two main categories of smoke detectors: optical detection (photoelectric) and physical process (ionization). Photoelectric detectors are classified as either beam or refraction. Beam detectors operate on the principle of light and a receiver. Once enough smoke enters the room and breaks the beam of light, the alarm is sounded. The refraction type has a blocker between the light and the receiver. Once enough smoke enters the room, the light is deflected around the beam to the signal. Finally, we have the ionization type detector; these detectors monitor the air around the sensors constantly. Once there is enough smoke in the room, the alarm will sound.

There are three main types of fire detectors: flame detectors, smoke detectors, and heat detectors. There are two main types of flame detectors and they are classified as infrared (IR) and ultraviolet (UV) detectors. IR detectors primarily detect a large mass of hot gases that emit a specific spectral pattern in the location of the detector; these patterns are sensed with a thermographic camera and an alarm is sounded. Additional hot surfaces in the room may trigger a false response with this alarm. UV flame detectors detect flames at speeds of 3–4 milliseconds due to the high-energy radiation emitted by fires and explosions at the instant of their ignition. Some of the false alarms of this system include random UV sources such as lightning, radiation, and solar radiation that may be present in the room.

There are heat detectors, which include fixed temperature or rate of rise detectors. The user will set a predetermined temperature level for the alarm to sound. If the room temperature rises to that setting, the alarm will sound. Rate of rise temperature will detect a sudden change of temperature around the sensor. Usually this setting is at around 10–15 degrees per minute. Nothing more is required of the consumer except routine checks for battery life and operation status. Heat detectors should not be used to replace smoke detectors; each component in fire safety serves its purpose and should be taken seriously. The combination of devices and the knowledge of procedures are the only way to achieve success during a possible fire.

Fire Suppression

All buildings should be equipped with an effective fire suppression system, providing the building with around the clock protection. Traditionally, fire suppression systems employed arrays of water sprinklers that would douse a fire and surrounding areas. Sprinkler systems are classified into four different groups: wet, dry, pre-action, and deluge.

- *Wet Systems* - have a constant supply of water in them at all times; these sprinklers once activated will not shut off until the water source is shut off.

- *Dry Systems* - do not have water in them. The valve will not release until the electric valve is stimulated by excess heat.

- *Pre-Action Systems* - incorporate a detection system, which can eliminate concerns of water damage due to false activations. Water is held back until detectors in the area are activated.

- *Deluge Systems* - operate in the same function as the pre-action system except all sprinkler heads are in the open position.

Water may be a sound solution for large physical areas such as warehouses, but it is entirely inappropriate for computer equipment. A water spray can irreparably damage hardware more quickly than encroaching smoke or heat. Gas suppression systems operate to starve the fire of oxygen. In the past, Halon was the choice for gas suppression systems; however, Halon leaves residue, depletes the ozone layer, and can injure nearby personnel.

There are several gas suppression systems that are recommended for fire suppression in a server room or anywhere electronic equipment is employed:

- *Aero-K* - uses an aerosol of microscopic potassium compounds in a carrier gas released from small canisters mounted on walls

1349

near the ceiling. The Aero-K generators are not pressurized until fire is detected. The Aero-K system uses multiple fire detectors and will not release until a fire is "confirmed" by two or more detectors (limiting accidental discharge). The gas is non-corrosive, so it does not damage metals or other materials. It does not harm electronic devices or media such as tape or discs. More important, Aero-K is nontoxic and does not injure personnel.

- ***FM-200*** - is a colorless, liquefied compressed gas. It is stored as a liquid and dispensed into the hazard as a colorless, electrically non-conductive vapor that is clear and does not obscure vision. It leaves no residue and has acceptable toxicity for use in occupied spaces at design concentration. FM-200 does not displace oxygen and, therefore, is safe for use in occupied spaces without fear of oxygen deprivation.

Support the Protection and Securing of Equipment

Environmental Alarms

Most alarm or access control systems are capable of monitoring environmental alarms. The best way to protect sensitive electronic devices is to constantly monitor the temperature or humidity in the data center, computer room, or server room and be notified immediately about an air-conditioning system, power failure, or water leaks. If an organization maintains a central station, this is one way of achieving an early warning that allows you to take corrective action before the servers melt down, bringing the enterprise to a halt. If the organization does not have a 24/7 control center for alarm monitoring, there are systems available that will call phone numbers or pagers to notify key personnel of a problem with any computer room, server room, or equipment room.

Equipment Protection

Security and monitoring equipment warrants special protection. Tamper protection is the means of protecting the physical devices associated with the alarm system through line supervision, encryption or alarming of enclosures and components. All intrusion detection, access control, and their associated data transmission media must be protected commensurate with the classification of the asset being protected. All intrusion detection sensors and access control readers must have tamper-resistant enclosures and integral tamper protection switches. All enclosures, cabinets, housings, and boxes, having hinged doors or removable covers that contain processors or connections must have tamper protection switches. These are pressure switches, so when the cover of a card reader is removed or an alarm panel is opened, a signal will be sent to the central station. All tamper alarm signals must be monitored continuously whether the system is in the access or secure mode of operation.

Security of Devices

Line security or line supervision is a term used to describe the various techniques that are designed to detect or inhibit manipulation of communication networks. All alarm systems must provide a means to incorporate refinements in electric apparatus and circuit arrangement to guard against an attempt to compromise the connecting line or communications channel between the central receiving station and the protected area. All signal and data transmission lines must incorporate some level of line supervision. Line supervision for security systems must detect and annunciate communication interruptions or compromised communications between field devices and the associated CPU. Field device signals must be supervised by monitoring the circuit and initiating an alarm in response to opening, closing, shorting, or grounding of the signal.

Encryption

Encryption is protecting the transmission of the signal by employing a data-encryption standard that applies a specific algorithm to alter the appearance of the data. For high security areas such as data centers, which fall into the category of controlled access areas, the encryption standard should be a strong and validated format, such as one that complies with the National Institute for Standards and Technology (NIST), Federal Information Processing Standards (FIPS) Publication 140-2. Systems protecting all other assets should meet UL 1076 Section 64A[1] line security standards.

Physical Protection of Exterior Devices

All exterior intrusion detection sensors and access control readers must have tamper-resistant enclosures and integral tamper protection switches. All enclosures, cabinets, housings, boxes, and fittings having hinged doors or removable covers that are protected by employed sensors must be locked, welded, brazed, or secured with tamper-resistant security fasteners and be tamper-alarmed.

---

1   http://ulstandardsinfonet.ul.com/scopes/scopes.asp?fn=1076.html

Physical Protection of Interior Devices

All interior intrusion detection sensors and access control readers must have integral tamper protection switches. All intrusion detection sensors, access control readers, and assessment equipment located outside controlled areas must have tamper-resistant enclosures. All intrusion detection sensors and access control system cabling should be routed within the controlled area. If the cables transverse an uncontrolled area, the cables must be encased in tamper-proof conduits.

Inventory Standards

To ensure compliance with generally accepted accounting principles and prudent financial management, an asset valuation, property capitalization, and inventory control policy for the organization needs to be developed and implemented. This is also a common sense approach to normal business practices. A property control specialist or similar role should tag equipment and sensitive items with a property control bar code tag and add the property to the inventory.

Periodically, property control will do an inventory count to ensure that the property is accounted for, and the recorded location of the property is current. It should be the policy that property should not be moved, transferred, sold, traded in, or disposed of in any fashion without the written approval of the property control section. This policy covers equipment with a threshold asset value before it is put into the inventory, and mobile media, such as a laptop or anything that holds proprietary information, regardless of dollar value.

Tracking Equipment

Radio-Frequency Identification (RFID)

Installing a RFID chip in expensive and portable media equipment will allow security to detect and record when the equipment is being taken out of the facility. This is very similar to a shopping center where an alarm sounds when an item is being shoplifted. If a person walks through the doorway (*Figure 10.35*) without paying for something, the radio waves from the transmitters, which are hidden in one of the door gates, are picked up by the coiled metal antenna in the label. This generates a tiny electrical current that activates a concealed chip or other electronic component buried in the label. The chip modifies the incoming radio waves and sends them back out again in a slightly different form. The receiver (hidden in the other door gate) picks up the modified signal and sounds the alarm.

Figure 10.37 - **RFID used in retail security**
(**Courtesy of Bosch Security Systems**)

In the corporate world, this device can be used either as an alarm trigger or as an identifier of when the equipment was removed and who removed it. It will be time stamped and along with video equipment can identify who removed the device.

At a basic level, each tag works in the same way:

- Data stored within an RFID tag's microchip waits to be read.
- The tag's antenna receives electromagnetic energy from an RFID reader's antenna.

- Using power from its internal battery or power harvested from the reader's electromagnetic field, the tag sends radio waves back to the reader.

- The reader picks up the tag's radio waves and interprets the frequencies as meaningful data.

- Passive RFID tags rely entirely on the reader as their power source (*Figure 10.38*). These tags are read up to 20 feet away, and they have low production costs, meaning that they cost pennies.

Figure 10.38 - **Small and inexpensive Passive RFID tags**
(Courtesy of Bosch Security Systems.)

Portable Media Protection

When using a piece of portable computer equipment or media, regardless of being used inside the facility or being removed for legitimate business outside of the facility, simple protection methods need to be employed in order to maintain the security of the equipment.

- *Use a Cable Lock:* Cable locks easily make up for their added travel weight by deterring casual thefts in both hotels and at workplaces. As long as the users pick something secure to lock their laptop to, they will not have to worry about it at work when they leave for lunch or back at the hotel when they head out to dinner. However, users should be reminded a cable

1355

can be cut and they should still use a safe or concealment in addition to the cable when possible.

- **Do not Leave a Laptop or Device Unattended:** For example, when going through security at the airport put the laptop through the X-ray machine last. Then stand there and wait for it so no one can grab it while you are taking off your shoes and so forth.

- **Use Strong Passwords:** Do not use an easily guessable password. The stronger a password is or better yet, if multi-factor authentication is used, the less likely an attacker is to gain access to the machine. Make up of a combination of numbers, letters, and symbols for a password that will make guessing more difficult for malicious users and password guessing programs.

- **Encrypt your Data:** If a computer gets stolen or hacked, it will be tough to impossible for thieves and hackers to access the sensitive data. Besides, from the potentially painful expense of replacing a laptop, a user might have lost some very expensive corporate data or personal information that far outweighs the cost of the hardware.

Personnel Privacy and Safety

Personnel are often the greatest assets when designing physical and environmental security. Personnel are becoming more mobile and more concerned regarding their privacy. An information security professional must be aware of privacy laws and expectations that can influence environmental monitoring and ensure personnel are aware of physical concerns when traveling. Finally, personnel under duress represent a special situation that requires forethought and training.

Privacy

All individuals have an expectation of privacy. This expectation varies by culture and people, but the security professional must understand the limits of monitoring individuals within the law of a country. While it is generally considered acceptable to place CCTV cameras in public parking lots, most of the world would not approve of CCTV cameras in a private area such as a shower or locker room. While these examples are extreme, others fall into a "grey" area. Such examples include a home office. Does an organization have a right to monitor any space work is performed on their behalf including a private home? Most privacy experts would side with a "no" answer for this question, but some security professionals or investigators may say "yes." This is largely due to a difference in perspective. The investigator is interested in collecting evidence and the security professional is interested in ensuring the safety of the individual and security of the organization's information.

In most instances communication about the organization's privacy policies is key to ensuring privacy related complaints are minimized. Many organizations place conspicuous signs that state CCTV or other types of monitoring are being conducted in an area. While some may argue this is alerting an attacker, in reality the attackers already assume or know there are cameras in the area. If they did not, a notice may very will deter or dissuade them. Either way, notifying or being conspicuous about monitoring can have advantages.

1357

Travel

Monitoring employees and trying to ensure their safety with the safety of the organization's information while abroad can be challenging. Many of the controls available in an organization's facility are not available while abroad so the information security professional must compensate with better personnel training and technical controls. The United States National Counterintelligence Executive provides the following tips for U.S. overseas travelers[1]:

YOU SHOULD KNOW

- In most countries you have no expectation of privacy in Internet cafes, hotels, offices, or public places. Hotel business centers and phone networks are regularly monitored in many countries. In some countries, hotel rooms are often searched.

- All information you send electronically – by fax machine, personal digital assistant (PDA), computer, or telephone – can be intercepted. Wireless devices are especially vulnerable.

- Security services and criminals can track your movements using your mobile phone or PDA and can turn on the microphone in your device even when you think it's off. To prevent this, remove the battery.

- Security services and criminals can also insert malicious software into your device through any connection they control. They can also do it wirelessly if your device is enabled for wireless. When you connect to your home server, the "malware" can migrate to your business, agency, or home system, can inventory your system, and can send information back to the security service or potential malicious actor.

- Malware can also be transferred to your device through thumb drives (USB sticks), computer disks, and other "gifts."

- Transmitting sensitive government, personal, or proprietary information from abroad is therefore risky.

---

1   http://www.ncix.gov/publications/reports/docs/traveltips.pdf

- Corporate and government officials are most at risk, but don't assume you're too insignificant to be targeted.

- Foreign security services and criminals are adept at "phishing" – that is, pretending to be someone you trust in order to obtain personal or sensitive information.

- If a customs official demands to examine your device, or if your hotel room is searched while the device is in the room and you're not, you should assume the device's hard drive has been copied.

BEFORE YOU TRAVEL

- If you can do without the device, don't take it.

- Don't take information you don't need,   i n c l u d i n g sensitive contact information.   Consider the consequences if your information were stolen by a foreign government or competitor.

- Back up all information you take; leave the backed-up data at home. If feasible, use a different mobile phone or PDA from your usual one and remove the battery when not in use. In any case, have the device examined by your agency or company when you return.

- Seek official cyber security alerts from:

    www.onguardonline.gov *and*
    www.us-cert.gov/cas/tips

Prepare your Device:

- Create a strong password (numbers, upper and   lower case letters, special characters – at least   8   characters   long). Never store passwords, phone numbers, or sign-on sequences on any device or in its case.

- Change passwords at regular intervals (and as soon as you return).

- Download current, up-to-date antivirus protection, spyware protection, OS security patches, and a personal firewall.

- Encrypt all sensitive information on the device. (But be warned: In some countries, customs officials may not permit you to enter with encrypted information.)

- Update your web browser with strict security settings.

- Disable infrared ports and features you don't need.

WHILE YOU'RE AWAY

- Avoid transporting devices in checked baggage.

- Use digital signature and encryption capabilities when possible.

- Don't leave electronic devices unattended. If you have to stow them, remove the battery and SIM card and keep them with you.

- Don't use thumb drives given to you – they may be compromised. Don't use your own thumb drive in a foreign computer for the same reason. If you're required to do it anyway, assume you've been compromised; have your device cleaned as soon as you can.

- Shield passwords from view. Don't use the "remember me" feature on many websites; retype the password every time.

- Be aware of who's looking at your screen, especially in public areas.

- Terminate connections when you're not using them.

- Clear your browser after each use: delete history files, caches, cookies, URL, and temporary internet files.

- Don't open emails or attachments from unknown sources. Don't click on links in emails. Empty your "trash" and "recent" folders after every use.

- Avoid Wi-Fi networks if you can. In some countries they're controlled by security services; in all cases they're insecure.

- If your device or information is stolen, report it immediately to your home organization and the local US embassy or consulate.

WHEN YOU RETURN

- Change your password.
- Have your company or agency examine the device for the presence of malicious software.
- For general travel alerts and information, see www.state.gov/travelandbusiness

These tips represent sound considerations for anyone traveling for business or anyone with access to sensitive information traveling for any reason. Personnel should be gently reminded through awareness and training that they can be targeted when abroad and even though they may be on vacation, they should remain vigilant while enjoying themselves.

Duress

Duress is a topic that relates to the concept of a person doing something or divulging something they normally would not under threat of harm. For example an intruder may break into a data center and demand the receptionist cancel the alarm and tell the police it is a false alarm or the attacker will harm the receptionist. These situations can occur quite quickly and proper training is crucial for ensuring personnel safety.

Bank tellers offer an excellent example of a position that is possibly subject to duress. During a bank robbery the teller is forced to commit an act (giving away the bank's money) they normally wouldn't perform to avoid harm. The key to understanding duress situations is knowing the assets, access and the alternatives of the organization. The assets of an organization should be identified to ensure the security professional understands where a duress situation may occur. This may be at a corporate building or with an executive on travel with special patents. Regardless of where the asset is the security professional must remember the protection and risk of duress follows the asset and the access to the asset. Personnel with access to the assets are typically the targets of duress situations. They can be the victims of verbal, physical and emotional abuse and harassment while the attacker attempts to access the asset. In all cases, the life and safety of the individual must be paramount when working with duress situations.

Scenario analysis can assist in determining the alternatives available and ensuring appropriate training and education can be conducted for individuals subject to duress. Scenario analysis is a type of risk analysis where assets, access and alternatives are mapped out in different "stories" to determine how a situation can play out. The more scenarios reviewed and the more knowledgeable the participants the better the results of the exercise. The results should be used to train personnel with access to assets. For example, bank tellers are often trained to put a dye pack with the money they give to the robber. This pack explodes rendering the money worthless and marks the robber with indelible ink for identification. Additionally a receptionist told to turn off a sounding alarm may enter a special duress code which not only turns off the alarm but silently alerts the police that there is a duress situation and to come immediately!

Duress situations are extremely challenging with sometimes deadly or life altering consequences. The information security professional should always seek the assistance of law enforcement or other professionals who specialize in this area when working through the design and implementation of duress training or mitigation controls.

More to Know **The following articles about Physical and Personnel security are freely available on the Internet:**

National Fire Protection Association Fact Sheets
*http://www.nfpa.org/itemDetail.
asp?categoryID=1867&itemID=44071&URL=Research/Fire%20statistics/
Printable%20fact%20sheets*

U.S. National Industrial Security Program Operating Manual
http://www.dss.mil/isp/odaa/nispom06.html

Privacy in Biometric Systems
*http://biometrics.nist.gov/cs_links/ibpc2012/presentations/Day2/Panell/223_1_
anderson.pdf*

Review Questions

1. The primary function of a physical protection system is?

    A. determine, direct and dispatch

    B. detection, delay and response

    C. display, develop, initiate and apprehend

    D. evaluate, dispatch and detain

2. To successfully complete a vulnerability assessment, it is critical that protection systems are well understood through:

    A. Threat definition, target identification and facility characterization

    B. Threat definition, conflict control and facility characterization

    C. Risk assessment, threat identification and incident review

    D. Threat identification, vulnerability appraisal and access review

3. Laminated glass is recommended for what type of locations:

    A. All exterior glass windows

    B. Interior boundary penetration and critical infrastructure facility

    C. Street-level windows, doorways and other access areas

    D. Capacitance proximity, intrusion detection locations and boundary penetration sites

4. The strategy of forming layers of protection around an asset or facility is known as:

    A. Secured Perimeter

    B. Defense-in-Depth

    C. Reinforced Barrier Deterrent

    D. Reasonable Asset Protection

5. What crime reduction technique BEST creates a physical environment that positively influences human behavior?

    A. Asset protection and vulnerability assessments

    B. Reducing vulnerability by protecting, offsetting or transferring the risk

    C. Crime prevention through environmental design

    D. Instituting employee screening and workplace violence programs

6. The key to a successful physical protection system is the integration of:

    A. people, procedures, and equipment

    B. technology, risk assessment, and human interaction

    C. protecting, offsetting, and transferring risk

    D. detection, deterrence, and response

7. What is the primary objective of controlling entry into a facility or area?

    A. Provide time management controls for all employees

    B. Ensure that only authorized persons are allowed to enter

    C. Keep potential hazards and contraband material out that could be used to commit sabotage.

    D. Identification purposes

8. For safety considerations in perimeter areas such as parking lots or garages what is the advised lighting?

    A. 3 fc

    B. 5 fc

    C. 7 fc

    D. 10 fc

9. What would be the most appropriate interior sensor used for a building that has windows along the ground floor?

    A. infrared glass-break sensor

    B. ultrasonic glass-break sensors

10

    C. acoustic/shock glass-break sensors

    D. volumetric sensors

10. Which of the following **BEST** describe three separate functions of CCTV?

    A. surveillance, deterrence, and evidentiary archives

    B. intrusion detection, detainment and response

    C. optical scanning, infrared beaming and lighting

    D. monitoring, white balancing and inspection

11. Although security technologies are not the answer to all organizational security problem, if applied appropriately what will they provide?

    A. the ability to reduce electrical costs

    B. they can enhance the security envelope and in the majority of cases will save the organization money

    C. government tax incentives for increased physical protection systems

    D. increased capital value of property with high-tech integrated technologies

12. A meaningful assessment of a facility or building should be used:

    A. to determine where all the fire exits are located

    B. within the context of the defined threats and the value of the organization's assets

    C. to count the number of employees within the facility

    D. to determine the structural strength of the perimeter walls

13. The **BEST** example of building a new facility for security is:

    E. limiting the number of entrances to the site that must be monitored, staffed and protected

    F. reducing the cost associated with energy needs in providing the physical protection system

    G. giving employees easy access to the facility without their knowledge of the security components used in monitoring their activities

    H. blast reinforcement film on all perimeter windows

14. All visitors entering the facility sign in and out on a visitor's log, this is established for what reasons?

    A. for the purpose of detection, accountability and the necessity for response

    B. access control and surveillance

    C. timeframe of the visit, who was visited, and in the case of an emergency have accountability of everyone for safety purposes

    D. for planning assessment and the requirements of proper designation

15. What is the **BEST** means of protecting the physical devices associated with the alarm system?

    A. Tamper protection

    B. Target hardening

    C. Security design

    D. UL 2050

16. When using a piece of portable computing equipment or media, regardless if it is being used inside the facility or is being removed for legitimate business outside of the facility, simple protection methods need to be employed in order to maintain the security of the equipment. These **BEST** consist of _____.

    A. cable locks, encryption, password protection and increased awareness

    B. reducing vulnerability by protecting, offsetting or transferring the risk

    C. operational readiness, physical protection systems, standard operating processes

    D. increase awareness, environmental design and physical security

17. Personal identity verification systems which use hand or fingerprint, handwriting, eye pattern, voice, face, or any other physical characteristics for authentication are:

    A. Biometric devices

    B. Technological systems

10

Physical (Enviromental) Security

    C. Physiometric devices

    D. Physical analysis devices

18. Physical security is applied by using _____ of physical protective measures to prevent or minimize theft, unauthorized access, or destruction of property.

    A. Layers

    B. Methods

    C. Varieties

    D. Types

19. What is a comprehensive overview of a facility to include physical security controls, policy, procedures and employee safety?

    A. Availability assessment

    B. Security survey

    C. Budgetary and financial performance

    D. Defense-in-depth

20. Which security control is most effective in curtailing and preventing "piggybacking" or "tailgating" as a means of unauthorized access?

    A. Cameras

    B. Turnstiles

    C. Keys

    D. Identification badges

Appendix

Answers to Review Questions

Domain 1 - Access Control

1. A preliminary step in managing resources is

    A. Conducting a risk analysis

    B. Defining who can access a given system or information

    C. Performing a business impact analysis

    D. Obtaining top management support

Correct answer is **B**. The first step to enabling an effective access control strategy is to specifically define the resources that exist in the environment for users to access. The next step in managing access control is defining who can access a given resource. The final step in the access control process is to specify the level of use for a given resource and the permitted user actions on that resource.

2. Which best describes access controls?

    A. Access controls are a collection of technical controls that permit access to authorized users, systems, and applications.

    B. Access controls help protect against threats and vulnerabilities by reducing exposure to unauthorized activities and providing access to information and systems to only those who have been approved.

    C. Access control is the employment of encryption solutions to protect authentication information during log-on.

    D. Access controls help protect against vulnerabilities by controlling unauthorized access to systems and information by employees, partners, and customers.

Correct answer is **B**. Access controls are the collection of mechanisms that work together to protect the assets of the enterprise. They help protect against threats and vulnerabilities by reducing exposure to unauthorized activities and providing access to information and systems to only those who have been approved.

    3. _____ requires that a user or process be granted access to only those resources necessary to perform assigned functions.

        A. Discretionary access control

        B. Separation of duties

        C. Least privilege

        D. Rotation of duties

Correct answer is **C**. The principle of least privilege is one of the most fundamental characteristics of access control for meeting security objectives. Least privilege requires that a user or process be given no more access privilege than necessary to perform a job, task, or function.

    4. What are the seven main categories of access control?

        A. Detective, corrective, monitoring, logging, recovery, classification, and directive

        B. Directive, deterrent, preventative, detective, corrective, compensating, and recovery

        C. Authorization, identification, factor, corrective, privilege, detective, and directive

        D. Identification, authentication, authorization, detective, corrective, recovery, and directive

Correct answer is **B**. The seven main categories of access control are directive, deterrent, compensating, detective, corrective, and recovery.

5. What are the three types of access control?

    A. Administrative, physical, and technical

    B. Identification, authentication, and authorization

    C. Mandatory, discretionary, and least privilege

    D. Access, management, and monitoring

Correct answer is **A**. For any of the access control categories, the controls in those categories can be implemented in one of three ways: administrative controls, technical (logical) controls, and physical controls

6. Which approach revolutionized the process of cracking passwords?

    A. Brute force

    B. Rainbow table attack

    C. Memory tabling

    D. One-time hashing

Correct answer is **B**. In 2003, Philippe Oechslin developed a faster method of organizing hash chains. The new chain structure developed from this method is called a rainbow chain or a rainbow table. The rainbow table attack has revolutionized password cracking and is being rapidly adopted by tool creators.

7. What best describes two-factor authentication?

    A. A hard token and a smart card

    B. A user name and a PIN

    C. A password and a PIN

    D. A PIN and a hard token

Correct answer is **D**. There are three fundamental types of authentication: authentication by knowledge—something a person knows, authentication by possession— something a person has, and authentication by characteristic—something a person is. Technical controls related to these types are called "factors." Something known can be a password or PIN, something physically possessed can be a token fob or smart card, and something a person is can usually be some form of biometrics. Single-factor authentication is the employment of one of these factors, two-factor authentication is using two of the three factors, and three-factor authentication is the combination of all three factors. The general term for the use of more than one factor during authentication is multifactor authentication.

8. A potential vulnerability of the Kerberos authentication server is

    A. Single point of failure

    B. Asymmetric key compromise

    C. Use of dynamic passwords

    D. Limited lifetimes for authentication credentials

Correct answer is **A**. There are some issues related to the use of Kerberos. For starters, the security of the whole system depends on careful implementation: enforcing limited lifetimes for authentication credentials minimizes the threats of replayed credentials, the KDC must be physically secured, and it should be hardened, not permitting any non-Kerberos activity. More importantly, the KDC can be a single point of failure, and therefore should be supported by backup and continuity plans.

9. In mandatory access control the system controls access and the owner determines

    A. Validation

    B. Need to know

    C. Consensus

    D. Verification

Correct answer is **B**. MAC is based on cooperative interaction between the system and the information owner. The system's decision controls access and the owner provides the need-to-know control.

10. Which is the least significant issue when considering biometrics?

    A. Resistance to counterfeiting

    B. Technology type

C. User acceptance

D. Reliability and accuracy

Correct answer is **B**. In addition to the access control elements of a biometric system, there are several other considerations that are important to the integrity of the control environment. These are resistance to counterfeiting, data storage requirements, user acceptance, reliability and accuracy, and target user and approach.

11. Which is a fundamental disadvantage of biometrics?

A. Revoking credentials

B. Encryption

C. Communications

D. Placement

Correct answer is **A**. When considering the role of biometrics, its close interactions with people, and the privacy and sensitivity of the information collected, the inability to revoke the physical attribute of the credential becomes a major concern. The binding of the authentication process to the physical characteristics of the user can complicate the revocation or decommissioning processes.

12. Role-based access control .

A. Is unique to mandatory access control

B. Is independent of owner input

C. Is based on user job functions

D. Can be compromised by inheritance

Correct answer is **C**. A role-based access control (RBA) model bases the access control authorizations on the roles (or functions) that the user is assigned within an organization. The determination of what roles have access to a resource can be governed by the owner of the data, as with DACs, or applied based on policy, as with MACs.

13. Identity management is

    A. Another name for access controls

    B. Technologies and processes intended to offer greater efficiency in the management of a diverse user and technical environment

    C. Technologies and processes focused on the provisioning and decommissioning of user credentials

    D. Technologies and processes used to establish trust relationships with disparate systems

Correct answer is **B**. Identity management is a much-used term that refers to a set of technologies intended to offer greater efficiency in the management of a diverse user and technical environment.

14. A disadvantage of single sign-on is

    A. Consistent time-out enforcement across platforms

    B. A compromised password exposes all authorized resources

    C. Use of multiple passwords to remember

    D. Password change control

Correct answer is **B**. One of the more prevalent concerns with centralized SSO systems is the fact that all of a user's credentials are protected by a single password: the SSO password. If someone were to crack that user's SSO password, they would effectively have all the keys to that user's kingdom.

15. Which of the following is incorrect when considering privilege management?

    A. Privileges associated with each system, service, or application, and the defined roles within the organization to which they are needed, should be identified and clearly documented.

    B. Privileges should be managed based on least privilege. Only rights required to perform a job should be provided to a user, group, or role.

    C. An authorization process and a record of all privileges allocated should be maintained. Privileges should not be granted until the authorization process is complete and validated.

D. Any privileges that are needed for intermittent job functions should be assigned to multiple user accounts, as opposed to those for normal system activity related to the job function.

Correct answer is **D**. An authorization process and a record of all privileges allocated should be maintained. Privileges should not be granted until the authorization process is complete and validated. If any significant or special privileges are needed for intermittent job functions, these should be performed using an account specifically allocated for such a task, as opposed to those used for normal system and user activity. This enables the access privileges assigned to the special account to be tailored to the needs of the special function rather than simply extending the access privileges associated with the user's normal work functions.

16. Threat modeling is the process of

A. Determining which threats to neutralize first

B. Developing access controls that compensate for vulnerabilities

C. A risk assessment approach in which decisions are based on risk and value.

D. Scenario analysis targeted towards determining the best approach for threat elimination.

Correct answer is **C**. Threat modeling is a risk assessment process. Threat modeling is a popular approach in determining risk and scoping in software development processes. Threat modeling relies on a strong understanding of the scope, threats, vulnerabilities, and compensating controls affecting a system.

17. When reviewing user entitlement the security professional must be **MOST** aware of

A. Identity management and disaster recovery capability

B. Business or organizational processes and access aggregation

C. The organizational tenure of the user requesting entitlement

D. Automated processes which grant users access to resources

Correct answer is **B**. Business and organizational processes and access aggregation are the most significant concerns with user entitlement. As individuals move through the organization, they accumulate access unless deliberately revoked. Additionally, the business process should always drive the need for entitlement and revocation of access.

18. Which formula represents ALE or annual loss exposure?

    A. ALE=SLE x ARO

    B. SLE=ARO x ALE

    C. SLE=ARO x EF

    D. ALE=EF x SLE

Correct answer is **A**. The annual loss expectancy is calculated by multiplying the single loss expectancy times the annual rate of occurrence.

19. In constructing a continuous monitoring system, numerous feeds from several systems must be correlated and analyzed. Which of the following **BEST** provides this capability?

    A. Intrusion Prevention System (IPS)

    B. Identity Management and Access Control System

    C. Intrusion Detection System (IDS)

    D. Security Information and Event Management (SIEM)

Correct answer is **D**. Security information and event management (SIEM) is a term used to describe a group of technologies that aggregate information about access controls and selected system activity to store for analysis and correlation. Logs and system information may be collected for a variety of reasons. SIEMs also present a attractive target for attackers as these systems are not only the repositories for current health information about the organization's information systems but also are the systems often first turned to when there is suspicion of an attack or infiltration. While SEIMs offer a great advantage, they also require extensive protection to ensure they do not become a liability.

20. A guard dog patrolling the perimeter of a data center is what type of a control?

    A. Recovery

    B. Administrative

    C. Logical

    D. Physical

Correct answer is **D**. A guard dog is an operational component of physical security.

Domain 2 - Telecommunications and Network Security

1. In the OSI reference model, on which layer would Ethernet (IEEE 802.3) be placed?

    A. Layer 1—Physical layer

    B. Layer 2—Data-link layer

    C. Layer 3—Network Layer

    D. Layer 4—Transport Layer

Correct answer is **B**. Layer 2, the data-link layer, describes data transfer between machines, for instance, by an Ethernet.

2. Which tactic would **BEST** be considered a part of a proactive network defense?

    A. Redundant firewalls

    B. Business Continuity planning

    C. Disallowing P2P traffic

    D. Perimeter surveillance and intelligence gathering

Correct answer is **D**. Ideally to counter an attack, network security must also be proactive, anticipate, and oppose the attack against their infrastructure by interdicting and disrupting an attack preemptively or in self-defense. This requires intelligence on the threat, active surveillance at the perimeter and beyond, and the ability to intercede upstream or disable a threat agent's tools.

3. In which situation is the network not the target of the attack?

    A. A denial-of-service attack on servers on a network

    B. Hacking into a router

    C. A virus outbreak saturating network capacity

    D. A man-in-the-middle attack

Correct answer is **D**. Although the modification of messages will often happen at the higher network layers, networks can be set up to provide robustness or resilience against interception and change of a message (man-in-the-middle attack) or replay attacks. Ways to accomplish this can be based on encryption or checksums on messages, as well as on access control measures for clients that would prevent an attacker from gaining the necessary access to send a modified message into the network.

4. Which of the following is **MOST** effective against a distributed denial-of-service attack?

    A. Secret fully qualified domain names (FQDNs)

    B. Redundant network layout

    C. Traffic filtering

    D. Network Address Translation (NAT).

Correct answer is **C**. Countermeasures to a denial-of-service attack include, but are not limited to: multiple layers of firewalls, careful filtering on firewalls, routers and switches, internal network access controls (NAC), redundant (diverse) network connections, load balancing, reserved bandwidth (quality of service, which would at least protect systems not directly targeted), and blocking traffic from an attacker on upstream router. However, traffic filtering has the most direct impact on improving resilience from DDOS attacks.

5. What is the optimal placement for network-based intrusion detection systems (NIDS)?

    A. On the network perimeter, to alert the network administrator of all suspicious traffic

    B. On network segments with business-critical systems

  C. At the network operations center (NOC)

  D. At an external service provider

Correct answer is **A**. Intrusion detection systems (IDS) monitor activity and send alerts when they detect suspicious traffic. There are two broad classifications of IDS: host-based IDS, which monitor activity on servers and workstations, and network-based IDS, which monitor network activity. Placing an IDS on the network perimeter monitors all traffic into an organization.

 6. Which of the following end-point devices would MOST likely be considered part of a converged IP network?

  A. File server, IP phone, security camera

  B. IP phone, thermostat, cypher lock

  C. Security camera, cypher lock, IP phone

  D. Thermostat, file server, cypher lock

Correct answer is **A**. See Figure 2.31

 7. Which of the following is an advantage of fiber-optic over copper cables from a security perspective?

  A. Fiber optics provides higher bandwidth.

  B. Fiber optics are more difficult to wiretap.

  C. Fiber optics are immune to wiretap.

  D. None—the two are equivalent; network security is independent from the physical layer.

Correct answer is **B**. From a security perspective, fiber optics' immunity to electromagnetic interference (EMI) and radio frequency interference (RFI) is important. Because fiber optics emit extremely small amounts of energy from the cable, data cannot be as easily intercepted as information is transported through electric current in wires.

A

Appendix
Answers to Review Questions

8. Which of the following devices should be part of a network's perimeter defense?

    A. A boundary router, A firewall, A proxy Server

    B. A firewall, A proxy server, A host based intrusion detection system (HIDS)

    C. A proxy server, A host based intrusion detection system (HIDS), A firewall

    D. A host based intrusion detection system (HIDS), A firewall, A boundary router

Correct answer is **B**. The security perimeter is the first line of protection between trusted and untrusted networks. In general, it includes a firewall and router that helps filter traffic. Security perimeters may also include proxies and devices, such as an intrusion detection system (IDS), to warn of suspicious traffic. The defensive perimeter extends out from these first protective devices, to include proactive defense such as boundary routers which can provide early warning of upstream attacks and threat activities. HIDS are associated with hosts behind the perimeter.

9. Which of the following is a principal security risk of wireless LANs?

    A. Lack of physical access control

    B. Demonstrably insecure standards

    C. Implementation weaknesses

    D. War driving

Correct answer is **A**. Wireless networks allow users to be mobile while remaining connected to a LAN. Unfortunately, this allows unauthorized users greater access to the LAN as well. In fact, many wireless LANs can be accessed off of the organization's property by anyone with a wireless card in a laptop, which effectively extends the LAN where there are no physical controls.

10. Which of the following configurations of a WLAN's SSID offers adequate security protection?

    A. Using an obscure SSID to confuse and distract an attacker

    B. Not using any SSID at all to prevent an attacker from connecting to the network

    C. Not broadcasting an SSID to make it harder to detect the WLAN

    D. An SSID does not provide protection

Correct answer is **D**. SSIDs are not for authentication.

11. IPSec

    A. provides mechanisms for authentication and encryption.

    B. provides mechanisms for nonrepudiation.

    C. will only be deployed with IPv6.

    D. only authenticates clients against a server.

Correct answer is **A**. IP Security (IPSec) is a suite of protocols for communicating securely with IP by providing mechanisms for authenticating and encryption. Standard IPSec authenticates only hosts with each other.

12. A Security Event Management (SEM) service performs the following function:

    A. Gathers firewall logs for archiving

    B. Aggregates logs from security devices and application servers looking for suspicious activity

    C. Reviews access controls logs on servers and physical entry points to match user system authorization with physical access permissions

    D. Coordination software for security conferences and seminars.

Correct answer is **B**. SEM/SEIM systems have to understand a wide variety of different applications and network element (routers/switches) logs and formats; consolidate these logs into a single database and then correlate events looking for clues to unauthorized behaviors that would be otherwise inconclusive if observed in a single log file.

13. Which of the following is the principal weakness of DNS (Domain Name System)?

  A. Lack of authentication of servers, and thereby authenticity of records

  B. Its latency, which enables insertion of records between the time when a record has expired and when it is refreshed

  C. The fact that it is a simple, distributed, hierarchical database instead of a singular, relational one, thereby giving rise to the possibility of inconsistencies going undetected for a certain amount of time

  D. The fact that addresses in e-mail can be spoofed without checking their validity in DNS, caused by the fact that DNS addresses are not digitally signed

Correct answer is **A**. Authentication has been proposed but attempts to introduce stronger authentication into DNS have not found wider acceptance. Authentication services have been delegated upward to higher protocol layers. Applications in need of guaranteeing authenticity cannot rely on DNS to provide such but will have to implement a solution themselves.

14. Which of the following statements about open e-mail relays is incorrect?

  A. An open e-mail relay is a server that forwards e-mail from domains other than the ones it serves.

  B. Open e-mail relays are a principal tool for distribution of spam.

  C. Using a blacklist of open e-mail relays provides a secure way for an e-mail administrator to identify open mail relays and filter spam.

  D. An open e-mail relay is widely considered a sign of bad system administration.

Correct answer is **C**. Although using blacklists as one indicator in spam filtering has its merits, it is risky to use them as an exclusive indicator. Generally, they are run by private organizations and individuals according to their own rules, they are able to change their policies on a whim, they can vanish overnight for any reason, and they can rarely be held accountable for the way they operate their lists.

15. A botnet can be characterized as

    A. An network used solely for internal communications

    B. An automatic security alerting tool for corporate networks

    C. A group of dispersed, compromised machines controlled remotely for illicit reasons.

    D. A type of virus

Correct answer is **C**. "Bots" and "botnets" are most insidious implementations of unauthorized, remote control of compromised systems. Such machines are essentially zombies controlled by ethereal entities from the dark places on the Internet.

16. A mesh network topology is rarely implemented in modern networks due to

    A. cost

    B. poor redundancy

    C. throughput

    D. optical fiber limits

Correct answer is **A**. Mesh networks are the most expensive of options as all nodes must connect to each other.

17. In installing an 801.11N wireless access point, which of the following provides the strongest wireless encryption?

    A. WPA

    B. WEP

    C. PKI

    D. WPA2

Correct Answer is **D**. WPA and WEP have been "broken" due to poor implementations and designs. Public Key Infrastructure (PKI) is used within several algorithms but only explains key exchange. WPA2 is the best answer.

18. A new installation requires a network in a heavy manufacturing area with substantial amounts of electromagnetic radiation and power fluctuations. Which media is best suited for this environment if little traffic degradation is tolerated?

    A. Coax cable

    B. Wireless

    C. Shielded twisted pair

    D. Fiber

Correct answer is **D**. Since fiber relies on light, electromagnetic and source power-based distortions do not affect it. Coax, wireless and shielded twisted pair rely and electromagnetic principles to operate and are therefore susceptible to electromagnetic interference.

19. Multi-layer protocols such as Modbus used in industrial control systems

    A. often have their own encryption and security like IPv6.

    B. are used in modern routers as a routing interface control.

    C. are often insecure by their very nature as they were not designed to natively operate over today's IP networks.

    D. have largely been retired and replaced with newer protocols such as IPv6 and NetBIOS.

Correct answer is **C**. Industrial control systems and their multi-layer protocols are largely insecure due to the original designs used to implement them. Given the life expectancy of the control systems, many are in use with inherently insecure designs, protocols and configurations.

20. A security professional needs to administer a server remotely. Assuming they can access the server from their location which is the BEST approach for access?

    A. TELNET

    B. SSHv2

    C. FTP

    D. TFTP

Correct answer is **B**. SSHv2 is the only protocol listed which supports strong encryption and is therefore the best choice.

Domain 3 - Information Security Governance and Risk

1. When determining the value of an intangible asset which is the **BEST** approach?

    A. Determine the physical storage costs and multiply by the expected life of the company

    B. With the assistance of a finance of accounting professional determine how much profit the asset has returned

    C. Review the depreciation of the intangible asset over the past three years.

    D. Use the historical acquisition or development cost of the intangible asset

Correct answer is **B**. Intangible asset value is challenging to determine. While there are several ways to determine the value of an intangible asset, the best approach involves seeking assistance from finance or accounting professionals to determine the impact of the asset to the organization.

2. Qualitative risk assessment is described by which of the following?

    A. Ease of implementation and it can be completed by personnel with a limited understanding of the risk assessment process

    B. Can be completed by personnel with a limited understanding of the risk assessment process and uses detailed metrics used for calculation of risk

1387

    C. Detailed metrics used for calculation of risk and ease of implementation

    D. Can be completed by personnel with a limited understanding of the risk assessment process and detailed metrics used for the calculation of risk

Correct answer is **A**. Qualitative risk assessments are a form of risk assessments that use stratified forms of risk such as "high, moderate and low." This simplified approach allows for those not as familiar with risk assessments the ability to perform risk assessments, which while not as specific as quantitative assessments are still meaningful.

    3. Single loss expectancy (SLE) is calculated by using:

        A. Asset value and annualized rate of occurrence (ARO)

        B. Asset value, local annual frequency estimate (LAFE), and standard annual frequency estimate (SAFE)

        C. Asset value and exposure factor

        D. Local annual frequency estimate and annualized rate of occurrence

Correct answer is **C**. The formula for calculating SLE is SLE = asset value (in $) × exposure factor (loss in successful threat exploit, as %).

    4. Consideration for which type of risk assessment to perform includes all of the following:

        A. Culture of the organization, likelihood of exposure and budget

        B. Budget, capabilities of resources and likelihood of exposure

        C. Capabilities of resources, likelihood of exposure and budget

        D. Culture of the organization, budget, capabilities and resources

Correct answer is **D**. It is expected that an organization will make a selection of the risk assessment methodology, tools, and resources (including people) that best fit its culture, personnel capabilities, budget, and timeline.

    5. Security awareness training includes:

        A. Legislated security compliance objectives

        B. Security roles and responsibilities for staff

    C. The high-level outcome of vulnerability assessments

    D. Specialized curriculum assignments, coursework and an accredited institution

Correct answer is **B**. Security awareness training is a method by which organizations can inform employees about their roles, and expectations surrounding their roles, in the observance of information security requirements. Additionally, training provides guidance surrounding the performance of particular security or risk management functions, as well as providing information surrounding the security and risk management functions in general.

6. A signed user acknowledgment of the corporate security policy:

    A. Ensures that users have read the policy

    B. Ensures that users understand the policy, as well as the consequences for not following the policy

    C. Can be waived if the organization is satisfied that users have an adequate understanding of the policy

    D. Helps to protect the organization if a user's behavior violates the policy

Correct answer is **D**. All users should sign an acknowledgement that they have read and understand the policies. While this does not ensure that they have read or understand the policies, it will help to protect the organization if a user's behavior violates the policy.

7. Effective security management:

    A. Achieves security at the lowest cost

    B. Reduces risk to an acceptable level

    C. Prioritizes security for new products

    D. Installs patches in a timely manner

Correct answer is **B**. There will always be residual risk accepted by an organization, and effective security management will minimize this risk to a level that fits within the organization's risk tolerance or risk profile.

1389

8. Availability makes information accessible by protecting it from:

    A. Denial of services, fires, floods, hurricanes, and unauthorized transactions

    B. Fires, floods, hurricanes, unauthorized transactions and unreadable backup tapes

    C. Unauthorized transactions, fires, floods, hurricanes and unreadable backup tapes

    D. Denial of services, fires, floods, and hurricanes and unreadable backup tapes

Correct answer is **D**. Availability is the principle that information is available and accessible by users when needed. The two primary areas affecting the availability of systems are (1) denial of service attacks and (2) loss of service due to a disaster, which could be man-made or natural.

9. To avoid bias, the security officer could report to any of the following:

    A. CEO, application development or CFO

    B. Chief information officer, CFO or application development

    C. CFO, CEO or chief information officer

    D. Application development, CFO or CEO

Correct answer is **C** The security officer must work with the application development managers to ensure that security is considered in the project cost during each phase of development (analysis, design, development, testing, implementation, and post implementation). To facilitate this best from an independence perspective, the security officer should not report to application development.

10. Tactical security plans are **BEST** used to:

    A. Establish high-level security policies

    B. Enable enterprise/entity-wide security management

    C. Reduce downtime

    D. Deploy new security technology

Correct answer is **D**. Tactical plans provide the broad initiatives to support and achieve the goals specified in the strategic plan. These initiatives may include deployments such as establishing an electronic policy development and distribution process, implementing robust change control for the server environment, reducing vulnerabilities residing on the servers using vulnerability management, implementing a "hot site" disaster recovery program, or implementing an identity management solution. These plans are more specific and may consist of multiple projects to complete the effort. Tactical plans are shorter in length, such as 6 to 18 months to achieve a specific security goal of the company.

11. Who is accountable for implementing information security?

A. Everyone

B. Senior management

C. Security officer

D. Data owners

Correct answer is **C**. The information security officer is responsible for ensuring the protection of all of the business information assets from intentional and unintentional loss, disclosure, alteration, destruction, and unavailability.

12. Security is likely to be most expensive when addressed in which phase?

A. Design

B. Rapid prototyping

C. Testing

D. Implementation

Correct answer is **D**. Security is much less expensive when it is built into the application design versus added as an afterthought at or after implementation.

13. Information systems auditors help the organization:

    A. Mitigate compliance issues

    B. Establish an effective control environment

    C. Identify control gaps

    D. Address information technology for financial statements

Correct answer is **C**. Auditors provide an essential role for maintaining and improving information security. They provide an independent view of the design, effectiveness, and implementation of controls. The results of audits generate findings that require management response and corrective action plans to resolve the issue and mitigate the risk.

14. Long-duration security projects:

    A. Provide greater organizational value

    B. Increase return on investment (ROI)

    C. Minimize risk

    D. Increase completion risk

Correct answer is **D**. Projects greater than 12 to 18 months are generally considered to be long term and strategic in nature and typically require more funding and resources or are more complex in their implementation.

15. Setting clear security roles has the following benefits:

    A. Establishes personal accountability, reduces cross-training requirements and reduces departmental turf battles

    B. Enables continuous improvement, reduces cross-training requirements and reduces departmental turf battles

    C. Establishes personal accountability, establishes continuous improvement and reduces turf battles

    D. Reduces departmental turf battles, Reduces cross-training requirements and establishes personal accountability

Correct answer is **C**. Establishing clear, unambiguous security roles has many benefits to the organization beyond providing information as to the responsibilities to be performed and who needs to perform them.

16. Well-written security program policies are **BEST** reviewed:

    A. At least annually or at pre-determined organization changes

    B. After major project implementations

    C. When applications or operating systems are updated

    D. When procedures need to be modified

Correct answer is **A**. Policies should survive two or three years even though they should be reviewed and approved at least annually.

17. Orally obtaining a password from an employee is the result of:

    A. Social engineering

    B. Weak authentication controls

    C. Ticket-granting server authorization

    D. Voice recognition software

Correct answer is **A**. Social engineering attacks occur when a potential intruder attempts to solicit confidential information that may be used for a subsequent attack.

18. 18.   A security policy which will remain relevant and meaningful over time includes the following:

    A. Directive words such as shall, must, or will, technical specifications and is short in length

    B. Defined policy development process, short in length and contains directive words such as shall, must or will

    C. Short in length, technical specifications and contains directive words such as shall, must or will

    D. Directive words such as shall, must, or will, defined policy development process and is short in length

Correct answer is **D**. Technical implementation details do not belong in a policy. Policies must be written technology independent. Technology controls may change over time as an organization's risk profile changes and new vulnerabilities are found.

1393

19. The ability of one person in the finance department to add vendors to the vendor database and subsequently pay the vendor violates which concept?

    A. A well-formed transaction

    B. Separation of duties

    C. Least privilege

    D. Data sensitivity level

Correct answer is **B**. Separation of duties ensures fraud or other undesirable behavior cannot occur without collusion between two or more parties. In this example, individuals could add himself or herself as a vendor and then pay themselves.

20. Collusion is **BEST** mitigated through:

    A. Job rotation

    B. Data classification

    C. Defining job sensitivity level

    D. Least privilege

Answer is **A**. Collusion involves multiple parties conspiring to perform an act harmful to the organization. By rotating jobs, collusion becomes more difficult as an increasing number of individuals must agree to harm the organization.

21. Data access decisions are **BEST** made by:

    A. User managers

    B. Data owners

    C. Senior management

    D. Application developers

Correct answer is **B**. Data owners are ultimately responsible for the information and therefore should determine access decisions.

Domain 4 - Software Development Security

1. The key objective of application security is to ensure

    A. that the software is hacker proof

    B. the confidentiality, integrity and availability of data

    C. accountability of software and user activity

    D. prevent data theft

Correct answer is **B**. The objective of application security is to make sure that the system and its resources are available when needed, that the integrity of the processing of the data and the data itself are ensured, and that the confidentiality of the data is protected. All of these purposes rely upon secure, consistent, reliable, and properly operating software. Ensuring confidentiality, integrity, and availability will mitigate the chances and impact of a hacking incident or data theft, but it must be recognized that total hacker proof software is utopian. Auditing (logging) functionality in software can help with detecting software and user activity, but this is not the key objective of application security. Software security controls can reduce the likelihood of data theft but they are not necessarily preventative.

2. For an application security program to be effective within an organization, it is critical to

    A. identify regulatory and compliance requirements.

    B. educate the software development organization the impact of insecure programming.

    C. develop the security policy that can be enforced.

    D. properly test all the software that is developed by your organization for security vulnerabilities.

Correct answer is **C**. The underlying foundation of software security controls is the organization's security policy. The security policy reflects the security requirements of the organization. The identification of regulatory and compliance requirements such as Sarbanes–Oxley (SOX), payment card industry data security standard (PCIDSS) are essential and must be factored into the security policy. Without a clear understanding of what

1395

the security requirements are, as defined in the security policy, educating software development teams may potentially be still inadequate. Testing for security vulnerability can provide some degree of software assurance, but with newer kinds of attacks against software being discovered, security testing does not directly indicate the effectiveness of an application security program.

3. The best defense against session hijacking and man-in-the-middle (MITM) attacks is to use which of the following in the development of software?

    A.   Unique and random identification

    B.   Use prepared statements and procedures

    C.   Database views

    D.   Encryption

Correct answer is **A**. Prepared statements and procedures protect against SQL injection. Data base views protect against unauthorized modification. Encryption protects the confidentiality of information but may not protect against a session hijacking attempt. Unique and random identifiers present a challenge for the attacker to guess what the next identifier may be.

4. An important characteristic of bytecode is that it

    A. has increased secure inherently due to sandboxing

    B. manages memory operations automatically

    C. is more difficult to reverse engineer

    D. is faster than interpreted languages

Correct answer is **D**. A programming language like Java compiles source code into a sort of pseudo-object code called bytecode. The bytecode is then processed by the interpreter (called the Java Virtual Machine, or JVM) for the CPU to run. Because the bytecode is already fairly close to object code, the interpretation process is much faster than for other interpreted languages. And because bytecode is still undergoing an interpretation, a given Java program will run on any machine that has a JVM. Memory management and sandboxing are important security aspects that apply to the programming language Java, but not to bytecode itself. The debate over whether a pseudo-object (bytecode) representation can be easily reverse engineered is debatable and inconclusive. Because bytecode is more pseudo-object representation of the source code, reversing to source code is in fact considered less difficult than from object or executable code.

5. Two cooperating processes that simultaneously compete for a shared resource, in such a way that they violate the system's security policy, is commonly known as

    A. Covert channel
    B. Denial of Service
    C. Overt channel
    D. Object reuse

Correct answer is **A**. A covert channel or confinement problem is an information flow issue. It is a communication channel allowing two cooperating processes to transfer information in such a way that it violates the system's security policy. There are two types of covert channels: storage and timing. A covert storage channel involves the direct or indirect reading of a storage location by one process and a direct or indirect reading of the same storage location by another process. Typically, a covert storage channel involves a finite resource, such as a memory location or sector on a disk that is shared by two subjects at different security levels. This scenario is a description of a covert storage channel. A covert timing channel depends upon being able to influence the rate that some other process is able to acquire resources, such as the CPU, memory, or I/O devices. Covert channels as opposed to what should be the case (overt channels) could lead to denial of service and object reuse has to do with disclosure protection when objects in memory are reused by different processes.

6. An organization has a website with a guest book feature, where visitors to the web site can input their names and comments about the organization. Each time the guest book web page loads, a message box is prompted with the message 'You have been P0wnd' followed by redirection to a different website. Analysis reveals that the no input validation or output encoding is being performed in the web application. This is the basis for which type of attack?

    A. Denial of Service
    B. Cross-site Scripting (XSS)
    C. Malicious File Execution
    D. Injection Flaws

Correct answer is **B**. A Web site that allows users to input information for later retrieval by other users, such as a guestbook comment page or blog, without proper input validation, may fail to detect when such input comes in is in the form of active scripting. Without appropriate output encoding, the script can be actively read and executed by the browser causing denial of service (Web site defacement) or other serious impacts. This is the basis of cross-site scripting attacks.

7. The art of influencing people to divulge sensitive information about themselves or their organization by either coercion or masquerading as a valid entity is known as

    A. Dumpster diving
    B. Shoulder surfing
    C. Phishing
    D. Social engineering

Correct answer is **D**. Social engineering is the art of getting people to divulge sensitive information to others either in a friendly manner, as an attempt to be "helpful," or through intimidation. Phishing is the form of social engineering using electronic means such as e-mail. Shoulder surfing is a disclosure attack wherein, an attacker stands over the shoulders of someone and reads the sensitive information they are viewing. Masking of information (asterisking password) can mitigate shoulder surfing.

Dumpster diving is another disclosure attack in which dumpsters are searched to glean sensitive information.

8. An organization's server audit logs indicate that an employee that was terminated in the morning was still able to access certain sensitive resources on his system, on the internal network, that afternoon. The logs indicate that the employee had logged on successfully before he was terminated but there is no record of him logging off before he was terminated. This is an example of which type of attack?

A. Time of Check/Time of Use (TOC/TOU)

B. Logic Bomb

C. Remote-access trojans (RATS)

D. Phishing

Correct answer is **A**. TOC/TOU is a common type of attack that occurs when some control changes between the time that the system security functions check the contents of variables and the time the variables actually are used during operations. For instance, a user logs on to a system in the morning and later is fired. As a result of the termination, the security administrator removes the user from the user database. Because the user did not log off, he or she still has access to the system and might try to get even. Logic bombs are software modules set up to run in a quiescent state, but to monitor for a specific condition or set of conditions and to activate their payload under those conditions. Remote access trojans are malicious programs designed to be installed, usually remotely, after systems are installed and working. Phishing attempts to get the user to provide information that will be useful for identity theft-type frauds.

9. The most effective defense against a buffer overflow attack is

    A. disallowing dynamic construction of queries
    B. bounds checking
    C. encoding output
    D. forced garbage collection

Correct answer is **B**. Buffer overflows can result when a program fills up the assigned buffer of memory with more data than its buffer can hold. When the program begins to write beyond the end of the buffer, the program's execution path can be changed, or data can be written into areas used by the operating system itself. A buffer overflow is caused by improper (or lacking) bounds checking on input to a program. By checking for the bounds (boundaries) of allowable input size, buffer overflow can be mitigated. Disallowing dynamic construction of queries is a defense against injection attacks and encoding the output mitigates scripting attacks. The collection of dangling objects in memory (garbage) can be requested but not necessarily forced and proper memory management can help mitigate buffer overflow attacks, but the most effective defenses against buffer overflow is bounds checking and proper error checking.

10. It is extremely important that as one follows a software development project, security activities are performed

    A. before release to production, so that the project is not delayed
    B. if a vulnerability is detected in your software
    C. in each stage of the life cycle
    D. when management mandates it

Correct answer is **C**. Security activities should be done in parallel with project initiation activities and, indeed, with every task throughout the project.

11. Audit logs are which type of control?

    A. Preventive
    B. Detective
    C. Compensating
    D. Corrective

Correct answer is **B**. Audit logs can be used to find out who (identity) did what (action), when (timestamp), and where (objects or resources affected) and are therefore detective in nature.

12. Who can enforce the separation of duties by ensuring that programmers do not have access to production code?

    A. Operations personnel

    B. Software librarian

    C. Management

    D. Quality assurance personnel

Correct answer is **B**. A software librarian ensures program or data library is controlled in accordance with policy and procedures.

13. The technical evaluation of assurance to ensure that security requirements have been met is known as?

    A. Accreditation

    B. Certification

    C. Validation

    D. Verification

Correct answer is **B**. Certification is the process of evaluating the security stance of the software or system against a predetermined set of security standards or policies. Management, after reviewing the certification, authorizes the software or system to be implemented in a production status, in a specific environment, for a specific period. Management authorization is known as accreditation.

14. Defect prevention rather than defect removal is characteristic of which of the following software development methodology?

    A. Computer Aided Software Engineering (CASE)

    B. Spiral

    C. Waterfall

    D. Cleanroom

Correct answer is **D**. In cleanroom software development methodology, the goal is to write code correctly the first time, rather than trying to find the problems once they are there. Essentially, it focuses on defect prevention rather than defect removal. The waterfall methodology is extremely structured and its key distinguishing characteristic is that each phase (stage) must be completed before moving on to the next, in order to prevent ad hoc scope creep. A distinguishing feature of the spiral model is that in each phase of the waterfall there are four substages, based on the common Deming PDCA (Plan-Do-Check-Act) model; in particular, a risk assessment review (Check). CASE is the technique of using computers and computer utilities to help with the systematic analysis, design, development, implementation, and maintenance of software.

15. A security protection mechanism in which untrusted code, which is not signed, is restricted from accessing system resources is known as?

> A. Sandboxing
> B. Non-repudiation
> C. Separation of Duties
> D. Obfuscation

Correct answer is **A**. One of the control mechanisms for mobile code is the sandbox. The sandbox provides a protective area for program execution. Limits are placed on the amount of memory and processor resources the program can consume. If the program exceeds these limits, the Web browser terminates the process and logs an error code. This can ensure the safety of the browser's performance. Non-repudiation is a security control mechanism in which the user or process cannot deny its action. Separation of duties is about ensuring that a security policy cannot be violated by a single user or process. Obfuscation is the process of rendering source code to be unreadable and unintelligible as a protection against reversing and IP issues.

16. A program that does not reproduce itself but pretends to be performing a legitimate action, while actually performing malicious operations in the background, is the characteristic of which of the following?

    A. Worms

    B. Trapdoor

    C. Virus

    D. Trojan

Correct answer is **D**. A Trojan is a program that pretends to do one thing while performing another, unwanted action. A Trojan does not reproduce itself as do worms and viruses in order to spread. A trapdoor or backdoor is a hidden mechanism that bypasses access control measures. It is an entry point into a program that is inserted in software by programmers during the program's development to provide a method of gaining access into the program for modification if the access control mechanism malfunctions and locks them out. Developers often refer to them as maintenance hooks.

17. A plot to take insignificant pennies from a user's bank account and move them to the attacker's bank account is an example of

    A. Social Engineering

    B. Salami Attack

    C. Pranks

    D. Hoaxes

Correct answer is **B**. A variant on the concept of logic bombs involves what is known as the salami scam. The basic idea involves siphoning off small amounts of money (in some versions, fractions of a cent) credited to a specific account, over a large number of transactions. Pranks are very much a part of the computer culture, so much so that you can now buy commercially produced joke packages that allow you to perform "stupid Mac (or PC or Windows) tricks." Hoaxes use an odd kind of social engineering, relying on people's naturally gregarious nature and desire to communicate, and on a sense of urgency and importance, using the ambition that people have to be the first to provide important new information.

18. Role-based access control to protect confidentiality of data in databases can be BEST achieved through which of the following?

    A. Views

    B. Encryption

    C. Hashing

    D. Masking

Correct answer is **A**. A view is a feature that allows for virtual tables in a database; these virtual tables are created from one or more real tables in the database. For example, a view can be set up for each user (or group of users) on the system so that the user can then only view those virtual tables (or views). Encryption, hashing, and masking can all provide confidentiality as well, but for databases, views based access control which is a content dependent access control mechanism is the best answer.

19. The two most dangerous types of attacks against databases containing disparate non-sensitive information are

    A. Injection and scripting

    B. Session hijacking and cookie poisoning

    C. Aggregation and inference

    D. Bypassing authentication and insecure cryptography

Correct answer is **C**. Aggregation is the ability to combine nonsensitive data from separate sources to create sensitive information. For example, a user takes two or more unclassified pieces of data and combines them to form a classified piece of data that then becomes unauthorized for that user. Thus, the combined data sensitivity can be greater than the classification of individual parts. Inference is the ability to deduce (infer) sensitive or restricted information from observing available information. Essentially, users may be able to determine unauthorized information from what information they can access and may never need to directly access unauthorized data. For example, if a user is reviewing authorized information about patients, such as the medications they have been prescribed, the user may be able to determine the illness. Inference is one of the hardest threats to control. All of the other attacks are primarily attacks on Web applications.

20. A property that ensures only valid or legal transactions that do not violate any user-defined integrity constraints in DBMS technologies is known as?

    A. Atomicity

    B. Consistency

    C. Isolation

    D. Durability

Correct answer is **B**. ACID test, which stands for atomicity, consistency, isolation, and durability, is an important DBMS concept. Atomicity is when all the parts of a transaction's execution are either all committed or all rolled back—do it all or not at all. Essentially, all changes take effect, or none do. Consistency occurs when the database is transformed from one valid state to another valid state. A transaction is allowed only if it follows user-defined integrity constraints. Illegal transactions are not allowed, and if an integrity constraint cannot be satisfied, the transaction is rolled back to its previously valid state and the user is informed that the transaction has failed. Isolation is the process guaranteeing the results of a transaction are invisible to other transactions until the transaction is complete. Durability ensures the results of a completed transaction are permanent and can survive future system and media failures, that is, once they are done, they cannot be undone. This is similar to transaction persistence.

21. Expert systems are comprised of a knowledge base containing modeled human experience and which of the following?

    A. Inference engine

    B. Statistical models

    C. Neural networks

    D. Roles

Correct answer is **A**. The expert system uses a knowledge base (a collection of all the data, or knowledge, on a particular matter) and a set of algorithms or rules that infer new facts from knowledge and incoming data. The knowledge base could be the human experience that is available in an organization. Because the system reacts to a set of rules, if the rules are faulty, the response will also be faulty. Also, because human decision is removed from the point of action, if an error were to occur, the reaction time from a human would be longer.

Domain 5 - Cryptography

1. Asymmetric key cryptography is used for the following:

    A. Encryption of data, Access Control, Steganography

    B. Steganography, Access control, Nonrepudiation

    C. Nonrepudiation, Steganography, Encryption of Data

    D. Encryption of Data, Nonrepudiation, Access Control

Correct answer is **D**. Steganography is the hiding of a message inside of another medium.

2. Which of the following supports asymmetric key cryptography?

    A. Diffie–Hellman

    B. Rijndael

    C. Blowfish

    D. SHA-256

Correct answer is **A**. The Diffie–Hellman asymmetric algorithm was the first of its kind and still one of the most commonly used today.

3. What is an important disadvantage of using a public key algorithm compared to a symmetric algorithm?

    A. A symmetric algorithm provides better access control.

    B. A symmetric algorithm is a faster process.

    C. A symmetric algorithm provides nonrepudiation of delivery.

    D. A symmetric algorithm is more difficult to implement.

Correct answer is **B**. Processing efficiency of asymmetric cryptography is less than symmetric cryptography due to relative computational processing resources needed. Its lower performance is a disadvantage of asymmetric cryptography.

4. When a user needs to provide message integrity, what option is **BEST**?

    A. Send a digital signature of the message to the recipient

    B. Encrypt the message with a symmetric algorithm and send it

    C. Encrypt the message with a private key so the recipient can decrypt with the corresponding public key

    D. Create a checksum, append it to the message, encrypt the message, then send to recipient

Correct answer is **D**. The use of a simple error detecting code, checksum, or frame check sequence is often used along with symmetric key cryptography for message integrity. A is meaningless without sending the message itself to compare hash results. B has a weakness if the attacker ever gets the symmetric key used to encrypt the message. C, while providing privacy, is, by itself, computationally inefficient relative to the objective of message integrity.

5. A CA provides which benefits to a user?

    A. Protection of public keys of all users

    B. History of symmetric keys

    C. Proof of nonrepudiation of origin

    D. Validation that a public key is associated with a particular user

Correct answer is **D**. A certificate authority (CA) "signs" an entities digital certificate to certify that the certificate content accurately represents the certificate owner. A is not a CA function because public keys are not meant to be secret. B is a function of key management. C is a function of a digital certificate.

6. What is the output length of a RIPEMD-160 hash?

    A. 160 bits

    B. 150 bits

    C. 128 bits

    D. 104 bits

Correct answer is **A**. The output for RIPEMD-160 is 160 bits.

7. ANSI X9.17 is concerned primarily with

    A. Protection and secrecy of keys

    B. Financial records and retention of encrypted data

    C. Formalizing a key hierarchy

    D. The lifespan of key-encrypting keys (KKMs)

Correct answer is **A**. Protection and secrecy of keys is the primary concern of ANSI 9.17. ANSI X9.17 was developed to address the need of financial institutions to transmit securities and funds securely using an electronic medium. Specifically, it describes the means to ensure the secrecy of keys.

8. When a certificate is revoked, what is the proper procedure?

    A. Setting new key expiry dates

    B. Updating the certificate revocation list

    C. Removal of the private key from all directories

    D. Notification to all employees of revoked keys

Correct answer is **B**. When a key is no longer valid, the certificate revocation list should be updated. A certificate revocation list (CRL) is a list of non-valid certificates that should not be accepted by any member of the PKI.

9. Which is true about link encryption?

    A. Link encryption is advised for high-risk environments, provides better traffic flow confidentiality, and encrypts routing information.

    B. Link encryption is often used for Frame Relay or satellite links, is advised for high-risk environments and provides better traffic flow confidentiality.

    C. Link encryption encrypts routing information, is often used for Frame Relay or satellite links, and provides traffic flow confidentiality.

    D. Link encryption provides better traffic flow confidentiality, is advised for high-risk environments and provides better traffic flow confidentiality.

Correct answer is **C.** Link encryption is not suitable for high-risk environments due to possible privacy weakness at each node. It is possible that an attacker could view decrypted data as encrypt decrypt function is performed at each node along the data path.

10. Which is the sequence that controls the operation of the cryptographic algorithm?

    A. Encoder

    B. Decoder wheel

    C. Cryptovariable

    D. Cryptographic routine

Correct answer is **C.** Cryptovariable or key controls the operation of the cryptographic algorithm.

11. The process used in most block ciphers to increase their strength is

    A. Diffusion

    B. Confusion

    C. Step function

    D. SP-network

Correct answer is **D.** The SP-network is the process described by Claude Shannon used in most block ciphers to increase their strength. SP stands for substitution and permutation (transposition), and most block ciphers do a series of repeated substitutions and permutations to add confusion and diffusion to the encryption process.

12. Which of the following **BEST** describes fundamental methods of encrypting data?

    A. Substitution and transposition

    B. 3DES and PGP

    C. Symmetric and asymmetric

    D. DES and AES

Correct answer is **C**. Data encryption relies on either symmetric or asymmetric designs to ensure the confidentiality of data. The vast majority of all encryption products algorithms or processes fall into one or the other methods.

13. Cryptography supports all of the core principles of information security except

    A. Availability

    B. Confidentiality

    C. Integrity

    D. Authenticity

Correct answer is **D**. Cryptography supports all three of the core principles of information security. Authenticity is not one of the cove principles.

14. A way to defeat frequency analysis as a method to determine the key is to use

    A. Substitution ciphers

    B. Transposition ciphers

    C. Polyalphabetic ciphers

    D. Inversion ciphers

Correct answer is **C**. The use of several alphabets for substituting the plaintext is called polyalphabetic ciphers. It is designed to make the breaking of a cipher by frequency analysis more difficult.

15. The running key cipher is based on

    A. Modular arithmetic

    B. XOR mathematics

    C. Factoring

    D. Exponentiation

Correct answer is **A**. The use of modular mathematics and the representation of each letter by its numerical place in the alphabet are the key to many modern ciphers including running key ciphers.

16. The only cipher system said to be unbreakable by brute force is

    A. AES

    B. DES

    C. One-time pad

    D. Triple DES

Correct answer is **C**. One-time pad is a key that is only used once and that must be as long as the plaintext but never repeats.

17. A message protected by steganography would most likely be found in a

    A. Public key

    B. Algorithm

    C. Private key

    D. Picture file

Correct answer is **D**. Steganography is the hiding of a message inside of another medium, such as a photograph, music, or other item. The message itself is not encrypted, but its existence is hidden so that only the intended recipient would know how to reveal the message.

18. Which is the **BEST** choice for implementing encryption on a smart card?

    A. Blowfish

    B. Elliptic Curve Cryptography

    C. TwoFish

    D. Quantum Cryptography

Correct answer is **B**. Smart cards have limited processing power and memory and therefore should use an approach which is light on processor demands. Elliptic Curve Cryptography is the only option provided which is highly efficient and therefore relies on little processing power.

19. An e-mail with an document attachment from a known individual is received with a digital signature. The e-mail client is unable to validate the signature. What is the **BEST** course of action?

    A. Open the attachment to determine if the signature is valid.

    B. Determine why the signature can't be validated prior to opening the attachment.

    C. Delete the e-mail

    D. Forward the e-mail to another address with a new signature.

Correct answer is **B**. When a digital signature cannot be validated, there may be several reasons. A system may not be able to reach a CA, but also the certificate used to sign the document may have been self-generated or worse forged.

20. The vast majority of Virtual Private Networks use

    A. SSL/TLS and IPSec.

    B. El Gamal and DES.

    C. 3DES and Blowfish

    D. TwoFish and IDEA.

Correct answer is **A**. Two major tools assist in both VPN and e-commerce secure networking. IPSec and SSL/TLS have become synonymous with network security. These protocols form the vast majority of secure network traffic and e-commerce enablement.

Domain 6 - Security Architecture and Design

1. A holistic lifecycle for developing security architecture that begins with assessing business requirements and subsequently creating a 'chain of traceability' through phases of strategy, concept, design, implementation and metrics is characteristic of which of the following frameworks?

    A. Zachman

    B. SABSA

    C. ISO 27000

D. TOGAF

Correct answer is **B**. SABSA (Sherwood Applied Business Security Architecture) is a holistic lifecycle for developing security architecture that begins with assessing business requirements. It generates a "chain of traceability" of security requirements to business functionality, through the phases of strategy, concept, design, implementation, and metrics. It represents any architecture using six layers, each representing a different perspective for the design and construction and use of the target system.

2. Which of the following component of ITIL's Service Portfolio is primarily focused on translating designs into operational services through a project management standard?

   A. Service Strategy
   B. Service Design
   C. Service Transition
   D. Service Operations

Correct answer is **C**. Service strategy is not necessarily part of service portfolio. It addresses new business needs and is used to generate the service portfolio, which includes the range of all the services that will be provided. Service design focuses on creating the services within the service portfolio. Service transition is primarily concerned with translating the service design into operational services and once these services have been deployed, they are transferred into steady-state service operations. The metrics that is collected for each service is used for continual service improvement.

3. Which of the following can **BEST** be used to capture detailed security requirements?

   A. Threat modeling, covert channels, and data classification
   B. Data classification, risk assessments, and covert channels
   C. Risk assessments, covert channels, and threat modeling
   D. Threat modeling, data classification, and risk assessments

Correct answer is **D**. Threat modeling can be used to determine the threats to your system or software, which can be used to generate detailed countermeasure requirements. Data classification can be used to determine appropriate levels of protection for the data that is transmitted or stored and this can be used to determine confidentiality, integrity or availability requirements. Determining residual and acceptable risk thresholds can be used to generate security requirements as well.

4. Which of the following security standards is internationally recognized as the standards for sound security practices and is focused on the standardization and certification of an organization's Information Security Management System (ISMS)?

    A. ISO 15408

    B. ISO 27001

    C. ISO 9001

    D. ISO 9146

Correct answer is **B**. ISO 27000 series will assist organizations of all types to understand the fundamentals, principles, and concepts to improve the protection of their information assets. ISO 15408 is the common criteria which includes the evaluation criteria for IT security. ISO 9001 provides the requirements for quality management system. ISO 9126 is an international standard for the evaluation of software quality.

5. Which of the following describes the rules that need to be implemented to ensure that the security requirements are met?

    A. Security kernel

    B. Security policy

    C. Security model

    D. Security reference monitor

Correct answer is **B**. Security policy documents the security requirements of an organization. Subsequently, a security model is a specification that describes the rules to be implemented to support and enforce the security policy. While the security policy provides the "What" requirements needs to be met, the security model provides "HOW" (the rules by which) the requirements will be met. The part of the operating system where security features are located is the security kernel. Security reference monitor is the tamperproof module that controls the access request of software to either the data or the system.

6. A two-dimensional grouping of individual subjects into groups or roles and granting access to groups to objects is an example of which of the following types of models?

    A. Multilevel lattice

    B. State machine

    C. Non-interference

    D. Matrix-based

Correct answer is **D**. While lattice-based models tend to treat similar subjects and objects with similar restrictions, matrix-based models focus on one-to-one relationships between subjects and objects. The best known example is the organization of subjects and objects into an access control matrix. An access control matrix is a two-dimensional table that allows for individual subjects and objects to be related to each other. A state machine model, describes the behavior of a system as it moves between one state and another, from one moment to another. A noninterference model maintains activities at different security levels to separate these levels from each other. In this way, it minimizes leakages that may happen through covert channels, because there is complete separation between security levels.

7. Which of the following models ensures that a subject with clearance level of 'Secret' has the ability to write only to objects classified as 'Secret' or 'Top Secret' but is prevented from writing information classified as 'Public'?

    A. Biba-Integrity

    B. Clark–Wilson

    C. Brewer–Nash

    D. Bell–LaPadula

Correct answer is **D**. Bell–LaPadula is a confidentiality model that deals with the prevention of information disclosure.

8. Which of the following is unique to the Biba Integrity Model?

    A. Simple property

    B. * (star) property

    C. Invocation property

    D. Strong * property

Correct answer is **C**. Both Biba and Bell–LaPadula have the simple and * (star) property and the strong * property is part of the confidentiality Bell–LaPadula model. The Invocation property is unique to the Biba integrity model, which considers a situation where corruption may occur because a less trustworthy subject was allowed to invoke the powers of a subject with more trust.

9. Which of the following models is **BEST** considered in a shared data-hosting environment so that the data of one customer is not disclosed to a competitor or other customers sharing that hosted environment?

    A. Brewer–Nash

    B. Clark–Wilson

    C. Bell–LaPadula

    D. Lipner

Correct answer is **A**. While the other models listed can provide confidentiality assurance, it is only the Brewer–Nash Model, which is also known as the Chinese wall model, that has a clear separation of access rights. The principle of Brewer–Nash model is that users should not be able to access the confidential information of both a client organization and one or more of its competitors. It is called the Chinese wall model because, like the Great Wall of China, once you are on one side of the wall, you cannot get to the other side.

10. Which of the following security models is primarily concerned with how the subjects and objects are created and how subjects are assigned rights or privileges?

    A. Bell–LaPadula

    B. Biba-Integrity

    C. Chinese Wall

    D. Graham–Denning

Correct answer is **D**. The Graham–Denning access control model has three parts: a set of objects, a set of subjects, and a set of rights. Bell–LaPadula is a confidentiality model. Biba is an integrity model. The Chinese Wall Model is also a confidential assurance model that deals with the about separation of access.

11. Which of the following ISO standards provides the evaluation criteria that can be used to evaluate security requirements of different products with different functions?

    A. 15408

    B. 27000

    C. 9100

    D. 27002

Correct answer is **A**. ISO/IEC 15408 is commonly referred to as the common criteria. It is an internationally recognized standard provided the first truly international product evaluation criteria. It has largely superseded all other criteria, although there continue to be products in general use that were certified under TCSEC, ITSEC, and other criteria.It takes a very similar approach to ITSEC by providing a flexible set of functional and assurance requirements, and like ITSEC, it is not very proscriptive as TCSEC had been. Instead, it is focused on standardizing the general approach to product evaluation and providing mutual recognition of such evaluations all over the world.

12. In the Common Criteria, the common set of functional and assurance requirements for a category of vendor products deployed in a particular type of environment are known as

    A. Protection Profiles

    B.   Security Target

    C. Trusted Computing Base

    D. Ring Protection

Correct answer is **A**. Protection profiles are the common set of functional and assurance requirements while security target is the specific functional and assurance requirements that the author of the security target wants a given product to fulfill. Trusted computing base and ring protection are not concepts of the common criteria.

13. Which of the following evaluation assurance level that is formally verified, designed and tested is expected for high risk situation?

    A. EAL 1

    B. EAL 3

    C. EAL 5

    D.   EAL 7

Correct answer is **D**. EAL 7 is the only one that given after the product is formally verified, designed, and tested. All the other levels of assurances are not formally verified.

14. Formal acceptance of an evaluated system by management is known as

    A. Certification

    B. Accreditation

    C. Validation

    D. Verification

Correct answer is **B**. In the accreditation phase, management evaluates the capacity of a system to meet the needs of the organization. If management determines that the needs of the system satisfy the needs of the organization, they will formally accept the evaluated system, usually for a defined period of time. During the certification phase, the product or system is tested to see whether it meets the documented requirements (including any security requirements). Validation and verification are usually part of the certification phase.

15. Which stage of the Capability Maturity Model (CMM) is characterized by having organizational processes that are proactive?

    A. Initial

    B. Managed

    C. Defined

    D. Optimizing

Correct answer is **C**. In the initial stage, the processes are unpredictable, poorly ¬controlled, and reactive. During the managed stage, the processes are characterized for projects (not the entire organization) and it is often reactive. In the defined stage, the processes are characterized for the entire organization and are proactive. In the optimizing stage the organization focuses on continuous process improvement.

16. Which of the following **BEST** provides a method of quantifying risks associated with information technology when validating the abilities of new security controls and countermeasures to address the identified risks?

    A. Threat/risk assessment

    B. Penetration testing

    C. Vulnerability assessment

    D. Data classification

Correct answer is **A**. Penetration testing, vulnerability assessments, and data classification may help with the identification of threats and countermeasures, but do not necessarily always translate or quantify the threats and vulnerabilities to risk.

17. The use of proxies to protect more trusted assets from less sensitive ones is an example of which of the following types of security services?

    A. Access control

    B. Boundary control

    C. Integrity

    D. Audit and monitoring

Correct answer is **B**. Access control services focus on the identification, authentication, and authorization of subject entities (whether human or machine) as they are deployed and employed to access the organization's assets. These services are concerned with how and whether information is allowed to flow from one set of systems to another, or from one state to another. Boundary control systems are intended to enforce security zones of control by isolating entry points from one zone to another (choke points). Integrity services focus on the maintenance of high-integrity systems and data through automated checking to detect and correct corruption. Audit and monitoring services focus on the secure collection, storage, and analysis of audited events through centralized logging as well as the events themselves through intrusion detection systems (HIDS and NIDS) and similar services.

18. Which of the following is the main reason for security concerns in mobile computing devices?

    A. The 3G protocol is inherently insecure

    B. Lower processing power

    C. Hackers are targeting mobile devices

    D. The lack of anti-virus software.

Correct answer is **B**. These devices share common security concerns with other resource-constrained devices. In many cases, security services have been sacrificed to provide richer user interaction when processing power is very limited. Also, their mobility has made them a prime vector for data loss since they can be used to transmit and store information in ways that may be difficult to control.

19. In decentralized environments device drivers that enable the OS to control and communicate with hardware need to be securely designed, developed and deployed because they are

    A. typically installed by end-users and granted access to the supervisor state

    B. typically installed by administrators and granted access to user mode state

      C. typically installed by software without human interaction.

      D. integrated as part of the operating system.

Correct answer is A. Device drivers that control input/output devices are typically installed by end-users (not necessarily administrators) and are often granted access to supervisor state to help them run faster. This may allow a malformed driver to be used to compromise the system unless other controls are in place to mitigate this risk. Drivers are not add-ons to the operating system and usually require human interaction for installation.

20. A system administrator grants rights to a group of individuals called "Accounting" instead of granting rights to each individual. This is an example of which of the following security mechanisms?

      A. Layering

      B. Data hiding

      C. Cryptographic protections

      D. Abstraction

Correct answer is **D**. In computer programming, layering is the organization of programming into separate functional components that interact in some sequential and hierarchical way, with each layer usually having an interface only to the layer above it and the layer below it. Data hiding maintains activities at different security levels to separate these levels from each other. Cryptography can be used in a variety of ways to protect sensitive system functions and data. By encrypting sensitive information and limiting the availability of key material, data can be hidden from less privileged parts of the system. Abstraction involves the removal of characteristics from an entity in order to easily represent its essential properties.

Domain 7 - Security Operations

1. In the event of a security incident, one of the primary objectives of the operations staff is to ensure that

      A. the attackers are detected and stopped.

      B. there is minimal disruption to the organization's mission.

C. appropriate documentation about the event is maintained as chain of evidence.

D. the affected systems are immediately shut off to limit to the impact.

Correct answer is **B**. While the operations staff may be able to detect the attack and in some cases the attackers, there is very little that the operations staff can do to stop them. All actions taken by the operations staff as they respond to handle the security incident must follow established protocols and documented, but this is not their primary objective. The affected systems must only be shut off after necessary data or evidence that will be admissible in court is collected. The best answer choice is that the operations staff must maintain operational resilience.

2. Assuming a working IDS is in place, which of the following groups is **BEST** capable of stealing sensitive information due to the absence of system auditing?

    A. Malicious software (malware)

    B. Hacker or cracker

    C. Disgruntled employee

    D. Auditors

Correct answer is **C**. Insiders (employees, contractors, etc.) can have access to ¬information that they should not be allowed to and in the absence of auditing (logging) their actions can go unnoticed. Encryption can provide controls over unauthorized disclosure. External attacker (hacker or cracker) activity and malware usually raise alerts on intrusion detection systems (IDS). Auditors may have the need and authorization for the disclosure of sensitive information and this access is often monitored.

3. Which of the following provides controlled and un-intercepted interfaces into privileged user functions?

    A. Ring protection

    B. Anti-malware

    C. Maintenance hooks

    D. Trusted paths

Correct answer is **D**. Ring protection can be used to enforce boundary control between kernel functions and end-user controls. Anti-malware software is used to protect against malicious software. Maintenance hooks are coding constructs written by the software developer for troubleshooting and impersonation purposes, but can be a potential backdoor for malicious software. Trusted paths provide trustworthy interfaces into privileged user functions and are intended to provide a way to ensure that any communications over that path cannot be intercepted or corrupted.

4. The doors of a data center spring open in the event of a fire. This is an example of
   A. Fail-safe
   B. Fail-secure
   C. Fail-proof
   D. Fail-closed

Correct answer is **A**. Fail-safe mechanisms focuses on failing with a minimum of harm to personnel while fail-secure focuses on failing in a controlled manner to block access while the systems is in an inconsistent state. For example, data center door systems will fail safe to ensure that personnel can escape the area when the electrical power fails. A fail-secure door would prevent personnel from using the door at all, which could put personnel in jeopardy. Fail-open and fail-closed are fail safe mechanisms.

5. Which of the following ensures constant redundancy and fault-tolerance?
   A. Cold spare
   B. Warm spare
   C. Hot spare
   D. Archives

Correct answer is **C**. A cold spare is a spare component that is not powered up but is a duplicate of the primary component that can be inserted into the system if needed. Warm spares are those that are already inserted in the system but do not receive power unless they are required. Hot spares stay powered on and waiting to be called upon as needed. Archives are data backups stored for historical purposes. To ensure constant redundancy and fault-tolerance, hot spare is the best option.

6. If speed is preferred over resilience, which of the following RAID configuration is the best choice?

    A. RAID 0
    B. RAID 1
    C. RAID 5
    D. RAID 10

Correct answer is **A**. In a RAID 0 configuration, files are written in stripes across multiple disks without the use of parity information. This technique allows for fast reading and writing to disk since all of the disks can typically be accessed in parallel. However, without the parity information, it is not possible to recover from a hard drive failure. This technique does not provide redundancy and should not be used for systems with high availability requirements.

7. Updating records in multiple locations or copying an entire database to a remote location as a means to ensure the appropriate levels of fault-tolerance and redundancy is known as

    A. Data mirroring
    B. Shadowing
    C. Backup
    D. Archiving

Correct answer is **B**. Data mirroring is a RAID technique that duplicates all disk writes from one disk to another to create two identical drives. Database shadowing is the technique in which updates are shadowed in multiple locations. It is like copying the entire database on to a remote location. Backups are to be conducted on a regular basis and are useful in recovering information or a system in the event of a disaster. Archiving is the storage of data that is not in continual use for historical purposes.

8. When the backup window is not long enough to backup all of the data and the restoration of backup must be as fast as possible, which of the following types of high-availability backup strategy is **BEST**?

    A. Full

    B. Incremental

    C. Differential

    D. Increase the backup window so a full backup can be performed

Correct answer is **C**. Full backup would not be possible since the backup window is not long ago for all the data to be backed up. Additionally, it is less likely that the backup window can be increased to allow for a full backup, which is both time consuming and costly from a storage perspective. In an incremental backup, only the files that changed since the last backup will be backed up. In a differential backup, only the files that changed since the last full backup will be backed up. In general, differentials require more space than incremental backups while incremental backups are faster to perform. On the other hand, restoring data from incremental backups requires more time than differential backups. To restore from incremental backups, the last full backup and all of the incremental backups performed are combined. In contrast, restoring from a differential backup requires only the last full backup and the latest differential.

9. At a restricted facility, visitors are requested to provide identification and verified against a pre-approved list by the guard at the front gate before being let in. This is an example of checking for

    A. Least privilege

    B. Separation of duties

    C. Fail-safe

    D. Psychological acceptability

Correct answer is **A**. Access to facilities should be limited to named individuals with a requirement for physical access following the principle of least privilege. Individuals who do not require frequent physical access to physical systems should not receive access to the facility. If occasional access is required, then temporary access should be granted and revoked when it is no longer required. It is recommended that you are familiar with the other principles mentioned.

10. The major benefit of information classification is to

    A. map out the computing ecosystem

    B. identify the threats and vulnerabilities

    C. determine the software baseline

    D. identify the appropriate level of protection needs

Correct answer is **D**. Information classification refers to the practice of differentiating between different types of information assets and providing some guidance as to how classified information will need to be protected. Vulnerability scans can be used to map out the computing ecosystem. Threat modeling is used to identify threats and vulnerabilities. Configuration management can be used to determine the software baseline.

11. When sensitive information is no longer critical but still within scope of a record retention policy, that information is **BEST**

    A. Destroyed

    B. Re-categorized

    C. Degaussed

    D. Released

Correct answer is **B**. Information categorization also includes the processes and procedures to lower the sensitivity label of information. For example, declassification may be used to downgrade the sensitivity of information. Over the course of time, information once considered sensitive may decline in value or criticality. In these instances, declassification efforts should be implemented to ensure that excessive protection controls are not used for nonsensitive information. When declassifying information, marking, handling, and storage requirements will likely be reduced. Organizations should have categorization or declassification practices well documented for use by individuals assigned with the task. Information may still be needed and so it cannot be destroyed, degaussed, or deleted.

12. The main benefit of placing users into groups and roles is

    A. Ease of user administration

    B. Increased security

C. Ease of programmatic access

D. Increased automation

Correct answer is **A**. While placing users into groups and roles can yield in increased security, ease of programmatic access, or automation, the main reason as to why this is done is for the ease of user administration. Efficient management of users requires the assignment of individual accounts into groups or roles. Groups and roles allow rights and privileges to be assigned to groups or a role as opposed to individual accounts. Individual user accounts can then be assigned to one or more groups depending on the access and privileges they require.

13. Which of the following **BEST** determines the suitability of an individual?

A. Job rank or title

B. Partnership with the security team

C. Role

D. Background investigation

Correct answer is **D**. A background investigation relevant to the role, job or access is the best approach for minimal security problems. While a background investigation will not guarantee the integrity or honesty of an individual it will give the organization a glimpse into the history of an individual and references.

14. Reports must be specific on both the message and which of the following?

A. Intended audience

B. Delivery options

C. Colors used

D. Print layout

Correct answer is **A**. Reporting is also fundamental to successful security operations. It can take a variety of forms depending on the intended audience. Technical reporting tends to be designed for technical specialists or managers with direct responsibility for service delivery. Management reporting will provide summaries of multiple systems as well as key metrics for each of the services covered by the report. Executive dashboards are intended for the executive who is interested in seeing only the highlights across multiple services, and provide simple summaries of current state, usually in a highly visual form such as charts and graphs.

15. Which of the following can help with ensuring that only the needed logs are collected for monitoring?

    A. Clipping level
    B. Aggregation
    C. XML Parsing
    D. Inference

Correct answer is **A**. Clipping levels are used to ensure that only needed logs are collected. This is mainly used, because even on a single system, logs can get to be very large. An example of a clipping level is that only failed access attempts are logged.

16. The main difference between a Security Event Information Management (SEIM) system and a log management system is that SEIM systems are useful for log collection, collation and analysis

    A. In real time
    B. For historical purposes
    C. For admissibility in court
    D. In discerning patterns

Correct answer is **A**. Security event information management (SEIM) solutions are intended to provide a common platform for log collection, collation, and analysis in real-time to allow for more effective and efficient response. Log management systems are similar in that, they also collect logs and provide the ability to report against them, although their focus tends to be on the historical analysis of log information, rather than real-time analysis. They may be combined with SEIM solutions to provide both

1429

historical and real-time functions. Evidence collections for admissibility in court and pattern discernment are not real-time functions.

17. When normal traffic is flagged as an attack, it is an example of

    A. Fail-safe

    B. Fail-secure

    C. False-negative

    D. False-positive

Correct answer is **D**. False-positives occur when the IDS or IPS identifies something as an attack, but it is in fact normal traffic. False-negatives occur when it failed to interpret something as an attack when it should have. In these cases, intrusion systems must be carefully "tuned" to ensure that these are kept to a minimum.

18. The best way to ensure that there is no data remanence of sensitive information that was once stored on a DVD-R media is by

    A. Deletion

    B. Degaussing

    C. Destruction

    D. Overwriting

Correct answer is **C**. Optical media such as CDs and DVD must be physically destroyed to make sure that there is no residual data that can be disclosed. Since the media mentioned in this context is a read-only media (burn-once) DVD, the information on it cannot be overwritten or deleted. Degaussing can reduce or remove data remanence in magnetic non-optical media.

19. Which of the following processes is concerned with not only identifying the root cause but also addressing the underlying issue?

    A. Incident management

    B. Problem management

    C. Change management

    D. Configuration management

Correct answer is **B**. While incident management is concerned primarily with managing an adverse event, problem management is concerned with tracking that event back to a root cause and addressing the underlying problem. Maintaining system integrity is accomplished through the process of change control management. Configuration management is a process of identifying and documenting hardware components, software, and the associated settings.

20. Before applying a software update to production systems, it is **MOST** important that

    A. full disclosure information about the threat that the patch addresses is available

    B. the patching process is documented

    C. the production systems are backed up

    D. an independent third party attests the validity of the patch

Correct answer is **C**. Prior to deploying updates to production servers, make certain that a full system backup is conducted. In the regrettable event of a system crash, due to the update, the server and data can be recovered without a significant loss of data. Additionally, if the update involved propriety code, it will be necessary to provide a copy of the server or application image to the media librarian. The presence or absence of full disclosure information is good to have but not a requirement as the patching process will have to be a risk-based decision as it applies to the organization. Documentation of the patching process is the last step in patch management processes. Independent third-party assessments are not usually related to attesting patch validity.

Domain 8 - Business Continuity & Disaster Recovery Planning

1. Which phrase best defines a business continuity/disaster recovery plan?

    A. A set of plans for preventing a disaster.

    B. An approved set of preparations and sufficient procedures for responding to a disaster.

1431

C. A set of preparations and procedures for responding to a disaster without management approval.

D. The adequate preparations and procedures for the continuation of all organization functions.

Correct answer is **D**. Business continuity planning (BCP) and Disaster recovery planning (DRP) address the preparation, processes, and practices required to ensure the preservation of the business in the face of major disruptions to normal business operations.

2. Regardless of industry, which element of legal and regulatory requirements are all industries subject to?

    A. Sarbanes–Oxley

    B. HIPAA

    C. Due care

    D.   BS25999

Correct answer is **C**. Regulatory risk is clearly defined by the industry the organization is a part of. However, no matter what industry the planner is in, due care applies.

3. Which of the following statements **BEST** describes the extent to which an organization should address business continuity or disaster recovery planning?

    A. Continuity planning is a significant organizational issue and should include all parts or functions of the company.

    B. Continuity planning is a significant technology issue and the recovery of technology should be its primary focus.

    C. Continuity planning is required only where there is complexity in voice and data communications.

    D. Continuity planning is a significant management issue and should include the primary functions specified by management.

Correct answer is **A**. Business continuity planning and Disaster recovery planning involve the identification, selection, implementation, testing, and updating of prudent processes and specific actions necessary to protect critical business processes from the effects of major system and network disruptions and to ensure the timely restoration of business operations if significant disruptions occur.

4. Business impact analysis is performed to **BEST** identify:

    A. The impacts of a threat to the organization operations.

    B. The exposures to loss to the organization.

    C. The impacts of a risk on the organization.

    D. The cost efficient way to eliminate threats.

Correct answer is **B**. The business impact analysis is what is going to help the company decide what needs to be recovered and how quickly it needs to be recovered.

5. During the risk analysis phase of the planning, which of the following actions could **BEST** manage threats or mitigate the effects of an event?

    A. Modifying the exercise scenario.

    B. Developing recovery procedures.

    C. Increasing reliance on key individuals

    D. Implementing procedural controls.

Correct answer is **D**. The third element of risk is mitigating factors. Mitigating factors are the controls or safeguards the planner will put in place to reduce the impact of a threat.

6. The **BEST** reason to implement additional controls or safeguards is to:

    A. deter or remove the risk.

    B. identify and eliminate the threat.

    C. reduce the impact of the threat.

    D. identify the risk and the threat.

Correct answer is **C**. Preventing a disaster is always better than trying to recover from one. If the planner can recommend controls to be put in place to prevent the most likely of risks from having an impact on the organization's ability to do business, then the planner will have fewer actual events to recover from.

7. Which of the following statements **BEST** describes business impact analysis?

    A. Risk analysis and business impact analysis are two different terms describing the same project effort.

    B. A business impact analysis calculates the probability of disruptions to the organization.

    C. A business impact analysis is critical to development of a business continuity plan.

    D. A business impact analysis establishes the effect of disruptions on the organization.

Correct answer is **D.** All business functions and the technology that supports them need to be classified based on their recovery priority. Recovery time frames for business operations are driven by the consequences of not performing the function. The consequences may be the result of business lost during the down period; contractual commitments not met resulting in fines or lawsuits, lost goodwill with customers, etc.

8. The term "disaster recovery" refers to the recovery of:

    A. organization operations.

    B. technology environment.

    C. manufacturing environment.

    D. personnel environments.

Correct answer is **B.** Once computers became part of the business landscape, it quickly became clear that we could not return to our manual processes if our computers failed. If those computer systems failed, there were not enough people to do the work nor did the people in the business still have the skill to do it manually anymore. Th is was the start of the disaster recovery industry. Still today, the term "disaster recovery" or "DR" commonly means recovery of the technology environment.

9. Which of the following terms **BEST** describes the effort to determine the consequences of disruptions that could result from a disaster?

    A. Business impact analysis.

    B. Risk analysis.

    C. Risk assessment.

    D. Project problem definition

Correct answer is **A**. The BIA is what is going to help the company decide what needs to be recovered and how quickly it needs to be recovered.

10. The **BEST** advantage of using a cold site as a recovery option is:

    A. is a less expensive recovery option.

    B. can be configured and made operational for any organization function.

    C. is preconfigured for communications and can be customized for organization functions.

    D. is the most available option for testing server and communications restorations.

Correct answer is **A**. Among the advantages of warm and cold site are that they are less expensive and available for longer recoveries.

11. The elements of risk are as follows:

    A. Natural disasters and man made disasters

    B. Threats, assets and mitigating factors

    C. Risk and business impact analysis

    D. business impact analysis and mitigating factors

Correct answer is **B**. There are three elements of risk: threats, assets, and mitigating factors.

12. The term "Recovery Time Objective" RTO means

    A. The maximum time a service or system can be unavailable.

    B. The amount of time a disaster recovery should take.

1435

    C. The time required to switch from a primary site to an alternate.

    D. The time which must elapse before enacting a crisis communication plan.

Correct answer is **A**. All applications need to be classified as to their time sensitivity for recovery even if those applications do not support business functions that are time sensitive. For applications, this is commonly referred to as recovery time objective (RTO) or maximum tolerable downtime (MTD).

13. The most efficient restore from tape back-up is:

    A. Full backup

    B. Incremental Backup

    C. Partial Backup

    D. Differential backup

Correct answer is **A**. If an organization wants the backup and recovery strategy to be as simple as possible, then they should only use full backups. They take more time and hard drive space to perform but they are the most efficient in recovery.

14. One of the advantages of a hot site recovery solution is that it

    A. is less expensive

    B. is highly available

    C. does not incur downtime

    D. no maintenance is required

Correct answer is **B**. Among the advantages of internal or external hot site are allows recovery to be tested, highly available, and site can be operational within hours.

15. Which of the following methods is not acceptable for exercising the business continuity plan?

    A. Table-top exercise.

    B. Call exercise.

C. Simulated exercise.

D. Halting a production application or function.

Correct answer is **D**. The only difference between a simulated and an actual exercise is that the first rule of testing is the planner will never create a disaster by testing for one. The planner must make every effort to make certain that what is being tested will not impact the production environment whether business or technical.

16. Which of the following is the primary desired result of any well-planned business continuity exercise?

A. Identifies plan strengths and weaknesses.

B. Satisfies management requirements.

C. Complies with auditor's requirements.

D. Maintains shareholder confidence

Correct answer is **A**. After every exercise the planner conducts, the exercise results need to be published and action items identified to address the issues that were uncovered by the exercise. Action items should be tracked until they have been resolved and, where appropriate, the plan updated. It is very unfortunate when an organization has the same issue in subsequent tests simply because someone did not update the plan.

17. A business continuity plan is best updated and maintained:

A. Annually or when requested by auditors.

B. Only when new versions of software are deployed.

C. Only when new hardware is deployed.

D. During the configuration and change management process.

Correct answer is **D**. The plan document and all related procedures will need to be updated after each exercise and after each material change to the production, IT, or business environment.

1437

18. Which of the following is **MOST** important for successful business continuity?

    A. Senior leadership support.

    B. Strong technical support staff.

    C. Extensive wide area network infrastructure.

    D. An integrated incident response team.

Correct answer is **A**. Without senior leadership support it is unlikely a business continuity program will succeed.

19. Which of the following is the **BEST** alternate site approach if the recovery time objective of a service is two months?

    A. Cold site.

    B. Reciprocal agreement.

    C. Warm site.

    D. Hot site.

Correct answer is **A**. If a service is not needed for several months a cold site is the correct tradeoff between time and speed for restoration.

20. A service's recovery point objective is zero. Which approach **BEST** ensures the requirement is met?

    A. RAID 6 with a hot site alternative.

    B. RAID 0 with a warm site alternative

    C. RAID 0 with a cold site alternative

    D. RAID 6 with a reciprocal agreement.

Correct answer is **A**. RAID 6 will provide a highly redundant storage situation while the hot site will stand ready to fail over should the primary site fail.

Domain 9 - Legal, Regulations, Investigations, and Compliance

1. Where does the greatest risk of cybercrime come from?

    A. Outsiders

    B. Nation-states

    C. Insiders

    D. Script kiddies

Correct answer is **C**. A word of caution is necessary: although the media has tended to portray the threat of cybercrime as existing almost exclusively from the outside, external to a company, reality paints a much different picture. The greatest risk of cybercrime comes from the inside, namely, criminal insiders.

2. What is the largest hindrance to fighting computer crime?

    A. Computer criminals are generally smarter than computer investigators.

    B. Adequate funding to stay ahead of the computer criminals.

    C. Activity associated with computer crime is truly international.

    D. There are so many more computer criminals than investigators that it is impossible to keep up.

Correct answer is **C**. The biggest hindrance to effectively dealing with computer crime is the fact that this activity is truly international in scope, and thus requires an international solution, as opposed to a domestic one based on archaic concepts of borders and jurisdictions.

3. Computer forensics is the marriage of computer science, information technology, and engineering with

    A. Law

    B. Information systems

    C. Analytical thought

    D. The scientific method

A

Appendix
Answers to Review Questions

1439

Correct answer is **A**. As a forensic discipline, this area deals with evidence and the legal system and is really the marriage of computer science, information technology, and engineering with law.

4. What principal allows an investigator to identify aspects of the person responsible for a crime when, whenever committing a crime, the perpetrator leaves traces while stealing assets?

   A. Meyer's principal of legal impunity
   B. Criminalistic principals
   C. IOCE/Group of 8 Nations principals for computer forensics
   D. Locard's principle of exchange

Correct answer is **D**. Locard's principle of exchange states that when a crime is committed, the perpetrators leave something behind and take something with them, hence the exchange. This principle allows an investigator to identify aspects of the persons responsible, even with a purely digital crime scene.

5. Which of the following is part of the five rules of evidence?

   A. Be authentic, be redundant and be admissible.
   B. Be complete, be authentic and be admissible.
   C. Be complete, be redundant and be authentic.
   D. Be redundant, be admissible and be complete

Correct answer is **B**. At a more generic level, evidence should have some probative value, be relevant to the case at hand, and meet the following criteria (often called the five rules of evidence): be authentic, be accurate, be complete, be convincing, and be admissible.

6. What is not mentioned as a phase of an incident response?

   A. Documentation
   B. Prosecution
   C. Containment
   D. Investigation

Correct answer is **B** The incident response and handling phase can be broken down further into triage, investigation, containment, and analysis and tracking.

7. Which **BEST** emphasizes the abstract concepts of law and is influenced by the writings of legal scholars and academics.

    A. Criminal law

    B. Civil law

    C. Religious law

    D. Administrative law

Correct answer is **B**. Civil law emphasizes the abstract concepts of law and is influenced by the writings of legal scholars and academics, more so than common law systems.

8. Which type of intellectual property covers the expression of ideas rather than the ideas themselves?

    A. Trademark

    B. Patent

    C. Copyright

    D. Trade secret

Correct answer is **C**. A copyright covers the expression of ideas rather than the ideas themselves; it usually protects artistic property such as writing, recordings, databases, and computer programs.

9. Which type of intellectual property protects the goodwill a merchant or vendor invests in its products?

    A. Trademark

    B. Patent

    C. Copyright

    D. Trade secret

Correct answer is **A**. Trademark laws are designed to protect the goodwill a merchant or vendor invests in its products.

10. Which of the following are computer forensics guidelines?

    A. IOCE, MOM and SWGDE.

    B. MOM, SWGDE and IOCE.

    C. IOCE, SWGDE and ACPO.

    D. ACPO, MOM and IOCE.

Correct answer is **C**. Like incident response, there are various computer forensics guidelines (e.g., International Organization of Computer Evidence (IOCE), Scientific Working Group on Digital Evidence (SWGDE), Association of Chief Police Officers (ACPO)). These guidelines formalize the computer forensic processes by breaking them into numerous phases or steps. MOM stands for means, opportunity, and motives.

11. Which of the following are categories of software licensing?

    A. Freeware, Open Source, and Commercial

    B. Commercial, Academic and Open Source

    C. Academic, Freeware and Open Source

    D. Freeware, Commercial and Academic

Correct answer is **D**. There are four categories of software licensing: freeware, shareware, commercial, and academic. Within these categories, there are specific types of agreements. Master agreements and end-user licensing agreements (EULAs) are the most prevalent.

12. What are the rights and obligations of individuals and organizations with respect to the collection, use, retention, and disclosure of personal information **BEST** related to?

    A. Privacy

    B. Secrecy

    C. Availability

    D. Reliability

Correct answer is **A**. Privacy can be defined as "the rights and obligations of individuals and organizations with respect to the collection, use, retention, and disclosure of personal information.".

13. Triage encompasses which of the following incident response subphases?

    A. Collection, transport, testimony

    B. Traceback, feedback, loopback

    C. Detection, identification, notification

    D. Confidentiality, integrity, availability

Correct answer is **C**. Triage encompasses the detection, identification, and notification subphases.

14. The integrity of a forensic bit stream image is determined by:

    A. Comparing hash totals to the original source

    B. Keeping good notes

    C. Taking pictures

    D. Encrypted keys

Correct answer is **A**. Ensuring the authenticity and integrity of evidence is critical. If the courts feel the evidence or its copies are not accurate or lack integrity, it is doubtful that the evidence or any information derived from the evidence will be admissible. The current protocol for demonstrating authenticity and integrity relies on hash functions that create unique numerical signatures that are sensitive to any bit changes. Currently, if these signatures match the original or have not changed since the original collection, the courts will accept that integrity has been established.

15. When dealing with digital evidence, the crime scene:

    A. Must never be altered

    B. Must be completely reproducible in a court of law

    C. Must exist in only one country

    D. Must have the least amount of contamination that is possible

The correct answer is **D**. Given the importance of the evidence that is available at a crime scene, the ability to deal with a scene in a manner that minimizes the amount of disruption, contamination, or destruction of evidence. Once a scene has been contaminated, there is no undo or redo button to push; the damage is done.

16. When outsourcing IT systems

    A. all regulatory and compliance requirements must be passed on to the provider.

    B. the outsourcing organization is free from compliance obligations.

    C. the outsourced IT systems are free from compliance obligations.

    D. the provider is free from compliance obligations.

Correct answer is **A**. An organization's obligations for due care extend to its business partners.

17. The (ISC)² code of ethics resolves conflicts between canons by:

    A. there can never be conflicts between canons.

    B. working through adjudication.

    C. the order of the canons.

    D. vetting all canon conflicts through the board of directors.

Correct answer is **C**. Conflicts are resolved through the order of the canons.

18. When dealing with digital evidence, the chain of custody:

    A. Must never be altered

    B. Must be completely reproducible in a court of law

    C. Must exist in only one country

    D. Must follow a formal documented process

Correct answer is **D**. The chain of custody must explain evidence from origin to destruction.

19. To ensure proper forensics action when needed, an incident response program must:

    A. avoid conflicts of interest by ensuring organization legal council is not part of the process.

    B. routinely create forensic images of all desktops and servers.

    C. only promote closed incidents to law enforcement.

    D. treat every incident as though it may be a crime.

Correct answer is **D**. An incident may be harmless but it may also be the start of an investigation. Therefore all incidents must be handled with care until proven benign.

20. A hard drive is recovered from a submerged vehicle. The drive is needed for a court case. What is the best approach to pull information off the drive?

    A. Wait for the drive to dry and then install it in a desktop and attempt to retrieve the information via normal operating system commands.

    B. Place the drive in a forensic oven to dry it and then use a degausser to remove any residual humidity prior to installing the drive in a laptop and using the OS to pull off information.

    C. While the drive is still wet use a forensic bit to bit copy program to ensure the drive is preserved in its "native" state.

    D. Contact a professional data recovery organization, explain the situation and request they pull a forensic image.

Correct answer is **D**. For heavily damaged media, professional data recovery services are the best chance for recovery.

Domain 10 - Physical (Environmental) Security

1. The primary function of a physical protection system is?

    A. determine, direct and dispatch

    B. detection, delay and response

    C. display, develop, initiate and apprehend

    D. evaluate, dispatch and detain

Correct answer is **B**. A well-designed system provides protection-in-depth, minimizes the consequences of component failures and exhibits balanced protection. The system itself typically has a number of elements that fall into the essence of deter–detect—delay–respond.

1445

2. To successfully complete a vulnerability assessment, it is critical that protection systems are well understood through:

   A. Threat definition, target identification and facility characterization
   B. Threat definition, conflict control and facility characterization
   C. Risk assessment, threat identification and incident review
   D. Threat identification, vulnerability appraisal and access review

Correct answer is **A.** At the beginning, a good assessment requires the security professional to determine specific protection objectives. These objectives include threat definition, target identification, and facility characteristics.

3. Laminated glass is recommended for what type of locations:

   A. All exterior glass windows
   B. Interior boundary penetration and critical infrastructure facility
   C. Street-level windows, doorways and other access areas
   D. Capacitance proximity, intrusion detection locations and boundary penetration sites

Correct answer is **C.** Laminated glass is recommended for installation in street-level windows, doorways, and other access areas.

4. The strategy of forming layers of protection around an asset or facility is known as:

   A. Secured Perimeter
   B. Defense-in-Depth
   C. Reinforced Barrier Deterrent
   D. Reasonable Asset Protection

Correct answer is **B.** In the concept of defense-in-depth, barriers are arraigned in layers with the level of security growing progressively higher as one comes closer to the center or the highest protective area. Defending an asset with a multiple posture can reduce the likelihood of a successful attack; if one layer of defense fails, another layer of defense will hopefully prevent the attack, and so on.

5. What crime reduction technique **BEST** creates a physical environment that positively influences human behavior?

    A. Asset protection and vulnerability assessments

    B. Reducing vulnerability by protecting, offsetting or transferring the risk

    C. Crime prevention through environmental design

    D. Instituting employee screening and workplace violence programs

Correct answer is **C**. Crime prevention through environmental design (CPTED) is a crime reduction technique that has several key elements applicable to the analysis of the building function and site design against physical attack. It is used by architects, city planners, landscapers, interior designers, and security professionals with the objective of creating a climate of safety in a community by designing a physical environment that positively influences human behavior.

6. The key to a successful physical protection system is the integration of:

    A. people, procedures, and equipment

    B. technology, risk assessment, and human interaction

    C. protecting, offsetting, and transferring risk

    D. detection, deterrence, and response

Correct answer is **A**. The key to a successful system is the integration of people, procedures and equipment into a system that protects the targets from the threat. A well-designed system provides protection-in-depth, minimizes the consequences of component failures and exhibits balanced protection.

7. What is the primary objective of controlling entry into a facility or area?

    A. Provide time management controls for all employees

    B. Ensure that only authorized persons are allowed to enter

    C. Keep potential hazards and contraband material out that could be used to commit sabotage.

    D. Identification purposes

Correct answer is **B**. The primary function of an access control system (ACS) is to ensure that only authorized personnel are permitted inside the controlled area. This can also include the regulation and flow of materials into and out of specific areas. Persons subject to control can include employees, visitors, customers, vendors, and the public. Access control measures should be different for each application to fulfill specific security, cost, and operational objectives.

8. For safety considerations in perimeter areas such as parking lots or garages what is the advised lighting?

    A. 3 fc
    B. 5 fc
    C. 7 fc
    D. 10 fc

Correct answer is **B**. Lights used for CCTV monitoring generally requires at least one to two footcandles of illumination, whereas the lighting needed for safety considerations in exterior areas such as parking lots or garages substantially greater (at least 5 fc).

9. What would be the most appropriate interior sensor used for a building that has windows along the ground floor?

    A. infrared glass-break sensor
    B. ultrasonic glass-break sensors
    C. acoustic/shock glass-break sensors
    D. volumetric sensors

Correct answer is **C**. Glass-break sensors are a good intrusion detection device for buildings with a lot of glass windows and doors with glass panes. The use of ¬dual-technology glass break sensors—acoustic and shock wave—is most effective. The reason is that if only acoustic is used and an employee pulls the window blinds up, it can set off a false alarm; but if it is set to a dual-alarm system both acoustic and shock sensors will need to be activated before an alarm is triggered.

10. Which of the following **BEST** describe three separate functions of CCTV?

    A. surveillance, deterrence, and evidentiary archives

    B. intrusion detection, detainment and response

    C. optical scanning, infrared beaming and lighting

    D. monitoring, white balancing and inspection

Correct answer is **A**. Uses of CCTV systems for security services include several different functions: surveillance, assessment, deterrence, and evidentiary archives.

11. Although security technologies are not the answer to all organizational security problem, if applied appropriately what will they provide?

    A. the ability to reduce electrical costs

    B. they can enhance the security envelope and in the majority of cases will save the organization money

    C. government tax incentives for increased physical protection systems

    D. increased capital value of property with high-tech integrated technologies

Correct answer is **B**. Businesses face new and complex physical security challenges across the full spectrum of operations. Although security technologies are not the answer to all organizational security problems, if applied appropriately, they can enhance the security envelope and in the majority of cases will save the organization money.

12. A meaningful assessment of a facility or building should be used:

    A. to determine where all the fire exits are located

    B. within the context of the defined threats and the value of the organization's assets

    C. to count the number of employees within the facility

    D. to determine the structural strength of the perimeter walls

Correct answer is **B**. The assessment of any vulnerability of a facility or building should be done within the context of the defined threats and the value of the organization's assets. That is, each element of the facility should be analyzed for vulnerabilities to each threat and a vulnerability rating should be assigned. A vulnerability assessment may change the value rating of assets due to the identification of critical nodes or some other factor that makes the organization's assets more valuable.

13. The **BEST** example of building a new facility for security is:

    A. limiting the number of entrances to the site that must be monitored, staffed and protected

    B. reducing the cost associated with energy needs in providing the physical protection system

    C. giving employees easy access to the facility without their knowledge of the security components used in monitoring their activities

    D. blast reinforcement film on all perimeter windows

Correct answer is **A**. Gates exist to facilitate and control access. Gates need to be controlled to ensure that only authorized persons and vehicles pass through. It is **BEST** to minimize the number of gates and access points because any opening is always a potential vulnerability. Each gate requires resources whether it uses electronic access control or a guard. The fewest number of entry points, the better the control of the facility.

14. All visitors entering the facility sign in and out on a visitor's log, this is established for what reasons?

    A. for the purpose of detection, accountability and the necessity for response

    B. access control and surveillance

    C. timeframe of the visit, who was visited, and in the case of an emergency have accountability of everyone for safety purposes

    D. for planning assessment and the requirements of proper designation

Correct answer is **C**. All visitors entering the facility should sign in and out on a visitor's log to maintain accountability of who is in the facility, the timeframe of the visit, who they visited, and in the case of an emergency have accountability of everyone for safety purposes.

15. What is the **BEST** means of protecting the physical devices associated with the alarm system?

    A. Tamper protection

    B. Target hardening

    C. Security design

    D. UL 2050

Correct answer is **A**. Tamper protection is the means of protecting the physical devices associated with the alarm system through line supervision, encryption, or tamper alarming of enclosures and components.

16. When using a piece of portable computing equipment or media, regardless if it is being used inside the facility or is being removed for legitimate business outside of the facility, simple protection methods need to be employed in order to maintain the security of the equipment. These **BEST** consist of _____.

    A. cable locks, encryption, password protection and increased awareness

    B. reducing vulnerability by protecting, offsetting or transferring the risk

    C. operational readiness, physical protection systems, standard operating processes

    D. increase awareness, environmental design and physical security

Correct answer is **A**. When using a piece of portable computer equipment or media, regardless if it is being used inside the facility or is being removed for legitimate business outside of the facility, simple protection methods need to be employed in order to maintain the security of the equipment: use a cable lock, do not leave the equipment unattended or unsecured, use strong passwords, and encrypt data.

17. Personal identity verification systems which use hand or fingerprint, handwriting, eye pattern, voice, face, or any other physical characteristics for authentication are:

    A. Biometric devices

    B. Technological systems

    C. Physiometric devices

    D. Physical analysis devices

Correct answer is **A**, Biometric devices rely on measurements of biological characteristics of an individual, such as a fingerprint, hand geometry, voice, or iris patterns.

18. Physical security is applied by using _____ of physical protective measures to prevent or minimize theft, unauthorized access, or destruction of property.

    A. Layers

    B. Methods

    C. Varieties

    D. Types

Correct answer is **A**. The primary goal of a physical protection program is to control access into the facility. In the concept of defense-in-depth, barriers are arraigned in layers with the level of security growing progressively higher as one comes closer to the center or the highest protective area. Defending an asset with a multiple posture can reduce the likelihood of a successful attack; if one layer of defense fails, another layer of defense will hopefully prevent the attack, and so on.

19. What is a comprehensive overview of a facility to include physical security controls, policy, procedures and employee safety?

    A. Availability assessment

    B. Security survey

    C. Budgetary and financial performance

    D. Defense-in-depth

Correct answer is **B**. Before any project begins there must be an assessment made in order to put together an operational plan and a practical approach to securing the facility. This security assessment can also be called a security survey, vulnerability assessment, or risk analysis.

20. Which security control is most effective in curtailing and preventing "piggybacking" or "tailgating" as a means of unauthorized access?

- A. Cameras
- B. Turnstiles
- C. Keys
- D. Identification badges

Correct answer is **B**. A common and frustrating loophole in an otherwise secure access control systems can be the ability of an unauthorized person to follow through a checkpoint behind an authorized person, called "piggybacking" or "tailgating." One solution is an airlock-style arrangement called a mantrap, in which a person opens one door and waits for it to close before the next door will open. Another system that is available is a turnstile, which can be used as a supplemental control to assist a guard or receptionist while controlling access into a protected area.

Index

I

Index

I

Index

I

Index

I

I

Index

I

Index

I

Index

I

Index

I

Index

X

Z